For full coverage of the constitutional and administrative law of the European Community:

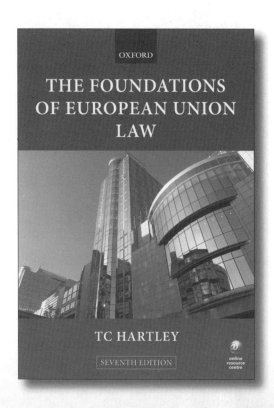

ISBN: 9780199566754

August 2010

Available from Oxford University Press.

Visit **http://www.oxfordtextbooks.co.uk/law** to find out more.

# THE SUBSTANTIVE LAW OF THE EU

## THE FOUR FREEDOMS

*Third Edition*

### CATHERINE BARNARD

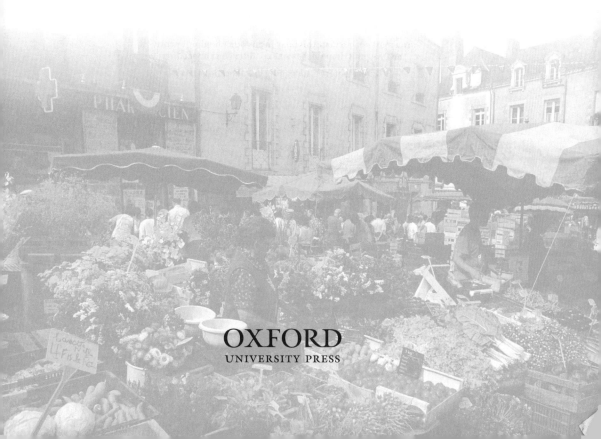

OXFORD
UNIVERSITY PRESS

# OXFORD
## UNIVERSITY PRESS

Great Clarendon Street, Oxford OX2 6DP

Oxford University Press is a department of the University of Oxford.
It furthers the University's objective of excellence in research, scholarship,
and education by publishing worldwide in

Oxford New York

Auckland Cape Town Dar es Salaam Hong Kong Karachi
Kuala Lumpur Madrid Melbourne Mexico City Nairobi
New Delhi Shanghai Taipei Toronto

With offices in

Argentina Austria Brazil Chile Czech Republic France Greece
Guatemala Hungary Italy Japan Poland Portugal Singapore
South Korea Switzerland Thailand Turkey Ukraine Vietnam

Oxford is a registered trade mark of Oxford University Press
in the UK and in certain other countries

Published in the United States
by Oxford University Press Inc., New York

British Library Cataloguing in Publication Data

Data available

Library of Congress Cataloging in Publication Data

Barnard, Catherine.
The substantive law of the EU : the four freedoms / Catherine Barnard.—3rd ed.
p. cm.
Includes bibliographical references and index.
ISBN 978–0–19–956224–4 (pbk.)
1. Freedom of movement—European Union countries. 2. Free trade—European
Union countries. 3. Law—European Union countries. 4. European Union. I. Title.
KJE5170.B37 2010
343.24′07—dc22                                                        2010019850

Typeset by Newgen Imaging Systems (P) Ltd, Chennai, India
Printed in Great Britain
on acid-free paper by
Ashford Colour Press Ltd, Gosport, Hampshire

ISBN 978–0–19–956224–4

5 7 9 10 8 6 4

# OUTLINE CONTENTS

# PART IV    FREE MOVEMENT OF CAPITAL

# PART V    COMPLETING THE SINGLE MARKET

# CONTENTS

## PART IV    FREE MOVEMENT OF CAPITAL

## PART V   COMPLETING THE SINGLE MARKET

# PREFACE

To entitle a book *The Substantive Law of the EU* inevitably offers a hostage to fortune. To do full justice to the sheer breadth of the subject requires several volumes, not just a single text. I am, therefore, more aware than most of the limitations imposed by producing a single volume. To keep the book within the bounds of the manageable, I have assumed that the reader has a basic knowledge of the institutional and constitutional structure of the EU. This allows this text to concentrate on an examination of the four freedoms, primarily in respect of the rules that regulate movement internally within the EU and, to a lesser extent, in respect of the rules that regulate movement from outside the EU. It is my hope that an understanding of the principles which underpin the four freedoms can be used as a guide to readers wishing to explore more closely specialist areas of EU substantive law. To assist with that process, I have used a number of free-standing case studies in the text, both to help illustrate the main points and to demonstrate how the general principles apply to more specialist areas.

When the first edition of the book was being written, the Constitutional Treaty was being negotiated. With the second edition, the French and Dutch 'no' votes had just put paid to the Constitutional Treaty. As the third edition was being put to bed, the Irish were persuaded to vote 'yes' to the Lisbon Treaty and, at the eleventh hour, the Czech president agreed to sign the text. The Treaty therefore came into force on 1 December 2009 and this edition of the book attempts to do justice to its contents. The most obvious impact is in respect of the change of numbers. I have used the Lisbon numbering throughout, even in respect of cases decided under the Rome or Amsterdam numbering, although on first use of the Lisbon number I have put its Amsterdam predecessor in brackets after it. Occasionally I have used the Rome or Amsterdam numbering, where I believe this helps to explain a particular decision of the Court or where the language of the text was significantly different to its Lisbon content. I have also decided to refer to the 'European Union' and 'Union law' throughout, except when talking historically where the distinction between EU, EC, and EEC was significant. I have also not changed titles of books and articles which use the pre-Lisbon terms. Finally, I have used the abbreviation 'TEU' after Treaty numbers to identify provisions of the Treaty on European Union after Lisbon, 'EU' to identify provisions of the Treaty on European Union before Lisbon. 'TFEU' is used to identify provisions of the Treaty on the Functioning of the European Union, 'EC' to indicate provisions of the European Community Treaty, and 'EEC' to identify provisions of the European Economic Community Treaty.

I have restructured some chapters of the book for its third edition, although the overall shape remains much the same. The largest changes can be found in Part II on goods. The discussion of the fiscal rules, Articles 28–30 TFEU (ex Articles 23–5 EC) on customs duties and Article 110 TFEU (ex Article 90 EC) on taxation, has now been placed in a single chapter, Chapter 3. Changes have also been made to the structure of the chapters on non-fiscal rules. Following an important decision in 2008, the case law on Articles 34 and 35 TFEU (ex Articles 28 and 29 EC) has been brought more closely into alignment and so the two Articles are now considered in Chapter 4. Another 2009 case has reduced the significance of the *Keck* line of case law and so Chapter 5 on certain selling arrangements has been shortened. The Article 36 TFEU (ex Article 30 EC) derogations and the mandatory requirements are now considered together in Chapter 6. The old Chapter 8 on intellectual property has been revised and placed on the companion website. Part III, concerning free movement of persons, follows the structure of the second edition: an introductory chapter sets out the common principles (Chapter 8), the subsequent chapters (Chapters 9–12) consider the law on workers, establishment, and services. Most of the discussion of the Citizens' Rights Directive 2004/38 can be found in the chapter on citizenship (Chapter 12) and in an expanded chapter on derogations, limitations, conditions, and justifications (Chapter 13). The rapidly evolving legal position of third-country nationals (TCNs) is considered in a revised Chapter 14. Chapter 15 concerns capital and monetary union. The structure of this chapter has been overhauled to reflect the growing importance of the cases on taxation, a development which is also evident in the expanded analysis of taxation in chapters in Part III. Chapter 16 considers how the internal market process is being 'completed' through the process of harmonisation. This chapter has been revised to reflect the introduction of the goods package.

I owe debts of gratitude to many people who helped me complete the various editions of this book. I am particularly grateful to those who have read and commented on various chapters for the different editions—Albertina Albors-Llorens, Cathryn Costello, Marise Cremona, Alan Dashwood, Simon Deakin, Michael Dougan, Julian Ghosh, Rosa Greaves, Elspeth Guild, Hannes Hofmeister, Steve Peers, Catherine Seville, Jukka Snell, John Tiley, Helen Toner, Takis Tridimas, Joanne Scott, Eleanor Spaventa, Stephen Weatherill, John Usher, Carsten Zatschler—as well as to the various anonymous referees provided by OUP and students who have written to me with suggestions. Their contributions have been invaluable, though, of course, any errors remain my own. Generations of students have helped shape my ideas, together with friends and colleagues in EU law both at Cambridge and elsewhere, in particular at Michigan, where I spent a productive sabbatical and enjoyed some lively discussions on EU and US law with Daniel Halberstam and Don Regan.

Matthew Cotton, Kate Salkild, and Penelope Woolf at OUP patiently saw the first edition through to completion; Melanie Jackson the second edition; Alex Clabburn, Jeremy Langworthy, Jonathon Price, and Anya Aghdam the third. I am very grateful to them all. However, my most heartfelt thanks go to my patient and understanding family, especially to my men—large, medium, and small—and to our wonderful, but non-sleeping, new addition.

Cambridge, January 2010

# TABLE OF LEGISLATION

*Resolutions*

# TABLE OF CASES

## EUROPEAN COURT OF HUMAN RIGHTS

## EFTA

## GERMANY

## IRELAND

## UNITED KINGDOM

# TABLE OF EQUIVALENCES[1]

## TREATY ON EUROPEAN UNION

| Old numbering of the Treaty on European Union | New numbering of the Treaty on European Union | Old numbering of the Treaty on European Union | New numbering of the Treaty on European Union |
|---|---|---|---|
| TITLE I | TITLE I | | Article 11 |
| Article 1 | Article 1 | | Article 12 |
| | Article 2 | TITLE III | TITLE III |
| Article 2 | Article 3 | Article 9 (repealed)[8] | Article 13 |
| Article 3 (repealed)[2] | | | Article 14[9] |
| | Article 4 | | Article 15[10] |
| | Article 5[3] | | Article 16[11] |
| Article 4 (repealed)[4] | | | Article 17[12] |
| Article 5 (repealed)[5] | | | Article 18 |
| Article 6 | Article 6 | | Article 19[13] |
| Article 7 | Article 7 | TITLE IV | TITLE IV |
| | Article 8 | Article 10 (repealed)[14] | |
| TITLE II | TITLE II | Articles 27a to 27e (replaced) | Article 20[15] |
| Article 8 (repealed)[6] | Article 9 | Articles 40 to 40b (replaced) | |
| | Article 10[7] | Articles 43 to 45 (replaced) | |

[1] Tables of equivalences as referred to in Article 5 of the Treaty of Lisbon. The original centre column, which set out the intermediate numbering as used in that Treaty, has been omitted.

[2] Replaced, in substance, by Article 7 of the Treaty on the Functioning of the European Union ("TFEU") and by Articles 13(1) and 21, paragraph 3, second subparagraph of the Treaty on European Union ("TEU").

[3] Replaces Article 5 of the Treaty establishing the European Community ("TEC").

[4] Replaced, in substance, by Article 15.

[5] Replaced, in substance, by Article 13, paragraph 2.

[6] Article 8 TEU, which was in force until the entry into force of the Treaty of Lisbon (hereinafter 'current'), amended the TEC. Those amendments are incorporated into the latter Treaty and Article 8 is repealed. Its number is used to insert a new provision.

[7] Paragraph 4 replaces, in substance, the first subparagraph of Article 191 TEC.

[8] The current Article 9 TEU amended the Treaty establishing the European Coal and Steel Community. This latter expired on 23 July 2002. Article 9 is repealed and the number thereof is used to insert another provision.

[9] – Paragraphs 1 and 2 replace, in substance, Article 189 TEC;
– paragraphs 1 to 3 replace, in substance, paragraphs 1 to 3 of Article 190 TEC;
– paragraph 1 replaces, in substance, the first subparagraph of Article 192 TEC;
– paragraph 4 replaces, in substance, the first subparagraph of Article 197 TEC.

[10] Replaces, in substance, Article 4.

[11] – Paragraph 1 replaces, in substance, the first and second indents of Article 202 TEC;
– paragraphs 2 and 9 replace, in substance, Article 203 TEC;
– paragraphs 4 and 5 replace, in substance, paragraphs 2 and 4 of Article 205 TEC.

[12] – Paragraph 1 replaces, in substance, Article 211 TEC;
– paragraphs 3 and 7 replace, in substance, Article 214 TEC.
– paragraph 6 replaces, in substance, paragraphs 1, 3 and 4 of Article 217 TEC.

[13] – Replaces, in substance, Article 220 TEC.
– the second subparagraph of paragraph 2 replaces, in substance, the first subparagraph of Article 221 TEC.

[14] The current Article 10 TEU amended the Treaty establishing the European Atomic Energy Community. Those amendments are incorporated into the Treaty of Lisbon. Article 10 is repealed and the number thereof is used to insert another provision.         [15] Also replaces Articles 11 and 11a TEC.

| Old numbering of the Treaty on European Union | New numbering of the Treaty on European Union | Old numbering of the Treaty on European Union | New numbering of the Treaty on European Union |
|---|---|---|---|
| TITLE V | TITLE V |  | Article 45 |
|  | Chapter 1 |  | Article 46 |
|  | Article 21 | TITLE VI (repealed)[17] |  |
|  | Article 22 | Article 29 (replaced)[18] |  |
|  | Chapter 2 | Article 30 (replaced)[19] |  |
|  | Section 1 | Article 31 (replaced)[20] |  |
|  | Article 23 | Article 32 (replaced)[21] |  |
| Article 11 | Article 24 | Article 33 (replaced)[22] |  |
| Article 12 | Article 25 | Article 34 (repealed) |  |
| Article 13 | Article 26 | Article 35 (repealed) |  |
|  | Article 27 | Article 36 (replaced)[23] |  |
| Article 14 | Article 28 | Article 37 (repealed) |  |
| Article 15 | Article 29 | Article 38 (repealed) |  |
| *Article 22 (moved)* | Article 30 | Article 39 (repealed) |  |
| *Article 23 (moved)* | Article 31 | Article 40 (replaced)[24] | *Article 20* |
| Article 16 | Article 32 | Article 40 A (replaced)[1] | *Article 20* |
| Article 17 (moved) | *Article 42* | Article 40 B (replaced)[1] | *Article 20* |
| Article 18 | Article 33 | Article 41 (repealed) |  |
| Article 19 | Article 34 | Article 42 (repealed) |  |
| Article 20 | Article 35 |  |  |
| Article 21 | Article 36 | **TITLE VII (replaced)[25]** | *TITLE IV* |
| Article 22 (moved) | *Article 30* | Article 43 (replaced)[2] | *Article 20* |
| Article 23 (moved) | *Article 31* | Article 43 A (replaced)[2] | *Article 20* |
| Article 24 | Article 37 | Article 43 B (replaced)[2] | *Article 20* |
| Article 25 | Article 38 | Article 44 (replaced)[2] | *Article 20* |
|  | Article 39 | Article 44 A (replaced)[2] | *Article 20* |
| *Article 47 (moved)* | Article 40 | Article 45 (replaced)[2] | *Article 20* |
| Article 26 (repealed) |  | **TITRE VIII** | **TITLE VI** |
| Article 27 (repealed) |  | Article 46 (repealed) |  |
| Article 27a (replaced)[16] | *Article 20* |  | Article 47 |
| Article 27b (replaced)[1] | *Article 20* | Article 47 (replaced) | *Article 40* |
| Article 27c (replaced)[1] | *Article 20* | Article 48 | Article 48 |
| Article 27d (replaced)[1] | *Article 20* | Article 49 | Article 49 |
| Article 27e (replaced)[1] | *Article 20* |  | Article 50 |
| Article 28 | Article 41 |  | Article 51 |
|  | Section 2 |  | Article 52 |
| *Article 17 (moved)* | Article 42 | Article 50 (repealed) |  |
|  | Article 43 | Article 51 | Article 53 |
|  | Article 44 | Article 52 | Article 54 |
|  |  | Article 53 | Article 55 |

[16] The current Articles 27a to 27e, on enhanced cooperation, are also replaced by Articles 326 to 334 TFEU.

[17] The current provisions of Title VI of the TEU, on police and judicial cooperation in criminal matters, are replaced by the provisions of Chapters 1, 5 and 5 of Title IV of Part Three of the TFEU.

[18] Replaced by Article 67 TFEU.

[19] Replaced by Articles 87 and 88 TFEU.

[20] Replaced by Articles 82, 83 and 85 TFEU.

[21] Replaced by Article 89 TFEU.

[22] Replaced by Article 72 TFEU.

[23] Replaced by Article 71 TFEU.

[24] The current Articles 40 to 40 B TEU, on enhanced cooperation, are also replaced by Articles 326 to 334 TFEU.

[25] The current Articles 43 to 45 and Title VII of the TEU, on enhanced cooperation, are also replaced by Articles 326 to 334 TFEU.

# TREATY ON THE FUNCTIONING OF THE EUROPEAN UNION

| Old numbering of the Treaty establishing the European Community | New numbering of the Treaty on the Functioning of the European Union | Old numbering of the Treaty establishing the European Community | New numbering of the Treaty on the Functioning of the European Union |
|---|---|---|---|
| PART ONE | PART ONE | Article 17 | Article 20 |
| Article 1 (repealed) | | Article 18 | Article 21 |
| | Article 1 | Article 19 | Article 22 |
| Article 2 (repealed)[26] | | Article 20 | Article 23 |
| | Title I—Categories and areas of union competence | Article 21 | Article 24 |
| | | Article 22 | Article 25 |
| | Article 2 | PART THREE | PART THREE |
| | Article 3 | | Title I—The internal market |
| | Article 4 | | |
| | Article 5 | *Article 14 (moved)* | Article 26 |
| | Article 6 | *Article 15 (moved)* | Article 27 |
| | Title II | Title I—Free movement of goods | Title II—Free movement of goods |
| | Article 7 | | |
| Article 3, paragraph 1 (repealed)[27] | | Article 23 | Article 28 |
| | | Article 24 | Article 29 |
| Article 3, paragraph 2 | Article 8 | Chapter 1—The customs union | Chapter 1—The customs union |
| Article 4 (moved) | *Article 119* | | |
| Article 5 (replaced)[28] | | Article 25 | Article 30 |
| | Article 9 | Article 26 | Article 31 |
| | Article 10 | Article 27 | Article 32 |
| Article 6 | Article 11 | *Part Three, Title X, Customs cooperation (moved)* | Chapter 2—Customs cooperation |
| *Article 153, paragraph 2 (moved)* | Article 12 | | |
| | Article 132[9] | *Article 135 (moved)* | Article 33 |
| Article 7 (repealed)[30] | | Chapter 2 | Chapter 3 |
| Article 8 (repealed)[31] | | Article 28 | Article 34 |
| Article 9 (repealed) | | Article 29 | Article 35 |
| Article 10 (repealed)[32] | | Article 30 | Article 36 |
| Article 11 (replaced)[33] | *Articles 326 to 334* | Article 31 | Article 37 |
| Article 11a (replaced)[1] | *Articles 326 to 334* | Title II | Title III |
| Article 12 (repealed) | *Article 18* | Article 32 | Article 38 |
| Article 13 (moved) | *Article 19* | Article 33 | Article 39 |
| Article 14 (moved) | *Article 26* | Article 34 | Article 40 |
| Article 15 (moved) | *Article 27* | Article 35 | Article 41 |
| Article 16 | Article 14 | Article 36 | Article 42 |
| *Article 255 (moved)* | Article 15 | Article 37 | Article 43 |
| *Article 286 (moved)* | Article 16 | Article 38 | Article 44 |
| | Article 17 | Title III | Title IV |
| PART TWO | PART TWO | Chapter 1 | Chapter 1 |
| *Article 12 (moved)* | Article 18 | Article 39 | Article 45 |
| *Article 13 (moved)* | Article 19 | Article 40 | Article 46 |

[26] Replaced, in substance, by Article 3 TEU.

[27] Replaced, in substance, by Articles 3 to 6 TFEU.     28  Replaced, in substance, by Article 5 TEU.

[29] Insertion of the operative part of the protocol on protection and welfare of animals.

[30] Replaced, in substance, by Article 13 TEU.

[31] Replaced, in substance, by Article 13 TEU and Article 282, paragraph 1, TFEU.

[32] Replaced, in substance, by Article 4, paragraph 3, TEU.

[33] Also replaced by Article 20 TEU.

| Old numbering of the Treaty establishing the European Community | New numbering of the Treaty on the Functioning of the European Union |
| --- | --- |
| Article 41 | Article 47 |
| Article 42 | Article 48 |
| Chapter 2 | Chapter 2 |
| Article 43 | Article 49 |
| Article 44 | Article 50 |
| Article 45 | Article 51 |
| Article 46 | Article 52 |
| Article 47 | Article 53 |
| Article 48 | Article 54 |
| Article 294 (moved) | Article 55 |
| Chapter 3 | Chapter 3 |
| Article 49 | Article 56 |
| Article 50 | Article 57 |
| Article 51 | Article 58 |
| Article 52 | Article 59 |
| Article 53 | Article 60 |
| Article 54 | Article 61 |
| Article 55 | Article 62 |
| Chapter 4 | Chapter 4 |
| Article 56 | Article 63 |
| Article 57 | Article 64 |
| Article 58 | Article 65 |
| Article 59 | Article 66 |
| Article 60 (moved) | Article 75 |
| **Title IV** | **Title V** |
|  | Chapter 1 |
| Article 61 | Article 67[34] |
|  | Article 68 |
|  | Article 69 |
|  | Article 70 |
|  | Article 71[35] |
| Article 64, paragraph 1 (replaced) | Article 72[36] |
|  | Article 73 |
| Article 66 (replaced) | Article 74 |
| Article 60 (moved) | Article 75 |
|  | Article 76 |
|  | Chapter 2 |
| Article 62 | Article 77 |
| Article 63, points 1 et 2, and Article 64, paragraph 2[37] | Article 78 |
| Article 63, points 3 and 4 | Article 79 |
|  | Article 80 |
| Article 64, paragraph 1 (replaced) | Article 72 |
|  | Chapter 3 |

| Old numbering of the Treaty establishing the European Community | New numbering of the Treaty on the Functioning of the European Union |
| --- | --- |
|  | Article 70 |
|  | Article 71[35] |
| Article 64, paragraph 1 (replaced) | Article 72[36] |
|  | Article 73 |
| Article 66 (replaced) | Article 74 |
| Article 60 (moved) | Article 75 |
|  | Article 76 |
|  | Chapter 2 |
| Article 62 | Article 77 |
| Article 63, points 1 et 2, and Article 64, paragraph 2[37] | Article 78 |
| Article 63, points 3 and 4 | Article 79 |
|  | Article 80 |
| Article 64, paragraph 1 (replaced) | Article 72 |
|  | Chapter 3 |
| Article 65 | Article 81 |
| Article 66 (replaced) | Article 74 |
| Article 67 (repealed) |  |
| Article 68 (repealed) |  |
| Article 69 (repealed) |  |
|  | Chapter 4 |
|  | Article 82[38] |
|  | Article 83[2] |
|  | Article 84 |
|  | Article 85[2] |
|  | Article 86 |
|  | Chapter 5 |
|  | Article 87[39] |
|  | Article 88[3] |
|  | Article 89[40] |
| **Title V** | **Title VI** |
| Article 70 | Article 90 |
| Article 71 | Article 91 |
| Article 72 | Article 92 |
| Article 73 | Article 93 |
| Article 74 | Article 94 |
| Article 75 | Article 95 |
| Article 76 | Article 96 |
| Article 77 | Article 97 |
| Article 78 | Article 98 |
| Article 79 | Article 99 |
| Article 80 | Article 100 |

[34] Also replaces the current Article 29 TEU.    [35] Also replaces the current Article 36 TEU.

[36] Also replaces the current Article 33 TEU.

[37] Points 1 and 2 of Article 63 EC are replaced by paragraphs 1 and 2 of Article 78 TFEU, and paragraph 2 of Article 64 is replaced by paragraph 3 of Article 78 TFEU.

[38] Replaces the current Article 31 TEU.    [39] Replaces the current Article 30 TEU.

[40] Replaces the current Article 32 TEU.

| Old numbering of the Treaty establishing the European Community | New numbering of the Treaty on the Functioning of the European Union | Old numbering of the Treaty establishing the European Community | New numbering of the Treaty on the Functioning of the European Union |
|---|---|---|---|
| Title VI | Title VII | Article 112 (moved) | Article 283 |
| Chapter 1 | Chapter 1 | Article 113 (moved) | Article 284 |
| Section 1 | Section 1 | Article 114 | Article 134 |
| Article 81 | Article 101 | Article 115 | Article 135 |
| Article 82 | Article 102 | | Chapter 4 |
| Article 83 | Article 103 | | Article 136 |
| Article 84 | Article 104 | | Article 137 |
| Article 85 | Article 105 | | |
| Article 86 | Article 106 | Article 111, paragraph 4 (moved) | Article 138 |
| Section 2 | Section 2 | Chapter 4 | Chapter 5 |
| Article 87 | Article 107 | Article 116 (repealed) | |
| Article 88 | Article 108 | | Article 139 |
| Article 89 | Article 109 | Article 117, paragraphs 1, 2, sixth indent, and 3 to 9 (repealed) | |
| Chapter 2 | Chapter 2 | | |
| Article 90 | Article 110 | | |
| Article 91 | Article 111 | Article 117, paragraph 2, first five indents (moved) | Article 141, paragraph 2 |
| Article 92 | Article 112 | | |
| Article 93 | Article 113 | Article 121, paragraph 1 (moved) | |
| Chapter 3 | Chapter 3 | Article 122, paragraph 2, second sentence (moved) | Article 140[41] |
| Article 95 (moved) | Article 114 | | |
| Article 94 (moved) | Article 115 | Article 123, paragraph 5 (moved) | |
| Article 96 | Article 116 | | |
| Article 97 | Article 117 | Article 118 (repealed) | |
| | Article 118 | Article 123, paragraph 3 (moved) | Article 141[42] |
| Title VII | Title VIII | | |
| Article 4 (moved) | Article 119 | Article 117, paragraph 2, first five indents (moved) | |
| Chapter 1 | Chapter 1 | Article 124, paragraph 1 (moved) | Article 142 |
| Article 98 | Article 120 | | |
| Article 99 | Article 121 | Article 119 | Article 143 |
| Article 100 | Article 122 | Article 120 | Article 144 |
| Article 101 | Article 123 | Article 121, paragraph 1 (moved) | Article 140, paragraph 1 |
| Article 102 | Article 124 | | |
| Article 103 | Article 125 | Article 121, paragraphs 2 to 4 (repealed) | |
| Article 104 | Article 126 | | |
| Chapter 2 | Chapter 2 | Article 122, paragraphs 1, 2, first sentence, 3, 4, 5 and 6 (repealed) | |
| Article 105 | Article 127 | | |
| Article 106 | Article 128 | | |
| Article 107 | Article 129 | Article 122, paragraph 2, second sentence (moved) | Article 140, paragraph 2, first subparagraph |
| Article 108 | Article 130 | | |
| Article 109 | Article 131 | Article 123, paragraphs 1, 2 and 4 (repealed) | |
| Article 110 | Article 132 | | |
| Article 111, paragraphs 1 to 3 and 5 (moved) | Article 219 | Article 123, paragraph 3 (moved) | Article 141, paragraph 1 |
| Article 111, paragraph 4 (moved) | Article 138 | Article 123, paragraph 5 (moved) | Article 140, paragraph 3 |
| | Article 133 | Article 124, paragraph 1 (moved) | Article 142 |
| Chapter 3 | Chapter 3 | | |

[41] – Article 140, paragraph 1 takes over the wording of paragraph 1 of Article 121.
  – Article 140, paragraph 2 takes over the second sentence of paragraph 2 of Article 122.
  – Article 140, paragraph 3 takes over paragraph 5 of Article 123.
[42] – Article 141, paragraph 1 takes over paragraph 3 of Article 123.
  – Article 141, paragraph 2 takes over the first five indents of paragraph 2 of Article 117.

| Old numbering of the Treaty establishing the European Community | New numbering of the Treaty on the Functioning of the European Union |
| --- | --- |
| Article 124, paragraph 2 (repealed) | |
| **Title VIII** | **Title IX** |
| Article 125 | Article 145 |
| Article 126 | Article 146 |
| Article 127 | Article 147 |
| Article 128 | Article 148 |
| Article 129 | Article 149 |
| Article 130 | Article 150 |
| **Title IX—(moved)** | *Part Five, Title II, common commercial policy* |
| Article 131 (moved) | *Article 206* |
| Article 132 (repealed) | |
| Article 133 (moved) | *Article 207* |
| Article 134 (repealed) | |
| **Title X (moved)** | *Part Three, Title II, Chapter 2* |
| Article 135 (moved) | *Article 33* |
| **Title XI** | **Title X** |
| Chapter 1 (repealed) | |
| Article 136 | Article 151 |
| | Article 152 |
| Article 137 | Article 153 |
| Article 138 | Article 154 |
| Article 139 | Article 155 |
| Article 140 | Article 156 |
| Article 141 | Article 157 |
| Article 142 | Article 158 |
| Article 143 | Article 159 |
| Article 144 | Article 160 |
| Article 145 | Article 161 |
| Chapter 2 | **Title XI** |
| Article 146 | Article 162 |
| Article 147 | Article 163 |
| Article 148 | Article 164 |
| Chapter 3 | **Title XII** |
| Article 149 | Article 165 |
| Article 150 | Article 166 |
| **Title XII** | **Title XIII** |
| Article 151 | Article 167 |
| **Title XIII** | **Title XIV** |
| Article 152 | Article 168 |
| **Title XIV** | **Title XV** |
| Article 153, paragraphs 1, 3, 4 and 5 | Article 169 |
| Article 153, paragraph 2 (moved) | *Article 12* |

| Old numbering of the Treaty establishing the European Community | New numbering of the Treaty on the Functioning of the European Union |
| --- | --- |
| **Title XV** | **Title XVI** |
| Article 154 | Article 170 |
| Article 155 | Article 171 |
| Article 156 | Article 172 |
| **Title XVI** | **Title XVII** |
| Article 157 | Article 173 |
| **Title XVII** | **Title XVIII** |
| Article 158 | Article 174 |
| Article 159 | Article 175 |
| Article 160 | Article 176 |
| Article 161 | Article 177 |
| Article 162 | Article 178 |
| **Title XVIII** | **Title XIX** |
| Article 163 | Article 179 |
| Article 164 | Article 180 |
| Article 165 | Article 181 |
| Article 166 | Article 182 |
| Article 167 | Article 183 |
| Article 168 | Article 184 |
| Article 169 | Article 185 |
| Article 170 | Article 186 |
| Article 171 | Article 187 |
| Article 172 | Article 188 |
| | Article 189 |
| Article 173 | Article 190 |
| **Title XIX** | **Title XX** |
| Article 174 | Article 191 |
| Article 175 | Article 192 |
| Article 176 | Article 193 |
| | **Title XXI** |
| | Article 194 |
| | **Title XXII** |
| | Article 195 |
| | **Title XXIII** |
| | Article 196 |
| | Title XXIV |
| | Article 197 |
| **Title XX (moved)** | *Part Five, Title III, Chapter 1* |
| Article 177 (moved) | *Article 208* |
| Article 178 (repealed)[43] | |
| Article 179 (moved) | *Article 209* |
| Article 180 (moved) | *Article 210* |
| Article 181 (moved) | *Article 211* |
| **Title XXI (moved)** | *Part Five, Title III, Chapter 2* |
| Article 181a (moved) | *Article 212* |

[43] Replaced, in substance, by the second sentence of the second subparagraph of paragraph 1 of Article 208 TFUE.

| Old numbering of the Treaty establishing the European Community | New numbering of the Treaty on the Functioning of the European Union | Old numbering of the Treaty establishing the European Community | New numbering of the Treaty on the Functioning of the European Union |
|---|---|---|---|
| **PART FOUR** | **PART FOUR** | **PART FIVE** | **PART SIX** |
| Article 182 | Article 198 | Title I | Title I |
| Article 183 | Article 199 | Chapter 1 | Chapter 1 |
| Article 184 | Article 200 | Section 1 | Section 1 |
| Article 185 | Article 201 | Article 189 (repealed)[45] | |
| Article 186 | Article 202 | Article 190, paragraphs 1 to 3 (repealed)[46] | |
| Article 187 | Article 203 | Article 190, paragraphs 4 and 5 | Article 223 |
| Article 188 | Article 204 | | |
| | **PART FIVE** | Article 191, first paragraph (repealed)[47] | |
| | **Title I** | Article 191, second paragraph | Article 224 |
| | Article 205 | Article 192, first paragraph (repealed)[48] | |
| *Part Three, Title IX (moved)* | **Title II** | Article 192, second paragraph | Article 225 |
| *Article 131 (moved)* | Article 206 | Article 193 | Article 226 |
| *Article 133 (moved)* | Article 207 | Article 194 | Article 227 |
| | **Title III** | Article 195 | Article 228 |
| *Part Three, Title XX (moved)* | Chapter 1 | Article 196 | Article 229 |
| *Article 177 (moved)* | Article 208[44] | Article 197, first paragraph (repealed)[49] | |
| *Article 179 (moved)* | Article 209 | Article 197, second, third and fourth paragraphs | Article 230 |
| *Article 180 (moved)* | Article 210 | Article 198 | Article 231 |
| *Article 181 (moved)* | Article 211 | Article 199 | Article 232 |
| *Part Three, Title XXI (moved)* | Chapter 2 | Article 200 | Article 233 |
| *Article 181a (moved)* | Article 212 | Article 201 | Article 234 |
| | Article 213 | | Section 2 |
| | Chapter 3 | | Article 235 |
| | Article 214 | | Article 236 |
| | **Title IV** | Section 2 | Section 3 |
| *Article 301 (replaced)* | Article 215 | Article 202 (repealed)[50] | |
| | **Title V** | Article 203 (repealed)[51] | |
| | Article 216 | Article 204 | Article 237 |
| *Article 310 (moved)* | Article 217 | Article 205, paragraphs 2 and 4 (repealed)[52] | |
| *Article 300 (replaced)* | Article 218 | Article 205, paragraphs 1 and 3 | Article 238 |
| *Article 111, paragraphs 1 to 3 and 5 (moved)* | Article 219 | Article 206 | Article 239 |
| | **Title VI** | Article 207 | Article 240 |
| *Articles 302 to 304 (replaced)* | Article 220 | Article 208 | Article 241 |
| | Article 221 | | |
| | **Title VII** | | |
| | Article 222 | | |

---

[44] The second sentence of the second subparagraph of paragraph 1 replaces, in substance, Article 178 TEC.

[45] Replaced, in substance, by Article 14, paragraphs 1 and 2, TEU.

[46] Replaced, in substance, by Article 14, paragraphs 1 to 3, TEU.

[47] Replaced, in substance, by Article 11, paragraph 4, TEU.

[48] Replaced, in substance, by Article 14, paragraph 1, TEU.

[49] Replaced, in substance, by Article 14, paragraph 4, TEU.

[50] Replaced, in substance, by Article 16, paragraph 1, TEU and by Articles 290 and 291 TFEU.

[51] Replaced, in substance, by Article 16, paragraphs 2 and 9 TEU.

[52] Replaced, in substance, by Article 16, paragraphs 4 and 5 TEU.

| Old numbering of the Treaty establishing the European Community | New numbering of the Treaty on the Functioning of the European Union | Old numbering of the Treaty establishing the European Community | New numbering of the Treaty on the Functioning of the European Union |
|---|---|---|---|
| Article 209 | Article 242 | Article 236 | Article 270 |
| Article 210 | Article 243 | Article 237 | Article 271 |
| Section 3 | Section 4 | Article 238 | Article 272 |
| Article 211 (repealed)[53] | | Article 239 | Article 273 |
| | Article 244 | Article 240 | Article 274 |
| Article 212 (moved) | *Article 249, paragraph 2* | | Article 275 |
| | | | Article 276 |
| Article 213 | Article 245 | Article 241 | Article 277 |
| Article 214 (repealed)[54] | | Article 242 | Article 278 |
| Article 215 | Article 246 | Article 243 | Article 279 |
| Article 216 | Article 247 | Article 244 | Article 280 |
| Article 217, paragraphs 1, 3 and 4 (repealed)[55] | | Article 245 | Article 281 |
| | | | Section 6 |
| Article 217, paragraph 2 | Article 248 | | Article 282 |
| Article 218, paragraph 1 (repealed)[56] | | *Article 112 (moved)* | Article 283 |
| | | *Article 113 (moved)* | Article 284 |
| Article 218, paragraph 2 | Article 249 | Section 5 | Section 7 |
| Article 219 | Article 250 | Article 246 | Article 285 |
| Section 4 | Section 5 | Article 247 | Article 286 |
| Article 220 (repealed)[57] | | Article 248 | Article 287 |
| Article 221, first paragraph (repealed)[58] | | Chapter 2 | Chapter 2 |
| | | | Section 1 |
| Article 221, second and third paragraphs | Article 251 | Article 249 | Article 288 |
| | | | Article 289 |
| Article 222 | Article 252 | | Article 290[60] |
| Article 223 | Article 253 | | Article 291[1] |
| Article 224[59] | Article 254 | | Article 292 |
| | Article 255 | | Section 2 |
| Article 225 | Article 256 | Article 250 | Article 293 |
| Article 225a | Article 257 | Article 251 | Article 294 |
| Article 226 | Article 258 | Article 252 (repealed) | |
| Article 227 | Article 259 | | Article 295 |
| Article 228 | Article 260 | Article 253 | Article 296 |
| Article 229 | Article 261 | Article 254 | Article 297 |
| Article 229a | Article 262 | | Article 298 |
| Article 230 | Article 263 | Article 255 (moved) | *Article 15* |
| Article 231 | Article 264 | Article 256 | Article 299 |
| Article 232 | Article 265 | | Chapter 3 |
| Article 233 | Article 266 | | Article 300 |
| Article 234 | Article 267 | Chapter 3 | Section 1 |
| Article 235 | Article 268 | Article 257 (repealed)[61] | |
| | Article 269 | | |

[53]  Replaced, in substance, by Article 17, paragraph 1 TEU.

[54]  Replaced, in substance, by Article 17, paragraphs 3 and 7 TEU.

[55]  Replaced, in substance, by Article 17, paragraph 6, TEU.

[56]  Replaced, in substance, by Article 295 TFEU.

[57]  Replaced, in substance, by Article 19 TEU.

[58]  Replaced, in substance, by Article 19, paragraph 2, first subparagraph, of the TEU.

[59]  The first sentence of the first subparagraph is replaced, in substance, by Article 19, paragraph 2, second subparagraph of the TEU.

[60]  Replaces, in substance, the third indent of Article 202 TEC.

[61]  Replaced, in substance, by Article 300, paragraph 2 of the TFEU.

| Old numbering of the Treaty establishing the European Community | New numbering of the Treaty on the Functioning of the European Union | Old numbering of the Treaty establishing the European Community | New numbering of the Treaty on the Functioning of the European Union |
|---|---|---|---|
| Article 258, first, second and fourth paragraphs | Article 301 | Article 280 | Article 325 Title III |
| Article 258, third paragraph (repealed)[62] | | *Articles 11 and 11a (replaced)* | Article 326[65] |
| Article 259 | Article 302 | *Articles 11 and 11a (replaced)* | Article 327[1] |
| Article 260 | Article 303 | | |
| Article 261 (repealed) | | *Articles 11 and 11a (replaced)* | Article 328[1] |
| Article 262 | Article 304 | | |
| Chapter 4 | Section 2 | *Articles 11 and 11a (replaced)* | Article 329[1] |
| Article 263, first and fifth paragraphs (repealed)[63] | | *Articles 11 and 11a (replaced)* | Article 330[1] |
| Article 263, second to fourth paragraphs | Article 305 | *Articles 11 and 11a (replaced)* | Article 331[1] |
| Article 264 | Article 306 | *Articles 11 and 11a (replaced)* | Article 332[1] |
| Article 265 | Article 307 | | |
| Chapter 5 | Chapter 4 | *Articles 11 and 11a (replaced)* | Article 333[1] |
| Article 266 | Article 308 | | |
| Article 267 | Article 309 | *Articles 11 and 11a (replaced)* | Article 334[1] |
| **Title II** | **Title II** | **PART SIX** | **PART SEVEN** |
| Article 268 | Article 310 | Article 281 (repealed)[66] | |
| | Chapter 1 | Article 282 | Article 335 |
| Article 269 | Article 311 | Article 283 | Article 336 |
| Article 270 (repealed)[64] | | Article 284 | Article 337 |
| | Chapter 2 | Article 285 | Article 338 |
| | Article 312 | Article 286 (replaced) | *Article 16* |
| | Chapter 3 | Article 287 | Article 339 |
| *Article 272, paragraph 1 (moved)* | Article 313 | Article 288 | Article 340 |
| Article 271 (moved) | *Article 316* | Article 289 | Article 341 |
| Article 272, paragraph 1 (moved) | *Article 313* | Article 290 | Article 342 |
| | | Article 291 | Article 343 |
| Article 272, paragraphs 2 to 10 | Article 314 | Article 292 | Article 344 |
| Article 273 | Article 315 | Article 293 (repealed) | |
| *Article 271 (moved)* | Article 316 | Article 294 (moved) | *Article 55* |
| | Chapter 4 | Article 295 | Article 345 |
| Article 274 | Article 317 | Article 296 | Article 346 |
| Article 275 | Article 318 | Article 297 | Article 347 |
| Article 276 | Article 319 | Article 298 | Article 348 |
| | Chapter 5 | Article 299, paragraph 1 (repealed)[67] | |
| Article 277 | Article 320 | | |
| Article 278 | Article 321 | Article 299, paragraph 2, second, third and fourth subparagraphs | Article 349 |
| Article 279 | Article 322 | | |
| | Article 323 | Article 299, paragraph 2, first subparagraph, and paragraphs 3 to 6 (moved) | *Article 355* |
| | Article 324 | | |
| | Chapter 6 | | |

[62] Replaced, in substance, by Article 300, paragraph 4 of the TFEU.

[63] Replaced, in substance, by Article 300, paragraphs 3 and 4, TFEU.

[64] Replaced, in substance, by Article 310, paragraph 4, TFEU.

[65] Also replaces the current Articles 27a to 27e, 40 to 40b, and 43 to 45 TEU.

[66] Replaced, in substance, by Article 47 TEU.     [67] Replaced, in substance by Article 52 TEU.

| Old numbering of the Treaty establishing the European Community | New numbering of the Treaty on the Functioning of the European Union | Old numbering of the Treaty establishing the European Community | New numbering of the Treaty on the Functioning of the European Union |
|---|---|---|---|
| Article 300 (replaced) | *Article 218* | Article 310 (moved) | *Article 217* |
| Article 301 (replaced) | *Article 215* | Article 311 (repealed)[68] | |
| Article 302 (replaced) | *Article 220* | *Article 299, paragraph 2, first subparagraph, and paragraphs 3 to 6 (moved)* | Article 355 |
| Article 303 (replaced) | *Article 220* | | |
| Article 304 (replaced) | *Article 220* | | |
| Article 305 (repealed) | | Article 312 | Article 356 |
| Article 306 | Article 350 | Final Provisions | |
| Article 307 | Article 351 | Article 313 | Article 357 |
| Article 308 | Article 352 | | Article 358 |
| | Article 353 | | |
| Article 309 | Article 354 | Article 314 (repealed)[69] | |

[68] Replaced, in substance by Article 51 TEU.          [69] Replaced, in substance by Article 55 TEU.

# ABBREVIATIONS

| | |
|---|---|
| ACT | Advance corporation tax |
| All ER | All England Law Reports |
| AFSJ | Area of freedom, security, and justice |
| AVMS | Audiovisual Media Services |
| BAA | British Airports Authority |
| BEPG | Broad economic guidelines |
| BVerfG | Bundesverfassungsgericht (German Federal Constitutional Court) |
| CCC | Customs Co-operation Council |
| CCM | Classic Community Method |
| CCP | Common Commercial Policy |
| CCT | Common Customs Tariff |
| CD | Customs Duties |
| CEEs | Charges having an equivalent effect to customs duties |
| CEN | *Comité européen de normalisation* |
| CENELEC | *Comité européen de normalisation électronique* |
| CFC | Controlled foreign company |
| Ch. | Reports from the Chancery Division of the English High Court of Justice |
| *CLJ* | *Cambridge Law Journal* |
| *CLP* | *Current Legal Problems* |
| *CM* | *Common Market* |
| CMLR | Common Market Law Reports |
| CMLRev. | Common Market Law Review |
| CN | Combined Nomenclature |
| CoOP | Country-of-origin principle |
| CPC | Community Patent Convention |
| CRD | Citizens' Rights Directive |
| CSA | Certain selling arrangements |
| CU | Customs Union |
| CUP | Cambridge University Press |
| *CYELS* | *Cambridge Yearbook of European Legal Studies* |
| Dec. | Decision |
| Dir. | Directive |
| DKr | Danish Kroner |
| DSU | Dispute Settlement Understanding (of the WTO) |
| *EBLRev.* | *European Business Law Review* |
| EC | European Communities |
| EC | BEuropean Central Bank |
| ECHR | European Convention on Human Rights and Fundamental Freedoms |

| | |
|---|---|
| ECtHR | European Court of Human Rights |
| *ECLR* | *European Competition Law Review* |
| ECR | European Court Reports |
| ECSC | European Coal and Steel Community (now defunct) |
| ECU | European Currency Unit |
| EEA | European Economic Area |
| *EFSA Journal* | European Food Safety Authority Journal |
| EFTA | European Free Trade Area |
| EFTA Ct Rep | European Free Trade Area Court Reports |
| *EIPR* | *European Intellectual Property Review* |
| *EIRR* | *European Industrial Relations Review* |
| *EJIL* | *European Journal of International Law* |
| *ELJ* | *European Law Journal* |
| *ELRev.* | *European Law Review* |
| EMI | European Monetary Institute |
| EMS | European Monetary System |
| EMU | Economic and Monetary Union |
| EP | European Parliament |
| *EPL* | *European Public Law* |
| ERM | Exchange Rate Mechanism |
| ERTA | European Road Transport Agreement |
| ESCB | European System of Central Banks |
| ESF | European Social Fund |
| ETA | The Basque terrorist organization |
| ETMR | European Trade Mark Reports |
| ETSI | European Telecommunications Standards Institute |
| EU | European Union |
| *EuZW* | *Europäische Zeitschrift für Wirtschaftsrecht* |
| EWC | European Works Council |
| EWCA Civ | The official individual numbering system for judgments delivered by the English Court of Appeal (Civil Division) |
| EWHC Admin | The official individual numbering system for judgments of the English High Court (Administrative Court) |
| FF | French Francs |
| *Fordham Intl LJ* | *Fordham International Law Journal* |
| FTA | Free Trade Area |
| FU | Full Union |
| GATS | General Agreement on Trade in Services |
| GATT | General Agreement on Tariffs and Trade |
| GDP | Gross domestic product |
| IGC | Inter-Governmental Conference |
| *ICLQ* | *International and Comparative Law Quarterly* |
| *ILJ* | *Industrial Law Journal* |
| IPRs | Intellectual Property Rights |

| | |
|---|---|
| IR | Irish Reports |
| *JCMS* | *Journal of Common Market Studies* |
| *JEPP* | *Journal of European Public Policy* |
| *J.L. Econ. & Org.* | *Journal of Law, Economics and Organization* |
| *J. Law and Soc.* | *Journal of Law and Society* |
| LIEI | Legal Issues of European Integration |
| LJIL | Leiden Journal of International Law |
| LQR | Law Quarterly Review |
| MCT | Mainstream corporation tax |
| MEEs | Measures of equivalent effect |
| MFN | Most Favoured Nation |
| MJ | Maastricht Journal |
| MLR | Modern Law Review |
| m.r. | Mandatory requirements |
| MU | Monetary Union |
| NAFTA | North American Free Trade Area |
| *NLJ* | *New Law Journal* |
| OJ | Official Journal of the EU |
| *OJLS* | *Oxford Journal of Legal Studies* |
| OMC | Open method of co-ordination |
| OUP | Oxford University Press |
| PIC | Prior informed consent |
| *PL* | *Public Law* |
| PU | Political Union |
| QB | Queen's Bench Division Reports |
| QMV | Qualified majority vote |
| QRs | Quantitative restrictions on trade |
| Reg. | Regulation |
| RIIA | Royal Institute of International Affairs |
| SE | Societas Europea |
| SEA | Single European Act |
| SGP | Stability and Growth Pact |
| TARIC | General Integrated Tariff of the European Communities |
| TCN | Third country national |
| TFEU | Treaty on the Functioning of the European Union |
| TWF | Television without Frontiers |
| VAT | Value Added Tax |
| WCO | World Customs Organization |
| WHO | World Health Organization |
| WLR | Weekly Law Reports |
| WTO | World Trade Organization |
| *YEEL* | *Yearbook of European Environmental Law* |
| *YEL* | *Yearbook of European Law* |

# LIST OF TABLES AND FIGURES

# PART I

# INTRODUCTION

# 1
# INTRODUCTION TO
# THE ISSUES

## A. INTRODUCTION

This book is about the free movement of goods, persons, services, and capital. It focuses principally on the rules interfering with movement from one Member State to another. To a lesser extent, it also examines the rules regulating those producers or people wishing to enter the European Union. The aim of this chapter is to place these rules in context. Why has the EU set about this policy of facilitating free movement? Who benefits, and who loses? What are the conditions necessary for free movement? And what is the ultimate objective of such policies? To begin with we start by examining the age-old question, why is free trade important? In the interests of maintaining the economic, political, and social integrity of the nation state, why not simply seal off national borders, keep out foreign goods, and protect national industries and national jobs?

## B. THE IMPORTANCE OF FREE TRADE

### 1. INTRODUCTION

The benefits of free trade can be summarized briefly—free trade allows for specialization, specialization leads to comparative advantage, and comparative advantage leads to economies of scale which maximize consumer welfare and ensure the most efficient use of worldwide resources. In his famous treatise on the *Wealth of Nations*, the classical economist Adam Smith noted, 'It is the maxim of every prudent master of a family, never to attempt to make at home what it will cost him more to make than to buy... What is prudence in the conduct of every private family, can scarce be folly in that of a great kingdom.'[1] Two hundred years later, the Leutwiler report,[2] prepared for GATT, reflected similar sentiments: '[a] farmer may know how to sew and a tailor may know how to raise chickens—but each can produce more by concentrating on doing what each can do most

---

[1] A. Smith, *The Wealth of Nations* originally published in 1776, Bk IV, Ch. II cited in P. Kenen, *The International Economy*, 4th edn (Cambridge: CUP, 2000), 9. Kenen himself says (at 20) that 'In a world of competitive markets, trade will occur and will be beneficial whenever there are international differences in relative costs of production.'

[2] The Leutwiler report of 1985 prepared for GATT, *Trade Policies for a Better Future: Proposals for Action* (Geneva: GATT, 1985), 23, cited in J. H. Jackson, *The World Trading System: Law and Policy of International Economic Relations*, 2nd edn (Cambridge, Mass.: MIT Press, 1997), 12.

efficiently'. Since trade allows countries to concentrate on what they can do best and, since no two countries are exactly alike in natural resources, climate, or workforce, those differences give each country a comparative advantage over the others in the same products.[3] Trade translates the individual advantages for many countries into maximum productivity for all.

## 2. THE THEORY OF COMPARATIVE ADVANTAGE

The theory of comparative advantage was developed by Ricardo in 1817,[4] using the example of wine and cloth production in the UK and Portugal. Jackson explains the operation of the model in the following terms.[5] In the UK it takes five hours of labour to produce a yard of cloth and ten hours a gallon of wine; in Portugal it takes ten hours of labour to produce a yard of cloth and six hours a gallon of wine. In these circumstances the UK has an *absolute* advantage in cloth production and Portugal has an *absolute* advantage in wine production. In the absence of trade (the so-called 'autarky' case), both countries will have to produce a mix of wine and cloth even though the UK is better at producing cloth and Portugal better at producing wine. Assuming an availability of 90 hours' labour then the total amount of wine and cloth produced in the UK and Poland is 13 yards of cloth and 14 gallons of wine. This is summarized in table 1.1.

**Table 1.1** Absolute advantage (autarky case)

|         | UK                         | Portugal                    | Total      |
| ------- | -------------------------- | --------------------------- | ---------- |
| Cloth   | 10 yds                     | 3 yds                       | 13 yds     |
|         | (10 × 5 hrs = 50 hrs)      | (3 × 10 hrs = 30 hrs)       |            |
| Wine    | 4 gallons                  | 10 gallons                  | 14 gallons |
|         | (4 × 10 hrs = 40 hrs)      | (10 × 6 hrs = 60 hrs)       |            |

However, if trade is opened up between the UK and Portugal (the so-called 'cosmopolitan case') and each state is allowed to specialize, then 18 yards of cloth and 15 gallons of wine can be produced, again assuming 90 hours of available labour (table.1.2).

**Table 1.2** Absolute advantage (cosmopolitan case)

|         | UK                         | Portugal                    | Total      |
| ------- | -------------------------- | --------------------------- | ---------- |
| Cloth   | 18 yds                     | 0 yds                       | 18 yds     |
|         | (18 × 5 hrs = 90 hrs)      |                             |            |
| Wine    | 0 gallons                  | 15 gallons                  | 15 gallons |
|         |                            | (15 × 6 hrs = 90 hrs)       |            |

---

[3] Ibid.

[4] D. Ricardo, *On the Principles of Political Economy and Taxation*, 3rd edn (London: John Murray, 1821), Ch. 7 with the definitive version appearing in P. Sraffa (ed.), *The Works and Correspondence of David Ricardo* (New York: CUP, 1953).

[5] This is taken from Jackson, above n. 2, 15. A more detailed analysis can be found in Kenen, above n. 1, 47–61.

From this we can see that specialization results in higher total productivity.

Even where one country has an absolute advantage in respect of *both* goods there is still an advantage in specialization. For example, if, in the UK, it takes five hours of labour to produce a yard of cloth and ten hours to produce a gallon of wine, while in Portugal it takes ten hours of labour to produce a yard of cloth and ten hours to produce a gallon of wine then, again assuming 90 hours of labour, table 1.3 shows production levels in the autarky case.

**Table 1.3** Comparative advantage (autarky case)

|  | UK | Portugal | Total |
|---|---|---|---|
| Cloth | 10 yds | 5 yds | 15 yds |
|  | (10 × 5 hrs = 50 hrs) | (5 × 10 hrs = 50 hrs) |  |
| Wine | 4 gallons | 4 gallons | 8 gallons |
|  | (4 × 10 hrs = 40 hrs) | (4 × 10 hrs = 40 hrs) |  |

If trade is opened up between the UK and Portugal then table 1.4 shows production levels in the cosmopolitan case.

**Table 1.4** Comparative advantage (cosmopolitan case)

|  | UK | Portugal | Total |
|---|---|---|---|
| Cloth | 18 yds | 0 yds | 18 yds |
|  | (18 × 5 hrs = 90 hrs) |  |  |
| Wine | 0 gallons | 9 gallons | 9 gallons |
|  |  | (9 × 10 hrs = 90 hrs) |  |

Even in the case of the UK having an absolute advantage in respect of both wine and cloth, there is an advantage for the two countries to trade if the *ratio* of production costs of the two products differs. Thus, in the second example, a gallon of wine in the UK costs two yards of cloth, whereas in Portugal it costs only one yard of cloth. It is therefore worthwhile for the UK to produce cloth and trade its excess for wine. Thus, as Jackson points out,[6] it is not the difference of absolute advantages but of comparative advantage that gives rise to gains from international trade.

These examples show that with specialization comes greater productivity and that ultimately free trade should lead to cheaper products for the British and Portuguese consumer and greater choice. If supply and demand can be brought into equilibrium, then *static* or *allocative* efficiency will be maximized (the wants or preferences of the various parties will have been satisfied to the greatest possible extent). Putting it another way, the welfare of consumers is maximized since they spend less of their

---

[6] Above n. 2, 16.

finite resources on buying the goods they need. At a micro-level, employment is secure for workers making cloth in the UK and wine in Portugal, with the important social consequences that ensue from this security. It also means that employers should put in place good terms and conditions of employment in order to retain a skilled workforce who can meet the demand for their products. Thus, social benefits will arise as a consequence of free trade.[7] Indeed, going beyond Ricardo, specialization, competition, and access to larger markets should bring the incentive to invest in production facilities and thus greater economies of scale.

The economic benefits of operating in a wider market were spelled out in the Spaak report drawn up by the heads of delegation to the foreign affairs ministers prior to the signing of the Treaty of Rome. They noted that in such a market it would no longer be possible to continue with out-dated modes of production which lead to high prices and low salaries. Instead of maintaining a static position, enterprises would be subject to a constant pressure to invest in order to develop production, improve quality, and modernize methods of exploitation. It would be necessary to progress to stand still.[8]

Free trade produces another consequence of great importance: the two nations, Portugal and the UK, are now dependent on each other for goods. The prosperity of the countries is enhanced, boosting the prospects for peace at home and also peace between the two trading nations: countries trading peacefully are less likely to go to war. This was Monnet's vision for the European Union.

## 3. THE PROBLEMS WITH THE BASIC MODEL

Ricardo's model is premised on a situation of perfect competition with no state intervention in the market. Economists make a number of assumptions about such markets:[9] buyers and sellers act rationally, are numerous, have full information about products on offer, can contract at little cost, have sufficient resources to transact, can enter and leave the market with little difficulty, and will carry out the obligations which they agree to perform. Under these assumptions market participants should continue to trade until no gains can be realized from further exchange. The distribution is *allocatively efficient*: assets are being employed in their most highly valued use.

Of course, the real world is not like this; the conditions of perfect competition do not exist in any market, not just transnational markets such as the EU's. For example, information failure, transaction costs, and the tendency of actors to shirk commitments are issues in all markets, albeit that the problems are exacerbated in the transnational context. However, there are certain problems which are associated with transnational markets which do not affect national markets in the same way. For example, national regulators tend to respond to local concerns, ignoring the external costs of their regulation, by generating trade barriers and granting inefficient subsidies. This can be seen in the following illustration.

---

[7] This was recognized in Art. 151 TFEU (ex Art. 136 EC) which provides that Member States believe that an improvement in working conditions 'will ensue not only from the functioning of the internal market...but also...from the approximation of provisions laid down by law, regulation or administrative action.'

[8] Author's translation of the Spaak report, Brussels, 21 Apr. 1956, Mae 120 f/56, 14.

[9] These are summarized by B. Cheffins, *Company Law: Theory, structure and operation* (Oxford: Clarendon Press, 1997), 6.

In the process of achieving allocative efficiency, some, if not all, British wine makers go out of business, as do Portuguese cloth makers. This is the politically and socially difficult face of any free trade regime. In a democratic society governments, needing to be re-elected, respond to public pressure about the actual or potential loss of domestic jobs caused by cheap imports. In the absence of any external restraining factor, they may put up trade barriers. So, under pressure from the Portuguese cloth industry, the Portuguese government might try to prevent the import of British cloth or at least limit the quantity of British cloth imported from the UK by issuing a limited number of import licences. These are quantitative restrictions on trade (QRs). Alternatively, the Portuguese government might lay down quality or other standards for the cloth sold in Portugal or it might allow Portuguese cloth producers to register a trade mark. Such steps are referred to as measures having an effect equivalent to quantitative restrictions (MEEs). These so-called non-tariff barriers (NTBs) may serve protectionist purposes (which would be condemned in a free trade regime) or they may further other, more legitimate, objectives such as consumer protection.

Any such action taken by the state might be reinforced by action taken by private parties: Portuguese cloth manufacturers might agree that they will supply cloth to wholesalers who agree to stock only Portuguese cloth. Such restrictions will inevitably reduce the gains from free trade.

The UK government might decide to retaliate by adopting fiscal measures designed to impede the import of Portuguese wine. It might impose customs duties (CDs) or other charges on the imported goods which have an equivalent effect to customs duties (CEEs). These tariff barriers would have the effect of making the Portuguese wine more expensive, as would taxing Portuguese wine at a higher rate than British wine or a rival product widely produced and consumed in the UK, such as beer. At the same time the Portuguese government might try to prop up its ailing domestic cloth industry by giving it large financial handouts (state aids) paid for by Portuguese taxpayers. It might also adopt a government purchasing policy based on the idea of buying national goods in preference to the cheaper imports. Once again, the taxpayer is footing the bill for a policy dictated not by economic efficiency but political necessity.

One way to remove such barriers is for the Portuguese and British governments to enter a bilateral agreement removing trade restrictions and requiring each Member State to recognize the goods produced by the other. If more states are involved, they might decide to set up a central institution to check that all participants are playing by the rules, a body whose decisions are binding on the national governments and take precedence over conflicting national laws. Ultimately, this body might begin to set the rules to deal with the problems of market failure which are specific to the transnational context. This then raises questions about the role of law in such an institutional arrangement and the legitimacy and accountability of the rule-making body. To maximize the benefits of free trade, such grouping needs to be global. The World Trade Organization (WTO) represents an important step in this direction. However, in the absence of global free trade, regional groupings (such as the EU) have formed which have tried to obtain the benefits of free trade from among a smaller number of states.[10] The classical thinking is that since worldwide free trade will

---

[10] This is recognized by Art. XXIV (8) of GATT.

maximize global welfare, so a smaller grouping must be the next best thing.[11] We turn now to consider what form these groupings might take.

## C.  THE DIFFERENT STAGES OF INTEGRATION

### 1.  INTRODUCTION

Economists have developed a number of labels to describe different levels of intensity of market integration (see Box 1).[12] Each of these forms of integration can be introduced in its own right; they are not necessarily stages in a process which eventually leads to full union.[13]

---

**Box 1**  DIFFERENT STAGES OF INTEGRATION[14]

- *Free Trade Area (FTA)*—Member States remove all impediments to free movement of goods among themselves but each state retains the autonomy to regulate its trading relations with non-Member States
- *Customs Union (CU)*—FTA + common external policy in respect of non-Member States (e.g., single customs tariff)
- *Common Market (CM)*—CU + free movement of persons, services, and capital
- *Monetary Union (MU)*—CM + single currency
- *Economic Union*—MU + single monetary and fiscal policy controlled by a central authority
- *Political Union (PU)*—Economic Union + central authority sets not only monetary and fiscal policies but is responsible to a central parliament with the sovereignty of a nation's government. Such a parliament might also set foreign and security policies
- *Full Union (FU)*—the complete unification of the economies involved and a common policy on matters such as social security, income tax.

---

We shall now consider where the EU fits into these stages of integration.

---

[11] This does not always occur if a Customs Union leads to trade diversion (replacement of cheaper imports from the outside world by more expensive imports from a partner): W. Molle, *The Economics of European Integration: Theory, Practice and Policy*, 5th edn (Aldershot: Dartmouth, 2006), 84.

[12] On the need to provide an economics analysis of issues of international trade, see R. Cass, 'Introduction: Economics and international law' in J. Bhandari and A. Sykes (eds.), *Economic Dimensions in International Law: Comparative and empirical perspectives* (Cambridge: CUP, 1997).

[13] A. El-Agraa, *The Economics of the European Community*, 4th edn (Hemel Hempstead: Harvester Wheatsheaf, 1994), 2.

[14] These stages are all derived from B. Balassa, *The Theory of Economic Integration* (London: Allen and Unwin, 1961). See also W. Molle, above n. 11, 10–11; P. VerLoren van Themaat, 'Some preliminary observations on the IGC: The relations between the concepts of a common market, a monetary union, an economic union, a political union and sovereignty' (1991) 28 *CMLRev.* 291.

## 2. FREE TRADE AREA AND CUSTOMS UNION

An FTA is characterized by a common internal policy (the free movement of goods between participating states) but different external policies (each state retains the competence to regulate trade with non-members). Loosely speaking, this describes the position in the European Free Trade Area (EFTA) and the North American Free Trade Area (NAFTA). The disadvantage of a free trade area is that goods coming from non-Member States will enter the area via the state with the most favourable trading regime (usually the one with the lowest tariffs) and then, taking advantage of the rules on free movement, benefit from the free circulation of its goods within the area.[15] A CU can overcome these problems. It is similar to an FTA internally but differs from an FTA externally because participating states have a common policy in respect of the non-members.

According to Article 28(1) TFEU (ex Article 23(1) EC), the EU comprises a CU where customs duties are prohibited between Member States and a common customs tariff (CCT) is adopted in respect of third countries. However, EU law has gone further than classical economic theory might expect by also prohibiting the use of non-tariff barriers, i.e. quantitative restrictions (QRs) which in welfare terms can be just as damaging to free trade without the revenue-producing benefits, and measures having equivalent effect (MEEs) (Articles 34–5 TFEU (ex Articles 28–9 EC)). The EU also prohibits anti-competitive behaviour by private actors which might attempt to resurrect barriers to trade which partition the market on national lines (Articles 101–2 TFEU (ex Articles 81–2 EC)), as well as state aids (Article 107 (ex Article 87 EC)).

## 3. COMMON MARKET, SINGLE MARKET, AND BEYOND

### 3.1 The Common Market

An FTA and a CU focus on the free movement of *products*. A common market allows for free movement of *production* factors (workers and capital) as well as products. The idea is that the liberalization of factors of production allows for the optimum allocation of labour and capital. If production factors are missing from a place where production would be most economical, entrepreneurs in a common market can shift their capital from places of low return to states which have more potential.[16] Similarly, labour can move from areas of high unemployment to areas of high employment. Ultimately this should lead to the equalization of prices.

This can be seen in the following example. Let's imagine that in Portugal labour is plentiful but capital is scarce and in the UK capital is plentiful but labour is scarce. Assuming that wine is relatively labour-intensive and cloth relatively capital-intensive, then wine will be cheaply produced in Portugal and cloth in the UK. In an FTA or CU, Portugal will export wine and the UK will export cloth. As we saw from table 1.2 above, Portugal will shift resources from the manufacture of cloth to wine while the UK will shift resources from the manufacture of wine to cloth. However, in a *common market* the

---

[15] This can be addressed in part through a system of certificates of origin. See, further, Molle, above n. 11, 10.

[16] Molle, above n. 11, 13.

goods *or* the factors of production can move. If the factors of production move then work-ers migrate from Portugal to the UK where they can earn more, and capital flows from the UK to Portugal. This will alter the relative scarcities of the two production factors in the UK and Portugal and thus equalize their prices.[17] This will reduce the cost differences between the two countries in the production of wine and cloth, thus removing the stimu-lus to trade in these goods.

This suggests that there is a relation of substitution between the movement of products and the movement of factors of production. Yet, as Molle points out, however interesting the results of substitution in theory, it is not very helpful for practical purposes, since its assumptions rarely hold good: markets are not characterized by perfect competition, fac-tors are not perfectly mobile, and countries are differently endowed with natural resources. Thus, it is more likely that free movement of products and free movement of production factors are *complements*, not substitutes. As we shall see, free movement of goods is par-ticularly important to the EU since in practice it is easier for goods to move to people than people to goods.

The creation of a common market lay at the heart of the European Community (now European Union) project. Article 2 EC (now repealed) said that the (then) Community had as its task the establishment of a common market (Article 3(3) TEU continues to provide that 'The Union shall establish an internal market' which is defined in Art. 26 TFEU), and one of the activities of the Community listed in Article 3 EC (now repealed) was the creation of 'an internal market characterized by the abolition, as between Member States, of obstacles to the free movement of goods, persons, services and capital'.

The detail of these four freedoms are found in specific Articles of the Treaty: Articles 34–5 TFEU on goods, Article 45 TFEU on workers, Article 49 TFEU on estab-lishment, Articles 56–7 TFEU on services, and Article 63 TFEU on capital. These Articles are based on the principle of *negative* integration—removing barriers to trade. As the Court put it in *Gaston Schul*,[18] the aim of the provisions of the Treaties is to eliminate 'all obstacles to intra-[Union] trade in order to merge the national markets into a single mar-ket bringing about conditions as close as possible to those of a genuine [domestic][19] market'.

### 3.2 The Single Market

By the mid 1980s Euro-sclerosis had set in and the failure of the common market was plain for all to see. In 1985 Jacques Delors, the president of the European Commission, responded with his ambitious plan for the single market.[20] A White Paper, *Completing the Internal Market*,[21] was drawn up under the direction of the British commissioner, Lord Cockfield, which focused on removing barriers which continued to prevent free

---

[17] Ibid., 169.

[18] Case 15/81 *Gaston Schul Douane Expediteur BV v. Inspecteur der Invoerrechten en Accijnzen, Roosendaal* [1982] ECR 1409, para. 33.

[19] The original quotation reads 'internal'. Earlier case law (e.g., Case 270/80 *Polydor* v. *Harlequin* [1982] ECR 329, para. 16) talks of 'domestic' market, and this term has been used for the sake of clarity.

[20] C. Grant, *Delors: Inside the house that Jacques built* (London: Nicholas Brealey Publishing, 1994), 66.

[21] COM(85)310. See H. Schmitt von Sydow, 'The basic strategies of the Commission's White Paper' in R. Bieber et al., *1992 One European Market? A critical analysis of the Commission's internal market strategy* (Baden-Baden: Nomos Verlagsgesellschaft, 1988).

movement.[22] It identified three principal obstacles to the completion of the single market:

- physical barriers to trade—e.g., intra-EU border stoppages, customs controls, and associated paperwork
- technical barriers to trade—e.g., meeting divergent national product standards adopted for health and safety reasons or for consumer and environmental protection, other technical regulations, conflicting business laws, entering nationally protected public procurement markets[23]
- fiscal barriers to trade—especially differing rates of VAT and excise duties.

The Cecchini Report on the Cost of Non-Europe[24] anticipated that the growth resulting from the single market would put between four and seven percentage points on the Union's domestic product and the creation of between two and five million new jobs.

The White Paper then identified 300 measures (the final count was actually 282) necessary to complete the single market. The Single European Act (SEA) 1986,[25] the first significant Treaty amendment after the Treaty of Rome, provided the necessary means to achieve these objectives. It introduced a new legal basis, Article 114 TFEU (ex Article 95 EC and originally Article 100a EEC), which provided for qualified majority voting when enacting measures for the approximation of Member States' laws which have as 'their object the establishment and functioning of the internal market'. While the original EEC Treaty had also envisaged a role for *positive integration* (harmonization) the legal bases provided, notably Articles 115 and 352 TFEU (ex Articles 94 and 308 EC), required unanimous voting in Council, and this hindered their utility as a means of adopting a large number of often controversial measures deemed necessary to complete the internal market. The introduction of Article 114 TFEU emphasized that the single market was essentially a law-making project. This raises the issue as to the type of (supranational) laws the EU requires. This question is considered in detail in Chapter 16.

The SEA also introduced Article 100b EEC into the Treaty of Rome which required the Commission, together with each Member State, to draw up an inventory of national measures which fell under Article 100a EEC (now Article 114 TFEU) and which had not been harmonized. The Council could then decide whether the provisions in force in a Member State could be recognized as being equivalent to those in another Member State. This power was not used and Article 100b was abolished by the Amsterdam Treaty.

---

[22] Lord Cockfield, *The European Union: Creating the single market* (Chichester: Wiley Chancery, 1994), 39.

[23] P. Cecchini, *The European Challenge 1992: The benefits of a single market* (Aldershot: Wildwood House, 1988), 4. These problems persist: see the Commission's Internal Market Package (COM(2007) 35) discussed in Ch. 4.

[24] Ibid., xvii–xviii.

[25] Much has been written on the background to the SEA—see, *inter alia*, P. Craig, 'The nature of the Community integration, democracy and legitimacy' in P. Craig and G. de Búrca (eds.), *The Evolution of EU Law* (Oxford, OUP, 1999). For critical comment on the SEA see P. Pescatore, 'Some critical remarks on the Single European Act' (1987) 24 *CMLRev.* 9: 'the implementation of the Act [represents]...on the whole a major setback for the European Communities...It...[would be] better for our future together...if we were to abandon this ill-fated experiment.' For a more positive reaction, see D. Edwards, 'The impact of the Single Act on the Institutions' (1987) 24 *CMLRev.* 19. See also J. De Zwann, 'The Single European Act: Conclusion of a unique document' (1986) 23 *CMLRev.* 747.

For presentation purposes, the SEA repackaged the four freedoms into the renamed 'internal' or 'single' market and, in Article 7a EEC (now Article 26 TFEU, ex Article 14 EC), set a new deadline by which they were to be achieved: 31 December 1992.[26] While the deadline was psychologically and politically significant,[27] it had no legal effect.[28] The name change, from 'common' to 'single' or 'internal' market, also had little effect. At first glance, the term 'single market' appears narrower than 'common market' because the single market is defined by reference only to the four freedoms while the common market combines the four freedoms with flanking measures such as agriculture, competition, and social matters. In reality, the realization of the single market was, and is, dependent on further policy action in an ever-wider range of fields, including competition and social policy.[29] For this reason it is likely that the terms common, single, and internal market are largely synonymous.[30]

Although the deadline for the completion of the single market was 1992, in fact the single market is not yet complete. As the Commission puts it, creating a genuinely integrated market is not a finite task, but rather an ongoing process, requiring constant effort, vigilance, and updating. With technological and political developments, the environment in which the single market functions is changing all the time. Although many obstacles have been removed, others come to light and will continue to do so[31] and need to be addressed. For this reason the realization of the single market is an ongoing project, not a historical artefact.

### 3.3 Area of Freedom, Security and Justice

The Amsterdam Treaty introduced a new concept, the area of freedom, security and justice (AFSJ). Article 67(1) TFEU says:

The Union shall constitute an area of freedom, security and justice with respect for fundamental rights and the different legal systems and traditions of the Member States.

---

[26] The deadline is merely noted in Case C–9/99 *Echirolles Distribution SA* v. *Association du Dauphiné* [2000] ECR I–8207. The deadline of 31 Dec. 1992 has been removed from Art. 26 TFEU. Article 26 remains significant for steering the interpretation of the four freedoms: Case C–102/09 *Camar* v. *Presidenza del Consiglio dei Ministri* [2010] ECR I–000, para. 33

[27] It represented the life span of two four-year Commissions. The original EC Customs Union was to be completed over three periods of four years. It was in fact completed in just over ten years in 1967.

[28] The declaration attached to the Article by the SEA said that the participants expressed their 'firm political will' to complete the internal market before 1 Jan. 1993 but that setting the date of 31 Dec. 1992 did not create 'an automatic legal effect'. See H. Schermers, 'The effect of the date 31 December 1992' (1991) 28 *CMLRev.* 275. See also A. Toth, 'The legal status of the declarations attached to the Single European Act' (1987) 24 *CMLRev.* 803. In Case C–378/97 *Criminal Proceedings against Wijsenbeek* [1999] ECR I–6207, para. 40, the Court observed that Art. 14 EC (now Art. 26 TFEU) could 'not be interpreted as meaning that, in the absence of measures adopted by the Council before 31 Dec. 1992 requiring the Member States to abolish controls of persons at the internal frontiers of the Community, that obligation automatically arises from expiry of that period'.

[29] The terminology of 'single market' has in fact been used by the Court since the early 1960s: e.g., Case 32/65 *Italy* v. *Council and Commission* [1966] ECR 389, 405; Case 15/81 *Gaston Schul* [1982] ECR 1409, para. 33.

[30] See P. Oliver and M. Jarvis, *Free Movement of Goods in the European Community*, 4th edn (London: Sweet and Maxwell, 2003). K. Mortelmans, 'The Common Market, the internal market and the single market, what's in a market?' (1998) 35 *CMLRev.* 101, 107. See also Tesauro AG in Case C–300/89 *Commission* v. *Council (titanium dioxide)* [1991] ECR I–2867: 'the concept of the "internal market" [is based] on that of the "common market"'.

[31] <http://www.ec.europa.eu/internal_market/top_layer/index_3_en.htm> and COM(2007)35, 6.

The rest of the Article explains the meaning of the three terms. 'Freedom' means the absence of *internal* border controls for persons and a common policy—on asylum, immigration, and external border control—in respect of third-country nationals (TCNs). 'Security' is about measures to prevent and combat crime, racism, and xenophobia, coordination and cooperation between police and judicial authorities and other competent authorities, as well as mutual recognition of judgments in criminal matters. Finally, the 'justice' element concerns access to justice, in particular through the principle of mutual recognition of judicial and extrajudicial decisions in civil matters.

The introduction of the AFSJ shows how the EU has undergone a shift from 'merely' establishing an internal market to creating an area of freedom, security, and justice which complements and overcomes the stages of economic integration defined in Box 1.[32] The elision between the two policy objectives can be seen in Article 3(2) TEU which talks of the EU maintaining and developing 'an area of freedom justice and security *without internal frontiers*'[33] in which 'the free movement of persons is ensured in conjunction with appropriate measures with respect to external border controls, asylum, immigration and the prevention and combating of crime'. The AFSJ is considered in more detail in Chapters 12 and 14.

## 4. ECONOMIC, MONETARY, AND POLITICAL UNION

The common market is at the heart of any economic, monetary, and political union. However, as Molle explains,[34] economic union also requires a high degree of coordination of economic policy, including macro-economic and monetary policies and possibly redistributive policies; while in a monetary union (MU) the currencies of the Member States are either linked through irrevocably fixed exchange rates and are fully convertible, or one common currency circulates in all Member States. Economic and monetary union combines the characteristics of economic union and monetary union and presupposes a high degree of coordination of macro-economic and budget policies. A political union (PU) goes further still, with integration extending beyond economics to include police, foreign policy, and security policy. Finally, the closest form of integration is full union (FU) which implies the 'complete unification' of the policies involved, and a common policy on such sensitive issues as social security and income tax. In these circumstances the situation of the union is virtually indistinguishable from that of a nation state.

The Maastricht Treaty provided the Union with the powers to achieve economic and monetary union. Chapter 1 of Title VIII TFEU concerns economic policy. It requires Member States to conduct their economic policies with a view to contributing to the achievement of the objectives of the Union[35] and in the context of the broad economic guidelines laid down annually by the Council.[36] Monetary policy is dealt with in Chapter 2 of Title VIII and applies to those countries which have satisfied the criteria for the single currency and have not opted out of the process. They are subject to the continuous duty of avoiding excessive government deficits[37] with the risk of being subject to a number of sanctions, including being fined. EMU is considered in greater detail in Chapter 15.

---

[32] S. Iglesias Sánchez, 'Free movement of third country nationals in the European Union? Main features, deficiencies and challenges of the new mobility rights in the area of freedom, security and justice' (2009) 15 *ELJ* 791, 795.　　　　　　　　　　　　　　　　　　　　　　　　[33] Emphasis added.
[34] Molle, above n. 11, 17.　　　[35] Art. 120 TFEU (ex Art. 98 EC).
[36] Art. 121 TFEU (ex Art. 99 EC).　　　[37] Art. 126 TFEU (ex Art. 104 EC).

The Lisbon Treaty shows the extent to which the EU is moving towards political union with the introduction of a Union minister for foreign affairs[38] as well as a president of the European Council,[39] together with expanding powers over matters such as police and judicial cooperation, areas which are no longer confined to the intergovernmental processes of the third pillar.[40] Yet, full union seems an unlikely prospect, with the Member States unwilling to hand over powers to the EU concerning such sensitive issues as foreign policy and key elements of the welfare state.

## D.  UNDERSTANDING THE INTEGRATION PROCESS

Neo-functionalists argue that there is a spillover from one type of integration to another.[41] In other words, if states integrated one sector of their economies, usually an area of low controversy (e.g., harmonization of technical standards), technical pressures would push them to integrate other sectors which are increasingly controversial (e.g., monetary and political union).[42] The following example illustrates this point.

Cutting Edge manufactures a successful range of lawnmowers in the UK. It wishes to break into new markets to sell more of its lawnmowers, with resulting benefits in terms of economies of scale. However, in order to sell on these new markets Cutting Edge needs to have both the right to export its goods from the UK without restriction and the right to import its lawnmowers into the new markets without fiscal or non-fiscal barriers to trade. It also needs to be able to promote and sell its lawnmowers in the host states without restriction. The provisions of the EU Treaties—especially Article 30 TFEU on customs duties, Article 110 TFEU on taxation, and Articles 34–5 TFEU on freedom to import and export—provide these rights.

Yet, removing barriers is not sufficient. Cutting Edge soon discovers that the levels of noise emission from lawnmowers permitted in France is lower than that in the UK. It is lower still in Germany. For Cutting Edge to sell on these markets, it has to redesign its lawnmower for each market unless and until there is mutual recognition by each state of the standards prescribed by the other states or a single harmonized standard is enacted by the EU. In fact, the EU has now used its powers under Article 114 TFEU (ex Article 95 EC) to enact a directive on 'the approximation of the laws of the Member States relating to the noise emission in the environment by equipment for use outdoors'.[43] However, Cutting

---

[38]  Art. 18 TEU. The formal title is High Representative of the Union for Foreign Affairs and Security policy.

[39]  Art. 15 TEU.

[40]  See Chapters IV and V of Title V TFEU.

[41]  See the path-breaking work of E. Haas, *The Uniting of Europe: Political, social and economic forces 1950-1957* (Stanford, Calif.: Stanford University Press, 1958) discussed in Craig, above n. 25. Supplementing the technical logic of functional spillover, neo-functionalists added the idea of political spillover. This involved the build-up of political pressures by interest groups, trade unions, and other actors to encourage further integration, with the Commission acting as a catalyst for these pressures.

[42]  See S. George, *Politics and Policy in the European Union*, 3rd edn (Oxford: OUP, 1996), 37; J. Lodge, 'Preface: The challenge of the future' in J. Lodge (ed.), *The European Community and the Challenge of the Future* (London: Pinter, 1993), xx–xxi; and B. Rosamond, *Theories of European Integration* (Basingstoke: Palgrave, 2000).

[43]  EP and Council Dir. 2000/14/EC ([2000] OJ L162/1).

Edge still needs a reliable and predictable application of these rules and an ability to enforce them in all Member States in which it wishes to trade.

Even with a harmonized standard, Cutting Edge is faced with the problem that currency fluctuations, often caused by governments using the exchange rate as a tool of economic policy, make it difficult for it to price its lawnmowers effectively. For Cutting Edge, a single currency and thus monetary union is the only solution. But monetary union makes it almost impossible for governments to control their national economies since they have lost an important tool to do so: devaluation. Thus monetary union creates strong pressure for economic union with economic policy being regulated centrally for the whole area of the common market.[44] As we have seen, for the Euro-zone countries, economic and monetary union has become a reality. This in turn creates pressure for a political union to ensure political accountability of the economic actors.

This example of Cutting Edge shows how the process of integration involves a gradual reduction in the power of national governments and a commensurate increase in the ability of the centre—i.e. the EU's supranational[45] institutions (the Commission and the Parliament)—to deal with sensitive, politically charged issues. It is the logic which lies at the heart of the so-called 'Monnet method'. For Jean Monnet, (neo-)functionalism meant the creation of a supranational regime or organization—i.e., one with joint or pooled authority (the High Authority and subsequently the Commission)—initially with power over the production of coal and steel, and subsequently over other economic sectors, thereby creating 'the first concrete foundations of the European Federation which is indispensable to the maintenance of peace'.[46] However, his objective of creating a European federation was to be achieved by stealth, combining a mixture of *dirigisme* (removing existing tariff and non-tariff barriers) with market forces.[47]

Some commentators argue that the evolution of the EU from merely a coal and steel community to a major economic and monetary union in a period of less than 50 years, suggests that neo-functionalism is the best explanation for the integration process. However, others reject functionalism as an adequate explanation for what is actually occurring in the EU. For Moravcsik, in his theory of liberal intergovernmentalism,[48] the role of the European Council is central to understanding the integration process. He says that integration proceeds as far and as fast as the governments of the Member States allow.[49] He said that the Single European Act 1986 was the product of inter-state bargaining between the British, French, and German governments and that traditional

---

[44] George, above n. 42, 38.

[45] R. Keohane and S. Hoffman ('Conclusions: Community politics and institutional choice' in W. Wallace (ed.), *The Dynamics of European Integration* (London: RIIA, 1990), 280 note that 'supranationality refers to a process of decision-making in which the participants refrain from unconditionally vetoing proposals and instead seek to attain agreement by means of compromises upgrading common interests'.

[46] M. Holland, *European Community Integration* (London, Pinter Publishers, 1993), 7 and 8, citing J. Monnet, *Memoirs*, trans. R. Mayne (New York: Doubleday and Company, 1978), 298. For a strong endorsement of this view, see the Preamble to the ECSC Treaty 'to substitute for age-old rivalries the merging of their essential interests; to create by establishing an economic community, the basis for a broader and deeper community among people long divided by bloody conflicts'. See, further, W. Wallace, 'Introduction: The dynamics of European integration' in W. Wallace (ed.), *The Dynamics of European Integration* (London: RIIA, 1990).   [47] Holland, above n. 46, 13.

[48] A. Moravcsik, 'Negotiating the Single European Act: National interests and conventional statecraft in the European Community' (1991) 45 *International Organisation* 19.

[49] George, above n. 42, 52.

tools of international statecraft, such as threats of exclusion and side payments, explained the final composition of the 1992 programme and the SEA 1986.[50]

Keohane and Hoffman try to reconcile these approaches. In their reformulation of neo-functionalism they recognize that successful intergovernmental bargaining is a pre-requisite to any form of spillover.[51] They note that, without a turnaround in French eco-nomic policy in 1983, and the decision of the British government to accept Treaty amendments to institutionalize deregulation, no consensus could have been reached on a programme to dismantle barriers in Europe.[52] Thus, spillover does not occur in a vacuum: it requires positive action on the part of the Member States.

These theories focus on the activities of states, but there is much more to the dynamic of European integration than states. Take, for example, the period leading up to the SEA 1986. While the involvement of the European Council was crucial in securing agree-ment on the objective of attaining the single market, in particular by resolving the issue of British budgetary contributions at the Fontainebleu summit in June 1984,[53] other institutions played a key role, especially the Commission. It was responsible for the Internal Market White Paper which placed much emphasis on the principle of mutual recognition which had been developed by the Court.[54] Within the Commission certain key individuals played a decisive role, in particular Lord Cockfield and Jacques Delors.[55] This convergence of events and actors provides a clear demonstration that 'institutions matter'.[56] This lies at the heart of *new institutionalism* which involves the study of formal and informal institutions, conventions, the norms and symbols embedded in them, pol-icy instruments, and procedures.[57]

The emphasis so far on state actors risks overlooking the fact that private actors also play a key role. For example, in the period leading up to the SEA a coalition of business interests, especially the influential European Round Table of Industrialists (representa-tives from the largest European companies) strongly supported the renewed impetus to make the single market a reality.[58] Increasingly other actors, particularly those from civil

---

[50] Considered by A. Young and H. Wallace, 'The single market' in H. Wallace, W. Wallace, and M. Pollack (eds.), *Policy-Making in the European Union*, 5th edn (Oxford: OUP, 2005), 100.

[51] R. Keohane and S. Hoffman, 'Conclusions: Community politics and institutional choice' in W. Wallace (ed.), *The Dynamics of European Integration* (London: RIIA, 1990), 287.

[52] Ibid., 286.

[53] As early as Jun. 1981 the European Council expressed its concern about the undermining of the single market: EC Bull. 6/81. A specific Internal Market Council was created in Jan. 1983.

[54] See further P. Craig, 'The evolution of the single market' in C. Barnard and J. Scott (eds.), *The Law of the Single European Market: Unpacking the premises* (Oxford: Hart Publishing, 2002); M. Van Empel, 'The 1992 programme: Interaction between legislation and judiciary' [1992/2] *LIEI* 1; and R. Dehousse, *The European Court of Justice* (Basingstoke: Macmillan, 1998), 86–8.

[55] 'Much of the success of the 1992 programme depended on our relationship. Delors left me to get on with it. I fathered it, launched it and drove it to the point of success': Lord Cockfield, quoted in C. Grant, *Delors: Inside the house that Jacques built* (London: Nicholas Brealey Publishing, 1994), 68. On the impor-tance of Jacques Delors, see H. Drake, 'Political leadership and European integration: The case of Jacques Delors' (1995) 18 *Western European Politics* 140; and D. Dinan, *Ever Closer Union: An introduction to European integration*, 3rd edn (Basingstoke: Macmillan, 2005).

[56] K. Armstrong and S. Bulmer, *The Governance of the Single European Market* (Manchester: Manchester University Press, 1998).                                                                              [57] Ibid., 52.

[58] Ibid. For details on the influence of big business, in particular the European Round Table, see K. Middlemas, *Orchestrating Europe: The informal politics of European Union 1973–1995* (London: Fontana Press, 1995), 138–9.

society such as the social partners (management and labour), have been brought into the process of policy formation and implementation.[59] And, from the earliest days of the Union, individuals have been used to help make the common market a reality in their own states when the Court of Justice (quietly[60]) developed the fundamental principles of direct effect[61] and supremacy[62] of Union law.[63] In this way the Court has created an alliance between itself and individuals, thereby circumventing the Member States and the Union legislator. At the same time the Court of Justice has harnessed national courts into the process of enforcing EU law.

This brief description of actors and processes reflects the *multilevel* nature of the governance in the EU:[64] decision-making competencies are shared by actors at different levels rather than monopolized by governments. The multilevel governance model views political arenas as interconnected, with actors, both public and private, operating in both the national and supranational arenas creating transnational associations in the process.[65] In order to understand free movement, it is the multilevel governance model which perhaps has the most to tell us about policymaking and implementation in the EU. We return to this theme in the final chapter of this book. We turn now to consider the principles which underpin the four freedoms, principles which the Court has played a key role in developing.

## E. THE PRINCIPLES UNDERPINNING THE COMMON MARKET

According to the theory, there are two approaches to attaining a common market (1) the *decentralized* model, underpinned by the principles of non-discrimination, market access, and the concept of competitive federalism, and (2) the *centralized* model which concerns harmonization. The choice between these two models says much about the respective power of the centre (the 'federal' government) and the states. We begin by examining the decentralized model.

### 1. THE DECENTRALIZED MODEL

The essence of the decentralized model is that states retain the freedom to regulate matters as diverse as product standards, qualifications to practise, and employment law so

---

[59] This is considered further in Ch. 12.

[60] E. Stein, 'Lawyers, judges and the making of a transnational constitution' (1981) 75 *American Journal of International Law* 1: 'Tucked away in the fairyland Duchy of Luxembourg and blessed, until recently, with benign neglect by the powers that be and the mass media', the Court of Justice has 'fashioned a constitutional framework for a federal-type structure in Europe'.

[61] Case 26/62 *NV Algemene Transport—en Expeditie Onderneming van Gend & Loos* v. *Netherlands Inland Revenue Administration* [1963] ECR 1.

[62] Case 6/64 *Flaminio Costa* v. *ENEL* [1964] ECR 585. See also Decl. 17 of the Lisbon Treaty concerning primacy.

[63] See, generally, J. Weiler, 'The transformation of Europe' (1981) 100 *Yale LJ* 2403; and B. de Witte, 'Direct effect, supremacy and the nature of the legal order' in Craig and de Búrca (eds.), above n. 25.

[64] L. Hooghe and G. Marks, *Multi–Level Governance and European Integration* (Lanham, Md.: Rowman and Littlefield, 2001).

[65] Ibid., 3–4.

long as those national rules do not interfere with key principles of 'federal' law. In the early days of the EU, the key principle was non-discrimination. In more recent years the Court has developed the more intrusive 'market access' or 'restrictions' test to remove barriers to free movement. We shall now examine these two different approaches.

## 1.1 Non-discrimination

The principle of non-discrimination on the grounds of nationality is the cornerstone of the four freedoms. It adopts a comparative approach, requiring out-of-state goods, persons, services, and capital to enjoy the same treatment as their in-state equivalents.[66] This model presupposes that domestic and imported goods, and national and migrant persons, services, and capital are similarly situated[67] and that they should be treated in the same way. The advantage with the non-discrimination model is that it does not interfere with national regulatory autonomy. Member States remain free to regulate the way that goods are produced and services provided, on condition that their regulation applies equally to home and host state goods or persons. So, national rules which are genuinely non-discriminatory are lawful. However, if there is (unjustified) discrimination, Union law requires the discriminatory element of the national measure to be set aside, but the substance of the national rule remains intact. This can be seen in the following example.

Widgets are produced in the UK and Portugal. Each state regulates the standards governing the production of these goods. In Portugal, before widgets originating in the UK can be sold, they are required to satisfy higher standards than widgets produced in Portugal. Portugal is therefore directly discriminating against British goods. The application of the non-discrimination principle means that Portugal can continue to set quality standards for widgets but that the widgets produced in the UK must be subject to the same treatment as those produced in Portugal. So, Portugal has the choice of either requiring all of the UK's widgets to meet the same (lower) standards as those required of Portuguese widgets, or requiring all widgets produced in Portugal to be made to the same (higher) standards required by Portugal for British widgets. This example shows that the non-discrimination model says nothing about the level at which the standards should be set, merely that the imported and domestic goods must be treated in the same way. The result is that the diversity of national rules is preserved.[68]

However, this narrow approach to the principle of equal treatment may itself lead to discrimination, as the widgets example shows. Widgets produced in the UK have already been manufactured according to standards laid down by the UK. In order to be admitted to the Portuguese market they must also satisfy Portuguese standards. In practice, the effect of extending the principle of equal treatment to the British goods is to impose an additional burden on goods originating in the UK. One way of analysing this situation is to say that the Portuguese rule is in fact discriminatory: the discrimination arises because it involves treating identically goods which are actually differently situated.

---

[66] See M. Poiares Maduro, *We the Court: The European Court of Justice and the European Economic Constitution* (Oxford: Hart Publishing, 1998).

[67] Cf. D. Wilsher, 'Does *Keck* discrimination make any sense? An assessment of the non-discrimination principle within the European single market' (2008) 33 *ELRev.* 3.

[68] N. Bernard, 'Discrimination and free movement in EC law' (1996) 45 *ICLQ* 82, 103.

Another way of viewing this situation—and the one favoured by the Court of Justice[69]—is that Portugal's rule is indirectly discriminatory (or indistinctly applicable[70]): on the face of the measure the rule applies to both domestic and imported goods but in fact disadvantages the imported goods because of the double burden they must satisfy. Therefore, Portugal's rule is unlawful, even though equally applicable, unless Portugal can justify it by pointing to a reason which should take precedence over the free movement of goods, such as the need to protect consumers or the environment.

## 1.2 Market Access

### (a) Market access v. Discrimination tests

While the discrimination test has a number of advantages, there are drawbacks too. First, the model is premised on the fact that migrants and nationals are similarly situated when, by definition, they are not. Even if this intellectual hurdle can be surmounted, the choice of comparator is not always obvious and may be determinative of the outcome.[71] Secondly, the effect of the non-discrimination model is to allow barriers to movement to remain because it permits the host state to impose its own rules on imported goods/migrants provided those rules apply equally to domestic goods/persons. For this reason, some advocate that a broader market access test be applied. This provides that national rules preventing or hindering market access are unlawful, irrespective of whether they actually discriminate against imports or migrants. The market access approach therefore looks at the national rule solely from the perspective of the (usually out-of-state) claimants: does the national rule prevent or hinder their market access?

The Court of Justice increasingly favours the market access approach. For example, in *Gebhard*,[72] a case concerning national rules on the use of the title *avvoccato* in Italy, the Court abandoned the language of discrimination and said that the national measures were 'liable to hinder or make less attractive the exercise of fundamental freedoms guaranteed by the Treaty'. Such rules breached Article 49 TFEU on freedom of establishment unless they could be justified. In *Commission v Italy (trailers)*,[73] a goods case, the Court said that 'Any other measure which hinders access of products originating in other

---

[69] See Case 120/78 *Rewe Zentrale v. Bundesmonopolverwaltung für Branntwein ('Cassis de Dijon')* [1979] ECR 649 considered in detail in Ch. 4.

[70] This terminology is explored further in Ch. 8.

[71] See, e.g., Case 270/83 *Commission v. France (tax credits)* [1986] ECR 273. France granted tax credits to shareholders receiving dividends from a company with a registered office in France but not to those with only a branch or agency in France (and a registered office in another Member State). The Court said that because Art. 49 TFEU (ex Art. 43 EC) expressly left traders free to choose the appropriate legal form in which to pursue their activities in another Member State that freedom of choice could not be limited by discriminatory tax provisions (para. 22). The French rule therefore breached Art. 49 and could not be justified on the facts. Thus, in its application of the principle of non-discrimination, the Court required the French tax system to treat a branch or agency having no legal personality in the same way as a company registered in France. If, as Banks notes, the Court had selected the treatment of a branch or agency of a nationally based company as the appropriate comparator, the outcome might have been very different (K. Banks, 'The application of the fundamental freedoms to Member State tax measures: Guarding against protectionism or second-guessing national policy choices' (2008) 33 *ELRev.* 482, 488).

[72] Case C–55/94 *Gebhard v. Consiglio dell'Ordine degli Avvocati e Procuratori di Milano* [1995] ECR I–4165, para. 37, citing Case C–19/92 *Kraus v. Land Baden-Württemberg* [1993] ECR I–1663, para. 32; Case C–76/90 *Säger v. Dennemeyer & Co. Ltd* [1991] ECR I–4221, para. 12.

[73] Case C–110/05 *Commission v. Italy* [2009] ECR I–519, para. 50.

Member States to the market of a Member State' breaches Article 34 TFEU. In subsequent case law, particularly in the field of persons and capital, the Court has tended to simplify the terminology and increasingly the reference to market access is replaced by the language of 'obstacles' to, or 'restrictions' on, free movement.[74]

While the discrimination and market access tests use different language, there is considerable overlap between the two models.[75] For example, quantitative restrictions for goods, refusal of entry/deportation of persons, and directly and indirectly discriminatory measures, by definition, hinder market access.[76] However, the difference between these two models can be seen when dealing with non-discriminatory rules, as the facts of *Commission v. Greece (opticians)*[77] illustrate. Greek law prohibited qualified opticians from operating more than one optician's shop. Under a pure discrimination model, this rule would be lawful: both Greek opticians and out-of state opticians are being treated equally (albeit equally badly). However, under the market access approach such a rule would be unlawful unless justified and this is the approach the Court adopted. It said this rule 'effectively amounts to a restriction on the freedom of establishment of natural persons within the meaning of Article [49 TFEU], notwithstanding the alleged absence of discrimination on grounds of nationality of the professionals concerned'.[78] This demonstrates the point noted above that, while the discrimination approach focuses on a comparison between the treatment of the in-state and out-of-state person/trader, the market access test focuses solely on the perspective of the out-of-state traders or migrants: what stands in their way of getting onto the market? Market access, at least in the early days, was a way of challenging over-regulation by states which makes cross-border trade difficult (just as it makes domestic trade difficult).[79]

The advantage of the market access approach is that it goes a long way towards building a single market by removing any unjustified obstacles to trade. As Advocate General Jacobs noted in *Leclerc-Siplec*,[80] 'If an obstacle to trade exists it cannot cease to exist simply because an identical obstacle affects domestic trade.' The market access approach is

---

[74] Cf. J.Meulman and H de Wael, 'A retreat from *Säger*? Servicing or fine-tuning the application of Article 49' (2006) 33 *LIEI* 207, 210–19.

[75] In Case C–341/05 *Laval un Partneri Ltd* v. *Svenska Byggnadsarbetareförbundet* [2007] ECR I–11767, para. 228 Mengozzi AG noted that it is often difficult to decide whether a set of rules adopted by private persons should be seen as indirect discrimination based on nationality, a restriction, a barrier or a deterrent to the freedom to provide services. See also S. Enchelmaier, 'The ECJ's recent case law on the free movement of goods: Movement in all sorts of directions' (2007) 26 *YEL* 115, 126–7.

[76] See, e.g., P. Van den Bossche, *The Law and Policy of the World Trade Organisation: Text, cases and materials*, 2nd edn (Cambridge: CUP, 2008) who has one chapter entitled 'Principles of non-discrimination' and another entitled 'Rules on market access' which covers tariff barriers to trade (e.g., customs duties), non-tariff barriers (e.g., QRs, inspections, origin marking) and barriers to trade in services.

[77] Case C–140/03 *Commission* v. *Greece (opticians)* [2005] ECR I–3177. See Case C–568/07 *Commission* v. *Greece (opticians) II* [2009] ECR I–000 for the Art. 260 TFEU (ex Art. 228 EC) follow-up action.

[78] Para. 28. There is an argument that the Greek rule is indirectly discriminatory: there is a risk that it might operate to the particular detriment of out-of-state traders since they are more likely to want to establish a chain of opticians in Greece to justify the initial start-up costs. However, such arguments seem artificial (although this has not prevented the Court itself from relying on such artificiality: e.g., Case C–322/01 *Deutscher Apothekerverband eV* v. *0800 DocMorris NV* [2003] ECR I–14887, para. 74). A better analysis is that the rule should be regarded as non-discriminatory but still prevents or impedes market access.

[79] G. Davies, 'Services, citizenship and the country of origin principle', *Mitchell Working Paper Series* 2/2007, 3: As Davies puts it, 'There may be no identifiable inequality of effect, but there is a general suppression of economic activity.'

[80] Case C–412/93 *Leclerc-Siplec* v. *TF1 Publicité* [1995] ECR I–179.

based on the idea famously articulated in *Cassis de Dijon*[81] that goods lawfully produced in one Member State should presumptively have free and unrestricted access to the market in another Member State (the principle of equivalence or mutual recognition). This enables the trader to develop a pan-European strategy to expand its market, thereby creating greater economies of scale for the producer and greater choice and competition for the consumer. It is a win-win situation. Translating this to persons, those who are qualified to practise in one Member State should also, in principle, be free to practise in another Member State. Once again, this enables individuals to expand the market for their services or to move to a place where their skills are better rewarded/appreciated while offering greater choice to consumers in the receiving state.

The disadvantage with market access is that it is far more intrusive into national regulatory autonomy since Union law requires the national measure to be struck down, unless it can be justified, even though it may not discriminate against the non-national.[82] This has serious implications for national legislation adopted by democratically elected governments, not least because a case can be made that almost any national rule has some effect on inter-state movement, even if that was never the intention of the rule and the effect on inter-state trade is slight.[83] Take, for example, a national law on the minimum wage. This could be challenged under the restrictions model because it would prevent migrants from working for less than the minimum and this might discourage them from moving to that state (the rule would not be open to challenge under the non-discrimination approach provided the minimum wage rate was the same for all workers, domestic and migrant). There is some evidence that in recent cases the Court has recognized this risk that the market access model is too all encompassing and so it has experimented with different legal techniques to draw the line between those rules which should be caught by Union law and those which should fall outside it.[84]

(b) The meaning of 'market access'

A further disadvantage with the market access test is the uncertainty which surrounds this 'inherently nebulous'[85] concept. Spaventa offers three possible interpretations.[86] The first, and narrowest, is that barriers to market access are those created by circumstances or legislation that make it 'more costly for new firms to enter an industry'.[87] There is some

---

[81] Case 120/78 *Rewe Zentrale* v. *Bundesmonopolverwaltung für Branntwein ('Cassis de Dijon')* [1979] ECR 649.

[82] This question is discussed further in C. Barnard, 'Restricting restrictions: Lessons for the EU from the US?' (2009) 68 *CLJ* 575.

[83] Cf., e.g., Case C–353/06 *Grunkin-Paul* [2008] ECR I–7639, paras. 23, 24, and 29 where the Court talked of the 'serious inconvenience' caused by a discrepancy in surnames created an obstacle to free movement of citizens under Art. 21(1) TFEU (ex Art. 18(1) EC). In Case C–110/05 *Commission* v. *Italy (Trailers)* [2009] ECR I–519 the Court referred to the '*considerable* influence' that a prohibition on the use of a product has on the behaviour of consumers.

[84] See the discussion of the *Keck* (Joined Cases C–267 and 268/91 [1993] ECR I–6097) line of case law in Ch. 5 and the *Viacom* (Case C–134/03 [2005] ECR I–1167) line of case law in Ch. 8 discussed in A. Biondi, 'Recurring Cycles in the Internal Market: Some Reflections on the Free Movement of Services' in A. Arnull, P. Eeckhout, and T. Tridimas (eds), *Continuity and Change in EU Law* (Oxford: OUP, 2008).

[85] P. Oliver and S. Enchelmaier, 'Free movement of goods: Recent developments in the case law' (2007) 44 *CMLRev.* 649, 674.

[86] 'From *Gebhard* to *Carpenter*: Towards a (non-)economic European Constitution' (2004) 41 *CMLRev.* 743, 757–8. See also C. Barnard and S. Deakin, 'Market access and regulatory competition' in C. Barnard and J. Scott (eds.), *The Legal Foundations of the Single Market: Unpacking the Premises* (Oxford: Hart Publishing, 2002).

[87] Citing Folovary, *Dictionary of Free Market Economics* (Edward Elgar Publishing Inc., 1998), 48.

overlap between this approach and the discrimination model outlined above, especially if it is assumed, as the Court often does, that new market entrants come from out of state.[88] It is supported by *Commission* v. *Italy (motor insurance)*[89] where the Court said that an obligation on an insurance company to provide third-party insurance to cover any risks proposed to them and to moderate premium rates breaches Articles 49 and 56 TFEU 'inasmuch as it involves changes and costs on such a scale that the obligation to contract renders access to the Italian market less attractive and, if they obtain access to that market, reduces the ability of the undertakings concerned to compete effectively, from the outset, against undertakings traditionally established in Italy'.[90]

The second, and much broader, approach to market access is that *any* regulation can be seen as a potential barrier to access, since *any* regulation imposes and implies compliance costs. This approach can be seen in the golden-share case, *Commission v UK (British Airports Authority (BAA))*.[91] BAA's articles of association prevented any person from acquiring BAA shares carrying the right to more than 15 per cent of the equity in BAA. The Court said that 'Rules which limit the acquisition of shareholdings…constitute a restriction on the free movement of capital'.[92] The Court added that although the restrictions were non-discriminatory 'they affect the position of a person acquiring a shareholding as such and are thus liable to *deter* investors from other Member States from making such investments and, consequently, affect access to the market'.[93] The answer to the question 'What is the deterrence?' is presumably the very existence of the rule: had the rule not existed there would have been no breach.

The third approach is what Spaventa describes as 'intuitive': rules which interfere with intra-Union trade should be subject to judicial scrutiny while rules considered neutral as regards intra-Union trade should not. The intuitive approach can be seen in *Laval*.[94] The case concerned a Latvian company which won a contract to refurbish a school in Sweden using its own Latvian workers. It faced ruinous industrial action by the Swedish trade unions when it refused to apply Swedish collectively agreed terms and conditions. Although this industrial action was permissible under Swedish law, Laval brought proceedings in the Swedish labour court, claiming that the industrial action was contrary to Article 56 TFEU. The Court said:

> the right of trade unions of a Member State to take collective action by which undertakings established in other Member States may be forced to sign the collective agreement for the building sector…is *liable to make it less attractive, or more difficult*, for such undertakings to carry out construction work in Sweden, and therefore constitutes a *restriction* on the freedom to provide services within the meaning of Article [56 TFEU].[95]

But how, precisely, did the collective action impose costs which made it 'more difficult' or 'less attractive' for Laval to operate in Sweden? Deakin suggests that one answer might be 'more difficult' in relation to the situation which would have prevailed had Latvian law

---

[88]  Case C–322/01 *DocMorris NV* [2003] ECR I–14887, para. 74.

[89]  Case C–518/06 *Commission* v. *Italy (motor insurance)* [2009] ECR I–000.

[90]  Para. 70.          [91]  Case C–98/01 *Commission* v. *UK* [2003] ECR I–4641.          [92]  Para. 44.

[93]  Para. 47, emphasis added. Cf case C–542/08 *Barth* v. *Bundesministerium für Wissenschaft und Forschung* [2010] ECR I–000, para. 39.

[94]  Case C–341/05 *Laval un Partneri Ltd* v. *Svenska Byggnadsarbetareförbundet* [2007] ECR I–11767.

[95]  Para. 99, emphasis added.

and/or Latvian collective agreements applied.[96] If this is correct, it means that the effect of the restrictions analysis is to enable service providers to export their home country laws and have them applied extraterritorially. Another answer may be intuition: Laval was a Latvian company and it was having difficulty fulfilling a contract which it had legitimately won, largely due to its cheaper labour costs. The Swedish strike action therefore prevented it from doing the very thing that EU accession had promised to the new Member States, namely free access to the markets in services in other Member States; and that was enough to trigger Article 56.

But if the effect of *Laval* is to allow challenges to host-state rules which differ from those which apply at home, this suggests that a mere difference between the rules of two states is sufficient to constitute a restriction on free movement, an understanding that the Court has rejected in the past.[97] Following *Laval* there is no reason why German tourists might not argue that the requirement of having to drive on the left hinders their free movement since British rules are different to those in Germany. Here, the Court's 'intuition' might lead it to find that the rules are in fact neutral as regards intra-Union movement. This might explain why in *Burbaud*[98] the Court said that the requirement of passing an exam in order to take up a post in the public service could not 'in itself be regarded as an obstacle' to free movement.[99]

Despite the problems with the market access test, the Court continues to see it as the mainstay of its analysis, as demonstrated by two Grand Chamber decisions of 2009, *Commission* v. *Italy (trailers)*[100] and *Commission* v. *Italy (motor insurance)*.[101] In both these cases the Court endorsed the market access analysis and offered some guidance as to the meaning of the phrase. The *Trailers* case concerned an Italian prohibition on motorbikes towing trailers. The Court indicated that market access could be hindered by a rule which has 'considerable influence on the behaviour of consumers, which, in its turn, affects the access of that product to the market of that Member State'.[102] Thus, (significant) reduction in demand is sufficient to satisfy the market access test. In the *Motor Insurance* case the Court said that the obligation of an insurance company to provide third-party cover to every potential customer constituted a 'substantial' interference in the operators' freedom to contract,[103] and that the obligation was likely to lead, in terms of organization and investment to 'significant additional costs for such undertakings'.[104]

For Snell, however, the notion of market access conceals rather than clarifies.[105] He argues that it covers a range of situations including discrimination against free movers or free movement,[106] substantial or direct obstacles to trade or free movement,[107] and

---

[96] 'Regulatory competition after *Laval*' (2007–8) 10 *CYELS* 581, 585–7.

[97] Case C–177/94 *Criminal Proceedings against Gianfranco Perfili, civil party: Lloyd's of London* [1996] ECR I–161, para. 17; Case C–384/93 *Alpine Investments BV* v. *Minister van Financiën* [1995] ECR I–1141, para. 27.    [98] Case C–285/01 *Burbaud* v. *Ministère de l'Emploi et de la Solidarité* [2003] ECR I–8219.

[99] Para. 96. To emphasize the point, the Court said that inasmuch as all new jobs are subject to a recruitment procedure, the requirement of passing a recruitment competition could not 'in itself be liable to dissuade candidates who have already sat a similar competition in another Member State from exercising their right to freedom of movement as workers' (para. 97).    [100] Case C–110/05 [2009] ECR I–519.

[101] Case C–518/06 [2009] ECR I–000.    [102] Para. 56.    [103] Para. 66.    [104] Para. 68.

[105] J. Snell, 'The notion of market access: A concept or a slogan?' (2010) 47 *CMLRev.* 437.

[106] See, e.g., Poiares Maduro AG in Case C–446/03 *Marks & Spencer* v. *Halsey* [2005] ECR I–10837, para. 37 where he said national policies 'must not result in less favourable treatment being accorded to transnational situations than to purely national situations'.

[107] Case C–518/06 *Commission* v. *Italy (Motor Insurance)* [2009] ECR I–000.

substantial reductions in profitability.[108] He concludes 'As the term lacks a clear content, the Court may use it freely either to approve or to condemn measures that it happens to like or dislike. Market access may simply provide a sophisticated-sounding garb that conceals decisions based on intuition.'[109]

### (c) Market access v. Exercise

There is a further practical problem with the language of market access: it suggests that restrictions on initial access to the market (e.g., requiring individuals to have certain qualifications, linguistic skills, or a licence before they do a particular job) are more serious than restrictions imposed by the host state when the migrant has actually got on to the market but is trying to exercise his freedoms (e.g., rules restricting tax and social advantages).[110] Yet rules restricting exercise of a free movement right can have just as serious a consequence on free movement as the initial refusal of access.[111] This can be seen in *Steinhauser*,[112] where a German artist was permitted to work (access) but not to participate in a tendering process for the use of a boutique from which to sell his art works (exercise). The Court, rejecting the French argument that Article 49 TFEU applied only to conditions regulating *access*, said that 'The [Treaties] included the right not only to take up activities as a self-employed person but also to pursue those activities in the broadest sense, including renting business premises.' The effect of this decision is now enshrined in the Services Directive 2006/123:[113] the directive applies to 'requirements which affect access to *or* the exercise of a service activity'.[114]

Given that it is often difficult to distinguish market access situations from those concerning exercise, the Court increasingly says that the national rules are 'restrictions' or 'obstacles' to free movement rather than hindering market access. We saw this in *Laval*, discussed above, and can see it again in the *Motor Insurance* case where the Court said 'the concept of restriction covers measures taken by a Member State which, although applicable without distinction, affect access to the market for undertakings from other Member States and thereby hinder intra-[Union] trade'.[115] In cases involving free movement of natural persons and citizens, the Court tends to abandon the (more commercial) market access language altogether, talking instead of how the national rule is liable to dissuade or deter an individual from exercising his right of free movement.[116]

---

[108] Cf. Case C–518/06 *Commission* v. *Italy (Motor Insurance)* [2009] ECR I–000 with Joined Cases C–544/03 and C–545/03 *Mobistar SA* v. *Commune de Fleron* [2005] ECR I–7723.

[109] Some support for this view can be found in See A. Rosas, '*Dassonville* and *Cassis de Dijon*' in M. Poiares Maduro and L. Azoulai, *The Past and Future of EU Law: The classics of EU Law revisited on the 50th anniversary of the Rome Treaty* (Oxford: Hart Publishing, 2009).

[110] This is the view of Lenz AG in Case C–415/93 *Bosman* [1995] ECR I–4921, paras. 203 and 205. Cf. Alber AG in Case C–176/96 *Lehtonen* [2000] ECR I–2681, para. 48; and Fennelly AG's attempts in Case C–190/98 *Graf* [2000] ECR I–493 to reconcile the two.

[111] For a discussion on whether rules restricting market access and those restricting exercise of the freedoms are most serious, cf. Lenz AG in Case C–415/93 *Bosman* [1995] ECR I–4921, paras. 203 and 205 with Alber AG in Case C–176/96 *Lehtonen* [2000] ECR I–2681, para. 48.

[112] Case 197/84 *Steinhauser* v. *City of Biarritz* [1985] ECR 1819.      [113] OJ [2006] L376/26.

[114] 9th Recital, emphasis added. See also Art. 49(2) TFEU 'Freedom of establishment shall include the right to *take up and pursue* activities as self employed persons' (emphasis added).      [115] Para. 64.

[116] See, e.g., Case C–499/06 *Nerkowska* [2008] ECR I–3993: '31. With regard to the scope of Article [21(1) TFEU], the Court has already held that the opportunities offered by the [Treaties] in relation to freedom of movement cannot be fully effective if a national of a Member State can be deterred from availing himself of them by obstacles raised to his residence in the host Member State by legislation of his State of origin

### (d) The convergence or unity thesis

One of the debates which has bedeviled the area of free movement is whether a single principle (e.g., non-discrimination or market access) should cover all four freedoms. The arguments in favour relate to the need for clarity, certainty, and consistency in interpretation,[117] particularly as an increasing number of cases raise issues affecting a number of freedoms (for example, a restriction on advertising might engage both Article 34 on goods and Article 56 on services[118]).

On the other hand, there are significant differences between the freedoms, in particular those provisions relating to the movement of natural persons, where human rights have a more significant role to play than when, for example, free movement of goods are at stake. Further, there are differences between the freedoms in respect of which the state has particular responsibility for regulation; in respect of free movement of goods and services, the principal regulator is the home state so any requirements imposed by the host state must take into account the controls already imposed by the home state. By contrast, in respect of free movement of workers and freedom of establishment, the principal regulator is the host state which might suggest that there is more room for the host state to impose its requirements on the migrant.

The shift to the market access/restrictions test in respect of all the freedoms does suggest an increasing degree of convergence; the differences between the freedoms manifest themselves in respect of the crafting of the justifications, the role of fundamental human rights and the Court's approach to proportionality. However, in concentrating on market access rather than discrimination as the basic test for establishing whether there is a breach of the Treaties, the Court has subtly altered the balance of power between the Union and the Member States. While a non-discrimination approach creates a space in which national regulators are free to act, untrammeled by Union law, the market access test has shifted the balance back in favour of the Union, giving the Court the power to scrutinize an ever-wider category of national measures for their compatibility with Union law.

### 1.3 Competitive Federalism

Both the non-discrimination and market access tests are premised on a *decentralized* model to market-building: Member States retain the freedom to regulate provided that they do not overstep the limits laid down by the Treaties (non-discrimination/market access). The effect of the EU rules on free movement of goods, persons, services, and capital is to place the different national systems into competition because those individuals or companies not satisfied with the political/legal/social environment in which they find themselves are free to move to another Member State which has a regime which suits them better. This freedom for individuals/capital to move has the effect of forcing the

---

penalising the fact that he has used them…32. National legislation which places certain of the nationals of the Member State concerned at a disadvantage simply because they have exercised their freedom to move and to reside in another Member State is a restriction on the freedoms conferred by Article [21(1) TFEU] on every citizen of the Union.'

[117] A point recognized by Poiares Maduro AG in Joined Cases C–158/04 and C–159/04 *Alfa Vita Vassilopoulos AE* [2006] ECR I–8135, para. 33. Cf P. Oliver, 'Of Trailers and jet-skis: Is the case law on Article 34 TFEU (ex Article 28 EC) careering in a new direction' (2010) *Fordham Intl LJ*, forthcoming.

[118] See, e.g., Joined Cases C–34–36/95 *Konsumentombudsmannen (KO)* v. *De Agostini (Svenska) Förlag AB* and *TV-Shop i Sverige AB* [1997] ECR I–3843.

national systems to compete to produce the best rules to attract (or retain) valuable assets (capital and labour). This is known as competitive federalism or regulatory competition.[119]

For competitive federalism to function, two conditions need to be satisfied. First, the *federal* (central) authorities must lay down and enforce the rules giving goods, persons, and capital freedom to exit one Member State and enter another. Secondly, the *states* (the decentralized authorities) must remain free to regulate the production of goods and the qualifications of people according to their own standards so as to enable regulators to respond to the competition. The outcome of this process of regulatory competition should be to produce optimal, efficient, and innovative legislation (a race to the top) because state officials vie with one another to create increasingly attractive economic circumstances for their citizens, knowing that re-election depends upon their success.[120] Regulatory competition also promotes diversity and experimentation in the search for effective legal solutions by providing for comparative data to assist in regulatory reform. This reduces the risk of widespread adoption of flawed laws. This is the classic 'laboratory of democracy' theory[121] which recognizes that competition is a dynamic process where trial and error is the best means of finding the optimal solution to complex problems.[122] Company law in the United States is often held up as an example of the success of regulatory competition. The American state of Delaware has been extremely successful in attracting companies to incorporate there,[123] and from this Delaware benefits from substantial incorporation fees. Some commentators attribute Delaware's success to its ability to offer the most suitable corporation laws[124] which other states have tried to emulate by revising their acts along similar lines.

The model of competitive federalism, with an active role for state authorities (in shaping their laws to meet the demands of consumers) and a limited role for the central authorities (ensuring freedom of movement) influenced the thinking of the drafters of the Treaty of Rome. The original EEC Treaty owed much to the ordo-liberal school which

---

[119] This is based on Tiebout's famous 'pure theory' of fiscal federalism: C. Tiebout, 'A pure theory of local expenditure' (1956) 64/5 *Journal of Political Economy* 416. For further details see C. Barnard and S. Deakin, 'Market access and regulatory competition' in Barnard and Scott (eds.), above n. 54; and G. Wagner, 'The economics of harmonisation: The case of contract law' (2002) 39 *CMLRev*. 995.

[120] D. Tarullo, 'Federalism issues in the United States' in A. Castro, P. Méhaut, and J. Rubery (eds.), *International Integration and Labour Market Organisation* (London, Academic Press, 1992), 101.

[121] Ibid.

[122] R. Van den Bergh, 'The subsidiarity principle in European Community law: Some insights from law and economics' (1994) 1 *Maastricht Journal of European and Comparative Law* 337, citing F. A. von Hayek, 'Competition as a discovery process' in his *New Studies in Philosophy, Politics, Economics and the History of Ideas* (Chicago, Ill.: University of Chicago Press, 1978), 149.

[123] Over 40% of New York Stock Exchange-listed companies, and over 50% of Fortune 500 companies, are incorporated in Delaware: D. Charny, 'Competition among jurisdictions in formulating corporate law rules: An American perspective on the "race to the bottom" in the European Communities' (1991) 32 *Harvard International Law Journal* 422, 428.

[124] See, e.g., ibid., 431–2; D. Fischel, 'The "race to the bottom" revisited: Reflections on recent developments in Delaware's corporation law' (1982) 77 *Northwestern University Law Review* 913, 920; R. Romano, 'Law as a product: Some pieces of the incorporation puzzle' (1985) 1 *J.L.Econ & Org.* 225, 257–8. Romano explains the advantages offered by Delaware: it offers comprehensive statutes and case law; the continuity in and small size of Delaware's Courts of Chancery provide an experienced judiciary specialized in corporate matters; Delaware's large population of corporations quickly generates legal controversies and thereby new precedents and rules; Delaware's reliance on incorporation fees binds Delaware to maintaining the stability and serviceability of its system.

originated in Freiburg in the 1930s.[125] In simple terms, ordo-liberalists believed that the Constitution should protect economic freedoms (freedom of movement) from public (and private) intervention in the same way as it protects civil and political rights, and this would guarantee individual freedom.[126] Central to their idea was the concept of *Ordnungspolitik*, according to which individual government decisions should both flow from, and be constrained by, the principles embedded in an economic constitution.

However, some commentators say that the analogies between the EU Treaties and an economic constitution should not be pushed too far.[127] For example, Chalmers argues that ordo-liberalism assumes too rigid and too discrete a separation of the market from other policies.[128] Indeed, in the EU it is simply not possible to disentangle the four freedoms from social, consumer, health, and environmental policies. This is recognized in the Treaties themselves which provide express grounds for Member States to derogate from individual rights for reasons connected with wider public interests such as public health and public policy. These derogations have been supplemented by an ever-expanding range of public-interest or 'mandatory' requirements developed by the Court. Together they reflect a 'social market' tradition whereby state intervention in the operation of the markets is accepted and expected, not only to address market failures but also to secure social values which are seen as public goods in their own right. Some of these ideas are now reflected in Article 3(3) TEU which identifies the establishment of a 'highly competitive social market economy' as one of the aims of the Union.[129]

These derogations and public-interest requirements do, however, themselves create considerable barriers to trade which can be addressed only through centralized regulation, and the Treaties envisaged this too, by providing the EU with powers to harmonize conflicting national laws (initially Article 100 EEC (now Article 115 TFEU, ex Article 94 EC) on the establishment and functioning of the common market and Article 235 EEC (now Article 352 TFEU, ex Article 308 EC), the residual legal basis).

## 2. THE CENTRALIZED MODEL

The need to have centralized standards is largely premised on market failure. If regulatory competition worked effectively Member States would compete against each other for the best laws. In these circumstances the host state would not need to invoke the public-health derogation or the consumer protection mandatory requirement because the goods/services produced in the home state would already be of a very high standard. Yet, in order to ensure successful regulatory competition, certain conditions must be satisfied:[130] there must be full mobility of people and resources at little or no cost;

---

[125] D. Chalmers, and E. Szyszczak, *European Union Law, Volume Two: Towards a European polity?* (Aldershot: Ashgate, 1998), 39 and D. Chalmers, 'The single market: From prima donna to journeyman' in J. Shaw and G. More (eds.), *New Legal Dynamics of European Union* (Oxford: OUP, 1995), 56.

[126] D. Gerber, 'Constitutionalizing the economy: German neo-liberalism, competition law and the "New Europe"' (1994) 42 *American Journal of Comparative Law* 25, 45–6; M. Streit and W. Mussler, 'The economic constitution of the European Community: From "Rome" to "Maastricht"' (1995) 1 *ELJ* 5.

[127] N. Reich, 'The November Revolution of the Court of Justice: *Keck, Meng* and *Audi* revisited' (1994) 31 *CMLRev.* 459.  [128] Chalmers, above n. 125, 66.

[129] Note also the possible downgrading of the objective of ensuring that competition is not distorted by its removal from the list of objectives in Art. 3 TEU and its inclusion in Protocol No. 27.

[130] For the literature on the economics of federalism, see Tiebout, above n. 119; F. Easterbrook, 'Antitrust and the economics of federalism' (1983) 26 *Journal of Law and Economics* 23, 34.

migrants must have full knowledge of each jurisdiction's revenue and expenditure patterns; and there must be a wide choice of destination jurisdictions to enable citizens to make meaningful decisions about migration. In reality these conditions are never met. For individuals the chances of exit are slim because they are unlikely to leave their own jurisdiction for linguistic, cultural, financial, or personal reasons; and capital (direct investment in business operations) is unlikely to leave unless a variety of factors (market proximity, transport costs, infrastructure levels, labour costs, and productivity levels) justify the move. Even if these conditions could be met, state legislation is often insufficiently responsive to the needs of its consumers.[131] This creates the risk that the type of regulatory competition which emerges is undesirable.

The following example demonstrates this. The UK knows that in practice individuals are less mobile than capital and so it decides to gain a competitive advantage in the single market by reducing employment protection or environmental standards in order to remain attractive to capital.[132] While such a strategy might have short-term benefits (e.g., job creation or at least job retention) it undermines the longer-term interests of the citizenry as a whole (e.g., lower quality jobs and an inferior environment). Faced with such deregulation by the UK, Portugal—which risks losing capital and thus jobs to the UK—relaxes its own standards. The UK responds by lowering its standards still further and a race to the bottom ensues with the UK and Portugal now competing on the basis of low standards.

Some commentators argue that this is the true explanation for what is actually happening in Delaware: its success in attracting incorporation is due to its victory not in a race to the top but in a race to the bottom. As Cary graphically puts it, Delaware, 'a pygmy among the 50 States prescribes, interprets, and indeed denigrates national corporate policy as an incentive to encourage incorporation within its borders, thereby increasing its revenue'.[133] While there is much controversy about the likelihood of EU states engaging in a full-blown race to the bottom,[134] there is a perception that it may happen and that steps need to be taken by the central bodies to combat it. This is what Cary called for in the US—the enactment of a *Federal* Corporate Uniformity Act, allowing companies to incorporate in the jurisdiction of their own choosing but removing much of the incentive to organize in Delaware or its rival states.[135]

Centralization offers advantages in terms of economies of scale by establishing a single set of rules applying to a broad class of transactions. It also reduces the costs that stem from evasion, through forum shopping, externalization, and extraterritoriality.[136] On the other hand, it raises difficulties, both legal (e.g., does the central body have the power to act (competence), should it act (subsidiarity), and, if so, to what extent (proportionality)?), and practical (e.g., should the harmonized standard represent an arithmetical mean of

---

[131] J. Sun and J. Pelkmans, 'Regulatory competition in the single market' (1995) 33 *JCMS* 67.

[132] This point was expressly recognized by Poiares Maduro AG in Case C–438/05 *Viking* [2007] ECR I–10779, para. 70.

[133] W. Cary, 'Federalism and corporate law: Reflections upon Delaware' (1974) 83 *Yale Law Journal* 663, 701.

[134] C. Barnard, 'Social dumping revisited: Lessons from Delaware' (2000) 25 *ELRev.* 57.

[135] Cary, above, n. 133, 701.

[136] J. Trachtman, 'International regulatory competition: Externalization and jurisdiction' (1993) 34 *Harvard Int. LJ* 47.

existing national measures or the optimal solution?).[137] It also creates political problems: it does not leave room for national diversity (i.e., the result would be one centrally regulated standard for an EU sausage, replacing hundreds of different regional varieties of sausage); it loses the benefits associated with local accountability; and it may lead to 'market freezing', reducing legislative innovation and experimentation. It also assumes a developed system of enforcement capable of preventing more complex forms of evasion. These issues are considered in detail in Chapter 16.

## F. CONCLUSIONS

The driving force behind the European Union is, and has always been, the consolidation of a post-war system of inter-state cooperation and integration that would make pan-European armed conflict inconceivable. This has been promoted through a vigorous emphasis on free trade, with all the economic benefits this entails, albeit not to the exclusion of all other interests. As we have seen, the TFEU allows Member States to derogate from the rules of free trade where overriding national interests are at stake.[138] It also makes provision for structural funds to help those who are losers in the integration process, in particular the European regional development fund and the European social fund.[139] And as the EU's self-perception changed from a European *Economic* Community to a European Union, so its tasks and objectives have been broadened to take into account a wider range of policies which may complement, but may also obstruct, free trade. For example, Article 3 TEU identifies a number of tasks for the Union which were not found in the original Treaty of Rome including full employment and social progress, equality between men and women, environmental protection, and combating social exclusion and discrimination. The solidarity between citizens of the EU envisaged by these measures and the state/federal intervention they necessitate are a far cry from an ordo-liberal/neo-liberal agenda which underpinned the Treaty of Rome.

This change in orientation can be seen in the simple statement by the Court in *Deutsche Post*,[140] a case on Article 157 TFEU (ex Article 141 EC) on equal pay. Originally, Article 157 (then Article 119 EEC) was included in the EEC Treaty as a market-making measure. It was intended to stop French industry, which had to respect the principle of equal pay for men and women, from losing out to companies established in other states (such as Italy) where the principle of equal pay was not respected. This economic function of Article 157 was recognized by the Court in some of its earliest case law.[141] Yet by the time the Court decided *Deutsche Post* in 2000 the change in approach was clear. The Court said that 'the economic aim pursued by Article [157]..., namely the elimination of distortions of competition between undertakings established in different Member States, is *secondary* to the

---

[137] A. Dashwood, 'Hastening slowly' in H. Wallace, W. Wallace, and C. Webb (eds.), *Policy Making in the European Community* (Chichester: Wiley, 1983), 178.

[138] See, e.g., Arts. 36, 45(3), and 52 considered in Chs. 6 and 13.

[139] Reg. 1083/2006 ([2006] OJ L210/25) laying down general provisions on the European Regional Development Fund, the European Social Fund and the Cohesion Fund. See generally J. Scott, *Development Dilemmas in the European Community: Rethinking regional development policy* (Buckingham, Open University Press, 1995).

[140] Joined Cases C–270/97 and C–271/97 *Deutsche Post* v. *Sievers* [2000] ECR I–929.

[141] Case 43/75 *Defrenne* v. *Sabena II* [1976] ECR 455.

social aim pursued by the same provision, which constitutes the expression of a funda-mental human right'.[142] This is significant for it marks an important shift in emphasis—from a pure market-based, neo-liberal vision premised on deregulation, efficiency, and the assumption of formal equality between individuals—to one which recognizes the need to accommodate and indeed value a wider range of interests. This change is encap-sulated by the reference introduced by the Lisbon Treaty in Article 3(3) TEU to a 'highly competitive *social market* economy'. This observation has already prompted Advocate General Cruz Villalón in *Santos Palhota* to suggest that the pre-Lisbon orthodoxy needs to be reconsidered.[143]

Since the 1970s the Court has tried to balance market rights with traditional civil, political, and social rights. This approach has now been legitimized by the adoption of the Charter of Fundamental Rights in 2000 which has now been incorporated by reference into the Treaties.[144] This rights-based approach has increasingly shaped the contours of the Court's case law, particularly in the field of citizens' rights.[145] At a time when global movements are mobilizing forces against free trade which they see as both wasteful to sustainable resources and producing inequality (where the rich—both people and regions—do better out of free trade than the poor),[146] the EU would find itself signifi-cantly out of step with its citizens if it did not recognize the broader social and environ-mental interests at stake. While this book focuses on the four freedoms, it also considers how the free-trade imperative is counterbalanced by these broader interests. It begins by considering the free movement of goods. Chapter 2 provides an introduction to the dif-ferent Treaty provisions on goods and places them in the broader context of the WTO in which the EU must operate.

---

[142] Para. 57, emphasis added. See also Case C–438/05 *Viking* [2007] ECR I–10779, para. 79: 'Since the [Union] has thus not only an economic but also a social purpose, the rights under the provisions of the [Treaties] on the free movement of goods, persons, services and capital must be balanced against the objec-tive pursued by social policy.'

[143] Case C–515/08, opinion of 5 May 2010, paras 51–53. See also the Monti Report, 'A new strategy for the simple market', 9 May 2010. See also C. Joerges and F. Rödi, 'The "Social Market Economy" as Europe's Social Model' EUI workup paper 2004/8.

[144] Art. 6(1) TEU. The 2007 version is the one included by the Lisbon Treaty.

[145] Case C–60/00 *Mary Carpenter* v. *Secretary of State for the Home Department* [2002] ECR I–6279; Case C–413/99 *Baumbast and R* v. *Secretary of State for the Home Department* [2002] ECR I–7091.

[146] Protests have arrived at the doors of the EU: L. Kirk, 'Protests at EU summit in Rome erupt in vio-lence', <http://www.euobserver.com>, 6 Oct. 2003. See further, e.g., E. Bircham and J. Charlton (eds.), *Anti–Capitalism: A guide to the movement* (London: Bookmarks Publications, 2001); Friends of the Earth, 'What's wrong with world trade?', <http://www.foe.co.uk/resource/briefings/wrong_with_world_trade.pdf>. For a more academic account, see H. Daly and J. Cobb, *For the Common Good: Redirecting the economy toward community, the environment, and a sustainable future*, 2nd edn (Boston, Mass.: Beacon Press, 1994).

# PART II

# FREE MOVEMENT OF GOODS

# 2

# INTRODUCTION TO THE FREE MOVEMENT OF GOODS

## A. INTRODUCTION

For the European Commission, 'free movement of goods is one of the success stories of the European project'.[1] This chapter is intended to provide an overview of the rules on free movement of goods, looking at how the various provisions interrelate both within the EU and on the wider international scene.

The core of the rules on goods can be found in Article 28 TFEU (ex Article 23(1) EC):

The Union shall comprise a *customs union* which shall cover all trade in goods and which shall involve the prohibition between Member States of customs duties on imports and exports and of all charges having equivalent effect, and the adoption of a common customs tariff in their relations with third countries.[2]

From this we can see that the free movement of goods has an internal and external dimension: goods originating *within* the EU enjoy the rights of free movement between the Member States, while goods originating *outside* the EU enjoy free movement only once they have paid the common customs tariff (CCT), if one is due.

## B. THE SCOPE OF THE PROVISIONS ON GOODS

For the Treaty provisions on goods to be engaged three conditions need to be satisfied:

1. The product at issue must be considered a good.
2. It must be used in cross-border trade between Member States of the EU and EEA.
3. The person to whom the provision is being applied must be an addressee of the Treaties.

We shall examine these conditions in turn.

---

[1] Commission, *Free Movement of Goods: Guide to the application of Treaty provisions governing free movement of goods (Articles 28–30 EC [Articles 34–6 TFEU])* (the 'Commission guide'), SEC(2009) 673, 7.
[2] Emphasis added.

## 1. THE DEFINITION OF GOODS

Goods are defined as products which 'can be valued in money and which are capable, as such, of forming the subject of commercial transactions'.[3] As Advocate General Fennelly put it in *Jägerskiöld*,[4] goods 'possess tangible physical characteristics'. So the Court has found products as diverse as paintings and other works of art,[5] petroleum products,[6] animals,[7] coins which are no longer legal tender,[8] and waste (whether recyclable or not, even though it has no market value)[9] to constitute goods. More surprisingly, it has found electricity to be a good,[10] by reference to its treatment as goods in Union law and in the laws of the Member States as well as in the Union's tariff nomenclature. Goods can be imported either for commercial or personal use.[11]

Where goods are merely ancillary to the main activity, then other provisions of the TFEU will apply. Therefore, in *Schindler*[12] the Court said that the organization of lotteries did not constitute an activity relating to 'goods', even though lotteries necessarily involved the distribution of advertising material and tickets. Because the main activity was a service, the Treaty provisions on services (Articles 56 TFEU *et seq.*) applied instead.[13] In *Weigel*,[14] a case concerning a German couple moving to Austria for work, the Court found that the provisions of Article 45 TFEU on free movement of workers applied even though the couple were contesting the legality of the tax payable on registering their car in Austria. Where it is not possible to detect the 'main focal point of the national measure',[15] the Court will apply the goods provisions together with, say, the provisions on services.[16]

However, unlike the Treaty provisions on persons and services, the Court has not expressly required the exchange of the goods needs to form part of an economic activity.[17] In this way, free movement of goods has more in common with free movement of capital: the Court assumes a movement of goods to be economic.

---

[3] Case 7/68 *Commission* v. *Italy (the art treasures case)* [1968] ECR 423, 428–9.

[4] Case C–97/98 *Jägerskiöld* v. *Gustafsson* [1999] ECR I–7319, para. 20.　　　[5] Ibid.

[6] Case 72/83 *Campus Oil Ltd and others* v. *Minister for Industry and Energy and others* [1984] ECR 2727, para. 17. As the Court explained, such goods could not be exempted from the Treaties just because of their importance for the life or the economy of a Member State.

[7] Case C–67/97 *Bluhme* [1998] ECR I–8033.

[8] Case 7/78 *Thompson* [1978] ECR 2247. Cf. donations in kind which are not goods: Case C–318/07 *Persche* [2009] ECR I–359, para. 29.

[9] Case C–2/90 *Commission* v. *Belgium* [1992] ECR I–4431, para. 28; Case C–221/06 *Stadtgemeinde Frohnleiten* v. *Bundesminister für Land- und Forstwirtschaft, Umwelt und Wasserwirtschaft* [2007] ECR I–9643, paras. 36–8.

[10] Case C–393/92 *Almelo* v. *Energibedriff Ijsselmij* [1994] ECR I–1477, para. 28; Case C–158/94 *Commission* v. *Italy (electricity)* [1997] ECR I–5789, para. 17.　　　[11] Case 218/87 *Schumacher* [1989] ECR 617.

[12] Case C–275/92 *Customs Excise* v. *Schindler* [1994] ECR I–1039. See also Case C–97/98 *Jägerskiöld* v. *Gustafsson* [1999] ECR I–7319: while fish are goods, fishing rights and angling permits derived from them did not constitute 'goods'; the services provisions applied instead. Cf. Case C–124/97 *Läärä* v. *Kihlakunnansyyttäjä* [1999] ECR I–6067, where the Court said that slot machines constituted goods.

[13] Case C–452/04 *Fidium Finanz* [2006] ECR I–9521, para. 32 made clear that, contrary to the apparent wording of Art. 57 TFEU (ex Art. 50 EC) which suggests that services are a residual category, Art. 57 does not establish any order of priority between free movement of services and the other freedoms.

[14] Case C–387/01 [2004] ECR I–4981.　　　[15] Commission guide, above n. 1, 47.

[16] Joined Cases C–34–36/95 *Konsumentombudsmannen (KO)* v. *De Agostini (Svenska) Förlag AB* and *TV-Shop i Sverige AB* [1997] ECR I–3843, noted by J. Stuyck (1997) 34 *CMLRev.* 1445, 1465.

[17] O. Odudu, 'Economic activity as a limit to Community law' in C. Barnard and O. Odudu (eds.), *The Outer Limits of European Union Law* (Oxford: Hart Publishing, 2009), 238–9.

## 2. THE TERRITORIAL ELEMENT

For any of the Treaty provisions on goods to apply there must be a cross-border element, i.e. there must be trade between Member States. Member States covers the members of the EU,[18] together with the states of the EEA. The cross-border element is satisfied even when the goods are merely transiting the territory.[19] Generally, where there is no movement of goods between states then Union law does not apply.[20] This means that Member States can treat domestically produced goods less favourably than imports. This is known as the principle of reverse discrimination. As we shall see below, goods with an EU origin, together with goods originally manufactured outside the EU which are in 'free circulation' in the EU, enjoy the right of free movement of goods.

## 3. ADDRESSEES OF THE TREATY PROVISIONS

According to the TFEU, the provisions on goods apply to the Member States. The phrase 'state' is broadly construed to include central and local government,[21] as well as other arms of government in whatever capacity they are acting (e.g legislative, or executive).[22] In addition, as we shall see in Chapter 4, the Treaty provisions on goods have also been deemed to apply to professional regulatory bodies and private bodies supported by the state whether through finance or other forms of supervision.[23] The corollary of this is that the Treaty provisions on goods do not appear to apply to private parties acting in a purely private capacity. In other words, the goods provisions have vertical but not horizontal direct effect.

In contrast to the dormant commerce clause in the US Constitution,[24] the nearest equivalent to the EU's free movement provisions, the Treaty provisions on goods also apply to the measures adopted by the Union institutions. However, given the broad margin of discretion left to the Union legislature, the standard set is higher: Union institutions will not be liable unless the measure is manifestly inappropriate to the objective pursued.[25]

Having established the meaning of the term goods, the aim of this chapter is to present an overview of the TFEU's rules relating to goods and briefly explain how the provisions interrelate.

---

[18] It also applies to European territories for whose external relations a Member State is responsible and to overseas territories dependent on or otherwise associated with a Member State. For full details see Annex B to the Commission Guide, above n. 1.

[19] Case C–320/03 *Commission* v. *Austria* [2005] ECR I–9871, para. 65.

[20] Cf. the position under Art. 30 TFEU (ex Art. 25 EC) considered in Ch. 3.

[21] Joined Cases C–1 and 176/90 *Aragonesa de Publicidad Exterior SA* v. *Departmento de Sanidad y Seguridad Social de la Generalitat de Cataluña* [1991] ECR I–4151, para. 8. See also Case 45/87 *Commission* v. *Ireland (Dundalk Water)* [1988] ECR 4929.

[22] See, e.g., Case C–5/94 *R* v. *MAFF, ex p. Hedley Lomas (Ireland) Ltd* [1996] ECR I–2553.

[23] See, e.g., Case 249/81 *Commission* v. *Ireland ('Buy Irish campaign')* [1982] ECR 4005.

[24] Art. 1, section 8, clause 3 of the US Constitution provides: 'The Congress shall have Power...to regulate Commerce with foreign Nations, and among the several States...'. This 'Commerce Clause' gives the federal government the power to *legislate* in respect of commerce (very broadly defined); it does not prohibit state-created restrictions on inter-state commerce. However, the Supreme Court has long read into the commerce clause the negative power (the so-called 'dormant' or 'negative' commerce clause) to restrict 'permissible state regulation of interstate commerce' (*Wyoming* v. *Oklahoma* 502 US 437, 454–5).

[25] Joined Cases C–154/04 and 155/04 *Alliance for Natural Health* [2005] ECR I–6451, paras. 47 and 52.

## C.  THE INTERNAL DIMENSION: THE RULES ON FREE MOVEMENT OF GOODS

Goods originating in one EU Member State have the right to be exported from that state under Article 35 TFEU (ex Article 29 EC) and the right to be imported into another Member State under Article 34 TFEU (ex Article 28 EC). Articles 34–5 prohibit both quantitative restrictions (such as quotas) on imports and exports and measures having equivalent effect to quantitative restrictions (MEEs). These MEEs concern other barriers to trade, such as national rules on packaging and labelling.

Both Articles 34–5 are subject to the exhaustive list of derogations found in Article 36. These derogations concern matters such as public policy, public security, and health, and can be invoked by the home or host state to justify a refusal to allow the import or export of particular goods. While cases where Member States prevent exports are rare, host states are willing to invoke Article 36 to try to keep imported goods out of their country, given that imports may well threaten the viability of national production. For this reason, the Court has adopted a narrow interpretation of the derogations listed in Article 36. If the Court does recognize that there is a public interest at stake, it requires that any action taken by the Member State be proportionate.

Where a Member State successfully invokes one of the express derogations, it creates a barrier to inter-state trade which can be eliminated through Union harmonization. As we saw in Chapter 1, the power to harmonize is provided by a number of legal bases contained in the Treaties, most notably Articles 114–15, and 352 TFEU (ex Articles 95, 94, and 308 EC). If the Union measure exhaustively harmonizes the field, Member States can no longer rely on the Article 36 derogations. If the measure only partly harmonizes the area, the national legislation in the unharmonized area is still subject to scrutiny under Articles 34–6, as the jam and chocolate case study (4.1) demonstrates in Chapter 4.

While Articles 34–6 address 'non-fiscal' or 'non-tariff' barriers to trade, Articles 28–30 TFEU (ex Articles 23–5 EC) and Article 110 TFEU (ex Article 90 EC) concern 'fiscal' or 'tariff' barriers to trade.[26] There is no equivalent to the express derogations found in Article 36 in respect of Articles 30 and 110. Article 30, which prohibits customs duties and charges having equivalent effect to customs duties (CEEs), concerns charges which are levied at the *frontier* of the state. By contrast, Article 110 concerns charges which are levied *internally* within the state on imported, exported, and domestic products. While Article 30 contains an absolute prohibition on customs duties and CEEs, Article 110 prohibits only discriminatory or protectionist taxation.[27] In other words, Article 110 allows Member States to tax a product (provided the tax does not discriminate against foreign goods and is not protectionist of national production) whereas Article 30 prohibits the state from levying any charge whatsoever. For this reason Member States prefer their

---

[26] These Treaty provisions are mutually exclusive. As the Court said in Case 74/76 *Ianelli & Volpi SpA* v. *Ditta Paolo Meroni* [1977] ECR 557: 'However wide the field of application of Article [34] may be, it nevertheless does not include obstacles to trade covered by other provisions of the [Treaties]...Thus obstacles of a fiscal nature or have equivalent effect...do not fall within the prohibition in Article [34].' See also Joined Cases C–34/01 to C–38/01 *Enirisorse SpA* v. *Ministero delle Finanze* [2003] ECR I–14243, para. 58.

[27] Joined Cases C–441 and 442/98 *Kapniki Michaïlidis AE* v. *Idryma Kinonikon Asfaliseon (IKA)* [2000] ECR I–7145, para. 22.

fiscal regime to be considered under Article 110. Nevertheless, the combined effect of Articles 30 and 110 is to prevent host states from making imported goods more expensive than domestic goods by imposing an additional financial burden on the imports, thereby removing their competitive advantage.[28]

## D. THE EXTERNAL DIMENSION

### 1. THE COMMON COMMERCIAL POLICY

As Article 28 makes clear, a key component of the external dimension of the Customs Union (CU) is the Common Customs Tariff (CCT) which in turn forms part of the EU's Common Commercial Policy (CCP). The CCT demonstrates an obvious distinction between the internal and external dimensions of EU trade policy. While Article 30 TFEU prohibits tariffs (customs duties) on goods crossing an internal frontier, tariffs are permitted at the EU's external frontier.[29] This distinction between the internal and external dimensions of the CU was emphasized in *Bouhelier*,[30] where the Court said that the characteristic feature of intra-Union relations was a complete liberalization of trade, as a result of the abolition of all obstacles to imports and exports, but that such provisions could not be transposed to relations with non-member countries. In a similar vein, the Court said in *EMI*[31] that the Treaty provisions on the CCP did not lay down any obligation on the part of the Member States to extend the binding principles governing the free movement of goods between Member States to trade with third countries. As the Court explained in *Polydor*,[32] this is because the aim of the EU Treaties is to create a single market. Agreements with third countries do not have the same objectives.

Once 'third country' goods (i.e., goods from a non-Member State) have legally entered the EU, after paying the CCT where necessary, the situation changes. The goods are described as being in 'free circulation' which means that they now benefit from the same rights as goods originating in the EU. However, the CCP is more than just the CCT. As Article 207(1) TFEU (ex Article 133(1) EC) explains, it also covers 'the conclusion of tariff and trade agreements, and the commercial aspects of intellectual property...the achievement of uniformity in measures of liberalization, export policy and measures to protect trade such as those to be taken in the event of dumping or subsidies'. Article 207(2) gives the European Parliament and Council power, acting by means of the ordinary legislative procedure, to adopt measures defining the framework for implementing the common commercial policy. The Union has therefore adopted regulations concerning tariffs, most notably Council Regulation 2913/92[33] on the Common Customs Code which was repealed and replaced by the Modernised Customs Code (MCC) in Regulation 450/2008.[34] It has also enacted measures concerning non-tariff barriers to

---

[28] Case 252/86 *Bergandi* [1988] ECR 1343, para. 24.

[29] Case 70/77 *Simmenthal SpA v. Amministrazione delle Finanze dello Stato* [1978] ECR 1453, para. 2.

[30] Case 225/78 *Procureur de la République de Besançon v. Bouhelier and others* [1979] ECR I–3151, para. 6.

[31] Case 51/75 *EMI Records Limited* v. *CBS United Kingdom Limited* [1976] ECR 811, para. 17.

[32] Case 270/80 *Polydor Limited and RSO Records Inc.* v. *Harlequin Records Shops Limited and Simons Records Limited* [1982] ECR 329, paras. 16–18.

[33] [1992] OJ L302/1 as amended.     [34] [2008] OJ L145/1.

external trade: Regulation 1061/2009[35] and Regulation 260/2009[36] respectively concern freedom to export and import without quantitative restrictions. In addition, the Council has adopted defensive measures designed to protect Union industry, in particular the regulations combating dumping by third-country importers[37] and subsidies by third-country governments.[38]

## 2.  THE EFFECT OF THE WTO

While this book will focus primarily on the internal dimension to trade and, to a more limited extent, on the EU's external trade policy, it is important to see the EU's approach to trade rules against the broader international background, in particular the World Trade Organization (WTO), the successor to the General Agreement on Tariffs and Trade (GATT) 1947. The WTO was set up as a result of the Uruguay Round of trade negotiations (1986–93).[39] The WTO, itself established by a charter,[40] administers the Understanding on Rules and Procedures Governing the Settlement of Disputes (Annex 2) and the Trade Policy Review Mechanism (Annex 3). Its objective is to 'facilitate the implementation, administration and operation, and further the objectives' of the WTO Agreement and the Multilateral Trade Agreements.[41]

The Uruguay Round also led to the conclusion of a number of multilateral agreements (agreements between all the parties)[42] and plurilateral agreements (agreements between certain parties). For our purposes, the three most important multilateral agreements concern:

- trade in goods (including GATT 1994, replacing GATT 1947) (Annex 1A)
- trade in services (GATS) (Annex 1B)
- Trade-Related Aspects of Intellectual Property Rights (TRIPS) (Annex 1C).

GATT 1947,[43] and now the WTO, have played a significant role in shaping the key trade provisions of the EU Treaties. For example, the national treatment clause in Article III (which prohibits discriminatory internal taxation and regulation) and Article XI (which prohibits quantitative restrictions on imports and exports)[44] are reflected in Articles 110,

---

[35]  [2009] OJ L291/1.

[36]  [2009] OJ L84/1. This regulation applies to states which are members of the WTO. See also Council Reg. (EC) No. 625/2009 on common rules for imports from state trading countries ([2009] OJ L185/1).

[37]  Council Reg. 384/96 on protection against dumped imports from countries not members of the European Community ([1996] OJ L56/1).

[38]  Council Reg. (EC) No. 597/2009 on protection against subsidized imports from countries not members of the European Union ([2009] OJ L188/93).

[39]  The full text of these agreements can be found at <http://www.wto.org/english/docs_e/legal_e/final_e.htm> and World Trade Organization, *The Legal Texts: The results of the Uruguay Round of multilateral trade negotiations* (Cambridge: CUP, 1999).

[40]  Properly known as the Agreement establishing the World Trade Organization discussed in J. Jackson, *The World Trade Organization: Constitution and jurisprudence* (London: RIIA, 1998), Ch. 3.

[41]  Art. III.1.　　　　[42]  Art. II.2.

[43]  The EU has been represented in GATT since the Dillon Round of 1960–1 (see T. Lyons, *EC Customs Law* (Oxford: OUP, 2001), 11–12). As a result of the Kennedy Round negotiations between 1964 and 1967 which achieved substantial cuts in tariff rates (the Protocol giving effect to these tariff cuts was ratified by Council Dec. 411/68 ([1968] OJ L305/2)), the Union was able to introduce the CCT 18 months early. With the CCT in place the Union has replaced the Member States in respect of the obligations imposed by GATT.

[44]  See also Art. XI.

34, and 35 TFEU, while Article VIII (on fees and formalities connected with importation and exportation) was incorporated into the notion of charges having equivalent effect under Article 30. Much of the wording from Article XX on general exceptions was borrowed verbatim by the Article 36 derogations.[45] In addition, Article VI (which permits the imposition of anti-dumping and any countervailing duties)[46] and Article XIX (on emergency action on imports of particular products) directly influenced the Union regimes on dumping, subsidies, and safeguards.[47]

The key provision of the GATT is the Most-Favoured Nation (MFN) clause contained in Article I.1. This provides that:

any advantage, favour, privilege or immunity granted by any contracting party to any product originating in or destined for any other country shall be accorded immediately and unconditionally to the like product originating in or destined for the territories of all other contracting parties.

This provision, also known as the external non-discrimination principle, means that if, in the course of trade negotiations, State A agrees to reduce the tariff on widgets from 10 per cent to 5 per cent provided that State B removes the tariffs on gadgets altogether, then all other contracting states will gain the benefit of a 5 per cent tariff on widgets when imported into State A and a zero tariff on gadgets when imported into State B. However, in a Free Trade Area (FTA) and CU, where there are no tariffs between the states, the effect of the application of the MFN clause would be to apply this benefit to all other WTO members. This would not be the intention of the members of the FTA or CU. For this reason Article XXIV of GATT[48] contains an important exception to the MFN clause. It allows for the creation of customs unions and FTAs to which the MFN principle does not apply, provided that certain conditions are satisfied. FTAs and CUs therefore achieve a high degree of trade liberalization between the parties at the expense of differential treatment of their trading partners.[49]

The rationale for the acceptance of such arrangements is based on the theory that the benefits of greater liberalization between some countries will outweigh the discriminatory effects of these preferential agreements on non-parties.[50] This reasoning was encapsulated in Article XXIV:4 which provides:

The contracting parties recognise the desirability of increasing free trade by the development, through voluntary agreements, of closer integration between the economies of the countries parties to such agreements. They also recognise that the purpose of a customs union or of a free trade area should be to facilitate trade between the constituent territories and not to raise barriers to the trade of other contracting parties with such territories.

---

[45] Art. 345 TFEU (ex Art. 296 EC) on national security and trade in arms draws directly on Art. XXI of GATT.

[46] The details of this Article are fleshed out by the Agreement on Implementation of Article VI (anti-dumping) and the Agreement on Subsidies and Countervailing Measures.

[47] This Article is fleshed out by the Agreement on Safeguards.

[48] See also the 'Understanding on the Interpretation of Article XXIV of GATT 1994' agreed during the Uruguay Round.

[49] See *Turkey: Restriction on imports of textiles and clothing products* WT/DS34/AB/R, 22 Oct. 1999 (and the panel body report WT/DS34/R, 31 May 1999). See further M. Cremona, 'Rhetoric and reticence: EU external commercial policy in a multilateral context' (2001) 38 *CMLRev.* 359, 362.

[50] Ibid., 363.

Although Customs Unions derogate from the MFN clause, the Member States *and* the European Union continue to be bound by the provisions of WTO. As the Court noted in *International Fruit*,[51] the *Member States* were committed to the GATT 1947 when they negotiated the Treaty of Rome[52] and the *Union*, assumed the functions inherent in the tariff and trade policy on the expiry of the transitional period, by virtue of Article 207. It continued that, insofar as the Union has assumed the powers previously exercised by the Member States, the provisions of the WTO bind the Union.[53]

Such binding effect does not, however, extend to giving rights to individuals. As the Court said in *International Fruit*, Article XI of GATT (prohibiting quantitative restrictions) was not 'capable of conferring on citizens of the [Union] rights which they can invoke before the courts'.[54] Therefore the provisions of GATT could not be invoked to challenge the validity of Union regulations. In this respect the Court appeared to equate direct effect with the possibility of review of legality and to rule out the latter unless the former was present.[55] In *Germany* v. *Council*[56] the Court went further. It said that GATT did not contain *any* provisions which could be invoked in a court, a view subsequently endorsed by *Portugal* v. *Council*[57] with respect to the WTO.

In *International Fruit* the Court tried to explain why it had ruled out direct effect of the GATT when it had found provisions of other international agreements to be directly effective.[58] It said that GATT was based on the principle of negotiations undertaken on the basis of 'reciprocal and mutually advantageous arrangements'.[59] For this reason GATT was characterized by great flexibility, particularly in respect of the provisions conferring

---

[51] Joined Cases 21–24/72 *International Fruit Company NV* v. *Produktschap voor Groenten en Fruit* [1972] ECR 1219.

[52] See Art. 206 TFEU (ex Art. 131 EC), which seeks the adherence of the Union to the same aims as those sought by the GATT, as well as the first paragraph of Art. 351 TFEU (ex Art. 307 EC) which provides that the rights and obligations arising from agreements concluded before the entry into force of the Treaties are not affected by the provisions of the EU Treaties.                              [53] Para. 18.

[54] Para. 27. See generally, E. Petersmann, 'Application of GATT by the Court of Justice of the European Communities' (1983) 20 *CMLRev.* 397 and F. Snyder, 'The gatekeepers: The European Courts and WTO law' (2003) 40 *CMLRev.* 313.

[55] P. Craig and G. de Búrca, *EU Law: Text, Cases and Materials*, 4th edn (Oxford: OUP, 2008), 208, considering para. 8 of the judgment.

[56] Case C–280/93 *Germany* v. *Council* [1994] ECR I–4973, para. 109.

[57] Case C–149/96 *Portugal* v. *Council* [1999] ECR I–8395, para. 47. Repeating its earlier case law, the Court said that 'the WTO agreements are not in principle among the rules in the light of which the Court is to review the legality of measures adopted by the [Union] institutions'. Cf. Tesauro AG in Case C–53/96 *Hermès International* v. *FHT Marketing Choice* [1998] ECR I–3603, paras. 22–37. For criticism of the Court's reasoning in *Portugal* v. *Council*, see S. Peers, 'Fundamental right or political whim? WTO law and the ECJ' in G. de Búrca and J. Scott (eds.), *The EU and the WTO: Legal and constitutional issues* (Oxford: Hart Publishing, 2001). See also the final recital in the Preamble to Dec. 94/800 ([1994] OJ L336/1), according to which 'by its nature, the Agreement establishing the World Trade Organization, including the Annexes thereto, is not susceptible to being directly invoked in [Union] or Member State courts'. In Joined Cases C–300 and 392/98 *Parfums Christian Dior SA* v. *TUK Consultancy BV* [2000] ECR I–11307, para. 44, the Court said that the provisions of TRIPs did not create rights for individuals enforceable in the national court.

[58] See, e.g., Case 104/81 *Hauptzollamt Mainz* v. *C.A. Kupferberg & Cie KG* [1982] ECR 3641 (Portuguese Free Trade Agreement). Cf. Case 270/80 *Polydor Ltd and RSO Records Inc.* v. *Harlequin Record Shops Ltd and Simons Records Ltd* [1982] ECR 329.

[59] Para. 21, referring to the Preamble to GATT. This was confirmed in Case 266/81 *Società Italiana per l'Oleodotto Transalpino (SIOT)* v. *Ministère italien des finances* [1983] ECR 731; Joined Cases 267–269/81 *Amministrazione delle Finanze dello Stato* v. *Società Petrolifera SpA (SPI) and SpA Michelin Italiana (SAMI)* [1983] ECR 801.

on the contracting party the possibility of derogation, the measures to be taken in the case of exceptional difficulty, and the settlement of conflict.[60] In *Portugal* v. *Council* the Court added that because the most important commercial partners of the Union did not make the WTO Agreements enforceable in their own legal systems[61] it did not wish to tie the hands of the Union legislature or executive.[62]

Despite the case law on direct effect, the Court will review the legality of Union measures in the light of WTO rules in two situations: first, where the Union intended to implement a particular obligation assumed in the context of the WTO[63] and, secondly, where the Union measure refers expressly to the precise provisions of the WTO agreements.[64] The Court has also extended the doctrine of harmonious interpretation to the WTO, which means that it will take account of the WTO when interpreting Union legislation. Therefore, in *Germany* v. *Council*[65] the Court said that:

the primacy of international agreements concluded by the [Union] over provisions of secondary [Union] legislation means that such provisions must, so far as possible, be interpreted in a manner that is consistent with those agreements.

# E.  CONCLUSIONS

This chapter has provided a brief introduction to the specific provisions of the Treaties on the free movement of goods. It has also given a taste of the broader international environment in which they operate. We shall now consider the specific EU rules, first by examining the provisions which prohibit fiscal barriers to trade (Articles 30 and 110) in Chapter 3 and then those which concern non-fiscal barriers to trade (Articles 34–6) in Chapters 4–6. This part of the book concludes with an examination of the rules regulating goods coming into the EU from third countries.

---

[60]  Joined Cases 21–24/72 *International Fruit Company NV* [1972] ECR 1219, para. 21.

[61]  Para. 43.

[62]  Para. 46. J. Trachtmann, 'Bananas, direct effect and compliance' (1999) 10 *EJIL* 655. For criticisms of the Court's political motivation, see G. Zonnekeyn, 'The status of WTO law in the Community legal order: Some comments in the light of the Portuguese Textiles Case' (2000) 25 *ELRev.* 293; for a defence of the Court's position, see A. Rosas (2000) 37 *CMLRev.* 797.

[63]  Case C–69/89 *Nakajima All Precision Co. Ltd* v. *Council* [1991] ECR I–2069.

[64]  Case 70/87 *Federation de L'Industrie de l'Huilerie de la CEE (Fediol)* v. *Commission* [1989] ECR 1781. The Court has not ruled out the possibility of an action for damages under Art. 340 TFEU (ex Art. 288 EC) for the Union's failure to respect WTO rules: Case C–93/02 P *Biret* v. *Council* [2003] ECR I–10497; Case T–19/01 *Chiquita Brands International* v. *Commission* [2005] ECR II–315; and Joined Cases C–120/06 P and C–121/06 P *Fabbrica italiana accumulatori motocarri Montecchio SpA and Fabbrica italiana accumulatori motocarri Montecchio Technologies LLC (FIAMM) and Giorgio Fedon & Figli SpA and Fedon America, Inc. (Fedon)* v *Council and Commission* [2008] ECR I–6513 considered in Ch. 7.

[65]  Case C–280/93 *Germany* v. *Council* [1994] ECR I–4973, paras. 110–11.

# 3

# FISCAL MEASURES: CUSTOMS DUTIES AND INTERNAL TAXATION

## A. INTRODUCTION

This chapter focuses on the Treaty provisions concerning fiscal rules, namely Articles 30 and 110 TFEU. As we saw in Chapter 2, these provisions are complementary but mutually exclusive. Article 30 contains an absolute prohibition and applies at the frontier. Article 110 applies to discriminatory or protective charges levied internally within a state. We begin by considering Article 30.

## B. ARTICLE 30: CUSTOMS DUTIES AND CHARGES HAVING EQUIVALENT EFFECT

### 1. INTRODUCTION

In the early days of the Union, fiscal barriers to trade hampered the creation of a single market. However, with the completion of the internal market came the abolition of customs controls[1] and so opportunities for states to demand fees, duties, and other levies diminished. Nevertheless, Article 30 still retains its importance.[2]

It will be recalled that the definition of a customs union (CU) found in Article 28 TFEU (ex Article 23 EC) contained both an internal and an external element. The internal dimension, the subject matter of this chapter, provides that the CU 'shall involve the prohibition between Member States of customs duties on imports and exports and of all charges having equivalent effect'. This must be read in conjunction with Article 30

---

[1] One of the key pillars of the single market was the abolition of all internal economic borders between Member States unless specific suspicion gave rise to individual control. Such controls could not be systematic or concentrated on the border between states (COM(2001) 51, 6). The abolition of internal frontier controls has increased the importance of controls at the external borders. In the past such controls were largely physical. Today, the emphasis is on computerization, post-import and audit controls, and risk analysis which allows the selection of those consignments which constitute the greatest risk, while physical controls are often carried out at the trader's premises. Frontier controls are largely devoted to combating smuggling and fraud.

[2] See, e.g., Case C–163/90 *Administration des Douanes et Droits Indirectes* v. *Legros* [1992] ECR I–4625; Case C–363/93 *Lancry* v. *Direction Général des Douanes* [1994] ECR I–3957.

TFEU (ex Article 25 EC and, before that, Article 12 EEC). The original Treaty provision, Article 12 EEC, was drafted as a standstill clause:

Member States shall refrain from introducing between themselves *any new customs duties* on imports or exports or any charges having equivalent effect, and from *increasing* those which they already apply in their trade with each other.[3]

Therefore Article 12 EEC prohibited states from both introducing new duties[4] and increasing existing charges.[5] Article 12 EEC was at issue in *Van Gend en Loos*,[6] where customs duties on a product called ureaformaldehyde were increased from 5 per cent to 8 per cent. The Dutch government argued that this was due, not to an increase in the rate, but to a new classification of the product. Rejecting this argument, the Court said that it was of little importance how the increase in customs duties occurred: the fact was that customs duties on ureaformaldehyde were now higher than when the EEC Treaty came into force and so the charge contravened Article 12 EEC.[7]

The Amsterdam Treaty replaced the standstill clause in Article 12 EEC with an absolute prohibition, now found in Article 30 TFEU:

Customs duties on imports and all charges having equivalent effect shall be prohibited between Member States. This prohibition shall also apply to customs duties of a fiscal nature.

So Article 30 prohibits both customs duties (CDs) and charges having equivalent effect to a customs duty (CEEs). We shall examine these in turn.

## 2. CUSTOMS DUTIES

A customs duty is a charge, determined on the basis of a tariff, specifying the rate of duty to be paid by the importer to the host state. Customs duties are prohibited because they are protectionist: they make the imported good more expensive than the rival domestic product.[8] *Van Gend en Loos*, considered above, is one of the few cases where the Court has considered customs duties.

## 3. CHARGES HAVING EQUIVALENT EFFECT TO CUSTOMS DUTIES

### 3.1 Introduction

Article 30 also prohibits charges having equivalent effect to customs duties (CEEs), thereby preventing Member States from circumventing the prohibition on customs duties by dressing up the charge as something else.[9] This was recognized in *Deutschmann*[10] where the Court said that a charge, imposed on the issue of an import licence, which applied

---

[3] Emphasis added.

[4] Joined Cases 90 and 91/63 *Commission* v. *Luxembourg and Belgium* [1964] ECR 625.

[5] Case 26/62 *Van Gend en Loos* [1963] ECR 1.     [6] Ibid.

[7] Arts. 13 and 16 EEC provided for the abolition of *existing* customs duties and charges having equivalent effect and exports respectively. As a result of the Acceleration Dec. 66/532 ([1966] JO 2971), all customs duties were to be abolished by 1 Jul. 1968. Since these Treaty provisions are now of historical significance only, they were removed as part of the Amsterdam clean up and renumbering.

[8] Case 7/68 *Commission* v. *Italy (the art treasures case)* [1968] ECR 423, 429.

[9] Joined Cases 2 and 3/62 *Commission* v. *Luxembourg and Belgium (the gingerbread case)* [1962] ECR 425, 432.     [10] Case 10/65 *Deutschmann* v. *Germany* [1965] ECR 469, 474.

only to imported goods and not to similar domestic products had, 'by altering its price, the same effect upon the free movement of goods as a customs duty'.

The Court gave a fuller definition of CEEs in the *Statistical Levy* case.[11] It said:

Any pecuniary charge, however small and whatever its designation and mode of application, which is imposed unilaterally on domestic or foreign goods by reason of the fact that they cross a frontier...constitutes a charge having equivalent effect...even if it is not imposed for the benefit of the State, is not discriminatory or protective in effect and if the product on which the charge is imposed is not in competition with the domestic product.

We shall examine each aspect of the definition in turn.

### 3.2 'Any pecuniary charge, however small...'

The reference to 'any pecuniary charge' reminds us that Articles 28 and 30 apply only to fiscal measures; non-fiscal rules relating to goods are likely to be covered by Articles 34–6. The reference to 'however small' indicates there is no *de minimis* rule in Article 30. As the Court said in the *Statistical Levy* case:[12]

The very low rate of the charge cannot change its character with regard to the principles of the [Treaties] which for the purpose of determining the legality of those charges, do not admit of the substitution of quantitative criteria for those based on the nature of the charge.

On the facts of the case, the Court found that a (very small) charge of 10 lire on each importer to cover the cost of collecting trade statistics breached Article 30 because it 'hampers the interpenetration at which the [Treaties aim] and thus has an effect on the free circulation of goods equivalent to a customs duty'.[13]

### 3.3 '...whatever its designation and mode of application...'

The reference to 'whatever its designation and mode of application' reinforces the point that, no matter how a Member State describes the charge, the Court is likely to consider it a CEE. So the Court has found a statistical levy to be a CEE,[14] as was a charge for health inspections on products from other Member States.[15] Similarly, a postal charge for the presentation of a parcel sent from another Member State for customs clearance was a CEE,[16] as was a tax on the export of a work of art to another Member State.[17] However, the Court has said that Value Added Tax (VAT) was not a CEE.[18]

### 3.4 '...imposed unilaterally on domestic or foreign goods by reason of the fact that they cross a frontier...'

The reference to crossing a frontier emphasizes the distinction between Article 30 and Article 110. While Article 110 applies to a charge borne by imported, exported, and

---

[11] Case 24/68 *Commission* v. *Italy (statistical levy case)* [1969] ECR 193. See generally R. Barents, 'Charges of equivalent effect to customs duties' (1978) 15 *CMLRev.* 415.

[12] Case 24/68 *Commission* v. *Italy* [1969] ECR 193, para. 14.     [13] Ibid.     [14] Ibid.

[15] E.g, Case 39/73 *Rewe-Zentralfinanz* v. *Direktor der Landwirtschaftskammer Westfalen-Lippe* [1973] ECR 1039; Case 314/82 *Commission* v. *Belgium* [1984] ECR 1543, para. 16. However, health inspection charges on goods coming from a non-Member State are permitted: Case 138/77 *Ludwig* v. *Freie und Hanseatische Stadt Hamburg* [1978] ECR 1645.     [16] Case 39/82 *Donner* v. *Netherlands* [1983] ECR 2305, para. 13.

[17] Case 7/68 *Commission* v. *Italy* [1968] ECR 423. The Commission argued that the tax was a CEE but the Court did not make a clear distinction between customs duties and CEEs. See also Case 18/71 *Eunomia* v. *Italy* [1971] ECR 811.     [18] Case 39/82 *Donner* v. *Netherlands State* [1983] ECR 2305.

domestic products internally within the Member State,[19] Article 30 applies to charges levied at the frontier.[20] It had been assumed that the reference to crossing a 'frontier' meant levies on goods crossing *national* frontiers (i.e. the frontier between State A and State B).[21] However, as the Court made clear in *Legros*,[22] Articles 28 and 30 also apply to charges levied on the crossing of a frontier *internal* to a particular Member State (i.e. from one part of State A to another). In *Legros* a charge (dock dues) was levied on all goods imported into Réunion, a French overseas territory, from Germany via Metropolitan France. All goods originating in Réunion were exempt from the dues; all other goods, including those from Metropolitan France and from other French overseas territories, had to pay the dues. The Court ruled:[23]

A charge levied at a *regional* frontier by reason of the introduction of products into a region of a Member State constitutes an obstacle to the free movement of goods which is at least as serious as a charge levied at the national frontier by reason of the introduction of the products into the whole territory of a Member State.

It continued that 'the effect of such a regional levy on the unity of the [Union] customs territory is not altered by the fact that it is also charged on goods from the other parts of the territory of the Member State in question'. Therefore the dock dues constituted a CEE, notwithstanding that the charge was also imposed on goods entering Réunion from another part of France. The Court said that this was not a situation of reverse discrimination[24] since it affected goods from other Member States as well as those from France.[25] In *Simitzi*[26] the Court said that the *Legros* principle applied equally to goods moving from one part of a Member State to another.[27] This led to the ruling in *Carbonati Apuani*[28] that a charge imposed on a specific good—marble—leaving Carrara, the town in Italy famous for the quarrying of marble, heading for other Member States as well as other parts of Italy, was a CEE.[29]

These rulings, while explicable in terms of ensuring the effectiveness of the provisions on customs duties and charges having equivalent effect, are controversial for two reasons. First, as Oliver and Enchelmaier point out,[30] these decisions were given without the benefit of any authority in support of the proposition. Secondly, they overlook the fact that Article 28(1) expressly states that the principle of free movement applies exclusively *between* the Member States. Undeterred, the Court in *Carbonati* buttressed its argument that Article 30 applied to intra-state free movement by reference to the fact that Article 28

---

[19] Joined Cases C–441 and 442/98 *Kapniki Michaïlidis AE* v. *Idryma Koinonikon Asfaliseon (IKA)* [2000] ECR I–7145, para. 22.

[20] This was emphasized in Joined Cases C–393/04 and C–41/05 *Air Liquide Industries Belgium SA* v. *Ville de Seraing* [2006] ECR I–5293, paras. 52–3.

[21] This understanding was strengthened by the fact that Art. 30 talks of the prohibition of customs duties and CEEs 'between Member States'.       [22] Case C–163/90 *Legros* [1992] ECR I–4625, paras. 16–18.

[23] Paras. 16–17, emphasis added.       [24] See further Ch. 4.

[25] See also Case C–363/93 *Lancry* [1994] ECR I–3957, para. 30, concerning the same dock dues, where the Court extended this ruling to goods which originated in France. See also Case C–37/96 *Sodiprem* v. *Direction Générale des Douanes* [1998] ECR I–2039.

[26] Joined Cases C–485/93 and C–486/93 *Simitzi* v. *Dimos Kos* [1995] ECR I–2655.       [27] Para. 21.

[28] Case C–72/03 *Carbonati Apuani Srl* v. *Comune di Carrara* [2004] ECR I–8027.

[29] See also Case C–293/02 *Jersey Produce Marketing Organisation* [2005] ECR I–9543.

[30] P. Oliver and S. Enchelmaier, 'Free movement of goods: Recent development in the case law' (2007) 44 *CMLRev.* 649, 652.

had to be read with Article 26(2) TFEU (ex Article 14(2) EC) which defines the internal market as 'an area without internal frontiers in which the free movement of goods, persons, services and capital is ensured'.[31] It noted that Article 26(2) did not draw any distinction between inter-State frontiers and frontiers within a state. If this is the case, then, given that Article 26(2) applies to the other free movement provisions, the same reasoning should apply to Articles 45, 49, 56 on free movement of persons and Article 63 on free movement of capital. However, the Court has steadfastly resisted such an extension.[32]

### 3.5  '… even if it is not imposed for the benefit of the State, is not discriminatory or protective in effect and if the product on which the charge is imposed is not in competition with the domestic product.'

The absolute prohibition on CEEs applies even where the money is not used for a protectionist purpose. This can be seen in *Diamantarbeiders*,[33] where the charge of 0.33 per cent of the value of imported diamonds was used to fund additional social benefits for workers in the diamond industry. The Court said that customs duties were prohibited independently of any consideration of the purpose for which they were introduced and the destination of the revenue obtained.[34] Thus, under Article 30 the Court is concerned with the *effect* of the charge—by imposing additional costs on the imported goods, the imports become less competitive. No account is taken of either the potentially beneficial purpose to which the charge is put[35] or the fact that the money is not used to benefit the national treasury.[36] The Court believes that if a state wants to achieve welfare objectives, the revenue for this should come from a general system of taxation which is applied to all goods (to which Article 110 may apply).

Given that charges which do not have a protectionist effect are caught by Article 30, *a fortiori* charges which do have protectionist effect will also be caught by Article 30. Therefore, in the *Gingerbread* case[37] the Court rejected as 'absurd' the Belgian government's argument that the charge on the imported product was needed to 'equate the price of the foreign product with the price of the Belgian product'.

## 4.  REMEDIES

### 4.1  Direct Effect

*Van Gend en Loos*[38] established that Article 30 was (vertically) directly effective[39] and so could be enforced in the national court. Given that, by their very nature, customs duties are levied by the state, the question of horizontal direct effect does not arise in respect of

---

[31]  Paras. 23–4.

[32]  See, e.g., Case C–212/06 *Government of French Community and Walloon Government* v. *Flemish Government* [2008] ECR I–1683 discussed in Ch. 8.

[33]  Joined Cases 2 and 3/69 *Sociaal Fonds voor de Diamantarbeiders* [1969] ECR 211. See also Joined Cases C–441 and 442/98 *Kapniki Michaïlidis AE* [2000] ECR I–7145, para. 17.      [34]  Ibid., 222.

[35]  See also Case C–173/05 *Commission* v. *Italy (environmental protection tax on gas pipelines)* [2007] ECR I–4917, para. 42: the fact that the tax was introduced with the 'sole aim' of protecting the environment in the light of the requirements of the precautionary principle was irrelevant.

[36]  See also Case 7/68 *Commission* v. *Italy (the art treasures case)* [1968] ECR 423.

[37]  Joined Cases 2 and 3/62 *Commission* v. *Luxembourg and Belgium* [1962] ECR 425, 434.

[38]  Case 26/62 [1963] ECR 1.

[39]  See also Cases 2 and 3/69 *Sociaal Fonds voor de Diamantarbeiders* [1969] ECR 211, 223.

Article 30. But what if private parties are responsible for collecting the duties? In *Dubois* v. *Garanor Exploitation*[40] the Court said that Article 30 would still apply. Garanor was the manager of an international road station where the customs authorities had an office at which all customs formalities, normally completed at state frontiers, could be carried out. Dubois had used the facilities but did not pay the transit charge provided for in the contract between Garanor and Dubois. On the issue that the charge was imposed not by the state but by a private individual, the Court ruled that a Member State was still in breach of its obligations if it charged for the costs of inspections and administrative formalities carried out by customs offices. It made no difference whether the charge resulted from a unilateral measure adopted by the authorities or, as here, from a series of private contracts.

## 4.2  Repayment of Unlawful Charges

In *San Giorgio*[41] the Court ruled that a *restitutionary* claim was available to the trader who had paid a customs duty or a charge having equivalent effect contrary to Union law. The Court said that this was a consequence of, and an adjunct to, the rights conferred on individuals by the Union provisions prohibiting such charges. However, the Court said that there would be no restitutionary claim if it led to the trader being unjustly enriched (see point (1) on fig. 3.1), as a result of having passed the cost on to others.[42] As the Court explained in *Comateb*,[43] to repay the trader the amount of the charge already received from the purchaser would be tantamount to paying him twice over while in no way remedying the consequences for the purchaser of the illegality of the charge. The Court continued that it was for the national courts to determine whether the burden of the charge had been transferred in whole or in part by the trader to others and, if so, whether reimbursement to the trader would amount to unjust enrichment. If the burden of the charge had been passed on only in part, it was for the national authorities to repay the trader the amount which had not been passed on.[44]

In *Comateb*[45] the Court developed its ruling in *San Giorgio* further and said that if the charge had been passed on to third parties (e.g. the final consumer), they could obtain reimbursement from either the trader or the state. If reimbursement was obtained from the trader, the trader had in turn to be able to obtain reimbursement from the state (see point (2) on fig. 3.1). If, on the other hand, the third party could obtain repayment directly from the national authorities (see point (3) on fig. 3.1) the question of reimbursing the trader would not arise.

---

[40] Case C–16/94 *Edouard Dubois* v. *Garanor Exploitation SA* [1995] ECR I–2421. See also Case C–206/06 *Essent Netwerk Noord BV* v. *Aluminium Delfzijl BV* [2008] ECR I–5497, para. 45, where legislation implemented an agreement concluded by various economic operators. Arts. 30 and 110 in principle still applied.

[41] Case 199/82 *San Giorgio* [1983] ECR 3595, para. 12.      [42] Ibid., para. 13.

[43] Case C–192/95 *Comateb* [1997] ECR I–165. For a full analysis, see M. Dougan, 'Cutting your losses in the enforcement deficit' (1998) 1 *CYELS* 233.

[44] Case C–192/95 *Comateb* [1997] ECR I–165, para. 28. See also Case C–147/01 *Weber's Wine World Handels-GmbH* v. *Abgabenberufungskommission Wien* [2003] ECR I–11365, paras 100–1. In Joined Cases C–441 and 442/98 *Kapniki Michaïlidis* [2000] ECR I–7145, para. 42 the Court ruled that Union law precluded any presumption or rule of evidence intended to shift to the trader the burden of proving that the charges unduly paid had not been passed on to other persons and preventing him from adducing evidence to refute any allegation that the charges have been passed on.

[45] Case C–192/95 *Comateb* [1997] ECR I–165, para. 24.

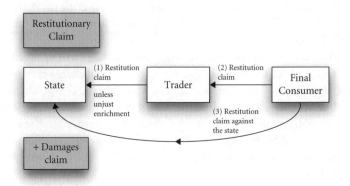

**Fig. 3.1** The effect of *Comateb*

The likelihood of final consumers actually reclaiming the money is minimal. They are more likely to vote with their wallets and buy the rival (probably national) product which is not subject to these additional costs. For this reason, the Court added in *Comateb* that the trader could also have a claim for damages for loss of sales brought about by having to pass on the unlawfully levied charge.[46] If domestic law permitted the trader to plead such damage, the national court had to give effect to such a claim. If, on the other hand, national law did not provide such a remedy, then the state could still be liable for reparation of loss caused by the levying of charges not due, irrespective of whether those charges had been passed on,[47] in accordance with the principles laid down in *Brasserie du Pêcheur and Factortame III*.[48]

The principle of national procedural autonomy applies to the claims for restitution and damages with the result that national procedural rules govern the cause of action providing they are not less favourable than those relating to similar claims regarding national charges (the principle of non-discrimination) and are not framed so as to render virtually impossible the exercise of rights conferred by Union law (the principle of effectiveness).[49] National time limits will also apply to these claims, provided they are reasonable[50] and do not breach the principles of equivalence and effectiveness.[51]

## 5. 'PERMISSIBLE' CHARGES

As we have seen, since the TFEU provides no defence to a breach of Article 30, the customs duty or CEE will not be allowed to stand, no matter how beneficial the purpose. The Court has firmly resisted attempts by Member States to invoke the Article 36 derogations

---

[46] Para. 31.      [47] Para. 34.

[48] Joined Cases C–46 and 48/93 *Brasserie du Pêcheur and Factortame III* [1996] ECR I–1029.

[49] Case 199/82 *San Giorgio* [1983] ECR 3595, para. 12.

[50] Case C–231/96 *Edis* v. *Ministero delle Finanze* [1998] ECR I–4951. See also Case C–260/96 *Ministero delle Finanze* v. *Spac* [1998] ECR I–4997 and Joined Cases C–279, 280, and 281/96 *Ansaldo Energia* v. *Amministrazione delle Finanze dello Stato* [1998] ECR I–5025.

[51] See further Case C–62/00 *Marks & Spencer plc* v. *Commissioners of Customs and Excise* [2002] ECR I–6325; Joined Cases C–216 and 222/99 *Riccardo Prisco Srl* v. *Amministrazione delle Finanze dello Stato* [2002] ECR I–6761; Case C–255/00 *Grundig Italiana SpA* v. *Ministero delle Finanze* [2002] ECR I–8003.

and apply them by analogy to Article 30.[52] Nevertheless, the Court has recognized that a charge can be lawful in the three circumstances listed in *Commission* v. *Germany*:[53]

if it relates to a general system of internal dues applied systematically and in accordance with the same criteria to domestic products and imported products alike..., if it constitutes payment for a service in fact rendered to the economic operator of a sum in proportion to the service..., or again, subject to certain conditions, if it attaches to inspections carried out to fulfil obligations imposed by [Union] law...

These three situations are not judicially developed derogations to Article 30; rather, they do not fall within the definition of a customs duty or a CEE at all and so escape the prohibition in Article 30 altogether.

We shall consider each situation in turn.

### 5.1 Payments for Genuine Administrative Services Rendered to the Importer/Exporter

If the payment is consideration for a genuine service of direct benefit to the importer or exporter then it is not a CEE. As the Court put it in *Commission* v. *Belgium (warehousing)*,[54] Article 30 will not apply if the national court[55] considers that 'the charge in question is the consideration for a service actually rendered to the importer and is of an amount commensurate with that service'.[56] However, the Court is wary about abuse of this rule. For example, in *Commission* v. *Italy*[57] the Italian authorities charged traders for opening customs posts beyond the normal business hours worked by Italian civil servants. The Italian government argued that because this was a service to the traders the charge was legitimate. The Court disagreed, reasoning that because, under a Union directive, the customs posts should have been open at these hours anyway, the charge constituted a CEE.

The Court has emphasized that, for the charge to fall outside Article 30, the services must confer a specific benefit on the individual importer/exporter.[58] Usually, however, the Court finds that this is not the case on the facts. So, when in the *Statistical Levy* case[59] the Italian government argued that the 10 lire levy constituted consideration for a service (because the information supplied afforded importers a better competitive position on the Italian market and exporters enjoyed a similar advantage abroad), the Court disagreed. It said that because the statistical information was beneficial to the public as a whole it should have been paid for by the public (through general taxation), and not by the individual importer/exporter. It added that because the connection between any competitive advantage gained by the importers and exporters and the collection of the statistics was

---

[52] Case 7/68 *Commission* v. *Italy (the art treasures case)* [1968] ECR 423, 430 where the Court said that the derogations contained in Art. 36 applied 'clearly and solely' to Arts. 34–5 and could not be applied to Art. 30.

[53] Case 18/87 *Commission* v. *Germany* [1988] ECR 5427, para. 6.

[54] Case 132/82 *Commission* v. *Belgium (warehousing)* [1983] ECR 1649.

[55] Case 39/82 *Donner* [1983] ECR 2305, para. 12.

[56] See also Case 170/88 *Ford España* v. *Estado español* [1989] ECR 2305.

[57] Case 340/87 *Commission* v. *Italy* [1989] ECR 1483. See also Case C–209/89 *Commission* v. *Italy* [1991] ECR I–1575 and the follow up in Case C–125/94 *Aprile Srl* v. *Ammininstrazione delle Finanze dello Stato* [1995] ECR I–2919.

[58] Case 18/87 *Commission* v. *Germany* [1988] ECR 5427, para. 7.

[59] Case 24/68 *Commission* v. *Italy* [1960] ECR 193. See also Case C–389/00 *Commission* v. *Germany (waste shipment)* [2003] ECR I–2001.

so difficult to assess, the charge could not be regarded as the consideration for a specific benefit actually conferred.[60] In a similar vein, the Court ruled in *Bresciani*[61] that because compulsory veterinary health inspections on imported raw cowhides were imposed in the public interest they could not be regarded as a service rendered to the importer so as to justify the imposition of a pecuniary charge. Because the public as a whole benefited, the costs had to be met out of the public purse.

However, there are borderline situations. In the *Warehousing* case[62] Belgium charged for the use of a special warehouse within the state where customs formalities could be completed instead of at the frontier. The Commission argued that these storage charges contravened Articles 28 and 30. Advocate General Mancini disagreed. He thought that the warehousing facilities constituted a specific benefit for the importer because the goods had customs clearance closer to their intended destination and the importer did not have to pay commercial warehousing costs. However, the Court agreed with the Commission and found that when payment of storage charges was demanded solely in connection with the completion of customs formalities, it could not be regarded as the consideration for a service actually rendered to the importer.

### 5.2  Charges for Inspections Required by Union Law

According to *Commission* v. *Germany*,[63] costs for compliance with mandatory[64] inspections required by *Union* law[65] can be passed on to the importer. They do not constitute a CEE providing four conditions are satisfied:[66]

(a)  they do not exceed the actual costs of the inspections in connection with which they are charged

(b)  the inspections are obligatory and uniform for all the products concerned in the Union

(c)  they are prescribed by Union law in the general interest of the Union

(d)  they promote the free movement of goods, in particular by neutralizing obstacles which could arise from unilateral measures of inspection adopted in accordance with Article 36.

Therefore, the German *Länder* were entitled to charge a fee to cover the costs of veterinary inspections on imported live animals carried out under Directive 81/389[67] concerning the protection of animals during international transport.

By contrast, charges for inspections required by *national* law do constitute a CEE.[68] Therefore, the importer cannot be required to pay for the inspection even if the inspection

---

[60]  Para. 16.

[61]  Case 87/75 *Bresciani* [1976] ECR 129. See also Case 63/74 *Cadsky SpA* v. *Istituto nazionale per il Commercio Estero* [1975] ECR 281, para. 8; Case 314/82 *Commission* v. *Belgium* [1984] ECR 1543, para. 12.

[62]  Case 132/82 *Commission* v. *Belgium* [1983] ECR 1649.

[63]  Case 18/87 *Commission* v. *Germany* [1988] ECR 5427.

[64]  This does not apply to inspections merely *permitted* by Union law: Case 314/82 *Commission* v. *Belgium* [1984] ECR 1543, para. 8.

[65]  The same rule applies where the inspection, and thus the charge, is required by an International Convention: Case 89/76 *Commission* v. *Netherlands* [1977] ECR 1355, para. 16, drawing parallels with the Union directive at issue in Case 46/76 *Bauhuis* [1977] ECR 5.                    [66]  Para. 8.

[67]  [1981] OJ L150/1 repealed and replaced by Council Dir. 91/628/EC ([1991] OJ L340/17 which in turn was repealed and replaced by Council Reg. (EC) 1/2005 [2005] OJ L3/1.

[68]  Case 46/76 *Bauhuis* [1977] ECR 5.

itself (which is considered to be a measure having equivalent effect under Article 34[69]) is justified under Article 36.[70] The explanation for this different treatment of charges levied in respect of inspections required by Union and national law lies in the fact that harmonization of inspection requirements by Union law removes an impediment to the free movement of goods that would otherwise arise as a result of a divergence between the national systems. As the Court noted in *IFG*,[71] if a public-health inspection is carried out in the state of origin, valid for the whole Union, this facilitates free movement of goods by reducing duplication of inspections at the frontier.[72]

### 5.3  Charges Falling within the Scope of Internal Taxation

If the charge 'relates to a general system of internal dues applied systematically and in accordance with the same criteria to domestic products and imported products alike' then the legality of the charge falls to be considered under Article 110 and not Article 30 because Articles 30 and 110 are mutually exclusive.[73] The relationship between Articles 30 and 110 will be explored more fully below. It is to Article 110 that we now turn.

## C.  ARTICLE 110: INTERNAL TAXATION

### 1.  INTRODUCTION

While Article 30 addresses fiscal barriers to trade levied at the *frontier*, Article 110 deals with fiscal rules which apply *internally* within a Member State.[74] Article 110 addresses two separate issues. Article 110(1) prohibits discriminatory taxation in respect of goods which are *similar*, such as one type of beer and another. It provides:

No Member State shall impose, directly or indirectly, on the products of other Member States any internal taxation of any kind in excess of that imposed directly or indirectly on similar domestic products.

If the Court finds that the products are not similar, it then considers Article 110(2) which concerns products *in competition* such as beer and (cheap) wine:

Furthermore, no Member State shall impose on the products of other Member States any internal taxation of such a nature as to afford indirect protection to other products.

---

[69]  See further Ch. 4.

[70]  Case 46/76 *Bauhuis* [1977] ECR 5, para. 13, Case 251/78 *Denkavit Futtermittel* v. *Minister für Ernährung* [1979] ECR 3369, para. 31.          [71]  Case 1/83 *IFG* v. *Freiestaat Bayern* [1984] ECR 349, para. 9.

[72]  Case 89/76 *Commission* v. *Netherlands* [1977] ECR 1355, para. 13.

[73]  Joined Cases C–34/01 to C–38/01 *Enirisorse SpA* v. *Ministero delle Finanze* [2003] ECR I–14243, para. 59.

[74]  Despite its close relationship with the rules on customs duties, the provisions on internal taxation were placed in the original Part Three of the EEC Treaty on policies of the Community, while the provisions on customs duties were found in the original Part Two entitled 'Foundations of the Community'. This led some to suggest that the provisions on internal taxation were subsidiary to those on customs duties: see Case 193/85 *Cooperativa Co-Frutta Srl* v. *Ammininstrazaione delle Finanze dello Stato* [1987] ECR 2085. Post Lisbon, both customs duties and internal taxation fall under Part Three entitled 'Union policies and internal actions'. However, Art. 110 falls under Title VII entitled 'Common rules on competition, taxation and approximation of laws' while Art. 30 falls under Title II entitled 'Free movement of goods'.

Together these provisions are intended to guarantee 'the complete neutrality of internal taxation as regards competition between domestic products and products imported from other Member States'[75] in order to ensure the free movement of goods between Member States in normal conditions of competition.[76]

Article 110 applies to *indirect* taxation (taxation on products[77]); it does not affect direct taxation (such as income tax on the producer), although any discrimination in respect of direct taxation may offend against other Treaty provisions, notably those on the free movement of persons.[78] We shall now turn to consider the detail of Article 110, beginning with the basic rule that Member States are free to determine their own schemes of taxation.

## 2. MEMBER STATE AUTONOMY TO DETERMINE ITS OWN TAXATION POLICIES

Article 110 gives Member States considerable discretion to determine the content of their own taxation policy (which products to tax, on what basis, and at what level). This is known as the principle of fiscal autonomy or fiscal sovereignty. This (relative) freedom was emphasized in the *Johnnie Walker* case,[79] where the question was raised whether Denmark could tax whisky at a higher rate than fruit wine. The Court said that Union law did not restrict the freedom of each Member State to lay down tax arrangements which differentiated between certain products on the basis of objective criteria, such as the nature of the raw materials used or the production processes employed. It continued that such differentiation was legitimate under Union law 'if it pursues objectives of economic policy[80] which are themselves compatible with the requirements of the [Treaties]'.[81]

Thus any scheme of taxation which makes a distinction between products based on objective criteria (unrelated to origin) is compatible with Article 110. Therefore, in *Bergandi*[82] the Court ruled that a French system of taxation which taxed games machines, the use of which the French government wished to discourage, at a higher rate than other games machines, was compatible with Article 110. Similarly, the Court said in *Commission* v. *France*[83] that it was legitimate for France to tax natural sweet wines whose production in regions with poor soil and low rainfall was 'traditional and customary' more favourably than other liqueur wines, provided that such preferential treatment

---

[75]  Case 193/85 *Co-frutta* [1987] ECR 2085, para. 25.

[76]  Case 252/86 *Bergandi* [1988] ECR 1343, para. 24.

[77]  The importance of this point was stressed in Joined Cases C–393/04 and C–41/05 *Air Liquide Industries Belgium SA* v. *Ville de Seraing* [2006] ECR I–5293, para. 57 where the Court said that Art. 110 did not apply since the tax is not 'imposed specifically on exported or imported products or in such a way as to differentiate them, given that it applies to economic activities carried out by industrial, commercial, financial or agricultural undertakings and not to products as such'.

[78]  See, e.g., Case C–204/90 *Bachmann* v. *Belgium* [1992] ECR I–249 considered further in Ch. 9.

[79]  Case 243/84 *Johnnie Walker* [1986] ECR 875.

[80]  In Case 252/86 *Bergandi* v. *Directeur Général des Impôts* [1988] ECR 1343, para. 29 the Court talked of 'legitimate economic or social purposes'.

[81]  Para. 22. See also Case C–221/06 *Stadtgemeinde Frohnleiten* v. *Bundesminister für Land- und Forstwirtschaft, Umwelt und Wasserwirtschaft* [2007] ECR I–2613, para. 56.

[82]  Case 252/86 *Bergandi* [1988] ECR 1343, para. 32.

[83]  Case 196/85 *Commission* v. *France* [1987] ECR 1597, para. 7.

was extended to imported products. In much the same way the Court said in *Chemial Farmaceutici*[84] that the Italian government was free to tax denatured synthetic alcohol which had petroleum as its base at a higher rate than denatured alcohol obtained by fermentation. This pattern of taxation was intended to promote agriculture and to reserve petroleum for other 'more important uses'.[85]

These cases demonstrate that national taxation policy[86] is, by its very nature, discriminatory. It is a matter for an elected government to decide whether to tax product X (e.g., natural sweet wines grown in disadvantaged regions) at a lower rate than product Y (e.g., other liqueur wines). Provided that such discrimination or, to use a more neutral term, differentiation, is based on objective criteria[87] unrelated to the origin (nationality)[88] of the goods, the tax does not fall within the purview of Article 110 (stage 1 of the enquiry—fig. 3.2). This highlights a key difference between Article 110 and the other Treaty provisions discussed in this book: Article 110 is essentially *permissive*; it allows Member States both to raise revenue by taxation and to determine the content of their own taxation policy. The other Treaty provisions are essentially *restrictive*: states cannot impose customs duties (Article 30), prohibit imports or exports etc. (Articles 34–5).

If, however, the Court senses that the policy choices guiding the taxation decisions are underpinned by discrimination on the grounds of *origin*, it will apply Article 110 (stage 2 of the enquiry—fig. 3.2).[89] Whether cases are dealt with at stage 1 or stage 2 of the enquiry seems to owe much to the Court's intuition. In *Bergandi*, *Commission v. France*, and *Chemial Farmaceutici* the Court clearly thought that the Member State's policy choices were legitimate and so found that the rules fell outside Article 110 (stage 1). This can be contrasted with the line of cases concerning the taxation of alcoholic drinks where, for example, the UK taxed beer more leniently than wine;[90] and France taxed fruit-based spirits (cognac, calvados, and armagnac), of which it was a major producer, more favourably than grain-based spirits (whisky, rum, and gin).[91] In these cases the Court suspected that the national taxation schemes favoured national products to the detriment of similar or potentially equivalent products produced elsewhere, and so applied Article 110 (stage 2).

## 3. THE SCOPE OF ARTICLE 110

Given its importance to the attainment of the single market, the Court has interpreted Article 110 widely 'so as to cover all procedures which, directly or indirectly, undermine the equal treatment of domestic products and imported products'.[92] For example, in *Bergandi* the Court said that Article 110 will apply 'whenever a fiscal levy is likely

---

[84] Case 140/79 *Chemial Farmaceutici SpA v. DAF SpA* [1981] ECR 1. See also Case 46/80 *SpA Vinal v. SpA Orbat* [1981] ECR 77.    [85] Para. 13.

[86] Whether imposed by law or administrative practice: Case 17/81 *Pabst & Richarz* [1982] ECR 1331.

[87] For criticism, see M. Hedemann-Robinson, 'Indirect discrimination: Article 95(1) EC back to front and inside out' (1995) 1 *EPL* 439.

[88] In this chapter the terms will be used synonymously. 'Origin' is the more correct term but 'nationality' is the term used in respect of the other freedoms.

[89] See A. Easson, 'Fiscal discrimination: New perspectives on Article 95 of the EEC Treaty' (1981) 18 *CMLRev.* 521, 540–1.    [90] Case 170/78 *Commission v. UK* [1980] ECR 417.

[91] Case 168/78 *Commission v. France* [1980] ECR 347.

[92] Case C–221/06 *Stadtgemeinde Frohnleiten* [2007] ECR I–2613, para. 40.

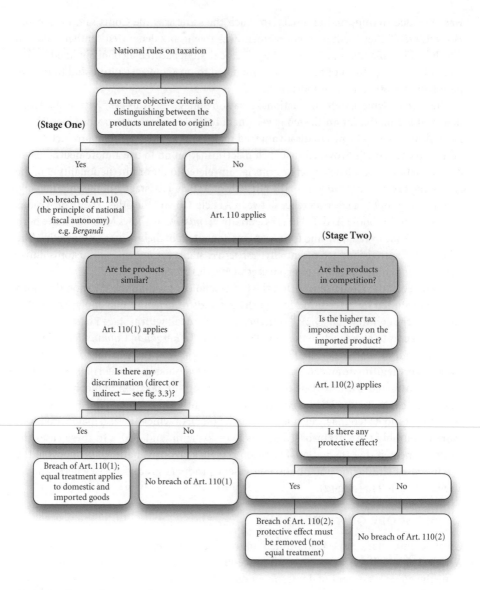

**Fig. 3.2** The application of Art. 110

to discourage imports of goods originating in other Member States to the benefit of domestic production'.[93] Therefore, Article 110 applies to tax imposed on imported (and exported[94]) products as well as to tax imposed on the *use* of those products.[95] It also covers charges 'going beyond classic levies directly imposed on goods'[96] such as fees for

---

[93] Para. 25.

[94] Art. 110 does apply to tax on exports even though this is not expressly provided on its face: Case 142/77 *Staten Kontrol v. Larsen* [1978] ECR 1787. See also Art. 111 TFEU (ex Art. 91 EC) which provides that where products are exported to the territory of any Member State, any repayment of internal taxation shall not exceed the internal taxation imposed on them directly or indirectly.

[95] Case 252/86 *Bergandi* [1988] ECR 1343, para. 27.

[96] Sharpston AG's Opinion in Case C–221/06 *Stadtgemeinde Frohnleiten* [2007] ECR I–2613, para. 32.

health inspections[97] and for roadworthiness testing of cars.[98] In addition, it applies to a charge on a specific activity of an undertaking in connection with products (i.e., a necessary[99] service associated with the product) which is calculated according to, for example, the weight of the product.[100] Therefore, in *Stadtgemeinde Frohnleiten*, the Court ruled that a levy imposed on an operator of a waste disposal site amounted to internal taxation for the purposes of Article 110 because it was imposed indirectly on waste being deposited.[101]

The prohibition in Article 110 on discriminatory and protective taxation is accompanied by the power contained in Article 113 to harmonize legislation 'concerning turnover taxes, excise duties and other forms of indirect taxation to the extent that such harmonization is necessary to ensure the establishment and functioning of the internal market'. Such harmonization is subject to a unanimous vote in Council and simple consultation with the European Parliament. Despite the extension of qualified majority voting (QMV) to many other areas of the Treaties, it is a sign of the highly sensitive nature of taxation that the procedure laid down by Article 113 has not been changed since 1957. The principal area where harmonization has occurred is in respect of VAT[102] and excise duties on manufactured tobacco,[103] alcohol,[104] and mineral oils.[105] Together these measures formed key components of the single market programme aimed at eliminating fiscal barriers to trade.

Article 110 applies independently of Article 113.[106] It is to the content of Article 110 that we now turn.

## 4. GOODS WHICH ARE SIMILAR (ARTICLE 110(1))

### 4.1 Definition of 'Similar'

Article 110(1) prohibits the host Member State from imposing a higher tax on goods imported into the Member State than on similar domestic goods. The key question is whether goods are 'similar'. Over the years the Court has used two tests to determine similarity. At first it applied a formal test, examining whether the products in question

---

[97] Case 29/87 *Denkavit* v. *Danish Ministry of Agriculture* [1988] ECR 2965.

[98] Case 50/85 *Schloh* [1986] ECR 1855.

[99] Case C-206/06 *Essent Netwerk Noord BV v. Aluminium Delfzijl BV* [2008] ECR I-5497.

[100] Case C-221/06 *Stadtgemeinde Frohnleiten* [2007] ECR I-2613, para. 43.      [101] Ibid., para. 47.

[102] Sixth Council Dir. 77/388/EEC on the harmonization of the laws of the Member States relating to turnover taxes ([1977] OJ L145/1) as amended.

[103] Council Dir. 92/79/EEC on the approximation of taxes on cigarettes ([1992] OJ L316/8), Council Dir. 92/80/EEC on the approximation of taxes on manufactured tobacco other than cigarettes ([1992] OJ L316/10), Council Dir. 95/59/EEC on taxes other than turnover taxes which affect the consumption of manufactured tobacco ([1995] OJ L291/40). The first two directives concern rates; the third, structures of taxation. These directives have all been amended, most significantly by Council Dir. 2002/10/EC as regards the structure and rates of excise duty applied on manufactured tobacco ([2002] OJ L46/26).

[104] Council Dir. 92/83 on the harmonization of the structures of excise duties on alcohol and alcoholic beverages ([1992] OJ L316/21), Council Dir. 92/84 on the approximation of the rates of duties on alcohol and alcoholic beverages ([1992] OJ L316/29).

[105] Council Dir. 92/81/EEC on the harmonization of the structures of excise duties on mineral oils ([1992] OJ L316/12) and Council Dir. 92/82/EEC on the approximation of the rates of excise duties on mineral oil ([1992] OJ L316/19). These directives were repealed and replaced by Council Dir. 2003/96/EC restructuring the Union framework for the taxation of energy products and electricity ([2003] OJ L283/51).

[106] Case 55/79 *Commission* v. *Ireland* [1980] ECR 481, para. 12.

normally come within the same fiscal, customs,[107] or statistical classification.[108] Subsequently, the Court adopted a broader test[109] which combined a factual comparison of the products with an economic analysis of their use. As the Court said in *Commission v. Denmark*:[110]

it is necessary first to consider certain objective characteristics of both categories of beverages, such as their origin, the method of manufacture and their organoleptic properties, in particular taste and alcohol content, and secondly to consider whether or not both categories of beverages are capable of meeting the same need from the point of view of consumers.

Thus, the scope of Article 110(1) is determined not on the basis of the strictly identical nature of the products but on their similar and comparable use.[111]

*Commission v. Denmark* considered the question whether fruit wines and wines made from grapes were similar. The Court found that table wines, whether made from grapes or fruit, were manufactured from the same kind of basic product (agricultural produce) and by the same process (natural fermentation). Their organoleptic properties, in particular their taste and alcohol content, were also similar. Furthermore, both drinks met the same needs for both present and future consumers, as they could be consumed in the same way (to quench thirst, as refreshments, and at meal times), even though fruit wine had always been less popular with consumers than wine made from grapes.[112] For these reasons the Court considered the two products to be similar.[113]

The Court also adopted this broader approach in *Commission v. France (tobacco)*[114] where it said that dark and light tobacco cigarettes were similar. It noted, first, that they were manufactured from different types of the same base product (tobacco), using comparable processes. Secondly, it said that their organoleptic characteristics, such as taste and smell, were similar, albeit that they contained different quantities of certain types of tobacco. Thirdly, it said they satisfied the same needs of consumers, given their similar properties. The fact that the average age of consumers of dark tobacco was higher than the average age of consumers of light tobacco did not affect this conclusion. Finally, it noted that the Union legislature treated both types of cigarettes in the same way and they fell in the same subheading of the Combined Nomenclature of the CCT.[115]

However, just because products contain the same raw ingredients does not always mean they will be similar. This can be seen in the *Johnnie Walker* case[116] where the question was raised whether whisky and fruit liqueur wines were similar. Under Danish law,

---

[107] A more detailed discussion of customs classification is found in Ch. 7.

[108] Case 27/67 *Fink-Frucht* [1968] ECR 223, 232; Case 45/75 *Rewe v. HZA Landau* [1976] ECR 181, para. 12.

[109] There are parallels here with the Court's approach to determining the relevant product market under Art. 102 TFEU (ex Art. 82 EC) on the abuse of a dominant position.

[110] Case 106/84 *Commission v. Denmark* [1986] ECR 833, para. 12, which was delivered on the same day as Case 243/84 *Johnnie Walker* [1986] ECR 875.

[111] Case 168/78 *Commission v. France* [1980] ECR 347, para. 5.

[112] See also Case 277/83 *Commission v. Italy* [1985] ECR 2049 where the Court said that marsala was similar to fruit liqueur wines.

[113] Para. 22. See also Case C–221/06 *Stadtgemeinde Frohnleiten* [2007] ECR I–2613, para. 60: domestic and imported waste deemed to be similar.

[114] Case C–302/00 *Commission v. France* [2002] ECR I–2055, paras. 24–8.

[115] The Combined Nomenclature is discussed in Ch. 7.

[116] Case 243/84 *Johnnie Walker* [1986] ECR 875.

whisky (40 per cent proof and manufactured exclusively abroad) was taxed at a much higher rate than fruit liqueur wines (up to 20 per cent proof and manufactured almost exclusively in Denmark). The Court found that the two drinks were not similar since they exhibited 'manifestly different characteristics'.[117] It noted that fruit wine of the liqueur type was a fruit-based product obtained by natural fermentation, whereas Scotch whisky was a cereal-based product obtained by distillation. The alcohol content of the two drinks also differed significantly. The Court said that, for the products to be regarded as similar, the raw material had to be present in 'more or less equal proportions in both products'. It added that the fact that whisky could be diluted 'would not be sufficient to render Scotch whisky similar to fruit wine of the liqueur type, whose intrinsic characteristics are fundamentally different'.[118]

### 4.2  Types of Discrimination

If the goods are similar then the taxation applied to those goods must be the same.[119] In other words it must not discriminate against foreign goods on the grounds of their origin, either directly or indirectly.[120]

### (a)  Direct discrimination

Direct discrimination involves less favourable treatment of the imported product on the ground of its origin. It can come about in a number of ways. For example, direct discrimination may arise because only the imported product is subject to the tax. This was the situation in *Lütticke*[121] where powdered milk from Luxembourg imported into Germany was subject to a tax not payable by the German product. Direct discrimination may also occur because the imported product is taxed at a different (usually higher) rate than the domestic product or the Member State uses different methods for calculating tax for the domestic and imported goods. Therefore, the Court found in *Haahr Petroleum*[122] that the national rule subjecting international transport to a tax 40 per cent higher than that imposed on domestic transport breached Article 110(1),[123] as did the rule in *Bobie*[124] where a Member State imposed a flat rate of tax on the domestic product but a graduated

---

[117]  Para. 12.

[118]  It then looked at Art. 110(2) and found that, since whisky was taxed within the general framework of taxation of spirits, including many Danish-produced goods, the scheme also did not breach Art. 110(2).

[119]  Case 106/84 *Commission* v. *Denmark* [1986] ECR 833, para. 22. If there is no discrimination the tax is lawful: Joined Cases C–34/01 to C–38/01 *Enirisorse SpA* v. *Ministero delle Finanze*, [2003] ECR I–14243, para. 60.

[120]  These terms are interpreted broadly: Case 28/67 *Molkerei-Zentrale Westfalen* v. *Hauptzollamt Paderborn* [1968] ECR 143, 155.

[121]  Case 57/65 *Lütticke* v. *Hauptzollamt Saarlouis* [1966] ECR 205.

[122]  Case C–90/94 *Haahr Petroleum* v. *Åbenrå Havn* [1997] ECR I–4085. See also Joined Cases C–114/95 and C–115/95 *Texaco A/S* v. *Middelfart Havn and others* [1997] ECR I–4263; Case C–242/95 *GT-Link A/S* v. *De Danske Statsbaner* [1997] ECR I–4449. See also Case C–47/88 *Commission* v. *Denmark* [1990] ECR I–4509.

[123]  See also Joined Cases C–290/05 and C–333/05 *Ákos Nádasdi* v. *Vám- és Pénzügyarség Észak-Alföldi Regionális Parancsnoksága and Ilona Németh* v. *Vám- és Pénzügyarség Dél-Alföldi Regionális Parancsnoksága* [2006] ECR I–10115: Hungarian law imposed a heavier tax burden on imported used vehicles than on similar used vehicles already registered in Hungary. In the Polish context see Case C–313/05 *Brzezinski* v. *Dyrektor Izby Celnej w Warszawie* [2007] ECR I–513.

[124]  Case 127/75 *Bobie* v. *Hauptzollamt Aachen-Nord* [1976] ECR 1079, para. 4; Case C–213/96 *Outokumpu Oy* [1998] ECR I–1777; Case C–101/00 *Tulliasiamies and Antti Siilin* [2002] ECR I–7487, para. 54.

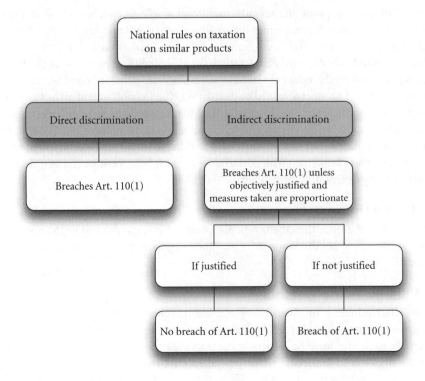

**Fig. 3.3** Discriminatory taxation under Art. 110(1)

tax on the imported product. Likewise, in *Stadtgemeinde Frohnleiten*[125] a national law reserving the benefit of an exemption from internal taxation to certain domestic products only, breached Article 110(1).

The conditions under which the tax is paid or tax relief granted may also lead to direct discrimination. For example, in *Commission* v. *Ireland*[126] Irish producers had longer to pay a tax than foreign producers. The Court said that although the benefit was small, 'the discrimination against products imported from other Member States is none the less obvious'.[127]

Since there are no express defences to Article 110 any directly discriminatory tax breaches Article 110 and cannot be saved[128] (see fig. 3.3). This means that the Member State must remove the discriminatory element of the taxation policy and so equalize the tax.

Reverse discrimination is, however, permitted by the Treaties. It occurs where the national law treats *domestic* products less favourably than imported products. This can

---

[125] Case C–221/06 *Stadtgemeinde Frohnleiten* [2007] ECR I–2613, para. 52. Similarly, in Case 21/79 *Commission* v. *Italy* [1980] ECR 1 the Court found discrimination where Italy charged lower taxes on regenerated oil than ordinary oil but did not extend this benefit to imported regenerated oil. See also Case 277/83 *Commission* v. *Italy (marsala)* [1985] ECR 2049.

[126] Case 55/79 *Commission* v. *Ireland* [1980] ECR 481; Case C–68/96 *Grundig Italiana* v. *Ministero delle Finanze* [1998] ECR I–3775.                                                    [127] Para. 9.

[128] Case C–302/00 *Commission* v. *France (tobacco)* [2002] ECR I–2055, para. 33.

be seen in *Peureux*,[129] where French distillers were required by French law to pay a tax which was not payable by the distillers of equivalent imported alcohol. The Court said:

Although Article [110] prohibits any Member State from imposing internal taxation on products imported from other Member States in excess of that on national products, it does not prohibit the imposition on national products of internal taxation in excess of that on imported products.

The Court justified the continued existence of reverse discrimination on the ground that such disparities 'result from special features of national laws which have not been harmonized in spheres for which the Member States are responsible'.[130] Therefore France was entitled to tax its own spirits at a higher rate than imported spirits.

## (b) Indirect discrimination

### (i) *Establishing a* prima facie *case of discrimination*

Direct discrimination is overt: it is clear on the face of the measure ('in law') that there is less favourable treatment of the imported goods. By contrast, a measure is indirectly discriminatory where on its face (in law) it makes no reference to the origin of the product, but in reality (in fact) it imposes a particular burden on the imported goods (sometimes referred to as disparate impact).

*Commission v. France (tobacco)*[131] provides a good illustration of such discrimination. Dark-tobacco cigarettes were taxed more favourably under French law than light-tobacco cigarettes. The system was found to be indirectly discriminatory because, although the law made no reference to the origin of the product, in fact dark-tobacco cigarettes were almost exclusively domestically produced while light-tobacco cigarettes came from other Member States. The Court added that this finding was not affected by the fact that a small fraction of dark-tobacco cigarettes came from other Member States and a certain proportion of light-tobacco cigarettes were domestically produced. It concluded that '[i]t appears, therefore, that the system of taxation is designed in such a way as to benefit a typical domestic product and handicaps imported cigarettes to the same extent'.

In *Humblot*[132] the Court found French car tax to be indirectly discriminatory. The French taxation system imposed a gradually increasing tax on all cars up to an engine size of 16 cv with a ceiling of 1,100 FF. A flat rate of tax (5,000 FF), known as the special tax, then applied to cars with an engine capacity of over 16 cv. The system was found to be indirectly discriminatory: on the face of the measure—in law—there was no discrimination, but in fact the special tax disadvantaged cars manufactured in other Member States because no cars with an engine capacity of over 16 cv were made in France. The Court noted that, in the absence of considerations relating to the amount of the special tax, consumers seeking comparable cars would naturally choose from among cars above and below the 16 cv rating. However, the French law affected their choice, especially because the special tax was payable for several years.[133] Therefore, the

---

[129] Case 86/78 *SA des Grandes Distilleries Peureux* v. *Directeur des Services Fiscaux de la Haute-Saône et du Territoire de Belfort* [1979] ECR 897, para. 32.

[130] Para. 33.

[131] Case C–302/00 [2002] ECR I–2055, para. 30.    [132] Case 112/84 *Humblot* [1985] ECR 1367.

[133] Para. 15.

Court said that the special tax reduced competition faced by domestic cars, contrary to Article 110(1).[134]

The Greek government operated a similar taxation scheme imposing a higher rate of tax on cars with an engine capacity in excess of 1,800cc. Greece produced cars only with an engine capacity of less than 1,600cc. However, in enforcement proceedings against Greece[135] the Court found that the Commission had failed to show that the Greek taxation system might have the effect of favouring the sales of Greek cars. Because no *prima facie* case of discrimination had been made out, there was no breach of Article 110. This case demonstrates that where indirect discrimination is alleged under Article 110(1), the Court requires the complainant to demonstrate *actual* (as opposed to potential[136]) disparate impact on the imported goods or actual benefit to the domestic producer.[137]

### (ii) Objective justification

While a *directly* discriminatory tax breaches Article 110, with no chance of being justified,[138] an *indirectly* discriminatory tax breaches Article 110 unless it can be objectively justified by the defendant Member State (see fig. 3.3). This means that where a *prima facie* case of discrimination is made out, the Member State can point to a national interest to justify its taxation policy. Provided that the national interest is (1) unconnected with the origin of the product, (2) pursues an objective recognized by the EU as legitimate, and (3) the steps taken to protect that interest are proportionate, then there is no breach of Article 110.[139] One potential justification is environmental protection and this would have been the ground put forward by the Greek government in *Commission* v. *Greece*[140] had a *prima facie* case of indirect discrimination been established. The government said that '[i]n view of the poor infrastructure of the road network and the problems of pollution prevailing in Greece, tax legislation discouraging the purchase of large-engined cars was justified'.

Various commentators have suggested that other potential justifications have been recognized by the Court: the discouragement of certain types of games machines in

---

[134] After *Humblot* France revised its tax system and replaced the 5,000 FF tax with nine more specific bands, depending on the power of the car. This system was challenged in Case 433/85 *Feldain* v. *Directeur des Services Fiscaux* [1987] ECR 3536 and also found to be indirectly discriminatory because the tax rate still increased significantly over 16 cv.

[135] Case 132/88 *Commission* v. *Greece* [1990] ECR I–1567.

[136] Cf. the case law on Arts. 34 and 45 TFEU: Joined Cases C–321/94 to C–324/94 *Pistre and others* [1997] ECR I–2343; and Case C–237/94 *O'Flynn* v. *Adjudication Office* [1996] ECR I–2617, para. 19.

[137] See also Case 252/86 *Bergandi* [1988] ECR 1343; Case 196/85 *Commission* v. *France* [1987] ECR 1597; and Case 140/79 *Chemial Farmaceutici* [1981] ECR 1. The Court also demands this in the case of indirect *sex* discrimination: Case C–167/97 *R* v. *Secretary of State for Employment, ex p. Seymour-Smith and Perez* [1999] ECR I–623.

[138] Although cf. the possibility, gradually being introduced in Art. 34 TFEU whereby distinctly applicable measures can be objectively justified: Case C–54/05 *Commission* v. *Finland* [2007] ECR I–2473 where the Court allowed an import licence to be justified, at least in principle, by 'mandatory requirements' (the language used in Art. 34 to describe objective justifications) and again in Case C–297/05 *Commission* v. *Netherlands (roadworthiness testing of cars)* [2007] ECR I–7467, paras. 73–4 where the Court allowed roadworthiness tests of imported cars to be potentially justified by mandatory requirements.

[139] The justifications are not defences because there are no express defences in respect of Art. 110. If the national rule can be justified then there is no breach of Art. 110 (see fig. 3.2) so there is no need to look for defences, since the defences, if available, apply only if there is a breach of the Treaty provision.

[140] Case 132/88 *Commission* v. *Greece* [1990] ECR I–1567; considered above n. 135.

*Bergandi*[141] (a type of consumer protection/public morality justification); regional development in the *Natural Sweet Wines* case;[142] and promoting agriculture and reserving petrol for other 'more important uses' in *Chemial Farmaceutici*[143] (a type of public-security justification). However, as we saw above, these grounds were all successfully invoked by the Member States to justify tax arrangements which differentiated between certain products on the basis of objective criteria (stage 1 of the enquiry—see fig. 3.2). In none of the cases did the Court ever reach stage 2 of the enquiry, requiring it to consider the issue of discrimination and thus of justification in the strict sense of the term. However, in the light of the Court's developing jurisprudence in other fields, notably Article 34 on goods, and Articles 45, 49, and 56 on persons, it is safe to say that indirectly discriminatory taxation schemes breach Article 110 unless justified. Justifications based on environmental protection, regional development, and saving scarce resources are likely to be accepted by the Court,[144] provided that the steps taken are proportionate. However, given that a *prima facie* case of discrimination has been established, the level of scrutiny by the Court of the justification in stage 2 is likely to be more intense than at stage 1.

## 5. GOODS WHICH ARE IN COMPETITION (ARTICLE 110(2))

If goods are deemed not to be sufficiently similar for the purposes of Article 110(1), the Court will then examine whether they are in competition with each other under Article 110(2),[145] even if only partially, indirectly, or potentially.[146] If so, the Court will consider whether the domestic goods benefit from some kind of 'indirect fiscal protectionism'. If this is the case, the prohibition in Article 110(2) applies (see fig. 3.2).

### 5.1 The Court's Approach To Article 110(2)

The Court has used a number of tests to determine whether goods are in competition. Sometimes it applies an economic test based on cross-elasticity of demand. With this test, the Court considers whether, if the price of one product goes up, sales of another increase. If so, there is substitutability and cross-elasticity of demand and so the two products are in competition.

The Court also takes into account factors such as the manufacture and composition of the product, and consumer preference, both present and future. In this way the test is not so different from that to establish similarity under Article 110(1). Ultimately the Court's approach is impressionistic: in view of its inherent characteristics, is a given tax mechanism *likely* to bring about the protective effect referred to by Article 110(2)?[147]

The British wine and beer case, *Commission* v. *UK*,[148] provides a good example of how the Court addresses the question whether two goods (beer and wine) are in competition. The Commission argued that British taxation policy contravened Article 110 because, if judged by equal volume, wine was subject to a tax burden approximately five times

---

[141] Case 252/86 *Bergandi* [1988] ECR 1343, para. 32.

[142] Case 196/85 *Commission* v. *France* [1987] ECR 1597, para. 7.

[143] Case 140/79 *Chemial Farmaceutici* [1981] ECR 1, para. 8. See also Case 46/80 *Vinal* [1981] ECR 77.

[144] See the parallel cases on free movement of goods discussed in Ch. 6.

[145] Case 193/85 *Co-frutta* [1987] ECR 2085, para. 19 (the importation of bananas); Case 27/67 *Fink-Frucht* [1968] ECR 223, 232; see also Case 168/78 *Commission* v. *France* [1980] ECR 347, para. 12.

[146] Case 356/85 *Commission* v. *Belgium* [1987] ECR 3299, para. 7.

[147] Case 170/78 *Commission* v. *UK* [1980] ECR 417, para. 10.      [148] Ibid.

that imposed on beer.[149] The Commission said that the two drinks belonged to the same category of alcoholic beverages: both were the product of natural fermentation and both could be used for the same purposes, as thirst-quenching drinks or to accompany meals. It also argued—and the Court accepted[150]—that there was a competitive relationship between wine and beer, and therefore Article 110(2) applied: in the case of certain consumers the two drinks could actually be substituted for one another, and in the case of other consumers they might, at least potentially, be substituted.

In judging substitutability the Court emphasized that account needed to be taken of potential substitutes brought about by increased free trade:[151]

For the purpose of measuring the possible degree of substitution, it is impossible to restrict oneself to consumer habits in a Member State or in a given region. In fact, those habits, which are essentially variable in time and space, cannot be considered to be a fixed rule; the tax policy of a Member State must not therefore crystallize given consumer habits so as to consolidate an advantage acquired by national industries concerned to comply with them.[152]

In other words, since tax is lower on beer than on wine, consumers can buy more beer for their money than wine. The taxation policy therefore reinforced the already advantageous position of beer on the market. In that respect it served to 'crystallize' consumer habits.

Despite its agreement with the Commission about substitutability, the Court also recognized the validity of the UK government's arguments that there were differences between wine and beer. For example, the alcohol content of wine is approximately four times that of beer, wine is appreciably more expensive than beer,[153] and wine and beer are produced according to different processes. Moreover, the Court recognized the different circumstances in which the two drinks are consumed. As the UK government argued:[154]

in accordance with long-established tradition in the United Kingdom, beer is a popular drink consumed preferably in public-houses or in connexion with work; domestic consumption and consumption with meals is negligible. In contrast, the consumption of wine is more unusual and special from the point of view of social custom.[155]

Although the Court thought that the British tax system showed a 'protective trend', when considered by reference to alcoholic strength rather than by volume (which the Court thought to be a more reliable measure[156]), it asked the parties to try to resolve the matter and report back.[157] Unable to reach an amicable settlement, the case returned to the Court three years later,[158] where it ruled that the decisive competitive relationship was between

---

[149] Ibid, para. 17.        [150] Ibid, para. 14.

[151] Ibid, para. 6: 'it is necessary to consider not only the present state of the market but also the possibilities for development within the context of free movement of goods at the [Union] level and the further potential for the substitution of products for one another which may be revealed by intensification of trade, so as fully to develop the complementary features of the economies of the Member States in accordance with the objectives laid down by Article [3 TFEU]'.        [152] Ibid, para. 14.

[153] Ibid, para. 13.

[154] This proved to be a matter of some dispute in the subsequent case, Case 170/78 *Commission* v. *UK* [1980] ECR 2265, where the Court recognized that none of the criteria of comparison (volume, alcoholic strength, and the price of the products) was capable of yielding reliable results on its own (para. 18).

[155] Case 170/78 *Commission* v. *UK* [1980] ECR 417, para. 13.        [156] Ibid, para. 19.

[157] Ibid, para. 24.        [158] Case 170/78 *Commission* v. *UK* [1983] ECR 2265.

beer, 'a popular and widely consumed beverage', and the most accessible wines, namely the 'lightest and cheapest varieties'.[159]

Having considered that these goods were in competition, the Court then examined the question of protective effect. It said that the UK's tax system had the effect of subjecting imported wine to an additional tax burden of at least 100 per cent by reference to alcoholic strength and 400 per cent by reference to volume[160] so as to afford protection to domestic beer production, thereby suppressing any potentially competitive relationship. As the Court said, 'the effect of the United Kingdom tax system is to stamp wine with the hallmarks of a luxury product which, in view of the tax burden which it bears, can scarcely constitute in the eyes of the consumer a genuine alternative to the typical domestically produced beverage'.[161] The UK taxation scheme therefore breached Article 110(2).

But what should the UK do about it? If the taxation scheme had been found to be discriminatory under Article 110(1), equalized tax rates would have been the solution (see fig. 3.2). In *Beer and Wine*, however, the complaint concerned the protective effect of the scheme, and Article 110(2) merely required its removal (see fig. 3.2).[162] In fact, the Chancellor of the Exchequer lowered the tax on wine and raised it on beer. As Weatherill concluded, the increasing consumption of wine suggests that the Court might have been right and that the British public had been deterred from buying wine by high taxes.[163]

Nearly thirty years later, similar issues were litigated in *Commission v Sweden*[164] but this time the Court found Sweden not to be in breach of Article 110. As with *Beer and Wine*, the Commission thought that the difference in the tax treatment of beer and wine was liable to afford indirect protection to beer (mainly produced in Sweden) to the detriment of wine (mainly imported from other Member States). The Court adopted a three-stage approach.[165] First, it considered whether the goods were in competition with each other. It pointed out that wine and beer were, to a certain extent, 'capable of meeting identical needs, which meant that a certain measure of mutual substitutability must be acknowledged', and so the decisive competitive relationship between wine and beer had to be established by reference to those wines which were the most accessible to the public at large (i.e., 'the lightest and least expensive varieties').[166] So, the Court said that wines with an alcoholic strength of between 8.5% vol. and 15% vol. and a final selling price ranging between SEK 49 and SEK 70 shared a sufficient number of characteristics with 'strong' beer with an alcoholic strength equal to or higher than 3.5% vol. to represent an alternative choice for the consumer and thus to be in competition with strong beer. Secondly, the Court considered whether the higher tax rate applied chiefly to the imported product. It found that wine with an alcoholic strength of 12.5% vol. was subject to taxation per percentage of alcohol by volume approximately 20 per cent higher per litre than beer with which it was in competition.[167]

Thirdly, it considered the question of protective effect: was the higher tax on wine liable to influence the market in question by reducing the potential consumption of imported

---

[159] Para. 12.    [160] Paras. 19–21.    [161] Para. 27.
[162] See A. Easson, 'The spirits, wine and beer judgments: A legal Mickey Finn?' (1980) 5 *ELRev.* 318 and 'Cheaper wine or dearer beer?' (1984) 9 *ELRev.* 57.
[163] S. Weatherill and P. Beaumont, *EU Law* (London: Penguin, 1999), 482.
[164] Case C–167/05 [2008] ECR I–2127.
[165] See also Case E–6/07 *HOB vín ehf v. Faxaflóahafnir*, judgment of EFTA Court 5 Mar. 2008, para. 52.
[166] Para. 43.    [167] Para 50.

products so as to advantage competing domestic products.[168] It took into account the difference between the selling prices of the products per litre and the impact of that difference on the consumer's choice, as well as looking at changes in the consumption of those products.[169] The Court pointed out that the price difference between the two products was virtually the same before taxation as after it (a litre of wine of 12.5% vol. cost just over twice the price of a litre of beer).[170] So, the Court found that the Commission had not shown that the difference between the price of strong beer and the price of wine in competition with that beer was so great that the difference in the excise duty was likely to influence consumer behaviour.[171]

So why the difference in outcome? The Court's approach in the *Sweden* case demonstrates more rigour in respect of analysis of the market than had been seen in *Commission v United Kingdom*. And because the burden of proof was on the Commission to show something close to actual protective effect,[172] the Commission had failed to make the case to the requisite legal standard and so the action was dismissed.

## 5.2 The Globalized Approach To Article 110?

In some cases, particularly those in the 1980s, the Court did not distinguish clearly between whether the goods were similar under Article 110(1) or in competition under Article 110(2). Instead, it adopted a globalized approach,[173] considering Article 110(1) and 110(2) together. From one perspective, this makes some sense: as the *Beer and Wine* case shows, the tests applied to both provisions do overlap. From another, it presents problems because the remedies under the two provisions are different.[174] Nevertheless, the Court adopted the globalized approach in three 'spirits' cases: *Commission v. Denmark,*[175] where Danish tax law favoured acquavit over other competing spirits; *Commission v. Italy,*[176] where Italian tax law favoured grappa over rum; and *Commission v. France,*[177] where French law favoured cognac over whisky. The Court said that Article 110 'taken as a whole, may apply without distinction to all the products concerned'.[178]

Subsequently, the Court has become more rigorous in distinguishing between Article 110(1) and (2).[179] For example, in *Commission v. Italy (bananas)*[180] Italy taxed bananas[181] (largely from the French overseas territories) at a higher rate than other table fruit typically produced in Italy (such as apples, pears, peaches, and plums). The Court decided that bananas and other soft fruits were not similar under Article 110(1) because the organoleptic characteristics and the water content of the two categories of products differed.[182] The Court

---

[168] Para 52.      [169] Para. 53.      [170] Para. 57.      [171] Para. 58.

[172] Cf. para. 60 where the Court said that 'it is impossible to require, in each case...that the protective effect of internal tax arrangements be shown statistically, but that it is sufficient for it to be shown that a given tax mechanism is likely, in view of its inherent characteristics, to bring about such an effect'.

[173] A. Easson, 'Fiscal discrimination: New perspectives on Article 95 of the EEC Treaty' (1981) 18 *CMLRev.* 521, 535.                      [174] This is considered in more detail below at text attached to nn. 184–88.

[175] Case 171/78 *Commission v. Denmark* [1980] ECR 447.

[176] Case 169/78 *Commission v. Italy* [1980] ECR 385.

[177] Case 168/78 *Commission v. France* [1980] ECR 347. See subsequently Case C–230/89 *Commission v. Greece* [1991] ECR I–1909 (Greek law taxed ouzo at a lower rate than whisky).                      [178] Para. 13.

[179] See, e.g., Case 243/84 *Johnnie Walker* [1986] ECR 875.

[180] Case 184/85 *Commission v. Italy (bananas)* [1987] ECR 2013.

[181] Italy had only a negligible production of bananas in Sicily which was ignored by the Court.

[182] It said: 'by way of example, the higher water content of pears and other fruit typically grown in Italy give them thirst-quenching properties which bananas do not possess. Moreover, the observation of the

then looked at Article 110(2) and found that the goods were in competition.[183] It also found that the tax on bananas had a protective effect: the tax was equivalent to half the import price of the bananas; most domestic soft fruit was subject to no tax at all.

## 6. REMEDIES

As we have already seen, the nature of the remedy depends on whether the case is considered under Article 110(1) or 110(2) (see fig. 3.2). If the case falls within Article 110(1) then the discrimination must be eliminated by, depending on the circumstances, equalizing the taxes imposed on the domestic and imported goods or extending a benefit enjoyed by domestic goods to imported goods. Therefore, in *Hansen*[184] the Court said that where national tax law favoured spirits produced by small and collective farms, those advantages had to be extended to imported Union spirits which fulfilled the same conditions.[185] While *Hansen* suggests a levelling up of benefits (the imported goods obtain the benefit accorded to domestic goods) the principle of formal equality merely requires equality of treatment. This means that there is nothing to prevent a levelling down of benefit (domestic goods lose the benefit accorded to them, bringing their treatment into line with that of imported goods),[186] as well as a levelling up.

If the case falls within Article 110(2) the state must remove the protective effect from its taxation scheme. This does not necessarily mean equalizing the tax burden on the imported goods.[187] Therefore, as we saw in the *Wine and Beer* case,[188] the Court did not require the wine to be taxed at the same rate as beer, merely that the protection enjoyed by beer be removed so that the tax reflected the objective differences between the products.

The remedies considered so far are particularly relevant where the Commission brings enforcement proceedings against a Member State. By contrast, where individuals invoke Article 110—which they can do because Article 110 is directly effective[189]—they may want the state to repay any tax unlawfully levied (see fig. 3.2). The availability of a restitutionary claim was confirmed by the Court in *Hans Just*,[190] where it said that Member States had to ensure the repayment of charges levied contrary to Article 110, subject to the principle of national procedural autonomy and unjust enrichment.[191] Damages are also payable for loss of sales. National time limits will apply to these claims, provided they are not such as

---

Italian government, which has not been challenged by the Commission, that the banana is regarded, at least on the Italian market, as a foodstuff which is particularly nutritious, of a high energy content and well-suited for infants must be accepted' (para. 10).

[183] See also Case 193/85 *Co-frutta* [1987] ECR 2085, judgment delivered on the same day. Cf. Case 27/76 *United Brands* v. *Commission* [1978] ECR 207.

[184] Case 148/77 *H. Hansen jun. & O.C. Balle GmbH & Co.* v. *Hauptzollamt de Flensburg* [1978] ECR 1787, para. 20.

[185] See also Case 68/79 *Hans Just I/S* v. *Danish Ministry for Fiscal Affairs* [1980] ECR 501, para. 16.

[186] This is permitted in the field of sex equality: Case C–408/92 *Smith* v. *Avdel Systems* [1994] ECR I–4435.

[187] A. Easson, 'Fiscal discrimination: New perspectives on Article 95 of the EEC Treaty' (1981) 18 *CMLRev.* 521, 535.

[188] Case 170/78 *Commission* v. *UK* [1983] ECR 2265.

[189] Art. 110(1): Case 57/65 *Lütticke GmbH* [1966] ECR I–205 and Case 28/67 *Molkerei-Zentrale Westfalen* [1968] ECR 143, 153; Art. 110(2): Case 27/67 *Fink-Frucht* [1968] ECR 223, 232.

[190] Case 68/79 *Hans Just I/S* [1980] ECR 501, para. 27.

[191] See the discussion of Case 199/82 *San Giorgio* [1983] ECR 3595 and Case C–192/95 *Comateb* [1997] ECR I–165 above (fig. 3.1).

to make the claim less favourable than those governing similar domestic actions and do not render the exercise of the rights virtually impossible or excessively difficult.[192]

## D.  THE BOUNDARY BETWEEN ARTICLE 110 AND OTHER TREATY PROVISIONS

### 1.  INTRODUCTION

According to the theory, Articles 110 and 30 are mutually exclusive[193] (as we have seen, Article 30 applies to charges levied at the frontier; Article 110 to charges levied within the Member State[194]), as are Articles 110 and 34 (Article 110 concerns fiscal measures; Article 34 non-fiscal). However, this division is not always so straightforward, as *Commission* v. *Denmark*[195] shows. Under Danish law the rate of duty applicable to private vehicles, calculated by reference to the value of the vehicle, was 105 per cent on the first DKr 20,000 and 180 per cent on the balance. The Court said that although Article 110 did not provide a basis for censuring the excessiveness of the level of taxation, charges of such a (high) level might impede the free movement of goods contrary to Article 34. However, when, in *DBI*,[196] a professional association of car importers relied on this ruling to challenge the level of duty applied to cars imported into Denmark, the Court, having looked at the figures,[197] found that free movement of vehicles was not impeded.[198] Subsequently, in *Brzezinski*[199] the Court appeared to rule out entirely the application of Article 34 to fiscal situations when it said that 'obstacles of a fiscal nature or having an effect equivalent to customs duties, which are covered by Articles [28 TFEU], [30 TFEU] and [110 TFEU], do not fall within the prohibition laid down in Article [34 TFEU]'.

In the final section of this chapter we consider cases on the borderline between Articles 30 and 110: the situation of a charge imposed on a product not produced in the Member State (the so-called exotic import); para-fiscal charges (those charges which apply to all goods but are then refunded in some form to the domestic producer); and other levies which appear to apply to all goods but are in fact targeted at the imported good.

### 2.  THE 'EXOTIC' IMPORT

If there is no similar or competing domestic product (or a very low domestic production of the particular goods[200]) Member States are still free to tax the imported goods. As the

---

[192]  Case C–90/94 *Haahr Petroleum* v. *Åbenrå Havn* [1997] ECR I–4085. The Court said a five-year limitation period was reasonable.

[193]  Case 10/65 *Deutschmann* v. *Germany* [1965] ECR 469.

[194]  Case C–313/05 *Brzezioski* v. *Dyrekto Izby Celnej w Warszawie* [2007] ECR I–513, paras 22–3.

[195]  Case C–47/88 *Commission* v. *Denmark* [1990] ECR I–4509, para. 10.

[196]  Case C–383/01 *De Danske Bilimportører* v. *Skatteministeriet, Told—og Skattestreisen* [2003] ECR I–6065. DBI bought a new Audi for its director at a total price of just under DKr 500,000 which included just under DKr 300,000 in registration duty.

[197]  During the period from 1985 to 2000 the total number of registered vehicles in Denmark rose from 1.5 million to 1.854 million and the number of new registrations varied between 78,000 and 169,000 per year.

[198]  Para. 41.

[199]  Case C–313/05 *Brzezinski* v. *Dyrektor Izby Celnej w Warszawie* [2007] ECR I–513, para. 50.

[200]  Case 193/85 *Co-frutta* v. *Amministrazione delle Finanze dello Stato* [1987] ECR 2085, para. 11. See also Case C–313/05 *Brzezioski* v. *Dyrekto Izby Celnej w Warszawie* [2007] ECR I–513, paras 22–3.

Court said in *Co-frutta*,[201] any such charge does not constitute a CEE under Article 30 but internal taxation within the meaning of Article 110, provided the tax fits within the general scheme of taxation applied systematically to categories of products in accordance with objective criteria irrespective of the origin of the products.[202] Therefore, an Italian tax on bananas, a fruit hardly grown in Italy, could be regarded as an integral part of a general system of internal dues within the meaning of Article 110 since it formed one of 19 consumer taxes of which three were charged on tropical products (coffee, cocoa, and bananas).[203]

This rule makes sense—if it were otherwise and Article 30 applied, Member States would not be able to tax products they did not produce themselves. However, even though the permissive regime under Article 110 applies, the Court will still consider the tax to ensure that it is neither discriminatory nor protective. In *Co-frutta*, decided the same day as *Commission v. Italy (bananas)*,[204] the Court found the tax on bananas to have protective effect.

## 3. PARA-FISCAL CHARGES

Para-fiscal charges wholly or partially offset the burden borne by domestic products but not imports. These may fall under Article 30 or 110 depending on the extent to which the charge is offset. As the Court explained in *Compagnie Commerciale*,[205] if the proceeds of the charge *fully* offset the burden borne by the domestic product when it is placed on the market, it has an effect equivalent to customs duties, contrary to Article 30. If, on the other hand, those advantages only *partly* offset the burden borne by domestic products, the charge is subject to Article 110. However, in this case the charge will breach Article 110 and is prohibited to the extent that it discriminates against imported products (i.e., the extent to which it partially offsets the burden borne by the taxed domestic product). It is for the national court to determine whether the charge imposed on the domestic product is wholly or partly offset.[206]

The application of these rules can be seen in *Capolongo*[207] and in *Nygård*.[208] *Capolongo* concerned an Italian law which established a body called ENCC.[209] This body had the

---

[201] Ibid., para. 13. Case 27/67 *Fink-Frucht* [1968] ECR 223, 231. See also Case C–109/98 *CRT France International SA v. Directeur régional des impôts de Bourgogne* [1999] ECR I–2237, para. 21; Case 90/79 *Commission v. France* [1981] ECR 283, para. 14, where a levy of 3% was charged on the sales of reprographic equipment and paid into the National Book Fund to subsidize the publication of quality works and to buy (French and foreign) books for libraries. French production of such equipment was extremely small. On the facts the Court found that this charge did fall within the scope of Art. 110 because it was levied in part to address the problems of breach of copyright.                                         [202] Para. 10.

[203] Para. 12.          [204] Case 184/85 [1987] ECR 2013 considered above, n. 180.

[205] Joined Cases C–78–83/90 *Compagnie Commerciale de l'ouest* [1992] ECR I–1847, paras. 27–8. See also Case 105/76 *Interzuccheri SpA v. Società Rezzano e Cavassa* [1977] ECR 1029, para. 10, and Case C–72/92 *Scharbatke v. Germany* [1993] ECR I–5525, para. 10; Case C–17/91 *Lornoy en Zonen v. Belgian State* [1992] ECR I–6523; and Case C–347/95 *Fazenda Publica v. UCAL* [1997] ECR I–4911; Joined Cases C–149/91 and C–150/91 *Sanders Adour v. Directeur des Services Fiscaux des Pyrenées-Atlantique* [1992] ECR I–3899.

[206] If the money goes into the national exchequer and is used for the benefit of a particular national *industry*, this may be considered a state aid: Joined Cases C–78–83/90 *Compagnie Commerciale de l'ouest* [1992] ECR I–1847.          [207] Case 77/72 *Capolongo v. Azienda Agricole Maya* [1973] ECR 611, para. 13.

[208] Case C–234/99 *Niels Nygård v. Svineafgiftsfonden* [2002] ECR I–3657. See also Case C–517/04 *Visserijbedrijf D.J. Koonstr & Zn. Vof v. Productschap Vis* [2006] ECR I–5015.

[209] Ente Nazionale per la Cellulosa e per la Carta.

task of promoting the development of cellulose production in Italy, largely by providing subsidies to the national industry.[210] It was funded by a government charge on domestically produced and imported cellulose, paper, and cardboard. The importer of egg boxes from Germany argued that this charge contravened Article 30; the Italian government said that since the charge applied to both domestic and imported goods it fell within Article 110. The Court agreed with the importer. It said that a duty within the general system of internal taxation could constitute a CEE within the meaning of Article 30 when the charge was 'intended exclusively to support activities which specifically benefit the taxed domestic product'.[211]

While *Capolongo* concerned a national rule which *fully* offset the burden borne by domestic products, *Nygård* involved a charge which only *partly* offset that burden. The case concerned a levy charged by the Danish authorities on pigs produced in Denmark for slaughter for the domestic market and on those intended for live export to other Member States. However, 60 per cent of the revenue generated was used to subsidize activities relating to slaughtering and processing on the domestic market and the marketing of the domestic product, while only 40 per cent of the revenue was used to finance activities concerning primary production which would benefit the production of pigs for export. The Court said that although the levy did not fall within Article 30 (because it was not a case of full offsetting), it could be considered discriminatory taxation prohibited by Article 110 to the extent that the advantages deriving from the use made of the revenue partially compensated for the charge imposed on pigs produced for slaughter in Denmark, thereby placing the production of pigs for export at a disadvantage.[212]

## 4. OTHER 'LEVIES'

As we saw above, levies on goods crossing a frontier are usually considered to be CEEs under Article 30 and so are prohibited. Arguments, such as those raised in *Bresciani*[213] that domestic goods are subject to similar charges, are not usually enough to trigger Article 110. Bresciani imported raw cowhides into Italy from France. These cowhides were subject to a health inspection for which a fee was charged to cover the costs of the examination and laboratory tests. Similar products of domestic origin were not subject to the same duty, although when animals were slaughtered they were subject to a veterinary inspection to determine whether the meat was fit for human consumption, for which a charge was levied. The Court said this was irrelevant: the fact that the domestic production was subjected to a similar financial burden mattered little unless the charges on the domestic and imported goods were applied according to the same criteria and at the same stage of production.[214] If these conditions were satisfied the charges would be considered as falling within a general system of taxation to which Article 110 would apply. This was the situation in *Denkavit*,[215] where the Court found that an annual levy charged in a like manner to importers and national producers of foodstuffs containing additives (intended to cover the costs incurred by the state in checking samples) was covered by Article 110 since it related to a general system of internal dues applied systematically

---

[210] See Roemer AG's Opinion in Case 77/72 *Capolongo* v. *Azienda Agricole Maya* [1973] ECR 611, 625.
[211] Para. 14.
[212] See also Case C–206/06 *Essent Netwerk Noord BV* v. *Aluminium Delfzijl BV* [2008] ECR I–5497, para. 57.                                                                [213] Case 87/75 *Bresciani* [1976] ECR 129.
[214] Para. 11.      [215] Case 29/87 *Denkavit* v. *Danish Ministry of Agriculture* [1988] ECR 2965.

and in accordance with the same criteria to domestic and imported products alike.[216] Furthermore, the charge was compatible with Article 110 since it did not discriminate against the imported goods in any way.

By contrast, in *Mikhailides*,[217] the Court found that a charge imposed on exported tobacco to compensate for a charge imposed on similar domestic products, but at a production stage prior to that at which the exported products were taxed, did not fall under Article 110. Instead, the charge fell within Article 30 because it was not applied 'at the same rate, at the same marketing stage and on the basis of an identical chargeable event'.[218]

# E.  CONCLUSIONS

Article 110 serves as a valuable complement to Article 30, while at the same time ensuring income to the national exchequer. However, as we saw in Chapter 1, the removal of fiscal barriers to trade is not sufficient in itself to realize free trade. Non-fiscal barriers can easily represent serious obstacles to trade. It is to this subject that we now turn.

---

[216] Para. 33.        [217] Joined Cases C–441/98 and C–442/98 [2000] ECR I–7145.        [218] Para. 24.

# 4

# NON-FISCAL MEASURES: QUANTITATIVE RESTRICTIONS AND MEASURES HAVING EQUIVALENT EFFECT

## A. INTRODUCTION

In the last chapter we considered *fiscal* barriers to trade. Now we move on to examine *non-fiscal* barriers to trade.[1] Such barriers can range from quotas to national measures prescribing the content and presentation of a product. Three Treaty provisions are relevant: Article 34 TFEU (ex Article 28 EC) on *imports*, Article 35 TFEU (ex Article 29 EC) on *exports*,[2] and Article 36 TFEU (ex Article 30 EC) containing derogations from Articles 34–5.[3]

Article 34 provides: 'Quantitative restrictions on imports and all measures having equivalent effect shall be prohibited between Member States.' Article 35 is drafted in the same terms but concerns exports. Both provisions prohibit two types of national measure: (1) quantitative restrictions on imports/exports (in essence quotas or bans) and (2) measures having an equivalent effect to a quantitative restriction (for example, rules on licences, and, particularly in respect of Article 34, regulations on the presentation of the product such as packaging).

Despite the similarity in drafting of Articles 34–5, the case law on the two Treaty provisions has diverged quite markedly since 1979: while Article 34 prohibited both distinctly and indistinctly applicable measures (broadly equivalent to directly and indirectly discriminatory measures), Article 35 prohibited distinctly applicable measures only. This aspect of the Court's case law on Article 35 has long been subject to criticism. However, in a landmark decision in 2008, *Gysbrechts*,[4] the Court appeared to make a significant move towards bringing the case law under the two Treaty provisions back into line, at

---

[1] For further details see L. Gormley, *Prohibiting Restrictions on Trade within the EEC* (Oxford: Elsevier/North Holland, 1985) and P. Oliver with M. Jarvis, *Free Movement of Goods in the EC*, 4th edn (London: Sweet and Maxwell, 2003).

[2] Art. III–153 of the Constitutional Treaty merged these two Articles into one. This change did not survive the Lisbon Treaty.

[3] See generally Commission, *Free Movement of Goods: Guide to the application of Treaty provisions governing free movement of goods (Articles 28–30 EC)* SEC(2009) 673.

[4] Case C–205/07 *Gysbrechts and Santurel Inter BVBA* [2008] ECR I–9947.

least in respect of distinctly and indistinctly applicable measures. Yet, full convergence between the case law on the two Treaty provisions has not been achieved: in *Commission v. Italy (trailers)*,[5] decided shortly after *Gysbrechts*, the Court extended the definition of MEEs under Article 34 to include 'Any other measure which hinders access of products originating in other Member States to the market of a Member State'. The significance of this development is considered in detail below.

Given the overlap between Articles 34–5 both are considered in this chapter. The focus will, however, be on the case law under Article 34 which is more extensive than that on Article 35. There is a practical explanation for this difference: because Member States have an interest in encouraging exports, with the exception of economically sensitive exports such as essential raw materials (e.g., oil) and politically sensitive exports (e.g., cultural goods, weapons, and even wine), they are unlikely to create barriers to exports. By contrast, in respect of imports, Member States may be more willing to impose barriers to trade, especially when those imports threaten the domestic product and thus national jobs.

This chapter will focus on the meaning of the terms 'quantitative restrictions' (QRs) and 'measures having equivalent effect' (MEEs). A new category of measure, 'certain selling arrangements' (CSAs), introduced by the Court of Justice in its (in)famous decision in *Keck*,[6] is considered in Chapter 5. The derogations and judicially developed justifications are considered in Chapter 6.

## B. QUANTITATIVE RESTRICTIONS

In *Geddo*[7] the Court defined quantitative restrictions as 'measures which amount to a total or partial restraint of, according to the circumstances, imports, exports or goods in transit'. Therefore QRs include (non-tariff[8]) quotas limiting the quantity of goods coming into a state or leaving the state. This can be seen in *Delhaize*.[9] A Belgian company ordered 3,000 hectolitres of Rioja wine from Spain, contrary to Spanish rules limiting the quantity of wine available for export in bulk to other Member States. The Court said that the Spanish rules breached Article 35.

QRs also cover the situation where the state generally allows the import but can prevent the import in specific cases. This can be seen in *Rosengren*[10] concerning Swedish rules prohibiting private individuals from buying alcoholic drinks by mail order or over the web. Instead they had to buy them from the 'Systembolaget', the state-owned company with a monopoly over retail sales in wine, beer, and spirits in Sweden. Because the Systembolaget could refuse an order from a customer, the Swedish law constituted a QR.[11]

---

[5] Case C–110/05 *Commission v. Italy* [2009] ECR I–000, para. 50.

[6] Joined Cases C–267 and 268/91 *Keck and Mithouard* [1993] ECR I–6097.

[7] Case 2/73 *Geddo v. Ente Nationale Risi* [1973] ECR 865, para. 7.

[8] Tariff quotas are covered by Art. 30 TFEU.

[9] Case C–47/90 [1992] ECR I–3669. See also the follow up in Case C–388/95 *Belgium v. Spain* [2000] ECR I–3123.

[10] Case C–170/04 *Rosengren v. Riksåklagaren* [2007] ECR I–4071. See also Case C–185/05 *Commission v. Sweden* [2007] ECR I–129*. Cf the case law on certain selling arrangements considered in Ch. 5.

[11] Para. 33.

QRs also include a ban on imports or exports which, as the Court noted in *Henn and Darby*,[12] is the most 'extreme form of prohibition'. This meant that the UK's ban on the import of pornographic material breached Article 34. Often a Member State will concede that its ban breaches the Treaties. For example, in *Hedley Lomas*[13] the UK accepted that its refusal to issue an export licence for a quantity of live sheep intended for slaughter in a Spanish slaughterhouse was a QR contrary to Article 35, as was a ban on the export of live calves in *CWF*.[14] In these cases the focus was instead on the Article 36 derogations. According to the orthodoxy, Member States can justify imposing a QR only by reference to one of the Article 36 derogations (see fig. 4.1). The first sentence of Article 36 provides:

The provisions of Articles 34–5 shall not preclude prohibitions or restrictions on imports, exports or goods in transit justified on grounds of public morality, public policy or public security; the protection of health and life of humans, animals or plants; the protection of national treasures possessing artistic, historic or archaeological value; or the protection of industrial and commercial property.

This is an exhaustive list of derogations which must be read in conjunction with the proviso in the second sentence of Article 36. This says that '[s]uch prohibitions or restrictions shall not, however, constitute a means of arbitrary discrimination or a disguised restriction on trade between Member States'.

Thus, the Treaties allow national measures to take precedence over the free movement of goods where they serve important interests recognized by the Union as valuable (public policy, security, health, the protection of national treasures and protection of industrial and commercial property), provided that the national measures are proportionate and do not constitute a means of arbitrary discrimination or a disguised restriction on trade between Member States. The detail of this provision is considered in Chapter 6.

## C. MEASURES HAVING EQUIVALENT EFFECT

### 1. INTRODUCTION

Articles 34–5 prohibit not only QRs but also measures having equivalent effect to quantitative restrictions (MEEs). In respect of national measures affecting imports, MEEs include rules on the shape,[15] content,[16] packaging,[17] and labelling[18] of goods—all of which may hinder inter-state trade but which cannot be described as QRs.[19] In this section we examine the definition of MEEs and how the Court has developed a sophisticated case law around MEEs, distinguishing between distinctly and indistinctly applicable measures and, more recently, any other measure which hinders market access.

---

[12] Case 34/79 *R. v. Henn and Darby* [1972] ECR 3795, paras. 12–13.
[13] Case C–5/94 *R v. MAFF, ex p. Hedley Lomas (Ireland) Ltd* [1996] ECR I–2553, para. 12.
[14] Case C–1/96 *R v. MAFF, ex p. Compassion in World Farming* [1998] ECR I–1251, para. 39.
[15] Case 16/83 *Criminal Proceedings against Prantl* [1984] ECR 1299.
[16] Case 286/86 *Minstère Public v. Deserbais* [1988] ECR 4907.
[17] Case C–315/92 *Verband Sozialer Wettbewerb ev v. Clinique Laboratories SNC* [1994] ECR I–317.
[18] Case C–463/01 *Commission v. Germany (deposit and return)* [2004] ECR I–11705.
[19] In Case 2/73 *Geddo v. Ente* [1973] ECR 865 the Court said 'whatever the description or technique employed, [MEEs] can also consist of encumbrances having the same effect' as QRs.

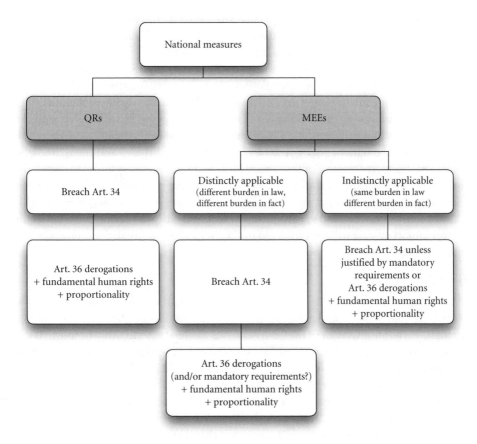

**Fig. 4.1** QRs and MEEs: The traditional approach under Art. 34

## 2. WHAT ARE MEASURES HAVING EQUIVALENT EFFECT?

### 2.1 The *Dassonville* Formula

The original definition of MEEs is found in *Dassonville*:[20]

All trading rules enacted by Member States which are capable of hindering, directly or indirectly, actually or potentially, intra-[Union] trade are to be considered as measures having an effect equivalent to quantitative restrictions.

In *Bouhelier*[21] the Court extended the *Dassonville* formula to Article 35.[22]

The potential breadth of the *Dassonville* formula is striking. In principle, measures having only an *indirect*, *potential* effect on trade fall within the formula's scope and therefore breach the Treaties. *Dassonville* thus tends to support an approach to Article 34 (and Article 35) as the basis for an economic constitution for the EU:[23] maximizing the right for individuals to participate on the market on whatever terms they choose, and

---

[20] Case 8/74 *Procureur du Roi* v. *Dassonville* [1974] ECR 837, para. 5.
[21] Case 53/76 *Procureur de la République de Besançon* v. *Les Sieurs Bouhelier* [1977] ECR 197; Case 68/76 *Commission* v. *France* [1977] ECR 515, paras. 15–16.
[22] Cf. Case C–412/97 *ED Srl* v. *Italo Fenocchio* [1999] ECR I–3845.          [23] See further Ch. 1.

providing them with a vehicle to challenge any national rule which—even potentially and indirectly—stands in their way. In other words, *Dassonville* supports a market access reading of Articles 34–5 rather than a discrimination approach.[24]

Looked at in its historical context, *Dassonville* was an effective tool to cull the dead wood of centuries of accumulated legislation. However, taken to extremes, a broad reading of *Dassonville* might mean that Article 34 could be used to challenge national rules limiting Sunday trading or development in the green belt or age restrictions on who can buy alcohol. While such legislation does circumscribe general commercial freedom in various ways, the national rules serve a variety of social purposes and their effects on *inter-state* trade are remote. For this reason the Court was eventually forced to curtail the broad sweep of the *Dassonville* formula when, in its judgment in *Keck*,[25] it recognized that non-discriminatory national measures restricting certain selling arrangements (CSAs) did not constitute MEEs and so fell outside the scope of Article 34 (see fig. 5.1). The details of this important case will be considered in Chapter 5. For now we shall examine the elements of the *Dassonville* formula.

## 2.2 'All Trading Rules'

According to *Dassonville*, Article 34 applies to 'all trading rules', which means that Article 34 concerns the marketing stage, and not the production stage, of the economic process. Therefore, in *Kramer*[26] the Court said that national rules limiting fishing in order to conserve fish stocks did not concern a trading rule and so did not constitute an MEE. In subsequent cases the Court has dropped the emphasis on the need to show a *trading* rule. For example, when defining MEEs in *Keck* the Court talked only of 'rules' that lay down requirements to be met by goods coming from other Member States.[27]

But even the reference to 'rules' is misleading. Article 34 itself refers to the more general term 'measures' and the Court has insisted that these measures need not be legally binding. Therefore in *Commission* v. *Ireland ('Buy Irish')*[28] the Court said that a campaign sponsored by the Irish government encouraging its citizens to buy Irish goods amounted to the establishment of a 'national *practice* introduced by the Irish government and prosecuted with its assistance'.[29] It continued that by influencing the conduct of traders and consumers in Ireland the campaign's potential effect on imports was comparable to that resulting from government measures of a binding nature.[30]

Thus, *Buy Irish* shows that the term 'rules' includes practices and policies. *Commission* v. *France (postal franking machines)*[31] takes the definition one stage further. It says that

---

[24] See J. H. H. Weiler, 'The constitution of the common market place' in P. Craig and G. de Búrca (eds.), *The Evolution of EU Law* (Oxford: OUP, 1999), 351–64, and A. Arnull, *The European Union and its Court of Justice*, 2nd edn (Oxford: OUP, 2006), 398–403.

[25] Joined Cases C–267 and 268/91 *Keck and Mithouard* [1993] ECR I–6097.

[26] Case 3/76 *Kramer* [1976] ECR 1279.

[27] Joined Cases C–267 and 268/91 *Keck* [1993] ECR I–6097, para. 15.

[28] Case 249/81 *Commission* v. *Ireland ('Buy Irish campaign')* [1982] ECR 4005. See also Case 45/87 *Commission* v. *Ireland (Dundalk Water)* [1988] ECR 4929.     [29] Emphasis added.

[30] Paras. 27–8.

[31] Case 21/84 *Commission* v. *France (postal franking machines)* [1985] ECR 1355, para. 13. See also Joined Cases 266 and 267/87 *R.* v. *Royal Pharmaceutical Society of Great Britain, ex p. Association of Pharmaceutical Importers* [1989] ECR 1295 where a 'Code of Ethics and Guidance Notes' constituted 'measures'.

'rules' also include administrative regulations and action[32] which show 'a certain degree of consistency and generality'. Therefore an administrative practice requiring prior approval to be given to postal franking machines, where approval was given to French machines but not those produced in the UK, breached Article 34.[33]

### 2.3 'Enacted by Member States'

#### (a) 'Enacted'

The next element of the *Dassonville* formula, 'enacted by Member States', is also misleading. As the previous section showed, the national measure does not need to be 'enacted' to fall within the scope of Article 34: a consistent policy or practice will suffice. The rules also do not need to be 'enacted' by the central government of a Member State. Article 34 applies to measures adopted by the authorities of a federal state and other territorial authorities.[34] It also applies to bodies for whose acts the national government is responsible, as *Commission* v. *Ireland*[35] demonstrates. The 'Buy Irish' campaign was administered by the Irish Goods Council (IGC), a registered company. Nevertheless, the Court said that Article 34 still applied because the aims and broad outline of the campaign were set by the government, the management committee of the IGC was made up of ten people appointed by the Minister for Industry, and most of the funding for the council's activities came from the government.[36]

Not only does Article 34 (and 35) apply to government or quasi-government bodies but it also applies to bodies which regulate the conduct of a particular profession. For example, in *Ex p. Association of Pharmaceutical Importers (API)*[37] the Court ruled that Article 34 applied to the Royal Pharmaceutical Society of Great Britain, the professional body for pharmacy. Following *Viking*,[38] Article 34 may also apply to bodies, such as trade unions, which have sufficient power to interfere with the free movement provisions.

---

[32] See also the preamble to Dir. 70/50: 'Whereas for the purpose of Article [34] et seq. "measures" means laws, regulations, administrative provisions, administrative practices and all instruments issuing from a public authority, including recommendations'. It adds that 'administrative practices' means 'any standard and regularly followed procedure of a public authority' and 'recommendations' means 'any instruments issuing from a public authority which, while not legally binding on the addressees thereof, cause them to pursue a certain conduct'.

[33] See also Case C–192/01 *Commission* v. *Denmark* [2003] ECR I–9693, para. 40; Case C–212/03 *Commission* v. *France (homeopathic medicines)* [2005] ECR I–4213, para. 17; Case C–88/07 *Commission* v. *Spain (medicinal herbs)* [2009] ECR I–000, para. 54.

[34] Joined Cases C–1 & 176/90 *Aragonesa de Publicidad Exterior SA* v. *Departmento de Sanidad y Seguridad Social de la Generalitat de Cataluña* [1991] ECR I–4151, para. 8. See also Case 45/87 *Commission* v. *Ireland (Dundalk Water)* [1988] ECR 4929.

[35] Case 249/81 *Commission* v. *Ireland ('Buy Irish campaign')* [1982] ECR 4005. See also Case 222/82 *Apple and Pear Development Council* v. *Lewis* [1983] ECR 4083, para. 17; and Case C–325/00 *Commission* v. *Germany (label of origin and quality)* [2002] ECR I–9977, paras. 19–20.

[36] M. Quinn and N. Macgowan, 'Could Article 30 impose obligations on individuals?' (1987) 12 *ELRev.* 163, 167 note that the Buy Irish Campaign was subsequently relaunched and exists through private sponsorship by means of a private company, Guaranteed Irish Limited, set up with the intention of promoting Irish goods through the use of the 'Guaranteed Irish' symbol.

[37] Joined Cases 266 and 267/87 *R.* v. *Royal Pharmaceutical Society of Great Britain, ex p. Association of Pharmaceutical Importers* [1989] ECR 1295, paras. 14–15. See also Case C–292/92 *Hünermund* v. *Landesapothekerkammer Baden-Württemberg* [1993] ECR I–6787, para. 14.

[38] Case C–438/05 [2007] ECR I–10779 considered further in Ch. 8.

(b)  Direct effect: Vertical and horizontal?

These rulings support the view that Article 34 has *vertical* direct effect[39] and can be enforced against a broad category of state or quasi-state defendants. This raises a further question: can or should Article 34 also have *horizontal* direct effect?[40] This question has assumed a renewed importance since the decision in *Angonese*,[41] where the Court ruled that Article 45 TFEU (ex Article 39 EC) on the free movement of workers has horizontal (as well as vertical) direct effect, at least in respect of a breach of the fundamental principle of non-discrimination.

From the perspective of ensuring the effectiveness of Article 34, there are good policy reasons for giving Article 34 horizontal direct effect. If a large British supermarket chain were to refuse to stock French products on the ground that it objected to certain policies pursued by the French government, then the supermarket's decision would have a damaging effect on inter-state trade. On the other hand, Article 34 is addressed to the Member States[42] and not to private parties who should be able to contract freely, unconstrained by Article 34. This was the view taken by the Court in *Sapod-Audic*,[43] where it said that a contractual obligation to affix the 'Green dot' recycling logo to packaging could not be regarded as a barrier to trade for the purposes of Article 34 'since it was not imposed by a Member State but agreed between individuals'. For these reasons Article 34 should not have horizontal direct effect.

Most commentators consider that, outside the field of intellectual property,[44] Article 34 (and Article 35[45]) have only vertical direct effect and so do not apply to action between individuals. Their action is constrained by the (less demanding) regime of the competition rules (Articles 101–2 TFEU (ex Articles 81–2 EC)).[46] Article 101 applies only in the

---

[39]  Case 74/76 *Ianelli & Volpi* v. *Meroni* [1977] ECR 557, para. 13; Case 83/78 *Pigs Marketing Board* v. *Redmond* [1978] ECR 2347, paras. 66–7; Case 222/82 *Apple and Pear Development Council* v. *Lewis* [1983] ECR 4083, para. 37; Case C–319/91 *Ligur Carni* v. *Unità Sanitaria Locale* [1993] ECR I–6621, para. 39.

[40]  For a fuller discussion on this point, see S. Van den Bogart, 'Horizontality' in C. Barnard and J. Scott (eds.), *The Law of the Single European Market: Unpacking the premises* (Oxford: Hart Publishing, 2002); M. Quinn and N. McGowan, 'Could Article 30 impose obligations on individuals?' (1987) 12 *ELRev*. 163; and J. Baquero Cruz, *Between Competition and Free Movement: The economic constitutional law of the European Community* (Oxford: Hart Publishing, 2002), Ch. 7; E. Lohse, 'Fundamental freedoms and private actors' (2007) 13 *EPL* 159.

[41]  Case C–281/98 *Angonese* v. *Cassa di Risparmio di Bolzano* [2000] ECR I–4139.

[42]  See also Case 7/68 *Commission* v. *Italy* [1968] ECR 428, 430: 'The subject of that chapter [the elimination of quantitative restrictions] is State intervention'; and Warner AG in Joined Cases 55 and 57/80 *Musik-Vertrieb Membran* v. *Gema* [1981] ECR 147, 175, talking of measures under Art. 34 which means 'a measure taken by a Member State; it does not mean a measure taken by a private person'. Cf. Arts. 157 and 45 TFEU (ex Arts. 141 and 39 EC) which are also addressed to Member States but nevertheless have been found to be binding on private individuals.

[43]  Case C–159/00 *Sapod-Audic* v. *Eco-Emballages SA* [2002] ECR I–5031, para. 74. See further G.Davies, ' "Process and production method"-based trade restrictions in the EU' (2007–8) 10 *CYELS* 69, 78–9.

[44]  See the separate chapter on the website.

[45]  Case 83/78 *Pigs Marketing Board* v. *Redmond* [1978] ECR 2347, para. 66, and Case C–47/90 *Etablissements Delhaize Frères et Compagnie Le Lion SA* v. *Promalvin SA and AGE Bodegas Unidas SA* [1992] ECR I–3669, paras. 28–9.

[46]  See Capotorti AG in Case 82/77 *Openbaar Ministerie of the Netherlands* v. *van Tiggele* [1978] ECR 25. This view is supported by Case 65/86 *Bayer AG* v. *Süllhöfer* [1988] ECR 5249 and Joined Cases 177 and 178/82 *Criminal Proceedings against Van de Haar* [1984] ECR 1797, para. 114, which suggest that Arts. 101 and 34 are mutually exclusive. Cf. Poiares Maduro AG in Case C–438/05 *Viking* [2007] ECR I–10779, paras. 31–56.

case of agreements between undertakings (so a unilateral decision by a supermarket is unlikely to be covered); Article 102 applies only if there is an abuse of a dominant position. Even the largest supermarket is unlikely to satisfy the criteria of dominance (40 per cent of market share). In these circumstances, our fictitious supermarket chain's conduct is likely to fall outside the scope of Union law.

That said, the state may have to take responsibility for the action of individuals either directly or indirectly. An example of direct responsibility can be seen in *A.G.M.-COS. MET.*[47] An expert advising the Finnish Ministry of Social Affairs and Health said in the press that vehicle lifts made by an Italian company, AGM, were not safe, even though they were certified as conforming to the relevant directive. This resulted in AGM losing sales in Finland. The Court said that if AGM could reasonably suppose that the statements were positions taken by the official with the authority of his office, they could be an obstacle to inter-state trade within the meaning of *Dassonville.*[48]

States may also take indirect responsibility for activities of individuals who have been disrupting the application of Article 34, even though the activity of the individuals is not itself caught by Article 34. This principle was established in *Commission v. France (Spanish strawberries).*[49] For many years French farmers sabotaged imported agricultural produce while the French authorities simply stood back and turned a blind eye. Eventually, the Commission brought Article 258 TFEU (ex Article 226 EC) enforcement proceedings against the French government 'for failing to take all necessary and proportionate measures'[50] to prevent the free movement of goods from being obstructed by the actions of private individuals. The Commission argued that the French government's failure to act contravened Article 34 TFEU read in conjunction with Article 4(3) TEU (ex Article 10 EC) on the duty of cooperation. The Court agreed, saying that Article 34 prohibited not only state action but also inaction:

The fact that a Member State abstains from taking action or, as the case may be, fails to adopt adequate measures to prevent obstacles to the free movement of goods that are created, in particular, by actions by private individuals on its territory aimed at products originating in other Member States is just as likely to obstruct intra-[Union] trade as is a positive act.[51]

However, it seems that liability will arise only where the state has 'manifestly and persistently abstained from adopting appropriate and adequate measures' to put an end

---

[47] Case C–470/03 *A.G.M.-COS.MET Srl v. Soumen valtio, Tarmo Lehtinen* [2007] ECR I–2749, para. 56. For criticism, see N. Reich, '*AGM-COS.MET* or: who is protected by EC Safety regulation?' (2008) 33 *ELRev.* 85.

[48] Paras. 56–7 and 60. In determining whether the statements were attributable to the state, the Court said (para. 58) the national court should take into account whether: the official has authority generally within the sector in question; the official sends out his statements in writing under the official letterhead of the competent department; the official gives television interviews on his department's premises; the official does not indicate that his statements are personal or that they differ from the official position of the competent department; and the competent state departments do not take the necessary steps as soon as possible to dispel the impression on the part of the addressee that they are official positions taken by the state.

[49] Case C–265/95 *Commission v. France (Spanish strawberries)* [1997] ECR I–6959. K. Muylle, 'Angry farmers and passive policemen: Private conduct and free movement of goods' (1998) 23 *ELRev.* 467, 469.

[50] See also para. 32 of the judgment.

[51] Paras. 30–1. See also Case C–309/02 *Radlberger Getränkegesellschaft mbH & Co. v. Land Baden-Württemberg* [2004] ECR I–11763, para. 80 where the state was liable under Art. 34 for its failure to ensure that private parties could effectively participate in a take-back system for beverage repackaging.

to individual action which jeopardizes free movement.[52] Less serious interference by individuals will not attract this sanction.[53]

## 2.4 'Directly or Indirectly, Actually or Potentially'

### (a) 'Actually or potentially'

Given the problems associated with the first two limbs of the *Dassonville* formula, it is not perhaps surprising that the Court has, in more recent decisions, increasingly referred to 'any *measure* capable of hindering, directly or indirectly, actually or potentially, intra-[Union] trade' as an 'obstacle' to free movement,[54] thereby dropping the first two limbs of *Dassonville*.[55] However, the third limb ('directly or indirectly, actually or potentially') remains good law and is the most important element of the formula since it emphasizes that the Court is concerned with the *effect* of the measure, not the intention behind it.

While most of the cases concern measures which have an actual effect on trade, the Court has recognized that it is sufficient for the measure to have a potential effect to breach Article 34. This can be seen in *Commission v. France (foie gras)*[56] concerning French rules on the composition of *foie gras*. Although very little *foie gras* was produced in other Member States,[57] the Court still found that because the French rule was 'capable of hindering, at least *potentially*, inter-state trade'[58] it breached Article 34.

The *foie gras* case also demonstrates the point made explicitly elsewhere that no *de minimis* rule applies to Article 34.[59] For this reason, the Court has said that national rules need apply only to part, and often a very small part, of the market to trigger the

---

[52] Para. 65. See also Council Reg. (EC) No. 2679/98 on the functioning of the internal market in relation to the free movement of goods among the Member States ([1998] OJ L337/8), considered in Ch. 6.

[53] See Case C–112/00 *Eugen Schmidberger, Internationale Transporte und Planzüge* v. *Republic of Austria* [2003] ECR I–5659, considered in Ch. 6.

[54] See, e.g., Case C–470/03 *A.G.M.-COS.MET Srl* [2007] ECR I–2749, para. 60 and Case C–319/05 *Commission* v. *Germany (Garlic Capsule)* [2007] ECR I–9811, para. 80. See also Case C–143/06 *Ludwigs-Apotheke München Internationale Apotheke* v. *Juers Pharma Import-Export GmbH* [2007] ECR I–9623, para. 26 which talks more narrowly of 'all legislation'.

[55] Cf. Case C–244/06 *Dynamic Medien Vertriebs GmbH* v. *Avides Media AG* [2008] ECR I–505, para. 26 and Case C–110/05 *Commission* v. *Italy (trailers)* [2009] ECR I–519, para. 33 where the Court used the original *Dassonville* formula.

[56] Case C–184/96 *Commission* v. *France (foie gras)* [1998] ECR I–6197, para. 17.

[57] Although cf. Case 118/86 *Openbaar Ministerie* v. *Nertsvoederfabriek Nederland BV* [1987] ECR 3883, para. 10: 'Since the rules described do not disclose any prohibition of imports, there is no need to consider Article [34].'

[58] Emphasis added. See also Case C–325/00 *Commission* v. *Germany (label of origin)* [2002] ECR I–9977, para. 25. Cf. Art. 110 TFEU where actual disparate impact must be shown: Case 132/88 *Commission* v. *Greece* [1990] ECR I–1567 and Case 252/86 *Bergandi* v. *Directeur général des impôts* [1988] ECR 1343, considered further in Ch. 3.

[59] Joined Cases 177 and 178/82 *Criminal Proceedings against Van de Haar* [1984] ECR 1797, para. 13: 'If a national measure is capable of hindering imports it must be regarded as a measure having an effect equivalent to a quantitative restriction, even though the hindrance is slight and even though it is possible for the imported product to be marketed in other ways' (emphasis added). See also Case C–126/91 *Schutzverband gegen Unwesen in der Wirtschaft ev* v. *Yves Rocher GmbH* [1993] ECR I–2361, para. 21, and Case C–67/97 *Criminal Proceedings against Ditlev Bluhme* [1998] ECR I–8033 where Fennelly AG said 'the slight effect of the Decision, in volume terms, cannot in itself prevent the application of Article [34]'. Cf. Case C–110/05 *Commission* v. *Italy (trailers)* [2009] ECR I–519, para. 56 considered below where the Court appeared to suggest the need for some form of threshold requirement. See also competition law where it is well-established that Art. 101 TFEU is subject to a *de minimis* rule: Case 5/69 *Völk* v. *Vervaeke* [1969] ECR 295.

Article 34 prohibition. Therefore, in *Bluhme*[60] the Court said that Article 34 applied to a rule which affected the Danish island of Læsø which covered only 0.3 per cent of Danish territory.

However, in cases which fall on the perimeter of free movement of goods, the Court has applied a remoteness test,[61] especially where the case does not concern a trading rule in the narrow sense of the term.[62] This can be seen in *Krantz*[63] concerning a Dutch law, allowing the collector of taxes to seize goods if purchasers failed to discharge their tax debts. The Court said the possibility that nationals of other Member States would hesitate to sell goods on instalment to purchasers in the Netherlands because such goods were liable to be seized by the collector of taxes was 'too uncertain and indirect' to warrant the conclusion that a national provision authorizing such seizure was liable to hinder trade between Member States,[64] and so Article 34 did not apply.[65]

## (b) 'Directly or indirectly'

*Dassonville* also provides that the national measure must 'directly or indirectly' hinder intra-Union trade. Increasingly this was interpreted to mean that both direct and indirect discrimination against imported goods were prohibited. The need to show some discrimination was emphasized in *Keck*. However, as we shall see, following *Commission v. Italy (trailers)*,[66] the importance of showing discrimination appears to have diminished, thereby bringing the case law back to the original market access approach found in *Dassonville*.

*Dassonville* concerned Belgian law requiring importers of Scotch whisky to hold a British certificate of authentication. This rule favoured those importing whisky directly from the UK over traders importing Scotch whisky into Belgium from other Member States where the whisky was already in free circulation. Such 'indirect' importers could obtain this certificate only with great difficulty. The Court did not analyse this problem in terms of discrimination; instead it merely said that the requirement to hold the certificate constituted an MEE. This effects-based approach to Article 34[67] stands in stark contrast to the narrower protectionist approach to the dormant commerce clause advocated by much of the US Supreme Court's jurisprudence.[68] Protectionist measures will, of course,

---

[60] Case C–67/97 *Bluhme* [1998] ECR I–8033. See also, e.g., Joined Cases C–277, 318 and 319/91 *Ligur Carni v. Unità Sanitaria Locale* [1993] ECR I–6621 (rule applied by a municipality to its slaughterhouse).

[61] See La Pergola AG in Case C–44/98 *BASF* [1999] ECR I–6269, para. 18.

[62] See E. Spaventa, 'The outer limits of the Treaty free movement provisions: Some reflections on the significance of *Keck*, remoteness and *Deliège*' in C. Barnard and O. Odudu, *The Outer Limits of European Union Law* (Oxford: Hart Publishing, 2009).

[63] Case C–69/88 *Krantz* [1990] ECR I–583. This is considered further in Ch. 5.

[64] Para. 11. See also e.g. Case C–93/92 *CMC Motorradcenter GmbH* v. *Pelin Baskiciogullari* [1993] ECR I–5009, para. 12; Case C–44/98 *BASF* v. *Präsident des Deutschen Patentamts* [1999] ECR I–6269, paras. 16 and 21.

[65] See also Case C–412/97 *ED Srl* v. *Italo Fenocchio* [1999] ECR I–3845 for an example under Art. 35.

[66] Case C–110/05 *Commission* v. *Italy* [2009] ECR I–519.

[67] See A. Rosas, *Dassonville* and *Cassis de Dijon*' in M. Poiares Maduro and L. Azoulai (eds.), *The Past and Future of EU Law: The Classics of EU law Revisited on the 50th anniversary of the Rome Treaty* (Oxford: Hart Publishing, 2010).

[68] D. Regan, 'The Supreme Court and state protectionism: Making sense of the dormant commerce clause' (1985) 84 *Mich. L. Rev.* 1091. He argues that the Court has rightly been exclusively concerned with preventing states from engaging in purposeful economic protectionism, which he defines to mean: (1) the statute was adopted for the purpose of improving the competitive position of local economic actors, just

be caught by Article 34 but so will a much wider range of measures, including those that are discriminatory and those that hinder market access.

The Commission has always recognized that Article 34 prohibits discrimination. In Commission Directive 70/50[69] it distinguished between measures which discriminate directly against imports ('distinctly applicable measures') and measures that indirectly affect imports ('indistinctly applicable measures' or 'equally applicable measures').[70] This directive applied only to the Union's transitional period (now expired)[71] but continues to be an important source to help understand this terminology.[72] Up until the early 2000s the case law followed the distinction drawn by the directive,[73] but more recent cases have paid less attention to whether the measure is discriminatory, focusing instead on the obstacle created by the rule to market access. This shift was confirmed in *Commission* v. *Italy (trailers)*. It now seems that Article 34 prohibits not only distinctly and indistinctly applicable rules but also those that hinder market access. We shall now consider these categories in turn.

# D.  DISTINCTLY APPLICABLE MEASURES

## 1.  INTRODUCTION

Distinctly applicable measures are loosely equivalent to directly discriminatory measures: the imported goods are treated less favourably than the domestic product when, in objective terms, they should be treated in the same way.[74] Putting it another way, the national measure has a different burden in law and in fact on the domestic and imported good. The need to show differential impact was emphasized by Article 2 of Directive 70/50:

This Directive covers measures, other than those applicable equally to domestic or imported products, which hinder imports which could otherwise take place, including measures which make importation more difficult or costly than the disposal of domestic production.

As fig. 4.1 demonstrates, according to the orthodox approach, distinctly applicable measures breach Articles 34 or 35 and, due to their obvious impact on inter-state trade, can be saved only by reference to Article 36. However, more recent case law suggests that in certain circumstances the Court will, on occasion, allow distinctly applicable measures to be saved by a broader range of judicially developed justifications,[75] known as 'mandatory'

---

because they are local, vis-à-vis their foreign competitors; and (2) the statute is analogous in form to the traditional instruments of protectionism (the tariff, quota, or embargo).

[69]  [1970] OJ L13/29 ([1970] OJ/Spec Ed. 17).

[70]  While this book will use the terms 'distinctly' and 'indistinctly applicable', it should be noted that there are many definitions and classifications of the measures. See, e.g., N. Bernard, 'Discrimination and free movement in EC law' (1996) 45 *ICLQ* 82 and C. Hilson, 'Discrimination in Community free movement law' (1999) 24 *ELRev.* 445.                                                          [71]  1 Jan. 1970.

[72]  See, e.g., Case 12/74 *Commission* v. *Germany* [1975] ECR 181, para. 14.

[73]  See Van Gerven AG in Joined Cases C–401 and 402/92 *Criminal proceedings against Tankstation 't Heukske vof and J.B.E. Boermans* [1994] ECR I–2199, para. 19.

[74]  The Court tends to use a variety of formulas to describe 'distinctly applicable' measures. It might say that the measure is 'discriminatory' or it might note, as in Case C–320/93 *Ortscheit* [1994] ECR I–5243, para. 9, that the national measure 'applies solely' to the foreign products.

[75]  See eg Case C–54/05 *Commission* v. *Finland* [2007] ECR I–2473 where the Court of Justice allowed an import licence to be justified, at least in principle, by mandatory requirements, and again in Case C–297/05

or 'public-interest' requirements, more usually associated with indistinctly applicable measures.

## 2. EXAMPLES OF DISTINCTLY APPLICABLE MEASURES

### 2.1 Imposing an Additional Requirement on the Imported/Exported Goods

Distinctly applicable measures include those which, as Article 2 of Directive 70/50 puts it, place conditions on imported products only, or demand higher standards of imports than of domestic products. Therefore, a requirement that imported goods be inspected breaches Article 34[76] due to the delays inherent in the inspection process[77] and the additional transport costs which the importer may incur.[78] So, in *Rewe* phytosanitary inspections of imported apples to control the spread of the apple disease San José scale in principle breached Article 34.[79]

Other unlawful conditions relate to the requirement for the imported goods (but not the domestic goods) to have a licence[80] or other official approval,[81] such as a certificate of fitness.[82] Alternatively the condition may relate instead to the composition of the goods. So, in *Weinvertriebs*[83] the Court said that a German law specifying the minimum alcohol content for imported (but not domestic) vermouth breached Article 34. The condition may also concern the circumstances under which the goods are promoted. Hence, a ban or other restriction on advertising foreign products, but not their domestic equivalents, breached Article 34.[84]

However, direct discrimination should not be too readily assumed, at least not in the context of Article 35. As always with the discrimination model, the prohibition on discrimination applies only if the goods for the domestic market and the goods for export are similarly situated. If there are objective differences between the two situations then the different treatment is not considered discriminatory.[85] This can be seen in

---

*Commission v. Netherlands (roadworthiness testing of cars)* [2007] ECR I–7467, paras. 73–4 where the Court allowed roadworthiness tests of imported cars to be potentially justified by mandatory requirements.

[76] Case 251/78 *Firma Denkavit Futtermittel GmbH v. Minister für Ernährung* [1979] ECR 3369, para. 10; Case 50/85 *Schloh v. Auto contrôle technique SPRL* [1986] ECR 1855 (roadworthiness testing).

[77] Case 132/80 *United Foods v. Belgian State* [1981] ECR 995, para. 28 (24 hours' notice to be given in writing for health inspection of imported fish).

[78] Case 4/75 *Rewe-Zentralfinanz eGmbH v. Landwirtschaftskammer* [1975] ECR 843, para. 4.

[79] For an example of such cases under Art. 35, see Case C–293/02 *Jersey Produce Marketing Organisation Ltd v. States of Jersey* [2005] ECR I–9543, paras. 75–6 and Case C–12/02 *Grilli* [2003] ECR I–11585, para. 48.

[80] Even if the licence is granted automatically: Joined Cases 51–54/71 *International Fruit (No. 2)* [1971] ECR 1107, para. 9. See also Case 40/82 *Commission v. United Kingdom (turkeys)* [1984] ECR 2793, para. 24, and Case 124/81 *Commission v. United Kingdom (UHT milk)* [1983] ECR 203, para. 9. For an equivalent case concerning exports, see Case 53/76 *Procureur de la République v. Bouhelier* [1977] ECR 197, para. 11.

[81] Case 21/84 *Commission v. France (postal franking machines)* [1985] ECR 1355; Case C–434/04 *Ahokainen* [2006] ECR I–9171, para. 22 (prior authorization required for the import of undenatured ethyl alcohol of an alcoholic strength of more than 80 per cent).

[82] Case 251/78 *Firma Denkavit Futtermittel GmBH* [1979] ECR 3369, para. 11.

[83] Case 59/82 *Schutzverband gegen Unwesen in der Wirtschaft v. Weinvertriebs-GmbH* [1983] ECR 1217, paras. 7–8.

[84] Case 152/78 *Commission v. France* [1980] ECR 2299, para. 13 (alcohol); Case C–320/93 *Ortscheit v. Eurim-Pharm Arzneimittel* [1994] ECR I–5243, para. 9 (medicinal products).

[85] See the parallel analysis in the context of discriminatory taxation under Art. 110 TFEU, considered in Ch. 3.

*Denkavit*,[86] concerning financial aid paid later for feedingstuffs exported in bulk than for inland deliveries. Although apparently a case of direct discrimination, the Court said that because the paperwork took longer for exported goods than for domestic goods there were objective differences between the two situations and so there was no discrimination.[87]

## 2.2 Rules Limiting Channels of Distribution

A second group of situations considered to be distinctly applicable concerns national rules limiting channels of distribution. We have already seen in *Dassonville*[88] how a national rule requiring the production of a certificate of authenticity favoured direct importers over indirect importers and so breached Article 34. This can also be seen in *De Peijper*,[89] where a parallel importer, who was not appointed to sell certain medicines directly on the Dutch market, bought them instead from a British wholesaler, and then imported them into the Netherlands. The parallel importer could not obtain the necessary authorization from the Dutch authorities because the appointed importer refused to give it access to the relevant documentation. The Court said that 'rules or practices which result in imports being channelled in such a way that only certain traders can effect these imports, whereas others are prevented from doing so' constitute an MEE.[90]

A number of Article 35 cases also concern national rules interfering with channels of trade,[91] particularly disposing of hazardous waste. For example, in *Inter-Huiles*[92] the Court said that national rules establishing a system for the collection and disposal of waste oils which prohibited export to a disposal or regenerating company in another Member State breached Article 35. Similarly, in *FFAD*[93] the Court said that municipal rules which prevented even qualified intermediaries from participating in the collection of waste with a view to reselling it in other Member States breached Article 35,[94] as did national rules requiring producers to deliver poultry offal to their local authority in *Nertsvoederfabriek*.[95]

## 2.3 National Rules Giving Preference to Domestic Goods

### (a) 'Buy national' rules

A third group of distinctly applicable measures involve national rules which give preference to, or an advantage for, domestic products. This can be seen in *Dundalk*

---

[86] Case 15/83 *Denkavit Nederland BV* v. *Hoofdproduktschap voor Akkerbouwprodukten* [1984] ECR 2171.  [87] Para. 18.

[88] Case 8/74 *Dassonville* [1974] ECR 837. See also Case 247/81 *Commission* v. *Germany* [1984] ECR 1111 (requirement to have a representative in the host state in which the goods were sold).

[89] Case 104/75 *De Peijper* [1976] ECR 613.  [90] Para. 13.

[91] See also Case C–350/97 *Wilfried Monsees* v. *Unabhängiger Verwaltungssenat für Kärnten* [1999] ECR I–2921, para. 29 (national rule making all international transit by road of animals for slaughter almost impossible in Austria).

[92] Case 172/82 *Syndicat national des fabricants raffineurs d'huile de graissage* v. *Groupement d'intérêt économique 'Inter-Huiles'* [1983] ECR 555. See also Case 295/82 *Groupement d'intérêt économique 'Rhône-Alpes Huiles'* v. *Syndicat national des fabricants raffineurs d'huile de graissage* [1984] ECR 575.

[93] Case C–209/98 *Entreprenørforeningens Affalds/Miljøsektion (FFAD)* v. *Københavns Kommune* [2000] ECR I–3743.  [94] Para. 42.

[95] Case 118/86 *Openbaar Ministerie* v. *Nertsvoederfabriek Nederland BV* [1997] ECR 3883, para. 11.

*Water*[96] concerning a clause in a tender to supply pipes for drinking water which specified that the pipes had to be made according to an Irish standard by a firm approved by
the Irish standards body as a supplier of pipes complying with the Irish standard. Only
one (Irish) firm had been approved by the body. The authorities rejected a tender from
an Irish/Spanish consortium proposing to supply pipes manufactured according to an
alternative international standard. The Court said that the terms of the tender discouraged those producing pipes to equivalent standards from tendering. This had 'the *effect* of
restricting the supply of the pipes needed for the Dundalk scheme to Irish manufacturers
alone'[97] and therefore breached Article 34.

'Buy national' campaigns are also considered distinctly applicable since, by their very
nature, they are intended to encourage the purchase of national products in preference
to imported products. Therefore, in *Commission* v. *Ireland ('Buy Irish')*[98] the Court condemned the Irish campaign since it reflected the Irish government's desire to achieve
'the substitution of domestic products for imported products and was liable to affect the
volume of trade between Member States'.[99] It reached this conclusion even though trade
had actually fallen by 6 per cent over the three years of the campaign.

*Commission* v. *Ireland* needs to be compared with the decision in *Apple and
Pear Development Council ('buy British fruit')*[100] where the Court said that a British
government-supported development council was under a duty not to run advertising
designed to discourage the purchase of products from other Member States, nor to dis-
parage those products in the eyes of the consumers, nor to advise consumers to purchase
domestic products solely by reason of their national origin. However, the Court did say
that such a body could draw attention in its publicity to the specific qualities of fruit
grown in the UK and could organize campaigns to promote the sale of certain varieties,
mentioning their particular properties, even if those varieties were typical of national
production.[101] This case law highlights the fine line between state-sponsored promotion
of national goods generally, which is unlawful, and state-sponsored promotion of specific
goods having distinctive qualities, which is permissible.

If 'buy national' campaigns are considered distinctly applicable, *a fortiori* national rules
requiring the purchase of certain quantities of the domestic product will be distinctly
applicable. In *PreussenElektra*[102] the Court ruled that an obligation placed on electricity

---

[96] Case 45/87 *Commission* v. *Ireland* [1988] ECR 4929. See also Case C–67/97 *Criminal Proceedings
against Ditlev Bluhme* [1998] ECR I–8033.

[97] Para. 20, emphasis added. Cf. Case C–254/05 *Commission* v. *Belgium (automatic fire detection systems)*
[2007] ECR I–4269, where the Court considered the requirement to apply a Belgian standard was 'applicable
without distinction to all products' and could be justified by a mandatory requirement (para. 31).

[98] Case 249/81 *Commission* v. *Ireland* [1982] ECR 4005. See also Case C–255/03 *Commission* v. *Belgium
(Walloon label of quality)*, judgment of 17 Jun. 2004, unreported. The problem of 'buy national' continues:
A. Willis, 'Cheap loan if car makers 'buy French', *euobserver.com*, 2 Apr. 2009.

[99] Para. 25.

[100] Case 222/82 *Apple and Pear Development Council* v. *Lewis* [1983] ECR 4083, para. 18.

[101] Ibid., para. 19. As a result of these two cases the Commission has offered 'Guidelines for the Member
States' involvement in Promotion of Agricultural and Fisheries Products—Article [34] Aspects' ([1986] OJ
C27/3). See also Reg. 3/2008 on information provision and promotion measures for agricultural products on
the internal market and in third countries (OJ [2008] L3/1).

[102] Case C–379/98 *PreussenElektra AG* v. *Schleswag AG* [2001] ECR I–2099, para. 70. See also Case 72/83
*Campus Oil* [1984] ECR 2727, para. 16 and Case C–398/98 *Commission* v. *Greece* [2001] ECR I–7915, para. 26.
These cases are considered in Ch. 6.

suppliers to purchase all of the renewable electricity produced in their region was an MEE since it limited the supplies those traders could obtain from producers in other Member States. The Court reached a similar conclusion in *Du Pont de Nemours*[103] where Italian law reserved 30 per cent of public supply contracts to companies established in certain regions of Italy. In its defence Italy argued that Italian regions not covered by the preferential system also suffered. The Court rejected the argument, saying that 'although not all the products of the Member State in question benefit by comparison with products from abroad, the fact remains that all the products benefiting by the preferential system are domestic products'. The measure therefore breached Article 34.

## (b)　Origin marking rules

Origin marking cases are also considered distinctly applicable, as *Commission v. Ireland (Irish souvenirs)*[104] demonstrates. Irish law required that all imported (but not domestic) jewellery depicting motifs suggesting that they were souvenirs of Ireland (for example, an Irish character, wolfhound, or shamrock) had to bear an indication of the country of origin or the word 'foreign'. The Irish government justified its rule on the ground that the appeal of souvenirs lay in the fact that they were manufactured in the place where they were bought. The Court rejected these arguments, favouring instead the Commission's view that buyers did not need to know where a product came from unless the product implied a certain quality (which was not the case here).[105] Rather dismissively, the Court said that since the souvenirs were of little commercial value, bought by tourists on the spot as 'pictorial reminders' of the place visited, they did not have to be manufactured in the country of origin.[106] Therefore, the Irish law *requiring* an indication of origin was a distinctly applicable MEE and breached Article 34. However, the Court added that Article 34 did allow domestic manufacturers to *choose* whether to attach the mark of origin to their goods.[107] This might be to the manufacturers' commercial advantage for the very reasons given by the Irish government.

It might be thought that a rule concerning origin marking did serve the interests of consumers since, as the Court said in *GB-INNO-BM*,[108] the provision of information to the consumer is a fundamental right. However, in *Commission v. UK (origin marking)*,[109] a case concerning a British law that certain imported goods be marked with an indication of origin, the Court explained why this might not always be so. It said that the UK law breached Article 34 because the origin marking requirement enabled consumers to distinguish between domestic and imported products, allowing them to assert any prejudices which they might have against the foreign product. In a single market an origin marking rule not only made the marketing of imported goods more difficult but it also had 'the effect of slowing down economic interpenetration in the [Union] by

---

[103] Case C–21/88 *Du Pont de Nemours Italiana SpA v. Unità sanitaria locale No. 2 di Carrara* [1990] ECR I–889, para. 11.

[104] Case 113/80 *Commission v. Ireland* [1981] ECR 1625. See also Case C–30/99 *Commission v. Ireland (hallmarking of precious metals)* [2001] ECR I–4619, para. 74.

[105] Cf. Spiteri, 'EU ponders "Made in the EU" label', euobserver.com, 13 Jan. 2004.　　　[106] Para. 15.

[107] Para. 16.

[108] Case C–362/88 *GB-INNO-BM v. Confédération du commerce luxembourgeois* [1990] ECR I–667, para. 18.

[109] Case 207/83 *Commission v. UK* [1985] ECR 1202.

handicapping the sale of goods produced as the result of a division of labour between Member States'.[110]

As the Court suggested in the *Buy Irish* and *Origin Marking* cases, indications of provenance[111] and designations of origin[112] are lawful only where the product genuinely has distinguishing qualities and characteristics which are due to the fact that it originated in a specific geographic area.[113] This was confirmed in *Commission v. Germany (Weinbrand)*[114] where the Court found that a German law reserving the well-known, but generic,[115] names 'Sekt' and 'Weinbrand' to products originating in Germany or coming from countries where German was the official language breached Article 34. The Court said that an area of origin defined on the basis of the national territory (Germany) or a linguistic criterion (German-speaking) could not constitute a geographic area capable of justifying an indication of origin[116] because the production of these drinks did not involve specific grapes or production methods. In other words, because the products did not have any qualities and characteristics rendering them typically German,[117] Germany could not reserve the generic names 'Sekt' and 'Weinbrand' to these national products.[118] Furthermore, the Court said that by reserving these names to domestic products, products from other Member States were compelled to employ names which were 'unknown or less esteemed by the consumer'.[119] As a result, the German legislation was 'calculated to favour the disposal of the domestic product on the German market to the detriment of the products from other Member States'.[120]

A common theme running through this line of case law is the Court's insistence on examining the effect of the measure.[121] If, in reality, the measure has a different burden in law and in fact on the imported goods it is considered to be distinctly applicable, no matter that the measure might be drafted in an indistinctly applicable (same burden in law, different burden in fact) manner. This can be seen most clearly in *Commission v. UK*

---

[110] Para. 17.

[111] Indications of provenance are intended to inform the consumer that the product bearing that indication comes from a particular place, region, or country: Case C–3/91 *Exportur* [1992] ECR I–5529, para. 11. Therefore, in Joined Cases C–321–4/94 *Pistre* [1997] ECR I–2343, para. 36, the description 'mountain' was not an indication of provenance. See further Ch. 6.

[112] Designations of origin guarantee not only the geographical provenance of the product but also that the goods have been manufactured according to quality requirements or manufacturing standards prescribed by an act of a public authority: Case C–3/91 *Exportur* [1992] ECR I–5529, para.11, citing the example of Case C–47/90 *Etablissements Delhaize Frères et Compagnie le Lion SA v. Promalvin SA and AGE Bodegas Unidas SA* [1992] ECR I–3669 (rioja wine).

[113] Case 12/74 *Commission v. Germany* [1975] ECR 181, para. 7.          [114] Ibid.

[115] This term is considered further in Case Study 6.1.

[116] Para. 8. In Case 286/86 *Minstère Public v. Deserbais* [1988] ECR 4907, para. 9, the Court said that the designation 'Edam' was not an appellation of origin.                     [117] Para. 10.

[118] Para. 16. In response to concerns that the Court's case law was having the effect of diminishing the quality of foodstuffs, the Commission adopted Reg. 2098/92 ([1992] OJ L208/1) which established a registration procedure for foodstuffs which have a link between their characteristics and geographical origins. This is considered further in Ch. 6. See also C. MacMaolain, 'Free movement of foodstuffs, quality requirements and consumer protection: Have the Court and the Commission both got it wrong?' (2001) 26 *ELRev.* 413, 417ff.                     [119] Para. 14.

[120] Case 12/74 *Commission v. Germany* [1975] ECR 181, para. 14.

[121] See esp. Case 45/87 *Commission v. Ireland (Dundalk Water)* [1988] ECR 4929.

*(origin marking)*[122] where, in response to the UK's argument that the rule was actually indistinctly applicable, the Court said:[123]

The requirements relating to the indication of origin of goods are applicable without distinction to domestic and imported products *only in form* because, by their very nature, they are intended to enable the consumer to distinguish between those two categories of products, which may thus prompt him to give his preference to national products.

## 3. DEFENDING DISTINCTLY APPLICABLE MEASURES

According to the orthodoxy, the significance for the defendant Member State of having its rule classified as a distinctly applicable measure is that it could justify it only by reference to one of the Article 36 derogations, not by the broader list of mandatory requirements which apply only to indistinctly applicable measures (see fig. 4.1).[124] However, there are signs that the Court is in the process of diluting, if not abandoning altogether, this well-established rule. This change has come about in two ways. First, in certain cases the Court has conveniently overlooked the fact that the rule was in fact directly discriminatory to enable the defending state to have recourse to the mandatory or imperative requirements. Perhaps the most blatant example of this is *Walloon Waste*,[125] which concerned a decree of the Walloon Regional Council prohibiting the storage or dumping in Wallonia of waste originating in another Member State or in a region of Belgium other than Wallonia. Most commentators consider this rule to be directly discriminatory[126] and so it should have been justified only by one of the express derogations. Instead, the Court applied the 'imperative requirements of environmental protection'.[127]

Secondly, in more modern cases the Court rarely expressly classifies a measure as distinctly applicable, describing the rule instead simply as an MEE. For example, in *Commission v Austria (roadworthiness of cars)*[128] the Court said that national rules making the registration of *imported* used vehicles previously registered in other Member States contingent upon compliance with certain technical requirements, although used vehicles already on the national market and having the same characteristics were not subject to such requirements in cases of re-registration, constituted an MEE. However, the Court said the Austrian rule could be justified on the grounds of public health (An express derogation) or environmental protection (a mandatory requirement).[129] As the Commission notes, this reflects a 'greening' of free movement of goods that has taken

---

[122] Case 207/83 *Commission v. UK* [1985] ECR 1202. For a similar approach see Case 177/83 *Kohl KG v. Ringelhan & Rennett SA and Ringelhan Einrichtungs GmbH* [1984] ECR 3651, para. 15.

[123] Para. 20, emphasis added.

[124] The Art. 36 derogations and the mandatory requirements are discussed in detail in Ch. 6.

[125] Case C-2/90 *Commission v. Belgium* [1992] ECR I-4431.

[126] The Commission argued this before the Court. See also, e.g., Bernard, above n. 70, 93; N. Notaro, 'The new generation case law on trade and environment' (2000) 25 *ELRev.* 467, 478–9, and 482. However, this is a difficult area because Art. 191(2) TFEU (ex Art. 174(2) EC) recognizes that 'damage should as a priority be rectified at source'.

[127] Para. 32.

[128] Case C-524/07 [2008] ECR I-187*, paras. 54 and 55. For an earlier example, see Case C-67/97 *Bluhme* [1998] ECR I-8033, para. 19. See also Case C-120/95 *Decker* v. *Caisse de Maladie des Employés Privés* [1998] ECR I-1831.

[129] See also Case C- 142/05 *Mickelsson* [2009] ECR I-000 where, given the facts, the Court appeared to dovetail the public health derogation and the mandatory requirements (para. 33)

place in recent years, underlining the fact that certain grounds of justification may be viewed differently over time.[130]

But it is not just in cases concerning the environment where the Court is bending (ignoring?) its own rules. For example, in *Commission v. Finland*[131] the Court permitted a Finnish law requiring import licences for vehicles, traditionally a distinctly applicable measure, to be justified by a road-safety mandatory requirement.[132] Likewise, in *LIBRO*[133] the Court allowed a distinctly applicable book price-fixing scheme to be justified by the 'overriding requirement in the public interest', namely the 'protection of books as cultural objects'.

Such cases have prompted some to call for the abolition of the distinction between the express derogations and mandatory requirements.[134] For example, in *Preussenelektra*[135] Advocate General Jacobs pointed to a number of decisions where the court has 'relied on imperative requirements in cases in which it was at least doubtful whether the measure could be considered as applying without distinction'.[136] He called on the Court to clarify the situation, especially because 'it is desirable that even directly discriminatory measures can sometimes be justified on grounds of environmental protection'.[137] As cases such as *Commission v. Finland* and *LIBRO* show, the Court does seem to be moving in this direction,[138] without expressly acknowledging what it is doing. However, it may well be that, as in *LIBRO*, the Court will be more likely to find the rule disproportionate since it is directly discriminatory.[139] A more carefully tailored (indirectly or non-discriminatory) rule might survive proportionality review more easily.

## 4. DISCRIMINATION ARISING FROM TREATING NATIONAL AND IMPORTED GOODS ALIKE: PRICE FIXING

So far we have considered discrimination which arises from treating national and imported goods *differently*. This is referred to as formal discrimination. Sometimes discrimination

---

[130] Commission, *Free Movement of Goods: Guide to the application of Treaty provisions governing free movement of goods*, SEC(2009) 673, 8.

[131] Case C–54/05 *Commission* v. *Finland* [2007] ECR I–2473.

[132] See also Case C–297/05 *Commission* v. *Netherlands (roadworthiness testing of cars)* [2007] ECR I–7467. The Court has finessed this change by merging the terminology: e.g., Case C–239/02 *Douwe Egberts NV* v. *Westrom Pharma* [2004] ECR I–7007, para. 55: 'Such a fetter may be justified only by one of the public interest grounds set out in Article [36] ... or by one of the overriding requirements ensuring inter alia consumer protection.'

[133] Case C–531/07 *Fachverband der Buch- und Medienwirtschaft v. LIBRO Handelsgesellschaft mbH* [2009] ECR I–000, para. 34.

[134] P. Oliver, 'Some further reflections on the scope of Articles 28–30 (ex 30–36)' (1999) 36 *CMLRev.* 738. See also Commission, *Free Movement of Goods: Guide to the application of Treaty provisions governing free movement of goods*, SEC(2009) 673, 42 which argues that the separation between the express derogations and the mandatory requirements is 'artificial and the Court is moving towards simplification and treating mandatory requirements in the same way as Article [36] justifications'.

[135] Case C–379/98 *PreussenElektra AG* v. *Schleswag AG* [2001] ECR I–2099, para. 226. See also his comments in Case C–203/96 *Chemische Afvalstoffen Dusseldorp* v. *Minister van Milieubeheer* [1998] ECR I–4075 and in Case C–136/00 *Rolf Dieter Danner* [2002] ECR I–8147.

[136] Citing Case C–389/96 *Aher-Waggon* v. *Germany* [1998] ECR I–4473, considered in Ch. 6.

[137] Para. 226.

[138] Some support for this view can be found in See A. Rosas, *Dassonville* and *Cassis de Dijon'* in M. Poiares Maduro and L Azoulai (eds.), above n. 67.

[139] Para. 35. Note the very brief discussion of the (dis)proportionality of the national rule.

can arise when national and imported goods are treated in the *same* way, where such equal treatment is not objectively justified. This is sometimes described as material discrimination. The price fixing cases—where the Member State sets either a maximum or minimum price for a particular good—provide an example of this. Fixing a maximum price may discriminate against imported goods, because if the maximum price is set too low it does not take into account the transport costs borne by the importer. Fixing a minimum price may also discriminate against imported goods because it removes any competitive advantage they may have. These issues were considered in *van Tiggele*[140] and *Tasca*.[141]

In *Tasca* the Court said that although a *maximum* price applicable to both domestic and imported goods did not in itself constitute an MEE, it could have such an effect when it was fixed at a level such that the sale of the imported products became, if not impossible, then at least more difficult than for domestic products. The Court therefore said that a maximum price constituted an MEE if it was fixed at such a low level that dealers wishing to import the product into the Member States could do so only at a loss. In a similar vein, the Court ruled in *Danis*[142] that a national rule imposing a price freeze could also constitute an MEE where it prevented the increased prices of imported goods from being passed on to the consumer. However, in *LIBRO*,[143] the Court appeared to change tack. It initially classified a maximum price fixing rule as a certain selling arrangement under *Keck*.[144] It would therefore benefit from the presumption of legality. However, because the rule was directly discriminatory the Court ruled that it was in fact an MEE.

In *van Tiggele* the Court said that price control rules applicable to both domestic and imported goods did not in general constitute an MEE but could do so where, for example,[145] imports could be impeded when a national authority fixed prices or profit margins at such a level that imported products were placed at a disadvantage in relation to identical domestic products, either because they could not profitably be marketed in the conditions laid down or because the competitive advantage conferred by lower cost prices was cancelled out. The Court then identified two types of minimum sale prices which were legitimate: first, a national provision prohibiting the retail sale of products at prices below the purchase price paid by the retailer and, secondly, the fixing of a minimum profit margin at a specific amount, and not as a percentage of the cost price.

## 5. 'REVERSE DISCRIMINATION'

So far we have concentrated on the situation where the national rule has (overtly) discriminated against *imported* goods. We now turn to the (rarer) situation where the national rule discriminates against *domestic* goods. This is known as reverse discrimination.

---

[140] Case 82/77 *Openbaar Ministerie* v. *van Tiggele* [1978] ECR 25.

[141] Case 65/75 *Criminal Proceedings against Riccardo Tasca* [1976] ECR 291.

[142] Joined Cases 16–20/79 *Criminal Proceedings against Danis* [1979] ECR 3327, para. 7.

[143] Case C–531/07 *LIBRO Handelsgesellschaft mbH* [2009] ECR I–000, para. 20–2. See also Case C–63/94 *Belgapom* [1995] ECR I–2467 where the Court ruled that Art. 34 did not apply where a Member State prohibited any sale which yielded only a very low profit.          [144] See further Ch.5.

[145] Para. 14. See also Case 231/83 *Cullet* [1985] ECR 305 and Case C–287/89 *Commission* v. *Belgium* [1991] ECR I–2233 on goods and Case C–442/02 *Caixa-Bank* v. *Ministère de l'Économie, des Finances and de l'industrie* [2004] ECR I–8961 (establishment); Joined Cases C–94/04 and C–202/04 *Cipolla* v. *Fazari* [2006] ECR I–2049 (services).

Because Article 34 does not apply to wholly internal situations,[146] reverse discrimination is compatible with Union law. Therefore, in *Mathot*[147] the Court said that a Belgian law requiring butter produced in Belgium to have certain details listed on its packaging, without imposing the same requirement on butter produced in other Member States, did not breach Article 34. As the Court explained in *Jongeneel Kaas*,[148] reverse discrimination is permitted because it encourages national rules which, while leaving imported products unaffected, have as 'their purpose to improve the quality of domestic production so as to make it more attractive to consumers'. In other words, although the national producers must bear additional costs as a result of their own government's action they may gain a competitive advantage in terms of quality. The effect of these decisions is to prevent national traders faced with more onerous national laws from complaining that they suffer a competitive disadvantage in respect of goods produced by their foreign rivals and that only the standards of the lowest state should apply to them in the name of equal treatment.

Given the broad scope of the *Dassonville* formula it is in fact rare for a situation of reverse discrimination to arise because most national measures have at least a 'potential' effect on trade.[149] This can be seen in *Pistre*,[150] where a French national was prosecuted for making unauthorized use of the word 'mountain' on a label. In his defence he said that the French law on the development and protection of mountain regions breached Article 34. However, the French government argued that Union law did not apply since the case occurred on French territory, concerning French nationals marketing French products.[151] Advocate General Jacobs agreed and urged the Court to decline jurisdiction, but the Court insisted that Article 34 did apply. Citing the *Dassonville* formula, it said that while the application of a national measure having *no actual link* to the importation of goods did not fall within the ambit of Article 34, 'Article [34] cannot be considered inapplicable simply because all the facts of the specific case before the national court are confined to a single Member State.'[152] The Court said that the measure facilitated the marketing of domestic goods to the detriment of imported goods,[153] and so created and maintained a difference of treatment between domestic and imported goods, 'hindering, at least *potentially*, intra-[Union] trade'.[154]

---

[146] Art. 34: 'Quantitative restrictions on imports and all measures having equivalent effect shall be prohibited *between* Member States' (emphasis added). Cf. Case C–363/93 *Lancry* v. *Direction genérale des Douanes* [1994] ECR I–3957 where the Court said that Art. 30 TFEU applied to duties levied on goods moving within the state (in casu from mainland France to French overseas territories) and P. Oliver, 'Some further reflections on the scope of Articles 28–30 (ex 30–36)' (1999) 36 *CMLRev.* 738, 787–8, and K. Mortelmans, 'The Common Market, the internal market and the single market, what's in a market?' (1998) 35 *CMLRev.* 101, 132–3.

[147] Case 98/86 *Criminal Proceedings against Mathot* [1987] ECR 809. See also Case 355/85 *Cognet* [1986] ECR 3241 (change in French law following ruling of Court in Case 229/83 *Leclerc* v. *Au Blé Vert* [1985] ECR 1, a ruling confirmed in Case C–9/99 *Échirolles Distribution SA* v. *Association du Dauphiné* [2000] ECR I–8207, para. 24). *Leclerc* makes clear that Art. 34 does not apply to a re-import situation (i.e., a domestic product leaves the Member State and then is re-imported, where the sole purpose of the re-import is to circumvent domestic rules).

[148] Case 237/82 *Jongeneel Kaas BV* v. *State of the Netherlands* [1984] ECR 483, para. 20.

[149] See Case C–184/96 *Commission* v. *France (foie gras)* [1998] ECR I–6197 considered above n. 56.

[150] Joined Cases C–321–4/94 *Pistre* [1997] ECR I–2343.   [151] Para. 41.   [152] Para. 44.

[153] Para. 45. See also Case C–293/02 *Jersey Produce* [2005] ECR I–9543.

[154] Ibid., emphasis added. See also Joined Cases C–158/04 and C–159/04 *Alfa Vita Vassilopoulos AE* [2006] ECR I–8135.

# E. INDISTINCTLY APPLICABLE MEASURES

## 1. INTRODUCTION

So far we have considered national measures which are overtly discriminatory: the discrimination is clear on the face of the measure. We now turn to consider the more covert type of discrimination which is found in indistinctly applicable measures. Indistinctly applicable measures are primarily those rules and practices which in law apply to both national and domestic products but in fact have a particular burden on the imported goods.[155] This different burden may arise because, while the national producer has to satisfy only one regulator (the home state), the imported goods have to satisfy a dual regulatory burden (home state and host state regulation), with the additional costs that this entails.[156] Such rules may have been introduced with the purpose of protecting national markets[157] or may have that effect.[158] Article 3 of Directive 70/50 makes no reference to the purpose of the measure. It merely provides:

This Directive also covers measures governing the marketing of products which deal, in particular, with shape, size, weight, composition, presentation, identification or putting up and which are equally applicable to domestic and imported products.[159]

Indistinctly applicable measures—whether they constitute an absolute barrier or a mere hindrance to the import of the foreign goods[160]—may constitute effective barriers to the free movement of goods and the Court has been assiduous in declaring them unlawful, unless they can be justified by the Member State in some way. The classic example of indistinctly applicable measures concern 'product requirements',[161] i.e. rules relating to designation, form, size, weight, composition, presentation, labelling, and packaging.[162]

---

[155] Case C–14/02 *ATRAL SA* v. *Etat belge* [2003] ECR I–4431, para. 63. Sometimes this is described in terms of protective effect: see, e.g., Case 16/83 *Prantl* [1984] ECR 1299, para. 21. Generally, however, the Court does not consider the protective effect of national legislation in the case of either distinctly or indistinctly applicable measures. Cf. G. Marenco, 'Pour une interpretation traditionelle de la notion de mesure d'effet equivalent à une restriction quantitative' (1984) 20 *Cahiers de Droit Européen* 291, who argues that protective effect is the rationale behind Art. 34; and the criticisms of this view in D. Chalmers, 'Repackaging the internal market: The ramifications of the *Keck* judgment' (1994) 19 *ELRev*. 385, 393–4. Clearly, measures which have as their purpose the regulation of trade in goods are caught by Art. 34 (*Keck, a contrario*, para. 12).

[156] See, e.g., Case C–239/90 *Boscher* v. *SA British Motors Wright* [1991] ECR I–2023, para. 15. For a fuller discussion of the issues raised here see Ch. 8.

[157] Case 788/79 *Gilli and Andres* [1980] ECR 2071, para. 10.

[158] Case 16/83 *Prantl* [1984] ECR 1299, para. 21.

[159] The Article continues: 'where the restrictive effect of such measures on the free movement of goods exceeds the effects intrinsic to trade rules. This is the case, in particular, where:
— the restrictive effects on the free movement of goods are out of proportion to their purpose;
— the same objective can be attained by other means which are less of a hindrance to trade.' The case law has tightened up the 'loose proportionality' aspect of this definition (W. H. Roth (1994) 31 *CMLRev*. 845, 850).

[160] Case 261/81 *Walter Rau* v. *De Smedt* [1982] ECR 3961, para. 13; Case C–448/98 *Criminal Proceedings against Jean-Pierre Guimont* [2000] ECR I–10663, para. 26.

[161] In Joined Cases C–401 and 402/92 *Criminal proceedings against Tankstation 't Heukske vof and J.B.E. Boermans* [1994] ECR I–2199, para. 16, Van Gerven AG said: '"product requirements" relate...to the intrinsic or extrinsic characteristics of the product concerned'.

[162] Joined Cases C–267 and 268/91 *Keck* [1993] ECR I–6097, para. 15.

This list, found in paragraph 15 of *Keck*, is reminiscent of that contained in Article 3 of Directive 70/50. Measures concerning product requirements are assumed to affect inter-state trade, even where both parties to the case are nationals,[163] and this is often reflected in the language used by the Court. It replaces phrases such as discrimination and dispa-rate impact on imported goods with a broad reference to the fact that the national rule 'hinders'[164] or creates an 'obstacle' to the free movement of goods.

In the past other situations have also been considered indistinctly applicable, includ-ing rules regulating advertising and sales promotion techniques.[165] These cases are now largely dealt with under the *Keck* 'certain selling arrangement' formula and are consid-ered further in Chapter 5. In addition, there was a group of cases concerning, for example, rules on authorizations and inspections, which could not be easily classified as either product requirements or certain selling arrangements but, for want of a better classifica-tion, tended to be lumped under the indistinctly applicable heading.[166] Since *Commission v. Italy (trailers)* it is likely that such non-product-related requirements, provided that they are not directly discriminatory, will be dealt with under the separate heading of 'Any other measure which hinders access of products originating in other Member States to the market of a Member State' (see fig 4.3 and the discussion below).

So it now seems that the indistinctly applicable category is reduced to covering product requirements to which the seminal decision of *Cassis de Dijon*[167] applies. In *Cassis* the Court had to balance the need to secure greater free movement while at the same time allowing Member States to protect interests not identified in the exhaustive list of deroga-tions found in Article 36 (such as environmental considerations and consumer protec-tion). However, traders resented Member States' ability to impose additional technical requirements on their goods each time they tried to break into a new national market. If goods were lawfully produced according to the laws of one Member State, why could they not be sold on the markets of all other Member States?

## 2. CASSIS DE DIJON

### 2.1 Mandatory Requirements and the Principle of Mutual Recognition

*Cassis de Dijon* concerned a straightforward product requirement: the composition of fruit liqueurs. The German authorities refused to allow Cassis de Dijon, a blackcurrant fruit liqueur made in France, to be sold in Germany owing to its insufficient alcoholic strength. German law required fruit liqueurs to have a minimum alcohol content of 25 per cent, whereas the French cassis had an alcohol content of only 15–20 per cent. The Court said that '[i]n the absence of common rules [i.e., harmonization] it is for Member States to regulate all matters relating to the production and marketing of alcohol and alcoholic

---

[163] Joined Cases C–158/04 and C–159/04 *Alfa Vita Vassilopoulos AE* [2006] ECR I–8135.

[164] Case C–366/04 *Schwarz* v. *Bürgermeister der Landeshauptstadt Salzburg* [2006] ECR I–10139, para. 30; Joined Cases C–158/04 and C–159/04 *Alfa Vita Vassilopoulos AE* [2006] ECR I–8135, para. 20.

[165] See, e.g., Case 382/87 *Buet* v. *Ministère public* [1989] ECR 1235; Joined Cases C–1/90 and 176/90 *Aragonesa* [1991] ECR I–4151.

[166] See, e.g., Case C–319/05 *Commission* v. *Germany (Garlic Capsule)* [2007] ECR I–9811, para. 81. See also Case C–88/07 *Commission* v. *Spain (medicinal herbs)* [2009] ECR I–1353.

[167] Case 120/78 *Rewe Zentrale* v. *Bundesmonopolverwaltung für Branntwein ('Cassis de Dijon')* [1979] ECR 649.

beverages on their own territory'.[168] The Court then laid down a general principle and an exception. Somewhat oddly, it started by considering the exception. It said:

Obstacles to movement in the [Union] resulting from disparities between the national laws relating to the marketing of the products in question must be accepted in so far as those provisions may be recognised as being necessary in order to satisfy *mandatory requirements* relating in particular to the effectiveness of fiscal supervision, the protection of public health, the fairness of commercial transactions and the defence of the consumer.[169]

To this the Court added in *Rau*:[170]

It is also necessary for such rules to be proportionate to the aim in view. If a Member State has a choice between various measures to attain the same objective it should choose the means which least restricts the free movement of goods.

Thus, in the absence of harmonization legislation, Member States can regulate product requirements and insist that national rules be applied to imported goods provided that the national rules can be justified by showing one of the mandatory requirements (e.g., consumer protection) and that the steps taken are proportionate.

In *Cassis* the German government relied on two of the mandatory requirements: public health and the protection of the consumer against unfair commercial practices. It argued, first, that the minimum-alcohol-content rule prevented a proliferation of low-alcohol drinks on the national market since such drinks more readily induced tolerance towards alcohol than stronger drinks. Not surprisingly, the Court dismissed this argument. It said that German consumers could obtain a wide range of weaker alcoholic products and strongly alcoholic drinks were often consumed in a diluted form.

As far as the consumer protection/fair trading argument was concerned, the German government said that drinks with a lower alcohol content secured a competitive advantage over drinks with a higher alcohol content, since alcohol was the most expensive constituent of the product.[171] The Court rejected this too, saying that 'it is a simple matter to ensure that suitable information is conveyed to the purchaser by requiring the display of an indication of origin and of the alcohol content on the packaging of products'.[172] Therefore, the national rules constituted an obstacle to trade and breached Article 34; labelling would have been an adequate response.

Having discussed and rejected the justifications put forward by the German government, the Court then laid down the general principle:

There is therefore no valid reason why, provided that they have been lawfully produced and marketed in one of the Member States, alcoholic beverages should not be introduced into any other Member State.[173]

---

[168] Para. 8.     [169] Emphasis added.     [170] Case 261/81 *Rau* [1982] ECR 3961, para. 12.
[171] In Case 182/84 *Miro* [1985] ECR 3731 the Member State ran a similar argument that imported products could have a price advantage as a result of the application of national taxes and excise duties which were proportional to the alcohol content. The Court said this was irrelevant: such differences in taxes and excise duties were 'part of the objective conditions of competition of which every trader may freely take advantage, provided that purchasers are given information so that they can freely make their choice on the basis of the quality and price of the products'.     [172] Case 120/78 *Cassis de Dijon* [1979] ECR 649, para. 13.
[173] Para. 14.

This idea, known as the presumption of *equivalence* or *mutual recognition*, is of great importance. It means that goods lawfully produced and marketed in one Member State (France) can, in principle, be sold in another Member State (Germany) without further restriction. Putting it another way, Germany must recognize French standards as equivalent to its own. However, this presumption can be rebutted by the host state (Germany)[174] demonstrating that its laws can be justified under one of the mandatory requirements,[175] and that the national rules are proportionate. In other words, as fig. 4.1 shows, owing to the presumption of equivalence, indistinctly applicable national measures which prevent goods lawfully produced in State A from being sold on the market in State B constitute a *prima facie* breach of Article 34. However, if the host state (B's) rules can be justified by reference to one of the mandatory requirements (or by one of the Article 36 derogations) and the steps taken are proportionate, the national measure is lawful[176] with the result that the national interest takes precedence over the free movement of goods.[177]

## 2.2 The Implications of the Decision

The result of *Cassis* is to replace dual regulation of a product (by both the home and host states) with single regulation (home state)[178] which, under the principle of mutual recognition, the host state is required to respect. Thus, *Cassis* introduces the principle of home state control and, in so doing, gives extraterritorial effect to the laws and standards laid down by the home state. As we saw in Chapter 1, the effect of the principle of mutual recognition is to put the different legal systems in competition with one another. Goods produced in France can be sold in Germany; the German consumers then have the choice between French goods and German goods produced according to different standards. This maintains a diversity of national rules.

However, since in the common market there is also free movement of capital there is a risk that business might flee to France and set up there to produce fruit liqueurs according to the 'lower' French standards, with serious implications for German jobs. Alternatively, if capital does not move but the German consumers buy the cheaper French

---

[174] On the burden of proof, see the Mutual Recognition Reg. 764/2008 (OJ [2008] L218/21) considered further below.

[175] Case 120/78 *Cassis de Dijon*, para. 8, sometimes referred to as the 'rule of reason' approach which was first raised in Case 8/74 *Dassonville* [1974] ECR 837, para. 6: 'In the absence of a [Union] system guaranteeing for consumers the authenticity of a product's designation of origin, if a Member State takes measures to prevent unfair practices in this connexion, it is however subject to the condition that these measures should be reasonable and that the means of proof required should not act as a hindrance to trade between Member States and should, in consequence, be accessible to all [Union] nationals.' See also Case 33/74 *Van Binsbergen* [1974] ECR 1299, para. 12 for an equivalent case in the field of services.

[176] See, e.g., Joined Cases 60 and 61/84 *Cinéthèque SA* v. *Fédération nationale des cinémas français* [1985] ECR 2605, para. 24.

[177] Para. 14. It used to be thought that the mandatory requirements and Art. 36 derogations operated differently. If a national measure could be justified by a mandatory requirement then it did not breach Art. 34. If the national measures could not be justified then there was a breach of Art. 34 and the Member State could in principle have recourse to the derogations in Art. 36 (see, e.g., Case 25/88 *Criminal Proceedings against Bouchara* [1989] ECR 1105, para. 11, and Case 298/87 *Smanor* [1988] ECR 4489, para. 15). However, the Court does not always make the distinction between mandatory requirements and Art. 36 derogations, often simply saying that the national measure can be justified under both Art. 36 and the mandatory requirements (see, e.g., Joined Cases C-34–36/95 *De Agostini* [1997] ECR I-3843, para. 45).

[178] N. Bernard, 'Flexibility in the European single market' in C. Barnard and J. Scott (eds.), *The Law of the Single European Market: Unpacking the Premises* (Oxford: Hart Publishing, 2002).

Cassis, this outcome will also be detrimental to German jobs. One response would be for the German producers to lobby their government for lower standards. If successful, this might prompt the French producers to request their government to lower standards still further, leading to a race to the bottom and a convergence (rather than a diversity) of standards at this low level. This problem was raised by the German government in Cassis itself:[179]

to allow alcoholic products into free circulation wherever, as regards their alcohol content, they comply with the rules laid down in the country of production would have the effect of imposing as a common standard within the [Union] the lowest alcohol content permitted in any of the Member States, and even of rendering any requirements in this field inoperative since a lower limit of this nature is foreign to the rules of several Member States.

The mandatory requirements recognized by the Court in Cassis are intended to place a brake on any such race to the bottom. They allow for (residual) *host* state control where an important interest of the host state[180] is at issue. Therefore, if Germany could successfully invoke a mandatory requirement, this would require French products to comply with the higher German standards. However, as we shall see in Chapter 6, the Member States have experienced difficulties both in successfully invoking these mandatory requirements and in showing that the steps taken were proportionate. Cassis is therefore seen as a decision promoting the *Union* interest of market integration, but at the cost of potentially eroding diverse (high) national standards adopted by democratically elected national governments.[181] This may create a 'regulatory gap'—if national law is struck down and not replaced by an equivalent Union law, the market is left unregulated. However, if a Union law is enacted this will create a further brake on any race to the bottom.

While some have expressed concern about Cassis' deregulatory potential, Weatherill warns against too much sentiment.[182] He argues that the development of European market integration confronts the dead wood of centuries of regulatory tradition in all the Member States. He says that '[t]he whole point of the exercise is regulatory renovation and a bonfire of red tape on the pyre of Article [34]'. He continues that the Court is frequently asked to deal with the collision between, on the one hand, the making of a market for Europe and, on the other, national rules introduced for once sound reasons that lost their purpose generations ago, mixed together with other national rules cherished by national producers as a convenient means for insulating themselves from the threat of out-of-state competition.

The result of this collision in Cassis was to favour market-making over the interests of German producers while benefiting both German consumers, who now have access to a wider choice of products, and traders from other Member States who can sell to a wider market. Furthermore, it is not always the case that consumers will exercise their choice and buy the cheaper, probably lower-standard good; they might go for quality instead.

---

[179] Case 120/78 *Cassis de Dijon* [1979] ECR 649, para. 12.

[180] Or rather the host state's consumer whose interests are not represented in the home state.

[181] In practice, many legislatures will resist the pressure to lower standards because, while lower standards may suit one group of industrial interests, such a move might well be unpopular with the voting public as a whole. See further Ch. 16.

[182] S. Weatherill, 'Pre-emption, harmonisation and the distribution of competence' in Barnard and Scott (eds.), above n. 40, 49.

This can be seen in *3 Glocken*,[183] a case where Italy insisted that only pasta made from durum wheat could be sold in Italy and not pasta made from the cheaper common wheat. As the Court pointed out, trends in the export markets demonstrated that competition based on quality operates in favour of durum wheat.[184] Statistics supplied to the Court revealed a steady increase in the market share held by pasta products made exclusively from durum wheat.[185] This suggests a race to the top in terms of quality and not to the bottom.

## 2.3 The Commission's Response to *Cassis*

The Commission was quick to realize the importance of *Cassis*.[186] It issued an interpretative communication on the judgment,[187] which recognized that the presumption of equivalence obviated the need for much harmonization legislation. Because each national standard was presumed to be equivalent, goods produced according to that national standard would have access to the market of all other Member States. Therefore, there was no longer a need for a directive prescribing the content of a 'Euro' fruit liqueur; harmonization would be confined to areas where Member States legitimately invoked a mandatory requirement or an Article 36 derogation. Outside those areas of harmonization, the principle of mutual recognition would apply and goods lawfully produced in one Member State would enjoy access to the market in another state, with the result that different regulatory traditions and different products would continue to coexist.

Nevertheless, nearly 30 years after *Cassis* technical obstacles to the free movement of goods within the EU remained widespread and went unchallenged by traders. The Commission therefore launched a 'Package on the internal market for goods' in February 2007.[188] For present purposes, the most important part of the package is Regulation 764/2008 laying down procedures relating to the application of certain national technical rules to products lawfully marketed in another Member State,[189] the so-called 'Mutual Recognition' Regulation. It has two elements. First, it lays down a procedure to be followed by national authorities wanting to ban a product or requiring the product to

---

[183] Case 407/85 *Drei Glocken GmbH* v. *USL Centro-Sud* [1988] ECR 4233 considered further in Case Study 6.1.     [184] Para. 27.

[185] Ibid.

[186] K. Alter and S. Meunier-Aitsahalia, 'Judicial politics in the European Community: European integration and the pathbreaking *Cassis de Dijon* decision' (1994) 26 *Comparative Political Studies* 535. Cf. R. Barents, 'New developments in measures having equivalent effects' (1981) 18 *CMLRev*. 271: 'The *Cassis de Dijon* judgment, while constituting a continuation of the Court's policy outlined in the *Dassonville* case, is not quite so revolutionary as the Commission wishes to believe.' See also A. Mattera, 'L'Arrêt Cassis de Dijon: une nouvelle approche pour la réalisation et le bon functionnement du marché intérieur' [1980] *Revue du Marché Commun* 505, 513.

[187] Commission, 'Communication from the Commission regarding the *Cassis de Dijon* judgment' ([1980] OJ C256/2) considered by L. Gormley, '*Cassis de Dijon* and the Communication from the Commission' (1981) 6 *ELRev*. 454. Various commentators suggested that the Communication went further than the Court's original judgment: see, e.g., M. Egan, *Constructing a European Market* (Oxford: OUP, 2001), 109.

[188] COM(2007)35.

[189] OJ [2008] L218/21. The three other measures resulting from the package are Reg. 765/2008 (OJ [2008] L218/30) setting out requirements for accreditation and market surveillance relating to the marketing of products, the so-called 'RAMS' Regulation; Dec. 768/2008/EC ([2008] OJ L218/82) on a common framework for the marketing of products; and an interpretative communication on procedures for the registration of motor vehicles originating in another member state (2007/C 68/04). The RAMS Regulation and the decision are discussed further in Ch. 16.

be modified. They must give the economic operator written notice of why they are taking this action and provide sufficient technical or scientific supporting evidence. The effect of this rule is to make clear that the burden of proof is on the host state as to why it is denying market access rather than on the trader as to why its goods should be admitted. This aspect of the regulation is considered further in Chapter 6. The second element of the regulation concerns the establishment of product contact points in each Member State which must provide information on the technical rules applicable. The provision of easily accessible information is an increasingly popular approach in Union legislation, as the discussion on the Services Directive 2006/123 in Chapter 11 reveals.

## 3. PRODUCT REQUIREMENT CASES

As *Keck* and *Commission v. Italy (trailers)* subsequently made clear, the principles in *Cassis de Dijon* apply to rules regulating products themselves, so-called 'product requirement' cases. While *Cassis de Dijon* itself concerned the composition of a product,[190] most of the product-requirement cases concern packaging and presentation. For example, in *Rau*[191] the Court said that a Belgian law requiring margarine to be marketed in cube-shaped packages, to avoid confusion with butter, was an indistinctly applicable MEE because it had the effect of requiring imported margarine to be repackaged before being sold on the Belgian market. A similar situation arose in *Prantl*[192] where German law restricted the use of the traditional *Bocksbeutel* (a bulbous-shaped bottle with a long neck) to German producers of quality wine.[193] Italian wine, produced in a similar-shaped bottle, was excluded from the German market to prevent confusion. The Court noted that if Italian exporters wished to market their wine in Germany[194] they had to put their wine in bottles different from those traditionally used, which made the marketing of the imported wine more difficult or costly, and it also deprived Italian producers of the commercial advantages of using the bulbous-shaped bottle. The national rule was therefore an MEE which breached Article 34.

Similar reasoning underpinned the Court's ruling in *Mars*.[195] Mars ran a promotional campaign, printing '+10%' on a flash on its sweet wrappers. Because the flash exceeded 10 per cent of the surface area of the bar, this contravened German rules on fair trade. The Court said that since the German rules compelled the importer to adjust the presentation of its products according to the place where they were to be marketed

---

[190] See also Case 407/85 *Drei Glocken GmbH* [1988] ECR 4233; Case 90/86 *Criminal Proceedings against Zoni* [1988] ECR 4285; Case 274/87 *Commission v. Germany (meat only meat products)* [1989] ECR 229; Case 94/82 *Criminal Proceedings against De Kikvorsh Groothandel-Import-Export BV* [1982] ECR 947 (maximum acidity in beer); Case 216/84 *Commission v. France (milk only milk powder)* [1988] ECR 793; Case 130/80 *Kelderman* [1981] ECR 527 (dry matter in bread); Case C–358/95 *Tommaso Morellato v. Unità sanitaria locale (USL) n. 11 di Pordenone* [1997] ECR I–1431(national legislation prohibiting the marketing of bread with a moisture content exceeding 34% or an ash content lower than 1.40% or containing bran). In all of these cases the Court said the national rule was an indistinctly applicable MEE and in most the Court noted that the national rule concerning composition required the importer to vary the method of manufacture according to the place where the product is sold.

[191] Case 261/81 [1982] ECR 3961.

[192] Case 16/83 [1984] 1299, para. 21. See also Case 261/81 *Rau* [1982] ECR 3961, para. 14.

[193] Para. 21.        [194] Para. 23.

[195] Case C–470/93 *Verein gegen Unwesen in Handel und Gewerbe Köln ev v. Mars GmbH* [1995] ECR I–1923.

and consequently to incur additional packaging and advertising costs,[196] they breached Article 34. *Mars* demonstrates the Court's determination to allow companies to adopt a Europe-wide marketing strategy.[197] Each time a host state, like Germany, insists on imposing its own rules the importer incurs an additional financial burden. Even if the costs are passed on to the consumer, the Court considers that the initial outlay of these costs acts as a disincentive to those traders contemplating marketing the products in the host state.[198]

So far, we have considered rules relating to packaging and presentation. Other requirements concern the (generic) designation of a product. The Court has ruled that Member States cannot reserve a generic name for products that are manufactured out of specific raw ingredients or contain only a given proportion of raw ingredients. Therefore, in *Miro*,[199] a Dutch rule restricting the name 'jenever' to drinks containing at least 35 per cent alcohol, breached Article 34 because it excluded Belgian jenever which had been lawfully produced with an alcohol content of 30 per cent. And in *Commission v. Italy*[200] the Court said that an Italian rule limiting the name chocolate to products made without vegetable fats and requiring chocolate with vegetable fats (primarily British and Irish chocolate) to be described as 'chocolate substitute' contravened Article 34 (see further Case Study 4.1 below). Other labelling requirements, such as an age-limit label on videos and DVDs[201] or language requirements imposed on products sold to end users,[202] also constitute MEEs.

Finally, in *Alfa Vita*[203] the Court added rules relating to 'production conditions' to the list of situations where Article 34 applied. In that case anyone wishing to sell bread had to run a fully equipped bakery even where the bread was delivered half-cooked and needed only to be 'baked-off'. This was considered a barrier to imports which breached Article 34.

---

**Case Study 4.1** THE CASE OF JAM AND CHOCOLATE

One way of dealing with some of the problems about the use of names is through Union-level harmonization, identifying at Union level the permitted ingredients in a product before it can be called, say 'chocolate'. However, this is easier said than done, as the history of the directives on jam and chocolate show. The first, very basic problem relates to the definition of these products. According to research, French consumers

---

[196] Para. 13. See also Case C–315/92 *Verband Sozialer Wettbewerb ev* v. *Clinique Laboratories SNC* [1994] ECR I–317, para. 19.

[197] Case C–463/01 *Commission* v. *Germany (deposit and return)* [2004] ECR I–11705, para. 61.

[198] See, e.g., Case C–217/99 *Commission* v. *Belgium* [2000] ECR I–10251, para. 18.

[199] Case 182/84 *Criminal Proceedings against Miro BV* [1985] ECR 3731.

[200] Case C–14/00 *Commission* v. *Italy* [2003] ECR I–513, para. 77. See also Case C–12/00 *Commission* v. *Spain* [2003] ECR I–459, para. 81.

[201] Case C–244/06 *Dynamic Medien Vertriebs GmbH* [2008] ECR I–505.

[202] Case C–366/98 *Geffroy and Casino France* [2000] ECR I–6579. See also Case C–369/89 *Piageme* v. *Peeters* [1991] ECR I–2971 which led to COM(93)532 on the use of languages in the marketing of foodstuffs. See also Case 78/80 *Fietje* [1980] ECR 3839, para. 15.

[203] Joined Cases C–158/04 and C–159/04 *Alfa Vita* [2006] ECR I–8135 and Case C–82/05 *Commission* v. *Greece (Bake Off Products)* [2006] ECR I–93*.

only countenance jams with pulp in them; the Dutch, on the other hand, like smooth, sugary jams.[204] The accession of the UK, Europe's largest jam consumer, to the EU in 1973 introduced a new difficulty: marmalade (which also happened to be the German word for jam).[205] Against this background it comes as little surprise that Directive 79/693/EEC[206] on 'the approximation of the laws of the Member States relating to fruit jams, jellies and marmalades and chestnut purée' (the Jam Directive), adopted under Articles 43 and 115 TFEU (ex Articles 37 and 94 EC), took 14 years to negotiate. The accession of Portugal to the EU in 1986, with its fondness for carrot jam, saw carrots (and indeed tomatoes and sweet potatoes) designated as fruit for the purposes of the directive.[207]

The definition of chocolate proved even stickier. In countries such as Belgium chocolate is made using 100 per cent cocoa products. In the UK (and five other states) milk chocolate is made with a small proportion (up to 5 per cent) of vegetable fats. Both products are described as chocolate in the countries in which they are made. Directive 73/241,[208] adopted under, *inter alia*, Article 115 TFEU (ex Article 94 EC), approximated the laws of the Member States concerning the composition, manufacturing specifications, packaging, and labelling of cocoa and chocolate products in order to ensure their free movement.[209] Article 1 of the directive provided that 'cocoa and chocolate products' mean 'the products intended for human consumption defined in Annex 1'. The Annex essentially laid down the minimum cocoa content for any product to be described as chocolate. Article 10(1) contained a free movement clause:[210] 'Member States shall adopt all the measures necessary to ensure that trade in the products referred to in Article 1...cannot be impeded by the application of national non-harmonised provisions.'

But where did these provisions leave British chocolate? The preamble to the directive recognized that the use of vegetable fats other than cocoa butter was permitted in certain Member States (especially the UK, Ireland, and Denmark) and 'extensive use is made of this facility'. It continued that economic and technical data were not sufficient to enable 'a decision relating to the possibilities and forms of any extension of the use of these fats in the [Union] as a whole [to] be taken at the present time'. However, Point 7(a) of the Annex prohibited the addition to chocolate of fats and fat preparations not derived exclusively from milk. Yet, this provision was 'without prejudice to Article 14(2)(a)' which provided that the directive 'shall not affect the provisions of national laws' at present 'authorizing or prohibiting the addition of vegetable fats other than cocoa butter to the products defined in Annex I'. The provisional nature of these rules was confirmed by the fact that Article 14(2)(a) required the Union to review the possibility of 'extending the use of these fats to the whole of the [Union]'.[211]

[204] Derived from *Wall Street Journal*, 2 Sep. 1989, cited in M. Egan, *Constructing a European Market* (Oxford: OUP, 2001), 74.

[205] According to the *Daily Telegraph*, an Austrian farmer was prosecuted for selling apricot jam under the name 'apricot marmalade': M. Leidig and A. Evans Pritchard, 'Farmer in marmalade rebellion', *Daily Telegraph*, 21 Oct. 2003, 17.          [206] [1979] OJ L205/5, now consolidated on the Eur-lex website.

[207] Annex II A.1, para. 2, in the consolidated version.          [208] [1973] OJ L228/23.

[209] 4th recital of the preamble.          [210] This term is considered in more detail in Ch. 16.

[211] Case C–14/00 *Commission v. Italy (chocolate)* [2003] ECR I–513, para. 54.

Given the complexity of these rules, it is not perhaps surprising that countries like Italy took the opportunity to protect their prized national chocolate from competition from abroad. Under Italian law chocolate originating in the UK, Ireland, and Denmark could be sold in Italy, but only under the name 'chocolate substitute'. In *Commission v. Italy*[212] the Commission argued that this law contravened Directive 73/241 by preventing chocolate lawfully produced in the UK, in accordance with the requirements as to the minimum content of cocoa-based ingredients laid down by the directive (albeit with the addition of vegetable fats), from moving freely. The Commission also argued that the Italian law contravened Article 34 on the free movement of goods: the use of a pejorative term such as 'chocolate substitute' served to devalue the product in the minds of consumers. Italy, on the other hand, relying on Point 7(a) of the Annex, said that the free movement clause applied only to products which did not contain vegetable fats.

The Court said that Article 14(2)(a) made it clear that, as regards the use of vegetable fats, the directive did not 'seek to establish a fully harmonised system under which common rules completely replace existing national rules in the field, since it expressly authorises the Member States to lay down national rules which are different from the common rules which it provides for'.[213] Therefore, the free movement clause in Article 10 of the directive applied to goods which did not contain vegetable fats. However, under Article 14(2)(a) the directive allowed Member States to adopt national rules authorizing the addition of vegetable fats to cocoa and chocolate products manufactured within their territory. This meant that under the directive the UK, Ireland, and Denmark could authorize their own manufacturers to add vegetable fats to chocolate made there, but this chocolate could not benefit from the free movement clause. So it seemed that Italy had won.

However, the Court then turned to consider the effect of Article 34. It said that Article 34 applied to obstacles to the marketing of products (British chocolate) whose manufacture was not the subject of comprehensive harmonization but which were manufactured in conformity with national rules explicitly permitted by the harmonizing directive (the addition of vegetable fats as permitted by Article 14(2)(a)).[214] Having ruled that Article 34 in principle applied to the case, the Court found that a rule prohibiting the use of the name 'chocolate' by (British) products might compel traders to adjust the presentation of their products according to the place where the goods were to be marketed and to incur additional packaging costs. It said the use of the name 'chocolate substitute' could adversely affect the consumer's perception of the chocolate in that 'it denotes substitute, and therefore inferior, product'.[215] The Italian law therefore breached Article 34 unless it could be justified by reference to one of the mandatory requirements and the steps taken were proportionate. The Court recognized that consumers needed to be properly informed about the products offered

---

[212] See also Case C–12/00 *Commission* v. *Spain* [2003] ECR I–459.    [213] Para. 58.

[214] Paras. 67 and 70.

[215] See also Case C–166/03 *Commission* v. *France (gold)* [2004] ECR I–6535 (a French rule restricting the word 'gold' to products of a fineness of more than 750 parts per 1,000; products of a lower fineness could be called 'gold alloy' only. The rule breached Art. 34 because it had the effect of excluding products described as 'gold' in other states which had lower levels of fineness).

to them. It continued that where a product offered for sale under a particular name was so different in terms of its composition or production from the products generally understood as falling within that description in the Union, then the state could require the importer to alter the description of the product. However, where the difference was of minor importance, appropriate labelling would suffice. On the facts, the Court found that the addition of vegetable fats to cocoa and chocolate products which satisfy the minimum contents required by the directive did not substantially alter the nature of those products, transforming them into different products.[216] Therefore, it said, the addition of a label of a 'neutral and objective statement' informing consumers of the presence of vegetable fats would suffice; the obligation to change the sales name was not necessary to satisfy the overriding interest of consumer protection.[217]

The result of this decision was that through the interpretation of Article 34 the Court almost achieved the free movement that the 1973 directive had failed to secure. The Court may well have been influenced by the fact that, by the time of its judgment, Directive 2000/36[218] had been adopted which had finally replaced Directive 73/241. Directive 2000/36 resolved the issue of whether chocolate containing vegetable fats could still be called chocolate.[219] The negotiations for this directive were protracted and acrimonious, with those states which did not allow the use of vegetable fats fighting to reserve the term 'chocolate' to products containing 100 per cent cocoa products. Some helpfully suggested that British chocolate might be called 'vegelate', 'vegette', or 'household chocolate' instead.[220] Directive 2000/36 inevitably contained a compromise: the name chocolate could still be applied to products with no more than 5 per cent vegetable fat content. They would enjoy free movement provided that they were labelled with a 'clearly legible statement: contains vegetable fats in addition to cocoa butter'.[221] Thus 27 years after the first Chocolate Directive which only partially harmonized the field, the Union now has its own exhaustive definition of chocolate.[222]

## 4. ARTICLE 35 AND INDISTINCTLY APPLICABLE MEASURES

So far we have concentrated on the application of Article 34 to indistinctly applicable measures and to product requirements in particular. As far as Article 35 is concerned, the situation was—up until 2008—different. Previously, the rule had been that only distinctly applicable measures were caught by Article 35. This was made clear in the *Groenveld*[223] which concerned a Dutch law prohibiting all manufacturers of meat products from having

---

[216] Para. 87.        [217] Paras. 88–9.

[218] [2000] OJ L197/19. Parliament's report (A4–0310/97) provides an interesting taster to the chocolate market.

[219] It also addressed the problem of 'milk chocolate': the UK and Ireland can sell in their own countries a product labelled as 'milk chocolate' with higher milk and lower milk content than 'milk chocolate' made and sold in the rest of the Union. If exported, it has to be described as 'family milk chocolate'. See 13th recital and points 4 and 5 of the Annex 1.

[220] 'EU cannot be serious!', *The Journal* (Newcastle, UK), 22 Jul. 2000, 1.

[221] Art. 2(2). See also the 5th to 7th recitals in the preamble.

[222] J. Walsh, 'Only the crumbliest, flakiest chocolate…', *Independent*, 17 Mar. 2000, 7.

[223] Case 15/79 *P.B. Groenveld BV* v. *Produktschap voor Vee en Vlees* [1979] ECR 3409.

horsemeat in stock, even though the sale of horsemeat was not actually prohibited in the Netherlands. Since the presence of horsemeat is not detectable in other meat products, the ban was designed to safeguard the export of meat products to countries which prohibited the marketing of horseflesh. The Court said that Article 35 concerned:

national measures which have as their specific object or effect the restriction on the patterns of export and thereby the establishment of *a difference in treatment between the domestic trade of a Member State and its export trade* in such a way as to provide a particular advantage for national production or for the domestic market of the State in question at the expense of the production or of the trade of other Member States. [Emphasis added]

Because the rule in *Groenveld* was equally applicable (non-discriminatory) it did not breach Article 35. For the same reasons the Court found that the rule in *Oebel*[224] did not breach Article 35. The case concerned restrictions on night working in bakeries.[225] The Court said that since the national rules were part of 'economic and social policy which applied by virtue of objective criteria to all the undertakings in the particular industry…without leading to any difference in treatment whatsoever on the ground of nationality',[226] there was no breach of Article 35.

Various suggestions have been offered as to why the Court confined the prohibition of MEEs to distinctly applicable measures under Article 35 while developing a sophisticated framework for dealing with indistinctly applicable and non-discriminatory measures under Article 34. One explanation is that export and import restrictions are fundamentally different. Import restrictions breach Article 34 because they subject the importer to a dual-burden: importers have to satisfy the rules of State A (state of origin) *and* State B (host state). By contrast, exporters have to satisfy only one set of rules—the rules of the state of origin—which are applied equally to goods for the domestic and import market. Allowing exporters to challenge domestic regulation under Article 35 would essentially present them with a way of circumventing the wholly internal rule by allowing challenges to national rules which have no effect on inter-state trade. As Oliver and Enchelmaier point out, if Article 35 were to extend to all barriers to exports, regardless of discrimination or protective intent, it would cover a large number of restrictions on production, such as planning regulations for factories, which are far removed from inter-state trade, as well as catching measures properly the preserve of other freedoms such as Article 49 TFEU on freedom of establishment.[227]

Nevertheless, in *Gysbrechts*[228] the Court appeared to modify its approach in *Groenveld*. The case concerned a Belgian rule which prevented a supplier engaged in distance selling, often over the Internet, from requiring any payment in advance before the expiry of

---

[224] Case 155/80 [1981] ECR 1993, considered further in Ch. 6.

[225] See also Joined Cases 141–143/81 *Criminal Proceedings against Gerrit Holdijk* [1982] ECR 1299, para. 11 (national rules laying down minimum standards for enclosures for fattening cows); Case 237/82 *Jongeneel Kaas BV v. State of the Netherlands* [1984] ECR 483, para. 22 (national rules laying down minimum standards of quality for domestic cheese production and rules on the compulsory use of stamps, marks, and inspection documents).

[226] Para. 16. See also Case C–80/92 *Commission* v. *Belgium* [1994] ECR I–1019, para. 24, which permits reverse discrimination (para. 25).

[227] P. Oliver and S. Enchelmaier, 'Free movement of goods: Recent developments in the case law' (2007) 44 *CMLRev.* 649, 686.

[228] Case C–205/07 [2008] ECR I–9947. See further, A. Dawes, 'A freedom reborn? The new yet unclear scope of Art. 29' (2009) 34 *ELRev.* 639.

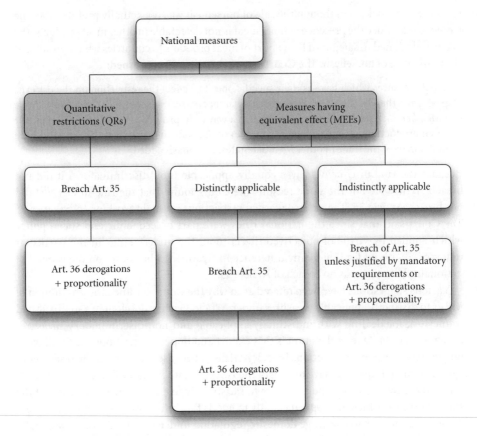

**Fig. 4.2** Art. 35 after *Gysbrechts*

a seven-day cooling-off period. In practice this meant that suppliers could not require consumers to provide their credit card number, even though the supplier undertook not to use it until after the cooling-off period. The effect of this rule was (as the Belgian government itself noted) to deprive the trader of an efficient tool to guard against non-payment.[229] The Court agreed, noting that the consequences of such a prohibition were generally more significant in cross-border sales made directly to consumers. This was due to the practical difficulty and commercial impracticality of bringing legal proceedings in another Member State against consumers who have received goods but not paid for them.[230] The Court concluded:

Consequently, even if a prohibition such as that at issue in the main proceedings is applicable to all traders active in the national territory, its actual effect is none the less greater on goods leaving the market of the exporting Member State than on the marketing of goods in the domestic market of that Member State.[231]

The measure was therefore an MEE contrary to Article 35.

A broad reading of this decision is that the Court has decided to bring its Article 35 case law fully into line with the Article 34 pre-*Commission* v. *Italy (trailers)* jurisprudence (see

---

[229] Para. 41.      [230] Para. 42.      [231] Para. 43.

fig 4.1), albeit with certain amendments to take into account the differences between rules on imports and those on exports. Certainly, this is what Advocate General Trstenjak had argued for in her opinion.[232]

A narrower reading of this decision, and one more consistent with the specific nature of Article 35, is that the Grand Chamber is merely modifying its ruling in *Groenveld*: Article 35 is still very much concerned with discrimination, albeit discrimination not just in object but also in effect.[233] Even from this narrow perspective, the modification is significant because the third limb of the *Groenveld* formula ('to provide a particular advantage for national production') has, apparently, been dropped. Furthermore, the Court allowed Belgium to defend its law not only by reference to the Article 36 derogations but also, for the first time, the mandatory requirements. On the facts the Court found that the rule could be justified on the grounds of consumer protection[234] but that it was disproportionate to prohibit suppliers from requiring that consumers provide their credit card numbers (although it was proportionate to prohibit the supplier to require an actual advance or any payment from the consumer before the expiry of the withdrawal period).

## F. THE MARKET ACCESS APPROACH

### 1. INTRODUCTION

In most of the case law considered so far, the Court has either explicitly or implicitly taken a three-stage approach. (1) it has identified a comparator product; (2) it has classified the measure as distinctly or indistinctly applicable and, (3) it has considered whether, in the case of distinctly applicable measures, one of the Article 36 derogations exists, or whether, in the case of indistinctly applicable measures, a mandatory requirement or an Article 36 derogation applies (see fig. 4.1). However, in some more recent cases the Court has replaced this three-stage approach with two stages. Harking back to the *Dassonville* formula, it has (1) simply noted that the national measure 'impedes', 'hinders', or creates an 'obstacle' to inter-state trade, making little or no reference to the question of discrimination, and then (2) considered whether a mandatory requirement or an Article 36 derogation applies.

This two-stage approach can be seen in *Monsees*[235] where the Court said that (1) Austrian rules laying down short maximum journey times and distances for the transport of animals for slaughter constituted an 'obstacle' to international transport and was therefore an MEE. It continued that (2) the rules could be justified on public-health grounds but were not proportionate. Likewise, the Court said in *Commission v. Austria*[236] that (1) by prohibiting heavy goods vehicles from being driven along a section of the A12 in the Austrian Tyrol (one of the main routes between southern German and northern Italy), Austrian law 'obstructs the free movement of goods' and therefore constituted an MEE.

---

[232] See esp. paras. 42–8.

[233] This is the view the Commission takes in its *Guidance*, above n. 3, 36: 'Article [35] catches trade barriers that have an actual and specific effect on exports and that create a difference in treatment between trade within a Member State and exports.'

[234] Paras. 47–9.

[235] Case C–350/97 *Monsees* v. *Unabhängiger Verwaltungssenat für Kärnten* [1999] ECR I–2921, para. 23.

[236] Case C–320/03 *Commission* v. *Austria* [2005] ECR I–7929, para. 67.

It added that (2) the rules could be justified on the grounds of environmental protection but were not proportionate.

This two-stage approach also assisted the Court in cases where the rules could not be easily classified as either a distinctly applicable measure or a product requirement. So, for example, it said that registration requirements were MEEs in *Commission* v. *France (reagents)*,[237] as were inspection requirements in *Celestini*,[238] and rules requiring prior approval for use of polyethylene pipes in *Commission* v. *Portugal*.[239] In *Commission* v. *Germany (Garlic Capsule)*[240] the Court said that the requirement for a marketing authorization as a medicinal product was an 'obstacle to intra-[Union] trade'; and in *Commission* v. *Netherlands* the Court said that a rule requiring cars to be subject to a roadworthiness-test regime was a 'restriction on the free movement of goods'.[241] These cases, in fact, presaged a more general change in approach signalled by *Commission* v. *Italy (trailers)*.[242]

## 2. *COMMISSION V. ITALY (TRAILERS)*

The *Trailers* case concerned an Italian rule prohibiting motorcycles from pulling trailers. The case thus concerned a ban on *use* of a product. This situation had been the subject of much discussion: should the *Keck* case law be applied by analogy and so the Italian rule would benefit from the presumption of legality (as Advocate General Kokott had argued in *Mickelsson*,[243] together with a number of Member States in their submissions to the Court of Justice in *Trailers*[244]), or should the rule be considered an MEE (as Advocate General Bot had argued in *Trailers*). The Court equivocated but concluded that the Italian rule was in fact an MEE.[245] It noted that while 'it was common ground' that the rule applied 'without regard to the origin of the trailers' (i.e., it was apparently non-discriminatory[246]) in fact the rule affected only imported goods[247] because Italian manufacturers did not manufacture trailers to be towed by motorcycles. The Court then identified three situations where a rule could be considered an MEE (see fig 4.3):[248]

(1) 'Measures adopted by a Member State the object or effect of which is to treat products coming from other Member States less favourably' (presumably distinctly applicable measures)]

(2) '[M]easures referred to in paragraph 35', namely for 'goods coming from other Member States where they are lawfully manufactured and marketed, rules that

---

[237] Case C–55/99 *Commission* v. *France (reagents)* [2000] ECR I–1149, para. 19, where the matter was conceded.

[238] Case C–105/94 *Celestini* v. *Saar-Sektkellerei Faber GmbH & Co. KG* [1997] ECR I–2971, para. 33.

[239] Case C–432/03 *Commission* v. *Portugal (polyethylene pipes)* [2005] ECR I–9665, para. 41. See also Case C–38/03 *Commission* v. *Belgium (wheelchairs)*, judgment of 13 Jan. 2005, not reported, para. 19.

[240] See also Case C–319/05 *Commission* v. *Germany (Garlic Capsule)* [2007] ECR I–9811, para. 81. See also Case C–88/07 *Commission* v. *Spain (medicinal herbs)* [2009] ECR I–1353, para. 83.

[241] Case C–297/05 *Commission* v. *Netherlands (roadworthiness testing of cars)* [2007] ECR I–7467, para. 74.               [242] Case C–110/05 *Commission* v. *Italy* [2009] ECR I–519.

[243] Case C–142/05 *Åklagaren* v. *Mickelsson* [2009] ECR I–000.        [244] Para. 22.

[245] A decision which had already been foreseen by Case C–265/06 *Commission* v. *Portugal* [2008] ECR I–2245, para. 36 concerning a ban on affixing of tinted film to the windscreen of cars. This confirms the earlier case, Case C–473/98 *Kemikalieinspketionen* v. *Toolex Alpha AB* [2000] ECR I–5681, where the Court said that the ban on the industrial *use* (not sale) of trichloroethylene, a substance with a known carcinogenic effect, constituted an MEE (para. 35).               [246] Para. 50.

[247] Para. 57.        [248] Para. 37.

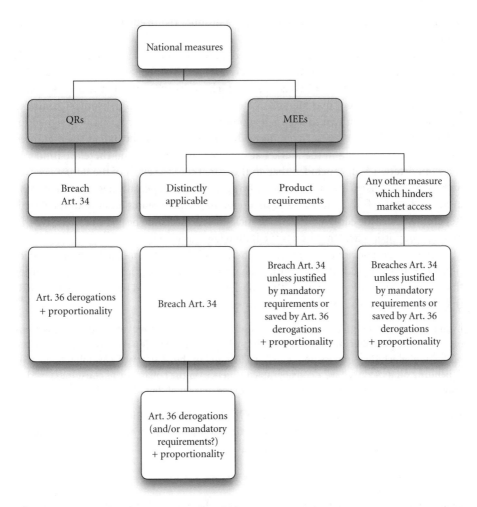

**Fig. 4.3** QRs and MEEs under Art. 34 after *Commission* v. *Italy*

lay down requirements to be met by such goods…even if those rules apply to all products alike' to which *Cassis de Dijon* applies (presumably indistinctly applicable product requirements)

(3) 'Any other measure which hinders access of products originating in other Member States to the market of a Member State is also covered by that concept'.

This third limb appears to have significant overlap with the other two: both distinctly and indistinctly applicable measures affect market access. It is perhaps better to regard the third limb as a 'catch-all'[249] for any other measure which cannot easily be

---

[249] For a summary of potential situations which might fall under this third heading, see Case C–219/07 *Nationale Raad van Dierenkwekers en Liefhebbers VZW* v. *Belgische Staat* [2008] ECR I–4475, para. 22: 'Any legal provision of a Member State prohibiting goods which have not been previously authorised from being marketed, acquired, offered, put on display or sale, kept, prepared, transported, sold, disposed of for valuable consideration or free of charge, imported or used constitutes a measure having an effect equivalent to a quantitative restriction within the meaning of Article [34]'.

classified as a distinctly applicable measure, a product requirement or a certain selling arrangement.

It was the third limb that the Court relied on in the *Trailers* case itself. It said that 'a prohibition on the use of a product in the territory of a Member State has a considerable influence on the behaviour of consumers, which, in its turn, affects the access of that product to the market of that Member State'.[250] It continued that 'Consumers, knowing that they are not permitted to use their motorcycle with a trailer specially designed for it, have practically no interest in buying such a trailer.'[251] Thus, the Italian law prevented a demand from existing in the market at issue for such trailers and therefore hindered their importation.[252] It concluded that, to the extent that the effect of the Italian law was 'to hinder access to the Italian market for trailers which are specially designed for motorcycles and are lawfully produced and marketed in Member States other than the Italian Republic', it constituted an MEE under Article 34 unless it could be justified objectively[253] and was proportionate. On the facts the Italian law was upheld.

While *Trailers* concerned a total prohibition, *Mickelsson*[254] concerned merely a restriction on the use of a product, this time personal watercraft (such as jet-skis) on waters other than general navigable waterways. The judgment closely followed the *Trailers* case, albeit that the language is somewhat more tentative:

Even if the national regulations at issue do not have the aim or effect of treating goods coming from other Member States less favourably, which is for the national court to ascertain, the restriction which they impose on the use of a product in the territory of a Member State may, depending on its scope, have a considerable influence on the behaviour of consumers, which may, in turn, affect the access of that product to the market of that Member State.[255]

The national rules therefore constituted an MEE contrary to Article 34 but could be justified on the grounds of environmental protection and public health. The question of proportionality was a matter for the national court.

## 3. THE IMPLICATIONS OF THE *TRAILERS* CASE

*Trailers* and *Mickelsson* send out a strong message that the market access test has returned to Article 34. Many would applaud this development since the need for a market access test has received weighty support in the past. Perhaps most famously, Advocate General Jacobs in *Leclerc-Siplec*[256] argued that all undertakings which engage in a legitimate economic activity in a Member State should have unfettered access to the whole of the Union market, unless there was a valid reason why not. However, he recognized that a pure market access test risked encompassing potentially too much national regulation in its net. He therefore suggested a threshold criteria: where the measure is liable 'substantially to restrict access to the market'[257] then it should breach Article 34 and need to be justified.

---

[250] Para. 56.

[251] Citing Case C–265/06 *Commission v Portugal* [2008] ECR I–2245, para. 33, above n. 245.

[252] Para. 57.    [253] Para. 58.

[254] Case C–142/05 *Aklagaren v Mickelsson, Roos* [2009] ECR I–000.    [255] Para. 26.

[256] Case C–412/93 *Leclerc-Siplec v. TF1 Publicité SA* [1995] ECR I–179. Cf E. Spaventa, 'Leaving *Keck* behind? The free movement of goods after the rulings in *Commission v Italy* and *Mickelsson and Roos*' (2009) *ELRev*. 914.

[257] Paras. 41 and 49. For academic support, see S. Weatherill, 'After *Keck*: Some Thoughts on How to Clarify the Clarification' (1996) 33 *CMLRev*. 885, 900; C. Barnard, 'Fitting the remaining pieces into the goods and services jigsaw?' (2001) 26 *ELRev*. 35.

The Court may have acknowledged the need for some sort of threshold in the *Trailers* case when it said that 'a prohibition on the use of a product...has a *considerable* influence on the behaviour of consumers, which, in its turn, affects the access of that product to the market of that Member State'.[258] This, however, raises questions as to how *Commission v. Italy* fits with the older case law which clearly states that no *de minimis* rule applies to Article 34. One answer may be that in the case of distinctly applicable measures and product requirement cases (limbs 1 and 2 of *Trailers*), no *de minimis* rule applies. Only in respect of the rump of cases falling in the third limb of *Trailers* will there be some threshold criteria.

Yet, resorting to the market access approach engages the problems outlined in Chapter 1. What is the meaning of hindering market access and how can it be shown?[259] It may be the Court will examine the evidence for *actual* interference with trade to demonstrate hindrance, as it did in *Commission v. Greece (computer games)*.[260] There the Court said that a Greek law prohibiting the installation and operation of electrical, electromechanical, and electronic games on all premises apart from casinos constituted an MEE, even though Greek law did not prohibit the import of the equipment, because in practice the importation of games machines stopped when the prohibition came into effect.[261]

Alternatively, the Court might rely on the fact that the national rule generates additional costs, as it did in *Commission v. Italy (foodstuffs for sportsmen and women)*.[262] There the Court said that the prior-authorization regime for high-energy foods and the payment of administrative costs rendered 'the marketing of such foods more difficult and expensive' and so was an MEE contrary to Article 34.[263] Likewise, in *Franzén*[264] the Court said that a Swedish rule permitting only holders of production licences or wholesale licences to import alcoholic drinks 'constituted an obstacle to the importation of alcoholic beverages from other Member States in that it imposes additional costs on such beverages'.[265] The rules therefore breached Article 34 and could not be saved under Article 36 since the licensing system was not proportionate.

However, the risk of relying simply on the fact that the national rules impose additional costs may not be enough. As Advocate General Poiares Maduro pointed out in *Alfa Vita*,[266] not every imposition of supplementary costs is wrongful. Some costs can arise from a mere divergence between the legislation of the state of production of the goods and the state where they are marketed. To be considered a restriction on trade, he said, 'the supplementary cost imposed must stem from the fact that the national rules did not take into account the particular situation of the imported products and, in particular, the fact that those products already had to comply with the rules of their State of origin'.

---

[258] Para. 56. See also *Mickelsson*, para. 26.

[259] For criticism of the Court's decision see P. Oliver, 'Of Trailers and Jet-Skis: is the Case Law on Article 34 TFEU (ex Article 28 EC) Careering in a New Direction?' (2010) *Fordham Journal of International Law*, forthcoming.

[260] Case C–65/05 *Commission v. Greece (computer games)* [2006] ECR I–10341, paras. 28–9.

[261] Para. 30.

[262] Case C–270/02 *Commission v. Italy (foodstuffs for sportsmen and women)* [2004] ECR I–1559. para. 19.

[263] However, where the authorization requirement concerns the retailer or the distributor of the goods then it seems there may be no breach of Art. 34: Case C–387/93 *Criminal Proceedings against Giorgio Domingo Banchero* [1995] ECR I–4663; Case C–189/95 *Criminal Proceedings against Franzén* [1997] ECR I–5909, para. 57; Case C–162/97 *Criminal Proceedings against Nilsson* [1998] ECR I–7477, para. 28.

[264] Case C–189/95 *Franzén* [1997] ECR I–5909.   [265] Para. 71, emphasis added.

[266] Joined Cases C–158/04 and C–159/04 *Alfa Vita* [2006] ECR I–8135, para. 44.

In his definition of a market access test,[267] a measure constitutes a 'barrier to access to a national market where it protects the acquired positions of certain economic operators on a national market or where it makes intra-[Union] trade more difficult than trade within the national market'. He then suggests that underpinning the market access approach is a discrimination test, based not on nationality or origin but free movement: 'It seems to me that a consistent approach emerges from the Court's case-law...identifying *discrimination against the exercise of freedom of movement.*' If he is correct, then the difference between the market access approach and the discrimination analysis is not as much as would first appear.

The *Trailers* case raises as many questions as it answers. It does, however, make clear that the footprint of *Cassis* still remains strong. Even in a third limb, market access case, the Court objected to the fact that trailers specially designed for motorcycles which were 'legally produced and marketed' in other Member States' could not, in practice be sold in Italy.[268] It also demonstrates an increasing convergence with the case law on the free movement of persons.[269]

## G. LITIGATION AVOIDANCE: DIRECTIVE 98/34 ON THE PROVISION OF INFORMATION IN THE FIELD OF TECHNICAL STANDARDS AND REGULATIONS

So far, this chapter has focused on decisions by the Court that a Member State has breached or may have breached Article 34. These rulings came about either from Article 258 enforcement proceedings brought by the Commission or Article 267 references from national courts which resulted from a challenge by a trader to the compatibility of a provision of national law with Article 34. However, by its very nature litigation is uncoordinated and reactive: individual litigants raise a Union law challenge when its suits their interests. The Commission can be more coordinated in its approach under Article 258 but it lacks the resources to bring proceedings in respect of every breach of Union law, and the procedure itself is subject to political intervention. To overcome some of these problems, the Union adopted Directive 98/34 (consolidating Directive 83/189 as amended),[270] requiring Member States to notify the Commission of any draft technical regulations *before* they are adopted and before they create barriers to trade so that they can be checked for their compatibility with Union law.[271] At first glance this directive seems dry and technical,

---

[267] Paras. 45–6.    [268] Para. 54.

[269] See further Ch. 1 and A. Tryfonidou, 'Further steps on the road to convergence among the market freedoms' (2010) 35 *ELRev.* 36.

[270] Dir. 98/34/EC of the European Parliament and of the Council laying down a procedure for the provision of information in the field of technical standards and regulations ([1998] OJ L204/37). This Dir. is itself due to be codified: COM(2010)179. For further information, see the TRIS (Technical Regulation Information System) website (<http://www.ec.europa.eu/enterprise/tris/about/index_en.htm>) and, in particular, *A Guide to the procedure for the provision of information in the field of technical standards and regulations and of rules on Information Society Services* (Luxembourg: OOPEC, 2005).

[271] L. Gormley, 'Some reflections on the internal market and free movement of goods' [1989/1] *LIEI* 9, 13.

but it has assumed considerable significance in the light of the Court's rulings in *CIA*,[272] *Unilever*,[273] and *Sapod-Audic*.[274]

For our purposes, Directive 98/34 contains two important provisions: Article 8 on the obligation to notify and the standstill provision in Article 9.[275] Article 8(1) requires Member States to notify the Commission of any draft 'technical regulations' which are due to be adopted, together with a statement of why they are needed.[276] The definition of technical regulations is loosely equivalent to the product requirements[277] listed by the Court in paragraph 15 of *Keck*.[278] Therefore, rules concerning the quality standards for flower bulbs,[279] prior approval for decoders for digitally broadcast television,[280] the compulsory marking or labelling of packaging,[281] the strength of soft-drink bottles, the prohibition on the marketing of cotton buds which were not made from biodegradable materials,[282] and the composition, classification, packaging, and labelling of pesticides[283] all constituted technical regulations which had to be notified.

Not only do rules concerning the products themselves have to be notified but so do rules concerning their use. Therefore in *Lindberg*[284] a Swedish prohibition on operators

---

[272] Case C–194/94 *CIA Security International SA* v. *Signalson SA and Securitel SPRL* [1996] ECR I–2201.

[273] Case C–443/98 *Unilever Italia SpA* v. *Central Food SpA* [2000] ECR I–7535.

[274] Case C–159/00 [2002] ECR I–5031.

[275] In addition to this formal procedure, many Member States notify their draft regulations informally to the Commission. As a result of these discussions, Member States often modify the original drafts and the file is closed (Gormley, above n. 271).

[276] Art. 1(9) defines 'technical regulation' as 'technical specifications and other requirements, including the relevant administrative provisions, the observance of which is compulsory, de jure or de facto, in the case of marketing or use in a Member State or a major part thereof, as well as laws, regulations or administrative provisions of Member States, except those provided for in Article 10, prohibiting the manufacture, importation, marketing or use of a product'. Art. 1(2) defines 'technical specification' as 'a specification contained in a document which lays down the characteristics required of a product such as levels of quality, performance, safety or dimensions, including the requirements applicable to the product as regards the name under which the product is sold, terminology, symbols, testing and test methods, packaging, marking or labelling and conformity assessment procedures'. For a discussion of the meaning of these terms, see Case C–159/00 *Sapod-Audic* [2002] ECR I–5031, paras. 26–30.

[277] Case C–267/03 *Lindberg* [2005] ECR I–3247, para. 60. *Lindberg* actually identifies three situations which constitute technical specifications: (1) technical specifications within the meaning of Art. 3(1) of the directive; (2) the 'other requirement' as defined in Art. 1(4); and (3) the prohibition of the manufacture, importation, marketing or use of a product referred to in Art. 1(11) (para. 34).

[278] See text attached to n. 162 above. The parallel between the definition of technical regulations and the Court's case law on Art. 34 is not exact. E.g., rules relating to language requirements are considered not to be technical regulations but they are measures having equivalent effect (Case C–33/97 *Colim NV* v. *Bigg's Continent Noord NV* [1999] ECR I–3175, para. 36). On other cases falling outside the definition, see Case C–37/99 *Roelof Donkersteeg* [2000] ECR I–10223; Case C–314/98 *Snellers Auto's BV* v. *Algemeen Directeur van de Dienst Wegverkeer* [2000] ECR I–863. Minor amendments do not need to be notified: Case C–433/05 *Sandström* [2010] ECR I–000, para. 49.

[279] Case C–52/93 *Commission* v. *Netherlands* [1994] ECR I–3591.

[280] Case C–390/99 *Canal Satélite Digital SL* v. *Administración General del Estado* [2002] ECR I–607.

[281] Case C–159/00 *Sapod-Audic* [2002] ECR I–5031, para. 32. See also Case C–20/05 *Schwibbert* [2007] ECR I–9447, paras. 36–7 (affixing the distinctive sign 'SIAE' to products to inform consumers that the reproductions are legal).

[282] Case C–303/04 *Lidl Italia* v. *Comune di Stradella* [2005] ECR I–7865.

[283] Case C–61/93 *Commission* v. *Netherlands* [1994] ECR I–3607. See also Case C–13/96 *Bic Benelux SA* v. *Belgian State* [1997] ECR I–1753.

[284] Case C–267/03 *Lindberg* [2005] ECR I–3247, para. 60. See also Case C–65/05 *Commission* v *Greece (computer games)* [2006] ECR I–10341, para. 61.

making certain types of gaming machines available to the players and thus to consumers also constituted a technical regulation and had to be notified. On the other hand, national measures restricting certain selling arrangements, considered by the Court in paragraph 16 of *Keck* to fall outside Article 34,[285] do not constitute technical regulations[286] and so do not need to be notified. The requirement to notify does, however, apply only to goods; it does not apply to requirements imposed on economic operators/service providers.[287]

On receipt of the Member State's notification, the Commission must inform the other Member States, as well as the relevant Standing Committee, which can then make comments. The Member State proposing the legislation must take these comments 'into account as far as possible in the subsequent preparation of the technical regulation' (see fig. 4.4).[288]

Article 9 of Directive 98/34 contains the standstill clause. The notifying Member State must postpone the adoption of the draft technical regulation for three months, pending its consideration by the Commission and the other Member States.[289] This period must be extended by a further three months if the Commission or another Member State delivers a 'detailed opinion' under Article 9(2) that the measure envisaged may create obstacles to the free movement of goods. The notifying Member State must respond to the Commission explaining the action it proposes to take in the light of these opinions, and the Commission must then respond to this. Article 9(3) requires the notifying Member State to postpone the adoption of the draft technical regulation for a further nine months if the Union announces its intention to adopt harmonization legislation, often based on the notified legislation.

So, Directive 98/34, with its procedural, as opposed to substantive, orientation is unusual in that it does not confer rights and obligations on individuals. Instead, it lays down a detailed procedure for a regulated dialogue between the Member State proposing the legislation, the Commission, and the other Member States.[290] This dialogue should result in the adoption of only those technical regulations which are compatible with EU law (although the Directive 98/34 procedure does not render the national legislation immune from subsequent challenge by a trader on the grounds that the measure breaches Article 34). Directive 98/34 therefore forms a key component in the programme of helping to 'promote the smooth functioning of the internal market'[291] and developing confidence between the national authorities.[292] However, the success of Directive 98/34 depends entirely on the willingness of the Member States to notify and comply with its provisions. In the early days of the operation of the directive the Commission, concerned about the low level of Article 8 notifications, started a series of enforcement proceedings against Member States for failing to notify.[293] The Court usually condemned

---

[285] See further Ch. 5.

[286] Case C–418/93 *Semeraro Casa Uno Srl* v. *Sindaco del Comune di Erbusco* [1996] ECR I–2975, para. 38.

[287] Case C–267/03 *Lindberg* [2005] ECR I–3247, para. 88.          [288] Art. 8(2).

[289] Art. 9(1), except in the case of urgency occasioned by 'serious and unforeseeable' circumstances: Art. 9(7). However, even in these circumstances the national rules remain subject to Art. 34: Case C–55/99 *Commission* v. *France (medical reagents)* [2000] ECR I–11499. At the height of the BSE crisis the UK used the emergency procedure in 24 cases (Commission, Report on the Operation of Dir. 98/34/EC from 1995 to 1998, COM(2000)429, 24).

[290] See 86/C 245/05 ([1986] OJ C245/4) and Case C–194/94 *CIA* [1996] ECR I–2201, para. 40. See also R. Dehousse, '1992 and beyond: The institutional dimension of the internal market programme' [1989/1] *LIEI* 109, 115.

[291] Preamble to Dir. 98/34, para. 3.          [292] Para. 40.

[293] These continue to this day: Case C–65/05 *Commission v Greece (computer games)* [2006] ECR I–10341, para. 64. The urgent need to introduce the law is no defence for failure to notify.

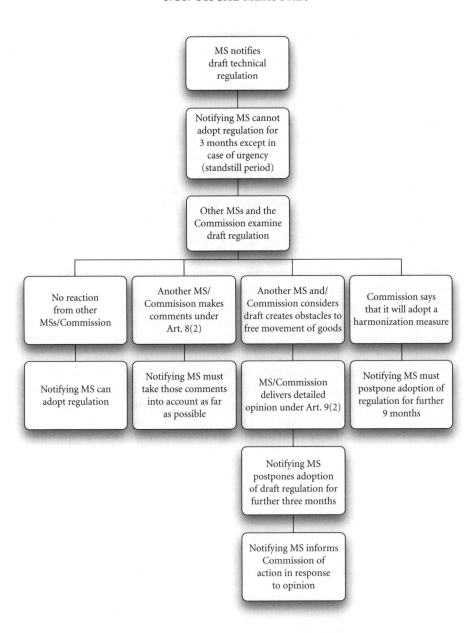

**Fig. 4.4** Arts. 8 and 9 of Dir. 98/34

the Member State for failing to notify as well as condemning the substance of the national regulations.[294] However, the Commission wanted the Court to go further and argued in a Communication of 1986[295] that:

when a Member State enacted a technical regulation falling within the scope of Directive [98/34] without notifying the draft to the Commission and respecting the standstill obligation, the regulation thus adopted is *unenforceable against third parties in the legal system of the*

---

[294] See, e.g., *Commission* v. *Germany* [1994] ECR I–2039.   [295] 86/C 245/05 ([1986] OJ C245/4).

*Member State in question.* The Commission therefore considers that litigants have a right to expect national courts to refuse to enforce national technical regulations which have not been notified as required by [Union] law.[296]

The Council did not share the Commission's views, and each time the directive was amended no reference to the unenforceability of the unnotified national measures was included in the text.[297]

At first, the Court shared the Council's reservations but, in *CIA*,[298] it changed its mind. The case concerned the failure by the Belgian government to notify its law on security systems to the Commission under Article 8 of Directive 98/34. This had an effect on private litigation involving two rival companies, CIA Security and Signalson. CIA sold a prize-winning burglar alarm system, Andromède, which had not been approved in accordance with Belgian law on security systems. Signalson, a commercial rival of CIA's, took advantage of this and said in a marketing campaign that the prize had been awarded on an improper basis and that the Andromède system did not work.[299] CIA then brought proceedings against Signalson alleging unfair trading practice, in particular libel. Signalson then counterclaimed, seeking an order restraining CIA Security from carrying on its business, on the ground that CIA was marketing an alarm system which had not been approved. In response, CIA claimed that the Belgian rules requiring prior approval of alarm systems breached Article 34 and that, in any event, the rules were invalid because they had not been communicated to the Commission under Article 8 of Directive 98/34 (see fig. 4.5).

The Court said that the Belgian rules on the quality and function tests which had to be fulfilled prior to an alarm system being approved and marketed in Belgium constituted technical regulations within the meaning of Directive 98/34 and so should have been notified under Article 8. The Court then said that Articles 8–9 of Directive 98/34 laid down a precise obligation on Member States to notify draft technical regulations to

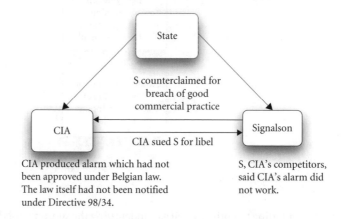

**Fig 4.5**  CIA and the effect of Dir. 98/34

---

[296]  Emphasis added.

[297]  See the views of Ruiz-Jarabo Colomer AG in Case C–273/94 *Commission* v. *Netherlands* [1996] ECR I–31, considered in detail in S. Weatherill, 'A case study in judicial activism in the 1990s: The status before national courts of measures wrongfully unnotified to the Commission' in D. O'Keeffe and A. Bavasso (eds.), *Liber Amicorum Gordon Slynn* (The Hague: Kluwer, 2000), 485.

[298]  Case C–194/94 *CIA* [1996] ECR I–2201.          [299]  P. Slot (1996) 33 *CMLRev.* 1035, 1036–7.

the Commission before they were adopted. Since these Articles were unconditional and sufficiently precise in terms of their content they could be relied on by individuals before national courts.[300]

The Court then considered the legal consequences of Belgium's failure to notify. Although a number of governments argued that, since the directive concerned only relations between the Member States and the Commission, it had no effect on relations between private parties, the Court disagreed. Referring to the Commission's 1986 Communication, to the directive's purpose of protecting free movement of goods, and to the elaborate procedure laid down by Articles 8–9, the Court said:

The effectiveness of [Union] control will be that much greater if the Directive is interpreted as meaning that breach of the obligation to notify constitutes a *substantial procedural defect* such as to render the technical regulations in question inapplicable to individuals.[301]

Therefore, CIA could rely on Articles 8–9 against Signalson and raise the Belgian government's failure to notify as a defence to the counterclaim.

This ruling seemed to suggest that CIA could rely on the provisions of Directive 98/34 horizontally (i.e., against a private party), thereby undermining the well-established principle that clear and sufficiently precise provisions of unimplemented or incorrectly implemented directives have vertical (but not horizontal) direct effect.[302] Although the Court did not address this issue directly it is unlikely that the Court intended covertly to overturn a rule of such constitutional significance.[303] If so, how can *CIA* be explained? One possibility is that CIA was relying on Articles 8–9 of the directive not aggressively (as a sword) but defensively (as a shield). In other words, Articles 8–9 were not imposing any legal obligation on Signalson; Signalson was merely suffering a disadvantage (that it could not rely on national law which would have helped it push CIA's alarm system off the market). Another view is that the Belgian law was a quasi-regulatory power, enabling individuals to take court action to secure the withdrawal from the market of a product not in conformity with the Belgian law.[304] In many states this type of power would have been exercised by a public body. To that extent Signalson was acting as an (unwitting) agent of the state: the form of the action was horizontal but the substance was vertical.[305] For this reason Signalson could not take advantage of the state's failure for its own purposes.

In *Unilever*,[306] the Court had the opportunity of clarifying its ruling in *CIA*. The case concerned a draft Italian law on olive-oil labelling which had been notified to the Commission in May 1998 under Article 8 of Directive 98/34. Although the Commission informed the Italian authorities that it intended to legislate in this area, thereby triggering the additional nine-month standstill provision under Article 9, Italy nevertheless adopted the legislation in August 1998. In September 1998, on receipt of an order from Central

---

[300] Para. 44.        [301] Para. 48, emphasis added.

[302] See, e.g., Case 152/84 *Marshall v. Southampton and South-West Area Health Authority (Teaching)* [1986] ECR 723, para. 48; Case C–91/92 *Faccini Dori v. Recreb Srl* [1994] ECR I–3325, paras. 22–5.

[303] See M. Dougan, 'The "disguised" vertical direct effect of directives?' (2000) 59 *CLJ* 586; K. Lackhoff and H. Nyseens, 'Direct effect of directives in triangular situations' (1998) 23 *ELRev.* 397; C. Hilson and A. Downes, 'Making sense of rights: Community rights in EC law' (1999) 24 *ELRev.* 121; M. Lenz, D. Sif Tynes, and L. Young, 'Horizontal what? Back to basics' (2000) 25 *ELRev.* 509. Cf. Bot AG's, opinion in Case C–555/07 *Kücükdeveci* [2010] ECR I–000.

[304] S. Weatherill, 'Breach of directives and breach of contract' (2001) 26 *ELRev.* 177, 180.

[305] Dougan, above n. 303, 602.        [306] Case C–443/98 [2000] ECR I–7535.

Food, Unilever supplied Central Food with 648 litres of olive oil. The next day, Central Food informed Unilever that, because the oil was not labelled in accordance with the contested Italian law, it would not pay for it. In response, Unilever argued that since the national law had been adopted in breach of the standstill clause in Article 9, the principle of non-enforceability laid down by *CIA* in respect of Article 8 applied equally to Article 9, and so it was not obliged to comply with the Italian labelling rules, and therefore Central Foods should pay what it owed.

Advocate General Jacobs disagreed with Unilever. He argued that the principle in *CIA* should not apply in this situation because it would have the effect of requiring traders to be experts, not only in their own contractual dealings but also in European Union law and, in particular, to know of the existence of Directive 98/34 and the judgment in *CIA*. They would also have to identify the technical regulation as such, and establish with certainty whether the Member State had complied with its obligations under Articles 8–9 of the directive. This last element, he noted, was particularly difficult, given the lack of publicity under the directive. He also thought that injustice could result: if a technical regulation was unenforceable in private proceedings an individual would lose a case in which such a regulation was at issue, not because of its own failure to comply with an obligation deriving from Union law, but because of a Member State's behaviour.[307] This was all because of the need to ensure effective enforcement of Union law.[308]

The Court rejected these arguments and applied *CIA*.[309] It said that 'breach of the obligations of postponement of adoption set out in Article 9 of Directive [98/34] also constitutes a *substantial procedural defect* such as to render technical regulations inapplicable'.[310] The Court then said that the inapplicability of the Italian law could be invoked in civil proceedings between individuals concerning contractual rights and obligations. It could not see a distinction between *Unilever* and *CIA* in this respect: there was no reason to treat disputes between individuals relating to unfair competition, as in *CIA*, differently from disputes between individuals concerning contractual rights and obligations. Then, in *Sapod-Audic*[311] the Court considered the consequences of a finding by the national court that an unnotified national technical regulation was inapplicable. It said that it was for national law to determine the severity of the sanction to be applied in these cases but the sanction could include the nullity or unenforceability of a contract, subject to the principles of non-discrimination and effectiveness.

In *Unilever* the Court also shed a little more light on the controversial question of 'horizontal' direct effect of Directive 98/34. While reasserting the orthodox rule laid down in *Faccini Dori* that there is no horizontal direct effect of directives, it carved out an exception to this rule in cases involving substantial procedural defects.[312] It distinguished between two types of directives. On the one hand, it said there are directives regulating relations between individuals, such as the Package Holiday Directive[313] which was at issue in *Faccini Dori*.[314] These sorts of directives approximate national laws and confer rights and obligations on individuals.[315] The orthodox rule (no horizontal direct effect) applies to these directives. On the other hand, it said there are directives involving institutional/

---

[307] See also Weatherill, above n. 304, 182.     [308] Paras. 100–3.     [309] Para. 39.
[310] Para. 45, emphasis added.
[311] Case C–159/00 [2002] ECR I–5031, para. 53, noted by M. Dougan (2003) 40 *CMLRev.* 193.
[312] Para. 50.        [313] Dir. 90/314/EEC ([1990] OJ L158/59).
[314] Case C–91/92 *Faccini Dori* [1994] ECR I–3325.
[315] See Jacob AG's comments in *Unilever*, para. 81.

Member State relations, like Directive 98/34, which is not intended to approximate laws but to protect free movement of goods by means of a preventive control mechanism.[316] Since Directive 98/34 merely requires notifications, it creates neither rights nor obligations for individuals.[317] As a result, it does not define the substantive scope of the legal rule on the basis of which the national court must decide the case before it and so the orthodox rule (no horizontal direct effect) does not apply.

The Court has imposed some limits on the *CIA/Unilever* rule of the inapplicability of national legislation in the event of non-notification. In *Lemmens*[318] it made clear that the *CIA* rule applies only to legislation which affects trade between Member States. Lemmens was charged with driving a vehicle under the influence of alcohol. Under domestic law, the breathalyser used had to comply with certain standards of quality, performance, and test methods. Lemmens argued that since the technical regulations in which those standards were set out had not been properly notified to the Commission under Directive 98/34, the results of the breathalyser test could not be used against him.

The Court disagreed. It said that while failure to notify technical regulations rendered the national regulations inapplicable inasmuch as they hindered the *marketing* of a product which was not in conformity with the regulations (*CIA*), it did not have the effect of rendering unlawful any *use* of a product which was in conformity with unnotified regulations.[319] It continued that the use of the breathalyser was not liable to create an obstacle to trade which could have been avoided if the notification procedure had been followed and therefore the directive did not preclude the use of the evidence.

Despite the limits imposed by *Lemmens*, the immediate practical effect of *CIA* on national governments was dramatic. For example,[320] the Dutch government drew up a list of 400 national regulations which should have been notified under the directive.[321] It unilaterally withdrew 96 technical regulations and subsequently withdrew a further 77 following discussions with the Commission. It then formally notified 227 texts, of which 70 were not considered significant, but the rest contained provisions contrary to Union law which needed to be rectified. This tale demonstrates the value of the Directive 98/34 procedure: without it, 330 technical regulations would have formed part of Dutch law and would have needed to have been addressed by Article 258 proceedings or individual challenge.

The ramifications of *CIA* extended beyond the Netherlands. The number of notifications increased generally from 29 in 1984 to 439 in 1995, 751 in 2000, and 710 in 2007,[322] as did the range of countries actually making notifications. In 1995 Germany, France, the Netherlands, and the UK accounted for the majority of notifications. By 2000 all Member States were regularly notifying draft regulations, including Ireland and Luxembourg which had taken little action in the past.[323] The Commission largely attributes this increase to the judgment in *CIA*, which prompted Member States to apply the directive with greater care.[324] As with *Cassis de Dijon*, the old allies—the Commission and the Court—worked together to ensure the effective application of Union law, with the Court drawing on the

---

[316] See para. 79.     [317] Para. 51.

[318] Case C–226/97 *Criminal proceedings against Johannes Martinus Lemmens* [1998] ECR I–3711.

[319] Para. 35.     [320] COM(2000)429, 35.

[321] For full details of the Dutch situation, see J. Jans, 'National legislative autonomy? The procedural constraints of European law' [1998/1] *LIEI* 25.

[322] These figures are taken from COM(2000) 429, Table VII in respect of 1999 and [2001] OJ C207/5 for 2000. More recent statistics can be found at <http://www.europa.eu.int/comm/enterprise/tris/statistics/index_en.htm>.

[323] Notably, by the accession of Austria, Finland, and Sweden and in part by an amendment to the directive which expanded its scope.

[324] COM(2000) 429, 22.

Commission's 1986 Communication and with the Commission proactively following up the Court's judgment.[325] There was a subsequent decline in notifications[326] but they picked up again in 2005 (the first year after the 10 new states acceded to the EU) with notifications up to 800 (30 per cent up on 2004 but including nearly 200 from the accession states), with the UK topping the table with 98 notifications. The Commission responded to around 35 per cent of the notifications and the Member States to about 16 per cent.[327]

# H.  CONCLUSIONS

Despite the apparent success of Directive 98/34, the Union has still introduced the Mutual Recognition Regulation 764/2008 to deal with continuing problems of market access for products'.[328] The Regulation's *Cassis de Dijon* heritage is clearly expressed:

Articles [34] and [36] of the [Treaties] entail *inter alia* that Member States of destination cannot forbid the sale on their territories of products lawfully marketed in another Member State and which are not subject to [Union] harmonisation, unless the technical restrictions laid down by the Member State of destination are justified on the grounds described in Article [36] ... or on the basis of overriding requirement of general public importance recognised by the Court of Justice's case law, and that they are proportionate.[329]

*Commission v Italy (trailers)* reinforces the importance of the market access approach, despite all the problems that this vexed term entails.

However, it would be a mistake to conclude that in *Cassis* the Court favoured free trade to the detriment of broader interests which are valued at national level. The development of mandatory requirements not only places a brake on any possible destructive regulatory competition (race to the bottom) but also recognizes that the European constitution is not merely economic but pluralistic, a constitution which embraces social and cultural values.[330] However, the broad scope of the *Dassonville* formula has forced the Court to recognize ever-more mandatory requirements to preserve a wide variety of national legislation. That said, in the majority of cases the Court either rejects the mandatory requirement put forward by the Member State on the facts or finds that the steps taken by the state to realize the objective are not proportionate. For these reasons, governments and commentators became increasingly concerned that the Court's interpretation of Article 34 was in fact leading to wide-scale destruction of national regulation, including rules which were non-discriminatory and which had little impact on cross-border trade. This led to the ruling in *Keck* where the Court carved out an area of national regulation, certain selling arrangements, and made it clear that Article 34 did not apply to it, even in principle. It is to the decision in *Keck* that Chapter 5 now turns.

---

[325] The Commission now refers to the Court's judgment at the bottom of each list of national notifications received (see, e.g., 98/C 177/02). At times the Commission finds it hard to disguise its glee at the ruling in *CIA* (see, e.g., COM(2000) 429, paras. 85 and 91).

[326] See, e.g., 508 drafts in 2002 (OJ [2003] C131/18). For a detailed analysis, see Commission Report, *Evaluation of the Application of Directive 98/34 in the Field of Information Society Services* COM(2003) 69 final, 10ff.                    [327] <http://www.ec.europa.eu/enterprise/tris/about/9834_in_2005.pdf>.

[328] MEMO/07/54, 14 Feb. 2007, 3.        [329] COM(2007)36, 2.

[330] M. Poiares Maduro, 'Striking the elusive balance between economic freedom and social rights in the EU' in P. Alston (ed.), *The EU and Human Rights* (Oxford: OUP, 1999).

# 5

# ARTICLE 34 AND CERTAIN SELLING ARRANGEMENTS

## A. INTRODUCTION

In the previous chapter we considered the Article 34 prohibition on measures having equivalent effect to quantitative restrictions (MEEs). We saw that originally MEEs fell into two categories: distinctly applicable measures (different burden in law and in fact) and indistinctly applicable measures (same burden in law, different burden in fact). Following *Commission* v. *Italy (trailers)*,[1] the second category was confined to product requirements and a third category was added: measures hindering market access. While the original, two-tiered classification was sufficient to address the relatively straightforward situations arising in the early case law, it proved a rather blunt instrument for later, more complex cases. In particular, the Court struggled to decide how rules concerning the time, place, and manner of marketing products[2]—so-called 'market circumstances' rules—fitted within this framework. The Court's attempts to reconcile market circumstances rules with Articles 34 and 36, the decision in *Keck*,[3] and the ramifications of this ruling form the focus of this chapter.

## B. MARKET CIRCUMSTANCES RULES AND ARTICLE 34

### 1. WHAT ARE MARKET CIRCUMSTANCES RULES?

Mortelmans defines market circumstances rules as those concerning, '[w]ho (pharmacist, door-to-door salesman, employee) sells the product, and when (Sundays, at night), where (shop, door-to-door) and how (with a gift)' he goes about it.[4] Such rules differ from MEEs in three main ways. First, while market circumstances rules, like MEEs, restrict

---

[1] Case C–110/05 [2009] ECR I–000.

[2] See E. White, 'In search of the limits to Article 30 of the EEC Treaty' (1989) 26 *CMLRev.* 235, 259 and his submissions on behalf of the Commission in Case C–145/88 *Torfaen BC* v. *B & Q plc* [1989] ECR 3851.

[3] Joined Cases C–267 and 268/91 *Keck and Mithouard* [1993] ECR I–6097.

[4] K. Mortelmans, 'Article 30 of the EEC Treaty and legislation relating to market circumstances: Time to consider a new definition' (1991) 28 *CMLRev.* 115, 116.

the volume of trade, unlike MEEs, they are neither *designed* to protect the home market[5] nor do they have the *effect* of protecting the home market. Secondly, while distinctly and indistinctly applicable MEEs are discriminatory in some way (e.g., same burden in law, different burden in fact), rules concerning market circumstances often affect the domestic producer and the importer in just the same way and so are non-discriminatory (same burden in law *and* same burden in fact).

A third difference relates to the regulatory burden and to whom that burden applies. MEEs, particularly product requirements, are prohibited by Article 34 because of the double burden they entail: the disparities between the different national rules oblige the producer/importer to comply with both the home and host states' rules, thereby increasing costs.[6] By contrast, market circumstances rules generally affect the retailer, not the producer/importer. Therefore dual regulation is not a problem because retailers have to satisfy only one set of rules (those of the home state). The reason why traders complain about market circumstances rules is that these rules limit the commercial freedom of traders to sell under the most liberalized conditions,[7] i.e. they prevent traders from selling goods exactly when, where, and how they choose. In other words, traders complain about the very existence of market circumstances rules, not the fact that they differ from state to state.

Given the remoteness of market circumstances rules from inter-state trade and the fact that they generally affect the *retailers* and not the producers/importers, it might be thought that such rules should fall outside Article 34 altogether and, in the name of subsidiarity, the detail be left to the Member States unhampered by Union law. However, the tentacles of the *Dassonville* formula, with its reference to measures which 'indirectly', 'potentially' hinder inter-state trade, are sufficiently all-embracing to bring national rules on market circumstances within the Article 34 prohibition.

This raises the fundamental question: what is the purpose of Article 34? As Advocate General Tesauro succinctly put it in *Hünermund*,[8] is Article 34 intended (1) to liberalize inter-state trade, as governments would argue (in which case Article 34 should not apply to market circumstances rules) *or* (2) to encourage the unhindered pursuit of commerce in the individual Member States, as some traders would argue (in which case Article 34 should apply to market circumstances rules)? Putting it more theoretically, is Article 34 there merely to mediate the relationship between market-liberalization on the one hand and national sovereignty on the other (so-called 'economic supranationalism'[9]), the view supported by Advocate General Tesauro's first approach, or is its purpose to give all traders the right to trade and thus to challenge any state norms that stand in their

---

[5] For an early recognition of this, see Slynn AG's approach in Joined Cases 60 and 61/84 *Cinéthèque SA and others* v. *Fédération nationale des cinémas français* [1985] ECR 2605.

[6] The Court emphasized this point in Case C–241/89 *SARRP* v. *Chambre syndicale des raffineurs et conditionneurs de sucre de France* [1990] ECR I–4695, para. 30.

[7] Van Gerven AG in Case C–145/88 *Torfaen* v. *B & Q plc* [1989] ECR 3851; Tesauro AG in Case C–292/92 *Hünermund and others* v. *Landesapothekerkammer Baden-Württemberg* [1993] ECR I–6787, para. 22; Van Gerven AG in Joined Cases C–401 and 402/92 *Criminal proceedings against Tankstation 't Heukske vof and J.B.E. Boermans* [1994] ECR I–2199, para. 20, and N. Reich, 'The November Revolution of the European Court of Justice: *Keck, Meng* and *Audi* revisited' (1994) 31 *CMLRev.* 459, 466–7.

[8] Case C–292/92 *Hünermund* [1993] ECR I–6787, para. 1.

[9] D. Chalmers, *European Union Law* (Cambridge: CUP, 2006), 665.

way (so-called 'economic constitutionalism'), the view supported by Advocate General Tesauro's second approach?

## 2. THE COURT'S EARLY APPROACH TO MARKET CIRCUMSTANCES RULES

For many years the Court struggled to fit market circumstance rules into its Article 34 case law.[10] It is possible to detect three different strands to the Court's early jurisprudence. The first reflected its methodology in *Cassis* (discussed in the previous chapter): market circumstances rules were MEEs and so breached Article 34 but were potentially justifiable. This can be seen in *Oosthoek*[11] where the Court said that a national law prohibiting the use of free gifts as an incentive to purchase a product—in this case encyclopaedias—could breach Article 34 because the producer might be required either to adopt an advertising or sales promotion scheme which differed from one Member State to another or to discontinue a scheme which it considered to be particularly effective.[12] In *Buet*[13] the Court said that its ruling in *Oosthoek* applied equally to rules depriving traders of a method of marketing whereby they realized almost all of their sales. Therefore, a national law prohibiting door-to-door selling of foreign-language teaching materials constituted an indistinctly applicable MEE but could be justified on the grounds of consumer protection.

In respect of advertising, the Court ruled in *Yves Rocher*[14] that a prohibition on eye-catching advertising of price comparisons (showing the old price crossed out and the new one in red next to it) was an indistinctly applicable MEE, as was a law in *Aragonesa* prohibiting the advertising of certain alcoholic drinks in public places.[15] The Court also said that measures limiting the types of shops which could sell certain goods, such as the rule in *LPO*[16] granting opticians the exclusive right to distribute glasses, also constituted an indistinctly applicable MEE, because it was capable of affecting the possibilities of marketing imported products in so far as they limited sales to certain channels. On the facts the rules could not be justified either by a mandatory requirement or an Article 36 derogation. As we shall see, the outcome in this line of cases will not be very different today post-*Keck*, albeit that the route to get there might be different.

The second approach adopted by the Court to market circumstances rules was to find that the national measure was not an MEE. It therefore fell outside Article 34, usually because it was not a 'trading rule' within the meaning of *Dassonville*, it was not

---

[10] As Tesauro AG admitted in Case C–292/92 *Hünermund* [1993] ECR I–6787, para. 11: 'Case law which—why conceal it?—is certainly not amenable to systematic interpretation'.

[11] Case 286/81 *Criminal Proceedings against Oosthoek's Uitgeversmaatschappi BV* [1982] ECR 4575.

[12] Para. 15. See also Case C–241/89 *SARRP* v. *Chambre syndicale des raffineurs et conditionneurs de sucre de France* [1990] ECR I–4695, para. 29 (national law prohibiting any statement in the advertising of artificial sweeteners alluding to the word sugar breached Art. 34 and could not be justified).

[13] Case 382/87 *Buet* v. *Ministère public* [1989] ECR 1235, para. 8.

[14] Case C–126/91 [1993] ECR I–2361. The case was brought by the extraordinarily named trade association, the Protective Association against Pernicious Economic Practices.

[15] Joined Cases C–1/90 and 176/90 *Aragonesa* [1991] ECR I–4151. See also Case C–362/88 *GB-INNO-BM* v. *Confédération du commerce luxembourgeois* [1990] ECR I–667.

[16] Case C–271/92 *Laboratoire de Prothèses and Groupement d'Opticiens Lunetiers Détaillants* [1993] ECR I–2899 (opticians' monopoly), para. 7. See also Case C–369/88 *Criminal Proceedings against Delattre* [1991] ECR I–1487, para. 51, and Case C–60/90 *Criminal proceedings against Jean Monteil and Daniel Samanni* [1991] ECR I–1547 (pharmacists' monopoly), para. 38.

discriminatory and it did not affect inter-state trade.[17] So in *Oebel*[18] the Court said that a German law forbidding night work in the bakery industry and transport and delivery before 5.45 a.m. did not breach Articles 34–5[19] because the restriction applied to all producers, wherever they were established, and trade within the Union remained possible at all times. In *Blesgen*[20] the Court said that a national rule prohibiting the sale of drinks over 22 per cent proof for consumption on public premises did not breach Article 34 because it had 'no connection with the importation of the products and for that reason [was] not of such a nature as to impede trade between Member States'.[21]

The decision in *Krantz*[22] is perhaps the most important in this line of case law. The Court had to consider whether a Dutch law, allowing the collector of taxes to seize goods if purchasers failed to discharge their tax debts, contravened Article 34. Having established that the national rule was non-discriminatory and did not seek to affect trade with other Member States,[23] the Court found that Article 34 was not breached. It said the possibility that nationals of other Member States would hesitate to sell goods on instalment to purchasers in the Netherlands because such goods were liable to be seized by the collector of taxes was 'too uncertain and indirect' to warrant the conclusion that a national provision authorizing such seizure was liable to hinder trade between Member States.[24] In this case the Court appeared to be applying a test based on causation[25] and found that the national rule was too remote to affect inter-state trade so Article 34 did not apply. As we shall see in Chapter 8, the approach adopted in this line of case law has had an increasing influence in the field of free movement of persons.

The third and most controversial approach adopted by the Court to the market circumstances rules can be found in the confused decisions in the Sunday trading cases. As was common in many states, British law required most shops to be closed on Sunday. Responding to customer demands, some do-it-yourself (DIY) stores, which cater for home-decorating enthusiasts with leisure time at weekends, began trading on Sundays and were prosecuted under the Shops Act 1950.[26] In their defence, they argued that the

---

[17] See also Joined Cases 60 and 61/84 *Cinéthèque* [1985] ECR 2605. According to a French law designed to encourage attendance at cinemas, videos of films could not be sold or hired within the first year of the film receiving its performance certificate. The legislation was non-discriminatory: it affected both French and imported videos equally. Slynn AG said that because the national rules were not specifically directed at imports, did not discriminate against imports and gave no protection to domestic producers, *prima facie* they did not breach Art. 34, even if imports were restricted or reduced.

[18] Case 155/80 *Summary proceedings against Sergius Oebel* [1981] ECR 1993.      [19] Para. 20.

[20] Case 75/81 *Blesgen v. Belgian State* [1982] ECR 1211.

[21] Para. 9. See also Case 148/85 *Direction générale des impôts et procureur de la République v. Marie-Louise Forest* [1986] ECR 3449, para. 19 (restriction on the quantity of wheat that could be milled has 'no effect on imports and is not likely to impede trade between Member States'); Case C–23/89 *Quietlynn v. Southend BC* [1990] ECR I–3059 (provisions prohibiting sale of sex articles from unlicensed sex shops have 'no connection with intra-[Union] trade' and so are not MEEs).

[22] Case C–69/88 *Krantz* [1990] ECR I–583, also discussed in Ch. 4.

[23] Para. 10. This is sometimes rephrased as 'its purpose is not to regulate trade in goods with other Member States': e.g., Case C–96/94 *Centro Servizi Spediporto Srl v. Spedizioni Marittima del Golfo Srl* [1995] ECR I–2883, para. 41.

[24] Para. 11. See also, e.g., Case C–93/92 *CMC Motorradcenter GmbH v. Pelin Baskiciogullari* [1993] ECR I–5009, para. 12; Case C–44/98 *BASF v. Präsident des Deutschen Patentamts* [1999] ECR I–6269, paras. 16 and 21.      [25] See La Pergola AG in Case C–44/98 *BASF* [1999] ECR I–6269, para. 18.

[26] P. Diamond, 'Dishonourable defence: The use of injunctions and the EEC Treaty; Case study of the Shops Act 1950' (1991) 54 *MLR* 72; R. Rawlings, 'The Euro-law game: Some deductions from a saga'

Shops Act breached Article 34 because goods could not be sold on Sunday, and those goods included goods made elsewhere in the EU.[27] The matter was first referred to the Court of Justice in *Torfaen*,[28] where the Court responded with one of its most opaque judgments. Without mentioning either *Dassonville* or *Cassis*, the Court said:

It is therefore necessary in a case such as this to consider first of all whether rules such as those at issue pursue an aim which is justified with regard to [Union] law...Such rules reflect certain political and economic choices in so far as their purpose is to ensure that working and non-working hours are so arranged as to accord with national or regional socio-cultural characteristics...[29]

Secondly, it is necessary to ascertain whether the effects of such national rules exceed what is necessary to achieve its aim in view. As is indicated in Article 3 of Commission Directive 70/50, '...the prohibition laid down in Article [34] covers national measures governing the marketing of products where the restrictive effects of such measures on the free movement of goods exceeds the effects intrinsic to trade rules. The question whether the effects of specific national rules do in fact remain within that limit is a question of fact to be determined by the national court.[30]

It was not clear whether *Torfaen* represented a mechanical application of the *Cassis* line of authority[31] or a new, two-stage test[32] based on establishing first whether the national measure pursued some objective consistent with Union law and then applying the 'superficial'[33] balancing act envisaged by Article 3 of Directive 70/50. Whatever *Torfaen* meant, it was left to the national courts to determine whether the restrictive effects of the Sunday trading ban exceeded its intrinsic beneficial effects. Because national courts reached different conclusions on the legality of the same piece of national legislation,[34] the Court of Justice took it upon itself to say in *Conforama* and *Marchandise*[35] that French rules prohibiting workers from working on Sunday (as opposed to the British rules requiring shops to be closed on Sunday) were not excessive and so were compatible with Article 34. Subsequently, in *Stoke-on-Trent*[36] the Court ruled that Article 34 did not apply to legislation prohibiting retailers from opening their shops on Sunday[37] because the restrictive effects on trade were not excessive to the social aim pursued by the legislation.[38]

---

(1993) 20 *J. Law and Soc.* 309; M. Jarvis, 'The Sunday trading episode: In defence of the Euro-defence' (1995) 44 *ICLQ* 451.

[27] The national court said that the ban on Sunday trading had the effect of reducing B & Q's total sales, that approximately 10% of the goods sold by B & Q came from other Member States and that a corresponding reduction of imports from other Member States would therefore ensue: Case C–145/88 *Torfaen Borough Council v. B & Q plc* [1989] ECR 3851, para. 7. [28] Ibid.

[29] Para. 13. [30] Para. 15 [31] See, e.g., L. Gormley (1990) 27 *CMLRev.* 141.

[32] C. Barnard, 'Sunday trading: A drama in five acts' (1994) 57 *MLR* 449; M. van der Woude, 'The limits of free circulation: The *Torfaen Borough Council* case' (1990) *LJIL* 62; and Tesauro AG in Case C–292/92 *Hünermund* [1993] ECR I–6787, para. 15. [33] Tesauro AG in ibid., para. 15.

[34] Cf. Northcote J in *B & Q v. Shrewsbury and Atcham BC* [1990] 3 CMLR 535 and Hoffmann J in *Stoke on Trent City Council v. B & Q* [1990] 3 CMLR 31 with Allen J in *Wellingborough BC v. Payless* [1990] 1 CMLR 773 and Mustill J in *Smiths-do-it-all v. Peterborough BC* [1990] 2 CMLR 577.

[35] Joined Cases C–312 and 332/89 *U.D.S. CGT de l'Aisne v. Sidef Conforama; Criminal proceedings against Marchandise* [1991] ECR I–1027.

[36] Case C–169/91 *Stoke on Trent and Norwich City Council v. B & Q plc* [1992] ECR I–6635.

[37] Para. 17.

[38] Para. 16. Meanwhile shoppers in the UK had grown so used to being able to shop on Sunday that the law was changed to allow this to happen: Sch. 1 to Sunday Trading Act 1994.

## 3. THE ACADEMIC RESPONSE

The Sunday trading episode revealed the inadequacy of the Court's analysis of measures relating to market circumstances. However, academics were also divided as to how to deal with the problem. Some argued that all such rules were MEEs and had to be justified under Article 36 or (more probably) by a mandatory requirement.[39] Others suggested that the solution lay in the wording of the *Dassonville* formula itself. Because *Dassonville* referred to rules which were capable of *hindering* (not merely affecting) inter-state trade,[40] measures with minimal effects on imports (such as those in *Blesgen*, *Krantz*, and *Oebel*) did not breach Article 34.[41] While there was much support for this view,[42] it sat uncomfortably with the decision in *Van de Haar*[43] that there was no *de minimis* rule in Article 34.[44]

White proposed another solution.[45] He argued that a distinction should be drawn between, on the one hand, rules relating to *product requirements* (i.e., rules concerning the composition, characteristics, and presentation of products) to which Article 34 should apply, and, on the other, rules concerning *market circumstances* (i.e., rules concerning place, time, manner, authorized person) which should fall outside the scope of Article 34, provided imported products enjoyed equal access to the market compared with national goods. Mortelmans[46] agreed with White's approach to product requirement rules but proposed a refinement of the market circumstances category. He distinguished between:[47]

- rules 'with a territorial element' (i.e., rules relating to activities situated in a *fixed* or *static* location),[48] such as town and country planning legislation,[49] or a ban on selling certain alcoholic beverages, or Sunday trading rules;[50]

- rules without a fixed location (sometimes referred to as *dynamic* rules), such as legislation prohibiting door-to-door selling (*Oosthoek*) and limiting the use of promotional gifts (*Buet*)).

He suggested that while static rules did not pose a real threat to the single market and so should fall outside Article 34, dynamic rules did pose a threat to the single market and so should be caught by Article 34.

---

[39]  See, e.g., L. Gormley (1990) 27 *CMLRev.* 141, 149; A. Arnull, 'What shall we do on Sunday?' (1991) 16 *ELRev.* 112.

[40]  See, e.g., Joined Cases C–321–4/94 *Criminal Proceedings against Jacques Pistre* [1997] ECR I–2343.

[41]  J. Steiner, 'Drawing the line: Uses and abuses of Article 30 EEC' (1992) 29 *CMLRev.* 749, 773.

[42]  See, e.g., Jacobs AG in Case C–412/93 *Leclerc-Siplec* v. *TFI Publicité SA* [1995] ECR I–179 and the references therein. For an earlier example, see Van Gerven AG in the pre-*Keck* decision in Case C–145/88 *Torfaen* [1989] ECR 3851, paras. 24–5.

[43]  Joined Cases 177 and 178/82 *Criminal proceedings against Jan van de Haar and Kaveka de Meern BV* [1984] ECR 1797.

[44]  Tesauro AG admitted this in Case C–292/92 *Hünermund* [1993] ECR I–6787, para. 21.

[45]  E. White, 'In search of the limits to Article 30 of the EEC Treaty' (1989) 26 *CMLRev.* 235.

[46]  Above n. 4, 115.        [47]  Ibid., 116 and 130.

[48]  Later (at 130) he talks of 'pub, shop, shopping centre, petrol station, bakery'.

[49]  Case 20/87 *Ministère public* v. *André Gauchard* [1987] ECR 4879.

[50]  Case C–145/88 *Torfaen* [1989] ECR 3851.

The White/Mortelmans distinctions have influenced the development of the *Keck* and post-*Keck* case law. The other point of influence was Advocate General Tesauro's Opinion in *Hünermund*.[51] The case concerned a German ban on pharmacists advertising para-pharmaceutical products outside their pharmacies.[52] The Advocate General noted that this measure was applicable without distinction to domestic and imported goods and made neither access to the market nor marketing of imported products more difficult than for domestic products.[53] He recognized that the measure could (hypothetically) reduce imports, but only because it could (equally hypothetically) reduce sales. For these reasons he concluded that the national measure had to be regarded as falling outside the field of application of Article 34—it had 'nothing to do with trade, still less with the integration of the markets'.[54] This Opinion paved the way for the Court's decision in *Keck and Mithouard*.[55]

## C. THE DECISION IN *KECK*

### 1. THE JUDGMENT

The facts of *Keck* were straightforward. Keck and Mithouard sold goods (Picon beer and Sati Rouge coffee) at a loss (i.e., at a price below that at which they had been purchased wholesale).[56] Since this was prohibited by French law they were prosecuted. In their defence they argued that because the French law deprived them of a method of sales promotion it restricted the volume of sales of imported goods and so was incompatible with Article 34. The Court disagreed. It began by noting that the purpose of the French law was not to regulate trade in goods,[57] even though such legislation could restrict the volume of sales (including sales of products from other Member States).[58] It then indicated that it wanted to stop dissatisfied traders from using Article 34 to challenge any restriction on their freedom to sell what they wanted, where they wanted, and when they wanted. It said that '[i]n view of the increasing tendency of traders' to invoke Article 34 of the Treaty as a means of 'challenging any rules whose effect is to limit their commercial freedom', even where such rules were not aimed at products from other Member States, it considered it 'necessary to re-examine and clarify its case law on this matter'.[59]

In this clarification the Court drew a distinction between 'product requirements' on the one hand, and 'certain selling arrangements' on the other. In respect of product

---

[51] Case C–292/92 [1993] ECR I–6787. This Opinion, rather than that of Van Gerven AG (the Advocate General in *Keck*), seems to have influenced the Court more in *Keck*: see Reich, above n. 7, 461.

[52] Pharmacists could advertise inside their shops but were not allowed to advertise in cinemas, on radio, or on television (Report for the hearing in Case C–292/92 *Hünermund* [1993] ECR I–6787, 6790).

[53] Para. 29.     [54] Para. 24.

[55] Joined Cases C–267 and 268/91 *Keck and Mithouard* [1993] ECR I–6097.

[56] See also the application of the decision in *Keck* to the prohibition of sales yielding very low profit in Case C–63/94 *Groupement National des Négociants en Pommes de Terre de Belgique* v. *ITM Belgium SA and Vocarex SA* [1995] ECR I–2467.

[57] Para. 12. By implication the outcome would be different if the legislation was designed to regulate trade: see Case C–158/94 *Commission* v. *Italy (electricity)* [1997] ECR I–5789, para. 31.     [58] Para. 13.

[59] Para. 14.

requirements, it reaffirmed in paragraph 15 that the principles in *Cassis* continued to apply:[60]

It is established by case law beginning with *Cassis de Dijon*...that, in the absence of harmonisation of legislation, obstacles to the free movement of goods which are the consequence of applying, to goods coming from other Member States where they are lawfully manufactured and marketed, rules that lay down requirements to be met by such goods (such as those relating to designation, form, size, weight, composition, presentation, labelling, packaging) constitute measures of equivalent effect prohibited by Article [34]. This is so even if those rules apply without distinction to all products unless their application can be justified by a public-interest objective taking precedence over the free movement of goods.[61]

The examples in the brackets are an indicative list of product requirement situations to which *Cassis de Dijon* will apply.

In paragraph 16 the Court turned its attention to 'certain selling arrangements'. It said that:

...contrary to what has previously been decided, the application to products from other Member States of national provisions restricting or prohibiting certain selling arrangements is not such as to hinder directly or indirectly, actually or potentially, trade between Member States within the meaning of the *Dassonville* judgment...provided those provisions apply to all affected traders operating within the national territory and provided that they affect in the same manner, in law and in fact, the marketing of domestic products and those from other Member States.

The Court continued in paragraph 17 that:

Where those conditions are fulfilled, the application of such rules to the sale of products from other Member States meeting the requirements laid down by that State is not by nature such as to *prevent* their [foreign goods'] access to the market or to *impede* access any more than it impedes the access of domestic products.[62]

Therefore overturning previous, unspecified case law, the Court said that national provisions restricting or prohibiting 'certain selling arrangements' do not fall within the *Dassonville* formula and so, unlike QRs, distinctly applicable MEEs and product requirements, do *not* breach Article 34 where the two conditions set out in paragraph 16 are satisfied (the so-called paragraph 16 proviso), namely:

(1)   the provisions apply to all affected traders operating in the territory

(2)   the provisions are non-discriminatory (same burden in law and in fact).

In *DocMorris*[63] Advocate General Stix-Hackl described the two limbs of the proviso respectively as (1) the principle of universality and (2) the principle of neutrality. Because in subsequent cases the Court has always found the principle of universality satisfied, this

---

[60] The language of 'product requirements' is taken from Van Gerven AG's Opinion in Joined Cases C–401 and 402/92 *Boermans* [1994] ECR I–2199, para. 16.

[61] See Case C–12/00 *Commission v. Spain* [2003] ECR I–459, para. 76, and generally G. Tesauro, 'The Community's internal market in the light of the recent case law of the Court of Justice' (1995) 15 *YEL* 1, 6.

[62] Emphasis added.

[63] Case C–322/01 *Deutscher Apothekerverband eV v. 0800 DocMorris NV* [2003] ECR I–14887, para. 59.

condition is largely redundant.[64] However, as we shall see, the second condition remains important.

National rules satisfying the two paragraph 16 conditions do not breach Article 34 (see fig. 5.1) because, according to the Court, such rules do not prevent access to the market (first limb of paragraph 17) nor do they impede access for foreign goods more than they impede access for domestic products (second limb of paragraph 17). Thus, in *Keck,* the market access test is presented not as a condition of its own, but rather as a consequence of the fact that the paragraph 16 proviso is satisfied.[65] As we shall see, in *Commission* v. *Italy (trailers)* the Court appears to have changed its mind on this point.

The bottom line in *Keck* is that national rules on certain selling arrangements do not breach Article 34. This contrasts with the situation of national rules on product requirements which *do* breach Article 34 and so need justifying by the Member States

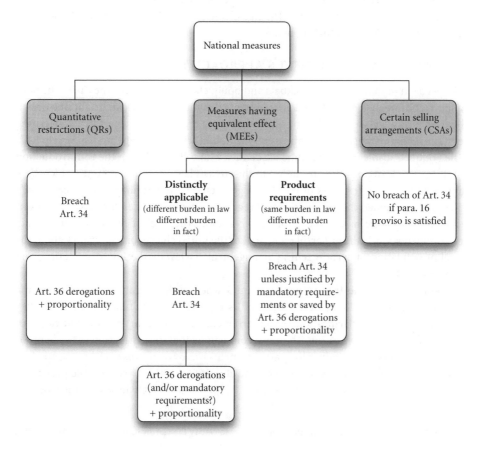

**Fig. 5.1** QRs, MEEs, and CSAs after *Keck* but before *Trailers*

---

[64] P. Oliver and S. Enchelmaier, 'Free movement of goods: Recent developments in the case law' (2007) 44 *CMLRev.* 649, 681.

[65] See A. Rosas, '*Dassonville* and *Cassis de Dijon*' in M. Poiares Maduro and L. Azoulai (eds.), *The Past and Future of EU Law: The classics of EU law revisited on the 50th anniversary of the Rome Treaty* (Oxford: Hart Publishing, 2010).

to be lawful. The ruling in *Keck* is significant because it confirms that there are outer limits to Article 34. The Court has carved out an area ('certain selling arrangements' (CSAs)) which is reserved for national regulators. The Court is not prepared to intervene unless there is evidence of discrimination. In so doing, it has recognized that some local regulatory choices do not damage the realization of economies of scale and wider consumer choice in an integrated market,[66] and so should not be subject to scrutiny under Articles 34 and 36. Read together, paragraphs 16 and 17 of *Keck* provide the Court's answer to Advocate General Tesauro's question in *Hünermund*: Article 34 is intended 'merely' to liberalize *inter-state* trade rather than encouraging the unhindered pursuit of commerce in the Member States. The Court therefore gave priority to the views of economic supranationalists over those of economic constitutionalists, thereby curtailing the individual 'right' to trade. And in reaching this conclusion the Court reintroduced the test of non-discrimination to Article 34, apparently in preference to the alternative, wider test based on market access. The significance of the difference between these two approaches is considered further below.

## 2. ANALYSIS OF THE COURT'S APPROACH IN *KECK*

The decision in *Keck* received brickbats and bouquets in almost equal measure. The bouquets came largely from national governments delighted by the clear, bright line drawn by the Court which rendered some of their national regulation—at least that concerning certain selling arrangements—apparently immune from challenge under Article 34.[67] The bouquets also came from some academics who welcomed both the re-introduction of the principle of non-discrimination to this area of law[68] and the certainty which *Keck* appeared to offer after years of confusion generated by the Sunday trading case law.[69] They also applauded the clear division of regulatory competence endorsed by the Court: the *producing* state makes the initial choices about the level of regulation of product requirements, while the *importing* state makes the initial choice for its territory about the level of regulation of certain selling arrangements (sales, marketing, distribution, and consumption).[70]

The brickbats came from other academics who, while broadly sympathetic to the Court's objectives in *Keck*, were critical of its realization. At the most basic level, they regretted that, in its 'clarification' of the earlier case law, the Court gave no indication of which cases it was overturning. They also complained that the distinction between product requirements and certain selling arrangements was by no means as clear as would first appear,[71] as the following example demonstrates. If national law requires the packaging of all power tools to bear a label indicating that power tools are dangerous, the labelling

---

[66] S. Weatherill, 'After *Keck*: Some thoughts on how to clarify the clarification' (1996) 33 *CMLRev.* 885, 886–7, and 895.

[67] In subsequent cases governments have regularly argued that the national rules should be considered 'certain selling arrangements' even where the Court subsequently disagrees: e.g., Case C–368/95 *Familiapress* [1997] ECR I–3843 considered at n. 101 below; Joined Cases C–158/04 and C–159/04 *Alfa Vita* [2006] ECR I–8135; Case C–244/06 *Dynamic Medien Vertriebs GmbH* [2008] ECR I–505.

[68] See, e.g., N. Bernard, 'Discrimination and free movement in EC law' (1996) 45 *ICLQ* 83; J. Snell, *Goods and Services in EC Law* (Oxford: OUP, 2002).

[69] Chalmers et al., *European Union Law* (Cambridge: CUP, 2006), 685.      [70] Ibid., 686.

[71] See, e.g., Case C–368/95 *Familiapress* [1997] ECR I–3843; Poiares Maduro AG in Joined Cases C–158/04 & C–159/04 *Alfa Vita* [2006] ECR I–8135, paras. 31–3.

obligation is a product requirement and presumptively unlawful under *Cassis*. If, by contrast, national law merely requires retailers to place a sign containing the same message on the counter next to the power tools, that would be a certain selling arrangement and presumptively lawful under *Keck*.[72]

More fundamentally, commentators bemoaned the introduction of a new, formulistic classification, 'certain selling arrangements', which, unlike well-established legal concepts such as direct and indirect discrimination, had never before seen the legal light of day. We turn now to consider how the Court has interpreted the phrase.

## 3. WHAT ARE 'CERTAIN SELLING ARRANGEMENTS'?

The Court has found a number of market circumstances rules to constitute certain selling arrangements.[73] For example, it said that national rules limiting the time at which goods could be sold were certain selling arrangements. Therefore, in *Boermans*[74] the Court said that national rules requiring petrol stations to close at night did not breach Article 34. Similarly, in *Punto Casa*[75] and *Semeraro Casa*[76] the Court found that Sunday trading rules were certain selling arrangements which did not breach Article 34 (and in so doing it laid to rest the ghost of *Torfaen*).

Other rules, directly affecting the retailers of goods, have also been considered certain selling arrangements. These include rules requiring retailers of particular goods to have actual premises in the locality (*Heimdienst*,[77] *DocMorris*,[78] *Commission v. Germany*[79]) and rules obliging retailers to be licensed (*Burmanjer*[80]). The Court has also said that national restrictions on the number or type of sales outlets constituted certain selling arrangements. Therefore, in *Commission v. Greece (infant milk)*[81] a Greek law requiring processed milk for infants be sold only in pharmacists' shops did not breach Article 34, nor, in *Banchero*,[82] did Italian legislation reserving the retail sale of tobacco products to authorized distributors.[83] In *A-Punkt*[84] the Court said that Austrian rules prohibiting selling in private homes (on the facts of the case cheap silver jewellery) also constituted certain selling arrangements. Restrictions on pricing, too, can constitute certain selling arrangements, as the facts of *Keck* itself show

[72] See, e.g., Case C–159/00 *Sapod-Audic* [2002] ECR I–5031, para. 75 (the national rule did not require a mark or label to be applied to the product itself but imposed a general obligation to identify, at the point of sale, that the packaging was recyclable. This constituted a selling arrangement.).

[73] Cf. May LJ in *The Countryside Alliance and others* v. *HM Attorney General* [2005] EWHC 1677, para. 212 'There is no magic in the label *certain selling arrangements*; that was merely a description of the measure in question in *Keck*'.

[74] Joined Cases C–401 and 402/92 [1994] ECR I–2199.

[75] Joined Case C–69 and 258/93 *Punto Casa SpA* v. *Sindaco del Commune di Capena and others* [1994] ECR I–2355.

[76] Joined Cases C–418/93, C–419/93, C–420/93, C–421/93, C–460/93, C–461/93, C–462/93, C–464/93, C–9/94, C–10/94, C–11/94, C–14/94, C–15/94, *Semeraro Casa Uno Srl and others* [1996] ECR I–2975.

[77] Case C–254/98 [2000] ECR I–151. Cf. Case C–323/93 *La Crespelle* [1994] ECR I–5077 rules on storage of semen treated as MEEs. [78] Case C–322/01 *0800 DocMorris* [2003] ECR I–14887.

[79] Case C–141/07 *Commission* v. *Germany (Pharmacies for Hospitals)* [2008] ECR I–6935, para. 31.

[80] Case C–20/03 *Burmanjer, Van der Linden, De Jong* [2005] ECR I–4133.

[81] Case C–391/92 *Commission* v. *Greece* [1995] ECR I–1621.

[82] Case C–387/93 *Criminal Proceedings against Banchero* [1995] ECR I–4663; cf. Case C–189/95 *Criminal Proceedings against Franzén* [1997] ECR I–5909, para. 57.

[83] See also Case C–162/97 *Criminal Proceedings against Nilsson* [1998] ECR I–7477, para. 28

[84] Case C–441/04 *A-Punkt Schmuckhandels GmbH* v. *Schmidt* [2006] ECR I–2093, para. 17.

(prohibition on resale at a loss). Similarly, a prohibition of sales yielding very low profit is a certain selling arrangement (*ITM*[85]), as is a rule fixing the retail price for books (*LIBRO*).[86]

In other cases the Court has said that restrictions on advertising constituted certain selling arrangements. So, in *Hünermund*[87] a German rule prohibiting pharmacies from advertising para-pharmaceutical products outside their premises did not breach Article 34, nor did a French rule in *Leclerc-Siplec*[88] which prohibited the fuel-distribution sector from advertising on television. Perhaps most esoteric is the Austrian rule in *Karner*[89] prohibiting retailers from indicating to consumers that goods came from an insolvent estate when they no longer constituted part of that estate. This rule constituted a CSA and did not breach Article 34. As we shall see, this line of case law on national rules restricting advertising and other forms of sales promotion techniques proved particularly problematic because, by now classifying the rules as selling arrangements, they benefited from the presumption of legality. This appeared to reverse pre-*Keck* decisions such as *Oosthoek*, *Buet*, and *Aragonesa* considered above[90] where the Court found equivalent rules to constitute MEEs and were presumptively unlawful.

In *Karner* the Court took the opportunity to summarize its case law on certain selling arrangements:[91]

[P]rovisions concerning *inter alia* the place and times of sale of certain products and advertising of those products as well as certain marketing methods [are] provisions governing selling arrangements within the meaning of *Keck and Mithouard*.

This suggests that, despite the lack of clarity over the precise meaning of the phrase 'certain selling arrangements', the Court is prepared to interpret it to cover any rules relating to sales and marketing methods,[92] the word 'certain' seemingly redundant.[93]

However, the use of the phrase raises a further problem in that it does not apparently catch national rules which the *Keck* formula might have been aimed at, such as non-discriminatory restrictions on planning and building in the green belt. There is a good argument that such rules should fall outside Article 34 (non-discriminatory rules not intended to affect inter-state trade) but linguistically it is difficult to argue that they concern 'selling arrangements'. How then should such situations be dealt with? Under *Keck* but shorn of the reference to certain selling arrangements (an approach which would seem to receive the support of Advocate General Kokott in *Mickelsson*[94]—see below)? Under the pre-*Keck*

---

[85] Case C–63/94 *Groupement National des Négociants en Pommes de Terre de Belgique v. ITM Belgium SA and Vocarex SA* [1995] ECR I–2467.

[86] Case C–531/07 *Fachverband der Buch- und Medienwirtschaft v. LIBRO Handelsgesellschaft mbH* [2009] ECR I–000, para. 20.     [87] Case C–292/92 *Hünermund* [1993] ECR I–6787.

[88] Case C–412/93 *Leclerc-Siplec* [1995] ECR I–179. The ruling in *Leclerc-Siplec* was confirmed in Case C–6/98 *ARD* v. *PRO Sieben Media* [1999] ECR I–7599, para. 46, where the Court said that since the restriction on advertising in this case (limitation on transmission time) is of a 'similar, but less extensive, kind, it also concerns certain selling arrangements' and the two conditions in para. 16 of *Keck* are 'clearly satisfied' (para. 48).

[89] Case C–71/02 *Herbert Karner Industrie-Auktionen GmbH* [2004] ECR I–3025.

[90] Nn. 11–16      [91] Para. 38.

[92] Case C–244/06 *Dynamic Medien Vertriebs GmbH* [2008] ECR I–505, para. 30. See also Geelhoed AG in Case C–239/02 *Douwe Egberts NV* v. *Westrom PharmaNV* [2004] ECR I–7007, para. 72: 'the qualification of selling arrangement should be reserved for rules which govern the general conditions under which products are marketed, i.e. when, where and by whom, and which do not specifically concern commercialisation as such'.     [93] Cf. Tesauro AG in Case C–368/95 *Familiapress* [1997] ECR I–3843, para. 9.

[94] Case C–142/05 *Åklagaren* v. *Mickelsson* [2009] ECR I–000.

cases such as *Krantz* (that the effect on inter-state trade is too uncertain and indirect for Article 34 to apply)?[95] Or as an MEE which can be justified?[96]

Following *Commission* v. *Italy (trailers)*, the last approach might be the favoured one. In borderline cases which have already come before the Court, where there is uncertainty as to whether the rule is a certain selling arrangement or an MEE, the Court tends to classify it as an MEE. This can be seen in *Dynamic Medien*.[97] A German law on the protection of young people prohibited the sale by mail order of 'image storage media' (DVDs and video cassettes) unless they had been examined by the relevant authorities in Germany and given an age classification. Advocate General Mengozzi considered the German rules to be a CSA because he focused on ' "how" and "where" the products may be sold' and on 'the personality of the purchaser, that is to say, "to whom" the products may be sold'.[98] By contrast, the Court focused on the fact that in order to be sold by mail order, 'image storage media had to be subject to a national examination and classification procedure' regardless of whether those DVDs had already been classified in the state of export[99] and they had to be labelled. Because such rules made imports 'more difficult and more expensive' they constituted MEEs and so breached Article 34[100] but could be justified on the grounds of protecting children.

The Court's conclusion in *Dynamic Medien* is unsurprising in the light of its earlier decision in *Familiapress*.[101] The case concerned an Austrian law prohibiting magazines containing prize competitions. This meant that the German magazine 'Laura', which contained prize competitions, could not be sold in Austria. In defending the legislation, the Austrian government argued that because the national law concerned a restriction on sales promotions, this constituted a selling arrangement within the meaning of *Keck* and so fell outside Article 34. The Court disagreed, saying that:

even though the relevant national legislation is directed against a method of sales promotion, in this case it bears on the *actual content of the products*, in so far as the competitions in question form an integral part of the magazine in which they appear.[102]

---

[95] See by analogy Joined Cases C–418/93 etc., *Semeraro Casa Uno Srl and others* [1996] ECR I–2975, para. 32.

[96] Support for this view can be found in Case C–65/05 *Commission* v. *Greece (computer games)* [2006] ECR I–10341, paras. 28–9 (Greek law prohibited the installation and operation of electronic games on all premises apart from casinos. Even though Greek law did not prohibit the import of the equipment, merely the prohibition of installation, the measure constituted an MEE, because the importation of games machines stopped when the prohibition came into effect).

[97] Case C–244/06 *Dynamic Medien* [2008] ECR I–505. See also Case C–416/00 *Tommaso Morellato* v. *Comune di Padova* [2003] ECR I–9343; Joined Cases C–158/04 and C–159/04 *Alfa Vita* [2006] ECR I–8135; and Case C–82/05 *Commission* v. *Greece (Bake Off Products)* [2006] ECR I–93* where anyone wishing to sell bread had to run a fully equipped bakery even where the bread was delivered half-cooked. Because the rules related to 'production conditions', not product requirements or CSAs, Art. 34 applied.          [98] Para. 49.

[99] Para. 33.          [100] Paras. 34–5.

[101] Case C–368/95 *Familiapress* [1997] ECR I–3689. The reasoning in this case may now be different following the Unfair Commercial Practices Dir. 2005/29 considered below in section E. This issue has been raised directly in Case C–540/08 *Mediaprint Zeitungs- und Zeitschriftenverlag GmbH & Co KG* v. *"Österreich"-Zeitungsverlag GmbH*, case lodged 4 Dec. 2008.

[102] Para. 11. See also Case C–390/99 *Canal Satélite Digital SL* v. *Administración General del Estado* [2002] ECR I–607, para. 30, 'the need in certain cases to *adapt the products* in question to the rules in force in the Member State in which they are marketed' prevented the requirements from being treated as selling arrangements within the meaning of para. 16 of *Keck*.

It continued that the legislation required traders established in other Member States to 'alter the contents of the periodical'.[103] As a result, the case did not concern a selling arrangement but a product requirement.[104] Similarly, in *Schwarz*,[105] the Court said an Austrian rule requiring chewing gum sold in vending machines to be packaged, while the same goods sold in Germany could be marketed without packaging, constituted an MEE because German producers had to package their goods 'which makes their importation into [Austria] more expensive'.[106] In all three cases, the Court focused on the centre of gravity of the rule, namely to modify the product.[107] The national rule was therefore more akin to a product requirement to which *Cassis* applied, than a CSA to which *Keck* applied.

The meaning and scope of the phrase 'certain selling arrangement' was not the only problem thrown up by the *Keck* decision. *Keck* and its progeny also created uncertainty in respect of (1) discriminatory rules regulating sales; (2) rules preventing or (severely) restricting the *use* of goods; (3) rules preventing or (severely) restricting an *activity*; and (4) non-discriminatory selling arrangements preventing or restricting access to the market. We shall consider these situations in turn.

## D.  PROBLEM SITUATIONS

### 1.  DISCRIMINATORY CERTAIN SELLING ARRANGEMENTS

#### 1.1  The Nature of the Problem

In the cases immediately following *Keck* (e.g., *Hünermund* and *Leclerc-Siplec*), the Court failed to apply paragraph 16 of its own judgment in *Keck* properly. Rather, it unthinkingly equated a finding that a national measure constituted a certain selling arrangement with a ruling that there was no breach of Article 34. This unthinking approach, while perhaps understandable on the policy ground of the Court's desire to remove certain types of rules altogether from the scope of Article 34, was subject to much criticism. It is here that Mortelmans' distinction between 'fixed' and 'dynamic' rules (considered above in section B) becomes useful to help understand the nature of that criticism.

While the Court's approach in *Keck* was largely uncontroversial in respect of 'fixed' location situations, it was much criticized in respect of dynamic situations. In respect of *fixed* location situations—rules concerning the time and place in which goods are sold—there is little effect on inter-state trade because the rules apply to *retailers* rather than to the producers/importers of goods, i.e. the rules apply after the goods have gained access to the market in the host state.[108] For this reason, the Treaty provisions

---

[103]  Para. 12.

[104]  See also Joined Cases C–158/04 and C–159/04 *Alfa Vita Vassilopoulos AE* [2006] ECR I–8135, para. 19 considered above n. 97.

[105]  Case C–366/04 *Schwarz* v. *Bürgermeister der Landeshauptstadt Salzburg* [2006] ECR I–10139.

[106]  Para. 29.

[107]  Case C–416/00 *Morellato* [2003] ECR I–9343, para. 28: '[T]he Court has never held that where national provisions, whilst regulating certain aspects of the sale of products, also require the products to be modified, these provisions are concerned with selling arrangements within the meaning of *Keck and Mithouard*.'

[108]  Stix-Hackl AG in Case C–322/01 *DocMorris* [2003] ECR I–14887, para. 77.

on establishment (Article 49 TFEU) are more relevant than those on goods,[109] and the principle of subsidiarity suggests that such matters should be left to the Member States, unconstrained by Article 34. Commentators were therefore broadly content with the finding in cases such as *Boermans* and *Punto Casa* that there was no breach of Article 34. As Advocate General Tesauro put it in *Familiapress*:[110]

[T]he only measures excluded from the scope of Article [34] are those which are absolutely general in nature, which apply—needless to say—without distinction, which do not impede imports and which might lead to a (hypothetical) reduction in the volume of imports only as a consequence of an equally hypothetical reduction in the volume of sales.

However, as regards *dynamic* situations, controversy surrounded the automatic finding in *Hünermund, Leclerc-Siplec, Commission* v. *Greece, Banchero* and even *Keck* itself that Article 34 did not apply. This is because the rules at issue in these cases—such as national measures restricting the sales outlets for particular goods[111] and restricting advertising and other forms of sales promotion, including resale at a loss[112]—were more closely linked to the activities of the actual producer/importer. This is because, as the pre-*Keck* cases demonstrated (for example *Oosthoek, Buet, Aragonea*, and *LPO*, considered in section B), such rules do pose a particularly serious threat to market integration because they interfere with access to the market for new (usually imported) goods. The following example illustrates this point.

Water plc, a British company, wants to break on to the French market with its bottled mineral water, $H_2O$. Given that French consumers all buy the familiar French brands, Evian and Vittel, Water plc will need to run an effective marketing campaign to raise awareness of its product in France. Such a campaign might include advertising, selling the product at a loss for a while, or offering some other sales incentive, such as a free gift or a 2-for-1 offer. $H_2O$ might also consider selling its product in a different way, by, for example, marketing it through non-traditional retail outlets or in bulk over the Internet. If French law prohibits such strategies then, according to *Hünermund* and *Leclerc-Siplec*, French law does not breach Article 34 because it concerns certain selling arrangements.

However, a ban on these different types of sales techniques may in fact be discriminatory (same burden in law, different burden in fact) because it is the new, imported product ($H_2O$) which is particularly affected by any such prohibition. French consumers will continue buying the well-established French brands, Evian and Vittel, in ignorance of the existence of $H_2O$ on the market and in the absence of any incentive to try it. Although any new French products will suffer from a similar disadvantage,[113] the majority of products

---

[109] Tesauro AG recognized this in Case C–292/92 *Hünermund* [1993] ECR I–6787, para. 27, citing Case 20/87 *Gauchard* [1987] ECR 4879. See also Joined Cases C–418/93 etc. *Semeraro Casa Uno Srl and others* [1996] ECR I–2975, para. 32.

[110] Case C–368/95 [1997] ECR I–3698, para. 10.

[111] As Jacobs AG pointed out in Case C–412/93 *Leclerc-Siplec* [1995] ECR I–179, paras. 38–9, severely restricting sales outlets can substantially restrict the access to the market of goods from other Member States.

[112] Van Gerven AG had argued in his Opinion in *Keck* that the French prohibition of resale at a loss could, in some cases, impede imported products' access to the French market more than that of domestic products: para. 5.

[113] The Court has dismissed this argument in other contexts: Case C–319/91 *Ligur Carni* v. *Unità Sanitaria Locale* [1993] ECR I–6621, para. 37, where it said '[when] a national measure has limited territorial scope because it applies only to a part of the national territory, it cannot escape being categorized as

affected are likely to come from other Member States as barriers to inter-state trade are removed.[114]

The $H_2O$ example therefore suggests that not all rules concerning certain selling arrangements are non-discriminatory, as the Court assumed in *Hünermund* and the other early cases. They might at least be discriminatory in fact, as the $H_2O$ example shows[115] and so should breach Article 34 unless justified by Article 36 or one of the mandatory requirements. If the Court reached this conclusion it would bring the post-*Keck* case law back into line with its pre-*Keck* jurisprudence (*Oosthoek*, *Buet*, *Aragonesa*, and *LPO*). It could do this simply by applying the proviso in paragraph 16, instead of assuming, as it seems to have done in *Hünermund* and the other early cases, that once it had classified the measure as a certain selling arrangement, the proviso in paragraph 16 of *Keck* was automatically satisfied, leading to a finding of no breach of Article 34.

Some of the Advocates General, in particular Advocate General Jacobs in *Leclerc-Siplec* and Advocate General Lenz in *Commission* v. *Greece*, urged the Court to look at the effect of dynamic national rules on imported products to see whether they were discriminatory in fact. At first the Court was reluctant, but in *De Agostini*[116] it changed its mind.

### 1.2 *De Agostini* and Beyond

#### (a) Discriminatory measures which prevent market access

In *De Agostini* the Court had an opportunity to revisit its decision in *Leclerc-Siplec*, this time in respect of a prohibition on advertising which *prevented* access to the foreign market (as opposed to merely impeding access as in *Leclerc-Siplec*). The case concerned a Swedish ban on television advertising directed at children under 12 and a ban on misleading commercials for skin-care products and detergents. The Swedish consumer ombudsman brought proceedings against two traders for (1) advertising a magazine, *Everything You Need to Know about Dinosaurs*, targeted at children under 12 and (2) marketing a soap, Body De Lite, in breach of the rules on misleading adverts. Like *Leclerc-Siplec* the Court recognized that these restrictions constituted certain selling arrangements; unlike *Leclerc-Siplec*, the Court specifically addressed the proviso in paragraph 16 of *Keck*. It said that while the first condition of the paragraph 16 proviso (the measure applied to all traders operating within the national territory) was clearly fulfilled, the second condition (the measure affected all traders in the same manner in law and in fact) might not be. It said that an outright ban on a type of promotion for a product which is lawfully sold there

---

discriminatory or protective for the purposes of the rules on the free movement of goods on the ground that it affects both the sale of products from other parts of the national territory and the sale of products imported from other Member States'. See also Joined Cases C–1 and 176/90 *Aragonesa de Publicidad and Publivía* [1991] ECR I–4151, para. 24.

[114] See Joined Cases C–34-36/95 *Konsumentombudsmannen (KO)* v. *De Agostini (Svenska) Förlag AB and others* [1997] ECR I–3843, para. 42. As Lenz AG put it in Case C–391/92 *Commission* v. *Greece (infant milk)* [1995] ECR I–1621, dynamic rules make product marketing more onerous and expensive for importers because 'the development of new manners of marketing may in these circumstances prove more difficult for foreign manufacturers than for domestic ones, who are familiar with conditions on the home market'. See now the effect of the Unfair Commercial Practices (UCP) Dir. 2005/29 ([2005] OJ L149/22) on such marketing practices.

[115] A point confirmed by the first limb of para. 17 in *Keck*.

[116] Joined Cases C–34–36/95 *De Agostini (Svenska) Förlag AB* [1997] ECR I–3843, noted by J. Stuyck (1997) 34 *CMLRev.* 1445, 1465.

might have 'a greater impact on products from other Member States'.[117] It continued that, while the efficacy of various types of promotion was a question of fact to be determined by the national court, 'in its observations De Agostini stated that television advertising was *the only effective form* of promotion enabling it to penetrate the Swedish market since it had no other advertising methods for reaching children and their parents'.[118]

These paragraphs contain a strong hint that the Court thought that the Swedish measure had the same burden in law but a different burden in fact, a point reinforced by its reference to the fact that television advertising was the only effective form of sales promotion available to De Agostini. The Court concluded that if an unequal burden in law or fact was found, then the national restriction would be caught by Article 34 as an MEE[119] and the burden would shift to the Member State to justify it under one of the mandatory requirements[120] or by an Article 36 derogation (see fig. 5.2).[121]

The decision in *De Agostini* is the outcome the Advocates General had predicted and sits more comfortably with the pre-*Keck* case law.[122] However, where *De Agostini* differs from the pre-*Keck* case law is that in *De Agostini* the Court took *Keck* as a starting point and decided that the measure constituted a certain selling arrangement. The measure therefore did not breach Article 34 *unless*, as the Court indicated in *De Agostini*, it was shown that the ban did not affect in the same manner—in fact or in law—the marketing of national products and products from other Member States.[123] In this situation there would be a breach of Article 34 which could be justified.

## (b) Discriminatory measures which impede market access

*Heimdienst*[124] extended the ruling in *De Agostini* to any discriminatory selling arrangement which, while not actually *preventing* market access as in *De Agostini* itself, did nevertheless *hinder or impede* that access.[125] *Heimdienst* concerned an Austrian rule

---

[117] Para. 42.

[118] Para. 43, emphasis added. Cf. Case C–412/93 *Leclerc-Siplec* [1995] ECR I–179, para. 19, where the Court noted that the French law which prohibited televised advertising in the distribution sector did not prevent distributors from using other forms of advertising.

[119] Case C–322/01 *DocMorris* [2003] ECR I–14887, para. 68.

[120] Para. 45, although compare the apparently contradictory wording in para. 47. See also Case C–376/98 *Germany* v. *Parliament and Council (Tobacco Advertising)* [2001] ECR I–8419, para. 113: 'By imposing a wide-ranging prohibition on the advertising of tobacco products, the Directive would in the future generalise that restriction of forms of competition by limiting, in all the Member States, the means available for economic operators to enter or remain in the market.'          [121] Para. 45.

[122] See the post-*Keck* case, Case C–239/02 *Douwe Egberts* [2004] ECR I–7007, para. 52 concerning a national law prohibiting references to 'slimming' in adverts. In reaching the conclusion that the law breached Art. 34 the Court cited one of the pre-*Keck* advertising cases, C–241/89 *SARPP* [1990] ECR I–4695.

[123] See now the effect of the UCP Dir. 2005/29 considered in section E below. *A fortiori*, if the measure has a different burden in law as well as in fact then there will also be a breach of Art. 34: Case C–320/93 *Ortscheit* v. *Eurim-Pharm Arzneimittel* [1994] ECR I–5243, para. 9 which concerned a distinctly applicable measure which fell within the scope of Art. 34 (citing *Keck*, para. 16).

[124] Case C–254/98 [2000] ECR I–151, considered by P. Koutrakos in 'On groceries, alcohol and olive oil: More on free movement of goods after *Keck*' (2001) 26 *ELRev*. 391. For an earlier example of a pre-*Keck* case with similar facts, see Joined Cases 87 and 88/85 *Société coopérative des laboratoires de pharmacie Legia and Lousi Gyselinx* v. *Minister for Health* [1986] ECR 1707.

[125] See also Case C–141/07 *Commission* v. *Germany (pharmacies for hospitals)* [2008] ECR I–6935, paras. 35 and 37 where German law required external pharmacies wishing to supply medicinal products to a hospital to have a 'degree of geographical proximity between the pharmacy...and the hospital for which those products are intended'. These rules constituted a discriminatory certain selling arrangement (paras. 31 and 35) and so breached Art. 34 (para. 43).

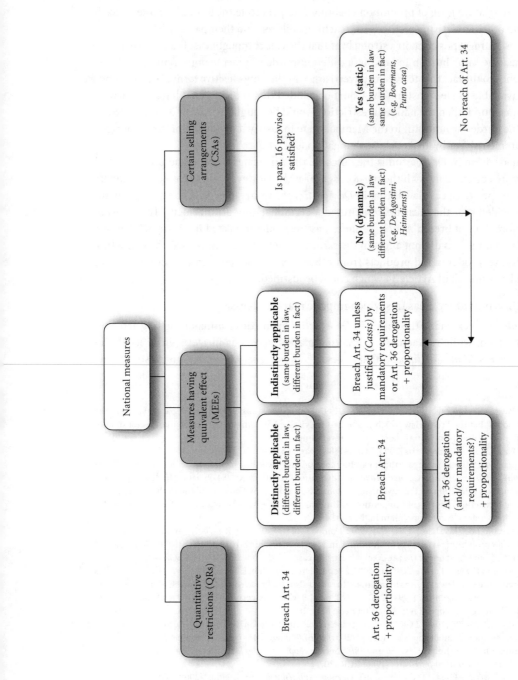

**Fig. 5.2** QRs, MEEs, and discriminatory CSAs before *Commission v. Italy* (*trailers*)

permitting bakers, butchers, and grocers to sell their produce door-to-door using a delivery van, but only if they also traded from a shop in that, or an adjacent, area.[126] Having classified the measure as a selling arrangement because 'it lays down the geographical areas in which each of the operators concerned may sell his goods by that method',[127] the Court then considered the *Keck* paragraph 16 proviso. It found that the legislation did not 'affect in the same manner the marketing of domestic products and that of products from other Member States'.[128] This was because the legislation obliged traders with a shop in another Member State to establish a shop in the locality (with the additional costs this entailed) before they could sell their goods door-to-door. Since traders established in other Member States suffered a disadvantage in comparison with local economic operators who already met the requirement of having a shop in the area, the Austrian rule breached Article 34 and needed to be justified. On the facts, the Court found the requirement to be disproportionate.[129]

*Heimdienst* influenced the Court's important decision in *DocMorris*.[130] DocMorris had a pharmacy in the Netherlands and also offered medicines for sale over the Internet. Both activities were licensed in the Netherlands. In Germany medicinal products could be sold but only in pharmacists' shops; sales by mail order were prohibited. The German pharmacists' association therefore tried to prevent DocMorris selling medicines to German consumers over the Internet. In paragraph 74 the Court found that the prohibition of Internet sales was 'more of an obstacle to the pharmacies outside Germany than to those within it'. While German pharmacies also could not sell their products over the Internet, for them this was an 'extra or alternative method' of gaining access to the German market: they could still sell their products in their dispensaries. However, for pharmacies not established in Germany, the Court noted that 'the internet provides a more significant way to gain direct access to the German market'. It concluded that '[a] prohibition which has a greater impact on pharmacies established outside German territory could impede access to the market for products from other Member States more than it impedes access for domestic products'. Because the prohibition did not affect the sale of domestic medicines in the same way as it affected the sale of those coming from other Member States, the German rule breached Article 34. While the breach could not be justified on public-health grounds in respect of non-prescription medicines,[131] it could be justified in respect of prescription medicines.

*DocMorris* is an important ruling from a practical and legal perspective. Viewed practically, it is a particularly significant decision for opening up the single market. New market entrants, however small, can now gain a foothold on markets in other states, via the Internet, without having to incur the significant costs of setting up their own distribution and retail networks in the host state.

From a legal perspective, the striking feature of the case is that, while couched in the language of discrimination, in fact the need to secure market access pervades the

---

[126] Although note the unusual feature of the case in that the dispute concerned two Austrian traders.
[127] Para. 24.     [128] Para. 25.     [129] See further Ch. 6.
[130] Case C–322/01 *DocMorris* [2003] ECR I–14887.
[131] See also Case C–497/03 *Commission* v. *Austria*, judgment of 28 Oct. 2004, not reported: ban on mail order sale of food supplements breached Art. 34, with the Court citing *DocMorris* to support this finding.

judgment,[132] as paragraph 74 (drawing on paragraph 17, rather than paragraph 16, of *Keck*) makes clear.[133] The Court is therefore more likely to find discrimination and thus a breach of Article 34 where the measure prevents or significantly impedes market access (*De Agostini, DocMorris*)[134] than where the impediment to market access is slight (*Hünermund, Leclerc-Siplec*[135] and two cases considered below, *Karner* and *Burmanjer*).[136] This emphasis on market access is now reinforced by *Commission* v. *Italy (trailers)*.[137]

Finally, *LIBRO*[138] considered the situation where the national rule was a distinctly applicable certain selling arrangement. In that case Austrian law prohibited importers of German language books from fixing a price lower than the retail price fixed or recommended by the publisher in the state of publication (Germany). Because the rule provided for less favourable treatment for imported goods the paragraph 16 and 17 proviso was not satisfied and so the rule was an MEE contrary to Article 34.[139] On the facts, even though the rule was directly discriminatory, the Court said it could be justified not by Article 36, since none of the derogations applied, but by need to protect 'books as cultural objects', an overriding requirement in the public interest. However, the Court found that the rule was disproportionate.[140]

### 1.3 Presumptions and the Burden of Proof

The reasoning in *De Agostini, Heimdienst,* and *DocMorris* suggests that certain discriminatory selling arrangements breach Article 34 unless justified—in just the same way as indistinctly applicable MEEs (product requirements). This could be expected because both discriminatory selling arrangements and indistinctly applicable MEEs concern rules which have the same burden in law and a different burden in fact (see fig. 5.2). If this is the case, does it really matter then whether the Court classifies the measure as a product requirement or a certain selling arrangement? The answer is probably yes: there is a difference between the two approaches in respect of presumptions and the burden of proof.[141] If the measure is classified as a product requirement, it is presumed to impede market access (*Cassis*), no matter how small the impediment is or might be[142]—the *per se* illegal approach. If, on the other hand, the measure is classified as a certain selling

---

[132] Staetmans (2002) 39 *CMLRev.* 1407, 1418. See also the influence of Stix-Hackl AG's Opinion: 'The decisive factor should therefore be whether or not a national measure significantly impedes access to the market' (para. 78).      [133] See also Case C–405/98 *Gourmet* [2001] ECR I–1795, paras. 21 and 24.

[134] This is particularly so given that these cases, viewed from a services perspective, would involve a breach of Art. 56 TFEU due to the fact that the prohibition creates a hindrance to the provision of cross-border services (see, e.g., Case C–405/98 *Gourmet* [2001] ECR I–1795) considered below n. 146 and Ch. 12.

[135] See discussion in paras. 71–2 of *DocMorris*.

[136] Case C–71/02 *Karner* [2004] ECR I–3025; Case C–20/03 *Burmanjer* [2005] ECR I–4133, paras. 29 and 31.      [137] Case C–110/05 *Commission* v. *Italy* [2009] ECR I–519 considered below at n. 169, para. 50.

[138] Case C–531/07 *LIBRO* [2009] ECR I–000, para. 20.      [139] Paras. 20–2.      [140] Para. 35.

[141] See Van Gerven AG in Joined Cases C–401 and 402/92 *Boermans* [1994] ECR I–2199. See also Fennelly AG in Case C–190/98 *Graf* v. *Filzmozer Maschinenbau GmbH* [2000] ECR I–493, para. 19: 'It is legitimate for the Court to develop presumptions about the market effects of different broadly defined categories of rules, provided that, in concrete cases, the validity of the presumption may be tested against the underlying criterion of market access, rather than automatically being taken as being sufficient in itself to dispose of the case.'

[142] Joined Cases 177/82 and 178/82 *Van de Haahr* [1984] ECR 1797, more recently confirmed by the Grand Chamber in Case C–463/01 *Commission* v. *Germany (deposit and return)* [2004] ECR I–11705, para. 62. See also Case C–67/97 *Bluhme* [1998] ECR I–8033.

arrangement then the presumption is that it does not hinder access to the market and so does not breach Article 34—the *per se* legal approach.[143] In the case of a certain selling arrangement the trader will (usually[144]) need to work hard to rebut the presumption of legality, possibly by producing statistical or other evidence to prove disadvantage which is *actual*, rather than merely potential, and *substantial*.

## (a) Actual disadvantage

The Swedish case *Gourmet*[145] shows the efforts needed by the trader to demonstrate actual disparate impact. The case concerned a total ban on advertising alcohol on the radio, on television, and in magazines. Following *De Agostini* (which concerned only a partial ban on advertising), the Court assumed that this measure was a certain selling arrangement. The question in *Gourmet* was whether the measure was discriminatory. The Swedish government had argued that since there had been a constant increase in sales of, for example, wines (overwhelmingly imported, principally from other Member States) the ban on advertising did not have a disparate impact on importers.

However, Advocate General Jacobs was more persuaded by Gourmet's statistics, indicating Swedish domination of the domestic market in strong beer, and its arguments that ingrained consumer habits would always tend to favour national beverages, so that, without advertising, products from other Member States were at a disadvantage; that daily press information on other (for example economic) topics would keep the names of national producers to the forefront of consumers' minds; and that the lack of any restriction on the advertising of light beer enabled Swedish brewers of such beer to promote their brand names (which were the same as for their strong beers) and thus gain an advantage over brewers of imported beer, who generally did not produce a light beer.[146]

The Court broadly followed its Advocate General,[147] concluding that:

> in the case of products like alcoholic beverages, the consumption of which is linked to traditional social practices and to local habits and customs, a prohibition of all advertising directed at consumers...is liable to impede access to the market by products from other Member States more than it impedes access by domestic products, with which consumers are instantly more familiar.[148]

The ban therefore breached Article 34 but could be justified on public-health grounds, subject to a decision by the national court on the proportionality of the measure. The Court also said that the ban, a 'non-discriminatory' restriction having a particular effect on the cross-border supply of advertising space, breached Article 56 TFEU (ex Article 49 EC) on the free movement of services—without feeling it necessary to apply its certain

---

[143] K. Armstrong, 'Regulating the free movement of goods' in J. Shaw and G. More (eds.), *Dynamics of European Integration* (Oxford: Clarendon Press, 1998), 482–3.

[144] Cf. Case C–322/01 *0800 DocMorris NV* [2003] ECR I–14887 where the Court glossed over all of these issues, although cf. para. 74: 'A prohibition which *has* a greater impact on pharmacies established outside German territory *could* impede access to the market for products from other Member States more than it impedes access for domestic products' (emphasis added). However, in Case C–441/04 *A-Punkt Schmuckhandels GmbH* v. *Schmidt* [2006] ECR I–2093, paras. 25–6 the Court again seems to require actual disparate impact.

[145] Case C–405/98 *Konsumentombudsmannen* v. *Gourmet International Products (GIP)* [2001] ECR I–1795.          [146] Para. 33.

[147] Paras. 21–4. See also Case E–4/04 *Pedicel* v. *Sosial- og helsdirektoratet* [2005] EFTA Court Reports 1.

[148] Para. 21. See also Case C–239/02 *Douwe Egberts* [2004] ECR I–7007, para. 53.

selling arrangement case law to free movement of services as well—but again could be justified on the grounds of public health.

### (b) Substantial disadvantage

In subsequent cases the Court has gone further and demanded not only that there be an *actual* disparate impact but that the disparate impact be *substantial* or at least not too remote. This can be seen in *Burmanjer*[149] where the Court said that even though insufficient information had been provided by the national court, the national rules prohibiting itinerant sales without a licence did not appear to affect the marketing of products from other Member States more than products from the host state, and even if those rules did have such effect, 'it would be too insignificant and uncertain to be regarded as being such as to hinder or otherwise interfere with trade between Member States'.[150]

   If no actual, substantial disparate impact is found then the national measure does not breach Article 34. This was the situation in *Karner*[151] concerning the Austrian rule prohibiting retailers from indicating to consumers that goods came from an insolvent estate when they no longer formed part of that estate. Once again, the Court applied the paragraph 16 proviso of *Keck*. Having found that the first limb was satisfied (the Austrian law applied without distinction to all the operators concerned who carried on their business on Austrian territory, regardless of whether they were Austrian nationals or foreigners),[152] it turned to the second limb. The Court noted that, unlike the national rules at issue in *De Agostini* and *Gourmet*, the Austrian law did not lay down a total prohibition on all forms of advertising in a Member State for a product which was lawfully sold there;[153] it merely prohibited any reference in the advert to the origins of the good. The Court concluded that although such a prohibition was likely to limit the total volume of sales:

[I]t nevertheless does not affect the marketing of products originating from other Member States more than it affects the marketing of products from the Member State in question. In any event, there is no evidence in the file forwarded to the Court by the national court to permit a finding that the prohibition *has had* such an effect.[154]

The Austrian law, being non-discriminatory, was therefore not caught by the prohibition in Article 34.[155]

### (c) Conclusions

While in these cases of discriminatory certain selling arrangements the Court does now appear to be applying broadly common principles, in fact the Court's approach still contains a number of inconsistencies. Take the advertising cases as an example. While it is clear that a total ban on all advertising of alcohol (*Gourmet*) and on television advertising where that deprives the trader of the only effective form of sales promotion which would have enabled it to penetrate a national market (*De Agostini*) breach Article 34, a limitation on where an advert can be placed (outside a pharmacists' shop

---

[149] Case C–20/03 [2005] ECR I–4133.          [150] Para. 31. This does not appear in the dispositif.
[151] Case C–71/02 *Karner* [2004] ECR I–3025.          [152] Para. 41.
[153] Case C–20/03 *Burmanjer* [2005] ECR I–4133, para. 29.          [154] Para. 42, emphasis added.
[155] Para. 43. What is less clear is why the Court, having established that the case fell outside the scope of Art. 34 and thus presumably the scope of Union law, nevertheless went on to consider the compatibility of the Austrian law with fundamental human rights (para. 52).

in *Hünermund*), who can advertise (a ban on the distribution sector from advertising on television—*Leclerc*) and what they can say (*Karner*[156]) does not. Is it so easy to draw such a clear line? When do limits on the wording become so extensive that in practice the advert is banned?

## 2. RULES PREVENTING OR (SEVERELY) RESTRICTING THE USE OF GOODS

Discriminatory certain selling arrangements were not the only area of difficulty. There were other problem areas too: non-discriminatory restrictions on *use* (such as a prohibition on driving cross-country vehicles off-road in a forest or speed limits on motorways[157]) posed particular challenges for the Court.[158] Advocate General Kokott in *Mickelsson*[159] and Advocate General Bot in *Commission* v *Italy (trailers)*[160] presented the Court of Justice with two starkly different alternatives as to how to tackle this situation.[161]

Advocate General Kokott favoured extending the *Keck* principle to restrictions on use[162] but with the caveat that if the national rule prevented or severely restricted access to the market Article 34 would nevertheless apply.[163] Advocate General Bot, on the other hand, proposed a narrow reading of *Keck,* a case he clearly did not like[164] but felt constrained by.[165] Adopting a strong integrationist perspective[166] and a deep-felt desire for convergence across the freedoms,[167] he urged the Court to apply a market access test: national legislation is likely to constitute an MEE if it 'hinders a product's access to the market, whatever the purpose of the measure'.[168]

His views appear to have won the day, at least for now. As we saw in Chapter 4, the Court said in *Commission* v *Italy (trailers)*[169] that a non-discriminatory rule prohibiting the use of a product (trailers for motorcycles) has a 'considerable influence on the behaviour of consumers, which, in turn, affects the access of that product to the market of that state'.[170] It therefore constituted an MEE and so contravened Article 34, unless

---

[156]  Although cf. Case C–239/02 *Douwe Egberts* [2004] ECR I–7007, paras. 49 and 54 and Case C–470/93 *Mars* [1995] ECR I–1293 considered in Ch. 4.

[157]  Case C–142/05 *Åklagaren* v. *Mickelsson* [2009] ECR I–000, Kokott AG's Opinion para. 45.

[158]  Cf. the earlier case, Case C–473/98 *Kemikalieinspketionen* v. *Toolex Alpha AB* [2000] ECR I–5681, para. 35 where the Court said that the ban on the industrial *use* of trichloroethylene, a substance with a known carcinogenic effect, constituted an MEE. The Court made no reference to the *Keck* line of case law.

[159]  Case C–142/05 *Åklagaren* v. *Mickelsson* [2009] ECR I–000.

[160]  Case C–110/05 *Commission* v. *Italy (trailers)* [2009] ECR I–519.

[161]  For a more detailed discussion, see T. Horsley, 'Anyone for *Keck*?' (2009) 46 *CMLRev.* 2001.

[162]  Paras. 55–6.          [163]  Paras. 66–7.

[164]  He thinks that a distinction between different categories of measures is not appropriate (para. 79); that the demarcation line is artificial and may be uncertain (para. 81); and that it has led to a differentiation between the goods regime and that for the other freedoms (para. 82).

[165]  Para. 85. See also Poiares Maduro AG in C–158/04 *Alfa Vita* [2006] ECR I–8135, paras. 31–5.

[166]  Para. 91.

[167]  Para. 118. He also said that the access to the market test should not involve an appraisal of complex economic data (para. 116)

[168]  Para. 136. Léger AG, who gave the first opinion in the case (5 Oct. 2006) assumed the rule was an MEE (para. 41) without any analysis. See also Case C–65/05 *Commission* v. *Greece (computer games)* [2006] ECR I–10341, paras. 41–2.          [169]  Case C–110/05 *Commission* v. *Italy (trailers)* [2009] ECR I–519.

[170]  Para. 56.

justified.[171] And in reaching this conclusion the Court appears to have adopted a new category of measure (see fig. 4.3) which is neither a product requirement nor a certain selling arrangement: measures which hinder 'access of products originating in other Member States to the market of a Member State'.[172] As the facts of the *Trailers* case demonstrates, this new category certainly covers bans on use and so the Italian rule breached Article 34 but could be justified on grounds of road safety. The Court relied extensively on this ruling in the follow-up case, *Mickelsson*,[173] concerning a restriction on the use of personal watercraft. Once again, the Court found the rule to be an MEE but one which could be justified on health and environmental grounds.

*Commission* v. *Italy (trailers)* and *Mickelsson* (probably) do not reverse *Keck*[174] but suggest a narrow reading of the decision—that it should be confined to situations which concern arrangements for sale (*modalités de vente*) and should not be extended any further. Other types of measures will therefore not benefit from the *Keck* presumption of legality, are likely to be considered rules hindering market access and so will breach Article 34, leaving Member States to justify their existence. If this analysis is correct then it means that the Court has now indirectly offered its solution to the next problem area: a ban on an activity.

## 3. RULES PREVENTING OR (SEVERELY) RESTRICTING AN ACTIVITY

In *R (on the application of the Countryside Alliance)* v. *Her Majesty's Attorney General*[175] the British House of Lords (now Supreme Court) had to consider whether a ban on an activity, namely hunting wild mammals with dogs, introduced in the controversial Hunting Act 2004, breached Article 34. The Countryside Alliance argued that the Act had an indirect effect on the movement of goods (by significantly reducing the trade in horses and hounds coming from Ireland). Lord Bingham expressed his bewilderment as to how to apply Article 34 to the case. He recognized that the ban could not be characterized as a selling arrangement but, he said, 'I have difficulty in recognising it as a trading rule or a product rule either'. He supported the view of the Divisional Court and the Court of Appeal that the 2004 Act did not engage Article 34 but 'I find it hard to say, on the present state of the [Court of Justice] authorities... that this conclusion is clear beyond the bounds of reasonable argument.'

Following *Commission* v. *Italy (trailers)*, it could be argued by the opponents of the Hunting Act that a non-discriminatory ban on an activity has a considerable influence on the behaviour of consumers (purchasers of horses and hounds), which, in turn, affects the access of those 'products' to the market in the UK. On the other hand, the facts of the *Countryside Alliance* case reveal the problems of (re)introducing the market access test to Article 34: does the British law really affect market access? And if it does, it means the UK government must justify its legislation (presumably on the grounds of animal welfare, although this in itself is a contested assertion) and must show that its legislation is proportionate (as we shall see in the next chapter, bans are often not deemed to be proportionate).

---

[171] Para. 58. The same approach would presumably be applied to restrictions on *possession*.
[172] Para. 37.　　　[173] Case C–142/05 *Aklagaren* v *Mickelsson, Roos* [2009] ECR I–000.
[174] See Case C–531/07 *LIBRO* [2009] ECR I–000, para. 20 a case decided after *Commission* v. *Italy (trailers)* but where the Court classified the rule as a certain selling arrangement.
[175] In *R (on the application of the Countryside Alliance)* v. *Her Majesty's Attorney General* [2007] UKHL 52.

If, on the other hand, the Court had decided to extend its approach in *Keck* these problems would be avoided since the UK law would have been presumptively lawful.

## 4. NON-DISCRIMINATORY SELLING ARRANGEMENTS PREVENTING OR RESTRICTING ACCESS TO THE MARKET

### 4.1 Non-Discriminatory Selling Arrangements Preventing Access to the Market

*Commission* v. *Italy (trailers)* also appears to have provided the answer to another problem thrown up by *Keck*, namely certain selling arrangements which are genuinely *non-discriminatory* (same burden in law and in fact) but do *prevent* access by the imported goods to the market.[176] Examples include a total ban on the sale of a particular product such as cigarettes, pornography, alcohol, guns, or drugs.[177] According to the first limb of paragraph 17 in *Keck*, non-discriminatory selling arrangements do not breach Article 34 because they do not prevent access to the market. Yet, it is clear that a ban on the sale of a product does have serious implications for inter-state trade.[178] Following *Commission* v. *Italy*, it would seem that the Court could now tackle this situation in one of two ways. First it could say that the ban on the sale of a product falls under the third limb of the definition of an MEE, i.e. 'Any other measure which hinders access of products originating in other Member States to the market of a Member State is also covered by that concept.' The rule therefore breaches Article 34 and needs to be justified. The other possibility is that the rule is classified as a certain selling arrangement and, even though non-discriminatory, is subject to a market access test following *Commission* v. *Italy*.[179] If this latter analysis is correct then *Commission* v. *Italy* has modified (corrected?) the first limb of paragraph 17 in *Keck* to include a market access test (see fig 5.3). If market access is prevented or hindered then the rule breaches Article 34 and needs to be justified.

The more general introduction of a market access test has long been supported by Advocate General Jacobs. In *Leclerc–Siplec* he argued that all undertakings which engage in a legitimate economic activity in a Member State should have unfettered access to the whole of the Union market, unless there is a valid reason why not. His favoured test for determining whether non-discriminatory measures breach Article 34 is to ask whether

---

[176] Although *quaere* whether it can be argued there is a ban on market access when there is no market to access due to the national ban on the existence of that market. Cf. *Commission* v. *Italy (trailers)*, para. 57 where the Court said that the Italian rule 'prevents a demand from existing in the market at issue for such trailers and therefore hinders their importation'.

[177] There is an argument that bans on sales cannot be considered a 'selling arrangement'. However, para. 16 of *Keck* does talk of 'prohibitions or restrictions' on selling arrangements and it therefore appears to envisage a 'ban' situation. See also, by analogy, Case C–210/03 *R v Secretary of State for Health, ex p. Swedish Match* [2004] ECR I–11893; Case C–434/02 *Arnold André GmbH & Co KG v. Landrat des Kreises Herford* [2004] ECR I–11825 where the Court accepted that a measure banning the marketing of tobacco could be adopted under Art. 114 TFEU.

[178] See, by analogy, the services decision Case C–275/92 *Schindler* [1994] ECR I–1039. Some suggest that applying *Schindler* is unnecessary because the matter could be resolved by relying on Case 34/79 *R.* v. *Henn and Darby* [1972] ECR 3795, paras. 12–13 where the Court ruled that a ban on *imports* constituted a quantitative restriction (QR).

[179] A. Rosas, '*Dassonville* and *Cassis de Dijon*' in M. Poiares Maduro and L. Azoulai (eds.), above n. 65.

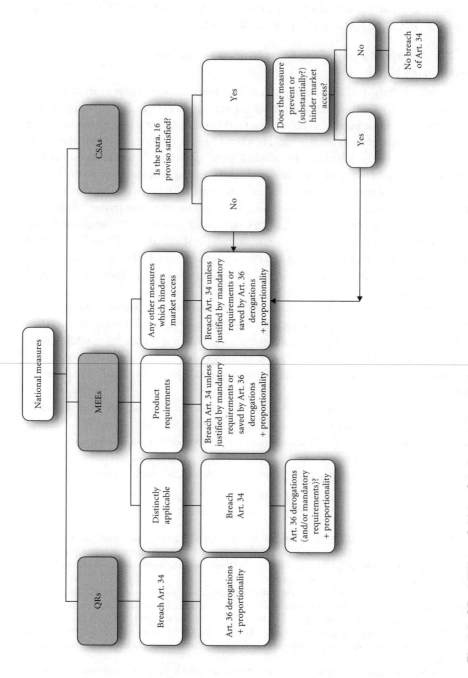

**Fig. 5.3** QRs, MEEs, and CSAs after *Commission v Italy*

the measure is liable 'substantially to restrict access to the market'?[180] He said that where a measure prohibits the sale of goods lawfully placed on the market in another Member State (as in *Cassis*), it is presumed to have a substantial impact on access to the market, since the goods are either denied access altogether or can gain access only after being modified in some way; the need to modify goods is itself a substantial barrier to market access.[181] On the other hand, he said, where a measure restricts certain selling arrangements, its impact will depend on whether it applies to some or all goods, the extent to which other selling arrangements remain available, and on whether the effect of the measure is 'direct or indirect, immediate or remote, or purely speculative and uncertain'. He continued that because the magnitude of the barrier to market access may vary enormously—from the insignificant to a quasi-prohibition—'a *de minimis* test could perform a useful function'.[182]

### 4.2 Non-Discriminatory Selling Arrangements Restricting Access to the Market

Advocate General Jacobs' suggestion of the need for some sort of threshold requirement might have been picked up by the Court in *Commission* v. *Italy* when it referred to the fact that a prohibition on the use of a product has a '*considerable* influence on the behaviour of consumers, which, in its turn, affects the access of that product to the market of that Member State'. A threshold requirement would also help to address another problem area, namely non-discriminatory measures which merely hinder or make less attractive free movement of goods. This was the *Punto Casa/Boermans* situation. Rules prohibiting Sunday trading (*Punto Casa*) or restricting the opening hours of shops (*Boermans*) do hinder access to the market for imported (as well as domestic) goods. However, according to the second limb of paragraph 17 such rules do not breach Article 34 because access by foreign goods to the market is not impeded more than access of domestic products (i.e., there is no discrimination). As we have already seen, the Court's approach to these static rules is largely uncontroversial because they have so little effect on access to the market. However, if we were to take a more extreme version of the rule, the conclusions might be different. For example, if a national law required shops to be closed six days a week (e.g., Sunday to Friday) instead of just one day (Sunday), then instinctively it seems that because such a rule—albeit non-discriminatory—substantially impedes access to the market it should breach Article 34 (see fig. 5.3).

*Commission* v. *Italy (trailers)* supports this view, as does the free movement of services case, *Alpine Investments*,[183] concerning a ban on cold-calling in the financial services industry. The Court, having noted that the measure was non-discriminatory, said that *Keck* did not apply because the national measure 'directly affects access to the markets in services in the other Member States and is thus capable of hindering intra-[Union] trade in services'.[184] The ban on cold-calling therefore breached Article 56 TFEU but could be

---

[180] Paras. 41 and 49. For academic support, see Weatherill, above n. 66, 900; C. Barnard, 'Fitting the remaining pieces into the goods and services jigsaw?' (2001) 26 *ELRev.* 35. See also Mortelmans' discussion (above n. 4, 128) of Van Gerven AG's implicit introduction of a *de minimis* rule in *Torfaen*. Cf. L. Gormley, 'Two years after *Keck*' [1996] *Fordham International Law Journal* 866, 882–3.          [181] Para. 44.

[182] Para. 45. See also Jacobs AG's Opinion in Case C–112/00 *Schmidberger* [2003] ECR I–5659. Cf. Weatherill, who objects to the term '*de minimis*' because it requires numerical quantification above n. 66, 900).          [183] Case C–384/93 [1995] ECR I–1141. See also Case C–275/92 *Schindler* [1994] ECR I–1039.

[184] Para. 38. Robert Walker LJ in *R. (on the application of Professional Contractors Group Ltd)* v. *Inland Revenue Commissioners* [2001] EWCA Civ 1945; [2002] 1 CMLR 46, para. 69 talked of 'indirect or debateable'

justified. Extending this case law to goods, as Advocate General Jacobs suggests, would mean that non-discriminatory national measures which are liable to prohibit or otherwise (substantially) impede the free movement of goods should breach Article 34 unless justified.[185] By contrast, if the measure does not substantially impede market access, or using the tortious language employed in the goods case *Krantz*[186] and the workers case, *Graf*,[187] if the effect of the national rule on free movement is 'too uncertain and indirect', the Treaties will not be breached.

A test based on 'substantial' hindrance of market access has been subject to three criticisms: first, that it is a statistical test which the courts are ill-equipped to apply;[188] secondly, that it effectively reverses the well-established rule that the *de minimis* principle does not apply to Article 34;[189] and thirdly, that the language of market access itself is far from clear: does it merely refer to barriers to market entry which make it more costly for new firms to enter an industry or does it refer to any regulation which imposes and implies compliance costs.[190] It is for these reasons that some prefer a more legal test based on causation and remoteness. For example, Advocate General La Pergola said in *BASF*[191] that the aim of Article 34 is to verify whether a causal link exists between the national measure and the pattern of imports. The language used in *Krantz* and *Graf*, examining whether the effect on trade is 'too indirect and uncertain', supports the remoteness test. However, Weatherill has argued that the remoteness test could equally be recast as an application of the notion that internal market law does not affect measures that cause no direct or substantial hindrance of access to the market of a Member State.[192]

The Court has not addressed this issue directly, and in practice its approach seems to be rather intuitive. It does not engage in any sophisticated economic analysis of (substantial) hindrance of market access (see, for example, in *DocMorris*) or any detailed legal analysis of remoteness (see, for example, *Krantz*). If it senses that some rules have little to do with market integration then it finds that they do not breach the Treaties (e.g., *Punto Casa*, *Boermans*, and *Graf*). If, on the other hand, it considers that other rules do prevent or substantially hinder access to the market it will find that they do breach the Treaties and need to be justified (*Trailers*, *Alpine Investments*). In the interests of clarity and consistency terminology based on 'substantial' hindrance of market access will be used throughout this book. It is supported by Advocate General Jacobs' Opinion in *Leclerc–Siplec* and it probably provides the best fit with the case law on persons, services, and capital. However, it will always be used subject to the caveats outlined here.

---

(para. 69) and 'direct and demonstrable' (para. 74). Cf. See also H. Toner, 'Non-discriminatory obstacles to the exercise of Treaty rights: Articles 39, 43, 49, and 18 EC' (2004) 23 *YEL* 275, 285–6 who argues that there are two possible thresholds: direct *or* significant. If the obstacle is direct then its effect needs only be perceptible; if the measure is significant or substantial then the obstacle does not need to be direct.

[185] The language is drawn from Case C–76/90 *Säger* v. *Dennemayer* [1991] ECR I–4221, para. 12.

[186] Cf. Spaventa's arguments that the Court uses the 'too indirect and uncertain' test only where the rule at issue is not a trading rule. She says that that provided they are not discriminatory, non-trading rules do not affect intra-Union trade unless a precise link of causation can be established: E. Spaventa, 'The outer limit of the Treaty free movement provisions: Some reflections on the significance of *Keck*, remoteness and *Deliège*' in C. Barnard and O. Odudu (eds.), *The Outer Limits of European Union Law* (Oxford: Hart Publishing, 2009), 263.         [187] Case C–190/98 *Graf* [2000] ECR I–493, paras. 24–5.

[188] See, e.g., V. Hatzopoulos, 'Recent developments of the case law of the ECJ in the field of services' (2000) 37 *CMLRev.* 43.         [189] Joined Cases 177 and 178/82 *van de Haar* [1984] ECR I–1797.

[190] See further Ch.1         [191] Case C–44/98 *BASF* [1999] ECR I–6269, para. 18.

[192] Above n. 66, 900. See also D. Doukas, 'Untying the market access knot: Advertising restrictions and the free movement of goods and services' (2006–7) 9 *CYELS* 177 who also sees convergence in the two tests (pp. 207–15).

# E. UNFAIR COMMERCIAL PRACTICES DIRECTIVE 2005/29

As we have seen, the interpretation of Article 34 TFEU given by the Court in *Trailers* has significantly reduced the areas of national law which benefit from the *Keck* presumption of legality. A further erosion to the *Keck* principle comes from a different quarter: the Unfair (business-to-consumer) Commercial Practices Directive 2005/29 (UCPD).[193] This directive marks a new stage in the evolution of consumer legislation because it adopts a maximum, not minimum, approach to harmonization.[194] The starting point of the directive is that commercial practices by traders are lawful. Therefore, any attempts by Member States to prohibit them contravene the directive. This was recognized by Advocate General Trstenjak in *VTB*:[195]

the Directive presupposes that commercial practices are fair as long as the precisely defined legal conditions for a prohibition are not fulfilled. It thus follows an...approach, in favour of the trader's entrepreneurial freedom, which accords essentially with the legal concept of '*in dubio pro libertate*'.

Article 2(d) UCPD defines unfair commercial practices broadly:[196]

'business-to-consumer commercial practices' (hereinafter also referred to as commercial practices) means any act, omission, course of conduct or representation, commercial communication *including advertising and marketing*, by a trader, directly connected with the *promotion, sale* or supply of a product to consumers.

As the italicized phrases show, this definition overlaps with 'certain selling arrangements' as defined in the *Keck* case law.

The directive prohibits unfair commercial practices.[197] It sets out the rules as to when the commercial practices are unfair. These fall into three categories:

1. an exhaustive list of 31 specific commercial practices, contained in the annex to the directive, (Article 5(5))

2. commercial practices which are misleading (by action or omission)[198] or aggressive[199] (Article 5(4))

3. commercial practices which contravene the requirements of professional diligence and materially distort (or are likely to materially distort) the economic behaviour of the average consumer[200] (Article 5(2)).

Categories 2 and 3 are principles-based: they apply only if the effect of the trader's practice is likely to alter consumers' decisions in relation to trading practices; in other words, they always take account of the impact on the consumer and hence this impact needs to

---

[193] OJ [2005] L149/22.

[194] Although the 1985 product liability Directive 85/374/EEC [1985] O.J. L210/29 also claimed to pursue total/maximum harmonization: for discussion, see H. Unberath and A. Johnston, 'The double-headed approach of the ECJ concerning consumer protection' (2007) 44 *CMLRev.* 1237, 1269ff.     [195] Para. 81.

[196] Art. 2(d), emphasis added.     [197] Art. 5(1).     [198] Arts. 6–7.     [199] Arts. 8–9.

[200] See S. Weatherill, 'Who is the "average consumer"?' in S. Weatherill and U. Bernitz, *The Regulation of Unfair Commercial Practices under EC Directive 2005/29* (Oxford: Hart Publishing, 2007). However, Art. 5(3) says 'Commercial practices which are likely to materially distort the economic behaviour only of a clearly identifiable group of consumers who are particularly vulnerable to the practice or the underlying product because of their mental or physical infirmity, age or credulity in a way which the trader could reasonably be expected to foresee, shall be assessed from the perspective of the average member of that group.'

be assessed on a case-by-case basis.[201] By contrast the first type of commercial practice caught by the prohibition is not principles-based (ie no case-by-case assessment is necessary) and is always unfair.

When assessing a national law banning a particular commercial practice (assuming that it falls within the scope of the directive[202]), the Court will first consider whether the commercial practice falls within one of the situations listed in the annex (category (1)). If so, the national law is compatible with the directive; the national prohibition does not depend on a further examination of, for example, its effects. If the annex does not apply, the Court will then examine whether the national authority has considered whether the commercial practice is misleading or aggressive within the meaning of Articles 6–9 (category (2)). If the practice is not misleading or aggressive, the Court will finally check whether the national authority has considered whether the commercial practice contravenes the requirements of professional diligence and whether it materially distorts the economic behaviour of the average consumer (category (3)). Category 3 therefore acts as a safety net for practices which do not come under the categories (1) and (2) and so is referred to as a general or residual clause.[203] If none of these three categories is satisfied, the national law contravenes the UCPD.

In other words, because the UCPD is a maximum harmonization measure,[204] only in the three categories of situation outlined above can a commercial practice be prohibited.[205] Member States cannot go further and ban other practices, as they could under most of the earlier consumer protection directives which were minimum harmonization measures. However, Article 3(5) UCPD does give Member States six years from June 2007 (and possibly longer[206]) to continue to apply (pre-existing) national provisions within the field approximated by the directive which are more restrictive or prescriptive than the UCPD, provided those national rules (1) implement directives containing minimum harmonization clauses, (2) are essential to ensure that consumers are adequately protected against unfair commercial practices, and (3) are proportionate.[207]

So what are the implications of this directive for the *Keck* case law?[208] As we have seen, under *Keck*, national legislation restricting or prohibiting certain selling arrangements, for example advertising or other sales promotion techniques such as free gifts, is presumptively *lawful* under EU law. In areas falling outside the scope of the UCPD, such as 'national rules relating to the health and safety aspects of products',[209] Article 34 TFEU

---

[201] Recital 17 says that the list in Annex I are 'the only commercial practices which can be deemed to be unfair without a case-by-case assessment against the provisions of Articles 5 to 9'.

[202] See Art. 3 considered below at n. 209.

[203] See also Trstenjak AG's Opinion in Joined Cases C–261/07 and C–299/07 *VTB-VAB NV* v. *Total Belgium NV* [2009] ECR I–000, para. 79.

[204] Art. 4 and 5th Recital UCPD, confirmed in Joined Cases C–261/07 and C–299/07 *VTB-VAB NV* [2009] ECR I–000, para. 52. This issue is raised again in Case C–540/08 *Mediaprint*, case lodged 4 Dec. 2008.          [205] Art. 5(1) 'Unfair commercial practices shall be prohibited.'

[206] This six-year period is subject to review (Art. 18). Art. 3(6) requires Member States to notify the Commission of any national provisions applied on the basis of Art. 3(5).

[207] Where Member States have taken advantage of Art. 3(5), then national rules which go beyond the directive remain subject to Art. 34, as interpreted in *Keck*.

[208] See further G. Anagnostaras, 'The Unfair Commercial Practices Directive in context: From legal disparity to legal complexity?' (2010) 47 *CMLRev.* 147, 152–161.

[209] Art. 3(3). See also Art. 3(9) on financial services and Art. 3(10) on the certification and indication of the standard of fineness of articles of precious metals. Recital 9 appears to go further: 'It is also without prejudice to [Union] and national rules on contract law, on intellectual property rights, on the health and

as interpreted by *Keck*, will continue to apply, including the presumption of legality of the national measure. However, for matters falling within the scope of the UCPD and not covered by the annex,[210] national laws drafted in general terms restricting or prohibiting commercial practices, including advertising and marketing, are presumptively *unlawful* unless, following a case-by-case assessment under Articles 5–9, the practice is unfair.[211]

The effect of the directive is therefore essentially to restore the pre-*Keck* position, as laid down in cases such as *Oosthoek, Buet* and *Aragonesa,* to national rules on commercial practices which fall within the scope of the directive. However, it is likely that now, following the UCPD, the litigation will focus not on Article 34 TFEU but on the directive. So if action is brought by the state against a trader for breaching a (national) rule prohibiting the use of promotional free gifts, the trader can invoke the UCPD (rather than Article 34) in its defence.[212] As *VTB-VAB*[213] (considered below) shows, by relying on the UCPD a trader can also defend itself against any action brought by a private party (if this is possible in the national system).[214]

The significance of the change in presumptions introduced by the UCPD can be seen in *VTB-VAB*. Belgian law prohibited vendors from making combined offers to consumers. This meant that commercial practices such as offering a free breakdown service to consumers buying certain quantities of petrol, or a money-off voucher in a magazine for a discount in certain shops, contravened Belgian law. Under *Keck* such a law would have been presumptively lawful unless actually and substantially discriminatory. However, following the UCPD the approach was different. The Court noted that Article 2(d) gave 'a particularly wide definition to the concept of commercial practices', and that combined offers constituted commercial practices within the meaning of Article 2(d).[215] Because

safety aspects of products, on conditions of establishment and authorization regimes, including those rules which, in conformity with [Union] law, relate to gambling activities, and to [Union] competition rules and the national provisions implementing them. The Member States will thus be able to retain or introduce restrictions and prohibitions of commercial practices on grounds of the protection of the health and safety of consumers in their territory wherever the trader is based, for example in relation to alcohol, tobacco or pharmaceuticals. Financial services and immovable property, by reason of their complexity and inherent serious risks, necessitate detailed requirements, including positive obligations on traders…'

[210] Where, however, the national legislation has prohibited one of the practices listed in the annex (e.g., claiming to be a signatory to a code of conduct when the trader is not or displaying a trust mark, quality mark or equivalent without having obtained the necessary authorization), then the legislation would be compatible with the UCPD and thus, by implication with the Treaties, without the need for going through the *Keck* analysis.

[211] Likewise, if a particular commercial practice is considered unfair after an assessment carried out under Arts. 5–9, the prohibition will be compatible with the directive and thus the Treaties.

[212] Given the structure of the directive, in that it does not confer rights as such on the trader, it will be more difficult for the trader to use the provisions of the UCPD as a sword against the state to challenge national regulations which exceed what is permissible under the UCPD. Perhaps there might be some residual scope here for Art. 34 TFEU—as interpreted in *Keck*. See also Case C–253/00 *Antonio Muñoz y Cia SA* v. *Frumar Ltd* [2002] ECR I–7289 considered in Ch. 16.

[213] Joined Cases C–261/07 and C–299/07 [2009] ECR I–000. See also Case C–522/08 *Telekomunikacja Polska SA w Warszawie* v *Prezes Urzędu Komunikacji Elektronicznej* [2010] ECR I–000, para. 33, on combined offers. For a further example, see Case C–304/08 *Zentrale zur Bekämpfung unlauteren Wettbewerbs eV* v. *Plus Warenhandelsgesellschaft mBH* [2010] ECR I–000 (UCPD precludes national legislation prohibiting in principle, without taking account of the specific circumstances of individual cases, commercial practices under which the participation of consumers in a prize competition or lottery is made conditional on the purchase of goods or use of services).

[214] See by analogy Case C–194/94 *CIA* [1996] ECR I–2201 concerning the Technical Standards Directive 98/34, discussed in Ch. 4, and the case law on triangular situations.        [215] Paras. 49–50.

combined offers did not fall within the annex to the directive, the Belgian legislation was precluded by the UCPD in so far as it prohibited combined offers without any verification of their unfairness in the light of the principles-based, case-by-case criteria (categories (2) and (3)).[216] Having found the Belgian law to be in breach of the directive, the Court saw no need to consider the compatibility of the national rule with the Treaties.

# F. CONCLUSIONS

The judgment in *Keck* represents a serious step towards establishing areas of national regulation where it is (and it is not) legitimate for Article 34 to intervene and, as the Court made clear in *Tobacco Advertising*,[217] over which the Union probably does not have the power to regulate under Article 114 TFEU (ex Article 95 EC).[218] Therefore, in the spirit of the subsidiarity principle, Member States retain their autonomy to regulate in areas which do not concern Union rules on free movement. However, in trying to delimit such an area, the Court reaffirmed the central place of the principle of non-discrimination in Article 34. Yet, as we have seen, in its attempts to resolve the problem of dealing with market circumstances rule, the Court created further difficulties, particularly in respect of those rules which did not fit the category of certain selling arrangements and those rules which were non-discriminatory but did hinder market access. Inevitably, this led the Court back to (re)considering the market access approach and in so doing probably narrowed the scope of *Keck*. The UCPD seems to have narrowed *Keck* still further.

However, as we saw in Chapter 1, the problem with a market access test is that almost any national measure can have some effect on market access, albeit indirect and potential, leading to a finding of a breach of Article 34. While such measures can be justified by Member States, this takes the courts (both European and national) into areas often involving sensitive choices of social policy, as the *Countryside Alliance* case shows. This is particularly true when it comes to assessing the proportionality of a particular measure. Generally, in the field of goods, the Court demands close scrutiny of the national measure. Yet, many national rules would not withstand close scrutiny, such as national rules imposing age restrictions on the purchase of cigarettes (why 16 and not 17?), alcohol, guns.

For these reasons, the Court has been reluctant to apply Article 34 to such cases. It now has a number of tools to achieve this: the *Keck* principle to deal with situations involving certain selling arrangements, the rule that the measure concerns a wholly internal situation, or arguments based on remoteness (that the effect of the measure on trade is too indirect and uncertain or not sufficiently substantial) to deal with other difficult cases. The Court is not always consistent or scientific in the application of these different tools, as it feels its way towards an appropriate solution to the problem of defining the outer limits of Article 34. These problems are more obvious in the field of free movement of persons where the market access test has a longer history. We consider this issue in more detail in Chapter 8. First, however, we consider the derogations to the principle of free movement and the judicially developed mandatory requirements.

---

[216] Para. 62.

[217] Case C–376/98 *Germany* v. *Parliament and Council* [2000] ECR I–8419, considered further in Ch. 16.

[218] Cf. G. Davies, 'Can selling arrangements be harmonised?' (2005) 30 *ELRev.* 371. See also I. Eriksson and U. Öberg, 'The Unfair Commercial Practices Directive in context' in Micklitz and Weatherill (eds.), above n. 200.

# 6

# DEROGATIONS AND JUSTIFICATIONS

## A. INTRODUCTION

As we have seen, Article 36 TFEU provides an exhaustive list of derogations from the principle of free movement of goods. This list, drawn directly from Article XX of the GATT reflected values deemed important in the 1950s. It has not, however, kept pace with the times and social interests deemed valuable now, such as environmental and consumer protection, are not reflected in Article 36. This has prompted the Court to develop an additional list of justifications—known as mandatory or public-interest requirements—which the Member States can invoke to justify the continued existence of their national rules. Traditionally, these mandatory requirements could be raised only where the measure was considered an indistinctly applicable MEE; they could not be used to justify distinctly applicable measures. Distinctly applicable measures could be saved only by the express Treaty derogations. However, as we saw in Chapter 4, the Court is increasingly recognizing that distinctly applicable measures can be saved by both the Article 36 derogations and the mandatory requirements. This is also the case with measures that interfere with market access following *Commission v Italy (trailers)*. The distinction between the Article 36 derogations and the mandatory requirements is therefore becoming less significant. Nevertheless, the Court still considers Member States' arguments separately under each heading but then applies common principles. In particular, it requires Member States to demonstrate the proportionality of the steps they have taken to serve the public-interest objective and, where necessary, show that these steps are compatible with fundamental human rights and principles of good governance. This chapter therefore examines the specific derogations under Article 36, the mandatory requirements developed by the Court, and the application of the principles of proportionality and fundamental rights.

## B. THE ARTICLE 36 DEROGATIONS

### 1. INTRODUCTION

The first sentence of Article 36 provides:

The provisions of Articles 34 and 35 shall not preclude prohibitions or restrictions on imports, exports or goods in transit justified on grounds of public morality, public policy or public security; the protection of health and life of humans, animals or plants; the protection of national treasures possessing artistic, historic or archaeological value; or the protection of industrial and commercial property.

This is an exhaustive list of derogations which must be read in conjunction with the proviso in the second sentence of Article 36. This says that '[s]uch prohibitions or restrictions shall not, however, constitute a means of arbitrary discrimination or a disguised restriction on trade between Member States'.

Thus, the Treaties allow national measures to take precedence over the free movement of goods where they serve important interests recognized by the Union as valuable (so-called 'public goods'), provided that the national measures are proportionate and do not constitute a means of arbitrary discrimination or a disguised restriction on trade between Member States. Eventually, restrictive national rules justified under Article 36 may be replaced by harmonized Union rules intended to protect the same interests at Union, rather than national, level.[1] In the absence of harmonization Member States remain free to invoke the derogations.

The Court has imposed two constraints on the Member States' freedom to invoke the Article 36 derogations. First, since Article 36 constitutes a derogation from the basic rule of free movement of goods it has to be interpreted strictly. Therefore, in *Irish Souvenirs*[2] the Court said that the exceptions listed in Article 36 could not be extended to include cases other than those specifically laid down. This meant that the Irish government could not rely on consumer protection and fairness in commercial transactions as a defence to its (directly) discriminatory conduct. Secondly, the derogations cannot be used to serve economic objectives.[3] Therefore, in *Commission* v. *Italy*,[4] Italy could not justify its ban on the import of pig meat because of economic difficulties with its own pig industry.[5]

Subject to these constraints, Member States can invoke any one of the derogations laid down in Article 36. The burden of proof is on the national authorities to 'demonstrate in each case that their rules are necessary to give effective protection to the interests referred to in Article [36]'.[6] We shall consider the different derogations in turn.

## 2. PUBLIC MORALITY

Member States enjoy a margin of discretion to determine what constitutes public morality in their own country. This can be seen in *Henn and Darby*,[7] where the UK banned the import of obscene films and magazines from the Netherlands on the grounds of public morality. The Court upheld the UK's decision, noting that 'it is for each Member State to determine in accordance with its own scale of values and in the form selected by it the

---

[1] These issues are considered in detail in Ch. 16.

[2] Case 113/80 *Commission* v. *Ireland* [1981] ECR 1625, para. 7.

[3] Case 95/81 *Commission* v. *Italy* [1982] ECR 2187, para. 27.

[4] Case 7/61 *Commission* v. *Italy* [1961] ECR 317, 329.

[5] See also Case C–324/93 *R.* v. *Secretary of State for the Home Department, ex p. Evans Medical Ltd (Generics (UK) Ltd intervening)* [1995] ECR I–563. In Case 238/82 *Duphar BV* v. *Netherlands* [1984] ECR 523, para. 23 the Court said Art. 36 could not justify a measure whose primary objective was budgetary (i.e., to reduce the costs of a sickness insurance scheme). Nor can the derogations be relied on to justify rules or practices which, albeit beneficial, contain restrictions explained primarily by a concern to lighten the administration's burden or reduce public expenditure: Case 104/75 *Adriaan de Peijper* [1976] ECR 613, para. 18.

[6] Case 227/82 *Criminal proceedings against Leendert van Bennekom* [1983] ECR 3883, para. 40.

[7] Case 34/79 [1979] ECR 3795.

requirements of public morality in its territory'.[8] Therefore, in principle the UK could invoke the first sentence of Article 36.

This decision can be contrasted with *Conegate*.[9] This time the UK prevented the import of sexy vacuum flasks and life-size inflatable dolls from Germany. Although the defendants argued that the dolls were to be used in window displays, their description as 'love-love dolls' and 'Miss World specials' suggested a different purpose.[10] This time the Court was more suspicious of the UK's justification based on public morality because the very same sort of goods could be manufactured in the UK. It said the fact that goods cause offence could not be regarded as sufficiently serious to justify restrictions on the free movement of goods where 'the Member State concerned does not adopt, with respect to the same goods manufactured or marketed within its territory, penal measures or other serious and effective measures intended to prevent the distribution of such goods in its own territory'.[11] Therefore the UK could not rely on the public-morality defence.

## 3. PUBLIC POLICY

### 3.1 Public Policy and the Import and Export of Goods

It is clear that the Union definition of public policy bears little resemblance to its broad common law equivalent. This derogation is narrowly construed and the Court has proved most resistant to all attempts to expand its scope. For example, in *Ringelhan*[12] the Court said, 'Whatever interpretation is to be given to the term "public policy" it cannot be extended so as to include considerations of consumer protection.'[13]

It is rare for the public-policy defence, as an independent free-standing defence,[14] to be successfully invoked in a goods case before the Court of Justice. *Thompson*[15] is the best known example. The case concerned a British ban on exporting silver coins, even though they were no longer legal tender, to prevent them from being melted down or destroyed. Because it was also a criminal offence in the UK to melt down coins, the Court said that a ban on exports was justified on grounds of public policy because it stemmed from 'the need to protect the right to mint coinage which is traditionally regarded as involving the fundamental interests of the State'.[16]

This decision can be compared with *Commission* v. *Italy*.[17] Italian law required that, when making a payment in advance, importers had to provide security of 5 per cent of the value of the goods. Italy justified its requirement on the grounds of public policy, citing in particular 'the defence of its currency'.[18] The Court rejected this argument.

---

[8] Para. 16.      [9] Case 121/85 *Conegate* v. *HM Customs and Excise* [1986] ECR 1007.
[10] Counsel for the customs authorities told the magistrates that 'it is almost certain that the dolls were intended to be used as sex aids. I don't know about the sexy vacuum flasks': *The Guardian*, 22 Jan. 1986, cited in S. Weatherill and P. Beaumont, *EU Law*, 3rd edn (London: Penguin, 1999), 529.      [11] Para. 15.
[12] Case 177/83 *Kohl* v. *Ringelhan & Rennett SA* [1984] ECR 3651.      [13] Para. 19.
[14] In Case C–434/04 *Ahokainen* v. *Virallinen syyttäjä* [2006] ECR I–9171, para. 28 it was invoked in conjunction with the public health defence when justifying Swedish measures used to control the consumption of alcohol.      [15] Case 7/78 *R.* v. *Thompson, Johnson, and Woodiwiss* [1978] ECR 2247.
[16] Para. 34.
[17] Case 95/81 [1982] ECR 2187. See also Case 7/61 *Commission* v. *Italy* [1961] ECR 317, 329.
[18] Para. 26.

### 3.2 Public Policy and the Right to Protest

(a) The position under the Treaties

The public-policy derogation has increasingly been invoked by Member States in the context of public protests and the fear of civil unrest. The public-policy arguments take one of two forms. In one line of case law the public-policy derogation has been invoked to justify the state allowing protesters to exercise their fundamental rights and, in so doing, interfere with free movement of goods. As we shall see in *Schmidberger*,[19] the Court has shown some sympathy with this argument.

In a second line of case law, the derogation has been invoked to prevent practices—usually by importers—which lead to civil unrest. Generally, the Court has not been sympathetic to such arguments, as *Cullet*[20] shows. When the Leclerc group started selling petrol at prices below those set by French law, a competitor brought proceedings against it claiming that Leclerc's pricing policy was unlawful. The Court found that the French law setting minimum petrol prices breached Article 34 because it allowed the authorities to manipulate prices which had the effect of preventing importers from entering the market.[21] The French government tried to justify the rule under Article 36, by referring to 'the threat to public order and security represented by the violent reactions which would have to be anticipated on the part of retailers affected by unrestricted competition'.[22] However, because the French government had not shown that it was unable, using the means at its disposal, to deal with the threat to public order and security represented by the protesters,[23] the Court said that France could not rely on Article 36.

Advocate General VerLoren Van Themaat adopted a different approach. He rejected the French government's arguments on principle. He said that there was no support for a wide interpretation of public policy to include civil unrest because private interest groups, rather than the Treaties and the Union institutions, would then determine the scope of Union freedoms. In such cases, he said that the concept of public policy requires effective action on the part of the authorities to deal with such disturbances.[24]

By turning the public-policy argument on its head, the Advocate General envisaged that public policy placed responsibility on the national authorities to deal with obstacles to free movement of goods created by interest groups. From a pure free movement perspective, he is right that interest groups objecting to the economic consequences of the single market, should not be able to interfere with the operation of the single market, nor should Member States be able to use civil disobedience as a pretext for protecting national interests. But if the Advocate General's views are taken to their logical conclusion this would mean that the national government would be obliged to apply all means at its disposal (the entire police force, the army?) to ensure the free movement of goods. Where would this leave fundamental rights to protest and how does this relate to the principle of proportionality?

---

[19] Case C–112/00 *Eugen Schmidberger, Internationale Transporte und Planzüge* v. *Republic of Austria* [2003] ECR I–5659. See also Case C–36/02 *Omega Spielhallen* [2004] ECR I–9609 discussed in Ch. 13.

[20] Case 231/83 *Cullet* v. *Centre Leclerc Toulouse* [1985] ECR 305. Cf. Case 42/82 *Commission* v. *France (the 'wine war')* [1983] ECR 1013, where violent demonstrations occurred when French *vinicolteurs* protested at the import of wine from Italy. However, France did not consider it worthwhile to raise the public order defence.                                                                                      [21] Para. 20.

[22] Para. 32.        [23] Para. 33.        [24] At 312.

The Court provided partial answers to these questions in *Commission* v. *France (Spanish strawberries)*.[25] The case arose out of a long history of violent attacks by French farmers directed against agricultural products from other Member States,[26] in particular Spanish strawberries and Belgian tomatoes.[27] Despite various tip-offs, the French police were either nowhere to be seen during these incidents or were present but did not intervene, even when they far out-numbered the perpetrators. Furthermore, the French authorities had prosecuted only a very small number of those involved, even though a number of the faces of the demonstrators had been caught on camera.[28] Eventually, the Commission brought enforcement proceedings against France, arguing that the failure by the French authorities to act breached Article 34 on the free movement of goods and Article 4(3) TEU (ex Article 10 EC) on the duty of cooperation.

The Court agreed, ruling that Article 34 required the Member States 'not merely themselves to abstain from adopting measures or engaging in conduct liable to constitute an obstacle to trade but also, when read with Article [4(3) TEU]..., to take all necessary and appropriate measures to ensure that that fundamental freedom is respected on their territory'.[29] The Court then acknowledged that:[30]

the Member States, which retain exclusive competence as regards the maintenance of public order and the safeguarding of internal security, unquestionably enjoy a margin of discretion in determining what measures are most appropriate to eliminate barriers to the importation of products in a given situation.

It is therefore not for the Union institutions to act in place of the Member States and to prescribe for them the measures which they must adopt and effectively apply in order to safeguard the free movement of goods on their territories.

Taking due account of Member State discretion, the Court continued that it could only verify 'whether the Member State concerned has adopted appropriate measures for ensuring the free movement of goods'.[31]

This case shows that the Court's control is residual, and any sanction is available only in cases involving 'manifest and persistent failure'[32] by the state. This would suggest that a national authority does have the discretion to balance the competing interests of the free movement of goods, the fundamental rights of freedom of expression and to protest (not mentioned by the Court but a general principle of law),[33] and the cost of funding such operations. Lord Slynn took these considerations into account when applying the Article 36 derogation in the British case of *ITF*.[34] ITF exported live animals from the port of Shoreham in West Sussex, but these exports were met with much opposition from animal rights protesters.[35] Ultimately the Chief Constable of the Sussex Police told ITF that he would permit ITF only two sailings a week, due to the expense of the policing operation. ITF argued that this decision made its business uneconomic and contravened Article 34.

---

[25] [1997] ECR I-6959.    [26] Para. 2.    [27] Paras. 4–6.    [28] Paras. 48–50.
[29] Para. 32.    [30] Paras. 33–4.    [31] Para. 35.    [32] Para. 65.
[33] Cases C–23/93 *TV10* v. *Commissariaat voor de Media* [1994] ECR I–4795; C–260/89 *ERT* v. *DEP* [1991] ECR I–2925; and C–368/95 *Vereinigte Familiapress Zeitungsverlags- und vertriebs GmbH* v. *Heinrich Bauer Verlag* [1997] ECR I–3689, para. 24.
[34] *R.* v. *Chief Constable of Sussex, ex p. International Trader's Ferry Ltd (ITF)* [1999] 1 All ER 129, noted by C. Barnard and I. Hare (1997) 60 *MLR* 394 and (2000) 63 *MLR* 581.
[35] Unlike *Cullet*, *ITF* concerned largely peaceful and lawful protest, not by those objecting to the consequences of the single market, but by those concerned about animal rights.

In considering the public-policy defence raised by the Chief Constable, Lord Slynn gave a broad definition of public policy, broader than any articulated by the Court of Justice. He said that quantitative restrictions 'justified on grounds of public policy include not just situations where there is something inherently bad about the activity itself which justifies the restriction but also where the broader requirements of public policy, here the maintenance of public order,[36] justify steps being taken which so long as proportionate may have a restrictive effect'.[37] The House of Lords accepted that the Chief Constable of Sussex had carried out this exercise effectively and that the restrictions on free movement were proportionate.

The Court of Justice itself was forced to engage in such a balancing act in *Schmidberger*.[38] An environmental association, Transitforum Austria Tirol, organized a demonstration blocking a stretch of the Brenner Motorway (the A13, the major transit route for trade between Northern Europe and Italy) for 30 hours, to draw attention to the threat to the environment and public health posed by the constant increase in the movement of heavy goods vehicles on the motorway.[39] Schmidberger, a German transport company, sought damages for the losses it suffered because its lorries were not able to use the motorway.

Following *Commission* v. *France*, the Court said the state's failure to ban this demonstration breached Articles 34–5 TFEU, read together with Article 4(3) TEU.[40] However, the Austrian authorities justified their (in)action on the ground of the fundamental rights of the demonstrators to freedom of expression and freedom of assembly guaranteed by the ECHR and the national constitution, principles which the Court recognized formed an integral part of the general principles of EU law.[41] The Court continued that 'since both the [Union] and its Member States are required to respect fundamental rights, the protection of those rights is a legitimate interest which, in principle, justifies a restriction of the obligations imposed by [Union] law, even under a fundamental freedom guaranteed by the [Treaties] such as the free movement of goods'.[42] In other words, the Court, like the House of Lords, took the need to protect the fundamental rights as the reason for restricting freedom of movement; unlike the House of Lords the Court did not see fundamental rights as constituting the express public-policy derogation.[43] Instead, it saw fundamental rights as a free-standing public-interest (or 'mandatory') requirement.

However, since the two human rights at stake, described by the Court as 'fundamental pillars of a democratic society',[44] were not absolute, the Court recognized that their exercise could be restricted, provided that 'the restrictions in fact correspond to objectives of general interest and do not, taking account of the aim of the restrictions, constitute disproportionate and unacceptable interference, impairing the very substance of the rights

---

[36] Reflecting the French '*ordre public*'. See also Lenz AG's Opinion and para. 56 of the judgment in Case C–265/95 *Commission* v. *France* [1997] ECR I–6959 (noted M. Jarvis (1998) 35 *CMLRev.* 1371, 1381).

[37] *R.* v. *Chief Constable of Sussex* [1999] 1 All ER 129, 143j.

[38] Case C–112/00 *Schmidberger* [2003] ECR I–5659.

[39] This is a matter of serious concern for the Tyrolean authorities which tried to ban all heavy goods vehicles over 7.5 tonnes carrying certain goods (e.g., logs, cork, stone, vehicles) from the A12 Inntal motorway (IP/03/984) but were stopped by the Court: Case C–320/03 R *Commission* v. *Austria* [2003] ECR I–7929; and the judgment in Case C–320/03 *Commission* v. *Austria* [2005] ECR I–9871.                        [40] Para. 64.

[41] Paras. 71–3.          [42] Para. 74.          [43] Cf. Case C–36/02 *Omega Spielhallen* [2004] ECR I–9609.

[44] Para. 79.

guaranteed'.[45] The Court then engaged in a balancing act to determine whether a fair balance had been struck between the competing interests.[46]

It noted a number of factors which distinguished *Schmidberger* from *Commission* v. *France*: the demonstration took place following a request for authorization as required by national law and after the Austrian authorities had decided to allow it to go ahead;[47] the obstacle to free movement was limited (a single event, on a single route, lasting for 30 hours) by comparison with 'both the geographic scale and the intrinsic seriousness' of the disruption caused in the French case;[48] the demonstrators were motivated by a desire to express their opinion on a matter of public importance and not by a desire to restrict trade in goods of a particular type or from a particular source;[49] and various administrative and supporting measures had been taken by the Austrian authorities to limit the disruption to road traffic, including an extensive publicity campaign launched well in advance by the media and the motoring organizations, both in Austria and in neighbouring countries, as well as the designation of alternative routes.[50] The Court concluded that this isolated incident did not give rise to a general climate of insecurity such as to have a dissuasive effect on intra-Union trade flows as a whole, by contrast to the serious and repeated disruptions to public order at issue in *Commission* v *France*.[51]

The Court also accepted the Austrian argument that all the alternative solutions (banning the protest altogether, limiting the location and duration of the protest) would have risked reactions which would have been difficult to control and would have been liable to cause much more serious disruption to intra-Union trade and public order, such as unauthorized demonstrations and confrontation between supporters and opponents of the group organizing the demonstration, or acts of violence on the part of the demonstrators who considered that the exercise of their fundamental rights had been infringed.[52] Therefore, the Court concluded that the fact that the Austrian authorities had not banned the demonstration was compatible with Articles 34–5 TFEU, read together with Article 4(3) TEU.[53]

## (b) The Monti Regulation

Following the Court's ruling in *Commission* v. *France*, the Council adopted the 'Monti' Regulation 2679/98,[54] which was designed to set up an intervention mechanism to safeguard free trade in the single market. This provides that State A can complain to the Commission about obstacles to the free movement of goods which are attributable to State B—either through action or inaction[55]—where the obstacles lead to serious disruption of the free movement of goods, cause serious loss to the individuals affected, and require immediate action.[56] State B must then explain the action it has taken, or proposes

---

[45] Para. 80.    [46] Para. 81.    [47] Para. 84.    [48] Para. 85.    [49] Para. 86.
[50] Para. 87.    [51] Para. 88.    [52] Para. 92.    [53] Para. 94.

[54] [1998] OJ L337/8. See also the Resolution of the Council and of the Representatives of the Governments of the Member States meeting within the Council of 7 Dec. 1998 ([1998] OJ L337/10) which encourages the Court to adopt an expedited procedure in respect of cases arising under Reg. 2679/98. For further details see <http://www.ec.europa.eu/enterprise/policies/single-market-goods/free-movement-non-harmonised-sectors/rapid-intervention-mechanism/#h2-regulation-2679/98---eliminating-obstacles-to-trade>.

[55] 'Inaction' is defined in Art. 1(2) as covering the case when the competent authorities of a Member State, in the presence of an obstacle caused by actions taken by private individuals, fail to take all necessary and proportionate measures within their powers with a view to removing the obstacle and ensuring the free movement of goods in their territory.    [56] Art. 1(1).

to take, to address the problem. State B must also 'take all necessary and proportionate measures so that the free movement of goods is assured in the territory of the Member State in accordance with the [Treaties]'. It must also inform the Commission of the action which its authorities have taken or intend to take.[57]

However, all of this is subject to the fundamental rights recognized in Article 2. This provides that:

This Regulation may not be interpreted as affecting in any way the exercise of fundamental rights, as recognised in Member States, including the right or freedom to strike. These rights may also include the right or freedom to take other actions covered by the specific industrial relations systems in Member States.

No reference is made in this regulation to compensation for those affected by these serious obstacles to trade.[58] *Schmidberger* suggests that the Court will give Member States a wide margin of discretion when deciding what action to take in such cases and will usually not try to second-guess Member States' decisions.

### 4. PUBLIC SECURITY

In the past the Court has been more sympathetic to arguments based on public security than to those based on public policy, as *Campus Oil*[59] demonstrates. Ireland, a country which is totally dependent on imports for its supplies of petroleum products, required importers of these products to buy a certain proportion of their needs from a state-owned oil refinery at prices fixed by the Irish government based on the costs incurred by the refinery. Ireland justified this requirement on the basis of public security. The Court agreed. It recognized that because of the exceptional importance of petroleum products as an energy source in the modern economy, an interruption in supplies, with the resultant dangers for the country's existence, could seriously affect public security.[60] Given that Ireland's law served the purpose of public security, the fact that it also served objectives of an economic nature was not important. The Court said that 'the aim of ensuring a minimum supply of petroleum products at all times was to be regarded as transcending purely economic considerations'.[61]

Yet, in a highly interdependent world, a nation's ability to hold its own petrol supplies would not be enough to make it independent in a time of crisis. The Court recognized this in *Commission* v. *Greece*,[62] where it was more sceptical of the public-security arguments raised by the Greek government. Greece wanted to have minimum holdings of petroleum products on its territory.[63] Rather than storing petrol itself, it required petrol companies to hold minimum stocks of petrol at their own installations. This extremely onerous obligation was mitigated by the fact that these companies could transfer the storage obli-

---

[57] Art. 3. The use of this procedure, 'which is designed to bring as speedy an end as possible to obstacles to the free movement of goods between Member States', is not a pre-condition to bringing an Art. 258 TFEU (ex Art. 226 EC) action: Case C–320/03 *Commission* v. *Austria* [2005] ECR I–7929, para. 35.

[58] See the Commission's Report on the application of Reg. 2679/98, <http://www.ec.europa.eu/enterprise/policies/single-market-goods/files/goods/docs/regl267998/finalreport-051207_en.pdf>.

[59] Case 72/83 *Campus Oil* [1984] ECR 2727. See also the *Golden Share* cases, Case C–503/99 *Commission* v. *Belgium* [2002] ECR I–4809; Case C–483/99 *Commission* v. *France* [2002] ECR I–4781; Case C–463/00 *Commission* v. *Spain* [2003] ECR I–4581 considered in Ch. 15.     [60] Para. 34.

[61] Para. 35.     [62] Case C–398/98 *Commission* v. *Greece* [2001] ECR I–7915.

[63] This law was based on Dir. 68/414/EEC ([1968] OJ Spec Ed (II) 586), now Dir 2006/67/EC ([2006] OJ L217/8).

gation to refineries established in Greece, but only on condition that the marketing companies had bought a large quantity of petroleum products from those refineries in the previous calendar year. This grandfather clause had the effect of making the marketing of petroleum products from other Member State more difficult, since, if the marketing companies bought their products from foreign refineries, the marketing companies would not be able to benefit from transferring the storage obligation. For this reason the Court of Justice found that the national rule breached Article 34.

The Greek government's defence was based on public security. It argued that the refineries' fundamental right to economic freedom would be excessively restricted if they were obliged to assume the marketing companies' obligation to store minimum stocks of petrol without benefiting from the marketing companies' obligation to purchase their supplies from the refinery in return. The Court rejected this defence, observing that these arguments were 'purely economic' which could never serve as a justification.[64]

However, the broad approach to public security seen in *Campus Oil* can also be detected in *Richardt*,[65] a case concerning strategically sensitive goods. Luxembourg law required a special transit licence for the import and export of goods of a strategic nature. Richardt imported a unit for the production of bubble memory circuits from the USA into France and then transported it into Luxembourg before exporting it to Russia. The unit was seized on public-security grounds by the Luxembourg authorities because Richardt did not have a transit licence. The Court said that because the concept of public security covered both a state's internal and external security, the importation, exportation, and transit of strategic goods could affect the public security of a Member State.[66] For this reason, Luxembourg was entitled to make the transit of goods, described as strategic material, subject to special authorization[67] in order to verify the nature of the goods. However, the Court did add that seizure of goods which did not have this authorization might be considered disproportionate in a case where the return of goods to their state of origin would have sufficed.[68]

In addition to the specific public-security derogation found in Article 36, the Treaties also contain some more general provisions in respect of public security. Article 346(1)(b) TFEU (ex Article 296(1)(b) EC) provides that Member States can take measures necessary for the protection of the essential interests of its security which are connected with the production of or trade in arms, munitions, and war material, although such measures cannot adversely affect the conditions of competition in the common market regarding products which are not intended for specifically military purposes.[69] As a derogation, this provision is narrowly construed.[70] Further, the Court has insisted that it is for a Member State seeking to take advantage of Article 346 to prove that it is necessary to have recourse

---

[64] Para. 30.

[65] Case C-367/89 *Criminal Proceedings against Aimé Richardt and Les Accessoires Scientifique SNC* [1991] ECR I-4621. See also Case C-70/94 *Fritz Werner Industrie-Ausrüstungen GmbH* v. *Federal Republic of Germany* [1995] ECR I-3189 concerning dual use goods, considered further in Ch. 7.  [66] Para. 22.

[67] Para. 23.  [68] Para. 24.

[69] For a full discussion see P. Koutrakos, 'The application of EC law to defence industries: Changing interpretations of Article 296 EC' in C. Barnard and O. Odudu (eds.), *The Outer Limits of European Union Law* (Oxford: Hart Publishing, 2009). See also the Commission's Interpretative Communication on the application of Art. 296 of the Treaty (now Art. 346) in the field of defence-related procurement, COM(2006) 779.

[70] Case C-239/06 *Commission* v. *Italy (duty-free imports of military equipment)* [2009] ECR I-000, para. 47. See also the earlier cases in the field of sex discrimination: Case C-273/97 *Sirdar* [1999] ECR I-7403; Case C-285/98 *Kreil* [2000] ECR I-69; and Case C-186/01 *Dory* [2003] ECR I-2479.

to that derogation to protect its essential security interests.[71] Therefore, in *Commission v. Italy* the Court ruled that Italy could not rely on Article 346 to justify its refusal to apply customs duties on imports of military material coming from third countries on the ground that that military material would cost more.

Article 347 TFEU (ex Article 297 EC) says that Member States must consult each other with a view to taking together the steps needed to prevent the functioning of the common market being affected by measures which a Member State may be called upon to take in the event of serious internal disturbances affecting the maintenance of law and order, in the event of war, serious international tension constituting a threat of war, or in order to carry out obligations it has accepted for the purpose of maintaining peace and international security.

If measures taken in the circumstances referred to in Articles 346–7 have the effect of distorting the conditions of competition in the common market, Article 348 TFEU (ex Article 298 EC) provides that, together with the state concerned, the Commission must examine how these measures can be adjusted to the rules laid down in the Treaties. By way of derogation from the procedure laid down in Articles 258–9 TFEU (ex Articles 226–7 EC), the Commission or any Member State may bring the matter directly before the Court of Justice if they consider that another Member State is making improper use of the powers provided for in Articles 346–7.

## 5. THE PROTECTION OF HEALTH AND LIFE OF HUMANS, ANIMALS, OR PLANTS

### 5.1 **Human Health**

#### (a) Level of scrutiny

The protection of health and life of humans, animals, or plants is the derogation most frequently invoked by the Member States. In the absence of harmonization,[72] the Court has ruled that each Member State has the right to determine the level of health protection desired for its citizens,[73] taking into account various factors such as the climate in the state,[74] the normal diet of the population, and its state of health.[75] However, while the Court recognizes that 'the health and life of humans rank foremost among the property interests protected by Article [36]',[76] it is suspicious of attempts by Member States to use health protection as a means of affording a disguised restriction on trade. It therefore requires Member States not only to produce evidence that they have genuine health concerns,[77]

---

[71] Ibid., para. 50. See also Case C–414/97 *Commission* v. *Spain* [1999] ECR I–5585.

[72] See, e.g., Case 97/83 *Criminal Proceedings against Melkunie* [1984] ECR 2367, para. 18.          [73] Ibid.

[74] Case 54/85 *Ministère public* v. *Mirepoix* [1986] ECR 1067, para. 15.

[75] Case 94/83 *Criminal Proceedings against Albert Heijn BV* [1984] ECR 3263, para. 16 (pesticides); cf. Case 178/84 *Commission* v. *Germany* [1987] ECR 1227, para. 48.

[76] See, e.g., Case C–320/93 *Lucien Ortscheit GmbH* v. *Eurim-Pharm Arzneimittel GmbH* [1994] ECR I–5243, para. 16; Case C–170/04 *Rosengren* v. *Riksåklagaren* [2007] ECR I–4071, para. 39.

[77] Case 90/86 *Criminal proceedings against Zoni* [1988] ECR 4285 (because there was no evidence that pasta made from common wheat contained chemical additives or colorants there was no need to exclude such pasta); Case 274/87 *Commission* v. *Germany* [1989] ECR 229 (because evidence that protein levels in Germany were more than adequate there was no need to restrict the import of a product with lower nutritional value to ensure a sufficient intake of protein); cf. Case 97/83 *Criminal Proceedings against Melkunie* [1984] ECR 2367 (because evidence that risk of active coliform bacteria in milk could be a real source of

which the Court will scrutinize carefully,[78] but also to demonstrate the existence of a seriously considered health policy.[79]

The intensity of this scrutiny can be seen in the *Beer Purity* case.[80] The German government banned the marketing of beer containing all additives (not just the additives for which there was concrete evidence of risks) on the grounds that Germans drank a lot of beer and the long-term effect of additives was not known. The Court said that the German rule could not be justified. Having examined the findings of international scientific research, the work of the Union's scientific committee for food, and the codex alimentarius of the United Nations and the World Health Organization (WHO), it found that the additives did not present a risk to public health. It also noted that the German government's policy was inconsistent because Germany permitted the use of these same additives in other drinks.

A similar degree of close scrutiny of the public-health defence can be found in *DocMorris*.[81] German law prohibited sales of medicinal products by mail order (in this case over the internet) with the result that in Germany prescription and non-prescription medicines could be sold only in pharmacists' shops. While the Court accepted that there were public-health grounds for restricting the provision of prescription medicines to pharmacies, this was not the case with non-prescription medicines. In the case of prescription medicines the Court said that given the risks attached to the use of these products, the need to be able to check the authenticity of doctors' prescriptions and to ensure that the medicine was handed over either to the customer directly or to another authorized person, Germany could justify a prohibition on mail-order sales. For good measure the Court added that given the real possibility of the labelling of a medicinal product bought in another Member State being in a language other than the buyer's, this might have more harmful consequences in the case of prescription medicines.[82]

Similar considerations did not apply in the case of non-prescription medicines. The Court noted the convenience of being able to place the order from the home or the office. It also recognized that, as regards incorrect use of the medicine, the risk could be reduced through an increase in the number of online interactive features which the customer had to use before being able to proceed to a purchase. As regards possible abuse, the Court said that it was not apparent that, for persons wishing to acquire non-prescription medicines unlawfully, purchase in a traditional pharmacy was more difficult than an internet purchase.

(b) Scientific uncertainty and the precautionary principle

If the scientific evidence about the health risks of a particular product is uncertain then Member States can decide what degree of health protection they intend to assure, having

---

danger to human health it was legitimate to impose a requirement seeking to exclude these bacteria); Case C–473/98 *Toolex Alpha AB* [2000] ECR I–5681 (there was 'hard' evidence that the carcinogenic effect of trichloroethylene upon the kidneys of a rat also occurs in humans).

[78] See, e.g., Case 118/86 *Openbaar Ministerie* v. *Nertsvoederfabriek Nederland BV* [1987] ECR 3883, para. 14.      [79] Case 40/82 *Commission* v. *United Kingdom (turkeys)* [1984] ECR 2793, para. 38.

[80] Case 178/84 *Commission* v. *Germany* [1987] ECR 1227.

[81] Case C–322/01 *0800 DocMorris NV* [2003] ECR I–14887. See further Ch. 5.

[82] Para. 119.

regard to the requirements of the free movement of goods within the Union.[83] This can be seen in *Sandoz*,[84] where the Dutch authorities refused to grant authorization for the importation of muesli bars with added vitamins from Germany (where they were lawfully sold). Given the uncertainties in scientific research about vitamins, albeit that vitamins are not harmful in themselves unless consumed in excess,[85] the Court said that the national rules were justified.

In *Commission v. Denmark*[86] the Court explained its approach in terms of the precautionary principle. It confirmed that, following a detailed assessment which reveals that scientific uncertainty persists as to the extent of the risk to human health,[87] Member States could rely on the precautionary principle to take protective measures,[88] without having to wait until the reality and seriousness of the risks were fully demonstrated.[89] These protective measures might be an authorization procedure based on a detailed assessment carried out on a case-by-case basis[90] or, in more extreme cases, a total ban. However, in *Mirepoix*[91] the Court required the Member State to review the prohibition and to allow, 'by means of a procedure that is easily accessible to traders', for exceptions to be made to the rules laid down where it appears that the use of the product is not dangerous to health.

---

[83] Case 174/82 *Officier van Justitie* v. *Sandoz* [1983] ECR 2445, para. 16; Case 53/80 *Officier van Justitie* v. *Koninklijke Kaasfabriek Eyssen BV* [1981] ECR 409; Case C–121/00 *Criminal proceedings against Walter Hahn* [2002] ECR I–9193, para. 45 (listeria).          [84] Case 174/82 [1983] ECR 2445.

[85] Para. 17.          [86] Case C–192/01 *Commission* v. *Denmark* [2003] ECR I–9693, para. 47.

[87] Purely hypothetical considerations' are not sufficient to justify measures being taken on the grounds of the precautionary principle: Case C–236/01 *Monsanto Agricoltura* [2003] ECR I–8105.

[88] According to the Commission's Communication on the precautionary principle, COM(2000) 1, 9, the principle will be applied where 'scientific evidence is insufficient, inconclusive or uncertain and there are indications through preliminary objective scientific evaluation that there are reasonable grounds for concern that the potentially dangerous effects on the environment, human, animal or plant health may be inconsistent with the chosen level of protection'. See also the discussion in J. Scott and E. Vos, 'The juridification of uncertainty: Observations on the ambivalence of the precautionary principle within the EU and the WTO' in C. Joerges and R. Dehousse (eds.), *Good Governance in Europe's Integrated Market* (Oxford: OUP, 2002) and G. Majone, 'The precautionary principle and its policy implications' (2002) 40 *JCMS* 89. See also Case C–157/96 *R.* v. *Ministry of Agriculture, Fisheries and Food (MAFF), ex p. NFU* [1998] ECR I–2211, para. 63, where the precautionary principle was first used by the Court, considered further in Ch. 16.

[89] Protective measures 'founded on mere suppositions which are not yet scientifically verified' cannot, however, justify Member State action: Case C–236/01 *Monsanto* [2003] ECR I–8105, para. 106. In Case T–13/99 *Pfizer Animal Health* v. *Council* [2002] ECR II–3305, when talking about the action that the *Union* could take on the ground of health protection, the General Court said 'under the precautionary principle the [Union] institutions are entitled, in the interests of human health to adopt, on the basis of as yet incomplete scientific knowledge, protective measures which may seriously harm legally protected positions' (para. 170) but the Union institution must examine carefully and impartially all the relevant aspects of the individual case (para. 171) basing any decision on 'scientific advice founded on the principles of excellence, transparency and independence' (para. 172). See K. Lenaerts, '"In the Union we Trust": Trust-Enhancing Principles of Community Law' (2004) 41 *CMLRev.* 317, 333.

[90] Case C–192/01 *Commission* v. *Denmark* [2003] ECR I–9693, para. 56. The Court will scrutinize any risk assessment carefully: Case C–319/05 *Commission* v. *Germany (Garlic Capsule)* [2007] ECR I–9811, paras. 91–95. The case law on vitamins has now been superseded by the Food Supplements Dir. 2002/46 ([2002] OJ L 183/51) challenged in Joined Cases C–154/04 & C–155/04 *Alliance for Natural Health* [2005] ECR I–6451 considered in Ch. 16.

[91] Case 54/85 *Ministère public* v. *Mirepoix* [1986] ECR 1067, paras. 16–17. See generally T. Van Rijn, 'A review of the case law of the Court of Justice on Articles 30 to 36 EEC in 1986 and 1987' (1988) 25 *CMLRev.* 593.

## (c) Healthcare services

The Court seems particularly sympathetic to public-health arguments when they are directly related to the functioning of the national healthcare system. For example, in *Evans Medical*[92] the British government refused to grant a licence to an importer of narcotic drugs on the ground that the imports might undermine the sole licensed manufacturer in the UK, jeopardizing the reliability of the supply of a particular drug in the UK. The Court said that such action could be justified on public-health grounds, provided there was no less restrictive way of achieving this objective and that the action was not being taken on economic grounds.

In *Monteil*[93] the Court went even further and raised the public-health derogation to a presumption of legality. It said that a pharmacists' monopoly in France on retail sales of medicinal products could be 'presumed to constitute an appropriate way of protecting public health'. However, it did add that importers should be able to produce evidence to show that its products did not involve any serious danger to public health. More recently, in *Commission v. Germany (pharmacies for hospitals)*,[94] the Court said a German rule requiring pharmacies supplying medicinal products to hospitals to be situated close to that hospital was a proportionate public-health requirement: the rules were appropriate because they ensured a reliable supply of good quality health products to the hospital,[95] and they were necessary because they ensured that there was a pharmacist responsible for the supply of the medicines who could be available quickly.[96]

But there are limits to the Court's sympathy with the demands experienced by national health systems, as *Decker*[97] shows. Under Luxembourg law the authorities were required to give prior authorization before any medical product (in this case glasses) could be bought abroad while no such authorization was required if the goods were purchased in Luxembourg. The Court said the rule breached Article 34 and rejected Luxembourg's public-health arguments based on ensuring quality of treatment. It said that the Directives on Mutual Recognition of Diplomas[98] meant that an optician in another Member State had equivalent qualifications to those in Luxembourg and so was properly qualified; and the fact that the glasses were bought on a prescription from an ophthalmologist guaranteed the protection of public health.[99]

### 5.2 Animal Health

Article 36 protects not only human health but also animal health.[100] This was the justification raised by Denmark in *Bluhme*[101] to prohibit the import of any bee onto the Danish

---

[92] Case C–324/93 [1995] ECR I–563. See also Case C–320/93 *Ortscheit v. Eurim-Pharm Arzneimittel GmbH* [1994] ECR I–5243; Joined Cases 266 and 267/87 *R. v. Royal Pharmaceutical Society of Great Britain, ex p. Association of Pharmaceutical Importers* [1989] ECR 1295.

[93] Case C–60/90 [1991] ECR I–1547, para. 43.

[94] Case C–141/07 *Commission v. Germany (pharmacies for hospitals)* [2008] ECR I–6935.

[95] Para. 49.    [96] Para. 56.

[97] Case C–120/95 *Decker v. Caisse de Maladie des Employés Privés* [1998] ECR I–1831.

[98] Considered further in Ch. 10.    [99] Paras. 42–4.

[100] Case C–323/93 *Société Civile Agricole du Centre d'Insémination de la Crespelle v. Coopérative d'Elevage et d'Insémination Artificielle du Département de la Mayenne* [1994] ECR I–5077; Case C–350/97 *Monsees v. Unabhängiger Verwaltungssenat für Kärnten* [1999] ECR I–2921.

[101] Case C–67/97 *Criminal Proceedings against Ditlev Bluhme* [1998] ECR I–8033, para. 19. See also Case C–510/99 *Tridon* [2001] ECR I–7777, para. 52.

island of Læsø except the Læsø brown bee. The Court said that measures to preserve an indigenous animal population with distinct characteristics contributed to the maintenance of biodiversity by ensuring the survival of the population of the Læsø brown bee. Because the prohibition on the import of other bees protected the life of the Læsø brown bee, the rules were justified under Article 36.[102]

In the light of *Bluhme*, can it be said that the protection of health derogation includes environmental protection? This was of particular significance when the Court maintained a clear distinction in the scope of application between the express derogations and the broader, judicially developed, mandatory requirements which include environmental protection (see fig. 4.1). The case law is not clear on this point. *FFAD*[103] suggests that environmental protection does not form part of the public-health derogation. The Court said that 'the protection of the environment cannot serve to justify any restriction on exports, particularly in the case of waste destined for recovery'. However, other cases point the opposite way. For example, in *Aher-Waggon*,[104] the Court said that a discriminatory German rule subjecting aircraft which had been registered in another Member State to stricter noise standards than those for equivalent domestic aircraft might be 'justified by considerations of public health *and* environmental protection'.[105]

*PreussenElektra*[106] also suggests that the public-health derogation might include environmental protection. The case concerned a national law requiring electricity supply undertakings to purchase all of the renewable electricity produced within their area of supply. The Court noted that the use of renewable energy sources for producing electricity was good for protecting the environment insofar as it contributed to the reduction in emissions of greenhouse gases. It then pointed to various Union documents which committed the EU to the greater use of renewable energy sources and added 'that policy is also designed to protect the health and life of humans, animals and plants'.[107] The Court also noted that Article 11 TFEU (ex Article 6 EC) requires environmental protection to be integrated into the definition and implementation of other Union policies. Without explaining whether the ruling was based on Article 36 or the mandatory requirements, the Court then concluded that 'in the current state of [Union] law' the national law was 'not incompatible with Article [34]'. Although the reasoning is not clear, *PreussenElektra* may be authority for the fact that environmental protection is a mandatory requirement, which has long been established, or, more radically, that environmental protection can be read into the Article 36 public-health derogation.

---

[102] Para. 33.

[103] Case C–209/98 *FFAD* v. *Københavns Kommune* [2000] ECR I–3473, para. 48, although cf. the ambiguity in para. 49. See also Case C–203/96 *Chemische Afvalstoffen Dusseldorp BV and others* v. *Minister van Volkshuisvesting, Ruimtelijke Ordening en Milieubeheer* [1998] ECR I–4075 where the Court seems to suggest that the Art. 36 derogations and the mandatory requirement of environmental protection are different (para. 49).

[104] Case C–389/96 *Aher-Waggon* v. *Germany* [1998] ECR I–4473, para. 19. See further N. Notaro, 'The new generation case law on trade and environment' (2000) 25 *ELRev.* 467.

[105] Emphasis added. The Court also noted that the German measures were proportionate because Germany was a densely populated state which attached special importance to ensuring that its population was protected from excessive noise emissions (para. 19); and that limiting noise emissions from aircraft was the most effective and convenient means of combating the noise pollution they created (para. 21). See also Case C–142/05 *Mickelsson* [2009] ECR I–000, para. 33.

[106] Case C–379/98 *PreussenElektra AG* v. *Schhleswag AG* [2001] ECR I–2099.

[107] Para. 75.

## 6. THE PROTECTION OF NATIONAL TREASURES POSSESSING ARTISTIC, HISTORIC, OR ARCHAEOLOGICAL VALUE

The Court has decided no case on the basis of the national treasures[108] derogation. The defence was, however, raised by the Italian government in *Commission v. Italy (art treasures)*.[109] The case concerned an Italian tax on exports of goods having an artistic, historic, archaeological, or ethnographic value. The Court found that since the tax was a charge having equivalent effect to a customs duty (CEE) under Article 30, and not an MEE, Article 36 did not apply.

The values recognized by this derogation were reinforced by the inclusion of the Title on Culture into the Treaties at Maastricht. Article 167(2) TFEU (ex Article 151(2) EC) provides that 'Action by the Union shall be aimed at encouraging cooperation between the Member States' including 'conservation and safeguarding of cultural heritage of European significance'. Nevertheless, the existence of Article 167 did not persuade the Court in *LIBRO*[110] to extend the national treasures derogation to cover the 'protection of cultural diversity in general'.

More specifically, the objectives of Article 36 have been buttressed by the adoption of Directive 93/7/EEC on the return of cultural objects unlawfully removed from the territory of a Member State.[111] This directive, along with Regulation 116/2009 on the export of cultural goods from the EU,[112] is not a harmonization measure. Instead, Directive 93/7 provides for cooperation between the states and a procedure for returning national treasures which have already left the territory of a Member State unlawfully. Regulation 3911/92, by contrast, goes further by setting up uniform preventive controls at the Union's external borders on the export of protected goods to third countries and requires the enforcement agencies to take account of the interests of other Member States.

## 7. THE PROTECTION OF INDUSTRIAL AND COMMERCIAL PROPERTY

The derogation on the protection of industrial and commercial property covers patents, trade marks, copyright, and other types of design rights. It is intended to protect private, as opposed to the public, interests found in the other derogations. In this area, the Court has engaged in a delicate balancing act between Article 34 and the first and second sentences of Article 36. Given its specialized nature, we shall consider the protection of IPRs in a separate chapter now found on the website accompanying this book. Protection of geographical denominations are also covered by this derogation and they are considered in Case Study 6.1 below.

---

[108] Guidance as to the meaning of this term may be derived from Dir. 93/7/EEC on the return of cultural objects unlawfully removed from the territory of a Member State [1993] OJ L74/74.

[109] Case 7/68 [1968] ECR 617.

[110] Case C–531/07 *LIBRO Handelsgesellschaft mbH* [2009] ECR I–000, paras. 32–3.

[111] [1993] OJ L74/74.

[112] [2009] OJ L39/1). See generally A. Biondi, 'The merchant, the thief and the citizen: The circulation of works of art within the EU' (1997) 34 *CMLRev.* 1173.

## 8. THE SECOND SENTENCE OF ARTICLE 36:
## ARBITRARY DISCRIMINATION AND
## A DISGUISED RESTRICTION ON TRADE

All measures for which an Article 36 derogation is claimed are justifiable only to the extent that they do not 'constitute a means of arbitrary discrimination or a disguised restriction on trade between Member States' under the second sentence of Article 36. The Court considered the meaning of this phrase in *Henn and Darby*,[113] the case concerning the ban on the import of pornographic material which the UK defended on the grounds of public morality. However, in the UK there was a discrepancy between the laws of the constituent parts of the UK on indecent or obscene articles. This, the defendants argued, breached the second sentence of Article 36. The Court disagreed.[114] It noted that the function of the second sentence of Article 36 was to prevent restrictions on trade based on one of the Article 36 derogations mentioned from being diverted from their proper purpose and used in such a way as either to create discrimination in respect of goods originating in other Member States or indirectly to protect certain national products. This was not the case with the UK's prohibition. The Court said that since the British laws, taken as a whole, had as their purpose the prohibition of the manufacture and marketing of publications or articles of an indecent or obscene character, there was no breach of the second sentence of Article 36.

The Court is particularly suspicious of the public-health defence being used as a disguised restriction on trade. At times this suspicion is justified, as the infamous *Turkeys* case[115] demonstrates. Shortly before Christmas 1981, the UK introduced a slaughter policy to deal with flocks infected with Newcastle disease, a contagious disease affecting poultry. Previously the UK had used a vaccination policy which the other Member States continued to use. At the same time, the UK introduced an import ban on poultry meat and eggs from all other Member States (except Denmark and Ireland) in order to protect animal health since, it said, in the absence of a vaccination policy the British flock would be susceptible to infection from imports.

Despite these apparently strong health arguments, the Court noted that the circumstances surrounding the ban revealed a rather different picture. It found that there had been a dramatic increase in the number of turkeys imported into the UK, especially from France, and that British turkey producers had lobbied the British government to take action to protect the domestic industry.[116] This action was deliberately timed to prevent imports of turkeys from France for the 1981 Christmas season.[117] Given the lack of consultation with the EU institutions about the change of policy and, in the absence of detailed background scientific work, the Court concluded that the UK measures did not 'form part of a seriously considered health policy'.[118] Instead, it said that the British measures constituted a disguised restriction on imports,[119] since 'the real aim of the 1981 measures was to block, for commercial and economic reasons, imports of poultry products from other Member States, in particular from France'.[120] The Court also considered that the measures were disproportionate: there were less stringent methods for achieving

---

[113] Case 34/79 [1979] ECR 3795.       [114] Para. 21.
[115] Case 40/82 *Commission v. United Kingdom* [1984] ECR 2793.       [116] Para. 22.
[117] Paras. 23 and 37.       [118] Para. 38.       [119] Para. 40.       [120] Para. 37.

the protection of animal health.[121] Subsequently the French turkey producers sued the British government for the losses they had suffered. Although the Court of Appeal struck out part of their claim,[122] they won £3.5 million in an out-of-court settlement.[123]

Generally, Member States must take equivalent action against their own producers to stand a chance of succeeding with a public-health defence. However, as the Court pointed out in *Rewe-Zentralfinanz*,[124] differential treatment is justifiable if there is a real risk affecting the import which is not present in the domestic product.[125] Therefore, the German authorities could conduct a phytosanitary inspection on imported apples to combat the apple disease, San José scale, where there was a real risk of the disease spreading to German apples in the absence of an inspection.[126] In these circumstances the inspection of imports, but not the domestic products which were unaffected by the disease, was lawful: it was discriminatory but not arbitrary.

Not only must the second sentence of Article 36 be respected by the Member States but any measure taken by States must respect the general principles of law, in particular proportionality and fundamental human rights. We consider these issues below. First, however, we shall examine the mandatory requirements.

# C. THE 'MANDATORY' REQUIREMENTS

## 1. INTRODUCTION

As we have seen, in *Cassis de Dijon* the Court developed an open-ended list of (confusingly named) 'mandatory requirements' to supplement the Article 36 derogations.[127] It did this to placate the Member States: its ruling on mutual recognition made significant inroads into states' competence to regulate products traded on their territory. The mandatory requirements were the states' compensation. Soon after *Cassis*,[128] the Court confirmed that mandatory requirements applied only to indistinctly applicable,[129] not

---

[121] Para. 41. Cf. Case 74/82 *Commission v. Ireland* [1984] ECR 317 (there, licensing of poultry imports was in principle lawful).

[122] *Bourgoin* v. *MAFF* [1986] QB 716, in a case which, following Joined Cases C–46 and 48/93 *Brasserie du Pêcheur and Factortame (No. 3)* [1996] ECR I–1029, is probably no longer good law.

[123] HC Debs. vol. 102 col. 116 (WA) 22 Jul. 1986 cited in Weatherill and Beaumont, above n. 10, 538.

[124] Case 4/75 *Rewe-Zentralfinanz* [1975] ECR 843 (San José scale), para. 8. See also Case 42/82 *Commission v. France (wine)* [1983] ECR 1013, para. 56; Case 50/85 *Schloh v. Auto Contrôle Technique SPRL* [1986] ECR 1855, para. 15.  [125] Case 4/75 *Rewe-Zentralfinanz* [1995] ECR 843, para. 8.

[126] The Court added that effective measures also had to be taken to prevent the distribution of contaminated domestic products.

[127] See generally J. Scott, 'Mandatory or imperative requirements in the EU and the WTO' in C. Barnard and J. Scott (eds.), *The Law of the Single European Market: Unpacking the premises* (Oxford: Hart, 2002), and E. Spaventa, 'On discrimination and the theory of mandatory requirements' (2001) 3 *CYELS* 457.

[128] Case 788/79 *Criminal Proceedings against Gilli and Andres* [1980] ECR 2071, para. 6. See also Case 6/81 *Beele* [1982] ECR 707, para. 7; Case C–67/88 *Commission v. Italy* [1990] ECR I–4285, para. 4; Case 94/82 *De Kikvorsch* [1983] ECR 947, para. 6; Case 182/84 *Miro* [1985] ECR 3731, para. 10.

[129] See Joined Cases C–1 and 176/90 *Aragonesa* [1991] ECR I–4151, para. 13: 'whereas according to the Court's case law the question of imperative requirements...cannot arise unless the measure in question applies without distinction to both national and imported products'; and Case C–2/90 *Commission v. Belgium (Walloon waste)* [1992] ECR I–4431, para. 34: 'Imperative requirements can indeed be taken into account only in the case of measures which apply without distinction to both domestic and imported products...'.

distinctly applicable, measures[130] (see fig. 4.1), although, as we have seen, this rigid distinction is breaking down.[131]

Mandatory requirements, now increasingly called 'imperative requirements'[132] or 'overriding requirements in the public interest'[133] to dovetail with the Court's jurisprudence on the free movement of persons,[134] are 'good' reasons put forward by the Member States to justify their conduct,[135] often based on Union policies identified in the Treaties.[136] They are the functional equivalents of the concept of objective justification developed in the context of indirectly discriminatory national taxes under Article 110 (see fig. 3.2). The mandatory requirements must be unrelated to the origin of the goods and they must serve objectives considered by the Court to be legitimate. They must also be accompanied by appropriate evidence showing that the rules genuinely serve the purposes for which they are intended;[137] mere assertion by the Member State is not sufficient.[138] Finally, like the Article 36 derogations, mandatory requirements are available only in the absence of harmonization.[139]

## 2. EXAMPLES OF 'MANDATORY' OR 'PUBLIC INTEREST' REQUIREMENTS

In *Cassis* the Court recognized four mandatory requirements:[140]

- the effectiveness of fiscal supervision[141]
- the protection of public health[142]

---

[130] Case 113/80 *Commission v. Ireland (Irish souvenirs)* [1981] ECR 1625, para. 11; Case 177/83 *Ringelhan* [1984] ECR 3651, para. 19; Case 59/82 *Schutzverband gegen Unwesen in der Wirtschaft v. Weinvertriebs-GmbH* [1983] ECR 1217, para. 11; Case C–21/88 *Du Pont de Nemours* [1990] ECR I–889, para. 14; Cases C–321–4/94 *Pistre* [1997] ECR I–2343, para. 52.

[131] Case C–524/07 *Commission v. Austria (roadworthiness of cars)* [2008] ECR I–187*, paras. 54–5.

[132] E.g., see Case 178/84 *Commission v. Germany* [1987] ECR 1227, para. 30, and Case C–239/90 *Boscher* [1991] ECR I–2023, paras. 17–18. As Weatherill and Beaumont point out, above n. 10, 575, the French term is *exigences impératives* and the Italian term is *esigenze imperative*. They note that neither 'mandatory' nor 'imperative' is entirely felicitous; the concept is closer to 'compelling' than 'compulsory'.

[133] Joined Cases C–267 and 268/91 *Keck and Mithouard* [1993] ECR I–6097, para. 15; Case C–368/95 *Familiapress* [1997] ECR I–3689, paras. 18 and 24; Joined Cases C–34–36/95 *De Agostini* [1997] ECR I–3843, paras. 45–6; Case C–3/99 *Cidrerie Ruwet SA v. Cidre Stassen SA and HP Mulmer Ltd* [2000] ECR I–8749, paras. 49–50.

[134] See Ch. 13.

[135] The burden of proof is on the Member State which cannot rely on the justification in the abstract but must specifically demonstrate its genuineness: Case C–14/02 *ATRAL SA v. Etat belge* [2003] ECR I–4431, para. 67.

[136] N. Nic Shuibhne, 'The free movement of goods and Article 28 EC: An evolving framework' (2002) 27 *ELRev.* 408, esp. 419ff.

[137] Case C–254/05 *Commission v. Belgium (automatic fire detection systems)* [2007] ECR I–4269, para. 36.

[138] E.g., Case C–265/06 *Commission v. Portugal (tinted windows)* [2008] ECR I–2245, paras. 40–7.

[139] See Case 120/78 *Cassis de Dijon* [1979] ECR 649, para. 8.      [140] Ibid.

[141] Case 823/79 *Criminal Proceedings against Carciati* [1980] ECR 2773, para. 9.

[142] See, e.g., Case 178/84 *Commission v. Germany (beer purity laws)* [1987] ECR 1227; Case C–123/00 *Bellamy and English Shop Wholesale SA* [2001] ECR I–2759; Case C–358/95 *Tommaso Morellato v. Unità sanitaria locale (USL), n. 11 di Pordenone* [1997] ECR I–1431; Joined Cases C–1 and 176/90 *Aragonesa* [1991] ECR I–4151, para. 13.

- the fairness of commercial transactions[143]
- the defence of the consumer.[144]

Subsequently, the Court recognized the following mandatory requirements:

- protection of the environment[145]
- protection of working conditions[146]
- protection of cinema as a form of cultural expression[147]
- protection of national or regional socio-cultural characteristics[148]
- maintenance of press diversity;[149] and, in a similar vein, the protection of books as cultural objects[150]
- preventing the risk of seriously undermining the financial balance of the social security system[151]
- protection of fundamental rights[152]
- preserving the maintenance of order in society[153]
- road safety[154]
- protection of children[155]

---

[143] See also Case 58/80 *Dansk Supermarked A/S* v. *A/S Imerco* [1981] ECR 181, considered further in the IPR chapter on the Internet website.

[144] Case 120/78 *Cassis de Dijon* [1979] ECR 649. In more recent cases the Court merges the two headings and talks of 'fair trading and the protection of the consumer'. See, e.g., Case C–448/98 *Guimont* [2000] ECR I–10663, para. 30.

[145] Case 302/86 *Commission* v. *Denmark* [1988] ECR 4607 and hints to that effect in Case 240/83 *Procureur de la République* v. *Association de Défense des Brûleurs d'Huiles Usagées* [1985] ECR 531; Case C–284/95 *Safety Hi-Tech Srl* v. *S & T. Srl* [1998] ECR I–4301, para. 64; Case C–389/96 *Aher-Waggon GmbH* v. *Germany* [1998] ECR I–4473; Case C–320/03 *Commission* v. *Austria* [2005] ECR I–7929, para. 35. See also Case 142/05 *Mickelsson* [2009] ECR I–000, para. 30 where the Court appeared to accept the Swedish government's argument that restricting the use of jet-skis on inland waterways could be justified on the grounds of environmental protection. It said that the use of personal watercraft had negative consequences for fauna, in particular where such craft are used for a lengthy period on a small area or driven at great speed. The noise as a whole disturbs people and animals and above all certain protected species of birds. Furthermore, the easy transport of personal watercraft facilitates the spread of animal diseases.

[146] Case 155/80 *Oebel* [1981] ECR 1993, para. 12: a prohibition on night working in the bakery industry 'constitutes a legitimate element of economic and social policy, consistent with the objectives of public interest pursued by the [Treaties]. Indeed this prohibition is designed to improve working conditions in a manifestly sensitive industry…'.

[147] Case 60/84 *Cinéthèque* v. *Fédération Nationale des Cinémas Français* [1985] ECR 2605.

[148] Case 145/88 *Torfaen Borough Council* v. *B & Q* [1989] ECR 3851.

[149] Case C–368/95 *Familiapress* [1997] ECR I–3689.

[150] Case C–531/07 *LIBRO* [2009] ECR I–000, para. 34.

[151] Case C–120/95 *Decker* v. *Caisse de Maladie des Employés Privés* [1998] ECR I–1831.

[152] Case C–112/00 *Schmidberger* [2003] ECR I–5659 para. 82. See also Case C–36/02 *Omega Spielhallen* [2004] ECR I–9609.

[153] Case C–65/05 *Commission* v *Greece (computer games)* [2006] ECR I–10341, paras. 32–4 referring to the services case law beginning with Case C–275/92 *Schindler* [1994] ECR I–1039, para. 58 considered further in Ch. 11.

[154] Case C–54/05 *Commission* v. *Finland* [2007] ECR I–2473, para. 40; Case C–265/06 *Commission* v. *Portugal (tinted film)* [2008] ECR I–2245, para. 36; Case C–110/05 *Commission* v. *Italy (trailers)* [2009] ECR I–519, para. 60.

[155] Case C–244/06 *Dynamic Medien Vertriebs GmbH* [2008] ECR I–505, para. 42.

- protection of animal welfare[156]
- the fight against crime.[157]

This non-exhaustive list demonstrates that the Court accepts most of the mandatory requirements put forward by the Member States provided that the national policies do not pursue aims of a purely economic nature.[158] The list also shows a recognition by the *EU* of non-commercial values[159] important to the *Member States*, and a confirmation by the Court that the Treaties are not purely about creating an economic constitution. The interests recognized range from protection of third parties (consumers, children, road users), protection of public order (effectiveness of fiscal supervision, maintenance of the plurality of the press, preservation of the social security system, preserving order in society, the fight against crime), and protection of fundamental rights. As we shall see in chapter 13, these fields of protected interests are broadly replicated in the context of free movement of persons and services. However, the problem facing the Court is that, each time it is called to adjudicate on any case where a mandatory requirement is invoked and the proportionality of the steps taken to achieve that objective are at issue, it has to rule on broad policy questions, thereby placing judges 'at the outer limits of their legitimate judicial role, where the judiciary risks substituting its assessment for that of the legislature'.[160]

We turn now to consider the mandatory requirements which have presented particular difficulties for the Court, consumer protection and fundamental rights.

## 3. CONSUMER PROTECTION

The two mandatory requirements most commonly invoked by the Member States are public health and consumer protection. Public health reflects the more carefully worded derogation found in Article 36 and the Court invariably refers to Article 36 when justifications based on public health are raised. As far as consumer protection is concerned, the Court has in mind 'the presumed expectations of an average consumer who is reasonably well-informed and reasonably observant and circumspect'.[161] This individual also reads labels on products.[162] In other words, Union law does not permit national laws protecting the unobservant and unintelligent consumer,[163] when such laws stand in the way of

---

[156] Case C–219/07 *Nationale Raad van Dierenkwekers en Liefhebbers VZW v. Belgische Staat* [2008] ECR I–4475, para. 27.

[157] Case C–265/06 *Commission v. Portugal* [2008] ECR I–2245, para. 38.

[158] Case C–254/98 *Schutzverband gegen unlauteren Wettbewerb v. TK-Heimdienst Sass GmbH* [2000] ECR I–151, para. 33.

[159] De Witte, 'Non-market values in internal market legislation' in N. Nic Shuibhne (ed.), *Regulating the Internal Market* (Cheltenham: Edward Elgar, 2006).

[160] D. Wyatt and A. Dashwood, *European Union Law*, 5th edn (London: Sweet and Maxwell, 2006), 587.

[161] Case C–210/96 *Gut Springenheide GmbH v. Oberkreisdirektor des Kreises Steinfurt* [1998] ECR I–4657, para. 31. The Court added that it was not necessary to order an expert's report or commission a consumer research poll on whether the consumer was likely to be misled. See also Case C–358/01 *Commission v. Spain (bleach)* [2003] ECR I–13145; Case C–446/07 *Severi v. Regione Emilia-Romagna* [2009] ECR I–000, para. 61.

[162] Case C–51/94 *Commission v. Germany* [1995] ECR I–3599, para. 34. H. von Heydebrand u.d. Lasa, 'Free movement of foodstuffs, consumer protection and food standards in the European Community: Has the Court of Justice got it wrong?' (1991) 16 *ELRev.* 391, 399, cites research suggesting that only 20% of consumers read labels.

[163] S. Weatherill, 'Recent case law concerning the free movement of goods: Mapping the frontiers of market deregulation' (1999) 36 *CMLRev.* 51, 54. Commission Communication, EU Consumer Policy

market integration which is of benefit to the consumer body as a whole.[164] The Court has taken the view that, in general, the consumer is better served by having access to a wider choice of products, some of which will be of better quality than others, than a narrower choice but with higher *national* standards of consumer protection. However, the Court has made this policy choice against a background of an increasing volume of *Union* level consumer legislation. The Court's approach can be seen in two references from Germany, *Clinique*[165] and *Mars*.[166]

In *Clinique* a German rule required that all 'Clinique' (cosmetic) products be sold under the name 'Linique' on the ground that the 'Clinique' name could mislead consumers into believing that the products had medicinal properties. Rejecting the consumer protection justification, the Court noted that the Clinique products were sold only in department stores, not in pharmacies, and they were presented as cosmetics and not as medicinal products. It concluded that the products were ordinarily marketed under the name Clinique in other countries where 'the use of that name apparently does not mislead consumers'.[167]

In *Mars* the German association against 'pernicious trading practices', which had complained about Mars' '+10%' promotion, argued that the campaign might conceal a price rise and that, since the '+10%' flash covered more than a tenth of the total surface area of the wrapping, consumers might be misled into thinking that they were receiving more than 10 per cent extra. The Court rejected both arguments. It said that Mars had not profited from the campaign by increasing its prices and that '[r]easonably circumspect consumers could be deemed to know that there was not necessarily a link between the size of publicity markings relating to an increase in a product's quantity and the size of that increase'.[168]

These cases show that, in defining a European approach to consumer protection, the Court rejected the German model based on the 'uninformed consumer' in favour of the model of the 'mature and prudent' consumer which dominates in other Member States.[169] In so doing, the Court adopted a 'majoritarian' approach, allowing the view of the majority of Member States to prevail over that of the (German) minority.[170] The Court is, however, prepared to relax its criteria for the average consumer in appropriate circumstances.

Strategy 2007–2013, COM(2007) 99, 3 which suggests more attention should be paid to the vulnerable (children and the old). See also Art. 5(3) of the Unfair Commercial Practices Directive 2005/29/EC ([2005] OJ L149/22) which makes special provision for 'consumers who are particularly vulnerable...because of their mental or physical infirmity'.

[164] This is the view of the other Union institutions: see, e.g., Council Res. concerning the future orientation of the policy of the EEC for the protection and promotion of consumer interests ([1986] OJ C167/1); Commission, Green Paper on European Union Consumer Protection, COM(2001)531, 3: 'It is the cross-border movement of goods and services that allows consumers to search out bargains and innovative products and services and thus ensures that they optimise their consumption decisions.' See generally G. Howells and T. Wilhelmsson, 'EC consumer law: Has it come of age?' (2003) 28 *ELRev.* 370.

[165] Case C–315/92 *Verband Sozialer Wettbewerb ev* v. *Clinique Laboratories SNC* [1994] ECR I–317.

[166] Case C–470/93 *Verein gegen Unwesen in Handel und Gewerbe Köln* v. *Mars GmbH* [1995] ECR I–1923. [167] Para. 21.

[168] Para. 24.

[169] H. Micklitz and S. Weatherill, *European Economic Law* (Aldershot: Ashgate, 1997), 271. See also H. Unberath and A. Johnston, 'The double-headed approach of the ECJ concerning consumer protection' (2007) 44 *CMLRev.* 1237.

[170] M. Poiares Maduro, *We the Court: The European Court of Justice and the European Economic Constitution* (Oxford: Hart Publishing, 1998), Ch. 3.

For example, it has conceded that account can be taken of 'social, cultural or linguistic factors'[171] when assessing consumer protection. It has also upheld national laws designed to protect the below average consumer where, as in *Buet*,[172] the product is targeted at the 'particularly vulnerable consumer', such as those who are 'behind with their education and are seeking to catch up'.[173]

The case concerned a French law prohibiting doorstep selling of educational materials which, the Court said, while constituting an obstacle to the free movement of goods could be justified on the ground of consumer protection. It said that since teaching material was not a consumer product in daily use, an ill-considered purchase could cause the consumer harm other than mere financial loss because the purchase of unsuitable or low-quality material could 'compromise the consumer's chances of obtaining further training and thus consolidating his position on the labour market'.[174] In these circumstances the Court said a right to cancel the contract[175] was not sufficient and the Member State was permitted to retain its more protective national laws.[176]

If the Court considers that there is a sufficiently serious risk of consumers being misled,[177] owing to linguistic, cultural, and social differences, then the marketing of the product can be prohibited on the ground of consumer protection. Therefore, in *Graffione*[178] the Court said that a Member State was justified in prohibiting the sale of toilet paper and paper handkerchiefs under the trade mark Cotonelle if there was a sufficiently serious risk of consumers thinking that they contained cotton. Generally, however, the Court tends to be rather sceptical of the claims by states for consumer protection because it fears that such arguments are a simple disguise for protectionism. This can be seen in *GB-INNO*[179] which concerned a Luxembourg rule prohibiting shops from advertising when their sales were due to take place and how long they would last. Because the effect of this rule was to deny consumers, particularly those in Belgium, access to certain kinds of information the Court said it could not be justified on the ground of consumer protection.[180] Thus the Luxembourg rule which was intended to protect consumers actually denied them a benefit and so contravened Union law.[181]

---

[171] Case C–220/98 *Estée Lauder Cosmetics GmbH & Co. OHG v. Lancaster Group GmbH* [2000] ECR I–117, para. 29.

[172] Case 382/87 *Buet* [1989] ECR 1235, para. 13. See also Case C–441/04 *A-Punkt Schmuckhandels GmbH v. Schmidt* [2006] ECR I–2093, para. 28 where the Court insisted that account be taken of the level of protection to be enjoyed by consumers in that case under Dir. 85/577 (OJ [1985] L372/31) on protecting the consumer in respect of contracts negotiated away from business premises.

[173] Conversely, if the consumer is 'specially informed' then lower standards of consumer protection are applied: Case C–239/90 *Boscher v. SA British Motors Wright* [1991] ECR I–2023, para. 20.

[174] Para. 14.

[175] As permitted by the Doorstep Selling Dir. 85/577 ([1985] OJ L372/31). See further Ch. 16.

[176] See also Case 286/81 *Oosthoek* [1982] ECR 4575 where the Court ruled that offering free gifts as a means of sales promotion could mislead consumers as to the real prices of certain products and distort the conditions on which genuine competition is based.

[177] There must be a high degree of consumer confusion: Case C–373/90 *Complaint against X* [1992] ECR I–131.　　　　　　　　　　　　　　　[178] Case C–313/94 *Fratelli Graffione SNC v. Ditta Fransa* [1996] ECR I–6039.

[179] Case C–362/88 *GB-INNO-BM* [1990] ECR I–667.

[180] Para. 19. This decision provided further stimulus for the need for a directive on comparative advertising to supplement the existing directive on misleading advertising. This led to EP and Council Dir. 97/55/EC ([1997] OJ L290/18) amending Dir. 84/450 ([1984] OJ L250/17) concerning misleading advertising so as to include comparative advertising. The directive has now been codified: EP and Council Dir. 2006/114 ([2006] OJ L376/21).

[181] On the essential role of advertising to provide users with information about the existence and availability of products see Case C–320/93 *Ortscheit* [1994] ECR I–5243, para. 10.

## 4. FUNDAMENTAL RIGHTS

The other mandatory requirement which has raised difficulties for the Court is the protection of fundamental rights. As we saw in *Schmidberger*,[182] fundamental rights, particularly guaranteeing freedom of expression and freedom of assembly, were successfully raised by the Austrian government to justify its failure to ensure the free movement of goods during the environmentalists' protest. Austria also raised a species of fundamental rights argument to explain why, in *Familiapress*,[183] it prevented newspapers and magazines from offering prize competitions. Its justification was to preserve press diversity[184] by preventing large publishers from driving smaller publishers off the market owing to their ability to offer larger prizes. This is, in essence, an argument based on freedom of expression under Article 10 ECHR.

However, the potential scope of the fundamental rights justification is not unlimited, as *A.G.M-COS.MET*[185] demonstrates. This case concerned a Finnish expert expressing doubt about the safety of some imported Italian lifts, albeit that the lifts were certified as conforming to the relevant directive. His remarks potentially breached Article 34 and the Finnish government relied on a human rights justification to escape liability. The Court rejected the justification:[186]

Under Article 10(1) of the European Convention on Human Rights, everyone within the jurisdiction of the Member States is guaranteed the right to freedom of expression. That freedom is an essential foundation of any democratic society. Member States, however, cannot rely on their officials' freedom of expression to justify an obstacle and thereby evade their own liability under [Union] law.

Even where a Member State is successful in invoking an Article 36 derogation or a mandatory requirement it must also show that the measures are proportionate to the risk presented by the import. It is to the question of proportionality that we now turn.

# D. PROPORTIONALITY

## 1. THE TEST

The principle of proportionality comprises essentially two tests: a test of suitability and a test of necessity. As Tridimas explains,[187] the first (suitability) refers to the relationship between the means and the ends: the means employed by the test must be suitable (or adequate or appropriate) to attain the ends (e.g., road safety). As the Court put it in *United Foods*,[188] there has to be a 'reasonable connexion' between the measures laid down by the authorities and the exercise of control. The second test (necessity) is one of weighing

---

[182] Case C–112/00 *Schmidberger* [2003] ECR I–5659, above n. 38.

[183] Case C–368/95 *Familiapress* [1997] ECR I–3689. See also P. Oliver, 'A review of the case law of the Court of Justice on Articles 30 to 36 EEC in 1985' (1986) 23 *CMLRev.* 325, 348–50.

[184] This was a particular problem in Austria where the market share of the largest press group was 55%, whereas in the UK it was 35%, and in Germany 24%.

[185] Case C–470/03 *A.G.M.-COS.MET Srl v. Soumen valtio, Tarmo Lehtinen* [2007] ECR I–2749, para. 72. This case is discussed further in Ch. 4. [186] Para. 72.

[187] T. Tridimas, 'Proportionality in Community law: Searching for the appropriate standard of scrutiny', in E. Ellis (ed.), *The Principle of Proportionality in the Laws of Europe* (Oxford: Hart Publishing, 1999), 68.

[188] Case 132/80 *NV United Foods and PVBA Aug. Van den Abeele v. Belgium* [1981] ECR 995, para. 28.

competing interests: the Court assesses the adverse consequences that the measure has on an interest worthy of legal protection and determines whether those consequences are justified in view of the importance of the objective pursued. Sometimes this second limb is viewed as having two distinct elements: whether there are other less restrictive means of producing the same result and, even if there are no less restrictive means, whether the measure, nevertheless, has an excessive effect on the applicant's interests.[189]

The burden of proof is on the national authorities to show that their rules satisfy the test of proportionality.[190] They must also show that they have pursued the stated objectives in a consistent and systematic manner.[191] However, as the Court pointed out in *Commission v. Italy (trailers)*,[192] 'that burden of proof cannot be so extensive as to require the Member States to prove, positively, that no other conceivable measure could enable that objective to be attained under the same conditions'.

Thus, using the medium of proportionality, the court (usually the national court in preliminary references[193] but sometimes the Court of Justice[194]) performs a balancing exercise between the objectives pursued by the national measure and its adverse effects on free movement. There is some evidence that if the proportionality review is performed by the Court of Justice, it tends to find the national measure disproportionate. By contrast, if the review is conducted by the national court it tends to uphold the validity of the measure.[195]

## 2. APPLYING THE PROPORTIONALITY TEST

The Court's approach to applying the proportionality principle can be seen in *Familiapress*.[196] It will be recalled that an Austrian rival sought to restrain sales of the magazine 'Laura' published in Germany on the ground that the magazine included prize competitions which contravened an Austrian law on unfair competition. The Court said that the rule breached Article 34 but could be justified on the grounds of press diversity (i.e., the need to protect small publishers who might be able to offer only smaller prizes from larger publishers able to offer larger prizes). It then left it to the national court to determine whether the national prohibition was 'proportionate to the aim of maintaining press diversity and whether that objective might not be attained by measures less restrictive of both intra-[Union] trade and freedom of expression'.[197] The Court then explained exactly how the national court should do this.

---

[189] For a variation on this theme, see Case C–170/04 *Rosengren* [2007] ECR I–4071, para. 50: 'they are necessary in order to achieve the declared objective, and that that objective could not be achieved by less extensive prohibitions or restrictions, or by prohibitions or restrictions having less effect on intra-[Union] trade'. See also Case C–141/07 *Commission v. Germany (pharmacies for hospitals)* [2008] ECR I–6935, para. 50.

[190] Case C–110/05 *Commission v. Italy* [2009] ECR I–519, para. 62.

[191] See, e.g., Case C–265/06 *Commission v. Portugal (tinted windows)* [2008] ECR I–2245, para. 43; Case C–500/06 *Corporación Dermostética* [2008] ECR I–5785, para. 39.

[192] Case C–110/05 *Commission v. Italy* [2009] ECR I–519, para. 66.

[193] See, e.g., Case 251/78 *Firma Denkavit Futtermittel GmbH* [1979] ECR 3369.

[194] See, e.g., Case C–189/95 *Criminal proceedings against Harry Franzén* [1997] ECR I–5909, para. 76.

[195] C. Barnard, 'Derogations, justifications and the four freedoms: Is state interest really protected?' in C. Barnard and O. Odudu (eds.), *The Outer Limits of EU Law* (Oxford: Hart Publishing 2009).

[196] Case C–368/95 *Familiapress* [1997] ECR I–3689. See also P. Oliver, 'A review of the case law of the Court of Justice on Articles 30 to 36 EEC in 1985' (1986) 23 *CMLRev.* 325, 348–50.

[197] Para. 27.

On the question of suitability, the Court said the national court had to commission a study[198] to determine: first, whether newspapers which offered the chance of winning a prize in competitions were actually in competition with those small press publishers who were considered unable to offer comparable prizes; and, secondly, whether the prospect of winning did constitute an incentive for potential consumers to purchase magazines and whether this was capable of bringing about a shift in demand. The Court continued that the national court also had to assess the extent to which, from the consumer's standpoint, the product concerned could be replaced by magazines which did not offer prizes. In making this assessment the national court had to take into account all the circumstances which might influence the decision to purchase, such as the presence of advertising on the front cover referring to the chance of winning a prize, the likelihood of winning, the value of the prize, or the extent to which winning depended on a test calling for a measure of ingenuity, skill, or knowledge.

The Court then turned to the question of necessity (whether the Austrian legislature could have adopted measures less restrictive of free movement of goods than an outright prohibition on the distribution of newspapers). It said the national court[199] had to consider whether national law could have required merely the removal of the page on which the prize competition appeared in copies intended for the Austrian market or the addition of a statement that readers in Austria did not qualify for the chance to win a prize.

*Familiapress* demonstrates that the application of the tests of suitability and necessity enables courts to review not only the legality, but also to some extent the merit, of legislative and administrative measures.[200] As Tridimas says, for this reason proportionality is often perceived as a far-reaching ground of review.[201] This view is reinforced by *Campus Oil*[202] where the Court said:

Article 36, as an exception to a fundamental principle of the [Treaties], must be interpreted in such a way that its scope is not extended any further than is necessary for the protection of the interests which it is intended to secure and the measures taken pursuant to that Article must not create obstacles to imports which are disproportionate to those objectives. Measures adopted on the basis of Article 36 can therefore be justified only if they are such as to serve the interest which that Article protects and if they do not restrict intra-Union trade more than is absolutely necessary.

The strict approach to proportionality can be seen in *Commission* v. *Portugal (tinted windows)*.[203] Portuguese law prohibited the fixing of tinted film on the inside of car

---

[198] Para. 30.

[199] Para. 32. See further W. Van Gerven, 'The effect of proportionality on the actions of the Member States of the European Community: National viewpoints from continental Europe' in Ellis (ed.), above n. 187, 42.

[200] T. Tridimas, 'Proportionality in Community Law: Searching for the appropriate standard of scrutiny' in Ellis (ed.), above n. 187, 68–9. See also, e.g., Case C–67/88 *Commission* v. *Italy* [1990] ECR I–4285 (requirement of adding colour-reactive sesame seed oil to edible vegetable oils to combat fraud not justified because there were no effective controls to see whether the sesame oil had been added).

[201] See further G. de Búrca, 'The principle of proportionality and its application in EC law' (1993) 13 *YEL* 105; G. Bermann, 'Proportionality and subsidiarity', in Barnard and Scott (eds.), above n. 127; F. G. Jacobs, 'Recent developments in the principle of proportionality in EC law' in Ellis (ed.), above n. 187 and 'Public law: The impact of Europe' [1999] *PL* 232.

[202] Case 72/83 [1984] ECR 2727, para. 37.

[203] Case C–265/06 *Commission* v. *Portugal* [2008] ECR I–2245. See also Case C–54/05 *Commission* v. *Finland (Import licences for cars)* [2007] ECR I–2473, paras. 45–6; Case C–297/05 *Commission* v. *Netherlands (Roadworthiness testing of imported cars)* [2007] ECR I–7467, paras. 78–9.

windscreens. Portugal justified this rule on the grounds of the fight against crime and road safety: the absence of film enabled the 'passenger compartment of motor vehicles to be immediately inspected by means of simple observation from outside the vehicle' to check that individuals are not criminals and are wearing seat belts.[204] The Court said that the measure was appropriate but not necessary:[205] a visual inspection was only one means available to the competent authorities for making these checks. The Court added that the Portuguese case was 'further undermined' by the fact that it allowed the marketing of motor vehicles pre-fitted with tinted windows within the limits laid down by the relevant Directive 92/22.[206] The Court concluded that the ban had to be regarded as 'excessive and, therefore, disproportionate with respect to the objectives pursued'.[207]

However, in areas of sensitivity the Court refers to the 'margin of discretion' left to the Member States when considering the question of necessity. This can be seen in *Dynamic Medien*[208] concerning the German authorities' insistence that they re-examine and classify imported DVDs aimed at young people (on the facts Japanese 'Animes' cartoons) which had already been classified by the British Board of Film Classification, the relevant British authority. Because the protection of children was at stake the Court deferred to the discretion of the German authorities and gave only the most cursory examination of the proportionality principle.[209]

## 3. THE MEASURES THAT CAN BE TAKEN BY THE DEFENDANT STATE

### 3.1 Bans, Licences, and Authorizations

In deciding how to protect the interest invoked, the host state has a range of possible steps it can take from, at the one extreme, banning the product, to licensing or authorizing its use on the other. Generally the Court finds that a national rule *banning* the import of a product is disproportionate because less restrictive alternatives exist.[210] So in *Rosengren*[211] the Court said that the ban on imports of alcohol by anyone, irrespective of age, 'goes manifestly beyond what is necessary for the objective sought', namely to protect younger people against the harmful effects of alcohol consumption. However,

---

[204] Para. 40.      [205] Para. 41.

[206] Now repealed and replaced by Reg. (EC) No. 661/2009 ([2009] OJ L200/1). The Commission also pointed out that due to the wide range of tinted film available—from transparent film to film which is almost opaque—at least some film would permit the desired visual inspection of the interior of motor vehicles.

[207] Para. 47.

[208] Case C–244/06 *Dynamic Medien Vertriebs GmbH* [2008] ECR I–505, para. 44; Case C–110/05 *Commission* v. *Italy (trailers)* [2009] ECR I–519, para. 65. See also Case C–284/95 *Safety Hi-Tech Srl* v. *S & T. Srl* [1998] ECR I–4301, para. 66 where the Court simply said that a prohibition on the use and marketing of Hydrochlorofluorocarbons (HCFCs) and halons to help protect the ozone layer could not be regarded as 'disproportionate to the aim pursued', without undertaking any of the analysis outlined in *Familiapress*.

[209] Paras. 47–8.

[210] See, e.g., Case 178/84 *Commission* v. *Germany* [1987] ECR 1227, para. 35; Case C–350/97 *Monsees* v. *Unabhängiger Verwaltungssenat für Kärnten* [1999] ECR I–2921. Case C–112/00 *Schmidberger* [2003] ECR I–5659, para. 89: 'an outright ban on the demonstration would have constituted unacceptable interference with the fundamental rights of the demonstrators to gather and express peacefully their opinion in public'.

[211] Case C–170/04 *Rosengren* [2007] ECR I–4071, para. 51.

there are exceptions: in *Toolex Alpha*[212] the Court found a Swedish ban on the import of trichloroethylene, a proven carcinogen, to be proportionate.

In some cases the Court will accept a more carefully tailored ban. So, in *Aragonesa*[213] the Court noted with approval that the ban on advertising of alcohol applied only to strong drink and to adverts placed in specified public places frequented by motorists and young people, the principal groups intended to be protected; and in the *Loi Evin* cases[214] the Court approved an advertising ban which affected one medium only, television. By contrast, in *Gourmet*[215] the national court was left to decide whether a Swedish law prohibiting advertising of alcoholic drinks in periodicals in order to combat alcohol abuse could be achieved by less extensive restrictions. This called for an analysis of the circumstances of law and fact which characterized the Swedish situation which, the Court of Justice said, the national court was better placed to assess.[216]

Generally, the Court prefers authorization (or equivalent) rules rather than bans. So, in *Schreiber*[217] the Court found that a system of prior authorization of biocidal products before they were placed on the market was proportionate. On the other hand, in *Franzén*[218] the Court said that a Swedish law requiring those selling alcohol to hold a licence, for which a high fee was charged, and to have sufficient storage capacity for that alcohol, was not proportionate to the public-health objective of reducing alcohol consumption. It said that this aim could have been attained by measures less restrictive of intra-Union trade.

Subsequently, in *Canal Satélite Digital*[219] the Court laid down four criteria for an authorization requirement to be justified and proportionate:

- it must be based on objective, non-discriminatory criteria known in advance
- it must not duplicate controls which have already been carried out
- any subsequent control would be too late to be genuinely effective
- it should not deter operators from pursuing their business plan due to its duration and disproportionate costs.

### 3.2 Labelling

Labelling is the Court's favoured solution to many proportionality problems connected with food. We can see this in *Rau*,[220] where the Court recognized that legislation designed to prevent butter and margarine from being confused was in principle justified, but said that the requirement to use only one specific type of packaging 'considerably exceed[ed] the requirements of the object in view'. It continued that consumers could be protected 'just as effectively by other measures, for example by rules on labelling, which hinder

---

[212] Case C–473/98 *Toolex Alpha AB* [2000] ECR I–5681.

[213] Joined Cases C–1 and 176/90 *Aragonesa de Publicidad Exterior SA* [1991] ECR I–4151, paras. 17–18.

[214] Case C–262/02 *Commission* v. *France* [2004] ECR I–6569 and Case C–429/02 *Bacardi France SAS* v. *Télévision française 1 SA* [2004] ECR I–6613.

[215] Case C–405/98 *Gourmet International Products* [2001] ECR I–1795, para. 33. See also Case C–434/04 *Anders Ahokainen* v. *Virallinen syyttäjä* [2006] ECR I–9171, para. 37.

[216] See also Case E–4/04 *Pedicel* v. *Sosial- og helsdirektoratet* [2005] EFTA Ct Rep 1.

[217] Case C–443/02 *Schreiber* [2004] ECR I–7275.

[218] Case C–189/95 *Criminal proceedings against Harry Franzén* [1997] ECR I–5909, para. 76.

[219] Case C–390/99 *Canal Satélite Digital* [2002] ECR I–607. See also the discussion at n. 305 below.

[220] Case 261/81 *Rau* [1982] ECR 3961, para. 12.

the free movement of goods less'.[221] This emphasis on the disclosure of information is intended to enable consumers to make an informed choice[222] rather than having that choice confined by government intervention.[223]

The benefits of labelling were emphasized in the *Beer Purity*[224] case. According to the sixteenth-century German *Biersteuergesetz*, the name 'Bier' could be used for products brewed with malted barley, hops, yeast, and water only. The use of other products, such as maize and rice (often found in foreign beers), meant that the product could not be described as 'Bier'. The German government attempted to justify restricting the name 'Bier' on the ground of consumer protection: since Germans linked the word 'Bier' to products manufactured with only the ingredients listed in the Biersteuergesetz they might be misled if the name was applied to products containing other ingredients. The Court rejected these arguments and, referring back to its case law on Article 110 on taxation, said that the legislation of a Member State should not 'crystallize given consumer habits so as to consolidate an advantage acquired by national industries concerned to comply with them'.[225] It continued that consumers could be protected 'by means which do not prevent the importation of products which have been lawfully manufactured and marketed in other Member States and, in particular, by the compulsory affixing of suitable labels giving the nature of the product sold'.[226] The Court noted that these labels could even be attached to the casks or the beer taps when beers were sold in draught.[227]

The *Biersteuergesetz* also banned the use of any additives in beer. The German government tried to justify this on the ground of public health: because of the amount of beer consumed by German drinkers (!), it was important to minimize the quantity of additives ingested for reasons of general preventive health.[228] The Court rejected this argument too, saying that the ban was disproportionate for two reasons: first, that additives were allowed in other German soft drinks and, secondly, that the ban was not limited to those additives where there was scientific evidence that they might cause harm.[229]

The *Biersteuergesetz* was eventually repealed: beers made in other Member States can be sold without restriction in Germany, provided all ingredients other than water, malt, hops, and yeast are clearly marked.[230] Subsequently, a French brewery sued the German government for damages for the loss it had suffered as a result of having to discontinue exports of beer to Germany since its beer did not comply with the Biersteuergesetz. In

---

[221] See also para. 17. See also Case C–448/98 *Guimont* [2000] ECR I–10663, para. 33.

[222] See Council Res. of 5 Apr. 1993 on future action on the labelling of products in the interest of the consumer ([1993] OJ C110/1).

[223] S. Weatherill, *EC Consumer Law and Policy* (Basingstoke: Longman, 1997), 49.

[224] Case 178/84 *Commission* v. *Germany* [1987] ECR 1227.

[225] Para. 32, referring to Case 170/78 *Commission* v. *United Kingdom (wine and beer)* [1980] ECR 417, considered in Ch. 3.

[226] See, more recently, Joined Cases C–158/04 and C–159/04 *Alfa Vita Vassilopoulos AE* [2006] ECR I–8135, para. 25.                                                                                     [227] Para. 36.

[228] Para. 48. See also Slynn AG's views that 'It seems to me disproportionate to seek to justify rules which exclude the whole of society from beer other than nationally produced beer because some additives may constitute a risk for a person who drinks in excess of 1,000 litres of beer a year or for an alcoholic already suffering from cirrhosis of the liver. Accepting that such persons may need protection there are other ways of achieving it, medical advice as to quantum and self-restraint to name only two.'

[229] See also Case 174/82 *Sandoz* [1983] ECR 2445.

[230] I. Murray, 'German beer law repealed', *The Times*, 2 Jun. 1990.

*Brasserie du Pêcheur*[231] the Court established the principle of state liability for breach of a Treaty provision. It said that in an area involving a wide discretion on the part of the legislature, such as laying down rules on the quality of beer put on the market, Union law conferred a right to reparation where three conditions were met: (1) the rule of law infringed had to be intended to confer rights on individuals; (2) the breach had to be sufficiently serious; and (3) there had to be a direct causal link between the breach of the obligation resting on the state and the damage sustained by the injured parties.[232] The Court suggested that the rules concerning the designation 'Bier' did constitute a serious breach, since the incompatibility of such rules with Article 34 was 'manifest' in the light of earlier decisions of the Court, in particular *Cassis de Dijon*. By contrast, in respect of the German prohibition on additives, the Court said that since Union guidance was significantly less clear, this aspect of the German law was unlikely to constitute a sufficiently serious breach. When the case returned to the German court it found that the complainants were not entitled to damages, even as regards the provisions governing the designation 'Bier', on the ground that there had been no direct causal connection between Germany's sufficiently serious breach and the damage suffered.[233]

The *Beer Purity* case demonstrates how intrusive the Court's proportionality review can be into the legislative choices made by the Member States. It also demonstrates the Court's pragmatic approach to proportionality: the Court itself came up with a suggestion for a more proportionate response to the problem of identifying the contents of beer (putting a label on the beer tap).[234] Similarly, in *Heimdienst* the Court suggested that, rather than requiring grocers who sold their goods from a van to have a shop in the locality as well, it would be more proportionate to require vans to have refrigeration equipment. In this way the Member State could ensure the hygiene of goods supplied to outlying areas.

If labelling is the preferred solution, then national rules regulating the content and language of the label themselves raise issues under Article 34 because the label may have to be altered[235] depending on the country in which the good is sold. For this reason, the Court has prevented unnecessary changes to any label, as *Geffroy*[236] demonstrates. The case concerned the sale in France of Coca-Cola which had been bought in the UK and was labelled in English, contrary to French law requiring all labels to be in French. The importer argued that Coca-Cola was such a well-known product that consumers would not have been inconvenienced by the labelling in English, and the Court agreed. While recognizing that a Member State was entitled to impose language requirements concerning the labelling of foodstuffs, it said that national law could not require the use of a

---

[231] Joined Cases C–46 and 48/93 *Brasserie du Pêcheur and Factortame III* [1996] ECR I–1029, developing the principle established in Joined Cases C–6 and 9/90 *Francovich and Bonifaci and others* v. *Italian Republic* [1991] ECR I–5357. *Factortame III* is considered further in Ch. 10. See also Case C–445/06 *Danske Slagterier* v. *Germany* [2009] ECR I–2119 (Danish association of slaughterhouse companies claiming compensation from Germany for its import ban on meat from uncastrated pigs which produced a sexual odour).

[232] Para. 51.    [233] [1997] 1 CMLR 971.

[234] See also Case C–254/98 *TK-Heimdienst Sass GmbH* [2000] ECR I–151. In some cases the Court will adopt a comparative approach seeing how other Member States have addressed a particular problem: Case C–126/91 *Yves Rocher* [1993] ECR I–2361, para. 18; cf. Case 286/81 *Oosthoek* [1982] ECR 4575, para. 20.

[235] See, e.g., Case 94/82 *De Kikvorsh* [1982] ECR 947, para. 10; Case C–217/99 *Commission* v. *Belgium* [2000] ECR I–10251, para. 17.

[236] Case C–366/98 *Geffroy and Casino France* [2000] ECR I–6579. See also Case C–369/89 *Piageme* v. *Peeters* [1991] ECR I–2971 which led to COM(93)532 on the use of languages in the marketing of foodstuffs. See also Case 78/80 *Fietje* [1980] ECR 3839, para. 15.

specific language for labelling of foodstuffs[237] without allowing for the use of another language easily understood by purchasers or ensuring that the purchaser was informed by some other means.

The Court's emphasis on labelling is not without its critics. For example, Von Heydebrand argues that the Court is wrong in thinking that consumers are adequately informed by labels.[238] He says that resources saved by forgoing harmonization are spent by national authorities determining whether the imported product is 'lawfully produced and marketed' in the Member State of origin.

---

### Case Study 6.1  NAMING FOODS

..............................................................................................................................

One of the most vexed questions facing the Union legislature and the Court is the naming of foods. Each state jealously guards the product names it uses, often allowing them to be registered in the national system, and swears that the way the product is made in its country is the best.[239] The arrival of a product bearing the same or similar name on to its market, usually produced according to different rules, invariably threatens the quality and reputation of the domestic product. States therefore allowed national producers to invoke the national registration to keep these imported goods off the market. This inevitably had the effect of partitioning the market along national lines and undermined the aim of the single market.

The EU's response has been twofold. First, it has introduced so-called 'Euro-foods', designating what ingredients can be included in certain products before the can be given a particular name. We saw this with chocolate and jam case study considered in Chapter 4. We also know how unpopular such moves tend to be. Secondly, the Union has recognized that the name of products typical of a particular region can actually be confined to products from that region. In the early days of the EU, this was largely done by the Court. However, the Court's approach has now been replaced by Union secondary legislation, originally adopted in 1992 but now found primarily in Regulation 510/2006.[240] This regulation allows national products to be registered in an *EU* register, thereby replacing the former national systems.[241]

As far as the Court's approach to national registration is concerned, its case law in the early 1970s recognized names which were (1) a designation or origin and (2) an

---

[237] Art. 34 and Art. 14 of Dir. 79/112/EEC ([1979] OJ L33/1) now Art. 17 of Dir. 2000/13 (OJ [2000] L109/29).                    [238] H. C. von Heydebrand u.d Lasa, above n. 162, 391.

[239] This patriotism is not confined to Member States: see Mancini AG's passionate opinion defending the need for pasta to be made only from durum wheat: Case 407/85 3 *Glocken GmbH* v. *USL Centro-Sud* [1988] ECR 4233, esp. para. 2. Particularly noteworthy is his lyrical argument that 'only pasta made with durum wheat does not become sticky during cooking and arrives on the plate as the Italians like it to be: "al dente" (and therefore, as André Gide put it in his journal, on 22 June 1942, "glissant des deux côtés de la fourchette")'.

[240] [2006] OJ L93/12. See also Commission Reg. (EC) No. 1898/2006 laying down detailed rules of implementation of Council Reg. (EC) No. 510/2006 on the protection of geographical indications and designations of origin for agricultural products and foodstuffs ([2006] OJ L369/1).

[241] Case C–478/07 *Budějovický Budvar* v. *Rudolf Ammersin* [2009] ECR I–000, para. 114: 'the aim of Regulation 510/2006 is not to establish, alongside national rules which may continue to exist, an additional system of protection for qualified geographical indications... but to provide a uniform and exhaustive system of protection for such indications'.

indication of provenance. Where a product possessed 'qualities and characteristics which are due to the fact that it originated in a specific geographical area',[242] the Court would allow the state to protect that name either as a consumer protection/fair trading mandatory requirement[243] or as an industrial or commercial property express derogation under Article 36.[244] That protection could be extended to the territory of another Member State.[245] However, having recognized this protection as a matter of principle, on the facts the Court generally ruled that its criteria for designating origin or indicating provenance were not satisfied and so found that the use of the name breached Article 34. This approach can be seen in *Commission v Germany*.[246]

German legislation confined the name 'Sekt' and 'Weinbrand' to products originating in Germany or other German-speaking countries. The Court said that 'An area or origin which is defined on the basis either of the extent of national territory or a linguistic criterion cannot constitute a geographical area' capable of justifying an indication or origin, particularly as the products might be produced from grapes of 'indeterminate origin'.[247] Germany was therefore in breach of Article 34. Likewise, Germany's insistence, in *Prantl*,[248] that only certain producers of domestic wine could use the traditional bulbous shape 'Bocksbeutel' bottle breached Article 34 because it kept Italian wine, also traditionally sold in similar shaped bottles, off the German market. The Court said that the consumer protection argument had to be fair to all sides.[249]

To help address some of the internal market problems created by a proliferation of names on national registers, the EU introduced an EU-wide register in 1992. This allowed three categories of names to be registered: PDOs (Protected Designation of Origin), PGIs (Protected Geographical Indication) and TSGs (Traditional Speciality Guaranteed). In March 2006 these registration systems were updated. The principal measure, Regulation 510/2006 on agricultural products and foodstuffs,[250] concerns PDOs and PGIs.[251]

As far as PDOs are concerned, Article 2(1)(a) provides that 'Designation of origin' means the name of a region, a specific place or, in exceptional cases, a country, used to

---

[242] Case 12/74 *Commission* v. *Germany* ('*Sekt*') [1975] ECR 181, para. 7.

[243] Case 16/83 *Criminal proceedings against Prantl* [1984] ECR 1299, para. 25.

[244] Ibid., para.34. Rules prohibiting false indications of origin are permissible: Case 207/83 *Commission* v. *UK* [1985] ECR 1201.     [245] Case C–3/91 *Exportur* [1992] ECR I–5529, para. 38.

[246] Case 12/74 *Commission* v. *Germany* ('*Sekt*') [1975] ECR 181.     [247] Para. 8.

[248] Case 16/83 *Prantl* [1984] ECR 1299.     [249] Case C–3/91 *Exportur* [1992] ECR I–5529, para. 32.

[250] A similar regime applies to wine (Reg. 479/2008) and spirits (Reg. 110/2008), although in spirits there is only one designation, 'geographic indication'. See also Council Reg. (EC) No. 3/2008 ([2008] OJ L3/1) on information provision and promotion measures for agricultural products on the internal market and in third countries. This provides for EU financial support for promoting Union products, in particular on PDOs, PGIs, TSGs, and quality wines.

[251] A separate regulation covers TSGs (Reg. 509/2006 (OJ [2006] L93/1), Implementing Reg. 1216/2007 (OJ [2007] L275/3). 'Traditional speciality guaranteed' means a traditional agricultural product or foodstuff with a 'specific character' ie a characteristic or set of characteristics which distinguishes an agricultural product or a foodstuff clearly from other similar products or foodstuffs of the same category where the name has a proven usage on the Union market for a time period showing transmission between generations (i.e., at least 25 years) (Art. 2(1)). Examples of TSGs include *Pizza Napoletana* and *Mozzarella* (cheese) from Italy (although Mozzarella di Bufala Campana is a PDO) and *Lambic, Gueuze Lambic, Gueuze/Lambiek, and Geuze-Lambiek, Geuze* (beers) from Belgium. A TSG does not refer to the geographic origin but highlights traditional character, either in the composition or means of production.

describe an agricultural product or a foodstuff which originates in that region, specific place or country, whose *quality or characteristics* are *essentially or exclusively* due to a particular geographical environment with its inherent natural and human factors; and the production, processing *and* preparation of which take place in the defined geographical area. Examples of registered PDOs include Cornish clotted cream, Jersey Royal potatoes, Scottish salmon,[252] West Country farmhouse Cheddar, Camembert de Normandie, Roquefort, Tuscan extra virgin olive oil, Gorgonzola, and Parmigiano di Reggiano.[253]

Parma ham is also a PDO[254] and the Consortium for Parma Ham has worked hard to defend the integrity of its product. Prior to the introduction of the 1992 legislation, the Consortium unsuccessfully brought a claim for passing-off in the English courts against Marks & Spencer, for marketing as 'genuine Parma ham' ham which had originated in Parma but had been sliced and packed in England.[255] However, the Consortium's hand was strengthened after the introduction of the 1992 Regulation when Parma Ham was registered as a PDO. The Consortium again brought proceedings in the UK, this time against the supermarket Asda, which, like M&S, sliced and packed Parma Ham in the UK. On a reference from the House of Lords,[256] the Court said that in principle the Consortium could rely on the regulation to protect its PDO. It said that while the requirement for the product to be sliced and packed in the region of production breached Article 35, that breach could be justified on the grounds of protection of industrial and commercial property, namely the need to control the quality and authenticity of the product,[257] and that the slicing and packaging requirement were proportionate.[258] However, on the facts of the case the Consortium could not rely on the regulation against Asda because the particular regulation where the PDO was registered did not expressly state that slicing and packing had to be done in Parma[259] with the result that, in the name of legal certainty, the regulation could not be invoked against Asda.

As far as PGIs are concerned, Article 2(1)(b) provides 'Geographical indication' means the name of a region, a specific place or, in exceptional cases, a country, used to describe an agricultural product or a foodstuff which originates in that region, specific place or country; which possesses a *specific quality, reputation or other characteristics attributable* to that geographical origin; and whose production *and/or* processing *and/*

---

[252] Note the lyrical description of the geographical area in the application for the PDO for Scottish salmon: 'The magical mix of climate, terrain, indigenous industries and the Scottish people's inherent love and respect for their surroundings has blended to create a unique environment. Pure coastal waters and sheltered lochs have sustained and nurtured each Scottish farmed salmon throughout its life cycle, while expert husbandry skills have ensured each salmon achieves and maintains prime condition.'

[253] For a full list see <http://www.ec.europa.eu/agriculture/quality/schemes/index_en.htm>. A number of these PDOs were registered by Commission Reg. 1107/96 (OJ [1996] L148/1).

[254] Commission Reg. 1107/96 (OJ [1996] L148/1).

[255] *Consorzio del Prosciutto di Parma* v. *Marks & Spencer Plc* [1991] RPC 351. N. Dawson, 'Case comment: The Parma ham case: Trade descriptions and passing off—shortcomings of English law?' (1991) *EIPR* 487.

[256] *Consorzio del Prosciutto di Parma* v. *Asda Stores Ltd* [2001] UKHL 7. S. Bennett and C. Thorne, 'Case comment: Parma ham labelling and repackaging' (2001) *EIPR* 592.                                              [257] Para. 76.

[258] Para. 79.

[259] Case C–108/2001 *Consorzio del Prosciutto di Parma* v. *Asda Stores Ltd* [2003] ECR I–5121.

*or* preparation take place in the defined geographical area. Registered PGIs include Melton Mowbray Pork Pie, Scottish beef, and Scottish lamb. Newcastle Brown Ale was one of the first products from the UK to be registered as a PGI.[260] However, when the Newcastle factory moved across the River Tyne to nearby Gateshead in 2004, it no longer satisfied the terms of the PGI, which required brewing to take place within the city limits of Newcastle-Upon-Tyne. The owners of the brewery, Scottish & Newcastle, therefore had to apply for their own PGI to be cancelled in order to allow beer from the Gateshead brewery to continue to be branded as Newcastle Brown Ale.[261]

Both PDOs and PGIs involve a clear link to a specific geographic region. As the Commission explains,[262] the main difference between the two is just how closely the product is linked to a specific geographical area. In general terms, a PDO product must derive its characteristics from the area (either from local raw materials, climate, soil quality, or other local factors) *and* it must be produced and processed in the locality. For PGIs it is sufficient that only one of the production stages takes place in the defined area. It is therefore much easier to satisfy the criteria for qualification as a PGI than a PDO yet the protection level against misuse is essentially the same.[263]

In order to initiate the registration process for a PDO or PGI, applicants—including applicants from third countries[264]—submit an application for registration to its own Member State[265] (or the Commission in the case of third-country applicants), specifying the name of the product for which they are seeking PDO or PGI status, providing a description of its organoleptic features, a definition of geographical area, evidence that the product originates in the defined area, and details of the link between the qualities of the product and its region of production. The Member State scrutinizes the application against the eligibility criteria, and if it considers that the eligibility criteria are met, it forwards the application to the Commission for a final decision. The Commission considers the application and, if it passes scrutiny, publishes the application in the Official Journal. Any person with a legitimate interest from any Member State other than the applicant's, may object within six months from publication. Thereafter the name is registered by Regulation. Registration commands a commercial advantage: the Commission estimates that registered products command a 30 per cent price premium over competing products.[266]

Once registered, the name is protected against direct or indirect commercial use by products not covered by the registration specification; any other false or misleading indication as to the provenance, origin, nature, or essential qualities of the product; and any other practice that is liable to mislead the public as to the true origin of the product.[267] Registration also protects against misuse, imitation, or evocation, even where the true origin of the product is indicated.[268]

---

[260] Commission Reg. 1107/96 (OJ [1996] L148/1).      [261] 2006/C 280/06.

[262] 'European Policy for Quality Agricultural Products', <http://www.ec.europa.eu/agriculture/publi/fact/quality/2007_en.pdf>.

[263] C. MacMaoláin, 'Waiter there's a beetle in my soup. Yes Sir, that's E120: Disparities between actual individual behaviour and regulating food labelling for the average consumer in EU Law' (2008) 45 *CMLRev.* 1147, 1154.      [264] Therefore Columbian coffee has a PGI registered in accordance with Reg. 510/2006.

[265] Arts. 4–7.      [266] <http://www.ec.europa.eu/agriculture/publi/fact/quality/2007_en.pdf>, 12.

[267] Art. 13.      [268] Ibid.

The scope of the protection can be seen in the *Gorgonzola* case.[269] The Court said that the name 'Cambozola' was an evocation of the PDO 'Gorgonzola', even though the names were different, because both names were used to market a soft blue cheese, and both names had four syllables where the third and fourth syllables of both names were identical.[270]

Names which have become generic may not, however, be registered. A generic name encompasses any product which, 'although it relates to the place or the region where this product or foodstuff was originally produced or marketed, has become the common name of an agricultural product or a foodstuff in the [Union]'.[271] To establish whether a name has become generic, Regulation 510/2006 provides that 'account shall be taken of all factors, in particular:

(a)  the existing situation in the Member States and in areas of consumption;

(b)  the relevant national or [Union] laws.'[272]

Examples of products whose names have become generic include Cheddar cheese (although 'West Country farmhouse Cheddar' is a PDO), Edam,[273] Dijon mustard, and Black Forest gateau.[274]

The name which has caused most difficulty in this respect is 'feta' cheese, a problem exacerbated by the fact that the name itself originated in Italy (*fetta* meaning slice), not Greece where the cheese is usually associated.[275] Greek feta is made from sheep's milk or a mixture of sheep and goats' milk by the traditional craft method of natural straining of the milk, without applying pressure. Feta production also commenced in the 1960s in Denmark, Germany, the Netherlands, and France but this cheese is made from cow's milk, which is more economical, and by an industrial ultra-filtration process, which is cheaper than the traditional method of straining. In *Canadane*[276] Advocate General Colomer considered the question whether Greece could insist on Danish feta bearing the less than attractive label 'white cheese in brine made in Denmark from pasteurized cows' milk', a requirement which the Danish producer thought would make its feta harder to sell, contrary to Article 34. The Advocate General found feta to be non-generic in Greece. In support, he referred to the defined status of feta cheese under Greek law, a Eurobarometer survey which demonstrated its geographical significance to Greek consumers and that Greece was the largest producer and consumer of feta in

[269]  Case C–87/1997 *Gorgonzola* [1999] ECR I–1301.

[270]  Paras. 27–8. See also Case C–132/05 *Commission* v. *Germany* [2008] ECR I–957, para. 46 where the Court said there was a phonetic and visual similarity between the names 'Parmesan' and 'Parmeggiano Reegiano'.                                                                                     [271]  Art. 3(1).

[272]  In Art. 3(1) of the original Reg. 2081/92 there was an additional indicator: 'the existing situation in other Member States'.                                    [273]  Case 286/86 *Minstère Public* v. *Deserbais* [1988] ECR 4907.

[274]  The Commission attempted to draw up a list of products considered generic: COM(96) 38 final. Its proposal for a decision contained the following names as generic: Brie, Camembert, Cheddar, Edam, Emmentaler, and Gouda (but not feta). The decision was never adopted due to the absence of agreement by the Council.

[275]  D. Gangjee, 'Say cheese! A sharper image of generic use through the lens of Feta' (2007) *EIPR* 172; C. MacMaolain, 'Eligibility criteria for protected geographical food names' (2006) *ELRev.* 579; B. O'Connor and I. Kireeva, 'What's in a name? The Feta cheese saga' (2003) *International Trade Law & Regulation* 110.

[276]  Case C–317/95 *Canadane* [1997] ECR I–4681.

the EU. He therefore argued that the Greek rules were protected under Article 36. The case was withdrawn before the Court ruled on the issue.

The Court did have to address the matter in *Denmark, Germany and France v Commission*[277] where the Northern European states successfully challenged registration of the name feta as a PDO on the grounds that the Commission, when registering the name 'feta', took no account of the fact that the name had been used for a considerable time in Member States other than Greece. The Commission then sent Member States a questionnaire on how well the name 'feta' was known among their consumers; its scientific committee unanimously concluded that the name feta was not generic and so the Commission re-registered feta as a PDO. Once again Denmark and Germany challenged the registration[278] but this time they were unsuccessful; the Commission had now identified various factors relating to the consumption of feta in the Member States to indicate that the name feta was not generic.[279]

Where the name has become generic (e.g., pasta, beer) but Member States continue to insist that its use be confined to products with certain ingredients or certain quantities of ingredients, the Court applies its traditional Article 34 case law, as it did in the *Beer Purity* case, considered above.[280] As we saw in *Beer Purity*, while recognizing that, in principle, the national rule might be justified on the grounds of consumer protection/fair trading, the Court usually finds the national measure disproportionate, insisting that clear labelling is more appropriate than prohibiting the sale altogether. Therefore, in *Deserbais*[281] the Court said that a French rule restricting the name 'Edam' to cheese with a minimum fat content of 40 per cent breached Article 34 because it had the effect of excluding from the French market German cheese which had been lawfully produced with a fat content of only 34 per cent.[282] The Court said that provided consumers had proper information, the German cheese could be sold in France. Similarly, in *3 Glocken*[283] the Court said that an Italian ban on the sale of pasta products made from common wheat or a mixture of common wheat and durum wheat was an obstacle to the import of pasta products from other Member States made from these ingredients, contrary to Article 34.[284] The 'compulsory affixing of suitable labels giving the nature of the product sold' was the proportionate response to Italian concerns about consumer protection.[285]

Where, however, the products are substantially different the Court may allow the national rules to stand. This was suggested in *Smanor*[286] where French law reserved

---

[277] Joined Cases C 289/96, 293/96 and 299/96 *Denmark, Germany and France v Commission* [1999] ECR I–1541.

[278] Joined Cases C–465/02 and C–466/02 *Germany and Denmark v. Commission* [2005] ECR I–9115.

[279] Para. 88.      [280] Above n. 224.

[281] Case 286/86 [1988] ECR 4907; Case C–210/89 *Commission v. Italy* [1990] ECR I–3697 (Italian rule restricting the name 'cheese' to products with a minimum fat content). See also Case C–448/98 *Guimont* [2000] ECR I–10663: a French rule restricting the name 'Emmenthal' to cheeses with a hard, dry rind was an indistinctly applicable MEE, as was a French rule restricting the name 'cider' to 'alcoholic drinks made of apples' in Case C–366/98 *Geffroy and Casino France* [2000] ECR I–6579.

[282] See generally L. Gormley, 'Recent case law on the free movement of goods: Some hot potatoes' (1990) 27 *CMLRev.* 825, 840–4.      [283] Case 407/85 *3 Glocken GmbH v. USL Centro-Sud* [1988] ECR 4233.

[284] Para. 11.      [285] Para. 16.

[286] Case 298/87 *Proceedings for compulsory reconstruction against Smanor SA* [1988] ECR 4489.

the name 'yoghurt' solely to fresh yoghurt; deep-frozen yoghurt could be sold but only under the name 'deep-frozen fermented milk'. The Court said that the French rules appear 'disproportionate in relation to the objective of consumer protection, when the characteristics of the deep-frozen products are not *substantially different*...from fresh products, and when appropriate labelling...would suffice to give consumers proper information'.[287] However, it was left to the national court to make the final decision whether the two products were sufficiently different to justify the difference in name.[288]

## 4. PROPORTIONALITY AND PUBLIC HEALTH

So far we have focused on the Court's general approach to proportionality. We turn now to consider the application of the proportionality principle in the specific context of public health, an area where, as the *Beer Purity* case shows, the Court fears that the derogation may be misused.[289] In some cases, the Court does uphold the host state's rule, as *Schwarz*[290] shows. Austrian law required chewing gum sold in vending machines to be packaged. The Court accepted the public health justification that 'in the past, non-packaged goods were impaired by moisture or insects, in particular ants, within vending machine containers'. The Court also accepted the argument that the requirement increased the safety of the chewing gum because 'consumers who buy non-packaged confectionery from vending machines must necessarily touch the goods and the delivery tray with their bare hands without having washed them beforehand'. It added that 'contamination of the delivery tray by pathogenic germs and their transmission onto the goods removed by the customer is by no means merely theoretical'.[291] The Austrian requirement therefore constituted an 'adequate and proportionate measure for the protection of public health'.[292]

In other cases the Court will intervene to declare the national measure invalid. The wine wars case, *Commission* v. *France*,[293] provides an example of this.[294] The early 1980s saw a large increase in imports of Italian table wine into France. This caused prices of wine to fall, prompting violent demonstrations by French wine growers. In response, the French authorities took a number of steps against the imported goods, which included subjecting every consignment of Italian wine to health inspections at the frontier. This whole process took weeks, sometimes months. By contrast, French wine was subject to only occasional checks. The Court considered the checks on Italian wine to constitute a 'disproportionate and discriminatory obstacle to imports'.[295] It said that, in the absence

---

[287] Para. 23.    [288] Para. 24.

[289] See also Case C–88/07 *Commission* v. *Spain (medicinal herbs)* [2009] ECR I–1353, para. 93 where the Court insisted on a 'detailed assessment, on a case by case basis, of the risk alleged by the Member States invoking Article [36]'.

[290] Case C–366/04 *Schwarz* v. *Bürgermeister der Landeshauptstadt Salzburg* [2006] ECR I–10139, para. 34.    [291] Para. 35.

[292] Para. 36. Cf. Case C–270/02 *Commission* v. *Italy (foodstuffs for sportsmen and women)* [2004] ECR I–1559, para. 24 where the Court found that Italy had failed to produce any evidence to explain the link between the authorization procedure and public health and the proportionality of the regime.

[293] Case 42/82 *Commission* v. *France (wine wars)* [1983] ECR 1013.

[294] See also Case C–420/01 *Commission* v. *Italy (energy drinks with caffeine)* [2003] ECR I–6445.

[295] Para. 61.

of any reasonable suspicion, the French authorities should have confined themselves to random checks.[296]

*Commission* v. *United Kingdom (UHT)*[297] provides a further example of this careful scrutiny of the proportionality of national measures justified on the grounds of public health. UHT milk could be imported into the UK only by a licence holder and could be marketed only by a licensed dealer who had packed the milk in a local dairy. The Court found that both measures breached Article 34. The UK justified the import licence requirement on the ground that it needed to know the origin of milk in order to regulate the temperature of its heat treatment which varied according to the disease status of the exporting country. The Court said that this objective could be achieved by less restrictive means, such as obtaining a declaration signed by the importer.

In respect of the dealers' licences, the UK argued that, owing to the disparities between the national laws on the production of UHT milk, this was the only effective means of protecting public health. Again the Court disagreed, saying that it would reject the public-health defence on the ground of proportionality if the same interests were already protected in the state of origin. It noted that UHT milk was made according to similar rules and using similar machines in all the Member States. It also recognized that UHT milk, by its very nature, could be kept for long periods, which obviated the need for control over the whole process. If it was concerned about protecting the health of humans, the Court said that the UK could ensure safeguards equivalent to those which it had prescribed for domestic production of UHT milk. However, the UK had to take into account certificates issued by the competent authorities of the exporting states. The Court said that these certificates would raise a presumption that the imported goods complied with the requirements of domestic health legislation, thereby enabling checks carried out on importation to be simplified.[298]

*UHT* shows how the principle of mutual recognition serves to limit the scope of the derogations by preventing the host state from replicating checks on imported products which have already been carried out by the state of origin. The Court says that such double-checks either constitute a disguised restriction on trade[299] or are disproportionate.[300] In *Biologische Producten*[301] the Court reminded the Member States of their duty 'to assist in bringing about a relaxation of the controls existing in intra-[Union] trade'.[302] It also said that while the host state was entitled to require the product to undergo a fresh examination, the authorities were not entitled to require unnecessary technical or chemical analyses or laboratory tests where those analyses or tests had already been carried out in another Member State and the results were available to the host state authorities.[303] In *Commission* v. *Portugal* the Court went further and said that '[s]trict compliance' with the obligation to cooperate required 'an active approach' on the part of the authorities in

---

[296] Para. 57.

[297] Case 124/81 *Commission* v. *United Kingdom* [1983] ECR 203. See also Case C–170/04 *Rosengren* v. *Riksåklagaren* [2007] ECR I–4071, paras. 43–56.                               [298] Para. 30.

[299] Case 272/80 *Frans-Nederlandse Maatschappij voor Biologische Producten* [1981] ECR 3277, para. 15.

[300] Case 132/80 *United Foods* [1981] ECR 995, para. 29; Case 188/84 *Commission* v. *France (woodworking machines)* [1986] ECR 419, para. 16.

[301] Case 272/80 [1981] ECR 3277. See also Case C–292/94 *Criminal Proceedings against Brandsma* [1996] ECR I–2159 and Case C–400/96 *Criminal Proceedings against Jean Harpegnies* [1998] ECR I–5121; Case C–212/03 *Commission* v. *France* [2005] ECR I–4213, paras. 42–3.

[302] Case 272/80 [1981] ECR 3277, para. 14.        [303] Ibid.

the host state. The Member States also had to ensure that the competent approval bodies cooperated with each other to facilitate the procedures to be followed to obtain access to the national market of the host state.[304]

## 5. PROCEDURALIZATION OF PROPORTIONALITY

Cases such as *UHT* and *Biologische Producten* suggest an increasing emphasis on 'good governance' in the states' approach to the question of proportionality, a point emphasized in *Greenham and Abel*.[305] Greenham was prosecuted for selling meal replacement food supplements ('Juice Plus + vegetable mixture' and 'Juice Plus + fruit mixture') which had been imported from other Member States where they had been lawfully manufactured and/or marketed. The substance coenzyme Q10 had been added to these products, a nutrient whose addition was not authorized in France for human consumption (although authorized in a number of other Member States). The Court said that the French rules breached Article 34 but could be justified under Article 36 provided the following conditions were satisfied:

- The national rules had to make provision for a procedure enabling economic operators to have a nutrient included on the national list of authorized substances. The criteria for inclusion had to be based on objective and non-discriminatory criteria.[306]

- The procedure had to be readily accessible and completed within a reasonable time.

- If the application was turned down, this decision had to be open to challenge before the courts.[307]

- An application to obtain the inclusion of a nutrient on the national list of authorized substances could be refused by the competent national authorities only if such substance posed a genuine risk to public health following a detailed assessment of the risk to public health, using the most reliable scientific data available and the most recent results of international research. The state also had to show that the steps taken were proportionate.[308]

In other words, to satisfy the principle of proportionality there needed to be a procedure available for the applicant to obtain authorization for its product and this procedure

---

[304] Case C–432/03 *Commission* v. *Portugal* [2005] ECR I–9665, para. 47. Cf. Case C–244/06 *Dynamic Medien* [2008] ECR I–505, where the Court did not take into account at the proportionality stage the fact that the British authorities had already classified the DVDs.

[305] Case C–95/01 *Greenham and Abel* [2004] ECR I–1333. See also Case C–24/00 *Commission* v. *France (nutrients)* [2004] ECR I–1277, noted M. Jarvis (2004) 41 *CMLRev.* 1395. The Court is also applying similar principles to Member States wishing to derogate from the other fundamental freedoms, such as services, as the healthcare cases demonstrate (considered in Ch. 13). By contrast, it has in the past been less stringent in its application of the procedural aspects of the proportionality principle to acts of the *Union* institutions: see, e.g., Joined Cases C–154/04 and C–155/04 *Alliance for Natural Health* [2005] ECR I–6451 considered in Ch. 16.

[306] This was added in Case C–219/07 *Nationale Raad van Dierenkwekers en Liefhebbers VZW* [2008] ECR I–4475, para. 34.

[307] *Greenham and Abel*, para. 35. See also Case C–244/06 *Dynamic Medien* [2008] ECR I–505, para. 50; Case C–219/07 *Nationale Raad van Dierenkwekers en Liefhebbers VZW* [2008] ECR I–4475, paras. 33–7.

[308] Ibid., para. 36.

had to comply with principles of good administration. In *Mickelsson*[309] the Court emphasized that the relevant national authorities also had to be proactive. The case concerned a Swedish rule limiting the use of jet-skis to general navigable waterways and not inland waterways unless those inland waterways had been specifically designated by the relevant authorities. The Court said the rule was proportionate on environmental protection grounds, provided that those authorities had actually made use of the power conferred on them to designate inland waterways suitable for jet-skis, and such measures had been adopted within a reasonable period after the entry into force of that law.[310]

The proceduralization of the requirements necessary to satisfy the proportionality test is also reflected in the Court's insistence that traders be given sufficient warning of changes in national regulation and adequate time to adapt. This can be seen in *Radlberger*[311] concerning the German deposit-and-return system. The Court accepted that the system, which had a discriminatory effect on importers,[312] could be justified on the grounds of environmental protection. It said that, while the measures were suitable for achieving that objective, they were disproportionate because of the manner in which they had been introduced: they did not afford the producers and distributors a transitional period sufficient to enable them to adapt to the requirements of the new system before the new system entered into force.[313]

The same argument about good governance influenced the Court in *Commission v. Austria (heavy lorries)*[314] where it found that the Austrian ban on heavy lorries using the A12 in the Tyrol on environmental grounds was disproportionate: a transitional period of only two months for introducing the ban was 'clearly insufficient'.[315] The Court also said that the Austrian authorities were 'under a duty to examine carefully the possibility of using measures less restrictive of freedom of movement'[316] before adopting a measure 'so radical as a total traffic ban on a section of motorway constituting a vital route of communication between certain Member States'.[317] This decision is not surprising because, if the Court were to find otherwise, it would threaten the viability of the very principle underpinning the single market, namely specialization and comparative advantage. If Member States could simply block a major transit route then the benefits of geographical specialization in the production of goods would be lost if these goods could not be transported elsewhere in the Union.[318]

---

[309] Case C–142/05 *Aklagaren* v *Mickelsson, Roos* [2009] ECR I–000. See also Case C–433/05 *Sandström* [2010] ECR I–000. [310] Para. 39.

[311] Case C–309/02 *Radlberger Getränkegesellschaft mbH & Co.* v. *Land Baden-Württemberg* [2004] ECR I–11763, para. 70. See also Case C–463/01 *Commission* v. *Germany (deposit and return)* [2004] ECR I–11705, para. 67.

[312] Para. 68.

[313] Case C–463/01 *Commission* v. *Germany (deposit and return)* [2004] ECR I–11705, para. 79; Case C–309/02 *Radlberger* [2004] ECR I–11763, para. 81.

[314] Case C–320/03 *Commission* v. *Austria (heavy lorries)* [2005] ECR I–7929, para. 35.

[315] Para. 90. [316] Para. 87.

[317] Ibid. The authorities also should have ensured there was sufficient rail capacity to allow a transfer from road to rail before implementing such a measure (para. 88).

[318] See further C. Hilson, 'Going local? EU law, localism and climate change' (2008) 33 *ELRev.* 194, 209. He argues that the theory of comparative advantage assumes the absence of externalities. Given that the climate change costs imposed by trade-related transport are not currently paid by producers and consumers, there is almost certainly too much long-distance trade at present. This might (but not always in the case of e.g., exotic produce grown out of season in greenhouses) favour local purchasing.

# E.  FUNDAMENTAL HUMAN RIGHTS

While proportionality has proved the most significant general principle of law limit-ing the Member States' right to take measures restrictive of free movement, the Court has also emphasized that fundamental human rights, including freedom of expression, the freedom to pursue a trade or profession, and the right to own property can limit a Member State's discretion (see fig 4.1). Thus, fundamental rights can serve a twofold func-tion in the jurisprudence on free movement of goods: (1) they can *constitute* a mandatory requirement, as in *Schmidberger*[319] (i.e., fundamental rights can be invoked defensively by a Member State to justify a restriction on trade); and (2) they can also be used to *limit* Member State action under a derogation or mandatory requirement.[320] It is this latter situation that we shall now consider.

In *Familiapress*[321] the Court said that, while a Member State can rely on overriding requirements to justify rules which may obstruct the exercise of free movement of goods, 'such justification must also be interpreted in the light of the general principles of law and in particular of fundamental rights', including freedom of expression.[322] The Court said that the Austrian prohibition on prize competitions in magazines, while justified on the grounds of the maintenance of the plurality of the press (in itself a human rights justification in the *Schmidberger* sense), could 'detract from freedom of expression'. However, most fundamental rights are not absolute and are subject to derogations, as the Court noted in *Familiapress*. It said that Article 10 of the European Convention did permit derogations for the purposes of maintaining press diversity, in so far as they are prescribed by law and are necessary in a democratic society.[323] The Court then said that it was for the national court to determine whether the national law was proportionate to the aim of maintaining press diversity and whether the objective could be attained by measures less restrictive of both intra-Union trade and freedom of expression.[324] In other words, as the Court said in *Metronome Musik*,[325] fundamental rights themselves may be restricted, provided that any restrictions 'correspond to objectives of the general interest pursued by the European Union and do not constitute in relation to the aim pursued a disproportionate and intolerable interference, impairing the very substance of the rights guaranteed'.

The introduction of the Charter of Fundamental Rights 2000—and now its incorpora-tion (by reference) into the Treaties[326]—helps legitimize the Court's increasing reference to human rights and gives it a further steer as to what constitutes 'Union' fundamen-tal rights.[327] Nevertheless, the balancing exercise is by no means straightforward. As the

---

[319] Case C–112/00 [2003] ECR I–5659, considered above n. 38.

[320] Case C–260/89 *Elliniki Radiophonia Tiléorassi AE v. Dimotiki Etairia Pliroforissis and Sotirios Kouvelas* [1991] ECR I–2925, para. 45.                    [321] Case C–368/95 [1997] ECR I–3689.

[322] Paras. 24–5. See further S. Weatherill, 'Free movement of goods' (2006) 22 *ICLQ* 457.

[323] Para. 26, citing the judgment of the ECtHR of 24 Nov. 1993 in *Informationsverein Lentia and others v. Austria*, Series A, No. 276.                    [324] Para. 27.

[325] Case C–200/96 *Metronome Musik GmbH v. Music Point Hokamp GmbH* [1998] ECR I–1953, para. 21.

[326] Art. 6(1) TEU.

[327] See Case C–244/06 *Dynamic Medien* [2008] ECR I–505, para. 41 where the Court expressly referred to the Charter to justify developing the new mandatory requirement, the protection of the child.

Court has said on a number of occasions, the economic freedom, free movement of goods, is deemed to be a fundamental right[328] in just the same way as more traditional civil and political fundamental rights. The hierarchy between the rights is therefore less obvious than in national systems.[329]

## F. HARMONIZATION AND TRUST

A Member State can invoke the Article 36 derogations and the mandatory require-ments[330] only in the absence of Union rules.[331] This can be seen in *Hedley Lomas*[332] where the Court said 'recourse to Article 36 is no longer possible where [Union] Directives provide for harmonisation of measures necessary to achieve the specific objective which would be furthered by reliance upon this provision'.[333] The case concerned a refusal by the UK to issue licences for the export of live animals intended for slaughter in Spain, contrary to Article 35, on the ground that the UK considered that Spanish slaughter houses did not respect the provisions of Directive 74/577/EEC[334] on stunning animals before slaughter. The UK justified its refusal on the ground of animal health under Article 36. The Court rejected this defence because Directive 74/577 already occupied the field, which meant that the Member States lost the right to act in this area.

The principles laid down in *Hedley Lomas* were reiterated in *CWF*.[335] The case con-cerned the export of live calves for rearing in veal crates. Since there was a harmonization directive which exhaustively regulated certain minimum standards, the UK could not rely on the public-health defence to justify preventing the export of the calves to states with standards which complied only with the minima laid down by the directive but not the high standards provided by British law. But the case raised the question whether the UK could rely on the public-policy or public-morality derogations instead, based on the fact that a section of public opinion believed that the system put in place by the direc-tive did not adequately protect animal health. The Court rejected this argument on the ground that the public policy and public morality arguments were not separate justifica-tions but were rather part of the (impermissible) public health arguments.[336] Consistently with *Cullet*, the Court argued that a Member State could not rely on the views or the

---

[328] See, e.g., Case C–265/95 *Commission* v. *France* [1997] ECR I–6959, para. 24; Case C–320/03 *Commission* v. *Austria* [2005] ECR I–7929, para. 63. This issue is considered further in Ch. 16.

[329] J. Coppel and A.O'Neill, 'The European Court of Justice: Taking rights seriously' (1992) 14 *Legal Studies* 227. For an example of this troubled relationship, see the discussion of Case C–438/05 *Viking* [2007] ECR I–10779 in Ch. 8.

[330] See Case 120/78 *Cassis de Dijon* [1979] ECR 649, para. 8.

[331] Cf. Case C–389/96 *Aher-Waggon* [1998] ECR I–4473; Case C–3/99 *Cidrerie Ruwet* v. *Stassen* [2000] ECR I–8749, Case 190/87 *Oberkreisdirektor* v. *Moorman* [1988] ECR 4689, para. 10 considered further in Ch. 16.                                          [332] Case C–5/94 [1996] ECR I–2553.

[333] Para. 18.

[334] [1974] OJ L316/10, repealed and replaced by Council Dir. 93/119 ([1993] OJ L340/21).

[335] Case C–1/96 *R.* v. *MAFF, ex p. Compassion in World Farming* [1998] ECR I–1251 considered further in Ch. 16.

[336] Para. 66. See also Case C–165/08 *Commission* v. *Poland (GMOs)* [2009] ECR I–000 where the Court rejected ethical and religious reasons raised to explain Poland's failure to respect the directive.

behaviour of a section of national public opinion unilaterally to challenge a harmonizing measure adopted by the Union institutions.[337]

But what happens if one Member State suspects that another is not enforcing the harmonization directive? The answer from the Court in *Hedley Lomas* is simple: a Member State cannot unilaterally adopt, on its own authority, corrective or protective measures designed to address any breach by another Member State of rules of Union law.[338] The Court added 'Member States must rely on trust in each other to carry out inspections on their respective territories.'[339] The importance of the concept of mutual trust has underpinned cases such as *Biologische Producten*[340] on double checks. But what happens if this trust has broken down?[341] The Union has tried to buttress the process of confidence-building in the field of customs and agriculture by passing Regulation 515/97[342] on mutual assistance between the administrative authorities of the Member States and cooperation between the Member States and the Commission to ensure the correct application of the law. However, as *Hedley Lomas* shows, considerable suspicion between different authorities still remains. Nevertheless, the Court means business: in *Hedley Lomas* it made clear that the UK would be liable in damages for state liability under *Factortame* principles[343] for refusing to issue the export licence in breach of Article 35. And because this was an area in which the UK had no discretion, the breach was deemed sufficiently serious.[344]

## G.  THE MUTUAL RECOGNITION REGULATION 764/2008

Despite the talk of trust on which the principle of mutual recognition depends, Member States still invoke Article 36 or the mandatory requirements to prevent goods coming on to their market. This, of course, creates significant barriers to free movement of goods, especially when the host state assumes that it can do so as of right rather than as an exception. Harmonization (considered in Chapter 16) is one response to the problem, as *Hedley Lomas* and *CWF* show. However, in the absence of harmonization legislation, the Union institutions have introduced administrative procedures to supplement judicial recourse

---

[337]  Para. 67. Case 231/83 *Cullet* [1985] ECR 305 is considered above n. 20.

[338]  Para. 20. As a last resort Member States could start enforcement proceedings under Art. 259 TFEU (ex Art. 227 EC) or could ask the Commission to act under Art. 258: Case C–11/95 *Commission* v. *Belgium* [1996] ECR I–4115, paras. 36–7 considered in Ch. 10.

[339]  Para. 19. In the context of external relations, see Case C–124/95 *R.* v. *HM Treasury and Bank of England, ex p. Centro-Com Srl* [1997] ECR I–81, para. 49, discussed in Ch. 7.

[340]  Case 272/80 [1981] ECR 3277 considered at n. 301 above, and Case 25/88 *Bouchara* [1989] ECR 1105, para. 18. See also Case 46/76 *Bauhuis* v. *Netherlands* [1977] ECR 5, para. 22 (inspections).

[341]  This was the central preoccupation of the Sutherland report. See further Ch. 16.

[342]  [1997] OJ L82/1.

[343]  Joined Cases C–46/93 and C–48/93 *Brasserie du Pêcheur and Factortame* [1996] ECR I–1029. See further Ch. 10.

[344]  Paras. 28–9. See also Case C–445/06 *Danske Slagterier* v. *Bundesrepublik Deutschland* [2009] ECR I–2119 concerning a state liability claim brought by a Danish association of slaughterhouse companies against Germany alleging that Germany had breached various EU directives and the Treaties. The Court makes clear, *inter alia*, that a successful state liability claim is not dependent on a prior successful Art. 258 TFEU (ex Art. 226 EC) action, nor do Art. 258 proceedings suspend national limitation periods.

aimed at improving the transparency of national measures taken against imported products.[345]

The first of those measures was Decision 3052/95/EC establishing a procedure for the exchange of information on national measures derogating from the principle of free movement of goods.[346] This was a direct result of the inventory of national measures which had not been harmonized under Article 114 TFEU (ex Article 95 EC and Article 100a EEC) drawn up by the Commission under the now defunct Article 100b EEC.[347] It was a catch-all measure[348] which applied in the absence of any more specific provisions, such as prior notification under the Information Directive 98/34 or the notification procedure laid down under the Product Safety Directive 2001/95 when a product is withdrawn.[349] Unlike the procedure under the Information Directive 98/34 (considered in Chapter 4), Decision 3052/95 required 'ex-post' notification to the Commission by a Member State which had taken measures[350] 'to prevent the free movement or placing on the market of a particular model or type of product lawfully produced or marketed in another Member State'. The Commission then informed the other Member States which could, along with the Commission, request further information. The decision did not, however, allow the other Member States to make comments or to interfere with the rules of the notifying Member State.

Given the low-key nature of the Decision and the lack of any incentive to notify, it is perhaps not surprising that levels of notification were low (102 measures were notified between 1995 and 1998) with notification coming from just five countries.[351] Failure by a state to notify the Commission could lead the state to be condemned by the Court in Article 258 TFEU (ex Article 226 EC) enforcement proceedings but again this was rare.[352] As a result, Decision 3052/95 was repealed and replaced by a strengthened procedure contained in Regulation 764/2008.[353] This so-called 'Mutual Recognition' Regulation was adopted as part of the Commission's 2007 'Package on Internal Market for Goods' (considered in Chapter 4). This regulation replaces the process of notifying the Commission with a dialogue between the national authorities of the host state and the 'economic operator' (i.e., the manufacturer of the product, if established in the Union, or the person who has placed, or wishes to place, the product on the market[354]). This dialogue is triggered when the host State has taken or intends to take, on the basis of a technical rule,[355] a decision prohibiting the placing of a product on the market, requiring the product's modification or additional testing, or requiring the product to be withdrawn from the market (the so-called Article 2(1) decision).[356]

---

[345] Third preambular para. to Dec. 3052/95 [1995] OJ L321/1.     [346] [1995] OJ L321/1.

[347] Commission Communication, 'Management of the mutual recognition of national rules after 1992: Operation conclusions reached in the light of the inventory drawn up pursuant to Article 100b of the EC Treaty' ([1993] OJ C353/4). See further Ch. 1.     [348] COM(2000) 194, 2.

[349] [2002] OJ L11/4.

[350] Dec. 3052/95 defines 'measure' as any measure taken by a Member State, except for judicial decisions, which has the effect of restricting the free movement of goods lawfully produced or marketed in another Member State, regardless of its form or the authority from which it emanates: Joined Cases C–388 and 429/00 Radiosistemi Srl v. Prefetto di Genova [2002] ECR I–5845, paras. 67–73.

[351] Report from the Commission on the implementation of Dec. 3052/95/EC: COM(2000) 194 final.

[352] Case C–432/03 Commission v. Portugal (polyethylene pipes) [2005] ECR I–9665, para. 60; Case C–88/07 Commission v. Spain (medicinal herbs) [2009] ECR I–1353, para. 115.     [353] OJ [2008] L218/21.

[354] Art. 8.     [355] As defined in Art. 2(2).     [356] Art. 2(1).

One of the key features of the regulation is that it clearly places the burden on the Member State to explain—in writing—to the economic operator the technical rule on which the Article 2(1) decision is to be based and setting out technical or scientific evidence to the effect that:[357]

- the intended decision is justified on one of the grounds of public interest set out in Article 36 TFEU or by reference to other overriding reasons of public interest;
- the intended decision is appropriate for the purpose of achieving the objective pursued and does not go beyond what is necessary in order to obtain that objective.

The regulation then lays down a time scale in which the economic operator must respond to defend its case. According to Article 6(2), if the host state persists with its decision it must notify the economic operator and the Commission, setting out why it is rejecting the arguments put forward by the economic operator and the technical or scientific evidence on which the decision is based, as well as identifying any remedies available under national law.[358] If the host state authority fails to follow the Article 6(2) procedure, 'the product shall be deemed to be lawfully marketed in that Member State'. The regulation also establishes 'product contact points' in each Member State providing information about technical rules on products and explaining the implementation of the mutual recognition principle.

## H.  CONCLUSIONS

One of the strengths of the new procedure under the Mutual Recognition Regulation is that it takes as its starting point the position that goods lawfully marketed in one of the Member States should be capable of being sold in another. It is for the host Member State to explain why this is not the case. It therefore makes very clear that the derogations and mandatory requirements are the exception and not the rule. This will represent a significant change in perspective for a number of Member States. Even more of a challenge to some Member States is the import of goods from third (non-Member States) countries. In the next chapter we consider how the EU has regulated this process.

---

[357] Art. 6(1).      [358] Art. 6(2).

# 7

# THE COMMON COMMERCIAL POLICY

## A. INTRODUCTION

So far, this book has concentrated on the internal rules regulating the free movement of goods. However, as Article 28(1) TFEU (ex Article 23(1) EC) makes clear, the customs union also includes the establishment of the Common Customs Tariff (CCT), an important element of the Common Commercial Policy (CCP) which is the subject of this chapter. This chapter aims to provide an introduction to this vast and complex area of law,[1] focusing on the main elements of the Union's external commercial policy concerning the movement of goods in and out of the EU.[2] The chapter concludes by highlighting the relationship between the EU's external policy and other areas of international trade law through a study of the banana dispute.

The key Treaty provisions on the CCP are Articles 206–7 TFEU (ex Articles 131 and 133 EC). Article 206 provides that:

By establishing a customs union in accordance with Articles 28 to 32, the Union shall contribute, in the common interest, to the harmonious development of world trade, the progressive abolition of restrictions on international trade and on foreign direct investment, and the lowering of customs barriers.

Article 207(1) then says:[3]

The common commercial policy shall be based on uniform principles, particularly with regard to changes in tariff rates, the conclusion of tariff and trade agreements relating to trade in goods and services, and the commercial aspects of intellectual property, foreign direct investment, the achievement of uniformity in measures of liberalisation, export policy and measures to protect trade such as those to be taken in the event of dumping or subsidies.[4] The

---

[1] A number of specific texts cover this area in detail: e.g S. Inama and E. Vermulst, *Customs and Trade Laws of the European Community* (Dordrecht: Kluwer, 1999); T. Lyons, *EC Customs Law* (Oxford: OUP, 2008); I. Macleod, I. Hendry, and S. Hyett, *The External Relations of the European Communities* (Oxford: Clarendon Press, 1996); F. Snyder, *International Trade and Customs Law of the European Union* (London: Butterworths, 1998).

[2] It therefore does not consider specific sectors such as textiles and agriculture.

[3] See further M. Cremona, 'The Draft Constitutional Treaty: External relations and external action' (2003) 40 *CMLRev.* 1347, esp. 1361–5.

[4] As the Court noted in *Opinion 1/78 (Natural Rubber)* [1979] ECR 2871, para. 45, this is a non-exhaustive list which must not 'close the door to the application in a [Union] context of any other process intended to regulate external trade'.

common commercial policy shall be conducted in the context of the principles and objectives of the Union's external action.

From this we can see that the CCP is based on two principles—uniformity and trade liberalization, now supplemented by the principles and objectives of the union's external action laid down in Chapter 1 of Title V TEU including advancing democracy, human rights, and respect for the principles of the UN Charter and international law.[5] These two principles manifest themselves in the two strands of the CCP.[6] First, the CCP concerns internal rules of Union law (sometimes referred to as autonomous or unilateral rules) which comprise, on the one hand, measures on tariffs (the CCT) and, on the other, non-tariff measures (the Union's export and import regimes and commercial defence instruments). These rules reflect the EU's international commitments and form the main focus for this chapter. Secondly, the CCP concerns bilateral and multilateral agreements with third countries (such as the Free Trade Agreement with Switzerland, the Association Agreements, and the Agreement establishing the WTO). These agreements are referred to as contractual or conventional arrangements and they will not be considered further in this chapter.

## B. TARIFF BARRIERS TO EXTERNAL TRADE: THE CCT

### 1. INTRODUCTION

Article 28(2) TFEU provides that products coming from third countries which are in free circulation in Member States will benefit from the rules on the free movement of goods, namely Articles 30, 34–7,[7] and 110[8] TFEU. Article 29 TFEU (ex Article 24 EC) explains that products coming from a third country are to be considered in free circulation in a Member State 'if the import formalities have been complied with and any customs duties or charges having equivalent effect which are payable have been levied in that Member State, and if they have not benefited from a total or partial drawback of such duties or charges'. These import formalities include the payment of a Common Customs Tariff (CCT). As the Commission puts it, through the tariff, the Union applies the principle that domestic producers should be able to compete fairly and equally on the internal market with manufacturers exporting from other countries.[9] Once the CCT is paid (if one is

---

[5] Cremona, above n. 3, 351.      [6] This typology is taken from I. Macleod et al., above n. 1, 274.

[7] The Lisbon Treaty has created a potential problem here. Art. 23(2) EC said that 'The provisions of Article 25 and of Chapter 2 of this Title shall apply to ... products coming from third countries which are in free circulation in the Member States.' Ch. 2 EC is entitled 'Prohibition of quantitative restrictions between Member States'. Art. 28 TFEU appears to have intended to replicate Art. 23. However, Ch. 2 is now entitled 'Customs cooperation' and contains one Article, Art. 33 TFEU (ex Art. 135 EC), giving competence to the Union to take measures to strengthen customs cooperation between Member State and between Member States and the Commission. The prohibition of quantitative restrictions between Member States is now found in Ch. 3. It is suggested that the continued reference to Ch. 2 is an oversight and goods in free circulation will continue to enjoy the rights under Ch. 3.

[8] Art. 28(2) TFEU does not make any reference to Art. 110 TFEU but, given that Art. 110 is the complement to Art. 30, it is accepted that goods in free circulation also benefit from this provision: Case 193/85 *Cooperativa Co-Frutta (Bananas)* [1987] ECR 2085, paras. 24–9. However, Art. 110 does not apply to goods on their initial import into the EU: Case C–228/90 *Simba SpA (bananas)* [1992] ECR I–3713, paras. 14–15.

[9] <http://www.ec.europa.eu/taxation_customs/customs/customs_duties/tariff_aspects/index_en.htm>.

due), the goods are considered to be in free circulation and so enjoy the same rights to free movement as goods originating in the EU.[10]

The CCT involves applying uniform customs duties to products imported from third countries, that is, the same tariff is levied irrespective of whether the goods enter the EU via Ireland or Italy. The importance of a uniform tariff was emphasized by the Court in *Aprile*[11] where it said that, in the absence of such uniformity, trade would be diverted through states where the tariff was the lowest, thus distorting the conditions of competition. Given this need for uniformity, the Court said in *Diamantarbeiders*[12] that, following the introduction of the CCT which was intended to achieve an equalization of customs charges levied at the frontiers,[13] Member States were prohibited from unilaterally introducing any new charges or charges having equivalent effect or raising those already in force.[14] For this reason it is the EU (and not the Member States) which negotiates on tariffs in the WTO.

In order to ensure that the same tariff is applied to the same goods across the EU, the national customs authorities need to know what the goods are, how much they are worth, and where they originate from.[15] The EU has therefore created a common set of rules on the CCT,[16] applied since July 1968, by which goods are classified and tariffs set according to a *uniform nomenclature*, *valued* according to uniform Union rules, and their *origin is determined* again according to Union rules.[17] These rules were originally found in a large number of regulations and directives which were amended over the years. For simplification much of this legislation was recast into the vast Community Customs Code (CCC) found in Council Regulation 2913/92[18] which was subsequently repealed and replaced by the Modernised Customs Code (MCC) in Regulation 450/2008,[19] and the implementing legislation, Commission Regulation 2454/93.[20] The Combined Nomenclature and the tariffs to be applied to those goods are contained in the Tariff Regulation, Council Regulation 2658/87.[21]

## 2. COMBINED NOMENCLATURE

### 2.1 The Process of Classification

The Combined Nomenclature (CN) sets detailed rules for determining the classification of goods. It is based on the International Convention on the Harmonized

---

[10] Case 119/78 *SA des Grandes Distilleries Peureux* v. *Directeur des Services fiscaux de la Haute-Saône et du territoire de Belfort* [1979] ECR 975, para. 26.

[11] Case C–125/94 *Aprile Srl* v. *Amministrazione dello Stato* [1995] ECR I–2919, para. 32. See further Ch. 1.

[12] Joined Cases 37 and 38/73 *Sociaal Fonds voor de Diamantarbeiders* v. *NV Indiamex et Association de fait De Belder* [1973] ECR 1609.                                        [13] Para. 9.

[14] Arts. 10–17 EEC.

[15] S. Inama and E. Vermulst, above n. 1, 136. Cf. P. Van der Schueren, 'Customs classification: One of the cornerstones of the single European market, but one which cannot be exhaustively regulated' (1991) 28 *CMLRev.* 855, 856 (on the question of 'tariff shopping').

[16] See Art. 33 of the MCC Reg. 450/2008 [2008] OJ L 145/1.

[17] For further details, see <http://www.ec.europa.eu/taxation_customs/customs/customs_duties/tariff_aspects/index_en.htm>.

[18] [1992] OJ L302/1 as amended, most notably by Reg. 2700/00 ([2000] OJ L311/17).

[19] [2008] OJ L145/1.        [20] [1993] OJ L253/1 as amended.

[21] Council Reg. 2658/87 on the Tariff and Statistical Nomenclature and on the CCT ([1987] OJ L256/1) as amended.

Commodity Description Coding System (the Harmonized System) 1983 administered by the World Customs Organization (WCO).[22] Regulation 2658/87[23] establishes the CN and empowers the Commission to adopt a complete version of the CN every year, together with the relevant rates of duty.[24] This takes effect as an amendment to Annex I of Regulation 2658/87.

The CN is divided into 99 chapters, each preceded by notes explaining what is (and is not) included in the chapter. Figure 7.1 contains an excerpt from Chapter 62 of the CN[25] on clothing which forms part of Section XI on textiles and textile articles.

CHAPTER 62

ARTICLES OF APPAREL AND CLOTHING ACCESSORIES,
NOT KNITTED OR CROCHETED

*Notes*

1. This chapter applies only to made-up articles of any textile fabric other than wadding, excluding knitted or crocheted articles (other than those of heading 6212).

2. This chapter does not cover:
   (a) worn clothing or other worn articles of heading 6309; or
   (b) orthopaedic appliances, surgical belts, trusses or the like (heading 9021).

| CN Code | Description | Conventional rate of duty (%)[26] | Supplementary unit |
|---|---|---|---|
| 6211 | Tracksuits, ski suits and swimwear; other garments: | | |
| | — Swimwear: | | |
| 6211 1100 | — Men's or boy's | 12 | p/st[27] |
| 6211 12 00 | — Women's or girls' | 12 | p/st |
| 6211 20 00 | — Ski suits | 12 | p/st |
| | ... | | |
| 6212 | Brassières, girdles, corsets, braces, suspenders, garters and similar articles and parts thereof, whether or not knitted or crocheted: | | |
| 6212 10 | Brassières: | | |
| 6212 10 10 | — In a set made up for retail sale... | 6.5 | p/st |
| 6212 10 90 | — Other | 6.5 | p/st |
| | ... | | |
| 6213 | Handkerchiefs: | | |
| 6213 20 00 | — Of cotton | 10 | p/st |
| 6213 90 00 | — Of other textile materials | 10 | p/st |

**Fig. 7.1** Excerpt from the Combined Nomenclature

---

[22] Properly known as the Customs Co-operation Council (CCC).

[23] ([1987] OJ L256/1) repealing the original Reg. 950/68 ([1968] OJ L172/1). See P. Oliver and X. Yataganas, 'The harmonised system of customs classification' (1988) 8 *YEL* 113.

[24] Art. 12.

[25] Commission Reg. (EC) 948/2009 ([2009] OJ L287/1) amending Annex I to Council Reg. (EEC) No. 2658/87 on the tariff and statistical nomenclature and on the CCT.

[26] Conventional duties are derived from an agreement between the EU and a third country.

[27] Number of items.

The CN Code in the first column comprises eight numbers: a four-digit 'heading' and an eight-digit 'subheading' (all eight numbers).[28] The first six numbers are based on the WCO harmonized system; the seventh and eighth numbers are used to make subdivisions not foreseen by the harmonized system.[29] The third column lists the tariff (rate of duty) and the fourth column identifies the unit of measurement. The whole text is accompanied by general rules for interpreting the CN which form part of the tariff.

The Tariff Regulation gives power to the Commission, with the involvement of the Customs Code Committee, to amend the CN as well as to use the CN to classify goods where there is uncertainty as to their precise classification.[30] Figure 7.2 provides an illustration of the Commission using these powers to classify a garment as a bra.

| Description of the goods | Classification (CN Code) | Reasons |
|---|---|---|
| 4. Self-coloured lightweight knitted article for women or girls (86% nylon, 14% elastane), to be worn next to the skin, reaching down to just below the bust, with narrow adjustable shoulder straps. It has a low-cut neckline at the front and the back, without opening.<br><br>There are bands of knitted fabric sewn onto the neckline and the armpits.<br><br>There are knitted side-panels of varying elasticity on the article, as well as an elasticated reinforcement at the front.<br><br>There is stitching just below the bust, reinforced on the inside, following the natural shape of the bust.<br><br>There is an elasticated band of a width of about 2 cm on the lower edge of the article, to make sure that the article clings to the body.<br><br>(Brassière) | 6212 10 90 | Classification is determined by general rules 1 and 6 for the interpretation of the Combined Nomenclature, note 2(a) to Chapter 61 and the wording of CN codes 6212, 6212 10 and 6212 10 90.<br><br>The elasticated reinforcement at the front, which gathers the fabric and contributes to the convex form of the cups, leads to the separation of the breasts which is characteristic of a brassiere.<br><br>The stitching follows the shape of the bust and gathers the fabric into the form of the cups.<br><br>The reinforcement of the stitching on the inside of the article serves as a stiffener and, together with the elasticated side panels, provides the support required for brassieres, in accordance with the Harmonised System explanatory notes to heading 6212, first paragraph. |

**Fig. 7.2** Excerpt from Commission Reg. 471/2002 ([2002] OJ L75/13) as amended concerning the classification of certain goods in the Combined Nomenclature

---

[28] Art. 3 of Reg. 2658/87.

[29] A 9th digit can be used by the Member State for its own purposes; and a 10th and 11th digit are used to form a TARIC (General Integrated Tariff of the European Communities) code. The TARIC is used to alert the customs authorities of the Member States to special customs regimes including, e.g. anti-dumping duties (Art. 5).

[30] Art. 9. The regulations in which it makes a classification are subject to judicial review. Non-privileged applicants may have standing: Case T–243/01 *Sony Computer Entertainment Europe Ltd* v. *Commission* [2003] ECR II–4189. If a national court has issued an incorrect binding tariff information (BTI), a national court is required under Art. 4(3) TEU (ex Art. 10 EC) to take, within its sphere of competence, all the measures necessary to ensure that that information is annulled and that new BTI, consistent with Union law is issued: Case C–206/03 *Commissioners of Customs & Excise* v. *Smith-Kline Beecham plc*, Order of 19 Jan. 2005 ([2005] OJ C106/10).

The Commission has classified this garment under the CN Code 6212 10 90.[31] The first four digits are the heading (6212) and the eight digits are the subheading (6212 10 90). As the third column explains, the classification of the product is determined by two of the six general substantive rules for the interpretation of the CN (rules 1 and 6),[32] together with the chapter notes to Chapter 61 (note 2(a)) which provides that Chapter 61 on articles of apparel and clothing accessories does not cover goods under heading 6212.

## 2.2 The Role of the Court of Justice

The Court of Justice has inevitably been involved with the interpretation of the successive regulations on the CCT. As Advocate General Jacobs noted in *Wiener*,[33] the Court's interpretation is indispensable, not only because the regulations are pieces of Union legislation directly applicable in all the Member States, but also in order to safeguard the uniform application of the CCT and thus to avoid deflections of trade. The Court has long held that, in the interests of legal certainty and ease of verification, the decisive criterion for the classification of goods for customs purposes is 'to be sought in their characteristics and objective properties as defined in the wording of the relevant heading of the CCT and of the notes to the sections or chapters'.[34] The Court has also held that, in interpreting the CCT, both the notes which head the chapters of the CCT and the Explanatory Notes to the Nomenclature of the WCO are important means for ensuring the uniform application of the tariff and as such could be regarded as useful aids to its interpretation,[35] albeit that they do not have legally binding force.[36] In addition, the intended use of a product may constitute an objective criterion for classification if it is inherent to the product, and that inherent character must be capable of being assessed on the basis of the product's objective characteristics and properties.[37]

The application of these principles can be seen in *Neckermann Versand*.[38] The case concerned garments which had been declared as pyjamas under heading 61.08 of the CCT ('women's or girls'…pyjamas,…knitted or crocheted') but were subsequently reclassified by the German authorities as upper garments and trousers, with the result that a higher rate of customs duty was chargeable. The Court of Justice noted that the wording of heading 61.08 did not provide a definition of pyjamas nor, on this occasion,

---

[31] For a similar conclusion by the Court, see Case C–80/96 *Quelle Schickedanz AG and Co.* v. *Oberfinanzdirektion Frankfurt am Main* [1998] ECR I–123, paras. 15–16.

[32] E.g., the first rule states that 'The titles of sections, chapters and sub-chapters are provided for ease of reference only; for legal purposes, classification shall be determined according to the terms of the headings and any relevant section or chapter notes…'. Rule 6 provides that 'For legal purposes, the classification of goods in the subheadings of a heading shall be determined according to the terms of those subheadings and any related subheading notes and, *mutatis mutandis* to the above rules, on the understanding that only subheadings at the same level are comparable'.

[33] Case C–338/95 *Wiener S.I. GmbH* v. *Hauptzollamt Emmerich* [1997] ECR I–6495, para. 9.

[34] Case 40/88 *Weber* v. *Milchwerke Paderborn-Rimbeck* [1989] ECR 1395, para. 13; Case C–196/05 *Sachsenmilch SA* v. *Oberfinanzdirektion Nürnberg* [2006] ECR I–5161, para. 22; Joined Cases C–362/07 and C–363/07 *Kip Europe* v. *Administration des Douanes* [2008] ECR I–9489, para. 26; Case C–150/08 *Siebrand* v. *Staatssecretaris van Financiën* [2009] ECR I–000, para. 24.

[35] Case 200/84 *Daiber* v. *Hauptzollamt Reutlingen* [1985] ECR 3363, para. 14.

[36] Case C–196/05 *Sachsenmilch SA* [2006] ECR I–5161, para. 23.

[37] Case C–396/02 *DFDS BV* v. *Inspecteur der Belastingdienst- Douanedistrict Rotterdam* [2004] ECR I–8439, para. 29. For a consideration of this rule in particular, see Case C–467/03 *Ikegami Electronics (Europe) GmbH* v. *Oberfinanzdirektion Nürnberg* [2005] ECR I–2389.

[38] Case C–395/93 *Neckermann Versand* v. *Hauptzollamt Frankfurt am Main-Ost* [1994] ECR I–4027.

did the CCT or WCO Explanatory Notes. The Court therefore examined 'the objective characteristics of pyjamas'.[39] It considered the use for which pyjamas were intended, concluding that they were exclusively or mainly 'worn in bed as nightwear'.[40] It added that in order to classify a garment as pyjamas, its sole and exclusive purpose did not have to be nightwear 'worn in bed' but that had to be the *main* use for which it was intended.[41] This case was followed by *Wiener*[42] concerning garments which had been classified as women's nightdresses under heading 60.04 but which were subsequently reclassified as 'dresses of synthetic textile fibres' under heading 60.05, and so subject to a higher customs duty. The Court said that since the goods were intended to be worn essentially in bed, they had to be regarded as nightdresses under heading 60.04, even though they could be used for other purposes.

These cases raise two more general constitutional points. First, although both decisions were the result of Article 267 TFEU (ex Article 234 EC) references, the Court not only gave the national court guidance on the interpretation of the law but also applied the law to the facts of the case. Under the principle of cooperation usually applied to Article 267, this is the task for the national court.[43] However, in *Wiener* Advocate General Jacobs applauded the Court's pragmatism, noting that the Court will give an interpretation tailored to the needs of the referring court. Such an interpretation may include applying the law to the facts.[44]

Secondly, these cases illustrate the potentially unlimited number of product classification questions that could be referred to the Court, raising the spectre of an already overloaded Court collapsing under the weight of references on matters apparently as banal as what constitutes pyjamas.[45] Given the importance of ensuring uniform interpretation, for Advocate General Jacobs the correct response was not to limit such references but to request that both national courts and the Court of Justice demonstrate 'a greater measure of self-restraint'.[46]

## 3. VALUATION

Once the goods have been classified, their value needs to be determined to assess *ad valorem* duties. The value is worked out according to the principles contained in the WTO Customs Valuation Agreement[47] which have been implemented by Articles 40–3 MCC. The valuation process is based on a 'fair, uniform, neutral system' which excludes the

---

[39] Para. 7.   [40] Ibid.

[41] Para. 9. These principles were applied in Case T–243/01 *Sony Computer Entertainment Europe Ltd* v. *Commission* [2003] ECR II–4189, para. 110 concerning the classification of Play Station®2.

[42] Case C–338/95 [1997] ECR I–6495.

[43] Joined Cases 28–30/62 *Da Costa en Schaake* v. *Nederlandse Belastingadministratie* [1963] ECR 31, 38.

[44] Cf. Case C–196/05 *Sachsenmilch SA* [2006] ECR I–5161, para. 19 where the Court left the national court to make the final decision on classification.

[45] Or, Case C–14/05 *Anagram International Inc.* v. *Inspecteur van de Belastingdienst- Douanedistrict Rotterdam* [2006] ECR I–6763: can gas-filled balloons made of aluminized, bonded plastic foil be classified as a toy? Yes, said the Court, they were intended 'essentially for the amusement of persons (children or adults)' even though the material they were made from was not resistant or durable. The 'fact that they do not last long and that they float in the air does not prevent children in particular from enjoying and playing with those objects' (paras. 23–4).   [46] Para. 18.

[47] Agreement on Implementation of Art. VII of GATT 1994 contained in Annex 1A. For guidance in the EU, see <http://www.ec.europa.eu/taxation_customs/resources/documents/customs/customs_duties/declared_goods/european/compendium_2008_en.pdf>.

use of 'arbitrary or fictitious customs values'.[48] The preferred method of valuation is the transaction value of the imported goods (i.e., the price actually paid or payable by the importer).[49] If the transaction value cannot be determined, then the agreement provides for four other methods of valuation. In order of preference they are: (1) the transaction value of identical goods; (2) the transaction value of similar goods; (3) the value based on the unit price at which the imported goods or identical or similar imported goods are sold within the Union in the greatest aggregate quantity to people not related to the sellers; and (4) the computed value.[50] In the Union context, the goods are valued at the point of entry into the EU which means that costs connected with the importation, such as transport and warehousing, are not included in the value.

## 4. DETERMINATION OF ORIGIN

The tariff, if any, to be applied to imports depends on their origin (Union or non-Union).[51] The determination of the origin of goods is laid down in Articles 35–9 MCC.[52] The rules considered below concern non-preferential origin. More detailed rules on the determination of origin are laid down in specific agreements made between the Union and non-Member States which give goods from those states preferential access to the EU.

Article 36(1) MCC (ex Article 23 CCC) provides that goods *wholly obtained* in a single country or territory shall be regarded as having their origin in that country or territory'. Examples of such 'wholly obtained' goods would be those identified in the original Article 23 CCC, namely 'natural products' and products derived from natural products (e.g., minerals extracted, vegetables harvested, and animals born and raised within that country). By contrast, Article 36(2) MCC (ex Article 24 CCC) concerns the origin of goods which are not wholly produced in one country or territory. It provides that they shall be deemed to originate 'in the country or territory where they underwent their last substantial transformation'.[53] Article 25 of the original CCC contained an anti-avoidance clause.[54] It said that any processing or working whose sole object is to circumvent the origin rules shall 'under no circumstances be deemed to confer on the goods thus produced the origin of the country where it is carried out within the meaning of Article 24'. Read together, the Court said that Articles 23–5 CCC constituted 'an indispensable means of ensuring the uniform application of the common customs tariff'.[55]

---

[48] Case C–306/04 *Compaq Computer International Cooperation* [2006] ECR I–10991, para. 30.

[49] Art. 41.        [50] Art. 42.

[51] As we saw in Ch. 2, under WTO rules the EU is not allowed to differentiate on the basis of origin in respect of WTO members, unless exceptionally allowed to do so (i.e., for the purposes of applying anti-dumping rules, or under WTO compliant preferences (Generalized System of Preferences (GSP) system or Art. XXV agreements).

[52] Customs authorities of the Member States can issue a decision relating to binding origin information (BOI) under Art. 20 MCC.

[53] Emphasis added. See also the Uruguay Round Agreement on (non-preferential) Rules of Origin contained in Annex 1A (multilateral agreements on the trade in goods) which is based on the notion of 'last substantial transformation'. Art. 24 CCC was more detailed. It provided the origin of goods which are not wholly produced in one country shall be deemed to originate in the country where they underwent their last, substantial economically justified processing or working in an undertaking equipped for that purpose and resulting in the manufacture of a new product or representing an important stage of manufacture'.

[54] This is not replicated in the MCC. However, the regulation does give the power to amend the regulation to avoid the circumvention of the tariff measures (Art. 54(c)).

[55] Case 49/76 *Gesellschaft für Überseehandel mbH v. Handelskammer Hamburg* [1977] ECR 41, para. 5.

The question, then, is how to determine what constitutes a 'substantial' last process or operation for the purposes of Article 36(2) MCC. The Commission identifies three main methods:[56]

- by a rule requiring a change of tariff (sub)heading in the HS nomenclature[57]
- by a list of manufacturing or processing operations that do or do not confer on the goods the origin of the country in which these operations were carried out
- by a value added rule, where the increase of value due to assembly operations and incorporation of originating materials represents a specified level of the ex-works price of the product.[58]

Further details are given in the Implementing Regulation 2454/93 and a table of 'list rules'.[59]

The Court has also been called on to rule what constitutes a 'substantial' last process. In *Überseehandel*[60] it said that a last process or operation was only substantial 'if the product resulting therefrom has its own properties and a composition of its own, which it did not possess before that process or operation'. However, if the activities affected only the presentation of the product for the purposes of its use but did not bring about a significant qualitative change in its properties, such a process did not determine origin. The case concerned the origin of untreated casein which was obtained in a third country but rendered fit for use by being ground up to various degrees of fineness in Germany where it was also graded and packed. The Court found that the casein did not have German origin. It said that the grinding of a raw material could not be considered as a process or operation because it resulted only in changing the consistency of the product and its presentation without bringing about a significant qualitative change in the raw material. The Court added that the grading and packaging was for marketing purposes only and did not affect its substantial properties. For similar reasons, the Court ruled in *Zentrag*[61] that the processing of the meat derived from beef quarters by boning, trimming, drawing the sinews, cutting into pieces, and vacuum-packing did not confer upon the meat the origin of the country in which those operations were carried out.

More difficult have been the cases involving so-called 'screwdriver operations' where the parts are manufactured in one country but assembled in another.[62] This presents the

---

[56] <http://www.ec.europa.eu/taxation_customs/customs/customs_duties/rules_origin/non-preferential/article_410_en.htm>.

[57] This must be one of the factors taken into account when making an overall assessment. It cannot be the only requirement: Case C–260/08 *Bundesfinanzdirektion West* v. *HEKO Industrieerzeugnisse GmbH* [2009] ECR I–000, para. 35.

[58] This test was supported by the Court in Joined Cases C–447/05 and C–448/05 *Thomson Multimedia Sales Europe* v. *Administration des douanes et droits indirects* [2007] ECR I–2049, para. 39.

[59] These list rules must be compatible with the rules of origin as set out in Art. 36(2) MCC and may not alter the scope of the rules: Case C–260/08 *HEKO Industrieerzeugnisse GmbH* [2009] ECR I–000, para. 21.

[60] Case 49/76 *Gesellschaft für Überseehandel* [1977] ECR 41. See also Case C–373/08 *Hoechst Metals and Alloys GmbH* v. *Hauptzollamt Aachen* [2010] ECR I–000, para. 51 where the Court ruled that sieving, crushing, and packaging did not confer origin.

[61] Case 93/83 *Zentralgenossenschaft des Fleischergewerbes eG (Zentrag)* v. *Hauptzollamt Bochum* [1984] ECR 1095.

[62] The assembly must be considered as a whole. As the Court put it in Case C–372/06 *Asda Stores Ltd* v. *Commissioners of HMRC* [2007] ECR I–11223, para. 58, Art. 36(2) and the implementing regulation 'do not envisage taking account, in the manufacturing process, of certain assembly operations to the detriment of certain others, or thereby artificially isolating such and such a part which itself comes from an assembly carried out by the same supplier'.

problem of determining which country actually confers origin, an issue raised in *Brother*[63] and *Yoshida*.[64] *Brother* was a dumping case concerning the origin of electronic typewriters where the parts were manufactured in Japan but assembled in Taiwan. Drawing on the (now revised) Kyoto Convention on the simplification and harmonization of customs procedures, which had been accepted on behalf of the Union,[65] the Court distinguished between 'simple' assembly operations and other assembly operations. 'Simple assembly' operations did not require staff with special qualifications for the work or sophisticated tools or specially equipped factories for the purposes of assembly. The Court said that such operations did not contribute to the essential characteristics or properties of the goods and so did not confer origin.

On the other hand, the Court recognized that other types of assembly operation could be regarded as conferring origin if they satisfied a technical test or, failing that, a value added test. In respect of the technical test, the Court ruled that an assembly process conferred origin where it represented, from a technical point of view and having regard to the definition of the goods in question, the decisive production stage during which the use to which the component parts were to be put became definite and the goods in question were given their specific qualities. The *technical* test was applied in *Yoshida* where the Court found that although the parts for slide fasteners (zips) were made in Japan, the slide fasteners themselves had German origin because the last substantial process took place in Germany. This involved attaching metal scoops to the tapes and joining the tapes together, attaching bottom and top stops and inserting the sliders.

In respect of the *value added* test, the Court said in *Brother* said that if the assembly operations as a whole involved 'an appreciable increase in the commercial value of the finished product at the ex-factory stage' then the assembly process conferred origin. In order to decide this, a comparison had to be made between the amount of the value added in the country of assembly and the value added in other countries. Where only two countries were concerned, the Court said that the mere assembly of those goods in one country from previously manufactured parts originating in the other was not sufficient to confer on the resulting product the origin of the country of assembly if the value added there was appreciably less than in the other country. In any event, the Court said that where a value of less than 10 per cent was added, this could not be regarded as sufficient to confer on the finished product the origin of the country of assembly.

By using the substantial transformation test, the Union has tried to prevent 'origin shopping' (i.e., attempts by importers to ensure that goods attain a favourable origin by means of as limited an activity as possible[66]). As we saw above, the original Article 25 CCC buttressed this aim by providing that where it was established or the facts justified the presumption that the processing had the 'sole aim' of circumventing Union provisions, then that processing did not confer origin. However, in *Brother* the Court said that the transfer of the assembly from the country where the parts were manufactured to another country where use was made of factories already in existence was no ground in itself for raising such a presumption. There might be other reasons to justify such a transfer. However, the Court said that where the transfer of the assembly coincided with the entry

---

[63] Case C–26/88 *Brother International GmbH v. Hauptzollamt Gießen* [1989] ECR I–4253.

[64] Case 114/78 *Yoshida GmbH v. Industrie-und Handelskammer Kassel* [1979] ECR 151.

[65] Council Dec. 77/415/EEC ([1977] OJ L166/1) in respect of the original Kyoto Convention and Council Dec. 2003/231/EC ([2003] OJ L162/113) in respect of the revised Convention.

[66] Lyons, above n. 1, 245.

into force of the relevant rules, the trader concerned had to prove that there were reasonable grounds, other than avoiding the consequences of the provisions in question, for carrying out the assembly operations in the country to which the goods were exported.

## 5. THE CUSTOMS TARIFF

The final stage in the process of customs classification is the application of the tariff itself.[67] Article 33 MCC (ex Article 20(1) CCC) provides that 'Import and export duties shall be based on the Common Customs Tariff.' The tariff levied was originally the arithmetic mean of the tariffs applied in 1957 by the Member States.[68] Since then, these tariffs have been amended, largely as a result of the various rounds of GATT. Loosely speaking, tariffs tend to be lower on raw materials and semi-manufactured goods and higher on finished products. This makes cheap raw materials available to EU manufacturers on the same competitive footing as to foreign processing companies. Low tariffs are also imposed in sectors where it is necessary to stimulate competition, such as in pharmaceuticals and information technology. However, even low tariffs in the 4–8 per cent range still represent a significant cost factor for importers and consequently a competitive benefit to EU producers.[69] The details of the rates of tariff are set out in the Tariff Regulation 2658/87 as amended (see fig. 7.1).

The tariff is collected by the state of import in accordance with national rules and conditions which must comply with the principles of non-discrimination and effectiveness.[70] The collecting state is allowed to retain 25 per cent of the customs duty to cover collection costs.[71] The remainder is paid over to the EU where it forms about 15 per cent of the Union's own resources.[72]

## 6. TARIFF QUOTAS

The EU may decide to impose tariff quotas on goods coming in from non-Member States (see, for example, the tariff quotas used as part of the new banana regime considered below in Section E). These are an exception to the normal rules since they permit the total or partial suspension of the normal duties applicable to imported goods for a given quantity of goods. *Preferential* tariff quotas enable a predetermined quantity of goods originating in a specific third country with which the EU has concluded an agreement, to be imported into the EU at a more favourable rate of duty than the normal third-country rate of duty specified in the combined nomenclature. *Autonomous* tariff quotas are used to stimulate economic activity in the EU. They are normally granted to raw materials, semi-finished goods or components not available or insufficiently available in the EU.[73]

Tariff quotas are administered in accordance with the rules laid down in Regulation 717/2008.[74] The Commission must publish a notice announcing the opening of the quotas

---

[67] According to Art. 31 TFEU (ex Art. 26 EC), 'Common Customs Tariff duties shall be fixed by the Council on a proposal form the Commission'.

[68] Originally Reg. 803/68 ([1968] OJ L148/6), now replaced by Reg. 2913/92 ([1992] OJ L302/1) on the CCC.

[69] Inama and Vermulst, above n. 1, 16.

[70] See, e.g., Joined Cases C–153 and 204/94 *R* v. *Commissioners of Customs and Excise, ex p. Faroe Seafood Co. Ltd and others* [1996] ECR I–2465, para. 66.          [71] Art. 2(3) of Dec. 728/94 ([1994] OJ L293/9).

[72] Lyons, above n. 1, 57.

[73] <http://www.ec.europa.eu/taxation_customs/customs/customs_duties/tariff_aspects/quotas/index_en.htm>.

[74] [2008] OJ L198/1.

in the Official Journal for which the trader may then apply. The releases for free circulation of products subject to a quota are usually made subject to a non-transferable licence issued by the Member State to which quota applications are made.[75]

## 7. THE ROLE OF THE MEMBER STATES

Once the goods have been classified by the customs authorities of the Member State of import, other Member States cannot levy additional import duties.[76] The importance of cooperation between the national customs authorities is made clear by the TFEU which contains a single-article Chapter headed customs cooperation. This Article, Article 33 TFEU (ex Article 135 EC), provides that the European Parliament and Council, acting in accordance with the ordinary legislative procedure (ex Article 251 EC co-decision procedure), must take measures 'to strengthen customs cooperation between Member States and between the latter and the Commission'.

With a *Union*-level CCT in place, the Member States are prohibited from levying their own customs duties on goods imported from non-Member States. Member States are also prohibited from levying charges having equivalent effect to customs duties on goods coming in from non-Member States. Although the Treaties do not make express provision to this effect, the Court ruled in *Aprile* that:[77]

Both the unicity of the [Union] customs territory and the uniformity of the common commercial policy would be seriously undermined if the Member States were authorised unilaterally to impose charges having equivalent effect to customs duties on imports from non-Member countries.

## C. NON-TARIFF BARRIERS TO EXTERNAL TRADE

So far we have been considering tariff barriers imposed on goods entering the EU from non-Member States. We shall now look at *non-tariff* measures which regulate both exports from and imports into the EU.

## 1. THE EXPORT REGIME: REGULATION 1061/2009

### 1.1 Freedom of export

The basic principle underpinning Regulation 1061/2009[78] (repealing the original Regulation 2603/69[79]) is freedom of export. Article 1 provides that:

The exportation of products from the European [Union] to third countries shall be free, that is to say, they shall not be subject to any quantitative restriction, with the exception of those restrictions which are applied in conformity with the provisions of this Regulation.

---

[75] Lyons, above n. 1, 119–24.

[76] Case C–384/89 *Criminal proceedings against Gérard Tomatis and Christian Fulichron* [1991] ECR I–127.                                                                [77] Case C–125/94 [1995] ECR I–2919, para. 34.

[78] [2009] OJ L291/1. The export and import of certain dangerous chemicals is covered by EP and Council Reg. (EC) No. 304/03 ([2003] OJ L63/1). Council Reg. (EC) No. 116/2009 ([2009] OJ L39/1) makes provision for the issuing of export licences in the case of the export of cultural goods. A notification procedure is also applied to certain substances to discourage their diversion to the illicit manufacture of narcotic drugs: Reg. 111/2005 ([2005] OJ L22/1).                                                [79] [1969] OJ L324/25 as amended.

This provision is directly effective.[80] Unlike Article 35 TFEU (ex Article 29 EC), Article 1 of the Export Regulation refers only to quantitative restrictions and not measures having equivalent effect. However, in *Werner*[81] the Court, relying on both a contextual interpretation and Article XI of GATT, said that a regulation based on Article 207 TFEU (ex Article 133 EC), whose objective was to implement the principle of free exportation at Union level, could not exclude from its scope measures adopted by the Member States whose effect was equivalent to a quantitative restriction where their application could lead to an export prohibition.[82]

## 1.2 Derogations

The principle of freedom of export is subject to certain limits. First, in order to prevent a critical situation from arising on account of a shortage of essential products, or to remedy such a situation, and where Union interests call for immediate intervention, Article 6 provides that the Commission, acting at the request of the Member State concerned or on its own initiative, can make the export of a product subject to the production of an export authorization. Such protective measures are subject to a Union information and consultation procedure before they can be implemented.[83] Article 7 allows the Council to take appropriate measures to prevent a critical situation form arising due to a shortage of essential products or to remedy such a situation and to allow international undertakings entered into by the Union or the Member States to be fulfilled.

Secondly, Article 9 specifically authorizes transitional provisions. It provides that in respect of products listed in the annex (e.g., crude oil and petrol),[84] Member States are authorized to implement an emergency sharing system introducing an allocation obligation vis-à-vis third countries provided for in international commitments entered into before the entry into force of the regulation. The Commission has to be notified of any such steps. This possibility exists until the EU has adopted appropriate measures pursuant to international commitments entered into by the Union or all of the Member States.

Thirdly, Article 10 permits Member States to introduce quantitative restrictions on exports on the grounds laid down in Article 36 TFEU (ex Article 30 EC) (public morality, public policy, or public security, public health, etc.). It will be recalled from Chapter 6 that the public-security derogation was at issue in *Richardt*[85] concerning strategic goods in transit. There the Court ruled that the concept of public security within the meaning of Article 36 covered both a Member State's internal and external security.[86] Referring to this decision, the Court said in *Werner*,[87] a case concerning dual-use goods (goods which can have both military and civilian uses), that Article 36 TFEU and Article 10 of the regulation had to be interpreted consistently[88] because, if the concept was interpreted more restrictively when used in Article 10, it would be tantamount to authorizing the Member States to restrict the movement of goods within the internal market more than movement between themselves and non-Member States.[89]

---

[80] Case C–83/94 *Criminal proceedings against Peter Leifer and others* [1995] ECR I–3231, para. 46.
[81] Case C–70/94 [1995] ECR I–3189.       [82] Para. 22.       [83] Arts. 2–5.
[84] The validity of this exclusion was upheld in Case 174/84 *Bulk Oil (Zug) AG* v. *Sun International Ltd and Sun Oil Trading Co.* [1986] ECR 559, para. 37.
[85] Case C–367/89 *Richardt and Les Accessoires Scientifiques* [1991] ECR I–4621.       [86] Para. 22.
[87] Case C–70/94 [1995] ECR I–3189.       [88] Ibid.       [89] Para. 25.

*Werner* concerned a decision by the German authorities to refuse to issue a German company with a licence to export a smelting and cast oven to Libya. The Court said that, given that it was increasingly difficult to look at the security of the state in isolation, since it was closely linked to the security of the international community at large,[90] the term 'public security' included 'the risk of a serious disturbance to foreign relations or to peaceful co-existence of nations'.[91] The Court added that although it was for the national court to decide whether Article 10 applied, 'it should, however, be observed that it is common ground that the exportation of goods capable of being used for military purposes to a country at war with another country may affect the public security of a Member State'.[92]

In *Leifer*,[93] a case decided the same day as *Werner*, a German national was prosecuted for having delivered plant, plant parts, and chemical products (capable of being used for making chemical weapons) to Iraq during the Iran–Iraq war without having the necessary export licences. The Court said that a Member State could, '*exceptionally*, adopt national measures restricting the export of dual-use goods to non-member countries' where necessary for public-security reasons.[94] Asking the applicant to prove that the goods would be used exclusively for civil purposes or refusing to issue a licence if the goods could objectively be used for military purposes was consistent with the principle of proportionality.[95]

The Court further developed the parallels between Article 36 TFEU and Article 10 of the Export Regulation in *Centro-Com*,[96] where it said that while a measure intended to apply sanctions imposed by a UN resolution to achieve a peaceful solution to the situation in Bosnia-Herzegovina fell within Article 10,[97] recourse to Article 10 by Member States ceased to be justified if Union rules provided the necessary measures to ensure protection of the interests listed in the Article.[98] The Union had issued a regulation on sanctions against the former Yugoslavia, implementing a UN resolution which banned the export of goods to the former Yugoslavia with the exception of essential medical supplies and foodstuffs. Export of these essential supplies had to be notified to the Sanctions Committee. Following reports of abuse of this procedure, the UK tightened up its own rules for allowing exports of these essential supplies: in order to ensure that exports actually matched their description and that the money was not being diverted to pay for goods which did not have a medical or humanitarian purpose, the British authorities permitted payment using Yugoslavian funds held by British banks but only where the exports were made from the UK.

The Court said these (additional) steps taken by the UK could not be justified, because effective application of the sanctions could be ensured by other Member States' authorization procedures, as provided for in the Sanctions Regulation, especially the procedures laid down by the Member State of exportation. Reflecting the principle of mutual trust laid down in *Hedley Lomas*,[99] the Court said that the Member States had to 'place trust in

---

[90] Para. 26. Cf. Case C–84/95 *Bosphorus Hava Yollari Turizm ve Ticaret* v. *Minister for Transport, Energy and Communications, Ireland and Attorney General* [1996] ECR I–3953, para. 26.     [91] Para. 27.

[92] Para. 28.

[93] Case C–83/94 *Criminal proceedings against Peter Leifer and others* [1995] ECR I–3231.

[94] Para. 30, emphasis added.     [95] Para. 36.

[96] Case C–124/95 *R.* v. *HM Treasury and Bank of England, ex p. Centro-Com Srl* [1997] ECR I–81.

[97] Para. 45.     [98] Para. 46.

[99] Case C–5/94 *Hedley Lomas* [1996] ECR I–2553, para. 19, considered in Ch. 6. Cf. Case C–230/98 *Amministrazione delle Finanze dello Stato* v. *Schiavon Silvano* [2000] ECR I–3547, para. 53.

each other as far as concerns the checks made by the competent authorities of the Member State from which the products in question are dispatched',[100] adding that there was no evidence that the procedure laid down by the Sanctions Regulation had not functioned properly. If it had doubts about the accuracy of descriptions of goods appearing in an export authorization issued by the competent authorities of another Member State, the UK could have had recourse to the system of collaboration established by the Regulation on Mutual Assistance.[101]

This case shows that once the Union has adopted measures harmonizing the conditions of export, then Member States must respect the relevant Union rules. This view is reinforced by the adoption of Council Regulation (EC) No. 1334/2000,[102] now repealed and recast by Regulation 428/2009,[103] setting up a Union regime for the control of exports of dual-use items and technology which is aimed at ensuring free movement of dual-use items inside the Union. It does not establish a common policy on export controls, replacing the national systems. Instead, it either requires or, in some cases, permits Member States to impose an authorization requirement in respect of the export of dual-use goods, which, subject to safeguard clauses, is valid throughout the Union.

## 2. THE IMPORT REGIME: REGULATION 260/2009

### 2.1 Freedom of import

Imports[104] into the European Union from non-Member States are covered by Regulation 260/2009[105] (repealing and codifying Regulation 3285/94[106]) which incorporates the Uruguay Round Agreement on Safeguards into EU law.[107] As with the Export Regulation, the basic rule is that products 'shall be freely imported into the [Union] and... shall not be subject to any quantitative restrictions'.[108] In the early case of *EMI*[109] the Court noted that a predecessor to Regulation 260/2009 related 'only to quantitative restrictions to the

---

[100] Case C–124/95 *Centro-Com* [1997] ECR I–81, para. 49. This is also the theme underpinning the Customs 2000/Customs 2002/Customs 2007 and now Customs 2013 (Dec 624/2007/EC ([2007] OJ L 154/25)). The Commission reported favourably on increase cooperation: COM(2008) 612.

[101] Council Reg. 1468/81 ([1981] OJ L144/1) now replaced by Council Reg. 515/97 ([1997] OJ L82/1).

[102] [2000] OJ L159/1, replacing the earlier regime. This has been amended and updated by Council Reg. 394/06 ([2006] OJ L74/1).

[103] [2009] OJ L134/1.

[104] This regulation does not cover the act of placing the goods on the market which is considered subsequent to the act of importation: Case C–296/00 *Prefetto Provincia di Cuneo* v. *Carbone* [2002] ECR I–4657, paras. 31–2.

[105] [2009] OJ L84/1. This regulation applies to states which are members of the WTO. See also Council Reg. (EC) No. 625/2009 on common rules for imports from state trading countries ([2009] OJ L185/1).

[106] [1994] OJ L349/53 as amended. This concerns imports from countries which are members of the WTO. Separate rules apply to imports from state trading countries. Reg. 3285/94 replaces Council Reg. 518/94 repealing Reg. 288/82. Special measures deal with, e.g., counterfeit goods: Council Reg. 1383/03 [2003] OJ L190/7.

[107] The regulation does not apply to textile products covered by Reg. 517/94 (other than those listed in Annex II which originate from a WTO Member State) and to products originating in certain third countries listed in Art. 1(1) of Reg. 519/94.

[108] Art. 1(2). The regulation governs importation and not placing on the market: Case C–296/00 *Prefetto Provincia di Cuneo* v. *Silvano Carbone* [2002] ECR I–4657, para. 35.

[109] Case 51/75 *EMI Records Ltd* v. *CBS United Kingdom Ltd* [1976] ECR 811, para. 20. See also Case 225/78 *Procureur de la République de Besançon* v. *Bouhelier and others* [1979] ECR 3151, para. 6.

exclusion of measures having equivalent effect'. In the light of the judgments in *Werner* and *Leifer* the Court might now be prepared to read the term 'quantitative restrictions' to include 'measures having equivalent effect'.

## 2.2 Derogations and Safeguard Measures

The freedom to import is also subject to a number of derogations provided by the regulation.[110] First, Article 24(2) permits Member States to derogate from the freedom to import on the same grounds as those laid down in Article 36 TFEU[111] if the Commission is given notice of the measures or formalities they intend to introduce or amend in accordance with this provision.[112] In the event of extreme urgency, the national measures or formalities must be communicated to the Commission immediately after their adoption.[113]

Secondly, Chapter V of the regulation,[114] based on Article XIX of GATT and the WTO Agreement on Safeguards, provides that where, according to Article 16(1),[115] 'a product is imported into the [Union] in such greatly increased quantities and/or on such terms or conditions as to cause, or threaten to cause, *serious* injury[116] to [Union] producers',[117] the Commission can, 'in order to safeguard the interests of the [Union]' take safeguard measures. These can take two forms:

- limiting the period of validity of import documents issued in respect of surveillance (see below)

- establishing an import authorization procedure and introducing a quota system for imports.[118]

Safeguard measures must apply to all such imports from all countries (the so-called *erga omnes* effect) and must not last longer than is necessary (and certainly not more than four years) to prevent or remedy serious injury and to give Union producers time to adjust.[119]

Safeguard measures may be preceded by surveillance measures,[120] a system of Union checks based on automatic import licensing, should market trends in this product threaten to cause serious injury to Union producers of like or competing products and

---

[110] Imports from third countries are also subject to general Union legislation on imports, e.g. product standards legislation generally.

[111] The Court expressly recognized the parallel between the derogations in Art. 24 of the Import Regulation concerning 'the external aspect of the common market' and Art. 36 TFEU concerning the 'internal aspect' in Case C–296/00 *Carbone* [2002] ECR I–4657, para. 34. Art. 24 also permits Member States to derogate on the grounds of special formalities concerning foreign exchange and of those introduced pursuant to international agreements.                                                                   [112] Art. 24(2).

[113] Ibid.          [114] Arts. 16–22.

[115] Art. 16(2) adds that 'As regards Members of the WTO, the measures referred to in paragraph 1 shall be taken only when the two conditions indicated in the first subparagraph of that paragraph are met', i.e. serious injury and greatly increased quantities.

[116] 'Serious injury' means a significant overall impairment in the position of [Union] producers: Art. 5(3)(a). Criteria for determining serious injury are listed in Art. 10, including an examination of the volume and price of imports, and the consequent impact on Union producers.

[117] '[Union] producers' mean the producers as a whole of the like or directly competing products operating within the territory of the Union or those whose collective output of the like or directly competing products constitutes a major proportion of the total Union production of those products: Art. 5(3)(c).

[118] See also similar powers for the Council contained in Art. 17.

[119] This is the so-called 'sunset clause' of Art. 20. There are certain exceptions to this rule, but even here the period must not exceed eight years.                                                               [120] Art. 11.

should the Union's interests require such checks. An example of one such surveillance measure is Commission Regulation (EU) No 1241/2009[121] continuing and updating the scope of prior surveillance of imports of certain iron and steel products originating in certain third countries. This regulation allows the EU, a major steel producer, to prolong the current import surveillance system covering trade in steel products until 31 December 2012. The data allows the EU to monitor sudden changes in the world steel market and deal with the potential volatility of the trade situation. As the Commission explains:

The surveillance system is particularly important in the present crisis situation marked by unprecedented uncertainties. The system will help shed light on global supply and demand trends. It will also provide information regarding the introduction of trade-restrictive measures by the EU's trade partners and the build-up of overcapacity by major steel producing countries.[122]

As the Commission notes, overcapacity is an increasing concern for the steel sector as the OECD foresees the gap between production and consumption continuing to grow. For 2010–12, the forecasted overcapacity will reach 500 million tons worldwide, 50 per cent of which is expected to come from Asia.[123]

   In respect of WTO members, surveillance measures are covered by the WTO Agreement on Import Licensing. Before safeguard or surveillance measures can be introduced, the Commission must be informed[124] and Member States or the Commission can request consultations with an Advisory Committee made up of representatives of each Member State.[125] An investigation may follow if the Commission considers there is sufficient evidence.[126] A decision to terminate the investigation or impose safeguard or surveillance measures must follow within nine months.[127] This investigation procedure does not have to be applied in an emergency situation, as envisaged by Article 8, which allows for provisional safeguard measures[128] to be applied in critical circumstances, where delay would cause damage which would be difficult to repair and where a preliminary determination provides clear evidence that increased imports have caused, or are threatening to cause, serious injury.[129] While safeguard measures take the form of a quota or equivalent, *provisional* safeguard measures will take the form of an increase in the existing level of a customs duty, if such action is likely to prevent or repair the serious injury.[130] The Commission must then conduct whatever investigation measures are necessary.[131] If it finds that the provisional safeguard measures need to be repealed, the customs duties collected have to be refunded.[132]

   There have been a very small number of EU safeguard cases.[133] As Inama and Vermulst point out, safeguard measures are less attractive in terms of relief than anti-dumping duties. Quotas do not affect the prices charged for imported goods which may continue to hurt domestic industry. Under the GATT rules, the Commission must also offer compensation to the main GATT suppliers affected by the protective measures. Furthermore, unlike anti-dumping measures, safeguard measures cannot be targeted at specific exporting countries or exporters. Both the Union institutions and the WTO Dispute

---

[121] [2009] OJ L332/54.          [122] <http://www.trade.ec.europa.eu/doclib/press/index.cfm?id=502>.
[123] Ibid.          [124] Art. 2.          [125] Arts. 3–4.          [126] Art. 6.          [127] Art. 7.
[128] See, e.g., Commission Reg. 560/02 which imposes provisional safeguard measures against imports of certain steel products ([2002] OJ L85/1).                              [129] Art. 8(1).
[130] Art. 8(2).          [131] Art. 8(3).          [132] Art. 8(4).          [133] Inama and Vermulst, above n. 1, 21–3.

Settlement Body consider that safeguard measures should be used only as an exceptional tool in emergency situations.[134]

## 3. THE COMMERCIAL DEFENCE INSTRUMENTS

Safeguard measures, designed to prevent disruptions caused by an unforeseen, sharp and sudden increase of imports of a particular product, are only one of three types of commercial policy instrument intended to protect the Union market from imports. The other two are:

- anti-dumping duties designed to protect the market from measures which are being unfairly traded
- countervailing duties designed to protect the market from subsidized measures.

The law on anti-dumping[135] is intended to deal with an unfair competitive advantage gained by a third-country exporter 'dumping' goods on the Union market to the detriment of the Union industry. A product is considered 'dumped' if its export price to the Union is less than a comparable price for the like product, in the ordinary course of trade, as established for the exporting country[136] (normally the country of origin).[137] A 'like product' is a product which is 'identical, that is to say, alike in all respects, to the product under consideration, or in the absence of such a product, another product which although not alike in all respects, has characteristics closely resembling those of the product under consideration'.[138]

Anti-dumping measures are governed by Regulation 384/96[139] which follows the text of the WTO Agreement on the implementation of Article VI of GATT. In essence, the regulation makes provision for an anti-dumping duty to be applied to any dumped product whose release for free circulation causes material injury[140] to the Union industry, threat of material injury to the Union industry, or material retardation of the establishment of such an industry.[141] An objective examination tests both the volume and the effect of the dumped imports on prices in the Union market for like products as well as on the consequent impact of those imports on the Union industry.[142] Dumping duties may be imposed only after a formal investigation.

Natural or legal persons, or a trade association acting on behalf of the Union industry, can make a written complaint about dumping, provided that they submit evidence of dumping, injury, and a causal link between the dumping and the injury.[143] After consulting an advisory committee the Commission can open an investigation and hear evidence from affected parties. If a preliminary investigation reveals that dumping has occurred, the Commission can impose provisional anti-dumping duties,[144] if these are shown to be in the broader Union interest. These provisional duties can be made definitive by a

---

[134] COM(2000)440.

[135] Reg. 384/96 ([1996] OJ L56/1. Since this is a specialist area of law, only an outline will be provided here. For further details, see Snyder, above n. 1.      [136] Art. 1(2) of Reg. 384/96 ([1996] OJ L56/1) as amended.

[137] Art. 1(3). Determination of 'dumping' is considered in Art. 2.      [138] Art. 1(4).

[139] Council Reg. 384/96 on protection against dumped imports from countries not members of the European Union ([1996] OJ L56/1); CONSLEG-96R0384.      [140] Art. 1(1).

[141] Art. 3.      [142] Union industry is defined in Art. 4.      [143] Art. 5.

[144] Art. 7. These measures usually take the form of an *ad valorem* duty but could also be a specific duty or a price undertaking (i.e., exporting producers could agree to sell for a minimum price).

decision from the Council, acting by qualified majority vote.[145] This can be avoided if the importer raises its prices to eliminate the dumping margin. A recent example of the use of this procedure is the imposition of duties from 0 to 85 per cent on imports of certain iron or steel fasteners originating in China.[146] The Commission's investigation found that Chinese producers of fasteners benefited from artificially low prices on raw materials. In line with the WTO Agreement on Anti-Dumping, the duties were imposed in order to re-establish fair trade in iron and steel fasteners. China has, however, challenged the duty before the WTO.[147]

Closely following the model of the Anti-dumping Regulation is Regulation 597/2009 on protection against subsidized imports from countries not members of the European Union,[148] which incorporates the WTO's Agreement on Subsidies and Countervailing Measures. Countervailing measures—usually duties—are intended to offset any subsidy granted, by the government of the country of origin of the imported product (or by the government of an intermediate country from which the product is exported), directly or indirectly, for the manufacture, production, export, or transport of any product whose release for free circulation in the Union causes material injury. The subsidy must be specific (i.e., it must be an export subsidy or a subsidy limited to a company, industry, or group of companies). The complaint and investigation procedures are similar to those laid down in the Anti-dumping Regulation.

## 4. TRADE BARRIERS

There is a fourth commercial policy instrument, the Trade Barriers Regulation (TBR) 3286/94,[149] which differs from the other three in that its purpose is aggressive rather than defensive. Its aim is to remove obstacles to trade created by third countries that have an effect on the market of the Union. An obstacle to trade means 'any trade practice adopted or maintained by a third country in respect of which international trade rules establish a right of action'. International trade rules are primarily those established under the auspices of the WTO and laid down in the annexes to the WTO Agreement. Once the Union has been alerted to the existence of a breach of a trade rule (as a result of an individual complaint or a referral from a Member State) and considers action to be necessary in the interests of the Union, the Council can take action under Article 207 TFEU once any relevant international dispute settlement procedure has been exhausted,[150] provided that such action is compatible with international (especially WTO) law.

Therefore, the TBR provides a vehicle for complaints of breaches of international obligations. It differs from the Anti-dumping and Countervailing Measures Regulations since it does not normally involve the imposition of measures at the EU's frontiers. Rather

---

[145] Art. 9.

[146] Council Reg. (EC) No. 91/2009 imposing a definitive anti-dumping duty on imports of certain iron or steel fasteners originating in the People's Republic of China ([2009] OJ L29/1).

[147] <http://www.trade.ec.europa.eu/doclib/press/index.cfm?id=442>.

[148] [2009] OJ L188/93.

[149] [1994] OJ L349/71 as amended. This replaces Reg. 2641/84 ([1984] OJ L252/1) on the protection against illicit commercial practices. The EU's guidance on the TBR can be found at <http://www.trade.ec.europa. eu/doclib/docs/2005/april/tradoc_122567.pdf>. See C. G. Molyneux, 'The Trade Barriers Regulation: The European Union as a player in a globalisation game' (1999) 5 *ELJ* 375 and M. Bronckers, 'Private participation in the enforcement of WTO law: The new EC Trade Barriers Regulation' (1996) 33 *CMLRev.* 299.

[150] Arts. 12–13.

it concerns problems encountered by EU exporters on third-country markets, as opposed to difficulties on the EU market, and paves the way for the EU to seek redress, whether by negotiated bilateral agreement, dispute settlement at the WTO, or retaliatory measures. For example, the TBR was used to challenge the American Anti-Dumping Act 1916 as being contrary to WTO rules.[151] The complaint arose because legal proceedings had been started under the Anti-Dumping Act against a subsidiary of an EU company, disrupting its activities and threatening its viability. As a result of these lawsuits, EU steel exporters could no longer rely on their long-established distribution network in the USA. Other companies also feared that they could become the target of further action by US competitors. A TBR investigation found that the 1916 Act was inconsistent with the US obligations under the WTO Agreement and its annexes. Having failed to reach a solution in informal consultations, the Commission initiated WTO dispute settlement proceedings and, in February 1999, a WTO panel found in favour of the EU.[152]

## D.  GOODS IN FREE CIRCULATION

### 1.  DEFINITIONS

As we have seen, Article 28(2) TFEU provides that products coming from third countries which are in 'free circulation' in Member States will benefit from the EU rules on free movement. Article 129(1) MCC says:

Non-[Union] goods intended to be put on the [Union] market or intended for private use or consumption within the [Union] shall be placed under release for free circulation.

Article 129(2) continues:

Release for free circulation shall entail the following:
  (a) the collection of any import duties due;
  (b) the collection, as appropriate, of other charges, as provided for under relevant provisions in force relating to the collection of those charges;
  (c) the application of commercial policy measures and prohibitions and restrictions insofar as they do not have to be applied at an earlier stage;
  (d) completion of the other formalities laid down in respect of the importation of the goods.

Article 129(3) also reiterates the right contained in Article 28 TFEU that '[r]elease for free circulation shall confer on non-[Union] goods the customs status of [Union] goods'.

The benefits enjoyed by goods in free circulation were highlighted by the early case of *Donckerwolcke*,[153] concerning cloth from Lebanon and Syria which had been put into free circulation in Belgium and then imported into France. In order to follow trends in

---

[151] 18th annual report from the Commission to the EP on the Community's anti-dumping and anti-subsidy activities. Overview of the monitoring of third country safeguard cases and of the implementation of the Trade Barriers Reg.: COM(2000)440.

[152] The USA has still not repealed the 1916 Act and the EU was allowed to retaliate.

[153] Case 41/76 *Suzanne Criel, née Donckerwolcke and Henri Schou* v. *Procureur de la République* [1976] ECR 1921, considered in J. Usher, 'The single market and goods imported from third countries' (1987) 7 *YEL* 159. For a more recent restatement, see Case C–405/03 *Class International Bv* v. *Colgate-Palmolive Company* [2005] ECR I–8735, para. 38.

imports, French law required importers both to declare the origin of goods and to have an import licence. In making the declaration on the French customs form, the importers in *Donckerwolcke* said that the cloth came from Belgium. When the French authorities discovered its true origin they prosecuted the importers for making a false declaration. The importers argued that the requirement to make a declaration constituted an MEE, breaching Article 34 TFEU. The Court confirmed that Article 34 applied to goods in free circulation as well as to those having Union origin, reasoning that the assimilation of goods in free circulation to products originating in the Member States could take full effect only if these goods were subject to the same conditions of importation irrespective of the state in which they were put in free circulation.[154] Therefore Article 34 applied 'without distinction' to products originating in the Union and to those which were put in free circulation in any one of the Member States, irrespective of the actual origin of those goods.[155] In this way goods in free circulation were 'definitively and wholly assimilated to products originating in Member States'.[156]

The same rules apply to goods which have been imported into the EU under a Union quota and subdivided into national quotas, as the Court made clear in *Commission v. Ireland (Cyprus Potatoes)*.[157] Potatoes originating in Cyprus were imported into the UK at a reduced rate of duty under a British quota which formed part of a Union tariff quota. They were then imported into Ireland. The Irish authorities required such imports to be made under licence. The Court said that this requirement contravened Article 34.[158] Once goods forming part of a quota had been duly imported into the Member State of destination (the UK), they were assimilated to the products which were in free circulation in that state, and so could be imported freely into other Member States.[159] Ireland also could not invoke the Article 36 TFEU derogations because Article 36 could not be relied on to protect its economic interests.[160]

## 2. RESTRICTIONS ON FREE CIRCULATION: ARTICLE 134 EC

In *Donckerwolcke* the Court made clear that the Community—and now the EU—had 'full responsibility' in the field of common commercial policy,[161] which meant that action by the Member States was pre-empted. The only time Member States can take unilateral action is where they are specifically authorized by the Union to do so.[162] As we have seen, some of the CCP instruments expressly allow this,[163] as did Article 134 EC which protected the legitimate interests of Member States when faced with the damaging effects of free trade. So, for example, in *Donckerwolcke* the French authorities used the declaration of origin to follow trade patterns. If they found deflections in trade they would seek protective measures under Article 134(1) EC, which provided that '[i]n order to ensure that the execution of measures of commercial policy taken in accordance with this Treaty by any Member State is not obstructed by deflection of trade, or where differences

---

[154] Para. 25.      [155] Para. 18.      [156] Para. 17.

[157] Case 288/83 [1985] ECR 1761, para. 25. See also Case 218/82 *Commission v. Council* [1983] ECR 4063, para. 13, and Case 199/84 *Procuratore della repubblica v. Tiziano Migliorini and Tibor Tiburzio Fischl* [1985] ECR 3317, para. 18.                                                                              [158] Para. 27.

[159] Paras. 24–5.      [160] Para. 28. See further Ch. 5.      [161] Case 41/76 [1976] ECR 1921, para. 32.

[162] Ibid. See also Case C–70/94 *Werner* [1995] ECR I–3189, para. 12.

[163] See, e.g., Art. 10 of the Export Reg. 2603/69 (now Art. 9 of Reg. 1061/2009) which, according to the Court in Case 174/84 *Bulk Oil* [1986] ECR 559, para. 33, constitutes a 'specific authorization'.

between such measures lead to economic difficulties in one or more Member States' the Commission had to recommend the methods for the requisite cooperation between Member States. Failing this, 'the Commission may authorise Member States to take the necessary protective measures, the conditions and details of which it shall determine'.[164]

Thus, Article 134 EC made provision for a supervised derogation for individual states from the CCP but, as the Court said in *Donckerwolcke*, derogations have to be 'strictly interpreted and applied' because 'they constitute not only an exception to the provisions of Articles [28] and [34 TFEU] which are fundamental to the operation of the common market, but also an obstacle to the implementation of the common commercial policy provided for by Article [207 TFEU]'.[165] Theoretically, such individual action should not be necessary under a *common* commercial policy. However, as the Court pointed out in *Donckerwolcke*, at the end of the transitional period of the CCP, differences remained between the Member States which were 'capable of bringing about deflections of trade or of causing economic difficulties in certain Member States'.[166] The Article 134 EC derogation allowed difficulties of this kind to be avoided. However, since 1992 Article 134 EC derogations have fallen into abeyance and Article 134 was finally deleted by the Lisbon Treaty. Situations such as those arising in *Donckerwolke* would now be dealt with under the Import Regulation.

The use of derogations granted under Article 134 EC was a key feature of the old banana regime which was based on a strict partitioning of the EU market. In the name of creating a single banana regime, attempts at addressing these problems drew fire from national and international quarters. In the final part of this chapter we take bananas as a case study to demonstrate how the different legal regimes regulating external trade interact to influence the shape of EU external trade policy.

## E.  THE BANANAS DISPUTE

Europeans consume 40 per cent of the world's bananas and the EU is the world's biggest market for bananas. Regulating the banana market has proved one of the most intractable problems facing the EU, an issue which has triggered litigation in national, European, and international fora. It also raises issues about how to reconcile free trade from non-Member States with the conflicting demands of domestic producers and consumers, as well as the sometimes difficult interaction between trade and development policy, and between EU trade policy and WTO rules.

Bananas consumed in the EU come from three sources: the EU itself (mainly from its overseas territories such as Guadeloupe and Martinique), the ACP countries[167] (largely former colonies of the EU), and Latin American countries. Bananas grown in the Latin American countries, known as dollar bananas, are the cheapest to produce.

---

[164] Art. 134(2) EC dealt with emergency situations: in a case of urgency Member States had to request authorization from the Commission to take the necessary measures themselves. The Commission had to take a decision as soon as possible and the Member States had then to notify the measures to the other Member States. The Commission had the power to decide at any time whether the Member State concerned had to amend or abolish the measures. Art. 134(3) concluded that in the selection of such measures priority was to be given to those which caused the least disturbance to the functioning of the Common Market.

[165] Para. 29.        [166] Paras. 26–7.        [167] African, Caribbean, and Pacific countries.

Their marketing is controlled by three American multinationals, Chiquita, Dole, and Del Monte. Prior to 1992 three different regimes covered bananas entering the EU. Largely due to their colonial ties or geography, France, Italy, the UK, Spain, Portugal, and Greece sold bananas produced in the EU or in ACP countries. Under the Lomé Convention, bananas from the ACP countries entered the EU free of tariffs. By contrast, Denmark, Ireland, and the Benelux countries consumed dollar bananas which were subject to a tariff of 20 per cent. In Germany, the import of bananas was a sensitive political issue. In 1957 the imposition of tariffs on bananas nearly scuppered the negotiations for the original Treaty of Rome. It was only when a Protocol on Bananas was concluded, allowing Germany to import a quota of bananas free of tariffs,[168] that the crisis was averted and Germany signed up to the EEC Treaty.

These different markets were kept partitioned by decisions issued under Article 134 EC.[169] These decisions were regularly, but unsuccessfully, challenged by the affected parties under Article 263 TFEU (ex Article 230 EC). For example, in 1987 the Commission issued a decision under Article 134 EC authorizing France not to apply Union treatment to bananas originating in certain third countries and in free circulation in other Member States.[170] This decision was unsuccessfully challenged by a French importer: as a non-privileged applicant it lacked individual concern.[171]

This pre-1992 banana regime, based as it was on a partitioned market, was clearly incompatible with the idea of a single European market. The Commission therefore began to draw up a single banana regime, spurred on by a GATT panel report which, responding to a complaint made by five Latin American states, found that the original banana regime contravened GATT 1947.[172] However, the EU blocked the report.

In coming up with a single regime, the Commission had to balance a number of potentially conflicting interests, in particular its responsibilities to the ACP countries, the needs of EU consumers for a regular supply of reasonably priced bananas, and the EU's obligations under GATT.[173] Eventually, the EU adopted Regulation 404/93[174] which had three elements: first, it imposed a quota of 854,000 tonnes on EU producers and provided compensation to offset the loss of income resulting from the common trade regime. Secondly, it laid down a tariff quota of two million tonnes under which dollar bananas could be imported at 100 ECUs a tonne and traditional ACP bananas could be imported duty free. Thirdly, it subjected non-traditional ACP bananas (i.e., those imported over and above the quota for traditional bananas) to a prohibitive 750 ECU per-tonne levy and dollar bananas exceeding the quota were subject to a levy of 850 ECUs a tonne. Recognizing

---

[168] Protocol annexed to the Implementing Convention on the Association of the Overseas Countries and Territories with the Union provided for under Art. [203 TFEU] (ex Art.187 EC).

[169] Various unsuccessful challenges were made to these market partitioning devices, often raising ingenious, but ultimately unsuccessful, legal arguments. See, e.g., Case 247/87 *Star Fruit Company SA v. Commission* [1989] ECR 291.

[170] Commission Communication pursuant to Art. [134 EC] (87/C 127/03) ([1987] OJ C127/4).

[171] Case 206/87 *Lefebvre Frères et Soeurs SA v. Commission* [1989] ECR 275. See also Case 191/88 *Co-Frutta Srl v. Commission* [1989] ECR 793 concerning an unsuccessful challenge brought against a Commission decision not to apply to Italy the Union treatment of bananas.

[172] GATT Panel Report on EEC–Member States' Import Regimes for Bananas, DS32/R, 3 Jun. 1993.

[173] COM(92)359, 2–3.

[174] [1993] OJ L47/1. For a full discussion, see R. Thagesen and A. Matthews, 'The EU's common banana regime: An initial evaluation' (1997) 35 *JCMS* 615.

that this new banana regime might not be compatible with GATT, the Commission recommended that a waiver was needed under Article XXV(5).[175]

This regime offended many, in particular the Latin American states, the powerful American multinationals (especially Chiquita), and Germany which lost its duty-free quota.[176] As a result, Germany brought Article 263 TFEU judicial review proceedings challenging the validity of the regulation on a number of grounds, including breach of fundamental human rights, such as the right to own property. Its application for interim measures was unsuccessful[177] as was the case on the merits (*Germany* v. *Council*),[178] much to the dismay of a former judge at the Court of Justice.[179] Individual actions brought under Article 263 TFEU by companies affected were also unsuccessful because the applicants did not have *locus standi*.[180] Proceedings brought in the national courts by affected companies were received more sympathetically, but the Court of Justice set restrictive criteria for granting interim relief[181] or denied the right of the national court to grant interim relief at all.[182] In an Article 267 (ex Article 234) reference on the validity of Regulation 404/93 the Court repeated its ruling in *Germany* v. *Council*.[183]

An administrative court in Frankfurt was also dissatisfied with the Court of Justice's ruling on the merits of the original case brought by Germany.[184] In particular, it objected to the fact that Regulation 404/93 lacked a hardship clause for dollar banana traders who were especially affected. In the light of the German Constitutional Court's ruling in the Maastricht Decision,[185] the Frankfurt court referred the matter to the Federal Constitutional Court (BVerfG). Meanwhile in *T. Port*[186] the Court of Justice ruled that Article 30 of the regulation did authorize and, depending on the circumstances, require the Commission to lay down rules catering for hardship.[187] Subsequently the BVerfG declared the reference inadmissible.[188] Since its judgments in *Brunner* and *Solange II*,[189]

---

[175] There was also much debate in the academic literature as to whether the new regime was in fact more open than the old. See e.g. H. Guyomard, C. Laroche, and C. Le Mouël, 'Impacts of the common market organisation for bananas on European Union markets, international trade and welfare' (1999) 21 *Journal of Policy Modeling* 619.        [176] Art. 21(2) of Reg. 404/93.

[177] Case C–280/93R *Germany* v. *Council* [1993] ECR I–3667.

[178] Case C–280/93 *Germany* v. *Council* [1994] ECR I–4973.

[179] U. Everling, 'Will Europe slip on bananas? The bananas judgment of the Court of Justice and national courts' (1996) 33 *CMLRev.* 401.

[180] Case C–256/93 *Pacific Fruit* v. *Council* not reported but cited in J. Trachtmann, 'Bananas, direct effect and compliance' (1999) 10 *EJIL* 655.

[181] Case C–465/93 *Atlanta Fruchthandelsgesellschaft mbH and others* v. *Bundesamt für Ernährung und Forstwirtschaft* [1995] ECR I–3761.

[182] Case C–68/95 *T. Port GmbH & Co. KG* v. *Bundesanstalt für Landwirtschaft und Ernährung* [1996] ECR I–6065.

[183] Case C–466/93 *Atlanta Fruchthandelsgesellschaft mbH and others* [1995] ECR I–3799.

[184] VG Frankfurt, Dec. of 24 Oct. 1996 [1997] EuZW, 182 discussed in A. von Bogdandy, 'The European Union as a human rights organization? Human rights and the core of the European Union' (2000) 37 *CMLRev.* 1307, 1322.        [185] *Brunner*, BVerfGE 89, 155, reported in translation at [1994] 1 CMLR 57.

[186] Case C–68/95 *T. Port GmbH & Co. KG* [1996] ECR I–6065.

[187] In Case C–312/00P *Commission* v. *Camar Srl and Tico Srl* [2002] ECR I–11355 the Court held the Commission liable under Art. 340 TFEU (ex Art. 288 EC) for failing to act under Art. 30.

[188] BVerfGE 89, 155. See F. Hoffmeister (2001) 38 *CMLRev.* 791, 793–6; A. Peters, 'The bananas decision 2000 of the German Federal Constitutional Court: Towards reconciliation with the ECJ as regards fundamental rights protection in Europe' (2000) 43 *German Yearbook of International Law* 276; C. Schmid, 'All bark and no bite: Notes on the Federal Constitutional Court's "banana decision"' (2001) 7 *ELJ* 95.

[189] *Re Wünsche Handelsgesellschaft*, Dec. of 22 Oct. 1986 [1987] 3 CMLR 225.

where the BVerfG had ruled that human rights protection in the EU was broadly compatible with that in the German Basic Law, the BVerfG said that references from German courts challenging the validity of EU secondary law as being incompatible with German fundamental rights would be declared inadmissible unless it could be shown that EU standards of human rights protection had since declined. The Frankfurt administrative court had not done this and it had also failed to take into account the Court of Justice's ruling in *T. Port*.

On the international level, the same five Latin American states which had complained about the original banana regime also complained about the new one. The GATT panel agreed, finding a breach of Articles I, II, and III,[190] but again the EU blocked the report. However, the EU attempted to buy off these Latin American companies with greater access to the EU market by concluding a Framework Agreement[191] which was then incorporated into a schedule to GATT 94.[192] Yet, the Court of Justice found that part of this agreement contravened the principle of non-discrimination and so was unlawful.[193] Around the same time the USA started investigating the EU's new banana regime under section 301 of the Trade Act 1994 on a petition from Chiquita.[194] A further panel, created under the new Dispute Settlement Understanding (DSU) which had been introduced by the WTO Agreement, looked into the 1993 Regulation and found that it contravened the GATT—a view largely upheld by the Appellate Body.[195] This finding led to a lengthy series of challenges concerning the precise meaning of the DSU and the quantification of concessions available to the USA.[196]

In 1998 the EU came up with yet another banana regime, Regulation 1637/98,[197] but once again this was found to be contrary to Article XIII of GATT as well as Articles II

---

[190] GATT Panel Report on the European Economic Community—Report Regime for Bananas, 19 Jan. 1994, DS 38/R. See J. Trachtmann, 'Bananas, direct effect and compliance' (1999) 10 *EJIL* 655, 665.

[191] This was the result of Art. XXVII negotiations.

[192] This became part of Union law by virtue of Dec. 94/800 ([1994] OJ L336/1).

[193] Case C–122/95 *Germany* v. *Council* [1998] ECR I–973, para. 71. Earlier the Court had rejected Germany's request for an Opinion under Art. 218 (11) TFEU (ex Art. 300 EC) on the ground that the agreement had already been concluded: *Opinion 3/94 (Framework Agreement on Bananas)* [1995] ECR I–4577. On the same day it handed down its judgment in Case C–122/95, the Court decided in Joined Cases C–364 and 365/95 *T. Port GmbH & Co.* [1998] ECR I–1023, on a reference from the German Finance Court, that part of Reg. 478/95 on additional rules for the application of Reg. 404/93 was invalid. For unsuccessful direct actions, see, e.g., Case T–2/99 *T. Port GmbH & Co. KG* v. *Council of the European Union* [2001] ECR II–2093 and Case T–3/99 *Banatrading GmbH* v. *Council of the European Union* [2001] ECR II–2123, and damages actions: Case T–56/00 *Dole Fresh Fruit International Ltd* v. *Council and Commission* [2003] ECR II–577; Case C–122/01P *T. Port GmbH & Co. KG* v. *Commission* [2003] ECR I–4261.

[194] For a full description of the political background to the banana dispute, including Chiquita's role, see O. Cahot and D. Webber, 'Banana splits: Policy process, particularistic interests, political capture, and money in transatlantic trade politics' (2002) 4 *Business and Politics* 5. Chiquita unsuccessfully sued the Commission for damages (EUR 564.1 million plus interest) under Arts. 268 and 340 TFEU (ex Arts. 235 and 288 EC) for the losses arising from the application of Reg. 2362/98 in Case T–19/01 *Chiquita Brands International* v. *Commission* [2005] ECR I–315. The case contains a useful summary of the bananas dispute.

[195] WTO Appellate Body Report, European Communities—Regime for the Import and Sale of Bananas, WT/DS27/AB/R. See Trachtmann, above n. 180, 666. In Case C–377/02 *Van Parys* v. *Belgisch Interventie -en Restitutiebureau* [2005] ECR I–1465 the Court said that a legal person could not plead before a national court the incompatibility of Union legislation with certain rules of the WTO even where the DSB has declared there to be such incompatibility.

[196] For a full description, see Trachtmann, above n. 180, 667–75.

[197] [1998] OJ L210/28. Detailed rules on the implementation of the regime can be found in Commission Reg. 2362/98 [1998] OJ L293/32.

and XVII of GATT.[198] As a result, the DSB authorized the USA to levy customs duties in respect of trade amounting to up to USD 191.4 million per year on imports originating in the EU. The US acted immediately and imposed ad valorem import duty at a rate of 100 per cent on various products including stationary batteries and spectacle cases. Six EU companies selling these products brought proceedings before the Court of First Instance (now the General Court) claiming compensation from the Commission and the Council for the damage they suffered as a result of the application of these retaliatory measures. While the General Court supported the principle that that the EU institutions could be liable in tort towards economic operators who were required to bear a disproportionate part of the burden resulting from a restriction of access to export markets,[199] they lost before the Court of Justice which found that the EU could not be held liable in tort for the lawful pursuit of its legislative activities.[200]

The Commission then issued various Communications in its quest to resolve the dispute.[201] Finally, Regulation 216/2001[202] was agreed and hailed as a settlement to the dispute. It consisted of a two-stage approach: initially there was a transitional tariff quota regime based on a first-come, first-served system and then a flat-rate tariff to be applied from 2006,[203] with tariff-free access for ACP bananas.[204] However, nine Latin American countries complained that the EU's planned €230 per tonne tariff (an increase on the €75 a tonne tariff) would have a devastating effect on their exports, a view upheld by the WTO arbitrator. The EU therefore agreed to impose a new import tariff of €176 per tonne from 1 January 2006.[205] However, in November 2006 Ecuador lodged a further complaint before the WTO arguing that EU banana tariffs still discriminated again Latin American producers. The panel ruled in 2008 that the duty-free tariff quota for bananas originating in ACP countries and the MFN tariff of €176 per tonne were in violation of Articles I, II, and XIII of GATT. Colombia and Panama also filed new disputes. A further panel, established at the request of the US, ruled that the duty-free tariff quota for bananas of ACP origin was in violation of Article I and XII of GATT. The EU appealed both reports but the Appellate Body upheld the panel's findings.[206]

---

[198] European Communities—Regime for the Import and Sale of Bananas, Recourse to Arbitration by the European Communities under Art. 22.6 of the DSU, Decision by the Arbitrators, WT/DS27/ARB (99–1434), 9 Apr. 1999. See Trachtmann, above n. 180, 671.

[199] Case T-69/00 *FIAMM* [2005] ECR II–5393, para. 157.

[200] Joined Cases C–120/06 P and C–121/06 P *Fabbrica italiana accumulatori motocarri Montecchio SpA and Fabbrica italiana accumulatori motocarri Montecchio Technologies LLC (FIAMM) and Giorgio Fedon & Figli SpA and Fedon America, Inc. (Fedon) v Council and Commission* [2008] ECR I–6513.

[201] Communication from the Commission to the Council on the consultations undertaken by the Commission with the aim of resolving the banana dispute: COM(2000)431; Communication from the Commission to the Council on the 'First Come, First Served' method for the banana regime and the implications of a 'tariff only' system: COM(2000)621.

[202] [2001] OJ L31/2. See also Reg. 2587/01 ([2001] OJ L345/13).

[203] See IP/00/1502, Brussels, 20 Dec. 2000.

[204] Commission Communication on the Modification of the European Community's import regime for bananas: COM(2004)399.

[205] Reg. 1964/2005 [2005] OJ L316/1.

[206] For further details on the chronology of the dispute, see <http://www.wto.org/english/news_e/pres09_e/pr591_e.htm>.

Meanwhile WTO Director-General Pascal Lamy used his 'good offices' to help broker an agreement which was successfully concluded in December 2009.[207] As part of the deal, the EU agreed to:

- cut its import tariff on bananas—the EU will do so in stages, from the current rate of €176/tonne to €114/tonne in 2017, at the earliest
- make the biggest cut first—the EU will first cut its tariff by €28/tonne to €148/per tonne, once all parties sign the deal.

In return, Latin American countries have agreed:

- not to demand further cuts—the EU will not cut its tariff further once the Doha Round of talks on global trade resumes
- to drop cases against the EU—Latin American producers will settle several legal disputes pending against the EU at the WTO.

In addition, bananas from African, Caribbean and Pacific countries (ACP) will continue to enjoy duty- and quota-free access to the EU granted since 2008, thanks to Economic Partnership Agreements (EPAs). The phased implementation of the deal gives the ACP countries time to adjust to stiffer competition from Latin America. Further, the Commission will propose mobilizing up to €200 million from the EU budget to support the main ACP exporting countries' adaptation—in addition to existing aid. In parallel, the EU and the US have initialled a deal in which the US agrees to settle its WTO dispute on bananas with the EU. Once the EU Council approves the bananas agreement and the Parliament has given its consent, the EU will sign the deal with Latin American countries. It will also sign a settlement agreement with the US.

## F.  CONCLUSIONS

The bananas dispute tells us much about EU external relations. It demonstrates the difficulties of putting into practice the trade liberalization goals found in Article 206 TFEU. Trade liberalization has always been an *aim* rather than an obligation,[208] reflecting the GATT objectives of lowering trade barriers through reciprocal and staged negotiations. Therefore the EU Treaties do not oblige Member States to extend the binding principles governing the free movement of goods to trade with third countries.[209] For the same reason Article 206 does not compel the institutions to liberalize imports from non-Member States, where to do so would be contrary to the interests of the Union.[210] Yet even against this background of flexibility, trade liberalization has proved difficult to achieve in practice because the EU's external policy must be formulated against the backcloth of international obligations and political imperatives. Any decisions are therefore subject to challenge at all levels—local, national, and international.

---

[207] <http://www.trade.ec.europa.eu/doclib/press/index.cfm?id=500>. The description that follows is taken largely from this press release. Further details about the deal can be found in <http://www.trade.ec.europa.eu/doclib/docs/2009/december/tradoc_145605.pdf>. See Council Dec. 2010/314/EU (OJ [2010] L141/1).

[208] Case C–150/94 *UK v. Council (import quotas for toys from China)* [1998] ECR I–7235, para. 67.

[209] Case 51/75 *EMI Records Ltd v CBS United Kingdom Ltd* [1976] ECR 811, para. 17.        [210] Ibid.

The bananas litigation demonstrates in concrete terms the change in emphasis noted earlier: from the rigid demands of uniformity laid down in the Treaties and the case law on the CCT towards greater flexibility. This flexibility has always been permitted first through the (now defunct) supervised derogations allowed by Article 134 EC and the specific provisions (i.e., derogations, safeguard measures) contained in the Import and Export Regulations. Once again we see the parallels between the internal and external dimensions of free movement of goods: the flexibility which has emerged in the development of the internal market is now also reflected in EU external policy.[211]

---

[211] Cremona, above, n. 3, 353.

# PART III

# FREE MOVEMENT OF PERSONS AND SERVICES

# 8

# INTRODUCTION TO THE FREE MOVEMENT OF PERSONS

## A. INTRODUCTION

The right for people to move freely from one state to another is a distinguishing feature of a common market. Yet although Article 3(1)(c) EEC provided that the Community (as it then was) aspired to 'the abolition, as between Member States, of obstacles to freedom of movement for ... persons',[1] the reality—at least for the first 40 years of the EU's existence—was rather different. The substantive provisions of the original Treaty of Rome did not in fact provide a general right of free movement for all people and companies: to qualify the individual or company had to be both a *national* of a Member State[2] (with nationality being a matter for national—not Union—law[3]) *and* be engaged in an economic activity as a worker (Articles 45–8 TFEU, ex Articles 39–42 EC), a self-employed person/company/branch or agency (Articles 49–55 TFEU, ex Articles 43–8 EC), or as a provider or receiver of services (Articles 56–62 TFEU, ex Articles 49–55 EC). Those falling within the scope of these 'fundamental'[4] freedoms enjoyed—and continue to enjoy—the right to free movement subject to derogations on the grounds of public policy, public security, and public health, as well as a more tailored exception for employment in the public service.

Underpinning Articles 45, 49, and 56 is, at a minimum, the principle of non-discrimination on the ground of nationality (or seat in the case of corporations). Thus, the migrant has to enjoy the same treatment as nationals in a comparable situation. As we saw in Chapter 1, the principle of equal treatment gives Member States the autonomy to determine the substance of the rules applicable in their territory; Union law will not interfere with those rules provided that they do not discriminate directly or indirectly. However, in more recent case law the Court has moved beyond the discrimination model and, returning to the language of Article 3(1)(c) EEC (now repealed), it has focused

---

[1] See also Case 118/75 *Watson and Belmann* [1978] ECR 1185, paras. 16–17.

[2] The same applies to companies: Case C–452/04 *Fidium Finanz AG v. Bundesanstalt für Finanzdienstleistungsaufsicht* [2006] ECR I–9521, para. 47.

[3] See generally C. Greenwood, 'Nationality and the limits of free movement of persons in Union law' (1987) 7 *YEL* 185, esp. 187–93; A. Evans, 'Nationality law and the free movement of persons in the EEC: With special reference to the British Nationality Act 1981' (1982) 2 *YEL* 173.

[4] See, e.g., Case 222/86 *Union nationale des entraîneurs et cadres techniques professionnels du football (Unectef)* v. *Georges Heylens and others* [1987] ECR 4097, paras. 8 and 14 (Art. 45).

instead on removing discriminatory and non-discriminatory 'obstacles' or 'restrictions' to free movement. While such an approach poses a greater threat to the Member States' legislative autonomy, it is an important step towards removing barriers to the creation of a single market where persons and services can, in principle, move freely.

The original reason for including Articles 45–62 in the Treaties was to ensure that the so-called 'factors of production' (workers, the self-employed, and service providers) could move freely from regions where jobs were hard to find to those areas needing extra workers.[5] According to the theory, this would lead to an equalization in the price of labour across the EU and greater prosperity for all. In fact, in the early days of the EU few people took advantage of this opportunity to move, due to a variety of factors: social (the wish not to move without their families), economic (the fear of losing entitlements to social benefits, especially pensions, if individuals moved out of their home states), cultural (the familiarity and enjoyment of the way of life in their own states), and linguistic (individuals often lacked the necessary language skills).

The EU went some way towards overcoming these obstacles: through secondary legislation adopted in the late 1960s/early 1970s (legislation which has been broadly construed by the Court) and through various programmes like 'Socrates', facilitating the mobility of students. In 1990 the Union adopted three specific directives conferring a general right of movement and residence on the retired, students, and those with independent means. However, this right was subject to the requirement that the individual had sufficient resources and medical insurance,[6] limitations intended to stop benefit and healthcare tourism.[7] Nevertheless, these three directives demonstrated a gradual erosion of the link between *economic* activity and free movement and a shift in perception away from viewing migrants as merely factors of production to seeing them as individuals with rights against the host state. At Maastricht this change in perspective culminated in the recognition of the status of 'citizen of the Union' for every national of a Member State, with specific rights and duties attached (Articles 20–5 TFEU, ex Articles 17–22 EC). Recent judgments of the Court suggest that EU citizens—whether economically active or not[8]—now enjoy a more general, free-standing right to move and reside freely in the Union under Article 21(1), but still subject to the limitations and conditions laid down in the Treaties and secondary legislation. The significance of the citizenship provisions was emphasized in the leading case of *Grzelczyk*,[9] where the Court famously said:

Union citizenship is destined to be the fundamental status of nationals of the Member States, enabling those who find themselves in the same situation to enjoy the same treatment in law irrespective of their nationality, subject to such exceptions as are expressly provided for.

---

[5]  Although cf. 'Europeans move for love rather than jobs', *euobserver.com*, 29 Mar. 2006.

[6]  Council Dirs. 90/364/EEC ([1990] OJ L180/26) on the rights of residence for persons of sufficient means (the 'Playboy' Directive), 90/365/EEC on the rights of residence for employees and self-employed who have ceased their occupational activity ([1990] OJ L180/28), and 90/366/EEC ([1990] OJ L180/30) on the rights of residence for students, repealed and replaced by Council Dir. 93/96 ([1993] OJ L317/59).

[7]  That is, 'moving to a Member State with a more congenial social security environment': Case C–456/02 *Trojani* [2004] ECR I–7573, Geelhoed AG's Opinion, para. 13 (and para. 18).

[8]  Case C–413/99 *Baumbast and R.* v. *Secretary of State for the Home Department* [2002] ECR I–7091.

[9]  Case C–184/99 [2001] ECR I–6193, para.31, echoing La Pergola AG in Case C–85/96 *Martínez Sala* [1998] ECR I–2691, para.18.

Implicit in this language is the transformative nature of the citizenship provisions, not only for the lives of the beneficiaries but also in terms of prompting the Court to reconsider fundamental tenets of its earlier jurisprudence.[10]

The consolidation of citizen's rights came with the adoption of European Parliament and Council Directive 2004/38 on the right of citizens of the Union and their family members to move and reside freely within the territory of the Member States (the Citizens' Rights Directive (CRD)).[11] This directive, repealing and replacing most of the previous secondary legislation adopted in the 1960s, together with the 1990 Residence Directives, has radically altered and improved the rights of migrant EU citizens and their families. It is discussed in detail in Chapter 12. For the present it is sufficient to note that the directive is premised on the idea that the longer individuals reside in the host state the more rights they enjoy. In particular, during the first three months of migration and after five years of residence there is no need to show any economic activity at all. This illustrates the extent to which the link with economic activity has now been severed. This is a significant change in perspective, a change which serves to underline just how far the EU has moved from its common market origins. However, the enactment of this directive has also served to underline an increasing divergence between the rights given to natural persons—through the introduction of Union citizenship, the CRD, and the often generous application of fundamental human rights—and those given to legal persons.[12] The rights of legal persons are considered in Chapters 10 and 11.

The free movement of persons has always been an area of greater sensitivity than the free movement of goods. People raise security and welfare implications in a way that goods do not. This helps to explain why the original Treaty gave rights only to the economically active: they brought skills to the host state's economy and could support themselves financially. It also helps to explain why there is no equivalent to the Common Commercial Policy for people. Fearing the pressure generated by an open border policy on national job markets and welfare systems, governments of the Member States refused to allow individuals holding the nationality of a non-Member State (known as 'third-country nationals' (TCNs)) who have entered the EU to benefit from the rights of free movement laid down in Articles 45–62 TFEU. However, the conclusion of the Schengen Agreement in 1985 marked a move—among at least some of the Member States—towards a common policy in respect of the immigration of TCNs and asylum-seekers, a subject which is outlined in Chapter 14.[13] Yet the principal focus of this book is on the specific rights to free movement enjoyed by nationals of the Member States of the EU. We start by examining the principles common to the Treaty provisions on persons, beginning with the most fundamental question: does EU law apply at all?

---

[10] See, e.g., Case C–138/02 *Collins* v. *Secretary of State for Work and Pensions* [2004] ECR I–2703 considered in Ch. 9 and Case C–50/06 *Commission* v. *The Netherlands (criminal convictions)* [2007] ECR I–4383, para. 32 considered in Ch. 13.                    [11] [2004] OJ L158/77.

[12] See also D. Edwards, 'Guest editorial: Will there be honey still for tea?' (2006) 43 *CMLRev.* 623, 625; R. White, *Workers, Establishment and Services in the European Union* (Oxford: OUP, 2004), 255ff. At p. 261 he notes that people have the constitutional right to move while businesses have only a (lesser) Union right to move.

[13] Further pressure has been put on the EU to open its borders to TCNs with the conclusion of the General Agreement on Trade in Services (GATS).

## B. THE SCOPE OF APPLICATION OF THE TREATY PROVISIONS ON FREE MOVEMENT OF PERSONS

In order for the provisions on the free movement of persons to apply, the claimant must fall within the (1) personal, (2) material, and (3) territorial scope of the Treaty provision; in addition, (4) the claimant must be able to rely on the Treaty provision against the particular defendant. These questions are jurisdictional: if these four conditions are not satisfied, then Union law does not apply and the claimant will have recourse to national law only (if any).[14] We shall examine these conditions in turn.

### 1. PERSONAL SCOPE

The personal scope of Union law covers three elements:

- Is the individual or corporation a national of a Member State?
- Are they engaged in an economic activity (where necessary)?
- Can they be classified as a worker, a self-employed person/company, a service provider or a citizen?

The rights of free movement apply only to those holding the nationality of one of the Member States. This is made clear in Article 20(1) TFEU (ex Article 17(1) EC): '[e]very person holding the nationality of a Member State shall be a citizen of the Union'. Thus, it is the Member States, not the EU, which are the gatekeepers to Union citizenship since it is the Member States which determine nationality.[15] This was confirmed in *Kaur*,[16] where the Court said that 'under international law, it is for each Member State, having due regard to [Union] law, to lay down the conditions for the acquisition and loss of nationality'.[17] Furthermore, one Member State is not in a position to criticize another Member State's attribution of nationality.[18] In respect of companies, it is the company's 'seat'[19] which has the same function for companies as nationality does for individuals. A company's seat is the state in which the company or firm, formed in accordance with

---

[14] For a valiant—but ultimately unsuccessful—attempt by the defendant to argue that Union law does not apply to situations in addition to those outlined in this section, including matters involving fundamental rights, see Case C–438/05 *International Transport Workers' Federation* v. *Viking Line* [2007] ECR I–10779, paras. 38–55.

[15] This is confirmed by the Declaration on Nationality of a Member State appended to the TEU. In the case of a person with dual nationality, the Court ruled in Case C–369/90 *Micheletti* v. *Delagación del Gobierno en Cantabria* [1992] ECR I–4239, para.10 that if a person was able to produce one of the documents referred to in Council Dir. 73/148/EEC ([1973] OJ L172/14) (now CRD) to prove they were nationals of one Member State, other Member States were not entitled to dispute that status on the ground that the persons concerned were also nationals of a non-Member State, the nationality of which took precedence under the host state's law.

[16] Case C–192/99 *R.* v. *Secretary of State for the Home Department, ex p. Kaur* [2001] ECR I–1237.

[17] Para. 19. The conditions might include period of residence, birth, and family ties.

[18] Case C–200/02 *Chen* [2004] ECR I–9925. See also B. Kunoy, 'A Union of national citizens: The origins of the Court's lack of *avant-gardisme* in the *Chen* case' (2006) 43 *CMLRev.* 179.

[19] Case C–330/91 *R.* v. *Inland Revenue Commissioners, ex p. Commerzbank AG* [1993] ECR I–4017, para. 13. This issue is discussed further in Ch. 10.

the law of a Member State, has its registered office, central administration, or principal place of business.[20]

As we saw in the introduction, individuals and companies also need to be engaged in an 'economic activity' to take advantage Articles 45, 49 and 56.[21] This, according to the Court in *Jundt*,[22] a case under Article 56, is 'the decisive factor' which brings an activity within the ambit of the provisions of the Treaties. In many cases this is assumed, particularly where the individual or company is being remunerated for the activity performed. However, it does become an issue in respect of voluntary or semi-voluntary activities, especially those undertaken as part of a rehabilitation programme.[23] In *Jundt* the Court emphasized that 'the activity must not be provided for nothing', albeit that there is no need for the service provider 'to be seeking to make a profit'.[24]

The position is different under Article 21(1) TFEU (ex Article 18(1) EC). There, non-economically active individuals can enjoy rights to movement and residence, as the Court said in *Baumbast*:[25]

the [Treaties do] not require that citizens of the Union pursue a professional or trade activity, whether as an employed or self-employed person, in order to enjoy the rights provided in Part Two of the [TFEU] on citizenship of the Union.

Therefore, in the case of citizens wishing to exercise their rights under Article 21(1) it is sufficient that they merely hold the nationality of one of the Member States; unlike individuals wishing to invoke Articles 45, 49, or 56, they need not be engaged in an economic activity. The detailed rules determining whether an individual is a worker, self-employed person, service provider or recipient, or citizen are set out in Chapters 9–12.

## 2. MATERIAL AND TERRITORIAL SCOPE

### 2.1 The Need for an Inter-State Element

Individuals must move from one Member State (usually the home state) to another state (usually the host state)[26] in order to fall within the material scope of Articles 45, 49, 56,

---

[20]  Ibid. See also Case C–210/06 *Cartesio Oktató és Szolgáltató bt* [2008] ECR I–9641, para. 109.

[21]  For a full discussion, see O. Odudu, 'Economic activity as a limit to Union law' in C. Barnard and O. Odudu (eds.), *The Outer Limits of European Union Law* (Oxford: Hart Publishing, 2009).

[22]  Case C–281/06 *Jundt* v. *Finanzamt Offenburg* [2007] ECR I–12231, para. 32.

[23]  Case 344/87 *Bettray* v. *Staatssecretaris van Justitie* [1989] ECR 1621, para. 17 considered further in Ch. 9.

[24]  Case C–281/06 *Jundt* v. *Finanzamt Offenburg* [2007] ECR I–12231, para. 33.

[25]  Case C–413/99 [2002] ECR I–7091, para. 83. See also the views of Jacobs AG in Case C–148/02 *Garcia Avello* [2003], para. 61 and Cosmas AG's even grander claims in Case C–378/97 *Wijsenbeek* [1999] ECR I–6207, para. 85: 'Article [21] does not simply enshrine in constitutional terms the *acquis communautaire* as it existed when it was inserted into the [Treaties] and complement it by broadening the category of persons entitled to freedom of movement to include other classes of person not pursuing economic activities. Article [21] also enshrines a right of a different kind, a true right of movement, stemming from the status as a citizen of the Union, which is not subsidiary in relation to European unification, whether economic or not.'

[26]  The territorial scope of Union law is defined in Art. 355 TFEU (ex Art. 299 EC) to include all the states of the EU. Special provision is made for overseas territories. The free movement provisions also apply to the EEA states. For specific applications, see Case C–214/94 *Boukhalfa* v. *Germany* [1996] ECR I–2253 (EU law will apply to a national of a Member State (Belgium) who is permanently resident in a non-member country (Algeria) but employed by another Member State (Germany) in its embassy in Algeria; Case 237/83 *Prodest* v *Caisse Primaire d' Assurance Maladie de Paris* [1984] ECR 3153 (Union law may apply to professional

and 21(1).[27] This movement can take the form of individuals moving their residence to another Member State, usually for the purposes of employment,[28] or, in the case of frontier workers, retaining their residence in the home state and working in the host state.[29] In the case of services, the provider or the recipient may not move but the service moves instead.[30] The requirement of an inter-state element is made explicit in Article 49 which refers to 'the freedom of establishment of nationals of a Member State in the territory of *another* Member State'.[31]

## 2.2 The Wholly Internal Situation

The corollary of the requirement of an inter-state element is that the free movement provisions cannot be applied to situations which are 'wholly internal to a Member State'.[32] This can be seen in *Saunders* where a British woman could not use Union law to challenge an undertaking given to a criminal court in England that she return to Northern Ireland and that she did not visit England or Wales for three years. As the Court said, Union law does not apply to activities which have no factor linking them with any of the situations governed by Union law[33] and which are confined in all aspects within a single Member State.[34] This was also the situation in *Gauchard*[35] where the manager of a French supermarket, who was prosecuted for extending his supermarket without permission, argued that the French rules breached Union law. The Court disagreed, saying that Union law did not apply because the company operating the supermarket was French and established in France, and its manager was French and resided in France. Therefore the case was exclusively internal to a Member State.

A purely hypothetical prospect of employment in another Member State is not sufficient to trigger the application of Union law. This can be seen in *Moser*[36] where a German national was denied access to a teacher training course in Germany because he was a member of the Communist party. He argued that the refusal to admit him to the course prevented him from applying for teaching posts in schools in other Member States and was thus contrary to Union law. The Court said that this 'hypothetical' possibility did not establish a sufficient connection with Union law to justify the application of Article 45.[37] Similarly, in *Kremzow*[38] a retired Austrian judge, sentenced to life imprisonment after

---

activities pursued outside Union territory as long as the employment relationship retains a sufficiently close link with the Union).

[27] Case C–184/99 *Grzelczyk* [2001] ECR I–6193, para. 32.

[28] See, e.g., Case 53/81 *Levin* [1982] ECR 1035

[29] In the case of frontier workers this includes the situation where the individual resides in their home state and works in the host state (e.g., Case C–213/05 *Geven* v. *Land Nordrhein-Westfalen* [2007] ECR I–6347) or works in the home state but resides in another state (e.g., Case C–527/06 *Renneberg* v. *Staatssecretaris van Financiën* [2008] ECR I–7735; Case C–287/05 *Hendrix* v. *Raad van Bestuur van het Uitvoeringsinstituut Werknemersverzekeringen* [2007] ECR I–6909).

[30] Case C–384/93 *Alpine Investments* [1995] ECR I–1141.     [31] Emphasis added.

[32] Case 175/78 *R* v. *Saunders* [1979] ECR 1129, para. 11.     [33] Ibid.

[34] See, e.g., Case C–18/95 *Terhoeve* v. *Inspecteur van de Belastingdienst Particulieren* [1999] ECR I–345, para. 26; Joined Cases C–64 and 65/96 *Land Nordrhein-Westfalen* v. *Kari Uecker and Vera Jacquet* v. *Land Nordrhein-Westfalen* [1997] ECR I–3171, para. 16.

[35] Case 20/87 *Minstère public* v. *Gauchard* [1987] ECR 4879, para. 10. See also, e.g., Joined Cases C–330 and 331/90 *Ministerio Fiscal* v. *Lopez Brea* [1992] ECR I–323; Case 136/78 *Ministère public* v. *Auer (No. 1)* [1979] ECR 437; Joined Cases C–54 and 91/88 and C–14/89 *Criminal Proceedings against Niño* [1990] ECR I–3537.     [36] Case 180/83 *Moser* v. *Land Baden-Württemberg* [1984] ECR 2539, para. 15.

[37] Para. 18.     [38] Case C–299/95 *Friedrich Kremzow* v. *Republik Österreich* [1997] ECR I–2629.

having murdered another lawyer, could not invoke Union law on a question of fundamental human rights under the ECHR. The Court said that while any deprivation of liberty could impede the exercise of free movement, a purely hypothetical prospect of exercising the right of free movement did not establish a sufficient connection with Union law.[39]

Conversely, Union law can be invoked by nationals against their own Member State when they are exercising[40]—or have exercised[41]—their rights of free movement, as *Surinder Singh*[42] shows. In 1982 Mr Surinder Singh, an Indian national, married a British citizen. From 1983 to 1985 they lived in Germany where Mrs Singh was employed on a part-time basis, which meant that under Union law she was a worker who was entitled to be joined by her spouse.[43] In 1985 she returned to the UK to run a business. The question was whether Mrs.Singh's husband could join her in the UK under Union law. If the situation was considered wholly internal then domestic law only would apply, with the result that Mr Singh was likely to be refused entry. If, however, the situation was not considered wholly internal then Union law would apply and Mr Singh could enter and remain in the UK, relying on Articles 45 and 49 TFEU, read in conjunction with the secondary legislation which allows a Union national to be joined by a spouse.

The Court opted for the second approach.[44] It reasoned that a national like Mrs Singh might be deterred from exercising her Union law rights of free movement if, on returning to her state of origin (the UK), the conditions of entry or residence were not at least equivalent to those which she would enjoy on entering the territory of another state (e.g., France),[45] including the right to be accompanied by her spouse.[46] In this way *Singh* serves to confirm the earlier case of *Knoors*,[47] where the Court found that a Belgian-qualified Dutch plumber who had worked in Belgium was entitled to rely on his Union law rights to work in the Netherlands (his home state) using his Belgian qualifications. The Court said that his position was 'assimilated to that of another person enjoying their rights and liberties guaranteed by the [Treaties]'.[48]

### 2.3 Abuse and Fraud

*Singh* also shows how Union law might be abused. What if the couple had gone to another Member State only for a short period? What if it had been a marriage of convenience? In *Singh* the Court dealt only briefly with the point. It said that Member States could prevent abuse of EU law where there was evasion of national legislation.[49] However, subsequent case law made clear that merely taking advantage of Union rights to free movement does

---

[39] Para. 16.

[40] Case C–384/93 *Alpine Investments* [1995] ECR I–1141, paras. 15 and 20–2; Case C–60/00 *Carpenter* [2002] ECR I–6279, para. 29. This exercise might only be 'virtual': Case C–200/02 *Zhu and Chen* [2004] ECR I–9925 considered in Ch. 12.

[41] Case C–419/92 *Scholz* [1994] ECR I–505, para. 9. See also Commission Guidance for better transposition and application of Dir. 2004/38: COM(2009) 313, 3.

[42] Case C–370/90 *R v. IAT and Surinder Singh, ex p. Secretary of State for the Home Department* [1992] ECR I–4265. See also Case C–18/95 *Terhoeve* [1999] ECR I–345.

[43] Under what was then Art. 10 of Reg. 1612/68 [1968] JO L257/2, considered further in Ch. 12.

[44] Para. 21.     [45] Para. 19.     [46] Para. 21.

[47] Case 115/78 *Knoors* v. *Secretary of State for Economic Affairs* [1979] ECR 399. See also Case C–107/94 *Asscher* [1996] ECR I–3089.     [48] Para. 24.

[49] Case C–370/90 [1992] ECR I–4265, para. 24.

not constitute abuse,[50] whatever the motive.[51] Article 35 CRD attempts to deal with some of these problems. It provides:

Member States may adopt the necessary measures to refuse, terminate or withdraw any right conferred by this Directive in the case of abuse of rights or fraud, such as marriages of convenience.

In its Communication on the CRD,[52] the Commission says, 'Fraud may be defined as deliberate deception or contrivance made to obtain the right of free movement and residence under the Directive.' It continues that in the context of the directive, fraud is likely to be limited to forgery of documents or false representation of a material fact concerning the conditions attached to the right of residence. Persons who have been issued with a residence document only as a result of fraudulent conduct in respect of which they have been convicted, may have their rights under the directive refused, terminated, or withdrawn.[53] The Commission then considers abuse. It says that abuse may be defined as an artificial conduct entered into solely with the purpose of obtaining the right of free movement and residence under Union law which, albeit formally observing of the conditions laid down by Union rules, does not comply with the purpose of those rules.[54] This is problematic as guidance for Member States because, as we have seen, the Court has long made clear that the motive for moving is irrelevant. The Court's case law appears to have narrowed the principle of abuse rights down almost exclusively to marriages of convenience.[55]

Where there is an abuse of rights or fraud, the Member States can adopt the necessary measures—civil (e.g., cancelling the effects of a proven marriage of convenience on the right of residence), administrative, or criminal[56]—provided these sanctions are effective, non-discriminatory, proportionate and subject to the procedural safeguards provided for in the directive.[57] According to the Commission, these measures can be taken at any point of time and may entail the refusal to confer rights under Union law on free movement (e.g., to issue an entry visa or a residence card) or the termination or withdrawal of rights under Union law on free movement (e.g., the decision to terminate validity of a residence card and to expel the person concerned who acquired rights by abuse or fraud).

### 2.4 Reverse Discrimination

*Saunders, Gauchard, Moser,* and *Kremzow* demonstrate that nationals cannot invoke the free movement provisions against their own Member States if they have not exercised their rights of free movement in some way.[58] Migrants, like Mrs Singh and Mr Knoors who take advantage of their Union law rights, may therefore enjoy more favourable treatment than nationals who have not migrated, a situation referred to as 'reverse discrimination'.[59] Why

---

[50] Case C–212/97 *Centros* [1999] ECR I–1459, para. 27.

[51] Case C–109/01 *Secretary of State for the Home Department* v. *Akrich* [2003] ECR I–9607, paras. 55–7.

[52] COM(2009) 313, 15.

[53] Citing Case C–285/95 *Kol* [1997] ECR I–3069, para. 29 and C–63/99 *Gloszczuk* [2001] ECR I–6369, para. 75.

[54] Citing Case C–110/99 *Emsland-Stärke* [2000] ECR I–11569, para. 52 and Case C–212/97 *Centros* [1999] ECR I–1459, para.25.

[55] See Case C–127/08 *Metock and Others v Minister for Justice, Equality and Law Reform* [2008] ECR I–6241, para. 75 discussed in Ch. 12.          [56] COM(2009) 313, 19.

[57] COM(2009) 313, 14.          [58] Although cf. Joined Cases C–321–4/94 *Pistre* [1997] ECR I–2343.

[59] 'Reverse discrimination arises when a national of a Member State is disadvantaged because he or she may not rely on a protective provision of Union law when a national of another Member State in otherwise

does Union law allow this apparent discrepancy? The rationale for the rule is twofold. First, it acts as jurisdictional divide between the application of EU law and the application of domestic law: EU law will apply where there is an inter-state dimension; domestic law will apply to facts wholly internal to the Member State.

The second rationale relates to what American scholars refer to as 'virtual representation':[60] migrants cannot necessarily gain access to the host state's political processes so Union law intervenes on their behalf to correct laws which discriminate against them. Nationals, by contrast, do more easily enjoy access to the state's processes and so they can lobby to get the rules changed. This may be what the Court was referring to in *Uecker and Jacquet*[61] when it said 'Any discrimination which nationals of a Member State may suffer under the law of that State fall within the scope of that law and must therefore be dealt with within the framework of the internal legal system of that State.'[62]

Nevertheless, many are still critical of the 'wholly internal rule' and the reverse discrimination that results,[63] most prominently Advocate General Sharpston in the *Walloon* case.[64] Belgium is a divided country, both politically and linguistically.[65] The Flemish (Dutch-speaking) region is more affluent than its Walloon (French-speaking) neighbour. The Flemish government offered a care insurance scheme for people with disabilities. In order to benefit from the scheme, an individual had to be either resident in the Dutch-speaking region (or in the bilingual region of the capital, Brussels) or resident in another Member State (as a citizen of that Member State or a Belgian citizen who had made use of the free movement rights) but working in the Dutch-speaking region. By contrast, Belgian citizens living in the French-speaking region of Belgium but working in the Flemish-speaking region could not benefit from the scheme. This is a classic example of reverse discrimination (those living in the French region but working in the Flemish region were in a worse position than those living in other Member States and working in the Flemish region).

Advocate General Sharpston thought time had come for a reconsideration of the wholly internal rule, at least in the circumstances of this case.[66] She offered two reasons to

identical circumstances may rely on that same provision': D. Pickup, 'Reverse discrimination and freedom of movement for workers' ((1986) 23 *CMLRev.* 135, 137).

[60] For a further discussion of the theory of 'virtual representation', see Ch.1. See also M. Poiares Maduro, *We the Court: The European Court of Justice and the European economic constitution* (Oxford: Hart Publishing, 1998), 69.

[61] Joined Cases C–64 and 65/96 [1997] ECR I–3171, para. 23. See also Case C–253/01 *Krüger* v. *Directie van de rechtspersoonlijkheid bezittende Dienst Wegsverkeer* [2004] ECR I–1191, para. 36.

[62] Para. 23. See also Case C–212/06 *Government of French Community and Walloon Government* v. *Flemish Government* [2008] ECR I–1683, para. 40.

[63] See e.g., A. Tryfonidou, 'Reverse discrimination in purely internal situations: An incongruity in a citizens' Europe' (2008) 35 *LIEI* 43, 63–4; E. Spaventa, 'Seeing the wood despite the trees? On the scope of Union citizenship and its constitutional effects' (2008) 45 *CMLRev.* 13; C. Dautricourt and S. Thomas, 'Reverse discrimination and free movement of persons under Community law: All for Ulysses, nothing for Penelope?' (2009) 34 *ELRev.* 433.

[64] Case C–212/06 *Walloon Government* [2008] ECR I–1683.

[65] For a fuller description see Sharpston AG's Opinion and also the case note by T. Vandamme (2009) 46 *CMLRev.* 287.

[66] She confessed to 'finding something deeply paradoxical about the proposition that, although the last 50 years have been spent abolishing barriers to freedom of movement *between* Member States, decentralised authorities of Member States may nevertheless reintroduce barriers through the back door by establishing them *within* Member States' (para. 116).

support her view that Union law should apply. The first concerns the Court's case law on Article 30 on customs duties.[67] As we saw in Chapter 3, Article 30 applies both at national and regional frontiers in order to give effect to the edict in Article 26(2) that the internal market should be an 'area without internal frontiers'. Advocate General Sharpston argued that similar reasoning should apply to the *Walloon* case.

Her second argument was based on the citizenship provisions of the Treaties which 'challenge the sustainability in its present form of the doctrine on purely internal situations',[68] especially in the context of this case which comes 'as close to a classic cross-border situation as a supposedly internal situation can'.[69] She considered the Flemish rule to be indirectly discriminatory, contrary to Article 18 TFEU (ex Article 12 EC), which the Flemish government had to justify. She concluded that citizens of the Union should be able to:

rely upon that citizenship, in combination with the principle of non-discrimination, as against a decentralised authority that unquestionably exercises the *auctoritas* of the State, in order to access a benefit that [Union] law clearly intends should be available widely to all workers and that groups of fellow-workers can indeed access through the intervention of [Union] law.[70]

The Court was not, however, prepared to follow its Advocate General. Reasserting the orthodoxy that '[Union] law clearly cannot be applied to such purely internal situations',[71] it added that the citizenship case law does not change this view because 'citizenship of the Union is not intended to extend the material scope of the [Treaties] to internal situations which have no link with [Union] law'.[72] For many states with devolved administrations which treat nationals from elsewhere in the state less favourably than residents and EU migrants (think about the fact that students resident in Scotland and EU students do not have to pay tuition fees to attend Scottish universities while English and Welsh students do[73]), the Court's decision came as a relief but the Advocate General's Opinion reveals the problems generated by the doctrine of reverse discrimination.

### 2.5 Erosion of the Rule

Despite the Court's attempts to maintain the wholly internal situation rule, a number of cases suggest that the rule is being eroded due to the fact that it takes increasingly little to trigger the application of Union law: a 'potential' link with Union law may well be sufficient.[74] For example, in *Deliège*[75] the Court said that, in principle, Union law applied because there was 'a degree of extraneity, derived from the fact that an athlete participated in a competition in a Member State other than that in which he is established'. And in *Carpenter*[76] the Court said that Union law applied to (and prevented) the deportation from the UK of a Filipino woman married to a British man simply because her husband provided services to advertisers established in other Member States. By implication, the

---

[67] Esp. Case C–72/03 *Carbonati* [2004] ECR I–8027.          [68] Para. 140.          [69] Para. 141.

[70] Para. 157.          [71] Para. 38, although cf. para. 40.

[72] Para. 39. See also Case C–127/08 *Metock* [2008] ECR I–6241, para. 77, considered further in Ch. 12.

[73] See further <http://www.saas.gov.uk/student_support/eu_students/2001_or_later/index.htm>.

[74] See also Case C–281/98 *Angonese* [2000] ECR I–4139.

[75] Joined Cases C–51/96 and C–191/97 [2000] ECR I–2549, para. 58. See also Case C–281/98 *Angonese* [2000] ECR I–4139, paras. 17–18, and the comment by R. Lane and N. Nic Shuibhne (2000) 37 *CMLRev.* 1237, 1242–5.          [76] Case C–60/00 [2002] ECR I–6279.

presence of Mrs Carpenter in the UK, looking after Mr Carpenter's children from a previous marriage, enabled him to travel abroad to provide these services[77] and that was sufficient to provide a sufficient Union law element.

## 3. CAN THE TREATY PROVISION BE INVOKED AGAINST THE DEFENDANT?

Assuming the matter falls in the personal, material and territorial scope of the free movement rules, the next question is whether those rules can be invoked against this particular defendant. This brings us to the vexed question of direct effect.

It is clear that the free movement provisions are directly effective and have been since the expiry of the transitional period. In respect of Article 45 on workers, direct effect was first acknowledged by the Court in *French Merchant Seamen*[78] and confirmed in *Van Duyn*[79] where the Court ruled that, despite the derogations from the principle of free movement contained in Article 45(3), the provisions of Articles 45(1) and (2) imposed a sufficiently precise obligation to confer direct effect. The Court also ruled that Articles 49 on establishment, 56 on services, and 21(1) on citizenship were (vertically) directly effective in *Reyners*,[80] *Van Binsbergen*,[81] and *Baumbast*[82] respectively. Not only can the claimants[83] invoke their directly effective rights against the host state (the more usual situation)[84] but they can also do so against the home state,[85] provided the situation is not wholly internal.

For many years it was not clear whether the provisions of the Treaties on free movement of persons had both vertical and horizontal direct effect[86] or only vertical direct effect. In *Walrave and Koch*[87] the Court suggested that the Treaty provisions had both: it said 'the rule on non-discrimination applies in judging *all legal relationships* in so far as these relationships, by reason either of the place they are entered into or the place where they take effect, can be located within the territory of the [Union]'. The Court also said that in addition to public authorities, the ban on discrimination 'extends likewise to rules of any other nature aimed at collectively regulating gainful employment and services'.[88] Yet subsequent cases concerned action taken by public authorities[89] or professional regulatory

---

[77] See Mrs Carpenter's submissions to the Immigration Appeal Tribunal (para. 17).

[78] Case 167/73 *Commission* v. *France* [1974] ECR 359, para. 41.

[79] Case 41/74 [1974] ECR 1337, para. 8.          [80] Case 2/74 [1974] ECR 631, para. 32.

[81] Case 33/74 *van Binsbergen* v. *Bestuur van de Bedrijfsvereniging voor de Metaalnijverheid* [1974] ECR 1299, para. 27.          [82] Case C–413/99 *Baumbast* [2002] ECR I–7091.

[83] The applicants can be the workers, self-employed, or service providers themselves or employers applying on their behalf: Case C–350/96 *Clean Car* [1998] ECR I–2521, para. 24. See also Case C–232/01 *van Lent* [2003] ECR I–11525, para. 20. Recruitment agencies can also benefit from the rights laid down by Art. 45: Case C–208/05 *ITC Innovative Technology Center GmbH* v. *Bundesagentur für Arbeit* [2007] ECR I–181, para. 25.          [84] E.g., Case 41/74 *Van Duyn* [1974] ECR 1337.

[85] This arises in cases concerning impediments to the 'export' of the worker, self-employed person, or company and service: e.g., Case C–384/93 *Alpine Investments* [1995] ECR I–1141, para. 30; Case C–107/94 *Asscher* [1996] ECR I–3089, para. 32; Case C–18/95 *Terhoeve* [1999] ECR I–345, para. 39; and to cases about returners: e.g., Case C–19/92 *Kraus* [1993] ECR I–1663, para. 15.

[86] Cf. Case 43/75 *Defrenne* v. *Sabena* [1976] ECR 455 concerning Art. 157 TFEU (ex Art. 141 EC) on equal pay.          [87] Case 36/74 [1974] ECR 1405, dispositif, emphasis added.

[88] Para. 17.

[89] See, e.g., the Home Office in Case 41/74 *Van Duyn* [1974] ECR 1337 and local authorities in Case 197/84 *Steinhauser* v. *Ville de Biarritz* [1985] ECR 1819 and Case C–168/91 *Konstantinidis* v. *Stadt Altensteig-Standesamt* [1993] ECR I–1191.

bodies (e.g., the Bar Council,[90] the Italian football association,[91] and the International Cycling Union[92]). This suggested an extended form of vertical direct effect only, not because the state is controlling the actions of these bodies but rather because the effect of decisions made by professional regulatory bodies was equivalent to state intervention. Some describe this as *private* governance.

However, in *Clean Car*[93] the Court provided a strong hint that the free movement of *workers* provision might have both vertical and horizontal direct effect, and this was subsequently confirmed in *Angonese*.[94] Applicants applying for jobs in a private bank had to produce a certificate of bilingualism issued by the local authority.[95] The Court noted that since working conditions were governed not only by laws but also by agreements and other acts adopted by private persons, there would be inequality in the application of Article 45 if it applied only to acts of a public authority.[96] Drawing on the long-established case law interpreting Article 157 TFEU (ex Article 141 EC) on equal pay,[97] the Court then ruled that the prohibition of discrimination in Article 45 applied both to agreements intended to regulate paid labour collectively and to contracts between individuals.[98]

Therefore Article 45 has horizontal direct effect, at least where the fundamental principle of non-discrimination is breached,[99] but it is not clear whether this ruling will also apply to Articles 21(1) on citizenship, 49 on establishment and 56 on services. In *Viking*,[100] Advocate General Poiares Maduro argued that these provisions should have horizontal direct effect when the private action was capable of effectively restricting others from exercising their right to freedom of movement.[101] However, the Court did not go that far. It said that Article 49 could be 'relied on by a private undertaking against a trade union or an association of trade unions'.[102] It added that in 'exercising their autonomous power to negotiate pay and conditions of employment with employers, trade unions participate in the drawing up of agreements seeking to regulate paid work *collectively*'.[103] This tends to

---

[90] Case 71/76 *Thieffry* v. *Conseil de l'ordre des avocats à la cour de Paris* [1977] ECR 765; Case C–309/99 *Wouters* [2002] ECR I–1577, para. 120.　　　　　　　　　　　　　　　[91] Case 13/76 *Donà* [1976] ECR 1333.

[92] Case 36/74 *Walrave and Koch* [1974] ECR 1405.

[93] Case C–350/96 [1998] ECR I–2521, itself confirming the hint in Case C–415/93 *Bosman* [1995] ECR I–4921, para. 86.　　　　　　　　　　　　　　　[94] Case C–281/98 [2000] ECR I–4139.

[95] Paras. 6–7.　　　[96] Para. 33.　　　[97] Esp. Case 43/75 *Defrenne* v. *Sabena* [1976] ECR 455.

[98] Para. 34. See further, E. Lohse, 'Fundamental freedoms and private actors: Towards an "indirect horizontal effect"' (2007) 13 *European Public Law* 159.

[99] Para. 36. See also Case C–94/07 *Raccanelli* v. *Max-Planck Gesellschaft (MPG)* [2008] ECR I–5939, para. 46, where the Court held that 'the prohibition of discrimination based on nationality laid down by Article 45 applies equally to private-law associations such as MPG'.

[100] Case C–438/05 *Viking* [2007] ECR I–10779, para. 43.

[101] In Case C–58/08 *Vodaphone* v. *Secretary of State for Business, Enterprise and Regulatory Reform*, Opinion of 1 Oct. 2009, paras. 21–4, he argued that the Court should apply its case law on the horizontal application of the free movement rules to its analysis of the internal market legal basis Art. 114 TFEU (ex Art. 95 EC).

[102] Case C–438/05 [2007] ECR I–10779, para. 61. See also Case C–341/05 *Laval un Partneri Ltd* v. *Svenska Byggnadsarbetareförbundet* [2007] ECR I–11767 in respect of Art. 56. These rulings create problems for trade unions which have now been placed in the same position as states, with the same responsibilities, albeit that unlike states, trade unions have one principal objective, protecting the interests of their members. Further, while trade unions are subject to the same obligations as states, it is difficult for them ever to be able to invoke any of the defences in Art. 52 TFEU (ex Art. 46 EC), such as public policy, which were drafted with states in mind.

[103] Para. 65 emphasis added. See A. Dashwood, '*Viking* and *Laval*: Issues of horizontal direct effect' (2007–8) 10 *CYELS* 525. For a more detailed discussion on the other ways in which the horizontal application

suggest the Court is equating the role of trade unions with that of professional regulatory bodies[104] and is not yet advocating full horizontal direct effect.

A corollary to the principle of direct effect is the remedy available to the claimant. As we shall see in Chapter 10, *Factortame III*[105] makes clear that an action for damages is, in principle, available to an individual (in that case where there was a breach of Article 49) provided three conditions are satisfied:

- the rule of law is intended to confer rights on individuals
- the breach of Union law is sufficiently serious
- there is a direct causal link between the breach of the obligation by the State and the damage sustained by the injured parties.

In *Factortame III* the defendant was the state. The decision leaves open the question of whether a Union remedy in damages might also be available against a trade union or, in the context of Article 45, other private parties. There is support from the competition field that Union law requires such a remedy to exist.[106] The Court alluded to the point briefly in *Raccanelli*[107] concerning alleged discrimination against a foreign doctoral student by the Max Planck Institute (MPI), one of the foremost research institutes in Europe. MPI is established under German private law in the form of an association operating in the public interest. The Court said that that neither Article 45 nor Regulation 1612/68 prescribed 'a specific measure to be taken by the Member States or associations such as [MPI] in the event of a breach of the prohibition of discrimination, but leaves them free to choose between the different solutions suitable for achieving the objective of those respective provisions, depending on the different situations which may arise'.[108] It continued that 'it is for the referring court to assess, in the light of the national legislation applicable in relation to non-contractual liability, the nature of the compensation which the applicant in the main proceedings would be entitled to claim'.[109]

## C. THE SCOPE OF THE TREATY PROHIBITION

### 1. INTRODUCTION

Assuming Union law applies, the next question is what type of measure, conduct or requirement is prohibited by the various provisions of the Treaties. In this section, we shall see that, at least in principle, refusal of entry/deportation, discriminatory measures and non-discriminatory measures which impede market access (often referred to as

---

of these Articles might be extended, see D. Wyatt, 'Horizontal effect of fundamental freedoms and the right to equality after *Viking* and *Mangold*, and the implications for Community competence' (2008) 4 *Croatian Yearbook of European Law and Policy* 1.

[104] This lack of clarity is exacerbated by the fact that the Court somewhat surprisingly cited the decision in Case C–265/95 *Commission* v. *France (strawberries)* [1997] ECR I–6959, a case on omissions by the state, not acts. This case is considered further in Ch. 4.

[105] Joined Cases C–46 and 48/93 *Brasserie du Pêcheur SA* v. *Federal Republic of Germany* and *R.* v. *Secretary of State for Transport, ex p. Factortame and others (Factortame III)* [1996] ECR I–1029.

[106] See, e.g., Case C–453/99 *Courage* v. *Creehan* [2001] ECR I–6297 discussed by A. Albors-Llorens, '*Courage* v. *Creehan*: Judicial activism or consistent approach?' [2002] 61 *CLJ* 38.

[107] Case C–94/07 *Raccanelli* [2008] ECR I–5939.       [108] Para. 50.       [109] Para. 51.

'restrictions' or obstacles' to free movement) are all prohibited by the various provisions of the Treaties. The analysis that follows is based on the 'unitary' thesis: that a common approach applies across all Treaty provisions on free movement of persons. This approach can be justified by the fact that, although Articles 45, 49, and 56 are 'mutually exclusive',[110] the Court said in *Royer*[111] that common principles apply to all three provisions both as regards the entry into, and residence in, the territory of the Member States and as regards the application of the prohibition of all discrimination on the grounds of nationality.[112]

However, there are differences between the provisions. When viewed from the perspective of the regulator, Article 49 on establishment has more in common with Article 45 on workers than with Article 56 on services. In the case of both Articles 45 and 49 the individual leaves State A to work in State B and it is the host state (State B) which has primary control over the individual's activities. By contrast, in respect of free movement of services, the service provider continues to be based in State A while providing services in State B. This time the principal regulator is the home state (State A). In this respect free movement of services has more in common with the free movement of goods:[113] both services and goods are primarily subject to home-state control with only residual host-state control. This suggests that a different regulatory approach is required for workers and establishment on the one hand, and goods and services on the other. In fact, as we shall see, the Court appears to be moving towards convergence of approach under Articles 45, 49, 56, and now Article 21(1) on citizenship,[114] albeit nuanced to reflect the different interests at stake. The common principles are outlined below; the differences are highlighted in the chapters that follow.

## 2. REFUSAL OF ENTRY/DEPORTATION

Refusal of entry to a state,[115] or deportation from a state,[116] are the most draconian steps a state can take against migrants. Because, under international law, states cannot deport

---

[110] Case C–55/94 *Gebhard* v. *Consiglio dell'Ordine degli Avvocati e Procuratori di Milano* [1995] ECR I–4165, para. 20, although cf. Case C–70/95 *Sodemare SA et al* v. *Regione Lombardia* [1997] ECR I–3395.

[111] Case 48/75 *Procureur du Roi* v. *Royer* [1976] ECR 497, para. 23.

[112] Case C–107/94 *Asscher* v. *Staatssecretaris van Financiën* [1996] ECR I–3089, para. 29 (concerning Arts. 45 and 49). See also M. Poiares Maduro, 'Harmony and dissonance in free movement' and H. Jarass, 'A unified approach to the fundamental freedoms' in M. Adenas and W.-H. Roth (eds.), *Services and Free Movement in EU Law* (Oxford: OUP, 2002).

[113] For an early example, see Case 155/73 *Guiseppe Sacchi* [1974] ECR 409, paras. 6–7 (transmission of a TV signal is a service but trade in sound recordings, films, apparatus, concerns goods).

[114] See, e.g., Case C–19/92 *Kraus* v. *Land Baden Württemberg* [1993] ECR I–1663, para. 32, where the Court said that 'national measures liable to hinder or render less attractive the exercise of *fundamental freedoms* guaranteed by the [Treaties]' breach the relevant Treaty provisions (emphasis added); Case C–345/05 *Commission* v. *Portugal (transfer of property)* [2006] ECR I–10633 where the same law was found to breach Arts. 21, 45, and 49 TFEU. V. Hatzopoulos, 'Recent developments of the case law of the ECJ in the field of services' (2000) 37 *CMLRev*. 43, 70. See also K. Mortelmans, 'Towards convergence in the application of the rules on free movement and on competition?' (2001) 38 *CMLRev*. 613 For criticism of the 'globalized approach', see L. Daniele, 'Non-discriminatory restrictions on the free movement of persons' (1997) 22 *ELRev*. 191, and for criticism of the use of a model which is not based on non-discrimination, see G. Davies, *Nationality Discrimination in the European Internal Market* (The Hague: Kluwer, 2003).

[115] Case 41/74 *Van Duyn* v. *Home Office* [1974] ECR 1337, paras. 22–3.

[116] Case 30/77 *R* v. *Bouchereau* [1977] ECR 1999; Case C–348/96 *Criminal Proceedings against Calfa* [1999] ECR I–11.

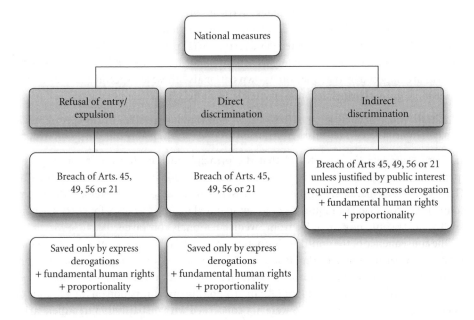

**Fig. 8.1** Refusal of entry/expulsion, direct and indirect discrimination

their own nationals, deportation orders can be made against migrants only.[117] Such orders are the equivalent in the field of persons to quantitative restrictions for goods. They therefore breach the Treaties and can be saved only by reference to one of the express derogations—public policy, public security, and public health.[118] The state must show that the measure taken is proportionate[119] and, where appropriate, compatible with fundamental human rights[120] (see fig. 8.1).

## 3. DISCRIMINATION ON THE GROUNDS OF NATIONALITY

### 3.1 Introduction

Once an individual (or company) has been admitted to the *territory* of a Member State he or she cannot be discriminated against on the grounds of nationality in respect of access to, or exercise of, a particular trade or profession. The principle of non-discrimination on the ground of nationality has been central to the operation of the Treaty provisions on the free movement of persons. For example, Article 45(2) provides that freedom of movement of workers 'shall entail the abolition of any discrimination based on nationality

---

[117] Case C–348/96 *Calfa* [1999] ECR I–11, para. 20.

[118] Case 2/74 *Van Duyn* [1974] ECR 6311, paras. 22–3; Case C–114/97 *Commission* v. *Spain* [1998] ECR I–6717, para. 42.

[119] Case C–100/01 *Ministre de l'Intérieur* v. *Olazabal* [2002] ECR I–10981, para. 43; Case C–108/96 *MacQuen* v. *Grandvision Belgium* [2001] ECR I–837, para. 31; Case C–3/88 *Commission* v. *Italy* [1989] ECR I–4035, para. 15; Case C–348/96 *Criminal Proceedings against Donatella Calfa* [1999] ECR I–11, para. 23.

[120] See Case C–260/89 *ERT* v. *DEP* [1991] ECR I–2925, para. 43 where the Court said that the application of the derogations in Arts. 52 and 62 TFEU (ex Arts. 46 and 55 EC) had to be appraised in the light of the general principle of freedom of expression in Art. 10 of the European Convention of Human Rights. See also Joined Cases C–482/01 and C–493/01 *Orfanopoulos and Oliveri* [2004] ECR I–5257 confirmed in Case C–441/02 *Commission* v. *Germany (Italian migrants)* [2006] ECR I–3449, paras. 108–9.

between workers of the Member States'; Article 49(2) says freedom of establishment occurs 'under the conditions laid down for its own nationals by the law of the country where such establishment is effected'; and Article 57(2) provides that the person providing a service may temporarily pursue his activity in the host state 'under the same conditions as are imposed by that State on its own nationals'. These are specific manifestations of the more general principle found in Article 18 TFEU (ex Article 12 EC):

Within the scope of application of the Treaties, and without prejudice to any special provisions contained therein, any discrimination on grounds of nationality shall be prohibited.[121]

In *Data-Delecta*[122] the Court said that the principle of non-discrimination required 'perfect equality of treatment in Member States of persons in a situation governed by [Union] law and nationals of the Member States in question'.[123] Therefore, the Court found that a Swedish law requiring a foreign national to lodge security for costs when no such security could be demanded from Swedish nationals contravened Article 18.[124]

The consequence of the non-discrimination approach is that a migrant will enjoy equal treatment with nationals of the host state. This means that if a migrant from State A moves to State B which has lower social standards the migrant will enjoy only those lower standards. As the Court said in *Perfili*,[125] in prohibiting discrimination on the grounds of nationality, Articles 18, 49, and 56 were not concerned with disparities in treatment arising from differences between the laws in the Member States so long as the laws affected all persons subject to them in accordance with objective criteria and without regard to nationality. The Court will intervene only if the rule is discriminatory, and even then it will require only that the discrimination be removed without interfering with the substance of the rule.

The principle of equal treatment also forms the basis of the Citizens Rights Directive 2004/38, albeit in a tailored form. The directive distinguishes between three groups of migrants: (1) those entering the host state for up to three months; (2) those resident for up to five years; and (3) those with permanent residence (usually because they have resided for more than five years in the host state). The first group—who do not need to be economically active—enjoy equal treatment with nationals in the host state but not in respect of social assistance or student benefits.

The second group comprises individuals who are engaged in gainful activity in the host state as a worker or a self-employed person (thereby bringing the worker and self-employed entitlements into close alignment); or they have sufficient medical and financial resources for themselves and their family members; or they are students with comprehensive sickness insurance and sufficient resources for themselves and their family members; or they

---

[121] In Case C–193/94 *Criminal Proceedings against Skanavi* [1996] ECR I–929 the Court said that Art. 18 TFEU applied independently only to situations governed by Union law in respect of which the Treaties lay down no specific prohibition on discrimination.

[122] Case C–43/95 *Data-Delecta v. MSL Dynamics* [1996] ECR I–4661. See also Case C–122/96 *Saldanha and MTS Securities Corporation v. Hiross Holding AG* [1998] ECR I–5325; and Case C–411/98 *Angelo Ferlini v. Centre hospitalier de Luxembourg* [2000] ECR I–8081.

[123] Joined Cases C–22/08 and 23/08 *Vatsouras v. Arbeitsgemeinschaft* [2009] ECR I–000, para. 52 makes clear that Art. 18 TFEU does not apply to possible differences in treatment between nationals of Member States and *non*-Member States.                    [124] Para. 22.

[125] Case C–177/94 *Criminal Proceedings against Gianfranco Perfili, civil party: Lloyd's of London* [1996] ECR I–161. See also Case C–387/01 *Weigel v. Finanzlandes direction für Vorarlberg* [2004] ECR I–4981.

are family members (including TCNs) accompanying or joining a Union citizen who satisfies one of the above situations. These individuals also enjoy the right to the same treatment as nationals of the host state, including in respect of social assistance. However, there is no right to equal treatment in respect of maintenance aid for studies, including vocational training, to individuals other than workers, self-employed persons, and members of their families. The third group—those with permanent residence—do not need to show they are workers, self-employed, students or adequately resourced. They enjoy equal treatment not only in respect of social assistance but also in respect of student maintenance in the form of grants or loans.

So what is meant by equal treatment or non-discrimination? The Court has recognized that Union law prohibits both direct discrimination and, unless objectively justified, indirect discrimination. We shall now consider each type of discrimination.[126]

## 3.2 Direct Discrimination/Distinctly Applicable Measures

Direct (or overt) discrimination means different and usually less-favourable treatment on the grounds of nationality. This can be seen in *Reyners*[127] where Belgian law permitted only nationals to become lawyers. Such measures (sometimes referred to as 'distinctly applicable') breach Articles 45, 49, 56, or 21 and/or Directive 2004/38. According to the orthodoxy, distinctly applicable measures may be lawful but only if they are saved by one of the express derogations provided by the Treaties and, once again, the state must show that the measure taken is proportionate[128] and, where appropriate, compatible with fundamental human rights (FHR)[129] (see fig. 8.1[130]). However, as with free movement of goods, there have been signs that the Court is contemplating a move towards allowing distinctly applicable measures to be justified not only by the express derogations but also by the judicially developed 'public-interest requirements',[131] although the case law is not consistent on this point.[132]

## 3.3 Indirect Discrimination/Indistinctly Applicable Measures

### (a) Definition

The Treaties also prohibit indirect (or covert) discrimination. This involves the elimination of requirements which, while apparently nationality-neutral on their face (same burden in law), have a greater impact on nationals of other Member States (different burden

---

[126] See generally C. Hilson, 'Discrimination in Community free movement' (1999) 24 *ELRev.* 445; C. Barnard, 'Fitting the remaining pieces into the goods and services jigsaw?' (2001) 26 *ELRev.* 35.

[127] Case 2/74 *Reyners* v. *Belgian State* [1974] ECR 631.

[128] Case C–100/01 *Ministre de l'Intérieur* v. *Olazabal* [2002] ECR I–10981, para. 43; Case C–108/96 *MacQuen* v. *Grandvision Belgium* [2001] ECR I–837, para. 31; Case C–3/88 *Commission* v. *Italy* [1989] ECR I–4035, para. 15; Case C–348/96 *Calfa* [1999] ECR I–11, para. 23. As Davies notes, in practical terms nationality has become a legally redundant concept (G. Davies, '"Any place I hang my hat?" or: Residence is the new nationality' (2005) 11 *ELJ* 43, 55).

[129] See Case C–260/89 *ERT* v. *DEP* [1991] ECR I–2925, para. 43.

[130] See fig. 4.1 for the equivalent approach in respect of goods.

[131] See, e.g., Joined Cases C–338/04, C–359/04, and C–360/04 *Placanica* [2007] ECR I–1891.

[132] See, e.g., Case C–341/05 *Laval un Partneri Ltd* [2007] ECR I–11767, paras. 116–117 where the Grand Chamber restated the orthodox position.

in fact).[133] As the Court explained in *Sotgiu*,[134] the Treaties prohibit all covert forms of discrimination which, by the application of other criteria of differentiation, lead in fact to the same result as direct discrimination. The Court has found national rules imposing requirements concerning residence[135] and language[136] to be indirectly discriminatory: while nationals almost always satisfy the condition, migrants do not.

Requirements as to holding particular qualifications[137] or licences[138] are also considered to be indirectly discriminatory, but in these cases the discrimination arises because the requirements create a double burden on migrants who have to satisfy two sets of rules (those of the home and host states) while nationals need to satisfy only one set of rules (those of the home state). Sometimes these requirements are referred to as indistinctly applicable measures.[139] While this double-burden theory helps to explain the services case law where the service provider, like the manufacturer of the goods, is subject to two regulators (those of the home and host states),[140] it is less satisfactory in respect of workers and establishment where in practice only one regulator (the host state) controls the migrant.

Nevertheless, the Court appears to gloss over this problem and the conceptual difficulty that double-burden rules are indirectly discriminatory but indirectly discriminatory measures (e.g., those concerning language and residence requirements) do not necessarily impose a double burden, by giving a broad definition to the phrase indirect discrimination. This can be seen in *O'Flynn*[141] concerning a British rule making payment by the state to cover funeral costs conditional on the burial taking place in the UK. The Court said:[142]

[C]onditions imposed by national law must be regarded as indirectly discriminatory where, although applicable irrespective of nationality, they affect essentially migrant workers...or the great majority of those affected are migrant workers,...where they are indistinctly applicable but can be more easily satisfied by national workers than by migrant workers...or where there is a risk that they may operate to the particular detriment of migrant workers...

---

[133] See, e.g., Case C–175/88 *Biehl* v. *Admininstration des Contributions* [1990] ECR I–1779, paras. 13–14; Case C–111/91 *Commission* v. *Luxembourg* [1993] ECR I–817, para. 9.

[134] Case 152/73 *Sotgiu* v. *Deutsche Bundespost* [1974] ECR 153.

[135] Case C–350/96 *Clean Car Autoservice GmbH* v. *Landeshauptmann von Wien* [1998] ECR I–2521; Case C–388/01 *Commission* v. *Italy (museums)* [2003] ECR I–721, para. 14. Cf. the case law on services, esp. Case C–288/89 *Stichting Collectieve Antennevoorziening Gouda* v. *Commissariaat voor de Media* [1991] ECR I–4007, paras. 10–11 considered in Ch. 11. In a similar vein, see also Case C–224/00 *Commission* v. *Italy (highway code)* [2002] ECR I–2965, para. 18: difference in treatment of persons contravening the highway code according to the place of registration of their vehicle found to be indirectly discriminatory—the great majority of offenders in possession of a vehicle registered in another Member State were not Italians.

[136] Case 379/87 *Groener* v. *Minister for Education* [1989] ECR 3967.

[137] Case C–340/89 *Vlassopoulou* v. *Ministerium für Justiz* [1991] ECR I–2357.

[138] Case 292/86 *Gullung* v. *Conseil de l'ordre des avocats* [1988] ECR 111.

[139] This reflects the Court's formulation of measures which are 'applicable without distinction to all'. See, e.g., Case 143/87 *Stanton* v. *INASTI* [1988] ECR 3877, para. 9.

[140] Cf. Case C–70/95 *Sodemare SA et al* v. *Regione Lombardia* [1997] ECR I–3395 and Case C–405/98 *Gourmet International Products AB (GIP)* [2001] ECR I–1795.

[141] Case C–237/94 [1996] ECR I–2617.

[142] Case C–237/94 *O'Flynn* v. *Adjudication Officer* [1996] ECR I–2617, paras. 18–19. See also Case E–3/05 *EFTA Surveillance Authority* v. *Norway* [2006] EFTA Ct Rep. 102, paras. 56–7 concerning a regional residence requirement.

The Court continued:

It is otherwise only if those provisions are justified by objective considerations independent of the nationality of the workers concerned, and if they are proportionate to the legitimate aim pursued by national law.

The Court found that the British rule constituted unjustified indirect discrimination (but did say that the UK could limit the allowance to a lump sum or reasonable amount fixed by reference to the normal cost of a burial in the UK).

From *O'Flynn* we can see that, unless objectively justified and proportionate to its aim (see fig. 8.1), the provision of national law must be regarded as indirectly discriminatory and contrary to Union law if it is *intrinsically liable* to affect migrant workers more than national workers and if there is a *risk* that it will place migrant workers at a particular disadvantage.[143] The Court added that it was not necessary to find that the measure did in practice affect a substantially higher proportion of migrant workers; it was sufficient that it was liable to have such an effect.[144] The broad formulation of indirect discrimination in *O'Flynn*, focusing on the *potential* effect on free movement means that, as with the case law on goods following *Dassonville*,[145] more national rules are liable to be caught by the Treaties. Three consequences flow from this: first, there is a risk that the rule that Union law does not apply to wholly internal situations is eroded; second, that the distinction between the market access approach considered in Chapter 1 and the discrimination approach is more apparent than real; and third, the broader the scope of measures caught under the heading of indirect discrimination, the greater the need for Member States to justify the continued existence of their national rules.

## (b) Justifications

In recognition of the need for Member States to be able to justify their rules on grounds other than the narrowly defined express derogations, the Court has allowed Member States to justify their indirectly discriminatory national rules by reference to 'objective justifications' (the language used in *O'Flynn* in the context of free movement of workers) or justifications in the 'public' or 'general interest' or 'imperative requirements' (the language more commonly used in the field of establishment and services).[146] These various terms appear synonymous[147] and are the equivalent of the 'mandatory requirements' in the field of goods. In all cases the Court recognizes that there exists a non-exhaustive

---

[143] Para. 20. The fact that nationals may also be affected by the rule does not prevent the rule from being indirectly discriminatory, provided that the majority of those affected are non-nationals: Case C–281/98 *Angonese* [2000] ECR I–4139, para. 41.

[144] Para. 21. Cf. the position in respect of Art. 110 on internal taxation where actual disparate impact must be shown: Case 132/88 *Commission* v. *Greece* [1990] ECR I–1567 considered in Ch. 3.

[145] Case 8/74 *Dassonville* [1974] ECR 837.

[146] Case C–76/90 *Säger* v. *Dennemeyer & Co. Ltd* [1991] ECR I–4221, para. 15; Case C–55/94 *Gebhard* [1996] ECR I–4165, para. 37.

[147] This view is supported by the workers case, Case C–195/98 *Österreicher Gewerkschaftsbund* v. *Republik Österreich* [2000] ECR I–10497, para. 45, where the Court reported that the Austrian government contends that the restrictions on free movement are 'justified by overriding reasons of public interest and are consistent with the principle of proportionality', and the services case, Case C–118/96 *Safir* v. *Skattemyndigheten i Dalarnas Län* [1998] ECR I–1897, para. 22: Article 56 TFEU 'precludes the application of any national legislation which, without objective justification, impedes a provider of services from actually exercising the freedom to provide them.'

list of national interests worthy of protection[148] (such as consumer protection, worker protection, cultural policy[149]) which are compatible with the objectives of the EU,[150] and which should take precedence over the free movement provisions, provided that the steps taken are proportionate and, where appropriate, compatible with fundamental human rights. These public-interest requirements are examined in more detail in Chapter 13.

### 3.4 Non-discriminatory Measures

#### (a) Pure non-discrimination

Since measures which discriminate on grounds of nationality (either directly or indirectly) breach the Treaties, it should follow that measures which do not discriminate do not breach the Treaties. This was the approach taken by the Court in the *Clinical Biology Laboratories* case.[151] Belgian law provided that for a laboratory to qualify for reimbursement from a sickness insurance scheme, all of its members, partners, and directors had to be doctors or pharmacists. The Court found that since the legislation applied without distinction to Belgian nationals and those from other Member States, it did not breach Article 49 (see fig. 8.2).[152]

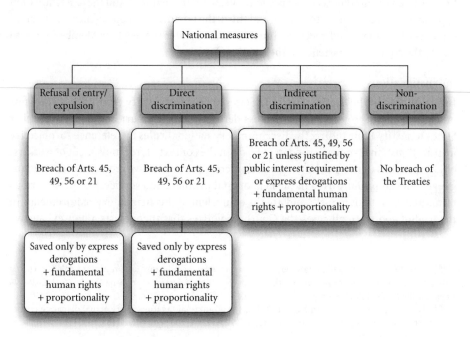

**Fig. 8.2** Pure non-discrimination model

---

[148] See Tesauro AG in Case C–118/96 *Safir* [1998] ECR I–1897, para. 29.

[149] Case C–288/89 *Gouda* [1991] ECR I–4007.

[150] Case C–464/02 *Commission v. Denmark (company vehicles)* [2005] ECR I–7929, para. 53.

[151] Case 221/85 *Commission v. Belgium* [1987] ECR 719.

[152] Cf. Joined Cases C–171/07 and C–172/07 *Apothekerkammer des Saarlandes v. Saarland* [2009] ECR I–000, considered in Ch. 10.

## (b) Non-discriminatory measures which prevent or hinder market access

However, a number of cases decided in the mid 1990s concerned measures which were not discriminatory (i.e., no discrimination either in law or in fact) but still hindered access to the market. Should these rules be caught by the Treaties? It will be recalled that the Court said in *Keck*[153] that non-discriminatory certain selling arrangements did not breach Article 34. This prompted various Member States to argue in the workers case, *Bosman*,[154] considered in Case Study 8.1 below, and in the services case, *Alpine Investments*,[155] that the *Keck* principle should apply equally to free movement of persons. *Alpine Investments* concerned a Dutch law prohibiting cold-calling to sell financial services both within and outside the Netherlands. The Court said that the Dutch law was 'general and non-discriminatory and neither its object nor effect [was] to put the national market at an advantage over providers of services from other Member States'.[156] The British and Dutch governments therefore argued that since this case was analogous to a non-discriminatory measure governing selling arrangements the principles of *Keck* should apply, with the result that the rule should not breach Article 56.

The Court disagreed. It emphasized that the Dutch law deprived operators of a 'rapid and direct technique for marketing and for contacting potential clients in other Member States'.[157] For this reason the Dutch law was not analogous to the selling arrangements in *Keck*:[158] while *Keck* concerned a situation where there was *no* hindrance of trade between Member States (i.e., access to the market was not affected), the prohibition on cold-calling in *Alpine* did '*directly affect access to the markets in services* in the other Member States and [was] thus capable of hindering intra-[Union] trade in services'.[159] Having established a breach (see fig. 8.3), due to the fact that the rule, while non-discriminatory, did affect market access, the Court then considered the question of justification. It accepted that the prohibition on cold-calling could be justified by the need to safeguard the reputation of the Dutch financial markets[160] and that the measures taken were proportionate.

Does *Alpine* mean then that the *Keck* ruling does not apply to free movement of persons?[161] The answer may well be no.[162] If *Keck* is removed from its specific 'goods' context (certain selling arrangements, a non-legal category developed to curb the excesses of *Dassonville*) and considered instead in terms of its purpose (the removal of non-discriminatory matters which do not substantially affect inter-state trade from the purview of Article 34), then it is possible to see how *Keck*-like principles can—and do—apply equally to the free movement of persons. *Graf*[163] provides a pointer in that direction. Graf,

---

[153] Joined Cases C–267 and 8/91 *Keck and Mithouard* [1993] ECR I–6097, considered in Ch. 5.

[154] Case C–415/93 *Union Royale Belge de Société de Football Association* v. *Bosman* [1995] ECR I–4921. See generally S. Weatherill (1996) 33 *CMLRev*. 991.

[155] Case C–384/93 *Alpine Investments BV* v. *Mininster van Financiën* [1995] ECR I–1141. See also Case C–275/92 *Customs and Excise* v. *Schindler* [1994] ECR I–1039, considered in Ch. 11.      [156] Para. 35.

[157] Para. 28.      [158] Para. 36.

[159] Para. 38, emphasis added. See also the Golden Shares cases: e.g. Case C–463/00 *Commission* v. *Spain* [2003] ECR I–4581 and Case C–98/01 *Commission* v. *UK* [2003] ECR I–4641 on the free movement of capital considered in Ch. 15.      [160] Para. 43.

[161] See D. O'Keeffe and A. Bavasso, 'Four Freedoms, One Market and National Competence. In Search of a Dividing Line' in D. O'Keeffe and A. Bavasso (eds), *Judicial Review in European Union Law: Liber Amicorum in Honour of Lord Slynn of Hadley* (The Hague, Kluwer, 2000).

[162] See, to that effect, Tizzano AG's views in Case C–442/02 *Caixa-Bank* v. *Ministère de l'Économie, des Finances and de l'Industrie* [2004] ECR I–8961, para. 73.

[163] Case C–190/98 *Graf* v. *Filzmozer Maschinenbau GmbH* [2000] ECR I–493.

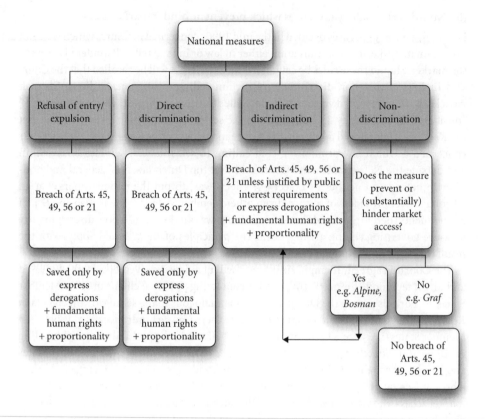

**Fig. 8.3** Non-discrimination model and market access

a German national, worked for his Austrian employer for four years when he terminated his contract in order to take up a job in Germany. Under Austrian law, a worker employed by the same employer for more than three years was entitled to compensation on termination of his contract provided that he was dismissed (and did not just resign). Graf argued that this rule contravened Article 45 because the effect of the rule was that, by moving to another state, he lost the chance of being dismissed in Austria and, with it, the chance of claiming compensation.

The Court disagreed: the Austrian law was genuinely non-discriminatory[164] and did not preclude or deter a worker from ending his contract of employment in order to take a job with another employer.[165] The Court explained that the entitlement to compensation when the employer dismissed an employee was not dependent on the worker's choosing whether to stay with his current employer but on a future and hypothetical event, namely being dismissed.[166] The Court concluded that '[s]uch an event is *too uncertain and indirect* a possibility for legislation to be capable of being regarded as liable to hinder free movement for workers'. Thus, the dismissal was too remote to be considered liable to affect free movement.[167] Putting it another way, and using more economic language,

---

[164] Para. 18.　　　[165] Para. 24. See also Case C–542/08 *Barth* [2010] ECR I–000, para. 39.
[166] Ibid.
[167] See also Joined Cases C–418/93, etc. *Semeraro Casa Uno Srl and others* [1996] ECR I–2975, para. 32 concerning Art. 49 TFEU. Cf. Case C–159/90 *SPUC* v. *Grogan* [1991] ECR I–4685, para. 24 where the Court noted that the link between the student associations and abortions carried out by clinics in other Member

non-discriminatory measures which do not substantially hinder access to the (labour) market[168] or whose effect on free movement is too remote,[169] fall outside Article 45[170] (and presumably the other Treaty provisions—see fig. 8.3) in much the same way as non-discriminatory certain selling arrangements cases (*Punto Casa*,[171] *Boermans*[172]) which do not substantially hinder access to the market fall outside Article 34.

Thus, it would seem that rules which merely *structure the market*[173] on which goods are sold and people carry out their economic activities do not generally breach the Treaties. They are the rules of the game, to which all of those conducting their activities in the state must comply. Some rules, like the labour laws at issue in *Graf*, or environmental or consumer laws, reflect social choices made by a democratically elected national government. Other rules actually make the market, as *Deliège*[174] demonstrates. A successful Belgian judo player complained that the Belgian judo federation's failure to select her for various international competitions breached Article 56. The Court disagreed, saying that, although selection rules inevitably had the effect of limiting the number of participants in a tournament, such a limitation was inherent in the conduct of an international high-level sports event. In other words, without any rules there would be no competition. The Court continued that such rules could not in themselves be regarded as constituting a restriction on the freedom to provide services prohibited by Article 56.[175]

Pulling the strands of the case law together, it could be said that *Graf* and *Deliège* and, in the context of goods, *Punto Casa* and *Boermans*, all concerned non-discriminatory rules which did not substantially hinder access to the market and so did not breach the Treaty provisions.[176] These rules stand at one stage removed from the individual good or person performing the economic activity. In the interests of subsidiarity, they are the very type

States was 'too tenuous' for the prohibition on the distribution of information to be regarded as a restriction within the meaning of Art. 56 TFEU; Case C–168/91 *Konstantinidis* [1993] ECR I–1191, para. 15.

[168] Cf. Case C–255/04 *Commission v. France (performing artists)* [2006] ECR I–5251, para. 38.

[169] In Case C–212/06 *Walloon Government* [2008] ECR I–1683 Sharpston AG supported this approach (paras. 55–6): 'A national measure can potentially constitute a prohibited obstacle even if it is non-discriminatory. However, in order actually to constitute an obstacle, such provision must affect access of workers to the labour market *and* their effect on freedom of movement must not be too indirect and uncertain.' On the facts, the Court found that the restrictive effects of the Flemish legislation—which confined affiliation to a care insurance scheme to those residing in the Dutch speaking region of Belgium and the bilingual speaking region of Brussels—were not 'too indirect and uncertain for it to be impossible to regard that legislation as constituting an obstacle contrary to Articles [49] and [56]' (para. 51). See also Joined Cases C–11/06 and C–12/06 *Morgan* [2007] ECR I–9161, para. 32 where the Court of Justice rejected the argument that the German first stage studies condition was 'too uncertain or too insignificant' to constitute a restriction on free movement under Article 21(1) TFEU. Cf Case C–211/08 *Commission v. Spain (unscheduled hospital treatment)* [2010] ECR I–000, para. 72.

[170] See also Case C–134/03 *Viacom Outdoor Srl v. Giotto Immobilier SARL (Viacom II)* [2005] ECR I–1167, para. 38 considered below n. 280. For a discussion of the debate about the merits of the legal test based on remoteness and the economic test based on 'substantial' hindrance of market access, see Ch. 5.

[171] Case C–69 and 258/93 *Punto Casa SpA* [1994] ECR I–2355.

[172] Joined Cases C–401 and 402/92 *Boermans* [1994] ECR I–2199.

[173] I am grateful to Michael Dougan for this phrase. See also the use of the solidarity principle in Case C–70/95 *Sodemare* [1997] ECR I–3395, para. 29, to justify excluding the application of Art. 49 to national rules which allow only non-profit-making private operators to participate in running old people's homes.

[174] Joined Cases C–51/96 and C–191/97 *Deliège v. Ligue Francophone de Judo et Disciplines Associés* [2000] ECR I–2549, para. 64. See *Wilander v. Tobin* [1997] 2 CMLR 346 for an English decision in the same vein.

[175] Para. 64.

[176] See also the views of Walker LJ, as he then was, in the Court of Appeal in *Professional Contractors' Group v. Commissioners of Inland Revenue* [2002] 1 CMLR 46, para. 69.

of measures which should fall outside the scrutiny of EU law. Just because they reduce the 'economic attractiveness' of pursuing the activity does not mean they should be caught by the Treaties.[177] But, if the non-discriminatory measures do substantially hinder access to the market, then they do breach the Treaty provision and need to be justified (see fig. 8.3). This was the outcome in *Alpine* and *Bosman*. It was also the outcome the Court appeared to be suggesting in the goods case *Commission* v. *Italy (trailers)*[178] (see fig. 4.3).

---

**Case Study 8.1** SPORT AND THE FREE MOVEMENT OF PERSONS

Sport, particularly the big money world of professional sport, provides an interesting case study of how the principles outlined above—of non-discrimination, market access, justification, and proportionality—have been used to remove barriers to the mobility of sportsmen and women. However, those running professional sport have not always seen the benefits of applying Union law. They have long claimed that 'sport is special', due to its social and educational function, and so should not be subject to Union law at all. Generally, the Court disagrees.[179]

Relatively early in its case law the Court made clear that sport was subject to Union law but only in so far as it constituted an economic activity.[180] Therefore, in *Donà* v. *Mantero*[181] the Court ruled that the activities of professional or semi-professional football players who were employed or provided a service fell within the scope of Articles 45 and 56. However, perhaps in recognition of the special nature of sport, the Court built in a *de facto* exception to this rule for *national* teams. Relying on the contentious justification that such national games were not commercial in nature, it said that Union law did not prevent the adoption of rules 'excluding foreign players from participation in certain matches for reasons which are not of an economic nature, which relates to the particular nature and context of such matches and are thus of sporting interest only, such as, for example, matches between national teams from different countries'.[182] The Court did add that '[t]his restriction on the scope of the provisions in question must however remain limited to its proper objective'. Therefore, in respect of the nationality of players that can be fielded, clubs (e.g., Manchester United and Chelsea) are subject to Union law, while national sides (e.g., England and France) are not.[183]

This national-team rule is not the only 'exception' carved out by the Court from the provisions on the free movement of persons. As we saw in *Deliège*,[184] the Court said that federation rules concerning the selection of athletes for international competitions did not constitute a restriction on the provision of services[185] and so fell outside

---

[177] Tizzano AG in Case C–442/02 *Caixa-Bank* [2004] ECR I–8961, para. 58.

[178] Case C–110/05 [2009] ECR I–519, considered in chapters 4 and 5.

[179] See generally, S. van den Bogaert and A.Vermeersch, 'Sport and the EC Treaty: A tale of uneasy bedfellows' (2006) 6 *ELRev*. 800.    [180] Case 13/76 *Donà* v. *Mantero* [1976] ECR 1333, para. 12.

[181] Ibid. See also Case 36/74 *Walrave and Koch* v. *Association Union Cycliste Internationale* [1974] ECR 1405, para. 4.    [182] Para. 14.

[183] Para. 15.

[184] Joined Cases C–51/96 and C–191/97 [2000] ECR I–2549, para. 64. See S. Van den Bogaert, 'The Court of Justice on the Tatami: Ippon, Waza-Ari or Koka?' (2000) 25 *ELRev*. 554.    [185] Para. 64.

Article 56.[186] In this way the Court has ensured a considerable degree of autonomy for sporting organizations to set their own rules.

For those sporting situations which do fall within the scope of Union law, the principle of non-discrimination on the grounds of nationality applies. The early cases concerned direct discrimination. For example, in *Donà*[187] the Court said that national rules providing that only those football players who were affiliated to the Italian Football Federation could play in professional matches, affiliation being open to Italian players only, breached Union law. This ruling led to a 'gentlemen's agreement' between the Commission and the Union of European Football Associations (UEFA) under which national associations had to allow each first division team to field at least three foreign players and two 'acclimatized'[188] foreigners in domestic league matches from the 1992 season—the so-called '3+2 rule'.[189] This was one of the rules challenged in *Bosman*.[190]

Bosman was a Belgian national employed by the Belgian first division club RC Liège. When his contract expired he wanted to play for the French second division club, US Dunkerque. Because no transfer certificate had been sent to the French Football Federation, Bosman was left without a club for the following season. He did manage to sign two short contracts with French clubs before ending up at Olympic de Charleroi, a Belgian third-division club. There was strong circumstantial evidence that Bosman was being boycotted by other clubs which might have employed him.[191] He argued that the 3+2 rule contravened Article 45. The Court agreed, arguing that the principle of non-discrimination applied to clauses contained in the regulations of sporting associations which restricted the rights of nationals of other Member States to take part in football matches. It said that the nationality clause related to the essence of the activity of professional players: if Union law did not apply to this situation, then Article 45 would be 'deprived of its practical effect and the fundamental right of free access to employment which the [Treaties confer] individually on each worker in the [Union] rendered nugatory'.[192]

---

[186] The Commission's Decision in the *Mouscron* case which anticipated the Court's ruling in *Deliège*. In *Mouscron* the Commission said that the UEFA Cup rule requiring each club to play its home match at its own ground (and not at a neighbouring ground) was a sports rule that did not fall within the scope of the Treaties competition rules ('Limits to application of Treaty competition rules to sport: Commission gives clear signal', IP/99/965).

[187] Case 13/76 [1976] ECR 1333. See also Case 36/74 *Walrave and Koch* [1974] ECR 1405.

[188] Players who have played in the country for an uninterrupted period of five years.

[189] *Financial Times*, 27 Jan. 1990 and 19 Apr. 1991.     [190] Case C–415/93 [1995] ECR I–4921.

[191] Para. 37.

[192] Para. 129. The Court reached the same conclusion in respect of an equivalent rule applied to a Slovakian handball player employed by a German club in the context of the Association Agreement between the Communities and Slovakia: Case C–438/00 *Deutscher Handballbund eV* v. *Maros Kolpak* [2003] ECR I–4135 noted by J.-P. Dubet (2006) 42 *CMLRev.* 499; S.Van den Bogaert (2004) 29 *ELRev.* 267. See also Case C–265/03 *Simutenkov* v. *Mininsterio de Educación y Cultura* [2005] ECR I–2579 where the Court (Grand Chamber) reached the same decision in respect of the Communities–Russia partnership agreement in respect of a Russian footballer playing in Spain (noted Hillion (2008) 45 *CMLRev.* 815); and Case C–152/08 *Real Sociedad de Fútbol SAD and Kahveci* v. *Consejo Superior de Deportes*, Order of 25 Jul. 2008 under the EEC–Turkey Association Agreement.

Despite losing on this point in *Bosman*, the football authorities insist that it is still necessary for some sort of national quota to be introduced because, they argue, in the absence of a quota young talent is not able to develop in the club at which they are trained because they cannot play in the first team, that the ability of tops clubs to buy up all of the talent means that competition at national level is not balanced, that national team managers see fewer nationals playing in national leagues which gives them less choice to select players, and with players moving from club to club there is a loss of national identity of clubs.[193] FIFA, the international football federation, therefore proposes introducing a 6+5 rule which would permit clubs to field a maximum of five players who are not eligible to play for the national team of the country of that club. Not surprisingly, the Commission has said that this rule is contrary to Union law.[194] The rule is also opposed by some football managers, like Arsenal's Arsène Wenger, who argues that spectators want to see the best football players and that the quality of English players is not enhanced by removing from them the incentive to improve their performance to win a place in the club side.[195]

By contrast, the European football association, UEFA, has introduced a 'Homegrown player rule' which applies to games in the Champions League and the UEFA cup.[196] Clubs competing in these competitions must include a minimum number of locally trained players in their squad (from the 2008–9 season the figure stands at 8 homegrown players in a squad of 25). Clubs are not obliged to play these home-grown players in any match. UEFA defines locally trained players as those who, regardless of their nationality, have been trained by their club or by another club in the same national association for at least three years between the age of 15 and 21. UEFA sees this rule as one step towards addressing the problem created by the *Bosman* ruling that 'the richest clubs have been able to stockpile the best players, which makes it easier for them to dominate both national and European competitions.'[197] The home-grown player rule, while potentially indirectly discriminatory,[198] is more carefully tailored than the 6+5 rule. The Commission has therefore indicated that it thinks the rule can be justified. It said the objectives of the rule, namely promoting training for young players and consolidating the balance of competitions, seem 'legitimate objectives of general interest, as they are inherent to sporting activity' and proportionate.

In more recent cases the Court has gone beyond the discrimination model, focusing instead on whether the measure has restricted the sportsperson's access to the

---

[193] 'FIFA: We'll convince the Commission on national quotas', *EurActiv* 11 Sep. 2008.

[194] 'UEFA rule on 'home-grown players': Compatibility with the principle of free movement of persons', <http://www.europa.eu/rapid/pressReleasesAction.do?reference=IP/08/807>.

[195] D. Pannick QC, 'Sports minister will lose his war against foreigners', *The Times*, 27 Nov. 2007.

[196] <http://www.uefa.com/uefa/footballfirst/protectingthegame/youngplayers/news/newsid=943393.html>.

[197] R. Williams and A. Haffner, 'FIFA quotas ruled offside?' [2008] *New Law Journal* 1017.

[198] Case 222/86 [1987] ECR 4097. See also Dec. 2000/12 *1998 Football World Cup* ([2000] OJ L5/55) on the distribution of tickets for the World Cup in France which was restricted to residents in France. The Commission said that this rule offended against 'fundamental [Union] principles' (para. 102). See also S. Weatherill, '0033149875354: Fining the organisers of the 1998 Football World Cup' [2000] *ECLR* 275.

market. This can be seen in respect of the other rule at issue in *Bosman* concerning transfer fees. According to federation rules, on the expiry of a contract with club A, a professional footballer could not play for club B until club A had released his registration. This was usually conditional on club B paying a transfer fee to club A. The Court said that these rules were not discriminatory because they applied equally to transfers between clubs belonging to different national associations within the same Member State and were similar to those governing transfers between clubs belonging to the same national association.[199] Nevertheless, the Court concluded that since the transfer rules 'directly affect players' access to the employment market in other Member States', they were capable of impeding free movement of workers and so breached Article 45 (see fig. 8.3).[200] For this reason the Court said that UEFA's rules could not be deemed comparable to those on selling arrangements for goods to which the principle in *Keck* applied.[201] The Court reached a similar conclusion in *Lehtonen*,[202] where the rules of a Belgian basketball association prohibited a basketball club from fielding players from other Member States (who had been transferred after a specific date) in national championship matches. The Court said that such rules were liable to restrict the freedom of movement of players which was contrary to Article 45.[203] Likewise, in *Olympique Lyonnais*[204] the Court said that a French collective agreement requiring a 'joueur espoir' (a player aged between 16 and 22 employed as a trainee by a professional club under a fixed-term contract) to sign, at the end of his training period, a professional contract with the club which trained him under pain of being sued for damages, was likely to discourage that player from exercising his right of free movement under Article 45 TFEU.

Having established a breach of Article 45 in *Bosman, Lehtonen* and *Olympique Lyonnais*, the Court then turned to the question of justification. In *Lehtonen* the Court recognized that transfer periods could be justified on the ground of ensuring the regularity of sporting competitions:[205] late transfers could substantially change the sporting strength of one or other team in the course of the championship. The Court noted that this would call into question the comparability of results between the teams taking part in that championship and consequently the proper functioning of the championship as a whole.[206] However, the Court said that such measures had to be proportionate and suggested that, on the facts, this was not the case because looser deadlines applied to players from non-European zone countries without that jeopardizing competitions.

---

[199] Para. 103.          [200] Ibid.

[201] Ibid. See also the discussion of Case C–384/93 *Alpine Investments* [1995] ECR I–1141, paras. 36–8, and Case C–275/92 *Schindler* [1994] ECR I–1039, para. 45.

[202] Case C–176/96 *Lehtonen and Castors Canada Dry Namur-Braine ASBL* v. *Fédération royale belge des sociétés de basket-ball ASBL (FRBSB)* [2000] ECR I–2681.          [203] Para. 49.

[204] Case C–325/08 *Olympique Lyonnais SASP* v *Olivier Bernard, Newcastle United FC* [2010] ECR I–000, para. 35.          [205] Para. 53.

[206] Para. 54.

In *Bosman* the Court also decided that the football federation rules were not proportionate on the facts. However, it began by recognizing that sport was special:[207]

> In view of the considerable social importance of sporting activities and in particular football in the [Union], the aims of maintaining a balance between the clubs by preserving a certain degree of equality and uncertainty as to results and of encouraging the recruitment and training of young players the transfer fees had to be accepted as legitimate.[208]

In other words, as Weatherill explains, unlike the widget market where producers aim to gain the largest market share, if necessary by driving their rivals off the market, sport is based on a notion of mutual interdependence. In sport, opponents are there to be beaten, but the whole point of the endeavour is destroyed if opponents are, literally, beaten out of sight;[209] and the Court recognized that steps taken to ensure this could be justified on the grounds of maintaining competitive balance between the teams, and encouraging training programmes.

However, the Court then considered the proportionality question. It said that the transfer rules were not an adequate means of maintaining financial and competitive balance in the world of football because they neither precluded the richest clubs from securing the services of the best players nor did they prevent the availability of financial resources from being a decisive factor in competitive sport, thus considerably altering the balance between clubs.[210]

In respect of the argument that transfer fees helped cover the cost of training new talent, the Court accepted that the prospect of receiving transfer fees was likely to encourage football clubs to seek new talent and train young players.[211] However, it said that, because it was impossible to predict with any certainty the sporting future of young players (only a limited number went on to play professionally), those fees were by nature contingent and uncertain. They were also unrelated to the actual cost borne by clubs of training both future professional players and those who would never play professionally. The Court therefore concluded that the prospect of receiving such fees could be neither a decisive factor in encouraging the recruitment and training of young

---

[207] The social importance of sport has assumed a growing importance as the Treaties have been amended. First, Decl. 29 on Sport was annexed to the Treaty of Amsterdam where the states emphasized the 'social significance of sport'. This was more fully articulated in the Declaration annexed to the Conclusions of the Nice European Council in Dec. 2000 which talked of 'the specific characteristics of sport and its social function in Europe'. The position was emphasized in the Lisbon Treaty. Art. 165(1) TFEU says 'The Union shall contribute to the promotion of European sporting issues, while taking account of the specific nature of sport, its structures based on voluntary activity and its social and educational function', a point recognized by the Court in Case C–325/08 *Olympique Lyonnais* [2010] ECR I–000, para. 40. See also Commission, 'White paper on sport' COM(2007) 391, 13: 'The case law of the European courts and decisions of the European Commission show that the specificity of sport has been recognised and taken into account...but it cannot be construed so as to justify a general exemption from the application of EU law.'

[208] Para. 106. See also Case C-325/08 *Olympique Lyonnais* [2010] ECR I–000, para. 41.

[209] S. Weatherill, '"Fair play please": Recent developments in the application of EC law to sport' (2003) 40 *CMLRev.* 51. See also Art. 165(2) TFEU which says that one of aspect of Union action is to develop 'the European dimension in sport, by promoting fairness and openness in sporting competitions and cooperation between bodies responsible for sports, and by protecting the physical and moral integrity of sportsmen and sportswomen, especially the youngest sportsmen and sportswomen'.     [210] Para. 107.

[211] Para. 108.

players nor an adequate means of financing such activities, particularly in the case of smaller clubs.

For these reasons the Court rejected the football authorities' arguments on the basis of suitability. For good measure, it also suggested that the transfer fee rules went beyond what was necessary to attain the objectives. Referring to Advocate General Lenz's Opinion, the Court accepted that the same aims could be achieved at least as efficiently by other means which did not impede freedom of movement of workers.[212] He had suggested two more proportionate possibilities: (1) to negotiate collectively specified limits for the salaries of the players; (2) to distribute the clubs' receipts among the clubs. Specifically, this meant that part of the income obtained by a club from the sale of tickets for its home matches should be distributed to other clubs. Similarly, the income received for awarding the rights to transmit matches on television could be divided up between all the clubs. The Court therefore concluded that Article 45 precluded the application of rules relating to transfer fees.

Similarly, in *Olympique Lyonnais*, the Court said that that a scheme providing for the payment of compensation for the costs of training where a young player (Olivier Bernard), at the end of his training, signs a professional contract with a club (Newcastle United) other than the one which trained him (Olympique Lyonnais) could, in principle, be justified by the objective of encouraging the recruitment and training of young players. However, once again, the Court found the scheme disproportionate because (1) the damages were not calculated in relation to the training costs actually incurred by Olympique Lyonnais but in relation to the total loss suffered by the club; and (2) the amount of that loss was established on the basis of criteria which were not determined in advance.

Although *Bosman* was decided on the basis of Article 45, rumbling in the background were Articles 101 and 102 TFEU (ex Articles 81 and 82 EC) on competition which had so influenced the Advocate General.[213] It is in the arena of competition law that most of the subsequent challenges to sport rules have been thrashed out including complaints to the Commission about FIFA rules on football player agents;[214] UEFA regulations allowing national football associations to block the broadcasting of football;[215] and UEFA's rule prohibiting multiple ownership of clubs.[216] In the world of competitive swimming two professional swimmers were banned for two years for

---

[212] Para. 110.

[213] The Court would have been forced to consider the issue in Case C–264/98 *Balog* v. *ASBL Royal Charleroi*, removed from the register on 2 Apr. 2001. Much of the AG's unpublished Opinion in that case can be found in A. Egger and C. Stix-Hackl, 'Sports and competition law: A never-ending story?' [2002] *ECLR* 81.

[214] The case was closed with the Commission recognizing that FIFA could regulate the profession in an attempt to promote good practice as long as access remained open and non-discriminatory: IP/02/585, 18 Apr. 02.

[215] The Commission permitted revised regulations allowing a block of two and a half hours on Saturday or Sunday (and not the weekend as a whole): IP/01/583, 20 Apr. 01. However, the Commission's views are not always correct: see Joined Cases T–185, 299 and 300/00 *M6* v. *Commission* [2002] ECR II–3805.

[216] The Commission found that the rule which provides that no two clubs participating in a club competition could be directly or indirectly controlled by the same entity or managed by the same person could be justified by the need to guarantee the integrity of the competitions: IP/02/942, 27 Jun. 2002. See also the Commission's Communication in [1999] OJ C363/2.

taking Nandrolone, a prohibited substance. They complained to the Commission that swimming's anti-doping rules infringed their economic freedoms under Article 56 on services and Articles 101 and 102 on competition law. The Commission rejected their complaints and the swimmers applied to the General Court for the Commission's decision to be annulled.[217] They lost before the General Court and again before the Court of Justice[218] which, while setting aside the General Court's decision, also dismissed the application for the annulment of the Commission's Decision. While the General Court adopted a generous approach towards the autonomy of sport, the Court of Justice took a stricter line:[219]

> The mere fact that a rule is purely sporting in nature does not have the effect of removing from the scope of the [Treaties] the person engaging in the activity governed by that rule or the body which has laid it down.

This is the enduring problem for the Court(s): as Weatherill puts it, 'Sporting rules have an economic effect. But without some fundamental rules there is no sport.'[220]

The *Bosman* judgment transformed professional football, changing the composition of many teams and putting an end to transfer fees for players out of contract.[221] Clubs have responded by hiring stars on longer contracts, with money previously used for transfer fees being diverted into wage packets, making millionaires out of many European players. But for Jean-Marc Bosman the litigation did not pay. He was left heavily in debt and, with his professional career over and his marriage in tatters, he moved back in with his parents.[222] In early 1997 some of the world's top players planned a testimonial for him in Barcelona. However, the Spanish FA and FIFA objected to the match, blaming Bosman for the large number of foreign players in the Spanish league.[223] The match did eventually go ahead but Bosman's name could not be officially connected with the event.[224] An out-of-court settlement of £312,000[225]

---

[217] Case T–313/02 *Meca-Medina and Majcen* v. *Commission* [2004] ECR II–3291.

[218] Case C–519/04P [2006] ECR I–6991. E.Szyszczak, 'Competition and sport' (2007) 32 *ELRev*. 95.

[219] Para. 57.

[220] S. Weatherill, 'Anti-doping revisited: The demise of the rule of "purely sporting interest"' [2006] *ECLR* 645.

[221] The *Bosman* ruling also applied to those players from states which had trade agreements with the EU: see, e.g., the case of the Polish basketball player Lilia Malaja who wished to move to France and the Russian football player Valery Karpin who wished to play in Spain, discussed by D. McAuley, 'They think it's all over... it might just be for now: Unravelling the ramifications for the European transfer system post-*Bosman*' (2002) 23 *ECLR* 331. See also Case C–264/98 *Balog* v. *ASBL Royal Charleroi*, removed from the register on 2 Apr. 2001.

[222] J. Northcroft, 'The abandoned pioneer', *Scotland on Sunday*, 15 Sep. 1996, 25. A. Dunn, 'Jean-Marc's the Boss Man: His fight for freedom was worth fortune to football stars', *The People*, 2 Jan. 2000, 54. On the ripple effect of the *Bosman* ruling on Eastern European players, see M. Butcher, 'Football: Transfer barriers come down and nationwide league action: Here come the Latvians', *Observer*, 3 Dec. 2000, 10.

[223] J. Webster, 'Spanish ire over Bosman fundraiser', *The European*, 20 Feb. 1997, 15; B. Oliver, 'Sport around the world: Bosman out in the cold in Spain', *Daily Telegraph*, 1 Mar. 1997, 18. See also D. Campbell, '"Foreigners killing football": UEFA chief's call for firm action against "global teams" at big clubs', *Observer*, 11 Mar. 2001, 1.

[224] B. Sutherland, 'Stars turn out for Bosman', *The Herald*, 28 Apr. 1997; J. Culley, 'Bosman reaps belated reward', *Independent*, 28 Apr. 1997.

[225] *Independent*, 23 Dec. 1998, 20, cited in Weatherill (2000) 25 *ELRev*. 282, 283. See also the essays on *Bosman* in M. Poiares Maduro and L. Azoulai (eds), *The Past and Future of EU Law* (Oxford: Hart Publishing, 2010).

was finally paid by the Belgian football authorities in December 1998—more than eight years after the expiry of his contract.

On a more positive note, the formula given by the Court in *Bosman* provided the framework for the football industry to negotiate new transfer rules. A breakthrough came in 2001[226] when rules were agreed by UEFA, FIFA, and the Commission which *inter alia* provided for:

- a system of training compensation to encourage and reward the training effort of clubs, in particular small clubs, for players aged under 23

- the creation of solidarity mechanisms redistributing a significant proportion of income to clubs involved in the training and education of a player, including amateur clubs

- the creation of one transfer period per season, and a further limited mid-season window, with a limit of one transfer per player per season

- minimum and maximum duration of contracts of respectively one and five years.

## 4. GOING BEYOND THE DISCRIMINATION MODEL

### 4.1 The Market Access Approach: Restrictions Liable to Prohibit, Impede, or Render Less Attractive Free Movement

So far we have concentrated on the fact that Articles 45, 49, 56 (and 21) prohibit discrimination on the ground of nationality. In cases such as *Alpine* and *Bosman* we have also seen how the Court has brought non-discriminatory national measures within the scope of the Treaties where they prevented or substantially hindered access to the market. These cases, decided in the mid 1990s, were indicative of a more general change of approach by the Court away from a three-stage discrimination analysis ((1) identifying a comparator group (this stage is often overlooked in practice except in tax cases); (2) classifying the measure as, e.g., directly or indirectly discriminatory and so finding a breach; and (3) examining justification/proportionality) towards a two-stage analysis based on market access ((1) identifying a restriction and thus a breach; and (2) examining justification/proportionality). This shift from a discrimination approach to a restriction approach can be traced back to *Säger*[227] where the Court said that Article 56 required:

*not only* the elimination of all discrimination against a person providing services on the ground of his nationality *but also* the abolition of any restriction, even if it applies without distinction to national providers of services and to those of other Member States, when *it is liable to prohibit or otherwise impede* the activities of a provider of services established in another Member State where he lawfully provides similar services.

The Court continued that any such restriction could be justified by imperative reasons relating to the public interest.[228]

---

[226] IP/01/314, 6 Mar. 2001.      [227] Case C–76/90 [1991] ECR I–4221, para. 12, emphasis added.
[228] Para. 15.

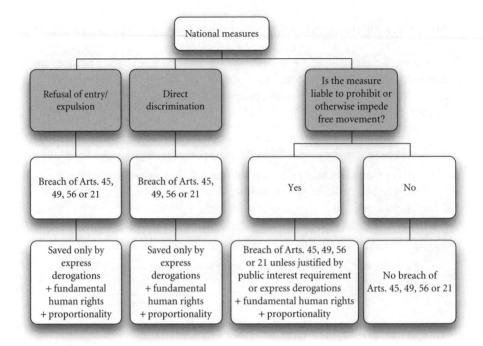

**Fig. 8.4** The *Säger* market access approach

*Säger* demonstrated a greater willingness by the Court to scrutinize national rules which, even potentially ('liable to'), prohibit, impede or restrict the individual's right to free movement. The Court is therefore making a more significant incursion into national regulatory autonomy than under its pure discrimination approach: unless Member States can justify their conduct, a national rule which is liable to prohibit or otherwise impede free movement will breach Union law, even if it does not discriminate against nationals.

The facts of *Kraus*[229] illustrate the importance of the change signalled by *Säger*. Kraus, a German student, complained that he was not allowed to use his British LLM title in Germany without prior authorization from the German authorities. If he had obtained an academic diploma from a German university, no such authorization would have been required. *Kraus* therefore concerned discrimination—not on the grounds of nationality (after all, Kraus was German)—but rather on the grounds that he had received training in another Member State which disadvantaged him when he returned to his country of origin (Germany).[230] Thus, he suffered discrimination based on the fact that he had exercised his rights of free movement and received some of his education in another Member State.[231] Focusing on the obstacles to free movement created by the German

---

[229] Case C–19/92 [1993] ECR I–1663. See also Case C–279/00 *Commission v. Italy (temp agencies)* [2002] ECR I–1425.

[230] See also Case C–370/90 *Surinder Singh* [1992] ECR I–4265, para. 23.

[231] See also Case C–224/98 *D'Hoop* v. *Office national de l'emploi* [2002] ECR I–6191, para. 34, where the Court said that by linking the grant of tideover allowances to the condition of having obtained the required diploma in Belgium, Belgian law thus '*places at a disadvantage certain of its nationals simply because they*

rule rather than on any discrimination, the Court said that Articles 45 and 56 precluded any national measure governing the conditions under which an academic title obtained in another Member State could be used, where that measure, even though applicable without discrimination on grounds of nationality (i.e., non-discriminatory), was '*liable to hamper or to render less attractive* the exercise by Union nationals, including those of the Member State which enacted the measure, of *fundamental freedoms* guaranteed by the [Treaties]'.[232] The Court then considered whether this national rule could be justi-fied. According to the Court it was legitimate for Germany to impose the restriction on the ground of 'the need to protect a public which will not necessarily be alerted to abuse of academic titles'.[233] It then considered the proportionality of the rule and, as with its more recent case law on goods, emphasized the need for good governance and fair pro-cedures to be applied.[234]

The *Kraus* judgment, focusing on the question of hindrance to the exercise of one of the fundamental freedoms rather than on discrimination, was not in any way an isolated decision. Its formulation has been more or less repeated in similar terms in numerous subsequent cases.[235] For example, in *Gebhard*,[236] a German national authorized to prac-tise as a '*Rechtsanwalt*' in Germany, opened chambers in Milan where he described him-self as '*avvocato*' without previously having registered with the Milan Bar as required by national law. The Court said that 'national measures liable to hinder or make less attrac-tive the *exercise* of *fundamental freedoms*' breached Article 49,[237] unless they could be justified by the general good, such as for reasons relating to organization, qualifications, professional ethics, supervision, and liability.[238]

At a push, the measures in both *Kraus* and *Gebhard* could have been considered indirectly discriminatory on the grounds of nationality: the requirement for the qual-ification to be authorized prior to use (*Kraus*) and to be registered with the Milan Bar before using the title '*avvocato*' (*Gebhard*) might have had a disparate impact on migrants.[239] The measure in *Kraus* could even have been considered directly discrimi-natory because only qualifications obtained in other Member States needed prior authorization.[240] Yet, in *Kraus*, *Gebhard*, and the subsequent case law the Court did not go down either route. This was probably sensible since it would have required an unnecessarily broad reading of the terms direct or indirect discrimination. Instead, the Court focused on the more general question of whether the measure was liable to prevent or hinder access to the market or exercise of the freedom and, finding it was,

---

*have exercised their freedom to move* in order to pursue education in another Member State' (considered fur-ther in Ch. 15). See Poiares Maduro AG's Opinion in Joined Cases C–158/04 and C–159/04 *Alfa Vita* [2006] ECR I–8135, para. 46 where he thought the test that applied to all Treaty provisions was 'discrimination against the exercise of freedom of movement'.

[232] Para. 32, emphasis added.      [233] Para. 35.      [234] Para. 42. See further Ch. 13.

[235] See, e.g., Joined Cases C–369 and 376/96 *Arblade, Leloup and Sofrage SARL* [1999] ECR I–8453, para. 33, Case C–3/95 *Sandker* [1996] ECR I–6511, para. 25.      [236] Case C–55/94 [1995] ECR I–4165.

[237] Para. 37.      [238] Para. 35.

[239] This was the approach adopted in Case C–281/98 *Angonese* [2000] ECR I–4139, paras. 40–6.

[240] However, this would have been discrimination based on the place where the service was provided and not on the nationality of the claimant: Case C–158/96 *Kohll* [1998] ECR I–1931, para. 33. See also Case C–55/98 *Skatteministeriet* v. *Bent Vestergaard* [1999] ECR I–7641, para. 22. These cases are considered fur-ther in Ch. 11.

required the measure to be justified. The Court's stance in these cases is sometimes referred to as its 'market access' approach (a phrase broad enough to include *exercise* of market freedoms, as *Gebhard* shows[241]), an approach it now applies not only to free movement of services and freedom of establishment but also to the free movement of workers,[242] free movement of citizens,[243] and, as we shall see in Chapter 15, free movement of capital.[244]

Perhaps because of the cumbersome language involved and the unsuitability of applying the language of 'market access' to certain groups—such as retired migrant citizens who have moved to another state—the Court has, in more recent cases, replaced the *Säger/Kraus/Gebhard* 'market access' formula in favour of the simpler wording, examining whether the national measure constitutes a 'restriction' on, or an 'obstacle' to, free movement (see fig. 8.5). The language of 'restrictions' reflects the text of Articles 49[245] and 56;[246]

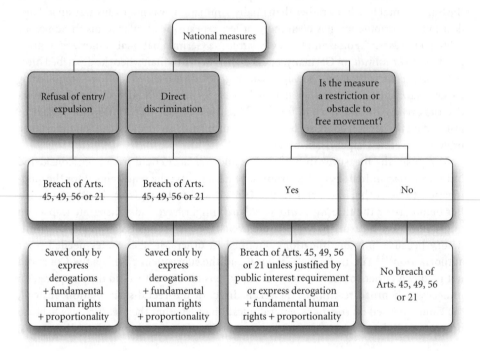

**Fig. 8.5** The restriction/obstacle approach

---

[241] In *Kraus* the Court said: 'the situation of a Union national who holds a postgraduate academic title which, obtained in another Member State, facilitates *access* to a profession or, at least, the *pursuit* of an economic activity, is governed by [Union] law' (para. 23, emphasis added).

[242] Case C–464/02 *Commission* v. *Denmark (company vehicles)* [2005] ECR I–7929, para. [45] (emphasis added).

[243] Case C–192/05 *Tas-Hagen* v. *Raadskamer WUBO van de Pensioen- en Uitkeringsrad* [2006] ECR I–10451, paras. 30–1.

[244] Case C–367/98 *Commission* v. *Portugal* [2002] ECR I–4731, paras. 44–5.

[245] See, e.g., Case C–250/95 *Futura Particpations SA* [1997] ECR I–2471; Case C–446/03 *Marks & Spencer* v. *Halsey* [2005] ECR I–10837, para. 34.

[246] See, e.g., Case C–255/04 *Commission* v. *France (performing artists)* [2006] ECR I–5251, para. 38.

the language of 'obstacles' reflects the original Article 3 EEC. Both terms are synonymous with the 'market access' test.[247]

Where the obstacle is created by the home state (state of origin) the Court sometimes uses a different formula, a formula based on disadvantages. This can be seen in *Kranemann*[248] concerning a German rule which provided that trainees who did their practical legal training in Germany were entitled to reimbursement of all their travel expenses, whatever the distance between their home and their place of training, but those who did their training in another Member State had to pay themselves for the part of the journey outside Germany. The Court said:

[T]he Treaty provisions relating to freedom of movement for persons…preclude measures which might place [Union] nationals at a disadvantage when they wish to pursue an economic activity[249] in the territory of another Member State…[250]

The Court continued that the German rule therefore constituted 'an obstacle' to the free movement of workers even if applied without regard to the nationality of the workers concerned.[251] Further, the rule could not be justified: aims of a purely economic nature could not constitute pressing reasons of public interest justifying a restriction on the fundamental freedom.[252]

### 4.2  Problems with the Restrictions Formula

As we have seen, there is little to choose between the *Säger* formula and that based on obstacles, and in cases such as *Kraus, Schindler,* and *Kranemann* the Court used both.[253]

---

[247] See, e.g., Joined Cases C–147/06 and C–148/06 *SECAP SpA* v. *Comune di Torino* [2008] ECR I–3565, para. 28: 'the automatic exclusion of abnormally low tenders to contracts of certain cross-border interest could deprive economic operators from other Member States of the opportunity of competing more effectively with operators located in the Member State in question and thereby *affect their access to the market in that State*, thus *impeding the exercise* of freedom of establishment and freedom to provide services, which constitutes a *restriction* on those freedoms'. See also Case C–190/98 *Graf* [2000] ECR I–493, para. 23: 'in order to be capable of constituting such an *obstacle*, [the provisions] must affect *access of workers to the labour market*'.

[248] Case C–109/04 *Kranemann* v. *Land Nordrhein-Westfalen* [2005] ECR I–2421, para. 25. See also Case C–232/01 *Van Lent* [2003] ECR I–11525, para. 15; Case C–345/05 *Commission* v. *Portugal (transfer of property)* [2006] ECR I–10633, paras. 20–2; Case C–192/05 *Tas-Hagen* [2006] ECR I–10451, paras. 30–1.

[249] E. Spaventa, *Free Movement of Persons in the EU: Barriers to movement and their constitutional context* (Hague: Kluwer, 2007), Ch. 7 argues that use of this language shows that the Court is actually developing a more general right not just to free movement but to 'exercise an economic activity in another Member State', a view supported by Case C–464/02 *Commission* v. *Denmark (Company Cars)* [2005] ECR I–7929, para. 34 where the Court declared that 'The provisions of the [Treaties] on freedom of movement for persons are intended to facilitate the pursuit by [Union] citizens of occupational activities of all kinds throughout the [Union].'

[250] Para. 25. In the context of services the rule may be phrased rather differently: Case C–17/00 *De Coster* v. *Collège des bourgmestre et échevins de Watermael-Boitsfort* [2001] ECR I–9445, para. 30: 'Article [56 TFEU] precludes the application of any national rules which have the effect of making the provision of services between Member States more difficult than the provision of services purely within one Member State.'

[251] Para. 26. For a similar approach in an establishment case, see Joined Cases C–151/04 and C–152/04 *Nadin* [2005] ECR I–11203, para. 34.

[252] Para. 34.

[253] Cf. paras. 28 and 32 in Case C–19/92 *Kraus* [1993] ECR I–1663 and paras. 43 and 45 in Case C–275/92 *Schindler* [1994] ECR I–1039. See also Case C–118/96 *Safir* [1998] ECR I–1897, paras. 23 and 25; Case C–79/01 *Payroll Data Services* [2002] ECR I–8923, paras. 26–7.

Both formulas raise problems. First, the meaning of the individual terms 'hindrance', 'obstacles', and 'restrictions'[254] is far from clear. Take, for example, the case of *Carpenter*. What was the obstacle which 'deterred' Mr Carpenter from exercising his freedom to provide cross-border services—the separation of husband and wife which would be 'detrimental to their family life',[255] the potential loss of child care,[256] or the emotional distress involved? Such cases come very close to saying the mere existence of a national rule constitutes a restriction. [257]

Secondly, the market access/restrictions approach makes no reference to the size or scale of the impediment: it is sufficient that there is an impediment or restriction or there is liable to be one.[258] While *Graf* would indicate that there needs to be more than a remote impediment to the free movement of persons to trigger an application of the Treaties, a view that appears to be enjoying support in some recent cases,[259] in most cases it still takes very little to engage the Treaties. For example, in *Bosal*[260] the Court found a breach of Article 49 due to its assessment that the Dutch tax rule 'might dissuade' a parent company from carrying on its activities through the intermediary of a subsidiary established in another Member State. This decision cost the Dutch treasury millions.

Once the Court finds the Treaties apply, the defendant (usually the Member State but not always) can of course, justify their national rules. However, where the national rules concern social policy the Court is forced to make difficult—and often political—decisions about the legitimacy and proportionality of these policy choices when it lacks the institutional capacity to gather and process the relevant economic/social/cultural information. This is the third problem with the restrictions approach, problems demonstrated by the Court's decision in *Viking*.[261]

In order to make costs savings, Viking, a Finnish company, wanted to reflag its vessel in Estonia. In response, the Finnish seamen's union (FSU) called their members out on strike. The Court found that the trade union's proposed strike action was a restriction on Viking's freedom of establishment. In its defence, the trade union argued that the strike was justified on the ground of worker protection, a position that the Court in

---

[254] Case C–464/02 *Commission v. Denmark (company vehicles)* [2005] ECR I–7929, para. 52; cf. paras. 35–7, where the emphasis is on 'obstacles'.                                                                          [255] Para. 39.

[256] Para. 44.

[257] See, e.g., Case C–98/01 *Commission v. UK (BAA)* [2003] ECR I–4641 considered in Ch. 15.

[258] Case C–49/89 *Corsica Ferries* [1989] ECR I–4441, para. 8: 'the Articles of the [TFEU] concerning the free movement of goods, persons, services and capital are fundamental [Union] provisions and any restriction, even minor, of that freedom is prohibited', a view repeated in Case C–212/06 *Walloon Government* [2008] ECR I–1683 para. 52.

[259] See, e.g., Case C–500/06 *Corporación Dermoestética* [2008] ECR I–5785, para. 33 where the Court said that a ban on national television advertising of medical and surgical treatments constituted a 'serious obstacle' to freedom of establishment and free movement of services; and in Case C–518/06 *Commission v. Italy (motor insurance)* [2009] ECR I–000, para. 66 the Court said that an obligation to contract constitutes a 'substantial interference in the freedom of contract'. As we saw above, in earlier cases the Court was more interested in the directness of the impediment rather than its significance: Case C–384/93 *Alpine Investments* [1995] ECR I–1141, para. 38 and Case C–415/93 *Bosman* [1995] ECR I–4921, para. 103. See H. Toner, 'Non-discriminatory obstacles to the exercise of Treaty rights: Articles 39, 43, 49, and 18 EC' (2004) 23 *YEL* 275, 285–6 who argues that there are two possible thresholds: direct *or* significant. If the obstacle is direct then its effect needs only be perceptible; if the measure is significant or substantial then the obstacle does not need to be direct.

[260] Case C–168/01 *Bosal Holding BV v. Staatssecretaris van Financiën* [2003] ECR I–9409.

[261] Case C–438/05 [2007] ECR I–10779.

principle accepted.[262] However, it then went on to curtail the circumstances in which that argument could be raised:

[E]ven if that action—aimed at protecting the *jobs and conditions of employment* of the members of that union *liable to be adversely affected* by the reflagging of the *Rosella*—could reasonably be considered to fall, at first sight, within the objective of protecting workers, such a view would no longer be tenable if it were established that the jobs or conditions of employment at issue were not jeopardised or under serious threat.[263]

The Court also gave a narrow reading to the proportionality principle. When considering the necessity limb of the proportionality test, the Court said that industrial action should be the last resort; and that national courts would have to verify whether the union had exhausted all other avenues under Finnish law before the industrial action was found proportionate. In reaching this conclusion the Court, apparently unwittingly, trampled over a range of social values. For example, it ignored the fact that the strike action was protected by the Finnish constitution; it seemed unaware that the criteria it prescribed for taking strike action (jobs and conditions of employment are under serious threat) limits the possibility of taking industrial action even in the UK where national laws are already strict; and it certainly rules out political strikes which are protected by various national systems.

Yet in other cases involving cultural issues the Court has taken a sensitive—and deferential—approach to the national rules. Consider, for example, *United Pan Europe Communications*,[264] a case decided at much the same time as *Viking*. In order to safeguard the pluralistic and cultural range of programmes on television networks, Belgium law required cable operators to broadcast certain television programmes which had 'must-carry' status transmitted by certain broadcasters in the French and Flemish communities. The Court said that a must-carry regime directly determined the conditions for access to the market for services, by requiring foreign providers to negotiate the conditions for access to the network, an obligation not imposed on the providers of services having must-carry status (primarily national providers). The legislation therefore breached Article 56 but could be justified on the grounds of cultural policy (safeguarding, in the audiovisual sector, the freedom of expression of the different social, cultural, religious, philosophical or linguistic components which exist in that region). On the question of proportionality, the Court said that the legislation was suitable (having regard to the bilingual nature of the Brussels-Capital region). On the question of necessity, the Court recognized a wide margin of discretion in the Member States but laid down certain conditions of good governance.[265] While many would laud this deference to the Member States, the Court's apparently diverging case law on justifications and proportionality generates considerable uncertainty and unpredictability.

---

[262]  *Viking*, para 77.

[263]  Ibid., para 81. This is a reference to the fact that Viking, presumably on good advice, had given an undertaking that neither it nor companies in the same group would 'by reason of the reflagging terminate the employment of any person employed by them'.

[264]  Case C–250/06 *United Pan-Europe Communications Belgium SA* v. *Etat belge* [2007] ECR I–11135.

[265]  Namely the award of must-carry status must first of all be subject to a transparent procedure based on criteria known by broadcasters in advance, it must be based on objective criteria which are suitable for securing pluralism and the criteria on the basis of which must-carry status is awarded must be non-discriminatory.

Fourthly, the shift away from a model focused on removing *discriminatory* obstacles to free movement to one based on removing any obstacles or restrictions to free movement paves the way for opportunistic challenges to a whole variety of national laws never intended to interfere with free movement. Take for example, the 70 mph speed limit on British motorways. A German tourist, probably in defence to a prosecution for speeding, might argue that the speed limit is a restriction on his freedom to receive services (as a tourist) under Article 56. Under the non-discrimination model such arguments would automatically fail because speed limits apply equally to nationals and migrants alike.[266] Under the market access approach, however, it is possible to see how such arguments might run and a breach of Article 56 might be found. Speed limits can of course be justified on the grounds of public safety.[267] But the problem lies with proportionality. While setting a speed limit might be a suitable means of achieving the public-safety objective, it is not obvious that a 70 mph limit is no more restrictive than necessary to achieve that objective (why not 69, 68 or 71 or 72 mph?).[268]

In the field of taxation the problem is even more acute. An Irish entrepreneur might argue that the higher rate of corporate tax in the UK deters him from establishing himself in the UK in breach of Article 49 (even though the tax rates apply equally to the British entrepreneurs). Now the principal reason for taxation is to raise revenue for national exchequers. However, as we have already seen in Chapter 6, economic arguments, such as the loss of tax revenue[269] or the cost to the national exchequer,[270] are not accepted as justifications and so the British tax rule might be considered unlawful.

Fifthly, and perhaps most fundamentally, as we noted in Chapter 1, the Treaties are based on an (ill-defined) model of competitive federalism: states are free to enact laws which respond to local choices but the free movement provisions of the Treaties put those laws into competition. Yet, the restrictions model threatens to jeopardize these very choices. As Johnston and Syrpis put it,[271] 'the Court has yet to develop a nuanced account of the circumstances under which regulatory diversity poses an obstacle to market integration'.

The problems with the restrictions model were noted by Advocate General Tizzano in his influential opinion in *Caixa-Bank*.[272] He expressed profound misgivings about the 'rather broad concept of restriction' in the case law covering all 'national measures *liable to hinder or make less attractive the exercise of fundamental freedoms* guaranteed by the [Treaties]'.[273] He said that such a broad approach to 'restrictions' allows economic opera-

---

[266] This point was recognized, albeit rather obliquely, in the 9th recital of the Services Dir. 2006/123 which is considered in detail in Ch. 11.

[267] Case C–55/93 *Criminal Proceedings against van Schaik* [1994] ECR I–4837; Joined Cases C–151/04 and C–152/04 *Nadin* [2005] ECR I–11203, para. 49.

[268] Cf Case C–110/05 *Commission v. Italy (Italian trailers)* [2009] ECR I–519, para. 67, 'Member States cannot be denied the possibility of attaining an objective such as road safety by the introduction of general and simple rules which will be easily understood and applied by drivers and easily managed and supervised by the competent authorities.'

[269] Case C–464/02 *Commission v. Denmark (company vehicles)* [2005] ECR I–7929, para. 45, citing the free movement of capital decision in Case C–319/02 *Manninen* [2004] ECR I–7477, para. 49.

[270] Case C–109/04 *Kranemann v. Land Nordrhein-Westfalen* [2005] ECR I–2421.

[271] A. Johnston and P. Syrpis, 'Regulatory competition in European company law after *Cartesio*' (2009) 34 *ELRev.* 378, 379.   [272] Case C–442/02 *Caixa-Bank* [2004] ECR I–8961.

[273] [278] Para. 39, emphasis in the original, criticizing, in particular, Case C–255/97 *Pfeiffer Großhandel* [1999] ECR I–2835.

tors, both national and foreign, to abuse Article 49 in order to oppose any national measure that, solely because it regulated the conditions for pursuing an economic activity,
could in the final analysis narrow profit margins and hence reduce the attractiveness
of pursuing that particular economic activity.[274] Echoing the sentiments expressed by
Advocate General Tesauro in his important opinion in the goods case *Hünermund*,[275] he
continued:[276]

> However, that would be tantamount to bending the [Treaties] to a purpose for which it was
> not intended: that is to say, not in order to create an internal market in which conditions are
> similar to those of a single market and where operators can move freely, but in order to estab
> lish a market without rules. Or rather, a market in which rules are prohibited as a matter of
> principle, except for those necessary and proportionate to meeting imperative requirements
> in the public interest.

He therefore advocated a return to a non-discrimination + market access approach[277]
(fig. 8.3): where the principle of non-discrimination is respected, a national measure
cannot be described as a restriction on the freedom of movement of persons unless the
measure 'directly affects market access'. He added that this approach makes it possible to
reconcile the objective of merging the different national markets into a single common
market with the continuation of Member States' general powers to regulate economic
activities.[278] Such an approach also resonates with the presumptions in the certain selling
arrangements case law (*Keck/De Agostini*): non-discriminatory restrictions do not breach
the Treaty *unless* it can be shown they interfere with market access.

## 5. TAXATION AND A REVERSION TO THE DISCRIMINATION MODEL?

Advocate General Tizzano's views marked something of a sea change in the Court's
approach, at least in the field of taxation where the Court is showing signs of retreating from its rigorous application of the market access approach.[279] This can be seen in
*Viacom II*.[280] At issue was a dispute between Giotto, a French estate agent, and Viacom,
an Italian bill-posting company employed to put up posters in the Italian town of Genoa
advertising Giotto's services. Giotto refused to reimburse Viacom for the sum of €226.92
paid to the Genoa authorities by way of an advertising tax on the grounds that the tax
contravened Article 56 TFEU. The Court began by citing the *Säger* formula[281] but then
noted the non-discriminatory nature of the tax: the rules on the levying of this tax did

---

[274] Para. 62. The Court itself acknowledged this in Case C–290/04 *FKP Scorpio* [2006] ECR I–9641, para.
46: 'the application of the host Member State's national rules to providers of services is liable to prohibit,
impede or render less attractive the provision of services to the extent that it involves expense and additional
administrative and economic burdens'.

[275] Case C–292/92 *Hünermund* [1993] ECR I–6787, para. 1 which led to the ruling in *Keck*, considered
further in Ch. 5.    [276] Para. 63.

[277] Para. 66.    [278] Para. 68.

[279] K. Banks, 'The application of the fundamental freedoms to Member State tax measures: Guarding
against protectionism or second-guessing national policy choices' (2008) 33 *ELRev.* 482, 504. See also
J. Snell, 'Non-discriminatory tax obstacles in Community law' (2007) 56 *ICLQ* 339.

[280] Case C–134/03 [2005] ECR I–1167. For further examples, see Case C–387/01 *Weigel v. Finanzlandes
direction für Vorarlberg* [2004] ECR I–4981, considered in Ch. 9, and Joined Cases C–544/03 and C–545/03
*Mobistar SA v. Commune de Fleron* [2005] ECR I–7723 considered in Ch. 11. See also Case C–453/04
*Innoventif* [2006] ECR I–4929 considered in Ch. 10 in respect of other charges.    [281] Para. 35.

not 'draw any distinction based on the place of establishment of the provider or recipient of the bill-posting services or on the place of origin of the goods or services that form the subject-matter of the advertising messages disseminated'.[282] The Court then added that because the tax was applied only to outdoor advertising activities involving the use of public space administered by the municipal authorities and its amount was fixed at a level which might be considered 'modest in relation to the value of the services provided which are subject to it',[283] the levying of the tax was not liable to prohibit or impede the provisions of services. It therefore did not breach Article 56. In other words, the tax regime was non-discriminatory and did not create a substantial impediment to the free movement of services.

Given that the Court has often relied on the non-discrimination model in respect of individual taxation, perhaps *Viacom II* is not so remarkable. It bears the hallmarks of the cases decided under Article 110 TFEU (ex Article 90 EC)[284] where the Court has long respected the principle of national fiscal autonomy and the territoriality of fiscal regimes, allowing Member States to tax (goods in the context of Article 110, the activity in the persons cases) as they choose, provided the tax does not discriminate on the grounds of origin and the effects of the tax are not protective.[285] However, as Banks shows,[286] the Court is far from consistent: a year after the *Viacom* line of cases, the Court made no mention of the discrimination analysis in other tax cases such as *Commission* v. *Belgium*[287] and *Commission* v. *Finland*.[288] Yet, she argues subsequent Grand Chamber decisions, notably *ACT Group Litigation*[289] and *FII Litigation*,[290] 'indicate a definite resurgence in discrimination reasoning in tax cases'.

# D.  CONCLUSIONS

The case law on free movement of persons ranges from the personal (as in *Carpenter*, where deportation risked breaking up the family unit) to the commercial (provision of TV signals by large companies). While common principles apply across this spectrum, the Court has adapted the principles to take account of the subject matter. In particular, the Court has in recent years used the principle of citizenship of the Union to shape the case law relating to these 'personal' cases, often prioritizing the protection of fundamental human rights.

The most important development in the case law is the shift from the discrimination model towards one based on market access. From the perspective of market integration, this is clearly an important development. However, by focusing on market access through the restrictions/obstacles approach, the Court has made an important policy shift away from respecting the autonomy of the Member States and the integrity of their rules (the

---

[282] Para. 37.        [283] Para. 38.

[284] Art. 110 was also considered in *Weigel*; in *Viacom II* Kokott AG referred to the Art. 110 case law. In Case C–313/05 *Brzezinski* v. *Dyrekto Izby Celnej W. Warszaure* [2007] ECR I–513, para. 28, on Article 110, the Court cited *Weigel*.                                                        [285] See further Ch. 3.

[286] K. Banks, above n. 279.

[287] Case C–433/04 *Commission* v. *Belgium (tax fraud)* [2006] ECR I–10653.

[288] Case C–232/03 *Commission* v. *Finland* [2006] ECR I–27.

[289] Case C–374/04 *Test Claimants in Class IV of the ACT Group Litigation* [2006] ECR I–11673.

[290] Case C–446/04 *Test Claimants in the FII Group Litigation* [2006] ECR I–11753.

effect of the non-discrimination model) towards greater Union intervention (the market access model). The result may well be deregulatory if a national rule is found to obstruct trade and no Union norm is put in its place. To avoid this outcome and to protect some state autonomy, the Court needs to be willing to interpret and apply the public-interest requirements broadly. This has not always been the case.

We turn now to consider the detailed rules in respect of workers, establishment, services, citizenship, and TCNs. We begin by examining the rules on workers.

# 9

# FREE MOVEMENT OF WORKERS

## A. INTRODUCTION

Article 45 TFEU (ex Article 39 EC) gives workers the right to move freely across the EU to seek and take up employment in another Member State on the same terms as nationals. The idea behind Article 45 was to enable workers from states with high levels of unemployment to move to other states where there was a demand for jobs. In the host state the migrant worker could find a job, probably benefit from higher wages than in their home state, and provide the skills needed by the host state. Furthermore, the principle of free movement meant that employers had a larger potential pool of workers from which to draw, and the principle of non-discrimination meant that employers selected candidates based on merit, not nationality. At least, this was the theory. In practice workers—at least those from the original Member States—often preferred to stay (unemployed) in a state they were familiar with, in the company of family and friends.

However, this was not the experience with workers from the EU-10[1]—the states which joined the EU in 2004—particularly those from the EU-8 who were keen to take advantage of free movement rights. The Accession Treaties made provision for transitional arrangements which allowed the 'old' Member States to decide whether they would permit free movement of workers (but not the self-employed or other categories of EU citizens) based on the '2+3+2' formula. This scheme obliged the Member States to declare in 2006, and again three years later in May 2009, whether they would open up their labour markets for workers from the Accession States. Any remaining restrictions end on 30 April 2011. A similar '2+3+2' scheme is in place in respect of workers from Romania and Bulgaria, which joined the EU on 1 January 2007. For these workers the restrictions will end on 31 December 2013.[2]

All the Member States, except Ireland, Sweden, and the UK, initially imposed labour-market restrictions on those coming from the EU-8 in 2004,[3] largely out of fear of benefit tourism and that an influx of 'cheap' Eastern European labour would displace local labour and drive down wages. However, according to the Commission, these fears have not been borne out: 'Practically all available research finds little impact of

---

[1] Poland, Lithuania, Latvia, Estonia, the Czech Republic, Slovakia, Hungary, and Slovenia (EU-8)—the former Eastern bloc countries—plus Cyprus and Malta.

[2] For country specific detail, see <http://www.ec.europa.eu/social/main.jsp?catId=466&langId=en>.

[3] For a summary, see Commission, 'The impact of free movement of workers in the context of EU enlargement', COM(2008) 765, 5.

post-enlargement labour mobility on wages and employment of local workers and no indication of serious labour market imbalances through intra-EU mobility, even in those Member States with the biggest inflows.'[4]

The UK is one such country. Its open-borders policy led to an estimated labour immigration of 450,000 to 600,000 within the two-and-a-half years following the May 2004 enlargement, significantly more migrants than had been expected.[5] Yet, the Commission observes that recent migration has had only a 'negligible or positive effect' on public finances and the welfare state (including its financing), citing data for the UK which shows that only a very small number of EU-8 nationals claim tax-funded benefits or housing support, although migration has created pressure on the provision of education, housing and health care services at the local level. And, since the economic downturn, there has been a 'substantial reduction in new entries and a parallel increase in return migration, prompting the Commission to conclude that free labour mobility provides a much needed flexibility in both directions: workers come when there is demand for labour and many leave again when employment conditions become less favourable.[6] Moreover, consistent with the objectives of the original drafters of the Treaties, the Commission has found that mobility by workers from the new Member States has had 'a clearly positive impact on economic growth in the EU', with one study suggesting that additional mobility from the EU-8 during the 2004–7 period boosted the aggregate GDP of the enlarged EU by about 0.17 per cent in the short-term and 0.28 per cent in the long run.[7]

Migration from the Eastern European countries was largely prompted by the significant wage differentials between the old and the new Member States. This was not the case with the original Member States which might help to explain why migration levels were low. The Union responded to this problem by adopting a series of measures giving rights not only to workers but also their families in an attempt to encourage them to move. Most notable in this respect was Regulation 1612/68. The legislature's approach was reinforced by judicial intervention. The Court has been instrumental in helping to secure the free movement of workers, by removing obstacles which impeded free movement and then by finding ways to ensure that workers and their families became integrated into the host state. And with these developments came a change in perspective. Workers were no longer simply viewed as factors of production needed to fulfil the objectives of the common market. Now they were seen as EU citizens with rights enforceable against the host state. Ultimately, this led to the adoption of the Citizens' Rights Directive (CRD) 2004/38 which gave rights not only to migrant workers and the self-employed but also to a range of other migrant citizens. This directive is discussed in detail in Chapter 12. In this chapter we focus on the rights given to workers, principally by the Treaties but also by Regulation 1612/68, some of which has not been repealed by the CRD. We begin by examining the fundamental question: who is a worker?

---

[4] Ibid., 12.

[5] For this reason, the UK and Ireland did not extend this liberal policy to Bulgarian and Romanian labour when these countries acceded to the EU in 2007.

[6] Commission, 'The impact of free movement of workers in the context of EU enlargement' COM(2008) 765, 9.

[7] Ibid., 11–12.

# B. THE DEFINITION OF A 'WORKER'

## 1. THE UNION DEFINITION

Although there is no definition of the term 'worker' in the Treaties, the Court has insisted that it be given a broad Union meaning, based on objective criteria to ensure uniform inter-pretation across the Member States.[8] In essence, where Union nationals are in a relation-ship of subordination—i.e., they are under the control of the employer—they are workers. As the Court put it in *Lawrie-Blum*,[9] the essential feature of an employment relationship is that 'for a certain period of time a person performs services for and under the direc-tion of another person in return for which he receives remuneration'. The national court must decide whether a relationship of subordination exists.[10] The sphere of employment[11] and the nature of the legal relationship between employer and employee (whether or not it involves public law status or a private law contract)[12] are immaterial. On the facts of *Lawrie-Blum* the Court found that a trainee teacher was a worker for the purpose of Article 45(1).

The worker must also be engaged in a 'genuine and effective' economic activity within the meaning of Article 2 EC (repealed by the Lisbon Treaty but much of the substance is repeated in Article 3 TEU). While most activities satisfy this requirement[13]—including playing professional football,[14] being a prostitute,[15] doing an apprenticeship,[16] and other types of training[17]—this may not always be the case. For example, work as part of a com-munity-based religion might not constitute an economic activity. This was at issue in *Steymann*[18] where a plumber worked for a Bhagwan community as part of its commercial activities. On the facts, the Court considered that since the community looked after his material needs and paid him pocket money this might constitute an indirect *quid pro quo* for genuine and effective work, and so Steymann could be considered a worker. On the

---

[8] See Case 75/63 *Unger v. Bestuur der Bedrijfsvereniging voor Detail handel en Ambachten* [1964] ECR 1977; Case 53/81 *Levin v. Staatssecretaris van Justitie* [1982] ECR 1035; paras. 11–12; Case 139/85 *Kempf v. Staatssecretaris van Justitie* [1986] ECR 1741, para. 15; Case 66/85 *Lawrie-Blum v. Land Baden-Württemberg* [1986] ECR 2121, para. 16. An earlier version of parts of this chapter first appeared in C. Barnard, *EC Employment Law*, 3rd edn (Oxford: OUP, 2006), Ch. 4.

[9] Case 66/85 [1986] ECR 2121, paras. 16–17.

[10] Case C–337/97 *Meeusen v. Hoofddirectie van de Informatie Beheer Groep* [1999] ECR I–3289, para. 15. In Case C–94/07 *Raccanelli v. Max-Planck Gesellschaft (MPG)* [2008] ECR I–5939, para. 37 the Court of Justice left it up to the national court to decide whether a researcher preparing a doctoral thesis on the basis of a grant contract concluded with the MPG satisfied the test of subordination and remuneration. Cf. Case C–107/94 *Asscher v. Staatssecretaris van Financiën* [1996] ECR I–3089, para. 26 where the Court said that a director and sole shareholder of a company was not a worker because company directors are not subordinate).

[11] Case 36/74 *Walrave and Koch* [1974] ECR 1405, para. 21.

[12] Case 152/73 *Sotgiu v. Deutsche Bundespost* [1974] ECR 153, para. 5.

[13] See, e.g., Case 13/76 *Donà v. Mantero* [1976] ECR 1333, para. 12.

[14] Case C–415/93 *Bosman* [1995] ECR I–4921, para. 73.

[15] Case C–268/99 *Aldona Malgorzata Jany and others v. Staatssecretaris van Justitie* [2001] ECR I–8615, para. 33, considered further in Ch. 10.

[16] Case C–188/00 *Kurz, née Yüce v. Land Baden-Württemberg* [2002] ECR I–10691, decided in the context of the EEC–Turkey Association Agreement.

[17] Case C–109/04 *Kranemann* [2005] ECR I–2421; Case C–10/05 *Mattern v. Mininstre du Travail et de l'emploi* [2006] ECR I–3145, para. 21.

[18] Case 196/87 *Steymann v. Staatssecretaris van Justitie* [1988] ECR 6159, para. 14. See further C. O'Brien, 'Social blind spots and monocular policy making: the ECJ's migrant worker model' (2009) 46 *CMLRev.* 1107.

other hand, in *Bettray*[19] the Court found that paid activity provided by the state as part of a drug rehabilitation programme did not represent a genuine and effective economic activity, since the work, which was designed for those who could not take up work under 'normal' conditions, was tailored to an individual's needs and was intended to reintegrate them into the employment market. By contrast, in *Trojani*[20] the Court of Justice left it to the national court to decide whether Trojani's work, performed for and under the direction of a Salvation Army hostel for about 30 hours a week as part of programme reintegrating individuals to the labour market, was 'real and genuine' paid activity, taking into account the status and practices of the hostel, the content of the social reintegration programme, and the nature and details of performance of the services.[21]

The economic activity must also not be on 'such a small scale as to be purely marginal and ancillary'.[22] Although this hurdle might raise particular difficulties for part-time workers, the Court has generally found that they are still workers. For example, in *Levin*[23] the Court found that a British woman working part-time as a chambermaid in the Netherlands could be a worker, even though she earned less than a subsistence wage, because, according to the Court, part-time work constituted an effective means of improving an individual's living conditions.[24] In *Kempf*[25] the Court also found that the work of a part-time music teacher was not on 'such a small scale as to be purely marginal and ancillary', even though his income was supplemented by social security benefits.[26] The Court said that once a finding of effective and genuine employment had been made, it was irrelevant whether the individual subsisted on his earnings or whether his pay was used to add to other family income[27] or was supplemented by public funds.[28] However, in *Raulin*[29] the Court again emphasized the role of the national court in making the final decision as to who is a worker. It said that an *'oproepkracht'* (an on-call worker) on a 'zero hours' contract, who was not actually guaranteed any work or obliged to take up any work offered and often worked only a very few days per week or hours per day, could be a 'worker' but that it was a matter for the national court to decide, taking into account the irregular nature and limited duration of the services provided.

This line of case law was usefully summarized in *Kurz*[30] where the Court said:

neither the sui generis nature of the employment relationship under national law, nor the level of productivity of the person concerned, the origin of the funds for which the remuneration is paid or the limited amount of remuneration can have any consequence in regard to whether or not the person is a worker.

This tends to suggest that the Court will find that an individual is a worker where possible, a view confirmed in *Vatsouras*.[31] The referring court had found that the 'brief minor'

---

[19] Case 344/87 *Bettray v. Staatssecretaris van Justitie* [1989] ECR 1621, para. 17. Cf. Case C–1/97 *Birden v. Stadtgemeinde Bremen* [1998] ECR I–7747, decided in the context of the EEC–Turkey Association Agreement, where a person employed under a job-creation scheme was considered a worker. See also Case C–14/09 *Genc v. Land Berlin* [2010] ECR I–000.

[20] Case C–456/02 *Trojani v. CPAS* [2004] ECR I–7573.       [21] Para. 24.

[22] See, e.g., Case C–357/89 *Raulin v. Minister van Onderwijs en Wetenschappen* [1992] ECR I–1027, para. 10. The mere fact that the employment is of short duration cannot of itself, exclude the employment from Art. 45: Case C–413/01 *Franca Ninni-Orasche v. Bundesminister für Wissenschaft, Verkehr und Kunst* [2003] ECR I–1187, para. 25.       [23] Case 53/81 [1982] ECR 1035, para. 17.

[24] Para. 15.       [25] Case 139/85 [1986] ECR 1741.       [26] See also Art. 14(4)(a) of Dir. 2004/38.

[27] Case 53/81 *Levin* [1982] ECR 1035.       [28] Para. 14.       [29] Case C–357/89 [1992] ECR I–1027.

[30] Case C–188/00 [2002] ECR I–10691, para. 32.

[31] Joined Cases C–22/08 and 23/08 *Vatsouras v. Arbeitsgemeinschaft* [2009] ECR I–000, para. 30.

professional activity engaged in by Mr Vatsouras 'did not ensure him a livelihood'.[32] Nevertheless, the Court of Justice said that:

independently of the limited amount of the remuneration and the short duration of the professional activity, it cannot be ruled out that that professional activity, following an overall assessment of the employment relationship, may be considered by the national authorities as real and genuine, thereby allowing its holder to be granted the status of 'worker' within the meaning of Article [45 TFEU].[33]

## 2. OTHERS CONSIDERED 'WORKERS'

The Court has extended the definition of 'worker' to include those seeking work.[34] While the period allowed for work-seekers to remain in the host state depends on the rules of that state, they must be given at least three months to look for work,[35] although if they are dependent on social security they may be asked to leave.[36] At the time of the decision in *Antonissen*[37] migrants in the UK had six months to look for work[38] which the Court found to be compatible with Union law. If, at the end of the six-month period, work-seekers can show that they have a genuine chance of being employed, they cannot be required to leave the host state. For this reason the Court said in *Commission* v. *Belgium*[39] that a Belgian law requiring a work-seeker to leave the state automatically on the expiry of the three-month period breached Article 45. Article 14(4)(b) of Directive 2004/38 (CRD) confirms this line of case law, making clear that Union citizen work-seekers (and their family members) cannot be expelled so long as they can 'provide evidence that they are continuing to seek employment and that they have a genuine chance of being engaged'. No time limit is specified.

Article 7(3) CRD also makes provision for those Union citizens who are no longer workers (or self-employed[40]) to retain worker (or self-employed) status in four situations:

(a) where the individual cannot work because s/he is temporarily incapacitated through illness or accident[41]

(b) where the individual has become *involuntarily* unemployed after having been employed for more than one year, and has registered as a job-seeker with the relevant employment office

(c) where the individual has become *involuntarily* unemployed after having completed a fixed-term contract of less than one year or after having become involuntarily unemployed during the first twelve months and after having registered as a

---

[32] Para. 25.     [33] Para. 30.

[34] Case C–85/96 *Martínez Sala* v. *Freistaat Bayern* [1998] ECR I–2691, para. 32; Case C–138/02 *Collins* v. *Secretary of State for Work and Pensions* [2003] ECR I–2703, para. 29. Cf. Art. 45(3), which envisages that the worker has already found a job before leaving for the host state.

[35] In certain circumstances work-seekers are entitled to social security benefits for three months under Art. 64 of Reg. 883/04 from 1 Mar. 2010.

[36] Declaration of the Council accompanying Dir. 68/360 and Reg. 1612/68 ([1968] OJ Spec Ed Series I–475).     [37] Case C–292/89 *R* v. *IAT, ex p. Antonissen* [1991] ECR I–745, para. 21.

[38] Statement of Changes to the Immigration Rules (HC 169).

[39] Case C–344/95 *Commission* v. *Belgium* [1997] ECR I–1035, para. 18.     [40] See further Ch. 10.

[41] Cf. Case C–43/99 *Leclere* [2001] ECR I–4265 considered below at n. 172.

job-seeker with the relevant employment office (in this situation the status of worker can be retained for no less than six months)

(d) where the individual embarks on vocational training (unless the individual is involuntarily unemployed, the retention of the status of worker requires the training to be related to the previous employment).[42]

In designating these individuals as workers, the CRD confirms and extends the case law of the Court.[43] It also means that they enjoy full equality of treatment under Article 24(1) CRD, for at least six months in the case of work-seekers satisfying the conditions in Article 7(3)(c) CRD, and are not subject to the derogation in Article 24(2) CRD.[44]

## C. THE RIGHTS CONFERRED ON WORKERS

### 1. INTRODUCTION

Article 45(1) provides that workers should enjoy the right of free movement which, according to Article 45(2), includes the abolition of any discrimination based on nationality between workers of the Member States, as regards employment, remuneration, and other conditions of work and employment. Article 45(3) then adds that free movement comprises the right to:

- accept offers of employment actually made
- move freely within the territory of the Member States for this purpose
- stay in the Member State for the purpose of the employment
- remain in the Member State after having been employed.

In addition, the Court has recognized that workers have the right, derived directly from the Treaties, to leave their state of origin,[45] to enter the territory of another Member State, and to reside and pursue an economic activity there.[46] The details of these rights were originally expanded by three secondary measures: Directive 68/360[47] on the rights of entry and residence, Regulation 1612/68 on the free movement of workers,[48] and

---

[42] Case 39/86 *Lair* [1988] ECR 3161 considered below at n. 218.

[43] See, e g., Case C–35/97 *Commission* v. *France* [1998] ECR I–5325, para. 41; Case C–413/01 *Ninni-Orasche* [2003] ECR I–13187, para. 34.

[44] Joined Cases C–22/08 and 23/08 *Vatsouras* [2009] ECR I–000, paras. 32–4.

[45] Case C–10/90 *Masgio* v. *Bundesknappschaft* [1991] ECR I–1119, paras. 18–19; Case C–415/93 *Bosman* [1995] ECR I–4921, para. 104; Case C–18/95 *Terhoeve* [1999] ECR I–345, paras. 37–8; Case C–190/98 *Graf* [2000] ECR I–493, para. 22; Case C–232/01 *Hans van Lent* [2003] ECR I–11525, para. 21; Case C–137/04 *Rockler* v. *Försäkringskassan* [2006] ECR I–1141, para. 18.

[46] Case C–363/89 *Roux* v. *Belgium* [1991] ECR I–273, para. 9; Case C–18/95 *Terhoeve* [1999] ECR I–345, para. 38.

[47] [1968] OJ Spec Ed (II) L485.

[48] [1968] OJ Spec Ed I–475. When enacting the regulation the Council took into account, first, the importance for the worker, from a human point of view, of having his entire family with him and, secondly, the importance, from all points of view, of the integration of the worker and his family into the host Member State without any difference in treatment in relation to nationals of that state (Case 249/86 *Commission* v. *Germany* [1989] ECR 1263, para. 11).

Regulation 1251/70[49] on the right to remain. Directive 68/360 and Regulation 1251/70,[50] along with a number of other Union directives, as well as the family rights provisions laid down in Articles 10–11 of Regulation 1612/68, have been repealed and replaced by the CRD 2004/38. This means that workers enjoy rights under Article 45 TFEU, the CRD and Regulation 1612/68 (see fig. 12.4). Often the Court will interpret the Treaties in the light of the secondary legislation.[51] However, in the event of a conflict with the secondary legislation, the Treaties will, of course, prevail. Therefore, a migrant worker can start working before completing the formalities to obtain any residence certificate because the right of residence is a fundamental right derived from the Treaties and is not dependent upon the possession of a residence permit.[52] Workers' employment rights are also derived from the Treaties[53] but further detail is provided by Regulation 1612/68 which applies exclusively to workers. It is this measure, as complemented by the CRD, that we shall focus on in this chapter.

## 2. EMPLOYMENT RIGHTS

Regulation 1612/68[54] was originally designed both to facilitate the free movement of workers and their families and to ensure their integration into the community of the host state. Regulation 1612/68 falls into two parts: (1) the right of *access* to a post on non-discriminatory terms (Title I); and (2) the right to equal treatment while doing that job (i.e., while *exercising* the rights of free movement) (Title II). The basic principle of equal treatment is also enshrined in Article 24(1) CRD which also applies to these situations.

### 2.1 Access to Employment

Article 1 of Regulation 1612/68 reiterates the substance of Article 45: any national of a Member State 'has the right to take up an activity as an employed person, and to pursue such activity, within the territory of another Member State', enjoying the same priority as a national. The worker may conclude and perform contracts of employment in accordance with the laws of the host state.[55] Any provisions which discriminate against foreign nationals or hinder foreign nationals from obtaining work are not permissible.[56]

### (a) Direct discrimination

As we saw in Chapter 8, the prohibition against discrimination applies both to directly and indirectly discriminatory measures. Measures are directly discriminatory where the migrant worker is treated less favourably than the national worker. This was the case

---

[49] OJ SE [1970] L142/24, 402.

[50] This was repealed by Commission Reg. 635/2006 (OJ [2006] L112/9).

[51] Case C–278/03 *Commission* v. *Italy (recruitment of teaching staff)* [2005] ECR I–3747, para. 15. Case C–341/05 *Laval* [2007] ECR I–11767 provides a particularly good illustration of this in the field of services, considered in Ch. 11.          [52] Case 118/75 *Watson and Belmann* [1976] ECR 1185, paras. 15–16.

[53] Case C–208/05 *ITC Innovative Technology Center GmbH* [2007] ECR I–181, para. 36, where the Court decided the case purely under Art. 45, consideration of the regulation being 'unnecessary'.

[54] [1968] OJ Spec Ed I–475, amended by Reg. 312/76 ([1976] OJ L3/2) and Council Reg. 2434/92 ([1992] OJ L25/1). This Reg. is due to be codified: COM(2010)204.          [55] Art. 2.

[56] Art. 3(1). Some examples of prohibited practices are listed in Art. 3(2): prescribing a special recruitment procedure for foreign nationals, restricting the advertising of vacancies in the press, and imposing additional requirements on applicants from other Member States of subjecting eligibility for employment to conditions of registration with employment offices.

with the '3+2 rule' in *Bosman*,[57] considered in Chapter 8, and the law in *Commission v. Italy*[58] providing that private security work could be carried out only by Italian security firms employing Italian nationals. Such directly discriminatory measures breach Article 45 (and the regulation and the CRD) and can be saved (probably) only by reference to one of the express derogations laid down by the Treaties or the secondary legislation (see fig. 8.1).

Regulation 1612/68 itself also identifies and seeks to eliminate other directly discriminatory barriers to access to employment. For example, Article 4(1) provides that national provisions which restrict, by number or percentage, the employment of foreign nationals in any undertaking do not apply to nationals of the other Member States. Therefore in *Commission v. France*[59] the Court said that a French rule requiring a ratio of three French seamen to one non-French seaman on a merchant ship contravened Article 4(1). Article 4(2) says that if there is a requirement that an undertaking has to employ a minimum percentage of national workers, then nationals of the other Member States count as national workers. Article 6 says that the engagement and recruitment of a worker must not depend on medical, vocational, or other criteria which are discriminatory on the grounds of nationality. However, it does permit the employer to require the migrant worker to take a vocational test when offering employment.

## (b) Indirect discrimination

Indirectly discriminatory measures also breach Article 45 and the regulation unless objectively justified[60] or saved by one of the express derogations (see fig. 8.1). As we have seen, indirect discrimination focuses on the effect of a measure, a point confirmed by Article 3(1) of Regulation 1612/68,[61] which 'makes explicit the principles formulated in Article [45 TFEU] with regard, specifically, to access to employment'.[62] Article 3(1) says that provisions laid down by national law, regulation, or administrative action or practices will not apply where, 'though applicable irrespective of nationality, their exclusive or principal aim *or effect* is to keep nationals of other Member States away from employment offered'.[63] Common examples of indirectly discriminatory rules are those requiring either a period of service or residence in the host state before enjoying a particular benefit. Therefore in *Scholz*,[64] the Court found the refusal by an Italian selection board to take into account a German applicant's previous employment in Germany to be unjustified indirect discrimination.[65] Similarly, a British rule in *Collins*[66] that entitlement to a jobseeker's allowance was conditional upon a requirement of being habitually resident in the UK

---

[57] Case C-415/93 [1995] ECR I-4921.

[58] Case C-283/99 *Commission v. Italy* [2001] ECR I-4363.

[59] Case 167/73 *Commission v. France (French merchant seamen)* [1974] ECR 359.

[60] See, e.g., Case C-15/96 *Kalliope Schöning-Kougebetopoulou v. Freie und Hansestadt Hamburg* [1998] ECR I-47. See also Case C-187/96 *Commission v. Greece* [1998] ECR I-1095; Case C-350/96 *Clean Car* [1998] ECR I-2521.

[61] According to Case C-281/98 *Angonese* [2000] ECR I-4139, para. 22, this provision applies only to states, not to employers.

[62] Case C-278/03 *Commission v. Italy (recruitment of teaching staff)* [2005] ECR I-3747, para. 15.

[63] Emphasis added.

[64] Case C-419/92 *Scholz v. Opera Universitaria di Cagliari and Cinzia Porcedda* [1994] ECR I-505.

[65] Para. 11.

[66] Case C-138/02 *Collins* [2004] ECR I-2703 considered further below at n. 178. See also Case C-346/05 *Charteignier v. ONEM* [2006] ECR I-10951.

was indirectly discriminatory. However, the Court found that the British rule could be justified; the question of proportionality was left to the national court.[67]

Language requirements may well be indirectly discriminatory measures but can usually be justified. This is expressly recognized by the second paragraph of Article 3(1) of Regulation 1612/68, which provides that the principle of equal treatment does not apply in respect of 'conditions relating to linguistic knowledge required by reason of the nature of the post to be filled'. This provision was successfully relied on by the Irish government in *Groener*.[68] The case concerned a Dutch woman who was refused a permanent post at a design college in Dublin, where she had already been teaching, because she did not speak Gaelic. Even though she did not need to use Gaelic for her work, the Court upheld the language requirement because it formed part of government policy to promote the use of the Irish language as a means of expressing national culture and identity.[69] It said that since education was important for the implementation of such a policy, the requirement for teachers to have an adequate knowledge of the Irish language was compatible with Article 3(1), provided that the level of knowledge was not disproportionate to the objective pursued.[70]

The Court did say in *Groener* that the Irish government could not require that the linguistic knowledge be acquired in Ireland.[71] This point was developed in *Angonese*.[72] The case concerned a requirement imposed by a bank operating in Bolzano (the Italian and German-speaking province of Italy) that admission to its recruitment competition was conditional on possession of a certificate of bilingualism. Because this certificate could be obtained only in Bolzano, Angonese, an Italian national who had studied in Austria, was not able to compete for a post on the ground that he lacked the Bolzano certificate, even though he submitted other evidence of his bilingualism. The Court found the bank's rule to be indirectly discriminatory,[73] even though the requirement affected Italian nationals resident in other parts of Italy as well as nationals from other Member States. It said that since the majority of residents of the province of Bolzano were Italian nationals, the obligation to obtain the certificate put nationals of other Member States at a disadvantage compared with residents of the province, making it difficult, if not impossible, for them to get jobs in Bolzano.[74] On the question of justification, the Court said that while the bank could justify requiring job applicants to have a certain level of linguistic knowledge, the fact that it was impossible to show proof of this knowledge by any other means—in particular by equivalent qualifications from other Member States—was disproportionate,[75] and so the bank's requirement breached Article 45.

---

[67] Subsequently the national court found the rule to be proportionate, a view that other UK courts have followed in respect of challenges to other social security benefits which impose a residence requirement (e.g., *Patmalniece* v. *Secretary of State for Work and Pensions* [2009] EWCA Civ 621 where the Court of Appeal said that the residence requirement could be justified on the grounds of ensuring that the individual was economically or socially integrated with the country whose social assistance they sought for the purpose of protecting the public finances of that country, and the requirement was proportionate).

[68] Case 379/87 *Groener* v. *Minister for Education* [1989] ECR 3967.      [69] Paras. 18–19.

[70] Para. 21.      [71] Para. 23.      [72] Case C–281/98 [2000] ECR I–4139.

[73] The Court reasoned that 'in order for a measure to be treated as being discriminatory on grounds of nationality, it is not necessary for the measure to have the effect of putting at an advantage all the workers of one nationality or of putting at a disadvantage only workers who are nationals of other Member States, but not workers of the nationality in question' (para. 41).      [74] Para. 39.

[75] Para. 44.

## (c) Non-discriminatory measures which hinder market access/obstacles approach

Non-discriminatory national measures which (substantially) impede access to the market also breach Article 45 and Regulation 1612/68 (and, presumably, the CRD) unless objectively justified (see fig. 8.3). We saw this in *Bosman*[76] where the Court found that the football transfer fee rules, albeit non-discriminatory, 'directly affect[ed] players' access to the employment market in other Member States'[77] and therefore constituted an unjustified 'obstacle to the freedom of movement of workers'.[78] If, on the other hand, the effect of the national legislation is 'too uncertain and indirect...to be capable of being regarded as liable to hinder free movement for workers', as in *Graf*,[79] then the measure does not breach Article 45 or the regulation.[80]

In the area of free movement of workers, the discrimination language is most firmly entrenched. However, as we saw in Chapter 8, the general trend in the field of free movement of persons is to move from the non-discrimination approach to the 'restrictions'/'obstacles' test,[81] even in cases where previously the Court would have categorized the measure as being indirectly discriminatory.[82] If the Court finds there is an 'obstacle', 'barrier', 'restriction' or 'impediment' to free movement, it then examines whether the rule can be objectively justified and whether the steps taken are proportionate. Free movement of workers has not been immune from this development, as *Lyyski*[83] demonstrates.

The case concerned a Swedish rule requiring an individual wanting to follow a special teacher training course at a designated university in Sweden to be employed at a Swedish school in order to complete the practical component of their training. The Court said that the rule placed those, like Mr Lyyski who was employed in a Swedish-speaking school in Finland, 'at a disadvantage'.[84] The legislation was thus 'liable to restrict the freedom of movement of workers' which was prohibited by Article 45. The Court continued that the requirement to be employed in a Swedish school constituted an 'obstacle to freedom of movement'[85] which could be justified on the grounds of preserving or improving the education system (Sweden had introduced this programme because it foresaw a shortage of qualified teachers). The Court also thought the Swedish requirement was proportionate: the programme was temporary and the requirement to be employed in a Swedish school assisted in the process of monitoring and assessing the practical training stage of the training.[86] However, the Court said the requirement had to be applied flexibly and on a case-by-case basis; account had to be taken of the merits of each individual applicant and whether the individual could be exempted from the practical part of the training.[87]

---

[76] Case C–415/93 [1995] ECR I–4921, considered in detail in Ch. 11.    [77] Para. 103.

[78] Para. 104. See E. Johnson and D. O'Keeffe, 'From discrimination to obstacles to free movement: Recent developments concerning the free movement of workers 1989–1994' (1994) 31 *CMLRev*. 1313.

[79] Case C–190/98 [2002] ECR I–493.    [80] Paras. 24–5.

[81] Case C–464/02 *Commission* v. *Denmark (company vehicles)* [2005] ECR I–7929, paras. 46 and 52. For an equivalent case under Art. 49 TFEU, see Joined Cases C–151/04 and C–152/04 *Nadin* [2005] ECR I–11203, para. 36.

[82] Cf. Case C–15/96 *Schöning-Kougebetopoulou* [1998] ECR I–47 (discrimination analysis of length of service provisions) with Case C–224/01 *Köbler* v. *Republik Österreich* [2003] ECR I–10239 (restrictions analysis of service provisions).    [83] Case C–40/05 *Lyyski* v. *Umeå universitet* [2007] ECR I–99.

[84] Para. 37.    [85] Para. 38.    [86] Paras. 42–3.    [87] Para. 49.

In most cases where the Court applies the restrictions approach it finds a breach of the Treaties. However, occasionally it considers that the rule does not restrict free movement and so there is no breach of Article 45.[88] This can be seen in *Burbaud*[89] where the Court said that the requirement of passing an exam in order to take up a post in the public service could not 'in itself be regarded as an obstacle' to free movement.[90]

## 2.2 Equal Treatment (or Removal of Obstacles) during the Employment Relationship

### (a) Equal treatment in respect of the terms and conditions of employment

While Title I of Regulation 1612/68 concerns initial access to employment, Title II concerns the 'exercise' of (as opposed to access to) employment, i.e. rules concerning terms and conditions of employment. Article 7(1) states that a migrant worker must not be treated:

differently from national workers in respect of any conditions of employment and work, in particular as regards remuneration, dismissal, and should he become unemployed, reinstatement or reemployment.[91]

Most of the case law concerns indirectly discriminatory measures. For example, in *Allué and Coonan*[92] an Italian law limited the duration of contracts of employment of foreign-language assistants, without imposing the same limitation on other workers. Since only 25 per cent of foreign-language assistants were Italian nationals, the law essentially concerned nationals of other Member States. It was indirectly discriminatory[93] and could not be justified.

As we have already seen, residence requirements are also likely to be indirectly discriminatory. So, in *Clean Car*[94] the Court found that an Austrian rule requiring business managers to be resident in Austria before they could work in Vienna breached Article 45. It noted that the rule was liable to operate mainly to the detriment of nationals of other Member States since the majority of non-residents were foreigners.[95] Austria sought to justify the residence requirement on the grounds that the manager needed to be resident to be effective in the business, to be served with a notice of any

---

[88] Case C–33/99 *Fahmi and Cerdeiro-Pinedo Amado* v. *Bestuur van de Sociale Verzekeringsbank* [2001] ECR I–2415, para. 43.

[89] Case C–285/01 *Isabel Burbaud* v. *Ministère de l'Emploi et de la Solidarité* [2003] ECR I–8219.

[90] Para. 96. To emphasize the point, the Court said that inasmuch as all new jobs are subject to a recruitment procedure, the requirement of passing a recruitment competition could not 'in itself be liable to dissuade candidates who have already sat a similar competition in another Member State from exercising their right to freedom of movement as workers' (para. 97). In a similar vein see Joined Cases C–51/96 and C–191/97 *Deliège* [2000] ECR I–2549, para. 64, discussed in Ch. 8.

[91] Art. 7(1) applies only to payments made by virtue of statutory or contracted obligations incumbent on the employer as a condition of employment: see Case C–315/94 *Peter de Vos* v. *Stadt Bielefeld* [1996] ECR I–1417.

[92] Case 33/88 *Allué and Coonan* v. *Università degli studi di Venezia* [1989] ECR 1591. See also Case 41/84 *Pinna* v. *Caisse d'allocations familiales de la Savoie* [1986] ECR 1 and Case C–272/92 *Spotti* v. *Freistaat Bayern* [1993] ECR I–5185. The Court extended this ruling to nationals of a non-EU state in the context of Art. 37(1) of the Europe Agreement: Case C–162/00 *Land-Nordrhein-Westfalen* v. *Beata Pokrzeptowicz-Meyer* [2002] ECR I–1049, para. 44.          [93] Para. 12.

[94] Case C–350/96 [1998] ECR I–2521. See also Case C–472/99 *Clean Car* [2001] ECR I–9687 on the issue of costs following the Court's earlier judgment.          [95] Para. 29.

fines imposed, and to have those fines enforced against him. The Court found these justifications disproportionate: the residence requirement was either inappropriate to achieve the aim pursued or went beyond what was necessary for that purpose.[96] It also noted that other, less restrictive measures were available to achieve the objective, such as serving a notice of the fines at the registered office of the company employing the manager.

Length of service requirements may also be indirectly discriminatory.[97] In *Schöning-Kougebetopoulou*,[98] the Court found that a collective agreement providing for promotion on grounds of seniority, but which took no account of service performed in another Member State, 'manifestly' worked to the detriment of migrant workers and so breached Article 45. The Court rejected the justifications based on rewarding loyalty to the employer and motivating employees because, on the facts, service with other legally separate employers was taken into account and so the loyalty argument could not be sustained.[99]

Article 7(4) of Regulation 1612/68 provides that clauses from a collective agreement or contract which discriminate against workers from other Member States, are null and void in so far as they lay down or authorize discriminatory conditions.[100] Until the parties amend the agreement to eliminate the discrimination, the migrant workers enjoy the same rules as those which apply to nationals.[101]

### (b) Equal treatment in respect of tax advantages

Article 7(2) of Regulation 1612/68 provides that a worker will enjoy the same social and tax advantages as national workers.[102] Both limbs of Article 7(2) have caused serious problems for the Court as it struggles to reconcile its jurisprudence on free movement and the creation of a single market with two of the most sensitive areas of national competence—the welfare state and taxation, matters which traditionally have a strongly territorial dimension. We begin by considering taxation, an area which has generated an extraordinary volume of case law during the 2000s. In order to understand this case law and the problems generated we start with a brief explanation of some of the internationally recognized principles of the rules governing taxation.

---

[96] Para. 34.

[97] Case 15/69 *Württembergische Milchverwertung Südmilch AG v. Ugliola* [1969] ECR 363 (German law provided that a period spent performing military service in Germany—but not in other Member States—had to be taken into account by an employer when calculating periods of service for the purposes of pay or other benefits).

[98] Case C-15/96 [1998] ECR I-47. See also Case C-187/96 *Commission v. Greece* [1998] ECR I-1095; Case C-195/98 *Österreichischer Gewerkschaftsbund, Gewerkschaft öffentlicher Dienst v. Republik Österreich* [2000] ECR I-10497; Case C-27/91 *URSSAF v. Le Manoir* [1991] ECR I-5531 and Case C-419/92 *Scholz* [1994] ECR I-505. [99] Para. 27.

[100] Case C-400/02 *Merida v. Bundesrepublik Deutschland* [2004] ECR I-8471.

[101] Case C-15/96 *Kalliope Schöning-Kougebetopoulou* [1998] ECR I-47, para. 33, applying by analogy the Art. 157 TFEU (ex Art. 141 EC) case law on equal pay: e.g., Case C-184/89 *Nimz v. Freie und Hansestadt Hamburg* [1991] ECR I-297, para. 18; Case C-33/89 *Kowalska v. Freie und Hansestadt Hamburg* [1990] ECR I-2591, para. 20.

[102] For a detailed examination of this provision see D. O'Keeffe, 'Equal rights for migrants: The concept of social advantages in Article 7(2), Reg. 1612/68' (1985) 5 *YEL* 92.

### (i) Principles of tax law in cross-border situations

Direct taxation remains one of 'the fundamental sacrosanct bastions of national sovereignty'.[103] Member States remain free to identify:

- the tax unit (those over whom they wish to assert legislative fiscal jurisdiction, usually those resident in the state and the profits which arise in that state)

- the tax base (i.e., the nature and quantum of the receipts it wishes to tax and the identification of the entitlement to and nature of tax reliefs[104])

- the tax rate

- how they wish to administer, assess, collect and recover tax.[105]

In other words, states enjoy fiscal autonomy[106] which means, as the Court has now recognized, that Member States are 'not obliged therefore to adapt their own tax systems to the different systems of tax of the other Member States' in order to eliminate, for example, any double taxation (see below), arising from 'the exercise in parallel by those Member States of their fiscal sovereignty'.[107]

Thus, the *existence* of tax law is a matter for Member State competence. However, how the Member State decides to *exercise* that competence remains subject to Union law.[108] The application of Union law to national systems of tax is problematic. In the field of free movement of workers, most of the cases concern the situation where national rules treat residents differently from non-residents. As we have already seen, it is classic single market case law that residence is a suspect ground of differential treatment and usually constitutes unlawful indirect discrimination against migrants.[109] However, under international (and thus national tax law) residence is *the* legitimate ground of differentiation. Under international tax law, *residents* of a taxing state are taxed on their worldwide profits ('unlimited taxation'), while *non-residents* are taxed on profits arising from sources located in that taxing state ('limited taxation').[110] This distinction is referred to as the principle of territoriality. As Ghosh explains, unlimited taxation is predicated on a progressive system of taxation. If it is right that individuals who obtain greater profits should pay more tax, then the objective of a progressive system would be frustrated if the state could levy tax only on sources of profits located within its territory.[111] This is why

---

[103] S. Kingston, 'The boundaries of sovereignty: The ECJ's controversial role applying the internal market rules to taxation' (2006–7) 9 *CYELS* 287.

[104] See the attempts at a Union 'common consolidated corporate tax base': <http://www.ec.europa.eu/taxation_customs/taxation/company_tax/common_tax_base/index_en.htm>.

[105] J. Ghosh, *Principles of the Internal Market and Direct Taxation* (Oxford: Key Haven, 2007), 1–14. See also Case C–374/04 *Test Claimants in Class IV of the ACT Group Litigation v. Commissioners of Inland Revenue* [2006] ECR I–11673, para. 50: 'It is for each Member State to organise, in compliance with Union law, its system of taxation of distributed profits and, in that context, to define the tax base as well at the tax rates which apply to the company making the distribution and/or the shareholder to whom the dividends are paid, in so far as they are liable to tax in that State.' See also Case C–194/06 *Staatssecretaris van Financiën v. Orange European Smallcap Fund* [2008] ECR I–3747, para. 48.

[106] Case C–298/05 *Columbus Container Services BVBA & Co v. Finanzamt Bielefeld-Innenstadt* [2007] ECR I–10451, para. 53. See also the discussion of the principle in respect of Art. 110 in Ch. 3.

[107] Case C–67/08 *Block v. Finanzamt Kaufbeuren* [2009] ECR I–883, para. 31.

[108] See, e.g., Case C–246/89 *Commission v. UK* [1991] ECR I–4585.

[109] Case C–175/88 *Biehl v. Administration des contributions du grand-duché de Luxembourg* [1990] ECR I–1779, para. 14.

[110] See further Ghosh, above n. 105, 4.          [111] Ibid.

residents are taxed on their worldwide profits. Underpinning the principle of unlimited taxation of residents is the idea that residents owe a personal allegiance to the state. Because *non*-residents are deemed to have less personal allegiance to the taxing State, the progressive system of taxation is mitigated by having taxed only those profits located within the legislative jurisdiction of the taxing state.[112]

The corollary of the distinction between residents and non-residents is that generally the state of residence grants taxpayers all the tax advantages relating to their personal and family circumstances because their personal and financial interests are centred there and so the state of residence can best assess the taxpayers' ability to pay tax.[113] The same will not apply to non-residents.

The problem for individuals resident in State A but receiving profits in State B is that they risk being taxed twice: once by the source state (State B) and then again in the home state (State A) where they are taxed on worldwide profits. To avoid this problem, a vast network of bilateral Double Taxation Conventions (DTCs) have been drawn up between states agreeing on which state enjoys priority in cross-border situations.[114] International tax law lays down the general rule that priority of taxation lies with the source state, meaning that it is up to home state (State A) to alleviate the double taxation. However, as we saw above, given the principle of fiscal sovereignty, the home state is not obliged to alleviate the double taxation, nor is it required to do so under Union law.[115]

Yet, as Kingston points out, if the home state decides not to alleviate the double taxation, this is certainly 'liable to hinder' free movement. However, each of these restrictions is simply 'an inevitable result of Member States' tax sovereignty, which can be eliminated only by (at present unforthcoming) legislation'.[116] As we shall see in the next chapter, for a while the Court viewed these hindrances as unlawful restrictions on free movement, rather than the inevitable consequence of the co-existence of 27 national tax systems, and so applied its restrictions jurisprudence with full vigour. When it found the legislation not to be justified, it threatened the viability of much national tax legislation which applied in cross-border situations. The decisions in *Marks & Spencers*[117] and *FII*[118] marked a turning point where the Court first took a more nuanced view towards the question of justifications (*M&S*) and then adopted a narrower view of what constituted a restriction which took far greater account of the realities of international tax law, including the legitimate difference in treatment between resident and non-resident tax payers (*FII*).

---

[112] Ibid, 4–5.

[113] Case C–279/93 *Finanzamt Köln-Altstadt* v. *Schumacker* [1995] ECR I–225, para. 32.

[114] S. Kingston, 'A light in the darkness: Recent developments in the ECJ's direct tax jurisprudence' (2007) 44 *CMLRev*. 1321, 1331. See also Case C–376/03 *D* v. *Inspecteur van de Belastingdienst/Particulieren/Ondernemingen buitenland te Heerlen* [2005] ECR I–5821, para. 51 where the Court rejected arguments based on the WTO principle of most favoured nation (MFN) status: a German resident with 10% of his wealth in the Netherlands could not be treated in the same way as a Belgian national under the Belgium-Netherlands DTC.

[115] Case C–194/06 *Orange European Smallcap Fund* [2008] ECR I–3747, paras. 37–41. In this respect the Court's case law on double *taxation* stands in stark contrast to its approach to double *regulation* in cases such as *Cassis de Dijon* (Case 120/78 [179] ECR 649. See further J. Snell, 'Non-discriminatory tax obstacles in Community Law' (2007) 56 *ICLQ* 339.   [116] Kingston, above n. 114, 1331

[117] Case C–446/03 *Marks & Spencer plc* v. *Halsey (Her Majesty's Inspector of Taxes)* [2005] ECR I–10837 considered in Ch. 10.

[118] Case C–446/04 *Test Claimants in the FII Group Litigation* v. *Commissioner of Inland Revenue* [2006] ECR I–11753 considered in Ch. 10.

### (ii) Differential treatment of residents and non-residents

Given that international tax law generally envisages that residents and non-residents can and should be treated differently in terms of taxation, how does this fit with Union law principles of non-discrimination? The Court of Justice has tried to square the circle[119] by saying that the circumstances of residents and those of non-residents are generally not comparable and so the principle of equal treatment should not apply.[120] However, if, on the facts of the case, the situations of the resident and non-resident taxpayers can be considered comparable, then it would be discriminatory to treat the two situations differently. This is particularly so in the case of frontier workers such as Mr Schumacker,[121] a Belgian national who lived in Belgium with his family but worked in Germany. As a non-resident worker his wages were subject to German income tax but he was denied certain benefits which were available to resident taxpayers. The Court ruled that a non-resident taxpayer who received all or almost all of his income in the state of employment was objectively in the same situation as a resident in that state who did the same work there. Because the situation of residents and non-residents was comparable, the Court ruled that the German rules gave rise to discrimination because the non-resident taxpayer did not have his personal and family circumstances taken into account either in his state of residence (where he received no income) or in his state of employment (where he was not resident).[122] Consequently, his overall tax burden was greater than that of a resident taxpayer.[123] The German rules therefore breached Article 45 and could not be justified.

While the Court required Germany to take Schumacker's personal and family circumstances into account, *Renneberg*[124] went further by requiring the state asserting unlimited taxation to extend to non-residents, considered to be in a comparable situation to residents, all tax advantages on the same terms as residents. The case concerned a Dutch

---

[119] In Case C–414/06 *Lidl Belgium GmbH & Co.KG* v. *Finanzamt Heilbronn* [2008] ECR I–3601, para. 22, the Court said that 'for the purposes of the allocation of fiscal competence, it is not unreasonable for the Member States to draw guidance from international practice and, particularly, the model conventions drawn up by the OECD'.

[120] Case C–279/93 *Schumacker* [1995] ECR I–225; Case C–376/03 *D* [2005] ECR I–5821, para. 37; Case C–336/96 *Gilly* v. *Directeur des services fiscaux du Bas-Rhin* [1998] ECR I–2793, para. 49.

[121] Case C–279/93 [1995] ECR I–225. See also Case C–383/05 *Talotta* v. *Etat belge* [2007] ECR I–2555 where the Court reached a similar conclusion in the context of Art. 49 TFEU. See generally M. Wathelet, 'The influence of free movement of persons, services and capital on national direct taxation: Trends in the case law of the European Court of Justice' (2001) 20 *YEL* 1.

[122] Para. 38. Cf. Case C–391/97 *Gschwind* v. *Finanzamt Aaachen-Außenstadt* [1999] ECR I–5451, para. 32, because the state of residence (the Netherlands) could take the personal and family circumstances of the individual into account, Art. 45 did not preclude the application of German legislation under which resident married couples were granted favourable tax treatment while the same treatment of non-resident married couples was made subject to the condition that at least 90% of their total income had to be subject to tax in Germany.

[123] Para. 28. See also Case C–152/03 *Ritter-Coulais* v. *Finanzamt Germersheim* [2006] ECR I–1711, para. 38 concerning the failure by the state of employment (Germany), when determining income tax liability in Germany, to take rental income losses incurred in France into account. This case was decided solely under Art. 45 TFEU, which was found to be breached, with no reference to Reg. 1612/68 (Cf. Case C–269/07 *Commission* v. *Germany (savings pension bonus)* [2009] ECR I–000 where both the Treaties and the regulation were referred to). See also Case C–182/06 *Etat du Gran-Duché de Luxembourg* v. *Lakebrink* [2007] ECR I–6705, para. 19, where, following the developments particularly in the field of establishment considered in Ch. 10, the Court rooted its reasoning firmly in the discrimination approach.

[124] Case C–527/06 *Renneberg* v. *Staatssecretaris van Financiën* [2008] ECR I–7735.

citizen working in the Netherlands but living in Belgium where he obtained more than 90 per cent of his income. Had he been a Dutch resident he would have enjoyed tax relief on his home based on the difference between the rental value of the house and the interest paid on the mortgage. Since he lived outside the Netherlands he enjoyed some tax relief on his home but at a lower rate. He argued that, following *Schumacker*, his situation was comparable to that of a resident and so he should have enjoyed the higher level tax relief. The Court agreed and found that the Dutch rules breached Article 45.

The effect of the ruling is that Mr Renneberg managed to have his cake and eat it.[125] While the Dutch tax system provides a generous subsidy for owner-occupied housing through its tax system, the Belgian system does not. In the Netherlands the tax subsidy was ultimately reflected in higher house prices, estimated at between 15 and 30 per cent, which was not the case in Belgium.[126] Therefore, the consequence of the Court's decision was to give Mr. Renneberg the benefit of the higher Dutch tax advantage while he enjoyed living in cheaper Belgian housing. As Vording put it, 'The chances are that the market had already compensated Mr Renneberg for his loss of tax relief before he went to the courts.'[127] This is an illustration of the problem identified above of the Court applying its single market case law to a situation which arises because of a disparity between national tax systems,[128] a problem exacerbated by the application of the restrictions-based approach.

### (iii) The restriction/obstacle approach

While most of the tax cases concerning Article 45 are considered under the non-discrimination model, the Court started to apply the restrictions model, especially where the home state rule was under challenge. This can be seen in *Commission v. Germany (subsidy on dwellings)*[129] which concerned a German rule granting a subsidy for owner-occupied dwellings to which individuals liable to unlimited taxation of income in Germany were entitled, provided that the dwellings built or purchased were situated in Germany. The Court found that 'Provisions preventing or deterring a national of a Member State from leaving his country of origin in order to exercise his right to freedom of movement constitute an obstacle to that freedom... prohibited by Articles [45 TFEU] and [49 TFEU].'[130] The Court said that while the aim of encouraging the building of dwellings in its territory in order to ensure an adequate supply of housing was a justification, it went beyond what was necessary to attain the objective pursued.[131]

However, as we saw in Chapter 8, the restrictions line of case law is open to misuse. For example, a migrant might argue that the fact that income tax rates are higher in State B than State A (a difference due to the Member States' freedom to set their own tax rates) discourages an individual from moving from State A to State B to seek work. *Weigel*[132] shows that the Court is trying to put a stop to such arguments. The case concerned a German husband and wife who transferred their residence to Austria where Mr Weigel had a job. They both brought their cars with them which had to be re-registered in

---

[125] H. Vording, '*Renneberg v. Staatssecretaris van Financiën*: The problem of an extended *Schumacker* rule' [2009] *British Tax Review* 67.                                                    [126] Ibid., 73.

[127] Ibid.          [128] See the Dutch government's arguments to that effect at para. 74.

[129] Case C–152/05 [2008] ECR I–39. See also Case C–345/05 *Commission v. Portugal (exemption from capital gains tax)* [2006] ECR I–10633; Case C–104/06 *Commission v. Sweden (deferral of capital gains tax)* [2007] ECR I–671.                                                              [130] Paras. 22 and 29.

[131] Para. 27.

[132] Case C–387/01 *Weigel v. Finanzlandes direction für Vorarlberg* [2004] ECR I–4981.

Austria for which a hefty tax was charged. The Court rejected their arguments that this tax breached Article 45(2), noting that the Austrian rule applied 'without regard to the nationality of the worker concerned to all those who registered a car in Austria and, accordingly, it is applicable without distinction'.[133] The Court then added that 'It is true that [the tax] is likely to have a negative bearing on the decision of migrant workers to exercise their right to freedom of movement.'[134] Under the *Säger* formula, this observation would have been enough for a finding of a breach of Article 45 which the Member State would then have to justify.[135] However, in *Weigel* the Court resorted to the pure non-discrimination approach (see fig. 8.2) and said that, provided that nationals and migrants were treated in the same way, the fact that the tax regimes of the different Member States were different was compatible with Union law.[136]

### (iv) Justification

Having established that the situations are comparable and that the national rule is discriminatory (or a restriction on free movement of workers), the next question is whether the rule can be justified. The Court rejects pure economic justifications such a reduction in tax revenue[137] or the cost to the national exchequer.[138] However, in *Bachmann*[139] the Court recognized the 'need to preserve the cohesion of the tax system' as a justification.

*Bachmann* concerned a Belgian law according to which the cost of life insurance premiums could not be deducted from taxable income where the premiums were paid in other Member States. This was because Belgian tax law gave the individual the choice of either having tax deducted on the premiums and then paying tax on future benefits or not having tax deducted on the premiums and then not paying tax on future benefits. If Bachmann was able to deduct tax on premiums paid in Germany, the Belgian authorities would have no way of being able to tax future benefits also payable in Germany.[140] For this reason the Court said that the Belgian rules were justified because there was a 'direct link' between the right to deduct contributions and the taxation of sums payable by insurers under pension and life assurance contracts; and that preserving that link was necessary to safeguard the cohesion of the tax system.[141]

---

[133] Para. 52.     [134] Para. 54.

[135] See, by analogy, the Art. 56 TFEU case, Joined Cases C–430 and 431/99 *Sea-Land Service* [2002] ECR I–5235 considered in Ch. 11.

[136] Para. 55. The Court reached the same conclusion under Art. 21 TFEU in Case C–365/02 *Lindfors* [2004] ECR I–7183. See also Geelhoed AG's discussion in Case C–374/04 *ACT Group Litigation* [2006] ECR I–11673, paras. 43–7.

[137] Case C–464/02 *Commission* v. *Denmark (company vehicles)* [2005] ECR I–7929, para. 45, citing the free movement of capital decision Case C–319/02 *Manninen* [2004] ECR I–7477, para. 49. See also C–422/01 *Försäkringsaktiebolaget Skandia (publ)* v. *Riksskatteverket* [2003] ECR I–6817, paras. 51–2 where the Court rejected arguments based on the need to preserve the tax base.

[138] Case C–109/04 *Kranemann* [2005] ECR I–2421.

[139] Case C–204/90 *Bachmann* v. *Belgian State* [1992] ECR I–249, para. 21, and Case C–300/90 *Commission* v. *Belgium* [1992] ECR I–305, para. 14.     [140] Para. 23.

[141] Paras. 21–3. In Case C–35/98 *Verkoiijn* [2000] ECR I–4071, paras. 57–8 the Court insisted that there had to be a direct link in respect of one and the same taxpayer, although this limitation has since been dropped: e.g., Case C–319/02 *Manninen* [2004] ECR I–7477.

Since *Bachmann* Member States have regularly invoked fiscal cohesion as a justification for their tax policies, but almost always without success.[142] The Court has insisted that the cohesion justification requires a direct link between the discriminatory tax rule and the compensating tax advantage and this has not been found in subsequent cases,[143] with the exception of *Krankenheim Ruhesitz*,[144] a freedom of establishment case. Germany taxed the profits of a German company but also allowed losses made by the German company's Austrian establishment to be taken into account as part of the calculation. However, when the Austrian company subsequently made profits, the German authorities added these profits to those of the German company and taxed both, even though those profits had already been taxed in Austria. The Court said that by reintegrating the losses of the Austrian establishment into the basis of assessment for the German company, albeit only up to the amount of profits made by the Austrian establishment, the German tax system subjected resident companies with permanent establishments in Austria to less favourable treatment than that enjoyed by resident companies with permanent establishment situated in Germany. This constituted an unlawful restriction on freedom of establishment but one which could be justified:

the reintegration of losses provided for by the German tax system...cannot be dissociated from their having earlier been taken into account. That reintegration, in the case of a company with a permanent establishment in another State in relation to which that company's State of residence has no power of taxation...reflects a logical symmetry. There was thus a direct, personal and material link between the two elements of the tax mechanism at issue in the main proceedings, the said reintegration being the logical complement of the deduction previously granted.[145]

Another justification recognized by the Court is the effectiveness of fiscal supervision[146] but again Member States have generally had little success in actually relying on it.[147] For instance, in *Schumacker* Germany said that administrative difficulties prevented the state of employment (Germany) from determining the income received by non-residents in their state of residence (Belgium). The Court rejected this argument, reasoning that this difficulty could be overcome through the application of Directive 77/799[148] on mutual assistance in the field of direct taxation.[149] By contrast in *X and Passenheim-van Schoot*,[150] the Court did uphold the justification in the case of taxpayers who had deliberately hidden details of their bank accounts in other Member States. They were subject to additional assessments and were fined. The Court said that the national rules constituted a restriction of both the freedom to provide services and of the free movement of capital[151]

---

[142] See, e.g., Case C–80/94 *Wielockx* v. *Inspecteur der Directe Belastingen* [1995] ECR I–2493; Case C–107/94 *Asscher* [1996] ECR I–3089; Case C–264/96 *Imperial Chemical Industries (ICI)* v. *Colmer* [1998] ECR I–4695.

[143] See M. Gammie, 'The role of the European Court of Justice in the development of direct discrimination in the European Union' (2003) 57 *Bulletin for International Fiscal Documentation* 86, 93.

[144] Case C–157/07 *Finanzamt für Körperschaften III in Berlin* v. *Krankenheim Ruhesitz am Wannsee-Seniorenheimstatt GmbH* [2008] ECR I–8061. [145] Para. 42.

[146] Case 120/78 *Cassis de Dijon* [1979] ECR 649.

[147] See, e.g., Case C–254/97 *Baxter and others* v. *Premier Ministre and others* [1999] ECR I–4809; Case C–55/98 *Skatteministeriet* v. *Bent Vestergaard* [1999] ECR I–7641. [148] [1977] OJ L336/15.

[149] Para. 45.

[150] Joined Cases C–155/08 and C–157/08 *X and E.H.A. Passenheim-van Schoot v Staatssecretaris van Financiën* [2009] ECR I–000. [151] Paras. 32–3.

but the measures could be justified on the grounds of the effectiveness of fiscal supervision and the prevention of tax evasion. On the question of proportionality, the Court said that where taxable items were concealed from the tax authorities of the taxing state, which meant that it could not request information from the competent authorities of the other Member State to establish correctly the amount of tax due, an extended recovery period of 12 years (as opposed to 5 years if the assets had been in the taxing state) did not go beyond what was necessary to guarantee the effectiveness of fiscal supervision and to prevent tax evasion. Nor did Union law preclude the fine imposed for concealment of the foreign assets and income from being calculated as a proportion of the amount to be recovered and over that longer period.[152]

### (c)  Equal treatment in respect of social advantages

#### (i)  Definition

Not only does Article 7(2) of Regulation 1612/68 require equal treatment in respect of tax advantages but it also requires 'social advantages' to be provided on a non-discriminatory basis. In *Even*[153] the Court defined social advantages broadly to include all benefits:[154]

which, whether or not linked to a contract of employment, are generally granted to national workers primarily because of their objective status as workers *or by virtue of the mere fact of their residence on the national territory* and the extension of which to workers who are nationals of other Member States therefore seems suitable to *facilitate their mobility* within the [Union].

The concept of social advantage includes benefits granted as of right[155] or on a discretionary basis,[156] and those granted after employment has terminated.[157] It also covers benefits not directly linked to employment, such as language rights,[158] death benefits,[159] and rights to be accompanied by unmarried companions.[160] These benefits do not necessarily 'facilitate mobility', as the *Even* formula requires, but do assist in integrating the migrant worker into the host state.[161] *Hartmann*[162] offered a new perspective on the justification for extending social advantages to migrant workers, in this case frontier workers. The Court said that the Austrian wife of a German worker, both of whom resided in Austria while he continued to work in Germany, could claim a German child-raising allowance

---

[152] Para. 76.        [153] Case 207/78 *Criminal Proceedings against Even* [1979] ECR 2019.

[154] Para. 22, emphasis added.

[155] See, e.g., Case C–111/91 *Commission* v. *Luxembourg* [1993] ECR I–817; Case C–85/96 *Martínez Sala* [1998] ECR I–2691, para. 28.

[156] Case 65/81 *Reina* v. *Landeskreditbank Baden-Württemberg* [1982] ECR 33, para. 17.

[157] See, e.g., Case C–57/96 *Meints* v. *Minister van Landbouw, Natuurbeheer en Visserij* [1997] ECR I–6689, para. 36 (payment to agricultural workers whose employment contracts are terminated); Case C–35/97 *Commission* v. *France (supplementary retirement pension points)* [1998] ECR I–5325; Case C–258/04 *Office national de l'empoli v Ioannidis* [2005] ECR I–8275, para. 34.

[158] Case 137/84 *Criminal proceedings against Mutsch* [1985] ECR 2681, para. 18 (criminal proceedings in the defendant's own language).

[159] Case C–237/94 *O'Flynn* [1996] ECR I–2617 (social security payments to help cover the cost of burying a family member).        [160] Case 59/85 *Netherlands* v. *Reed* [1986] ECR 1283, para. 28.

[161] E. Ellis, 'Social advantages: A new lease of life' (2003) 40 *CMLRev*. 639, 648.

[162] Case C–212/05 *Hartmann v Freistaat Bayern* [2007] ECR I–6303. For discussion, see A. Tryfonidou, 'In search of the aim of the EC free movement of persons provisions: Has the Court of Justice missed the point?' (2009) 46 *CMLRev*. I–1591.

because receipt of a child-raising allowance reduced the worker's obligation to contribute to family expenses.[163]

These cases suggest that the Court will give the widest possible reading to Article 7(2) in order to establish the 'greatest possible freedom of movement for migrant workers'.[164] This approach prompted the Court in *Hendrix* to re-examine the fundamental tenets of the complex Social Security Regulation 1408/71 (Regulation 883/04 from 1 March 2010). This regulation does not harmonize social security arrangements but coordinates them instead. In so doing, it contains a careful, politically negotiated balance between those benefits which can be exported and those which cannot. *Hendrix* threatened to undermine this balance. It concerned incapacity benefit payable to young people in the Netherlands, a special non-contributory benefit which was non-exportable (i.e., a benefit reserved to people residing in the territory of the state granting the benefit). Previously, that would have been conclusive and the case should have ended there.

However, in *Hendrix* the Court went on to consider the position of Mr Hendrix under Article 45 TFEU and Regulation 1612/68 when payment of the benefit was terminated after he changed his residence from the Netherlands to Belgium while continuing to work in the Netherlands. The Court said that the benefit was also a social advantage under Article 7(2) of Regulation 1612/68 which in turn is the 'specific expression, in the specific area of the grant of social advantages, of the principle of equal treatment enshrined in Article [45(2) TFEU]'.[165] Therefore the residence requirement was subject to review under Article 45 and Article 7(2) of Regulation 1612/68 and found to constitute unlawful indirect discrimination[166] unless justified (see below).

The effect of this decision is to reverse the standard presumption of the legality of the territoriality of social welfare benefits (i.e., Member States can restrict payment to those resident within the state). Following *Hendrix*, the presumption is that a state's refusal to allow the export of those benefits is unlawful unless justified.[167] And in reaching this conclusion the Court has been criticized because, in using purely legal tools which may well possess their own internal logic and doctrinal consistency, the Court is 'taking away from the political institutions an appreciable part of their power to decide on important questions of public expenditure and social solidarity'.[168] More positively, the development in *Hendrix* can be seen as a way of facilitating free movement by encouraging the home state to bear some of the costs of the emigration of its citizens, and not just the host state.

### (ii) Family members

The decision in *Even*, with its reference to 'residence on the national territory', shows that Article 7(2) applies to benefits granted by the host state not just to its workers[169] but also

---

[163] Para. 26.

[164] Case C–287/05 *Hendrix* v. *Raad van Bestuur van het Uitvoeringsinstituut Werknemersverzekeringen* [2007] ECR I–6909, para. 52. [165] Para. 53.

[166] See also Case C–57/96 *Meints* [1997] ECR I–6689, para.51. Subsequently, in Joined Cases C–396/05, C–419/05, and C–450/05 *Habelt* v. *Detscher Rentenversicherung Bund* [2007] ECR I–11895, para. 79 the Court talked about a restriction on the free movement of persons.

[167] M. Dougan, 'Expanding the frontiers of EU citizenship by dismantling the territorial boundaries of the national welfare states' in C. Barnard and O. Odudu (eds.) *The Outer Limits of EU Law* (Oxford: Hart Publishing, 2009). [168] M. Dougan, 'Legal developments' (2008) 46 *JCMS* 127, 137.

[169] This includes those who are not resident in the territory of the providing state: Case C–57/96 *Meints* [1997] ECR I–6689, para. 50; Case C–337/97 *Meeusen* [1999] ECR I–3289, para. 21.

to its residents.[170] This means that both migrant workers *and* their families can enjoy the social advantages offered by the home state.[171] The Court justified this development on the ground that Article 7(2) was essential not only to encourage free movement of workers as well as their families,[172] but also to ensure 'the best possible conditions for the integration of the Union worker's family in the society of the host Member State'.[173] This is now confirmed by Article 24(1) CRD which says that the benefit of the right to equal treatment 'shall be extended to family members who are non-nationals of a Member State and who have the right of residence or permanent residence'.

*Christini*[174] and *Castelli*[175] show just how wide-reaching the principle of equal treatment is in respect of social advantages, and how its beneficiaries are not only workers but also their family members. In *Christini* the French railways had a scheme which offered a fare reduction for people with large families. Christini, an Italian mother resident in France and the widow of an Italian who had worked in France, was refused the fare reduction on the ground of her nationality. SNCF, the French railway company, justified its decision on the ground that Article 7(2) applied only to advantages connected with the contract of employment. The Court disagreed, arguing that in view of the equality of treatment Article 7(2) was designed to achieve, the substantive area of application had to be delineated to include all social and tax advantages, regardless of any connection with an employment contract, including fare reductions for large families. It added that Article 7(2) applied to those lawfully entitled to remain in the host state, irrespective of whether the 'trigger' for the rights—the worker—was alive.

The Court adopted a similarly broad approach in *Castelli* concerning an Italian woman who lived in Belgium with her son. She had never worked and was refused a pension on the ground that she was not Belgian and that no reciprocal agreement existed between Belgium and Italy. Nevertheless, the Court found that the concept of social advantages in Article 7(2) should include a pension, reasoning that the principle of equal treatment in Article 7(1) of Regulation 1612/68 was also intended to prevent discrimination against a worker's dependent relatives.[176]

### (iii) Work-seekers

If family members can enjoy social advantages on the same terms as nationals, does the same rule apply to work-seekers? Early case law suggested that work-seekers did not enjoy access to social advantages in the same way as employed workers[177] but *Collins*[178] changed this position. Collins was an Irish work-seeker who came to the UK looking for employment. A week after his arrival he claimed Jobseeker's Allowance but was turned down on

---

[170] Jacobs AG in Case C–43/99 *Leclere* [2001] ECR I–4265, para. 96; S. Peers, '"Social advantages" and discrimination in employment: Case law confirmed and clarified' (1997) 22 *ELRev.* 157, 164.

[171] Cf. the early decision in Case 76/72 *Michel S.* v. *Fonds national de reclassement social des handicapés* [1973] ECR 457, para. 9, where the Court limited social advantages to workers.

[172] See, e.g., Case 94/84 *ONEM* v. *Deak* [1985] ECR 1873, para. 23.

[173] Case C–413/99 *Baumbast and R* v. *Secretary of State for the Home Department* [2002] ECR I–7091, para. 50.

[174] Case 32/75 *Fiorini (née Christini)* v. *SNCF* [1975] ECR 1085. See also Case C–278/94 *Commission* v. *Belgium (tideover benefits)* [1996] ECR I–4307; Case C–185/96 *Commission* v. *Greece (attribution of large family status)* [1998] ECR I–6601.          [175] Case 261/83 *Castelli* v. *ONPTS* [1984] ECR 3199.

[176] Ibid., concerning dependent relatives in the ascending line; in Case 94/84 *Deak* [1985] ECR 1873 the Court extended the benefit to dependent descendants, even though the descendant was a TCN.

[177] Case 316/85 *Centre public d'aide sociale de Courcelles (CPAS)* v. *Lebon* [1987] ECR 2811 and Case C–3/90 *Bernini* [1992] ECR I–1071.          [178] Case C–138/02 *Collins* [2004] ECR I–2703.

the grounds that he was not habitually resident in the UK. The Court began by stating the orthodox position that, as a work-seeker, the rights Collins enjoyed under Article 45 and Regulation 1612/68 were limited to equal treatment in respect of access to employment; he did not enjoy equal treatment in respect of social (financial) advantages. However, the Court then said that 'in view of the establishment of citizenship of the Union', it was no longer possible to exclude from the scope of Article 45 benefits of a 'financial nature intended to facilitate access to employment in the labour market of a Member State'.[179] *Collins* therefore sent out a clear message: orthodox tenets of the Court's earlier case law (in particular on workers) must now be given a 'citizenship' reading which might lead to a different result.

At first sight, the Court's approach to the Treaty provisions in *Collins* sits uncomfortably with Article 24(2) CRD, which provides that Member States are not obliged to provide social assistance during the citizen's first three months of residence or longer in the case of work-seekers under Article 14(4)(b) CRD. The term 'social assistance' is not defined in the directive although it is likely to be given an EU meaning. Traditionally it is used by way of contrast to 'social security'.[180] Originally, 'social security' was based on ideas of social insurance against the occurrence of risks facing those in work (sickness, unemployment and accidents) and other 'risks' in life which were likely to occur (childbirth, retirement and the needs of survivors on the death of the breadwinner). Having paid insurance contributions (in the UK through national insurance) the individual would become entitled to the benefit on the occurrence of the particular risk, without the application of any means test. By contrast, social assistance looked to need, and was more likely to be discretionary, requiring a decision of some authority on the suitability of the applicant for support.[181]

Returning to the dilemma presented by *Collins*, the Court managed to square this circle by declaring in *Vatsouras*[182] that 'Benefits of a financial nature which, independently of their status under national law, are intended to facilitate access to the labour market cannot be regarded as constituting "social assistance" within the meaning of Article 24(2) of Directive 2004/38.' In other words, such benefits are considered social advantages and not social assistance and so do not fall within the derogation under Article 24(2) but remain subject to the principle of equal treatment in Article 45(2) TFEU[183] (and Article 7(2) of Regulation 1612/68). However, as we shall see below, the combined use of objective justification, in particular the real link test, reasserted in *Vatsouras*,[184] and the application of the principle of proportionality may go some way towards protecting national welfare systems from 'benefit tourists'.

---

[179] See also Joined Cases C–22/08 and 23/08 *Vatsouras* [2009] ECR I–000, para. 37.

[180] R. White, *EC Social Security Law* (Longman: Harlow, 1999), 5–6. Cf. Case C–578/08 *Chakroun* [2010] ECR I–000, para. 45 where the Court, when interpreting the Family Reunification Dir. 2003/86, said 'social assistance' refers to assistance granted by public authorities, whether at national, regional or local level, which can be claimed by an individual who does not have stable and regular resources sufficient to maintain himself and his family.

[181] The distinction became blurred, first, because entitlement to social assistance has tended to become a matter of right rather than discretion, and second, because the burden of funding social insurance has resulted in moves to require a test of means even for some insurance-based benefits: while above, n. 180, 6.

[182] Joined Cases C–22/08 and 23/08 [2009] ECR I–000, para. 45.

[183] This reasoning also enabled the Court to conclude that by interpreting Art. 24(2) CRD in the light of Art. 45(2) TFEU this has 'not disclosed any factor capable of affecting the validity of Article 24(2)' (para. 46).

[184] Paras. 38–40.

*(iv) Limits*

Despite the Court's apparently broad approach to social advantages, it has recognized that there are some limits to the scope of Article 7(2), as the facts of *Even* itself demonstrate.[185] The case concerned Belgian regulations providing that a retirement pension could begin, if requested, up to five years prior to the normal pension age of 65, albeit with a reduction for early payment. This reduction was not made in the case of Belgians who had served in the Allied Forces during the Second World War and who had received an invalidity pension granted by an Allied country. Mr Even, a French national living in Belgium, received an invalidity pension from the French government, and he wished to receive the full Belgian state pension when he took early retirement. The Court said that the relevant Belgian legislation could not be considered a social advantage granted to a national worker because it benefited those who had given wartime service to their own country and 'its essential objective is to give those nationals an advantage by reason of the hardships suffered for that country'.[186] *Even* can perhaps be explained on the basis of the sensitive issues at stake: the Court did not want to face a future claim made by a migrant who was a former soldier but who had not served with the Allied Forces.

In *Leclere*[187] the Court gave a more detailed statement of the limits of Article 7(2). Leclere and his wife were Belgian. He was a frontier worker who lived in Belgium but worked in Luxembourg. When he had an accident in Luxembourg, the Luxembourg authorities paid him an invalidity pension. However, when his wife subsequently had a child he was refused a child birth allowance under Article 7(2) on the ground that he was no longer a worker. The Court upheld this decision. It said that as a former worker Leclere retained his status as worker in respect of the invalidity pension which was linked with his previous employment. He was therefore protected against any discrimination affecting rights acquired during the former employment. On the other hand, since he was not currently engaged in an employment relationship, he could not claim *new* rights which had no link with his former occupation.[188]

*(v) Non-discrimination and justification*

If the benefit does constitute a social advantage, then it must be provided on a non-discriminatory basis. While a number of the early cases concerned direct discrimination, the more recent cases concern indirect discrimination which is also prohibited unless justified. This can be seen in *Collins*,[189] the work-seeker case, where the Court noted that the British 'habitual residence' requirement disadvantaged those who had exercised their rights of free movement. However, the rule could be justified as a legitimate way of ensuring that there was a 'genuine link'[190] between the person applying for the

---

[185] Case 207/78 [1979] ECR 2019. See also Case C–315/94 *De Vos* [1996] ECR I–1417. Cf. Case 15/69 *Ugliola* [1970] ECR 363.

[186] Para. 23. See also Case C–386/02 *Baldinger* v. *Pensionsversicherungsanstalt der Arbeiter* [2004] ECR I–8411, para. 19 where the Court said that an Austrian allowance granted to Austrian prisoners of war was also not a social advantage. It was not granted to national workers because of their status as either workers or residents.                                                                [187] Case C–43/99 [2001] ECR I–4265.

[188] Para. 59. Cf. Art. 7(3) CRD.

[189] Case C–138/02 *Collins* [2004] ECR I–2703. See also Case C–237/94 *O'Flynn* [1996] ECR I–2617 considered in Ch. 8.

[190] Para. 67. See also Case C–258/04 *Office national de l'emploi* v *Ioannidis* [2005] ECR I–8275, paras. 30–3.

benefit.[191] The Court added that while the residence requirement was appropriate to attain the objective it was only proportionate if it rested on clear criteria known in advance, judicial redress was available and the period of residence could not be excessive.[192]

In *Geven*[193] the Court developed further the requirement of a real link between the claimant, in this case a Dutch woman residing in the Netherlands but doing 'minor' employment in Germany, and the territory in which she was claiming the benefit, in this case a German child-raising allowance. In order to obtain this benefit, the individual had to be resident in Germany, an indirectly discriminatory requirement. The Court permitted the German government to raise a wide range of justifications to defend the breach, in particular encouraging the birth rate, allowing parents to care for their children themselves by giving up or reducing their employment and benefitting individuals who, by their choice of residence have 'established a real link with German society'. Germany was also flexible in its requirements for showing a real link: it could be done through residence or, in the case of frontier workers, by showing a substantial contribution to the German labour market. This pitted Mr Hartmann[194] (whose position was considered above) and Ms Geven against one another: neither could show residence but while Mr Hartmann worked full time in Germany and therefore made a substantial contribution to the national labour market, Ms Geven did not. Mr Hartmann's wife therefore received the benefit; Ms Geven did not.[195]

Finally, in *Hendrix* (considered above) the Court found the residence requirement could be justified on two grounds.[196] First, it noted that the benefit was 'closely linked to the socio-economic situation' of the Netherlands since it was based on the minimum wage and standard of living there. Secondly, and more significantly, in the light of the fit between Social Security Regulation 1408/71 (now Regulation 883/04) and Regulation 1612/68, the Court pointed to the principle of non-exportability in the Social Security Regulation, to justify the residence requirement.[197] However, in contrast to the pre-*Hendrix* situation, the Court emphasized that these justifications were now subject to a proportionality review which was a matter for the national court.

These cases are good examples of how the court has used the 'real link' test to help reconcile the traditionally territorial approach to the payment of benefits and the need to facilitate free movement.[198] While a territorial restriction is presumptively unlawful, it

---

[191] Para. 70.

[192] Para. 72. The proportionality of the measure was upheld by the national court: [2005] UKSSCSC CJSA_4065_1999 (4 Mar. 2005).

[193] Case C-213/05 *Geven v Land Nordrhein-Westfalen* [2007] ECR I-6347.

[194] Case C-212/05 *Hartmann v Freistaat Bayern* [2007] ECR I-6303.

[195] For discussion, see S. O'Leary, 'Developing an ever closer union between the peoples of Europe? A reappraisal of the case law of the Court of Justice on the free movement of persons and EU citizenship' (2008) 27 *YEL* 167, 188–9.

[196] Cf. Case C-228/07 *Petersen v. Arbeitsmarktservice Niederösterreich* [2008] ECR I-6989 where the Court found the residence criteria could not be objectively justified after careful scrutiny of potential justifications.

[197] The Court adopted a similar approach in Case C-341/05 *Laval un Partneri Ltd v. Svenska Byggnadsarbetareförbundet* [2007] ECR I-11767 where the Court looked to see if the provisions of the Posted Workers Dir. 96/71 had been satisfied to see if a justification had been made out.

[198] C. O'Brien 'Real links, abstract rights and false alarms: The relationship between the ECJ's "real link" case law and national solidarity' (2008) 33 *ELRev.* 643. See also R. White, 'Free movement, equal treatment and citizenship of the union' (2005) 54 *ICLQ* 885, 905.

can be justified by requiring the migrant to show a genuine connection with the territory of the paying state but the proportionality of the conditions used to demonstrate that link will be carefully scrutinized. Because, in *Geven* and *Hartmann,* Germany was flexible in the ways that the 'real link' could be demonstrated, the Court was generally sympathetic towards its legislation. Nevertheless, the EU's approach still stands in sharp contrast to that adopted by the US Supreme Court: it has consistently found unconstitutional state laws which grant social welfare benefits only to individuals who have resided in the state for a year.[199]

### (d)  Equal treatment and vocational training

#### (i)  Access to training

Not only does Regulation 1612/68 require equal treatment in respect of tax and social advantages but the principle also applies in respect of access to vocational training. Article 7(3) provides that a worker shall 'have access to training in vocational schools and retraining centres' under the same conditions as national workers. In *Gravier*[200] the Court defined 'vocational training' broadly to include any form of education which prepares an individual for a qualification or which provides the necessary training or skills for a particular profession, trade, or employment. In *Blaizot*[201] the Court confirmed that vocational training could be received at universities, except in the case of courses intended for students 'wishing to improve their general knowledge rather than prepare themselves for a particular occupation'.[202]

Access to training is one thing; the level of fees for that training is another. In *Gravier* the Court said that since access to training was likely to promote free movement of persons by enabling them to obtain a qualification in the Member State where they intended to work,[203] the conditions of access to vocational training fell within the scope of the Treaties. Therefore, if a host state charged a registration fee to migrant students but not to its own students, there was a breach of Article 18 TFEU (ex Article 12 EC).[204]

The principle that migrant students must have access to higher education on the same terms as nationals and to be charged the same fees has started to pose significant problems for states, such as the UK and Ireland, which are net recipients of students. In respect of the availability of places, in the UK at least, every incoming migrant EU student will take a place which might have been occupied by a domestic student.[205] These issues were

---

[199]  See, e.g., *Shapiro v. Thompson* 394 US 618 (1969); *Saenz v. Roe* 526 US 489 (1999). See also G. Rosberg, 'Free movement of persons in the United States' in T. Sandalow and E. Stein (eds.) *Courts and Free Markets: Perspectives form the United States and Europe* (Oxford: Clarendon Press, 1982).

[200]  Case 293/83 *Gravier v. Ville de Liège* [1985] ECR 593, para. 30. For background see K. Lenaerts, 'Education in European Community law after "Maastricht"' (1994) 31 *CMLRev.* 7; J. Shaw, 'From the margins to the centre: Education and training law and policy' in P. Craig and G. de Búrca (eds.), *The Evolution of EU Law* (Oxford: OUP, 1999).

[201]  Case 24/86 *Blaizot v. Université de Liège and others* [1988] ECR 379.

[202]  Paras. 19–20. See also Case C–40/05 *Lyyski* [2007] ECR I–10025, paras. 28–30 (teacher training course constituted vocational training).                                                                    [203]  Para. 24.

[204]  Para. 26.

[205]  See the comments of Sir Howard Newby, chief executive of the Higher Education Funding Council for England reported by L. Lightfoot, 'Students face EU fight for places', *Daily Telegraph*, 4 Mar. 2004, 1. He said

considered directly by the Court in *Commission* v. *Austria*.[206] Austrian law allowed broad access to higher education for holders of Austrian school leaving certificates but subjected those with comparable certificates from other Member States to more stringent requirements. The principal ground offered by Austria to justify its indirectly discriminatory rules[207] was to preserve the 'homogeneity of the Austrian higher or university education system'. It argued that if it did not impose some limitation, Austria, with its policy of unrestricted access to all levels of education,[208] could expect a large number of students with diplomas awarded in other states (especially Germany), who had failed to be admitted to higher education courses in those states, to try to attend higher education courses in Austria. Such a situation, it argued, would cause 'structural, staffing and financial problems'.[209]

The Court found that there was little evidence that this was in fact a problem[210] and even if it was, the justification based on preserving the homogeneity of the Austrian higher education system was not, in fact, made out by the Austrian government.[211] Even if it was a problem, the Court offered a simple solution: excessive demand for access to specific courses could be met by the adoption of specific non-discriminatory measures such as the establishment of an entry examination or the requirement of a minimum grade.[212] It also noted that the risks alleged by the Austrian government were not exclusively an Austrian problem 'but have been and are suffered by other Member States'[213] (including Belgium which had introduced similar restrictions which were also found to breach Union law[214]).[215]

---

that 'We expect to admit students on their merit. Most universities take the view that they want the most talented students almost irrespective of their origins. If they come from Estonia as opposed to Egham [in the UK], that is a matter for them.' This problem has been brought into sharp focus by enlargement. A report from the Higher Education Policy Institute (<http://www.hepi.ac.uk/files/10AnUpdate-Supplyand Demandto2010.pdf>) predicted that 30,000 students will arrive from the new Member States and that this is 'likely to increase competition for places…If the government does not provide the extra places, some of these will be displacing UK students'. See also M.Dougan, 'Fees, grants, loans and dole cheques: Who covers the costs of migrant education within the EU? (2005) 42 *CMLRev.* 943.

[206] Case C–147/03 [2005] ECR I–5969, noted Rieder (2006) 43 *CMLRev.* 1711. See also Case C–73/08 *Bressol* v. *Gouvernement de la Communauté française* [2010] ECR I–000.

[207] Para. 47.

[208] According to the AG's Opinion, this policy was introduced to improve the percentage of Austrian citizens with a higher education qualification, which was one of the lowest in the EU (para. 26).

[209] Para. 50, citing the Court's case law on access to healthcare services (Case C–158/96 *Kohll* [1998] ECR I–1931, para. 41 and Case C–368/98 *Vanbraekel* [2001] ECR I–5363) by analogy.          [210] Para. 65.

[211] Para. 66.          [212] Para. 61.          [213] Para. 62.

[214] Case C–65/03 *Commission* v. *Belgium* [2004] ECR I–6427. Nevertheless, in Mar. 2006 the Minister for Higher Education proposed capping the number of foreign students to 30% in areas dominated by foreign students such as veterinary medicine where French students count for 86% of the total students studying in Belgium. The minister said that the reform could save 15 million euros that could be reinvested in Belgian education: *euobserver.com*, 22 Mar. 2006.

[215] See Austrian Chancellor Wolfgang Schussel's subsequent criticism of the Court of Justice for extending its competence into areas where there is 'decidedly no [Union] law such as on access of foreign students to Austrian universities'. He called for the debate on the future of the EU to focus not only on the fate of the Constitution but also on the role of the Court of Justice: *euobserver.com*, 3 Jan. 2006.

*(ii) Funding*

*Gravier* concerned fees, not grants. Maintenance grants can constitute 'social advantages' within the meaning of Article 7(2).[216] In *Matteucci*[217] an Italian worker working in Belgium applied for a scholarship available on a bilateral (Belgium–Germany) basis to study singing in Berlin. Her application was rejected on the ground that she was not Belgian. The Court said that this was contrary to Article 7(2): a bilateral agreement reserving scholarships for nationals of the two Member States which were the parties to the agreement could not prevent the application of the principle of equality under Union law.

Matteucci's case was a strong one: she had lived and worked in Belgium all her life. But the case law on Article 7(2) is open to exploitation by those who do short-term casual work in another Member State and then claim entitlement to social advantages in the form of a grant for further study in the host state. The Court had to address this problem in two important cases, *Lair*[218] and *Brown*.[219] *Lair* concerned a French woman who had moved to Germany where she worked on a series of part-time contracts. Having decided to study for a languages degree at the University of Hanover she sought a maintenance grant from the German authorities. The Court recognized that people who had previously pursued an effective and genuine activity in the host state could still be considered workers and so could receive a maintenance grant under Article 7(2) but only on condition that there was a link between the previous occupational activity[220] and the studies.[221] However, the Court added that where a migrant worker became involuntarily unemployed no link between the studies and the occupational activity was required before a maintenance grant was awarded.[222] The result in *Lair* has now been incorporated into Article 7(3)(d) CRD.

*Brown* was rather different. He was a student with dual French and British nationality who lived in France for many years before getting a place at Cambridge University to read engineering. He was sponsored by Ferranti and worked for the company in the UK for eight months before starting his course. He then claimed that he was a worker and so was entitled to a grant from the British authorities under Article 7(2). The Court refused to recognize him as a worker, viewing his work for Ferranti as merely ancillary to his studies.[223] Therefore, he could not receive a maintenance grant under Article 7(2), nor could he rely on the general prohibition of discrimination in Article 18 TFEU to obtain the grant. The Court said that at that stage of development of Union law the assistance

---

[216] Case C–3/90 *Bernini* v. *Minister van Onderwijs en Wetenschappen* [1992] ECR I–1071, para. 23, where the Court ruled that descendants of workers could rely on Art. 7(2) to obtain study finance under the same conditions as children of national workers. This also applies to non-resident children of migrant workers (Case C–337/97 *Meeusen* [1999] ECR I–3289, para. 25) but not to workers who have returned to their states of origin (Case C–33/99 *Fahmi* [2001] ECR I–2415, para. 46).

[217] Case 235/87 *Matteucci* v. *Communauté française de Belgique* [1988] ECR 5589.

[218] Case 39/86 *Lair* v. *Universität Hannover* [1988] ECR 3161. See also Case C–357/90 *Raulin* [1992] ECR I–1027, para. 21.          [219] Case 197/86 *Brown* v. *Secretary of State for Scotland* [1988] ECR 3205.

[220] The host state cannot make the right to the same social advantages conditional upon a minimum period of prior occupational activity (Case 39/86 *Lair* [1988] ECR 3161, para. 44). In Case C–413/01 *Ninni-Orasche* [2003] ECR I–13187, para. 42, the Court added that the mere fact the individual is employed on a fixed-term contract does not mean that when the contract expires the employee is automatically to be regarded as voluntarily unemployed.

[221] If no link exists between the study and the previous occupational activities, the person does not retain the status of migrant worker (Case C–357/89 *Raulin* [1992] ECR I–1027).          [222] Para. 37.

[223] Para. 27.

given to students for maintenance and training fell outside the scope of the Treaties.[224] This view was confirmed by Article 3 of the Students' Directive 93/96, which provided that the directive did not establish any right to payment of maintenance grants by the host state for students who benefit from the right of residence. Article 3 has been repealed and replaced by Article 24(2) CRD, which provides that, prior to the acquisition of permanent residence (primarily, under Article 16 CRD, after five years' residence), the host state is not obliged to grant maintenance aid for studies, including vocational training, consisting of student grants or loans to persons other than workers, the self-employed, persons who retain such status and members of their families.

However, *Brown* and the directive(s) left open the question whether *only* maintenance grants were excluded from the scope of Union law or whether *all* assistance given to students (maintenance grants *and* income support, housing benefit, and child support) was excluded. This issue was addressed in *Grzelczyk*.[225] A French national studying in Belgium supported himself financially during the first three years of study, as required by Article 1 of Directive 93/96 (now Article 7(1)(c) CRD). He then applied to the Belgian authorities for a minimex (a guarantee of minimum income) to fund his fourth and final year. This was refused on the ground that he was not Belgian. Had he been a worker, such (direct) discrimination in respect of access to a social advantage would have contravened Article 7(2).[226] However, the national court thought that he was not a worker so the Court of Justice considered his position as an EU citizen under Articles 20–1 TFEU (ex Articles 17–18 EC)[227] and as a student under the Students' Directive 93/96. The Court noted that while Article 1 of Directive 93/96 (now Article 7(1)(c) CRD) required the student to have sufficient resources to avoid becoming a burden on the social assistance system,[228] there were no provisions in the directive precluding students from receiving social security benefits.[229] The Court therefore concluded that Article 21 TFEU on the citizen's right to move and reside freely, read in conjunction with Article 18 TFEU on non-discrimination, precluded Belgium from requiring migrants to be workers before they could receive the minimex, when no such condition applied to nationals.[230]

*Grzelczyk* therefore suggested that *Brown* continued to be good law in respect of maintenance grants but the principle of equal treatment applied in respect of all other benefits classified as general social assistance which were provided to national students.[231] This understanding was subject to further qualification by *Bidar*.[232] Bidar, a French national, came to the United Kingdom in 1998 to live with his grandmother. Having attended the local secondary school, he started reading economics at University College London in September 2001. While he received assistance with his tuition *fees* following *Gravier*, his application for financial assistance to cover his *maintenance* costs, in the form of a student loan, was refused on the grounds that he did not satisfy the conditions laid down (i.e., resident in the UK for three years prior to starting the course plus having 'settled' status in the UK, a status that was, in practice, impossible for students to attain).

---

[224] Para. 18.    [225] Case C–184/99 *Grzelczyk* [2001] ECR I–6193.

[226] Case 249/83 *Hoeckx v. Openbaar Centrum voor Maatschappelijk Welzijn* [1985] ECR 973, para. 25.

[227] These are considered further in Ch. 12.    [228] Para. 38.    [229] Para. 39.    [230] Para. 46.

[231] A. Iliopoulou and H. Toner (2002) 39 *CMLRev.* 609, 612.

[232] Case C–209/03 *R (on the application of Danny Bidar) v. London Borough of Ealing, Secretary of State for Education and Skills* [2005] ECR I–2119.

While the UK government thought that it was on safe ground denying Bidar a maintenance grant and loan due to the decisions in *Brown* and *Lair* and Article 3 of Directive 93/96, the Court of Justice had other ideas. It noted that Bidar, a citizen of the Union, was lawfully resident in the UK due to Article 21 TFEU read in conjunction, not with the Students' Directive 93/96, but the Persons of Independent Means Directive 90/364 (now Article 7(1)(b) CRD), the conditions of which he was deemed to have satisfied. And because he was lawfully resident in the UK, he was entitled to equal treatment under Article 18 TFEU in respect of social assistance benefits. The Court said that these benefits did now include assistance with maintenance costs whether through subsidized loans or grants. It said that given the changes that had occurred at EU level in respect of education and training since *Lair* and *Brown*, and now confirmed by Article 24 CRD, social assistance for a student 'whether in the form of a subsidised loan or a grant, intended to cover his maintenance costs' fell within the scope of application of the Treaties. Bidar was therefore entitled to have the principle of non-discrimination on the grounds of nationality applied to him. The Court then said that the English rules were indirectly discriminatory: requiring students to be settled in the UK and to satisfy certain residence conditions risked placing nationals of other Member States at a disadvantage since both conditions were likely to be more easily satisfied by UK nationals. However, the Court also accepted that while, in the organization and application of their social assistance schemes, Member States had to show a certain degree of financial solidarity with nationals of other Member States, it was legitimate for a Member State to grant assistance only to students who had demonstrated a certain degree of integration into the society of that state.[233] This integration could be shown through a period of residence. The Court suggested that a three-year residence requirement was compatible with Union law but that the requirement to be settled was not, since it was impossible for a student from another Member State ever to obtain settled status.

This case shows that the limits laid down by Article 3 of the Students' Directive (now Article 24(2) CRD) did not apply to those who are students but come to the host state in a capacity other than that of a student (e.g., where, as in *Bidar*, they come as persons of independent means). The decision also shows that the spirit of the distinction drawn in *Brown* between fees (where full equal treatment was required from day one) and maintenance (where it was not) is still maintained. Had the Court ruled that maintenance grants were to be provided to all migrant students on day one of their arrival in the host state, this would have had a dramatic effect on the education budgets of host states, particularly states which are net recipients of students. The Court staved off this possibility by allowing host states to impose a proportionate residence requirement on all students prior to entitlement to maintenance grants and loans, a position now confirmed by Article 24(2)

---

[233] Cf. Joined Cases C–11/06 and C–12/06 *Morgan v Bezirksregierung Köln and Iris Bucher v Landrat des Kreises Düren* [2007] ECR I–9161, considered in Ch. 12, concerning the obligations of the *home* state to provide educational grants for its students studying in a host state. It concluded that (para. 28) 'where a Member State provides for a system of education or training grants which enables students to receive such grants if they pursue studies in another Member State, it must ensure that the detailed rules for the award of those grants do not create an unjustified restriction of the right to move and reside within the territory of the Member States'. In other words, if states do decide to fund studies in other Member States they must not impose arbitrary conditions. See M. Dougan, 'Cross-border educational mobility and the exportation for student financial assistance' (2008) 33 *ELRev* 723, 730.

CRD which provides for a five-year residence period.[234] The five-year residence period was upheld in *Förster*[235] where the Court said that a condition of five years' continuous residence could not be seen as excessive in order to ensure the degree of integration of migrants in the host Member State.[236] The Court added that since the residence requirement was applied by the national authorities on the basis of clear criteria known in advance, this guaranteed 'a significant level of legal certainty and transparency' in the context of the award of maintenance grants.[237]

### (e) Equal treatment and other benefits

Equality is not confined to tax and social advantages and vocational training. Article 8(1) of Regulation 1612/68 provides that migrant workers must also enjoy equality of treatment with nationals in respect of trade union membership and the exercise of rights related to trade union membership, 'including the right to vote and to be eligible for the administration or management posts of a trade union'.[238] In *ASTI I* and *ASTI II*[239] the Court ruled that Article 8 applied to the right to vote and to stand in elections held by bodies such as occupational guilds to which workers were required to belong, to which they had to pay contributions and which were responsible for defending and representing their interests. However, Article 8 does provide that workers can be excluded from taking part in the management of bodies governed by public law and from holding office governed by public law.[240] The Austrian government relied on this clause in *Commission v. Austria (workers' chambers)*[241] to justify its exclusion of all non-Austrians from standing for election to workers' chambers. Unsurprisingly, the Court said that, as a derogation to a fundamental freedom, the public law exception had to be interpreted narrowly.[242] Since there was little difference between the role of workers' chambers in *Commission v. Austria* and the role of the guilds in the *ASTI* cases, the *Austria* case fell within the scope of Article 8 of Regulation 1612/68 (and Article 45 TFEU)[243] and Austria was in breach of the principle of equal treatment.

Finally, Article 9 of Regulation 1612/68 provides that workers must enjoy all the rights and benefits accorded to national workers in matters of housing, including ownership, and the right to put their names on housing lists in the region where they are employed. Therefore in *Commission v. Greece*[244] the Court found a rule restricting a foreigner's right

---

[234] Respecting the non-regression clause in the CRD, the UK has maintained its three-year rule.

[235] Case C–158/07 *Förster v Hoofddirectie van de Informatie Beheer Groep* [2008] ECR I–8507, para. 52.

[236] It added that Member States remained free to award maintenance grants to students from other Member States without the five-year residence requirement (para. 59). [237] Paras. 56–7.

[238] See further A. Evans, 'Development of European Community law regarding the trade union rights and related rights of migrant workers' (1979) 28 *ICLQ* 354.

[239] Case C–213/90 *Association de Soutien aux Travailleurs Immigrés v. Chambre des Employés Privés (ASTI I)* [1991] ECR I–3507 and Case C–118/92 *Commission v. Luxembourg (ASTI II)* [1994] ECR I–1891.

[240] Art. 8.      [241] Case C–465/01 [2004] ECR I–8291.      [242] Para. 39.

[243] The Austrian law had already been condemned in Case C–171/01 *Wählergruppe, 'Gemeinsam Zajedno/Birlikte Alternative und Grüne Gewerkschafter Innen/UG' and others* [2003] ECR I–4301 which concerned Art. 10 of the EEC–Turkey Agreement which is interpreted in the same way as Art. 8 of Reg. 1612/68.

[244] Case 305/87 *Commission v. Greece* [1989] ECR 1461. See also Case 63/86 *Commission v. Italy (social housing)* [1988] ECR 29, considered in Ch. 10.

to own property in Greece breached the free movement rules, since access to housing and ownership of property was the corollary of free movement.[245]

# D. CONCLUSIONS

In the case law on workers it is possible to detect the embryo of what later became EU citizenship. In particular, the Court's decisions on social advantages under Article 7(2) of Regulation 1612/68 went far beyond what was necessary to ensure the mobility of workers. The ever-expanding rights given to the worker's family members in cases such as *Christini* and *Castelli* provided the testing ground for the Court's more ambitious jurisprudence on rights for EU citizens who are not economically active.[246] And now, in cases such as *Collins*, we see how the Court is using its citizenship case law to justify removing limitations on the exercise of Union rights.

The human rights orientation which underpins much of the Court's case law on workers is less visible in respect of freedom of establishment. In this area we see a greater preoccupation with ensuring that individuals and, increasingly, companies gain access to the host state's market and do not suffer impediments once on that market. It is to this subject that we now turn.

---

[245] Para. 18.

[246] See, e.g., Case C–184/99 *Grzelczyk* [2001] ECR I–6193, considered further in Ch. 12.

# 10

# FREEDOM OF ESTABLISHMENT

## A. INTRODUCTION

While Article 45 concerns workers, Article 49 TFEU (ex Article 43 EC) concerns the self-employed and companies. Both individuals and companies have the right to take up and pursue activities in other Member States without discrimination. As the Court put it in *Factortame II*,[1] the essence of Article 49 is 'the actual pursuit of an economic activity through a fixed establishment in another Member State for an indefinite period'. In this chapter we consider restrictions on both access to, and exercise of, freedom of establishment, particularly in the light of the Services Directive 2006/123.[2] However, we begin by considering the beneficiaries of the right of establishment.

## B. THE SCOPE OF THE PROVISIONS ON FREEDOM OF ESTABLISHMENT

### 1. THE FREEDOM OF ESTABLISHMENT FOR INDIVIDUALS

Article 49 provides that 'restrictions on the freedom of establishment of nationals of a Member State in the territory of another Member State shall be prohibited'. In practice this means that the self-employed nationals of a Member State have the right to establish themselves in another Member State.[3] The Treaties do not define 'self-employed', but in *Jany*[4] the Court explained that, unlike workers, the self-employed work outside a relationship of subordination, they bear the risk for the success or failure of their employment, and they are paid directly and in full.[5] The case concerned Czech and Polish women working as prostitutes in the Netherlands.[6] They paid rent to the owner of the premises

---

[1] Case C–221/89 *R.* v. *Secretary of State for Transport, ex p. Factortame (Factortame II)* [1991] ECR I–3905, para. 20.

[2] [2006] OJ L376/36. While this directive is more typically associated with temporary service provision under Art. 56, many individuals and companies establishing themselves on a permanent basis in the host state are actually service providers (e.g., lawyers, accountants) to whom the Services Dir. may apply.

[3] But not a third country: Case C–102/05 *Skatteverket* v. *A and B*, Order of 10 May 2007; Case C–157/05 *Holböck* v. *Finanzamt Salzburg-Land* [2007] ECR I–4051, para. 28.

[4] Case C–268/99 *Jany and others* v. *Staatssecretaris van Justitie* [2001] ECR I–8615, noted by C. Hillion (2003) 40 *CMLRev.* 465. See also Joined Cases C–151/04 and C–152/04 *Nadin* [2005] ECR I–11203, para. 31.

[5] Paras. 34 and 70–1.

[6] The case was decided under the Europe Agreements but in this regard the Court said that the principles were the same as those under Art. 49 (para. 38).

and received a monthly income (of between FL. 1,500 and 1,800) which they declared to the tax authorities. The Court considered them to be self-employed. The fact that prostitution was considered immoral by some did not alter the Court's conclusions: recognizing the margin of discretion allowed to the Member States in these sensitive areas, the Court said that it would not substitute its own assessment for that of the Member States where an allegedly immoral activity was practised legally.[7]

*Jany* suggests that Article 49 permits individuals to engage in a wide range of economic activities in other Member States and still be considered self-employed. As the Court put it in *Barkoci and Malik*,[8] a self-employed person could conduct 'activities of an industrial or commercial character, activities of craftsmen, or activities of the professions of a Member State'.[9] Individuals can also exercise their right of establishment in another way: by participating in the formation of a company in another Member State[10] within the meaning of Article 54 TFEU (ex Article 48 EC) (by, for example becoming a shareholder in a company[11] or a director[12]). Finally, a Union citizen who is no longer self-employed will retain the status of being self-employed in the circumstances laid out in Article 7(3) of the Citizens' Rights Directive (CRD).[13]

The breadth of Article 49 was emphasized by the Court in *Gebhard*:

the concept of establishment within the meaning of the [Treaties] is therefore a very broad one, allowing a [Union] national to participate, on a stable and continuous basis, in the economic life of a Member State other than his state of origin and to profit therefrom, so contributing to social and economic penetration within the [Union] in the sphere of activities as self-employed persons.[14]

## 2. THE FREEDOM OF ESTABLISHMENT FOR COMPANIES

In respect of companies, the Treaties contemplate two forms of establishment:

- the right to set up and manage undertakings, in particular companies or firms within the meaning of the second paragraph of Article 54 (primary establishment)[15]

---

[7] Para. 56. However, the Court could not resist adding: 'Far from being prohibited in all Member States, prostitution is tolerated, even regulated, by most of those States, notably the Member State concerned in this case [the Netherlands]' (para. 57).

[8] Case C–257/99 *R.* v. *Secretary of State for the Home Department, ex p. Barkoci and Malik* [2001] ECR I–6557, para. 50. This was in the context of Art. 45(3) of the Association Agreement which has wording 'similar or identical to' Art. 49.

[9] See also Case C–55/94 *Gebhard* [1995] ECR I–4165, para. 23, 'all types of self-employed activity'.

[10] Art. 49(2).

[11] Case 182/83 *Fearon* v. *Irish Land Commission* [1985] ECR 3677, para. 9; Case C–251/98 *Baars* v. *Inspecteur der Belastingdienst Particulieren/Ondernemingen Gorinchem* [2000] ECR I–2728, para. 22; Case C–212/97 *Centros* v. *Erhvervs- og Selskabsstyrelsen* [1999] ECR I–1459, para. 19.

[12] Case C–221/89 *Factortame II* [1991] ECR I–3905.     [13] These are discussed in Ch. 9.

[14] Para. 25. This is the establishment equivalent of the requirement in the field of workers to be engaged in a genuine and effective economic activity which is not ancillary or purely marginal. See also Art. 4(5) of the Services Dir. 2006/123/EC ([2006] OJ L376/36) considered further in Ch. 11.

[15] Art. 49, para. 2. Art. 54 provides that '"Companies or firms" means companies or firms constituted under civil or commercial law, including cooperative societies, and other legal persons governed by public or private law, save for those which are non-profit making' (para. 2). The non-profit making exclusion was emphasized in Case C–70/95 *Sodemare* v. *Regione Lombardia* [1997] ECR I–3395, an exclusion consistent with the equivalent provision in Art. 56 that services are 'normally provided for remuneration'.

- the right to set up agencies, branches, or subsidiaries by nationals of any Member State established in the territory of any Member State (secondary establishment);[16] provided there is a permanent establishment, the establishment does not need to have separate legal personality.[17]

As the Court emphasized in *Cadbury's Schweppes*,[18] in both situations Article 49 presupposes (1) actual establishment of the company in the host state (i.e., permanent presence) and (2) the pursuit of a genuine economic activity there. Both conditions must be fulfilled for Article 49 to apply. This can be seen in *Stauffer*.[19] An Italian charitable foundation had commercial premises in Germany which it rented out, the letting being managed by a German property agent. The Court said that Article 49 did not apply because, while holding immovable property indicated permanent presence, there was no genuine economic activity because the property was not actively managed. The Court said that Article 63 TFEU (ex Article 56 EC) on free movement of capital applied instead. However, the Court has insisted that the provisions on establishment, not capital, will apply where:

- national provisions apply to existing holdings[20]—or the acquisition of holdings[21]—by nationals of State A in the capital of a company established in State B, giving them a definite influence on the company's decisions and allowing them to determine its activities
- national rules which affect relations within a group of companies.[22]

The rights for legal persons are discussed in detail below. First we turn to the rights enjoyed by individuals under Article 49.

## C. THE RIGHTS CONFERRED ON NATURAL PERSONS: THE SELF-EMPLOYED

### 1. RIGHTS OF DEPARTURE, ENTRY, AND RESIDENCE

Directive 73/148/EEC on the abolition of restrictions on movement and residence within the Union for nationals of Member States with regard to establishment and the provision of services[23] provided that Member States had to abolish restrictions on the movement and residence of nationals (but not of companies[24]) wishing either:

- to establish themselves in another Member State as self-employed persons

---

[16] Art. 49, para. 1.

[17] Case C-414/06 *Lidl Belgium GmbH & Co.KG v. Finanzamt Heilbronn* [2008] ECR I-3601, para. 15.

[18] Case C-196/04 *Cadbury's Schweppes v Commissioners of the Inland Revenue* [2006] ECR I-7995, para. 54.

[19] Case C-386/04 *Centro di Musicologia Walter Stauffer* [2006] ECR I-8203, para. 19. See also Case C-451/05 *ELISA v. Directeur general des impost* [2007] ECR I-8251, paras. 65-7.

[20] Case C-231/05 *Oy AA* [2007] ECR I-6373, para.20.

[21] Case C-251/98 *Baars* [2000] ECR I-2787, paras. 21-2, and Case C-208/00 *Überseering* [2002] ECR I-9919, para. 77.

[22] Case C-446/04 *FII Group Litigation* [2006] ECR I-11753, para. 118; Case C-231/05 *Oy AA* [2007] ECR I-6373, para. 23.     [23] [1973] OJ L172/14.

[24] Case 81/87 *R. v. HM Treasury, ex p. Daily Mail and General Trust* [1988] ECR 5483, para. 28.

- to provide services in another Member State
- to enter another Member State to receive services.

The directive also imposed the same obligations on Member States in respect of members of the self-employed person's family. This directive has now been repealed and replaced by the Citizens' Rights Directive 2004/38 in respect of freedom of establishment (but not free movement of services), the details of which are considered in Chapter 12. However, as the Court has observed, the provisions of the directive(s) merely spell out the rights already protected by Article 49 itself. So Article 49 prohibits a home State from hindering the establishment of one of its own nationals in another Member State.[25] Article 49 also prohibits a requirement that a migrant be registered with the relevant authorities before obtaining the right of residence,[26] since the grant of a residence permit has merely probative value—it is not constitutive of the right of residence.[27] Likewise, a rule providing that failure to register results in deportation breaches Article 49, since this would negate the right of residence conferred by the Treaties.[28]

Having left State A and entered State B, what rights does an individual enjoy once in State B? According to Article 49, freedom of establishment includes the 'right to take up *and* pursue' activities as a self-employed person 'under the conditions laid down for its own nationals by the law of the country where such establishment is effected'. In its application of the principle of equal treatment. In its application of the principle of equal treatment, Article 49 therefore distinguishes between (1) the right to take up an activity (access—i.e., the initial right to take up work as a self-employed person), and (2) the right to pursue that activity once in the host state (exercise—i.e., the terms and conditions of employment and the facilities necessary to exercise that profession). We shall consider these in turn.

## 2. THE RIGHT OF ACCESS TO SELF-EMPLOYMENT

### 2.1 Primary and Secondary Establishment

Article 49 applies to both primary and secondary establishment. With *primary* establishment, an individual leaves State A to set up a permanent establishment in State B; with *secondary* establishment, an individual maintains an establishment in State A[29] while setting up a second professional base (e.g., an office or chambers) in State B. This was the situation in *Klopp*,[30] where a German national and member of the Düsseldorf Bar wished to practise in Paris as an *avocat* while remaining a member of the Düsseldorf Bar and retaining his residence and chambers there. His application was rejected by the Paris Bar on the ground that an *avocat* could have only one set of chambers which had to be in the region of Paris. The effect of the French rules was to allow *avocats* to have a

---

[25] Case C–251/98 *Baars* [2000] ECR I–2787, para. 28. See also Case 81/87 *Ex p. Daily Mail* [1988] ECR 5483, para. 16.

[26] Case C–363/89 *Roux* [1991] ECR I–273, para. 11.

[27] Case 48/75 *Royer* [1976] ECR 497, para. 31; Case C–363/89 *Roux* [1991] ECR I–273, para. 12.

[28] Case C–363/89 *Roux* [1991] ECR I–273, para. 11.

[29] Either as an employee or a self-employed person in State A: Case 143/87 *Stanton* v. *Inasti* [1988] ECR 3877, para. 12.

[30] Case 107/83 *Ordre des Avocats au Barreau de Paris* v. *Klopp* [1984] ECR 2971, para. 19. See also Case C–53/95 *Inasti* v. *Kemmler* [1996] ECR I–703; Case C–162/99 *Commission* v. *Italy (dentists)* [2001] ECR I–541, para. 20.

primary, but not a secondary, establishment. For lawyers established in other Member States this meant that they could exercise their rights of establishment but only by giving up their first place of establishment. The Court said that in principle French law breached Article 49: Article 49 entitled individuals to maintain more than one establishment.[31] In the interests of the administration of justice, the Court said that France was justified in requiring lawyers to abide by its rules of professional ethics and to practise in such a way as to maintain sufficient contact with their clients and the courts, but this could be facilitated by 'modern methods of transport and telecommunications',[32] without the need for living in the locality and giving up their primary establishment.

## 2.2 Equal Treatment and Beyond

### (a) The discrimination approach

The principle of equal treatment laid down in Article 49 means that, in the absence of specific Union rules, each Member State is free to regulate access to a profession in its territory,[33] provided it does not directly or indirectly discriminate on the grounds of nationality (see fig. 8.1). A directly discriminatory measure (one which treats migrants less favourably than nationals) breaches Article 49 and can be saved (probably) only by reference to one of the express derogations. Therefore, in *Reyners*[34] the Court said that a Belgian rule preventing a qualified Dutch national from practising as a lawyer on the grounds of his nationality in Belgium breached Article 49.[35] Similarly, in *Commission* v. *Austria (certification)*[36] Austrian legislation introduced in the light of the EU's enlargement in 2004, requiring nationals of the eight new Member States to prove that they would not be working as employees (and thus excluded from the free movement of workers provisions under the transitional arrangements[37]) by producing a certificate showing that, for example, they were a member of a partnership or a limited liability company, enshrined 'a difference in treatment on the grounds of nationality which is prohibited, in principle, by Article [49]'.

Indirectly discriminatory measures (those which ostensibly treat the migrant and the national in the same way but in fact disadvantage the migrant) also breach Article 49 unless they can be objectively justified or saved by an express derogation. Such measures include national laws requiring professionals to hold a licence before they can practise and/or to be registered with a professional body,[38] usually after having passed the relevant examinations and holding certain qualifications. These rules can be considered indistinctly applicable because they require migrants to shoulder the dual burden of having to satisfy first the home, and then the host, state authorities of their suitability to practise, while nationals have to satisfy only one authority (that of the home state). This reading holds true in the case of secondary establishment (where the requirements of the home and host states apply simultaneously) but less so in the case of primary establishment where only one set of registration requirements applies at any given time (those of the home state followed by those of the host state).

---

[31] Para. 19.  [32] Paras. 21–2.  [33] Case 107/83 *Klopp* [1984] ECR 2971, para. 17.

[34] Case 2/74 *Reyners* v. *Belgian State* [1974] ECR 631.

[35] See also Case 38/87 *Commission* v. *Greece* [1988] ECR 4415; Case C–252/99 *Commission* v. *Italy* [2001] ECR I–4195.  [36] Case C–161/07 [2008] ECR I–10671.

[37] See further Ch. 9.

[38] E.g., Case 292/86 *Gullung* v. *Conseils de l'ordre des avocats du barreau de Colmar* [1988] ECR 111.

The Court usually finds that indirectly discriminatory requirements can in principle be justified. For example, in *Gullung*[39] the Court said a French requirement for all lawyers to be registered at the Bar before practising, could be justified on the ground of ensuring 'the observance of moral and ethical principles and the disciplinary control of the activity of lawyers'[40] or, as the Court put it in *Vlassopoulou*,[41] for reasons relating to the organization of the profession, qualifications, professional ethics, supervision, and liability. The steps taken must, however, be proportionate.

## (b) The 'restrictions' approach

In respect of non-discriminatory national rules, the Court has changed its position. As we saw in Chapter 8, while in the early days the Court thought that non-discriminatory rules did not breach Article 49,[42] subsequent case law focused more on whether the rule nevertheless hindered market access or constituted a restriction on free movement. This can be seen in *Gebhard*,[43] an Article 49 case. Gebhard, a German lawyer (*Rechtsanwalt*) with chambers in Stuttgart, established a set of chambers in Milan and called himself *avvocato*. He was eventually suspended by the Milan Bar because he had been practising under the title *avvocato* without being registered. The Court focused on the obstacles to freedom of establishment created by the Italian rules. It said:[44]

national measures liable to *hinder or make less attractive* the exercise of fundamental freedoms guaranteed by the [Treaties] must fulfil four conditions: they must be applied in a non-discriminatory manner; they must be justified by imperative requirements in the general interest; they must be suitable for securing the attainment of the objective which they pursue; and they must not go beyond what is necessary in order to attain it...

Since *Gebhard* the emphasis of the case law has generally been on whether the national measure is liable 'to prohibit, impede or render less attractive'[45] access to, or exercise of, the right of establishment (the so-called 'hindrance', 'obstacle', or 'restriction' cases) rather than the elimination of discrimination. So, for example, in *Haim II*[46] the Court found that a language requirement imposed on dentists wishing to practise in Germany restricted establishment under Article 49. In *Wouters*[47] the Court assumed that a Dutch rule prohibiting multi-disciplinary partnerships between members of the Bar and accountants constituted a restriction on the right of establishment. In *Commission v Greece (computer games)*[48] the Court said a prohibition on traders from other Member States

---

[39] Case 292/86 *Gullung* [1988] ECR 111.        [40] Para. 29.

[41] Case 340/89 *Vlassopoulou v. Ministerium für Justiz, Bundes- und Europaangelegenheiten Baden-Württemberg* [1991] ECR I–2357, para. 15.

[42] Case 221/85 *Commission v. Belgium (Clinical Laboratories)* [1987] ECR 719.

[43] Case C–55/94 [1995] ECR I–4165.

[44] Para. 37. See also Case C–19/92 *Kraus* [1993] ECR I–1663, considered further in Ch. 8.

[45] Case C–79/01 *Payroll Data Services (Italy) Srl, ADP Europe SA and ADP GSI SA* [2002] ECR I–8923, para. 26.

[46] Case C–424/97 *Haim v. Kassenzahnärtzliche Vereinigung Nordrhein (Haim II)* [2000] ECR I–5123, para. 57.

[47] Case C–309/99 *J.C.J. Wouters, J.W. Savelbergh and Price Waterhouse Belastingadviseurs BV v. Algemene Raad van de Nederlandse Orde van Advocaten* [2002] ECR I–1577, para. 122, and Art. 25 of the Services Dir. 2006/123 considered in Section E below.

[48] Case C–65/05 *Commission v. Greece (computer games)* [2006] ECR I–10341, paras. 50–2. See Case C–109/08 *Commission v. Greece (computer games) II* [2009] ECR I–000 for the Art. 260 TFEU (ex Art. 228 EC) follow-up action.

operating electronic and computer games breached Article 49; and in *Apothekerkammer des Saarlandes*[49] the Court said that a rule excluding non-pharmacists from operating pharmacies, 'denying other economic operators access to this self-employed activity' constituted a restriction within the meaning of Article 49. In all four cases the focus then shifted to the question of whether the national measure could be justified and the steps taken were proportionate.

The Court has tended to recognize a broad range of justifications put forward by the Member State. So, for example, in *Haim II* where the Court found that, while the German-language requirement could be justified on the ground that dentists had to be able to communicate with their patients and the relevant authorities,[50] there did need to be a certain number of dentists capable of communicating in Turkish to serve the needs of the Turkish community.[51] However, the Court indicated that the requirement to speak German could be justified on the facts. In *Commission* v. *Greece* the Court accepted in principle the Greek government's arguments that because computer games are easy to adapt to become games of chance this can lead to serious social problems such as the addiction of the players, the waste of considerable economic resources, and the easy and illegal enrichment of those involved in the operation, installation and trade of electronic games and the loss of large sums of money by the players and of considerable tax revenue. However, the Court found the rules disproproation because Greece had not established that it had implemented 'all the technical and organisational measures likely to have achieved the objective pursued by that Member State using measures which were less restrictive of intra-[Union] trade'.

## 3. THE EXERCISE OF ACTIVITIES AS A SELF-EMPLOYED PERSON

### 3.1 Equal Treatment and Beyond

So far we have considered the application of both the non-discrimination principle and the *Gebhard* hindrance/obstacle approach to national rules affecting *access* to self-employment. We turn now to consider the application of these principles to measures which interfere with the *exercise* of the profession, in particular in respect of the terms and conditions under which it is performed.[52] As we have already seen, national measures which discriminate—either directly or indirectly—on the ground of nationality in respect of access to a profession are prohibited. The same applies to the exercise of a profession. *Commission* v. *Italy (dentists)*[53] is a good example of a directly discriminatory rule. Italian law provided that dentists who transferred their residence to another Member State lost their registration with the Italian dental association. Since this rule did not apply to Italian nationals the Court found that it breached Article 49. Similarly, in *Commission* v. *Belgium (air traffic)*[54] the Court said that a Belgian law requiring 'foreigners' (i.e., non-Belgians) to have been resident in Belgium for at least one year in order to register an aircraft breached Article 49. The Court said the rule 'clearly constitute[s]

---

[49] Joined Cases C–171/07 and C–172/07 *Apothekerkammer des Saarlandes* v. *Saarland* [2009] ECR I–000, paras. 23–4.  [50] Case C–424/97 *Haim II* [2000] ECR I–5123, para. 59.

[51] Para. 60. Cf. Case 379/87 *Groener* [1989] ECR 3967.

[52] See by analogy Art. 7(1) of Reg. 1612/68 considered in Ch. 9.

[53] Case C–162/99 [2001] ECR I–541, para. 36.

[54] Case C–203/98 *Commission* v. *Belgium* [1999] ECR I–4899.

discrimination on the grounds of nationality which impedes the exercise of the freedom of establishment of those persons'.[55]

Indirect discrimination is also prohibited, as *Fearon*[56] shows. The Court said that an exemption from an Irish rule on the compulsory acquisition of land for those who had resided for more than a year within three miles of the land was indirectly discriminatory but could be justified on grounds of preserving the ownership of land to those who worked on it.

As with the cases on access to the market, increasingly the Court has abandoned the equal treatment principle in favour of the formula based on removing obstacles or restrictions to the exercise of the freedom of establishment. This can be seen in *Konstantinidis*.[57] Konstantinidis, a Greek national, worked in Germany as a self-employed masseur and assistant hydrotherapist. Although his name was entered into the marriage register as Konst*ad*inidis, he argued that the correct transcription of his name from the Greek should have been Konst*ant*inidis. He sought to have the register corrected because, he said, the distortion of his name could cause potential clients to confuse him with other masseurs, and this interfered with his business contrary to Article 49.[58]

Having noted that the Treaties did not prevent the transcription of a Greek name into Roman characters,[59] the Court began by using the discrimination framework to determine whether the national rules on transliteration were capable of placing Konstantinidis 'at a disadvantage in law or in fact, in comparison with the way in which a national of that Member State would be treated in the same circumstances'.[60] The Court then moved on to examine whether there were any obstacles or impediments to Konstantinidis' free movement. It said that the German rules breached Article 49 only in so far as their application caused a Greek national 'such a degree of inconvenience as in fact to interfere with his freedom to exercise the right of establishment'.[61] It continued that the interference would be sufficiently substantial if, as a result of the transcription, the spelling of Konstantinidis' name led to a modification of the pronunciation with the risk that clients might confuse him with others.[62]

While Advocate General Jacobs reached much the same conclusion, his approach was inspired by fundamental human rights[63] and not market values. He said that a Union national who goes to another Member State as a worker or a self-employed person was entitled not just to pursue his trade or profession and to enjoy the same living and working conditions as nationals of the host state but also to assume that:

wherever he goes to earn a living in the European [Union], he will be treated in accordance with a common code of fundamental values, in particular those laid down in accordance with the European Convention on Human Rights. In other words, he is entitled to say 'civis

---

[55] Para. 13.          [56] Case C–182/83 [1985] ECR I–3677, paras. 10–11.

[57] Case C–168/91 *Christos Konstantinidis* v. *Stadt Altensteig* [1993] ECR I–1191.

[58] For a similar case in the field of citizenship, but without the emphasis on interference with business, see Jacobs AG's Opinion in Case C–148/02 *Carlos Garcia Avello* v. *Etat Belge* [2003] ECR I–11613 considered further in Ch. 12.          [59] Para. 14.

[60] Para. 13.          [61] Para. 15.          [62] Para. 16.

[63] See, e.g., para. 40: 'A person's right to his name is fundamental in every sense of the word. After all, where are we without our name? It is our name that distinguishes each of us from the rest of humanity. It is our name that gives us a sense of identity, dignity and self-esteem. To strip a person of his rightful name is the ultimate degradation, as is evidenced by the common practice of repressive penal regimes which consists in substituting a number for a prisoner's name.'

europeus sum' [I am a European citizen] and to invoke the status in order to oppose any violation of his fundamental rights.[64]

This Opinion, delivered just as the Treaty on European Union was being concluded, contained an important recognition of the changing attitude towards migrants: they were
not only factors of production but were also citizens with fundamental (civil and political) rights. This approach eventually inspired the seminal decisions such in *Martínez
Sala*[65] and *Baumbast*[66] on the free movement of citizens, cases considered in detail in
Chapter 12.

In *Skanavi*[67] the Court was also encouraged to decide an establishment case under
the citizenship provisions, but it declined. Mrs Skanavi, a Greek national working in
Germany, had failed to exchange her Greek driving licence for a German one within one
year of residence, as required by Union law. As a result, she was prosecuted for driving
without a licence and fined. The Court said that while Member States were competent
to impose penalties for a breach of such rules, they could not impose a penalty so disproportionate to the gravity of the infringement that this became an obstacle to the free
movement of persons. For this reason the Court said that it would be disproportionate
to treat a person who had failed to exchange her driving licence as if she were driving
without a licence[68] because a criminal conviction would damage her ability to exercise
certain trades or professions which would constitute a further, lasting restriction on free
movement.[69]

## 3.2 Enjoyment of Social Advantages

The principle of equal treatment also applies in respect of the enjoyment of various general facilities necessary to pursue self-employed activity—i.e., the enjoyment of social
advantages, to use the term found in Article 7(2) of the Workers' Regulation 1612/68.[70]
While the original Establishment Directive did not contain any equivalent provision to
Article 7(2), the Court has used Article 49 TFEU to achieve the same result (a position
now supported by Article 24(1) CRD). This can be seen in *Steinhauser*,[71] a case concerning a German artist who was not allowed to participate in a tendering process for the
use of an art and craft boutique in the French city of Biarritz, on the ground that he
was not French. He claimed that he had been directly discriminated against contrary to
Article 49. The defendant local authority argued that Article 49 applied only to conditions
regulating *access* to a profession and so did not apply to this case. The Court disagreed,
ruling that Article 49 included the right not only to take up activities as a self-employed
person but also to pursue those activities in the broadest sense,[72] including renting business premises.[73]

---

[64] Para. 46.      [65] Case C–85/96 *Martínez Sala v. Freistaat Bayern* [1998] ECR I–2691.
[66] Case C–413/99 *Baumbast and R v. Secretary of State for the Home Department* [2002] ECR I–7091.
[67] Case C–193/94 *Criminal Proceedings against Sofia Skanavi and Konstantin Chryssanthakopoulos*
[1996] ECR I–929. See also Case C–476/01 *Kapper* [2004] ECR I–5205, para. 36.      [68] Para. 37.
[69] Para. 38.      [70] This is considered further in Ch. 9.
[71] Case 197/84 *Steinhauser v. City of Biarritz* [1985] ECR 1819.
[72] The Court referred to the General Programme for the Abolition of Restrictions on the Freedom of
Establishment which expressly excluded the imposition of conditions on the power to exercise rights normally attached to the activity of a self-employed person, including submitting of tenders (OJ Spec Ed 2nd
Series IX, 7 Restrictions, A).      [73] Para. 16.

In other words, Mr Steinhauser should have enjoyed a social advantage (a boutique for selling his wares) on the same terms as nationals. Likewise, a migrant should enjoy housing 'under the same conditions as his competitors' who are nationals.[74] Therefore, in *Commission* v. *Italy (social housing)*[75] the Court said an Italian law allowing only Italians to purchase or lease housing built with the help of public funds and to obtain a reduced-rate mortgage breached Article 49. In a similar vein the Court found in *Commission* v. *Greece (housing)*[76] that a rule allowing Greek nationals, but not migrants, to purchase immovable property breached Article 49.

### 3.3 Taxation, Equal Treatment, and Beyond

The Court has interpreted Article 49 to require equal treatment not only in respect of social advantages but also tax advantages for the self-employed (see also Article 24(1) CRD). Many of the cases concern claims by non-residents that they are being treated differently from residents. In these cases the Court looks to see if the situation of the claimant is in fact similar to the position of a resident. If the situations are not similar then the Court finds no breach of Article 49.[77] If the situations are similar—particularly the case with 'frontier' self-employed—the Court then examines the question of discrimination. For example, *Wielockx*[78] concerned a Dutch law which provided that non-residents were not allowed to set up a pension reserve qualifying for deductions under the same tax conditions as those of a resident taxpayer. Wielockx was a self-employed Belgian national residing in Belgium who received his whole income from a partnership in a physiotherapy practice in the Netherlands. For this reason he was considered to be in objectively the same situation as a resident. The Court said that excluding him from favourable pension arrangements amounted to indirect discrimination contrary to Article 49. It also found that such discrimination could not be justified on the ground of fiscal cohesion.[79]

*Asscher*[80] confirms that a residence criterion can be indirectly discriminatory. Asscher was a Dutch national who worked in Belgium while residing in the Netherlands and then moved to Belgium. Although he worked in a self-employed capacity in both countries, he was treated as a non-resident in the Netherlands and taxed at a higher rate than residents. The Court noted that a residence criterion was 'liable to act mainly to the detriment of nationals of other Member States, since non-residents are most frequently

---

[74]　Case 63/86 *Commission* v. *Italy (social housing)* [1988] ECR 29, para. 16.

[75]　Case 63/86 [1988] ECR 29, para. 14.　　　[76]　Case 305/87 [1989] ECR 1461, para. 23.

[77]　See further the discussion in Ch. 9 on the distinction between residents and non-residents in international tax law.

[78]　Case C–80/94 *Wielockx* v. *Inspecteur der Directe Belastingen* [1995] ECR I–2493. See also Case C–346/04 *Conijn* v. *Finanzamt Hamburg-Nord* [2006] ECR I–6137.

[79]　The question of justifications in respect of taxation is considered further in Ch. 9. See generally F. Vanistendael, 'The consequences of *Schumacker* and *Wielockx*: Two steps forward in the tax procession of Echternach' (1996) 33 *CMLRev*. 255; and M. Wathelet, 'The Influence of free movement of persons, services and capital on national direct taxation' (2001) 20 *YEL* 1.

[80]　Case C–107/94 *Asscher* v. *Staatssecretaris van Financiën* [1996] ECR I–3089, para. 38; Case C–329/05 *Finanzamt Dinslaken* v. *Meindl* [2007] ECR I–1107, para. 28, Case C–440/08 *Gelen* v. *Staatssecretaris van Financiën* [2010] ECR I–000, para. 48. Cf. Case C–104/06 *Commission* v. *Sweden (sale of residential property)* [2007] ECR I–671, para. 25, where the Court used the *Gebhard* language of hindrance to describe the residence criteria.

non-nationals'.[81] The rule therefore breached Article 49[82] and, once again, could not be justified on the ground of ensuring cohesion of the tax system.[83]

While in most of the tax cases concerning the self-employed (or small family businesses[84]) the Court has relied on the traditional concepts of discrimination, in some cases the Court has resorted to the *Gebhard* hindrance/restriction formula, noting as it did in *Kemmler*[85] that the national rule 'inhibits the pursuit of occupational activities outside the Member State'. Therefore, the Court said that a host-state rule requiring that social security contributions be made to a national scheme when the self-employed person already contributed to benefits in his home state where he habitually resided, breached Article 49 unless the requirement could be justified.[86]

The hindrance/restriction formula also helps address those national rules which discourage individuals from leaving their home state to establish themselves elsewhere. This can be seen in *De Lasteyrie du Saillant*.[87] Under French law, a taxpayer wishing to leave France and establish himself elsewhere became liable to tax on income which had not yet been realized; had he stayed in France there would have been no such liability until increases in value were actually realized. The Court said that such a rule was liable to hinder freedom of establishment,[88] 'even if it is of limited scope or minor importance',[89] and could not, on the facts, be justified by generalized concerns to prevent tax avoidance.[90]

## 4. QUALIFICATIONS

The refusal by a host state to recognize qualifications acquired in other EU states has represented a serious practical obstacle to freedom of establishment. Although Article 53 TFEU (ex Article 47 EC) allows the Council to adopt directives for the mutual recognition of diplomas, for many years the requirement of unanimity in Council[91] slowed the process. As a result the Court was left with the task of reconciling the host state's legitimate need for qualified people to do certain jobs with the fundamental principle of freedom of movement.

### 4.1 Where There Is No Union Legislation

At first the Court gave effect to the non-discrimination principle contained in Article 49. It said that if Union law had not laid down provisions to secure the objective of freedom of establishment, the Member States and legally recognized professional bodies[92]

---

[81] Para. 38.     [82] Para. 49.

[83] See also Case C–168/01 *Bosal Holding BV* v. *Staatssecretaris van Financiën* [2003] ECR I–9409, paras. 30–1. Case C–478/98 *Commission* v. *Belgium (Eurobond)* [2000] ECR I–7587, para. 35 in respect of capital considered in Ch. 15.

[84] Case C–464/05 *Geurts* v. *Administratie van de BTW* [2007] ECR I–9325, paras. 20–2.

[85] Case C–53/95 *Kemmler* [1996] ECR I–703, para. 12.     [86] Para. 12.

[87] Case C–9/02 *De Lasteyrie du Saillant* v. *Ministère de l'Economie, des Finances et de l'industrie* [2004] ECR I–2409. See also Case C–314/08 *Filipiak* v. *Dyrektor Izby Skarbowej w Poznaniu* [2009] ECR I–000, para. 67.     [88] Para. 48.

[89] Para. 43.

[90] The same applies to those wishing to receive services such as insurance from another Member State: Case C–150/04 *Commission* v. *Denmark (insurance)* [2007] ECR I–1163, para. 76.

[91] Now the ordinary legislative procedure applies.

[92] Case 71/76 *Thieffry* v. *Conseil de l'ordre des avocats à la cour de Paris* [1977] ECR 765.

retained the jurisdiction to adopt the necessary measures,[93] provided that they complied with the obligations of cooperation laid down by Article 4(3) TEU (ex Article 10 EC)[94] and the principle of non-discrimination.[95] This point was made in *Patrick*,[96] where a British architect applied for authorization to practise in France but his application was rejected on the ground that there was neither a diplomatic convention between the UK and France concerning the mutual recognition of certificates nor an EU directive on recognition of architectural qualifications.[97] However, the Court said that the need for directives had 'become superfluous with regard to implementing the rule on nationality since this is henceforth sanctioned by the [Treaties] itself with direct effect'.[98] Therefore the French authorities could not, on the grounds of nationality, deny Patrick the right to establish himself, nor could they require him to satisfy additional conditions (such as being authorized to practise) which were not applicable to nationals.

However, the principle of non-discrimination may itself be an obstacle to free movement. If an individual has taken six years to qualify as a lawyer in State A, the principle of non-discrimination would probably allow the authorities in State B to permit the individual to practise but on the same terms as nationals (i.e., by recommencing their studies in State B, thus taking several further years to qualify). For this reason, in *Thieffry*[99] the Court began to shift its focus from the principle of non-discrimination to one of mutual recognition. The case concerned a Belgian lawyer who held a Belgian diploma of Doctor of Laws which had been recognized by a French university as equivalent to the French first degree in law. He subsequently obtained a French *avocat*'s certificate, having passed the French Bar exams. However, he was refused admission to the Paris Bar on the ground that he lacked a French degree. The Court held that this requirement constituted an unjustified restriction on the freedom of establishment because Thieffry held a diploma recognized as an equivalent qualification by the competent authority in France and had passed the French Bar exams.

The real importance of the principle of mutual recognition was made clear in the seminal case of *Vlassopoulou*[100] concerning a Greek lawyer who worked in Germany advising on Greek and EU law. Her application to join the local German Bar was rejected on the ground that she had not pursued her university studies in Germany, had not sat the two German state exams, and had not completed the preparatory stage, although she did hold a German doctorate. The Court ruled that:[101]

national requirements concerning qualifications may have the effect of *hindering nationals of the other Member States in the exercise* of their right of establishment guaranteed to

---

[93] Case 292/86 *Gullung* [1988] ECR 111.

[94] Case 222/86 *UNECTEF v. Heylens* [1987] ECR 4097, para. 10.

[95] Case C–61/89 *Criminal proceedings against Marc Gaston Bouchoucha* [1990] ECR I–3551.

[96] Case 11/77 *Patrick v. Ministre des affaires culturelles* [1977] ECR 1199.

[97] However, see Council Dir. 85/384/EEC ([1985] OJ L223/15) on the mutual recognition of formal qualifications in architecture now repealed and replaced by EP and Council Dir. 2005/36 ([2005] OJ L255/22).

[98] Para. 13.     [99] Case 71/76 [1977] ECR 765.

[100] Case C–340/89 [1991] ECR I–2357, noted J. Lonbay (1991) 16 *ELRev.* 507. See also N. Hopkins, 'Recognition of teaching qualifications: Community law in the English context' (1996) 21 *ELRev.* 435. This approach was approved in respect of a Union national with a Turkish dental qualification who had practised in a Member State but lacked the qualifications required by Council Dir. 78/686/EEC: see Case C–319/92 *Haim I* [1994] ECR I–425.

[101] Para. 15, emphasis added. See also Case C–19/92 *Kraus* [1993] ECR I–1663, para. 32.

them by Article [49]. That could be the case if the national rules in question took no account of the knowledge and qualifications already acquired by the person concerned in another Member State.

The Court then elaborated on the principle of mutual recognition. It said that the host state had to compare a migrant's qualifications and abilities with those required by the national system to see whether the applicant had the appropriate skills to join the equivalent profession. If the comparison revealed that the holder had the knowledge and qualifications which were, if not identical, then at least equivalent to the national diploma, then the host state was obliged to recognize the diploma. If, on the other hand, the comparison revealed that the applicant only partially fulfilled the necessary qualifications, then the host Member State could require the applicant to demonstrate that she had acquired the relevant knowledge and qualifications which then had to be taken into account.[102] The Court added that to ensure that the Member States complied with the obligations inherent in the principle of mutual recognition, the decision-making body had to give reasons for its decisions which also had to be reviewable by the courts to verify compatibility with Union law.[103]

*Vlassopoulou* effectively pre-empted the 'diabolically complex and completely unnecessary'[104] Council Directive 89/48/EEC on mutual recognition of higher education diplomas and the complementary Directive 92/51/EEC[105] (now repealed and replaced by Directive 2005/36[106]). Nevertheless, the Union proceeded with the adoption of these two 'horizontal' directives to complement and gradually replace the existing vertical directives. It is to these directives and the earlier 'vertical' directives that we now turn. However, where the directives do not apply, the principles in *Vlassopoulou* are still used by the Court to fill the gap.[107]

### 4.2 Where There Is Union Legislation

#### (a) Introduction

In its first wave of harmonization legislation, the Council adopted a vertical approach, harmonizing the diverse national rules profession by profession. This led to directives on doctors, nurses, dentists, and vets,[108] as well as a number of directives concerning a

---

[102] Paras. 17–21. In Case C–345/08 *Krzystof Peśla* v *Justizministerium Mecklenburg-Vorpommern* [2009] ECR I–000 the Court said that EU law required the host State to carry out the examination of equivalence in the light of the academic and professional training and experience as a whole before requiring a candidate to take an aptitude test. The knowledge to be taken as a reference point for the purposes of assessing whether a candidate can be admitted directly to a legal traineeship, was that attested by the qualification required in the host state.

[103] C–104/91 *Colegio Oficial de Agentes de la Propriedad Inmobiliaria* v. *José Luis Aguirre Borrell and others* [1992] ECR I–3003, para. 16.    [104] Lonbay, above n. 100, 516.

[105] [1989] OJ L19/16 and [1992] OJ L209/25.

[106] [2005] OJ L255/22. For full details, see <http://www.ec.europa.eu/internal_market/qualifications/future_en.htm#modif>.

[107] The principles still apply where the directives do not: Case C–164/94 *Georgios Aranitis* v. *Land Berlin* [1996] ECR I–135; Case C–456/05 *Commission* v. *Germany (psychotherapists)* [2007] ECR I–10517; Case C–586/08 *Rubino* v. *Mininstero dell'Università e della Ricerca* [2009] ECR I–000, para. 34; Case C–345/08 *Peśla* [2009] ECR I–000, paras. 24–5.

[108] See Dirs. 75/362/EEC ([1975] OJ L167/1) and 75/363/EEC ([1975] OJ L167/14) on doctors, 77/452/EEC ([1977] OJ L176/1) on nurses responsible for general care, 78/686/EEC ([1978] OJ L233/1) on dentists,

range of industries such as manufacturing and processing, small craft, food and retail,[109] the activities of intermediaries, and the building industry.[110] These directives laid down minimum standards on training. The advantage of these directives was that once the individual had completed the training and acquired the qualification then recognition was automatic:[111] the host state had to accept the equivalence of the qualifications and could not require the individual to comply with requirements other than those laid down by the relevant directives.[112]

However, the process of negotiating these directives was interminably slow (the Directive on Architects[113] alone took 17 years to agree), and they were also limited in scope (for example, the Directive on Lawyers' Services[114] applied only to services and not to establishment).[115] To tackle these problems, the single market programme heralded a new approach: horizontal harmonization based on the principle of mutual recognition derived from the Court's rulings in *Cassis de Dijon*[116] and *Vlassopoulou*.[117] The result of this initiative was Directive 89/48[118] on the mutual recognition of higher education diplomas—the first 'general system' or 'horizontal' directive for 'higher level training (i.e., qualifications attained beyond degree level). This was followed by the second general-system Directive 92/51/EEC[119] for professions for which the level of training was lower, and a third general-system directive, Directive 99/42/EC,[120] extending the mutual recognition approach to the industrial and professional sectors previously covered by earlier vertical directives. This directive also gave recognition not only to formal qualifications but also to experience and skills.

Directives 89/48 and 92/51 differed markedly from their sectoral forbears: they applied to all regulated professions rather than to a single profession;[121] recognition was based

---

78/1026/EEC ([1978] OJ L362/1) on vets, 80/154/EEC ([1980] OJ L33/1) on midwives, 85/432/EEC ([1985] OJ L253/34) on pharmacists, 86/457/EEC ([1986] OJ L267/26) on general practitioners, and 87/540/EC ([1987] OJ L322/20) on carriers of goods by waterway. These directives have now been repealed and replaced by the Recognition of Professional Qualifications (RPQ) Dir. 2005/36 ([2005] OJ L255/22).

[109] See, e.g., Dirs. 64/427/EEC ([1963–4] OJ Spec Ed Series I–148), 75/369/EEC ([1995] OJ L167/29), and 68/367 ([1968] Series I Ch. II–513). These directives have now been repealed and replaced by the RPQ Dir. 2005/36 ([2005] OJ L255/22).

[110] Dir. 64/224/EEC ([1963–4] OJ Spec Ed Series I–126). This directive has now been repealed and replaced by the RPQ Dir. 2005/36.

[111] Case C–154/93 *Abdullah Tawil-Albertini* v. *Ministre des Affaires Sociales* [1994] ECR I–451, para. 11.

[112] Case C–238/98 *Hocsman* v. *Ministre de l'Emploi et de la Solidarité* [2000] ECR I–6623, para. 33.

[113] Council Dir. 85/384/EEC ([1985] OJ L223/15) (now repealed and replaced by the RPQ Dir. 2005/36 ([2005] OJ L255/22)) and Communication 2002/C 214/03 considered in Case C–310/90 *Nationale Raad van de Orde der Architecten* v. *Egle* [1992] ECR I–177; Case C–447/93 *Dreessen* v. *Conseil national de l'ordre des architectes* [1994] ECR I–4087. See also Council Recommendation 85/386/EEC concerning the holders of a diploma in architecture awarded in a third country ([1985] OJ L223/28).

[114] Council Dir. 77/249/EEC ([1977] OJ L78/17). See Case 427/85 *Commission* v. *Germany (Re Lawyer's Services)* [1988] ECR 1123; Case C–294/89 *Commission* v. *France* [1991] ECR I–3591.

[115] However, see now EP and Council Dir. 98/5/EC ([1998] OJ L77/36) to facilitate practice of the profession of lawyer on a permanent basis in a Member State other than that in which the qualification was obtained, which is considered below nn. 189–94.

[116] Case 120/78 [1979] ECR 649, considered in Ch. 4.　　　[117] Case C–340/89 [1991] ECR I–2357.

[118] [1989] OJ L19/16 as amended.

[119] [1992] OJ L209/25 as amended. Council Res. of 18 Jun. 1992 ([1992] OJ C187/1) accompanying Dir. 92/51 EEC invites the Member States to allow EU nationals who have been awarded diplomas, certificates, or other qualifications by third countries to take up and pursue professions in the Union by recognizing these diplomas and certificates in their territories.　　　[120] [1999] OJ L201/77.

[121] Bull. EC 6-1988, 11.

on the principle of mutual trust without prior coordination of the preparatory and educational courses for the various professions;[122] and recognition was granted to the 'end product'—to fully qualified professionals who have already received professional training.[123] As the Court put it in *Commission* v. *Greece*,[124] the general-system directives essentially establish 'a presumption that the qualifications of an applicant entitled to pursue a regulated profession in one Member States are sufficient for the pursuit of that profession in the other Member States'. Most significantly, the general-system directives were not intended to harmonize the conditions for taking up or pursuit of the various professions; this remained a matter for Member States' competence 'within the limits imposed by [Union] law'.[125] Although this approach avoided some of the problems associated with the negotiation of sector-specific directives, the gain came at a price. The general-system directives did not guarantee automatic recognition;[126] they merely required the host state authorities to consider the migrant's qualifications and, if the qualifications proved to be lacking in terms of duration and content, the host state could impose additional requirements.

In an attempt to reorganize, rationalize, and standardize the principles which applied across both the vertical and horizontal directives, the Parliament and Council adopted a single directive, Directive 2005/36/EC, repealing and replacing the earlier directives on the recognition of professional qualifications (RPQ Directive). The aim of the RPQ Directive 2005/36 is 'to introduce a more flexible and automatic procedure based on common platforms established by professional associations at European level, stemming from increased co-operation between the public and private sectors'.[127] It is a complicated directive, running to 120 pages including annexes. The section that follows gives an outline of some of the key principles underpinning the directive.

## (b) The basic rules

The directive applies to all nationals of a Member State wishing to pursue a 'regulated profession' in a Member State other than that in which they obtained their professional qualifications on either a self-employed or employed basis.[128] A regulated profession involves the pursuit of a 'professional activity'[129] access to which is subject to the possession of specific professional qualifications[130] which, in turn, are defined as qualifications attested by evidence of formal qualifications, an 'attestation of competence' and/or professional experience.[131] In principle, the host state must recognize qualifications obtained in one

---

[122]  Ibid. See also Case C–274/05 *Commission* v. *Greece* [2008] ECR I–7969, para. 30.

[123]  Bull. EC 6–1988, 11. In Case C–274/05 *Commission* v. *Greece* [2008] ECR I–7969, para. 37 the Court emphasized that the directive did not concern the recognition of the prior academic qualifications on which the professional qualifications were based.

[124]  Case C–274/05 *Commission* v. *Greece* [2008] ECR I–7969, para. 30.

[125]  Case C–274/05 *Commission* v. *Greece* [2008] ECR I–7969, para. 38. The directives also do not concern the choice of recruitment and selection procedure for filling posts and they cannot be relied on as the basis for the right actually to be recruited: Case C–586/08 *Rubino* v. *Mininstero dell'Università e della Ricerca* [2009] ECR I–000, para. 27.

[126]  Case C–39/07 *Commission* v. *Spain (hospital pharmacists)* [2008] ECR I–3435, para. 39.

[127]  IP/02/393.     [128]  Art. 2(1).     [129]  Art. 1(c).     [130]  Art. 3(1)(a).

[131]  Art. 3(1)(b). In Case C–39/07 *Commission* v. *Spain (hospital pharmacists)* [2008] ECR I–3435, para. 33 the Court has added that 'a profession is deemed regulated . . . where access to the professional activity constituting that profession or its exercise is governed by laws, regulations or administrative provisions creating a system under which that professional activity is expressly reserved to those who fulfil certain conditions and access to it is prohibited to those who do not fulfil them'.

or more other states which allow their holder to pursue the same qualification there.[132] Article 4(1) adds:

The recognition of professional qualifications by the host Member State allows the beneficiary to gain access in that Member State to the same[133] profession as that for which he is qualified in the home state and to pursue it in the host Member State under the same conditions as its nationals.

The directive then distinguishes between those providing services on a temporary basis (Title II) and those wishing to establish themselves on a permanent basis (Title III). We shall consider these two situations in turn.

### (c)  Free provision of services

According to Article 5(1), any Member State national legally established in a Member State (State A) may provide services on a temporary and occasional basis,[134] account being taken of the duration, frequency, regularity, and continuity of the provision of services, in another Member State (State B) under their original professional title without having to apply for recognition of their qualifications. However, if service providers relocate outside of their Member State of establishment (State A) in order to provide services, they must also provide evidence of two years' professional experience if the profession in question is not regulated in State A.[135] Conversely, if the profession is regulated, then the two years' practice cannot be required.[136]

The directive lays down a number of administrative provisions, including the possibility for the host state, State B, to require the service provider to make a declaration prior to providing any services on its territory, to renew it annually, and to give details of any insurance cover or other means of personal or collective protection with regard to professional liability.[137] State B can also require that the first application be accompanied by certain documents listed in Article 7(2), such as proof of the nationality of the service provider, of their legal establishment, and of their professional qualifications. State B can also require that, where the service is provided under the professional title of the Member State of establishment or under the formal qualification of the service provider, service providers furnish the recipient of the service with certain information, particularly with regard to insurance coverage against the financial risks connected with any challenge to their professional liability.[138]

### (d)  Freedom of establishment

The directive also makes provision for a professional to become established in another Member State in order to conduct a professional activity there on a stable basis. The directive comprises the three existing systems of recognition:

- the general system for the recognition of professional qualifications (Chapter I)
- the system of automatic recognition of qualifications attested by professional experience in certain industrial, craft and commercial sectors (Chapter II)
- the system of automatic recognition of qualifications for specific professions (doctor, nurse, dentist, vet, midwife, pharmacist and architect (Chapter III)).

---

[132] Art. 1.          [133] I.e., 'the activities covered are comparable': Art. 4(2).
[134] Art. 5(2). These principles are considered further in Ch.11.          [135] Art. 5(1)(b).          [136] Ibid.
[137] Art. 7(1).          [138] Art. 9.

However, as the Court has made clear in *Commission v. Spain (pharmacists)*, 'the right to recognition of diplomas is guaranteed as an expression of the fundamental right of freedom of establishment',[139] so any interpretation of the directive must be read subject to Article 49 TFEU. We shall now consider the three situations envisaged by the directive.[140]

### (i) The general system for the recognition of professional qualifications

This 'general' system applies as a fallback to all the professions not covered by specific rules of recognition (Chapters II and III considered below) and to certain situations where the migrant professional does not meet the conditions set out in other recognition schemes.[141] As with Directives 89/48 and 92/51, this general system is based on the principle of mutual recognition, subject to the application of compensatory measures if there are substantial differences in the levels of training between the home and host states.[142]

The basic rules are set out in Article 13 which distinguishes between two situations. The first concerns access to, or pursuit of, a 'regulated profession' (i.e., a professional activity access which is subject to one of the five levels[143] of professional qualifications[144] considered below) in the both the home state (State A) and the host state (State B).[145] Here the competent authority in State B may not refuse, on the grounds of inadequate qualifications, to authorize a national of another Member State access to and pursuit of the profession under the same conditions as for nationals, provided that the applicant holds a training qualification obtained in another Member State (State A), issued by a competent authority, which attests to a level of training at least equivalent to the level immediately below[146] that required in the host Member State.[147] There are five levels of qualifications identified in Directive 2005/36, reflecting the levels in the three original general-system directives. These range from the lowest (level (a) 'attestation of competence') to the highest (levels (d) and (e) 'diplomas'[148] which require three- or four-year university degrees or equivalents plus professional training).[149] Any of the qualifications must be issued by a competent authority in a Member State, designated in accordance with the legislative, regulatory or administrative provisions of that Member States'.[150] It is

---

[139] Case C–39/07 *Commission* v. *Spain (pharmacists)* [2008] ECR I–3435, para. 37.

[140] SCADPlus contains a helpful explanation of the directive: <http://www.europa.eu/legislation_summaries/internal_market/living_and_working_in_the_internal_market/free_movement_of_workers/c11065_en.htm>.                                                                     [141] Art. 10.

[142] In accordance with recital 14 in the preamble to Dir. 2005/36, the recasting by that directive does not affect the mechanism of recognition established by Dirs. 89/48 and 92/51. See also Case C–586/08 *Rubino* [2009] ECR I–000, para. 27.                                                          [143] Art. 11.

[144] Art. 3(1)(a).        [145] Art. 13(1).

[146] This requirement, while at first sight surprising, reflects the fact that in some states acquiring qualification takes longer then others without in any way reflecting the quality of the qualification. So in the UK it takes on average three years to obtain a degree; in other states it takes four to five years.

[147] Art. 13(1).

[148] Diplomas may be composed of a set of documents evidencing formal qualifications: Case C–286/06 *Commission* v. *Spain* [2008] ECR I–8025, para. 55. It is sufficient that the education and training were received 'mainly' in the Union. The education and training may have been received wholly or partly in a Member State other than the one which awarded the qualification (see also Case C–274/05 *Commission* v. *Greece* [2008] ECR I–7969, para. 28).

[149] Art. 11. Therefore, a solicitor awarded the title by the Law Society, having completed a three-year university degree followed by a vocational training course (the legal practice course) and who has completed a two-year training contract, holds a 'diploma' for the purpose of the directive.

[150] Art. 13(1) and (2).

up to the competent authorities of the awarding state to ensure the quality of the training and education and to verify, in the light of the rules applicable within the framework of their professional education and training system, whether the conditions necessary for their award are fulfilled.[151] This means, for example, that State B cannot refuse to recognize a diploma awarded by a competent authority in State A because the education and training in State A or B leading to the award of the diploma was provided by a body which could not have been recognized as an educational establishment in State B.[152]

The second situation identified in Article 13 of the directive is where the profession concerned is not regulated in State A[153] but it is regulated in State B and subject to the possession of specific professional qualifications. In this situation State B must grant access to and pursuit of the profession to applicants who have pursued that profession for two years full-time in State A over the preceding ten years.

In either the first or second situations, the host Member State can make recognition of qualifications subject to the applicant's completing compensatory measures,[154] namely an aptitude test[155] or an adaptation period[156] of up to three years if:[157]

- the training is one year shorter than that required by the host Member State, or

- the training received covers substantially different matters to those covered by the formal training required in the host Member State, or

- the profession as defined in the host Member State comprises one or more regulated professional activities which do not exist in the corresponding profession in the applicant's home Member State, and that difference consists of specific training which covers substantially different matters from those covered by the migrant.

The host Member State must, in principle, offer the applicant the choice between an adaptation period and an aptitude test[158] but it can derogate from this requirement in respect of those professions requiring a precise knowledge of national law and in respect of which the provision of advice and/or assistance concerning national law is an essential and constant aspect of the professional activity.[159] It can also derogate with the Commission's permission.[160]

---

[151] Case C–151/07 *Khatzithanansis* v. *OEEK* [2008] ECR I–9013, paras. 30–1.          [152] Para. 34.
[153] Art. 13(2).
[154] Art. 14. However, states must have legislated to this effect: Case C–142/04 *Aslanidou* v. *Ypourgas Ygeias & Pronoias* [2005] ECR I–7181, para. 35. See also Case C–141/04 *Peros* v. *Techniko Epimelitirio* [2005] ECR I–7163.          [155] Art. 3(1)(h).
[156] Adaptation period means a period of supervised practice in the host state under the responsibility of a qualified member of the profession, possibly accompanied by further training; the period of supervised practice is the subject of an assessment (Art. 3(1)(g)).          [157] Art. 14(1).
[158] Art. 14(2), first para.
[159] Art. 14(3). For a consideration of the meaning of this phrase, see Case C–149/05 *Price* v. *Conseil des ventes voluntaries de meubles aux enchères publiques* [2006] ECR I–7691 (voluntary sales of chattels by auction). In Case C–197/06 *Confederatie van Immobiliën-Beroepen van België VZW* v. *Van Leuken* [2008] ECR I–2627, paras. 35–8, the Court indicated that a profession which is, in the host Member State, open to persons who have not received significant education and training in law cannot be considered to be one 'whose practice requires precise knowledge of national law' and the derogation did not apply to the profession of estate agent in Belgium. The situations listed in the derogation are exhaustive: Case C–274/05 *Commission* v. *Greece* [2008] ECR I–7969, para. 44.
[160] Art. 14(2), paras. 2–3.

In *Colegio de Ingenieros*[161] the Court noted that compensatory measures had to be restricted to those cases where they were proportionate to the objective pursued because, due to the time and effort involved, they could be a 'highly dissuasive factor for a national of a Member State exercising his right under the Directive'. For this reason the Court ruled that the directive did permit the 'partial' taking up of a regulated profession, thereby allowing the migrant professional to dispense with the requirement of having to comply with the compensatory measures and allowing him to take up his professional activities immediately. This meant that in principle an Italian engineer qualified only in hydraulics could take up the more general profession of civil engineer in Spain. Although this might lead to some confusion on the part of the consumer, the Court said this could be avoided by requiring migrants to mention the names and locations of the bodies or examining board which awarded them their academic titles and/or require the migrant to use their titles in the original language form as well as in translation.[162]

The 2005 directive also introduces the concept of 'common platforms', drawn up by representative professional associations, which are suitable for compensating for substantial differences which have been identified between the training requirements existing in the various Member States for a given profession.[163] If such a platform is likely to make the mutual recognition of qualifications easier, the Commission can submit it to the Member States and adopt an implementing measure.[164] In these circumstances, the host state must waive the imposition of compensatory measures on applicants who meet the platform's conditions.

### (ii) System of automatic recognition of qualifications attested by professional experience in certain industrial, craft, and commercial activities

As we have seen, Chapter I of the directive offers a qualified version of mutual recognition: mutual recognition applies subject to the application of compensatory measures if there are substantial differences between the training acquired by the migrant and the training required in the host Member State. Chapter II contains the second approach to mutual recognition found in the original sector specific directives. The industrial, craft, and commercial activities listed in the directive[165] are subject to the *automatic* recognition of qualifications attested by professional experience provided that conditions concerning the duration and form of professional experience (in a self-employed or employed capacity) are satisfied.[166] Account is also taken of previous training and this may reduce the amount of professional experience required. All previous training should, however, be proven by a certificate recognized by the Member State or judged by a competent professional body to be fully valid. Thus, Chapter II of the directive offers an unqualified version of mutual recognition.

---

[161] Case C–330/03 *Colegio de Ingenieros de Caminos, Canales y Puertos* v. *Adminstración del Estado* [2006] ECR I–801, para. 24. See also Case C–197/06 *Van Leuken* [2008] ECR I–2627, paras. 40–1.

[162] Para. 25.    [163] Art. 15(1).    [164] Art. 15(2).

[165] I.e., those sectors previously covered by professional activity covered by the former 'transitional' directives (Dirs. 64/222/EEC, 64/427/EEC, 68/364/EEC, 68/366/EEC, 68/368/EEC, 70/523/EEC, 75/368/ EEC, 75/369/EEC, 82/470/EEC, and 82/489/EEC, already consolidated by Dir. 1999/42/EC).

[166] Arts. 17–19.

### (iii)  System of automatic recognition of qualifications for specific professions

Chapter III deals with specific professions. As with the previous sector specific directives, each Member State must automatically recognize certificates of training, on the basis of coordination of the minimum training conditions, covering the professions of doctors, nurses responsible for general care, dental practitioners, specialized dental practitioners, veterinary surgeons, midwives, pharmacists, and architects.[167] For the qualification to be recognized, the directive lays down minimum training conditions and the minimum duration of studies for each of these professions. The formal qualifications conforming to the directive issued by the Member States are listed in an annex (Annex V). Holders of these qualifications can practise their profession in any Member State. The effect of Chapter III is therefore unqualified mutual recognition combined with partial harmonization (of the training requirements).

### (iv)  Common provisions

Chapter IV of Title III contains the procedure for submitting a request for mutual recognition of professional qualifications.[168] It also permits migrant professionals to use the title conferred on them by the home state as well as the professional title of the corresponding host Member State.[169] If a profession is regulated in the host Member State by a private association or organization, the migrant must also be able to become a member of that organization or association and thus be able to use the corresponding title.[170]

Title IV contains detailed rules for pursuing the profession, including the possibility for the host state to require migrants to have knowledge of the relevant language necessary for practising the profession. It also requires close collaboration between the competent authorities in the host Member State and the home Member State,[171] by, for example, requiring each Member State to designate a coordinator to facilitate the uniform application of the directive[172] and to designate contact points which must provide citizens with information on the recognition of professional qualifications and to assist them in enforcing their rights, particularly through contact with the competent authorities to rule on requests for recognition.[173]

### (v)  Abuse

States have long expressed a concern about the provisions of the directives being abused, a concern the Court acknowledged in *Commission* v. *Spain (engineers)*[174] but ultimately dismissed; the fact that a national of a Member State wishing to pursue a regulated profession chooses to qualify for that profession in his preferred Member State cannot of itself constitute an abuse. Therefore, Spain's refusal to recognize an engineering qualification granted by the Italian authorities on the basis of studies carried out solely in Spain but coordinated by an Italian university, and involving an exam in Italy, meant that Spain breached the directive.

---

[167]  The directive also recognizes the principle of automatic recognition for medical and dental specializations common to at least two Member States under existing law but limits future additions to Dir. 2005/36 to those that are common to at least two-fifths of the Member States.          [168] Arts. 50–1.

[169]  Art. 52(1).          [170] Art. 52(2).          [171] Art. 56(1).          [172] Art. 56(4).          [173] Art. 57.

[174]  See, e.g., Case C–286/06 *Commission* v. *Spain* [2008] ECR I–8025, paras. 69–72. See below nn. 284–312.

The issue arose again, in a more blatant case of bootstrapping in *Consiglio degli Ingegneri*.[175] In both Italy and Spain the profession of engineer is conditional on possession of a university diploma and registration in the register of the relevant professional body. In addition, the Italian, but not the Spanish, system provides for a state examination which a candidate must pass in order to be entitled to pursue the profession. Cavallera held a first degree in mechanical engineering awarded by the University of Turin (Italy) after three years' education. He then applied for, and obtained, homologation in Spain of his Italian qualification (i.e., certification that his Italian degree was equivalent to a corresponding Spanish degree); this in turn allowed him to accede to the regulated profession in Spain, because Spain did not require an additional state examination. On the basis of the certificate of homologation, Cavallera enrolled in the register of one of the 'colegios de ingenieros técnicos industriales' in Catalonia, in order to pursue the regulated profession of industrial technical engineer in Spain, specializing in mechanical engineering. However, he never worked in Spain, nor did he follow any course of study or take any exams under the Spanish education system, nor did he take the state examination provided for under Italian legislation for the purpose of being entitled to pursue the profession of engineer. Nevertheless, he wanted to rely on the mutual recognition of diplomas directive to gain access to the profession of engineer in Italy, even though he had not sat the state examination required under Italian law.

Without relying on the abuse of law doctrine, the Court said Cavallera could not rely on the directive. It said that a 'diploma' did not include a certificate issued by a Member State (Spain) which did not attest to any education or training covered by the education system of that Member State and was not based on either an examination taken or professional experience acquired in that Member State.[176] Were the directive to apply, this would be tantamount to allowing a person who had merely obtained a qualification in the Member State in which he studied (Italy), which did not in itself provide access to that regulated profession, nonetheless to gain access to that profession, even though the homologation certificate obtained elsewhere (Spain) provided no evidence that the holder had acquired an additional qualification or professional experience.[177] That would be contrary to the principle, enshrined in the directive, that Member States reserve the option of fixing the minimum level of qualification necessary to guarantee the quality of services provided within their territory.[178]

The line between legitimate exercise of free movement, such as in the *Commission v. Spain (engineers)* case, and situations deemed to fall outside the ambit of the directive, as illustrated by *Consiglio degli Ingegneri*, is clearly a thin one. In both situations, the applicants had spent the entirety of their studies in the Member State in which they later sought to work as engineers. Similarly, in both cases, the academic qualifications as between the relevant systems (Spain and Italy) were deemed equivalent by competent authorities, the only difference being that in *Commission v. Spain (engineers)*, an Italian university certified the Spanish course as equivalent to its own before the students took up their studies, whereas in *Consiglio degli Ingegneri*, the Spanish ministry of education merely certified the equivalence between Cavallera's Italian degree and the degrees awarded in the Spanish system *ex post*. The only distinction of any significance that it seems to be possible to draw

---

[175] Case C–311/06 *Consiglio degli Ingegneri* v. *Ministero della Giustizia, Marco Cavallera* [2009] ECR I–000.                                                                                  [176] Para. 56.
[177] Para. 57.         [178] Ibid.

between the two situations is that the students in the *Commission* v. *Spain (engineers)* case also went to Italy to pass the Italian State exam for engineers at the end of their studies, whereas Cavallera could not point to any qualification or experience obtained in Spain. The outcome of the *Consiglio degli Ingegneri* case would have been different if Cavallera had worked, even for a very short time, in Spain before returning to Italy.[179]

### (e) The legal profession

The recognition of legal qualifications has proved to be a particularly thorny issue given the major differences between the legal systems of the Member States. For this reason, the legal profession has been more regulated by EU law than most.[180] The first directive, 77/249 on the provision of services,[181] enabled lawyers to provide services in other Member States under the control of their home state and using their home state title, but subject to the same conditions laid down for lawyers established in the host state, with the exception of any conditions requiring residence or registration of a professional activity in that state.[182] The directive also makes provision for lawyers providing services to be introduced to the presiding judge and the president of the relevant Bar and to work in conjunction with a local lawyer.[183]

The rules laid down in the directive are, of course, subject to the Treaty provisions, including Article 56 TFEU. The importance of this can be seen in *AMOK*,[184] where German law provided that the unsuccessful litigant in proceedings before a German court did not have to pay the costs of the local lawyer as well as the lawyer providing the service. The Court said that the German rule requiring the hiring of a local German lawyer had the effect of discouraging parties from having recourse to lawyers established in other Member States: 'The freedom of such lawyers to provide their services would thereby be obstructed and the harmonisation of the sector, as initiated by the Directive, adversely affected.'[185]

The influence of Article 56 can also be seen in *Cipolla*.[186] The Court said that national law setting a professional scale of charges which permitted no derogation was liable to render access to the Italian legal services market more difficult for lawyers established in other Member States and was therefore likely to restrict the exercise of their activities providing services in breach of Article 56. However, the Court recognized that the Italian government might be able to justify the restriction on the grounds of consumer protection and safeguarding the proper administration of justice[187] but it was for the national court to assess the proportionality of the measure, bearing in mind the specific context of the Italian legal market (an extremely large number of lawyers who might be encouraged to compete against each other on price, with the risk of deterioration on the quality of the services provided).[188]

---

[179] I am grateful to Carsten Zatschler for this point.

[180] See further S.Claessens, *Free Movement of Lawyers in the European Union* (Nijmegen: Wolf Legal Publishers, 2008).                    [181] Dir. 77/249/EC ([1977] OJ L78/17).

[182] Art. 4(1).

[183] This ensures that the service providing lawyer can act within the local judicial system, has the necessary support and can comply with local procedural and ethical rules: Case 427/85 *Commission* v. *Germany* [1988] ECR 1123 but such requirements cannot be disproportionate: Case C–294/89 *Commission* v. *France* [1991] ECR I–3591.

[184] Case C–289/02 *AMOK Verlags GmbH* v. *A & R Gastronomie Gmbh* [2003] ECR I–15059.

[185] Para. 39.        [186] Joined Cases C–94/04 and C–202/04 *Cipolla* v. *Fazari* [2006] ECR I–2049.

[187] Para. 64.        [188] Para. 67.

While Directive 77/249 made no provision for mutual recognition of diplomas, Directive 89/48/EEC—and now the RPQ Directive 2005/36 considered above—requires lawyers trained in a system which differs from that of the host state either to sit an aptitude test or to complete an adaptation period in order for their diplomas to be recognized by another Member State.

The final piece in the lawyers' jigsaw is Directive 98/5. While Directive 77/249 concerns lawyers' *services*, Directive 98/5/EC[189] concerns lawyers' *establishment*. It represented a new phase in the recognition of qualifications because it specifically provides that a person's *authorization* to practise in their home Member State must be taken into account by the host state. The directive gives lawyers two options. First, it enables them to practise permanently and without restriction under their *original* professional title[190] in another Member State and on the same basis as the host state's own lawyers,[191] giving advice on the laws of the home and host state as well as on EU and international law. Lawyers who are fully qualified in one Member State will simply have to register with the Bar or other competent authority in the host state on the basis of their registration in the home state,[192] without the need for either an aptitude test or an adaptation period or any language test.[193]

Secondly, the directive makes it easier to acquire the professional title of the host state. A migrant lawyer who has 'effectively and regularly' practised in the law of the host state, including Union law, for at least three years under his home state title can seek admission to the profession of lawyer in the host state (i.e., can use both the host state's and the home state's title) without having to undergo an aptitude test or adaptation period.[194]

### (f) Non-application of horizontal directives

If the activity does not fall within the scope of Directive 2005/36, then, as *Bobadilla*[195] demonstrates, the principles laid down in *Gebhard* and *Vlassopoulou* continue to apply. Bobadilla, a Spanish national, undertook a postgraduate course in fine arts restoration in the UK with financial help from the leading Spanish museum, the Prado. Although she then worked in the Prado on a temporary contract, she was refused a permanent job on the ground that her British qualification had not been recognized as equivalent to a Spanish degree. The Court said that if the national court found that the profession was not regulated within the meaning of the then two horizontal directives, the Prado nevertheless had to investigate whether Bobadilla's diploma and professional experience were regarded as equivalent to the qualification required. The Court added that the Prado was 'ideally placed' to assess Bobadilla's actual knowledge and abilities, given that it had helped to fund her course and had already employed her.[196]

---

[189] [1998] OJ L77/36. The validity of this directive was unsuccessfully challenged in Case C–168/98 *Luxembourg* v. *European Parliament and Council* [2000] ECR I–9131.     [190] Art. 2.

[191] Arts. 6–7.     [192] Art. 3(1).

[193] Case C–506/04 *Wilson* v. *Ordre des avocats du barreau de Luxembourg* [2006] ECR I–8613.

[194] Art. 10. Concerns about whether three years' practice is enough to really qualify the individual in the law of the host state underpinned Luxembourg's unsuccessful challenge to the directive in Case C–168/98 *Luxembourg* v. *European Parliament and Council* [2000] ECR I–9131.

[195] Case C–234/97 *Fernández de Bobadilla* v. *Museo Nacional del Prado* [1999] ECR I–4773 was in fact decided under Art. 45 on free movement of workers, not Art. 49 on establishment. See also Case C–108/96 *Criminal proceedings against Mac Quen and others* [2001] ECR I–837, paras. 24–6; Case C–313/01 *Morgenbesser* [2003] ECR I–13467.     [196] Para. 35.

Similarly, in *Rubino*,[197] the Court reiterated that Articles 45 and 49 TFEU guarantee to the nationals of the Member States access to activities, in a self-employed or employed capacity, without discrimination based on nationality. Consequently, national authorities had to ensure that qualifications obtained in other Member States were accorded their proper value and were duly taken into account in the context of any recruitment procedures.

In the absence of harmonization, the host Member State remains competent to define the exercise of those activities,[198] including the power to impose criminal penalties on a national of another Member State for the illegal pursuit of a regulated profession,[199] provided that the host state respects Article 49. In practice this means that any requirement imposed by the host state is liable to hinder or make less attractive the exercise of the right of establishment and so will breach Article 49 unless it can be justified on public-interest grounds or under one of the express derogations.[200] In *Bouchoucha*[201] the Court said that the French authorities could prevent a French national with a British qualification in osteopathy from practising on public-health grounds because the qualification enjoyed no mutual recognition in the Union and the activity was confined to doctors in France. For much the same reason the Court ruled in *Mac Quen*[202] that a Belgian law restricting the conduct of eye examinations to ophthalmologists, to the exclusion of opticians who were not qualified medical doctors, could also be justified on the grounds of public health.

### (g) Qualifications obtained in third countries

A particular problem has arisen in respect of Union nationals who, after acquiring professional qualifications in a third country, return to work in Member State A which does recognize their qualification before going to work in State B which does not. Does Union law require the authorities in State B to apply the directives or the *Vlassopoulou* principles? At first the answer seemed to be no. For example, in *Tawil-Albertini*[203] a French national obtained Lebanese dentistry qualifications which were subsequently recognized by the Belgian authorities. Relying on this fact and on the provisions of the Dentists' Directive 78/686/EEC, he applied to the French Ministry to practise in France. His application was refused, and this decision was upheld by the Court, which said that the recognition by one Member State of qualifications awarded by non-Member States did not bind the other Member States.[204]

However, in *Haim I*[205] the Court qualified *Tawil-Albertini*. Haim was an Italian national who had acquired Turkish dentistry qualifications which had been recognized by the Belgian authorities. Haim was not, however, allowed to practise in Germany on the ground that he had not completed the two-year preparatory training required by German law. This time the Court said that, while the German authorities had not breached the

---

[197] Case C–586/08 *Rubino* [2008] ECR I–000, para. 34.
[198] Case C–108/96 *Mac Quen* [2001] ECR I–837, para. 24.
[199] Case C–104/91 *Borrell* [1992] ECR I–3003, para. 19.
[200] Case C–108/96 *Mac Quen* [2001] ECR I–837, paras. 24–6.
[201] Case C–61/89 [1990] ECR I–3551. See also J. Lonbay, 'Picking over the bones: Rights of establishment reviewed' (1992) 17 *ELRev.* 507, 509.
[202] Case C–108/96 [2001] ECR I–837. See also Case C–294/00 *Deutsche Paracelsus Schulen für Naturheilverfahren GmbH* v. *Kurt Gräbner (Heilpratikers)* [2002] ECR I–6515.
[203] Case C–154/93 [1994] ECR I–451.     [204] Para. 13.     [205] Case C–319/92 [1994] ECR I–425.

directive (since the directive did not require Germany to recognize Turkish qualifications recognized by Belgium), they had breached Article 49 by failing to do a *Vlassopoulou*-type comparison, examining whether and to what extent the *experience* already acquired in another Member State corresponded to that required by German law.[206]

In *Hocsman*[207] the Court went one stage further. It required State B to take account of all of the *formal qualifications* acquired elsewhere as well as practical experience when making the *Vlassopoulou* comparison. Hocsman, an Argentinian, acquired Spanish nationality in 1986 and then became a French citizen in 1998. His Argentine medical diploma was recognized by the authorities in Spain where he was authorized to practise as a specialist in urology in 1986. He was, however, refused permission to practise in France owing to the fact he held an Argentine diploma. Clarifying its earlier case law,[208] the Court said that the French authorities had to take into consideration:

all the diplomas, certificates and other evidence of formal qualifications of the person concerned and his relevant experience, by comparing the specialised knowledge and abilities so certified and that experience with the knowledge and qualifications required by the national rules.[209]

Similar principles are applied to highly qualified third-country national (TCN) employees wishing to work in the EU under the new blue card scheme.[210] This is considered further in Chapter 14.

## D. THE RIGHTS CONFERRED ON LEGAL PERSONS: COMPANIES

### 1. INTRODUCTION

So far we have focused on rights for individuals (natural persons). We turn now to the application of Article 49 to legal persons. Article 49 includes the right to set up and manage companies or firms (primary establishment) and the abolition of restrictions on the setting up of agencies, branches, or subsidiaries by nationals of any Member State in the territory of another Member State (secondary establishment). Article 54 provides that companies or firms formed in accordance with the law of a Member State and having their registered office, central administration, or principal place of business within the Union are to be treated in the same way as natural persons. In this way, the Treaties aim to assimilate the position of legal persons with that of natural persons. However, because of the artificial nature of the corporate entity, it is difficult simply to extrapolate to companies principles (such as non-discrimination) which are relatively easy to apply to individuals.[211]

---

[206] Para. 29. Haim then sued the German Association of Dental Practitioners of Social Security Schemes for *Factortame III* damages for the loss suffered by being denied the possibility of practising as a dentist for the scheme: Case C–424/97 *Haim II* [2000] ECR I–5123.       [207] Case C–238/98 [2000] ECR I–6623.

[208] Para. 30.       [209] Para. 35.

[210] Dir. 2009/50 [2009] OJ L155/17 adopted under Art. 63(3)(a) and (4) EC (now Arts. 79–80 TFEU). The UK, Ireland, and Denmark are not taking part.

[211] See Case 81/87 *Ex p. Daily Mail* [1988] ECR 5483, para. 19. See V. Edwards, 'The secondary establishment of companies: The case law of the Court of Justice' (1998) 18 *YEL* 221, 221–2.

## 2. THE RIGHT OF DEPARTURE

The problem of extending the case law on individuals to companies was highlighted by one of the earliest decisions in this field, *Daily Mail*.[212] We have already seen how Article 49 and the original Directive 73/148 (now CRD) grant individuals the right to leave their home state without restriction in order to take up self-employment in another state. However, in *Daily Mail* the Court said that the same rule did not apply to companies. Daily Mail, an investment company incorporated under English law with its registered office in London, wanted to avoid paying UK tax when selling a significant part of its assets. It therefore decided to transfer its central management and control to the Netherlands prior to the sale of the shares, while maintaining its legal personality and status as a UK company.[213] Before it could change residence, the UK Treasury needed to give its approval but, although Daily Mail had applied for permission to relocate, it moved its office to the Netherlands without waiting for the Treasury's response.

Daily Mail subsequently sought a declaration that the requirement to obtain consent was unnecessary under Articles 49 and 54 TFEU. The Court disagreed. Having pointed to the wide variety of national laws on the factors providing a connection to the national territory and the absence of coordination directives, it concluded that neither Article 49 nor Article 54 conferred on companies incorporated in State A the right to transfer— without any restriction or impediment from State A—their central management, control, and administration to State B while at the same time retaining their status as companies in State A.[214] This judgment does not mean that companies cannot move their residence but that—at the present stage of development of Union law—restrictions can be imposed on emigrating companies by the home state.

Some commentators saw the case as a prompt either to the Union legislature to make use of its powers under Article 50(2) TFEU (ex Article 44(2) EC) to coordinate and/ or harmonize company law[215] or to the Member States to enter into agreements under Article 293 EC (repealed by the Lisbon Treaty) on the mutual recognition of companies or firms and the retention of legal personality in the event of transferring their seat from one state to another.[216] Others questioned the compatibility of this ruling with the case law on capital and services where the Treaty provisions cover both exit (emigration) and entry (immigration).[217] They argued that the case might now need reconsideration in light of the general shift in the case law towards the restrictions approach: since the requirement of Treasury consent hindered the exercise of the freedom of establish-

---

[212] Case 81/87 [1988] ECR 5483. See generally T. Tridimas, 'The case law of the European Court of Justice on corporate entities' (1993) 13 *YEL* 335.

[213] For this reason under the incorporation theory the case did not concern the transfer of the company's seat, merely its fiscal residence.                                                         [214] Para. 24.

[215] Cf. Case C–212/97 *Centros* [1999] ECR I–1459, para. 28: 'the fact that company law is not completely harmonised in the [Union] is of little consequence. Moreover, it is always open to the Council, on the basis of the powers conferred upon it by Article [50(2)(g) TFEU], to achieve complete harmonisation.' For details on EU company law legislation, see V. Edwards, *EC Company Law* (Oxford: OUP, 1999) and J. Wouters, 'European Community law: Quo vadis?' (2000) 37 *CMLRev.* 257. The EU has also enacted a regulation establishing a European Company ('Societas Europea'), Reg. 2157/2001 on the Statute for a European Company ([2001] OJ L294/1) accompanied by Dir. 2001/86 on the involvement of employees ([2001] OJ L294/22).

[216] J. Lever (1989) 26 *CMLRev.* 327, 331.

[217] See, e.g., E. Wymeersch, 'The transfer of the company's seat in European company law' (2003) 40 *CMLRev.* 661, 677.

ment it should breach Article 49 and need justification under one of the public-interest requirements.

This view was shared by Advocate General Poiares Maduro in *Cartesio*.[218] The case concerned a limited partnership seeking to transfer its operational headquarters from Hungary to Italy while remaining registered in Hungary, so that its legal status could continue to be governed by Hungarian law.[219] The Hungarian commercial court refused to enter the new address in the local register on the ground that the transfer was not possible under Hungarian law. It held that a firm (partnership or company) that wished to transfer its operational headquarters to another Member State first had to be wound up in Hungary and then reconstituted under the law of the new Member State (Italy). However, the Advocate General said 'Articles [49 TFEU] and [54 TFEU] preclude national rules which make it impossible for a company constituted under national law to transfer its operational headquarters to another Member State.' He also thought the rules could not be justified.

The Court offered a more nuanced perspective. It distinguished between two situations: (1) where the seat of a company incorporated under the law of one Member State is transferred to another Member State with *no* change as regards the law which governs that company (the situation in *Daily Mail* and *Cartesio*); and (2) where a company governed by the law of one Member State moves to another Member State with an attendant change as regards the national law applicable (reincorporation).[220]

In respect of the first situation, the Court said the matter fell outside the scope of Union law because the company no longer satisfied the pre-conditions of being a company formed under national law. In the absence of harmonization, it was for *national law* to define the connecting factor (i.e., registered office only (for those states applying the incorporation theory) or registered office and real seat (for those states applying the *siège réel* theory))[221] required for a company to be regarded as incorporated under the law of that Member State (thereby mirroring the situation with natural persons where national law decides whether the individual holds the nationality of the Member State).[222] National law also determines the conditions required for the company to maintain its status as a company incorporated under the law of that Member State. This includes the possibility for that Member State not to permit a company governed by its law to retain that status if the company intends to reorganize itself in another Member State by moving its seat to the territory of the latter, thereby breaking the connecting factor required under the national law of the Member State of incorporation.[223] If a company reorganizes itself in this way then it is no longer a company formed and existing under (Hungarian) law and so falls outside the scope of Article 54 and so Union law does not apply.[224] This means that in the circumstances of Cartesio, Hungarian law could insist on the Hungarian company being wound up prior to being reconstituted in Italy without this constituting a restriction on freedom of establishment.

By contrast, in the second situation the Court said that the company is converted into a form of company which is governed by the law of the Member State to which it has moved (Italy). The Court said that the power of Member States to determine the connecting

---

[218] Case C–210/06 *Cartesio Oktató és Szolgáltató bt* [2008] ECR I–000.
[219] Hungarian company law is based on the real seat theory.     [220] Para. 111.
[221] For a discussion of these theories, see below.     [222] Para. 109.     [223] Para. 110.
[224] For criticisms see M. Szydło (2009) 46 *CMLRev.* 703, 714–19.

factor cannot justify the Member State of incorporation (Hungary) preventing that company from converting itself into a company governed by the law of the new Member State (Italy) to the extent that it is permitted by that (Italian) law to do so, by requiring the company's winding-up or liquidation. The Court said that such a barrier (the winding-up or liquidation) to the actual conversion of a company 'constitutes a restriction on the freedom of establishment of the company concerned which, unless it serves overriding requirements in the public interest, is prohibited under Article [49 TFEU]'.[225]

Although the applicants were not successful in *Daily Mail* or *Cartesio*, it seems likely that, had they wanted to establish only a branch, agency, or subsidiary in the host state, they could have relied on Article 49 against the home state to enable them to exercise their freedom of establishment in another Member State. This was confirmed in *X and Y AB*,[226] where the Court said Article 49 prohibited the state of origin 'from hindering the establishment in another Member State of...a company incorporated under its legislation which comes within the definition contained in Article [54]'.[227] Therefore, a Swedish law preventing Swedish companies with subsidiaries in other Member States from receiving certain types of tax concessions breached Article 49 unless justified.

## 3. ACCESS TO THE MARKET OF THE HOST STATE

### 3.1 Primary and Secondary Establishment

#### (a) The basic rules

As we have seen, Articles 49 and 54 contemplate both primary and secondary establishment.[228] In respect of primary establishment, a company (or an individual) can exercise its right of establishment by taking part in the incorporation of a company in another Member State (see also Case Study 10.1 below). In that regard, Article 55 TFEU (ex Article 294 EC)[229] ensures that the out-of-state company will enjoy the same treatment as nationals of that Member State as regards participation in the capital of the new company.[230] Primary establishment can also occur where a company transfers its seat[231] from one state to another. In practice, this is rare,[232] and some states actually forbid it.[233] More common is the situation where companies create a *secondary* establishment in the host state by setting up branches, agencies, or subsidiaries. It is in this area that the Court has been most active in eliminating obstacles to such establishment.

---

[225] Para. 113. Presumably, the facts of *Viking* would also fall into this category: Case C–438/05 *Viking* [2007] ECR I–10779 (considered in Ch. 8).

[226] Case C–200/98 *X AB and Y AB* v. *Riksskatteverket* [1999] ECR I–8261.        [227] Para. 26.

[228] Some commentators suggest that these terms have become virtually 'meaningless' due to the Court's broad interpretation in Case C–212/97 *Centros* [1999] ECR I–1459 and Case C–208/00 *Überseering* [2002] ECR I–9919. See Colomer AG in Case C–212/97 *Centros* [1999] ECR I–1459, para. 36 and Wymeersch, above n. 217, 680.

[229] Art. 55 TFEU (ex Article 294 EC) provides that 'Member States shall accord nationals of the other Member States the same treatment as their own nationals as regards participation in the capital of companies or firms within the meaning of Article [54], without prejudice to the application of other provisions of the [Treaties].'        [230] Case 81/87 *Ex p. Daily Mail* [1988] ECR 5483, para. 17.

[231] The controversial meaning of 'seat' is discussed below.

[232] Cf. M. Siems, 'Convergence, competition, *Centros* and conflicts of law: European company law in the 21st century' (2002) 27 *ELRev.* 47.        [233] E.g., Germany and Austria: E. Wymeersch, above n. 217, 668.

In particular, the Court has prevented host states from insisting that business can be conducted only through a primary establishment (with a registered office, headquarters, and principal place of business in the host state) since this would negate the very right of secondary establishment. This can be seen in *Commission v. Italy (Foreign Securities Dealing).*[234] In order to set up as a securities dealer in Italy, Italian law required that the dealer had to be constituted in the form of a limited company with its registered office in Italy. The Commission successfully argued that this requirement prevented dealers from other Member States from making use of other forms of establishment, especially branches or agencies, and discriminated against them by obliging them to bear the expense of setting up a new company. The Court said that Article 49 expressly left traders free to choose the appropriate legal form in which to pursue their activities in another Member State.[235] In seeking to justify the breach, the Italian authorities argued that the requirement was necessary for supervising and effectively sanctioning the dealer in question. The Court disagreed, reasoning that Italy had failed to show that this was the 'only means' of achieving the objective.

The Court's wish to make the provisions on secondary establishment effective has been extended to the case of discrimination against *employees* on the ground that the company has its registered office in another Member State. Therefore, in *Segers*[236] the Court ruled that Articles 49 and 54 prohibited a Member State from excluding the director of a company from a national sickness insurance scheme on the ground that the company had its registered office in another Member State, even though it did not conduct any business there. The Court said that discrimination against employees in connection with social security protection 'indirectly restricts the freedom of companies of another Member State to establish themselves through an agency, branch or subsidiary in the Member State concerned'.[237]

---

**Case Study 10.1** THE *FACTORTAME* LITIGATION
..................................................................................................

The Court's desire to ensure both primary and secondary establishment of companies is central to an understanding of the Court's ruling in *Factortame II*. To the press and politicians, the name Factortame provokes a range of emotions: patriotism, xenophobia, Europhobia. To lawyers, the *Factortame* litigation provides a good case study of the effects of EU law on national law and politics and, for the purposes of this chapter, the importance of Article 49. In order to understand this litigation it has to be placed in context.

At the heart of the problem lay the Common Fisheries Policy (CFP),[238] which divided up fishing quotas on national lines,[239] and the Act of Accession of Spain to the EU,

---

[234] Case C–101/94 *Commission v. Italy (Re Restrictions on Foreign Securities Dealing)* [1996] ECR I–2691.                [235] Case 270/83 *Commission v. France (tax credits)* [1986] ECR 273, para. 22.

[236] Case 79/85 *Segers v. Bedrijfsvereniging voor Bank-en Verzekeringswegen, Groothandel en Vrije Beroepen* [1986] ECR 2375.                [237] Para. 15.

[238] For full details, see R. Churchill, 'The EEC's fisheries management system: A review of the first five years of its operation' (1988) 25 *CMLRev.* 369, C. Noirfalisse, 'The Community system of fisheries management and the Factortame case' (1992) 12 *YEL* 325, and R. Churchill, 'Quota hopping: The common fisheries policy wrongfooted?' (1990) 27 *CMLRev.* 209.

[239] The CFP was based on total allowable catches (TACs), prescribing the amount of fish which could be caught from a particular stock over a particular period, and quotas allocated among the Member States

which restricted the number of Spanish vessels allowed to fish in the EU. In order to circumvent these restrictions Spanish fishing companies started 'quota-hopping', i.e. registering their boats as British and then fishing under the British quota even though they lacked any genuine link with the UK.[240] The British government tried to prevent this by imposing nationality and residence requirements on the owners and crew of fishing vessels to ensure that there was a real economic link between the ship and the country of registration. For example, in 1983 the UK required 75 per cent of the crew of a British fishing boat to be EU nationals (Spain was not then a member of the EU). The Irish government replicated these British rules, fearing that the Spanish quota-hoppers might turn their attention to Ireland once the restrictive British rules were in place. Equivalent Irish legislation was found compatible with EU law in *Pesca Valentia*.[241]

In 1986 the UK imposed new licence conditions for vessels fishing under the UK quota, relating first to the crew of the vessel (75 per cent EU nationals, 75 per cent resident in the UK and all contributing to the UK social security scheme) and, secondly, to the operation of the vessel (for example at least 50 per cent of the catch had to be landed and sold in the UK). In *Ex p. Agegate*[242] the Court upheld the nationality and social security conditions but found that the residence condition could not be justified. In *Jaderow*[243] the Court said that Member States could require vessels to operate from national ports,[244] provided the vessels were not required to depart from a national port on all their fishing trips.

Despite these various steps, quota-hopping continued, and following a further wave of Spanish registrations in 1986–7,[245] the Merchant Shipping Act 1988 was passed, together with the Merchant Shipping (Registration of Fishing Vessels) Regulations 1988.[246] The 1988 Act created a new register for all British fishing vessels, including those already registered under the Merchant Shipping Act 1894. According to section 14(1) of the 1988 Act, a fishing vessel could be registered in the new register only if all the following applied:

(a)  the vessel was British-owned[247]

---

dividing up the TACs. The CFP also envisaged various long-term conservation measures, including closed seasons, closed areas, and minimum fish sizes.

[240] Noirfalisse, above n. 238, 334–5.

[241] Case 223/86 *Pesca Valentia Ltd* v. *Minister for Fisheries and Forestry, Ireland and the Attorney General* [1988] ECR 83.

[242] Case C–3/87 *The Queen* v. *Minister of Agriculture, Fisheries and Food, ex p. Agegate Ltd* [1989] ECR 4459.

[243] Case C–316/87 *The Queen* v. *Minister of Agriculture, Fisheries and Food, ex p. Jaderow Ltd* [1989] ECR 4509. See also the enforcement proceedings brought by the Commission: Case C–279/89 *Commission* v. *UK* [1992] ECR I–5785.

[244] Evidenced by the landing of a proportion of its catches or the vessel's periodic presence in the national port.      [245] Noirfalisse, above n. 238, 337.

[246] SI 1988/1926.

[247] According to s.14(2), a fishing vessel was deemed to be British-owned if the legal title to the vessel was vested wholly in one or more qualified persons or companies and if the vessel was beneficially owned by one or more qualified companies or, as to not less than 75%, by one or more qualified persons.

(b)   the vessel was managed, and its operations directed and controlled, from within the United Kingdom

(c)   any charterer, manager, or operator of the vessel was a qualified (British) person or company.[248]

Despite its obviously discriminatory nature, the UK was advised that:

> any discrimination that arises out of the proposed measures [what became the 1988 Act] is a natural consequence of the [common fisheries policy] itself which divides quotas along national lines... We consider that rules on nationality of fishing vessels are the most appropriate way of establishing a genuine link between the Member States and the vessel intending to fish for the Member State's quota.[249]

Nevertheless, the 1988 Act precipitated challenges at both Union and national levels. At Union level, the Commission brought enforcement proceedings against the UK under Article 258 TFEU (ex Article 226 EC) for a declaration that section 14 of the 1988 Act breached Article 49.[250] It also successfully applied for an interim order under Article 278 TFEU (ex Article 242 EC) requiring the UK to suspend the application of the nationality requirements laid down in section 14.[251] The UK complied with effect from November 1989.

At national level, judicial review proceedings were brought by the owners or operators of 95 fishing vessels which had been registered as British under the Merchant Shipping Act 1894[252] but could not satisfy one or more of the conditions laid down the 1988 Act and so were deprived of the right to fish from April 1989.[253] The Divisional Court made an Article 267 TFEU (ex Article 234 EC) reference on the substantive issues of Union law raised in the proceedings (the case which became *Factortame II*). The Divisional Court also ordered that, by way of interim relief, the application of the 1988 Act[254] and the 1988 Regulations had to be suspended. However, this was overturned by a unanimous Court of Appeal which held that under *national* law the courts had no power to suspend the application of Acts of Parliament because, at common law, an interim injunction could not be granted against the Crown.[255] The House of Lords agreed with the Court of Appeal's interpretation of

---

[248]   According to s.14(7) 'qualified person' meant a person who was a British citizen resident and domiciled in the UK and 'qualified company' meant a company incorporated in the UK and having its principal place of business there, at least 75% of its shares being owned by one or more qualified persons or companies and at least 75% of its directors being qualified persons.

[249]   Quoted by Lord Slynn in *Factortame (No. 5)* [2000] 1 AC 524, 543E.

[250]   Case C–246/89 *Commission* v. *UK* [1991] ECR I–4585.

[251]   Case C–246/89 R *Commission* v. *UK* [1989] ECR 3125, Order of the President of the Court.

[252]   These facts are set out in detail in Case C–213/89 *R.* v. *Secretary of State for Transport, ex p. Factortame Ltd (Factortame I)* [1990] ECR I–2433, paras. 3–13.

[253]   Some fishing vessels had originally been registered in Spain but were subsequently registered in the UK; others had always been registered in the UK but had been purchased by the complainant companies. For a fuller exposition of the parties, see N. Green, 'Proportionality and the supremacy of Parliament in the UK' in E. Ellis (ed.), *The Principle of Proportionality in the Laws of Europe* (Oxford: Hart, 1999), 159.

[254]   In particular Part II laying down the registration conditions.

[255]   [1989] 2 CMLR 353. As Bingham LJ explained, to decide otherwise would be a 'constitutional enormity' (at 407).

national law[256] but referred the case to the Court of Justice on the interpretation Union law. In *Factortame I*,[257] the Court of Justice said that *Union* law required the granting of interim relief to secure effective interim protection of directly effective rights. For this reason the national rule (no injunction against the Crown) had to be set aside; the House of Lords obliged and granted interim relief on the facts.[258]

On the issue of substance, the Court of Justice ruled in *Factortame II*,[259] and again in the enforcement proceedings brought by the Commission,[260] that the conditions laid down for the registration of vessels should not form an obstacle to freedom of establishment within the meaning of Article 49.[261] Beginning by defining the conditions for the grant of 'nationality' to a ship, the Court said that each Member State had to comply with the prohibition on discrimination against nationals of other Member States on grounds of their nationality. Therefore, the Court ruled that the nationality condition on the owners or charterers of a vessel, or the shareholders and directors of a company, was contrary to Article 49.[262] The Court added that such a condition was also contrary to Article 55, under which Member States had to accord nationals of the other Member States the same treatment as their own nationals as regards participation in the capital of companies or firms.

The Court then turned to the requirements that the owners, charterers, managers, and operators of the vessel or, in the case of a company, the shareholders and directors be resident and domiciled in the UK. It found these requirements to be unjustifiably indirectly discriminatory: while the majority of UK nationals satisfied these requirements automatically as they were resident and domiciled in the UK, nationals of other Member States would in most cases have to move their residence and domicile to the UK in order to comply with them.[263] The requirements therefore breached Article 49.

By contrast, the Court found that the rule that a vessel had to be managed and its operations directed and controlled from within the UK was compatible with Union law since it 'essentially coincides with the actual concept of establishment' within the meaning of Article 49 'which implies a fixed establishment'.[264] On the other hand the Court said that such a requirement would not be compatible with Article 49 if it precluded registration of a secondary establishment.

---

[256] R. v. *Secretary of State for Transport, ex p. Factortame Ltd* [1990] 2 AC 85, 151–3. See further, N. Gravells, 'Disapplying an Act of Parliament pending a preliminary ruling: Constitutional enormity or Community law right?' [1989] *Public Law* 568.

[257] Case C–213/89 [1990] ECR I–2433, noted by A. Toth (1990) 27 *CMLRev.* 573. For discussion, see P. Oliver, 'Interim measures: Some recent developments' (1992) 29 *CMLRev.* 7, 10–19.

[258] R. v. *Secretary of State for Transport, ex p. Factortame Ltd* [1991] 1 AC 603, noted by P. Allott (1990) 49 *CLJ* 377. The Law Lords were also influenced by the fact that the Court of Justice had granted interim relief in Case C–246/89R *Commission* v. *UK* [1989] ECR 3125. See further N. Gravells, 'Effective protection of Community law rights: Temporary disapplication of an Act of Parliament' [1991] *Public Law* 180 and D. Oliver, 'Fishing on the incoming tide' (1991) 54 *MLR* 442.          [259] Case C–221/89 [1991] ECR I–3905.

[260] Case C–246/89 *Commission* v. *UK* [1991] ECR I–4585. Other states also attempted to address the problems of quota-hopping. Their measures were equally unsuccessful: e.g., Case C–93/89 *Commission* v. *Ireland* [1991] ECR I–4569, para. 15: 'by requiring nationals of other Member States to set up an Irish company before obtaining a licence to fish at sea, Ireland has failed to fulfil its obligations under Article [49]'; Case C–151/96 *Commission* v. *Ireland* [1997] ECR I–3327 (nationality requirement for owner); Case C–334/94 *Commission* v. *France* [1996] ECR I–1307 (nationality requirement for owner and crew).

[261] Para. 23.          [262] Para. 30.          [263] Para. 32.          [264] Para. 34.

Although the ruling in *Factortame II* seems complex, in essence the Court accepted the Commission's argument that the conditions laid down by the 1988 Act breached Article 49 in two ways:[265]

- by preventing *nationals* of other Member States from setting up and acting as directors of companies in the sea fisheries sector in the UK (i.e., by interfering with primary establishment)[266]

- by restricting the possibility for *companies* of other Member States to pursue sea-fishing activities from the UK through agencies, branches, or subsidiaries (i.e., by interfering with secondary establishment).

However, in reaching its conclusions Noirfalisse[267] suggests that the Court blurred the distinction between the grant of nationality and the freedom of establishment. She argues that the prohibition of discrimination on the ground of nationality in Articles 18 and 49 presupposes the existence of the concept of nationality; a national of a Member State cannot invoke Article 49 to *obtain* the nationality of another Member State where he wishes to establish.[268] Under international law each state can fix the conditions for granting its nationality to its ships: there must exist a genuine link between the state and the ship.[269] She therefore argues that the 1988 Act was merely the expression of the exclusive power of a Member State to define its own ships. It did not concern the exercise of the right to establishment at all.

When *Factortame II* returned to the UK, the Divisional Court made an order giving effect to the Court's judgment and also directed the claimants to give particulars of their claims for damages, covering expenses and losses incurred between 1 April 1989 (when the 1988 Act came into force) and 2 November 1989 (when it was repealed). It then made a further reference to the Court of Justice on the question of State liability. In *Factortame III*[270] the Court said that the principle of state liability—where a state could be held responsible for loss and damage caused to individuals as a result of breaches of Union law—was inherent in the system of the Treaties, whatever organ of the state was responsible for the breach.[271] In an area such as the registra-

---

[265] Case C–246/89 *Commission* v. *UK* [1991] ECR I–4585, para. 19, and Mischo AG's Opinion, paras. 29–33. See also Art. 14(1) of the Services Dir. considered in Section E below.

[266] Cf. Case C–299/02 *Commission* v. *Netherlands (registration of ships)* [2004] ECR I–9761, paras. 20–1 where the Court ruled that national measures requiring as a condition for being able to register a ship in the Netherlands that the shareholders, directors, and natural persons responsible for day-to-day management of the Union company owning the ship have Union or EEA nationality constituted an obstacle to freedom of establishment and was not a proportionate means of attaining the goal of exercising effective control and jurisdiction over ships flying the Dutch flag.

[267] Noirfalisse, above n. 238, 344–6.

[268] See also Art. 54 'Companies or firms formed in accordance with the law of a Member State' enjoy equal treatment (emphasis added).

[269] See Art. 5(1) of the Convention of the High Seas of 1958 referred to by the Court.

[270] Joined Cases C–46 and 48/93 *Brasserie du Pêcheur SA* v. *Federal Republic of Germany* and *R.* v. *Secretary of State for Transport, ex p. Factortame and others (Factortame III)* [1996] ECR I–1029. For detailed analysis of the case see P. Craig, 'Once more unto the breach: The Community, the state and damages liability' (1997) 113 *LQR* 67; and the essays in J. Beatson and T. Tridimas (eds.), *European Public Law* (Oxford: Hart, 1998) and J. Lonbay and A. Biondi (eds.), *Remedies for Breach of EC Law* (Chichester: Wiley, 1997).

[271] Para. 32.

tion of vessels and fisheries which conferred a wide discretion on the legislature, the Court said that Union law conferred a right to reparation where three conditions were met:[272]

- the rule of law was intended to confer rights on individuals
- the breach of Union law was sufficiently serious
- there was a direct causal link between the breach of the obligation by the state and the damage sustained by the injured parties.

The Court ruled that the first condition was 'manifestly satisfied' in the case of Article 49.[273] Regarding the second condition, the Court said that the decisive test was whether the Member State manifestly and gravely disregarded the limits on its discretion.[274] It then listed a number of factors which the national court could take into consideration[275] and gave a strong hint that it considered the UK's breach to be sufficiently serious. In particular, it noted that the nationality condition constituted 'direct discrimination manifestly contrary to [Union] law' and that the residence and domicile conditions were unjustifiable. It did add that in making its assessment, the national court had to take into account the legal disputes relating to particular features of the common fisheries policy, the attitude of the Commission which had made its position known to the UK in good time, and the assessments as to the state of certainty of Union law made by the national courts in the interim proceedings brought by individuals affected by the Merchant Shipping Act.[276] Finally, in respect of the third condition the Court said that this was a matter for the national courts to decide.

The Divisional Court, the Court of Appeal, and the House of Lords[277] all found that the breaches of Union law resulting from the 1988 Act were in principle sufficiently serious to give rise to liability for any damage that might have been caused to the applicants. In his speech, Lord Slynn recognized that the Act had been passed after anxious consideration with the benefit of legal advice and that the government had acted in good faith with the intention of protecting British fishing communities rather than with the deliberate intention of harming Spanish fishermen. However, he found the UK liable[278] because the 'deliberate adoption of legislation which was clearly discriminatory on the grounds of nationality',[279] the shortness of the transitional period, the fact

---

[272] Para. 51, considered further in Ch. 6.

[273] 'The essence of Article [49] is to confer rights on individuals (Case 2/74 *Reyners* [1974] ECR 631, para. 25)'.                                                                      [274] Para. 55.

[275] These included: the clarity and precision of the rule breached, the measure of discretion left by that rule to the national or Union authorities, whether the infringement and the damage caused was intentional or involuntary, whether any error of law was excusable or inexcusable, the fact that the position taken by a Union institution may have contributed towards the omission, and the adoption or retention of national measures or practices contrary to Union law (para. 56).

[276] Para. 63. The 37th claimant argued that the UK failed to adopt the measures needed to comply with the Order of the President of the Court of 10 Oct. 1989 in *Commission* v. *UK* immediately and that this needlessly increased the loss it sustained. The Court said that if this allegation proved correct, it should be regarded by the national court as constituting in itself a manifest and, therefore, a sufficiently serious breach of Union law.                          [277] [1997] EuLR 475, [1998] EuLR 456, and [2000] 1 AC 524 respectively.

[278] *R.* v. *Secretary of State, ex p. Factortame (No. 5)* [2000] 1 AC 524, 542C–D per Lord Slynn (Arabic numbers reflects the numbering of English case law, Roman numerals that of the Court of Justice).

[279] Ibid., 545G.

that at the time there was no way of challenging the statute, and the requirement to re-register, all emphasized the determination of the government to press ahead with the scheme, despite the strong opposition of the Commission and doubts of some of its officials.[280] The rulings on damages precipitated a further outcry in the British press, with significantly varying estimates as to how much the claims would cost the British taxpayer.[281]

Following its comprehensive defeat in the *Factortame* litigation, the UK sought to have a protocol added to the EC Treaty at Amsterdam allowing Member States to impose requirements ensuring that vessels had a real economic link with the populations dependent on fisheries and related industries in that state.[282] The UK was unsuccessful.

## (b) Regulatory competition

Given the Court's enthusiasm to encourage secondary establishment, could those wishing to form a company take advantage of EU rules by incorporating a company in State A which has lenient incorporation rules and then, relying on Articles 49 and 54, set up a branch or agency in State B, thereby avoiding State B's more onerous rules of incorporation? Early cases on services suggested that this tactic would fail since it is a well-established principle that EU law cannot be relied on for abusive or fraudulent ends.[283] In *Centros*,[284] however, the Court appeared to reach the opposite conclusion.

Centros Ltd was a private company incorporated in the UK by two Danish citizens, Mr and Mrs Bryde, who were its sole shareholders. With a view to trading in Denmark, they applied to have a branch of the company registered in Denmark. At the time of the registration request, Centros had never traded in the UK, and for this reason the Danish

---

[280] Ibid., 545E. See A. Cygan (2000) 25 *ELRev.* 452.

[281] These ranged from £55 million to £100 million: G. Wilson, 'The final humiliation: Britain must pay Spanish fishermen "up to £100 million"', *Daily Mail*, 29 Oct. 1999; D. Bridgett, 'Britain to pay £55 million to Spanish fishermen', *Mail on Sunday*, 18 Feb. 2001. The case rumbled on: see e.g. *R. v. Secretary of State, ex p. Factortame (No. 7)* [2001] 1 CMLR 47 (QBD (T&CC)) on the legal nature of the claim, the applicable limitation periods, and the nature of the damages that could be awarded; *R. (Factortame Ltd and others) v. Secretary of State for Transport, Local Government and the Regions (No. 8)* [2002] EWCA Civ 932, [2002] 4 All ER 97, concerning the question whether an agreement made in July 1998 under which the claimants, Factortame Ltd, now in a 'parlous financial state', agreed to pay accountants, Grant Thornton, 8% of the damages awarded for services ancillary to the conduct of the litigation was champertous and therefore unenforceable. According to the ICC Directory of UK Companies, Factortame itself seems to have ceased trading and is now lying dormant on the register of companies (its last annual return was submitted on 9 May 2001).

[282] Draft Protocol to the EC Treaty: Quota Hopping Memo by the UK, IGC, Jul. 1996.

[283] See, e.g., Case 33/74 *Van Binsbergen v. Bedrijfsvereniging Metaalnijverheid* [1974] ECR 1299, para. 13; Case C–23/93 *TV10 v. Commissariaat voor de Media* [1994] ECR I–4795, para. 21, considered further in Ch. 12; Case C–367/96 *Kefalas v. Elliniko Dimosio* [1998] ECR I–2843, para. 20; and Case C–373/97 *Diamantis v. Elliniko Dimosio and Organismos Ikonomikis Anasygkrotisis Epicheiriseon AE (OAE)* [2000] ECR I–1705.

[284] Case C–212/97 [1999] ECR I–1459. These issues were raised again in Case C–86/00 *HSB-Wohnbau GMBH* [2001] ECR I–5353 but the Court found that it did not have jurisdiction to hear the case. See generally S. Deakin, 'Two types of regulatory competition: Competitive federalism versus reflexive harmonisation. A law and economics perspective on *Centros*' (1999) 2 *CYELS* 231 and C. Barnard and S. Deakin, 'Market access and regulatory competition' in C. Barnard and J. Scott (eds.), *The Law of the Single European Market: Unpacking the premises* (Oxford: Hart Publishing, 2002).

registrar of companies refused to register the branch. He considered that the company was actually seeking to register its principal business establishment in Denmark and not just a branch, and that the Brydes were seeking to evade Danish law on minimum capital requirements. In Denmark companies had to have at least DKr 200,000 (approximately £20,000)[285] when they were formed; the UK had no rules on minimum capital requirements.

The Court ruled that the registrar's refusal to grant the registration request constituted an obstacle to the freedom of establishment,[286] saying that it was 'immaterial' that the company was formed in the UK only for the purpose of establishing itself in Denmark where its main or entire business was to be conducted.[287] It also said that this was not a case of abuse because the national rules which the Brydes were trying to avoid were rules governing the formation of companies and not rules concerning the pursuit of certain trades, professions, or businesses.[288] In other words, they were not fraudulently taking advantage of the provisions of Union law[289] because they were doing what the Treaties expressly permit, namely incorporating in one Member State and setting up a secondary establishment in another.[290]

The Danish government sought to justify the refusal to register on the ground of the need to maintain its rules on minimum capital requirements. It said that the rules served two purposes: first, to reinforce the financial soundness of companies in order to protect public creditors against the risk of seeing the debts owed to them become irrecoverable (since, unlike private creditors, they could not secure debts by means of guarantees); and secondly, the law aimed at protecting all creditors from the risk of fraudulent bankruptcy due to the insolvency of companies whose initial capitalization was inadequate.

The Court ruled that the first justification offered was inadequate because it was inconsistent—the vital factor in the registrar's refusal to grant the registration request was the failure of the company to trade in the UK. This was immaterial to the protection of creditors since they would have been no better off had the company previously traded in the UK and been able to register its branch in Denmark.[291] Furthermore, EU company information disclosure directives put Danish creditors on notice that Centros Ltd was not a company governed by Danish law. The refusal to register was not only unjustifiable, it was also disproportionate. The Court said that the Danish authorities could have adopted less-restrictive measures by, for example, making it possible in law for public creditors to obtain the necessary guarantees.

The Court did, however, recognize the validity of the second justification put forward by the Danish government about abuse. It said that its ruling did not prevent Denmark from adopting measures for preventing or penalizing fraud, either in relation to the company itself or to its members, where it had been established that the members were in fact attempting to evade their obligations towards private or public creditors by means of the formation of the company. However, the Court added that combating fraud did not justify a practice of refusing to register a branch of a company which had its registered office

---

[285] See M. Siems, 'Convergence, competition, *Centros* and conflicts of law: European company law in the 21st century' (2002) 27 *ELRev.* 47, 49.          [286] Paras. 29–30.

[287] Para. 17, citing Case 79/85 *Segers* [1986] ECR 2375.          [288] Para. 26.          [289] Para. 24.

[290] Para. 27. See also Case C-196/04 *Cadbury's Schweppes* v *Commissioners of the Inland Revenue* [2006] ECR I-7995, para. 36 considered below at n. 405.          [291] Para. 35.

in another Member State[292]—but did not suggest what steps states could take to combat fraud, which would be compatible with Union law.[293]

In *Inspire Art*[294] the Court repeated its ruling in *Centros*, this time in respect of Dutch rules on minimum capital requirements and directors' liability which applied to companies deliberately established in another Member State (the UK) to avoid the Dutch rules but carrying on their activities exclusively or almost exclusively in the Netherlands through a branch.[295] The Court said that the Dutch rules had the effect of unjustifiably impeding the exercise by companies of freedom of establishment.[296] It added that the reasons why a company was formed in the UK and the fact that it carried on its activities exclusively in the Netherlands did not deprive the company of the right to invoke the freedom of establishment guaranteed by the Treaties, save where abuse was established on a case-by-case basis.[297]

For some, the decision in *Centros* gave the green light to a Delaware-style race to the bottom coming to the EU in the field of company law.[298] These commentators argue that companies are now free to incorporate in the state with the most lax incorporation standards and then, using branches or agencies, carry on the bulk of their operations in other states which apply 'higher' standards for incorporation. One brake on this race to the bottom—the use of the public-interest requirements—was not applied on the facts in *Centros*.[299] In company law there is another potential brake on any such race to the bottom, the *siège réel* ('real seat') doctrine, which is applied in countries such as France, Germany, and Italy. According to this doctrine, the national courts will view the reality of the situation rather than the legal form, and so will regard the applicable law as that of the Member State in which the company has its main centre of operations (head office or principal place of business) rather than that of the state of incorporation.[300] The effect of this doctrine is to prevent companies from doing what Centros did—that is, the doctrine limits freedom of incorporation.

By contrast, the UK, Ireland, the Netherlands, and, to a certain extent, Denmark operate a 'state of incorporation' rule,[301] according to which the applicable law is that of the state in which the company is incorporated or registered, irrespective of whether it has a physical presence there. Therefore, as the facts of *Centros* demonstrate, English law permits companies to be incorporated in the UK but with their residence or main operations

---

[292] Para. 38.

[293] P. Cabral and P. Cunha, '"Presumed innocent": Companies and the exercise of the right of establishment under Community law' (2000) 25 *ELRev.* 157, 162.

[294] Case C–167/01 *Kamer van Koophandel en Fabrieken voor Amsterdam* v. *Inspire Art Ltd* [2003] ECR I–10155.                                                                          [295] Para. 100.

[296] Para. 101.        [297] Para. 105.        [298] See further Ch.1.

[299] See C. Barnard and S. Deakin, 'Market access and regulatory competition' in Barnard and Scott (eds.) above n. 284; S. Deakin, 'Legal diversity and regulatory competition: Which model for Europe?' (2006) 12 *ELJ* 440.

[300] For a fuller discussion, see R. Drury, 'Migrating companies' (1999) 24 *ELRev.* 354; K. Sørensen, 'Prospects for European company law after the judgment of the European Court of Justice in *Centros Ltd*' (1999) 2 *CYELS* 203; W. Schön, 'Playing different games? Regulatory competition in tax and company law compared' (2005) 42 *CMLRev.* 331.

[301] Danish law was essentially applying the incorporation theory for corporate capacity and the real seat theory for recognition of foreign companies, based on the perceived abuse of Danish rules on minimum capital requirements: J. Hansen, 'A new look at *Centros*: From a Danish point of view' (2002) 13 *EBLRev.* 85.

in another Member State. This outcome would not be permitted by Member States which operate the *siège réel* doctrine.

*Centros* called into question the status of the *siège réel* doctrine under Union law. Although the judgment is far from clear on this point, it could be argued that the Court was suggesting that the validity of an incorporation in one Member State (the UK) could not be called into question in another (Denmark) on the grounds that the principal business presence or central administration of the company concerned was not located in the state of incorporation. However, since the *siège réel* doctrine was not clearly before the Court, this interpretation cannot be relied on with any certainty. Nevertheless, it is arguable that, after *Centros*, the *siège réel* doctrine does pose an obstacle to freedom of establishment which needs justification.

These questions were confronted more directly by the Court in *Überseering*.[302] Überseering, a Dutch company, sued a German company, NCC, for defective work carried out by NCC on Überseering's behalf in Germany. Prior to bringing the proceedings, all the shares in Überseering were acquired by two German nationals. The German court found that, since Überseering had transferred its centre of administration to Germany, as a company incorporated under Dutch law it did not have legal capacity in Germany because it had not been formed according to German law[303] and so could not bring proceedings.[304] German law thus refused to recognize the legal personality which Überseering enjoyed under Dutch law (and continued to enjoy under Dutch law even after its centre of administration had been moved),[305] with the result that the German courts effectively denied the company access to justice in Germany.

The Court began by distinguishing *Daily Mail* from the facts of *Überseering*. It noted that *Daily Mail* concerned *emigration*, i.e. a company wishing to invoke Union law rights against its state of incorporation (the UK) when transferring its centre of administration while at the same time retaining its status as a British company.[306] By contrast, *Überseering* concerned an *immigrating* company and, in particular, the recognition (or rather lack of it) by one Member State (Germany) of a company incorporated under the law of another Member State (the Netherlands).[307] The Court said that because Überseering was a company validly incorporated under the law of the Netherlands, where its registered office was established, it had no alternative under German law but to reincorporate in Germany if it wished to enforce its rights under a contract before a German court.[308] This contravened Articles 49 and 54 because '[t]he requirement of reincorporation of the same company in Germany is therefore tantamount to outright negation of freedom of establishment'.[309]

The Court then considered whether the restriction on freedom of establishment could be justified. It said that while it was conceivable that overriding requirements relating to the general interest (e.g., the protection of the interests of creditors, minority shareholders, employees, and even the taxation authorities) could—in certain circumstances and subject to certain conditions—justify *restrictions* on freedom of establishment, they could not justify an outright *negation* of freedom of establishment.[310]

The effect of this judgment may be to erode the *siège réel* doctrine still further. It requires German courts to recognize companies validly formed under Dutch law, even though

---

[302] Case C–208/00 *Überseering BV* v. *Nordic Construction Company Baumanagement GmbH (NCC)* [2002] ECR I–9919.          [303] For a full explanation, see Wymeersch, above n. 217, 674.
[304] Para. 9.          [305] Paras. 63 and 71.          [306] Para. 62.          [307] Para. 66.          [308] Para. 79.
[309] Paras. 80–1.          [310] Paras. 92–3.

they would not be recognized under German law. Indeed, a company with its 'registered office, central administration or principal place of business within the [Union]' cannot be denied access to any other Member State.[311] This does not necessarily mean that the Court is privileging the incorporation theory; rather that it is paying more attention to the state in which the company has been incorporated.[312]

### 3.2 Equal Treatment and Beyond

The first paragraph of Article 54 provides that:

Companies or firms formed in accordance with the law of a Member State and having their registered office, central administration or principal place of business within the Union shall, for the purposes of this Chapter, be treated in the same way as natural persons who are nationals of Member States.

Relying on this provision, the Court ruled in *Commission v. France (tax credits)*[313] that it is the company's 'seat'[314] which serves as the connecting factor with the legal system of a particular state. In other words, a company's seat has the same function for companies as nationality does for individuals. A company's seat is the state in which the company or firm, formed in accordance with the law of a Member State, has its registered office, central administration, or principal place of business.[315] Therefore direct discrimination is discrimination on the ground of the company's seat; indirect discrimination involves the use of criteria which, 'by the application of other criteria of differentiation, lead in fact to the same result'.[316] According to the orthodoxy, direct discrimination breaches Article 49 and can be saved only by reference to one of the express derogations in Article 52 TFEU (ex Article 46 EC); indirect discrimination breaches Article 49 unless justified by a public-interest requirement or one of the express derogations (see fig. 8.1).

Case study 10.1 (above) on the *Factortame* litigation provides some good examples of discriminatory situations. However, as with other areas of free movement, the Court is increasingly moving towards the restrictions/market access approach, as was seen in *Centros*,[317] the principal case where access to the market was denied. The Court found that the registrar's refusal to register a branch of the company was an obstacle to freedom of establishment and so breached Article 49.[318] This approach has been followed in a number of subsequent cases, both by the Court of Justice and the EFTA Court. For example, in *Commission v. Italy (trade fairs)*[319] the Court said that a national rule requiring the authorities to give their approval before a trade fair could take place constituted a restriction on the freedom of establishment. Likewise, in *EFTA Surveillance Authority* v. *Norway*[320] the EFTA Court said that Norway's decision to introduce an exclusive right for

---

[311] Wymeersch, above n. 217, 680.      [312] Ibid., 689.

[313] Case 270/83 [1986] ECR 273, para. 18.

[314] Case C–330/91 R. v. *Inland Revenue Commissioners, ex p. Commerzbank AG* [1993] ECR I–4017, para. 13, correcting the translation error found in Case 270/83 *Commission v. France (tax credits)* [1986] ECR 273: see Edwards, above n. 211, 225–6.                                      [315] Ibid.

[316] Case C–330/91 *Ex p. Commerzbank AG* [1993] ECR I–4017, para. 14.

[317] Case C–212/97 [1999] ECR I–1459, para. 34. See also Case C–221/89 *Factortame II* [1991] ECR I–3905.                        [318] See also Case C–208/00 *Überseering* [2002] ECR I–9919, para. 82.

[319] Case C–439/99 *Commission v. Italy* [2002] ECR I–305, para. 39. See also Case C–169/07 *Hartlauer Handelsgesellschaft mbH* v. *Wiener Landesregierung* [2009] ECR I–1721. See also Arts. 9–13 of the Services Dir. considered in section E below.                   [320] Case E–1/06 [2007] *EFTA Court Reports* 8.

one state–owned company to run all games of chance and gambling, thereby excluding private operators from the market, constituted:

a restriction on the freedom of establishment and the freedom to provide services, as it completely removes them from the market and insofar denies them access to that market...The restrictions are of a non-discriminatory nature, since the contested legislation applies without distinction to domestic and foreign operators of gaming machines.[321]

However, on the facts, the Court found the Norwegian rules justified and proportionate.

Finally, in *Commission v. Italy (motor insurance)*[322] the Court found that an Italian obligation to contract imposed on all insurance companies operating in the field of third party liability motor insurance and in relation to all vehicle owners constituted a restriction on freedom of establishment (and freedom to provide services). In this case the Court emphasized the significance of the restriction. It said the imposition by a Member State of an obligation to contract 'constitutes a *substantial* interference in the freedom to contract which economic operators, in principle, enjoy'.[323] It continued that in a sector like insurance, 'such a measure affects the relevant operators' access to the market, in particular where it subjects insurance undertakings not only to an obligation to cover any risks which are proposed to them, but also to requirements to moderate premium rates'.[324] It concluded that 'Inasmuch as it obliges insurance undertakings which enter the Italian market to accept every potential customer, that obligation to contract is likely to lead, in terms of organisation and investment, to significant additional costs for such undertakings.'[325] The rules therefore beached the Treaties but could be justified on the grounds of social protection for victims of road traffic accidents. The Court also said the rules were proportionate.

## 4. THE EXERCISE OF THE RIGHT OF ESTABLISHMENT

### 4.1 Equal Treatment and Beyond

Once the company has established itself or a branch in the host state then it must enjoy the same terms and conditions and other benefits available to national companies. Therefore, in *Commission v. Italy (data processing)*[326] the Court said that an Italian law, providing that only companies in which all or a majority of shares were directly or indirectly in public or state ownership could conclude agreements for data-processing systems for public authorities, 'essentially favour[ed] Italian companies'[327] and so breached Article 49. It could not be justified on the facts.

As we have seen elsewhere, in more recent case law, the Court has required not only discriminatory measures to be removed but also obstacles, restrictions, or hindrances to the enjoyment of the freedom of establishment. This can be seen in *Pfeiffer*.[328] Pfeiffer operated a large supermarket in Austria under the name Plus KAUF PARK.

---

[321] Para. 27.     [322] Case C–518/06 *Commission v. Italy (motor insurance)* [2009] ECR I–000.
[323] Para. 66.     [324] Para. 67.     [325] Para. 68.
[326] Case 3/88 [1989] ECR 4035. See also Case C–272/91 *Commission v. Italy* [1994] ECR I–1409.
[327] Para. 9.
[328] Case C–255/97 *Pfeiffer Großhandel GmbH v. Löwa Warenhandel GmbH* [1999] ECR I–2835. See also Ch. 9.

It obtained a court order restraining Löwa, a rival German discount store operating in Austria, from using the trade name 'Plus'. The Court of Justice ruled that such an order was 'liable to constitute an impediment' to Löwa's aim of realizing a uniform advertising concept across the EU, contrary to Article 49.[329] However, the Court said that because the primary aim of the national law was to safeguard trade names against the risk of confusion[330] it could be justified by overriding requirements in the general interest relating to the protection of industrial and commercial property interests, and the court's order was proportionate since there was a risk of confusion between the two trade names.

By contrast, in *Neri*[331] the Court found the steps taken by the Italian government to protect educational standards to be disproportionate. A British company, ESE, set up 12 branches in Italy where, for a fee, it provided courses which were validated by Nottingham Trent University (NTU) which also awarded a BA degree at the end of the course. Neri enrolled on one such course and then discovered that the Italian authorities had a practice of not recognizing the degree awarded on this course even though it was legally recognized in the UK. The Court noted that this Italian practice was 'likely to deter students from attending these courses and thus seriously hinder the pursuit by ESE of its economic activity' in Italy.[332] While the Court recognized that the professed aim of the Italian measure—to ensure high standards of university education—was legitimate, the steps taken were not proportionate because Italian law permitted similar arrangements to those between NTU and ESE and the Italian practice meant that the authorities refused to recognize any foreign degree.[333]

The proportionality question was also at issue in *Sevic*[334] where the Court considered the compatibility with Article 49 of a German law on company transformations providing for mergers only between companies established in Germany. It said that cross-border mergers constituted an exercise of the freedom of establishment[335] and that since such mergers could not be registered in the German commercial register, this was likely to deter the exercise of freedom of establishment.[336] The Court recognized that while the national rules could be justified on the grounds of protecting the interests of creditors, minority shareholders, and employees, as well as protecting the effectiveness of fiscal supervision and the fairness of commercial transactions, the German law was nevertheless disproportionate because it involved a 'general refusal to register a merger between an in-state and out-of-state company even where the protection of public interests, such shareholder protection, was not threatened.[337]

---

[329] Para. 20.

[330] This corresponded to the specific subject matter of the trade name: Case C–317/91 *Deutsche Renault* [1993] ECR I–6227, para. 37.

[331] Case C–153/02 *Valentina Neri v. European School of Economics (ESE Insight World Education System Ltd)* [2003] ECR I–13555.     [332] Para. 43.

[333] Paras. 47–9.

[334] Case C–411/03 *Sevic Systems* [2005] ECR I–10805. For the implications of this decision on company law directives see P. Behrens (2006) 43 *CMLRev.* 1669.

[335] The Court made no distinction between inbound and outbound mergers.     [336] Para. 22.

[337] Para. 30.

### 4.2 Taxation, Equal Treatment, and Beyond (and Back?)

#### (a) The discrimination approach

Equal treatment is also required in respect of tax advantages.[338] However, for the principle of equal treatment to apply, the two situations must be comparable.[339] If the different treatment of the comparator companies is based on the internationally accepted distinction in tax law between residents and non-residents then the matter should fall outside the Treaty prohibition on discrimination.[340] It will be recalled from Chapter 9 that international tax law and Union law both now recognize the principle of territoriality, namely that resident companies are taxed on their worldwide profits ('unlimited taxation'), while non-resident companies are taxed only on profits arising from sources located in that taxing state ('limited taxation').[341] This distinction can be seen in *Futura Participations*[342] concerning a Luxembourg rule that while all income earned by *resident* taxpayers was taxable, irrespective of where it was earned, for *non-resident* taxpayers only profits and losses arising from Luxembourg activities was taken into account when calculating tax payable in Luxembourg. The Court found that this rule was compatible with Article 49 because it conformed to the fiscal principle of territoriality.

However, *Futura Participations* also concerned a rule requiring taxpayers to keep their accounts in Luxembourg if they wished to carry forward losses in Luxembourg. The Court said that such a rule meant that if a company or firm with its primary establishment in another Member State wished to carry forward any losses incurred by its branch in Luxembourg, it had to keep two sets of accounts: one set complying with the accounting rules applicable in the state where it had its seat, another complying with the rules applicable in Luxembourg where it had its branch. The Court said that the rule constituted a 'restriction' on the freedom of establishment contrary to Article 49 (in fact, the rule was indirectly discriminatory) but could be justified on the ground of ensuring the effectiveness of fiscal supervision. However, the Court said that the rule was not proportionate because, although Luxembourg could legitimately require the non-resident taxpayer to demonstrate its losses clearly and precisely, it could not refuse the tax benefit simply because the company had not kept proper accounts in Luxembourg.

The preferential treatment by national tax law of companies established in a state over those with only a branch or agency in the state is a common feature of the case law in this area, as *Commission* v. *France (tax credits)*[343] shows. In order to avoid double taxation (which will occur where income is taxed once as corporation tax in the hands of the

---

[338] See, e.g., Case C–157/07 *Finanzamt für Körperschaften III in Berlin* v. *Krankenheim Ruhesitz am Wannsee-Seniorenheimstatt GmbH* [2008] ECR I–8061, para. 32: 'provisions which allow losses incurred by a permanent establishment to be taken into account in calculating the profits and taxable income of the principal company constitute a tax advantage. Granting or not granting such an advantage for a permanent establishment situated in a Member State other than that in which that company is established must therefore be regarded as a factor likely to affect the freedom of establishment.'

[339] See generally J. Wouters, 'Fiscal barriers and corporate establishment' (1994) 14 *YEL* 73.

[340] Case C–279/93 *Schumacker* [1995] ECR I–225.

[341] A point the Court recognized in Case C–446/03 *Marks & Spencer plc* v. *Halsey (Her Majesty's Inspector of Taxes)* [2005] ECR I–10837, para. 39.

[342] Case C–250/95 *Futura Participations SA and Singer* v. *Administration des Contributions* [1997] ECR I–2471, para. 22.

[343] Case 270/83 [1986] ECR 273. See also Case C–170/05 *Denkavit International BV* v. *Ministre de l'Economie, des Finances et de l'industrie* [2006] ECR I–11949, para. 29.

distributing company and again in the in the hands of the shareholder when distributed as dividends), France granted tax credits to recipients of dividends distributed by French companies. However, these tax credits were granted only where the recipient had a registered office in France. Therefore, in the case of a foreign parent, only a subsidiary—but not a branch or agency—could receive the tax credit. The Court said that Article 49 expressly left traders free to choose the appropriate legal form in which to pursue their activities in another Member State and that freedom of choice could not be limited by discriminatory tax provisions.[344] The rule therefore breached Article 49 and could not be justified on the facts. The Court reached the same conclusion in *Royal Bank of Scotland (RBS)*[345] where it found that a Greek law taxing company profits at a higher rate if its seat was in another Member State than if its seat was in Greece breached Article 49.

However, there is an important difference between *Commission v. France* and *RBS*. In *RBS* the Court considered the rule to be directly discriminatory since the discrimination was based on the location of the company's seat and, as we have seen, the seat gives a company its nationality.[346] Since the case concerned direct discrimination on the ground of nationality the Court looked only at the express derogations found in Article 52 and, because the Greek government had not relied on any of the grounds listed in Article 52, it could not justify its legislation.[347] By contrast, in *Commission v. France* the Court considered a rule based on the location of a company's registered office (and thus its seat under the real seat doctrine) to be indirectly discriminatory.[348] If the rule is considered indirectly discriminatory then it can be saved by both objective justifications and the express derogations (see fig. 8.1).

The waters are muddied further when the national rule distinguishes not on the basis of the location of a company's seat but on the basis of the residence of a company, the traditional basis on which taxation is levied. This was the situation in *Ex p. Commerzbank*[349] where the Court ruled that the use of the criterion of fiscal residence for the purpose of granting a repayment supplement on overpaid tax was liable to work 'more particularly to the disadvantage' of those companies having their seat in other Member States. In other words, the rule was indirectly discriminatory, it breached Article 49, and could in principle be justified although this was not the case on the facts.[350] When viewed from the perspective of the case law on natural persons, the Court's decision in *Commerzbank* is unsurprising, because the Court has long recognized that residence requirements

---

[344]  Para. 22.

[345]  Case C–311/97 *Royal Bank of Scotland plc v. Elliniko Dimosio (RBS)* [1999] ECR I–2651.

[346]  See also Case C–1/93 *Halliburton Services BV v. Staatssecretaris van Financiën* [1994] ECR I–1137, esp. para. 20.

[347]  Cf. Case C–105/07 *NV Lammers & Van Cleeff v. Belgische Staat* [2008] ECR I–173, para. 19 where the Court considered that discrimination on the basis of a company's seat could be justified (para. 25).

[348]  See the Commission's submission in para. 9.

[349]  Case C–330/91 [1993] ECR I–4017, para. 15. See also Case C–250/95 *Singer* [1997] ECR I–2471, para. 22; Case C–105/07 *Lammers* [2008] ECR I–1730, para. 19.

[350]  See also Case C–254/97 *Société Baxter v. Premier Ministre* [1999] ECR I–4809, para. 13, concerning a French rule which allowed pharmaceutical companies to deduct expenditure on research from tax, provided the research was carried out in France. Given that research was generally carried out at the headquarters of these companies, the Court found that the rule 'seems likely to work more particularly to the detriment of undertakings having their principal place of business in other Member States and operating in France through secondary places of business'. Such rules breached Art. 49 and in principle could have been justified on the ground of the effectiveness of fiscal supervision, but this was not the case on the facts.

are indirectly discriminatory.[351] However, when viewed from the perspective of those states which operate the *siège réel* doctrine, 'residence' coincides with 'seat',[352] and thus nationality.[353] Seen from this angle, discrimination on the grounds of residence should constitute direct discrimination on the ground of nationality which, according to the orthodox jurisprudence, can be saved only by one of the express derogations and not by the more general category of objective justifications. The same problem does not arise for states which apply the incorporation theory because the state of incorporation (its seat and hence its nationality) and the place of its main operations (residence) are not necessarily the same. Therefore, different treatment on the ground of place of incorporation constitutes direct discrimination (*RBS*),[354] while different treatment on the ground of residence constitutes indirect discrimination (*Commerzbank*). If, as has been suggested,[355] *Commission* v. *France* had been viewed as a case concerning discrimination based on residence rather than location of seat, the Court's approach to the question of justification would have sat more comfortably with *Commerzbank*.

## (b) The hindrance/restriction approach—and its reconsideration

### (i) *What is a restriction?*

To avoid some of the problems found in the *RBS* line of case law, the Court has tended to use the formula based on removing hindrances, obstacles, or restrictions to the freedom of establishment,[356] which can then be justified not only by reference to the express derogations but also by the broader (and more appropriate[357]) justifications. We can see this in *Lankhorst-Hohorst*[358] which concerned German 'thin capitalization' rules. Under these rules, a resident subsidiary company making loan repayments to a non-resident parent were treated as dividend payments and so subject to tax in the resident subsidiary's hands. Had these repayments been made to a resident parent company they would have been tax deductible by the subsidiary. The Court, without reference to the internationally recognized distinction between resident and non-resident companies, said the rules constituted an unjustified 'obstacle' to the freedom of establishment because they made it 'less attractive for companies established in other Member States to exercise freedom of

---

[351] See, e.g., Case C–145/99 *Commission* v. *Italy* [2002] ECR I–2235, para. 38.

[352] As the Court itself did in Case C–264/96 *Imperial Chemical Industries plc (ICI)* v. *Colmer* [1998] ECR I–4695, paras. 22–3, noted by N. Travers, 'Residence restraints on the transferability of corporate trading losses and the right of establishment in Community law' (1999) 24 *ELRev.* 403.

[353] Poiares Maduro AG in Case C–210/06 *Cartesio Oktató* [2008] ECR I–9641, para. 23 noted that the real seat theory 'inextricably entwines a company's nationality and residence'.

[354] This would apply equally to Case C–101/94 *Commission* v. *Italy (foreign securities)* [1996] ECR I–2691; and Case C–212/97 *Centros* [1999] ECR I–1459.

[355] Edwards, above n. 211. Cf. Case C–112/91 *Werner* v. *Finanzamt Aachen-Innenstadt* [1993] ECR I–429, para. 15.

[356] See M. Gammie, 'The role of the European Court of Justice in the development of direct discrimination in the European Union' (2003) 57 *Bulletin for International Fiscal Documentation* 86.

[357] A. Cordewener, G. Kofler, and S. Van Thiel, 'The clash between European freedoms and national direct tax law: Public-interest defences available to the Member States' (2009) 46 *CMLRev.* 1951.

[358] Case C–324/00 *Lankhorst-Hohorst GmbH* v. *Finanzamt Steinfurt* [2002] ECR I–11779, para. 32. See also Case C–436/00 *X, Y* v. *Riksskatteverket* [2002] ECR I–10829, para. 49 where the Court talked about a 'restriction on freedom of establishment', and for a broad, restriction-based approach, see Case C–168/01 *Bosal Holding* [2003] ECR I–9409, para. 27: 'a parent company *might be* dissuaded from carrying on its activities' through a subsidiary established in another state (emphasis added).

establishment and they may, in consequence, refrain from acquiring, creating or maintaining a subsidiary in the State that adopts the measure'.

However, as we saw in Chapters 8 and 9, there is an inherent tension between the 'restriction' approach and taxation regimes in the Member States which differ significantly in respect of tax rates, tax bases and accounting rules. Enterprising lawyers began to argue that because, say, the corporation tax rate was higher in the UK than in Ireland this constituted an 'impediment' or 'restriction' on an Irish company's ability to establish a subsidiary in the UK.[359] Such arguments forced states, like the UK, to justify their higher rate and show that it was proportionate. The problem is that the justification for levying tax is essentially economic—taxation is the principal source of revenue for all states which they then use to provide a range of public and other services—and the Court will not generally accept pure economic justifications. This resulted in substantial losses to national treasuries[360] which, as a result, increasingly began to express serious concerns about the Court's interference in this sensitive area.[361] Should the Court be applying the full force of its single market case law, based on a restrictions analysis, to an area with long established, internationally recognized principles based on a discrimination model? Indeed, was it legitimate for the Court to trespass at all in this area of state sovereignty?

In an important opinion in *ACT Group Litigation*,[362] Advocate General Geelhoed offered a potential solution. He suggested a distinction should be drawn between what he termed 'quasi-restrictions', on the one hand, and 'true restrictions' on the other.[363] Quasi-restrictions refer to restrictions resulting inevitably from the coexistence of national tax systems. Certain disadvantages for companies active in cross-border situations result directly and inevitably from this juxtaposition of systems, and in particular from: (1) the existence of cumulative administrative compliance burdens for companies active cross-border; (2) the existence of disparities between national tax systems; and (3) the necessity to divide tax jurisdiction, meaning dislocation of tax base. He said that while such rules may 'restrict' cross-border activity in a general sense, the term 'restriction'—although employed in the Court's case law—was misleading because, what was really at issue were distortions of economic activity resulting from the fact that different legal systems existed

---

[359] See, e.g., Case C–196/04 *Cadbury's Schweppes* [2006] ECR I–7995.

[360] E.g., when the Court struck down the national rule in Case C–168/01 *Bosal Holding BV* [2003] ECR I–9409 it was estimated that the direct costs of the case amounted to 1.2 billion euros between 2003 and 2010. Even after changing its legislation it is estimated that the cost to the Nethlerlands was 0.55 billion euros a year to comply with the judgment: S. Kingston, 'The boundaries of sovereignty: The Court's controversial role applying the internal market rules to taxation' (2006–7) 9 *CYELS* 287.

[361] This was recognized by Commissioner Kovács: 'But several Member States feel that the Court does not have sufficient regard in its decisions to specific national policies and particularly to the financial consequences of its judgements…In particular, I am not happy with the fact that EU tax policy is increasingly being made as a result of Court decisions rather than as a result of coordinated policy actions of Member States. I am convinced that the recent developments in this area could lead to a situation where it will become almost impossible for Member States to protect their tax bases at national level': <http://www.ec.europa.eu/commission_barroso/kovacs/speeches/51201TDI.pdf>. See also the introduction of Art. 65(4) TFEU by the Lisbon Treaty (considered in Ch. 15), first proposed by the Constitutional Treaty, which was seen as a direct rebuff to the Court.

[362] Case C–374/04 [2007] ECR I–11673.

[363] Paras. 37–40. See also his Opinion in Case C–524/04 *Thin Cap Group Litigation* [2007] ECR I–2107, para. 48 and the discussion by S. Kingston, above n. 360; and 'A light in the darkness: Recent developments in the ECJ's direct tax jurisprudence' (2007) 44 *CMLRev.* 1321.

side-by-side.[364] In certain cases, these distortions provide disadvantages for economic actors; in other cases, advantages.[365] In the first case, litigants describe them as 'restrictive'; in the second case, they stimulate cross-border establishment activity. He added dryly, 'In the latter case, the taxable subject concerned does not generally invoke [Union] law.' He concluded that 'In the absence of an EU-wide tax solution, therefore, such quasi-restrictions should be held to fall outside the scope of Article [49 TFEU].' He added that the Court should be cautious in intervening in areas involving fiscal-economic policy considerations which the legislator is better placed to deal with.

By contrast, in respect of 'true' restrictions, ie those going beyond the inevitable consequences of the coexistence of national tax systems, Advocate General Geelhoed argued that they should fall within the scope of Article 49. He continued that because the criteria determining direct tax jurisdiction are residence- or source-based, this essentially means that 'all "truly" restrictive national direct tax measures will also, in practice, qualify as directly or indirectly discriminatory measures'. In other words, in the context of tax, true restrictions can and should be analysed (only) under the discrimination approach. Therefore, if the rule is truly non-discriminatory it will not breach the Treaties.

The Court's response to the criticisms leveled at its tax jurisprudence took two forms. First, in decisions such as *Marks & Spencer's*,[366] a case with the potential to cost national treasuries billions if the decision went against them,[367] the Court maintained its restrictions case law but developed a more nuanced, state-friendly approach to justifications and proportionality. Secondly, in cases such as *FII*[368] the Court appeared to follow the advice of its Advocate General and moved towards the adoption of a more discrimination-based analysis.

### (ii) Marks & Spencer's

*Marks & Spencer's (M&S)*[369] concerned a British company which had subsidiaries in the United Kingdom and in a number of Member States. In 2001 it ceased trading in continental Europe owing to record losses in the 1990s. M&S then claimed group relief from the United Kingdom tax authorities for the losses incurred by its Belgian, German, and French subsidiaries. However, under British law, the resident companies in a group (i.e. UK-based subsidiaries) could set off their profits and losses among themselves but were not allowed do so where the losses were incurred by subsidiaries which had no establishment in the United Kingdom and did not trade there.

The Court said that the British rules on group relief breached Article 49 because they discouraged undertakings from setting up subsidiaries in other Member States[370] and

---

[364] The Court subsequently made a similar point in Case C–527/06 *Renneberg* [2008] ECR I–7735.

[365] This point was recognized by the Court in Case C–67/08 *Block* v. *Finanzamt Kaufbeuren* [2009] ECR I–883, para. 35.

[366] Case C–446/03 *Marks & Spencer plc* v. *Halsey (Her Majesty's Inspector of Taxes)* [2005] ECR I–10837.

[367] A. Cordewener and I. Dörr (2006) 43 *CMLRev*. 855; V. Houlder, G. Parker, and N. Tait, 'Ministers relieved at decision on M & S losses', *The Financial Times*, 14 Dec. 2005, 3. As Kingston pointed out (above n. 360), numerous Member States had laws similar to the UK's rules. The German government alone forecast possible losses of 30 billion euros if the Court found the rules incompatible with Union law.

[368] Case C–446/04 *Test Claimants in the FII Group Litigation* v. *Commissioner of Inland Revenue* [2006] ECR I–11753.          [369] Case C–446/03 [2005] ECR I–10837.

[370] Para. 31.

so constituted a restriction on freedom of establishment.[371] To this extent it followed the advice of its Advocate General Poiares Maduro who rejected a discrimination-based approach on the grounds that it was 'not sufficient to safeguard all the objectives comprised in the establishment of the internal market'[372] and argued in favour of applying the restriction-based approach: taxation should not be seen as distinct but should be subject to 'the same concept of restriction on freedom of establishment which is applicable to [non-tax] areas.'[373]

Yet in applying the restrictions approach, the Court appeared to confuse the distinction between the existence of a taxing jurisdiction (a matter for national law) and its exercise (a matter for Union law).[374] As Ghosh explains, following the well recognized distinction in treatment between residents and non-residents, the UK did not tax the non-resident subsidiaries on their profits because the non-UK subsidiaries did not fall in the scope of the UK's tax jurisdiction. The corollary of this is that the UK should not have been obliged to take into account the non-UK subsidiaries' losses and so the Court should have said that the UK group relief provisions did not breach Article 49 at all.[375] However, under the restrictions approach, the Court required the UK to take the non-resident subsidiaries' losses into account,[376] thereby extending the scope of the UK's tax jurisdiction.

However, having gone down the route of finding a breach the Court did recognize the necessary asymmetry between the treatment of profits and losses at the justification stage. The UK offered—and the Court accepted[377]—three justifications:[378]

- protecting a balanced allocation of the power to impose taxation between the various Member States concerned, so that profits and losses are treated symmetrically in the same tax system[379]

- avoiding the risk of the double use of losses which would exist if the losses were taken into account in the Member State of the parent company (the UK) and in the Member States of the subsidiaries (Belgium, France, Germany)

- avoiding the risk of tax avoidance which would exist if the losses were not taken into account in the subsidiaries' Member States; within a group of companies, losses might be transferred to the companies established in the Member States which apply the highest rates of taxation and in which the tax value of the losses is therefore the highest.[380]

This deference to Member State interest—and the implicit recognition that states need the revenue from taxation—is one of the striking and novel features of the case.

---

[371] Para. 34.    [372] Ibid.    [373] Para. 35.

[374] See Case C–385/00 *de Groot* v. *Staatssecretaris van Financiën* [2002] ECR I–11819, para. 94, which expressly recognizes this distinction.

[375] J. Ghosh, *Principles of the Internal Market and Direct Taxation* (Oxford: Key Haven Publications, 2007), 82–3. See more generally, M. Graetz and A. Warren, 'Dividend taxation in Europe: When the ECJ makes tax policy' (2007) 44 *CMLRev.* 1577.    [376] A matter the Court speedily dismissed at para. 40.

[377] Para. 51.    [378] Para. 43.

[379] See also Case C–182/08 *Glaxo Wellcome* [2009] ECR I–000, para. 88, where the justification was upheld on the facts in the context of an Art. 63 case.

[380] The provisions are not cumulative despite suggestions to the contrary in *M&S*: Case C–414/06 *Lidl Belgium GmbH & Co.KG* v. *Finanzamt Heilbronn* [2008] ECR I–3601, para. 40.

However, while the Court generally accepted the proportionality of the UK's rules it said that the measures were not proportionate where:[381]

- the non-resident subsidiary had exhausted the possibilities available in its state of residence of having the losses taken into account in its state of residence for the accounting period concerned by the claim for relief and also for previous accounting periods, and

- there was no possibility for the foreign subsidiary's losses to be taken into account in its state of residence for future periods either by the subsidiary itself or by a third party, in particular where the subsidiary has been sold to that third party.

Consequently, where the resident parent company demonstrated to the tax authorities that these conditions were fulfilled, it was contrary to freedom of establishment to prevent the parent from deducting from its taxable profits in that Member State (the UK) the losses incurred by its non-resident subsidiaries.[382] However, this exception was narrowly drawn and the *M&S* judgment by and large endorsed the legality of the UK's group relief scheme.

In *Oy AA*,[383] whose facts were broadly similar to those in *M&S*, albeit that this time it was the profits of a Finnish subsidiary being transferred to an out-of-state parent rather than the losses, the Court repeated its approach in *M&S* but this time found the Finnish group-relief rules proportionate, albeit without clearly distinguishing between *Oy AA* and *M&S*. *Oy AA* does, however, suggest that M&S's victory was a limited one[384] and indicates a more general shift to upholding the validity of national taxation schemes.

### (iii) A shift to the discrimination approach

While *M&S* and *Oy AA* demonstrated a more generous construction of the justifications in favour of upholding national tax laws, in other cases there were signs that the Court was rejecting a pure restrictions approach altogether in favour of a model more sensitive to the well recognized distinction between residents and non-residents. At heart, this model has discrimination at its core. In the field of establishment, this change was first identified in *Innoventif*,[385] a case concerning not a tax but a charge. The Court said that a German law, making registration of a branch of a limited company established in another Member State subject to the payment of an advance on the anticipated cost of the publication of the objects of the company, was 'not liable to place companies from other Member States in a less favourable factual or legal situation than companies from the Member States of establishment'.[386] The payment of an advance therefore did not 'constitute an obstacle to the pursuit of the company's activities'.

Confirmation of a more general move towards a discrimination-based approach can be found in two Grand Chamber decisions decided on the same day: *FII Group Litigation*[387]

---

[381] Para. 55.          [382] Para. 55.

[383] Case C–231/05 *Oy AA* [2007] ECR I–6373. See also Case C–337/08 *X Holding Bv* v. *Staatssecretaris van Franciën* [2010] ECR I–000, Case C–311/08 *SGI* v. *Belgium* [2010] ECR I–000.

[384] G. Airs, '*Oy AA*: Limitations on transfers of profits to domestic situations not preclded by EC Treaty' (2007) *British Tax Review* 597, 603.

[385] Case C–453/04 *Innoventif* [2006] ECR I–4929. See also the tax cases discussed in Ch. 8.

[386] Para. 39.

[387] Case C–446/04 *Test Claimants in the FII Group Litigation* v. *Commissioner of Inland Revenue* [2006] ECR I–11753.

and *ACT Group Litigation.*[388] *ACT* concerned 'outgoing' dividends, i.e. dividends paid by a UK subsidiary to a non-UK parent. Consistent with the principles of international tax law outlined above, the non-UK parent was not liable for UK tax on the dividends but nor was it entitled to a UK tax credit on those dividends. By contrast, UK parents receiving 'upstream' dividends from UK subsidiaries would have received a tax credit for the ACT paid by the UK subsidiary.

*FII* concerned the reverse situation—'incoming' dividends payable by a non-UK subsidiary to a UK parent. As Kingston succinctly puts it, in *FII* the UK parent company was liable to UK corporation tax on the incoming dividends. It was granted tax relief for any foreign tax which the non-UK subsidiary had paid on the dividends abroad but was not otherwise entitled to a UK tax credit on them. By contrast, a UK parent receiving dividends from a UK subsidiary would not be liable to corporation tax on the dividends and would have received a tax credit for the ACT which the UK subsidiary had paid. In both *ACT* and *FII* the claimants argued that the UK rules breached Article 49.

In *ACT* the Court found that the UK rules were compatible with Article 49. The Court said that the situation of a UK parent and a non-UK parent was not comparable because the non-UK parent was not subject to the tax charge while the UK parent was subject to the charge.[389] Therefore, the UK rules did 'not constitute discrimination prohibited by Article [49]'.[390] By contrast, in *FII*, the Court found that the rules did breach Article 49 because they were discriminatory. As the Court put it:[391]

Article [49 TFEU] precludes a national measure which allows a resident company which has received dividends from another resident company to deduct the amount of ACT paid by the latter company from the amount of ACT for which the former company is liable, whereas a resident company which has received dividends from a non-resident company is not entitled to make such a deduction in respect of the corporation tax which the last-mentioned company is obliged to pay in the State in which it is resident.

Putting it another way, because the UK had chosen to exercise tax jurisdiction over a resident parent company with or without a resident subsidiary, the discrimination arose because in one case (where the subsidiary was resident) a tax credit was given, in the other case (where the subsidiary was non-resident) it was not.[392] The Court concluded:

Such a difference in treatment has the effect of discouraging United Kingdom-resident companies from investing their capital in a company established in another Member State and also has a restrictive effect as regards companies established in other Member States in that it constitutes an obstacle on their part to the raising of capital in the United Kingdom.[393]

---

[388] Case C–374/04 *Test Claimants in Class IV of the ACT Group Litigation* v. *Commissioners of Inland Revenue* [2006] ECR I–11673. The discussion that follows draws extensively on S. Kingston, above n. 360.

[389] Para. 58. For a further example, see Case C–282/07 *Etat belge – SPF Finances* v. *Truck Center SA* [2008] ECR I–10767, para. 49.     [390] Para. 72.

[391] Para. 94.

[392] See also Case C–418/07 *Société Papillon* v. *Ministère du Budget, des comptes publics et de law function publique* [2008] ECR I–8947.

[393] Para. 97. For a further example of cases involving the taxation of residents where the Court requires foreign and domestically sourced income to be treated equally, see, e.g., Case C–347/04 *Rewe Zentralfinanz eG* v. *Finanzamt Köln-Mitte* [2007] ECR I–2647; Case C–201/05 *Test Claimants in the CFC and Dividend Group Litigation* v. *Commissioners of Inland Revenue*, Order of 23 April 2008, para. 42.

(c) Summary

Read together, the tax cases discussed in this chapter and in Chapter 9 are authority for the following propositions:[394]

- *Basic rule*: different treatment of resident and non-resident taxpayers is compatible with Union law (*Futura Participations*). If, however, the situations of the two are deemed comparable (for example, where the non-resident earns 90 per cent or more of their income in the source state[395]), the source state must taken their personal and family circumstances into account (*Schumacker*). Further, any other discrimination against the non-resident who is deemed to be in a comparable position to a resident is contrary to Article 49 unless it can be justified (*Asscher*).

- *Residents and incoming income*: in the case of *resident* taxpayers, home-state legislation which treats income or related losses coming from, for example, subsidiaries in another Member States differently and usually less favourably than those coming from the home state breach Articles 49 and 54 unless justified (*M&S, FII*).[396] However, where the non-resident subsidiary has the possibility of having its losses taken into account in its state of residence, then these can be ignored by the parent's home state (*M&S*). Where there is no difference in treatment the national legislation is lawful.[397] This principle can also be seen outside the shareholder context, especially in the field of services.[398]

- *Residents and outgoing income*: In the case of *resident* taxpayers, home-state legislation which treats income going to another Member States differently and usually less favourably than if the income had stayed in the home state breach Articles 49 and 54 unless justified (*De Lasteyrie du Saillant*)

- *Non-residents and expenditure*: while the source state is not generally obliged to treat non-residents in the same way as residents (unless non-residents receive 90 per cent of their income in the host state[399]), the source state must allow the non-resident to deduct business expenses (for example, tax advice[400]) which have a 'direct economic connection' to the income received from the business activity in the source state[401] and the same tax rate should be applied.[402]

---

[394] This analysis develops some of the ideas in S. Kingston, 'A light in the darkness: Recent developments in the ECJ's direct tax jurisprudence' (2007) 44 *CMLRev.* 1321, 1331–4.

[395] E.g., Case C–279/93 *Schumacker* [1995] ECR I–225.

[396] Case C–105/07 *NV Lammers & Van Cleeff* [2008] ECR I–173, paras. 20–4. In the field of free movement of capital see e.g., Case C–35/98 *Staatssecretasris van Financiën* v. *Verkooijen* [2000] ECR I–40711; Case C–319/02 *Manninen* [2004] ECR I–7477.

[397] Case C–298/05 *Columbus Container Services BVBA & Co* v. *Finanzamt Bielefeld-Innestadt* [2007] ECR I–10451, para. 40.

[398] See, e.g. Case C–55/98 *Bent Vestergaard* [1999] ECR I–7641; Case C–39/04 *Laboratoires Fournier SA* v. *Direction des verifications nationales et internationales* [2005] ECR I–2057, para. 15; Case C–150/04 *Commission* v. *Denmark (insurance)* [2007] ECR I–1163, para. 42, considered further in Ch. 11.

[399] Case C–346/04 *Conijn* v. *Finanzamt Hamburg-Nord* [2006] ECR I–6137, para. 18.

[400] Case C–346/04 *Conijn* [2006] ECR I–6137, para. 21.

[401] Case C–345/04 *Centro Equestre da Lezíria Grande* v. *Bundesamt für Finanzen* [2007] ECR I–1425, para. 38. See also Case C–290/04 *FKP Scorpio* [2006] ECR I–9461, para. 49.

[402] This principle is derived from the free movement of services case Case C–234/01 *Gerritse* v. *Finanzamt Neukölln-Nord* [2003] ECR I–5933, paras. 53–4.

- *Non-residents and outgoing resources*: while in the earlier cases differential treatment by the home state of money payable by a subsidiary to a non-resident parent than to a resident parent constituted a restriction on freedom of establishment (*Lankhorst-Hohorst*), the more recent case law considers the situation of the resident and non-resident parent as not being comparable and so the matter falls outside Article 49 (*ACT*).

### (d) Prevention of abuse of law: Wholly artificial arrangements

We have already examined a number of justifications which, following *M&S*, have been successfully raised by states to save their tax regimes. One justification which has started to assume considerable significance in the field of taxation[403] in recent years is prevention of abuse of law.[404] This can be seen in *Cadbury Schweppes*.[405]

In order to try to prevent companies setting up subsidiaries in states with more favourable tax regimes, the UK introduced the controlled foreign company (CFC) rules. Generally, UK parent companies are not taxed on non-resident subsidiaries' profits, consistent with the principle of territoriality.[406] However, there was an exception to this rule concerning CFCs, i.e. non-resident subsidiary companies in which a UK parent owned a holding of more than 50 per cent. The profits of the CFC were subjected to tax in the UK when the corporation tax in the country of the subsidiary's residence was less than three-quarters of the rate applicable in the UK. The resident parent did receive a tax credit for the tax paid by the CFC but the system was designed to make the resident company pay the difference between the tax paid in the foreign country and the tax which would have been paid had the company been resident in the United Kingdom. Unless their legislation fell within one of a number of exceptions to the legislation, parent companies wishing to avoid the CFC regime had to show that neither the main purpose of the transactions which gave rise to the profits of the CFC nor the main reason for the CFC's existence was to achieve a reduction in UK tax by means of the diversion of profits (the so-called motive test).

The UK applied its CFC rules to Cadbury Schweppes, which had established a subsidiary in Ireland where the tax rate was 10 per cent. It therefore charged Cadbury Schweppes corporation tax of nearly £9 million. Cadbury's challenged this decision as being incompatible with Article 49. Reiterating the principles established in *Centros*,[407] the Court said the fact that a company was established in a Member State for the purpose of benefiting from more favourable legislation did not in itself suffice to constitute an abuse of the freedom of establishment.[408] It therefore said that because the CFC legislation involved a difference in the treatment of resident companies on the basis of the level

---

[403] See also Commission Communication, 'The application of anti-abuse measures in the area of direct taxation—within the EU and in relation to third countries' COM(2007) 785. Cf. free movement of natural persons and the citizenship case law where the Court appears to reject the abuse doctrine regardless of the artificial nature of the transactions: e.g., Case C–200/02 *Chen* [2004] ECR I–9925; Case C–109/01 *Akrich* [2001] ECR I–9607.

[404] For a full discussion on this subject see R. de la Feria and S.Vogenauer, *Prohibition of Abuse of Law: A new general principle of EU Law* (Oxford: Hart Publishing, forthcoming).

[405] Case C–196/04 *Cadbury's Schweppes v. Commissioners of the Inland Revenue* [2006] ECR I–7995.

[406] See the discussion on this point in Case C–446/03 *Marks & Spencer* [2005] ECR I–10837.

[407] Case C–212/97 [1999] ECR I–1459.          [408] Para. 37.

of taxation imposed on the company in which they had a controlling holding, it constituted a restriction on freedom of establishment.[409]

On justification the Court said that the national measure restricting freedom of establishment could be justified on the ground of preventing abusive practices, i.e. 'the specific
objective of such a restriction must be to prevent conduct involving the creation of *wholly*
*artificial* arrangements which do not reflect economic reality, with a view to escaping the
tax normally due on the profits generated by activities carried out on national territory'.[410]
The question was whether the rules were disproportionate. Relying on its seminal decisions on abuse in *Emsland-Stärke*[411] and *Halifax and Others*,[412] the Court continued:[413]

In order to find that there is such an [artificial] arrangement there must be, in addition to a
subjective element consisting in the intention to obtain a tax advantage, objective circumstances showing that, despite formal observance of the conditions laid down by Union law, the
objective pursued by freedom of establishment... has not been achieved.

In other words, to be compatible with the Treaties, the tax legislation had to give parent companies the opportunity of showing that, despite the existence of tax motives, the
incorporation of a CFC reflected economic reality, i.e. that there was an actual establishment intended to carry on genuine economic activities in the host Member State. This
finding had to be based on 'objective factors which were ascertainable by third parties
with regard, in particular, to the extent to which the CFC physically exists in terms of
premises, staff and equipment' and not as a 'letterbox' or 'front' subsidiary.[414]

Despite the cautious terms in which the abuse doctrine is drafted, some, including
Advocate General Poiares Maduro in *Cartesio*,[415] think that the Court's ruling allowing
Member States to be 'wary' of 'letter box' companies 'represents a significant qualification
of the rulings in *Centros* and *Inspire Art*'. The Court continued its approach in *Cadbury
Schweppes* in the *Thin Cap* case.[416] This concerned a UK law targeting the practice of thin
capitalization (whereby, as we saw above, a group of companies seeks to reduce the taxation of profits made by one of its subsidiaries by electing to fund that subsidiary by way of
loan—rather than equity—capital, thereby allowing that subsidiary to transfer profits to a
parent company in the form of interest which is deductible in the calculation of its taxable
profits, and not in the form of (non-deductible) dividends). Where the parent company is
resident in a state in which the rate of tax is lower than that which applies in the state in
which its subsidiary is resident, the tax liability may thus be transferred to a state which

---

[409] Para. 46. See also Case C–471/04 *Finanzamt Offenbach am Main-Land* v. *Keller Holding GmbH* [2006]
ECR I–2107.
[410] Para. 55. Emphasis added. Cf. the field of VAT where the Court has applied the abuse test to 'mainly'
artificial transactions: Case C–255/02 *Halifax and others* [2006] ECR I–1609. Mengozzi AG in Case C–298/05
*Columbus Container Services BVBA & Co* v. *Finanzamt Bielefeld-Innestadt* [2007] ECR I–10451 saw no reason to relax the test in the field of direct taxation.
[411] Case C–110/99 *Emsland-Stärke* [2000] ECR I–11569, paras. 52–3.
[412] Case C–255/02 *Halifax* [2006] ECR I–1609, paras. 74–5. For more detailed discussion, see K. Sørensen,
'Abuse of rights in Community law: A principle of substance or merely rhetoric?' (2006) 43 *CMLRev.* 423;
P. Schammo, 'Arbitrage and abuse of rights in the EC legal system' (2008) 14 *ELJ* 351; and V. Edwards
and P. Farmer, 'The Concept of Abuse in the Freedom of Establishment of Companies: A Case of Double
Standards' in A. Arnull et al (eds), *Continuity and Change in EU Law* (Oxford: OUP, 2008).
[413] Para. 64.
[414] Paras. 65–8.     [415] Case C–210/06 [2008] ECR I–000, para. 29.
[416] Case C–524/04 *Test Claimants in the Thin Cap Group Litigation* v. *Commissioners of Inland Revenue*
[2007] ECR I–2107.

has a lower tax rate. By providing that the interest was to be treated as a distribution, the UK legislation was able to prevent practices the sole purpose of which was to avoid the tax that would normally be payable on profits generated by activities undertaken in its territory.[417]

Once again, the question was whether the UK rules were disproportionate. The Court said they were unless two conditions were satisfied. First, the legislation had to provide for a consideration of objective and verifiable elements which made it possible to identify the existence of a purely artificial arrangement, entered into for tax reasons alone, and allowed taxpayers to produce, if appropriate and without being subject to undue administrative constraints, evidence as to the commercial justification for the transaction in question. Secondly, if it was established that such an arrangement exists, that legislation had to treat that interest as a distribution only in so far as it exceeded what would have been agreed upon at arm's length.

More generally, the Court has made clear that national legislation cannot operate a 'general presumption of abusive practices'[418] and that it is usually more proportionate for a state to rely on Directive 77/799 to obtain from the competent authorities of another Member State[419] any information which is necessary to enable it to effect a correct assessment of the taxes covered by the directive.[420]

(e) Remedies

If the Court finds that the national taxation is discriminatory or constitutes an obstacle to the freedom of establishment, then the applicants need to have an effective remedy. The Court emphasized this point in *Metallgesellschaft*[421] concerning a British rule permitting subsidiaries resident in the UK to pay dividends to their parent company without having to pay advance corporation tax (ACT) on condition that the parent company was also resident in the UK. The subsidiaries still had to pay mainstream corporation tax (MCT) but they did this at the end of a particular period. However, if the parent company had its seat in another Member State the subsidiaries had to pay the ACT up front, although it could subsequently be set off against any liability to MCT. Subsidiaries with a parent company resident in the UK therefore had a cashflow advantage over those where the parent was not resident in the UK. The Court said that this rule constituted an unjustifiable breach of Article 49.

It then considered whether subsidiaries with a parent not resident in the UK could claim for the payment of interest covering the cost of loss of the use of the sums paid by way of the ACT. It said:

In such circumstances, where the breach of [Union] law arises, not from the payment of the tax itself but from its being levied prematurely, the award of interest represents the 'reimbursement' of that which was improperly paid and would appear to be essential in restoring the equal treatment guaranteed by Article [49 TFEU].[422]

---

[417] Paras. 76-7.     [418] Case C–105/07 *NV Lammers & Van Cleeff* [2008] ECR I–173, para. 27.

[419] But not from third countries: Case C–446/04 *FII* [2006] ECR I–11753, para. 170.

[420] Case C–451/05 *ELISA* v. *Directeur general des impost* [2007] ECR I–8251, para. 92. For an equivalent case in the field of services, see Case C–433/04 *Commission* v. *Belgium (tax fraud)* [2006] ECR I–10653, paras. 39–40. However, the same will not be true where third countries are involved: Case C–101/05 *Skatteverket* v. *A* [2007] ECR I–11531, paras. 61–3.

[421] Joined Cases C–397 and 410/98 *Metallgesellschaft Ltd and Hoechst* v. *Commissioners of Inland Revenue* [2001] ECR I–1727.     [422] Para. 87.

Following *Factortame I*, the Court dismissed the argument that under English law a claim in *restitution* might not be available. That rule had to be set aside because such a claim was essential to rectify the breach of Article 49.[423] However, the 'ancillary questions' relating to such a claim, such as the payment of interest, including the rate of interest and the date from which it must be calculated[424] were a matter for the Member States.

The Court then considered the situation if the claimants' claims were treated as claims for *compensation* for damage caused by breach of Union law. It said that breach of Article 49 entitled the taxpayer to payment of damages in a sum equal to the interest accrued on the tax which they had paid from the date of premature payment until the date on which it properly fell due. Citing *Factortame III*, the Court said that where national law excluded loss of profit as a head of damage this breached Union law because it made reparation of damage practically impossible—especially in the context of economic or commercial litigation.[425]

The key criteria for state liability claims is that the damage has to be sufficiently serious. In *FII*[426] the Court suggested that given the rapid evolution of the Court's case law in the field of taxation it was unlikely that any breach could be considered sufficiently serious[427] and so Member States would not be liable. For this reason, claimants prefer to argue that their remedy should be in restitution, not state liability, although the Court has refused to be drawn on this debate: 'it is not for the Court to assign a legal classification to the actions brought before the national court by the claimants in the main proceedings.'

Finally, *Thin Cap*[428] placed an additional hurdle in the way of claimants: 'the national court may, in order to establish the recoverable losses, determine whether the injured parties have shown reasonable diligence in order to avoid those losses or to limit their extent and whether, in particular, they availed themselves in time of all legal remedies available to them'. However, in order to prevent the exercise of the rights which Article 49 confers on individuals from being rendered impossible or excessively difficult, the national court may determine whether the application of that legislation, coupled, where appropriate, with the relevant provisions of double taxation conventions, would, in any event, have led to the failure of the claims brought by the claimants in the main proceedings before the tax authorities of the Member State concerned.

## E.  THE SERVICES DIRECTIVE

### 1.  INTRODUCTION

So far we have concentrated on the application of the EU Treaties to national restrictions on the freedom of establishment. This has resulted in the creation of a large body of case law fleshing out precisely what Article 49 means in specific contexts. The European Commission, in its controversial Services Directive 2006/123, has tried to codify this case law in Chapter III of the directive, which concerns the establishment of service providers. This proved to be the least controversial part of the directive and stayed largely intact

---

[423] Paras. 88–9.      [424] Case C–470/04 *N* [2006] ECR I–7409.      [425] Para. 91.

[426] Case C–446/04 [2006] ECR I–11753, para. 215.

[427] Case C–446/04 *FII* [2006] ECR I–11753, para. 201.

[428] Case C–524/04 *Thin Cap Group Litigation* [2007] ECR I–2107, para. 124.

throughout the drafting process. Chapter IV of the directive specifically concerns the free movement of services and this, together with a more general discussion of the scope of the directive, the exclusions and derogations from the directive, and the other regulatory techniques used by the directive to facilitate service provision, will be considered in the next chapter.

Drawing on the decision in *Gebhard*, Article 4(5) defines establishment as 'the actual pursuit of an economic activity, as referred to in Article [49] of the Treaties, by the provider for an indefinite period and through a stable infrastructure from where the business of providing services is actually carried out'.[429] The directive therefore covers the situation where providers of services wish to establish themselves in the state and provide services there either as a new business (primary establishment) or where an existing business wishes to set up a new establishment, such as a branch or agency (secondary establishment).

## 2. THE WHOLLY INTERNAL SITUATION

There is a debate as to whether Chapter III applies not only to out-of-state providers wishing to establish themselves in the host state but also to in-state providers wishing to establish themselves, either as primary or secondary establishment, in their own state.[430] In other words, does the establishment chapter apply not merely to cross-border service provision but also to wholly internal situations? Some support for a broad reading of Chapter III comes from the preamble which says that the concept of the provider should 'not be limited solely to cross-border service provision...but should also cover cases in which an operator establishes itself in *a* Member State in order to develop its service activities there'.[431] Further, Chapter III on establishment, unlike Chapter IV on Services, makes no reference to the need to be established in *another* Member State. Similarly, Article 2(1), on scope, does not refer to an inter-state element. It merely provides: 'This Directive shall apply to services supplied by providers established in *a* Member State' (emphasis added).[432] The issue was actually discussed during the negotiations: an amendment proposing that the directive should be confined to inter-state situations was rejected by the IMCO Committee of the European Parliament. This tends to suggest that the directive does apply to wholly internal, as well as inter-state, situations.

The argument against the directive applying to internal situations is twofold. First, the Court, albeit somewhat uncertainly, is holding the line that Union law on free movement of persons does not apply to wholly internal situations.[433] The counter argument to this is that the Services Directive achieves for establishment what harmonization directives do for goods: product standard directives cover all manufactured or marketed goods even though Article 34 TFEU applies only to cross-border situations. Secondly, while the legal bases of the directive (Articles 53 and 62 TFEU (formally the first and third sentences of

---

[429] Fuller details are provided in the 37th recital.

[430] Commission Handbook on the Services Dir., OPEC, 2007 ('Handbook') also available at <http://www.ec.europa.eu/internal_market/services/services-dir/index_en.htm>, 31.

[431] 36th recital. Emphasis added.

[432] The same language is used in the 16th recital. Cf. 5th recital: 'Since the barriers in the internal market for services affect operators who wish to become established in *other* Member States as well as those which provide a service in another Member State without being established there'.

[433] Case C–212/06 *Walloon Government* [2008] ECR I–1683 considered in Ch. 8.

Articles 47(2) and 55 EC)) make no reference to transnational situations, Article 53 is in the same chapter as Article 49 which refers to cross-border situations only.

Whatever the scope of the directive, the establishment chapter specifically deals with two groups of rules: (1) authorization schemes, and (2) requirements which are prohibited or subject to evaluation. We shall consider these in turn.

## 3. AUTHORIZATION SCHEMES

### 3.1 The Rules

Article 9(1) provides that authorization schemes, broadly defined as obligations on a service provider to be in some way authorized, accredited, licensed, or registered before it can operate in a particular country,[434] are not permitted.[435] In fact, this prohibition is subject to an 'unless' clause broadly replicating the Court of Justice's case law on justifications:[436] authorization schemes are permitted provided that:

- they do not discriminate (either directly or indirectly) against the provider in question
- the scheme is justified by an overriding reason relating to the public interest (ORRPI)
- the objective pursued cannot be attained by means of a less restrictive measure (e.g., monitoring the activities of the service provider or making a simple declaration).

This is the classic formulation found in cases such as *Gebhard*: non-discriminatory authorization schemes can be justified by public-interest requirements (ORRPI), provided the steps taken are proportionate. So what are the ORRPI?

### 3.2 ORRPI

The directive, following the lead given by the Court, adopts a broad and non-exhaustive approach to 'overriding reasons relating to the public interest'. According to Article 4(8), the phrase means:

reasons recognised as such in the case law of the Court of Justice, including the following grounds: public policy (which includes issues relating to human dignity, the protection of minors and vulnerable adults and animal welfare);[437] public security; public safety; public health; preserving the financial equilibrium of the social security system; the protection of consumers, recipients of services and workers; fairness of trade transactions; combating fraud; the protection of the environment and the urban environment; the health of animals; intellectual property; the conservation of the national historic and artistic heritage; social policy objectives and cultural policy objectives.

---

[434] BERR Consultation Paper 2007, 65.

[435] This is subject to the caveat in Art. 9(3) that 'This section shall not apply to those aspects of authorisation schemes which are governed directly or indirectly by other [Union] instruments'; cf. Art. 3(1).

[436] Case C–55/94 *Gebhard* [1995] ECR I–4165.

[437] See the 41st recital: 'The concept of "public policy", as interpreted by the Court of Justice, covers the protection against a genuine and sufficiently serious threat affecting one of the fundamental interests of society and may include, in particular, issues relating to human dignity, the protection of minors and vulnerable adults and animal welfare. Similarly, the concept of public security includes issues of public safety.' The inclusion of protection of minors and animal welfare was probably at the behest of the UK.

The list of overriding reasons relating to the public interest found in the 40th recital of the preamble[438] is even longer than that found in Article 4(8). Some of the additional headings do reflect the case law of the Court (e.g., the prevention of unfair competition, safeguarding the sound administration of justice) but some are new or have not appeared in this form before (e.g., 'cultural policy objectives, including safeguarding the freedom of expression of various elements, in particular social, cultural, religious and philosophical values of society; the need to ensure a high level of education, … the promotion of the national language; … and veterinary policy'.) With such extensive justifications available to the host state, the directive has not in fact adjusted 'the scope of host state regulatory competence'.[439]

### 3.3 The Criteria for Granting Authorization

Not only must authorization schemes themselves be justified but so must the criteria applied in granting the authorization. Once again, the criteria used must be non-discriminatory, justified by overriding reasons in the public interest and proportionate.[440] But, in addition, the criteria must be:

- clear and unambiguous
- objective
- made public in advance
- transparent and accessible.[441]

These conditions for essentially good governance had already begun to surface in the Court's case law.[442]

The influence of the Court's case law, in particular mutual recognition, can also be felt elsewhere: for example, conditions for granting authorization for a new establishment must not duplicate requirements and controls which are equivalent or essentially comparable to those already conducted in another Member State or in the same Member State.[443] Again, following the Court's case law, the directive provides that the authorization must enable the provider to have access to the service activity, or to exercise that activity, throughout the national territory unless there are good reasons why not (e.g., where separate planning permission is required for the opening of each shop).[444] In practical terms, the effect of the directive is that authorizations granted by one local authority bind other local authorities unless there are good reasons otherwise.[445]

---

[438] Cf. the 56th recital which appears to offer an alternative, shorter and exhaustive list of overriding reasons relating to the public interest.

[439] S. Weatherill, 'Promoting the consumer interest in an integrated services market', *Mitchell Working Paper Series*, 1/2007, 7.

[440] The definition of proportionality is not provided here. Cf. Art. 10(3)(c) where a strict proportionality test is applied.                                                                                    [441] Art. 10(2).

[442] See, e.g., Case C–95/01 *Greenham and Abel* [2004] ECR I–1333 considered in Ch. 6; C–157/99 *Geraets-Smits and Peerbooms* [2001] ECR I–5473 considered in Ch. 11; Case C–54/99 *Association Eglise de Scientologie de Paris* v. *The Prime Minister* [2000] ECR I–1335 considered in Ch. 15.

[443] Art. 10(3) and the 61st recital of the preamble. See, by analogy, the goods case, Case C–292/94 *Criminal Proceedings against Brandsma* [1996] ECR I–2159.

[444] Art. 10(4) and the 59th recital. See also Case C–134/05 *Commission* v. *Italy* [2007] ECR I–6251.

[445] Handbook, 36.

### 3.4 Procedural Protection

The directive guarantees a certain level of procedural protection. It provides that decisions relating to authorization (e.g., refusing or withdrawing authorization but not its granting), have to be fully reasoned and subject to review by the courts;[446] that the authorization should not be for a limited period, subject to certain public-interest justifications;[447] and that authorization procedures have to be clear, made public in advance,[448] not unduly complicated,[449] and dealt with expeditiously.[450] Likewise, where the number of authorizations is limited, due to scarcity of available natural resources or technical capacity, any selection procedure must also comply with principles of fairness.[451]

## 4. 'OTHER REQUIREMENTS'

The directive concerns not only authorization schemes but also 'other requirements'. In respect of these 'other requirements',[452] the directive distinguishes between (1) those which are prohibited, and (2) those which are 'suspect' and need to be evaluated.

### 4.1 Prohibited Requirements

Article 14 lists eight requirements which are *prohibited*. This means that there are no overriding reasons in the public interest (ORRPI) justifications or derogations provided by the directive available to Member States (subject to what the Court might say in respect of the application of the *Treaty* rules and justifications).The prohibited requirements draw extensively on the Court's case law. The first group concerns those rules which are discriminatory, either directly or indirectly. These include nationality requirements for the provider, his staff, individuals holding the share capital, or members of the provider's management or supervisory bodies;[453] or a requirement that these individuals be resident in the territory.[454]

The directive also rules out requirements forbidding a provider from having an establishment in more than one Member State,[455] or on being entered in the registers or enrolled with professional bodies in more than one Member State.[456] In addition, it prohibits restrictions on the freedom of a provider to choose between a principal or a

---

[446] Art. 10(6). See, by analogy, Case 222/86 *Heylens* [1987] ECR 4097.    [447] Art. 11(1).

[448] Art. 13(1). See, by analogy, Case C–503/99 *Commission* v. *Belgium* [2002] ECR I–4809.

[449] Art. 13(2).

[450] Art. 13(3). If no response is given within the set time, the authorization is deemed to have been granted: Art. 13(4) and 63rd recital.

[451] Art. 12(1). See also 62nd recital. In establishing the rules for the selection procedure Member States can take into account various public-interest requirements including social policy objectives, health and safety of employees and the self-employed and preservation of the environment as well as 'overriding reasons relating to the public interest': Art. 12(3). Any authorization must be granted for a limited period: Art. 12(2).

[452] Defined by Art. 1(7) to mean 'any obligation, prohibition, condition or limit provided for in the laws, regulations or administrative provisions of the Member States or in consequence of case-law, administrative practice, the rules of professional bodies, or the collective rules of professional associations or other professional organisations, adopted in the exercise of their legal autonomy; rules laid down in collective agreements negotiated by the social partners shall not as such be seen as requirements within the meaning of this Directive'.    [453] Case C–221/89 *Factortame II* [1991] ECR I–3905.

[454] Case C–350/96 *Clean Car* [1998] ECR I–2521.

[455] Case 96/85 *Commission* v *France* [1986] ECR 1475.

[456] See also Case 107/83 *Klopp* [1984] ECR 2971.

secondary establishment,[457] as well as the case-by-case application of an economic test making the granting of an authorization subject to proof of the existence of an economic need or market demand.[458] The directive also prohibits competing operators from being involved in the decisions of competent authorities in the granting of individual authorizations; it prevents states from obliging operators to obtain financial guarantees or insurance from operators established in that state;[459] and it also prohibits states from obliging providers to have been previously registered or to have previously exercised the activity for a given period in that state.[460]

### 4.2 Suspect Requirements

Article 15(2) identifies a further eight requirements which are 'suspect'. These include quantitative or territorial restrictions (e.g., a rule limiting the number of operators providing a service in a particular area or limiting the number of operators per head of population or setting a minimum distance between operators);[460A] an obligation on a provider to take a specific legal form (e.g., a requirement that only legal persons can provide particular service, thereby excluding natural persons from the market);[461] or a requirement that non-profit-making bodies only can provide a service[462]); a ban on having more than one establishment in the territory of the same state;[463] and requirements fixing a minimum number of employees[464] or fixing minimum or maximum tariffs with which the provider must comply (thereby depriving service providers the right to compete on price or quality).[465]

Unlike the prohibited requirements, the directive requires Member States to evaluate whether these suspect requirements are compatible with the conditions laid down in Article 15(3), namely checking whether they are (1) non-discriminatory (i.e., neither directly nor indirectly discriminatory on the grounds of nationality/location of registered office); (2) necessary[466] (i.e. the requirements must be justified 'by an overriding reason relating to the public interest'); and (3) proportionate (this is the strict proportionality test: 'requirements must be suitable for securing the attainment of the objective pursued; they must not go beyond what is necessary to attain that objective and it must not be possible to replace those requirements with other, less restrictive measures which attain the same result'[467]). The Commission's handbook places much emphasis on the need to apply the proportionality principle in respect of these suspect requirements. For

---

[457] Case C–212/97 *Centros* [1999] ECR I–1459.

[458] This provision does not apply to territorial planning requirements which do not pursue economic aims but serve overriding reasons relating to the public interest (Art. 14(5)).

[459] See also 67th recital.

[460] See also 68th recital and Case C–203/98 *Commission v. Belgium (aerial photography)* [1999] ECR I–4899.

[460A] Joined Cases C–570/07 and C–571/07 *Pérez and Gómez* [2010] ECR I–000.

[461] Case C–171/02 *Commission v. Portugal* [2004] ECR I–5645.

[462] Case C–439/99 *Commission v. Italy (trade fairs)* [2002] ECR I–305.

[463] Cf. Art. 14(2) prohibiting national rules preventing service providers from having an establishment in *more* than one state.

[464] See Case C–514/03 *Commission v Spain (security services)* [2006] ECR I–963.

[465] See also Joined Cases C–94/04 and C–202/04 *Cipolla* [2006] ECR I–11421. The other requirements listed in Art. 15 are: rules relating to shareholding of capital (e.g., requirements on companies to hold a minimum amount of capital); requirements reserving the right to provide certain services to particular providers; an obligation on the provider to supply other specific services jointly with the principal service.

[466] Confusingly so-called when what is actually meant is objective justification, the language used in e.g. Art. 10(2)(b).        [467] Cf. Art. 10(2)(c) where no such detail is provided.

example, in respect of the ban on having more than one establishment on the territory, the Commission argues that 'in many cases Member States will be able to ensure the objective of high quality of services by other less restrictive means, such as a requirement to have qualified staff providing the service'.[468]

It is likely that requirements which are not listed as prohibited or suspect and which are not considered as authorizations under Articles 9–10 will continue to be subject to the traditional review under Article 49 as interpreted by the Court in cases such as *Gebhard*.[469] Since the Services Directive broadly endorses the Court of Justice's case law on public-interest requirements, it is likely that the outcomes under the directive and the Treaties will not be very different, albeit that any case decided under Article 49 will certainly require a transnational element.

### 4.3 Reporting, Mutual Evaluation, and the Standstill Provision

Chapter III of the directive contains reporting provisions: Article 9(2) requires Member States to identify their authorization schemes and give reasons to show why they are justified and proportionate.[470] A similar provision applies to suspect requirements needing to be evaluated.[471] These reports feed into the process of mutual evaluation (considered in detail in Chapter 11).[472]

Article 15(6) introduces a partial standstill clause. This provides that Member States cannot introduce any new 'suspect' requirement of the kind listed in Article 15(2), from 28 December 2006, unless justified by an ORRPI under Article 15(3). Further, Article 15(7) applies a simplified notification procedure to such requirements: the Member State must notify the rules to the Commission, which must inform the other Member States. However, unlike the procedure under the Technical Standards Directive 98/34,[473] there is no standstill clause: the notifying state is free to adopt the requirement prior to any Commission decision.[474] The Commission then has three months to examine the compatibility of any new requirement with Union law and, where appropriate, adopt a decision requesting the notifying state to refrain from adopting the requirement or to abolish the requirement.[475] This is a significant innovation aimed at controlling *ex ante* the introduction of barriers to establishment but nevertheless less effective than the Directive 98/34 procedure where, following cases such as *Unilever*,[476] the standstill provisions have legal consequences.

## F.  CONCLUSIONS

In this chapter we have seen the strong parallels being developed in the case law on the freedom of establishment in respect of both individuals and companies. For many

---

[468] Handbook, 47.     [469] COM(2004) 2, 23.

[470] The reporting obligation does not apply to the criteria and conditions for the granting of an authorization: 58th recital.

[471] Art. 15(5). In this report the states need to specify (1) the requirements they intend to maintain and the reason why they consider that those requirements comply with Art. 15(3); (2) the requirements which have been abolished; and (3) the requirements which have been made less stringent.     [472] Art. 39(5).

[473] OJ [1998] L204/37 considered further in Ch. 4.

[474] It is therefore unlikely that the Case C–194/94 *CIA* [1996] ECR I–2201 will apply to Art. 15(7).

[475] Notification made under Dir. 98/34 is deemed to fulfil the obligation of notification provided for in the Services Dir.     [476] Case C–443/98 *Unilever* [2000] ECR I–7535.

years the principle of non-discrimination on the ground of nationality underpinned this jurisprudence. However, since *Gebhard*, the Court has shifted its focus from equal treatment to the removal of obstacles to access to the host state's market, and the exercise of the freedom—although in the field of taxation there is a move back to applying the discrimination approach. The emphasis on effective market access is also shaping the Court's development of free movement of services, and it is to this subject that we now turn.

# 11

# FREEDOM TO PROVIDE AND RECEIVE SERVICES

## A. INTRODUCTION

Articles 56–7 TFEU (ex Articles 49–50 EC) lay down the principle of freedom to provide services on a temporary basis by a person established in one Member State to a recipient established in another. Article 57 defines services and applies the principle of equal treatment to the service provider.[1]

While the structure of Articles 56–7 does not differ very much from the Treaty provisions on workers and establishment, for many years services were seen as the poor relation to the other freedoms because Article 57 suggested that the services provisions were subordinate:[2]

Services shall be considered to be 'services' within the meaning of the Treaties...insofar as they are not governed by the provisions relating to freedom of movement for goods, capital and persons.[3]

However, in reality, growth in the economy has essentially been driven by services,[4] which now account for 70 per cent of GDP and employment in the majority of the Member States. This has been reflected in the case law: an increasing number of cases were decided under Articles 56–7 in the 1990s.[5] Perhaps reflecting this change of perspective, the Court said in *Fidium Finanz*[6] that Article 57 did not establish any order of priority between the freedom to provide services and other freedoms; it merely related to the definition of the notion of services. It continued: 'The notion of "services" covers services which are not governed by other freedoms, in order to ensure that all economic activity falls within the

---

[1] See also General Programme for the Abolition of Restrictions of Freedom to Provide Services ([1961] OJ Spec Ed Second Series IX/3).     [2] E.g., Case C–55/94 *Gebhard* [1995] ECR I–4165, para. 22.

[3] Emphasis added.

[4] Commission, 'The state of the internal market for services', COM(2002) 441, 5. The Lisbon European Council said that a key part of the programme to make the EU the most competitive and dynamic knowledge-based economy in the world by 2010 was to make the internal market work for services (Press Release Lisbon (24 March 2000) No. 100/1/00).

[5] Sometimes alongside other Treaty provisions such as Art. 34 (e.g., Joined Cases C–34–36/95 *De Agostini* [1997] ECR I–3843) and sometimes instead of other Treaty provisions such as Art. 63 on capital (e.g., Case C–118/96 *Safir* v. *Skattemyndigheten i Dalarnas Län* [1998] ECR I–1897, para. 35).

[6] Case C–452/04 *Fidium Finanz AG* v. *Bundesanstalt für Finanzdienstleistungsaufsicht* [2006] ECR I–9521, para. 32.

scope of the fundamental freedoms.'[7] The Court will therefore determine the centre of gravity of the particular case before deciding which Treaty provision applies.[8]

However, services pose intellectual and practical problems not experienced with the other freedoms. 'Services' cover a vast range of situations: service providers can move from one state to another to provide professional services (as lawyers, accountants, or architects) or various trades (the infamous Polish plumber); service receivers might move between states in search of healthcare, tourism, or education; and, of increasing importance, neither provider nor receiver move but the service itself does (e.g., over the web, such as Internet gambling). Regulations in the states also vary: in some states it is the service itself which is regulated; in others it is the service provider which is regulated. With this variety of situations and methods of regulation it is difficult to have a 'one size fits all' model for addressing restrictions on freedom to provide services. This helps to explain why adopting a single 'Services' Directive presented significant difficulties (considered in section D below).

For the Court, the variety of services situations has also posed problems.[9] As Advocate General Jacobs pointed out in *Säger*,[10] where the provider of the service spends a substantial period of time in the host state (e.g., an architect supervising the execution of a large building project) there is a fine line between services and establishment. There is also a potential overlap with the free movement of goods, where the person providing the service transmits it in the form of a product (e.g., the provider of an educational service posts a series of books and CDs). In examining these difficulties, this chapter will follow the structure of those on workers and establishment: it will consider who is entitled to benefit from the services provisions and the rights they enjoy in respect of (1) initial access to the market; (2) the exercise of the freedom; and (3) the enjoyment of social advantages. The chapter concludes with a consideration of the Services Directive 2006/123.

## B. WHO CAN RELY ON ARTICLES 56 AND 57?

### 1. THE SCOPE OF ARTICLES 56 AND 57

#### 1.1 The Freedom to Provide Services

The first paragraph of Article 56 provides that:

[R]estrictions on freedom to provide services within the Union shall be prohibited in respect of nationals of Member States who are established in a State other than that of the person for whom the services are intended.[11]

Article 56 therefore envisages the situation where the service provider established in State A holding the nationality of one of the Member States[12] (not necessarily that of State A)

---

[7] Ibid.

[8] Para. 34. Cf the third chamber decision in Case C-384/08 *Attanasio Group Srl* v. *Comune di Carbognano* [2010] ECR I-000, para. 39 which appears to suggest that Art. 56 applies only if Art. 49 does not.

[9] Case C-215/01 *Schnitzer* [2003] ECR I-4847, para. 30.

[10] Case C-76/90 *Säger* [1991] ECR I-4221, paras. 25-6.

[11] Art. 56(2) allows the EP and Council, by the ordinary legislative procedure, to extend the provisions of the services chapter to nationals of a third country who provide services and are established in the EU.

[12] Both conditions need to be satisfied: Case C-290/04 *FKP Scorpio* [2006] ECR I-9461, paras. 67-8.

provides services in Member State B[13] and then returns to State A once the activity is completed.

Article 56 can be used to challenge rules laid down by both the host state (State B) and the home state (State A) which obstruct the provision of services. Most cases concern barriers raised by the host state (State B). For example, in *Van Binsbergen*[14] a Dutch national, Kortmann, living in Belgium, challenged a Dutch rule requiring legal representatives to be established in the Netherlands before they could represent a person in the Dutch courts. The Court found that in principle the Dutch rule breached Article 56. Similarly, in *Commission v. France (performing artists)*[15] the Court said that French law, which presumed artists had 'salaried status' resulting in them being subject to the social security scheme for employed workers, constituted a restriction on freedom to provide services. The Court said that the French system was 'likely both to discourage the artists in question from providing their services in France and discourage French organisers of events from engaging such artists'.[16]

However, an increasing number of cases concern obstacles to the provision of services created by the home state, State A. For example, in *Ciola*[17] the Court said that an Austrian company which provided moorings for boats on Lake Constance to boat owners resident in other Member States could rely on Article 56 against the Austrian authorities when they limited the number of moorings available for boat owners resident abroad. In *Gourmet*[18] the Court went further and said that a national rule preventing undertakings established in State A from offering advertising space in their publications to *potential* advertisers established in other Member States could be challenged in State A as contrary to Article 56.[19]

Perhaps the most remarkable decision in this line of case law is *Carpenter*[20] where a Filipino national married to a British husband successfully challenged British immigration rules which were going to result in her deportation on the ground that this would be detrimental to their family life and, therefore, to the conditions under which Mr Carpenter exercised the freedom to provide services.[21] Mr Carpenter ran a business selling advertising space in medical and scientific journals. Although the business was established in the UK, where the publishers of the journals were based, much of his work was conducted with advertisers established in other Member States. The Court found that

---

[13] Case C–452/04 *Fidium Finanz AG* [2006] ECR I–9521, para. 25 confirms that Art. 49 cannot be relied on by a company established in a third country.

[14] Case 33/74 *J.H.M. van Binsbergen v. Bestuur van de Bedrijfsvereniging voor de Metaalnijverheid* [1974] ECR 1299.

[15] Case C–255/04 *Commission v. France (performing artists)* [2006] ECR I–5251, para. 38. In Case C–154/89 *Commission v. France (tour guides)* [1991] ECR I–659 the Court clarified that the activities of a tourist guide from the home state (State A) who takes tourists on a tour from State A to a host state (State B) may be subject to two distinct sets of legal rules: (1) if a tour company from State A is established in State B and employs its own guides established in State A, then it is the tour company that provides the service; (2) if a tour company from State A hires self-employed tourist guides who are established in State B, then it is *the guide* who provides the service. Art. 56 applied to both situations (para. 10). [16] Para. 38.

[17] Case C–224/97 *Ciola v. Land Vorarlberg* [1999] ECR I–2517, paras. 11–12.

[18] Case C–405/98 *Gourmet International Products (GIP)* [2001] ECR I–1795, para. 35.

[19] See also Case C–384/93 *Alpine Investments BV v. Minister van Financiën* [1995] ECR I–1141, para. 19: prior existence of an identifiable recipient was not a condition for the application of the provisions on the freedom to provide services. [20] Case C–60/00 *Carpenter* [2002] ECR I–6279.

[21] Para. 39.

such services fell within Article 56, 'both in so far as the provider travels for that purpose to the Member State of the recipient and in so far as he provides cross-border services without leaving the Member State in which he is established'.[22] The Court said, '[t]hat freedom could not be fully effective if Mr Carpenter were to be deterred from exercising it by obstacles raised in his country of origin to the entry and residence of his spouse'.[23] Read together, *Ciola*, *Gourmet*, and *Carpenter* not only demonstrate that service providers can invoke Articles 56–7 against their home states but they also show that the Court has gone a long way towards eroding the principle that Union law does not apply to wholly internal situations in the field of services.

## 1.2 The Freedom to Travel to Receive Services

The text of Articles 56–7 is confined to giving rights for service providers only. However, if service providers can travel to the state of the recipient, then logic would suggest that the recipient should also be able to travel to the state of the provider. The Council took this view in (the now repealed) Directive 73/148 where Article 1(b) required the abolition of restrictions on the movement and residence of 'nationals wishing to go to another Member State as recipients of services'. Subsequently, the Court confirmed that the Treaties applied to this situation. In *Luisi and Carbone*[24] two Italians were fined for taking more money out of Italy than the (then) currency regulations permitted in order to go to other Member States both as tourists and to receive medical treatment. The Court said that the freedom to receive services from a provider established in another Member State was the 'necessary corollary' of the freedom to provide services.[25] Therefore the Court said that tourists, individuals receiving medical treatment, and those travelling for the purpose of (private) education[26] or business should have the right of free movement without being obstructed by restrictions, even in relation to payment.[27] This decision paved the way for various attempts at medical tourism, with a view to gaining access to treatment not available in the home state[28] or, at least, gaining access more quickly than would otherwise be the case (see Case Studies 11.1 and 11.2).[29]

## 1.3 Neither Provider nor Recipient Travels

The Court has also said that Articles 56–7 apply where neither the provider nor the recipient of the service travels but the service itself moves (e.g., by telephone, fax, email, the Internet, or cable).[30] Two cases illustrate this, *Alpine Investments*[31] and *Bond*.[32] In *Alpine Investments* the Dutch Ministry of Finance prohibited a Dutch company from telephoning individuals in the Netherlands or in other Member States to offer them various financial

---

[22] Para. 29.     [23] Para. 39.

[24] Joined Cases 286/82 and 26/83 *Luisi and Carbone* v. *Ministero del Tesoro* [1984] ECR 377.

[25] Para. 10.     [26] See further below n. 104.     [27] Para. 16.

[28] Case C–159/90 *The Society for the Protection of Unborn Children Ireland Ltd (SPUC)* v. *Stephan Grogan and others* [1991] ECR I–4685 (abortion); Case C–157/99 *H.T.M Peerbooms* v. *Stichting CZ Groep Zorgverzekeringen* [2001] ECR I–5473.

[29] Case C–157/99 *B.S.M Geraets-Smits* v. *Stichting Ziekenfonds VGZ*; *H.T.M Peerbooms* v. *Stichting CZ Groep Zorgverzekeringen* [2001] ECR I–5473 (neuro-stimulation). See nn. 348–366.

[30] See, e.g., Case 62/79 *SA Compagnie générale pour la diffusion de la télévision Coditel* v. *Ciné Vog Films* [1980] ECR 881; Joined Cases C–34–36/95 *De Agostini* [1997] ECR I–3843.

[31] Case C–384/93 *Alpine Investments* [1995] ECR I–1141. See also Case C–243/01 *Piergiorgio Gambelli* [2003] ECR I–13031, para. 54 (betting services provided over the Internet).

[32] Case 352/85 *Bond van Adverteerders and others* v. *Netherlands* [1988] ECR 2085.

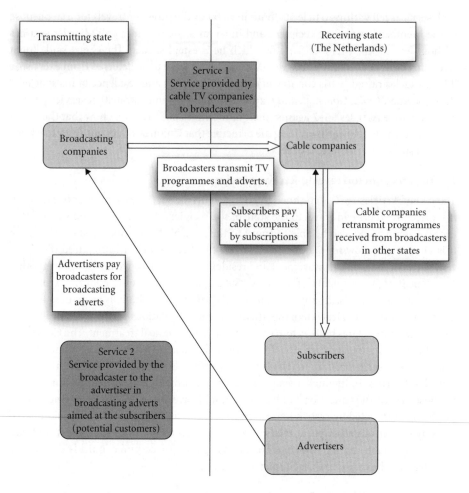

**Fig. 11.1** The transfrontier provision of services in *Bond van Adverteerders*

services (cold calling) unless they had the prior written consent of the clients. The Court ruled that Article 56 covered services which the provider offered by telephone to potential recipients established in other Member States without moving from the Member State in which the service provider was established.[33]

*Bond* demonstrates just how complex the case law on services can be. Dutch law prohibited the distribution by cable of radio and television programmes transmitted from other Member States which contained advertising aimed at the Dutch public (see fig. 11.1). The Court noted that the transmission of programmes across frontiers involved two distinct, cross-frontier services:[34] (1) the service provided by the cable companies in the receiving state (the Netherlands) to the broadcasting companies in the transmitting state (e.g., Luxembourg) by re-transmitting programmes to their subscribers; and (2) the

---

[33] Para. 42. See also the cases on cross-border advertising, e.g. Case C–405/98 *Gourmet International Products* [2001] ECR I–1795, para. 39.

[34] Paras. 14–15.

service provided by the broadcasting companies in the transmitting state to advertisers in the receiving state (the Netherlands) in broadcasting adverts aimed at potential customers in the Netherlands. The Court also noted that both services were provided for remuneration.[35] First, the cable network operators were paid in the form of fees which they charged their subscribers for the service they provided to the broadcasters. The Court said that it was irrelevant that the broadcasters did not generally pay the cable network operators for relaying their programmes because Article 57 did not require the service to be paid for by those for whom it was performed. Secondly, the broadcasters were paid by the advertisers for the service of broadcasting the adverts.

## 2. PERFORMANCE OF A SERVICE FOR REMUNERATION

Having considered who can rely on the services provisions, the next question is what is a service? Article 57 provides that services shall be considered 'services' within the meaning of the Treaties where they are 'normally provided for remuneration' and provided on a temporary basis. Article 57 therefore has three elements (1) services; (2) remuneration; and (3) temporary. We shall look at these in turn.

### 2.1 What Activities Constitute 'Services'?

Article 57(1) gives examples of what constitutes a service, including activities of craftsmen and the professions, and activities of an industrial and commercial character. The case law has significantly expanded on this rather anachronistic list. From *Luisi and Carbone* we have already seen how tourism,[36] medical,[37] financial,[38] business, and educational activities constitute services. We have also seen that the transmission of a television signal[39] and a signal by cable television constitutes a service.[40] In other cases the Court has said that the provision of people by an employment agency,[41] debt-collection work,[42] lotteries,[43] bank building loans,[44] insurance,[45] and sporting activities[46] are all services. Given the breadth of the subject matter included within the definition of services[47] and

---

[35] Para. 16.

[36] See also Case C–198/89 *Commission* v. *Greece* [1991] ECR I–727 (guiding by a tourist guide is a service).

[37] This applies to care provided both in and out of a hospital environment: Case C–157/99 *Geraets-Smits and Peerbooms* [2001] ECR I–5473, para. 53. See also Case C–159/90 *SPUC* v. *Grogan* [1991] ECR I–4685.

[38] Case C–384/93 *Alpine Investments BV* [1995] ECR I–1141.

[39] Case 155/73 *Sacchi* [1974] ECR 409, para. 6. However, the Court said that trade in material, sound recordings, films, apparatus, etc. used for the diffusion of television signals was subject to the rules relating to the free movement of goods.

[40] Case 52/79 *Procureur du Roi* v. *Debauve* [1981] ECR 833, para. 8; or, as the Court put it in Case 352/85 *Bond* [1988] ECR 2085 and Joined Cases C–34–36/95 *De Agostini* [1997] ECR I–3843, the service of transmitting programmes and advertisements from broadcasters in one Member State to cable networks in another.          [41] Case 279/80 *Criminal Proceedings against Alfred John Webb* [1981] ECR 3305.

[42] Case C–3/95 *Reisebüro Broede* v. *Sandker* [1996] ECR I–6511, para. 24.

[43] Case C–275/92 *Schindler* [1994] ECR I–1039.

[44] Case C–484/93 *Svensson* v. *Ministre du Logement et d'Urbanisme* [1995] ECR I–3955 (legal persons); Case C–222/95 *Société Civile Immobilière Parodi* v. *Banque H. Albert de Bary et Cie* [1997] ECR I–3899.

[45] Case C–118/96 *Safir* [1998] ECR I–1897, para. 22.

[46] Joined Cases C–51/96 and C–191/97 *Deliège* [2000] ECR I–2549.

[47] The Court has made clear that the special nature of certain services, e.g. social security, does not remove them from the scope of the fundamental principle of freedom of movement: Case 279/80 *Webb* [1981] ECR 3305, para. 10, Case C–158/96 *Kohll* v. *Union des Caisses de Maladie* [1998] ECR I–1931 paras. 20–1.

the scope of the Treaty provisions, it is hard to think of areas of activity excluded from its protection.[48]

## 2.2 Services Are 'Normally Provided for Remuneration'

### (a) The need for an economic link

The requirement in Article 57(1) that services are 'normally provided for remuneration' was introduced to exclude gratuitous services from the scope of the Treaties. This point was emphasized in *Jundt*[49] which concerned a German lawyer, resident in Germany, who taught a 16-hour course at the University of Strasbourg for which he received a small honorarium (about €500). The Court said that he was a service provider under Article 56, even thought the activity was carried out on a quasi-honorary basis. It added that for the Treaty provisions to apply, 'the activity must not be provided for nothing' although there is no need 'for the person providing the service to be seeking to make a profit'.[50]

The Court has used the requirement of 'remuneration' to exclude services without a direct economic link between the provider and the recipient from the scope of the Treaties. This can be seen in *SPUC* v. *Grogan*.[51] Handbooks prepared and distributed by various Irish students' unions included information about the availability of legal abortion in the UK and the identity and location of a number of abortion clinics in the UK. The Society for the Protection of the Unborn Child (SPUC), an anti-abortion group, argued that the distribution of such information contravened the Irish ban on abortion and so sought an injunction against Grogan, the president of the students' union, to restrain the distribution of the handbooks. In his defence, Grogan argued that because he was providing information about the availability of a service the injunction constituted an obstacle to the freedom to provide services contrary to Article 56.

Setting the moral debate about abortion to one side,[52] the Court agreed that abortion performed in accordance with the law of a particular Member State did constitute a service within the meaning of Article 57.[53] However, it said that Union law did not apply to the provision of information about the identity and location of clinics in another Member State providing abortions[54] because the information was not distributed on behalf of an economic operator established in another Member State.[55] The Court concluded that the information constituted a 'manifestation of freedom of expression and of the freedom to impart and receive information which is independent of the economic activity carried on by clinics in another Member State'.[56] This conclusion enabled the Court to avoid deciding a case where *EU* fundamental *economic* rights (freedom to travel to receive a service) appeared to collide with a fundamental tenet of a *national* constitution (the right to life of

---

[48]  For further examples, see Art. 4(1) of the Services Dir. and 34th recital considered below.

[49]  Case C–281/06 *Jundt* v. *Finanzamt Offenburg* [2007] ECR I–12231.     [50]  Paras. 32–3.

[51]  Case C–159/90 [1991] ECR I–4685. See further, T. Hervey and J. McHale, *Health Law and the European Union* (Cambridge: CUP, 2004), 144–56.

[52]  Para. 20.

[53]  Para. 21. This classification of abortion as a service (or by the language used) offended many: see, e.g., M. Kenny, 'The dilemma that won't go away', *The Sunday Telegraph*, 23 Feb. 1992, 13, who asked 'Is that all it is—[is abortion] like hairdressing or chiropody? Where is conscience? Where is feeling?'.

[54]  Para. 27.     [55]  Para. 26.     [56]  Ibid.

the unborn).[57] Eventually the European Court of Human Rights and the Member States in an Intergovernmental Conference were left to resolve some of the issues arising from the case (see Case Study 11.1).

The judgment in *SPUC* v. *Grogan* has been much criticized[58] because the Court's reasoning turned on the absence of an economic link between the information provider (Grogan) and the service provider (the abortion clinics). Had the abortion clinics paid the students' union—even a small sum—for providing the information the outcome would have been different. And even on the facts as they stood there was an indirect economic link in the relationship: although the clinics did not pay the students' union for distributing the information, the pregnant women who received the information would have paid the abortion clinics in England and Wales for the termination. According to (the admittedly more commercial case) *Bond*[59] (fig. 11.1), that might have been sufficient to bring the matter within the scope of Union law because the Court said that it was not relevant that 'some of those services are not paid for by those for whom they are performed'.[60]

With the benefit of hindsight, a better way of understanding the case might be to view it as a *Graf*-type situation,[61] where the effect on Union law of the Irish courts granting an injunction was too remote and so did not create a sufficiently substantial impediment to access to the market. The Court said as much, noting that the link between Grogan and the abortion clinics in other Member States was 'too tenuous for the prohibition on the distribution of information to be regarded as a restriction' falling within Article 56.[62]

The Advocate General adopted a different approach. He thought that the rule developed in the goods case, *GB-INNO*[63] (where consumers' freedom to shop in another Member State was compromised if they were deprived of access to advertising in their own state), should apply to services. He considered that the Irish ban on abortion constituted a non-discriminatory impediment to intra-Union trade in services, contrary to Article 56, but one that could be justified under Article 52 TFEU (ex Article 46 EC), to which Article 62 TFEU (ex Article 55 EC) refers, on the ground of public policy because it related to 'a policy choice of a moral and philosophical nature the assessment of which is a matter for the Member States'.[64] He also considered that the steps taken to pursue the objective of protecting the unborn life were proportionate and compatible with fundamental human rights.

---

[57] Ibid. See D. R. Phelan, 'The right to life of the unborn v Promotion of trade in services: The European Court of Justice and the normative shaping of the European Union' (1992) 55 *MLR* 670. The Court may have feared a supremacy challenge: see the veiled threats made by Walsh J in the Supreme Court in *Grogan*: 'any answer to the reference received from the European Court of Justice will have to be considered in the light of our own constitutional provisions', considered in S. O'Leary, 'The Court of Justice as a reluctant constitutional adjudicator: An examination of the abortion information case' (1992) 17 *ELRev*. 138, 154–7.

[58] See, e.g., ibid., 146.

[59] Case 352/85 [1988] ECR 2085, para. 16. See also Joined Cases C–51/96 and 191/97 *Deliège* [2000] ECR I–2549, para. 56. [60] Para. 16.

[61] Case C–190/98 *Graf* [2000] ECR I–493. See further Ch. 8.

[62] Para. 24. See T. Hervey, 'Buy baby: The European Union and regulation of human reproduction' (1998) 18 *OJLS* 207.

[63] Case C–362/88 *GB-INNO-BM* v. *Confédération du commerce luxembourgeois* [1990] ECR I–667, para. 8.

[64] Para. 26.

**Case Study 11.1** IRISH ABORTION, BRITISH IVF, AND EUROPEAN
UNION LAW
...............................................................................................

The decision in *SPUC* v. *Grogan* focused international attention on the Irish ban on abortion found in Article 40.3.3 of the Constitution. It provides:

> The State acknowledges the right to life of the unborn and, with due regard to the equal right to life of the mother, guarantees in its laws to respect, and, as far as practicable, by its laws to defend and vindicate that right.[65]

This provision was introduced in 1983[66] to copper-fasten the prohibition against abortion contained in the Offences Against the Person Act 1861 from any attempts by an activist judiciary to use the constitutional right to privacy[67] to legalize abortion in the manner of the US Supreme Court in *Roe* v. *Wade*.[68]

By contrast, in the UK abortion is legal and freely available (within the limits of the Abortion Act 1967). About 8,000 Irish women come to Britain for abortions each year,[69] often after receiving advice from welfare clinics in Ireland. These clinics were prevented from giving such information in *Attorney General (SPUC)* v. *Open Door Counselling and Dublin Well Woman Centre*[70] where, relying on Article 40.3.3, the Irish Supreme Court granted an injunction restraining welfare clinics from assisting pregnant women travelling abroad to obtain abortions. The clinics challenged this decision before the European Court of Human Rights,[71] where the majority of the Court upheld their complaint and found a breach of Article 10 on freedom of expression.[72] While recognizing that the injunction pursued 'the legitimate aim of the protection of morals of which the protection in Ireland of the right to life of the unborn is one aspect',[73] the Court found the restriction to be over-broad and disproportionate.[74]

While *Open Door Counselling* forced the Irish government to confront the potential conflict between the application of its abortion laws and human rights, the earlier case of *Grogan* (discussed above) had obliged the Irish government to address the potential conflict between Article 56 TFEU and Article 40.3.3 of the Irish Constitution. As we have seen, the Court of Justice fudged the issue but indicated that Irish law was compatible with Article 56. To put the matter beyond doubt, the Member States agreed

---

[65] Ss. 58–9 of the Offences Against the Person Act 1861 make it a criminal offence unlawfully to procure or to assist in the procurement of abortion. For a more detailed analysis of the background, see O'Leary, above n. 57, 138–41.

[66] 8th Amendment of the Constitution Act 1983. However, as the *Irish Times* noted, the turn-out in the referendum on the amendment was 53.6%. Of those, 66.45% voted in favour of the amendment, 35.79% of eligible voters: A. Murdoch, 'The Irish myth of a blinkered society', *Independent on Sunday*, 8 Mar. 1992, 8.

[67] This concern was triggered by the Irish Supreme Court's decision in *McGee* v. *Attorney General* [1974] IR 284. For a full discussion see G. Hogan and G. Whyte, *Kelly's The Irish Constitution*, 3rd edn (Dublin: Butterworths, 1994), 790–1.

[68] 410 US 113 (1973).

[69] A. Tate, 'Day trippers: The women forced to come to England for abortions', *The Mirror*, 20 Jul. 2002, 16 and 18.    [70] [1988] IR 593.

[71] *Open Door Counselling and Dublin Well Woman* v. *Ireland*, Series A, No. 246 (1993) 15 EHRR 244 (judgment of 29 Oct. 1992).

[72] Cf. Van Gerven AG's views in Case C–159/90 *SPUC* v. *Grogan* [1991] ECR I–4685.    [73] Para. 63.

[74] Para. 74.

at Maastricht to add the 'Abortion' Protocol protecting Article 40.3.3 from challenge under EU law. The Protocol provides:

> Nothing in the Treaty on European Union, or in the Treaties establishing the European Communities, or in the Treaties or Acts modifying or supplementing those Treaties, shall affect the application in Ireland of Article 40.3.3. of the Constitution of Ireland.[75]

This Protocol was included in the Treaty 'by stealth and without reference of the issue to the Dail [Irish lower house of Parliament]'.[76] While it was intended to satisfy the pro-life lobby,[77] the Protocol caused consternation among liberals who feared that it denied Irish women access to information[78] and removed the rights of EU citizens to travel to another Member State to receive services. Moreover, the Protocol did not actually succeed in its primary purpose of putting an end to challenges based on Union law, as the X case[79] showed. X was a 14-year-old girl who became pregnant after being raped by a friend's father. Her parents brought her to London for an abortion and hoped that tissue collected from the foetus would provide the necessary forensic evidence to convict the man. When the papers were sent to the Irish Attorney General[80] he successfully sought an injunction from the High Court in Dublin preventing the girl from travelling to London for the abortion.[81] This forced the family to return to Ireland,[82] with X threatening to kill herself. The Supreme Court reversed the High Court's decision and lifted the injunction,[83] thereby allowing the girl to return to London for the abortion. The majority ruled, not on EU law, but on the basis of the wording in Article 40.3.3, that abortion was permissible if there was a 'real and substantial risk to the life as distinct from the health of the mother, which can only be avoided by the termination of her pregnancy'.[84]

In the light of the confusion generated by the X case, and given the risk that in the Irish referendum on the ratification of the Maastricht Treaty liberals would vote

---

[75] Protocol No. 17 annexed to the TEU and to the Treaties establishing the European Communities. For a summary of the debate about the meaning and scope of this Protocol (esp. the phrase 'in Ireland'), see J. Kingston and A. Whelan, with I. Bacik, *Abortion and the Law* (Dublin: Round Hall, Sweet and Maxwell, 1997), esp. 167–70. See also N. Nic Shuibhne, 'Margins of appreciation: National values, fundamental rights and EC free movement law' (2009) 34 *ELRev.* 230, 247. See now Protocol No. 35 of the Lisbon Treaty which is drafted in broadly the same terms. In order to reassure the Irish people, with a view to persuading them to vote in favour of the Lisbon Treaty in Sep. 2009, the European Council adopted a Decision at its 18/19 Jun. 2009 meeting, which came into force on the same date as the TEU and TFEU, making clear that 'Nothing in the Treaty of Lisbon attributing legal status to the Charter of Fundamental Rights of the European Union, or in the provisions of that Treaty in the area of Freedom, Security and Justice affects in any way the scope and applicability of the protection of the right to life in Article 40.3.1, 40.3.2 and Article 40.3.3…'. This Decision will form a Protocol to be attached to the next accession Treaty.

[76] F. Murphy, 'Maastricht: Implementation in Ireland' (1994) 19 *ELRev.* 94.

[77] C. O'Brien, 'A constitutional change could get Ireland out of a tight spot on abortion', *The Times*, 1 Apr. 1992, 14.

[78] *EP News*, 9–13 Mar. 1992, 4. See also the Debates of the European Parliament, No. 3–416/207–218, 12 Mar. 1992.

[79] *Attorney General* v. *X* [1992] 2 CMLR 277.

[80] Cf. E. Gorman and T. Walker, 'Law chief regrets abortion trauma', *The Times*, 10 Apr. 1992.

[81] Judgment of the High Court of Costello J [1992] 2 CMLR 277, 281.

[82] J. Langton, 'Ireland's anguish', *Sunday Telegraph*, 23 Feb. 1992, 13.      [83] [1992] 2 CMLR 277, 290.

[84] Para. 38.

against the Treaty if the issue of the right to travel were not resolved,[85] the Irish government sought to have a 'ten-minute' IGC to amend its Maastricht Protocol.[86] Fearing that this would pave the way for other states to revisit aspects of the Treaty that they wished to change, the Heads of State refused the request but they did agree to the addition of a (non-binding) Declaration which provided:[87]

> That it was and is their intention that the Protocol shall not limit freedom to travel between Member State or, in accordance with conditions which may be laid down, in conformity with Union law, by Irish legislation, to obtain or make available in Ireland information relating to services lawfully available in Member States.[88]

The Irish people then voted in favour of the Maastricht Treaty which was ratified by Ireland in the summer of 1992.

However, the Declaration did not help Mr Grogan because the Irish High Court refused to allow it to be taken into account when deciding his case on its return from Luxembourg.[89] Morris J explained that since the Maastricht Treaty had not come into force at the time of the litigation it could not be relied on.[90] The High Court therefore concluded that the Irish prohibition on third parties providing a woman with information about abortion clinics in the UK did not contravene Union law and made permanent the injunction sought by SPUC against Grogan.[91]

SPUC's success was short-lived. As part of the deal to appease the liberals to secure a 'yes' vote in the Maastricht referendum, the Irish government committed itself to holding three referenda. The first two concerned the right of Irish citizens to travel abroad and to have free access to information about abortion. These were supported by a two-to-one majority. The third referendum on tightening up the Supreme Court's decision in X was defeated by a two-to-one majority.[92] As a result of these referenda, Article 40.3.3 of the Constitution was amended to read, first:

> This subsection shall not limit freedom to travel between the State and another State.[93]

---

[85] There was also concern that the pro-life groups would vote against the Treaty because, in their view, it paved the way for a more liberal abortion regime.

[86] T. Jackson and A. Murdoch, 'EC dashes Irish hopes of amending treaty', *Independent*, 6 Apr. 1992.

[87] Declaration of the High Contracting Parties to the TEU of 1 May 1992 ([1992] OJ C191/109).

[88] The Amendment continued: 'At the same time the High Contracting Parties solemnly declare that, in the event of a future constitutional amendment in Ireland which concerns the subject matter of Article 40.3.3 of the Constitution of Ireland and which does not conflict with the intention of the High Contracting Parties hereinbefore expressed, they will, following the entry into force of the Treaty on European Union, be favourably disposed to amending the said Protocol so as to extend its application to such constitutional amendment if Ireland so request.'  [89] *SPUC* v. *Grogan* [1993] 1 CMLR 197.

[90] Paras. 30–4.

[91] Para. 14. This was despite the fact that the Irish government had made a statement in Strasbourg that the right to information on abortion did exist in Irish law. See Murphy, above n. 76, 104.

[92] Ibid., 104.

[93] 13th Amendment of the Constitution Act 1992. A Dutch women's group tried to push the right to travel to receive an abortion one stage further. In Jun. 2001 Women on Waves sailed the *Aurora*, a 'floating reproductive health centre', into the international waters 12 miles off the Irish coast to offer abortions to Irish women (N. Byrne, 'Anti-abortionists charter boat to confront "Aurora"', *Independent*, 15 Jun. 2001, and S. O'Neill, 'Bouncers protect abortion ship', *Daily Telegraph*, 16 Jun. 2001). They failed to acquire the necessary licence under Dutch law to carry out abortions and so could not provide terminations.

and, secondly, that:

> This subsection shall not limit freedom to obtain or make available, in the State, subject to such conditions as may be laid down by law, information relating to services lawfully available in another State.[94]

Despite these amendments, five years later another case similar to X came to public attention, this time concerning a 13-year-old rape victim.[95] She was said to be suicidal, and eventually the High Court did allow her to travel to England for an abortion.[96] In March 2002 a further referendum was held on whether to reverse the Supreme Court's ruling in X in order to prevent abortion even if the mother threatened suicide or if there were legitimate threats to the life of the mother. The proposal was rejected by a narrow margin.[97]

Ireland has not been alone in struggling to reconcile aspects of its social policy with EU law. In the UK, Diane Blood became famous for her successful attempt to circumvent the restrictions laid down in the Human Fertilization Embryology Act 1990 by relying on Articles 56 and 57 TFEU. When the Bloods were trying to conceive a child Steven Blood contracted meningitis. While he was in a coma, Mrs Blood requested the doctors to take samples of his sperm. They did so but, since he was in a coma, they did not obtain his written consent as required by the 1990 Act. This meant that Diane Blood could not receive IVF treatment in the UK. Stephen died soon after. Subsequently Diane Blood sought IVF treatment using her husband's sperm which she wanted to take to Belgium where the consent rule did not apply. However, the UK authority, the HFEA, refused to grant permission because the conditions laid down in the 1990 Act had not been met.

In the Court of Appeal, the Master of the Rolls recognized that the refusal of permission to export the sperm made impossible the provision of fertilization services in another Member State.[98] Nevertheless, he said that given the ethical and moral considerations raised by artificial insemination, the UK was justified[99] in taking measures to prevent abuse and undesirable practices from occurring.[100] However, he found on the facts that the HFEA had failed to take two important considerations into account: it

---

[94] 14th Amendment of the Constitution Act 1992.

[95] M. Sheehan and J. Burns, 'Court stops girl's abortion trip' and 'For pity's sake', *Sunday Times*, 23 Nov. 1997.

[96] J. Kierans, 'Outrage as teenage rape victim prepares to abort pregnancy; Irish girl prepares for abortion in Britain', *People*, 30 Nov. 1997.

[97] 618,485 people voted for (45%) and 629,041 (50.4%) voted against with a turnout of around 45%: R. Cowan, 'Irish reject tougher abortion law: Tight result in referendum fails to clear up confusion', *Guardian*, 8 Mar. 2002, 2. The defeat of the amendment was attributed in part to Rosemary Scallan MEP (the singer Dana), a prominent anti-abortion campaigner, who campaigned against the amendment on the ground that it did not go far enough: D. McKittrick, 'Irish liberals head off change to abortion law', *Independent*, 8 Mar. 2002, 2.

[98] R. v. *Human Fertilisation and Embryology Authority, ex p. Diane Blood* [1997] 2 CMLR 591, para. 52. See generally T. Hervey, above n. 62, and D. Morgan and R. Lee, 'In the name of the father? *Ex parte Blood*: Dealing with novelty and anomaly' (1997) 60 *MLR* 840.

[99] Citing Cases C–384/93 *Alpine Investments* [1995] ECR I–1141 and C–275/92 *Schindler* [1994] ECR I–1039.

[100] Para. 54. Some of these issues were explored further in *U* v. *W* [1997] 2 CMLR 431.

had not given due consideration to the effect of Article 56, nor had it recognized that this case was unique (after this judgment there would be no further cases where sperm was preserved without consent).[101] The HFEA then reversed its decision and Diane Blood travelled to Belgium for the treatment. At the end of 1998 Diane Blood gave birth to a son, Liam,[102] and, after receiving further treatment, another son, Joel, in 2002.[103]

### (b) Services and the welfare state

Services provided as part of the welfare state have presented particular problems for Union law. Given that most are paid for out of the public purse but are free at the point of delivery, the absence of remuneration between the provider and the recipient suggests that they fall outside the scope of Articles 56–7. This is the case with state education. As the Court said in *Humbel*,[104] state education did not constitute a service because the state was not seeking to engage in gainful activity—it was merely fulfilling its duties towards its own population in the social, cultural, and educational fields, and was paid for by the public.[105] Because the same considerations do not apply to education in the private sector, the Court said in *Wirth*[106] that private education could constitute a service when it was financed essentially out of private funds, in particular by students or their parents, and where the provider sought to make an economic profit.[107]

In *Geraets-Smits and Peerbooms*[108] some of the Member States relied on *Humbel* to argue that hospital services were also 'special'[109] and so did not constitute an economic activity within the meaning of Article 57 because patients received care in a hospital without having to pay for it themselves (a benefits in kind system), albeit that in an insurance-based system, such as that in the Netherlands, all or part of the cost of the treatment was paid for directly by the relevant sickness scheme. The Court disagreed. It said that, despite the special nature of hospital services, Union law still applied.[110] Then, relying on the *Bond* line of case law (see fig. 11.1), the Court said that the payments made by the sickness insurance funds under contractual arrangements between the funds and the hospitals were consideration for the hospital services, even if payable at a flat rate. For this reason they 'unquestionably represent remuneration for the hospital which receives them and which is engaged in an activity of an economic character'.[111] In *Müller-Fauré*[112] the Court went further, focusing on the fact that the

---

[101] Para. 61.     [102] S. Oldfield, 'Liam is his Daddy to a T', *Daily Mail*, 31 Dec. 1998, 2.

[103] 'Overjoyed Diane Blood cradles her second son', *Daily Mail*, 19 Jul. 2002, 1. The HFEA 1990 prohibited the father's name from being used on the children's birth certificates. Subsequently, the government admitted that this rule contravened the Human Rights Act 1998 and this has now been rectified by the Human Fertilisation and Embryology (Deceased Fathers) Act 2003.

[104] Case 263/86 *Belgium* v. *Humbel* [1988] ECR 5365.     [105] Paras. 17–19.

[106] Case C–109/92 *Wirth* v. *Landeshauptstadt Hannover* [1993] ECR I–6447.     [107] Para. 17.

[108] Case C–157/99 [2001] ECR I–5473 considered below at nn. 352–66.

[109] Para. 54. See also the AGs' Opinions in Cases C–368/98 *Vanbraekel* v. *ANMC* [2001] ECR I–5363 and C–157/99 *Geraets-Smits and Peerbooms* [2001] ECR I–5473.     [110] Para. 54.

[111] Para. 58.

[112] Case C–385/99 *V.G. Müller-Fauré* v. *Onderlinge Waarborgmaatschappij oz Zorgverzekeringen UA* and *E.E.M. van Riet* v. *Onderlinge Waarborgmaatschappij oz Zorgverzekeringen UA* [2003] ECR I–4509.

treatment received abroad had been paid for by the patient. It did not refer to the relationship either between the patient and the sickness fund or the sickness fund and the health care provider.[113] This suggests, and *Watts*[114] confirms, that Article 56 applies equally to benefits-in-kind systems like the British one where healthcare is provided to patients directly, without the medium of sickness funds, and paid for by general taxation.[115] In reaching this conclusion the Court opened up a market[116]—healthcare— previously reserved almost exclusively to Member States.[117] This approach may spill over to other sectors, as states increasingly apply a market model to the provision of welfare services.[118]

## 2.3 The Temporary Nature of Services

The key factor distinguishing services from establishment is duration: while a person who stays in the host state permanently is likely to be covered by the rules relating to establishment,[119] a person staying there on a 'temporary'[120] basis is likely only to be providing services. How can the two situations be distinguished? In *Gebhard*[121] the Court said that the temporary nature of the activities has to be determined 'in the light, not only of the duration of the provision of the service but also of its regularity, periodicity or continuity'. Thus, as the Court indicated in *Schnitzer*,[122] there is no magic formula for determining whether the rules on services or those on establishment apply: it has to be decided by the national court on a case-by-case basis. However, in *Trojani*[123] the Court made clear that an activity carried out on a permanent basis, or at least without a foreseeable limit to its duration, would not fall within the services provisions. That said, service providers under Article 56 can equip themselves with some form of infrastructure in the host Member State (e.g., an office, chambers, or consulting rooms), provided it is necessary to perform the services.[124] However, a requirement by the state for a service provider to have premises would breach Article 56 since it negates the freedom to provide services.[125]

---

[113] Para. 39.

[114] Case C–372/04 *Watts* v. *Bedford Primary Care Trust* [2006] ECR I–4325. See further C. Newdick, 'Citizenship, free movement and health care: Cementing individual rights by corroding social solidarity' (2006) 43 *CMLRev.* 1645.

[115] E. Spaventa, 'Public services and European Law: Looking for boundaries' (2003) 6 *CYELS* 271.

[116] V. Hatzopoulos, '*Killing* national health and insurance systems but *healing* patients? The European market for healthcare services after the judgments of the Court in *Vanbraekel* and *Peerbooms*' (2002) 39 *CMLRev.* 683.

[117] G. Davies, 'Welfare as a service' [2002] *LIEI* 27.

[118] Ibid., 38–9. See also A. P. van der Mei, *Cross-border Access to Public Benefits* (Oxford: Hart Publishing, 2002).

[119] Case 2/74 *Reyners* v. *Belgium State* [1974] ECR 631; Case 11/77 *Patrick* v. *Belgian State* [1977] ECR 1119.

[120] Art. 57(2).

[121] Case C–55/94 [1995] ECR I–4165, para. 27 considered in Ch. 10. See also Case 63/86 *Commission* v. *Italy (social housing)* [1988] ECR 29, and Case C–298/99 *Commission* v. *Italy* [2002] ECR I–3129, para. 56.

[122] Case C–215/01 *Schnitzer* [2003] ECR I–4847, paras. 30–2.

[123] Case C–456/02 *Trojani* v. *CPAS* [2004] ECR I–7573, para. 28.    [124] Para. 27.

[125] Case C–134/05 *Commission* v. *Italy (extra-judicial debt recovery)* [2007] ECR I–6251, para. 43; Case C–404/05 *Commission* v. *Germany (inspection of organic production)* [2007] ECR I–10239, para. 34.

# C. THE RIGHTS CONFERRED ON SERVICE PROVIDERS AND RECEIVERS

## 1. RIGHTS OF DEPARTURE, ENTRY, AND RESIDENCE

### 1.1 The Rights of the Provider and Recipient

Article 56 TFEU, together with Directive 73/148,[126] originally regulated the rights of entry and residence for those who actually move to provide or receive a service. This directive was repealed but not altogether replaced by the Citizens' Rights Directive (CRD) 2004/38.[127] Natural persons who are service providers going to another Member State for less than three months will be covered by Article 6 CRD in the same way as any other migrant (see fig. 12.4) but legal persons and those providing services for a longer period are not expressly covered by the CRD. For most purposes, this is not significant because in the field of services the Court has always placed much reliance on the Treaty provisions— and not secondary legislation—to give rights to service providers. This can be seen in *Commission v. Belgium (private security firms)*[128] concerning a law requiring every staff member of a security firm to carry an identification card issued by the Belgian Minister for the Interior. The Court said that the formalities involved in obtaining such an identification card were likely to make the provision of services across frontiers more difficult and so breached Article 56.[129] The Court added that since the migrant service provider had to be in possession of an identity card or a passport, the requirement to obtain an additional identity document was disproportionate.

The same reliance on the Treaties can be seen in *Oulane.*[130] A French service recipient was arrested in a goods tunnel closed to the public in Rotterdam Central station, with a view to his deportation on the ground that he failed to present a valid identity card or passport. The Court, having cited the relevant provisions of rights of residence Directive 73/148 and noted that the conditions laid down were left unchanged by Directive 2004/38,[131] concluded that a detention order issued by the Dutch authorities constituted 'an unjustified restriction on the freedom to provide services and is therefore contrary to Article [56]'.[132]

### 1.2 The Position of the Provider's Workforce

The right of entry to a Member State to provide a service applies not only to the individual or company but also to its workforce, irrespective of nationality. The Court made this clear in *Rush Portuguesa*[133] where a Portuguese company used its own third-country

---

[126] Dir. 73/148 ([1973] OJ L172/14) on the abolition of the restrictions on movement and residence within the Union for nationals of Member States with regard to establishment and the provision of services.

[127] This directive is considered in detail in Ch. 12.

[128] Case C–355/98 *Commission v. Belgium (private security firms)* [2000] ECR I–1221, paras. 38–9.

[129] See also Case C–189/03 *Commission v. Netherlands (private security firms)* [2004] ECR I–9289, para. 27.

[130] Case C–215/03 *Oulane v. Minister voor Vreemdelingenzaken en Integratie* [2005] ECR I–1215, para. 38.                                                                [131] Para. 20.

[132] Para. 44.

[133] Case C–113/89 *Rush Portuguesa v. Office national d'immigration* [1990] ECR I–1417.

national (TCN) workforce[134] to carry out a contract building a railway line in France. Rush Portuguesa's use of a TCN workforce contravened French rules which provided that only the French Office d'Immigration could recruit non-Union workers. The Court ruled that Articles 56–7 'preclude a Member State from prohibiting a person providing services established in another Member State from moving freely on its territory *with all his staff*'.[135] The Court continued that Member States also could not make the movement of staff subject to restrictions such as a condition as to engagement *in situ* or an obligation to obtain a work permit because such conditions discriminated against guest service providers in relation to their competitors established in the host country who were able to use their own staff without restrictions.

The result of *Rush Portuguesa* is that Article 56 allows companies from State A (e.g., Portugal) to 'post' (i.e., send) their own workforce to provide a service in State B (e.g., France), even where the workforce includes TCNs, provided that the TCN workers do not seek access to the labour market in the host state and that they return to their country of origin or residence once the contract is finished.[136] This raised the spectre of what some term 'social dumping', where service providers take advantage of cheaper labour (and inferior labour standards) in their own state (Portugal) to win a contract in the host state (France).[137] However, the Court sought to address these concerns in *Rush Portuguesa* by ruling in paragraph 18 that:[138]

[Union] law does not preclude Member States from extending their legislation, or collective labour agreements entered into by both sides of industry, to any person who is employed, even temporarily, within their territory, no matter in which country the employer is established; nor does [Union] law prohibit Member States from enforcing those rules by appropriate means.

This suggests that the host state *can* apply all of its labour laws to the provider's workforce, thereby removing the competitive advantage enjoyed by the service provider, namely its cheaper labour.

The position in *Rush Portuguesa* was apparently reinforced by the enactment of Directive 96/71 on Posted Workers.[139] The directive no longer gives the host Member State the discretion as to whether to apply its labour standards to posted workers; instead it *requires* the host state to apply to posted workers a 'nucleus of mandatory rules'[140] listed in Article 3(1), in particular relating to wages (but only minimum wages), working time, and equal treatment, as laid down either by law or, in the case of the construction industry, collective agreements which satisfy certain conditions laid out in Article 3(8). At least initially, trade union lawyers, particularly from the wealthier Northern European states, welcomed the directive as a way of protecting labour standards in those states from being

---

[134] The workforce was actually Portuguese, but at the time the transitional arrangements for Portuguese accession to the EU were in place and Portuguese workers did not enjoy the rights of free movement. For our purposes the Portuguese workers constitute third-country nationals (see para. 4 of the judgment).

[135] Para. 12, emphasis added. See also Case C–43/93 *Vander Elst* v. *Office des Migrations Internationales* [1994] ECR I–3803.      [136] Case C–43/93 *Vander Elst* [1994] ECR I–3803, para. 21.

[137] Germany was particularly exercised by this problem. See W. Streeck, 'Neo-voluntarism: A new social policy regime' (1995) 1 *ELJ* 31, 42, and S. Simitis, 'Dismantling or strengthening labour law: The case of the European Court of Justice' (1996) 2 *ELJ* 156, 163.      [138] Para. 18.

[139] Dir. 96/71/EC ([1996] OJ L18/1). See P. Davies, 'Posted workers: Single market or protection of national labour law systems' (1997) 34 *CMLRev.* 571 and C. Barnard, *EC Employment Law* (Oxford: OUP, 2006), 280–9.      [140] 13th recital of the directive.

undermined by posted workers from southern and Eastern states. However, employers involved in posting staff argued that because the directive had the effect of requiring the out-of-state service provider to adapt its terms and conditions of employment each time it posted workers to another Member State, the directive interfered with, rather than promoted, the provision of services.[141]

It was against this backcloth that the *Laval*[142] dispute arose. The case concerned a Latvian company which won a contract to refurbish a school in Sweden using its own Latvian workers who earned about 40 per cent less than comparable Swedish workers. The Swedish construction union wanted Laval to apply the Swedish collective agreement but Laval refused, in part because the collective agreement was unclear as to how much Laval would have to pay its workers, and in part because it imposed various supplementary obligations on Laval such as paying a 'special building supplement' to an insurance company to finance group life insurance contracts. There followed a union picket at the school site, a blockade by construction workers, and sympathy industrial action by the electricians unions. Although this industrial action was permissible under Swedish law, Laval brought proceedings in the Swedish labour court, claiming that this action was contrary to *Union* law (in particular Article 56 TFEU on freedom to provide services) and the Posted Workers' Directive.

The Court insisted on a narrow reading of the directive: the host state could insist on applying its labour law rules to posted workers but only in respect of those matters exhaustively[143] listed in Article 3(1) of the directive, thus apparently reversing paragraph 18 of *Rush Portuguesa*. Because Article 3(1) did not cover matters such as the 'special building supplement' and the other insurance premiums, these could not be applied to the Latvian posted workers.[144] The Court also said that the requirement to pay Latvian workers Swedish rates of pay was not compatible with the directive. This was because Sweden had failed to comply with the precise terms of Article 3(1) and (8) of the directive by neither enacting minimum wage legislation nor expressly taking advantage of the complex provisions in Article 3(8) which allowed minimum wage rates to be set by collective agreements.[145] More generally, because the trade unions' demands fell outside the scope of the directive,[146] industrial action taken to enforce the terms of the Swedish collective agreement was incompatible with Article 56.[147]

*Laval* shows that the Posted Workers' Directive is primarily a measure to facilitate free movement of services and not a measure to realize social policy objectives, a point confirmed by its legal basis (Articles 53(2) and 62 TFEU (ex Articles 47(2) and 55 EC)).

---

[141] See, e.g., P. Davies, 'The Posted Workers Directive and the EC Treaty' (2002) 31 *ILJ* 298, 300.

[142] Case C–341/05, *Laval* [2007] ECR I–987.

[143] Case C–341/05 *Laval* [2007] ECR I–987, para. 71. This is more clearly expressed in Case C–319/06 *Commission* v. *Luxembourg* [2008] ECR I–4323, para. 26. For a full discussion, see C. Barnard, 'The UK and posted workers: The effect of *Commission v Luxembourg* on the territorial application of British labour law' (2009) 38 *Industrial Law Journal* 122.                                          [144] Para. 83.

[145] *Laval*, para 67. See A. C. L. Davies, 'One Step Forward, Two Steps Back, The *Viking* and *Laval* cases in the ECJ' (2008) 37 *ILJ* 126.

[146] *Laval* suggests that failure to comply with the terms of the directive means that a breach of Art. 56 cannot be justified (paras. 108–11). By contrast, Case C–346/06, *Dirk Rüffert v Land Niedersachsen* [2008] ECR I–1989, para. 36 suggests non-compliance with the directive amounts to a breach of Art. 56.

[147] By implication, in these situations the preambular paragraph in Dir. 96/71, to the effect that 'this Directive is without prejudice to the law of the Member States concerning collective action to defend the interests of trades and professions', becomes irrelevant.

This view is reinforced by the Court's observations that the directive is 'first' intended to 'ensure a climate of fair competition between national undertakings and undertakings which provide services transnationally',[148] and that the mandatory rules for minimum protection in Article 3(1) prevent a situation from arising where the out-of-state provider competes unfairly against the host state.[149] Only 'secondly' does the Court refer to the worker protection element of the directive.[150] It could, therefore, be argued that the Court has reached a careful compromise in these cases: posted workers will enjoy the better terms and conditions of employment in the host state but only if the host state has complied with the provisions of the directive to the letter. If it has not, then any attempt to apply the host-state rules will breach both the directive and Article 56. According to this analysis, the directive and Article 56 are mutually reinforcing: the restrictive interpretation of the directive is derived from Article 56 and the substance of Article 56 is derived from the directive.[151] In this way, the Court has sought to silence those critics who argued at the time when the directive was adopted that the directive was *ultra vires* Article 56 because it obstructed the freedom to provide services.

## 2. RIGHTS OF ACCESS TO THE MARKET IN SERVICES IN OTHER MEMBER STATES

*Laval* demonstrates just how closely linked the right of entry is with questions of access to the market more generally. This section examines in more detail the nature of the obstacles that prevent or impede access to the market in services.

### 2.1 Discriminatory Measures

#### (a) Distinctly applicable measures

Article 57 provides that 'the person providing the service may...temporarily pursue his activity in the Member State where the service is provided, under the same conditions as are imposed by that State on its own nationals'. It therefore prohibits discrimination on the ground of nationality against those wishing to provide/receive services. The problem with applying the principle of non-discrimination is the choice of comparator. The obvious candidate is a person providing equivalent services who is established in the host state. However, establishment connotes more permanence than the provision of services; and the service provider already has a place of establishment—in the home state. Recognizing this problem, the Court noted in *Säger*[152] that:

a Member State may not make the provision of services in its territory subject to compliance with all the conditions required for establishment and thereby deprive of all practical effectiveness the provisions of the [Treaties] whose object is, precisely, to guarantee the freedom to provide services.

This ruling helps to explain in part the Court's decision in *Laval*: host states cannot require service providers and their staff to comply with all of the host state's labour

---

[148] *Laval*, para 74.          [149] Ibid., para 75.          [150] Ibid., para 76.

[151] See esp. *Rüffert*, above n. 146, para. 36.

[152] Case C–76/90 [1991] ECR I–4221, para. 13. See also Case 33/74 *Van Binsbergen* [1974] ECR 1299, para. 11; Case 205/84 *Commission v. Germany (the insurance cases)* [1986] ECR 3755, para. 26, and Case C–484/93 *Svensson* [1995] ECR I–3955 (legal persons); Case C–118/96 *Safir* [1998] ECR I–1897, para. 30.

standards since they have already satisfied the standards in the home state. Applying both sets of rules imposes a double burden and this would deprive Article 56 of all practical effectiveness.[153]

The Court spelt out the meaning of the principle of direct discrimination in *Gouda*:[154]

Article [56 TFEU] entails, in the first place, the abolition of any discrimination against a person providing services on *the grounds of his nationality or the fact that he is established in a Member State other than the one in which the service is provided*.

Thus, Article 56 prohibits (direct) discrimination not only on the grounds of nationality as with the other Treaty provisions, but also on the grounds of the place of establishment (see fig. 11.2), a wider concept of discrimination than is found in the other freedoms. The Court continued that:[155]

national rules which are not applicable to services without discrimination as regards their origin are compatible with [Union] law only in so far as they can be brought within an express exemption, such as that contained in Article [52 TFEU].

Thus, in respect of direct discrimination on the ground of nationality, the Court reaffirmed the orthodox position that direct discrimination breaches Article 56 and can be saved only by reference to one of the express derogations. While the Court has wavered on this point over the years, it recently re-confirmed the orthodoxy in *Laval*[156] and again in *Commission* v. *Poland (Germany/Poland agreement)*.[157]

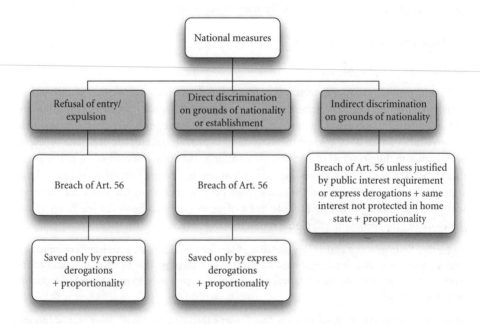

**Fig. 11.2** The discrimination approach to free movement of services

---

[153] See also Case C–164/99 *Portugaia Construções* [2002] ECR I–787.

[154] Case C–288/89 *Stichting Collectieve Antennevoorziening Gouda* v. *Commissariaat voor de Media* [1991] ECR I–4007, para. 10 (emphasis added).       [155] Para. 11.

[156] Case C–341/05, *Laval* [2007] ECR I–987, paras. 116–17. See also Case C–490/04 *Commission* v. *Germany (posted workers)* [2007] ECR I–6095, para. 86.

[157] Case C–546/07 [2010] ECR I–000, para. 47 (although cf. paras. 43 and 51).

*FDC* provides an example of direct discrimination.[158] Under Spanish law, film distributors would be granted a licence to dub foreign (mainly US) films on condition that they also distributed a Spanish film at the same time. The Court said that this rule breached Article 56 because it gave preferential treatment to the producers of Spanish films over producers established in other Member States, since only Spanish producers had a guarantee that their films would be distributed. The Spanish government then tried to justify the rule for reasons of cultural policy, but this was rejected by the Court on the ground that cultural policy was not one of the exhaustive list of derogations in Article 52 TFEU (ex Article 46 EC).

Where discrimination is based on the fact that the service provider is established in another Member State, the Court said in *Gouda* that such discrimination could also be saved only by reference to the express derogations found in Article 52.[159] However, the case law is not consistent on this point. If the national rule is drafted in terms of requiring a service provider to be established and/or to have a residence[160] in the host state, the mirror image of a rule discriminating against those established in another Member State, then the Court may treat this version of the rule as being indirectly discriminatory on the ground of nationality.[161] Such discrimination also breaches Article 56[162] but can be justified not only by the express derogations but also by the broader public-interest requirements.[163] However, given the serious consequences for the provision of services of a national rule requiring establishment, the Court will carefully scrutinize any justification offered. Therefore, in *Van Binsbergen*[164] the Court recognized that a Dutch rule requiring representatives before tribunals to be resident in the Netherlands could be justified on the ground of professional rules of conduct connected with the administration of justice (relating to organization, qualifications, professional ethics, supervision, and liability).[165] However, it found the residence requirement to be disproportionate because the administration of justice could be satisfactorily ensured by measures less restrictive to the freedom to provide services, such as choosing an address for service.[166]

---

[158] Case C-17/92 *Federación de Distribuidores Cinematográficos v. Estado Español et Unión de Productores de Cine y Televisión* [1993] ECR I-2239, para. 15.

[159] See also Case 352/85 *Bond* [1988] ECR 2085, para. 32; Case C-260/89 *ERT v. DEP* [1991] ECR I-2925, para. 24. For further discussion and a proposed reconciliation of the case law, see Tesauro AG's Opinion in Case C-118/96 *Safir* [1998] ECR I-1897, para. 31.

[160] See Case 39/75 *Coenen v. The Sociaal-Economische Raad* [1975] ECR 1547.

[161] Cf. Case C-546/07 *Commission v. Germany (Germany/Poland Agreement)* [2010] ECR I-000, paras. 39–40.

[162] See, e.g., Case C-294/97 *Eurowings Luftverkehrs AG v. Finanzamt Dortmund-Unna* [1999] ECR I-7447, para. 19. In more recent cases the Court describes such rules as having a 'dissuasive' effect on free movement of services amounting to 'a denial of that freedom': Case C-150/04 *Commission v. Denmark (insurance)* [2007] ECR I-1163, para. 40.

[163] For an illustration of complete conceptual and legal confusion, see Case C-484/93 *Svensson* [1995] ECR I-3955, para. 15: discrimination based on the place of establishment can 'only be justified on the *general interest* grounds referred to in Article [52(1)] to which Article [62] refers' (emphasis added). The Court then considers general interest grounds relating to the coherence of the fiscal regime and not the derogations listed in Art. 52 (paras. 16–18). [164] Case 33/74 [1974] ECR 1299.

[165] Para. 12.    [166] Para. 16.

## (b) Indistinctly applicable measures

In *Gouda*[167] the Court also confirmed that unjustified indistinctly applicable measures were prohibited by Article 56. It said:

12. In the absence of harmonisation of the rules applicable to services, or even of a system of equivalence, restrictions on the freedom guaranteed by the [Treaties] in this field may arise in the second place as a result of the application of national rules which affect any person established in the national territory to persons providing services established in the territory of another Member State who already have to satisfy the requirements of that State's legislation.

13.... [S]uch restrictions come within the scope of Article [56] if the application of the national legislation to foreign persons providing services is not justified by overriding reasons relating to the public interest or if the requirements embodied in that legislation are already satisfied by the rules imposed on those persons in the Member State in which they are established.

In other words, those measures which impose a dual burden on foreign service providers breach Article 56 unless they can be justified by overriding reasons relating to the public interest (see fig. 11.2).[168]

*Commission* v. *Germany (insurance cases)*[169] provides a good example of an indistinctly applicable rule. The Court found that German rules requiring insurance companies wishing to provide insurance in Germany to be both established and authorized in Germany breached Articles 56–7 because the rules increased costs for those providing services in Germany, especially when the insurer conducted business there only occasionally.[170] These requirements therefore constituted 'the very negation of the fundamental freedom to provide services'.[171] On the question of justification,[172] the Court noted the sensitivity of the insurance sector,[173] given the number of policyholders affected, the difficulty facing anyone taking out insurance to judge the financial viability of an insurance company, and the fact that insurance was based on future and often unpredictable events.[174] For these reasons the Court considered that the German restrictions on the freedom to provide services could be justified on the ground of consumer protection and that those interests were not adequately protected in the state of establishment. However, while it found that the authorization requirement was proportionate, it said the residence requirement was not.

---

[167] Case C–288/89 [1991] ECR I–4007, para. 12.

[168] Para. 13. See also Joined Cases 110 and 111/78 *Ministère public and 'Chambre syndicale des agents artistiques et impresarii de Belgique' ASBL* v. *Willy van Wesemael* [1979] ECR 35 and Case 279/80 *Webb* [1981] ECR 3305.        [169] Case 205/84 *Commission* v. *Germany (the insurance cases)* [1986] ECR 3755.

[170] Para. 28.

[171] Para. 19. See also Case C–279/02 *Commission* v. *Italy (temp agencies)* [2002] ECR I–1425, para. 18.

[172] Para. 27. See further Commission Interpretative Communication, Freedom to Provide Services and the General Good in the Insurance Sector, C(1999) 5046 and M. Tison, 'Unravelling the general good exception: The case of financial services' in M. Andenas and W. Roth (eds.), *Services and Free Movement in EU Law* (Oxford: OUP, 2002).

[173] Case 205/84 *Commission* v. *Germany (insurance cases)* [1986] ECR 3755 now Dir. 2009/138/EC on the taking-up and pursuit of the business of Insurance and Re-insurance ([2009] OJ L335/1): Case C–191/99 *Kvaerner* v. *Staatssecretaris van Financiën* [2001] ECR I–4447, para. 38.

[174] Paras. 30–1.

### (c) Non-discriminatory measures

The cases considered so far have all involved some form of discrimination which restricted the free movement of services. As with the early case law on establishment, there was a period when the Court said that a national measure which was genuinely non-discriminatory did not breach Article 56. For example, in *Debauve*[175] it said that a national ban on transmitting advertisements by cable television did not breach Articles 56–7 'if those rules are applied without distinction as regards the origin, whether national or foreign, of those advertisements, the nationality of the person providing the services, or the place where he is established'.[176]

However, as the Court's case law increasingly took market access into account,[177] it recognized that non-discriminatory measures did in principle breach Article 56 if they were liable to prevent or impede access to the market. We saw this in *Alpine Investments*,[178] considered in Chapter 8, and we can also see it in *Schindler*.[179] The Schindlers were agents of SKL, a public body responsible for organizing lotteries on behalf of four *Länder* in Germany. They sent advertisements and application forms to the UK inviting people to participate in the German lottery, and were prosecuted for breaching the (then) national law banning lotteries. The Court said that the national legislation prohibiting the holding of large lotteries was a non-discriminatory obstacle to the freedom to provide services which contravened Article 56 becuase it was liable to prohibit free movement of services.[180] However, it continued that, bearing in mind the moral, religious, and cultural aspects of gambling, the restriction could be justified on the ground of preventing the lottery from becoming 'a source of private profit', as well as avoiding 'the high risk of crime or fraud' and 'the incitement to spend which may have damaging individual and social consequences'.[181]

### 2.2 Measures 'Liable to Prohibit or Otherwise Impede' Freedom to Provide Services

Cases such as *Alpine* and *Schindler* marked a stepping stone towards a more general reliance on the market access test. In fact, reliance on the market access test had already been signalled by the Court in the early case of *Van Binsbergen*[182] and confirmed in its seminal decision of *Säger*[183] where it said that Article 56 requires:

*not only* the elimination of all discrimination against a person providing services on the grounds of his nationality *but also* the abolition of any restriction even if it applies without distinction to national providers of services and to those of other Member States, when it is liable to prohibit or otherwise impede the activities of a provider of services established in another Member State where he lawfully provides similar services.[184]

---

[175] Case 52/79 *Debauve* [1981] ECR 833.

[176] Para. 16. See also Case 15/78 *Société générale alsacienne de banque SA* v. *Koestler* [1978] ECR 1971, para. 6. For criticisms of this view see Van Gerven AG in Case C–159/90 *SPUC* v. *Grogan* [1991] ECR I–4685, paras. 19–22.

[177] The foundations of such jurisprudence can be traced back to the early case law: see, e.g., Case 39/75 *Coenen* [1975] ECR 1547, para. 6. See, esp., Case C–76/90 *Säger* [1991] ECR I–4221, para. 12.

[178] Case C–384/93 [1995] ECR I–1141. See also Case C–118/96 *Safir* [1998] ECR I–1897, para. 30.

[179] Case C–275/92 [1994] ECR I–1039.

[180] Paras. 47–8. See also Case C–36/02 *Omega* [2004] ECR I–9609, para. 25.     [181] Para. 60.

[182] Case 33/74 [1974] ECR 1299, paras. 10–11.

[183] Case C–76/90 [1991] ECR I–4221. Cf. Case 205/84 *Commission* v. *Germany (insurance cases)* [1986] ECR 3755, para. 25.     [184] Para. 12, emphasis added.

*Säger* concerned a German law requiring those monitoring patents to have a licence. This licence was granted on condition that the individual held certain professional qualifications (e.g., as a lawyer or patent agent). Dennemayer, a British company, monitored patents on behalf of clients, particularly in Germany, and informed them when the fees for renewing the patents became due. The commission charged by Dennemayer was lower than that charged by German patent agents who complained that Dennemeyer was breaching German law by trading without a licence; Dennemayer argued that the German law itself breached Article 56. The Court found that the German rule prevented undertakings established in other Member States from providing services to patent holders established in the national territory, and prevented patent holders from freely choosing the manner in which their patents were to be monitored.[185] The rule therefore breached Article 56 unless it could be justified (see fig. 11.3).[186]

The *Säger* formulation, often simplified to the question 'Does the national law constitute a restriction on the freedom to provide services?',[187] the test which the Court has applied in most subsequent services cases,[188] avoids the intellectual somersaults involved in deciding whether particular national rules are indistinctly applicable or non-discriminatory (direct discrimination is still usually treated separately as fig. 11.3 shows).

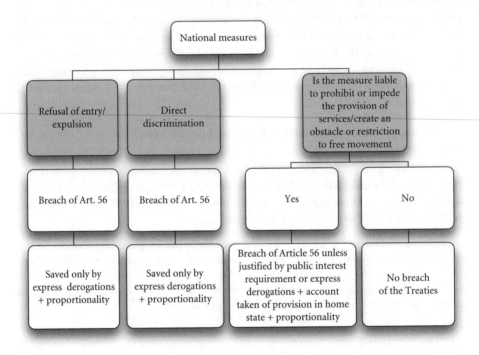

**Fig. 11.3** The effect of *Säger* on the services case law

---

185  Para. 14.

186  See also Case C–255/04 *Commission* v. *France (performing artists)* [2006] ECR I–5251, para. 29.

187  See, e.g., Case C–243/01 *Gambelli* [2003] ECR I–13031, para. 45.

188  See, e.g., Case C–43/93 *Vander Elst* [1994] ECR I–3803, para. 14; Case C–272/94 *Guiot* [1996] ECR I–1905, para. 10; Case C–222/95 *Parodi* [1997] ECR I–3899, para. 18; Case C–58/98 *Corsten* [2000] ECR I–7919, para. 33.

The influence of the change wrought by *Säger* can be seen in *Commission v. Italy*,[189] another case about patent agents. Italian law required patent agents established in another Member State to be entered on the Italian register of patent agents before providing a service there. Registration was conditional on having a residence or place of business in Italy. Instead of considering—as it would have done in the past— whether registration and residence requirements discriminated in some way, due to the additional expense and administrative and economic burdens for businesses established in another Member State,[190] the Court merely observed that the Italian rules constituted 'a *restriction* within the meaning of Article [56]'.[191] The focus then shifted to questions of justification and proportionality.

The Court has considered a wide variety of national rules to be restrictions on freedom to provide services. For example, it has said that authorization requirements are restrictions. Therefore, in *Commission v. Netherlands* the Court said that Dutch law requiring private security firms, detective agencies, and their managers to be authorized breached Article 56.[192] Where the authorization or licensing requirements are subject to a territorial limitation, the Court is particularly suspicious,[193] especially when used to prevent an 'excessive number of foreign undertakings from establishing themselves' in that area.[194] Translation requirements are also restrictions due to the 'additional expense and the administrative and financial burden for undertakings established in another Member State'.[195] An obligation to swear an oath of allegiance to the state where the service is provided is also an 'impediment to' the pursuit of an out-of-state operator's activities in the host state which 'impairs its access to the market',[196] as are conditions relating to maximum/minimum staffing levels,[197] and obligations to lodge guarantees with the relevant authorities.[198] Legislation setting compulsory minimum fees, or at least permitting control by the relevant authorities of the fees charged, have also been considered restrictions on freedom to provide services.[199]

In addition, the Court has classified a number of rules regulating gambling as 'restrictions'. For example, in *Anomar*[200] the Court said that Portuguese rules restricting the right to operate games of chance or gambling solely to casinos in permanent or temporary gam-

---

[189] Case C–131/01 *Commission v. Italy* [2003] ECR I–1659. See also Case C–465/05 *Commission v. Italy (private security activities)* [2007] ECR I–11091, para. 85; Case C–389/05 *Commission v. France (Insemination of bovine semen)* [2008] ECR I–5337, para. 66.

[190] Case C–49/98 *Finalarte* [2001] ECR I–7831, para. 70.

[191] Emphasis added, para. 27, and para. 42 on the residence requirement. See also Case C–165/98 *Mazzoleni* [2001] ECR I–2189, para. 24; Case C–215/01 *Schnitzer* [2003] ECR I–4847, para. 34; Case C–496/01 *Commission v. France (bio-medical analysis)* [2004] ECR I–2351, para. 64. The same applies to companies: Case C–452/04 *Fidium Finanz AG* [2006] ECR I–9521, para. 46.

[192] Case C–189/03 *Commission v. Netherlands (private security firms)* [2004] ECR I–9289, para. 17. See also Case C–43/93 *Vander Elst* [1994] ECR I–3803, para. 15; Case C–451/99 *Cura Anlagen GmbH v. Auto Service Leasing GmbH (ASL)* [2002] ECR I–3193, para. 37; Case C–205/99 *Analir and others v. Administración General del Estado* [2001] ECR I–1271, para. 22; Case C–410/96 *Criminal Proceedings against André Ambry* [1998] ECR I–7875, para. 30; Case C–288/02 *Commission v. Greece* [2004] ECR I–10071, para. 30.

[193] Case C–134/05 *Commission v. Italy (extra-judicial debt recovery)* [2007] ECR I–6251, para. 64; Case C–465/05 *Commission v. Italy (private security activities)* [2007] ECR I–11091, para. 58.

[194] Case C–465/05 *Commission v. Italy (private security activities)* [2007] ECR I–11091, para. 78.

[195] Case C–490/04 *Commission v. Germany (posted workers)* [2007] ECR I–6095, para. 69.

[196] Case C–465/05 *Commission v. Italy (private security activities)* [2007] ECR I–11091, para. 46.

[197] Ibid, para. 105.    [198] Ibid., para. 109.    [199] Ibid., para. 127.

[200] Case C–6/01 *Anomar v. Estado português* [2003] ECR I–8621, para. 66.

ing areas breached Article 56, as did a Greek prohibition on the installation of computer games in venues other than casinos in *Commission* v. *Greece*.[201] In *Placanica*[202] the Court said that an Italian rule prohibiting—on pain of criminal penalties—the pursuit of activities in the betting or gaming sector without a licence or police authorization constituted a restriction on the freedom to provide services as did a rule prohibiting Italian intermediaries from facilitating the provision of betting services on behalf of a British supplier.

Advertising restrictions also breach Article 56. So, in *Gourmet*[203] the Court said that a prohibition on advertising had a particular effect on the cross-border supply of advertising, given the international nature of the advertising market. It therefore constituted a restriction on the freedom to provide services. Similarly, in *Bacardi*[204] the Court found the French 'loi Evin' prohibiting direct and indirect television advertising of certain alcoholic drinks breached Article 56 because (1) the owners of the advertising hoardings had to refuse any advertising for alcoholic beverages if the sporting event was likely to be retransmitted in France; (2) the French rules impeded the provision of broadcasting services for television programmes because French broadcasters had to refuse all retransmission of sporting events in which hoardings bearing advertising for alcoholic beverages marketed in France might be visible; and (3) the organizers of sporting events taking place outside France could not sell the retransmission rights to French broadcasters if the transmission of the television programmes of such events was likely to contain indirect television advertising for those alcoholic beverages. The Court said that such restrictions could, however, be justified on the grounds of public health and that the steps taken were proportionate.[205]

### 2.3 Justification and Proportionality

#### (a) Grounds of justification

As we have seen, indistinctly applicable measures and measures which hinder the provision of services between Member States can be justified, using the language in *Säger*,[206] by 'imperative reasons relating to the public interest and which apply to all persons or undertakings pursuing an activity in the State of destination, *in so far as that interest is not protected by the rules to which the person providing the services is subject in the Member State in which he is established*'.

In *Gouda*[207] the Court listed a number of examples of imperative reasons in the public interest,[208] including consumer protection and worker protection. We shall consider these public-interest grounds in more detail in Chapter 13. For now it is sufficient to

---

[201] Case C–65/05 *Commission* v. *Greece* [2006] ECR I–10341, para. 56.

[202] Joined Cases C–338/04, C–359/04 and C–360/04 *Placanica* [2007] ECR I–1891, paras. 42 and 44. See also Case C–433/04 *Commission* v. *Belgium (tax fraud)* [2006] ECR I–10653, para. 32.

[203] Case C–405/98 [2001] ECR I–1795, para. 39. See also now the effect of the UCPD 2005/29 (OJ [2005] L149/22) considered in Ch. 5.

[204] C–429/02 *Bacardi* v. *Télévision Française 1 SA* [2004] ECR I–6613. See also Case C–262/02 *Commission* v. *France* [2004] ECR I–6569.

[205] Paras. 37–41.    [206] Case C–76/90 [1991] ECR I–4221, para. 15, emphasis added.

[207] Para. 13. See generally J. Fernández Martin and S. O'Leary, 'Judicial exceptions to the free provision of services' (1995) 1 *ELJ* 308 and the updated version in Andenas and Roth (eds.), above n. 193.

[208] Also described as 'overriding reasons in the public interest', 'justified by the general good' (Case 279/80 *Webb* [1981] ECR 3305, paras. 16–17) and 'mandatory grounds in the general interest' (Case C–224/97 *Ciola* [1999] ECR I–2517, para. 15).

note two points. First, there are still some hints in the case law that, as with the early case law on mandatory requirements, justifications and derogations serve a different legal function: derogations apply where the Treaties are actually breached. By contrast, where a justification is made out, and the measure is proportionate, there is no breach of Article 56. This distinction is alluded to in *Kattner Stahlbau*[209] where the Court said that 'Articles [56] and [57] are to be interpreted to the effect that they *do not preclude* national legislation' such as a German requirement that all employers in a certain industry and a certain territory be affiliated to the employers' liability insurance association on grounds that it can be justified by the principle of solidarity (spreading the cost of insurance over the good risks and the bad).

Secondly, the Court has applied these public-interest requirements with a considerable degree of flexibility. In some cases it is prepared to engage in a detailed scrutiny of the justifications advanced by the Member States and/or in the question of proportionality, as the broadcasting cases considered below indicate (Case Study 11.2). In other cases, particularly those touching upon sensitive socio-cultural issues, it has afforded Member States a considerable margin of appreciation.[210] *Schindler* is the prime example of this. There the Court accepted without question all the justifications advanced by the UK government about the social ills of gambling, despite the fact that the Court knew that the National Lotteries Act 1993 had gone through Parliament permitting the creation of the very type of lottery which the UK government had so forthrightly condemned in *Schindler*.[211]

However, the Court's extreme leniency in *Schindler* was not repeated in *Zenatti*.[212] The case concerned an Italian law prohibiting the taking of bets on sporting competitions except through specially appointed bodies which then used the funds to promote sporting activities, especially in deprived areas. The Court said that such a limitation on who could take bets was acceptable only if, from the outset, it reflected a concern to bring about a genuine diminution in gambling opportunities and if the financing of social activities constituted only an incidental beneficial consequence[213] and not the real justification for the restrictive policy. If the real aim of the limitation was to fund social activities, that motive could not in itself be regarded as an objective justification for restrictions on the freedom to provide services.

## (b) Home-state control

When considering whether the host state's action could be justified in the field of services, *Säger* added the additional criteria that the national court had to take into account the action already taken by the *home* state to protect that particular interest (see fig. 11.3). This is a reflection of the principle of home-state control or country of origin. The importance

---

[209] Case C–350/07 *Kattner Stahlbau GmbH* v. *Maschinenbau- und Metall- Berufsgenossenschaft* [2009] ECR I–1513, para. 92 emphasis added.

[210] This is the description used by the Court in Case C–67/98 *Questore di Verona* v. *Diego Zenatti* [1999] ECR I–7289, paras. 15 and 33.

[211] See, e.g., paras. 31 and 51.

[212] Case C–67/98 [1999] ECR I–7289, para. 36. See also Joined Cases C–338/04 and C–360/04 *Placanica* [2007] ECR I–1891, paras. 53–4. For a full discussion, see D. Doukas and J. Anderson, 'Commercial gambling without frontiers: When the ECJ throws the dice are loaded' (2008) 27 *Yearbook of European Law* 237.

[213] See also Case E–3/06 *Ladbrokes Ltd* v. *Government of Norway*, [2007] EFJA Court Report 86, para. 48; Case E–1/06 *EFTA Surveillance Authority* v. *Norway* [2007] *EFTA Court Report* 8, para. 39.

of this principle can be seen in *Guiot*.[214] The Court said that a national law requiring an employer providing a service in the host Member State to pay employer's contributions to the social security fund of the host Member State, in addition to the contributions paid to the social security fund in the state in which the employer was established, placed an additional financial burden on the employer which was liable to restrict the freedom to provide services. It said that the national legislation could be justified by the public interest relating to the 'social protection of workers in the construction industry'.[215] Then, reflecting the country-of-origin principle (CoOP), the Court said that if the workers enjoyed the same protection, or essentially similar protection, by virtue of employer's contributions already paid by the employer in the Member State of establishment,[216] which was a matter for the national court to decide,[217] then the justification was not made out. In other cases, the Court has said that failure to take into account supervision which has already been carried out in the home state means the national measure fails the test of proportionality.[218]

The requirement that the host state take account of the measures put in place by the home state to protect the relevant interest is important because, in respect of services, the primary regulator is the home state and the host state can impose only supplementary controls. In this regard, the services case law follows that on goods where, in cases such as *Biologische Producten*,[219] the Court ruled that the host state could require the product to undergo a fresh examination but had to take into account the results of tests already carried out by the state of origin. By contrast, the home state control rule does not apply to Articles 45 and 49 on the free movement of workers and establishment where the primary regulator is the host state and so the controls imposed by the home state are of little relevance. The CoOP lay at the heart of the debate about the Services Directive which is considered in Section D below.

### (c) Proportionality

Finally, the Court requires that the steps taken to protect the public interest must be proportionate, i.e. appropriate for securing the attainment of the objective which they pursue and must not go beyond what is necessary in order to attain it.[220] Once again it is possible to see how the intensity of the Court's review varies according to the sensitivity of the subject matter. Where national rules do not raise politically difficult issues, the Court's scrutiny tends to be quite intrusive. For example, in *Säger* itself the Court found that the licensing requirements for those monitoring patents exceeded what was necessary to protect the public interest because the services were straightforward (alerting clients when fees were due), the service provider gave no advice to the clients (who were themselves experts in the field), and there was no risk to clients if those monitoring the patents failed in their task (the German patent office itself also sent out official reminders).

---

[214] Case C–272/94 *Guiot* [1996] ECR I–1905. See also Case C–496/01 *Commission* v. *France (bio-medical analysis)* [2004] ECR I–2351, para. 71          [215] Para. 16.

[216] Para. 17. See also Joined Cases C–369/96 and C–376 *Arblade* [1999] ECR I–8453, para. 80.

[217] On the facts the Court observed that the Belgian and Luxembourg contributions at issue in practice covered the same risks and had a similar, if not identical, purpose (para. 19).

[218] Case C–465/05 *Commission* v. *Italy (private security activities)* [2007] ECR I–11091, para. 63.

[219] Case 272/80 *Criminal Proceedings against Biologische Producten BV* [1981] ECR 3277, para. 14, considered further in Ch. 6.

[220] Joined Cases C–369 and 376/96 *Arblade* [1999] ECR I–8453, para. 35.

Similarly, in the *Tourist Guide cases*[221] the Court found that while the requirement that tourist guides possess a licence could in principle be justified by 'the general interest in consumer protection and in the conservation of the national historical and artistic heritage', such a requirement was disproportionate.[222] The Court noted that the rule had the effect of reducing the number of tourist guides, leading tour operators to use local guides, with the drawback that the tourists 'do not have a guide who is familiar with their language, their interests and their specific expectations'. The Court added that the profitable operation of such group tours depended on the commercial reputation of the operator, who faced competitive pressure from other tour companies. These factors compelled companies to be selective in employing tourist guides and to exercise some control over the quality of their services.

Where cases do involve more politically sensitive issues the Court can adopt a much lighter touch. For example, in *Schindler* the Court did not consider proportionality at all when upholding the national rule banning lotteries; in *Läärä*[223] it did examine proportionality but its approach was remarkably hands-off.[224] The case concerned a Finnish law granting exclusive rights to run the operation of slot machines to a public body, with the revenue raised going into the public purse. This rule had the effect of preventing a British company from operating its slot machines in Finland. The Court said that the Finnish legislation involved no discrimination on grounds of nationality and applied without distinction to operators who might be interested in that activity, whether they were established in Finland or in another Member State.[225] However, it said that while such legislation constituted an impediment to freedom to provide services because it directly or indirectly prevented operators in other Member States from making slot machines available to the public,[226] it could be justified on the grounds laid down in *Schindler*,[227] and the steps taken were proportionate.[228] The Court said that it was for the Member States to decide whether to prohibit the operation of such machines or only to restrict their use.

This judicial deference towards the Member States may partly be explained by the fact that, in these cases involving an activity which is legal in one state but illegal in another, the Court is wary of imposing the values of the majority of the states (where lotteries are lawful, albeit highly regulated) on the minority (where lotteries are unlawful).[229] In this respect, the Court's approach stands in stark contrast to the majoritarian approach

---

[221] Case C–180/89 *Commission* v. *Italy* [1991] ECR I–709.

[222] Para. 24. See also Case C–11/95 *Commission* v. *Belgium* [1996] ECR I–4115, para. 55.

[223] Case C–124/97 [1999] ECR I–6067. See also Case C–6/01 *Anomar* v. *Estado português* [2003] ECR I–8621.

[224] See also Case C–36/02 *Omega* [2004] ECR I–9609 discussed in Ch. 13 and Joined Cases C–94/04 and C–202/04 *Cipolla* v. *Fazari* [2006] ECR I–2049 discussed in Ch. 10; Case C–250/06 *United Pan Europe Communications* v. *Belgium* [2007] ECR I–11135. Cf. Case C–65/05 *Commission v Greece (computer games)* [2006] ECR I–10341, paras. 37–41 where the Court distinguished the *Schindler* line of case law and applied a strict proportionality test.

[225] Para. 28.          [226] Para. 29.          [227] Para. 33.

[228] Para. 42. See also Case C–42/07 *Liga Portuguesa de Futebol Profissional (CA/LPFP) v Departamento de Jogos da Santa Casa da Misericórdia de Lisboa* [2009] ECR I–000 where the Court found the Portuguese ban on operators established in other Member States from offering gambling over the Internet was also proportionate to the objective of the fight against crime.

[229] See, e.g., Case C–275/92 *Schindler* [1994] ECR I–1039, para. 32.

detected by Poiares Maduro in respect of product requirements under Article 34.[230] Another explanation is that these cases concern the situation of a service which moves but the provider and recipient do not.[231] In these cases traditional frontier controls imposed on migrants to protect the interests of the state do not function, and for this reason the Court may be more willing to allow Member States greater scope to protect their own interests. Only if the value judgments of the Member State appear manifestly unfounded will the national rule breach EU law.[232] This might help to explain why, in *Gambelli*,[233] the Court indicated that an Italian law imposing criminal penalties, including imprisonment, on private individuals in Italy who collaborated over the web with a British bookmaker to collect bets—an activity normally reserved to the Italian state monopoly CONI—was disproportionate, although the Court said it was ultimately for the national court to decide bearing in mind that betting was encouraged in the context of games organized by licensed *national* bodies[234] and that the British supplier was already regulated in the UK.[235]

Shortly after its decision in *Gambelli*, the Court ruled in *Lindman*[236] that a Finnish law, which taxed lottery wins when the lottery took place in another Member State but not when they occurred in Finland, was not appropriate to achieve the objective of preventing wrongdoing and fraud, the reduction of social damage caused by gaming, the financing of activities in the public interest and ensuring legal certainty. The Court said that the file transmitted by the referring court disclosed 'no statistical or other evidence which enables any conclusion as to the gravity of the risks connected to playing games of chance or, *a fortiori*, the existence of a particular causal relationship between such risks and participation by nationals...in lotteries organised in other Member States'.[237]

These lottery cases demonstrate a further noteworthy feature: even though the national law was apparently directly discriminatory, the Court allowed the Member States to justify the discrimination by reference to the broad public-interest requirements laid down in *Schindler*, not just the express derogations, as the orthodox jurisprudence might suggest.[238] However, the Court's case law is not consistent on this point. In the more recent decision, *Commission* v. *Spain (lottery winnings)*[239] the Court was adamant that the discriminatory Spanish rule (lottery winnings from lotteries organized in Spain were tax exempt while those from lotteries in other Member States were not) could not be saved by overriding reasons in the public interest: 'the fact remains that those [overriding reasons] cannot be relied on to justify discriminatory restrictions'.[240] It continued that such a discriminatory restriction is compatible with Union law 'only if it is covered by an express derogating

---

[230]  M. Poiares Maduro, *We the Court: The European Court of Justice and the European economic constitution* (Oxford: Hart Publishing, 1998), 68, 72ff., citing cases such as Case 178/84 *Commission* v. *Germany (Beer Purity)* [1987] ECR 1227; and Case 407/85 *3 Glocken* [1988] ECR 4233 considered in Ch. 6.

[231]  See also Case C–384/93 *Alpine Investments* [1995] ECR I–1141.

[232]  See G. Straetmans (2000) 37 *CMLRev.* 991, 1001.

[233]  Case C–243/01 *Gambelli* [2003] ECR I–13031. See also Joined Cases C–338/04, C–359/04 and C–360/04 *Placanica* [2007] ECR I–1891, para. 58. Cf. Case E–1/06 *EFTA Surveillance Authority* v. *Norway* [2007] *EFTA Ct Rep.* 8, para. 51.                                                                                      [234]  Para. 72.

[235]  Para. 73.

[236]  Case C–42/02 *Lindman* [2003] ECR I–13519.          [237]  Para. 26.

[238]  Cf. this merging of the public-interest requirements with the express derogations can also be seen in the 40th recital in the preamble of the Services Dir. considered below in Section D and the briefer definition in Art. 4(8).                                                                            [239]  Case C–153/08 [2009] ECR I–000.

[240]  Para. 36, citing *inter alia*, Case C–243/01 *Gambelli* [2003] ECR I–13031, para. 65 and Joined Cases C–338/04, C–359/04 and C–360/04 *Placanica* [2007] ECR I–1891, para. 49.

provision...namely public policy, public security or public health'.[241] Tantalizingly, the Court left open the question whether the objective of preventing money laundering and combating tax evasion could fall within the definition of public policy.[242]

---

**Case Study 11.2** BROADCASTING, ADVERTISING, AND THE FREEDOM TO PROVIDE SERVICES

The application of the rules considered above on justification and proportionality is clearly demonstrated by the case law on the compatibility with Article 56 of restrictive (primarily Dutch and Belgian) national laws regulating broadcasting, retransmission of programmes, and advertising. For example, in *Bond*[243] the Court found that a Dutch law, the *Kabelregeling*, banning advertising intended specially for the Dutch public, breached Article 56 (see fig. 11.1). Even if it could be justified on the ground of maintaining 'the non-commercial and thereby pluralistic nature' of the Dutch broadcasting system, the Court found that the ban was not proportionate because there were less restrictive ways of achieving the objective by, for example, prohibiting the advertising of certain products or on certain days and limiting the duration and frequency of advertisements.

The successor regulations to the *Kabelregeling*, the *Mediawet*, were also condemned by the Court in *Gouda*.[244] Under the *Mediawet,* only those broadcasters having a non-commercial structure could advertise. The law also imposed the limits on advertising which the Court had indicated in *Bond* would be legitimate (ie limits concerning quantity, placement, and timing). The requirement relating to non-commercial structure of broadcasters was justified by the Dutch government on the ground of cultural policy. This argument was rejected by the Court because it thought that there was no connection between cultural policy and the structure of foreign broadcasting bodies. By contrast, the Court thought that the condition relating to advertising could in principle be justified on the grounds of consumer protection and cultural policy. However, it found on the facts that the rules did operate to limit competition in advertising and so breached Article 56.

The *Mediawet also* required national broadcasting bodies to use the technical resources of the Dutch public studio to make 75 per cent of their programmes. In *Commission* v. *Netherlands*[245] the Court found that because this rule prevented or limited national broadcasters from using the services of undertakings established in other Member States it breached Article 56. Once again the Dutch government relied on a justification based on cultural policy, and again the Court rejected it on the ground of proportionality: the measure was not suitable to achieve the objective.

The result of these cases was to favour the right of the broadcaster in the transmitting state to provide services. In this respect the case law on broadcasting fits within the general principle laid down in *Säger* of home-state control: the home state primarily regulates the activities of the broadcaster transmitting from its territory. The host (receiving) state can impose controls on broadcasters from other Member States but such controls are supplementary. And, as *Bond, Gouda,* and *Commission* v.

---

[241] Para. 37.  [242] Para. 39.  [243] Case 352/85 [1988] ECR 2085.
[244] Case C–288/89 [1991] ECR I–4007.  [245] Case C–353/89 [1991] ECR I–4069, para. 23.

*Netherlands* demonstrate, in practice the Court is unwilling to accept any interference with the broadcaster's freedom to provide services by the host state.

The Court's approach is reflected in Directive 2010/13/EU, originally called the Television without Frontiers (TWF) Directive 89/552[246] and now, since 2007, the Audiovisual Media Services (AVMS) Directive. The original version of the directive was intended to secure the freedom to provide television services.[247] The 2007 amendments distinguish between linear (TV transmissions) and non-linear services (e.g., web clips). While there are certain common rules—and this is reflected in changes to the language (for example, references to 'television broadcasts are replaced by 'audiovisual media services'[248] and 'broadcasters' have become 'media service providers')—non-linear services are subject to greater self-regulation. We shall focus primarily on linear services.

The directive is based on the 'transmitting-state' principle[249] which means, according to *De Agostini*,[250] that the transmitting state has the primary responsibility for ensuring that 'media service providers' (broadcasters[251]) established in that state comply with national rules coordinated by the directive on the 'organisation and financing of broadcasts and the content of programmes'.[252]

The corollary of the transmitting-state principle is that the receiving state must allow programmes received from the transmitting state to be shown in its territory with-

---

[246] [1989] OJ L298/23. It was subsequently amended by Dir. 97/36 ([1997] OJ L202/60) in order to 'clarify certain definitions or obligations on Member States under this Directive' (3rd recital). The TWF Dir. was overhauled by EP and Council Dir. 2007/65 [2007] OJ L332/27 and renamed the Audiovisual Media Services Dir. The codified version, Dir. 2010/13/EU ([2010] OJ L 95/1), repeals the earlier Directives. See M. Burri-Nenova, 'The New Audiovisual Media Services Directive: Television *without* frontiers, television without cultural diversity' (2007) 44 *CMLRev.* 1689. For a more general discussion on harmonization in the services sector, see W. Roth, 'The European Economic Community's law on services: Harmonisation' (1988) 25 *CMLRev.* 35.          [247] Case C–412/93 *Leclerc-Siplec* [1995] ECR I–179, para. 28.

[248] Explained in Art. 1(a)(i) as 'a service as defined by Articles 56 and 57 [TFEU] which is under the editorial responsibility of a media service provider and the principal purpose of which is the provision of programmes in order to inform, entertain or educate, to the general public by electronic communications networks within the meaning of [Article 2(a)] of Directive 2002/21/EC. Such an audiovisual media service is either a television broadcast…or an on-demand audiovisual media service… A 'television broadcast' '(i.e. a linear audiovisual media service) means an audiovisual media service provided by a media service provider for simultaneous viewing of programmes on the basis of a programme schedule. An 'on-demand audiovisual media service' '(i.e. a non-linear audiovisual media service) means an audiovisual media service provided by a media service provider for the viewing of programmes at the moment chosen by the user and at his individual request on the basis of a catalogue of programmes selected by the media service provider.

[249] Art. 2(1) provides that 'Each Member State shall ensure that all audiovisual media services transmitted by media service providers under its jurisdiction comply with the rules of the system of law applicable to audiovisual media services intended for the public in that Member State.' See also Case C–11/95 *Commission v. Belgium* [1996] ECR I–4115, para. 42; Case C–14/96 *Criminal Proceedings against Paul Denuit* [1997] ECR I–2785, para. 32. In addition Art. 4(6) makes the transmitting state responsible for ensuring that the media service provider complies with the provisions of the directive.

[250] Joined Cases C–34–36/95 [1997] ECR I–3843, para. 28.

[251] See Case C–89/04 *Mediakabel BV v. Commissariaat voor de media* [2005] ECR I–4891 on the meaning of television broadcasting services.

[252] Art. 2(2)–(5) lays down the rules to determine which media service providers are under the jurisdiction of a Member State. Prior to the 1997 amendments, the Court had to grapple with the issue of a Member State's jurisdiction *ratione personae* over a broadcaster: Case C–222/94 *Commission v. UK* [1996] ECR I–4025. The 1997 directive in part codified this judgment. For more details, see L. Woods and J. Scholes, 'Broadcasting: The creation of a European culture or the limits of the internal market?' (1997) 17 *YEL* 47.

out restriction.[253] Therefore, the principle of mutual recognition underlies Directive 2010/13: a television programme legitimately broadcast in one Member State can be rebroadcast in another without restriction.[254] Even if the receiving Member State considers that the transmitting state is not exercising proper control, the receiving state cannot unilaterally adopt corrective or protective measures but must bring infringement proceedings under Article 259 TFEU (ex Article 227 EC) or request the Commission to take action under Article 258 TFEU (ex Article 226 EC).[255]

Article 3(2) lists the circumstances in which the receiving state can derogate from the rule of home-state control. It provides that if a television broadcast[256] comes from another Member State which 'manifestly, seriously and gravely' infringes Article 27 concerning programmes which might seriously impair the physical, mental, or moral development of minors[257] and/or Article 6 concerning audiovisual media services containing 'incitement to hatred based on race, sex, religion or nationality' and the broadcaster has infringed Article 27 and/or Article 6 on at least two occasions in the previous 12 months then the Member State must notify the broadcaster and the Commission. If attempts at seeking an amicable settlement fail then the receiving state can provisionally suspend retransmission until the Commission determines whether the suspension is compatible with Union law. The UK has made more use of this provision than any other Member State.[258] In particular, it banned reception of the Red Hot Dutch channel, broadcast initially via satellite from the Netherlands and then from Denmark.[259] The UK also relied on it to suspend the transmission of Eurotica Rendez-Vous by a Danish satellite television company. The Commission upheld the UK's decision as being compatible with the directive.[260]

Having concentrated on cases concerning broadcasting, we turn now to advertising[261] or 'audiovisual commercial communication'[262] as it is now called. Although the

---

[253] Art. 3(1) provides that 'Member States shall ensure freedom of reception and shall not restrict retransmissions on their territory of audivisual media services from other Member States for reasons which fall within the fields co-ordinated by this Directive.'

[254] C. Jones, 'Television without frontiers' (1999/2000) 19 YEL 299, 308.

[255] Case C–11/95 Commission v. Belgium [1996] ECR I–4115, paras. 36–7, referring to Case C–5/94 Hedley Lomas [1996] ECR I–2553, para. 20, considered in Ch. 6.

[256] Member States can derogate from on-demand audiovisual media services on the grounds of public policy, public health, public security and the protection of consumers (Art. 3(4)).

[257] See also Rec. 2006/952/EC on the protection of minors and human dignity and on the right of reply in relation to the competitiveness of the European audiovisual and on-line services industry [2006] OJ L378/72.

[258] Information in this section comes from Jones, above n. 254, 318–19.

[259] R. v. Secretary of State for National Heritage, ex p. Continental Television [1993] 3 CMLR 387 and referred to the Court in Case 327/93 Red Hot Television. The reference was removed from the register on 29 Mar. 1996 because Red Hot Dutch went bankrupt.

[260] The Commission's decision was unsuccessfully challenged under Art. 263 TFEU (ex Art. 230 EC) in Case T–69/99 Danish Satellite TV (DSTV) v. Commission [2001] ECR II–4039. The Court found that DSTV did not have locus standi since it was not directly concerned by the Act and was therefore not entitled to seek its annulment.

[261] The indirect advertising rules at issue in C–429/02 Bacardi v. Télévision Française 1 SA [2004] ECR I–6613 did not fall under the AVMS Dir. so were considered solely by reference to Art. 56 TFEU.

[262] Art. 1(h) says ' "audiovisual commercial communication" means images with or without sound which are designed to promote, directly or indirectly, the goods, services or image of a natural or legal entity

basic rules are the same (i.e., the transmitting-state principle still applies), the advertising provisions of Directive 2010/13 are more prescriptive than those on broadcasting. So while the broadcasting provisions say little about content or quality (leaving that for the Member State where the broadcaster is established), the directive does lay down a number of more detailed rules concerning the content of television advertising,[263] prescribing the conditions under which advertisements can be broadcast, prohibiting the use of certain techniques, and limiting the amount of broadcast time which can be devoted to advertising.[264]

The provisions concerning both advertising and broadcasting are minimum requirements[265] which, according to Article 4(1), means that *transmitting* states can 'require media service providers under their jurisdiction to comply with more detailed or stricter rules' in the areas covered by the directive. This is, however, subject to the free movement clause[266] contained in Article 3(1), which provides that Member States must not 'restrict retransmissions on their territory of audiovisual media services from other Member States for reasons which fall within the fields coordinated by this Directive'. Therefore in *Leclerc-Siplec*[267] a French government ban on advertising in the distribution sector was compatible with Article 4(1) of the directive,[268] since it was applied by the *transmitting* state to broadcasters under its jurisdiction and did not affect the freedom of broadcasters established in other Member States, which met the minimum requirements laid down by the directive, from providing services.[269] Although a ban seems inconsistent with the directive's express aim of facilitating the provision of services, France could legitimately impose such a rule because the directive lays down only minimum standards. Apart from the free movement clause, the only ceiling constraining Member States when enacting the stricter requirements is compatibility with the Treaty provisions, in particular Articles 34 and 56. On the facts, the Court found that

pursuing an economic activity. Such images accompany or are included in a programme in return for payment or for similar consideration or for self-promotional purposes. Forms of audiovisual commercial communication include, inter alia, television advertising, sponsorship, teleshopping and product placement.' One of the more controversial features of the revised directive is that it allows for 'product placement' in television programmes (but not news or documentaries of children's programmes, i.e. 'any form of audiovisual commercial communication consisting of the inclusion of or reference to a product, a service or the trade mark thereof so that it is featured within a programme, in return for payment or for similar consideration'. The details are set out in Art. 11.

[263] E.g., Art. 9(c) requires that audiovisual commercial communications should not prejudice respect for human dignity, be discriminatory, encourage behaviour prejudicial to health and safety or the environment; Art. 9(d) prohibits the advertising of cigarettes and other tobacco products. Art. 9(e) concerns advertisements directed at minors and Art. 9(g) provides that audiovisual commercial communications must not cause moral or physical detriment to minors by, e.g., exploiting children's inexperience, credulity, or pester power.

[264] E.g., Art. Art. 9(1)(a) and (b) requires that TV advertising and teleshopping be readily recognizable and should not use subliminal techniques (see Case C–195/06 *KommAustria* v. *ORF* [2007] ECR I–8817 on the meaning of teleshopping in the context of prize games). Art. 23 concerns the quantity of advertising permitted, and Art. 24 gives details of when advertising and teleshopping spots can be used.

[265] Minimum standards directives are considered further in Ch. 16.

[266] Free movement clauses are considered further in Ch. 16.

[267] Case C–412/93 [1995] ECR I–179.     [268] Para. 44.     [269] Para. 41.

the French rules did not breach Article 34 because they were classified as certain selling arrangements and so, following the decision in *Keck*,[270] fell outside Article 34.[271]

The relationship between Directive 2010/13 and the Treaty provisions was explored further in *De Agostini*,[272] this time concerning the rights of the *receiving* state to limit the activities of an advertiser. De Agostini, a Swedish company belonging to an Italian group, advertised a children's magazine about dinosaurs on TV3 (broadcast to Scandinavia by satellite from the UK) and on TV4 (a Swedish television station). This magazine was printed in Italy in a number of languages and it formed part of a series. With each issue came one part of a model dinosaur: children buying the whole series would have collected all parts of the model. The consumer ombudsman argued that this campaign contravened the Swedish ban on advertising aimed at children. The case was joined with *TV Shop*. TV Shop, which specialized in teleshopping, broadcast 'infomercials' for Body de Lite skincare products and the detergent Astonish on TV3 and on a Swedish home-shopping channel. This time the consumer ombudsman sought to restrain misleading advertising for these products.

The logic of Directive 2010/13 suggests that, with the exception of the derogations laid down in the directive, the receiving state (Sweden) could not limit the advertisements broadcast by an out-of-state service provider. The Court disagreed. It noted that the directive, while coordinating national provisions on television advertising and sponsorship, did so only partially.[273] It continued that while the directive provided that Member States were to ensure freedom of reception and were not to impede retransmission on grounds relating to television advertising and sponsorship (the areas which had been harmonized), 'it does not have the effect of excluding completely and automatically the application of rules other than those specifically concerning the broadcasting and distribution of programmes'[274] (the area which had not been harmonized). Therefore, the receiving state could apply its general rules on misleading advertising to television advertisements broadcast from other Member States in order to ensure the overriding interest of consumer protection.[275] They could do this provided that those national rules did not involve secondary control of television broadcasts (i.e., control additional to that which the broadcasting Member State had to carry out)[276] and did not prevent retransmission of television broadcasts coming from other Member States.[277] In response to arguments from the Commission and De Agostini that this ruling would undermine the transmitting-state principle, the Court pointed to Directive 84/450 on misleading advertising[278] (now Directive 2006/114[279]) which would be 'robbed of its substance in the field of television advertising if the receiving Member State were deprived of all possibility of adopting measures against an advertiser'.[280]

The Court then considered whether the Swedish rules breached Article 34. As we saw in Chapter 6, the Court adopted a more sophisticated analysis to its own *Keck*

---

[270] Joined Cases C–267 and 268/91 [1993] ECR I–6097, para. 16.

[271] See also Case C–6/98 *ARD* v. *PRO Sieben Media* [1999] ECR I–7599, paras. 45–8 and Joined Cases C–320, 328, 329, 337, 338, and 339/94 *RTI* v. *Ministero delle Poste e Telecomunicazioni* [1996] ECR I–6471.

[272] Joined Cases C–34–36/95 [1997] ECR I–3843. See also now the effect of the UCPD 2005/29 (OJ [2005] L149/22 discussed in Ch. 5.

[273] Para. 32.      [274] Para. 33.      [275] Para. 28.      [276] Paras. 34–5.      [277] Para. 38.

[278] [1984] OJ L250/17.      [279] [2006] OJ L376/21.

[280] Para. 37. However cf. Case C–99/01 *Gottfried Linhart* v. *Hans Biffl* [2002] ECR I–9375, para. 24.

jurisprudence than it had done in *Leclerc-Siplec*. While recognizing that a prohibition on television advertising aimed at children constituted a certain selling arrangement,[281] it found that an outright ban might have a greater impact on products from other Member States (see fig. 5.2).[282] The ban therefore breached Article 34 and needed to be justified under either a *Cassis* mandatory requirement or an Article 36 derogation.[283] The Court reached a similar conclusion in respect of Article 56 but by a different route. There was no mention of certain selling arrangements. Instead, by applying *Bond* and *Gouda*, it found that the national rules prohibiting advertising constituted a restriction on the freedom to provide services, but that a receiving state (Sweden) could take measures against an advertiser in relation to television advertising, provided that those provisions were necessary for meeting overriding requirements of general public importance or one of the Article 52 TFEU (ex Article 46 EC) derogations, and that the steps taken were proportionate. The Court then returned to the directive and its application to the ban on advertising aimed at children. It said that, given the provisions specifically devoted to the protection of minors, Sweden could no longer apply rules specifically designed to control the *content* of advertising with regard to minors. In this field, at least, harmonization is total and the principle of transmitting-state control reasserted.[284]

Leaving aside the ruling on the compatibility with the directive of a ban on advertising aimed at children, *De Agostini* produces a paradoxical result: the application of two harmonization directives and two fundamental Treaty provisions gives the green light to the Member States to *hinder* free movement in advertising.[285] Any such restrictions on advertising may infringe the freedom of expression under Article 10(1) ECHR but, as the Court pointed out in *RTL Television*[286] (a case on the interpretation of the (then) TWF Directive), the restrictions could be justified under Article 10(2). The restrictions pursued a legitimate aim involving the protection of consumers as television viewers (citing *Gouda*), as well as their interest in having access to quality programmes, and the steps taken were proportionate.

It seems that the case law before and after the TWF/AVMS directive is less different than would at first appear. This is perhaps not so surprising: as the Court made clear in *UTECA*,[287] the directive does not completely harmonize the rules relating to the areas which it covers. Nevertheless, the Member States still have to satisfy the fundamental freedoms. The case concerned a Spanish rule requiring television operators to earmark 5 per cent of their operating revenue for the pre-funding of European cinematographic films and films made for television and, more specifically, to reserve 60 per cent of that 5 per cent for the production of works of which the original language is one of the official languages of that Member State. While the Court considered that the 5 per

[281] Para. 39.

[282] Para. 42. See the more assertive statement to that effect in Case C–405/98 *Gourmet International Products (GIP)* [2001] ECR I–1795, para. 21. [283] Paras. 45–6.

[284] A. Criscuolo, 'The "TV without frontiers" Directive and the legal regulation of publicity in the European Community' (1998) 23 *ELRev.* 357, 362.

[285] Ibid., 363. Cf UCPD 2005/29 considered in Ch. 5.

[286] Case C–245/01 *RTL Television GmbH* v. *Niedersächsische Landesmedienanstalt für proviaten Rundfunk* [2003] ECR I–12489, paras. 68–74.

[287] Case C–222/07 *UTECA* v. *Administracíon General del Estado* [2009] ECR I–000, para. 19.

cent earmarking was not a restriction, the 60 per cent rule was, but could be justified on the grounds of defending and promoting Spanish multilingualism[288] and the rule was proportionate.

## 2.4 Abuse

Although the Court has done much to encourage the provision of services, it is wary of the services rules being abused by individuals who deliberately establish themselves in State A in order to provide services to customers in State B, thereby avoiding State B's more restrictive rules. It therefore said in *Commission v. Germany (insurance cases)*[289] that a host state (State B) was allowed to take measures to prevent a person from directing its activity entirely or principally towards its territory, but doing so by services rather than establishment simply to avoid the professional rules of conduct which would be applicable to him had he been established in State B. The Court said that such a situation would be subject to judicial control under the provisions on establishment rather than on services.

As we saw in Case Study 11.2 above, the Netherlands, with its restrictive broadcasting laws, has been particularly affected by attempts to avoid its rules, with Dutch companies setting up commercial stations in Luxembourg and, relying on the services provisions, using the Luxembourg station to broadcast programmes back to the Netherlands. The Dutch government passed a law prohibiting broadcasting organizations established in the Netherlands from investing in a broadcasting company established in another Member State which provided services directed towards the Netherlands. In *Veronica*[290] the Court said that such a rule did not breach Article 56 where it had the specific effect of ensuring that those organizations could not improperly evade the obligations deriving from the national legislation concerning the pluralistic and non-commercial content of those programmes.[291] It reached a similar conclusion in *TV10*[292] where it said that a Member State (the Netherlands) could regard as a domestic broadcaster a radio and television organization which established itself in another Member State (Luxembourg) in order to provide services which were intended for Dutch territory. The Court said that the aim of the measure was to prevent organizations which established themselves in another Member State from being able, by exercising the freedoms guaranteed by the Treaties, wrongfully to avoid obligations under national law, in this case those designed to ensure the pluralist and non-commercial content of programmes. However, the *TV10* approach did differ in one respect from that in *Veronica* because the Court seemed to have classified the principle of abuse as a ground for justifying restrictions on the

---

[288] Paras. 26–7. For a similarly benign approach to Member State rules, see Case C–250/06 *United Pan-Europe Communications Belgium SA v. Etat belge* [2007] ECR I–11135.

[289] Case 205/94 [1986] ECR 3755, para. 22, reaffirming Case 33/74 *Van Binsbergen* [1974] ECR 1299, para. 13.

[290] Case C–148/91 *Vereniging Veronica Omroep Organisatie v. Commissariaat voor de Media* [1993] ECR I–487.

[291] Para. 13.

[292] Case C–23/93 *TV10 SA v. Commissariaat voor de Media* [1994] ECR I–4795 and the note by P. Wattel (1995) 32 *CMLRev.* 1257.

freedom to provide services, and no longer as a ground for precluding the Treaties' application.[293]

However, in *VT4*[294] the Court appeared to backtrack. VT4, a broadcaster established in the UK, made programmes aimed at the Flemish public and transmitted the signals from the UK to Belgium. The Belgian authorities thought VT4 had been established in the UK merely to circumvent the application of Flemish law. The Court said that just because all the broadcasts and advertisements were aimed at the Flemish public did not mean that VT4 could not be regarded as being established in the UK. Without referring to either *Veronica* or *TV10,* it continued that the Treaties did not 'prohibit an undertaking from exercising the freedom to provide services if it does not offer services in the Member State in which it is established'.[295] Therefore the pendulum seems to have swung back towards the Court's original stance supporting those wishing to provide services, a change which coincided with the adoption of the TWF/AVMS Directive which laid down criteria for determining in which state a broadcaster was established.[296] As *Centros*[297] subsequently confirmed, there is nothing abusive about simply taking advantage of the Treaty provisions on free movement.[298]

## 3. THE EXERCISE OF SERVICE ACTIVITY

### 3.1 Social Advantages

Having looked at rules which prevent or impede initial *access* to the services market in another Member State, we turn now to consider rules which impede the actual performance of, or the receipt of, a service in the host state. In the absence of provisions equivalent to Article 7(1)–(2) of Regulation 1612/68 on workers, the Court has read Article 56 so as to require equal treatment in respect of the terms and conditions on which the service is provided or received and equal treatment in respect of social and tax advantages. We begin by considering social advantages.

In *Cowan*[299] a British tourist had been attacked and robbed outside a *métro* station in Paris. He was refused criminal injuries compensation because he was neither a French national nor was he resident in France. The Court said that when Union law guarantees a person the right to go to another Member State, the corollary of the right is that the individual be protected from harm on the same basis as nationals and persons residing there. Consequently, the principle of non-discrimination applied to recipients of services, even where the compensation was financed by the treasury.[300]

---

[293] D. Doukas, 'Free movement of broadcasting services and abuse of law' in R. de la Feria and S. Vogenauer (eds.), *Prohibition on Abuse of Law* (Oxford: Hart Publishing, forthcoming).

[294] Case C–56/96 *VT4 Ltd* v. *Vlaamse Gemeenschap* [1997] ECR I–3143.          [295] Para. 22.

[296] See Art. 2 of Dir. 2010/13.

[297] Case C–212/97 *Centros* [1999] ECR I–1459 considered in Ch. 10.

[298] For a full discussion, see A. Kjellgren, 'On the border of abuse: The jurisprudence of the European Court of Justice on circumvention, fraud and abuses of Community law' in Andenas and Roth (eds.), above n. 193.

[299] Case 186/87 *Cowan* v. *Le Trésor Public* [1989] ECR 195. See also Case 63/86 *Commission* v. *Italy (social housing)* [1988] ECR 29, para. 19 and Case C–484/93 *Svensson* [1995] ECR I–3955.

[300] Para. 17. In a similar vein, see Case C–164/07 *Wood* v. *Fonds de garantie des victimes des actes de terrorisme et d'autres infractions* [2008] ECR I–4143. Cf. Case C–109/92 *Wirth* [1993] ECR I–6447 considered above, n. 106.

For similar reasons, in *Commission v. Spain (museums)*[301] the Court condemned a Spanish law providing for free admission to state museums for Spanish nationals and foreigners resident in Spain but not to tourists. The Commission pointed out that since visiting museums encourages tourists, as recipients of services, to go to another Member State, there was a close link between freedom of movement and museum admission. The Court found that the Spanish rules breached both Article 18 TFEU (ex Article 12 EC) and Article 56 TFEU.[302]

### 3.2 Tax Advantages

#### (a) The provision of services

Initially, the Court applied the equal treatment model to taxation. This can be seen in *De Coster*[303] where a Belgian tax on satellite dishes encouraged subscribers to receive their programmes by cable instead (no tax was levied on cable). Because Belgian distributors had unlimited access to cable distribution,[304] the Court found that this rule had a particular impact on broadcasters established in other Member States which could be received only by satellite.[305] The tax therefore breached Article 56 and could not be justified.[306]

However, as we have seen elsewhere, the Court subsequently moved away from the discrimination model and applied the restrictions approach. For example, in *Sea-Land Service*[307] the Dutch authorities levied a tariff to cover the cost of navigation services charged on sea-going vessels but not on inland waterway vessels. Sea-Land argued that the tariff was indirectly discriminatory because the majority of those operating inland waterway vessels were Dutch. The Court found that while there was no discrimination because the two means of transport were not comparable, the tariff imposed on sea-going vessels was liable to 'impede or render less attractive' the provision of those services and so breached Article 56.[308] However, it ruled that the tariff could be justified on the ground of public security provided there was a correlation between the amount of the tariff and the cost of the service from which the sea-going vessels benefit.

The facts of this case highlight the problem of applying the restrictions model to taxation. What is the impediment to out-of-state actors? It is the actual payment of the tax. While no one likes paying tax, if all sea-going vessels have to pay it, there is no particular impediment for the out-of-state vessel. The Court appears to have seen the force of this argument in *Viacom II*[309] and *Mobistar*[310] which suggest a return to a non-discrimination approach, at least in the field of tax (see fig. 8.2). In *Mobistar* the Court found that a munici-

---

[301] Case C–45/93 [1994] ECR I–911; Case C–388/01 *Commission v. Italy* [2003] ECR I–721, para. 12.

[302] See also Case C–20/92 *Hubbard v. Hamburger* [1993] ECR I–3777, para. 14.

[303] Case C–17/00 *François De Coster v. Collège des bourgmestre et échevins de Watermael-Boitsfort* [2001] ECR I–9445.

[304] Para. 31.          [305] Para. 35.

[306] See also Case C–169/08 *Presidente del Consiglio dei Ministri v. Regione Sardegna* [2009] ECR I–000.

[307] Joined Cases C–430 and 431/99 *Inspecteur van de Belastingdienst Douane, district Rotterdam v. Sea-Land Service Inc. and Nedlloyd Lijnen BV* [2002] ECR I–5235, para. 32.

[308] Para. 32. See also Case C–345/04 *Centro Equestre da Lezíria Grande v. Bundesamt für Finanzen* [2007] ECR I–1425, para. 29.

[309] Case C–134/03 [2005] ECR I–1167. See also Case C–222/07 *UTECA v. Administración General del Estado* [2009] ECR I–1407, para. 22.

[310] Joined cases C–544/03 and C–545/03 *Mobistar v. Commue de Fléron* [2005] ECR I–7723. Cf. Case C–17/00 *De Coster* [2001] ECR I–9445.

pal tax on transmission pylons, masts, and antennae for GSM, which applied 'without distinction to national providers of services and to those of other Member States and affects in the same way the provision of services within one Member State and the provision of services between Member States', did not breach Article 56.[311] In *Viacom II*[312] the Court found that a municipal tax on outdoor advertising, applied on a non-discriminatory basis and fixed at a level considered 'modest in relation to the value of the services provided' did not breach Article 56 since 'the levying of such a tax is not on any view liable to prohibit, impede or otherwise make less attractive the provision of advertising services to be carried out in the territory of the municipalities concerned'.[313]

### (b) Receipt of services

Most of the cases considered so far concern national rules which are intended to discourage service *providers* of other Member States from exercising their rights in the host state. Yet, there is also a group of cases concerning national rules, often concerning tax, intended to discourage potential national service *recipients* from receiving that service in another state. When considering the validity of these rules the Court often uses the language of discrimination. For example, in *Bent Vestergaard*[314] Danish tax law distinguished between professional training courses held at tourist resorts in other Member States and those taking place in Denmark. While Danish law presumed that courses held abroad were an excuse for a holiday, with the result that the costs were not tax-deductible, it did not apply the same presumption to courses held in Denmark. The Court found that such a rule involved an unjustifiable difference in treatment based on the place where the service was provided and therefore breached Article 56.[315] Similarly, in *Laboratoires Fournier*[316] the Court said that French law restricting the benefit of a tax credit only to research carried out in France, differentiated according to the place where the services were provided, contrary to Article 56. In other cases the Court says that national rules making the provision of services between Member States more difficult than the provision of services within just one Member State[317] also breach Article 56.[318]

While the language used in all these cases carries overtones of direct discrimination, the Court in fact seems to regard such rules as impeding, deterring[319] or constituting a restriction on[320] the exercise of the freedom to receive services[321] which can then be

---

[311] Para. 35.          [312] Case C–134/03 [2005] ECR I–1167.          [313] Paras. 37–8.

[314] Case C–55/98 *Skatteministeriet v. Bent Vestergaard* [1999] ECR I–7641.          [315] Para. 22.

[316] Case C–39/04 *Laboratoires Fournier SA v. Direction des verifications nationales et internationales* [2005] ECR I–2057, para. 15. See also Case C–150/04 *Commission v. Denmark (insurance)* [2007] ECR I–1163, para. 42 where the Court used the language of dissuasion.

[317] Case C–158/96 *Kohll* [1998] ECR I–1931, para. 33. See also Case C–381/93 *Commission v. France (maritime services)* [1994] ECR I–5154, para. 17; Case C–136/00 *Danner* [2002] ECR I–8147, para. 29; Case C–118/96 *Safir* [1998] ECR I–1897, para. 23; Case C–17/00 *De Coster* [2001] ECR I–9445, para. 30; Case C–422/01 *Försäkringsaktiebolaget Skandia (publ), Ola Ramstedt v. Riksskatteverket* [2003] ECR I–6817, para. 26;

[318] However, where the rules do not have the effect of making the provision of services more difficult between states than those offered purely within one Member State there is no breach of Art. 56: Case C–8/02 *Leichtle v. Bundesanstalt für Arbeit* [2004] ECR I–2641, para. 37; Case C–281/06 *Jundt* [2007] ECR I–12231, para. 52.

[319] Cases C–76/05 and C–318/05 *Schwarz and Gootjes-Schwarz v Finanzamt Bergisch Gladbach* [2007] ECR I–6847, para. 66.          [320] Case C–281/06 *Jundt* [2007] ECR I–12231, para. 55.

[321] See Case C–118/96 *Safir* [1998] ECR I–1897, paras. 25 and 30; Case C–290/04 *Scorpio* [2006] ECR I–9461, para. 33. See also the discussion of Case C–109/04 *Kranemann* [2005] ECR I–2421 in Ch. 8.

justified not only by the express derogations laid down in the Treaties but also by the broader public-interest requirements. This can be seen in *Skandia*[322] concerning Swedish rules which treated an occupational pension insurance policy taken out by a Swedish company with an out-of-state insurer less favourably than if the policy had been taken out with a Swedish company. The Court said that in view of the disadvantage to the employer in financial terms in the postponement of the right to deduction until the time the pension benefits were paid to the employee, the Swedish rules were 'liable both to dissuade Swedish employers from taking out occupational pension insurance with institutions established in other Member States and 'to dissuade those institutions from offering their services on the Swedish market'.[323] The rules breached Article 56 and could not be justified.

The approach, which looks to see whether the national rule under challenge has the effect of making the provision of services between Member States more difficult than the provision of services purely within one Member State, is the mainstay of the healthcare cases which we now consider.[324]

### 3.3 The Healthcare Cases

### (a) Introduction

Healthcare has traditionally been provided on a territorial basis. Patients contribute to a national system either through taxation or by paying premiums into an insurance scheme. In return, healthcare is available from a locally based provider. The only express provision made originally by Union law for treatment in other Member States was the Social Security Regulation 1408/71,[325] Article 22(1) required the home state (State A) to meet bills incurred by State A patients while in the host state (State B) in two situations: first, where they needed emergency medical treatment using what was the form E111 and now the European Health Insurance Card;[326] and, secondly, where they have been expressly authorized to receive non-emergency treatment in State B using the E112 form.[327] In respect of the second situation, Article 22(2) explained that authorization could not be refused where the treatment was among the benefits provided for in

---

[322] C–422/01 *Skandia* [2003] ECR I–6817. [323] Para. 28.

[324] See, e.g., Case C–158/96 *Kohll* [1998] ECR I–1931, para. 35; Case C–157/99 *Geraets-Smits and Peerbooms* [2001] ECR I–5473, para. 69.

[325] Consolidated version [1997] OJ L28/1.

[326] Art. 22(1)(a). See also Communication from the Commission concerning the introduction of a European health insurance card (COM(2003) 73 final), and its adoption by Commission Dec. 189/03 [2003] OJ L276/1. There was also special provision for pensioners and members of their families when they require treatment abroad in Art. 31 of Reg. 1408/71 (Case C–326/00 *Idryma Koinonikon Asfaliseon (IKA)* v. *Vasilios Ioannidis* [2003] ECR I–1703). However, Reg. 1408/71 itself has now been amended to bring the entitlements of the rights of other patients more closely into line with the rights of these pensioner patients (see Reg. 631/2004/EC [2004] OJ L 100/1). So all patients are now entitled, during a stay in another Member State for a reason other than the receipt of the treatment, to treatment 'which become[s] necessary on medical grounds during a stay in the territory of another Member State/the Member State other than the State of residence, taking into account the nature of the benefits and the expected length of the stay'.

[327] Art. 22(1)(c). Where authorization has been granted, concerns about the planning and organization of hospital care cannot be invoked by the competent state: Case C–145/03 *Heirs of Annette Keller* v. *INSS* [2005] ECR I–2529, para. 62. Case C–466/04 *Acereda Herrera* v. *Servicio Cántabro de Salud* [2006] ECR I–5431 added that authorization does not entitle the patient or any accompanying person to be reimbursed for costs of travel, accommodation, and subsistence when in the host state except for the costs of accommodation and meals in hospital.

State A[328] and where the patient could not be given the treatment within the time normally necessary for obtaining the treatment in State A,[329] taking into account the patient's current state of health and the probable course of the disease. If the costs of the treatment in State B were higher than those in State A, then the relevant body in State A had to meet those additional costs where authorization was granted.[330] However, Article 22(2) put the funder of the healthcare, and not the patient, in charge of the decision whether to authorize treatment abroad and, in the past, such authorizations were relatively rare.[331] Under Regulation 883/04,[332] which replaced Regulation 1408/71 from March 2010, emergency health treatment is provided under Article 19(1), travel for the purpose of receiving treatment is covered by Article 20 which still requires authorization.

How do Articles 56–7 TFEU fit into this framework?[333] Their relevance first became apparent in *Luisi and Carbone*[334] and *SPUC* v. *Grogan*[335] which showed that EU nationals could in principle travel to another Member State to receive medical treatment because medical services constituted 'services' within the meaning of Article 57. But who pays for the treatment? If patients cannot get the treatment they want within a reasonable time at home, can they be treated in another Member State and then, under Articles 56–7, expect their own Member State to foot the bill? If so, Union law would pose a considerable threat to careful planning for comprehensive healthcare provision at national level. The easiest way of avoiding such problems would have been for the Court to say that Union law did not apply to national healthcare provision since healthcare did not constitute an economic activity. However, as we have already seen, the Court rejected this approach[336] and said that Articles 56–7 did apply to healthcare. Instead, it has used the public-interest requirements to reconcile the individual's right to travel in order to receive treatment in another Member State with the home state's duty to provide adequate healthcare to the population as a whole.

## (b) *Kohll* and *Decker*: Opening up the market

This process of reconciliation began with *Kohll*,[337] which concerned the Luxembourg healthcare system according to which medical services were offered on a reimbursement basis. The insurance rules permitted treatment to be received in other Member States

---

[328] This limitation was upheld in Case C–157/99 *Geraets-Smits and Peerbooms* [2001] ECR I–5473, para. 45.

[329] This requirement was interpreted in Case C–372/04 *Watts* v. *Bedford Primary Care Trust* [2006] ECR I–4325 to mean whether the hospital treatment required by the patient's medical condition could be provided in the home state within 'an acceptable time which ensures its usefulness and efficiency'.

[330] Art. 36 of Reg. 1408/71.

[331] For a full discussion, see T. Hervey, 'The current legal framework on the right to seek health care abroad in the European Union' (2006–7) 9 *CYELS* 261. She emphasizes that individual authorized treatment differs from block purchasing agreements, for which the High Level Group on Health Services and Medical Care has drafted the 2005 EU Guidelines for Purchase of Treatment Abroad.

[332] [2004] OJ L166/1.

[333] A useful summary of the implications of the cases considered below can be found in T. Hervey and L. Trubek, 'Freedom to provide healthcare services in the EU: An opportunity for "hybrid governance"' (2007) 13 *Columbia Journal of European Law* 623, 631–4.

[334] Joined Cases 286/82 and 26/83 [1984] ECR 377, above n. 24.

[335] Case C–159/90 [1991] ECR I–4685 above n. 51.

[336] Case C–157/99 [2001] ECR I–5473, paras. 52–9.

[337] Case C–158/96 [1998] ECR I–1931. Cf. Case C–120/95 *Decker* v. *Caisse de maladie des employés privés* [1998] ECR I–1831 (on goods) in which no prior authorization was sought.

but required prior authorization from the sickness fund which was meeting the cost. No requirement for prior authorization was imposed in respect of treatment received domestically. When Kohll's daughter was refused permission to receive orthodontic treatment in Germany he argued that the Luxembourg rules breached Article 56. In principle the Court agreed, arguing that because the rules had the effect of making the provision of services between Member States more difficult than the provision of services purely within one Member State,[338] they breached Article 56 unless they could be justified.

The Luxembourg authorities put forward two justifications for the authorization requirement: first, that it constituted the only effective and least restrictive means of controlling expenditure on health and balancing the budget of the social security system. While the Court accepted this argument in principle,[339] it rejected it on the facts. Because Kohll sought reimbursement for the treatment in Germany at the same rate that applied in Luxembourg and according to the tariff laid down by the insurance scheme, there was no significant effect on the financing of healthcare or the social security scheme.[340]

Secondly, Luxembourg argued that the rule could be justified on public-health grounds in order to ensure both the quality of the medical treatment and a balanced medical and hospital service open to all. Once again, the Court accepted the argument in principle, but rejected it on the facts. It said that since the conditions for taking up and pursuing the professions of doctor and dentist had been the subject of several coordinating and harmonizing directives, Luxembourg could not raise such public-health concerns.[341] It also said that Luxembourg had failed to produce any evidence showing that the rules were indispensable for the maintenance of an essential treatment facility or medical service in Luxembourg. Since the rules could not be justified, the authorization requirement breached Articles 56–7, despite the fact that Article 22(2) of Regulation 1408/71 expressly envisaged prior authorization.[342]

*Kohll* therefore suggested that Articles 56–7 were able to reshape the contours of Article 22 (now Article 20). The importance of what the Treaty provisions could achieve was again seen in *Vanbraekel*.[343] In that case prior authorization was wrongfully withheld from a patient insured in Belgium who had received treatment in France. The question raised was at what level the reimbursement should be made—according to the higher tariffs payable if the treatment had been provided in Belgium or the lower tariffs payable if the treatment was received abroad. Article 56 was used to fill the gap. The Court noted that if a patient had a lower level of cover when receiving hospital treatment in another Member State (France) than when undergoing the same treatment in the state where he was insured (Belgium), this could 'deter, or even prevent, that person from applying to providers of medical services established in other Member States and constitutes, both for insured persons and service providers, a barrier to freedom to provide services'.[344] The Court also rejected the justifications put forward by the Belgian government. It said that reimbursement of the higher amount which would have been payable had the treatment been carried out in Belgium neither jeopardized a balanced medical and hospital service open to all nor had a significant effect on the functioning

---

[338] Para. 33.     [339] Para. 41.     [340] Paras. 40 and 42.     [341] Paras. 47–9.

[342] In Case C–56/01 *Patricia Inizan v. Caisse primaire d'assurance maladie des Hauts-de-Seine* [2003] ECR I–12403, para. 26, the Court nevertheless still found Art. 22(2) to be valid.

[343] Case C–368/98 [2001] ECR I–5363.     [344] Para. 45.

of the social security scheme.[345] Article 56 therefore required reimbursement at the higher rate.

*Kohll* and the related case *Decker*, on goods, created 'lively' reactions in the healthcare world[346] because they suggested that in respect of non-hospital (extramural) care, a prior authorization requirement could not be justified, with the result that patients (as opposed to the healthcare service or sickness funds) could demand treatment in other Member States and be reimbursed for the costs of that treatment. As Van der Mei put it, reimbursement of the costs of cross-border healthcare no longer seemed a rarely granted privilege but a judicially enforceable right.[347] However, *Decker* and *Kohll* left open two questions: first, whether the same rules applied to hospital (intramural) healthcare and, secondly, whether the principles laid down in those cases applied to a system based on benefits in kind rather than on reimbursement. These questions were considered by *Geraets-Smits and Peerbooms*[348] and *Müller-Fauré and van Riet*.[349]

### (c) Intramural care

Both cases concerned the Dutch healthcare system, which is funded through a sickness insurance scheme. Unlike the Luxembourg scheme which provides a right for the insured to be reimbursed for medical bills paid to providers, the Dutch scheme provides benefits in kind. This means that the sickness funds enter into agreements with (local) healthcare providers (usually hospitals in the Netherlands)[350] and the insured patient must go to one of the contracted providers for treatment. Unlike the Luxembourg system, the patient does not pay and then get reimbursed. Instead, the contracted providers are paid directly by the sickness funds.[351]

While the basic rule was that patients receive treatment from contracted providers, the Dutch sickness funds did authorize treatment from non-contracted providers (both at home and abroad) on two conditions: first, that the treatment was 'normal in the professional circles concerned' and, secondly, that the treatment by the non-contractual provider was necessary for the patient, having first assessed the treatment available in the Netherlands, and whether it could be obtained without undue delay. The compatibility of these conditions with Union law was at issue in two Dutch cases: *Geraets-Smits and Peerbooms* which largely concerned the question of the availability of the treatment, and *Müller-Fauré and van Riet* concerning undue delay.[352]

Mrs Geraets-Smits, a Dutch national suffering from Parkinson's disease, sought reimbursement for the costs of her medical treatment in Germany which she claimed was better than that provided in the Netherlands. Mr Peerbooms, a Dutch national in a persistent vegetative state, was transferred to Austria for neurostimulation treatment. He could not have obtained this treatment in the Netherlands where the technique was used only experimentally. In both cases reimbursement was refused on the ground that satisfactory and adequate treatment was available in the Netherlands.

---

[345] Paras. 51–2.

[346] W. Palm, et al., *Implications of Recent Jurisprudence on the Co-ordination of Health Care Protection Systems* (Brussels: Association Internationale de la Mutualité, 2000).

[347] A. P. van der Mei, 'Cross-border access to health care within the European Union: Some reflections on *Geraets-Smits and Peerbooms* and *Vanbraekel*' (2002) 9 *MJ* 189.

[348] Case C–157/99 [2001] ECR I–5473.      [349] Case C–385/99 *Müller-Fauré* [2003] ECR I–4509.

[350] Para. 66.      [351] See C–385/99 *Müller-Fauré* [2003] ECR I–4509, para. 105.

[352] E. Spaventa, 'Public services and European Law: Looking for boundaries' (2003) 6 *CYELS* 271.

The Court found that the prior-authorization rules laid down by the insurance schemes for treatment by non-contracted providers 'deter, or even prevent, insured persons from applying to providers of medical services established in another Member State and constitute, both for insured persons and service providers, a barrier to freedom to provide services'.[353] In principle the rules therefore breached Article 56.

The Court then considered the justifications for the authorization requirement. It noted that the Dutch system was planned to ensure sufficient and permanent access to a balanced range of high-quality hospital treatment (i.e., by establishing and equipping an appropriate number of hospitals evenly distributed throughout the country)[354] while at the same time trying to control costs and prevent wastage of financial, technical, and human resources.[355] Allowing patients to go to any non-contracted hospital would jeopardize this careful planning at a stroke.[356] For these reasons the Court found that a system of prior authorization for intramural care was in principle 'both necessary and reasonable' on public-health grounds in order to guarantee a 'rationalised, stable, balanced and accessible supply of hospital services'[357] provided that the conditions under which the authorization was granted—both substantively and procedurally—could themselves be justified.[358]

Looking first at the *procedural* conditions,[359] the Court said that these could be justified provided the procedural system was easily accessible for patients; that the decision whether to grant authorization was based on objective, non-discriminatory, and pre-determined criteria; that the request was dealt with objectively and impartially and within a reasonable time; and that refusals to grant authorization were capable of being challenged in judicial or quasi-judicial proceedings.[360]

The Court then turned to the *substantive* conditions for attaining authorization, beginning with the requirement that the treatment had to be 'normal in the professional circles concerned'. It found this to be justified provided it took account of what was sufficiently tried and tested[361] by *international* science (as opposed to simply national science which would tend to favour national treatment).[362] The Court thought that the second condition, necessity of the proposed treatment, could also be justified on grounds both of public health and of ensuring the financial stability of the sickness insurance system,[363] provided that the condition was construed as meaning that authorization to receive treatment in another Member State could be refused only if the same or equally effective treatment could be obtained without undue delay from a contracted provider in the home state.[364] The Court recognized that if contracted providers were not given priority, this would put at risk the very principle of having contractual arrangements with hospitals and so

---

[353] Para. 69. Cf. Case C–444/05 *Stamatelaki* v. *OAEE* [2007] ECR I–3185 (total ban on treatment abroad breached Art. 56).                                                                                   [354] Para. 76.

[355] Paras. 78–9. All this at a time when the healthcare sector has to satisfy increasing needs with limited funding.                                       [356] Case C–385/99 *Müller-Fauré* [2003] ECR I–4509, para. 82.

[357] Paras. 80–1.           [358] As elaborated by Case C–385/99 *Müller-Fauré* [2003] ECR I–4509, para. 66.

[359] On the importance of the procedural requirements, see Case C–205/99 *Analir* [2001] ECR I–1271, paras. 37–8.                                                                                                [360] Para. 90.

[361] I.e., the authorities must take into consideration all the relevant available information, e.g. existing scientific literature and studies, the authorized opinions of specialists, and whether the proposed treatment is covered by the sickness insurance system of the Member State in which the treatment is provided (para. 98).                                                                                          [362] Para. 97.

[363] Paras. 105–6.          [364] Para. 104.

'undermine all the planning and rationalisation carried out in this vital sector'.[365] Thus, while rejecting the territorial nature of healthcare services, the Court did recognize the value of a 'closed' system based on a number of contracted providers.[366]

However, when considering whether the treatment could be granted without undue delay from a contracted provider, the Court said that the national authorities had to consider all the circumstances of each specific case, taking into account both the patient's medical history and condition and the degree of pain or the nature of the patient's disability which might make it impossible or extremely difficult for the patient to carry out a professional activity.[367] This subjective approach, based on the individual patient's state of health, means that a state cannot refuse permission for treatment abroad simply because it would mean that the patient would jump the waiting list. Therefore, in *Van Riet* the Dutch sickness fund could not refuse to pay for Mrs van Riet's treatment (an arthroscopy) in Belgium where it was available much sooner than in the Netherlands simply because appropriate treatment was available in the Netherlands without undue delay. In deciding whether to authorize treatment the fund had to take into account Mrs van Riet's medical condition and medical history (she had been suffering pain for eight years).

### (d) Extramural care

The cases we have considered so far (*Geraets-Smits and Peerbooms* and *Van Riet*) concerned hospital services. We turn now to non-hospital services which were considered in *Müller-Fauré*. While on holiday in Germany, Müller-Fauré underwent major dental treatment. When the Dutch sickness fund refused to reimburse her because she had not received prior authorization for the treatment, she argued that this requirement breached Article 56. The Court agreed, but this time found no justification for the authorization rule. It said that no evidence had been produced to show that if patients were allowed to travel to another Member State for non-hospital treatment without authorization, this would seriously undermine the financial balance of the Dutch scheme.[368] As the Court noted, care is generally provided near the patient's residence, in a cultural environment familiar to the patient, and allows a relationship of trust to build up with the treating doctor.[369] For these reasons the Court anticipated that the numbers taking advantage of the possibility of (non-hospital) treatment in other Member States would be small due to the barriers of language, geography, the cost of staying abroad, and the lack of information about the care provided there.[370]

However, the Court did add an important caveat to its ruling, which it had already mentioned in *Kohll*[371] and *Decker*:[372] patients from State A travelling to State B for extramural treatment but without prior authorization could claim reimbursement of the treatment cost, but only within the limits of the cover provided by the sickness insurance scheme in State A[373] (rather than for all expenses incurred, which would be the case under Article 22 of Regulation 1408/71). The Court also said that State A could impose other conditions on reimbursement in so far as they were neither discriminatory nor an

---

[365] Para. 106. The Court added that if the contracted provider could not provide the treatment, the sickness fund could not give priority to a non-contracted national provider (para. 107).

[366] Van der Mei, above n. 118, 201.    [367] C–385/99 *Müller-Fauré* [2003] ECR I–4509, para. 90.

[368] Para. 93.    [369] Para. 96.    [370] Para. 95.    [371] Para. 42.    [372] Para. 40.

[373] Paras. 98 and 106.

obstacle to free movement (e.g., requiring that a GP should refer a patient to a specialist consultant).[374]

This case law tells us that medical services fall within the scope of Articles 56–7. Prior authorization requirements in principle breach Article 56 but are likely to be justified for intramural care (where there seems to be a presumption of legality) but not for extramural care (where there seems to be a presumption of illegality)[375] or (possibly) for systems based on reimbursement (following *Kohll*).[376] This largely institutional distinction between intra- and extramural care creates a number of difficulties. Does it turn on the physical location of the treatment (GP's surgery or hospital out-patient department) or the type of treatment (minor or major surgery)?[377] Cross-border access to *hospital* care, therefore, remains governed by Regulation 1408/71 and now Regulation 883/04, but insured persons may be entitled to get authorization in a greater number of cases than the few falling within the ambit of Article 22(2) of Regulation 1408/71.[378] For example, following *Van Riet* account should be taken not only of the patient's current state of health (as required by Article 22(2)) but also the past medical record. And, in respect of waiting lists, account should not just be taken of 'the time normally necessary' for the treatment in State A but consideration must also be given to 'all circumstances of each specific case', which may include the circumstances of the patient[379] as well as a more objective reading of what constitutes a 'normal' waiting time.[380] It therefore seems that Article 56 TFEU and Article 22 of Regulation 1408/71 run in parallel.[381]

### (e) Application of these principles to the British NHS

The parallelism between Article 56 and the Regulation is supported by *Watts*,[382] a case concerning the British National Health Service (NHS), where care is basically free at the point of delivery but paid for out of taxation. Watts suffered from severe arthritis of the hips but was told in October 2002 that, since her case was 'routine', there would be a one-year wait for surgery. She therefore applied to the Bedford Primary Care Trust (PCT) for authorization to undergo surgery abroad under the E112 scheme but this was refused, on the ground that treatment could be provided to the patient 'within the Government's NHS Plan targets' and so 'without undue delay'. She therefore sought judicial review of the PCT's decision. Subsequently, her health deteriorated and she was re-examined in January 2003 when she was listed for surgery within three or four months. Although Bedford PCT repeated its refusal to issue an E112, in March 2003 Mrs Watts nevertheless underwent a hip replacement operation in France for which she paid £3,900. She continued with her judicial review application, claiming in addition reimbursement of the medical fees incurred in France, but her application was dismissed on the ground that she had not had to face undue delay after the re-examination of her case in January 2003. The Court of Appeal referred the matter to the Court of Justice.

---

[374] Para. 106.      [375] Van der Mei, above n. 118, 200.

[376] P. Cabral, 'The internal market and the right to choose cross border medical care' (2004) 29 *ELRev.* 673, 686.

[377] E. Steyger, 'National health systems under fire (but not too heavily)' (2002) 29 *LIEI* 97, 106.

[378] Van der Mei, above, n. 118, 200 and 206.

[379] See G. Davies, 'Medical treatment abroad' (2003) 153 *NLJ* 938, 939.

[380] See also Case C–385/99 *Müller-Fauré* [2003] ECR I–4509, para. 92.

[381] See Ruiz-Jarabo Colomer AG's Opinion in Case C–56/01 *Inizan* [2003] ECR I–12403.

[382] Case C–372/04 *Watts* v. *Bedford Primary Care Trust* [2006] ECR I–4325.

In *Watts* the Court was less concerned with the Article 56 aspect of the case than with the application of the Regulation. It said that, in order to be entitled to refuse authorization on the ground of waiting time, the competent institution (essentially the PCT) had to establish that:

the waiting time, arising from objectives relating to the planning and management of the supply of hospital care...does not exceed the period which is acceptable in the light of an objective medical assessment of the clinical needs of the person concerned in the light of his medical condition and the history and probable course of his illness, the degree of pain he is in and/or the nature of his disability at the time when the authorization is sought.[383]

It adopted a similar approach under Article 56.[384] Furthermore, it added, the setting of waiting times should be done 'flexibly and dynamically', so that the period initially notified to the person concerned could be reconsidered in the light of any deterioration in the patient's state of health occurring after the first request for authorization. For good measure it added that Article 56 required the UK to reimburse Mrs Watts' travel and accommodation costs where it would have reimbursed those costs had the travel occurred in the UK.

*Watts* shows that the Court's case law in the Dutch and Luxembourg cases applies to public systems such as the British NHS even though there is no mechanism for reimbursement in a non-insurance-based system such as the UK's. It also shows that the UK practice of the blanket use of waiting lists as a way of managing limited NHS resources cannot be justified if account is not taken of the individual circumstances of the applicant. *Watts* also means that the NHS regulations will have to set out the criteria for the granting or refusal of prior authorization necessary for reimbursement of the cost of hospital treatment provided in another Member State, in order to circumscribe the exercise of the national competent authorities' discretionary power and permit effective judicial review of decisions refusing to grant authorization.

While cases like *Geraets-Smits and Peerbooms* may not have revolutionized the cross-border provision of intramural care, they have certainly raised awareness, at least in the UK, of the possibility of using foreign hospitals to cut waiting lists. When *Geraets-Smits and Peerbooms* was decided, there were about a million people waiting for surgery on the NHS and more than 200,000 had been waiting at least six months.[385] The Labour government had committed itself to reducing that number to zero. Less than six months after *Geraets-Smits and Peerbooms*, the first group of British patients who had been waiting for surgery for over a year travelled by Eurostar to France for hip and knee replacements and cataract operations.[386] Although the Department of Health based its decision on *Geraets-Smits and Peerbooms* and *Vanbraeckel*,[387] *Geraets-Smits* in fact concerned treatment which was not available in the Netherlands and did not concern undue delay.

---

[383] Para. 68.      [384] Paras. 119–20.

[385] R. Mendick, 'Thousands to get NHS ops abroad', *Independent on Sunday*, 28 Jul. 2002.

[386] N. Hawkes and C. Bremner, 'English patients take French cure', *The Times*, 19 Jan. 2002, which also notes the patients were promised 'explanations in English, British newspapers, "and a decent cup of tea"'; J. Mulkerrins, 'Britain's best new hospital (it's in France)', *Sunday Times*, 20 Jan. 2002.

[387] <http://www.dh.gov.uk/en/Healthcare/Entitlementsandcharges/OverseastreatmentguidanceforNHS/index.htm>.

All these developments have, however, forced the Commission to explore the implications of the Court's decisions on patient mobility and healthcare in the EU[388] to work out ways, for example, of reaching a 'common understanding on patients' rights, entitlements and duties', and working out methods of sharing spare capacity and transnational care. The Commission originally intended to include healthcare services in the Services Directive 2006/123 (see below) but this proved too controversial. Instead the Commission put forward a specific proposal, entitled 'A Community framework on the application of patients' rights to cross-border healthcare'.[389] Its proposal falls into three parts. First, it prescribes common principles to be embedded in all health systems including common standards on quality and safety. Secondly, it establishes a framework for cooperation with regard to issues such as recognition of prescriptions, European centres of excellence and E-health. Thirdly, it aims to systematize the Court's healthcare case law. As with the case law, it distinguishes between extramural care in other Member States for which authorization by the home state is not required, and intramural care which still requires authorization. Patients with rare diseases will be allowed to travel abroad for treatment even if the treatment is not covered by the home state, but long-term care and transplants will not fall under the new rules. The proposed directive is intended as an alternative to the framework provided under Regulation 883/04.[390]

## D. THE SERVICES DIRECTIVE

### 1. INTRODUCTION

So far we have concentrated on the application of the Treaty provisions on services. We turn now to consider the adoption of the controversial Services Directive 2006/123[391] by the Council and European Parliament at the end of 2006. The aim of the directive was to open up the market in services, which accounts for over two thirds of Europe's GDP. There were two main drafts of the directive: the 'Bolkestein' draft of 2004[392] and the McCreevy draft of 2006 which reflected the significant changes introduced by the European Parliament. The original 'Bolkestein' provided a legal framework that would (1) eliminate the obstacles to the freedom of establishment for service providers; (2) remove the obstacles to temporary service provision between the Member States; and (3) lay down detailed rules on mutual assistance between Member States as well as requiring Member States to establish a point of single contact (PSC). The provisions on establishment (which were discussed in Chapter 10) and mutual assistance remained largely intact throughout the process of negotiation. However, the rules on temporary service

---

[388] Commission Communication, 'Follow-up to the high level reflection process on patient mobility and healthcare developments in the European Union' (COM(2004) 301 final). See also Commission Communication, 'Modernising social protection for the development of high-quality, accessible and sustainable health are and long term care: support for the national strategies using the "open method of coordination"' (COM(2004) 304 final) and the Commission's consultation paper regarding 'Community action on health services' (SEC(2006) 1193/4) 26 Sep. 2006.　　　　　[389] COM(2008) 415.

[390] For a discussion on how the two regimes will fit, see Editorial Comments, 'Towards an improved framework for cross-border healthcare' (2008) 45 *CMLRev.* 1325.

[391] [2006] OJ L376/36. The following draws on the more extensive discussion in C. Barnard, 'Unravelling the Services Directive' (2008) 45 *CMLRev.* 323.　　　　　[392] COM(2004) 2 final/3.

provision, based as they were on the CoOP, proved particularly controversial and were subject to significant revision.

## 2. SCOPE

We turn now to examine the content of the directive, a vexed but important question because if the national rule falls within the scope of the directive, the rules in the directive will apply. If the rules fall outside the scope of the directive, the provisions of the Treaties and the case law discussed above will apply. This leads to the unfortunate result that a directive intended to provide some clarity for small and medium sized enterprises (SMEs) has actually introduced an increasingly complex and fragmented regime.

### 2.1 The Meaning of Services

According to Article 2(1), the directive applies to 'services supplied by providers established in a Member State'. Services are defined in accordance with the GATS definition: '"Service" means any self-employed economic activity, normally provided for remuneration, as referred to in Article [57] of the [Treaties]'.[393] The list of services found in Article 57 has been updated by the Directive to include:

- business services such as management consultancy, certification and testing; facilities management, including office maintenance; advertising; recruitment services; and the services of commercial agents
- services provided both to businesses and to consumers, such as legal or fiscal advice; real estate services such as estate agencies; construction, including the services of architects; distributive trades; the organization of trade fairs; car rental; and travel agencies
- consumer services such as those in the field of tourism, including tour guides; leisure services, sports centres and amusement parks; and, to the extent that they are not excluded from the scope of application of the directive, household support services, such as help for the elderly.[394]

The striking feature about this list is that the services identified are relatively uncontroversial and are often provided by small operators (SMEs).

### 2.2 Requirements, Restrictions, and Barriers

Assuming the activity is a service within the meaning of the directive then the directive can be used to challenge 'requirements which affect access to or the exercise of a service activity'.[395] The word 'requirement' is broadly construed by Article 4(7) of the directive:

any obligation, prohibition, condition or limit provided for in the laws, regulations or administrative provisions of the Member States or in consequence of case-law, administrative practice, the rules of professional bodies, or the collective rules of professional associations or other professional organisations, adopted in the exercise of their legal autonomy...

While the broad definition of 'requirement' is intended to give the Services Directive the widest possible reach, for the over-zealous, it will catch rules never intended to be covered

---

[393] Art. 4(1).    [394] 33rd recital.    [395] 9th recital.

by Union law. As we saw in Chapter 5, the breadth of the *Dassonville* formula[396] eventually led to the Court's ruling in *Keck*[397] (certain non-discriminatory selling arrangements did not breach Article 34). In the field of persons, the use of the restrictions/obstacles jurisprudence has generated similar anxieties[398] and the Court has experimented with different formulae to try to identify the outer limits of the Treaty provisions in these areas, including specifying that rules, such as those in *Graf*,[399] whose effect on free movement is too remote or insubstantial do not breach the Treaties. Some have suggested that it is necessary to carve a *Keck*-style certain selling arrangements (CSAs) exception out of Article 56. However, in *Omega*[400] Advocate General Stix-Hackl counselled against any such development, arguing that the transposition of the distinction made in *Keck* to freedom to provide services was unpersuasive because:

> where there are sufficient international implications, a rule on arrangements for the provision of any service—irrespective of location—must constitute a restriction of relevance to [Union] law simply because of the incorporeal nature of services, without any distinction at all being permissible in this respect between rules relating to arrangements for the provision of services and rules that relate directly to the services themselves.[401]

The 'requirement' formula used in the Services Directive also generated concerns in the European Parliament: could British service providers argue that the requirement to drive on the right in all Continental European countries restricted their ability to provide services there? The 9th recital was included in the preamble to try to put a stop to such arguments. The recital distinguishes between two situations. The first sentence provides that where requirements affect the access to, or the exercise of,[402] a service activity, the directive will apply. This also suggests that the directive supports a market access, rather than a discrimination, reading of the directive.

However, the second sentence of the 9th recital says that the directive does not apply:

> to requirements, such as road traffic rules, rules concerning the development or use of land, town and country planning, building standards as well as administrative penalties imposed for non-compliance with such rules which do not specifically regulate or specifically affect

---

[396] Case 8/74 *Procureur du Roi v. Dassonville* [1974] ECR 837.

[397] Joined Cases C–267/91 and C–268/91 *Keck and Mithouard* [1993] ECR I–6097, paras. 16–17.

[398] See, e.g., Geelhoed AG in Case C–374/04 *ACT Group Litigation* [2006] ECR I–11673 and Tizzano AG in Case C–442/02 *Caixa-Bank* [2004] ECR I–8961 considered in Chs. 10 and 8 respectively.

[399] Case C–190/98 *Graf v. Filzmozer Maschinenbau GmbH* [2000] ECR I–493.

[400] Case C–36/02 *Omega* [2004] ECR I–9609, para. 36. See also Case C–356/08 *Commission v. Austria* [2009] ECR I–000 where the Court avoided the Austrian government's arguments that the requirement to open a bank account with a bank in the region concerned a method of use to which *Keck* applied (although see now Case C–110/05 *Commission v. Italy (trailers)* [2009] ECR I–519 discussed in Ch. 6).

[401] Case C–287/03 *Commission v. Belgium (loyalty bonus)* [2005] ECR I–3761 lends support to the Advocate General's view that the concept of CSA should not be applied to services. Belgian law prevented vendors from making a 'linked offer', through its customer loyalty programme, of products and services dissimilar to those principally sold. While the Court dismissed the Art. 258 TFEU (ex Article 226 EC) application on the grounds that the Commission had failed to establish a breach of Art. 56, at no stage did the Court suggest that Art. 56 would not apply because the national rule affected selling arrangements. Cf now the effect of the UCPD 2005/29 considered in Ch. 5 and Joined Cases C–261/07 and C–299/07 *VTB-VAB* [2009] ECR I-000.

[402] Case 197/84 *Steinhauser v. City of Biarritz* [1985] ECR 1819 had already established that Art. 49 covered both access to and exercise of the freedom of establishment.

the service activity but have to be respected by providers in the course of carrying out their economic activity in the same way as by individuals acting in their private capacity.

Thus, certain non-discriminatory 'rules of the game', using the language of *Deliège*, are presumptively lawful. This view is reinforced by the unusual phrase 'in the same way as by individuals acting in their private capacity'. So, if the rules apply to all individuals, irrespective of their nationality or the status in which they are acting, they are lawful. However, if the service provider can show that the rules do 'specifically regulate or specifically affect the service activity' then they may be unlawful and need to be justified. Therefore, because the Belgian requirement of driving on the right is non-discriminatory and applies to all Belgians including those acting in their private capacity, it is presumptively compatible with the directive.

However, as the Court itself has discovered with *Keck*, trying to define a rule that weeds out the unmeritorious claims while leaving the door open to genuine claims is not easy, and the second sentence of the 9th recital suffers from similar shortcomings as the 'certain selling arrangement' formula in *Keck*. The reference in the recital to planning is instructive. Most people would agree that green-belt legislation or listed-building legislation should, in principle, fall outside the scope of Union law. The second sentence of the 9th recital is intended to achieve this. On the other hand, planning restrictions can interfere with an individual's freedom of establishment or freedom to provide services, especially when the planning rules are more akin to an authorization requirement (e.g., the requirement to get planning permission prior to building a new office).[403] The Commission's handbook seeks to address this difficulty by saying that the mere fact that rules are labelled in a specific way, for example as town planning rules, or that requirements are formulated in a general way, i.e. are not specifically addressed to service providers, is not sufficient to determine that they are outside of the scope of the Services Directive.[404]

### 2.3 Exclusions, Limitations, and Derogations

#### (a) Exclusions and limitations

We have already seen that the directive does not cover non-economic activity, matters which are not considered as services (such as goods) and non-discriminatory rules of the game. The directive also contains more specific exclusions, limitations, and derogations. The principal *exclusions* can be found in Article 2(2)–(3). These provisions list those service sectors to which the directive 'does not apply'. The list is long and broad,[405] including services of general interest,[406] financial services,[407] electronic communication services and networks,[408] temporary work agencies,[409] and private security services.[410] Most importantly, from the perspective of this chapter, healthcare services,[411] audiovisual services,[412] and gambling activities,[413] including lotteries, gambling in casinos and

---

[403] See the 47th and 59th recital.

[404] OPEC, 2007, also available at <http://www.ec.europa.eu/internal_market/services/services-dir/index_en.htm>, 17.

[405] Cf. the Commission's original proposal which listed only three excluded services (financial services, electronic communications, and transport).          [406] Art. 2(2)(a).

[407] Art. 2(2)(b).          [408] Art. 2(2)(c).          [409] Art. 2(2)(e).          [410] Art. 2(2)(k).

[411] Art. 2(2)(f).          [412] Art. 2(2)(g).          [413] Art. 2(2)(h). See also the 25th recital of the preamble.

betting transactions, are excluded from the scope of the directive. In addition, Article 2(3) adds that 'This Directive shall not apply to the field of taxation.' The Treaty provisions on services will continue to apply to these areas.

Article 1(2)–(7) of the directive spells out a further group of *limitations*. Of perhaps most interest is Article 1(6)–(7). Introduced to appease the trade union movement which had expressed grave concern over the implications of the Services Directive (concerns embodied in the figure of the Polish plumber seen as threatening Northern European jobs and labour standards), Article 1(6) makes clear that the directive *does not affect* labour law and social security legislation of the Member States. This observation was particularly important in the light of the disputes in *Viking*[414] and *Laval*[415] then progressing through the courts. These cases highlighted the fact that, absent any exclusion for labour law, national labour laws risked being challenged under the Services Directive and that the posted workers provisions in the original (2004) draft services directive were inadequate to address these concerns. Moreover, the Posted Workers Directive had nothing to say about the right to take collective action—at issue in both *Viking* and *Laval*—to protect the workers' interests. An attempt to address this point can be found in Article 1(7) of the directive which adds that:

This Directive does not affect the exercise of fundamental rights as recognised in the Member States and by [Union] law. Nor does it affect the right to negotiate, conclude and enforce collective agreements and to take industrial action in accordance with national law and practices which respect [Union] law.[416]

Originally modelled on the fundamental rights clause in so-called Monti Regulation 2679/98,[417] Article 1(7) indicates that a right to take industrial action is only a legitimate exception to the freedom to provide services insofar as this is consistent with Union law.[418] Therefore industrial action which the Court deems inconsistent with Union law— such as the situation identified in *Viking* where strike action was taken even though no jobs were 'jeopardised or under serious threat'[419]—is covered by the Services Directive (and Article 56 TFEU).[420]

## (b) Other derogations

There are other derogations which apply to specific parts of the directive, most importantly Article 17, entitled 'additional derogations', and Article 18, 'case-by-case derogations', both of which derogate from Chapter IV on the free movement of services. We shall consider these later. In addition, some of the requirements in Chapter III on establishment are subject to the full range of public-interest requirements (ORRPI) developed by the Court of Justice ('broad justifications'), while some of the requirements in Chapter IV are subject to the express derogations provided in the Treaties plus environmental protection ('narrow justifications). These are considered further below.

---

[414] Case C–438/05 *International Transport Workers' Federation* v. *Viking Line ABP* [2007] ECR I–10779.
[415] Case C–341/05 *Laval* [2007] ECR I–987.
[416] See also the 15th recital which expressly refers to the Charter and the accompanying explanations.
[417] OJ [1998] L337/8 considered in Ch. 6.
[418] See also the similar drafting in Art. 28 of the Charter of Fundamental Rights 2000.
[419] Para. 84. At para. 44 the Court said the right to strike may be 'subject to certain restrictions. As is reaffirmed by Article 28 of the Charter...those rights are to be protected in accordance with Union law and national law'.      [420] T. Novitz, 'EU labour rights as human rights' (2006–7) 9 CYELS 357, 374.

## 3. FREEDOM TO PROVIDE SERVICES

Following its radical overhaul by the McCreevy draft, Chapter IV on free movement of services, especially section 1, contains some of the most opaque provisions of the directive. This problem is exacerbated by the awkward mismatch between the original draft (Country of origin principle (CoOP) + derogations) and the final version (no CoOP + derogations), and between the directive and the case law under the Treaties.[421] We start by considering the most controversial provision of the Directive, Article 16.

### 3.1 Article 16(1): Freedom to Provide Services v. The CoOP

The first and second paragraphs of Article 16(1) contain the general statements that:

Member States shall respect the right of providers to provide services in a Member State other than that in which they are established.

The Member State in which the service is provided shall ensure free access to and free exercise of a service activity within its territory.

The third paragraph of Article 16(1) adds that 'Member States shall not make access to or exercise of a service activity in their territory subject to compliance with any requirements' which do not satisfy the principle of non-discrimination, a narrow range of justifications, and proportionality.

The three parts of Article 16(1), based essentially on the Treaty language of freedom to provide services, replaced the controversial CoOP found in the original Article 16(1) of the Bolkestein draft. This said:

Member States shall ensure that providers are subject only to the national provisions of their Member State of origin which fall within the coordinated field.

It continued that Article 16(1) covered national provisions relating to access to and the exercise of a service activity, in particular those requirements governing the behaviour of the provider, the quality or content of the service, advertising contracts, and the provider's liability. The original Article 16(2) then made clear that the Member State of origin was to be responsible for supervising the provider and the services provided by him, including services provided by him in another Member State. Article 16 was then subject to the three express derogations (general, transitional, and case-by-case derogations—see below).

For the Commission, the use of the country-of-origin principle in the Bolkestein version of the Services Directive was a logical extension of, for example, the TWF (now AVMS) Directive 2010/13 (considered above in Case Study 11.2),[422] and the E-commerce Directive 2000/31,[423] both of which had the country-of-origin principle at their core.[424] However, the Services Directive was considerably more ambitious than its sectoral forebears, since its horizontal approach meant that it covered all the sectors in its scope[425] not just specific sectors. Further, while the TWF/AVMS Directive 2010/13 contained a mix of deregulation (country-of-origin principle) and re-regulation through minimum

---

[421] Art. 3(3) expressly provides that 'Member States shall apply the provisions of this Directive in compliance with the rules of the Treaty on the right of establishment and the free movement of services.'

[422] OJ [1989] L298/23.      [423] OJ [2000] L178/1

[424] For a discussion on the three generations of the CoOP in the legislative practice of the EU: V. Hatzopoulos, 'Legal aspects in establishing the internal market for services' College of Europe Research Paper in Law 6/2007, 27–9.                          [425] See, e.g., COM(2004) 2, 8.

harmonization (e.g., rules on protection of minors, prohibition of racism), the Bolkestein proposal concerned deregulation (country-of-origin principle) and only very limited re-regulation. Given the broad and unidentified nature of services covered, more extensive re-regulation was not possible.

For this reason, among others, a large number of states lined up against the CoOP and the original Article 16 was doomed to fail in its pure CoOP form. The European Parliament's intervention secured the removal of the CoOP wording and replaced it with something apparently more anodyne now found in the current Article 16(1). But how great, in fact, is the difference between the CoOP and the freedom to provide services? Under the country-of-origin principle, the principal regulator would have been the home state, reinforced by the presumption that the host state could not impose any additional requirements unless there were very good reasons (listed in the derogations in the original Articles 17–19). On one view, the present Article 16 comes close to a country-of-origin principle: while the original version of Article 16 defined the law which could be applied (the home-state law), the current version defines the law that cannot be applied (the host-state law).[426] Another reading is that the current approach appears to reverse the country-of-origin principle:[427] it accepts that the host state can impose its own restrictions on the service provider, where there are good reasons for so doing, account being taken of the protection already provided in the home state.[428] This latter reading broadly reflects the case law of the Court where the CoOP is not as firmly embedded in respect of services as it is in free movement of goods. As we have seen,[429] the CoOP does exist, but not in terms of establishing the breach (as is the case for goods), but in terms of justifying the breach where the Court requires the host state to take into account requirements already imposed by the home state.

In practice, the difference between the original and current version of Article 16 may well be one of emphasis rather than substance: the country-of-origin principle raises a strong presumption of illegality of the host-state measure; the current approach may raise a weaker presumption of illegality. This may mean that service providers will continue having to investigate the rules (justified under Article 16(1), third sentence and Article 16(3)) in each state in which they provide services, although their task will be made easier by the establishment of PSCs to provide recipients, in their state of residence, clear, easily accessible information, including by electronic means, about requirements applicable to service activities.[430]

## 3.2 Article 16(2): Particularly Suspect Requirements

In its original version, Article 16 contained a list of *prohibited* requirements which could not be saved by any general justifications but to which the express derogations (see below) in Articles 17–19 applied. This approach was changed in the final version of the directive. Article 16(2) identifies seven requirements (including an obligation on the provider to

---

[426] This reading is supported by looking at the three sentences of Art. 16(1) together.

[427] However, despite the change of wording in Art. 16(1), elements of the country-of-origin principle remain elsewhere in the directive, provisions which came almost unamended from the Bolkestein draft. See, e.g., Art. 29 which requires the authorities in the state of *establishment* to provide information to the host state about the legitimacy of the services provider. If the host state has reason to think that the service provider does not comply with the laws of the home state, the state of *establishment* must carry out checks, inspections, or investigations.     [428] This reading is supported by Art. 16(1), third sentence.

[429] See e.g. Case C–76/90 *Säger* [1991] ECR I–4221, para. 15.     [430] Art. 21.

have an establishment in the territory of the host state[431] or to obtain an authorization from the host state's competent authorities, including an entry in a register;[432] and a ban on the provider setting up a certain form or type of infrastructure, including an office or chambers[433]) which can be saved not only by the express derogations in Article 17 and the case-by-case derogations in Article 18, but also by a narrow list of public-interest requirements provided for by the directive. In practice, it is likely that states will find the seven requirements hard to justify. Therefore, we might term these requirements 'particularly suspect'.

The narrow list of public-interest requirements can be used to justify not only the seven requirements listed in Article 16(2) but also, according to Article 16(1), 3rd paragraph, 'any [other] requirements' which affect access to or exercise of a service activity in another Member State, such as a rule requiring the use of a particular language in the host state.

### 3.3 (Narrow) Justifications

The narrow justifications are listed in Article 16(1), third paragraph, and largely repeated in Article 16(3).[434] According to Article 16(1), third paragraph, Member States shall not, 'make access to or exercise of a service activity in their territory subject to compliance with any requirements' which do not respect the principles of (a) non-discrimination, (b) necessity, and (c) proportionality.

Article 16(1) explains 'non-discrimination' in the following terms: 'the requirement may be neither directly nor indirectly discriminatory with regard to nationality or, in the case of legal persons, with regard to the Member State in which they are established'. This is fairly standard fare, although no reference is made to discrimination on the grounds of establishment which, as we have seen, is a well-established prohibited ground of discrimination in the Court's case law on services.[435]

The language of 'necessity' is misleading.[436] It does not in fact refer to the first limb of a proportionality test but rather to justifications: 'the requirement must be justified for reasons of public policy, public security, public health or the protection of the environment'. In fact, even the language of justifications is misleading because the list contained in heading (b) is actually an expanded list of express derogations found in the Treaties; environment has been added. No reference is made to the judicially developed overriding reasons relating to the public interest (ORRPI) used in Chapter III on establishment. It must therefore be assumed that the drafters of the directive deliberately decided not to apply the full gamut of ORRPI to the seven requirements listed in Article 16(2) of the directive and 'any [other] requirements'.[437] In this way the directive reflects the long-established idea that the host state has more right to intervene in respect of establishment (hence the broad ORRPI justifications) than it does in respect of services, where the principal regulator is the home state (hence the narrow justifications).

---

[431]  Case 33/74 *van Binsbergen* [1974] ECR 1299.

[432]  Case C-390/99 *Canal Satélite* [2003] ECR I-607.

[433]  Case C-55/94 *Gebhard* [1995] ECR I-4165.

[434]  The McCreevy draft (COM(2006) 160) did not dare address this overlap: the version of Art. 16 that got through the European Parliament was treated as almost sacred: J. Flower, 'Negotiating the Services Directive' (2006–7) 9 *CYELS* 217, 229.          [435]  Case 33/74 *van Binsbergen* [1974] ECR 1299.

[436]  See also Art. 15(3)(b).

[437]  See also Handbook, 50 and BERR Consultation Paper 2007, 68: 'No other justifications will be sufficient.'

Heading (c), proportionality, is more straightforward. Here the directive adopts the traditional two-pronged approach—the requirement must be suitable for attaining the objective pursued, and must not go beyond what is necessary to attain that objective. Integral to the proportionality review in the case law is a requirement on the host state to take account of the levels of protection provided to secure that interest in the home state.[438] This is not referred to in Article 16(1) but is implicit in the provisions on mutual assistance in Chapter VI.

### 3.4 Derogations

In the original version of the directive, the country-of-origin principle was flanked by general derogations, transitional derogations, and case-by-case derogations. This basic structure has remained largely intact in the final version of the directive, despite the (apparent) removal of the country-of-origin principle, but it is now supplemented by the justifications considered in section 3.3 above. The derogations are now divided into two: the 'additional derogations' found in Article 17 and the case-by-case derogations found in Article 18.

The 'additional derogations' in Article 17 concern matters such as services of general economic interest in the utility sector and judicial recovery of debts[439] as well as matters covered by specific Union measures, including the Posted Workers Directive 96/71,[440] the Lawyers' Directive 77/249,[441] Title II of the Professional Qualifications Directive 2005/36,[442] and the Citizens' Rights Directive 2004/38.[443] Article 16 will not apply to these areas.

The 'case-by-case' derogations found in Article 18 apply 'in exceptional circumstances only'.[444] Article 18(1) permits Member States to 'take measures relating to the safety of services' in respect of a particular provider established in another Member State. Article 18(2) adds two further caveats. First, a derogation can be made only after the mutual assistance procedure laid down in Article 35 has been complied with. The second caveat is that before the host state can take measures relating to the safety of a particular service, it must ensure: first, that there has been no harmonization in the field; secondly, that the measures provide for a higher level of protection of the recipient than would be the case in a measure taken by the home state; thirdly, that the home state has not taken any measures or has taken measures which are insufficient as compared with those referred to in Article 35(2); and fourthly, that the measures are proportionate.[445]

Given this elaborate procedure, it is hard to imagine a Member State ever making use of Article 18 when they can invoke the (narrow) justifications in Article 16(1) without having to go through any of this complex and time-consuming procedure.

### 3.5 The Reporting Provisions

Buried in Article 45(5), and not in the Chapter on Services, are the reporting provisions: the Member States must, by 28 December 2009, present a report to the Commission

---

[438] Case C–76/90 *Säger* [1991] ECR I–4221, para. 15.        [439] See also 85th recital.
[440] This is probably unnecessary given the exclusion in Art. 3(1)(a). See also the 86th and 87th recitals.
[441] OJ [1977] L78/17.        [442] OJ [2005] L 255/22.        [443] OJ [2004] L158/77
[444] See also 91st recital.
[445] Finally, Art. 18(3) makes clear that the case-by-case derogations under Art. 18 do not affect other Union instruments in which the freedom to provide services is guaranteed and where case-by-case derogations are provided, notably the E-commerce Dir.

on the national requirements whose application can be justified, giving reasons.[446] By implication, all Member States will first have had to screen their national legislation. After the 2009 deadline, Member States must inform the Commission of any changes in their requirements or any new requirements, together with the reasons for them (presumably based on Article 16(1) and (3), although this is not stated). The Commission must inform the other Member States but the Member States remain free to adopt the provisions in question. The Commission is then to provide annual 'analyses and orientations on the application of these provisions in the context of this Directive'.

These screening provisions were introduced in the 2006 draft of the directive, possibly to offset some of the consequences of removing the CoOP. At first blush these provisions appear to mirror the procedure for evaluating suspect requirements under Article 15 on establishment. There are, however, some significant differences. In particular, the services provisions are not subject to the full mutual evaluation procedure (despite the fact that the Commission says that the two procedures are in fact similar[447]); neither are they subject to either the same quasi-standstill provision found in Article 15(6) of the directive, nor to the equivalent of the procedure in the Technical Standards Directive 98/34.

## 4. RIGHTS OF RECIPIENTS OF SERVICES

Recipients of services also enjoy rights under the directive. Article 19 says that *home* states cannot impose requirements on recipients which restrict their use of a service supplied by a provider established in the host state. It then offers two examples of such restrictions:

- an obligation on the recipient to obtain authorization from, or to make a declaration to, the competent authorities of the home state (however, non-discriminatory authorization schemes are permitted[448])

- discriminatory limits on the grant of financial assistance by reason of the fact that the provider is established in another Member State or by reason of the location of the place at which the service is provided.[449]

The striking feature of these examples is that they are firmly rooted in the discrimination model while the case law under Article 56 has moved beyond that.[450]

Article 20 is directed at the *host* state. Article 20(1) contains the general prohibition against discrimination (not restrictions/obstacles): 'Member States shall ensure that the recipient is not made subject to discriminatory requirements based on his nationality or place of residence.' This sentiment is amplified in Article 20(2) which says that 'Member States shall ensure that the general conditions of access to a service, which are made available to the public at large by the provider, do not contain discriminatory provisions relating to the nationality or place of residence of the recipient.' However, the obligations in Article 20(2) go beyond the state; all providers are under an obligation not to discriminate.

---

[446] This is possibly a narrower reporting obligation that that under, e.g., Art. 9(2).
[447] Handbook, 79.        [448] 92nd recital.
[449] See Case C–55/98 *Bent Vestergaard* [1999] ECR I–7641 considered above.
[450] See, e.g., Case C–158/96 *Kohll* [1998] ECR I–1931, para. 33. See also Case C–381/93 *Commission* v. *France (maritime services)* [1994] ECR I–5154, para. 17; Case C–136/00 *Danner* [2002] ECR I–8147, para. 29; Case C–118/96 *Safir* [1998] ECR I–1897, para. 23.

This is a far-reaching provision which shows how the regulation of the provision of services can penetrate deep into the private sphere.

Article 20(2) contains the intriguing caveat that the principle of non-discrimination does not preclude 'the possibility of providing for differences in the conditions of access where those differences are directly justified by objective criteria'. This might mean that providers can impose different prices for postage and packaging depending on the location of the client.[451] It is not clear whether this means that all discrimination, direct or indirect, can be objectively justified, contrary to well-established case law, or whether it means that, in order to establish discrimination, the two situations have to be comparable and if there are objective differences between the situation of the service recipient and the migrant then no prima facie case of discrimination can be established.

Finally, Article 21 is intended to encourage potential recipients of a service to use services provided in other Member States by imposing requirements on the *home* state to provide information about consumer protection, the availability of dispute settlement in the providing state, and contact details of consumer bodies which can provide practical assistance.[452]

## 5. QUALITY OF SERVICES

It might be thought that a chapter on the quality of services would be the core of any directive on services and that it would contain detailed rules on how quality might be achieved. This is not, in fact, the case with the Services Directive, not least because this would not be feasible in a horizontal directive spanning over 80 sectors. Instead, much of Chapter V is actually devoted to the requirement of providing clear, timely information with a view to creating transparency in the transnational services market and building confidence.[453] For example, Article 22(1) lists 'indispensable' information which must be provided by the provider,[454] including information about the provider (e.g., name, legal status, form, contact details) and about the service (e.g., the price of the service, and insurance guarantees).[455]

Further, albeit voluntary, confidence building measures can be found in Article 23. Article 23(1) provides that Member States 'may' ensure[456] that providers established in their territory, whose services present a direct and particular risk to the health and safety of the recipient/third party/financial security of the recipient,[457] subscribe to professional liability insurance appropriate to the nature and the extent of the risk, or provide a guarantee or similar.[458]

Only in Article 26 does the chapter turn to the real question of quality of services and this is on a non-mandatory basis: 'Member States shall, in cooperation with the

---

[451] BERR Consultation Paper 2007, 61.   [452] Art. 21(2).

[453] See the equivalent provisions in Art. 5 of the E-commerce Dir. 2000/31 discussed by Lopez-Tarruella, 'A European Community regulatory framework for electronic commerce' (2001) 38 *CMLRev.* 1337,

[454] Art. 22(2) explains how this can be done. See also the 96th recital.

[455] See also the overlap in Art. 27(1).

[456] In the 2004 version of the directive, the obligation was mandatory. Note the more mandatory language in the 98th and 99th recitals but the important caveat in the 99th recital: 'there should be no obligation for insurance companies to provide insurance cover'.   [457] These terms are all defined in Art. 23(5).

[458] This provision does not affect professional insurance or guarantee arrangements provided for in other Union instruments Art. 23(4). The Commission has powers to flesh out the details of this provision, under the comitology procedures: Art. 23(4).

Commission, take accompanying measures to encourage providers to take action on a *voluntary basis* in order to ensure the quality of service provision[459] in particular through certification or assessment of their activities by independent or accredited bodies; and drawing up their own quality charter or participation in quality charters or labels (e.g., the star classification system for hotels[460]) by professional bodies at Union level. This is the softest of the provisions in Chapter V.

## 6. THE ROLE OF THE STATE

One of the distinctive features of the directive concerns the onerous obligations it places on the states. These are found primarily in Chapter II concerning administrative simplification (which require states to get their own houses in order) and Chapter VI on administrative cooperation (which require states to cooperate with each other).

### 6.1 Administrative Simplification

In respect of administrative simplification, Article 5(1) requires Member States to 'examine the procedures and formalities' applicable to the access to, and exercise of, a service activity (e.g., submission of documents and filing a declaration or registration to the relevant authorities) and simplify them where they are not sufficiently simple.[461] These few words, especially when read in conjunction with the specific screening obligations resulting from Chapters III and IV, impose a dramatic and onerous requirement not only on the Member States but also on the professional bodies, organizations and associations[462] to verify that all national laws and other professional rules are compatible with the directive. If carried out thoroughly, and in the spirit of cooperation required by Article 4(3) TEU (ex Article 10 EC), the directive requires states and professional bodies to trawl through the many thousands of pages of their rule books to check whether the rules fall within the scope of the directive and, if they do, which rules may constitute barriers to the provision of services or the establishment of service providers. States must then either remove these barriers or justify them where appropriate and/or simplify the procedures, and then report back to the Commission on what they have done.[463] This legislative spring clean fits well with the Better Regulation agenda advocated by the Barroso Commission.[464]

Of more practical importance to service providers is the obligation on the Member States to establish a—real or virtual—point of single contact (PSC) through which it is possible to *complete*[465] all procedures and formalities (e.g., authorizations, declarations,

---

[459] Emphasis added.

[460] According to Art. 26(3) information on the significance of certain labels and the criteria for applying labels and other quality marks relating to services must be easily accessed by providers and recipients. See also 102nd recital with the additional powers to the Commission to issue a mandate for the drawing up of specific European standards under Dir. 98/34 (OJ [1998] L204/37).

[461] This reflects the Union's own expressed intention to simplify its legislation: the Institutional Agreement on Better Law Making (OJ [2003] C321/1), para. 35.    [462] Art. 4(7) and Handbook, 77.

[463] Art. 39(1) and (5) considered above.

[464] See, e.g., Commission Communication, 'Strategic review of better regulation in the European Union': COM(2006) 689; 'A single market review': COM(2007) 60, 6. This is considered further in Ch. 16.

[465] Cf. Art. 57 of Recognition of Professional Qualifications Dir. 2005/36 (OJ [2005] L255.22) where the contact point merely provides information and assistance about having professional qualifications recognized. The PSC will allow individuals to have their qualifications actually recognized.

notifications, the allocation of a company registration number[466]), whether imposed by central, regional or local level.[467] These PSCs must, according to Article 7, provide providers and recipients of services with certain key information in a variety of Union languages.[468]

Chapter II does not 'draw any distinction between domestic and foreign providers'.[469] Therefore, its provisions apply in the same way to service providers established in another Member State, and to service providers established (or wishing to establish) in the territory of their own Member State.[470] The thinking behind this is pragmatic. In the same way that domestic providers will benefit from any programme of legislative/administrative simplification which will also assist out of state providers, so should domestic providers also benefit from administrative support through use of PSCs.

## 6.2 Administrative Cooperation

Chapter VI on administrative cooperation returns to a theme familiar from free movement of goods: mutual assistance 'in order to ensure the supervision of providers and the services they provide'.[471] This is the corollary of the mutual recognition provisions found in the directive. Article 5(3) is one of the relatively few examples of mutual recognition provisions. It requires host states to accept documents from other Member States which serve equivalent purposes. Mutual recognition thus has the potential to avoid a proliferation of rules applicable to service providers but it only works if there is confidence between states and a willingness on the part of the host state to engage proactively with the home state and to cooperate. Mutual assistance is therefore intended to foster trust in the legal framework and supervision in other Member States.

To persuade states to cooperate, the directive designates which state is responsible in particular situations.[472] This is supported by a 'clear, legally binding obligation for Member States to cooperate effectively'.[473] In this way the Services Directive builds on Regulation 2006/2004 on the cooperation between consumer protection authorities.[474] In practical terms, Member States have to designate one or more liaison points[475] as well as facilitating both operational cooperation and the provision of information by providers established in the home state to the competent authorities in other Member States.[476]

The success of the directive will, of course, depend on Member States' enthusiasm to comply with their screening obligations. The initial signs were not that encouraging. There was no fanfare on 28 December 2009, the date for the implementation of the directive, because, according to press reports, only 11 Member States had completed the steps necessary to put the directive onto their national statute books, still fewer have completed all the necessary operational steps in time, although business associations do report that many Member States have made substantial changes to national rules and procedures implementing the directive.[477]

---

[466] Handbook, 26.    [467] This is largely repeated in Art. 8(1).    [468] Art. 7(5).
[469] Handbook, 20–1.    [470] Ibid.    [471] Art. 28(1). See also 108th recital.
[472] Arts. 29–35.    [473] Ibid.
[474] OJ [2004] L364/1, referred to in 104th recital. For discussion, see Micklitz, 'Transborder law enforcement: Does it exist?' in U. Bernitz and S. Weatherill (eds.), *The Regulation of Unfair Commercial Practices under EC Directive 2005/29: New rules and new techniques* (Oxford: Hart Publishing, 2007).
[475] Art. 28(2).    [476] Art. 28(3)–(7).
[477] 'Services law needs robust application', *European Voice*, 7 Jan. 2010.

# E. CONCLUSIONS

The case law discussed in this chapter helps to demonstrate the problems posed by the sheer variety, nature, and duration of services. Another facet of the problem concerns the broad matrix of interests at stake: the interests of the state of establishment and those of the state where the service is provided, both of which may (or may not) want to encourage the export and import of the service; the interests of the potential providers and recipients of the service, especially when the recipient travels to receive a service (e.g., tourist and healthcare services), and the interests of those who might lose out when chasing scarce resources (e.g., those still on waiting lists). Given such a spectrum of interests, national regulation of services tends to be more detailed and complex because, unlike goods, it is not just the service itself but also the service provider, its staff, and equipment which are being regulated. This has posed a tremendous challenge to the Court in balancing the Union interest in opening up the services market with the need to preserve the often legitimate interests of the state. Because one size does not fit all, the standard model of non-discrimination on the grounds of nationality—possibly suitable in the early days of the Union when the provision of services was less complex—does not readily resolve issues raised by the different barriers to the provision and receipt of services. Increasingly the Court falls back on the *Säger* hindrance/obstacle model, finds most national measures to breach Article 56, and then focuses on the question of justification. As the healthcare cases demonstrate, the Court's analysis of justification can be extremely detailed, but in cases where this proves to be too politically difficult it accepts the justification raised by the Member State without question.

# 12

# UNION CITIZENSHIP

## A. INTRODUCTION

So far we have considered the position of those nationals who have exercised their rights of free movement as workers, the self-employed, and the providers and recipients of services. These migrants have been described as market citizens (*homo economicus* or the *bourgeois*) who participate in, and benefit from, the common market as economic actors.[1] Yet, they constitute only a small percentage of the EU's working population: prior to the 2004 enlargement, approximately 1.5 per cent of EU-15 citizens lived and worked in a different Member State from their country of origin (less than 3 million people)—a proportion that had hardly changed for the last 30 years.[2] Post enlargement, the figure stands at about 8 million[3] (out of a total population of about 500 million), albeit that many more millions of EU citizens exercise their right to travel to other Member States temporarily—particularly as tourists or as students.

This means that the vast majority of Union nationals who are economically active have never exercised their rights of free movement under Articles 45, 49, and 56 (except possibly in their capacity as tourists); by definition, those who are not economically active cannot enjoy the rights of free movement (although they have been assisted by decisions of the Court on work-seekers, tourists, and students as well as by the original 1990 Residence Directives[4]). Yet, Union law continues to affect many aspects of the daily lives of those nationals who do not, or cannot, exercise their rights of free movement. Such individuals often feel at best removed, and at worst alienated, from those taking decisions in their name. This legitimacy gap has presented a major challenge for the EU: what can be done to enable all nationals to identify with, and feel loyalty to, the EU?

The concept of 'Citizenship of the Union', introduced at Maastricht, formed a key part of the Union's response, aiming to provide the glue to help bind together nationals of all

---

[1] M. Everson, 'The legacy of the market citizen' in J. Shaw and G. More (eds.), *New Legal Dynamics of the European Union* (Oxford: Clarendon Press, 1995).

[2] <http://www.ec.europa.eu/employment_social/workersmobility_2006>. See also A. Taylor, 'Skilled staff reluctant to move in Europe', *Financial Times*, 11 Dec. 2006. As we have seen, obstacles included differences in tax systems, healthcare, benefits, lack of EU-wide integrated employment legislation, patchy cross-border recognition of professional qualifications, difficulty finding work for spouses, and availability of housing and schools.　　　　　[3] 5th Report on Citizenship of the Union: COM(2008) 85.

[4] Council Dir. 90/364/EEC ([1990] OJ L180/26) on the rights of residence for persons of sufficient means; Council Dir. 90/365/EEC on the rights of residence for employees and self-employed who have ceased their occupational activity ([1990] OJ L180/28) and Council Dir. 93/96 on the rights of residence for students ([1993] OJ L317/59). These directives have been repealed and replaced by the Citizens' Rights Dir. 2004/38 ([2004] OJ L158/77).

the Member States. Union citizenship is both a retrospective and prospective concept: retrospective in that it contains a recognition that the EU has its own people; prospective in that it is through citizenship that communities and identities are constituted.[5] However, the concept of Union citizenship is itself subject to an important limitation: it can be enjoyed only by those holding the nationality of one of the Member States. It has therefore not helped the 18.5 million (and rising) third-country nationals (TCNs) who are legally resident in the EU.[6] Many contribute to the economies of the host country and so, indirectly, to the EU, but they are excluded from the rights granted to citizens.[7] This chapter will examine the concept of Union citizenship and the rights EU citizens enjoy; in Chapter 14 the position of TCNs is considered.

## B.  CITIZENSHIP OF THE UNION

While a desire to create a 'Europe for Citizens'[8] or a 'People's Europe'[9] dates back to the early 1970s, it was not until the Spanish pressed the issue at Maastricht[10] that the idea of Union citizenship took concrete form. A new Part Two, entitled 'Citizenship of the Union', was added to the EC Treaty by the Maastricht Treaty in 1992, establishing 'Citizenship of the Union' and listing a number of specific rights which citizens can enjoy.

The inclusion of the citizenship provisions into the Treaties started a lengthy and ongoing debate about the nature of EU citizenship, focusing on two interrelated questions. First, what model of citizenship can and should the Union adopt? The copious literature is full of suggestions, including market citizenship (focusing on the rights of economic actors), social citizenship (emphasizing the social-welfare rights of citizenship), or republican citizenship (based on active citizen participation in the decision-making process). Secondly, given that the EU is a *sui generis*, transnational polity, should EU citizenship aim to replicate citizenship of a nation state (so that European citizenship means citizenship of a European nation state), or should the EU aim to create a new, post-national form of citizenship based on multiple-level associations and identifications at regional, national, and European level. If the latter model, this raises the further question of the extent to which it is legitimate to draw on the literature and ideas relating to the development of citizenship of a nation state in mapping and analysing what is occurring at EU level.

In practice, many writers do take this literature as their starting point since this informs most individuals' understanding of citizenship. This chapter draws on one particular strand of the literature, examining whether the term citizenship is or should be

---

[5] See J. Shaw, *Citizenship of the Union: Towards post-national membership*, specialized course delivered at the Academy of European Law, Florence, Jul. 1995.

[6] Commission, *First Annual Report on Migration and Integration*, COM(2004) 508.

[7] They are sometimes described as 'denizens'. See, e.g., K. Groenendijk, 'The Long Term Residents Directive, denizenship and integration' in A. Baldaccini, E. Guild, and H. Toner (eds.), *Whose Freedom, Security and Justice? EU immigration and asylum law and policy* (Oxford: Hart Publishing, 2007), 429.

[8] See the Tindemans Report on the European Union which contained a chapter entitled 'Towards a Europe for citizens' (Bull. EC (8) 1975 II no. 12, 1) which was drawn up at the request of the Paris summit in 1974.

[9] See the two Adonnino Reports of 1985 to the European Council on a People's Europe (Bull. EC Suppl. 7/85).

[10] For a full discussion of the background see S. O'Leary, *The Evolving Concept of Community Citizenship* (The Hague: Kluwer, 1996), Ch. 1. See also the Spanish memorandum on citizenship, 'The road to European citizenship', Co.SN 3940/90, 24 Sep. 1990.

based on ideas of inclusion or exclusion.[11] An approach to citizenship based on inclusionary ideologies casts the net of potential beneficiaries widely, including not only nationals (whether economically active or not) but also those TCNs who are lawfully resident. It envisages that these citizens enjoy a broad range of civil, political, economic, and social rights. This version of citizenship is sometimes referred to as 'social citizenship'[12] and has some resonance in the EU as the EU develops, albeit in a piecemeal fashion, a broad range of social policies.[13]

By contrast, the exclusionary approach to citizenship constructs the identity of the citizen through the 'Other': the TCN who needs to be excluded to make the citizen 'secure'.[14] For a while this model seemed to be in the ascendancy in the EU. At Amsterdam a new objective was introduced into (now) Article 3(2) TEU of maintaining and developing 'an area of freedom justice and security without internal frontiers' in which 'the free movement of persons is ensured in conjunction with appropriate measures with respect to external border controls, asylum, immigration and the prevention and combating of crime'. This idea is developed further by Title V of Part Two TFEU. Yet the reality is inevitably more complex than this and, as we shall see in Chapter 14, the need to welcome TCN migrant workers to fill jobs in areas where there are skills gaps and to help address problems created by an ageing population has forced the EU to rethink any exclusionary agenda suggested by Article 3 TEU.

We begin by examining the citizenship offered by the EU to its nationals, taking Held's understanding of citizenship as our starting point:[15]

Citizenship has meant a reciprocity of rights against, and duties towards, the community. Citizenship has entailed membership, membership of the community in which one lives one's life. And membership has invariably involved degrees of participation in the community.

Held's definition suggests that there are three interconnected strands to citizenship: rights and duties, membership, and participation. These ideas will form the framework in which we examine EU citizenship.

## C. RIGHTS AND DUTIES

### 1. INTRODUCTION

#### 1.1 The Main Treaty Provisions

In his classic work on (British) citizenship,[16] Marshall argued that citizenship involves full membership of the community which has gradually been achieved through the

---

[11] See, e.g., J. D'Oliveira, 'European citizenship: Its meaning, its potential' in R. Dehousse (ed.), *Europe after Maastricht: An ever closer union?* (Munich: Law Books in Europe, 1994), 141–6; J. Shaw, 'The many pasts and futures of citizenship in the European Union' (1997) 22 *ELRev*. 554.

[12] M. Dougan, 'Free movement: The workseeker as citizen' (2001) 4 *CYELS* 93, 103.

[13] C. Barnard, 'EU social policy: From Employment Law to Labour Market Reform' in P. Craig and G. de Búrca (eds.), *The Evolution of EU Law* (Oxford: OUP, forthcoming).

[14] Shaw, above n. 11, 571. See also G. de Búrca, 'The quest for legitimacy in the European Union' (1996) 59 *MLR* 349, 356–61.

[15] D. Held, 'Between state and civil society: Citizenship' in G. Andrews (ed.), *Citizenship* (London: Lawrence and Wishart, 1991), 20, cited in Shaw, above n. 11.

[16] T. H. Marshall, *Citizenship and Social Class* (Cambridge: CUP, 1950), 28–9.

historical development of individual rights, starting with civil rights (basic freedoms from state interference), followed by political rights (such as electoral rights), and, most recently, social rights (including rights to education, health care, unemployment insurance, and old-age pensions—the rudiments of a welfare state). Where does the EU stand against this yardstick? Article 20(2) TFEU provides that 'Citizens of the Union shall enjoy the rights and be subject to the duties provided for in the Treaties. They shall have, *inter alia*':[17]

- the right to move and reside freely within the territory of the Member States[18]
- the right to vote in local and European elections in the host state and stand as a candidate
- the right to diplomatic and consular protection from the authorities of any Member State in third countries[19]
- the right to petition the European Parliament and the right to apply to the ombudsman and to address the institutions and advisory bodies of the Union in any one of the official languages of the EU.

These rights are to be exercised in accordance with the conditions and limits defined by the Treaties and by the measures adopted thereunder.

This rather motley collection of rights falls far short of the full panoply envisaged by Marshall. In part this is due to the Union's lack of competence, particularly in fields connected with the welfare state, and in part due to the principle of subsidiarity—can and should the Union be attempting to replicate welfare-state provision which is already extensively and expensively provided for at national level? This demonstrates the problem of using literature written in the context of the nation state as a measure by which to assess the EU. For this reason, it might be fairer to say that the rights contained in Part Two supplement and complement rights granted at national level.[20]

It is also a mistake to look at the four substantive rights listed in Part Two in isolation. Article 20(2) makes clear that the four rights listed are merely examples ('*inter alia*'). The reference to the fact that '[c]itizens shall enjoy the rights…provided for in the Treaties' means that *migrant* citizens also enjoy the right to non-discrimination on the ground of

---

[17] Art. 25 TFEU requires the Commission to report every three years on the application of these provisions. On this basis, the Council, acting unanimously in accordance with the special legislative procedure and after obtaining the consent of the European Parliament, may adopt provisions to strengthen or to add to the rights listed in Art. 20(2) TFEU. These provisions will enter into force only after their approval by the Member States in accordance with their respective constitutional requirements (Art. 25, para. 2 TFEU).

[18] See also Art. 45(1) of the Charter.

[19] See also Art. 46 of the Charter. Of 166 countries outside the EU, there are only three where all 27 Member States are represented (COM(2009) 262). An estimated 8.7% of EU citizens (7 million people) travelling outside the EU do so to countries where their Member State is not represented (COM(2009) 263). The implementation of this provision can be found in Dec. 95/553/EC of the Representatives of the Governments of the Member States meeting within the Council of 19 Dec. 1995 regarding protection for citizens of the EU by diplomatic and consular representations ([1995] OJ L314/73). See also the Commission's Green Paper, 'Diplomatic and consular protection of Union citizens in third countries' COM(2006) 712. The Lisbon Treaty added a new Art. 23(2) giving powers to the Council to adopt directives to facilitate diplomatic and consular protection in accordance with the special legislative procedure and after consulting the European Parliament.

[20] See also Art. 9 TEU: 'Citizenship of the Union shall be additional to national citizenship and shall not replace it', repeated in Art. 20(1) TFEU.

nationality found in Article 18 TFEU,[21] while all citizens (not just those who have exercised their rights of free movement) can enjoy the right to equal treatment, originally on the ground of sex, now on other grounds,[22] along with other social, environmental, and consumer rights.[23] This prompted Advocate General La Pergola in *Stöber and Pereira* to describe Part Two TFEU as progress of 'major significance in the construction of Europe'.[24]

## 1.2 The Charter

Given that a number of citizens' rights do exist, albeit scattered across primary and secondary sources, the Cologne European Council decided that the fundamental rights should be consolidated into a charter and so become more visible.[25] Eventually the Charter on Fundamental Rights was signed in 2000, bringing together in a single text both civil and political rights on the one hand and economic and social rights on the other.[26] The Charter, which draws on the European Convention on Human Rights, the constitutional traditions of the Member States, and general principles of Union law, is grouped around six fundamental values shared by the 'peoples' (not just the citizens) of Europe:[27] dignity (Articles 1–5); freedoms (Articles 6–19); equality (Articles 20–6); solidarity (Articles 27–38); citizens' rights (Articles 39–46); and justice (Articles 47–50).[28] The Charter's significance is all the greater following the Lisbon Treaty's entry into force giving the Charter legal effect,[29] albeit subject to the special position of the UK and Poland as laid down by the protocol.[30] The protection of human rights will be further reinforced

---

[21] See, e.g., Case C–274/96 *Bickel and Franz* [1998] ECR I–7637 considered below n. 47.

[22] See Art. 19 TFEU (ex Art. 13 EC) and the directives adopted under it: Dir. 2000/43 on Race and Ethnic Origin ([2000] OJ L180/22) and the Framework Dir. 2000/78 ([2000] OJ L303/16) prohibiting discrimination on grounds of age, religion, belief, disability and sexual orientation.

[23] See, e.g., N. Reich, 'A European constitution for citizens: Reflections on the rethinking of Union and Community law' (1997) 3 *ELJ* 131, 142–57 and 'Union citizenship: Metaphor or source of rights?' (2001) 7 *ELJ* 4, 7.

[24] Joined Cases C–4 and 5/95 *Stöber and Pereira* v. *Bundesanstalt für Arbeit* [1997] ECR I–511, para. 50.

[25] See the conclusions of the Cologne European Council setting up a Convention to draft a human rights Charter: <http://www.ue.eu.int/newsroom/newmain.asp?lang=1>, Annex IV, para. 44. Academics have long called for this: e.g. K. Lenaerts, 'Fundamental rights to be included in a Community catalogue' (1991) 16 *ELRev.* 367; P. Alston and J. Weiler, 'An "ever closer union" in need of a human rights policy: The European Union and human rights' in P. Alston (ed.), *The EU and Human Rights* (Oxford: OUP, 1999).

[26] See, e.g., I. Hare, 'Social rights as fundamental human rights' in B. Hepple (ed.), *Social and Labour Rights in a Global Context: International and comparative perspectives* (Cambridge: CUP, 2002); J. Kenner, 'Economic and social rights in the EU legal order: The mirage of indivisibility' in J. Kenner and T. Hervey (eds.), *Economic and Social Rights under the EU Charter of Fundamental Rights* (Oxford: Hart Publishing, 2003). Cf. S. Smismans, 'The European Union's fundamental rights myth' (2010) 48 *JCMS* 45.

[27] 1st recital.

[28] For criticism see J. H. H.Weiler, 'Editorial: Does the European Union truly need a charter of rights?' (2000) 6 *ELJ* 95.

[29] See Art. 6(1) TEU. Prior to 1 Dec. 2009, the Charter was not legally binding, described instead as a 'solemn proclamation'. However, a number of AGs referred to it in their Opinions (see, e.g., Jacobs AG's Opinion in Case C–50/00 *Unión de Pequeños Agricultores* v. *Council of the European Union* [2002] ECR I–6677; Geelhoed AG's Opinion in Case C–224/98 *D'Hoop* v. *Office National d'Emploi* [2002] ECR I–6191), as did the General Court (Case T–177/01 *Jégo Quéré et Cie SA* v. *European Commission* [2002] ECR II–2365) and the Court of Justice: Case C–540/03 *EP v Council (Family Reunification Directive)* [2006] ECR I–5769, paras. 38 and 58. So far the position following the entry into force of the Lisbon Treaty is not so different: Case C–555/07 *Kücückdeveci* v. *Swedex GmbH* [2010] ECR I–000.

[30] Protocol No. 30 on the application of the Charter of Fundamental Rights of the European Union to Poland and the United Kingdom. The Heads of States have agreed to extend that protocol to the Czech

by the EU's accession to the European Convention on Human Rights provided for by Article 6(2) TEU.[31]

However, the Charter's existence serves to highlight an ongoing tension that pervades the area of law concerning citizenship. Fundamental rights are seen as universal, capable of being enjoyed by all human beings. By contrast, the majority of the rights in Part Two TFEU on citizenship of the Union can be enjoyed only by EU citizens who benefit from them by virtue of their nationality. It might also be thought that the rights outlined by Part Two TFEU and the Charter are all enforceable vertically against the body bestowing the title 'citizen', i.e. the EU. In fact, most are enforced vertically but against the state—either the citizen's own state (in the case of social, consumer, and environmental rights) or the host state (in respect of the free movement rights). Only a few rights are enforceable vertically against the EU (the right to petition the Parliament and to contact the ombudsman).[32] Therefore, one of the conundrums of EU citizenship is that rights intended to foster a commitment to the Union are actually being exercised against the Member States.

The relationship between the Union citizen and the Member States also explains another potential tension. The Union gives rights but—despite the wording of Article 20(2)—demands little by way of duties from its citizens (e.g., to pay taxes, to participate in the defence of the country, to obey the law, to vote, willingness to work).[33] These duties are owed to the Member States and thus it is the Member States which bear the burden—using national taxpayers' money—of the rights. And because the Member States hold the purse strings, and ultimately the decision-making power, they are not prepared to relinquish their sovereignty fully. Therefore, while, under international law, citizens of a state cannot be deported, no matter how mad, bad, or impecunious they might be, migrant EU citizens can still be deported from the host state.[34] In this respect EU citizenship is more partial than would first appear.

## 1.3 Article 21(1) TFEU

Of the rights laid down in Articles 20–5 TFEU, Article 21(1) (ex Article 18(1) EC) is considered the 'primary'[35] right. It gives EU citizens the right to move *and* reside freely within

---

Republic: Conclusions of the European Council of 29 and 30 Oct. 2009 (Doc. 15265/09 Concl. 3). For a discussion of the protocol, see C. Barnard, 'The 'opt-out' for the UK and Poland from the Charter of Fundamental Rights: Triumph of rhetoric over reality?' in S. Griller and J. Ziller (eds.), *The Lisbon Treaty: EU Constitutionalism without a Constitutional Treaty* (New York: SpringerWien), 2008, 257.

[31] See also the Commission's Communication 'An area of freedom, security and justice serving the citizen', COM(2009) 262, 7. The fundamental rights agency (established by Council Reg. 168/2007 ([2007] OJ L53/1)) assists the EU institutions and Member States through research projects and data collection. See also the complementary programme, 'Fundamental rights and citizenship' adopted by Council Dec. 2007/252/ JHA ([2007] OJ L110/33).

[32] See S. O'Leary, 'The relationship between Community citizenship and the protection of fundamental rights in Community law' (1995) 32 *CMLRev.* 519.

[33] See, e.g., C. Closa, 'Citizenship of the Union and nationality of the Member States' (1995) 29 *CMLRev.* 487, 509.

[34] This issue is considered in more detail in Ch. 13. Note, in the same spirit, that Member States can still reserve certain senior jobs in the public service to nationals only (Art. 45(4) TFEU and Arts. 51 and 62 TFEU).

[35] La Pergola AG in Case C–85/96 *Martínez Sala* v. *Freistaat Bayern* [1998] ECR I–2691, para. 18. See also 1st recital to CRD 2004/38.

the territory of the Member States,[36] subject to the limitations and conditions laid down in the Treaties and by the measures adopted to give them effect.[37] The initial question facing the Court was whether Article 21(1) merely codified the existing law (as the drafters had intended), in which case it was largely unremarkable,[38] or whether it went beyond the existing law and created a free-standing right to movement for *all* Union citizens, irrespective of their economic or financial standing. If so, then Article 21 was of considerable importance. After a certain amount of prevarication, when the Court made passing reference to the citizenship provisions but only to reinforce its interpretation of Articles 45, 49, or 56,[39] the Court finally decided on the importance of citizenship when it declared in *Grzelczyk*[40] that:

Union citizenship is destined to be the fundamental status of nationals of the Member States, enabling those who find themselves in the same situation to enjoy the same treatment in law irrespective of their nationality, subject to such exceptions as are expressly provided for.[41]

This paved the way for the Court in *Baumbast*[42] to sever the link between migration and being economically active:

the Treaty on European Union does not require that citizens of the Union pursue a professional or trade activity, whether as an employed or self-employed person, in order to enjoy the rights provided in Part Two [TFEU], on citizenship of the Union.

This resulted in the finding in *Chen*[43] that a baby, born to Chinese parents in Northern Ireland which gave the baby the nationality of the Republic of Ireland (i.e., Irish nationality), enjoyed the rights of Union citizenship. She therefore enjoyed the right to reside in the UK under Article 21(1), subject to the limitations and conditions laid down by the Person of Independent Means Directive 90/364 (now Article 7(1)(b) of the CRD 2004/38) which had to be interpreted narrowly.

---

[36] As La Pergola AG said in Case C–85/96 *Martínez Sala* [1998] ECR I–2691, para. 18 in emphasizing the right to move *and* the right to reside, Art. 21(1) extracted the kernel from the other freedoms of movement.

[37] The European Parliament and Council, acting in accordance with the ordinary legislative procedure, may 'adopt provisions with a view to facilitating the exercise of the rights referred to in paragraph 1' (Art. 21(2)) where the Treaties have not provided the necessary powers. However, in respect of social security or social protection Art. 21(3) TFEU provides that the Council can act in accordance with the special legislative procedure.

[38] Even prior to Maastricht there were a number of decisions which can be seen with the benefit of hindsight to have a citizenship component: e.g., Case 186/87 *Cowan* [1989] ECR 195; Case 293/83 *Gravier* v. *City of Liège* [1985] ECR 593.

[39] See, e.g., Case C–193/94 *Skanavi* [1996] ECR I–929; Case C–274/96 *Bickel and Franz* [1998] ECR I–7637.

[40] Case C–184/99 [2001] ECR I–6193, para. 31, echoing La Pergola AG in Case C–85/96 *Martínez Sala* [1998] ECR I–2691, para. 18. For a full discussion, see D. Kostakopoulou, 'Ideas, norms and European citizenship: Explaining institutional change' (2005) 68 *MLR* 233.

[41] See also La Pergola AG in Case C–85/96 *Martínez Sala* [1998] ECR I–2691, para. 20., who said the introduction of Union citizenship creates a new status for the individual, 'a new individual legal standing in addition to that already provided for', and Art. 21 attaches to that new status the right to move and reside freely.

[42] Case C–413/99 *Baumbast and R.* v. *Secretary of State for the Home Department* [2002] ECR I–7091, para. 83.

[43] Case C–200/02 *Chen* v. *Secretary of State for the Home Department* [2004] ECR I–9925. Cf. *McCarthy v. Secretary of State* [2008] EWCA 641 now on appeal to the House of Lords.

From the case law it is now possible to say that, subject to the limitations and conditions laid down in the Treaties and the secondary legislation, all EU citizens enjoy under Article 21(1) TFEU:[44]

- the initial right of entry into another Member State[45]
- a free standing and directly effective right of residence in another Member State[46]
- the right to enjoy social advantages on equal terms with nationals[47] for those lawfully resident[48] in another Member State.

## 2. THE CITIZENS' RIGHTS DIRECTIVE 2004/38

### 2.1 Introduction

The rights provided by Article 21(1) must now be viewed in the context of the Citizens' Rights Directive (CRD) 2004/38,[49] which repeals and replaces the directives facilitating the migration of the economically active: Directive 68/360[50] on the rights of entry and residence; Regulation 1251/70[51] on the right to remain; the two Union directives on establishment and services;[52] and the three 1990 Residence Directives, together with the provisions on family rights laid down in Articles 10 and 11 of Regulation 1612/68. At the heart of the directive lies the basic idea that the rights enjoyed by the migrant citizen and their family members increase the longer a person is resident in another Member State.[53]

Because the Court sees this directive as central to citizens' rights it insisted in *Metock*[54] that it must not be interpreted restrictively nor must the provisions of the CRD be interpreted so as to deprive them of their effectiveness. Furthermore, the Court notes that there is a continuum between the pre- and post-CRD,[55] as well as a raising of standards. It said that the CRD 'aims in particular to strengthen the right of free movement and residence of all Union citizens, so that citizens cannot derive less rights from that directive than from the instruments of secondary legislation which it amends or repeals'.[56]

---

[44] A full discussion of the development of this case law can be found in Ch. 15 of the first edition of this book.

[45] Case C–357/98 *Ex p. Yiadom* [2000] ECR I–9265.

[46] Case C–413/99 *Baumbast* [2002] ECR I–7091, para. 84.

[47] Case C–274/96 *Bickel and Franz* [1998] ECR I–7637 (translation facilities); Case C–85/96 *Martínez Sala* [1998] ECR I–2691 (child allowance); Case C–184/99 *Grzelczyk* [2001] ECR I–6193 (minimex).

[48] Case C–85/96 *Martínez Sala* [1998] ECR I–2691; Case C–456/02 *Trojani* [2004] ECR I–7573.

[49] In its Report on the Application of the Directive (COM(2008) 840/3, 3) the Commission notes that 'The overall transposition of Directive 2004/38 is rather disappointing. Not one Member State has transposed the Directive effectively and correctly in its entirety. Not one Article of the Directive has been transposed effectively and correctly by all Member States.'

[50] [1968] OJ SE (II) L257/13/485.

[51] This was repealed by Commission Reg. 635/2006 (OJ [2006] L112/9).

[52] Dir. 73/148 OJ [1973] L172/14 and Dir. 75/34 (OJ [1975] L14/10).

[53] The cross-border element remains essential: Case C–127/08 *Metock and others v Minister for Justice, Equality and Law Reform* [2008] ECR I–6241, para. 77. See also 3rd recital of CRD: 'Union citizenship should be the fundamental status of nationals of the Member States *when* they exercise their right of free movement and residence' (emphasis added).

[54] Case C–127/08 *Metock* [2008] ECR I–6241, paras. 84 and 93.

[55] Para. 59.     [56] Ibid.

## 2.2 The Personal Scope of the Citizens' Rights Directive

### (a) The rules

The directive applies to Union citizens, defined, as with Article 20(1) TFEU, as 'any person having the nationality of a Member State'[57] who moves to, or resides in, a Member State other than that of which he or she is a national.[58] In fact, as we shall see, for the first five years, it really applies only to those Union citizens who have sufficient resources, either through employment or independently, who will not become an unreasonable burden on the host state.

The directive also applies to family members, irrespective of nationality,[59] who 'accompany *or* join them'.[60] As with the original Article 10 of Regulation 1612/68, the family members fall into two groups: (1) those who must be admitted[61] and (2) those whose entry and residence the host state must merely facilitate[62] (see fig. 12.1). In respect of the first group, the definition of family members is drafted more broadly than in the original Regulation 1612/68. According to Article 2(2) CRD, family member means:[63]

(a)  spouse

(b)  the partner with whom the Union citizen has contracted a registered partnership, on the basis of the legislation of a Member State, if the legislation of the host Member State treats registered partnerships as equivalent to marriage and in accordance with the conditions laid down in the relevant legislation of the host Member State

(c)  the direct descendants who are under the age of 21 or are dependants and those of the spouse or partner as defined in (b)

(d)  the dependent direct relatives in the ascending line and those of the spouse or partner as defined in (b).

In respect of the second group (those whose admission must be facilitated), according to Article 3(2) two sorts of family members fall into this category:

(a)  any other family members,[64] not falling under Article 2(2) who, in the country from which they have come,[65] are dependants or members of the household of the Union citizen having the primary right of residence, or where serious health grounds strictly require the personal care of the family member by the Union citizen[66]

(b)  the partner with whom the Union citizen has a durable relationship, duly attested.[67]

---

[57]  Art. 2(1).          [58]  Art. 3(1).

[59]  See also the fifth recital to the directive: 'The right of all citizens to move and reside freely within the territory of the Member States should, if it is to be exercised under objective conditions of freedom and dignity, be also granted to their family members, irrespective of nationality.'          [60]  Ibid. Emphasis added.

[61]  Art. 3(1).          [62]  Art. 3(2).          [63]  Art. 2.

[64]  The degree of relatedness is not specified: COM(2009) 313, 5.

[65]  The meaning of this phrase was considered by the British Court of Appeal in *KG (Sri Lanka)* v. *Secretary of State for the Home Department* [2008] EWCA Civ 13.

[66]  The fact that these conditions are satisfied must be proved by a document issued by the relevant authority in the country of origin or country from which they are arriving in the case of those seeking residence under Art. 7: Art. 8(5)(e).

[67]  By contrast, the fact that a 'durable relationship, duly attested' exists is satisfied merely by 'proof' for those seeking residence under Art. 7: Art. 8(5)(f).

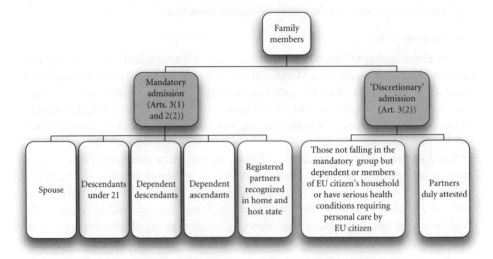

**Fig. 12.1** Family members under the CRD

While Article 3(2) requires the host state merely to 'facilitate entry and residence' of this second group, the directive provides a strong steer that the normal rule will be to permit entry. Article 3(2)(b) provides: 'The host Member State shall undertake an extensive examination of the personal circumstances and shall justify any denial of entry or residence to these people.'

We shall now consider the meaning of the various terms to describe family members, particularly in the light of the Court's case law under (the now repealed) Article 10 of Regulation 1612/68.

### (b) Spouses, registered partners, and partners in a durable relationship duly attested

#### (i) Spouses

*Who is a 'Spouse'?* The Court has approached the term 'spouse' in a conventional manner:[68] it is the person to whom the EU citizen is married under the laws of the state where the marriage was entered into. In *Diatta*[69] the Court considered the situation of a couple who were married but separated. The case concerned a Senegalese woman married to a French national who lived and worked in Germany. Eventually she separated from her husband and lived in separate accommodation with the intention of divorcing. The authorities refused to renew her residence permit on the ground that she was no longer a family member of an EU national and did not live with her husband. The Court ruled that the (then) Article 10 of Regulation 1612/68 did not require members of a migrant's family to live permanently together. It reasoned that if cohabitation of spouses was a mandatory condition for a residence permit, the worker could cause his spouse to be expelled from the Member State at any moment, simply by throwing her out of the house.

---

[68]  Although cf. Case C–117/01 *KB* v. *National Health Service Pensions Agency* [2004] ECR I–541, paras. 33–4 interpreting Art. 157 TFEU (ex Art. 141 EC) on equal pay where the Court held that national legislation preventing a transsexual man from marrying a woman interfered with the right to marry under Art. 12 ECHR, thereby preventing the man from receiving a survivor's pension, and so breached Art. 157.

[69]  Case 267/83 *Diatta* v. *Land Berlin* [1985] ECR 567.

*Diatta* therefore suggests that separated couples must be allowed to remain in the host state, a decision compatible with the Court's approach in *Commission v. Germany*[70] that Regulation 1612/68 had to be interpreted in the light of the requirement of the respect for family life set out in Article 8 ECHR. However, the position under the CRD may be different. To enjoy a right of residence under Article 7(1)(d) the family members must be 'accompanying or joining a Union citizen', and to acquire permanent residence under Article 16(2) the family members must have 'legally resided with the Union citizen in the host state for a continuous period of five years'.[71] This suggests a requirement of actual cohabitation.

A divorced spouse's position is different again. In *Diatta*[72] the Court said that a 'marital relationship cannot be regarded as dissolved so long as it has not been terminated by the competent authority'.[73] This would suggest that only on the completion of all the formal stages of divorce proceedings, including the grant of a decree absolute, will the spouse's dependent right of residence in the Member State cease. However, as we shall see, Article 13 of Directive 2004/38 does give certain legal protection to divorcees.[74]

The term 'spouse' does not include cohabitees. This was shown in *Reed*[75] where the Court ruled that an English woman wishing to join her cohabitee in the Netherlands could not rely on Article 10 of Regulation 1612/68 because she was not a spouse. However, on the facts of the case Reed was successful because under *Dutch* law foreigners in a stable relationship with a Dutch national were entitled to reside in the Netherlands. If Ms Reed were not allowed to remain in the Netherlands, this would be discriminatory, contrary to Articles 18 and 45 TFEU and Article 7(2) of Regulation 1612/68. The position of cohabitees is now also covered, at least in part, by the discretionary admission provisions in Article 3(2)(b) CRD, provided the relationship is durable and duly attested (see below).

*Forced, arranged and polygamous marriages*: To date the Court has not willingly looked behind the marriage 'veil' to see whether the marriage is valid. However, Article 35 CRD provides:

Member States may adopt the necessary measures to refuse, terminate or withdraw any right conferred by this Directive in the case of abuse of rights or fraud, such as marriages of convenience.

This provision comes with the caveat that any measure taken has to be proportionate and subject to the procedural safeguards provided in the directive.[76] In its guidance on the directive,[77] the Commission is more expansive: 'Marriages validly contracted anywhere in the world must be in principle recognized for the purpose of the application of the Directive.' It continues that:

Forced marriages, in which one or both parties is married without his or her consent or against his or her will, are not protected by international or Union law. Forced marriages must be distinguished from arranged marriages, where both parties fully and freely consent to the

---

[70] Case 249/86 [1989] ECR 1263, para. 10.

[71] Cf. the more favourable position under the Long Term Residents Dir. 2003/109 ([2003] L16/44, adopted under Art. 63(3)(a) and (4) EC discussed in Ch. 14. The TCN family member will enjoy a right to permanent residence and equal treatment rights in the first state without having to move to a second Member State.

[72] Case 267/83 [1985] ECR 567.    [73] Para. 20.    [74] See below, text attached to nn. 183–185.

[75] Case 59/85 [1986] ECR 1283.    [76] Arts. 30–1, considered in detail in Ch. 13.

[77] Commission Guidance for better transposition and application of Dir. 2004/38: COM(2009) 313, 4.

marriage, although a third party takes a leading role in the choice of partner, and from marriages of convenience.

This suggests that the host state is not obliged to admit the spouse of a forced marriage but must admit the spouse of an arranged marriage. The Commission also says that Member States are not obliged to recognize polygamous marriages, contracted lawfully in a third country, which may be in conflict with their own legal order. It adds 'This is without prejudice to the obligation to take due account of the best interests of children of such marriages.'

*Marriages of convenience*: Marriages of convenience are given special attention in the guidance in the section on abuse and fraud. The Commission says:[78]

Recital 28 defines marriages of convenience for the purposes of the Directive as marriages contracted for the *sole* purpose of enjoying the right of free movement and residence under the Directive that someone would not have otherwise. A marriage cannot be considered as a marriage of convenience simply because it brings an immigration advantage, or indeed any other advantage. The quality of the relationship is immaterial to the application of Article 35.[79]

The Commission lists a set of indicative criteria for cases where there is *unlikely* to be an abuse of Union rights (e.g., the third-country spouse would have no problem obtaining a right of residence in his/her own capacity or has already lawfully resided in the EU citizen's Member State beforehand; the couple had been in a relationship for a long time; or they had a common domicile/household) and some criteria which indicate the possible intention to abuse the rights conferred by the directive (e.g., the couple have never met before their marriage; they are inconsistent about their respective personal details; they do not speak a language understood by both).

The Commission says that these criteria are possible triggers for investigation only; they are not in anyway conclusive. It continues that due attention has to be given to all the circumstances of the individual case and that the investigation may involve a separate interview with each of the two spouses but any investigation must respect fundamental rights, in particular Articles 8 ECHR (right to respect for private and family life) and 12 ECHR (right to marry) (Articles 7 and 9 of the EU Charter). The burden of proof lies on the Member States seeking to restrict rights under the directive. On appeal, it is for the national courts to verify the existence of abuse in individual cases, evidence of which must be adduced in accordance with the rules of national law, provided that the effectiveness of Union law is not undermined.

### (ii) Registered partners and partners in a durable relationship duly attested

So far we have examined the position of spouses. We turn now to consider the position of 'partner', a new category introduced by the directive. In respect of registered partners,[80] the CRD follows the approach adopted in *Reed*. It gives rights to 'the partner

---

[78] Ibid., 15 (emphasis in the original).

[79] It adds: 'The definition of marriages of convenience can be extended by analogy to other forms of relationships contracted for the sole purpose of enjoying the right of free movement and residence, such as (registered) partnership of convenience, fake adoption or where an EU citizen declares to be a father of a third country child to convey nationality and a right of residence on the child and its mother, knowing that he is not its father and not willing to assume parental responsibilities.'

[80] See generally, H. Toner, *Partnership Rights, Free Movement and EU Law* (Oxford: Hart Publishing, 2004).

with whom the Union citizen has contracted a registered partnership, on the basis of legislation of a Member State' provided that 'the legislation of the host Member State treats registered partnerships as equivalent to marriage and in accordance with the conditions laid down in any such legislation'.[81] In other words, only if the partnership is recognized by both the home and host state will the registered partner enjoy the rights laid down by the CRD.

While unmarried heterosexual couples may be able to benefit from this provision if they are able to enter into a 'registered partnership' recognized in both the home and host state, the most immediate beneficiaries will be homosexual couples. Therefore a British man who has entered into a civil partnership under the British Civil Partnership Act 2004 with a Brazilian man, would be able to go with his Brazilian civil partner to Sweden to reside and work there under the CRD since Swedish law recognizes registered partnerships of homosexual couples. By contrast, this couple will not be able to rely on the directive to reside and work in Greece since Greece does not recognize registered partnerships. Partners in this situation, as well as unmarried heterosexual couples whose relationship is not formally recognized by law, will have to rely on the discretionary provisions in Article 3(2)(b) in order to persuade the host state to admit the Union citizen's partner. However, Article 3(2)(b) is dependent on the individuals showing that the relationship is durable and duly attested, terms not defined in the directive, although the Commission suggests that it could be determined by reference to a certain minimum period of being together. If partners cannot satisfy these requirements, their only avenue of recourse is to rely on the principles in *Reed* (outlined above).

### (iii) First point of entry principle and the principle of abuse

It had long been thought that the family provisions of Regulation 1612/68 and now the CRD meant that TCN spouses could either accompany the migrant spouse when moving from Member State A to B, or join the migrant spouse in State B directly from a third country.[82] *Akrich*[83] cast doubt on this orthodoxy.

Akrich, a Moroccan national, was convicted of theft in the UK and deported to Algeria. He then returned to the UK on a false French identity card, was deported again, and again clandestinely returned to the UK. He then married a British national, who went to work in Ireland; he was deported to Ireland. Relying on the principles in *Surinder Singh*,[84] Mrs Akrich wanted to return to the UK, bringing her husband with her. The Court said that Union law did not apply. At paragraphs 50–1 the Court said that in order to benefit from the rights under Article 10 of Regulation 1612/68 a TCN spouse (Mr Akrich) could move to another Member State with the migrant citizen (Mrs Akrich) only once the TCN spouse/registered partner had lawfully entered one EU state under national law (the first point of entry principle) and lawfully resided there (the prior lawful residence (PLR) principle). This suggested that Mr and Mrs Akrich could not return together to the UK. However, the Court added that where the marriage was genuine, the UK had to have regard to respect for Mrs Akrich's family life under

---

[81] [81] Art. 2(2)(b).    [82] See, e.g., M. Elsmore and P. Starup, case note on *Jia*, (2007) 44 *CMLRev*. 787.
[83] Case C–109/01 *Secretary of State for the Home Department* v. *Akrich* [2001] ECR I–9607, noted by E. Spaventa (2005) 42 *CMLRev*. 225.    [84] Case C–370/90 [1992] ECR I–4265, see Ch. 8.

Article 8[85] which suggested that the UK should admit husband and wife on human rights grounds.

The decision, particularly in respect of the PLR principle, was subject to much criticism. Although based on the idea of separation of competence between Member States (deciding who could enter their territory) and the EU (guaranteeing movement between states after initial entry),[86] the PLR principle rested on shaky foundations, particularly in the light of decisions such as *MRAX*[87] (Member States cannot deny entry to TCN spouses on the sole ground that the TCN has not obtained the required visa) and *Carpenter*[88] (TCN visa overstayer who subsequently married EU citizen allowed to stay in UK to enable citizen to provide services).

The Court responded to this criticism in *Jia*[89] by limiting *Akrich* to the situation where the TCN spouse was not lawfully resident in one Member States before he moved to another.[90] However, in *Metock*[91] the Court expressly reversed the PLR principle, as laid down in paragraphs 50–1 in *Akrich* (but not the rest of the judgment), following a careful textual analysis of the directive.[92] *Metock* concerned four TCNs who arrived in Ireland and unsuccessfully applied for asylum. While still resident in Ireland they married migrant EU citizens who were also resident in Ireland. None of the marriages was a marriage of convenience. The TCN spouses were all refused a residence card by the Irish authorities on the ground that they did not satisfy the PLR principle.

Relying on the 'restrictions' approach used extensively in respect of free movement of persons, the Court said that 'if Union citizens were not allowed to lead a normal family life in the host Member State, the exercise of the freedoms they are guaranteed by the [Treaties] would be seriously obstructed'.[93] It continued that the directive applied to all Union citizens who moved to, or resided in, a Member State other than that in which they were a national, and to their family members who accompanied *or* joined them in that Member State, regardless of whether the TCN has already been lawfully resident in another Member State.[94]

Thus, by giving a broad interpretation to the verb 'joined', the Court abandoned the PLR principle. However, the Court went further than that since it also gave rights not only to pre-existing couples but also to couples that met in the home state.[95] The reason for this was that the refusal of the host state to grant TCN family members a right of residence might discourage Union citizens from continuing to reside in the host state.[96] As Costello points out, in reaching this conclusion, the Court rejects the usual conception of spousal dependency underpinning family reunification law, where the trailing spouse follows the worker to another Member State.[97] Instead, 'the Directive becomes an instrument for both family formation and family reunification, two modes of family migration that Member States often seek to differentiate'.[98]

---

[85] Para. 58.    [86] Para. 49.

[87] Case C–459/99 *Mouvement contre le racisme l'antisémeitisme et la xénophobie ASBL (MRAX)* v. *Belgium* [2002] ECR I–6591, para. 61.    [88] Case C–60/00 [2002] ECR I–6279.

[89] Case C–1/05 *Jia* v. *Migrationsverket* [2007] ECR I–1.    [90] Para. 26.

[91] Case C–127/08 *Metock* [2008] ECR I–6241, para. 58. See A. Tryfonidou, 'Family reunification rights of (migrant) Union citizens: Towards a more liberal approach' (2009) 15 *ELJ* 634.    [92] Paras. 49–55.

[93] Para. 62.    [94] Para. 70.

[95] Para. 99. See also Case C–551/07 *Sahin*, Reasoned Order of 19 Dec. 2008.    [96] Para. 92.

[97] C. Costello, '*Metock*: Free movement and "normal family life" in the Union' (2009) 46 *CMLRev.* 587, 601.

[98] Ibid.

A number of Member States, especially Denmark,[99] were deeply worried about the implications of the Court's rights-based approach for their conception of discretionary migration control.[100] The Court tried to assuage these concerns by pointing out that first, its ruling applied not to TCNs generally but only to TCN family members of migrant EU citizens.[101] Secondly, it said that Member States could still control migration using the express derogations (public policy, public security, and public health) laid down by the directive.[102] It added that even if the personal conduct of the TCN did not justify the adoption of measures of public policy or security, 'the Member State remains entitled to impose other penalties on him which do not interfere with freedom of movement and residence, such as a fine, provided that they are proportionate'.[103] Thirdly, the Court pointed out that, in accordance with Article 35 CRD, Member States could adopt the necessary measures to refuse, terminate or withdraw any right conferred by that directive in the case of abuse of rights or fraud, such as marriages of convenience,[104] 'it being understood that any such measures must be proportionate and subject to procedural safeguards provided for in the directive'.[105]

The Commission also responded to Member State concerns by issuing guidance[106] on when Union law is being abused in the case of family reunification. It says that abuse occurs 'when EU citizens, unable to be joined by their third country family members in their Member State of origin because of the application of national immigration rules preventing it, move to another Member State with the *sole* purpose to evade, upon returning to their home Member State, the national law that frustrated their family reunification efforts'. It continues that the defining characteristics of the line between genuine and abusive use of Union law should be based on the assessment of whether the exercise of Union rights in a Member State from which the EU citizens and their family members return was genuine and effective, an assessment made on a case-by-case basis. If, in a concrete case of return, the use of Union rights was genuine and effective, the Member State of origin should not inquire into the personal motives that triggered the previous move.

### (c) Dependants

Directive 2004/38 gives rights to the Union citizen's direct descendants under the age of 21 and dependent descendants, as well as to those of the spouse or registered partner.[107]

---

[99] COM(2008) 840/3, 4. See also A. Willis, 'New guidelines will reduce fake marriages, Brussels says', <http://www.euobserver.com/22/28407>.

[100] Costello, above n. 97, 588. See e.g., Justice and Home Affairs Council Conclusions Press release 16325/1/08, 27 and 28 Nov. 2008: 'The Council considers that, in compliance with and in the interests of the right of free movement, every effort must be made to prevent and combat any misuses and abuses, as well as actions of a criminal nature, with forceful and proportionate measures with due regard to the applicable law, against citizens who break the law in a sufficiently serious manner by committing serious or repeated offences which cause serious prejudice.'                                                           [101] Para. 73.

[102] These derogations are considered further in Ch. 13.           [103] Para. 97.

[104] The 28th recital adds 'or any other form of relationships contracted for the sole purpose of enjoying the right of free movement or residence'. See also Council Res. 97/C382/01 of 4 Dec. 1997.

[105] Para. 75.           [106] COM(2009) 313, 17–18.

[107] The children do not need to be blood relatives: Case C–275/02 *Ayaz* v. *Land Baden-Württemberg* [2004] ECR I–8765, para. 45, a case under the EU–Turkey Association Agreement which the Court said was to be interpreted in line with Reg. 1612/68 and the CRD. The Court ruled that stepchildren are also covered. The Commission's Guidance (COM(2009) 313, 5) adds that the provision includes 'relationships or minors in custody of a permanent legal guardian. Foster children and foster parents who have temporary custody

It also gives rights to the dependent ascendants (e.g., parents, grandparents) of the Union citizen and the Union citizen's spouse or registered partner.[108] In *Lebon*[109] the Court made clear that dependency was a question of fact. It said that a dependant is 'a member of the family who is supported by the worker',[110] adding that there was no need to determine the reasons why the dependant needed the worker's support or to enquire whether the dependants could support themselves by working.[111]

In *Jia*[112] the Court developed the definition of dependency in the context of dependent relatives in the ascending line (Chinese mother-in-law (Mrs Jia) of German self-employed migrant (Mrs Li) working in Sweden). It said that, in order to determine dependency, an individual assessment was necessary. This meant that the host state (Sweden) had to assess whether, having regard to the applicant's 'financial and social conditions', she was not in a position to support herself. The need for material support from the Union national or her spouse had to exist in Mrs Jia's state of origin (China) (or the country from which she came) when she applied to join the Union national.[113] The Court said that the host state could require proof of dependency, adduced by 'appropriate means',[114] but that did not necessarily mean a document from the Chinese authorities. On the other hand, a mere undertaking from a Union national or his spouse to support the family member 'need not be regarded as establishing the existence of that family member's situation of real dependence'.[115]

In respect of the Union citizen's other family members (e.g., aunts, uncles, cousins) who are dependants *or* members of his household, the state must 'facilitate their entry and residence'. The same applies to those whose 'serious health grounds strictly require the personal care of the family member of the Union citizen'.

## 2.3 Rights of Departure, Entry, and Return

### (a) The right to depart from the home state

National rules which preclude or deter nationals of a Member State from leaving their state of origin interfere with freedom of movement, even if they apply to all migrants.[116] Directive 2004/38 reinforces, and the case law confirms,[117] the Treaty right to depart from a Member State—not necessarily the state of origin—where Union citizens and

may have rights under the Directive, depending upon the strength of the ties in the particular case. There is no restriction as to the degree of relatedness.'

[108]  In respect of all of these categories of family members 'documentary evidence that the conditions laid down' are met is required for those seeking a right of residence: Art. 8(5)(d).

[109]  Case 316/85 [1987] ECR 2811.

[110]  Para. 22. The support must be material rather than emotional: COM(2009) 313, 5.     [111]  Para. 22.

[112]  Case C–1/05 *Jia* [2007] ECR I–1.

[113]  Para. 37. The Commission's Guidance (COM(2009) 313, 5) adds 'The Directive does not lay down any requirement as to the minimum duration of the dependency or the amount of material support provided, as long as the dependency is genuine and structural in character.'     [114]  Para. 41.

[115]  Paras. 42–3.

[116]  See, e.g., the workers' cases: Case C–10/90 *Masgio v. Bundesknappschaft* [1991] ECR I–1119, paras. 18–19; Case C–415/93 *Bosman* [1995] ECR I–4921, para. 104; and Case C–232/01 *Hans van Lent* [2003] ECR I–11525, para. 21.

[117]  See Case C–33/07 *Ministerul Administrației și Internelor v. Jipa* [2008] ECR I–5157, paras. 17–20; Case C–127/08 *Metock* [2008] ECR I–6241, para. 68.

their families currently live.[118] According to the directive, Union citizens and their family members may leave the Member State by producing a valid identity card or passport (passport only for TCN family members) which the Member State is obliged to issue or renew.[119] The passport[120] must be valid for all Member States and for any states through which the holder must pass when travelling between Member States.[121] Expiry of the identity card or passport on the basis of which the person entered the host state and was issued with a registration certificate or card (see below) is not to constitute a ground for expulsion from the host state.[122]

## (b) The right to enter the host state

Host states must allow Union citizens and their families to enter their territory but, in order to find out who is on their territory,[123] host states can ask the migrant to produce an identity card or passport (passport only for TCN family members).[124] No visa or other entry formality can be demanded from Union citizens[125] but they can be demanded from a member of the worker's family who is not an EU national.[126] This is one of the many examples of the way in which the CRD distinguishes between the treatment of EU and non-EU national family members. However, in *MRAX*[127] the Court said that a refusal to allow entry due to the non-production of valid passports/identity cards, and where necessary a visa, would be disproportionate if TCN spouses were able to prove their identity and marital ties in other ways and there was no evidence that they represented a risk to public policy, security, or health. This position is now confirmed in Article 5(4) CRD.

Although Member States are entitled to check passports/identity cards (and visas where necessary) at the frontier, the compatibility of such border formalities with the notion of a 'Europe without internal frontiers' laid down in Article 26 TFEU has been questioned in two cases brought by the Commission. In the first, *Commission v. Belgium*,[128] non-Belgian EU nationals residing in Belgium were required to produce their residence or establishment permits in addition to their passports or identity cards. The Court said that

---

[118] Art. 4(1).     [119] Art. 4(3). No exit visa or equivalent formality may be imposed.

[120] If the passport is the only document with which the person may lawfully leave the country, it must be valid for at least five years: Art. 4(4).

[121] Art. 4(4). Having produced a passport or identity card, the Member State may not demand from the worker an exit visa or similar document (Art. 4(2)).     [122] Art. 15(2).

[123] Case C–265/88 *Messner* [1989] ECR 4209.

[124] Art. 5(1). Art. 5(4) provides that where an EU citizen or a TCN family member does not have the necessary travel documents (or visas), the Member State must give them every reasonable opportunity to obtain the documents or to corroborate or prove by other means that they are covered by the right to freedom of movement and residence.     [125] Art. 5(1), 2nd para.

[126] Art. 3(2). Case 157/79 *R v. Pieck* [1980] ECR 2171, para. 10. The list of third countries whose nationals need visas when crossing the external border of the Member States is determined by Council Reg. 539/2001 ([2001] OJ L81/1). Member States must grant TCN family members 'every facility' to obtain the necessary visas which must be issued free of charge and on the basis of an accelerated procedure. The Commission considers that delays of more than four weeks are not reasonable. Citing Case C–503/03 *Commission v. Spain* [2006] ECR I–1097, the Commission also says (COM(2009) 313, 6) that TCN family members have a right to obtain a visa on presentation of a valid passport and evidence of the family link only. Member States can also encourage integration of EU citizens and their TCN family members by offering language course on a voluntary basis but no consequence can be attached to their refusal to attend them (COM(2009) 313, 7). Possession of a valid residence card issued under Art. 10 CRD exempts family members from the visa requirement.

[127] Case C–459/99 *MRAX v. Belgium* [2002] ECR I–6591, para. 61.

[128] Case 321/87 *Commission v. Belgium* [1989] ECR 997.

such controls could constitute a barrier to free movement if carried out in a systematic, arbitrary, or unnecessarily restrictive manner.[129] In the second case, *Commission v. Netherlands*,[130] the Court ruled that national legislation requiring citizens to answer questions put by border officials regarding the purpose and duration of their journey and the financial means at their disposal was incompatible with Directive 68/360. In these two cases the Court has curtailed the level of checks that can occur at an internal frontier. Nevertheless, it said in *Wijsenbeek*[131] that, despite Article 26 TFEU (ex Article 14 EC) (on the single market) and Article 21 TFEU (on the free movement of citizens), Member States could still require individuals, whether EU citizens or not, to establish their nationality on entering a Member State at an internal frontier of the EU.[132] Therefore, a Dutch MEP was required to hand over his passport to immigration control when he arrived in the Netherlands on a flight from Strasbourg. Further, Member States could impose penalties for breach of the requirement to present an identity card or passport, provided that the penalties are comparable to those which apply to similar national infringements and are proportionate.[133]

Finally, Article 5(5) CRD permits the host Member State to require the migrant to report his/her presence to the authorities within a reasonable and non-discriminatory period of time. Failure to comply may make the migrant 'liable to proportionate and non-discriminatory sanctions'. In this regard the directive confirms the decision in *Watson and Belmann*[134] where the Court found that an Italian law providing for migrants to be deported if they failed to register with the Italian authorities within three days of entering Italy was unlawful.[135]

### (c) The right to return to the home state

The right to return to the home state is not expressly dealt with by the CRD but is covered by the Treaties, as interpreted by the Court. The issue was considered in *Surinder Singh*,[136] examined in Chapter 8, and arose again in *Eind*.[137] The case concerned a Dutch worker who was employed in the UK where he was joined by his 11-year-old Surinamese daughter. The UK gave her a right to reside as a family member of a worker under what is now Article 2(2) CRD. Less than two years later, father and daughter returned to the Netherlands but Mr Eind could not work because he was ill and so received social

---

[129] Para. 15.    [130] Case C–68/89 *Commission* v. *Netherlands* [1991] ECR I–2637.

[131] Case C–378/97 *Criminal Proceedings against Florus Ariël Wijsenbeek* [1999] ECR I–6207. The facts of *Wijsenbeek* occurred in Dec. 1993 before the provisions of Title IV of Part Three of the Treaty of Amsterdam came into force (now Title V of Part Three TFEU). However, the Schengen provisions were operative at that time and these allowed for the crossing of internal borders without checks. Yet, because this freedom is subject to derogations on the grounds of public policy and national security, the Court said that until common rules were adopted checks could be made (para. 43): C. Jacqueson, 'Union citizenship and the Court of Justice: Something new under the sun? Towards social citizenship' (2002) 27 *ELRev.* 260, 264.

[132] Para. 45.    [133] Case C–215/03 *Oulane* [2005] ECR I–1215, para. 38.

[134] Case 118/75 *Watson and Belmann* [1976] ECR 1185. In Case C–357/98 *Ex p. Yiadom* [2000] ECR I–9265, para. 25: provisions protecting Union nationals who exercise the fundamental freedom of movement under Art. 21(1) TFEU had to be interpreted in their favour.

[135] See also Case C–265/88 *Messner* [1989] ECR 4209. In respect of a TCN spouse of a migrant worker, see Case C–459/99 *MRAX* [2002] ECR I–6591, para. 78.

[136] Case C–370/90 [1992] ECR I–4265.

[137] Case C–291/05 *Minister voor Vreemdelingenzaken en Integratie v Eind* [2007] ECR I–10719.

assistance. The daughter's application for a residence permit was turned down on the ground that since her father was not economically active, he was no longer covered by Union law and so neither was she.

The Court said that while Article 2(2) gave the TCN daughter a right to install herself with the worker in the UK,[138] it did not entail an autonomous right to free movement for the family member.[139] However, following references to the citizenship provisions,[140] the Court did say that the right of the migrant worker to return and reside in the Netherlands, after having been gainfully employed in the UK, was 'conferred by [Union] law, to the extent necessary to ensure the useful effect of the right to free movement for workers under Article [45]'.[141] The Court said that Eind would be deterred from exercising his right of free movement if he could not return to the Netherlands, economically active or not.[142] Likewise he would also be deterred from exercising his rights of free movement if he could not continue living together with close family members on his return to the Netherlands. So, under (unspecified) Union law, the daughter had the 'right to install herself with her father' in the Netherlands, even though her father was not economically active, provided that she was under 21 or dependent.[143]

### 2.4 The Right of Residence in the Host State

Not only does the directive guarantee the right to leave the home state and enter the host state, it also grants the migrant the right of residence. The directive essentially envisages three tiers of residence (see fig 12.2): up to three months; three months to five years; and (generally) five years and beyond.

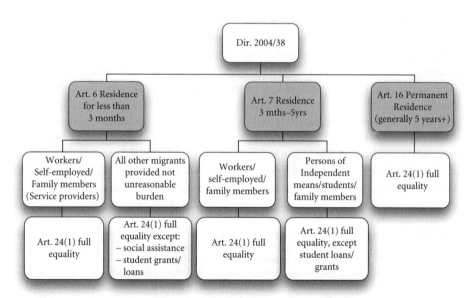

**Fig. 12.2** Residence and equality under Dir. 2004/38. (On the meaning of equality see fig. 8.1.)

---

[138] Para. 21.     [139] Para. 23.     [140] Paras. 28–32.     [141] Para. 32.     [142] Para. 35.
[143] Paras. 38–9.

### (a)  Right of residence for up to three months

Those resident for up to three months enjoy a 'right of residence'. According to Article 6, if Union citizens (whether economically active or not)[144] can produce a valid identity card or passport, and they wish to stay for up to three months only, Member States must grant them the right of residence.[145] The same applies to TCN family members, including TCNs accompanying or joining the Union citizen, on production of a valid passport.[146] However, this right of residence is not unlimited: apart from the general derogations, it is also subject to the condition that the migrants do not become 'an unreasonable burden on the social assistance system of the host state'.[147]

### (b)  Right of residence for more than three months and up to five years

#### (i)  Citizens' and family members' rights

Those resident for more than three months but less than five years also enjoy a 'right of residence'. According to Article 7(1) CRD, all Union citizens have the right of residence on the territory of another Member State for more than three months if they are workers, self-employed,[148] have sufficient resources and medical insurance, or they are students, also with sufficient resources and medical insurance.[149] The same right also applies to family members accompanying or joining the Union citizen,[150] whether they are nationals of a Member State or not.[151] Only where the host state has a reasonable doubt as to whether a Union citizen or his/her family members satisfies these conditions can the Member States verify whether the conditions are fulfilled. This verification cannot be carried out systematically.[152]

The host state can require Union citizens to register with the relevant authorities.[153] The deadline for registration may not be less than three months from the date of arrival.[154] A registration *certificate* must then be issued[155] on production of a valid identity card or passport,[156] a confirmation of engagement from the employer or certificate of employment or proof that they are self-employed, or proof that they satisfy the conditions of being of independent means or a student.[157] Failure to comply with the registration requirement may render the person concerned liable to 'proportionate and non-discriminatory sanctions'. The issuing of a registration certificate or equivalent (see below) gives the host state the opportunity to check not only whether the migrant satisfies the conditions laid down in the CRD but also whether the migrant is a 'desirable' person. This is confirmed by Article 27(3) which provides the host state may request the Member State of origin and, if

---

[144] In this respect the directive does not depart so much from the position under the case law when, following Case 186/87 *Cowan* [1989] ECR 195, all tourists were recipients of services.          [145] Art. 6(1).

[146] Art. 6(2).          [147] Art. 14(1). This term is considered further in Ch. 13.

[148] Union citizens retain the right of residence so long as they remain workers/self-employed persons: see Art. 7(3) considered further in Ch. 9.

[149] The conditions as to sufficient resources and medical insurance are considered in more detail in Ch. 13.

[150] A more limited range of family members can enjoy the Art. 7 rights where the Union citizen is a student: Art. 7(4).          [151] Art. 7(1)(d) and Art. 7(2).

[152] Art. 14(2).          [153] Art. 8(1).          [154] Art. 8(2).

[155] Ibid. The issuing of these certificates or equivalent documents must be free of charge or for a charge not exceeding that imposed on nationals for the issuing of similar documents: Art. 25(2).

[156] The expiry of the identity card/passport which was the basis for entering the host state and the issuing of a registration certificate or registration card (see below) cannot constitute a ground for expulsion: Art. 15(2).          [157] Art. 8(3).

necessary, other Member States to provide information concerning any previous police record the migrant may have. However, this is the exception not the rule: the Article makes clear that the host state may request this information only if it considers it 'essential' and '[s]uch enquiries shall not be made as a matter of routine'.

A registration certificate is also issued to family members of Union citizens who are themselves Union citizens. The host Member State may, however, require the EU family members to produce not only a valid identity card or passport but also the Union citizen's registration certificate, together with documentary evidence that the family members fall within a relationship covered by Article 2(2).[158] By contrast, TCN family members must[159] be issued with a 'residence *card*'[160] provided they produce broadly equivalent documents to those required for EU national family members.[161] The residence card (but not the registration certificate) is valid for five years from the date of issue (or for the envisaged period of residence of the Union citizen if that is less than five years)[162] but will expire as a result of prolonged absences.[163] The renewal requirement makes it easier for the host state to monitor the activities of TCNs. In respect of both the registration certificate and the residence card, the host state can carry out checks on compliance with any requirement deriving from national legislation for non-nationals to carry these documents, provided the same requirement applies to their own nationals as regards identity cards.[164]

A migrant worker can reside and start working before completing the formalities to obtain a residence permit[165] because the right of residence is a fundamental right derived from the Treaties and is not dependent upon the possession of particular documents;[166] residence permits have only probative value,[167] as *Martínez Sala*[168] shows. A Spanish national living in Germany since 1968 held various residence permits which had expired and a series of documents saying that she had applied for an extension of her permit. She then had a baby and applied for a child allowance but her application was rejected on the grounds that she had neither German nationality, nor a residence entitlement, nor a residence permit. The Court said that it was discriminatory to require a national of another Member State to produce a document (the residence permit) to obtain the benefit when

---

[158] Art. 8(5).

[159] The obligation to issue the residence card is mandatory because European Union—not national—immigration law applies.

[160] This exempts TCN family members from the visa requirement under Art. 5(2).

[161] Arts. 9–10. The list of documents to be produced is exhaustive: recital 14 and Case C–127/08 *Metock* [2008] ECR I–6241, para. 53. Member States may require that documents be translated, notarised or legalised where the national authority concerned cannot understand the language in which the particular document is written, or have a suspicion about the authenticity of the issuing authority (COM(2009) 313, 7).

[162] Art. 11(1).

[163] The validity of the residence card is not affected by temporary absences not exceeding six months or longer absences up to 12 months for important reasons such as pregnancy and childbirth (Art. 11(2)).

[164] Art. 26. See also Case C–327/02 *Panayotova* v. *Mininster voor Vreemdelingenzaken en Integratie* [2004] ECR I–11055, para. 27: the granting of residence permits must be based on a procedural system which is easily accessible and capable of ensuring that the persons concerned will have their applications dealt with objectively and within a reasonable time, and refusals to grant a permit must be capable of being challenged in judicial or quasi-judicial proceedings. According to the Commission (COM(2009) 313, 7), the residence card for a TCN must be issued within six months. [165] Art. 25.

[166] Case 118/75 *Watson and Belmann* [1976] ECR 1185, paras. 15–16. This is now confirmed in Art. 25(1) CRD and recital 11. See also Poiares Maduro AG's Opinion in Case C–524/06 *Huber* v. *Germany* [2008] ECR I–9705, para. 19.

[167] To this effect, see Case 48/75 *Royer* [1976] ECR 497, para. 50. The same rule also applies to a TCN spouse of a migrant worker: Case C–459/99 *MRAX* [2002] ECR I–6591, para. 74.

[168] Case C–85/96 [1998] ECR I–2691.

its own nationals were not required to do the same.[169] In *Oulane* the Court added that since the right of residence was derived directly from the Treaties, it was not legitimate for the host state to require the EU migrant to produce a passport when he could prove his identity by other means.[170] Further, it said that detention and deportation based solely on the failure of the person to comply with legal formalities concerning the monitoring of aliens 'impair the very substance of the right' and are 'manifestly disproportionate to the seriousness of the infringement'.[171]

Once Union citizens have registered themselves, what use can the host-state authorities make of the information supplied? This question arose in *Huber*[172] concerning a centralized register held by the German authorities which contained certain personal data relating to foreign nationals who were resident in Germany for more than three months. The register was used for statistical purposes and by the security and police services and by the judicial authorities. Mr Huber, an Austrian national, worked in Germany as a self-employed insurance agent. He asked for his data to be deleted from the register, alleging discrimination since no similar database existed for German nationals.

The Court ruled that the use of a register of data for the purpose of providing support to the authorities responsible for applying the rules on residence was, in principle, legitimate and compatible with the prohibition of discrimination on grounds of nationality laid down by Article 18(1) TFEU (ex Article 12(1) EC).[173] However, the Court said that such a register should not contain any information other than what was 'necessary', within the meaning of Article 7(e)[174] of the Data Protection Directive 95/46.[175] The Court then distinguished between personal data contained in the documents referred to in Articles 8(3) (proof of (self)employment) and 27(1) CRD (derogations), which it considered was 'necessary' for applying the rules on residence,[176] and personal data containing individualized personal information for statistical purposes, which was not.[177] The Court also said that, as a citizen who had migrated under Article 21 TFEU, Mr Huber enjoyed the right to non-discrimination under Article 18 TFEU.[178] Because Union citizens were treated differently to nationals in respect of the systematic processing of personal data for the purposes of fighting crime, this constituted discrimination prohibited by Article 18(1) TFEU.[179]

### (ii) Family members' rights on the death or departure of the Union citizen or on divorce

Articles 12–13 of the Citizens' Rights Directive 2004/38 give family members the right to retain their residence in the host state on the death or departure of the EU citizen or in the event of divorce, annulment of marriage, or termination of registered partnership. In the case of the death or departure of the Union citizen, family members who are EU nationals[180] will continue to enjoy the right of residence.[181] In the case of the death (but

---

[169] For an extension of this principle to the member of a Turkish worker's family legally residing in a Member State, see Case C–262/96 *Sürül* v. *Bundesanstalt für Arbeit* [1999] ECR I–2685.

[170] Case C–215/03 *Oulane* [2005] ECR I–1215 Para. 25.     [171] Para. 40.

[172] Case C–524/06 *Huber* v. *Germany* [2008] ECR I–9705.     [173] Para. 58.

[174] 'Member States shall provide that personal data may be processed only if:... (e) processing is necessary for the performance of a task carried out in the public interest or in the exercise of official authority vested in the controller or in a third party to whom the data are disclosed'.     [175] OJ [1995] L281/31.

[176] Para. 59.     [177] Para. 68.     [178] Para. 73.     [179] Para. 80.

[180] Art. 12(1), para. 1.

[181] From the way Art. 12(1) is drafted, it would appear that the conditions to be a worker/self-employed/otherwise self-supporting/student/family member do not apply to the right of residence under Art. 7. They apply only to the right to acquire permanent residence.

not departure) of the EU citizen, the TCN family members retain the right of residence provided that they have been residing in the host state as family members for at least a year before the citizens' death.[182] In order to attain permanent residence they must be workers/self-employed/have independent means or be members of the family, already constituted in the host Member State, of a person satisfying these requirements.

In the case of divorce or equivalent, the CRD makes new provision for 'legal safeguards to people whose right of residence is dependent on a family relationship by marriage and who could therefore be open to blackmail with threats of divorce'.[183] Article 13(2) therefore says that TCN family members do not lose the right of residence where:

- prior to the divorce or equivalent, the marriage or registered partnership lasted at least three years including one year in the host Member State, or

- by agreement between the spouses or partners or by court order, the TCN spouse or partner has custody of the Union citizen's children, or

- this is warranted by particularly difficult circumstances, such as having been a victim of domestic violence while the marriage or registered partnership was subsisting, or

- by agreement between the spouses or partners or by court order, the TCN spouse or partner has the right of access to a minor child, provided that the court has ruled that such access must be in the host state and for as long as is required.[184]

In addition, in order to obtain *permanent* residence the TCN family members must show that they are workers/self-employed/have independent means (but not a student) or they are members of the family already constituted in the host Member State of a person satisfying these requirements. These conditions laid down in Article 13(2) do not apply to family members who are nationals of a Member State[185] who will continue to enjoy a right of residence, no matter how short the original marriage or equivalent. However, they will also need to show they are economically active or self-sufficient or be a student or family member to obtain *permanent* residence.

Despite the strictness of the rules in relation to TCN family members, there is one important exception: if the EU citizen leaves the host state or dies his/her children will not lose their right of residence, nor will the parent with actual custody of the children irrespective of nationality, provided that the children reside in the host state and are enrolled at an educational establishment for the purposes of studying there, until the completion of their studies.[186]

### (c) Right of permanent residence

The third 'tier' of residence rights is the right to permanent residence. There are two ways of acquiring permanent residence: (1) through five years' continuous legal residence; or (2) through a shorter period for those who were economically active either as a worker or as a self-employed person who satisfy the conditions under what was Regulation 1251/70[187] and Directive 75/34.[188] In both situations the directive considers the migrants to be so

---

[182] Art. 12(2), para. 1.
[183] COM(2001) 257, 15.      [184] Art. 1.2(2).      [185] Art. 12(1).
[186] Art. 12(3) reflecting the decisions in Joined Cases 389/87 and 390/87 *Echternach and Moritz* [1989] ECR I–723, Case C–413/99 *Baumbast and R* [2002] ECR I–7091.
[187] On the right of workers to remain in the territory of the host state after having been employed there [1970] OJ L142/24.      [188] On the right of the self-employed to remain [1975] OJ L14/10.

assimilated into the host state that they are regarded and treated as nationals in all but name. This is a remarkable development. We shall examine the two situations in turn.

### (i) Article 16: Five years' residence

Union citizens and their family members, including TCNs,[189] who have resided legally for a continuous period of five years in the host state, have the right of permanent residence there.[190] This right is not dependent on the Union citizen being a worker/self-employed person or having sufficient resources/medical insurance,[191] albeit that in most cases[192] the migrant will have been a worker/self-employed/student/person of independent means/ family member under Article 7 during the previous five years in order to accrue the five-year period of residence. The family members of a Union citizen to whom Article 12(2) (death/departure of the Union citizen) or Article 13(2) (divorce or equivalent) apply, who satisfy the conditions laid down in those Articles (e.g., the family members are workers/ self-employed etc.) will also acquire the right of permanent residence after residing legally for a period of five consecutive years in the host state.[193]

Continuity of residence is not affected by temporary absences not exceeding a total of six months a year, or by absences of a longer duration for compulsory military service, or by one absence of a maximum of 12 consecutive months for important reasons such as pregnancy and childbirth, serious illness, study or vocational training, or a posting in another Member State or a third country.[194] On the other hand, continuity of residence is broken by any expulsion decision duly enforced against the person concerned.[195] Once acquired, the right of permanent residence is lost only through absence from the host Member State for a period exceeding two consecutive years.[196]

### (ii) Article 17: Other ways of acquiring permanent residence

While five years' residence is the usual way for acquiring a right to permanent residence, it is also possible for a migrant or their family members to acquire a right to permanent residence before they have completed a continuous period of five years' residence in the situations which were originally laid down in Regulation 1251/70[197] and Directive 75/34. This made provision for workers and their family members to remain in a Member State after having been employed there. This regulation has now been repealed[198] and replaced by Article 17 of Directive 2004/38 which maintains the existing *acquis* but changes the language from the 'right to remain' to the 'right of permanent residence'. Article 17(1) provides that workers and the self-employed have the right to permanent residence in three situations:

(a) retirement at the pension age[199] or through early retirement, provided they have been employed in the host state for the preceding 12 months[200] and resided in the host state continuously for more than three years

---

[189] Art. 16(2).    [190] Art. 16(1).    [191] Ibid., 2nd sentence.

[192] Cf. Case C–456/02 *Trojani* [2004] ECR I–7573. Cf. also Art. 12(1) para. 2 which expressly requires EU national *family members* to be economically active/student/have sufficient resources before they acquire the right of permanent residence.    [193] Art. 18.

[194] Art. 16(3).    [195] Art. 21.    [196] Art. 16(4).    [197] [1970] OJ SE L142/24, 402.

[198] Commission Reg. 635/2006 (OJ [2006] L112/9). Dir. 75/34 was repealed by the CRD.

[199] If the law of the host state does not grant the right to an old-age pension to certain categories of self-employed persons, the age condition is deemed to have been met once the person has reached the age of 60.

[200] Periods of involuntary unemployment duly recorded by the relevant employment office, periods not worked for reasons not of the person's own making and absences from work or cessation of work due to illness, or accident are to be regarded as periods of employment: Art. 17(1), para. 3.

(b)  incapacity, provided they have resided for more than two years in the host state[201] and have ceased to work due to some permanent incapacity

(c)  frontier workers, provided after three years of continuous employment and residence in the host State A, they work in an employed or self-employed capacity in State B, while retaining their residence in State A to which they return each day or at least once a week.

The conditions as to length of residence and employment in (a) and (b) do not apply if the worker/self-employed person's spouse or partner[202] is a national of the host state or has lost the nationality of the host state through marriage to the worker/self-employed person.[203]

The worker/self-employed person's family members residing with him in the host state (irrespective of nationality) are also entitled to benefit from the reduced period of residence. According to Article 17, they too can enjoy permanent residence in the host state where either (1) the worker/self-employed person is entitled to permanent residence under Article 17(1);[204] or (2) under Article 17(4) the worker/self-employed person dies during his working life but before having acquired the right to permanent residence under 17(1) and:

(a)  the worker/self-employed person had resided continuously in the host state for two years at the time of death, or

(b)  the death resulted from an accident at work or occupational disease, or

(c)  the surviving spouse lost the nationality of the host state through marriage to the worker/self-employed person.

In *Givane*[205] the Court showed that it will interpret these requirements strictly. Givane, a Portuguese national, worked in the UK as a chef for three years before going to India for ten months. He then returned to the UK with his Indian wife and three children but died less than two years later. The Court upheld the British authorities' decision refusing Givane's family indefinite leave to remain on the grounds that Givane had not satisfied the requirements of what is now Article 17(4) which required him to have resided in the UK for the two years immediately preceding his death.[206] Such a literal reading of the requirement stands in stark contrast to the generous approach to the interpretation of other provisions of Union law based on the right to family life in cases such as *Carpenter*.[207] More striking still is the fact that the Court uses the integration argument to justify *excluding* Givane's family from the UK. It said that the two-year requirement was intended to establish a significant connection between the Member State and the worker and his family and 'to ensure a certain level of their integration in the society of that state'.[208]

As we saw above, in the case of those family members faced with the death or departure of the Union citizen in circumstances not covered by Article 17, and in the case of those

---

[201]  If the incapacity is due to an occupational accident or disease entitling the worker to a pension for which an institution of the state is entirely or partially responsible, then no condition to length of residence is imposed.                                           [202]  Partner as defined in Art. 2(2)(b) CRD.

[203]  Art. 17(2).          [204]  Art. 17(3).

[205]  Case C–257/00 *Givane and others* v. *Secretary of State for the Home Department* [2003] ECR I–345.

[206]  Para. 46.

[207]  Case C–60/00 *Carpenter* [2002] ECR I–6279, para. 38. See also Case C–413/99 *Baumbast* [2002] ECR I–7091; Case C–459/99 *MRAX* [2002] ECR I–6591, paras. 53–61.                          [208]  Para. 46.

family members faced with divorce or equivalent, they can acquire permanent residence only if they meet the requirements laid down in Article 7(1) (i.e., they must be workers/self-employed/persons of independent means/student[209]/family member[210]) and have resided legally for a period of five consecutive years in the territory of the host state.[211]

### (iii)  Administrative formalities

Proof of permanent residence is given by the Member State issuing, as soon as possible, a 'document certifying permanent residence', having verified the Union citizen's duration of residence.[212] Article 21 provides that continuity of residence is attested by any means of proof in use in the host Member State. In respect of the family members who are not nationals of a Member State, the host state must issue a permanent residence card, renewable automatically every ten years,[213] within six months of the submission of the application.[214] According to Article 20(3), interruption in residence not exceeding two consecutive years will not affect the validity of the permanent residence card.

### 2.5  The Right to Equal Treatment

### (a)  Introduction

The cornerstone of the CRD is Article 24(1) laying down a general right of equal treatment (ie no direct or indirect discrimination) 'within the scope of the [Treaties]' for all Union citizens residing on the basis of the directive in the territory of the host state. The Article continues that the benefit of this right is to be extended to family members who are not nationals of a Member State but who have the right of residence or permanent residence. However, Article 24(1) expressly makes the principle of equal treatment '[s]ubject to such specific provisions as are expressly provided for in the [Treaties] and secondary law'. Therefore, it is possible to derogate from the principle of equal treatment on the grounds, *inter alia* of public policy, public security, public health and employment in the public service as well as in respect of the conditions as to sufficient resources and medical insurance found in the original 1990 Residence Directives, now replicated in the CRD (see Chapter 13).

As we saw in the Workers' Regulation 1612/68, the principle of equal treatment will apply in respect of both initial access to a job as well as the exercise of that position. It will also apply in respect of enjoyment of social advantages and tax advantages. However, here Article 24(2) contains an important limitation (see fig. 12.2). In respect of *social assistance* (defined in *Chakroun* in the context of the Family Reunification Directive 2003/86 as assistance granted by public authorities which can be claimed by individuals not having stable and regular resources sufficient to maintain himself and his family), the host state is not obliged to confer entitlement to it during the first three months of residence or, in the case of a work seeker, the period during which Union citizens can provide evidence that they are continuing to seek employment and that they have a genuine chance of being

---

[209] This does not apply to TCN family members: Art. 12(2), para. 2 concerning death or departure; Art. 13(2), para. 2 concerning divorce or equivalent.

[210] With the added condition in the case of TCN family members that they are members of the family already constituted in the host Member States, of a person satisfying those requirements: Art. 12(2), para. 2 concerning death or departure; Art. 13(2), para. 2 concerning divorce or equivalent.

[211] Art. 18 referring to Art. 12(2) concerning death or departure; Art. 13(2) concerning divorce or equivalent.          [212] Art. 19.

[213] Details of the re-application process are found in Art. 20(2).          [214] Art. 20(1).

engaged.[215] Therefore, students and persons of independent means can call on equal treatment in respect of social assistance only after the first three months of residence; job-seekers entering the state to look for work under Article 14(4)(b) will not enjoy entitlement to social assistance at all.[216] This restriction, a 'derogation from the principle of equal treatment',[217] does not apply to workers, self-employed persons, persons who retain such status and members of their families. If Union citizens do have recourse to social assistance, 'An expulsion measure shall not be the automatic consequence'.[218] Furthermore, except on the grounds of public policy, security, and health, an expulsion measure may not be adopted against Union citizens or their family members if the Union citizens are workers/self-employed/work-seekers with a genuine chance of being engaged.[219]

In respect of *maintenance aid* for studies, including vocational training, the host state is not obliged to give grants or student loans to Union citizens or their family members until they have acquired permanent residence except to those who are economically active and their family members.

What then is meant by the principle of equal treatment? As yet, there is no case law under Article 24(1) CRD, although there are many decisions under Regulation 1612/68 which were discussed in Chapter 9. There are, however, a number of cases decided under Article 21(1) TFEU in respect of social advantages for citizens lawfully resident[220] in the host state and it is these cases that we shall consider in determining the meaning of equal treatment.

## (b) Social advantages and equal treatment

### (i) Direct and indirect discrimination

*Martínez Sala*[221] is the first case on equal treatment in respect of social advantages decided under Article 21(1) TFEU. She was a Spanish national who had been living in Germany since 1968 when she was 12. She had various jobs and various residence permits in that time. When she gave birth in 1993 she did not have a residence permit but she did have a certificate saying that an extension of the permit had been applied for. The German authorities refused to give her a child-raising allowance on the grounds that she was neither a German national nor did she have a residence permit. If she had been a worker she would have been entitled to the benefit as a social advantage under Article 7(2) of Regulation 1612/68. Given her background, it was unlikely that she was a worker (or an employed person within the meaning of Regulation 883/04 (ex Regulation 1408/71)).[222] The Court therefore considered her situation under Part Two TFEU on non-discrimination and citizenship.

It said that, as a national of a Member State lawfully residing in the territory of another Member State,[223] Martínez Sala came within the personal scope of the citizenship

---

[215] Art. 14(4)(b). See Case C–578/08 *Chakroun* [2010] ECR I–000, para. 46.

[216] Joined Cases C–22/08 and 23/08 *Vatsouras* [2009] ECR I–000, para. 35. This case also considers the meaning of the terms social assistance and social advantage, considered in Ch. 9.        [217] Ibid, para. 34.

[218] Art. 14(3). If they are expelled, the procedural protection provided in Arts. 30 (notification) and 31 (judicial/administrative redress) apply to any such decision: Art. 15(1).        [219] Art. 14(4).

[220] See generally, A. P. van der Mei, *Free Movement of Persons within the European Community: Cross-border access to public benefits* (Oxford: Hart Publishing, 2003).

[221] Case C–85/96 [1998] ECR I–2691.        [222] It was for the national court to make the final decision.

[223] This was merely probative and not constitutive of the right to residence: see above n. 167.

provisions.[224] She therefore enjoyed the rights laid down by Article 20(2) TFEU, including the right not to suffer discrimination on grounds of nationality under Article 18 TFEU[225] in respect of all situations falling within the material scope of the Treaties.[226] This included the situation where a Member State delayed or refused to grant a benefit provided to all persons lawfully resident in the territory of that state on the ground that the claimant did not have a document (a residence permit) which nationals were not obliged to have.[227] On this basis the Court concluded that Martínez Sala was suffering from direct discrimination on the ground of nationality contrary to Article 18[228] and, since it was direct discrimination, it could not be objectively justified (see fig.12.3).[229]

The Court fudged the issue of what was meant by 'all situations' falling within the material scope of Union law.[230] It seems that the Court thought that because the child-raising allowance constituted a social advantage within the meaning of Article 7(2) of Regulation 1612/68[231] it fell within the material scope of Union law, even though the judgment was premised on the fact that Martínez Sala was not a worker. The Court also did not make clear on what basis Martínez Sala was lawfully resident in Germany. Although the Court of Justice left it to the national court to decide whether Martínez Sala was a worker or an employed person, she did not appear to be economically active, nor did she seem to fulfil the conditions of (then) Directive 90/364 on persons of independent means (now Article 7(1)(b) CRD). As a result, she did not appear to be lawfully resident under Union law. Her lawful residence may have derived from national law and specifically from her actual presence and that the German authorities had not requested her to leave.[232] In other words, because she was not *un*lawfully resident in Germany she was entitled to equal treatment. This view is supported by *Trojani*.[233]

*Trojani* was a French national who had been living in a Salvation Army hostel in Belgium where, in return for board and lodging and some pocket money, he did various jobs for about 30 hours a week. He was denied the minimex (the Belgian minimum income guarantee) on the grounds that he was neither Belgian nor a worker under Regulation 1612/68. In respect of his rights as a citizen, the Court said that while Trojani did not derive from Article 21 the right to reside in Belgium due to his lack of resources,[234] since he was lawfully resident in Belgium, as was shown by the residence permit which the Belgian authorities had issued to him, he could benefit from the fundamental principle of equal treatment laid down in Article 18 TFEU.[235] This is the significant feature of the case:[236] as the Court pointed out in *Trojani*,[237] and subsequently confirmed in *Bidar*,[238] 'a citizen of the Union who is not economically active may rely on Article [18 TFEU] where he has been lawfully resident in the host state for a certain period of time *or* possesses a residence permit'.[239] Thus, legal residence can come about in one of two ways: by having a residence permit or actual presence in the host state for a certain period of time. *Trojani*

---

[224] Para. 61. See the essays on this case in M. Poiares Maduro and L. Azoulai (eds), *The Past and Future of EU Law* (Oxford: Hart Publishing, 2010).

[225] It also includes the right to free movement under Art. 21(1) TFEU: Case C–221/07 *Zablocka-Wehrmüller* v. *Land Baden-Württemberg* [2008] ECR I–9029, para. 25.          [226] Para. 62.

[227] Ibid.          [228] Para. 64.          [229] Ibid.          [230] Para. 63.          [231] See further Ch. 9.

[232] See also Art. 6(a) of the Council of Europe Convention on Social and Medical Assistance 1953 which provides that the Contracting Parties shall abstain from expelling an alien lawfully resident 'on the sole ground that he is in need of assistance'.          [233] Case C–456/02 *Trojani* [2004] ECR I–7573.

[234] Para. 36.          [235] Paras. 37 and 40.          [236] Para. 43.          [237] Para. 37.

[238] Case C–209/03 [2005] ECR I–2119. See also Case C–158/07 *Förster* [2008] ECR I–8507, para. 39.

[239] Case C–456/02 *Trojani* [2004] ECR I–7573, para. 43. Emphasis added.

itself concerned a residence permit; *Bidar*, considered below, concerned lawful residence based on actual presence.[240]

Mr Trojani therefore suffered direct discrimination on the grounds of his nationality in respect of the minimex. The same legal issue was raised in the seminal case of *Grzelczyk*[241] which also concerned direct discrimination. Grzelczyk, a French national studying at a Belgian university, supported himself financially for the first three years of his studies but then applied for the minimex (the Belgium minimum income guarantee) at the start of his fourth and final year. While Belgian students could receive the benefit, migrant students could not,[242] and so Grzelczyk suffered (direct) discrimination contrary to Article 18 TFEU.[243] The question was whether Article 18 TFEU applied to his case. Referring to *Martínez Sala*, the Court said that because Grzelczyk, a citizen of the Union, was lawfully resident in Belgium he could rely on Article 18 TFEU in respect of those situations which fell within the material scope of the Treaties,[244] including those situations involving 'the exercise of the fundamental freedoms guaranteed by the [Treaties] and those involving the exercise of the right to move and reside freely in another Member State, as conferred by Article [21(1) TFEU]'.[245] Therefore, in *Grzelczyk* the Court defined the material scope of Union law, not by reference to the fact that the benefit fell within the scope of Regulation 1612/68 as it had suggested in *Martínez Sala*,[246] but by reference to the fact that Grzelczyk had actually moved.[247] This significantly broadened the scope of the principle of equal treatment.

A question was raised whether the fact that he had applied for the minimex meant that he no longer satisfied the requirements in the Students' Directive 93/96 (now Article 7(1) (c) CRD) of having sufficient resources.[248] The Court said that the Belgian authorities had to provide some temporary support to the migrant citizen, as they would to nationals, given that there exists 'a certain degree of financial solidarity' between nationals of a host Member State and nationals of other Member States,[249] but only for so long as they do not become an unreasonable burden on public finances. While this decision could be seen as opening up social welfare systems of host Member States to migrants,[250] the actual reasoning in the case presents migrants with a dilemma: lawful residency entitles the migrant to equal treatment within the host state; but exercise of that right to equal treatment might enable the host state to consider that the claimant has become an unreasonable financial burden.[251]

Student finance was also at issue in *Bidar*,[252] this time in a case concerning indirect discrimination. It will be recalled from Chapter 9 that Bidar, a French national, had lived in the UK with his grandmother after his mother's death. He subsequently went

---

[240] As did Case C–85/96 *Martínez Sala* [1998] ECR I–2691.

[241] Case C–184/99 [2001] ECR I–6193.     [242] Para. 29.     [243] Para. 30.     [244] Para. 32.

[245] Para. 33, citing Case C–274/96 *Bickel and Franz* [1998] ECR I–7637.

[246] Although it had already established that the minimex was a social advantage (paras. 27–9): Case 249/83 *Hoeckx* [1985] ECR 973.

[247] There must be actual—as opposed to hypothetical—movement: Case C–299/95 *Kremzow* v. *Republik Österreich* [1997] ECR I–2629. Cf. E. Spaventa, 'Seeing the wood despite the trees? On the scope of Union citizenship and its constitutional effects' (2008) 45 *CMLRev.* 13.

[248] This question is considered further in Ch. 13.     [249] Para. 44.

[250] S. Giubboni, 'Free movement of persons and European solidarity' (2007) 13 *ELJ* 360.

[251] M. Dougan and E. Spaventa, 'Educating Rudy and the (non-)English patient: A double bill on residency rights under Article 18 EC' (2003) 28 *ELRev.* 697.     [252] Case C–209/03 [2005] ECR I–2119.

to university but was turned down for financial assistance to cover his maintenance costs, in the form of a student loan, on the grounds that he did not satisfy the criteria of being settled in the UK nor did he satisfy the residence requirements laid down by British law. The Court found these conditions to be indirectly discriminatory since they risked placing nationals of other Member States at a disadvantage. However, the Court also accepted that while, in the organization and application of their social assistance schemes, Member States had to show a degree of financial solidarity with nationals of other Member States, it was legitimate for a Member State to grant assistance only to students who had demonstrated a certain degree of integration into the society of that state. This integration could be shown through a period of residence. The Court suggested that a three-year residence requirement was compatible with Union law[253] but that the requirement to be settled was not, since it was impossible for a student from another Member State ever to obtain settled status.[254]

In reaching this conclusion, the Court relied on *D'Hoop*[255] which concerned a Belgian national who completed her secondary education in France where she obtained the *baccalauréat* in 1991.[256] She then returned to Belgium for her university education. At the end of her university studies she applied to the Belgian authorities for a tide-over allowance—a type of unemployment benefit granted to young people who have just completed their studies and are seeking their first job. Her application was rejected on the ground that she had not received her secondary education in Belgium. The Court said that, as a Belgian national, she fell within the personal scope of the citizenship provisions,[257] and that as a free mover she fell within the material scope of the Treaty provisions. The Court therefore said that she could rely on the principle of equal treatment even against her own state after having studied abroad.[258]

But what discrimination had she suffered?[259] It could be argued that the national rule was indirectly discriminatory: in order to obtain a tide-over allowance individuals had to receive their secondary education in Belgium. This had a disparate impact on non-nationals (as well as some nationals like D'Hoop) and so breached Article 21 unless objectively justified.[260] Alternatively, the national rule could be seen as discriminatory, not on the ground of nationality but on the ground of the individual having exercised her rights of free movement. Both the Advocate General and the Court seemed to support this interpretation. Advocate General Geelhoed said that Ms D'Hoop had been 'placed at a disadvantage by discriminatory provisions of the Member States of which they are nationals,

---

[253] Cf. the five-year residence requirement in Art. 24(2) CRD which was upheld as proportionate in Case C–158/07 *Förster* [2008] ECR I–8507, para. 53.

[254] See generally K. Hailbronner, 'Union citizenship and access to social benefits' (2005) 42 *CMLRev.* 1245.

[255] C–224/98 *D'Hoop* v. *Office national de l'emploi* [2002] ECR I–6191.

[256] The Court said that the provisions on citizenship of the Union were applicable as soon as they entered into force and so they applied to the present discriminatory effects of situations arising prior to the citizenship provisions coming into force (citing Case C–195/98 *Österreichischer Gewerkschaftsbund* v. *Republik Österreich* [2000] ECR I–10497, paras. 54–5, and Case C–290/00 *Duchon* v. *Pensionsversicherungsanstalt der Angestellten* [2002] ECR I–3567, paras. 43–4).          [257] Para. 27.

[258] Para. 31.

[259] See also A. Iliopoulou and H. Toner, 'A new approach to discrimination against free movers' (2003) 28 *ELRev.* 389.          [260] Para. 36.

which penalise them retrospectively for a period of residence in another Member State'.[261] The Court agreed:[262]

By linking the grant of tideover allowances to the condition of having obtained the required diploma in Belgium, the national legislation thus *places at a disadvantage certain of its nationals simply because they have exercised their freedom to move* in order to pursue education in another Member State.

The Court continued that '[s]uch inequality of treatment is contrary to the principles which underpin the status of citizen of the Union, that is, the guarantee of the same treatment in law in the exercise of the citizen's freedom to move'.[263] In subsequent cases, the Court said such disadvantage constituted a 'restriction' on free movement,[264] an analysis the Court has subsequently used, particularly where it is the rules of the home state that create the obstacles to free movement.[265] The national rule therefore breached Article 21(1) unless it could be objectively justified.

The Court examined the question of justification in *D'Hoop* even though no evidence had been submitted to it on this point. It said that since the tide-over allowance aimed at facilitating the transition from education to the employment market it was legitimate for the national legislature to ensure that a 'real link' existed between the applicant for that allowance and the geographic employment market concerned.[266] However, the Court found that the condition concerning the place of secondary education was 'too general and exclusive in nature' and that it unduly favoured an element which was not necessarily representative of a real and effective degree of connection between the applicant for the tide-over allowance and the geographic employment market, to the exclusion of all other representative elements. It therefore went beyond what was necessary to attain the objective pursued.[267]

*(ii) Discrimination caused by similar treatment*

The cases considered so far all concern discrimination caused by the different treatment of similarly situated groups. *Garcia Avello*[268] concerns the opposite: discrimination arising from the fact that differently situated groups were being treated similarly. Carlos Garcia Avello, a Spanish national, married Isabelle Weber, a Belgian national, and they lived together in Belgium. They had two children, dual nationals, who were given their father's surname (Garcia Avello). He then applied to the Belgian authorities to have the

---

[261] Para. 53.      [262] Para. 34, emphasis added.

[263] Para. 35. Case C–135/99 *Ursula Elsen* v. *Bundesversicherungsanstalt für Angestellte* [2000] ECR I–10409. See also Case C–28/00 *Kauer* v. *Pensionsversicherungsanstalt der Angestellten* [2002] ECR I–1343, para. 44; Case C–302/98 *Sehrer* v. *Bundesknappschaft* [2000] ECR I–4585, para. 32.

[264] See, e.g., Case C–499/06 *Nerkowska* [2008] ECR I–3993; Case C–221/07 *Zablocka-Wehrmüller* [2008] ECR I–9029, para. 35. The 'restriction' approach is considered below.

[265] M. Cousins, 'Citizenship, residence and social security' (2007) 32 *ELRev.* 386, 394.

[266] Dougan and Spaventa (above n. 251) suggest that the requirement of a 'real link' is inspired by the same spirit as the requirement in *Grzelczyk* of an 'unreasonable financial burden', recognizing that there are limits to solidarity which Union law can superimpose on national welfare states. This requirement may be generously construed in favour of the Member State.

[267] Para. 39. See also Case C–258/04 *Office national de l'empoli* v. *Ioannidis* [2005] ECR I–8275, paras. 30–3.

[268] Case C–148/02 *Carlos Garcia Avello* v. *Etat Belge* [2003] ECR I–11613, noted by T. Ackermann, (2007) 44 *CMLRev.* 141.

children's surnames changed to Garcia Weber, reflecting the Spanish pattern for surnames which comprise the first element of the father's surname (Garcia) followed by the mother's maiden name (Weber). While Belgian law did permit a change of surname when serious grounds were given, the Belgian authorities did not apply this exception to Garcia Avello because usually 'children bear their father's surname'.

The Court confirmed that the citizenship provisions applied to this case. It noted that since Mr Garcia Avello's children held the nationality of two Member States, they enjoyed the status of citizen of the Union.[269] This meant that they enjoyed equal treatment with nationals of the host state in respect of situations falling within the material scope of the Treaties, in particular those involving the freedom to move and reside in the territory of the Member States.[270] Therefore the children could not suffer discrimination on the ground of nationality in respect of their surname. Because the Garcia Avello children, holding both Spanish and Belgian nationality, were in a different situation from Belgian nationals holding just one (Belgian) nationality,[271] they had a 'right to be treated in a manner different to that in which persons having only Belgian nationality are treated, unless the treatment in issue can be justified on objective grounds'.[272] Since the Court rejected the justifications put forward by the Belgian government (the immutability of surnames as a founding principle of the social order and integration of nationals from other Member States) the Court concluded that Articles 18 and 20 TFEU precluded the Belgian authorities from refusing a name change to the Garcia Avello children.[273]

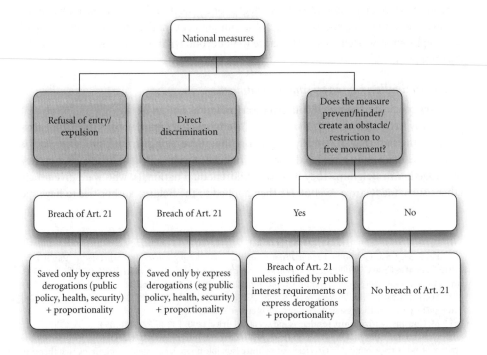

**Fig. 12.3** The restrictions approach to Art. 21

---

[269] Para. 21.    [270] Para. 24.    [271] Paras. 34 and 37.    [272] Para. 34.
[273] Para. 44. The Court may now apply the 'restrictions' approach to such cases: see, e.g., Case C–353/06 *Grunkin-Paul* [2008] ECR I–7639 considered below, n. 298.

## (iii) Restrictions approach

Although most of the landmark citizenship cases were decided under the non-discrimination/equal treatment model, the more general shift to a restrictions/market access based approach seen elsewhere in the free movement case law can now also be seen in the field of citizenship.[274] It was first seriously raised by Advocate General Jacobs in *Pusa*[275] where he argued that 'discrimination on grounds of nationality, whether direct or indirect, is not necessary in order for Article [21] to apply'.[276] He noted that although freedom of movement was originally guaranteed by a prohibition of discrimination on grounds of nationality, 'there has been a progressive extension of that freedom in the Court's case-law so that non-discriminatory restrictions are also precluded'.[277] He said that the wording of Article 21 was not limited to a prohibition of discrimination,[278] concluding that:[279]

subject to the limits set out in Article [21] itself, no unjustified burden may be imposed on any citizen of the European Union seeking to exercise the right to freedom of movement or residence. Provided that such a burden can be shown, it is immaterial whether the burden affects nationals of other Member States more significantly than those of the State imposing it.[280]

Following the lead of its Advocate General, the Court in *Pusa*[281] appeared to move towards the restrictions/obstacle approach. It confirmed the shift in *Tas-Hagen*.[282] The case concerned a Dutch law that made payment of a benefit to civilian war victims conditional on the applicants being resident in the Netherlands at the time that they made their application. This law, said the Court, was liable to dissuade Dutch nationals such as Mrs Tas-Hagen from exercising her freedom to move and reside outside the Netherlands.[283] It therefore constituted a 'restriction on the freedoms conferred by Article [21(1)] on every citizen of the Union'.[284] The Court recognized that the Dutch law could be justified on the grounds of solidarity with the population of the Netherlands both before and after the war but thought the requirement of residence to be disproportionate. While acknowledging that, in respect of benefits not covered by Union law, Member States enjoyed a wide margin of appreciation in deciding what criteria were to be used in assessing connection to society,[285] a residence criterion was not a satisfactory indicator of the degree of connection of civilian war victims to the Netherlands when it was liable to lead to different

---

[274] See Editorial Comments, 'Two-speed European citizenship? Can the Lisbon Treaty help close the gap?' (2008) 45 *CMLRev.* 1, 2.

[275] Case C–224/02 *Pusa* v. *Osuuspankkien Keskinäinen Vakuutusyhtiö* [2004] ECR I–5763. See also F. Jacobs, 'Citizenship of the European Union: A legal analysis' (2007) 13 *ELJ* 591.   [276] Para. 18.

[277] Para. 20.   [278] Ibid.   [279] Para. 22.

[280] See also Jacobs AG's views in Case C–96/04 *Niebüll* [2006] ECR I–3561, para. 54: 'While the practical difficulties which he is likely to encounter may not stem from discrimination on the grounds of nationality, they constitute a clear obstacle to his right as a citizen to move and reside freely.'

[281] Case C–224/02 *Pusa* [2004] ECR I–5763. Compare para. 19 (restrictions based) and para. 20 (discrimination based).

[282] Case C–192/05 *Tas-Hagen* v. *Raadskamer WUBO van de Pensioen- en Uitkeringsrad* [2006] ECR I–10451, paras. 30–1. See also Case C–345/05 *Commission* v. *Portugal (transfer of property)* [2006] ECR I–10633, para. 24.   [283] Para. 32.

[284] Para. 31.   [285] Para. 36.

results for individuals resident abroad whose integration into Dutch society was in all respects comparable.[286]

The careful scrutiny of the proportionality of the national rules is the hallmark of subsequent case law. For example, *Nerkowska*[287] shows how the Court has insisted that the personal circumstances of each individual be taken into account, despite the administrative burden this might entail.[288] Ms Nerkowska, a Polish national, was a product of her country's tumultuous history. Born in 1946 in the territory of present-day Belarus, her parents were deported to Siberia where they died. She was then deported in 1951 to the former USSR where she lived under 'difficult conditions'. She returned to Poland in 1957 and lived there until 1985 when she moved to Germany. She was denied payment of a disability pension granted by Poland to civilian victims of war and repression because she was resident in another Member State. The Court said that the Polish rule constituted a restriction on free movement of citizens[289] but could be justified on the grounds of (1) ensuring that there was a connection between the society of the Member State concerned and the recipient of a benefit and (2) the necessity of verifying that the recipient continued to satisfy the conditions for grant of that benefit.[290]

However, the Court found the Polish rule requiring residence throughout the period of payment of the benefit was disproportionate: the fact that a person was a national of the Member State granting the benefit and had lived in Poland for more than 20 years was sufficient to establish a connection between that State and the recipient of the benefit. Furthermore, the objective of verifying that the recipient of a disability pension continued to satisfy the conditions for its grant could be achieved by other means which, although less restrictive, were just as effective.[291]

This robust—and case-by-case—approach to proportionality was also emphasized in *Morgan*.[292] Under German law the award of education and training grants for studies in another Member State was subject to a twofold obligation (the 'first-stage studies condition'): (1) to have attended an education or training course for at least one year in Germany and (2) to continue only that same education or training in another Member State. The application of these conditions meant that Rhiannon Morgan, a German national, who

---

[286] Para. 38. Cf. Case C–103/08 *Gottwald* v. *Bezirkshautmannschaft Bregenz* [2009] ECR I–000, para. 36. See further G. Davies, '"Any place I hang my hat?" or: Residence is the new nationality' (2005) 11 *ELJ* 43 who laments challenges to a residence requirement for the damage it does to a community's ability to offer benefits to local residents.

[287] Case C–499/06 *Nerkowska Zakład Ubezpieczeń Społecznych Oddział w Koszalinie* [2008] ECR I–3993.

[288] Cf. the Art. 110 TFEU (ex Art. 90 EC) case, Case C–74/06 *Commission* v. *Greece (registration tax on imported cars)* [2007] ECR I–7585, para. 29, where the Court was mindful of the administrative burden imposed in assessing the depreciation of each and every car. The Court therefore said it was sufficient to use fixed scales calculated on the basis of criteria such as a vehicle's age, mileage, general condition to determine value.                                                                                  [289] Para. 34.

[290] Paras. 37–9.

[291] Para. 46. See also Case C–221/07 *Zablocka-Wehrmüller* [2008] ECR I–9029, para. 41. Cf. Case C–103/08 *Gottwald* [2009] ECR I–000, para. 32 where the Court found that a residence criterion could be justified as a condition for the granting of a free annual road toll disc for people with disabilities in Austria and was proportionate since there was no minimum period of residence required, the term residence was interpreted broadly and the disc was also provided to non-residents who regularly travelled in Austria.

[292] Joined Cases C–11/06 and C–12/06 *Morgan v Bezirksregierung Köln and Iris Bucher v Landrat des Kreises Düren* [2007] ECR I–9161.

moved to the UK where she worked for a year as an au pair before commencing her studies at a British university, was refused a grant by the German authorities.

The Court found that because of the personal inconvenience, additional costs and possible delays which it entailed, the first stage studies condition was liable to discourage citizens of the Union from leaving Germany in order to pursue studies in another Member State.[293] It therefore constituted a restriction on freedom of movement for citizens of the Union contrary to Article 21(1).[294] The German government put forward a number of justifications for its rule, all of which were subject to a strict proportionality review. For example, it said that the condition was justified as a way of showing integration into German society.[295] However, the Court noted the personal situation of the applicant: she had been raised in Germany and completed her schooling there. This demonstrated her integration into German society. Therefore, the first-stage studies condition as a proxy for showing integration was too general and exclusive and so was disproportionate.[296]

There is, however, a risk attendant on such an individualized approach. As the healthcare cases considered in Chapter 11 show, the emphasis on protecting the individual over the interests of the community reflects what Newdick terms an 'institutional "asymmetry" within the EU, in which the Court of Justice favours private "economic" interests over the public "welfare" policies identified by national governments'.[297] He argues that this market citizenship is consistent with inequality because individual choice, rather than government policy, is the dominant influence.

### (iv) The implications of the restrictions approach

As *Tas-Hagen*, *Nerkowska*, and *Morgan* show, the Court has made effective use of the restrictions approach to strike down state rules that deter departure from the state. Traditional discrimination analysis can be difficult to apply in this context, as we saw in *D'Hoop*. The Court also recognized this in *Grunkin-Paul*.[298] Leonhard Matthias Grunkin-Paul was born in Denmark to Mr Grunkin and Dr Paul, a German husband and wife. Their child was also German but had always lived in Denmark. The child was given the surname Grunkin-Paul which was entered on his Danish birth certificate. However, the German authorities refused to register his surname because under German law a German child cannot bear a double-barrelled surname composed of the surnames of both the father and mother. Because Grunkin-Paul and his parents were German, he could not allege discrimination on grounds of nationality, a point the Court acknowledged.[299] However, in applying the restrictions model[300] the Court may have implicitly recognized the risk that it could be all-embracing. It therefore added a threshold requirement: it said that a discrepancy in surnames is likely to result in 'serious inconvenience'[301] in the child's day-to-day life as he moved between Denmark and Germany. The Court found that the German rule could not be justified.

---

[293] Para. 30.        [294] Para. 32.

[295] See also Case C–209/03 *Bidar* [2005] ECR I–2119, paras. 56–7.        [296] Paras. 42–6.

[297] C. Newdick, 'The European Court of Justice, Trans-national health care, and social citizenship: Accidental death of a concept' (2008) 26 *Wisconsin International Law Journal* 844, 864.

[298] Case C–353/06 *Grunkin-Paul* [2008] ECR I–7639.        [299] Paras. 19–20.        [300] Para. 21.

[301] Paras. 23 and 29.

While the 'restrictions' approach might serve to simplify analysis, it has been used in rather unexpected ways—as *De Cuyper*[302] shows. The case concerned the withdrawal of an unemployment allowance payable by the Belgian government to a Belgium national on the ground that he no longer resided in Belgium. Article 10 of the then Social Security Regulation 1408/71[303] (now Regulation 883/04) allows certain benefits to be subject to a residence requirement and so the case should have stopped there. Instead, the Court subjected the residence requirement to review under Article 21 TFEU and found that since the Belgian legislation 'places at a disadvantage certain of its nationals simply because they have exercised their freedom to move and to reside in another Member State [it] is a restriction on the freedoms conferred by Article [21]'.[304] However, the Court did find that the residence requirement could be justified by the need to monitor the employment and family situation of the unemployed[305] and that no less-restrictive monitoring measures existed to achieve the objective of allowing inspectors to check whether the situation of, for example, a person who had declared that they were living alone and unemployed had changed which might have an effect on the benefit granted.[306] In reaching this conclusion, the Court appeared to protect the integrity of the complex Social Security Regulation 1408/71 (Regulation 883/04 from 1 March 2010) from challenge.[307] However, subsequent cases, like *Hendrix*,[308] suggest that opening up the Social Security Regulation to review under the restrictions model has the potential to undermine the carefully negotiated settlement reached by (democratically accountable) political actors.

### (v) Quantitative and qualitative approach

The Article 21(1) cases considered so far might suggest that migrant citizens who are not economically active now have the right to claim all benefits available in the host State (whether classified as social assistance or social advantages) on the same terms as nationals, unless the benefits are expressly excluded by Union law or there are objectively justified reasons why not. If this analysis is correct, then the creation of citizenship of the Union leads to what Iliopoulou and Toner describe as the 'perfect assimilation' approach, where the treatment of Union migrants is placed on an equal footing with that of nationals of the host Member State unless Union law specifically provides otherwise.[309] But, when looked at carefully, the cases do not support the full assimilationist approach and actually suggest an incremental approach to residence and equality—the longer migrants reside in the Member State, the greater the number of benefits they receive on equal terms with nationals.

But on what basis are non-economically active migrants entitled to (financially expensive) maintenance on equal terms with nationals? Unlike migrant workers, it

---

[302] Case C–406/04 *De Cuyper* v. *Office national de l'emploi* [2006] ECR I–6947.     [303] Para. 37.
[304] Para. 39.     [305] Para. 41.     [306] Paras. 43–4.
[307] As Geelhoed AG noted in para. 116. Although cf. Joined Cases C–502/01 and C–31/02 *Gaumain-Cerri* v. *Kaufmännische Krankenkasse-Pflegekasse* [2004] ECR I–6483, para. 36.
[308] Case C–287/05 [2007] ECR I–6909 considered in Ch. 9. See also M. Dougan, 'Expanding the frontiers of European Union citizenship by dismantling the territorial boundaries of the national welfare states' in C. Barnard and O. Odudu (eds.), *The Outer Limits of European Union Law* (Oxford: Hart Publishing, 2009).
[309] A. Iliopoulou and H. Toner (2002) 39 *CMLRev.* 609, 616. This is what Léger AG had in mind in Case C–214/94 *Boukhalfa* v. *Bundesrepublik Deutschland* [1996] ECR I–2253, para. 63. See also S. Friess and J. Shaw, 'Citizenship of the Union: First steps in the European Court of Justice' (1998) 4 *EPL* 533.

cannot be argued that they have contributed to the economy of the host state[310] through taxation.[311] Instead, the answer appears to lie in the degree to which the migrant is integrated into the community of the host state combined with a notion of social solidarity between members of that community.[312] At national level, welfare states are legitimized at least in part by a diffuse sense of solidarity: national taxpayers pay their taxes to help look after their fellow citizens in need. This solidarity is founded on some sense of shared interests which in turn is based on a shared nationality[313] and/or a shared identity. Thus *national* citizenship leads to the evolution of a sense of *national* solidarity. The striking feature of both *Grzelczyk* and *Bidar* is that the Court has taken the concept of *European Union* citizenship, the 'fundamental status of nationals of the Member States',[314] to justify the creation of a sense of *transnational* solidarity between (taxpaying) nationals of a host Member State and (impoverished migrant) nationals of other Member States, with the result that the migrant needs to be treated in the same way as nationals in respect of access to certain social advantages.

However, the reference in *Grzelczyk* and *Bidar* to merely 'a *certain degree* of financial solidarity'[315] indicates that the notion of solidarity is limited. *Grzelczyk* suggests that the limits to the solidarity—and thus the equality—principle are related to the degree to which the migrant is integrated into the society of the host state. *Bidar* makes this point expressly. Having referred to the need for Member States to show 'a certain degree of financial solidarity with nationals of other Member States' in the organization and application of their *social assistance* systems, the Court continued that 'In the case of assistance covering the maintenance costs of students, it is thus legitimate for a Member State to grant such assistance only to students who have demonstrated a certain degree of integration into the society of that State.'[316] And length of residence is a key indicator of integration: 'the existence of a certain degree of integration may be regarded as established by a finding that the student in question has resided in the host state for a certain length of time'.[317]

---

[310] Although the Court's case law on the definition workers, to include migrants who received only limited wages and work a small number of hours (e.g., Case 139/85 *Kempf* [1986] ECR 1741 and Case C–357/89 *Raulin* [1992] ECR I–1027), rather undermines the substance of this rationale.

[311] For a criticism of such arguments see Geelhoed AG's Opinion in Case C–209/03 *Bidar* [2005] ECR I–2119, para. 65.

[312] In his opinion in Case C– 70/95 *Sodemare SA* [1997] ECR I–3395, para. 29, Fennelly AG defined solidarity as the 'inherently uncommercial act of involuntary subsidization of one social group by another'. The meaning of solidarity in the EU context is considered further in C. Barnard, 'Solidarity as a tool of new governance' in G. De Búrca and J. Scott (eds.), *New Governance and Constitutionalism in Europe and the US* (Oxford: Hart Publishing, 2006).

[313] See D. Miller, 'In defence of nationality' in D. Miller, *Citizenship and National Identity* (Cambridge: Polity Press), 2000, cited in N. Barber, 'Citizenship, nationalism and the European Union' (2002) 27 *ELRev*. 241, 250 who notes that it is an observable fact that nationality is the principal source of solidarity.

[314] Case C–184/99 *Grzelczyk* [2001] ECR I–6193, paras. 30–1; Case C–148/02 *Garcia Avello* [2003] ECR I–11613, paras. 22–3 and Case C–209/03 *Bidar* [2005] ECR I–2119, para. 31.

[315] *Grzelczyk*, para. 44; *Bidar*, para. 56 (emphasis added). Case C–413/99 *Baumbast* [2002] ECR I–7091, a case decided under Dir. 90/364 (now CRD), can also be explained in terms of solidarity, as Geelhoed AG noted in *Bidar*, para. 31.

[316] Para. 57.

[317] Para. 59. See also Geelhoed AG's remarks in Case C–413/01 *Ninni-Orasche* [2003] ECR I–13187, paras. 90–1. For an emphasis on the contextual approach which takes account of length of residence and degree of integration, see Ruiz-Jarabo Colomer AG's opinion, in Case C–138/02 *Collins* [2003] ECR I–2703, paras. 65–7.

Thus, the Court seems to be adopting a 'quantitative' approach to equality:[318] the longer migrants reside in the Member State, the more integrated they are in that state and the greater the number of benefits they receive on equal terms with nationals.[319] So, the cases appear to span a spectrum: at one end is *Martínez Sala*, a long-term resident (she had lived in Germany for 25 years and had two children there), fully integrated into the host state. She enjoyed full equal treatment (the payment of the child benefit on exactly the same terms as nationals). Having spent most of her life in Germany, she benefited from the principle of solidarity, possibly even national solidarity, and thus enjoyed full equal treatment on the same terms as nationals.

At the other end of the spectrum are those migrant citizens, like *Collins*[320] who have just arrived in the host state. While Article 21(1) gives them the right to move and reside freely in the host state,[321] they are not entitled to equal treatment in respect of social assistance benefits (e.g., the minimex) because they are not yet integrated into the host state's community and thus no solidarity exists (of either the national or transnational variety), although they might receive some social advantages on a non-discriminatory basis.[322] In the middle of this spectrum lies Grzelczyk who was only partially integrated into the society of the host state and so enjoyed only limited equal treatment (he received the minimex on the same terms as nationals but only until he became an unreasonable burden on public funds when his right of residence could be terminated).[323] *Bidar* probably falls somewhere between *Martínez Sala* and *Grzelczyk* on the spectrum. Like Grzelczyk, Bidar had been resident in the UK for three years; unlike Grzelczyk his integration was qualitative as well as quantitative: his surviving family lived in the UK, he had attended a British school, and he was about to go to a British university. His life was in the UK, just as Martinez Sala's was in Germany. When viewed in this light, the decision in *Bidar* that he should enjoy access to maintenance grants and loans on the same terms as nationals seems fair and right.

The 'quantitative' approach to equality is reflected in the Citizens' Rights Directive 2004/38 which, as we have seen, envisages three groups of migrants (fig. 12.2).[324] The first group (up to three months)[325] enjoy a general right to equal treatment[326] but not in respect of social assistance and student finance.[327] The second group (three months to five years) enjoys equal treatment even in respect of social assistance (albeit subject to the justification of requiring a real link with the territory of the host state in the case of an indirectly discriminatory rule).[328] However, host Member States are not obliged to provide them

---

[318] This is sometimes referred to as the 'affiliation model': see O. Golynker, 'Job Seekers' Rights in the European Union: Challenges of Changing the Paradigm of Social Solidarity' (2005) 30 *ELRev*. 111, 118–119.

[319] Kokott AG, 'EU citizenship: Citoyens sans frontiers', *Durham European Law Institute European Law Lecture* 2005, 13.

[320] Case C–138/02 *Collins* [2003] ECR I–2703, especially para. 69. See esp. Ruiz-Jarabo Colomer AG's Opinion (para. 76): Union law did not require the benefit to be provided to a citizen of the Union who entered the territory of a Member State with the purpose of seeking employment while lacking any connection with the state or link with the domestic employment market.

[321] See also Geelhoed AG Case C–413/01 *Ninni-Orasche* [2003] ECR I–13187.

[322] E.g., Case C–274/96 *Bickel and Franz* [1998] ECR I–7637 translation services for a court hearing.

[323] See also Case C–413/99 *Baumbast and R* [2002] ECR I–7091.

[324] Cf. A.Somek, 'Solidarity decomposed: Being and time in European citizenship' (2007) 32 *ELRev*. 787.          [325] Art. 6.

[326] Art. 24(1).          [327] Art. 24(2).

[328] Art. 24(1). On the 'real link' test: Joined Cases C–22/08 and 23/08 *Vatsouras* [2009] ECR I–000, paras 38–40 and C. O'Brien 'Real links, abstract rights and false alarms: The relationship between the ECJ's "real

with student grants or loans unless they are economically active or assimilated thereto.[329] The third group (generally those residing in the host state for more than five years) enjoy full equal treatment,[330] including equal treatment in respect of student maintenance.

The qualitative approach to integration can also be found in the directive, albeit not in the context of establishing rights to equal treatment in respect of length of residence but in respect of an expulsion decision. Under Article 28 the host State must take account of considerations such as 'how long the individual concerned has resided on its territory, his/her age, state of health, family and economic situation, social and cultural integration into the host Member State and the extent of his/her links with the country of origin'[331] when deciding whether to expel an individual.

### (c) Tax advantages

It was only in the mid 2000s that cases began to arise concerning EU citizens alleging that tax rules, often those of the state of origin, constituted an impediment to/restriction on their rights of free movement. These arguments coincided with a more general shift by the Court from the discrimination model towards the restrictions approach in the field of taxation, a move documented in detail in Chapters 9 and 10. As we saw above, *Pusa*,[332] a tax case, appeared to endorse this development in the field of citizenship.

*Pusa* concerned a Finnish pensioner living in Spain who owed money in Finland. An attachment order was made against his pension for the purpose of recovering the debt. Had he resided in Finland, the income tax he owed would have been deducted first in order to calculate what was left of his monthly pension to which an attachment order could have been made. However, since he resided in Spain, no such initial deduction was made. The Court ruled that the difference in treatment unjustifiably resulted in Mr Pusa being 'placed at a disadvantage by virtue of exercising his right to move and reside freely'[333] contrary to Article 21(1). This reasoning was also followed in *Schwarz*[334] concerning German children attending a school for the exceptionally gifted and talented in Scotland. Their parents did not get tax relief on the schooling; had the children been educated in Germany, the parents would have received the tax relief. The Court said that the German rule disadvantaged the children of nationals merely by reason of the fact that they had exercised their freedom of movement and this obstacle could not be justified.

---

link" case law and national solidarity' (2008) 33 *ELRev.* 643.

[329] Art. 24(2). The Dir. draws no distinction between those coming to the host state *qua* student and those not coming in this capacity.

[330] Art. 24(1).

[331] See also Joined Cases C–482/01 and C–493/01 *Orfanopoulos* v. *Land Baden-Württemberg* [2004] ECR I–5257, para. 99: 'To assess whether the interference envisaged is proportionate to the legitimate aim pursued, in this instance the protection of public policy, account must be taken, particularly, of the nature and seriousness of the offences committed by the person concerned, the length of his residence in the host Member State, the period which has elapsed since the commission of the offence, the family circumstances of the person concerned and the seriousness of the difficulties which the spouse and any of their children risk facing in the country of origin of the person concerned.'

[332] Case C–224/02 *Pusa* [2004] ECR I–5763.

[333] Para. 31. See also Case C–520/04 *Turpeinen* [2006] ECR I–10685. See also Case C–152/05 *Commission* v. *Germany (subsidy on dwellings)* [2008] ECR I–39, para. 30

[334] Cases C–76/05 and C–318/05 *Schwarz and Gootjes-Schwarz* v *Finanzamt Bergisch Gladbach* [2007] ECR I–6847. See also Case C–318/05 *Commission* v. *Germany (School Fees)* [2007] ECR I–6957.

*Pusa* and *Schwarz* concerned challenges by nationals who had exercised their rights of free movement against the home state; *Rüffler*[335] concerned a challenge by a migrant citizen to host state tax laws. It concerned a German claimant who retired to Poland where he lived on his German pension. Under Polish law only contributions paid to a Polish health insurance body were tax deductible. Because Mr Rüffler paid his contributions to a German body he did not benefit from the tax advantage. The Court found that the situation of a retired (German) taxpayer resident in Poland and receiving pension benefits paid under the compulsory health insurance scheme of another Member State, and that of a Polish retired person also resident in Poland but receiving his pension under a Polish health insurance scheme, were comparable since both were subject to an unlimited liability to tax in Poland. The Court then found that because the Polish rules disadvantaged taxpayers, like Mr Rüffler, who had exercised their freedom of movement to take up residence in Poland,[336] they therefore constituted 'a restriction on the freedoms conferred by Article [21(1)] on every citizen of the Union'[337] which could not be justified.

While the restrictions approach is an effective way of subjecting national tax rules which hinder free movement to review under Union law, this model sits uncomfortably with the international tax law principles of fiscal sovereignty and territoriality. As previous chapters have shown, the Court has more recently developed its understanding of the implications of these principles for its analysis,[338] with the result that it has tended to revert to the discrimination approach. The citizenship tax cases are no exception, as *Lindfors*[339] and *Schempp*[340] made clear. In these cases the Court said that mere difference between the tax regime of one Member State and another was not sufficient to trigger Article 21(1); migrant citizens had to show that they had suffered disadvantage in comparison with nationals. *Schempp* also emphasized that the claimant and the comparator had to be similarly situated. On the facts the Court ruled that the situation of Mr Schempp, a German national, who made maintenance payments to his former spouse now resident in Austria which were not tax deductable, was not comparable with the situation of a German national who made equivalent payments to a former spouse resident in Germany which were tax deductible. There was therefore no breach of the principle of non-discrimination.

### 2.6  Specific Rights for Family Members

So far we have concentrated on the meaning of equal treatment in the general context of Article 24 CRD and under Article 21(1) TFEU. The CRD, together with Regulation 1612/68, lays down specific rights for families. Not only will they enjoy the right to equal treatment in respect of social advantages, as we have already seen, but also in respect of the right to work, schooling, and housing.

### (a)  Equal treatment and the right to work for family members

Article 23 of Directive 2004/38 permits the Union citizen's family members who have the right of residence or the right of permanent residence to take up employment

---

[335]  Case C–544/07 *Rüffler v. Dyrektor Izby Skarbowej we Wrocławiu Ośrodek Zamiejscowy w Wałbrzychu* [2009] ECR I–000.                                                                        [336]  Para. 72.
[337]  Para. 73.        [338]  See further Chs. 9 and 10.
[339]  Case C–365/02 *Lindfors* [2004] ECR I–7183, para. 34.
[340]  Case C–403/33 *Schempp v. Finanzamt München* [2005] ECR I–6421, para. 45.

or self-employment in the host state (but not in any other state[341]), irrespective of the nationality of the family member.[342] These family members will enjoy equal treatment in respect of their terms and conditions of employment, as well as dismissal rights under Article 24(1) CRD.

## (b) Equal treatment and schooling

With a view to encouraging the integration of migrant children into the society of the host state,[343] Article 12 of Regulation 1612/68 requires the children of an EU national who is, or has been, employed in another Member State to be admitted to that state's general educational, apprenticeship, or vocational training courses.[344] This provision remains in Regulation 1612/68 and has not been replicated in the CRD 2004/38. Strictly speaking, the right therefore extends only to the children of *workers*.

Member States are obliged to encourage these children to attend such courses and, if necessary, make special efforts to ensure that the children can take advantage of educational and training facilities on an equal footing with nationals.[345] The reference to 'children' includes not only school age children but also those over the age of 21 who are no longer dependent on the working parent. In *Gaal*[346] the Court refused to make a link between the limitations imposed in the original Article 10 (identification of family members) and the rights contained in Article 12. It said that the principle of equal treatment required that the children of migrant workers should be able to continue their studies in order to be able to complete their education successfully.

Article 12 says that admission for migrant workers' children to education and training must be on the same conditions as for nationals. The reference to 'same conditions' is broadly construed. In the early case of *Casagrande*[347] the Court ruled that the term 'conditions' extended to 'general measures intended to facilitate educational attendance', including a grant for maintenance and training. Therefore, it was unlawful for the German authorities to refuse a monthly maintenance grant payable to school age children to the daughter of an Italian working in Germany. The right to a maintenance grant applies even where the children decide to receive their education in their state of origin. For this reason the Court ruled in *Di Leo*[348] that the German authorities could not refuse a grant to the daughter of an Italian migrant worker employed in Germany for 25 years on the grounds that she wished to study medicine in her state of origin (Italy).[349]

The importance of the right to education was emphasized in *Baumbast*[350] which concerned a German national who had been working in the UK. Relying on his rights under Regulation 1612/68 he had brought his Colombian wife and children with him to the UK.

---

[341] Case C–10/05 *Mattern v. Ministre du travail et de l'Emploi* [2006] ECR I–3145, para. 27.

[342] Case 131/85 *Gül v. Regierungspräsident Düsseldorf* [1986] ECR 1573.

[343] Case 9/74 *Casagrande v. Landeshauptstadt München* [1974] ECR 773, para. 7.

[344] These are to be read disjunctively: Joined Cases 389 and 390/87 *Echternach and Moritz* [1989] ECR 723.

[345] Case 9/74 *Casagrande* [1974] ECR 773, para. 8. Council Dir. 77/486/EEC ([1977] OJ L199/139) on the education of migrant workers' children requires that free tuition is available, including the teaching of the official language of the host state (Art. 2) and that the host state must promote the teaching of the children's mother tongue and culture (Art. 3). This applies equally to children with a disability: Case 76/72 *Michel S.* [1973] ECR 457, paras. 15–16.

[346] Case C–7/94 *Landesamt für Ausbildungsforderung Nordrhein-Westfalen v. Gaal* [1995] ECR I–1031.

[347] Case 9/74 [1974] ECR 773.     [348] Case C–308/89 *Di Leo v. Land Berlin* [1990] ECR I–4185.

[349] Para. 12.     [350] Case C–413/99 [2002] ECR I–7091.

However, when he ceased working the British authorities refused to renew his residence permit or those of his family with the result that the children could not complete their education in the UK. The Court found that the UK's decision breached Article 45 because, as the Court explained, to prevent a child of an EU citizen from continuing his education in the host state might 'dissuade that citizen from exercising the rights to freedom of movement laid down in Article [45] and would therefore create an obstacle to the effective exercise of the freedom thus guaranteed by the [EU Treaties]'.[351] For much the same reason in R[352] the children of an American woman and her French husband who worked in the UK were entitled to carry on their education in the UK, even though the parents were divorced and the children were living with their mother (a non-EU national).[353]

If the children of migrants can continue receiving their education in the host state, then in order to be able to enjoy that right they need someone to look after them. This was confirmed in *Baumbast and R*. Reading Article 12 of Regulation 1612/68 in the light of the requirement of respect for family life under Article 8 ECHR, the Court said the right conferred by Article 12 'necessarily implies' that the child has the right to be accompanied by the person who is his primary carer and who is entitled to reside with the child during his studies,[354] notwithstanding that the carers might not have had independent rights under EU law[355] because they are TCNs.[356] This case law has now been codified by Article 12(3) CRD.

In *Ibrahim*[357] the Court put together *Gaal* and *Baumbast* to conclude that the children of a national of a Member State (Denmark), who works or has worked in the host Member State (the UK), and the TCN parent who is their primary carer can claim a right of residence in the UK on the sole basis of Article 12, without such a right being conditional on their having sufficient resources and comprehensive sickness insurance cover in that State. In *Teixeira*[358] the Court added that the right of residence in the host Member State of the parent who was the primary carer for a child of a migrant worker, where that child was in education in that State, was not conditional on one of the child's parents having worked as a migrant worker on the date on which the child started in education. It also said that the right of residence in the host Member State of the parent who was the primary carer for a child of a migrant worker, where that child was in education, ended when the child reached the age of majority, unless the child continued to need the presence and care of that parent in order to be able to pursue and complete his or her education.

## (c) Equal treatment and housing

Originally, Article 10(3) of Regulation 1612/68 provided that workers were obliged to have available for their families 'housing considered as normal' for national workers in the region where they are employed. According to *Diatta*,[359] the purpose of Article 10(3) was both to implement public policy and to protect public security by preventing immigrants from living in precarious conditions.[360] In *Commission* v. *Germany*[361] German law required family members of EU migrant workers to have appropriate housing not only

---

[351] Para. 50.      [352] Case C–413/99 [2002] ECR I–7091.      [353] Paras. 60–2.      [354] Para. 73.
[355] Para. 71.
[356] See also Case C–200/02 *Chen* v. *Secretary of State for the Home Department* [2004] ECR I–9925.
[357] Case C–310/08 *London Borough of Harrow* v. *Ibrahim* [2010] ECR I–000.
[358] Case C–480/08 *Teixeira* v. *London Borough of Lambeth* [2010] ECR I–000.
[359] Case 267/83 [1985] ECR 567.      [360] Ibid., para. 10.      [361] Case 249/86 [1989] ECR 1263.

upon their arrival but also for the duration of their residence. The Court said that the German law went too far and that Article 10(3) applied solely when the worker and his family were first reunited. Once the family had been brought together the position of the migrant worker was no different from that of a national. Article 10(3) was deleted by the CRD and not replaced.

## 2.7 The Relationship between the CRD and the Treaties

It is clear that Directive 2004/38 lays down some significant rights for migrants and their families. However, the relationship between the CRD, the relevant Treaty provisions, and the case law is by no means clear, especially in the field of services. Of course, any interpretation of the Treaties—the principal source of rights—will prevail over the directive but, as we saw in Chapter 11, in the field of healthcare services the Court may try to steer its interpretation of the Treaties so as to bring them in line with the requirements of the directive. Alternatively, the Court might say, as it has on several occasions in respect of, for example Regulation 1612/68 on workers,[362] that the secondary measure merely makes explicit the principles formulated by the Treaties and so simply applies the Treaties.

Figure 12.4 shows how the various Treaty provisions and the directive might interact:

- If a worker's case is at issue, Article 45 is the relevant Treaty provision, supplemented by Regulation 1612/68 and, to a certain extent, the CRD.[363]

- If an establishment case is at issue, Article 49 is the relevant Treaty provision, supplemented by the CRD.

- If a services case is at issue, Article 56 is the relevant Treaty provision. Strictly speaking the CRD has no direct relevance in the field of services. However, for service providers/ recipients migrating to another Member State for less than three months, their position is indistinguishable from any other migrant citizen who can rely on Article 6 CRD.[364] Beyond three months, service providers could argue that they are persons of independent means and so rely on the provision in Article 7 CRD.

- If the migrant is a person of independent means or a student then they will enjoy rights under Article 21(1) TFEU and Article 7 CRD provided that they satisfy the conditions concerning sufficient resources and sickness insurance.

- A non-economically active migrant continues to be in the most precarious position. For the first three months of their stay they will enjoy the rights laid down by Article 6 CRD, albeit with limits on the rights to equality that they will enjoy (see fig. 12.3) and on condition they do not become an unreasonable burden on the social assistance system of the host state. Over and above three months but less than five years, they will be dependent on any rights given by Article 21(1) TFEU.

---

[362] See, e.g., Case C–278/03 *Commission* v. *Italy* [2005] ECR I–3747, para. 15; Case C–465/01 *Commission* v. *Austria* [2001] ECR I–8291, para. 25.

[363] The continued application of Reg. 1612/68 after the coming into force of the CRD is confirmed in Case C-310/08 *Ibrahim* [2010] ECR I–000, para. 45.

[364] This is the view the Court appears to take in Case C–215/03 *Oulane* v. *Mininster voor Vreemdelingenzaken en Integratie* [2005] ECR I–115, paras. 19–20. See Art. 17(8) of the Services Dir. 2006/123 ([2006] OJ L376/36) which gives precedence to the CRD.

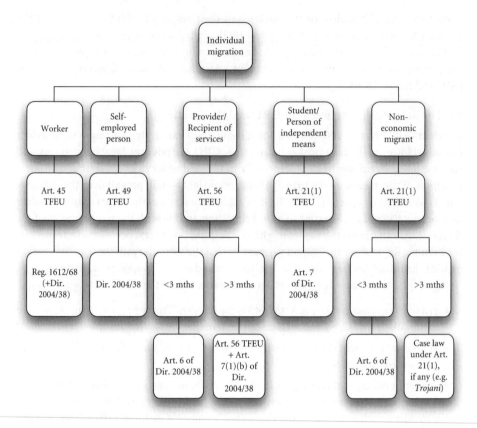

**Fig. 12.4** Summary of the sources of legal rights for individuals who move to another Member State

This analysis suggests that the CRD fills in some of the interstices between the Treaty provisions but its coverage is far from complete. For this reason, litigants will inevitably invoke Article 21(1) in the hope that it may offer greater protection than the directive. As we have already seen, the Court has in the past been prepared to make creative use of the status of Union citizenship to ensure that it is 'not merely a hollow or symbolic concept'.[365] In particular, it has used the advent of Union citizenship to require a rethink of the orthodox case law on the Union provisions on free movement of persons,[366] as well as to strike down national rules which distinguish between nationals and migrants,[367] and between nationals who have migrated and those who have not.[368] It has also used citizenship to justify limiting the limits to the 1990 Residence Directives (now Article 7 CRD) by applying the principle of proportionality in a rigorous fashion.[369]

[365] Per Geelhoed AG in Case C–209/03 *Bidar* [2005] ECR I–2119, para. 28.

[366] Case C–138/02 *Collins* [2003] ECR I–2703, para. 63.

[367] Case C–456/02 *Trojani* v. *CPAS* [2004] ECR I–7573.

[368] Case C–224/98 *D'Hoop* [2002] ECR I–6191.

[369] See also Case C–413/99 *Baumbast* [2002] ECR I–7091 and Case C–200/02 *Chen* [2004] ECR I–9925 considered in detail in Ch. 13.

That said, if experience to date is anything to go by, the Court will decide cases, as far as possible, on the basis of Articles 45, 49, and 56;[370] only where this proves impossible will it resort to Articles 20 and 21(1) (e.g., *Martínez Sala, Grzelczyk, Baumbast*).[371] In some cases it provides an answer based on Articles 45, 49, or 56 in respect of economic actors and Article 21 in respect of non-economic actors (e.g., *Morgan*).[372] Yet even where the case is decided on the basis of Articles 45, 49, and 56 the Court may take into account citizen-ship-type principles. For example, its decision in *Carpenter*[373] (concerning the position of the Filipino wife of a British service provider), handed down shortly before *Baumbast* and *Akrich*,[374] can probably best be seen as a citizenship case, with its strong overlay of human rights protection.

## D. MEMBERSHIP

So far we have concentrated on the first strand of David Held's citizenship matrix, rights (and duties). The rights for migrants are extensive. It is, however, surprising, how little reference is made to duties for those migrants. This suggests a structural imbalance in the EU's notion of citizenship. However, it may be that some elements of the notion of duty can be detected through the third strand of citizenship, participation, particularly in respect of getting involved in the process of holding the administration to account. It is less apparent in respect of the second strand, membership to which we now turn.

As far as membership is concerned, it has a legal and psychological dimension. The formal, legal indicator of membership is nationality. Nationality demarcates the national from the alien; it is the manifestation of citizenship to the outside world and the juridical tie between the individual and the community.[375] Two consequences flow from national-ity: the state assumes certain responsibilities for the individual holding its nationality and the individual is subject to the government of that particular state.

Nationality is also the principal indicator of membership for the EU. According to Article 20(1) TFEU, '[e]very person holding the nationality of a Member State shall be a citizen of the Union'. From this it is clear that it is the Member States, and not the EU,

---

[370] Case C–100/01 *Olazabal* [2002] ECR I–10981, considered further in Ch. 13 where the Court noted that Art. 21 'finds specific expression in Article 45 of the [Treaties]' in relation to the free movement of workers. The Court said that since the facts of the case fell within the scope of Art. 45, it was not necessary to rule on the interpretation of Art. 21. See also Case C–348/96 *Calfa* [1999] ECR I–11, para. 30; Case C–392/05 *Alevizos* v. *Ipourgos Ikonomikon* [2007] ECR I–3505, para. 80; Case C–152/05 *Commission* v. *Germany (sub-sidy for housing)* [2008] ECR I–39, para. 18.

[371] Although cf. Case C–274/96 *Bickel and Franz* [1998] ECR I–7637; Case C–135/99 *Elsen* [2000] ECR I–10409. See N. Reich and S. Harbacevica, 'Citizenship and family on trial: A fairly optimistic overview of recent court practice with regard to free movement of persons' (2003) 40 *CMLRev*. 615, 627.

[372] See also Case C–345/05 *Commission* v. *Portugal (exemption from capital gains tax)* [2006] ECR I–10633; Case C–104/06 *Commission* v. *Sweden (deferral of capital gains tax)* [2007] ECR I–671.

[373] Case C–60/00 [2002] ECR I–6279, paras. 40–1, considered further in Ch. 8; Case C–291/05 *Eind* [2007] ECR I–10719. See, in a similar vein, Case C–117/01 *KB* v. *National Health Service Pensions Agency* [2004] ECR I–541.

[374] Case C–109/01 *Akrich* [2003] ECR I–9607, paras. 58–9 (where *Carpenter* was cited).

[375] C. Closa, 'Citizenship of the Union and nationality of Member States' (1995) 32 *CMLRev*. 487.

which are the gatekeepers to EU citizenship.[376] This was confirmed in *Kaur*,[377] where the Court said 'under international law, it is for each Member State, having due regard to [Union] law, to lay down the conditions for the acquisition and loss of nationality'.[378] Furthermore, the host Member State is not in a position to criticize another Member State's attribution of nationality.[379]

The significance of the additional observation made by the Court in *Kaur* that, when exercising their powers in the sphere of nationality, the Member States must have due regard to EU law, can be seen in *Rottmann*.[380] An Austrian national was accused of serious fraud in Austria. He moved to Germany and applied for naturalisation, without mentioning the proceedings against him in Austria. He was granted German nationality and, as a result, he lost his Austrian nationality under Austrian law. However, when the German authorities learned that he was the subject of judicial investigation in Austria, they sought to withdraw his naturalisation with retroactive effect. This decision risked rendering him stateless, as well as depriving him of his status as a citizen of the Union. The Court ruled:[381]

A decision withdrawing naturalisation because of deception corresponds to a reason relating to the public interest. In this regard, it is legitimate for a Member State to wish to protect the special relationship of solidarity and good faith between it and its nationals and also the reciprocity of rights and duties, which form the bedrock of the bond of nationality.

However, the Court continued that the national court had to ascertain whether the withdrawal decision observed the principle of proportionality in respect of the consequences for Rottmann in the light of EU law. It added that the principle of proportionality might include giving Rottmann a reasonable period of time to try to recover Austrian nationality.[382]

So far we have concentrated on the legal indicators of membership. The psychological dimension of membership is harder to articulate, but at its core lies a sense of belonging and identity. To a certain extent legal links can help foster a sense of 'common identity and shared destiny',[383] particularly in the EU where law has been so central to the

---

[376] This is confirmed by the Declaration on Nationality of a Member State appended to the TEU. In the case of a person with dual nationality, the Court ruled in Case C–369/90 *Micheletti* v. *Delagación del Gobierno en Cantabria* [1992] ECR I–4239, para. 10 that if a person was able to produce one of the documents referred to in Council Dir. 73/148/EEC ([1973] OJ L172/14) (now CRD) to prove they were nationals of one Member State, other Member States were not entitled to dispute that status on the ground that the persons concerned were also nationals of a non-Member State, the nationality of which took precedence under the host state's law.

[377] Case C–192/99 R. v. *Secretary of State for the Home Department, ex p. Kaur* [2001] ECR I–1237 noted by H. Toner (2002) 39 *CMLRev.* 881.

[378] Para. 19. The conditions might include a period of residence, birth, and family ties. See J. Shaw, 'Citizenship and enlargement: The outer limits of EU political citizenship' in C. Barnard and O. Odudu (eds.), *The Outer Limits of European Union Law* (Oxford: Hart Publishing, 2009) who describes the difficulties facing the substantial populations of non-nationals in the new EU states following the break-up of former states (the Soviet Union and Yugoslavia) resulting in minorities not holding national citizenship of the host state and thus not benefitting from EU rights. She also points out that in Estonia, Latvia, and Lithuania there are high barriers to becoming a national citizen for a resident non-national, including strict language tests.

[379] Case C–200/02 *Chen* [2004] ECR I–9925. See also B. Kunoy, 'A union of national citizens: The origins of the court's lack of *avant-gardisme* in the *Chen* case' (2006) 43 *CMLRev.* 179.

[380] Case C–135/08 *Rottmann* v. *Freistaat Bayern* [2010] ECR I–000.          [381] Para. 51.

[382] Paras. 55–9.

[383] Jacobs AG in Case C–92/92 and 326/92 *Phil Collins* [1993] ECR I–5145, para. 11.

integration process.[384] The EU has also been proactive in taking other steps to develop a sense of belonging—the EU flag, EU day (9 May), EU motto (United in diversity), and EU anthem ('Ode to Joy' from Beethoven's Ninth Symphony),[385] the red passport, the pink driving licence, town-twinning, and student mobility programmes (Erasmus/Socrates). Some commentators are dismissive of these top-down attempts to create a true European citizenship, arguing that they cannot overcome the historical legacy of market citizenship, which is essentially premised on self-interest.[386] Others are concerned that the continued emphasis on market citizenship excludes those who do not conform[387] and so, for many, citizenship undermines, rather than creates, a sense of identity at EU level. And for those who do not hold the nationality of one of the Member States exclusion may be total.

A further criticism of the creation of EU citizenship is that it comes at the expense of national or regional identity. The EU is at least aware of these concerns. Article 4(2) TEU requires the Union to respect 'the national identities of the Member States, inherent in their fundamental structures, political and constitutional, inclusive of regional and local self-government',[388] while Article 167 TFEU (ex Article 151 EC) requires the Union to contribute to the 'flowering of the cultures of the Member States, while respecting their national and regional diversity'.[389] Advocate General Jacobs picked up on the diversity theme in *Garcia Avello*,[390] noting that the intention of Article 21 TFEU was to allow free, and possibly repeated or even continuous, movement within a single 'area of freedom, security and justice' (AFSJ), in which 'both cultural diversity and freedom from discrimination' are ensured. The Court reached similar conclusions in the same case, reasoning that the Belgian practice of refusing to change a child's surname to reflect the Spanish pattern was 'neither necessary nor even appropriate for promoting the integration within Belgium of the nationals of other Member States'.[391]

The AFSJ introduced at Amsterdam, to which Advocate General Jacobs referred, is part of the EU's response to concerns about exclusion, especially of TCNs, and failure to recognise the diversity of states in the EU. According to Article 67(1) TFEU:

The Union shall constitute an area of freedom, security and justice with respect for fundamental rights and the different legal systems and traditions of the Member States.

The subsequent paragraphs of Article 67 then consider freedom, security and justice in turn. Article 67(2) TFEU concerns freedom. It provides that the Union shall 'ensure the

---

[384] See M. Cappelletti, M. Seccombe, and J. H. H. Weiler (eds.), *Integration through Law* (Berlin: De Gruyter, 1985).

[385] These were listed in Art. I–8 of the Constitutional Treaty under the heading 'The symbols of the Union'. Many thought that the EU had gone too far with these trappings of statehood and the symbols were dropped from the Lisbon Treaty.

[386] S. Douglas-Scott, *Constitutional Law of the European Union* (Harlow: Longman, 2002), 492.

[387] Everson, above n. 1.

[388] See also the Union's approach to subsidiarity as laid down in Art. 5(3) TEU and Protocol (No. 2) on the application of the principles of subsidiarity and proportionality, and Protocol (No. 3) on the role of national parliaments in the European Union. See further Ch.16.

[389] See also Art. 3(3) TEU: The Union shall 'respect its rich cultural and linguistic diversity, and shall ensure that Europe's cultural heritage is safeguarded and enhanced'. In Case C–288/89 *Stichting Collectieve Antennevoorziening Gouda* v. *Commissariaat voor de Media* [1991] ECR I–4007, para. 13 the Court took the 'social, cultural, religious and philosophical' diversity of the Netherlands into account (see Case Study 11.2). See also Case 379/87 *Groener* v. *Minister for Education* [1989] ECR 3967, considered in Ch. 9.

[390] Case C–148/02 *Garcia Avello* [2003] ECR I–11613, para. 72.     [391] Para. 43.

absence of internal border controls for persons and shall frame a common policy[392] on asylum, immigration and external border control, based on solidarity between Member States, which is fair towards third-country nationals'.[393] Thus 'freedom' means free movement of EU nationals as well as 'fair' Union-based migration policies for TCNs. These latter policies are considered further in Chapter 14

Article 67(3) TFEU (ex Article 29 EU) concerns security:

The Union shall endeavour to ensure a high level of security through measures to prevent and combat crime, racism and xenophobia,[394] and through measures for coordination and cooperation between police[395] and judicial authorities[396] and other competent authorities,[397] as well as through the mutual recognition of judgments in criminal matters and, if necessary, through the approximation of criminal laws.

As we shall see in Chapter 14, the Hague Programme 2004–9 has prioritized the security agenda and is used to justify keeping out TCNs who might pose a threat to the security of EU insiders. This exclusionary policy serves to undermine the more integrationist stance envisaged by Article 67(2). Finally, Article 67(4) concerns justice and this is considered below.

The Commission is now attempting to locate the citizen more firmly at the heart of the AFSJ. In its 2009 Communication, *An Area of freedom, security and justice serving the citizen*,[398] it outlines a programme 'building a citizen's Europe' where 'All action taken in future should be centred on the citizen', focusing on four priorities: first, 'promoting citizens rights', emphasizing the role of fundamental rights, especially respect for the 'human person and human dignity, and for the other rights enshrined in the Charter. Data protection is particularly emphasized. Secondly, the Commission talks of a 'Europe of justice'. This is considered below. Thirdly, the priority of 'a Europe that protects' emphasizes the need for a domestic security strategy. The final strand, 'Promoting a more integrated society for the citizen—a Europe of solidarity', largely concerns the position of TCNs and is considered in the next chapter. These different policy strands fed into the adoption by the European Council of the Stockholm programme 2010–14,

---

[392] This language is new but reflects the fact that the Tampere and Hague programmes have already called for this.

[393] The reference to the need to be fair to TCNs is also new. The para. continues that 'For the purpose of this Title, stateless persons shall be treated as third-country nationals'.

[394] See, e.g., Council Framework Decision 2008/913 ([2008] OJ L328/55) on combating certain forms and expressions of racism and xenophobia by means of criminal law.

[395] See, e.g., Council Dec. 2002/630/JHA establishing a framework programme on police and judicial cooperation in criminal matters (AGIS) ([2002] OJ L203/5); Council Dec. 2003/170/JHA on the common use of liaison officers posted abroad by the law enforcement agencies of the Member States ([2003] OJ L67/27); Council Dec. 2008/615/JHA on the stepping up of cross-border cooperation, particularly in combating terrorism and cross-border crime ([2008] OJ L210/1 and Council Dec. 2008/616/JHA implementing Dec. 2008/615/JHA ([2008] OJ L210/12) incorporating the Prüm Treaty into EU legislation, providing indirect access to Member States' databases on fingerprints and DNA information and access to vehicle registration data. See K. Lachmeyer, 'European police cooperation and its limits: From intelligence-led to coercive measures' in C. Barnard and O. Odudu (eds.), *The Outer Limits of European Union Law* (Oxford: Hart Publishing, 2009).

[396] See eg the Council Framework Dec. 202/584/JHA on the European Arrest Warrant ([2002] OJ L190/20).

[397] See, e.g., Council Framework Dec. 2006/960/JHA ([2006] OJ L386/89) on simplifying the exchange of information and intelligence between law enforcement authorities of the Member States.

[398] COM(2009) 262.

which is considered in Chapter 14. For present purposes, it is sufficient to note the European Council's continued emphasis on security. It says: 'The challenge will be to ensure respect for fundamental rights and freedoms and integrity while guaranteeing security in Europe.'[399] It continues: 'An internal security strategy should be developed in order to further improve security in the Union and thus protect the lives and safety of European citizens and tackle organized crime, terrorism and other threats.'[400] Thus, membership means for citizens that safety is the real priority.

## E. PARTICIPATION

An important way of fostering a sense of belonging comes through participation in the life of the community. This is the third strand in Held's matrix of citizenship. In the Greek city state (polis) all citizens (for which read free men with property) actively participated in the legislative process. This is the fullest, richest, and most active kind of citizenship, underpinned by ideas of equality (at least among those allowed to participate). Viewed in this light, citizenship is a status, different from nationality, which requires active involvement by the citizen in shaping the polity. In the modern state the concept of democracy has evolved from participative democracy in the republican style (with all men participating) to representative democracy (where the people elect their representatives). Now the only active participation expected of citizens is to vote and possibly to stand as a candidate in elections.[401]

### 1. REPRESENTATIVE DEMOCRACY

#### 1.1 Introduction

One of the distinguishing features of the Constitutional Treaty was its expressed commitment to democracy. This has survived in the Lisbon Treaty. The title on democratic principles begins, in Article 9 TEU, with a statement of commitment to the principle of democratic equality:

In all its activities, the Union shall observe the principle of the equality of its citizens, who shall receive equal attention from its institutions, bodies, offices and agencies.

Article 10(3) TEU adds 'Every citizen shall have the right to participate in the democratic life of the Union.' The centrality of representative democracy to the EU is stated in Article 10(1) TEU: 'The functioning of the Union shall be founded on representative democracy.' Article 10(2) TEU then identifies the two routes by which the citizen's voice is heard at EU level: (1) directly, through their MEPs ('Citizens are directly represented at Union level in the European Parliament'); and (2) indirectly via Member State participation ('Member States are represented in the European Council by their Heads of State

---

[399] European Presidency Conclusions 11 Dec. 2009, para. 26.    [400] Ibid., para. 29.
[401] Although cf. Dec. 2010/37/EC on the European Year of Voluntary Activities promoting Active Citizenship [2010] OJ L17/43.

or Government and in the Council by their governments, themselves democratically accountable either to their national parliaments,[402] or to their citizens').

Article 10(2) thus emphasizes the multi-faceted nature of representative democracy in the EU: while recognizing that the EU gains some legitimacy through direct elections to the European Parliament, the Article makes express the parallel legitimacy derived from elections to national parliaments which hold government ministers representing Member State interests in the EU to account. This indirect route to legitimacy is important since the turnout in elections to the European Parliament is so low. Article 10(4) TEU is intended to help to address this problem by encouraging the creation of pan-European political parties. It says 'Political parties at European level contribute to forming European political awareness and to expressing the will of citizens of the Union.' Furthermore, the extension of the use of the 'ordinary legislative procedure' which gives equal say to the Parliament and Council,[403] including in controversial areas such as most of the AFSJ and the common commercial policy, means that the European Parliament does now really does count.

## 1.2 Elections to the European Parliament

The only democratically elected body in the EU is the European Parliament.[404] Article 8 of the Act concerning the election of the representatives of the European Parliament by direct universal suffrage[405] provides that 'the electoral procedure shall be governed in each Member State by its national provisions'. However, neither the EU Treaties nor the 1976 Act defines who is entitled to vote and to stand as a candidate in elections to the European Parliament—questions which go to the core of 'the principles of democracy on which the Union is based'.[406] This was at issue in two important and complementary cases decided on the same day: *Spain v. United Kingdom* and *Eman*.[407] *Spain v. United Kingdom*, a rare example of an Article 259 TFEU (ex Article 227 EC) action, raised the question whether a Member State (the UK) was entitled to extend the right to vote in elections to the European Parliament to nationals of non-member countries resident in Europe (Gibraltar, a British Crown Colony which does not form part of the UK and to which only parts of Union law apply). The European Court of Human Rights had condemned the UK for failing to hold elections to the European Parliament in Gibraltar contrary to Article 3 of Protocol No. 1 of the Convention.[408] In response, the UK established a new electoral region which combined Gibraltar with an existing region in England (the South West) and created a special electoral register. Spain argued that the extension of the right

---

[402] National parliaments, too, have a greater role, especially in respect of ensuring compliance with the principle of subsidiarity: see Arts. 5(3) and 12 TEU and Protocol (No. 1) on the Role of National Parliaments in the European Union. See further S. Weatherill, 'Competence and legitimacy' in C. Barnard and O. Odudu (eds.), *The Outer Limits of European Union Law* (Oxford: Hart Publishing, 2009), 30–1.

[403] The procedure is laid down in Art. 294 TFEU. The Council acts by qualified majority vote (QMV) save where Arts. 293–4 TFEU provide otherwise.

[404] Art. 223 TFEU (ex Art. 190(4) EC).

[405] Annexed to Council Dec. 76/787/ECSC, EEC, Euratom ([1976] OJ L278/1) as amended by Council Dec. 2002/772/EC, Euratom ([2002] OJ L283/1). See also Art. 39(2) of the Charter.

[406] Tizzano AG in his Joined Opinion in Cases C–145/04 and C–300/04 *Kingdom of Spain v. United Kingdom of Great Britain and Northern Ireland; M.G. Eman and O.B. Sevinger v. College van burgemeester en wethouders van Den Haag* [2006] ECR I–7917.

[407] Cases C–145/04 *Spain v. United Kingdom* [2006] ECR I–7917; C–300/04 *Eman and Sevinger* [2006] ECR I–8055 (noted L. Besselink (2008) 45 *CMLRev.* 787).

[408] *Matthews v. United Kingdom*, no. 24833/94 [1999] ECHR I–251.

to vote in elections to the European Parliament to people who were not citizens of the Union breached Union law. The Court disagreed. It said that the definition of those entitled to vote and stand as a candidate in elections to the European Parliament fell within the competence of each Member State and that EU law did not preclude a Member State from granting those rights to individuals who had close links to it, as well as to their own nationals or citizens of the Union resident in their territory.[409]

While *Spain* v. *UK* concerned a state extending the right to vote to non-nationals, *Eman* concerned the opposite situation: a state (the Netherlands) excluding certain categories of its own nationals resident in an overseas territory associated to the Union (OCT),[410] in this case Aruba, from the right to vote and to stand as a candidate in European elections. The Court said that individuals who held the nationality of a Member State and who lived or resided in a territory which was one of the OCTs could rely on the rights conferred on citizens of the Union.[411] However, the Court said that Article 22(2) TFEU on voting rights of *migrants* did not apply to a citizen of the Union residing in an OCT who wished to exercise his right to vote in the Member State of which he was a national.[412] On the other hand, the Court said that the Dutch authorities were nevertheless in breach of the principle of equal treatment because Dutch nationals resident in a non-member state did have the right to vote in European elections but Dutch nationals resident in the Netherlands Antilles or Aruba did not,[413] and that the Dutch had failed to offer an objective justification for such difference in treatment.[414] For good measure, the Court also suggested that a remedy in damages should be available as a result of the breach of Union law.[415]

So far we have concentrated on the rights of *nationals* to vote and stand as a candidate in elections.[416] Article 22 TFEU permits *migrant* EU citizens to vote and stand as a candidate in elections for local[417] and European elections,[418] subject to 'derogations where warranted by problems specific to a Member State'. Two directives have been adopted to implement these rights which provide for equal treatment: migrant EU citizens have the right to vote and stand as a candidate in municipal or European elections provided they

---

[409] Para. 78. See also Case C–535/08 *Pignataro* [2009] ECR I–50*: the provisions on Union citizenship permit a national rule requiring a candidate for election to a regional assembly to reside in that region at the time of nomination.

[410] Art. 355 TFEU (ex Art. 299(3) EC).    [411] Paras. 27–9.

[412] The Court justified this decision by reference to the case law of the European Court of Human Rights which had ruled that the criterion linked to residence was acceptable to determine who were entitled to the right to vote and to stand as a candidate in elections: *Melnychenko* v. *Ukraine*, no. 17707/02 ECHR 2004–X, paras. 56–7.                                                                        [413] Para. 58.

[414] Para. 60.    [415] Para. 70.

[416] Cases C–145/04 *Kingdom of Spain* v. *United Kingdom of Great Britain and Northern Ireland* [2006] ECR I–7917, para. 76.

[417] See also Art. 40 of the Charter; Dir. 94/80/EC ([1994] OJ L368/38), as amended by Dir. 96/30/EC ([1996] OJ L122/14), laying down detailed arrangements for the exercise of the right to vote and to stand as a candidate in municipal elections by citizens of the Union residing in a Member State of which they are not nationals. See further J. Shaw, *The Transformation of Citizenship in the European Union: Electoral rights and the restructuring of political space* (Cambridge: CUP, 2007).

[418] See also Art. 40 of the Charter; Dir. 93/109/EC ([1993] OJ L329/34) on the right to vote and stand as a candidate in elections to the European Parliament for citizens of the Union residing in a Member State of which they are not nationals. This directive provides that entitlement to vote and to stand as a candidate in the Member State of residence is conferred on people, who are citizens of the Union but who are not nationals of the Member State where they reside and who satisfy the conditions applicable to nationals of that state in respect of the right to vote and to stand as a candidate, and are not deprived of those rights in their home Member State. See P. Oliver, 'Electoral rights under Article 8b of the Treaty of Rome' (1996) 33 *CMLRev.* 473 and H. Lardy, 'The political rights of Union citizenship' (1996) 2 *EPL* 611.

satisfy the same conditions as the host state imposes on its own nationals.[419] The flip side of the coin is that migrant citizens cannot participate in the most important elections— those for the national parliaments. This is a further example of the partial nature of EU citizenship.

### 1.3 Deliberative or Participatory Democracy

Many argue that, with turnout for European Parliament elections being so low, the EU still suffers from a serious democratic deficit. As part of its response, the Commission[420] issued a White Paper on Governance identifying five principles underpinning good governance: openness, participation, accountability, effectiveness, and coherence.[421] The White Paper also placed much emphasis on citizen participation as a way of supplementing representative democracy.[422] In the absence of an identifiable public space and a common language the chances of this happening are slim. More realistic is the possibility of citizen participation through alternative intermediaries, primarily 'civil society'.[423] According to the White Paper, it is civil society that 'plays an important role in giving voice to the concerns of citizens' and delivers 'services that meet people's needs'.[424] The value of the involvement of civil society is now acknowledged by Article 11 TEU (originally entitled 'The principle of participatory democracy' in Article I–47 of the Constitutional Treaty). Article 11(1) TEU provides that 'The institutions shall, by appropriate means, give citizens and representative associations the opportunity to make known and publicly exchange their views in all areas of Union action.' Article 11(2) TEU adds that the institutions must maintain an 'open, transparent, and regular dialogue with representative associations and civil society'.[425]

The Commission is now keen to formalize links with other bodies and, as part of this process, it has issued a Communication on minimum standards for consultation of interested parties by the Commission.[426] This is reinforced by Article 11(3) TEU which

---

[419] In practice, few take advantage of this possibility: only 11.9% of EU citizens resident in another Member State voted in the 2004 elections to the European Parliament: MEMO/06/484, Brussels, 13 Dec. 2006.

[420] Partly to lay to rest its own ghosts: see, e.g., Committee of Independent Experts, *First Report on Allegations Regarding Fraud, Mismanagement and Nepotism in the EC*, presented to the EP, 15 Mar. 1999. See also A. Tomkins, 'Responsibility and resignation in the European Commission' (1999) 62 *MLR* 744 and V. Mehde, 'Responsibility and accountability in the European Commission' (2003) 40 *CMLRev.* 423. See also Commission Communication, 'On a comprehensive EU policy against corruption' (COM(2003) 317).

[421] COM(2001) 428. For a detailed discussion of this document, see C. Joerges, Y. Mény, and J. H. H. Weiler (eds.), *Mountain or Molehill? A critical appraisal of the Commission White Paper on Governance*, Jean Monnet Working Paper No. 6/01 and the special edition of the *European Law Journal* (2002) vol. 8(1).

[422] Commission Discussion Paper, 'Commission and non-governmental organisations: Building a stronger partnership', COM(2000) 11: 'The decision-making process in the EU is first and foremost legitimized by the elected representatives of the European people. However, NGOs can make a contribution in fostering a more participatory democracy both within the European Union and beyond.'

[423] According to the Governance White Paper COM(2001) 428, 14, civil society includes the following: trade unions and employers' organizations ('social partners'); non-governmental organizations; professional associations; charities; grass-roots organizations; organizations that involve citizens in local and municipal life with a particular contribution from churches and religious communities. See K. Armstrong, 'Rediscovering civil society: The European Union and the White Paper on Governance' (2002) 8 *ELJ* 102.

[424] COM(2001) 428, 14.

[425] The Church and non-confessional organizations are singled out in Art. 17(3) TEU.

[426] Commission Communication, 'Towards a reinforced culture of consultation and dialogue: General principles and minimum standards for consultation of interested parties by the Commission' COM(2002) 704 upon which it had previously consulted (COM(2002) 277). See D. Obradovic and Alonso Vizcaino,

requires the Commission to carry out broad consultations with parties concerned in order to ensure that the Union's actions are coherent and transparent.[427] In some sectors, dialogue with representative associations has already been formalized. For example, the Sixth Environment Action programme (2002–12) expressly recognized the need to empower citizens, and the measures proposed included extensive and wide-ranging dialogue with stakeholders in environmental policymaking.[428] This led to specific Union action programmes promoting non-governmental organizations active in the field of environmental policy.[429]

In the field of employment law and labour market regulation, the social partners (management and labour) are the interlocutors.[430] Their involvement was constitutionalized by Articles 154–5 TFEU[431] (ex Articles 138–9 EC) requiring the Commission to consult management and labour about whether there should be any legislation in the field and, if so, its content. Social partners can also negotiate collective agreements which can be given legislative effect by a Council 'decision'.[432] The European Parliament has no formal role in this process except the right to be 'informed'.[433] A number of directives have been adopted using this 'collective' route to legislation, including directives on parental leave, part-time work and fixed-term work.[434] When the validity of the Parental Leave Directive 96/34 was challenged in *UEAPME*[435] by an organization representing small and medium-sized enterprises which had been excluded from the negotiation process, the General Court (formerly the Court of First Instance) endorsed this alternative 'collective' approach to lawmaking. It said that, in respect of measures adopted by the Council under the traditional legislative route, the democratic legitimacy was derived from the European Parliament's participation.[436] However, in respect of measures adopted under the collective route where the European Parliament had no role, the 'principle of democracy on which the Union is founded requires…that the participation of the people be otherwise ensured, in this instance through the parties representative of management

'Good governance requirements concerning the participation of interest groups in EU consultations' (2006) 43 *CMLRev.* 1049.

[427] See also Art. 15 TFEU: 'In order to promote good governance and ensure the participation of civil society, the Union institutions, bodies, offices and agencies shall conduct their work as openly as possible.'

[428] EP and Council Dec. 1600/2002 ([2002] OJ L242/1).

[429] See, e.g., EP and Council Dec. No. 466/2002/EC ([2002] OJ L75/1). See also Dir. 2003/35 ([2003] OJ L156/17), amending Dir. 85/337 ([1985] OJ L216/40) providing for public participation in respect of the drawing up of certain plans and programmes relating to the environment and improving public participation and for provisions on access to justice contributing to the obligations arising under the Århus Convention considered in, e.g., Case C–427/07 *Commission* v. *Ireland* [2009] ECR I–000 and Case C–263/08 *Djurgården-Lilla Värtans Miljöskyddsförening* v. *Stockholms kommun genom dess marknämnd* [2009] ECR I–000.

[430] C. Barnard, 'Governance and the social partners' (2002) 8 *ELJ* 80.

[431] See also Art. 152 TFEU: 'The Union recognises and promotes the role of the social partners at its level, taking into account the diversity of the national systems. It shall facilitate dialogue between the social partners respecting their autonomy.'

[432] Art. 155(2) (ex Art. 139(2)). The term 'decision' is used in Art. 155(2) but has been interpreted to mean any legally binding act, in particular, directives.

[433] Art. 155(2) TFEU.

[434] Council Dir. 96/34/EC on Parental Leave ([1996] OJ L145/4) repealed and replaced by Council Dir. 2010/18/EU ([2010] OJ L68/13); Council Dir. 97/81/EC on Part-time Work ([1998] OJ L14/9); and Council Dir. 99/70/EC on Fixed-Term Work ([1999] OJ L175/43). See further C. Barnard, *EC Employment Law* (Oxford: OUP, 2006), Ch. 2.

[435] Case T–135/96 *Union Européenne de l'artisanat et des petites et moyennes entreprises (UEAPME)* v. *Council* [1998] ECR II–2335.        [436] Para. 88.

and labour who concluded the agreement which is endowed by the Council...with a legislative foundation at [Union] level'.[437]

But this broadening of the consultation and legislative process raises further problems of representativity (and accountability) of the interlocutors. To what extent do they really represent the views of their members and to what extent are these views more generally representative? This issue lay at the heart of UEAPME's challenge to the Parental Leave Directive.[438] The agreement on parental leave had been negotiated by the intersectoral social partners—UNICE (the European employers' association, now called BUSINESSEUROPE), CEEP (the public sector employers' association), and ETUC (the European trades union confederation). UEAPME argued that since the interests of small and medium-sized undertakings differed from those represented by UNICE, UEAPME should also have been at the negotiating table.

The General Court disagreed. It said that it was for the Commission to examine the representativity of the signatories to collective agreements and the Council had to verify whether the Commission had fulfilled this task. Where the degree of representativity was lacking the Commission and Council had to refuse to implement the agreement at Union level.[439] On the facts, the General Court found that the Commission and Council had fulfilled their task. Since the signatories were *general* cross-industry organizations with a general mandate, as distinct from cross-industry organizations representing *certain* categories of workers and undertakings with a specific mandate (the subgroup in which UEAPME was placed), they were sufficiently representative.[440] However, in the light of the problems in *UEAPME* the Commission said in its Governance White Paper that, in return for developing more extensive partnership arrangements, civil society organizations had to 'tighten up their internal structures, furnish guarantees of openness and representativity, and prove their capacity to relay information or lead debates in the Member States'.[441]

Broadening the range of actors involved in the legislative process has also been reflected in the debates leading to the two key constitutional developments in recent years, the Charter of Fundamental Rights and the Constitutional Treaty. For example, membership of the Convention, the body responsible for drafting the Charter was relatively broad, comprising representatives of the Member State governments (15), the Commission (1), the European Parliament (16), and national Parliaments (30), with observer status for representatives of the Council of Europe and the Court of Justice. Documents related to the process were available on the web, submissions were taken from NGOs, and the methods of working were more deliberative[442] (rather than secretive and intergovernmental

---

[437] Para. 89. See N. Bernard, 'Legitimising EU law: Is the social dialogue the way forward? Some reflections around the *UEAPME* case' in J. Shaw (ed.), *Social Law and Policy in an Evolving European Union* (Oxford: Hart Publishing, 2000).

[438] See G. Britz and M. Schmidt, 'The institutionalised participation of management and labour in the legislative activities of the European Community: A challenge to the principle of democracy under Community law' (2000) 6 *ELJ* 45, esp. 66–7 and A. Adinolfi, 'Admissibility of action for annulment by social partners and "sufficient representativity" of European agreements' (2000) 25 *ELRev.* 165.          [439] Para. 90.

[440] Paras. 95–6.          [441] COM(2001) 428, 17.

[442] For an overview of the historical development of 'deliberative democracy' see 'Introduction' in J. Bohman and W. Rehg (eds.), *Deliberative Democracy: Essays on reason and politics* (Cambridge, Mass.:, MIT Press, 1997) and J. Elster, 'Introduction' in J. Elster (ed.), *Deliberative Democracy* (Cambridge: CUP, 1998).

which has been characteristic of intergovernmental conferences (IGCs)).[443] However, as De Búrca notes, while the process may have been 'aimed at' the citizen, and a virtue made of the openness and novel nature of the process, this was not to be a genuinely participative process but one which, albeit deliberative in nature, was to be composed only of institutional representatives from the national and European level.[444] By contrast, the conclusion of the Lisbon Treaty bore all the hallmarks of a return to intergovernmentalism.

### 1.4 Direct Participation

Perhaps the most striking example of direct citizen participation is the introduction by the Lisbon Treaty of Article 11(4) TEU which provides that:

Not less than one million citizens who are nationals of a significant number of Member States may take the initiative of inviting the Commission, within the framework of its powers, to submit any appropriate proposal on matters where citizens consider that a legal act of the Union is required for the purpose of implementing the Treaties.[445]

Inserted as a last-minute addition to the text, this 'Citizens initiative' envisages active and direct participation of EU citizens in a way never before experienced in the EU. However, this provision itself poses a challenge to representative democracy. What if those million, a miniscule percentage of the EU's total population,[446] make a proposal (e.g., the expulsion of all black immigrants) wholly unacceptable to the liberal values on which the EU is based? Will this provision in fact expose the legislative system to unnecessary and undesirable influence?[447]

### 1.5 Conclusions

Despite the various attempts to make the EU more explicitly democratic many EU citizens were not convinced. The rejection of the Constitutional Treaty by the voters of France and the Netherlands in 2005 caused profound shock waves to reverberate across the EU. The voters of these two countries—founding members of the European project— sent out a strong message of their discontent. It is difficult to say for sure why the voters turned against a text whose aims were, according to the Laeken declaration,[448] to respond to citizens' calls for a 'clear, open, effective, democratically controlled [Union] approach' and to bring citizens closer to the 'European design'. Nevertheless, surveys have indicated that for those voting on the European issues (as opposed to those giving a

---

[443] Similarly, the Convention on the Future of Europe involved in drafting the Constitutional Treaty was comprised of a president and two vice presidents, representatives of the Member States (15), the European Parliament (16), national Parliaments (30), the Commission (2), the accession countries (13) and from their Parliaments (26) and observers from the Committee of the Regions, the European ombudsman, and the social partners (13).

[444] G. de Búrca, 'The drafting of the European Union Charter of Fundamental Rights' (2001) 26 *ELRev.* 126, 131. See also A. Arnull, 'The future of the convention method' (2003) 28 *ELRev.* 573.

[445] The operational detail of this Article, including the minimum number of Member States involved, is to be fleshed out in accordance with the first para. of Art. 24 TFEU.

[446] See D. Chalmers, Editorial, 'Constitutional treaties and human dignity' (2003) 28 *ELRev.* 147 and Editorial Comments, 'Direct democracy and the European Union…is that a threat or a promise' (2008) 45 *CMLRev.* 929.

[447] The Commission seeks views on some of these thorny questions in its Green Paper on a European Citizens' Initiative: COM(2009) 622.

[448] <http://www.consilium.europa.eu/ueDocs/cms_Data/docs/pressData/en/ec/68827.pdf>.

bloody nose to the incumbent national government), their concerns ranged from specific fears generated by reading the text, in particular its perceived excessive market liberalism (i.e., it was 'too British'[449]), to more general concerns about the EU's expansion, both geographically and in terms of competence. Following a period of reflection,[450] the states decided to repackage the Constitutional Treaty, stripping it of its most overt 'constitutional' garb, and readopt largely the same content as the Lisbon Treaty in 2007. This did not satisfy the Irish who rejected the revised Treaty in 2008. Following the second—and now positive—vote in Ireland in September 2009 and after prevarication in the Czech Republic, the Lisbon Treaty came into force in December 2009.

The whole saga does not reflect well on the Union's own democratic structures, despite various attempts by the Commission to engage with EU citizens, in particular through its 'Plan D for democracy dialogue and debate',[451] dovetailing with its 'Action plan to improve communicating Europe'.[452] This focuses on stimulating wider public debate and promoting citizens' participation in the democratic process. A decision has been adopted, now entitled 'Europe for citizens'[453] (replacing the original title 'Citizens for Europe',[454] a shift deemed psychologically significant in the light of the ratification crisis), establishing a programme promoting active European citizenship. This has been backed up by 'A citizens' agenda: Delivering results for Europe'[455] and attempts to engage the citizen in respect of social policy through the Commission's *Renewed Social Agenda: Opportunities, access and solidarity.*[456] However, many citizens remain to be convinced, a problem exacerbated by the deep financial crisis many states now find themselves in and a perception that the EU's response is not helping.

## 2. ACCESS TO JUSTICE

### 2.1 Access to Information

#### (a) Regulation 1049/2001

There is a further dimension to the right to participate: the need for citizens to have access to courts and other bodies to challenge decisions taken by the lawmakers.[457] First, however, they need to know what is going on. The right for citizens to gain access to information was given a Treaty basis at Amsterdam.[458] Article 15 TFEU (ex Article 255 EC)

---

[449] T. Garton-Ash, 'What is to be done: Blairism is the answer to Europe's ills but we need someone else to deliver it', *The Guardian*, 2 Jun. 2005, describing the French perception of the Constitutional Treaty as 'too much enlarged to include new countries, too Anglophone, and too enamoured of liberal-free market economics'.

[450] Declaration by the Heads of State or Government of the Member States of the European Union on the ratification of the Treaty establishing a Constitution for Europe, European Council, 16 and 17 Jun. 2005.

[451] COM(2005) 494.      [452] SEC(2005) 985.

[453] COM(2006) 542; EP and Council Dec. 1904/2006 establishing for the period 2007 to 2013 the programme 'Europe for Citizens' to promote active European citizenship ([2006] OJ L378/32), as amended.

[454] COM(2005) 116.      [455] COM(2006) 211.

[456] COM(2008) 412. See C. Barnard, 'Solidarity and the Commission's "renewed social agenda"' in M. Ross and Y. Borgmann-Prebil (ed.), *Promoting Solidarity in the European Union* (Oxford: OUP, 2010).

[457] For the importance of this dimension, see A. Wiener and V. della Sala, 'Constitution-making and citizenship practice: Bridging the democracy gap in the EU?' (1997) 35 *JCMS* 595, 602–3.

[458] See also the Final Act of the Treaty on European Union signed at Maastricht on 7 Feb. 1992 where the Member States incorporated Decl. 17 on the right of access to information: 'The Conference considers that transparency of the decision-making process strengthens the democratic nature of the institutions and the

provides that any citizen of the Union *and* any natural or legal person residing or having a registered office in a Member State has a right of access to the documents of the Union institutions, bodies, offices, and agencies, whatever their medium,[459] subject to the principles laid down in Regulation 1049/2001[460] which are supplemented by rules of procedure for each institution.[461]

In *Svenska Journalistförbundet*[462] the Court said that the objective of (the predecessor to) Regulation 1049/2001 was to give effect to the 'principle of the largest possible access for citizens to information with a view to strengthening the democratic character of the institutions and the trust of the public in the administration'.[463] This point was emphasized in *Sweden v Council*[464] concerning the refusal by the Council to give access to an opinion of its legal service on a proposal for a directive laying down minimum standards for the reception of applicants for asylum. The General Court upheld the Council's decision; the Court of Justice set aside the General Court's judgment. In so doing, it noted the need for the Council to balance the particular interest to be protected by non-disclosure of the document against the public interest in the document being made accessible in the light of the advantages stemming 'from increased openness, in that this enables citizens to participate more closely in the decision-making process'[465] and confers 'greater legitimacy on the institutions in the eyes of European citizens'.[466] It said those considerations are clearly of particular relevance where the Council is acting in its legislative capacity, as is apparent from recital 6 of the preamble to Regulation 1049/2001, according to which wider access must be granted to documents in precisely such cases. It continued:

Openness in that respect contributes to strengthening democracy by allowing citizens to scrutinize all the information which has formed the basis of a legislative act. The possibility for citizens to find out the considerations underpinning legislative action is a precondition for the effective exercise of their democratic rights.

---

public's confidence in the administration.' In Case C–58/94 *Netherlands* v. *Council* [1996] ECR I–2169, para. 35 the Court noted that Decl. 17 links the public's right of access to documents to the 'democratic nature of the institutions'.

[459] See also Art. 1(1) TEU; Art. 42 of the Charter of Fundamental Rights. This issue is considered further in D. Curtin, 'Citizens' fundamental right of access to EU information: An evolving digital *passepartout*' (2000) 37 *CMLRev.* 7.

[460] [2001] OJ L145/43. The regulation concerns access to *documents*, not to information more generally: Case T-264/04 *WWF European Policy Programme* v. *Council* [2007] ECR II–911, para. 76. A proposal for a revised measure can be found at COM(2008) 229. See M. de Leeuw, 'The regulation on public access to European Parliament, Council and Commission documents in the European Union' (2003) 28 *ELRev.* 324. For the Commission's own perspective, see its Green Paper, 'Public access to documents held by institutions of the European Community: A review' (COM(2007) 185).

[461] In addition, the EU has given effect to the Århus Convention to Union Institutions and Bodies (Reg. (EC) No. 1367/2006 (OJ [2006] L264/13)), which guarantees the public the right of access to environmental information held by the Union institutions and bodies. These must also make environmental information available to the public in easily accessible electronic databases.

[462] Case T-174/95 *Svenska Journalistförbundet* v. *Council of the European Union* [1998] ECR II–2289.

[463] Para. 66. The europa website (<http://www.europa.eu.int/>) provides free access to information about the EU and its policies; <http://www.eur-lex.europa.eu/en/index.htm> provides free access to all legislation, consultation documents, and the judgments of the Court of Justice.

[464] Joined Cases C–39/05 and C–52/05 *Sweden v Council* [2008] ECR I–4723.      [465] Para. 45.

[466] Para. 59. See also Case C–64/05 P *Sweden* v. *Commission* [2007] ECR I–11389, para. 54. For a more sceptical perspective, see D. Curtin, 'Through the looking glass: The myths of transparency in the European Union', *Durham European Law Institute Lecture* 2004.

However, a problem may arise where the information requested relates specifically to an individual. Regulation 45/2001[467] protects individuals with regard to the processing of personal data by the Union institutions and bodies. The interaction between this regulation and Regulation 1049/2001 was considered in *Bavarian Lager*.[468] Due to exclusive purchasing contracts binding a large number of operators of pubs in the UK requiring them to obtain supplies of beer from certain breweries, Bavarian Lager was not able to sell its product and complained to the Commission. A meeting was held with British officials, who agreed to amend their rules, but the Commission refused to allow Bavarian Lager to attend. Under Regulation 1049/2001 the Commission disclosed the minutes of the meeting to Bavarian Lager but blanked out the names of five people who had attended that meeting, arguing that Bavarian Lager had not established either an express and legitimate purpose or any need for such disclosure, as was required by the Regulation on the protection of personal data, and therefore, the exception concerning the protection of private life, laid down by the regulation on public access to documents, applied. However, the General Court annulled the Commission's decision and said that while the list of participants named in the minutes contained personal data, since the people who participated at that meeting did so as representatives of their organizations and not in a private capacity, the protection of privacy or integrity of the persons concerned was not compromised.[469]

### (b) The principle of good administration

Article 9 TEU says that citizens shall 'receive equal attention from its institution, bodies, offices and agencies'. Article 10(3) TEU adds that decision-making process needs to be based on the principles of transparency and subsidiarity. This is operationalised in Article 15(2) TFEU which says that 'The European Parliament shall meet in public, as shall the Council when it is discussing and adopting a legislative proposal.'[470] The Council has put this into practice by amending its rules of procedure.[471]

Article 41 of the Charter of Fundamental Rights, entitled 'Right to good administration',[472] is more explicit. Article 41(1) contains the general principle that 'Every person [not just an EU citizen] has the right to have his or her affairs handled impartially, fairly and within a reasonable time by the institutions, bodies, offices and agencies of the Union.' Article 41(2) spells out more precisely what the right includes:

- the right of every person to be heard before any individual measure which would affect him or her adversely is to be taken

- the right of every person to have access to his or her file, while respecting the legitimate interests of confidentiality and of professional and business secrecy

- the obligation of the administration to give reasons for its decisions.

---

[467] OJ [2001] L8/1. See also Art. 16 TFEU (ex Art. 286 EC).

[468] Case T–194/04 *The Bavarian Lager Co. Ltd v Commission of the European Communities* [2007] ECR II–4523. Currently on appeal (Case C–28/08P).

[469] Paras. 125–6.

[470] See also Art. 16(8) TEU: 'The Council shall meet in public when it deliberates and votes on a draft legislative act'. By implication, the same transparency does not apply to non-legislative acts.

[471] For discussion on the merits of the change, see M. de Leeuw, 'Openness in the legislative process in the European Union' (2007) 32 *ELRev.* 295.

[472] See also Joined Cases C–154/4 and C–155/04 *R* v. *Secretary of State for Health, ex p. Alliance* [2005] ECR I–8419, para. 82.

When things go wrong, Article 41(3) provides that every person has the right to have the Union make good any damage caused by the institutions or servants in the performance of their duties, in accordance with the general principles common to the laws of the Member States.

## 2.2 Non-judicial Avenues

In practice, there are few cases where the Court has, in fact, been prepared to award compensation. This makes the non-judicial routes more important. EU citizens—together with natural or legal persons residing or having their registered office in a Member State—have the right under Article 24 TFEU (ex Article 21 EC) both to petition the European Parliament in accordance with Article 227 TFEU (ex Article 194 EC)[473] and to apply to the ombudsman in accordance with Article 228 TFEU (ex Article 195 EC).[474] They can write in any one of the Union languages and receive a reply in that language.[475] As with a complaint based on good administration under Article 41 of the Charter, a petition to the European Parliament is confined to matters affecting the complainant directly. There is no such limitation in respect of applications to the European ombudsman (nor in respect of access to information) which allows public-spirited citizens to raise matters of more general concern via this route. This range of rights and remedies is available in respect of breaches committed by *Union* institutions. The Treaty appears to offer no specific protection to citizens when faced with maladministration by *national* authorities exercising Union law powers.

## 2.3 Judicial Avenues

In respect of the courts, the EU envisages access at two levels: at European level to enable citizens to challenge decisions of the Union institutions and at domestic level to challenge decisions of the national authorities which interfere with Union law rights or to challenge the decisions of the EU institutions indirectly. In respect of remedies against national authorities, the Court has been active in guaranteeing Union rights, by developing the principles of direct effect and supremacy of Union law,[476] and the principles of effective judicial protection.[477] These proceedings complement the power to bring Article 258 TFEU (ex Article 226 EC) enforcement proceedings initiated by the Commission but often as a result of complaints by individuals about (in)action by Member States.[478] The

---

[473] See also Art. 44 of the Charter. The Charter applies to residents as well as citizens.

[474] See also Art. 43 of the Charter. See generally K. Heede, 'Enhancing the accountability of Community institutions and bodies: The role of the European Ombudsman' (1997) 3 *EPL* 587.

[475] Art. 24(4) TFEU. See also Art. 41(4) of the Charter.

[476] Case 26/62 *NV Algemene Transport en Expeditie Onderneming Van Gend en Loos* v. *Nederlands Administratie de Belastingen* [1963] ECR 1; Case 6/64 *Costa* v. *ENEL* [1964] ECR 585. See also Decl. 17 concerning primacy added by the Lisbon Treaty.

[477] See, e.g., Joined Cases C–6/90 and C–9/90 *Francovich and Bonifaci* v. *Italy* [1991] ECR I–5357, Case 222/84 *Johnston* v. *RUC* [1986] ECR 1651; Joined Cases C–46 and 48/93 *Brasserie du Pêcheur and Factortame* [1996] ECR I–1029; Case C–432/05 *Unibet* v. *Justitiekanslern* [2007] ECR I–2271.

[478] See, e.g., Commission's 5th Report on Citizenship: COM(2008) 85, 9 where the Commission also emphasizes the value of the SOLVIT mechanism. SOLVIT helps EU citizens and businesses find fast and pragmatic solutions to problems arising from the incorrect application of EU law by national administrations, within a deadline of ten weeks. SOLVIT's case flow has increased from 12 to 70 new cases per month. The average resolution rate is around 80%.

Commission has made the complaints process more user-friendly.[479] However, the Court of Justice has been far more reticent about ensuring such full access to the Court by citizens when seeking to challenge the acts of the Union institutions directly. In its now (in)famous line of cases on *locus standi* for non-privileged applicants under Article 263 TFEU (ex Article 230 EC), the Court has ensured that only in the most exceptional circumstances will an individual be granted standing.[480] Interest groups, acting as intermediaries, have fared little better.[481] While the Court has emphasized that proceedings can be started in the national court and then a preliminary reference sought under Article 267 TFEU (ex Article 234 EC), as Advocate General Jacobs explained in *UPA*,[482] in certain circumstances this possibility is not available, leaving individuals without a remedy. While the amendments introduced by the Treaty of Lisbon to Article 263(4) have relieved the situation somewhat, in particular by allowing natural or legal persons to challenge 'regulatory acts' without having to show 'individual concern', the key phrase 'regulatory acts' remains undefined. The Lisbon Treaty has, however, re-emphasized the role of the Member States to provide 'remedies sufficient to ensure effective legal protection in the fields covered by Union law'.[483] It therefore looks like Article 267 TFEU (ex Article 234 EC) references from the national court will remain the main route for natural and legal persons to challenge legislative acts.

The AFSJ deals with a third dimension to the question of justice: access to justice in cross-border disputes. Article 67(4) TFEU says: 'The Union shall facilitate access to justice, in particular through the principle of mutual recognition of judicial and extra-judicial decisions in civil matters.'[484] This policy strand now goes by the name of 'a Europe of justice'. In its AFSJ Communication,[485] the Commission says that priority must be given to mechanisms that facilitate people's access to the courts so that they can enforce their rights, especially their contractual rights, throughout the Union.[486]

---

[479] A notice containing a standard form for complaints to be submitted to the Commission ([1999] OJ C119/5) and a consolidated version of the internal procedural rules applicable to its relations with the complainant in the context of the infringement proceedings (COM(2002) 141) have been published by the Commission.

[480] Case C–50/00P *UPA* v. *Council* [2002] ECR I–6677. Cf. the strong Opinion of Jacobs AG to the contrary and the decision of the General Court in Case T–177/01 *Jégo Quéré & Cie SA* v. *Commission* [2002] ECR I–2365. For a general discussion see A. Albors-Llorens, 'The standing of private parties to challenge Community measures: Has the European Court missed the boat?' (2003) 62 *CLJ* 72.

[481] Case C–312/95P *Stichting Greenpeace Council (Greenpeace International)* v. *Commission* [1998] ECR I–1651.

[482] Case C–50/00P *UPA* v. *Council* [2002] ECR I–6677. See also Case C–131/03P *R.J. Reynolds Tobacco Holdings Inc.* v. *Commission* [2006] ECR I–7795, paras. 81–2.

[483] Art. 19(1), 2nd para TEU.

[484] This reflected Art. 61(c) EC but is expressed in wider terms to reflect current practice. Legislation has already been adopted under this provision. See, e.g., Council Reg. 743/2002 establishing a general Community framework of activities to facilitate the implementation of judicial cooperation in civil matters ([2002] OJ L115/1) (the UK and Ireland gave notice of their wish to participate in the adoption of the regulation; Denmark is not taking part); Council Dir. 2002/8/EC ([2003] OJ L26/41) on improving access to justice in cross-border disputes by establishing minimum common rules relating to legal aid for such disputes. The UK and Ireland gave notice of their wish to participate in the adoption of the directive; Denmark is not taking part.

[485] COM(2009) 262, 2.

[486] See, e.g., Reg. (EC) No. 861/2007 establishing a European Small Claims Procedure ([2007] OJ L199/1); Reg. 1896/2006 creating a European order for payment procedure ([2006] OJ L399/1); Reg (EC) No. 593/2008 ([2008] OJ L177/6) on the law applicable to contractual obligations (Rome I); Reg (EC) No. 1393/2007 ([2007]

# F. CONCLUSIONS

As Preuß put it, Union citizenship began as a terminological pooling of the few rights which the individual enjoyed in other Member States. It neither generated an inner bond between the Union and the individual nor did it presuppose such an inner connection as a precondition for acquiring it.[487] The recent developments, both legislative and judicial, suggest that the time may have come to reconsider this initial assessment. While it cannot be said that these developments have generated a 'European citizenry' which could 'pave the way for the transition to a European Federal State', they have certainly enriched the status of citizenship, by creating some bonds between individuals and the Union different from (but not stronger than) those which exist between individuals and their own Member States.[488] European citizenship does now allow individuals a multiplicity of associative relations based on manifold economic, social, cultural, scholarly, and even political activities, irrespective of the traditional territorial boundaries of the European nation states, without binding individuals to a particular nationality.[489]

The principle of solidarity has been particularly influential in that regard and here we can see a process of boot-strapping taking place—citizenship (imposed from above) is used to justify taking limited steps in the name of solidarity and solidarity is being used from the bottom up to foster a growing sense of citizenship. However, the Court has shown some awareness of the sensitivities of the issue, in particular concerns about 'benefit tourism'.[490] As a result, it has allowed Member States to insist on a demonstrable link with the host state's territory before an individual becomes entitled to benefits, whether it is through a period of residence as in *Bidar*, or a genuine link with the employment market of the host state as in *D'Hoop*. If it were otherwise then any enforced equality would have the potential to generate such hostility and anti-migrant feeling among host state nationals that, far from fostering a sense of Union citizenship, it could do the reverse. There is a risk that this is already happening in the field of higher education.[491]

There are increasing signs of this alienation from the EU which citizens have expressed in various referenda, in particular the French and Danish votes on the Maastricht Treaty, the initial Irish 'no' to the Nice Treaty, the French and Dutch 'no' votes to the Constitutional Treaty, and the initial Irish 'no' to the Lisbon Treaty. Weiler puts this point succinctly: 'as the [Union] has grown in size, in scope, in reach and despite a high rhetoric including the very creation of "European citizenship" there has been a distinct disempowerment of the individual European citizen, the specific gravity of whom continues to decline as the

---

OJ L324/79) on the service in the Member States of judicial and extrajudicial documents; Dir. 2008/52/EC ([2008] OJ L136/3) on certain aspects of mediation in civil and commercial maters.

[487] U. Preuß, 'Problems of a concept of European citizenship' (1995) 1 *ELJ* 267.     [488] Ibid., 268.

[489] Ibid.

[490] That is 'moving to a Member State with a more congenial social security environment': Case C–456/02 *Trojani* [2004] ECR I–7573, Geelhoed AG's Opinion, para. 13 (and see para. 18). See also his Opinion in *Bidar* in para. 66.

[491] C. Barnard, 'EU citizenship and the principle of solidarity' in Dougan and Spaventa (eds.), *Social Welfare and EU Law* (Oxford: Hart Publishing , 2005). See also C. Newdick, 'Citizenship, free movement and health care: Cementing individual rights by corroding social solidarity' (2006) 43 *CMLRev.* 1645.

Union grows'.[492] Is there a way forward? Weiler advocates that EU citizenship should be understood as a supranational construct grounded in belonging simultaneously to two different *demoi* based on different subjective factors of identification.[493] At one and the same time, he argues, individuals can, say, be British nationals, based on a strong sense of cultural identification and belonging, and also European citizens, based on, first, an acceptance of the legitimacy and authority of decisions made by fellow European citizens (underpinned by the 'social contract' of the common Treaties) and, secondly, shared values which transcend ethno-national diversity. These shared values include a commitment to principles of solidarity expressed through the welfare state, the European social model,[494] and human rights as embodied in the ECHR and now the Charter. Yet his suggestions have themselves been criticized for being too assimilationist, excluding those who do not share these values.[495]

Others have argued that the EU should aim at decoupling the concepts of state, nation, national identity, and nationality in favour of a form of post-national membership radically different from a (nation) statist concept of citizenship.[496] Underpinning this idea is active participation, as well as the more traditional passive conferral of rights, and it is here that the EU is engaged in some of its most elaborate citizenship-building. The advantage of such an understanding of citizenship is that nationality becomes increasingly unimportant. In this interpretation of citizenship there should be a place for legally resident TCNs. The legal position of TCNs is the subject of Chapter 14. Before that, in Chapter 13, we shall consider the limits to the rights of free movement which, as we shall see, have been significantly influenced by the case law on citizenship.

---

[492] J. H. H. Weiler, 'The European Union belongs to its citizens: Three immodest proposals' (1997) 22 *ELRev.* 150.

[493] J. H. H. Weiler, 'To be a European citizen—Eros and civilization' (1997) 4 *JEPP* 495.

[494] The Nice European Council offered a definition of the European social model (Annex I, para. 11): 'The European Social Model, characterised in particular by systems that offer a high level of social protection, by the importance of the social dialogue and by services of general interest covering activities vital for social cohesion, is today based...on a common core of values.' These values are outlined in para. 11, 'solidarity and justice as enshrined in the Charter of Fundamental Rights' and para. 23, 'Social cohesion, the rejection of any form of exclusion or discrimination and gender equality'.

[495] N. Barber, 'Citizenship, nationalism and the European Union' (2002) 27 *ELRev.* 241.

[496] Shaw, above n. 5, 47.

# 13

# DEROGATIONS, LIMITATIONS, CONDITIONS, AND JUSTIFICATIONS

## A. INTRODUCTION

Chapters 9–12 concerned the specific rights enjoyed by migrant workers, the self-employed, providers/receivers of services, and citizens in the host state. We turn now to examine the express powers given to the Member States by Union law to prevent or restrict migrants from enjoying those rights in full. The express derogations laid down by the Treaties fall into two categories: general derogations (public policy, public security, and public health) and specific derogations (employment in the public service). In principle, the *general* derogations are used to justify a decision to refuse a person entry or to expel them, as well as justifying any discriminatory measure or other conduct which prevents or impedes access to the market or exercise of the freedom (see fig. 8.1). In practice, however, because the general derogations are used as a means of controlling migration they are invoked more commonly by states than other actors. The *specific* derogation applies only to the initial refusal of access to employment in the public sector.

In addition to these express derogations the three directives on the rights of residence adopted in the 1990s contained limitations and conditions. In particular, they required those seeking residence (students, persons of independent means, and the retired) to have sufficient resources and medical cover. With the repeal of the three directives, the conditions have been incorporated into the Citizens' Rights Directive 2004/38. As a result of the case law on citizenship, the limitations and conditions laid down by these directives have been subject to an increasingly strict proportionality review.

Supplementing the express derogations are the 'public-interest' requirements developed by the Court. Initially, these public-interest requirements could be invoked by the Member States to justify indirectly discriminatory and non-discriminatory national rules, together with those rules which prevent or impede market access. In more recent cases there are signs that these justifications can also be invoked to defend directly discriminatory measures too, although the case law is not consistent. In this chapter we shall examine the express derogations, the limitations and conditions, and the public-interest justifications. We begin by considering the express derogations.

# B.  PUBLIC POLICY, PUBLIC SECURITY, AND PUBLIC HEALTH

## 1.  INTRODUCTION

Article 45(3) TFEU allows Member States to derogate from the principle of free movement of workers on the grounds of public policy, public security, and public health. Articles 52 and 62 TFEU (ex Articles 46 and 55 EC) contain the same derogations for establishment and services. The burden of proof is on the defendant state to prove that one of the derogations justifies its rule.[1] Member States use express derogations to preserve their sovereign rights to control who enters their territory and who resides there. However, as we saw in Chapter 5, derogations to fundamental freedoms are interpreted strictly so that their scope cannot be determined unilaterally by a Member State without being subject to control by the Court.[2] In *Orfanopoulos*[3] the Court went so far as to say that 'a particularly restrictive' interpretation of the derogations is required in the case of citizens of the Union. The derogations are therefore read subject to the general principles of law, in particular proportionality[4] and fundamental human rights.[5] Further, the list of derogations is exhaustive and the Court is not prepared to add any further headings to it.[6] The derogations will also not apply where Union directives provide for exhaustive harmonization of the field.[7] Finally, derogations cannot be used to serve economic purposes.[8] Therefore, a Member State cannot rely on a derogation to justify excluding foreign nationals from its labour market simply because unemployment is high in the state and there is a political need to preserve jobs for nationals.[9]

The bare bones of the general derogations were originally fleshed out by the provisions of Directive 64/221[10] which regulated the state's response to the conduct by

[1]  See, e.g., Case C–260/04 *Commission v. Italy (horse race betting licences)* [2007] ECR I–7083, para. 33.

[2]  See, e.g., Case 41/74 *Van Duyn* v. *Home Office* [1974] ECR 1337, para. 18; Case C–348/96 *Calfa* [1999] ECR I–11, para. 23; Case C–114/97 *Commission v. Spain* [1998] ECR I–6717, para. 34. Case C–441/02 *Commission v. Germany* [2006] ECR I–3449, paras. 32–5 contains a useful summary of the rules applicable to the express derogations.

[3]  Joined Cases C–482/01 and C–493/01 *Orfanopoulos* v. *Land Baden-Württemberg* [2004] ECR I–5257, para. 53.

[4]  Case C–100/01 *Ministre de l'Intérieur* v. *Olazabal* [2002] ECR I–10981, para. 43; Case C–108/96 *Mac Quen* [2001] ECR I–837, para. 31; Case C–3/88 *Commission* v. *Italy* [1989] ECR I–4035, para. 15; Case C–348/96 *Calfa* [1999] ECR I–11, para. 23.

[5]  See Case C–260/89 *ERT* v. *DEP* [1991] ECR I–2925, para. 43 where the Court said that the application of the derogations in Arts. 52 and 62 had to be appraised in the light of the general principle of freedom of expression in Art. 10 of the ECHR.

[6]  Case C–17/92 *Federación de Distribuidores Cinematográficos* v. *Estado Español et Unión de Productores de Cine y Televisión* [1993] ECR I–2239, para. 20 (cultural policy is not one of the derogations set out in Art. 52); Case C–388/01 *Commission v. Italy* [2003] ECR I–721, para. 20 (cohesion of the tax system not one of the derogations under Art. 52).

[7]  Case C–421/98 *Commission* v. *Spain (architects)* [2000] ECR I–10375, paras. 41–2.

[8]  See, e.g., Case 352/85 *Bond* v. *Netherlands* [1988] ECR 2085, para. 34; Case C–384/08 *Attanasio Group* [2010] ECR I–000, para. 55; and Art. 27(1) CRD.

[9]  Cf. the transitional limitations on free movement of workers contained in the Accession Agreements.

[10]  [1963–64] OJ Spec Ed Series I, 117. See also Commission Communication to the Council and the European Parliament on the Special Measures concerning the movement and residence of citizens of the Union which

*individuals.*[11] Directive 64/221 was repealed by the Citizens' Rights Directive 2004/38 (CRD).[12] Article 27(1) CRD makes clear that Member States may restrict the freedom of movement and residence of Union citizens (i.e., any person having the nationality of a Member State, not just workers and the self-employed) and their family members (irrespective of nationality), on grounds of public policy, public security, or public health. However, while apparently reiterating the provisions of the Treaties, in fact the directive has actually limited the circumstances in which the host state can invoke the derogations because the CRD is premised on the idea that the longer individuals reside in the host state, the harder it is for that state to deport them (see fig. 13.2 below). Because the provisions of the CRD draw on Articles of Directive 64/221, as interpreted by the Court, this chapter examines the CRD with reference to the position under Directive 64/221.

## 2. PUBLIC POLICY AND PUBLIC SECURITY

### 2.1 Introduction

Despite the fact that the Treaties suggest that public policy and public security are separate derogations, the Court's case law has largely subsumed public security under the heading of public policy.[13] The Court has given Member States a certain margin of discretion to determine what constitutes public policy in the light of their national needs.[14] For example, in *Van Duyn*[15] the Court said that the particular circumstances in which a Member State could rely on the concept of public policy might 'vary from one country to another and from one period to another'. It was therefore 'necessary to allow the competent national authorities an area of discretion within the limits imposed by the [Treaties]'. Similarly, in *Jany*[16] the Court said that '[Union] law does not impose on Member States a uniform scale of values as regard the assessment of conduct which may be considered to be contrary to public policy'.[17] Yet, in respect of individuals this margin of discretion

---

are justified on the grounds of public policy, public security, or public health 1999: COM(99) 372.

[11] According to Art. 2, Dir. 64/221 applied to all measures (legislative measures and individual decisions taken in applying the legislation (Case 36/75 *Rutili* [1975] ECR 1219, para. 21) as well as to judicial decisions (Case 30/77 *R* v. *Bouchereau* [1977] ECR 1999) concerning entry into the territory, issue or renewal of residence permits, and expulsion from the territory). This suggests that the directive did not apply to restrictions on access to employment or the general regulation of employment relations. By contrast, it was thought that the Treaty derogations applied both to exclusion/expulsion and to discrimination in respect of access to employment and discrimination in respect of the terms and conditions on which employment is granted or exercised (see, e.g., Case C–350/96 *Clean Car Autoservice* v. *Landeshauptmann von Wien* [1998] ECR I–2521, para. 24, referring to Case C–415/93 *Bosman* [1995] ECR I–4921, paras. 84–6). Although cf. Case C–114/97 *Commission* v. *Spain* [1998] ECR I–6717, para. 42; Case C–355/98 *Commission* v. *Belgium* [2000] ECR I–1221, para. 29, which suggested that the Treaty derogations applied to exclusion/expulsion only.

[12] OJ [2004] L158/77.

[13] Cf. The UK's decision to refuse entry to the UK to Dutch MP Geert Wilders on public-security grounds: 'Dutch MP banned from entering the UK', <http://www.news.bbc.co.uk/1/hi/uk_politics/7882953.stm>.

[14] Joined Cases 115 and 116/81 *Adoui and Cornuaille* v. *Belgian State* [1982] ECR 1665, para. 8.

[15] Case 41/74 *Van Duyn* [1974] ECR 1337, para. 18.

[16] Case C–268/99 [2001] ECR I–8615, para. 60.

[17] See also Case C–36/02 *Omega* [2004] ECR I–9609, para. 31.

is limited by the provisions of what is now the CRD 2004/38 and also by a 'citizenship' reading of the national law. This point was made in *Commission* v. *The Netherlands (criminal convictions)*[18] where the Court said that the safeguards provided by what was then Directive 64/221 called for 'a broad interpretation as regards the persons to whom they apply', including EU citizens who are not lawfully resident on the territory of the host state.

### 2.2 Public Policy and the Individual

#### (a) Personal conduct

The starting point for determining what constitutes public policy and public security in respect of the individual was Article 3(1) of Directive 64/221,[19] now Article 27(2) CRD, first paragraph, which says that measures taken on the grounds of public policy must be 'based exclusively on the *personal conduct* of the individual concerned'.[20] The corollary of this is, as the Court pointed out in *Bonsignore*,[21] that extraneous matters unrelated to the individual may not be taken into account. Bonsignore was convicted of a firearms offence and of causing the death of his brother by negligence when handling a pistol for which he had no licence. A deportation order was made against him for reasons of a 'general preventive nature'. In other words, faced with a resurgence of violence among immigrant communities,[22] the national court wanted to make an example of Bonsignore to deter others. The Court of Justice said that deportation in these circumstances would contravene the directive; deportation could be ordered, but only in the case of breaches of the peace and public security actually caused by the individual defendant himself.[23]

The question of what constitutes personal conduct was considered in detail in *Van Duyn*.[24] Mrs Van Duyn was refused entry into the UK to work as a secretary for the Church of Scientology. Although membership of this church was not prohibited by the British authorities, the church's activities were considered to be 'socially harmful'.[25] The Court said that the personal conduct did not need to be unlawful before a Member State could invoke the public-policy exception. It was sufficient that the conduct be deemed

---

[18]  Case C–50/06 [2007] ECR I–4383, paras. 32–5.

[19]  This provision is directly effective: Case 41/74 *Van Duyn* [1974] ECR 1337, para. 15.

[20]  Emphasis added. See also F. Wooldridge, 'Free movement of EEC nationals: The limitation based on public policy and public security' (1977) 2 *ELRev.* 190. While the category of public policy and public security is usually considered from the perspective of personal conduct, the annex to Dir. 64/221 also listed diseases and disabilities which might threaten public security or public policy. It identified drug addiction, profound mental disturbance, and manifest conditions of psychotic disturbance with agitation, delirium, hallucinations, or confusion as falling within this category. This list is not contained in the CRD.

[21]  Case 67/74 *Bonsignore* v. *Oberstadtdirektor of the City of Cologne* [1975] ECR 297 confirmed in Case C–441/02 *Commission* v. *Germany (Italian migrants)* [2006] ECR I–3449, para. 93.

[22]  Mayras AG doubted the basis for such an order. He expressed himself to be 'rather sceptical' of the deterrent effect of a deportation order. He feared it masked xenophobia ([1975] ECR 297, 315).

[23]  Paras. 6–7.    [24]  Case 41/74 [1974] ECR 1337.

[25]  On 25 Jul. 1968 the Minister of Health said in the House of Commons that 'Scientology is a pseudo-philosophical cult...[It] is socially harmful. It alienates members of families from each other and attributes squalid and disgraceful motives to all who oppose it...There is no power under existing law to prohibit the practice of Scientology; but the government have concluded that it is so objectionable that it would be right to take all steps within their power to curb its growth.' These steps included preventing foreign nationals from entering to study or work there. As Mayras AG noted, the UK's lack of power to take measures against the Church is 'one consequence of a particularly liberal form of government'.

'socially harmful' and that the state had taken administrative measures to counteract these particular activities.[26]

The Court was also asked to decide in *Van Duyn* whether membership of a particular organization could constitute personal conduct. It ruled that a person's past association could not, in general, justify a decision refusing him the right to move freely; but a person's present association with an organization could constitute personal conduct, because present association reflected a voluntary participation in the activities of an organization, as well as an identification with its aims and designs.[27]

More controversially, the Court also suggested in *Van Duyn* that the host state could refuse a national of another Member State the benefit of the rules on the free movement of persons, even though the state did not place a similar restriction on its own nationals.[28] Therefore, the UK could refuse to allow a Dutch national to enter the UK to work for the Church of Scientology on public-policy grounds while permitting, albeit with disapproval, a British national to do the very same job. The Court justified this decision by reference to the principle of international law[29] that Member States have no authority to refuse entry or to expel their own nationals from the territory of their own state.[30]

However, this aspect of the ruling in *Van Duyn* sits uncomfortably with the general principle of non-discrimination on the ground of nationality and subsequent case law has implicitly reversed this aspect of the judgment. It is now clear that Member States must apply the doctrine of non-discrimination in so far as it is consistent with the principles of international law. Therefore, if equivalent conduct on the part of the state's own nationals is not subject to 'repressive measures or other genuine and effective measures intended to combat such conduct',[31] it cannot be a cause for expelling migrants. This can be seen in *Adoui and Cornuaille*[32] where two French prostitutes[33] were refused permission to reside in Belgium on public-policy grounds, despite the fact that prostitution was not prohibited by Belgian legislation.[34] The Court said that Member States were not entitled to base the exercise of their discretion on 'assessments of certain conduct which would have the effect of applying an arbitrary distinction to the detriment of nationals of other Member States'.[35] Therefore, Member States must be consistent in their conduct towards nationals

---

[26] Para. 19.      [27] Para. 17.

[28] Para. 21. See G. F. Mancini who described this aspect of the ruling as a 'false step' in 'The free movement of workers in the case law of the European Court of Justice' in D. Curtin and D. O'Keeffe (eds.), *Constitutional Adjudication in EC and National Law: Essays for the Hon. Mr Justice T. F. O'Higgins* (Dublin: Butterworths, 1992), 75. For further consideration of the 'double penalty' rule, see E. Guild, 'Security of residence and expulsion of foreigners: European Community law' in E. Guild and P. Minderhoud (eds.), *Security of Residence and Expulsion: Protection of aliens in Europe* (The Hague: Kluwer, 2000), 68–9.

[29] Para. 22.

[30] See further Case C–171/96 *Pereira Roque* v. *Governor of Jersey* [1998] ECR I–4607, paras. 49–50; Case C–348/96 *Calfa* [1999] ECR I–11, para. 20. This principle is reinforced by Art. 27(4) CRD: the Member State which issued the migrant's passport or identity card (usually the state of origin) must allow the migrant who has been expelled on the grounds of an express derogation to re-enter its territory without any formality, even if the document is no longer valid or the nationality of its holder is in dispute.

[31] Joined Cases 115 and 116/81 *Adoui and Cornuaille* [1982] ECR 1665, para. 8.      [32] Ibid.

[33] Or, as the Court delicately put it, they worked at a bar that was 'suspect from the point of view of morals'.

[34] Para. 6, although certain incidental activities, such as the exploitation of prostitution by third parties and various forms of incitement to debauchery, were unlawful.

[35] Para. 7.

and migrants. As the Court put it succinctly in *Jany*,[36] conduct by migrants (prostitution) which a Member State (the Netherlands) accepts on the part of its own nationals cannot be regarded as constituting a genuine threat to public order.

The concept of personal conduct adopted in *Van Duyn* was further narrowed in *Bouchereau*.[37] The Court said that the public-policy exception could be invoked to justify restrictions on the free movement of workers only if 'there was a genuine and sufficiently serious threat affecting one of the fundamental interests of society'.[38] Therefore, a simple infringement of the social order by breaching the law (possessing drugs) would not be enough to justify steps taken on public-policy grounds. For similar reasons, in *Adoui*[39] the Court said that being a prostitute did not constitute sufficiently serious personal conduct to justify applying the derogations, Likewise, in *Jipa*[40] the Court said that the mere fact that a national of a Member State (Romania) had been deported from another state (Belgium) on the grounds of being an illegal resident there did not constitute sufficiently serious personal conduct to justify restricting his right to travel.

The Court has since repeatedly emphasized just how strictly it applies the 'genuine and sufficiently serious threat' test. In *Commission* v. *Germany (Italian migrants)*[41] Germany was condemned for expelling EU migrants on 'serious' public-policy grounds, a lower standard than the EU test of 'genuine and sufficiently serious threat affecting a fundamental interest of society'. This tough line can also be seen in *Commission* v. *Spain (SIS)*.[42] Two Algerians married to EU citizens were refused entry into Spain because of a Schengen 'alert' which had been issued against them.[43] The Schengen Contracting States had agreed that they would issue an 'alert' concerning a TCN spouse on grounds of public policy and public security, terms which were more loosely defined than their equivalents in the EU directive. The Court said that the existence of an alert against a TCN was evidence that there were reasons for refusing entry to the TCN but such evidence had to be corroborated by information enabling the host state to verify whether the individual constituted a present and sufficiently serious threat affecting the fundamental interests of society. Because the Spanish authorities had failed to verify whether the two Algerians did satisfy the *Bouchereau* test, Spain was in breach of Union law. This case therefore shows that, in the case of conflict between Schengen rules and the Treaties/CRD, the Treaties/CRD will take precedence.

Article 3(2) of Directive 64/221 and now Article 27(2) CRD provides that previous criminal convictions will not themselves constitute reasons for taking measures on the ground of public policy. This issue was considered in *Bouchereau*[44] where a French national working in England was convicted of unlawful possession of drugs. Six months earlier he had pleaded guilty to a similar offence and had been given a 12-month conditional discharge. The magistrate now wished to deport him on the ground of public policy. The Court decided that the existence of a criminal conviction could be taken into

---

[36] Case C–268/99 *Jany* [2001] ECR I–8615, para. 61. This case concerned the Association Agreements with Poland and the Czech Republic.        [37] Case 30/77 [1977] ECR 1999.

[38] Para. 35, emphasis added. This test has also been applied in the context of the EU-Turkey Association Council Decision (considered further in Ch. 14): Case C–340/97 *Nazli* [2000] ECR I–957, paras. 56–61.

[39] Joined Cases 115 and 116/81 [1982] ECR 1665.

[40] See also Case C–33/07 *Ministerul Administraţiei şi Internelor* v. *Jipa* [2008] ECR I–5157, para. 25.

[41] Case C–441/02 *Commission* v. *Germany (Italian migrants)* [2006] ECR I–3449.

[42] Case C–503/03 *Commission v Spain* [2006] ECR I–1097 noted Bouwer (2008) 45 *CMLRev.* 1251.

[43] Further details about Schengen can be found in Ch. 14.        [44] Case 30/77 [1977] ECR 1999.

account only in so far as the circumstances which led to that conviction were evidence of 'personal conduct constituting a *present threat* to the requirements of public policy' by showing a propensity to commit the similar acts again.[45] This was a matter for the national court to decide.

The importance of showing that the individual constituted a present threat to public policy was emphasized in *Calfa*.[46] Greece had expelled Calfa for life on the ground that she had been convicted of obtaining and being in possession of drugs for personal use. The Court ruled that Calfa could be expelled for having committed a criminal offence provided that her personal conduct created a genuine and sufficiently serious threat affecting one of the fundamental interests of society.[47] Under Greek law foreign nationals convicted under the drugs law were automatically expelled for life.[48] The Court said that because no account was taken of the personal conduct of the offender or of the danger which she represented to the requirements of public policy, Greek law breached the directive.[49] This case therefore makes clear that states can only take measures against individuals who have committed a criminal offence if, *in addition*, they constitute a present, genuine, and sufficiently serious threat to one of the fundamental interests of society.[50] In *Orfanopoulos*[51] the Court added that Member States also had to take into account factual matters which occurred after the final decision of the competent authorities which might point to the cessation or the substantial diminution of the present threat that the individual posed to public policy.[52]

This case law on personal conduct, starting with *Van Duyn*, has been incorporated into Article 27(2) of the Citizens' Rights Directive 2004/38. It provides:

Measures taken on grounds of public policy or public security shall comply with the principle of proportionality and shall be based exclusively on the personal conduct of the individual concerned.

Previous criminal convictions shall not in themselves constitute grounds for taking such measures.

The personal conduct of the individual concerned must represent a genuine, present and sufficiently serious threat affecting one of the fundamental interests of society. Justifications that are isolated from the particulars of the case or that rely on considerations of general prevention shall not be accepted.

Figure 13.1 illustrates how Article 27(2) shapes the host state's decision-making process.

### (b) Measures which can be taken against the migrant

#### (i) Exclusion or expulsion

Neither the Treaties nor Directive 2004/38 specify what measures can be taken against a migrant by the state on the grounds of public policy or public security. One possibility is exclusion (the refusal to allow an individual to enter the country), as in *Van Duyn*, or

---

[45] Paras. 28–9.    [46] Case C–348/96 [1999] ECR I–11.    [47] Para. 25.

[48] See also Joined Cases C–482/01 and C–493/01 *Orfanopoulos* [2004] ECR I–5257, para. 53.

[49] Para. 27. See also Case C–50/06 *Commission* v. *The Netherlands (criminal convictions)* [2007] ECR I–4383, para. 46.

[50] Case C–441/02 *Commission* v. *Germany (Italian migrants)* [2006] ECR I–3449, para. 35.

[51] Joined Cases C–482/01 and C–493/01 *Orfanopoulos* [2004] ECR I–5257, para. 82.

[52] See also Case C–467/02 *Cetinkaya* v. *Land Baden-Württemberg* [2004] ECR I–10895, para. 47 concerning the EU–Turkey Association Agreement considered further in Ch. 14.

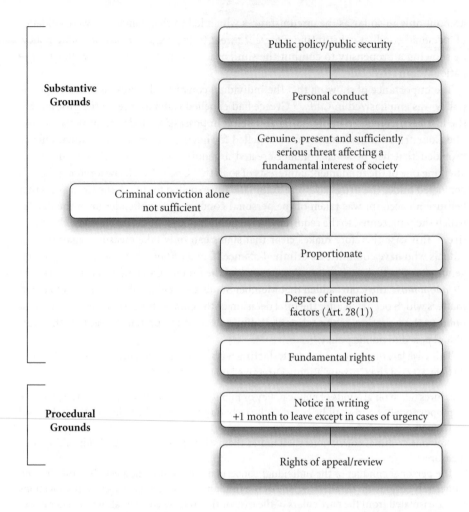

**Fig. 13.1** Factors to be considered before individual can be deported on grounds of public policy or public security

expulsion (the removal of an individual who has already entered the state), as in *Calfa*,[53] but these are draconian responses. As the Court said in *Watson and Belmann*,[54] deportation 'negates the very right conferred and guaranteed by the [Treaties]'.[55]

---

[53] See A. Barav, 'Court recommendation to deport and the free movement of workers in EEC law' (1981) 6 *ELRev.* 139. If expulsion/deportation is ordered, the state which issued the identity card or passport must allow the holder to re-enter its territory, even if the document is no longer valid or the nationality of its holder is in dispute (Art. 27(4) of Dir. 2004/38). See also Case C–459/99 *MRAX* [2002] ECR I–6591 on the position of TCNs. N. Nic Shuibhne, 'Derogating from the free movement of persons: When can EU citizens be deported?' (2005–6) 8 *CYELS* 187.

[54] Case 118/75 [1976] ECR 1185; Case 157/79 *R* v. *Pieck* [1980] ECR 2171, paras. 18–19; Case C–265/88 *Criminal Proceedings against Messner* [1989] ECR 4209, paras. 14–15. See also Case C–329/97 *Ergat* [2000] ECR I–1487 in respect of Turkish workers.

[55] Para. 20.

Deportation can also have a significant effect on the individual's life, particularly family life if the migrant is a long-time resident. For this reason Directive 2004/38 introduces additional protection against expulsion. Article 28(1) provides that when deciding whether to deport an individual on the grounds of public policy or public security, the host state must take into account length of residency, age, health, family and economic situation, social and cultural integration into the host state, and enduring ties with the individual's country of origin.[56] Furthermore, citizens and their family members who have permanent residence (i.e., more than five years) cannot be deported, according to Article 28(2), save on serious grounds of public policy or public security. Minors[57] and citizens who have resided[58] in the host state for the previous ten years cannot be deported at all, according to Article 28(3), except if the decision is based on 'imperative grounds of public security' (not public policy), as defined by Member States (see fig. 13.2). This very strict approach to derogations for those with permanent residence status means that the migrant EU citizen is treated like a national in all but name. Under international law, states cannot deport their own nationals; under the CRD the same is almost true for EU permanent residents.

However, the new gradations found in Article 28(2)–(3) introduce distinctions which may prove hard to apply in practice. It is difficult to distinguish between deportation for 'ordinary' public-policy reasons which applies to individuals with less than five years' residence who represent a 'genuine, present and *sufficiently serious* threat affecting one of the fundamental interests of society' (Article 27(2)) and deportation for '*serious* grounds of public policy or public security' which applies to those migrants with permanent residence (Article 28(2)). Even the phrase 'imperative grounds of public security' in Article 28(3) is not so clear. Presumably this refers to migrants who are convicted terrorists, serial rapists, or killers.

Whether deportation (as opposed to some lesser restriction) can be justified turns largely on the question of proportionality.[59] Deportation cannot be automatic,[60] nor can there be a presumption that the migrant should be expelled.[61] Deportation for 'technical' infringements of the host state's law is also not permissible, as *Watson and Belmann* demonstrates. The Court said that the deportation of a migrant for failing to have reported to the police the place where she was staying within three days of entering the country was 'so disproportionate to the gravity of the infringement that it becomes an obstacle to the free movement of persons'.[62] In much the same vein, Article 15(2) of Directive 2004/38 provides that the expiry of an identity card or passport is not sufficient to justify deportation.

---

[56] See also Joined Cases C–482/01 and C–493/01 *Orfanopoulos* [2004] ECR I–5257, para. 99, couching this right in terms of the right to family life under Art. 8 ECHR, which had to be weighed in the balance.

[57] Except if the expulsion is necessary for the best interests of the child as provided for in the UN Convention on the Rights of the Child 1989.

[58] Unlike Art. 16, there is no requirement of having 'legally' resided. However, the British Court of Appeal said that time spent in prison did not count towards the ten year period of residence: *HR (Portugal) v. Secretary of State for the Home Deparment* [2009] EWCA Civ 371.      [59] Art. 27(2).

[60] Case C–408/03 *Commission* v. *Belgium* [2005] ECR I–2647.

[61] Joined Cases C–482/01 and C–493/01 *Orfanopoulos* [2004] ECR I–5257, para. 92.

[62] Case 118/75 *Watson & Belmann* [1976] ECR 1185, para. 21. See also Case C–215/03 *Oulane* [2005] ECR I–1215, paras. 38 and 40.

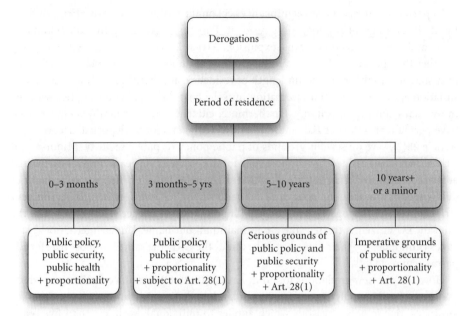

**Fig. 13.2** When the different derogations can be invoked

Article 33 adds that expulsion orders cannot be issued by the host Member State as a penalty or legal consequence of a custodial penalty unless they comply with the general principles concerning sufficiently serious threat laid down in Article 27, protection against expulsion under Article 28, and the rules concerning public health under Article 29.[63] Furthermore, if an expulsion order is enforced more than two years after it was issued, the Member State must check whether the individual is currently and genuinely a threat to public policy or public security and must assess whether there has been any material change in the circumstances since the expulsion order was issued.[64]

### (ii) Other measures

The national system can, of course, impose other, less severe, sanctions for breaches of national law. For example, in *Pieck*[65] the Court said the host state could fine or imprison a migrant for breaching national laws on immigration formalities, provided that the penalties were comparable to those for equivalent offences committed by nationals. In *Rutili*[66] the Court said that restricting a person's right of residence to a limited area in the country was also possible under Article 18 TFEU[67] (not under Article 45(3) TFEU[68]), provided that the Member State could impose similar restrictions on its own nationals.[69] Therefore, the French minister could prohibit Rutili, an Italian national who had spent all his life in France, from living in certain regions of France due to his political and trade union activities if the minister could do the same to a national.

---

[63]  Art. 33(1).        [64]  Art. 33(2).        [65]  Case 157/79 *R* v. *Pieck* [1980] ECR 2171, paras. 18–19.
[66]  Case 36/75 [1975] ECR 1219.        [67]  Para. 49.
[68]  The Court made clear that Art. 45(3) applied to prohibitions on residence only in respect of the whole territory and not by reference to its internal subdivisions (paras. 46–8).
[69]  Para. 50.

The approach based on non-discrimination in *Rutili* was confirmed in Article 22 CRD:

The right of residence and the right of permanent residence shall cover the whole territory of the Member State. Member States may impose territorial restrictions on the right of residence and the right of permanent residence only where the same restrictions apply to their own nationals.

Nevertheless, the Court diluted the non-discrimination approach in *Olazabal*[70] where it upheld legislation allowing for movement restrictions, the very same sort of rules it had found unlawful in *Rutili*. Olazabal, a Spanish national of Basque origin, was a member of ETA, 'an armed and organised group whose activity constitute[d] a threat to public order'.[71] As a result of his involvement in the kidnapping of a Spanish industrialist he was sentenced to 18 months' imprisonment in France followed by a four-year ban on residing in the vicinity of the Spanish border. He argued that the residence ban was discriminatory since nationals could not be subject to any such limitation. The Court rejected his arguments. It said that because Union law allowed migrants to be subject to the ultimate sanction (deportation) they could therefore be subject to less-severe measures—such as facing restrictions on their right of residence—without it being necessary for identical measures to be applied to nationals.[72]

Thus, by examining the facts of *Olazabal* through the lens of proportionality rather than non-discrimination the Court reached an entirely different conclusion from the one in *Rutili*. It distinguished the two cases on factual grounds: Rutili was, to all intents and purposes, French; Olazabal was a migrant worker. Furthermore, there was some suspicion in *Rutili* that the action taken against him was on the ground of his trade union activities which itself would have contravened Article 8 of Regulation 1612/68. By contrast Olazabal was a terrorist and could have been deported for that reason.[73]

The Court also clarified the criteria laid down in *Rutili*. It said that a Member State could—under Article 45(3) TFEU—limit a worker's right of residence to a part of the national territory provided that:[74]

- such action was justified by reasons of public order or public security based on his individual conduct
- those reasons were so serious that otherwise he would have been prohibited from residing in, or banished from, the whole of the national territory
- the conduct which the Member State concerned wished to prevent gave rise, in the case of its own nationals, to punitive measures or other genuine and effective measures.

This case highlights one of the (many) questions raised as to the compatibility of the directive with the Treaties: *Olazabal* concerned the interpretation of the Treaties while Article 22 CRD on territorial scope is a provision in a directive.

### (iii) Fundamental human rights

When taking the decision whether to deport a migrant, the host state must take into account not only the principle of proportionality but also fundamental human rights, a

---

[70] Case C–100/01 *Olazabal* [2002] ECR I–10981, para. 45.   [71] Para. 35.   [72] Para. 41.
[73] Paras. 34–6.   [74] Para. 45.

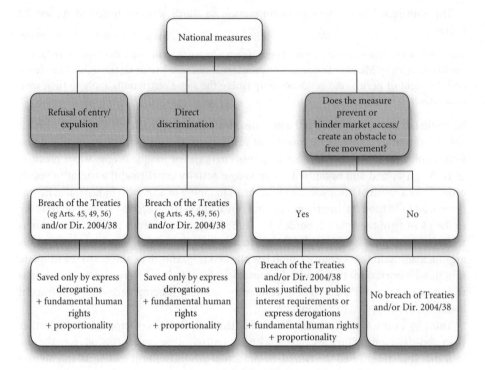

**Fig. 13.3** Free movement, derogations, justifications, fundamental human rights (FHR), and proportionality

fact that the Court has emphasized in a number of recent cases, notably *Carpenter*[75] and *Orfanopoulos*.[76] *Carpenter* concerned a decision by the UK to deport Mrs Carpenter, a Filipino national, who, having overstayed her entry permit to the UK, married a British national. Faced with the threat of deportation, Mrs Carpenter argued that this would restrict her husband's ability to carry on business as a service provider in other Member States since she looked after his children while he was away.[77] The Court said that a Member State could 'invoke reasons of public interest to justify a national measure which is likely to obstruct the exercise of the freedom to provide services only if that measure is compatible with the fundamental rights whose observance the Court ensures'.[78] On the question of fundamental rights, the Court said that the decision to deport Mrs Carpenter constituted:

an interference with the exercise by Mr Carpenter of his right to respect for his family life within the meaning of Article 8 of the [ECHR]...which is among the fundamental rights

---

[75] Case C–60/00 *Carpenter* [2002] ECR I–6279, paras. 40–1, considered further in Ch. 8.

[76] Joined Cases C–482/01 and C–493/01 *Orfanopoulos* [2004] ECR I–5257 confirmed in Case C–441/02 *Commission v. Germany (Italian migrants)* [2006] ECR I–3449, paras. 108–9.

[77] Para. 17.

[78] Para. 40, citing Case C–260/89 *ERT* [1991] ECR I–2925, para. 43, and Case C–368/95 *Familiapress* [1997] ECR I–3689, para. 24. Cf. Art 51(1) of the Charter which applies to the Member States 'only when they are implementing Union law'. No reference is made to derogations.

which, according to the Court's settled case-law, restated by the Preamble to the Single European Act and by Article 6(2) EU, are protected in [Union] law.[79]

Drawing on the case law of the European Court of Human Rights, the Court then said that even though no right of an alien to enter or to reside in a particular country was guaranteed by the Convention, 'the removal of a person from a country where close members of his family are living may amount to an infringement of the right to respect for family life as guaranteed by Article 8(1) of the Convention'. It continued that such an interference would infringe the Convention if it did not meet the requirements of Article 8(2) ECHR, namely that the deportation had to be in accordance with the law, motivated by one or more of the legitimate aims under Article 8(2) and 'necessary in a democratic society' (justified by a pressing social need and proportionate).[80] The Court concluded that the decision to deport Mrs Carpenter did not 'strike a fair balance' between the competing interests of the right of *Mr* Carpenter to respect for his family life on the one hand and the maintenance of public order and public safety, on the other.[81] Even though Mrs Carpenter had infringed UK immigration laws by overstaying her visa she did not constitute a danger to public order and safety. Therefore, the decision to deport her was not proportionate (see fig. 13.3).

In *Orfanopoulos*[82] the Court also emphasized that the state needed to take into account fundamental human rights in deciding whether to deport a migrant, in this case a Greek national convicted of drugs and violence offences but who had lived most of his life in Germany where he had a wife and children. The Court said that the assessment had to be made by the national authorities, on a case-by-case basis, to decide where a fair balance lay between the legitimate interests in complying with the general principles of Union law and the protection of fundamental rights such as the right to family life.[83]

### (c) The right to reapply

In *Adoui*[84] the Court made clear that excluded or expelled individuals must have the chance to reapply. This point was more recently confirmed in *Shingara*[85] where the Court said that, because a decision excluding migrants from entering a Member State was a derogation from the fundamental principle of freedom of movement, it could not be of unlimited duration.[86] Therefore a Union national expelled from a Member State could apply for a fresh residence permit.[87] If that application was made after a reasonable time, the competent administrative authority in the host state had to consider whether there

---

[79] Para. 41. See also Case C–63/99 *R* v. *Secretary of State for the Home Department, ex p. Gloszczuk* [2001] ECR I–6369, para. 85; Case C–235/99 *R* v. *Secretary of State for the Home Department, ex p. Kondova* [2001] ECR I–6427, para. 90; Case C–413/99 *Baumbast* [2002] ECR I–7091, para. 72; Case C–109/01 *Akrich* [2003] ECR I–9607, paras. 58–9.

[80] Para. 42, citing *Boultif* v. *Switzerland*, No. 54273/00, paras. 39, 41, and 46, ECHR 2001–IX.

[81] Para. 43.     [82] Joined Cases C–482/01 and C–493/01 *Orfanopoulos* [2004] ECR I–5257.

[83] Para. 100. Fundamental rights and proportionality are not the only general principles of law that the Court has to take into account. It will also look at, e.g., legitimate expectations and legal certainty: Case C–97/05 *Gattoussi* v. *Stadt Rüsselsheim* [2006] ECR I–11917, para. 42.

[84] Joined Cases 115 and 116/81 [1982] ECR 1665, para. 12; Case C–348/96 *Calfa* [1999] ECR I–11, para. 27.

[85] Joined Cases C–65/95 and C–111/95 *R.* v. *Secretary of State for the Home Department, ex p. Mann Singh Shingara and ex p. Abbas Radiom* [1997] ECR I–3343.

[86] Para. 40. See also Case C–235/99 *ex p. Kondova* [2001] ECR I–6427, para. 90; Case C–63/99 *ex p. Gloszczuk* [2001] ECR I–6369, para. 85.     [87] Para. 39.

had now been a material change in the circumstances which had justified the first decision ordering expulsion.[88]

Article 32(1) CRD confirms that a Member State cannot issue orders excluding individuals from their territory for life. Individuals must be able to submit an application to
lift an exclusion order after a reasonable period and, in any event, after three years, establishing a material change in their circumstances from those which justified the decision
ordering their exclusion in the first place. Member States then have six months to reach a
decision during which time the applicant remains excluded.[89]

### 2.3 Public Policy and Legal Persons

Until *Omega*[90] there had been little case law where states invoked the public-policy derogation to restrict the activities of corporate bodies. In *Centros*[91] the Danish government
tried to justify its rules on minimum capitalization on the public-policy ground of protecting creditors from the risk of fraudulent bankruptcy due to the insolvency of companies whose initial capitalization was inadequate. The Court simply said 'that the reasons
put forward do not fall within the ambit of Article [52] of the [Treaties]'. However, in
*Segers*[92] the Court recognized that the need to combat fraud might fall within the express
derogations although on the facts it found that the refusal to accord sickness benefit to a
director of a company formed in accordance with the law of another Member State could
not be justified.

In subsequent cases, the Court has drawn on the rules developed in the context of
natural persons to other situations in which public policy is invoked. For example, in
*Commission* v. *UK (open skies)*[93] concerning the power to refuse operating authorizations
to an airline where that airline represented a threat to public policy, the Court referred
to the *Bouchereau* formula, in its definition of public policy.[94] In *Commission* v. *Austria
(certification)*[95] the Court said that it was not sufficient for a state to make general asser-
tions of the public-policy interest at stake (in this case 'the danger of circumvention by
supposed bogus self-employed persons of the transitional rules governing the freedom of
movement for workers'). States had to put forward 'precise evidence' capable of establishing that the potential infringement of those rules constituted a genuine and sufficiently
serious threat to a fundamental interest of society. The *Open Skies* decision confirmed the
approach taken in the free movement of capital case, *Église de Scientologie*,[96] where the
Court also said that any person affected by a restrictive measure based on such a derogation had to have access to legal redress.

However, it was only in *Omega*[97] that the Court really got to grips with the public-policy
derogation in the context of corporate conduct. The case concerned a decision by the Bonn

---

[88] Ibid.          [89] Art. 32(2).          [90] Case C–36/02 [2004] ECR I–9609.

[91] Case C–212/97 *Centros* [1999] ECR I–1459, para. 34. See also Case C–260/89 *ERT* v. *DEP* [1991] ECR
I–2925, para. 25.          [92] Case 79/85 *Segers* [1986] *ECR* 2375, para. 17.

[93] Case C–466/98 *Commission* v. *UK* [2002] ECR I–9427.

[94] Para. 57. See also Case C–168/04 *Commission* v. *Austria* [2006] ECR I–9041, para. 64; Case C–465/05
*Commission* v. *Italy (private security activities)* [2007] ECR I–11091, para. 50

[95] Case C–161/07 [2008] ECR I–10671, para. 37.

[96] Case C–54/99 *Association Eglise de Scientologie de Paris* v. *The Prime Minister* [2000] ECR I–1335,
paras. 17–18.

[97] Case C–36/02 [2004] ECR I–9609. See also Case C–319/06 *Commission* v. *Luxembourg* [2008] ECR
I–4323.

Police Authority to ban Omega, a German company using British equipment, from running a laserdrome where, through the use of laser guns fired at fixed sensory tags attached to players' jackets, it was possible to 'play at killing'. The decision was taken on public-policy grounds: 'the commercial exploitation of games involving the simulated killing of human beings infringed a fundamental value enshrined in the national [German] constitution, namely human dignity'.[98] The Court appeared to recognize that the protection of fundamental rights, including the protection of human dignity, actually constituted the public-policy derogation.[99] Therefore, a fundamental principle of particular resonance in Germany[100] was successfully invoked by the German government to limit the free movement of services. Furthermore, the Court found the German prohibition to be proportionate because it prohibited only the variant of the laser game which fired on human targets—i.e., playing at killing people.[101] This conclusion is unsurprising given the strong emphasis generally placed by the Court on margin of discretion given to Member States.[102]

## 3. PUBLIC HEALTH

### 3.1 Public Health and the Individual

The annex to Directive 64/221 provided an exhaustive list of diseases or disabilities which could trigger action against an individual on public-health grounds: those subject to quarantine listed in International Health Regulation No. 2 of the World Health Organization of 25 May 1951; tuberculosis (TB); syphilis; and other infectious or contagious diseases or contagious parasitic diseases if they are subject to provisions for protection of nationals of the host country. Migrants who were HIV positive or who suffered from AIDS found themselves in a particularly invidious position.[103] Some Member States tried to deny them admission[104] although there was no express provision for this in the directive.[105] However, in its 1999 Communication the Commission rejected the use of any measures which could lead to 'social exclusion, discrimination or stigmatisation of persons with HIV/AIDS'.[106] More generally, the Commission observed that the public-health grounds

---

[98] Para. 32.

[99] Paras. 33–4, 36, and 41, as well as Stix-Hackl AG's Opinion, although cf. para. 35, where the Court appears to be discussing human rights in terms of the public-interest justification.

[100] Although it had been recognized by the Court in Case C–377/98 *Netherlands* v. *Parliament and Council* [2001] ECR I–7079.                                               [101] Para. 39.

[102] Para. 31.

[103] See W. Van Overbeek, 'AIDS/HIV infection and the free movement of persons within the Community' (1990) 27 *CMLRev.* 791.

[104] Ibid., 792. Guild notes that in Bavaria there was an attempt to use HIV/AIDS as a public health ground for expulsion but it was quickly stopped as illegal under the directive: E. Guild, 'Security of residence and expulsion of foreigners: European Community law' in Guild and Minderhoud (eds.), above n. 28, 64.

[105] In this context of the Union's treatment of its own staff or job applicants with HIV is instructive. The Court has ruled that the requirement that every person undergo a medical examination did not infringe Art. 8 of the ECHR provided that the individual consented: Case C–404/92P *X* v. *Commission* [1994] ECR I–4737, para. 17. The Court has examined the conclusions of the Council of the Ministers of Health which said that employees who are HIV positive but who do not show any symptoms of AIDS should be looked on as normal employees fit for work ([1989] OJ C28/2). The Court said that the administration must treat these conclusions as rules of practice, otherwise the principle of equal treatment would be infringed: see Case T–10/93 *A* v. *EC Commission* [1994] ECR II–179, IA–119, II–387.

[106] 'Special measures concerning the movement and residence of citizens of the Union which are justified on the grounds of public policy, public security, or public health' (COM(99) 372, 12).

were 'somewhat outdated'. It concluded that 'restrictions of free movement can no longer be considered a necessary and effective means of solving public health problems'.

The public-health derogation contained in Directive 64/221 has been updated by Article 29(1) CRD which now refers to diseases with epidemic potential, as defined by the relevant instruments of the World Health Organization, and other infectious diseases or contagious parasitic diseases but with the additional condition that they must be the subject of protection provisions applying to nationals of the host state.

Unlike the public-policy and public-security derogations, which can be invoked in respect of the migrant's initial entry to the territory or at any time during the first five years of the migrant's stay, the public-health derogation can be invoked only to justify the initial refusal of entry or the refusal to issue a first residence certificate or card (i.e., diseases occurring after a three-month period from the date of arrival cannot constitute grounds for expulsion from the territory)[107] (see fig. 13.2). Thus, once recognized, the right of residence cannot be contested on health grounds. In exceptional cases (i.e., only in cases where 'there are serious indications that it is necessary') the host state can require those entitled to the right of residence to undergo a (free) medical examination, within three months of the date of arrival.[108]

### 3.2 Public Health and Welfare Policies

When a Member State tries to justify its welfare policies on public-health grounds, the Court has not referred to Directive 64/221 or the CRD. Instead, it applies principles similar to those developed in the context of Article 36 TFEU,[109] including scrutinzing carefully whether the public-health derogation invoked by the state is supported by the facts. This can be seen in *Corporación Dermoestética*[110] where the Italian government relied on public-health grounds to justify its ban on advertising medical and surgical treatments on national television by private healthcare clinics. However, because clinics could advertise on local television the Court said that the rules exhibit 'an inconsistency ... and cannot therefore properly attain the public health objective which they seek to pursue'.

Generally, however, the Court takes a sympathetic view of a state's freedom to organize its own healthcare system, as *Kohll*,[111] *Geraets-Smits*,[112] and *Müller-Fauré*[113] show. As we saw in Chapter 11, in all three cases national law required individuals to obtain prior authorization before they could receive non-emergency medical treatment in other Member States. In each case the Court ruled that this requirement breached Article 56[114] and the question was then whether the 'exporting' state (usually the state where the patient was insured, the state of origin) could justify the restriction. In each case the exporting state argued that the authorization requirement was necessary in order to maintain a high-quality, balanced medical hospital service open to all.[115]

---

[107] Art. 29(2).          [108] Art. 29(3).

[109] For example in Joined Cases C–171/07 and C–172/07 *Apothekerkammer des Saarlandes* v. *Saarland* [2009] ECR I–000, para. 30 the Court cited Case C–170/04 *Rosengren* [2007] ECR I–4071, para. 49. See Ch. 6. See also Case C–73/08 *Bressol* v. *Gouvernement de la communauté française* [2010] ECR I–000, paras. 62–74.

[110] Case C–500/06 *Corporación Dermoestética* [2008] ECR I–5785, para. 39.

[111] Case C–158/96 *Kohll* [1998] ECR I–1931. For the parallel case on goods, see Case C–120/95 *Decker* [1998] ECR I–1831.          [112] Case C–157/99 *Geraets Smits and Peerbooms* [2001] ECR I–5473.

[113] Case C–385/99 *Müller-Fauré and van Riet* [2003] ECR I–4509.

[114] This issue is considered in detail in Ch. 11.

[115] *Kohll*, para. 50, *Geraets-Smits*, para. 73, *Müller-Fauré*, para. 67.

The Court recognized that such an objective, 'even if intrinsically linked to the method of financing the social security system', could fall within the derogations on grounds of public health under Article 52 insofar as it contributed to the attainment of a high level of health protection.[116] The Court also held that Article 52 permitted Member States 'to restrict the freedom to provide medical and hospital services in so far as the maintenance of treatment capacity or medical competence on national territory is essential for the public health, and even the survival of, the population'.[117] Disregarding, or at least modifying,[118] the well-established principle that derogations cannot be used to serve economic objectives,[119] the Court said in *Geraets-Smits*[120] that the authorization requirement helped to meet 'a desire to control costs and to prevent, as far as possible, any wastage of financial, technical and human resources'. It added that such wastage was all the more damaging because 'it is generally recognised that the hospital care sector generates considerable costs and must satisfy increasing needs, while the financial resources which may be made available for health care are not unlimited, whatever the mode of funding applied'. The Court therefore concluded that in principle a system of prior authorization was both 'necessary and reasonable' on public-health grounds to guarantee a 'rationalised, stable, balanced and accessible supply of hospital services'.[121]

However, in *Müller-Fauré* the Court made clear that a refusal to grant prior authorization based, not on fear of wastage resulting from hospital overcapacity, but solely on the ground that there were waiting lists for the hospital treatment concerned, could not amount to a properly justified restriction on freedom to provide services.[122] It could not see how waiting times were necessary to safeguard the protection of public health—quite the contrary. If the only reason related to 'considerations of a purely economic nature' they could not 'as such justify a restriction on the fundamental principle of freedom to provide services'.[123]

The general deference to a Member State's assessment of its own health policy seen in the 'healthcare tourism' cases can also be found in *Mac Quen*.[124] Belgian law provided that only ophthalmologists could perform eye examinations, excluding opticians who were not qualified medical doctors. Noting the importance of protecting public health,[125] the Court said that reserving the right to carry out eye tests to ophthalmologists could be regarded as an appropriate means of ensuring a high level of health protection. The restriction was therefore lawful provided that the national court considered the steps proportionate. However, the Court did add that while the Belgian authorities might be justified in concluding that at present there might be a risk to public health if opticians were authorized to carry out certain eyesight examinations, 'an assessment of this kind is

---

[116] *Kohll*, para. 50, *Geraets-Smits*, para. 73.  [117] *Kohll*, para. 51, *Geraets-Smits*, para. 74.

[118] A point recognized in the goods case Case C–141/07 *Commission v. Germany (pharmacies for hospitals)* [2008] ECR I–6935, para. 60.

[119] A principle that the Court expressly refers to in *Kohll*, para. 41.  [120] Para. 79.

[121] In *Kohll* this approach underpinned the Court's reasoning in respect of the overriding requirement of excluding the risk of seriously undermining the financial balance of the social security system and not the public-health derogation.

[122] Para. 92.

[123] Ibid. See also Case C–372/04 *Watts* [2006] ECR I–4325 considered further in Ch. 11, and Case C–115/08 *Land Oberösterreich v ČEZ* [2009] ECR I–000, para. 109.

[124] Case C–108/96 *Mac Quen* [2001] ECR I–837, paras. 28–30.  [125] Art. 3(1)(p).

liable to change with the passage of time, particularly as a result of technical and scientific progress'.[126]

In a similar vein the Court upheld a rule excluding non-pharmacists from running pharmacies on public-health grounds in *Apothekerkammer des Saarlandes*.[127] Referring to the precautionary principle,[128] the Court said that a Member State could take the measures that reduce, as far as possible, a public-health risk including, more specifically, a risk to the reliability and quality of the provision of medicinal products to the public, products whose therapeutic effects distinguish them substantially from other goods due to the serious harm they can cause to patients if they are consumed unnecessarily or incorrectly.[129] The Court concluded that given the power accorded to the Member States to determine the level of protection of public health, Member States could require that medicinal products be supplied by pharmacists enjoying genuine professional independence. While a pharmacist did have the objective of making a profit, this was 'tempered by his training, by his professional experience and by the responsibility which he owes, given that any breach of the rules of law or professional conduct undermines not only the value of his investment but also his own professional existence'.[130] Since non-pharmacists are not subject to the same professional obligations, the Court said that the operation of a pharmacy by a non-pharmacist could represent a risk to public health, in particular to the reliability and quality of the supply of medicinal products at retail level, because the pursuit of profit in the course of such operation was not tempered by moderating factors which characterized the activity of pharmacists.

## 4. PROCEDURAL REQUIREMENTS

### 4.1 General Provisions

Directive 64/221 laid down minimum procedural requirements to protect migrants faced with a decision refusing renewal of a residence permit or ordering expulsion on the grounds of public policy, public security, and public health. These requirements were much criticized because they were minimal but complex and consequently generated a large volume of case law. Directive 2004/38 has improved upon and simplified the procedural protection. It requires that migrants facing any decision taken against them on the grounds of public policy, public security, and public health must be informed in writing in such a way that they are able to comprehend its content and the implications for them.[131] They must also be told 'precisely and in full' of the grounds on which the decision in their case is based (unless this is contrary to the interests of the security of the state)[132] in order to enable the migrant to prepare an effective defence.[133] The notification must also specify the court or administrative authority with which the person concerned may lodge an appeal, the time limit for the appeal and, where applicable, the time allowed

---

[126] Para. 36.

[127] Joined Cases C–171/07 and C–172/07 *Apothekerkammer des Saarlandes* [2009] ECR I–000. For criticism, see L. Hancher and W. Sauter, 'One Step Beyond: from *Sodemare* to *DocMorris*: the EU's freedom of establishment case law concerning healthcare' (2010) 47 *CMLRev.* 117, 140–1

[128] See further Ch. 6.     [129] Paras. 30–2.     [130] Para. 37.

[131] Art. 30(1) CRD. See also Joined Cases 115 and 116/81 *Adoui and Cornuaille* [1982] ECR 1665, para. 13.     [132] Art. 30(2).

[133] Case 36/75 *Rutili* [1975] ECR 1219, para. 39; Joined Cases 115 and 116/81 *Adoui and Cornuaille* [1982] ECR 1665, para. 13.

for the person to leave the territory. Except in 'duly substantiated' cases of urgency, the period provided for leaving the country must not be less than one month from the date of notification (see fig. 13.1).[134]

### 4.2 Remedies

#### (a) The new rules

The directive then provides for the availability of certain remedies. In the original Directive 64/221, Article 8 required the individual to have the same legal remedies as nationals. Where no legal remedies were available (or the remedies were inadequate in some way), then Article 9 said that individuals had to be able to exercise their right of defence before a 'competent authority' which could not be the same as that which adopted the measure restricting his freedom.[135] While the original drafts of the CRD broadly followed the distinction between the Article 8 and 9 remedies contained in Directive 64/221, the final version of the CRD abandoned this approach. Instead, Article 31(1) provides that:[136]

The persons concerned shall have access to judicial and, where appropriate, administrative redress procedures in the host Member State to appeal against or seek review of any decision taken against them on the grounds of public policy, public security or public health.

In addition, Article 31(3) provides that the 'redress procedures shall allow for an examination of the legality of the decision, as well as of the facts and circumstances on which the proposed measure is based. They shall ensure that the decision is not disproportionate, particularly in view of the requirements laid down in Article 28 [concerning protection against expulsion].'

   Despite the fact that the content of Article 31 differs from that of Articles 8 and 9, it is likely that the Court will draw on its pre-existing case law to interpret the provision.[137] For this reason, we shall now examine the salient features of the Court's jurisprudence under Directive 64/221.

#### (b) Access to judicial redress: Appeal and review

While Article 31(1) of Directive 2004/38 talks of 'access to judicial…procedures in the host Member State to appeal against or seek review of any decision', Article 8 of Directive 64/221 gave the migrant the same legal remedies as nationals in respect of acts of the administration when the migrant was faced by a decision concerning entry, or the refusal to issue or renew a residence permit, or a decision ordering expulsion from the territory. Consistent with the principle of national procedural autonomy, the Court said

---

[134] Art. 30(3).    [135] Case 36/75 *Rutili* [1975] ECR 1219, para. 35.

[136] The importance of this provision and its implication for the more general right to effective judicial protection was noted by the General Court in Case T–228/02 *OMPI* v. *Council* [2006] ECR II–4665.

[137] The protection given to individuals was greater under Art. 9 than under Art. 8. Yet, while Art. 8 applied to decisions concerning entry, refusing to issue or renew a residence permit, or ordering expulsion from the territory, Art. 9 was more limited in scope and applied only to decisions refusing to issue or renew a residence permit or ordering expulsion. Therefore, Art. 9 did not lay down any requirements in relation to decisions refusing *entry* to the territory (Case C–357/98 *Ex p. Yiadom* [2000] ECR I–9265, para. 33) on the ground that individuals refused entry are usually not physically present in the territory and so cannot submit a defence in person before the competent authority. For this reason individuals refused entry were confined to the protection given by Art. 8.

that Article 8 did not govern the ways in which remedies were to be made available (for instance by stipulating the courts from which such remedies could be sought)[138] and this is likely to be extended to Article 31. However, the Court said in *Ex p. Shingara*[139] that Member States could not execute a decision ordering expulsion before the migrant was able to avail himself of the Article 8 remedy.

In *Ex p. Shingara* the Court was also asked whether the requirement on Member States to provide 'the same legal remedies' referred to (a) specific remedies available in respect of decisions concerning entry by *nationals* of the state concerned (*in casu* an appeal to an immigration adjudicator), or (b) only to remedies available in respect of acts of the administration generally (*in casu*, an application for judicial review, a less substantial remedy than an appeal). The Court said that no account could be taken of the remedies available to *nationals* concerning the right of entry because the two situations were not comparable. As we have already seen, with nationals the right of entry is a consequence of the status of being a national; by contrast, with migrants Member States have the discretion whether to invoke the public-policy derogation. Therefore, since an appeal to an immigration adjudicator was ruled out, migrants were left with the same remedies as those available against acts of the administration generally and the Court said that this satisfied the obligation under Article 8. Given that Article 31 expressly provides for appeal or review in the alternative, it is likely that *Shingara* will continue to apply.

In *Pecastaing*[140] the Court said that the 'same remedies' would include suspension of the acts challenged, if this remedy was available to nationals. However, it added that Article 8 did not oblige the host state to allow the migrant to remain in its territory throughout the entire proceedings, so long as he was able to obtain a fair hearing and to present his defence in full.[141] This is now confirmed in Article 31(4) which allows Member States to exclude the individual from their territory pending the redress procedure but adds that 'Member States may not prevent the individual from submitting his/her defence in person, except where his/her appearance may cause serious troubles to public policy or public security or when the appeal or judicial review concerns a denial of entry or residence.'

### (c) Administrative redress

Article 31 envisages that administrative redress must be available where appropriate *in addition* to judicial redress. This is a marked change from Article 9 of Directive 64/221 which applied where there were no legal remedies or where the legal remedies were inadequate in some way. So, for example, Article 9(1) said that where either:

- there was no right of appeal to a court of law
- the appeal was only in respect of the legal validity of the decision
- the appeal did not have suspensory effect

---

[138]  Case 48/75 *Royer* [1976] ECR 497, para. 60.
[139]  Joined Cases C–65/95 and C–111/95 [1997] ECR I–3343, para. 24.
[140]  Case 98/79 *Pecastaing* v. *Belgium* [1980] ECR 691, para. 12.
[141]  Case 98/79 [1980] ECR 691, para. 13; Case C–357/98 *Ex p. Yiadom* [2000] ECR I–9265, para. 35. On interim orders, see Art. 31(2) CRD.

then the authority making the final decision (refusing renewal of a residence permit or ordering expulsion of the holder of a residence permit) could not, save in cases of urgency, take a decision until a 'competent authority',[142] which differed from the decision-maker, had given its view.[143] Therefore, the competent authority had to give its opinion—based on an exhaustive examination of all the facts and circumstances of the case, including the expediency of the proposed measure[144]—*before* the decision-maker finally decided to expel or not to renew the residence permit.[145]

Some of the more general rules developed by the Court in the context of its case law under Article 9(1) are likely to be applied equally to administrative redress under Article 31 including the requirement that while Member States can decide on the procedure by which a person appears before the competent authority, the individual must enjoy 'the same rights of defence and assistance or representation as the domestic law of that country provides for',[146] and must be informed of the authority's decision.[147]

### 4.3 Assessment

Even with such changes in place, it is not at all clear how much attention is actually paid in practice to the (limited) procedural safeguards laid down by the Directive. For example, in Euro-2000 when large numbers of English football fans (EU citizens and recipients of services) were deported from Belgium, it seems they were given none of the basic protection provided by the then directive.[148] By contrast, in the British case of *Gough and Smith*,[149] where the appellants unsuccessfully challenged banning orders preventing

---

[142] Art. 9 did not define the term 'competent authority'. In Case 131/79 *Ex p. Santillo* [1980] ECR 1585 the Court recognized that a recommendation for deportation made by a criminal court at the time of conviction could constitute an opinion given by a competent authority, provided that the court has taken account of Art. 3(2) of Dir. 64/221, now Art. 27(2) of the CRD (that the mere existence of criminal convictions did not automatically constitute grounds for deportation). However, the Court has made clear that the competent authority does not have to be judicial in nature: all that Art. 9 requires is for the authority to perform its duties in absolute independence; that it is not directly or indirectly subject to any control by the administrative body empowered to take the measures provided for in the directive; and that the authority follow a procedure which enables the person concerned, on the terms laid down by the directive, effectively to present his defence and that all the factors to be taken into account by the administration are placed before it.

[143] Art. 9(1). See also Case 48/75 *Royer* [1976] ECR 497, para. 61.

[144] Joined Cases 115 and 116/81 *Adoui and Cornuaille* [1982] ECR 1665, para. 15.

[145] Case C–175/94 *R v. Secretary of State for the Home Department, ex p. John Gallagher* [1995] ECR I–4253, para. 20.

[146] Art. 9(1); Joined Cases C–297/88 and C–197/89 *Dzodzi v. Belgium* [1990] ECR I–3763, para. 62.

[147] Ibid.; Case C–175/94 *Gallagher* [1995] ECR I–4253.

[148] V. Chaudhary and A. Osborn, 'England's glory night marred by fans' riots', *The Observer*, 18 Jun. 2000; M. Hervey and D. Lister, 'More trouble expected after release of 500 supporters', *The Times*, 19 Jun. 2000. Addressing the problems of football hooliganism has been left to soft law measures (see, e.g., Res. on hooliganism and the free movement of football supporters ([1996] OJ C166/40); Council Res. concerning a handbook with recommendations for international police cooperation and measures to prevent and control violence and disturbances in connection with football matches with an international dimension, in which at least one Member State is involved ([2002] OJ C22/1 updated [2006] OJ C322/1); Council Rec. concerning a Handbook for police and security authorities concerning cooperation at major events with an international dimension [2007] OJ C313/4) or third-pillar measures (Joint Action 97/339/JHA on cooperation on law and order and security ([1997] OJ L147/1); Council Dec. 2002/348/JHA concerning security in connection with football matches with an international dimension ([2002] OJ L121/1) as amended by Council Dec. 2007/412/JHA ([2007] OJ L155/76). See also Council Res. on the use by Member States of bans on access to venues of football matches with an international dimension ([2003] OJ C281/1).

[149] *Gough and Smith* v. *Chief Constable of Derbyshire* [2002] 2 *CMLR* 11, noted E. Deards, 'Human rights for football hooligans?' (2002) 27 *ELRev.* 206.

them from attending certain football matches both in the UK and abroad, the Divisional Court[150] and the Court of Appeal did give careful consideration to the appellants' rights under both the Treaties and Directive 64/221.

## C.  PUBLIC SERVICE EXCEPTION

### 1.  INTRODUCTION

It has been traditional for Member States, as part of the exercise of their sovereignty,[151] to reserve certain public-service jobs to their own nationals.[152] Article 45(4) provides that the principles of free movement of workers and non-discrimination on the ground of nationality do not apply to 'employment in the public service'. Articles 51 and 62 TFEU (ex Articles 45 and 55 EC) contain an equivalent provision in respect of establishment and services, albeit drafted in rather different terms. Article 51 says that '[t]he provisions of this chapter shall not apply ... to activities which in that State are connected, even occasionally, with the exercise of official authority'. The justification for this derogation is that particular posts presume a 'special relationship of allegiance to the State' and a 'reciprocity of rights and duties which form the foundation of the bond of nationality'.[153]

Because Articles 45(4), 51, and 62 represent further exceptions to fundamental freedoms they must also be narrowly construed,[154] with their scope limited to what is 'strictly necessary for safeguarding the interests of the State which that provision allows the Member States to protect'.[155] Therefore, in *Sotgiu*[156] the Court said that Article 45(4) applied only to conditions of access to employment; it did not authorize discriminatory conditions of employment once access had been granted. This meant that the German postal service could not rely on Article 45(4) to justify its refusal to pay Sotgiu, an Italian national, a separation allowance granted to German workers, on the ground that he was employed in the public service. The Court said that the fact that Sotgiu had been admitted to the service denied the existence of those interests which justified the derogation.

### 2.  ARTICLE 45(4): 'EMPLOYMENT IN THE PUBLIC SERVICE'

The Court has insisted on a Union definition of the phrase 'employment in the public service'.[157] In *Commission v. Belgium*[158] it explained that the jobs envisaged by Article 45(4) 'involve direct or indirect participation in the exercise of powers conferred by public law and duties designed to safeguard the interests of the State or of other public authorities'. The Court continued that these jobs are 'characteristic of specific activities

---

[150]  Ibid., Laws LJ.

[151]  See Mancini AG in Case 307/84 *Commission* v. *France* [1986] ECR 1725, para. 2.

[152]  For further details see G. Morris, S. Fredman, and J. Hayes, 'Free movement and the public sector' (1990) 19 *ILJ* 20; C. Lenz, 'The public service in Article 48(4) EEC with special reference to the law in England and in the Federal Republic of Germany' [1989] 15 *LIEI* 75.

[153]  Case 149/79 *Commission* v. *Belgium* [1980] ECR 3881, para. 10. See also J. Handoll, 'Article 48(4) and non-national access to public employment' (1988) 13 *ELRev.* 223.

[154]  Case 152/73 *Sotgiu* v. *Deutsche Bundespost* [1979] ECR 153, para. 4.

[155]  Case 225/85 *Commission* v. *Italy* [1987] ECR 2625.        [156]  Case 152/73 [1979] ECR 153, para. 4.

[157]  See, e.g., Case C–473/93 *Commission* v. *Luxembourg* [1996] ECR I–3207, para. 26.

[158]  Case 149/79 [1982] ECR 1845, para. 7.

of public service insofar as [they are] invested with the exercise of public power *and* the responsibility for safeguarding the general interests of the State'.[159] It is not clear whether these requirements are to be read cumulatively or disjunctively.[160] A cumulative reading is consistent with the view that Article 45(4) must be interpreted restrictively; but support can be found in *Commission v. Italy*[161] for the argument that the requirements are to be read disjunctively.

The other question facing the Court is whether the phrase 'public service' requires an institutional or a functional approach. The *institutional* or organic approach, which is supported by the wording of Article 45(4), views the institution and its personnel as a whole, regardless of the specific functions carried out by individuals within the organization. This approach would allow a Member State to reserve all jobs in a particular organization, such as the civil service, to nationals even where some of those jobs are of a purely administrative or technical nature and involve no tasks designed to safeguard the interests of the state. This approach has been favoured by states keen to reserve as many posts as possible for their own nationals.[162] By contrast, the *functional* approach looks at the work required of a particular post to see if it involves direct or indirect participation in the exercise of powers conferred by public law and duties designed to safeguard the interests of the state. The functional approach would allow Member States to reserve only certain posts to nationals.

Consistent with the view that derogations are narrowly construed, the Court actually adopts the functional approach.[163] On a case-by-case basis, it examines the tasks and responsibilities inherent in the post[164] to see if they fulfil 'the very strict conditions'[165] of Article 45(4) rather than considering the nature of the legal relationship between the employee and the employing administration or the individual's job description.[166] This approach has led the Court to find that most jobs do not benefit from the Article 45(4) derogation. For example, it has said that of the jobs of a teacher in a state school,[167] a state nurse,[168] a foreign-language assistant in a university,[169] various posts on the state railways,[170] a local government employee,[171] a trainee lawyer,[172] a seaman,[173] a job in research not involving sensitive research work,[174] and a post in the lower echelons of the

---

[159] Emphasis added.

[160] Cf. Handoll, above, n. 153, Lenz, above, n. 152, Morris, Fredman, and Hayes, above, n. 152, 23.

[161] Case 225/85 [1987] ECR 2625, paras. 9–10.

[162] See the Belgian government's arguments in Case 149/79 *Commission v. Belgium* [1980] ECR 3881.

[163] Case C–473/93 *Commission v. Luxembourg* [1996] ECR I–3207, para. 27.

[164] Case 149/79 *Commission v. Belgium* [1982] ECR 1845, para. 8; Case C–473/93 *Commission v. Luxembourg* [1996] ECR I–3207, para. 27.

[165] Case C–473/93 *Commission v. Luxembourg* [1996] ECR I–3207, para. 33.

[166] Case 152/73 *Sotgiu* [1974] ECR 153.

[167] Case 66/85 *Lawrie-Blum* [1986] ECR 2121; Case C–4/91 *Bleis v. Ministère de l'education nationale* [1991] ECR I–5627.                [168] Case 307/84 *Commission v. France* [1986] ECR 1725.

[169] Case 33/88 *Allué and Coonan* [1989] ECR 1591.

[170] Case 149/79 *Commission v. Belgium* [1982] ECR 1845.

[171] Case 149/79 *Commission v. Belgium* [1980] ECR 3881 and [1982] ECR 1845 (plumbers, carpenters, electricians, gardeners).

[172] Case C–109/04 *Kranemann v. Land Nordrhein-Westfalen* [2005] ECR I–2421, para. 19 where the Court made clear that the concept of employment in the public service did not encompass employment by a private natural or legal person, whatever the duties of the employee.

[173] Case C–37/93 *Commission v. Belgium* [1993] ECR I–6295.

[174] Case 225/85 *Commission v. Italy* [1987] ECR 2625.

civil service, none constituted employment in the public service.[175] On the other hand, in the rather odd case of *Commission* v. *Belgium*[176] the Court found that local authority posts for architects, supervisors,[177] and night watchmen did fall within the Article 45(4) exception. Less controversially, it said in *Commission* v. *Italy*[178] that those involved in advising the state on scientific and technical questions were employed in the 'public service'.

While it is difficult to draw any clear principles from the case law, it seems that senior government jobs can be confined to nationals only even though this may mean that Article 45(4) represents a barrier to promotion for non-nationals.[179] However, where the exercise of public-law powers is purely marginal and ancillary to the principal function of the posts, then such jobs generally fall outside Article 45(4). This is the view taken by the Commission in its Communication designed to eliminate restrictions in areas of the public sector[180] where it listed jobs in the public sector to which, in normal circumstances, Article 45(4) did not apply. These included public healthcare services; employment in state educational institutions; research for non-military purposes in public establishments; and public bodies responsible for administering public commercial services, including public transport, gas or electricity distribution, air or maritime navigation, post and telecommunications, and broadcasting.

The Commission followed up its Communication on public-sector posts with enforcement proceedings against defaulting Member States. For example, Greece was condemned for maintaining for its own nationals posts in education, healthcare, the utilities, public transport, post and telecommunications, radio and television broadcasting, the Athens opera, and municipal and local orchestras;[181] and Luxembourg was condemned for restricting posts in the public sectors of research, education, health, inland transport, post, telecommunications, and the utilities to its own nationals.[182] In the field of education, the Luxembourg government argued that teachers had to be Luxembourg nationals in order to 'transmit traditional values' and that, in view of the size of the country and its specific demographic situation, the nationality requirement was an essential condition for preserving Luxembourg's national identity. While recognizing that the preservation of national identities was a legitimate aim, the Court said that the Luxembourg government's response was disproportionate. It argued that Luxembourg's interest could be effectively safeguarded otherwise than by a general exclusion of nationals from other Member States, in particular by imposing conditions relating to training, experience, and knowledge of the language.[183]

On the other hand, the Commission suggested that Article 45(4) would apply to the police and other forces of order, the armed forces, the judiciary, tax authorities, and the

[175]  Case 66/85 *Lawrie-Blum* [1986] ECR 2121.

[176]  Case 149/79 *Commission* v. *Belgium* [1982] ECR 1845, para. 8.

[177]  Namely head technical office supervisor, principal supervisor, works supervisor, and stock controller.                                        [178]  Case 225/85 *Commission* v. *Italy* [1987] ECR 2625, para. 9.

[179]  Ibid., para. 10.         [180]  88/C 72/02.

[181]  Case C–290/94 *Commission* v. *Greece* [1996] ECR I–3285.

[182]  Case C–473/93 *Commission* v. *Luxembourg* [1996] ECR I–3207. See also Case C–173/94 *Commission* v. *Belgium* [1996] ECR I–3265.

[183]  Case C–473/93 *Commission* v. *Luxembourg* [1996] ECR I–3263, paras. 32–5.

diplomatic service.[184] This approach was reflected in the Court's decisions in *Anker*[185] and the *Spanish Merchant Navy* case,[186] albeit subject to a proportionality review. In *Anker* the Court upheld in principle a German law requiring the post of master of a fishing vessel flying the German flag to be German. Because the job entailed duties connected to the maintenance of safety and to the exercise of police powers, particularly in the case of danger on board, together with powers of investigation, coercion, and punishment, the Court said that the post entailed direct participation in the exercise of powers conferred by public law for the purposes of safeguarding the general interest of the state.[187] It added that even though masters were employed by private bodies, this did not take the matter outside the scope of Article 45(4) because they were acting as 'representatives of public authority in the service of the general interests of the State'.[188]

However, the Court emphasized that, to benefit from the Article 45(4) derogation, the powers had to be exercised on a regular basis and did not represent only a 'very minor part of their activities'.[189] It therefore found that the post of master of small-scale deep-sea fishing vessels which involved skippering small boats with a small crew and participating in fishing and processing fish products did not benefit from the Article 45(4) derogation.[190] In the *Spanish Merchant Navy* case[191] the Court followed *Anker*, and found that the posts of master and chief mate in the Spanish merchant navy were also posts in which exercise of the duty of representing the flag state was in practice only occasional and so again did not benefit from the Article 45(4) derogation.[192]

## 3. THE EXERCISE OF 'OFFICIAL AUTHORITY'

In respect of establishment, Article 51 contains an equivalent derogation to that in Article 45(4); Article 62 extends this to services. Article 51 talks of the 'exercise of official authority' which more clearly suggests a functional approach than the Article 45(4) equivalent 'employment in the public service'. Since the Court applied the functional test to Article 45(4) and since the objectives of Article 51 are similar to those of Article 45(4), it is likely that the case law on Article 45(4) will apply equally to Article 51.[193]

The nature of what constitutes official authority was considered in *Reyners*,[194] where the Court examined whether the profession of *avocat* could be confined to nationals on the ground that *avocats* were connected with the public service of administration of justice. The Court said that Article 51 had to be narrowly construed: it applied only to those activities which had a 'direct and specific connection with official authority'.[195] It

---

[184] [1988] OJ C72/2; P. Watson, 'Free movement of workers: Recent cases' (1989) 14 *ELRev.* 415. And even in respect of these sectors, the Commission has since tightened up its approach: COM(2002) 694, 19.

[185] Case C–47/02 *Albert Anker, Klaas Ras, Albertus Snoek* v. *Bundesrepublik Deutschland* [2003] ECR I–10447.

[186] Case C–405/01 *Colegio de Oficiales de la Marina Mercante Española* v. *Administración del Estado* [2003] ECR I–10391. [187] Para. 61.

[188] Para. 62. [189] Para. 63. [190] Para. 64.

[191] Case C–405/01 *Colegio de Oficiales de la Marina Mercante Española* [2003] ECR I–10391.

[192] Para. 45. See also Case C–89/07 *Commission* v. *France* [2008] ECR I–45: requirement of French nationality for access to the posts of master (captain) and officer (chief mate) on all vessels flying the French flag could not be justified under Art. 45(4). See also Case C–447/07 *Commission* v. *Italy* [2008] ECR I–125; Case C–94/08 *Commission* v. *Spain* [2008] ECR I–160.

[193] Cf. Case C–283/99 *Commission* v. *Italy* [2001] ECR I–4363, para. 25.

[194] Case 2/74 [1974] ECR 631. [195] Para. 45.

continued that Article 51 would justify the exclusion of a whole profession only where those activities were linked to that profession in such a way that freedom of establishment would require the host Member State to allow the exercise by non-nationals, even occasionally, of functions related to official authority.[196] This would not be the case with the legal profession where contacts with the courts, although regular and organic, did not constitute the exercise of official authority because it was possible to separate tasks involving the exercise of official authority from the professional activity taken as a whole.[197]

In subsequent cases the Court has also rejected arguments based on Article 51. For example, it found that the job of road traffic accident expert, whose reports were not binding on the courts,[198] did not involve the exercise of official authority; nor did the technical job of designing, programming, and operating data-processing systems;[199] nor did the job of transport consultant;[200] nor did the task of vehicle inspection.[201] In *Commission v. Belgium (security guards)*[202] the Court said that the activities of private security firms, security-systems firms, and internal security services were not normally directly and specifically connected with the exercise of official authority. As the Court said in *Commission v. Spain*,[203] merely making a contribution to the maintenance of public security, which any individual could be called upon to do, did not constitute exercise of official authority. Similarly, in *Thijssen*[204] the Court held that the office of an approved Commissioner responsible for the monitoring of insurance companies did not constitute the exercise of official authority although it did recognize that the Insurance Inspectorate itself, which had the task of both supervising the application of the law and making new regulations, did exercise official authority because its supervisory function served to protect insured parties and the public interest.[205] These cases therefore suggest that derogations under Articles 51 and 62 must be restricted to activities which, in themselves, are directly and specifically connected with the exercise of official authority; functions that are merely auxiliary and preparatory, especially when carried out by a private body which are supervised by an entity which effectively exercises official authority by taking the final decision, are excluded from the definition of the exercise of official authority.[206]

## D.  OTHER LIMITATIONS AND CONDITIONS

### 1.  INTRODUCTION

So far we have concentrated on the express derogations laid down by the Treaties (public policy, public security, public health, and employment in the public service). In respect of

---

[196] Para. 46.  [197] Para. 51.

[198] Case C–306/89 *Commission* v. *Greece* [1991] ECR I–5863, para. 7.

[199] Case C–3/88 *Commission* v. *Italy* [1989] ECR I–4035, para. 13.

[200] Case C–263/99 *Commission* v. *Italy* [2001] ECR I–4195.

[201] Case C–438/08 *Commission* v. *Portugal* [2009] ECR I–000. In Case C–160/08 *Commission* v. *Germany* [2010] ECR I–000 ambulance service activities did not fall in Art. 51.

[202] Case C–355/98 *Commission* v. *Belgium* [2000] ECR I–1221, para. 26. See also Case C–283/99 *Commission* v. *Italy* [2001] ECR I–4363, para. 20; Case C–465/05 *Commission* v. *Italy* [2007] ECR I–11091, para.40.  [203] Case C–114/97 *Commission* v. *Spain* [1998] ECR I–6717, para. 37.

[204] Case C–42/92 *Thijssen* v. *Controldienst voor de verzekeringen* [1993] ECR I–4047.

[205] Para. 11.

[206] Case C–404/05 *Commission* v. *Germany (inspection of organic production)* [2007] ECR I–10239, para. 38; Case C–438/08 *Commission* v. *Portugal (vehicle inspection)* [2009] ECR I–000, para. 37.

workers, the self-employed, and service providers/receivers these are the only grounds on which they can be refused entry or deported. For those who do not fall within one of these classifications, the position has now changed. Prior to the CRD, refusal of entry/deportation could occur without the host state showing one of the express derogations and without the benefit of the procedural protection laid down in Directive 64/221. For example, states could deport work seekers who had not found a job in the host state after three months (unless they could show that they had genuine chances of being employed[207]) without any rights to notice or to be heard. The CRD has changed this. Article 15(1) extends the procedures laid down in Articles 30 (notification of decisions) and Article 31 (procedural safeguards) to 'all decisions restricting free movement of Union citizens and their family members on grounds other than public policy, public security or public health'. Article 15(1) now also applies to those given the rights of free movement under the original 1990 Residence Directives[208] (students, the retired, and persons of independent means)—now repealed and replaced by the CRD—who are refused entry or deported for not satisfying the criteria provided by the directive concerning adequate financial resources and sickness insurance.

## 2. THE LIMITATIONS: FINANCIAL RESOURCES AND SICKNESS INSURANCE

The original three 1990 Residence Directives, while all driven by the desire to allow those who were self-supporting to migrate, in fact differed in their detail. Persons of independent means and their family members, originally covered by the so-called 'Playboy' Directive 90/364 and now by Article 7(1)(b) of the CRD,[209] have the right of residence on the territory of another Member States for a period longer than three months if they:

have sufficient resources for themselves and their family members not to become a burden on the social assistance system of the host Member State during their period of residence and have comprehensive sickness insurance cover in the host Member State.[210]

According to Article 8(4) CRD, broadly replicating the equivalent provision of Directive 90/364, Member States may not lay down a fixed amount which they regard as 'sufficient resources' but they must take into account the personal situation of the person concerned. In all cases this amount must not be higher than the threshold below which nationals of the host Member State become eligible for social assistance, or, where this criterion is not applicable, higher than the minimum social security pension paid by the host Member State.[211] In *Commission* v. *Belgium (Portuguese migrants)*[212] the Court made

---

[207] See now Art. 14(4)(b) considered further in Ch. 9.

[208] Council Dir. 90/364/EEC ([1990] OJ L180/26) on the rights of residence for persons of sufficient means; Council Dir. 90/365/EEC on the rights of residence for employees and self-employed who have ceased their occupational activity ([1990] OJ L180/28) and Council Dir. 93/96/EC ([1993] OJ L317/59) on the rights of residence for students.

[209] See Art. 7(1)(d) and (2) in respect of the rights of residence of family members.

[210] Case C–209/03 *Bidar* [2005] ECR I–2119, para. 36 suggests that the burden of proof is on the state to show that the individual does not have sufficient resources or sickness insurance prior to removing the individual from the state rather than on the migrant citizen to show that he has sufficient resources/medical insurance to entitle him to stay.

[211] Art. 8(4) CRD. See also COM(2009) 313, 8.

[212] Case C–408/03 *Commission* v. *Belgium (Portuguese migrants)* [2006] ECR I–2647, para. 44.

clear that the authorities of the host Member State were entitled to undertake the necessary checks to ensure the 'existence, amount and availability' of those resources.

As far as sickness insurance is concerned, the Commission's guidance[213] provides that any insurance cover, private or public, contracted in the host Member State or elsewhere, is acceptable in principle, as long as it provides comprehensive coverage[214] and does not create a burden on the public finances of the host Member State. The guidance also says that pensioners fulfil the condition of comprehensive sickness insurance cover if they are entitled to health treatment on behalf of the Member State which pays their pension. The European Health Insurance Card offers comprehensive cover when the EU citizen does not move residence (in the sense of Regulation (EEC) No 1408/71 now Regulation 883/04) to the host Member State and intends to return to the home Member State.

The Retired Persons Directive 90/365 was drafted in similar terms to Directive 90/364, but it specified that the individual had to be in receipt of an invalidity or early retirement pension, or old age benefits or a pension in respect of an industrial accident or disease 'of an amount sufficient to avoid becoming a burden on the social security system of the Member State'. These requirements have now been wrapped up into the persons of independent means provisions (Article 7(1)(b) of the CRD).

The Students' Directive 93/96 differed somewhat from the other two Residence Directives and these differences have been reproduced in Article 7(1)(c) CRD. It provides that Union citizen students and their (reduced group of[215]) family members have the right of residence on the territory of another Member States for a period longer than three months if the students:

- are enrolled in a recognized educational establishment[216] for the principal purpose of following a course of study, including vocational training

- have comprehensive sickness insurance cover in the host state

- can assure the relevant national authority (but not prove), 'by means of a declaration or by such equivalent means as they may choose' that they have sufficient resources for themselves and their family members 'not to become a burden on the social assistance system of the host Member State during their period of residence'.

Because a student's financial position might change with the passage of time for reasons beyond his control, the Court said in *Grzelczyk*[217] that the truthfulness of his declaration was to be assessed only at the time when it was made. Article 8(3) adds that, for the purpose of getting a registration certificate, Member States cannot require the declaration to refer to any specific amount of resources. Unlike the other two Residence Directives, no minimum level of resource was specified in the original Students' Directive but Article 8(4) CRD on assessing sufficient resources appears to apply to students as well as to persons of independent means.

---

[213] COM(2009) 313, 9–10.

[214] Cf. Case C–413/99 *Baumbast* [2002] ECR I–7091 considered below n. 231.

[215] According to Art. 7(4)(d) only the spouse, the registered partner recognized by the law of both the home and host state, and dependent children have the right of residence as family members. Discretionary admission under Art. 3(2) shall apply to his/her dependent relatives in the ascending line and those of his/her spouse or registered partner.

[216] I.e., a private or public establishment, accredited or financed by the host Member State on the basis of its legislation or administrative practice.  [217] Case C–184/99 *Grzelczyk* [2001] ECR I–6193, para. 45.

In *Commission* v. *Italy*[218] the Commission gave two reasons for the difference between the financial provisions concerning students and those applying to persons of independent means (and retired persons). The first related to the planned length of stay—the student's stay in the host state was only temporary (since it was limited to the duration of the studies), whereas the stay of the other two groups was potentially indefinite. The second concerned the fact that students were more likely to find work to supplement their income than the other two groups. Therefore, the risk of students becoming a burden on social assistance was less than in the case of persons of independent means. Furthermore, under Article 2 of the Students' Directive (but not under the CRD), the validity of student residence permits could be limited to one year, renewable annually. Therefore, the Court said, the national authorities could intervene more rapidly where a student became a burden on national social assistance.

Finally, Article 3 of the original Students' Directive 93/96 made clear that the host state was not obliged to pay maintenance grants to migrant students. The essence of this provision was replicated in Article 24(2) CRD which says there is no right to equal treatment in respect of 'maintenance aid for studies... consisting in student grants or student loans' for those not having the right of *permanent* residence (i.e., usually after five years) or who are not engaged in an economic activity (workers, the self-employed), persons who retain their worker/self-employed status and members of their families.[219]

## 3. THE LIMITS TO THE LIMITATIONS

The conditions and limitations laid down by the original Residence Directives and now the CRD indicate that while Member States were willing to admit the economically active and their families, they would not admit others unless they were able to support themselves. This prompted one commentator to observe that the EU had not yet reached the stage where the peoples of the Member States were considered as just one community, mutually extending solidarity, where revenues and financial charges are shared irrespective of national boundaries.[220] However, this perspective was put to the test in *Grzelczyk*.[221] It will be recalled from the previous chapter that Grzelczyk was a French student studying at university in Belgium. Having supported himself during the first three years of his course, largely by working part-time, he applied to the Belgian authorities for the minimex (a non-contributory social security benefit paid to nationals in need) to help support him during his final year of study. He was refused the benefit on the ground that he was neither a Belgian national nor a migrant worker. The question for the Court was whether, as a migrant *citizen*, he was entitled to equal treatment in respect of the benefit,[222] or whether, as a migrant *student*, the limits laid down by the directive applied to him.

The Court struck a careful balance. While recognizing that Article 3 of the original Students' Directive 93/96 did not establish any right to payment of a maintenance grant, it noted that the directive did not preclude students from receiving other social security benefits.[223] The Court then said that while a Member State could withdraw or not renew

---

[218] Case C–424/98 [2000] ECR I–4001, paras. 40 and 45.    [219] See further Ch. 9.
[220] C. Tomuschat (2000) 37 *CMLRev.* 449, 454.    [221] Case C–184/99 [2001] ECR I–6193.
[222] This is considered further in Ch. 9.
[223] Para. 39. See A. P. Van Der Mei, 'EU law and education: Promotion of student mobility versus protection of education systems' in M. Dougan and E. Spaventa (eds.), *Social Welfare and EU Law: Essays in European law* (Oxford: Hart Publishing, 2005).

a residence permit of a student who had recourse to social assistance,[224] such measures could not be the *automatic* consequence of a migrant student having recourse to the host state's social assistance system.[225] Then, referring to the directive's preamble which said that beneficiaries of the right of residence could not become an 'unreasonable' burden on the public finances of the host Member State,[226] the Court said that the Students' Directive 93/96, like the two other Residence Directives (90/364 and 90/365), accepted 'a certain degree of financial solidarity' between nationals of a host Member State and nationals of other Member States, particularly if the difficulties which a beneficiary of the right of residence encountered were temporary.[227]

*Grzelczyk* therefore suggests that a state cannot withdraw a student's residence permit or refuse to renew it simply because he has become a temporary burden on public funds. It is only when the burden becomes unreasonable that this can occur. This is now confirmed in Article 14(3) CRD:

An expulsion measure shall not be the automatic consequence of a Union citizen's or his or her family member's recourse to the social assistance system of the host Member State.[228]

But when does a migrant become an unreasonable burden? In its guidance,[229] the Commission says that the authorities must carry out a proportionality test. To this end, it says that Member States may develop a points-based scheme as an indicator based on three sets of criteria:[230]

(1) duration

- For how long is the benefit being granted?
- Outlook: is it likely that the EU citizen will get out of the safety net soon?
- How long has the residence lasted in the host Member State?

(2) personal situation

- What is the level of connection of the EU citizen and his/her family members with the society of the host Member State?
- Are there any considerations pertaining to age, state of health, family and economic situation that need to be taken into account?

(3) amount

- What is the total amount of aid granted?
- Does the EU citizen have a history of relying heavily on social assistance?
- Does the EU citizen have a history of contributing to the financing of social assistance in the host Member State?

---

[224] Para. 42.

[225] Para. 43. See also Case C–408/03 *Commission* v. *Belgium (Portuguese migrants)* [2006] ECR I–2647, para. 68.                                    [226] Para. 44. See now Recital 10 CRD.

[227] Ibid. See N. Nic Shuibhne, 'Derogating from the free movement of persons' (2005–6) 8 *CYELS* 187 and 'The Outer Limits of EU Citizenship: Displacing EU Free Movement Rights' in C. Barnard and O. Odudu (eds), *The Outer Limits of European Union Law* (Oxford, Hart Publishing, 2009).

[228] If Union citizens/their family members are expelled on these grounds, the procedural protection provided in Arts. 30 (notification) and 31 (judicial/administrative redress) apply to any such decision: Art. 15(1). The host Member State cannot impose a ban on entry in the context of such an expulsion decision: Art. 15(3).                                    [229] COM(2009) 313, 8–9.

[230] See also Recital 16 CRD.

While the Court in *Grzelczyk* imposed limits on the requirement to have sufficient resources, in *Baumbast*[231] the Court imposed limits on the requirement to have medical insurance, this time in the context of the original Persons of Independent Means Directive 90/364 (now Article 7(1)(b) CRD). Baumbast, a German national, brought his family to the UK. They lived off private income and did not rely on financial assistance from the state. They also had comprehensive medical insurance in Germany and they travelled there when necessary for treatment. However, they did not have medical insurance providing emergency cover should they need it in the UK. For this reason, the Secretary of State refused to renew Mr Baumbast's residence permit and the residence documents of his Columbian wife and children. The question for the Court was whether the UK was entitled to insist upon Baumbast complying fully with the requirements of Directive 90/364. The Court said that the directive's limitations were subject to the principle of proportionality.[232] Because Mr Baumbast basically satisfied all the conditions of Directive 90/364,[233] it would amount to a disproportionate interference with the exercise of the right of residence if he were denied residence simply on the ground that his sickness insurance did not cover the emergency treatment given in the host Member State.[234]

*Baumbast* paved the way for the radical decision in *Chen*.[235] Chen's parents, who were Chinese, wished to have a second child but this was forbidden in China due to the single-child policy. With the benefit of good legal advice, Mrs Chen entered the UK when she was six months pregnant and moved to Belfast to give birth. Under the Irish Constitution as it then stood, the *ius soli* (law of the soil) was the sole criterion for the acquisition of Irish nationality so that any child born anywhere on the island of Ireland acquired Irish nationality, irrespective of any family connections with Ireland. So the baby, Catherine, was Irish. With her Irish passport, Catherine and her mother moved to Wales.[236]

The Court said that Catherine, even though only eight months old, enjoyed the rights of Union citizenship. She could therefore enjoy the right to reside under Article 21(1) TFEU, subject to the limitations and conditions laid down by the Person of Independent Means Directive 90/364 (Article 7(1)(b) CRD). These she satisfied: she had both sickness insurance and sufficient resources, so that she did not become a burden on the British state. The fact that these resources came from her mother was irrelevant: the Court noted that the directive laid down no condition as to the origin of the resources, merely that they

---

[231] Case C–413/99 *Baumbast and R.* [2002] ECR I–7091. For a fuller discussion of these judgments see COM(2003) 101.     [232] Para. 91.

[233] Para. 92.     [234] Para. 93.

[235] Case C–200/02 *Chen v. Secretary of State for the Home Department* [2004] ECR I–9925.

[236] In an attempt to put an end to such 'citizenship' or 'passport tourism', the Irish Constitution was amended (79% of those voting were in favour, 21% against), removing citizenship as a constitutional right and restoring to the *Oireachtas* (Irish Parliament) the power to legislate in relation to the acquisition of Irish nationality and citizenship. This led to the Irish Nationality and Citizenship Act 2004 granting citizenship now on the basis of a combination of not only *ius soli* but also *ius sanguinis* (in the case of non-national parents, one of the child's parents must have had a substantial connection with Ireland by being legally resident there for a number of years): A. Tryfonidou, 'Case C–200/02 *Chen*: Further cracks in the "great wall" of the European Union' (2005) 11 *EPL* 527, 531; A. Chrisafis, 'Ireland tightens ring of steel around fortress Europe: Referendum voters put limit on automatic citizenship law', *The Guardian*, 14 Jun. 2004, 10. According to press reports, the Chen family 'fled their luxury apartment in Wales' and returned to China: 'Voters' right to scrap this rule', *News of the World*, 13 Jun. 2004.

be sufficient.[237] In a similar vein, the Court said in *Commission* v. *Belgium (Portuguese migrants)*[238] that the provider of those 'sufficient resources' did not need to have a 'legal link' with the beneficiary (such as the link between parent and child in *Chen*).[239] Therefore, it was enough, for the purposes of the directive, for a Portuguese national living in Belgium with her daughters to be financially supported by her long-standing Belgian partner even though he was not legally obliged to provide for her; she 'had' sufficient resources.

The careful articulation of the proportionality principle in *Baumbast* and again in *Chen* and *Commission* v. *Belgium*,[240] limiting the Member State's right to rely on the limitations laid down in the Residence Directives, helps to explain *Grzelczyk*: Grzelczyk could not be refused a minimex under Article 1 of Directive 93/96 because he had been lawfully residing in Belgium for three years, during which time he had had sufficient resources (and medical insurance). Now that he was suffering 'temporary difficulties' it would be disproportionate to deny him the minimex; and paying him the minimex temporarily was certainly more proportionate than withdrawing his right of residence before the end of the course.

In all four cases the Court placed much emphasis on the fact that the individuals were citizens of the Union[241] and, in the words of *Grzelczyk*, could benefit from 'a certain degree of financial solidarity'[242] with nationals of a host Member State in 'emergency' situations (pressing financial or medical need). In this way the Court has used the citizenship principle to limit the limitations of the directives: all that is now required is sufficiently sufficient resources and health insurance.[243] Whatever the original intentions of the EU legislator, EU citizenship has helped to foster, at least to a limited extent, solidarity among citizens of the Union,[244] a solidarity nurtured by the Court.

---

# E.  JUSTIFICATIONS

## 1.  INTRODUCTION

The (general) express derogations are available in respect of any breach of Union law (refusal of entry as well as directly, indirectly, and non-discriminatory measures and

---

[237] Para. 33. In *W (China) and X (China)* v. *Secretary of State for the Home Department* [2006] EWCA Civ 1494, the British Court of Appeal ruled that both Chinese parents of an EU citizen child, together with the (four-year-old) child herself, had to satisfy the two conditions of possession of sickness insurance and sufficient resources in order to enjoy the right of free movement. In *Liu* v. *Secretary of State for the Home Department* [2007] EWCA 1275 the Court of Appeal said there was no obligation on states to adjust their laws to enable TCN parents of an EU citizen child to be able to work so as to provide sufficient resources for the child.          [238] Case C–408/03 [2006] ECR I–2647.

[239] Para. 46.

[240] See generally, M. Dougan, 'The constitutional dimension to the case law on Union citizenship' (2006) 31 *ELRev*. 613.          [241] See the discussion in Ch. 12.

[242] Case C–184/99 *Grzelczyk* [2001] ECR I–6193, para. 44.

[243] M. Dougan and E. Spaventa, 'Educating Rudy and the (non-) English patient: A double-bill on residency rights under Article 18 EC' (2003) 28 *ELRev*. 699. See also N. Nic Shuibhne, 'The outer limits of EU citizenship: Displacing economic free movement rights' in C. Barnard and O. Odudu (eds.), *The Outer Limits of European Union Law* (Oxford: Hart Publishing, 2009).

[244] M. Dougan and E. Spaventa '"Wish you weren't here…" New models of social solidarity in the European Union' in M. Dougan and E. Spaventa (eds.), *Social Welfare and EU Law: Essays in European law* (Oxford: Hart Publishing, 2005).

other restrictions on free movement). However, as we saw in Chapter 8, indirectly discriminatory and non-discriminatory measures which hinder free movement (see fig. 8.3), together with measures which prevent or impede market access (see fig. 8.4) and possibly even directly discriminatory measures, can be saved by a broader category of objective justifications/public-interest requirements. In *O'Flynn* we saw that the language of objective justification was used in the context of free movement of workers. In respect of establishment and services, the Court tends to talk about justifications in the 'public' or 'general interest' or 'imperative requirements'[245] but it seems likely that these terms are the functional equivalent of 'objective justifications',[246] which in turn are the persons' equivalent to mandatory requirements in the field of goods. In all cases the Court recognizes that there exist certain national interests which are worthy of protection[247] and should take precedence over the free movement provisions. However, the burden is on the defendant state to prove the existence of any such justification[248] and explain the link between the justification put forward and the measures taken to achieve it.[249] In other words, the justification must be actually made out; it is not sufficient for a state to invoke it without supporting evidence.[250]

In *Gebhard*,[251] a case on establishment, the Court elaborated on the requirements necessary for the national rule to satisfy the test of justification. It said that national measures liable to hinder or make less attractive the exercise of fundamental freedoms guaranteed by the Treaties had to fulfil four conditions in order not to breach (in that case) Article 49. They had to:

- be applied in a non-discriminatory manner
- be justified by imperative requirements in the general interest
- be suitable for securing the attainment of the objective which they pursued
- not go beyond what was necessary to attain it.[252]

The operative part of the judgment in *Gebhard* makes clear that this test also applies to the free movement of workers and services.[253]

---

[245] Case C–76/90 *Säger* [1991] ECR I–4221, para. 15; Case C–55/94 *Gebhard* [1996] ECR I–4165, para. 37.

[246] This view is supported by the workers case, Case C–195/98 *Österreicher Gewerkschaftsbund* [2000] ECR I–10497, para. 45, where the Court reported that the Austrian government contended that the restrictions on free movement were 'justified by overriding reasons of public interest and are consistent with the principle of proportionality', and the services case, Case C–118/96 *Safir* [1998] ECR I–1897, para. 22: 'Article [56 TFEU] precludes the application of any national legislation which, without objective justification, impedes a provider of services from actually exercising the freedom to provide them.'

[247] See Tesauro AG in Case C–118/96 *Safir* [1998] ECR I–1897, para. 29. In the context of social rights, see S. Giubboni, *Social Rights and Market Freedom in the European Constitution: A labour law perspective* (Cambridge: CUP, 2006).

[248] See, e.g., Case C–260/04 *Commission v. Italy (horse race betting licences)* [2007] ECR I–7083, para. 33.

[249] Joined Cases C–151/04 and C–152/04 *Nadin* [2005] ECR I–11203, para. 52; Case C–243/01 *Gambelli* [2003] ECR I–13031, para. 63. The Court may well scrutinize the stated objectives rigorously as in Case C–169/07 *Hartlauer Handelsgesellschaft mbH v. Wiener Landesregierung and others* [2009] ECR I–1721.

[250] See, e.g., Case C–389/05 *Commission v. France (Insemination of bovine semen)* [2008] ECR I–5337, para. 103 where the Court rejected the French government's justification based on town and country planning because its arguments were not 'substantiated by any statistical information or data'.

[251] Case C–55/94 [1995] ECR I–4165.       [252] Para. 37.       [253] Para. 6.

## 2. THE JUSTIFICATIONS RECOGNIZED BY THE COURT

So what are the justifications recognized by the Court so far? In the services case, *Gouda*,[254] the Court listed the public-interest grounds which it had already recognized:

- professional rules intended to protect the recipients of a service[255]
- protection of intellectual property[256]
- protection of workers[257]
- consumer protection[258]
- conservation of the national historic and artistic heritage[259]
- turning to account the archaeological, historical, and artistic heritage of a country and the widest possible dissemination of knowledge of the artistic and cultural heritage of a country[260]
- cultural policy.[261]

As with *Cassis*, the list in *Gouda* is not exhaustive. The Court has also recognized a number of other public-interest grounds. Chalmers loosely divides the justifications into four groups. The first group concerns market externalities (where a transaction fails to take account of somebody's interests and that person was not deemed to have a choice in the matter).[262] This heading includes justifications such as:

- guaranteeing the quality of skilled trade work and protecting those who have commissioned such work[263]
- the protection of the interests of creditors, minority shareholders, and employees[264]

---

[254]  Case C–288/89 [1991] ECR I–4007.

[255]  Joined Cases 110 and 111/78 *Ministère public* v. *Willy van Wesemael and others* [1979] ECR 35, para. 28. In Case C–3/95 *Sandker* [1996] ECR I–6511, para. 38, the Court spelled out this justification more fully: 'the application of professional rules to lawyers, in particular those relating to organization, qualifications, professional ethics, supervision and liability, ensures that the ultimate consumers of legal services and the sound administration of justice are provided with the necessary guarantees in relation to integrity and experience'.

[256]  Case 62/79 *Coditel* [1980] ECR 881.

[257]  Case 279/80 *Criminal Proceedings against Webb* [1981] ECR 3305, para. 19; Joined Cases 62 and 63/81 *Seco* v. *EVI* [1982] ECR 223, para. 14. Subsequently in Case C–272/94 *Criminal Proceedings against Guiot* [1996] ECR I–1905, para. 16, the Court stressed the importance of the social protection of workers in the construction industry. However, this did not entail strike action to enforce terms and conditions of employment which exceed the exhaustive list in Art. 3(1) of the Posted Workers Dir. 96/71: Case C–341/05, *Laval* [2007] ECR I–987, para. 110.

[258]  Case 220/83 *Commission* v. *France (co-insurance)* [1986] ECR 3663, para. 20; Case 252/83 *Commission* v. *Denmark (co-insurance)* [1986] ECR 3713, para. 20; Case 205/84 *Commission* v. *Germany (insurance)* [1986] ECR 3755, para. 30; Case 206/84 *Commission* v. *Ireland (co-insurance)* [1986] ECR 3817, para. 20; Case C–180/89 *Commission* v. *Italy (tourist guides)* [1991] ECR I–709, para. 20.

[259]  Case C–180/89 *Commission* v. *Italy* [1991] ECR I–709, para. 20.

[260]  Case C–154/89 *Commission* v. *France* [1991] ECR I–659, para. 17; Case C–198/89 *Commission* v. *Greece* [1991] ECR I–727, para. 21.

[261]  Case C–288/89 *Gouda* [1991] ECR I–4007, paras. 22–3; Case C–353/89 *Commission* v. *Netherlands* [1991] ECR I–4069 and Case C–23/93 *TV10* [1994] ECR I–4795.

[262]  D. Chalmers et al., *EU Law* (Cambridge: CUP, 2006), 833–4.

[263]  Case C–58/98 *Josef Corsten* [2000] ECR I–7919, para. 38.

[264]  Case C–208/00 *Überseering* [2002] ECR I–9919, para. 92.

- protection of the environment[265]
- promoting sustainable settlement in a designated area (essentially a regional policy goal) where there has been a decline in population due to harsh climate, vast distances, and sparse population[266]
- road safety[267]
- the need to safeguard the reputation of the Dutch financial markets (and to protect the investing public).[268]

A second group concerns civil liberties (i.e., ensuring that the economic freedoms do not compromise the political values which are central to protecting human dignity, autonomy, and equality) such as the protection of human dignity[269] or freedom of expression and assembly.[270] A third group concerns what Chalmers describes as protecting certain 'socio-cultural' practices (i.e., protecting local institutions which 'enable local or national markets to function, while securing reliability, trust and credibility'):

- ensuring the balance between sports clubs[271]
- prevention of social dumping[272] or unfair competition[273]
- prevention of abuse of free movement of services[274] or Union law more generally[275]
- avoiding disturbances on the labour market[276]
- the survival of small and medium-sized undertakings and the maintenance of employment[277]
- social protection of workers in respect of, for example, social security provision[278]
- combating illegal employment[279]
- ensuring the adequacy of regular maritime services to, from, and between islands[280]

---

[265] Case C–17/00 *De Coster* v. [2001] ECR I–9445, paras. 36–7; Joined Cases C–151/04 and C–152/04 *Nadin* [2005] ECR I–11203, para. 52.

[266] Case E–3/05 *EFTA Surveillance Authority* v. *Norway* [2006] EFTA Ct Rep 102 para. 57.

[267] Case C–55/93 *Criminal Proceedings against van Schaik* [1994] ECR I–4837; Joined Cases C–151/04 and C–152/04 *Nadin* [2005] ECR I–11203, para. 49.

[268] Case C–384/93 *Alpine Investments* [1995] ECR I–1141, para. 44. See also Case C–222/95 *Parodi* v. *Banque H. Albert de Bary* [1997] ECR I–3899, para. 22, where the Court noted that the banking sector was a particularly sensitive area from the perspective of consumer protection.

[269] Case C–36/02 *Omega* [2004] ECR I–9609.

[270] See the goods case Case C–112/00 *Schmidberger* [2003] ECR I–5659 discussed in Ch. 6. The Court tentatively also recognized the right to accommodation in Case C–345/05 *Commission* v. *Portugal (transfer of property)* [2006] ECR I–10663, para. 31.

[271] Case C–415/93 *Bosman* [1995] ECR I–4921, para. 106; Case C–176/96 *Lehtonen* v. *FRSB* [2000] ECR I–2681, para. 54.

[272] Case C–244/04 *Commission* v. *Germany* [2006] ECR I–885, para. 61; Case C–341/05 *Laval* [2007] ECR I–987, para. 103.

[273] Case C–60/03 *Wolff & Müller* v. *Pereira Félix* [2004] ECR I–9553, para. 41.

[274] Case C–244/04 *Commission* v. *Germany* [2006] ECR I–885, para. 38.

[275] Case C–147/03 *Commission* v. *Austria (higher education)* [2005] ECR I–5969, para. 70. For discussion, see R. de la Feria, 'Prohibition of abuse of Community law: The creation of a new general principle of EC law through tax' (2008) 45 *CMLRev.* 395, 416.

[276] Case C–445/03 *Commission* v. *Luxembourg* [2004] ECR I–10191, para. 38.

[277] Case C–464/05 *Geurts* v. *Administratie van de BTW* [2007] ECR I–9325, para. 26.

[278] Case C–255/04 *Commission* v. *France* [2006] ECR I–5251, para. 47.     [279] Ibid., para. 52.

[280] Case C–205/99 *Analir* [2001] ECR I–1271, para. 27.

- preserving or improving the education system[281]
- the promotion of mobility and integration of disabled people and the wish to ensure that there is a connection between the society of the Member State concerned and the recipient of the benefit.[282]

However, as with its case law under Article 258 TFEU (ex Article 226 EC) enforcement proceedings, Member States cannot plead 'provisions, practices or situations prevailing in its domestic legal order, including those resulting from the constitutional organization of that State, to justify the failure to observe obligations arising under [Union] law'.[283] Therefore, in the *Walloon* case the Flemish government could not plead the requirements inherent in the division of powers within the Belgian federal structure and, particularly, the fact that the Flemish Community could exercise no competence in relation to care insurance in respect of those residing in the territory of other linguistic communities, to justify excluding those French speaking non-residents who worked in the flemish part from access to the care insurance scheme.

A fourth group of justifications relates to the 'preservation of public order,[284] i.e. 'to supply services that are necessary for the government of its territory'. Here the Court is concerned with protecting certain values or interests as well as safeguarding the machinery of government that enables such protection. The list therefore includes the public interests recognized in *Schindler* to justify a ban on lotteries (e.g., preventing gambling and avoiding the lottery from becoming the source of private profit; avoiding the risk of crime or fraud; avoiding the risk of incitement to spend, with damaging individual and social consequences), as elaborated in the subsequent gambling cases to include 'moral, religious and cultural factors'.[285] In these sorts of cases the Court offers states a wide scope for discretion in areas deemed sensitive ideologically or associated with particular risks.[286] The 'machinery of government' justifications include:

- preserving the systems of administration of justice[287]
- the coherence of a scheme of taxation[288]

---

[281] Case C–40/05 *Lyyski* [2007] ECR I–99, para. 39. See also Case C–281/06 *Jundt* [2007] ECR I–12231, para. 58: 'promoting teaching, research and development'.

[282] Case C–103/08 *Gottwald* [2009] ECR I–000, para. 32.

[283] Case C–212/06 *Walloon Government* [2008] ECR I–1683, para. 58.

[284] This heading is expressly recognized in Case C–465/05 *Commission v. Italy (private security activities)* [2007] ECR I–11091, para. 74. In that case the Italian government justified its requirement to limit licences for security guards to a particular territory on the grounds of the protection of public order and security, to ensure that private security activities were carried out safe from infiltration by local criminal organizations. The justification failed on the ground that it was not proportionate.

[285] Case C–243/01 *Gambelli* [2003] ECR I–13031, para. 63.

[286] Van Gerven AG in Case C–145/88 *Torfaen Borough Council v. B & Q plc* [1989] ECR 3851, para. 102.

[287] Case C–3/95 *Sandker* [1996] ECR I–611. In a similar vein, in Joined Cases C–147/06 and C–148/06 *SECAP SpA v. Comune di Torino* [2008] ECR I–3565, para. 32 the Court endorsed a justification based on ensuring that the local administration can function without having its capacity so overwhelmed that might jeopardize the attainment of a project.

[288] Case C–204/90 *Bachmann* [1992] ECR I–249. This is considered further in Ch. 9. See also, e.g., Case C–300/90 *Commission v. Belgium* [1992] ECR I–305; Case C–294/97 *Eurowings Luftverkehrs AG* [1999] ECR I–7447, para. 19.

- the effectiveness of fiscal supervision[289]

- the balanced allocation of the power to impose taxes between the Member States[290]

- the need to ensure the effective collection of income tax,[291] and preventing wholly artificial arrangements aimed solely at escaping national tax normally due[292]

- preserving the financial balance of a social security scheme[293]

- preventing fraud on the social security system[294]

- controlling costs, and preventing wastage of financial, technical, and human resources[295]

- the obligation of solidarity which is 'characterised, in particular, by funding through contributions the amount of which is not strictly proportionate to the risks insured and by the granting of benefits the amount of which is not strictly proportionate to contributions'[296]

- the need for legal certainty.[297]

Some of the justifications recognised in this fourth category come close to the very type of economic justifications which the Court has rejected in other cases.[298] For example, in SETTG[299] the Court said that a Greek law requiring all tourist guides to have a particular employment relationship with their employer (which effectively prevented self-employed tourist guides from other Member States from providing services in Greece) could not be justified on the ground of 'maintaining industrial peace as a means of bringing a collective dispute to an end and thereby preventing any adverse effects on an economic sector and consequently on the economy of the State'.[300] The Court said that such a justification had to be regarded as an 'economic aim'[301] which could not constitute a reason relating

---

[289] Case C–55/98 *Bent Vestergaard* [1999] ECR I–7641, para. 23. However, a general presumption of tax avoidance or tax fraud is not sufficient to justify a fiscal measure which compromises the objectives of the Treaties: Case C–433/04 *Commission* v. *Belgium* [2006] ECR I–10653, para. 35.

[290] Case C–446/03 *Marks & Spencer plc v. Halsey* [2005] ECR I–10837, para. 51. This is considered further in Ch. 10. See also Case C–330/07 *Jobra Vermögensverwaltungs-Gesellschaft mbH v. Finanzamt Amstetten Melk Scheibbs* [2008] ECR I–9099, para. 32.

[291] Case C–290/04 *Scorpio* [2006] ECR I–9461, para. 35.

[292] Case C–196/04 *Cadbury's Schweppes* [2006] ECR I–7995, para. 51. This is considered further in Ch. 10.

[293] Case C–158/96 *Kohll* [1998] ECR I–1931, para. 41. This is considered further in Ch. 11.

[294] Case C–406/04 *De Cuyper* [2006] ECR I–6947, para. 41.

[295] Case C–157/99 *Geraets-Smits and Peerbooms* [2001] ECR I–5473, paras. 78–9.

[296] Case C–350/07 *Kattner Stahlbau GmbH* v. *Maschinenbau- und Metall- Berufsgenossenschaft* [2009] ECR I–1513, para. 87. See also Case C–192/05 *Tas-Hagen* [2006] ECR I–10451, paras. 34–5.

[297] Case C–347/06 *ASM Brescia SpA* v. *Comune di Rodengo Saiano* [2008] ECR I– 5641, para. 64.

[298] Even outside the economic justifications the Court has not been prepared to extend the list indefinitely: e.g., Case C–18/95 *Terhoeve* [1999] ECR I–345, para. 45, where the Court held that considerations of a purely administrative nature could not make lawful a restriction on the free movement of persons.

[299] Case C–398/95 *SETTG* v. *Ypourgos Ergasias* [1997] ECR I–3091.

[300] Para. 25. See also Joined Cases C–49/98, C–50/98, C–52/98 to C–54/98 and C–68/98 to C–71/98 *Finalarte and others* [2001] ECR I–7831, paras. 38–9 and Case C–164/99 *Portugaia Construções Lda* [2002] ECR I–787, paras. 25–6 where the Court rejected the justification for the imposition of national social legislation on posted workers of protecting the domestic construction industry and reducing unemployment to avoid social tensions.

[301] See also Case C–137/04 *Rockler* v. *Försäkringskassan* [2006] ECR I–1141, para. 24. The Court will look to see if the expressed aim is genuinely economic or whether, viewed objectively, the rules actually serve

to the general interest that justified a restriction on the freedom of establishment.[302] For similar reasons the Court has rejected arguments based on a reduction in tax revenue as an overriding reason in the public interest[303] or the cost to the national exchequer.[304] Hatzopoulos explains the different treatment between public-order justifications which have been accepted by the Court and other cases where the aim is considered economic on the ground that the former serve a 'structural' purpose and so are regarded more leniently than those which do not.[305] At times, the dividing line seems very fine.

## F.  PROPORTIONALITY

Once the Member State has identified an express derogation or a public-interest require-ment which the Court has accepted, a court (theoretically the national court but often the Court of Justice) will determine whether the steps taken by the Member State to realize that objective are, where appropriate, compatible with fundamental human rights (see above) and proportionate. The burden of proof is on the defending state.[306] The Court offers various formulations of the proportionality test[307] but, as we saw in Chapter 6, the proportionality issue essentially raises two questions: first, whether the measures are suit-able for securing the attainment of the objective and, secondly, whether they go beyond what is necessary in order to attain it.[308] As Straetmans observes,[309] the first question requires only a marginal control of the aptitude or suitability of the national legislation to obtain the aim pursued. By contrast, the second question requires courts to determine whether the interest pursued cannot be satisfied by other, less restrictive means.

The application of this two-stage approach can be seen in *De Coster*[310] concerning a decision by the Belgian authorities to tax satellite dishes. This had the effect of imposing a charge on the reception of television programmes by satellite while no equivalent charge was payable on those received by cable. The tax was found to interfere with the provision

---

another, legitimate objective. This approach can be seen in Joined Cases C–49, 50, 52, 54, 68, and 71/98 *Finalarte* [2001] ECR I–7831.

[302]  Para. 23. Cf. Jacobs AG's suggestion in Case C–147/03 *Commission* v. *Austria (students)* [2005] ECR I–5969 that if the Court said that migrant students were entitled to maintenance grants 'the financial bur-den of the free movement of students on state resources would become significant', and this would be a good reason for states to be allowed to invoke economic grounds, albeit narrowly tailored, to justify certain restrictions on their availability to migrants.

[303]  Case C–464/02 *Commission* v. *Denmark (company vehicles)* [2005] ECR I–7929, para. 45, citing the free movement of capital decision in Case C–319/02 *Manninen* [2004] ECR I–7477, para. 49. See also C–422/01 *Skandia* [2003] ECR I–6817, paras. 51–2 where the Court rejected arguments based on the need to preserve the tax base.

[304]  Case C–109/04 *Kranemann* [2005] ECR I–2421.

[305]  V. Hatzopoulos, 'Recent developments of the case law of the ECJ in the field of services' (2000) 37 *CMLRev*. 43, 79.

[306]  See, e.g., Case C–465/05 *Commission* v. *Italy (private security activities)* [2007] ECR I–11091, para.76.

[307]  See, e.g., Case C–288/89 *Gouda* [1991] ECR I–4007, para. 15: 'the application of national provisions to providers of services established in other Member States must be such as to *guarantee* the achievement of the intended aim and must not go beyond that which is necessary in order to achieve that objective. In other words, it must not be possible to obtain the same result by less restrictive rules' (emphasis added); Case C–157/99 *Geraets-Smits and Peerbooms* [2001] ECR I–5473, para. 75: 'to make sure that the measures do not exceed what is objectively necessary for that purpose and that the same result cannot be achieved by less restrictive rules'.                    [308]  See, e.g., Case C–67/98 *Zenatti* [1999] ECR I–7289, para. 29.

[309]  G. Straetmans (2000) 37 *CMLRev*. 991, 1002.          [310]  Case C–17/00 [2001] ECR I–9445.

of services because broadcasters from other states were not allowed the unlimited access to cable distribution which Belgian broadcasters enjoyed. However, the Belgian authorities argued that the tax could be justified on the ground of preventing 'the uncontrolled proliferation of satellite dishes in the municipality and thereby [preserving] the quality of the environment'. While the Court doubted whether the measure was *suitable* to attain that objective,[311] it was convinced that the tax exceeded what was *necessary* to achieve the objective of protecting the urban environment. It suggested that alternative, less-restrictive methods existed for achieving this objective,[312] such as laying down rules about the size of the dishes, their position, and the way in which they were fixed to a building, or the use of communal dishes.[313]

By contrast, the Court thought that the proportionality test had been satisfied in *Alpine Investments*. It agreed that the national law banning cold-calling was suitable, noting that the consumer was generally caught unawares by a cold call and so was in no position either to ascertain the risks inherent in the type of transactions or to compare the quality and price of the caller's services with competitors' offers. On the question of necessity, the Court found that the rules were no more restrictive than necessary: although cold-calling was prohibited, other techniques for making contact with clients were still permitted. It also noted that the rules applied only to potential clients but not to existing clients and that the prohibition was limited to the sector in which abuses had been found (the commodities futures market).[314] The Court added that just because other Member States imposed less strict requirements to achieve the same objectives[315] did not mean that the Dutch rules were disproportionate.[316]

As *De Coster* shows, the Court is prepared to offer guidance as to what measures it considers proportionate. It is prepared to accept authorization requirements provided that they satisfy the criteria in *Kraus*.[317] It will be recalled that the German authorities said that a migrant had to be authorized before he could use his LLM title awarded by a non-German university. The Court said it was legitimate for Germany to impose the restriction on the ground of 'the need to protect a public which will not necessarily be alerted to abuse of academic titles'[318] but required Germany to show that:

- the authorization procedure was intended solely to verify whether the postgraduate academic title was properly awarded
- the procedure was easily accessible and was not excessively expensive
- reasons were given for any refusal of authorization
- the refusal could be the subject of judicial procedures
- any penalty for non-compliance with the authorization procedure was not disproportionate to the gravity of the offence.[319]

---

[311] Para. 37. See also Case C–79/01 *Payroll Data Services* [2002] ECR I–8923, paras. 32–7.

[312] Ibid.

[313] For another good example of the Court applying the 'necessity' limb of the proportionality test, see Case 352/85 *Bond* [1988] ECR 2085, para. 37.

[314] Para. 54.

[315] E.g., in the UK broking firms were required to tape-record unsolicited phone calls (para. 50).

[316] Paras. 50–7.

[317] Case C–19/92 [1993] ECR I–1663. See also Case C–279/00 *Commission* v. *Italy (temp agencies)* [2002] ECR I–1425.  [318] Para. 35.

[319] Para. 42.

In *Commission* v. *Italy (private security activities)*[320] the Court recognized that a system of territorially unlimited prior authorization of private security guards could be justified on the grounds of maintaining public order accompanied by the establishment of regular administrative checks. For example, in *Commission* v. *Austria (certification)*,[321] the Court said that introducing a certification requirement for all nationals from the A-8 countries wishing to work in a self-employed capacity, to prevent circumvention of the transitional arrangements on free movement of workers, was disproportionate. The Court said that it would be less restrictive to put in place a system of regular administrative checks, 'possibly coupled with obligations concerning the communication of information on the part of the economic operators potentially affected'. This was particularly the case since the national provisions were in fact targeted at one sector only, the building industry. These cases highlight a point we have seen elsewhere that the Court requires Member States to show flexibility in the application of its rules[322] and take into account the individual circumstances of the migrant's case.[323]

## G.  CONCLUSIONS

Questions have been raised about the compatibility of the Treaty derogations with the objectives of the internal market, and more specifically with the notion of Union citizenship laid down by Articles 20–1 TFEU. In particular, Articles 45(4) and 51 represent a continued respect for national sovereignty at a time when efforts are being made to promote a European consciousness through Union citizenship, and when employers are being encouraged to appoint on merit and not nationality. However, no attempt has been made to amend these derogations and Directive 64/221 continues—only slightly modified—in the CRD 2004/38. Yet, as we saw in *Grzelczyk* and *Baumbast* the concept of citizenship has begun to impinge on the interpretation of the general derogations and the limitations and conditions laid down in what were the 1990 Residence Directives, an approach imbued with a strong fundamental rights orientation. As the notion of EU citizenship begins to take shape in the consciousness of the courts and the litigants (or at least their lawyers), a different light may well be cast on the cases interpreting the derogations. On the other hand, while the express derogations appear to become ever narrower, the justifications recognized by the Court are becoming ever broader. Often the Court finds that the states have not made out the justification on the facts or that, even if the justification is made out, the steps taken to achieve the particular goal are not proportionate. However, in its use of the justifications, the Court has found the necessary flexibility to help it reconcile market integration with the need to protect national interests.

---

[320]  Case C–465/05 *Commission* v. *Italy* [2007] ECR I–11091, para. 77.
[321]  Case C–161/07 [2008] ECR I–10671, paras. 38–40.
[322]  Case C–213/05 *Geven* [2007] ECR I–6347, considered in Ch. 9.
[323]  Case C–40/05 *Lyyski* [2007] ECR I–99, para. 49.

# 14

# THIRD-COUNTRY NATIONALS AND THE EU

## A. INTRODUCTION

According to Article 3 TEU, the Union shall 'offer its citizens an area of freedom, security, and justice without internal frontiers, in which free movement of persons is ensured in conjunction with appropriate measures with respect to external border controls, asylum, immigration and the prevention and combating of crime'.[1] Thus, in an area of freedom, security and justice (AFSJ) citizens have the right to move freely; but they also have a right to security. This is achieved principally at the external borders of the EU where there is greater emphasis on keeping out 'undesirable' third-country nationals (TCNs)[2] and managing the immigration that is permitted. The relationship between EU law and national law is complex. It used to be said that while *Union* law gives EU citizens the right to move freely, *national* immigration law determines the conditions under which TCNs can enter a Member State (either directly from the third country or from another Member State), have access to the labour market, be joined by their families, and become naturalized. However, as we shall see, increasingly EU law is occupying the traditional domain of national law, albeit subject to complicated derogations for certain Member States.

Yet, there remain key differences between Union citizens and TCNs: unlike EU citizens, TCNs generally do not enjoy free movement between Member States (secondary movement), subject to some notable exceptions (students, researchers and in future blue-card holders), and this causes fragmentation in the single market. Furthermore, for EU citizens the state's ability to exclude or expel is interpreted restrictively; for TCNs the relationship between the individual and the state is reversed. Because TCNs do not, as a rule, have a right of admission or protection from expulsion as a matter of EU law, the rights of the state to ensure security take precedence over the rights of the individual.[3]

---

[1] For detailed discussion, see, e.g., N. Walker, 'In search of the area of freedom, security and justice: A constitutional Odyssey' in N. Walker (ed.), *Europe's Area of Freedom, Security and Justice* (Oxford: OUP, 2004); D. Kostakopoulou, 'The Area of Freedom, Security and Justice and the European Union's Constitutional Dialogue' in C. Barnard (ed.), *The Fundamentals of EU Law Revisited* (Oxford: OUP, 2007).

[2] Commission Communication, 'Towards integrated management of the external borders of the Member States of the European Union', COM(2002) 233, 4. For an example of the Court putting up external frontiers, see Case C–109/01 *Akrich* [2003] ECR I–9607, considered in Ch. 8.

[3] E. Guild, 'Security of residence and expulsion of foreigners: European Community law' in E. Guild and P. Minderhoud (eds.), *Security of Residence and Expulsion: Protection of aliens in Europe* (The Hague: Kluwer, 2000), 63.

Migration, particularly of TCNs, is also a highly emotive, politically sensitive subject.[4] Mass migration is both a threat and an opportunity. It is an opportunity because TCNs can bring much-needed skills and youth to reinvigorate an ageing population. It is a threat because an influx of the 'other' poses a significant challenge economically (to jobs for nationals and to the welfare state), culturally (different religions, different values), and socially (how to integrate the TCNs into existing communities). More recently, any discussion about migration is inevitably overlaid by concerns about security, especially in the wake of the terrorist attacks of 9/11 and the London and Madrid bombings,[5] together with more general concern about organized crime. Depending on the economic and security situation of the time, the political discourse ebbs and flows: from encouraging migration (see, for example, the EU–Turkey Association agreement discussed in Section D below) to discouraging migration (see, for example, the central thrust of the Hague programme governing policy in the field of freedom, security and justice for the years 2005–10, now followed by the Stockholm programme).

This basic tension between the opportunities and threats posed by TCN migration gives rise to a number of questions: should there be limits on the numbers of TCNs admitted to a Member State? Once admitted, what rights should they enjoy? Should they enjoy the right to work, to equal treatment with nationals, to move to another Member State? Should they be encouraged (or even required) to integrate? This chapter considers the Union's answer to some of these questions. However, in order to understand the EU's position and any legislation it has adopted, we need first to examine the evolving competences of the EU, including the right to opt-out for certain Member States, and the changing policy domain.

## B. THE DEVELOPMENT OF AN AREA OF FREEDOM, SECURITY, AND JUSTICE

### 1. THE EVOLVING TREATY POSITION

#### 1.1 Introduction

Owing largely to their colonial past, the states of the Union have always had a large number of TCNs lawfully resident on the basis of national law: in 2006 there were 18.5 million non-EU nationals resident in the EU, about 3.8 per cent of the total population.[6] In recognition of this fact, the European Union has long given TCNs certain rights, albeit on an ad hoc basis. As the previous chapters of this book have shown, since the late 1960s Union law has allowed TCN family members of migrant nationals to accompany the migrant when moving to another state, and to enjoy rights once in residence.[7] It also allows com-

---

[4] COM(2000) 757, 5: 'The social conditions which migrants face, the attitudes of the host population and the presentation by political leaders of the benefits of diversity and of pluralistic societies are all vital to the success of immigration policies.'

[5] Albeit that the London bombers were actually British-born. EU Council, 'European Union plan of action on combating terrorism', Council Doc. 10010/3/04, 11 Jun. 2004. The Commission says that in 2007 almost 600 failed, foiled or successfully executed terrorist attacks were carried out in 11 Member States (COM(2009) 263).

[6] COM(2009) 262.

[7] See, e.g., Reg. 1612/68, discussed in Ch. 9 and Dir. 2004/38 discussed in Ch. 12.

panies providing services in other Member States to use their TCN workforce.[8] However, in both situations the rights of the TCN are derived from an EU (natural or legal) person; TCNs do not enjoy their own independent rights.

In addition, the Treaties have given some rights to TCNs who do not move from one state to another. For example, Article 227 TFEU (ex Article 194 EC) on the right to petition the European Parliament and Article 15 TFEU (ex Article 255 EC) on access to documents are enjoyed by those who are legally resident, irrespective of nationality. Article 157 TFEU (ex Article 141 EC) on equal pay for men and women and Article 169 TFEU (ex Article 153 EC) on rights of consumers to information go further still. They apply to all workers and consumers—the individual does not even need to be resident.[9] Furthermore, most of the rights enumerated in the Charter of Fundamental Rights are conferred on all persons regardless of their nationality or place of residence. As the Commission notes,[10] the Charter therefore 'reflects the European Union's traditions and positive attitude to equal treatment of citizens of the Union and third-country nationals'. This view was reinforced by the adoption of the two directives under Article 19 TFEU (ex Article 13 EC): Directive 2000/43 on equal treatment irrespective of racial and ethnic origin[11] and Directive 2000/78 on equal treatment in respect of religion or belief, age, disability, and sexual orientation[12] which apply to 'all persons', irrespective of nationality or residence. However, enjoyment of these EU rights is still dependent on a Member State's decision— still largely under national law—to admit a TCN to its territory in the first place and to allow them to reside and work there.

The EU has also entered various international agreements granting more favourable rights to certain TCNs. The most substantive agreement, on the European Economic Area (EEA), extends the EU's own *acquis* to Norway, Iceland, and Liechtenstein.[13] In addition, the EU has a number of agreements on migrant workers and social security with countries such as Morocco, Algeria, and Turkey.[14] Under these agreements, the Member States retain the right to admit the migrant to their territory but, once admitted, the agreements give migrants certain rights after they have been resident for a prescribed period. The most ambitious of these agreements is the one between the EU and Turkey, the key provisions of which are considered in section D below.

Title V of Part Three TFEU provides an alternative basis for the EU to regulate the position of TCNs independently of any relationship with an EU citizen. However, the sensitivities at play here mean that the relationship between EU rules and Member State discretion is complex. We turn now to consider the development of the European Union's competence to regulate immigration from third countries.

---

[8] Case C–113/89 *Rush Portuguesa* v. *Office national d'immigration* [1990] ECR I–1417.

[9] J. D'Oliveira, 'European citizenship: Its meaning, its potential' in R. Dehousse (ed.), *Europe after Maastricht: An ever closer union?* (Munich: Law Books in Europe, 1994), 141–6 and 'Union citizenship: Metaphor or source of rights?' (2001) 7 *ELJ* 4, 7.          [10] COM(2001) 127, 3.

[11] Dir. 2000/43 ([2000] OJ L180/22).

[12] Dir. 2000/78, the so-called horizontal directive; M. Bell, *Anti–discrimination Law and the European Union* (Oxford: OUP, 2002), R. Whittle and M. Bell, 'Between social policy and Union citizenship: The Framework Directive on equal treatment in employment' (2002) 27 *ELRev.* 677.

[13] [1994] OJ L1/1; [1995] OJ L86/58.

[14] See, further, S. Peers, 'Towards equality: Actual and potential rights of third country nationals in the European Union' (1996) 33 *CMLRev.* 7.

## 1.2 The Maastricht Treaty and the Third Pillar

Until 1992, the EU had no express competence to regulate the position of TCNs. Any legislation which affected TCNs (e.g., Regulation 1612/68 on the free movement of workers and the Posted Workers Directive 96/71 which was adopted after the Maastricht Treaty) were based on the free movement provisions in the (then) EC Treaty. However, the changing geo-political climate forced the Member States to re-examine their position. With the fall of the Berlin wall, EU Member States which had been pursuing 'zero' immigration policies became concerned about security issues caused by (potentially) mass migration from former Eastern-bloc countries.[15] Increasingly they insisted on greater controls at the external frontiers, with the result that many economic migrants sought entry to the EU either illegally or through asylum procedures.[16] In response, the Member States agreed at Maastricht that a third, intergovernmental, pillar (Title VI TEU) on cooperation in respect of justice and home affairs (JHA) should be included in the Treaty. This provided that matters concerning the crossing of external borders, immigration,[17] asylum, drug addiction, fraud, judicial cooperation in civil and criminal matters, customs, and police cooperation were matters of common interest for the Member States.[18] These were matters for EU law to which the classic Community method (CCM), including principles such as direct effect, did not apply. New powers were also added to the first pillar (i.e., the EC Treaty—areas in which the CCM did apply) to deal with migration issues, including Article 100c EC which empowered the Council to determine which TCNs needed visas.[19] Article 2(3) of the Social Policy Agreement (now Article 153(1)(g) TFEU) also gave the Council the power to adopt measures concerning the conditions of employment for third-country nationals.

Prior to the Maastricht Treaty, a separate, intergovernmental process—Schengen—was already underway. Under the Schengen Agreement of 1985 and the implementing Convention of 1990,[20] the now 25 participating states agreed to remove border formalities at common frontiers, approximate visa formalities, and ensure the cooperation of law

---

[15] E. Guild, 'The single market, movement of persons and borders' in C. Barnard and J. Scott (eds.), *The Law of the Single European Market: Unpacking the premises* (Oxford: Hart Publishing, 2002), 296.

[16] COM(2000) 757, 13.

[17] Cf. General Dec. (No. 6) on Arts. 13–19 of the Single European Act (SEA): 'Nothing in these provisions shall affect the right of the Member States to take such measures as they consider necessary for the purposes of controlling immigration from third countries and to combat terrorism, crime, the traffic in drugs and illicit trading in works of art and antiques', discussed in R. Plender, 'EC competence and non-Member States nationals' (1990) 39 *ICLQ* 599, 606. However, Decl. 43 annexed to the SEA did provide that the Member States would cooperate, without prejudice to the powers of the Community, in particular as regards the entry, movement, and residence of nationals of third countries. They would also cooperate in the combating of terrorism, crime, the traffic in drugs, and illicit trading in works of art and antiques.

[18] Points (1)–(3) of (then) Art. K.1. See D. O'Keeffe, 'Recasting the third pillar' (1995) 32 *CMLRev.* 893 and 'The emergence of a European immigration policy' (1995) 20 *ELRev.* 20.

[19] Council Reg. 1683/95 of 29 May 1995 laying down a uniform format for visas ([1995] OJ L164/1). Council Reg. 2317/95 ([1995] OJ L234/1) in respect of visa requirements for TCNs, now replaced by Reg. 539/2001 ([2001] OJ L81/1). Reg. 2317/95/EC was annulled for procedural reasons: Case C–392/95 *Parliament* v. *Council* [1997] ECR I–3213. See S. Peers, 'The Visa Regulation: Free movement blocked indefinitely' (1996) 21 *ELRev.* 150; *EU Justice and Home Affairs Law* (Oxford: OUP, 2006), 69–71; and K. Hailbronner, 'Visa regulation and third-country nationals in EC Law' (1994) 31 *CMLRev.* 969.

[20] Belgium, France, Germany, Luxembourg, and the Netherlands were the original signatories to the Agreement in 1985.

enforcement agencies, particularly in relation to drugs and firearms.[21] Often presented as the 'testing ground' for the free movement of persons, the Schengen *acquis* was intended to facilitate the application of Article 26 TFEU (ex Article 14 EC).[22]

The Schengen agreements cover all nationals of the Member States of the European Union, regardless of whether they are members of the Schengen area. All individuals are subject to the same (increased) checks when crossing one of Schengen's *external* frontiers but, once admitted to the Schengen area, they enjoy free movement across internal frontiers.[23] However, the abolition of border controls has not meant an end to the policing powers of the competent authorities, nor has it prevented individual Member States from requiring individuals to hold, carry, and present identity documents.

## 1.3 The Amsterdam Treaty and the AFSJ

### (a) Communitarization of the third pillar

The inevitable overlaps created by the Maastricht Treaty between the Community pillar (the EC Treaty) and the third pillar (JHA) created considerable practical and legal difficulties, not least because the Court of Justice had no jurisdiction to hear immigration and asylum cases arising under the third pillar. As a result, the Heads of State agreed at Amsterdam to 'communitarize' parts of the third pillar,[24] transferring key areas concerning the free movement of persons (asylum, immigration, and the rules governing the crossing of external borders) from the third to the first pillar. These provisions were placed in a new Title IV of Part Three of the EC Treaty entitled 'Visas, asylum, immigration and other policies related to free movement of persons'. EC measures adopted in these areas where intended to 'establish progressively an area of freedom, security and justice'.[25] Police cooperation and judicial cooperation in criminal matters remained in the third pillar, renamed 'Provisions on police and judicial cooperation in criminal matters' (PJC). This continued division generated considerable difficulties, first for the legislature in determining whether the measure was a first or third pillar one,[26] and subsequently for the Court.[27] The Court of Justice now had jurisdiction to hear preliminary

---

[21] See, generally, J. Schutte, 'Schengen: Its meaning for the free movement of persons in Europe' (1991) 28 *CMLRev.* 549.

[22] D. O'Keeffe, 'The Schengen Convention: A suitable model for European integration?' (1991) 11 *YEL* 185.

[23] See, esp., Art. 2 'Internal borders may be crossed at any point without any checks on persons being carried out.'

[24] J. Monar, 'Justice and home affairs in the Treaty of Amsterdam: Reform at the price of fragmentation' (1998) 23 *ELRev.* 320.    [25] Art. 61 EC.

[26] This led to the adoption of what became known as the '"double text practice", whereby the main substance of a given Community policy was included in an EC regulation or a directive (first pillar), while the criminal law aspects of such a policy were separated out and included in a separate framework decision (third pillar)' (E. Sharpston, 'The area of freedom, security and justice ("AFSJ") in the EU:– The story so far and (some of) the challenges ahead', Thomas More Lecture, delivered at Lincoln's Inn, 13 Nov. 2008).

[27] See, e.g., Case C–301/06 *Ireland v European Parliament and Council (retention of data)* [2009] ECR I–593. Perhaps better known is Case C–176/03 *Commission v Council (Criminal Penalties)* [2005] ECR I–7879; Case C–440/05 *Commission v Council (Ship source pollution)* [2007] ECR I–9097. To deal with the problems raised, Art. 83(2) TFEU was subsequently introduced by the Lisbon Treaty which provides: 'If the approximation of criminal laws and regulations of the Member States proves essential to ensure the effective implementation of a Union policy in an area which has been subject to harmonisation measures, directives may establish minimum rules with regard to the definition of criminal offences and sanctions in the area concerned.' The effect of Protocol No. 21 (see below) is that the UK can opt out from measures adopted under

references concerning matters under Title IV of Part Three EC, but only from courts of last resort.[28] It also had jurisdiction to hear references on the validity and interpretation of, for example, framework decisions under the third pillar,[29] but only where Member States had specifically declared that they were prepared to accept the Court's jurisdiction.[30] Even though the Court had reduced jurisdiction, the fact that it had jurisdiction at all is significant, not least for ensuring that Community measures adopted under Title IV were compatible with fundamental rights.[31]

Given the subject matter of the disputes that did arise, the cases often needed speedy resolution. As a result, a new fast-track procedure was introduced, the *procédure préalable d'urgence* (PPU)[32] which applies to cases referred in areas covered by Title VI TEU and Title IV of Part Three of the EC Treaty[33] (now Title V, Part Three TFEU[34]).

The communitarization of the third pillar raised serious problems for three states—the UK, Ireland, and Denmark—and they successfully secured opt-outs from its provisions. These opt-outs were contained in three protocols.[35] The first permitted the UK and Ireland (as a result of its common travel area with the UK[36]) not to apply some aspects

Art. 83(2) TFEU even in fields like criminal penalties for environmental matters (e.g., Dir. 2009/123 ([2009] OJ L280/52), in which it is currently bound.

[28] Art. 68(1) EC. In addition, Art. 68(3) EC gave the Council, the Commission, and the Member States the chance to request the Court to give a ruling on a question of interpretation of Title IV itself or acts taken under it.

[29] Art. 35(1) EU. It also had jurisdiction to review the legality of framework decisions and decisions (Art. 35(6) EU).

[30] Art. 35(2)–(3) EU. For a full discussion, see S. Peers, *EU Justice and Home Affairs Law* (Oxford: OUP, 2007).

[31] See, e.g., Case C–224/02 *Pupino* [2005] ECR I–5285, where the Court was also prepared to check the compatibility of third-pillar measures with human rights. See S. Prechal, 'Direct effect, indirect effect, supremacy and the evolving constitution of the European Union' in C. Barnard (ed.), above n. 1.

[32] Art. 1 Council Dec. 2008/79/EC, Euratom [2008] OJ L24/42; Art. 23a of the Protocol on the Statute of the Court of Justice and Art. 104b of its Rules of Procedure. The first case decided under the PPU was Case C–195/08 PPU *Inga Rinau* [2008] ECR I–5271. For discussion, see C. Barnard, 'The PPU: Is it worth the candle? An early assessment' (2009) 34 *ELRev.* 281.

[33] See the reference to the PPU in the new Art. 267(4) TFEU: 'If such a question is raised in a case pending before a court or tribunal of a Member State with regard to a person in custody, the Court of Justice of the European Union shall act with the minimum of delay.'

[34] Court of Justice's Information Note on references from national courts for a preliminary ruling', (2009/C 297/01) ([2009] OJ C297/1), para. 33.

[35] Art. 69 EC said that Title IV EC was subject to three protocols added by the Treaty of Amsterdam. See generally M. Hedemann-Robinson, 'The area of freedom, security and justice with regard to the UK, Ireland and Denmark: The "opt-in opt-outs" under the Treaty of Amsterdam' in D. O'Keeffe and P. Twomey (eds.), *Legal Issues of the Amsterdam Treaty* (Oxford: Hart Publishing, 1999); J de Zwaan, 'Opting in and opting out of rules concerning free movement of persons: Problems and practical arrangements' (1998–9) 1 *CYELS* 107.

[36] If Ireland had participated in Title IV measures, the common travel area would have meant that TCNs could have entered the UK via Ireland without any restrictions. Given that about 70% of all travel from Ireland is to the UK, Ireland was not prepared to surrender its common travel area with the UK and so it also opted out of Title IV. However, in Decl. 55 by Ireland on Art. 3 of the Protocol on the position of the UK and Ireland, Ireland declared that it intended to exercise its right under Art. 3 to take part in the adoption of measures pursuant to Title IV of Part Three EC to the maximum extent compatible with the maintenance of its Common Travel Area with the UK. It added that 'Ireland recalls that its participation in the Protocol on the application of certain aspects of Article 14 of the Treaty establishing the European Community reflects its wish to maintain its Common Travel Area with the United Kingdom in order to maximise freedom of movement into and out of Ireland.'

of Article 14 EC (now Article 26 TFEU) regarding the elimination of controls at internal borders.[37] In return for this concession, the protocol permitted the other Member States to exercise border controls on people seeking to enter their territory from the UK and Ireland.[38]

The second protocol, 'The Protocol on the position of the UK and Ireland', which to a certain extent overlaps with the first, exempted the UK and Ireland from measures taken under Title IV of Part Three EC, although Article 3 of the protocol permitted the UK and Ireland to notify their desire to participate in measures taken under Title IV.[39] This opt-in had to be exercised within three months after a proposal had been presented to the Council. If, after a reasonable period of time, such a measure could not be adopted with the UK or Ireland taking part, then the Council could adopt the measure without their participation.[40] In essence, the UK has been keen to support measures taken to buttress the external frontiers of the EU while refusing to participate in measures affecting the internal borders.

The third protocol, on the position of Denmark, provided that, with the exception of rules determining the third countries whose nationals had to hold a visa when crossing the external frontiers of the Member States or measures relating to a uniform format of visas (matters which had their origin in the now repealed Article 100c EC), Title IV did not apply to Denmark. Unlike those protocols on the UK and Ireland, the Danish Protocol made no provision for Denmark to opt in to the Title IV measures.

### (b) The incorporation of the Schengen *acquis*

The Amsterdam Treaty also incorporated the Schengen *acquis*[41] into the single institutional framework of the Union.[42] Until Amsterdam, Schengen was a purely intergovernmental process from which the EU's political actors were excluded. With the incorporation of Schengen by the Amsterdam Treaty, the Schengen *acquis* became part of EC and EU law. The Council determined the legal basis for each of the provisions of the Schengen Convention and the other *acquis* in the (then) EC and EU Treaties.[43] The Schengen Protocol also provided that future measures, proposals, and initiatives building on the Schengen *acquis* were to be subject to the relevant provisions of the EC and EU Treaties.

---

[37] Protocol on the application of certain aspects of Art. 14 EC to the UK and Ireland.          [38] Art. 3.

[39] Protocol on the Position of the UK and Ireland.

[40] The UK and Ireland can also sign up to the measures after they have been adopted, but in these circumstances the conditions governing general flexibility apply (Art. 4). Ireland can also denounce the protocol altogether (Art. 8).

[41] According to the annex to the protocol (repealed by the Lisbon Treaty), the Schengen *acquis* comprises the 1985 Agreement, the 1990 Convention, the Accession Protocols and Agreements, and the Decisions and Declarations adopted by the Executive Committee established by the 1990 Implementation Convention and acts adopted by bodies on which the Executive Committee has conferred powers. A more detailed list of the *acquis* subsequently appeared in Dec. 99/435/EC ([1999] OJ L176/1). The Schengen *acquis* which has been given a legal basis appears at [2000] OJ L239/1.

[42] Protocol Integrating the Schengen *Acquis* into the Framework of the EU. See S. Peers, 'Caveat emptor? Integrating the Scehngen acquis into the European Union legal order' (1999) 2 *CYELS* 87.

[43] Council Dec. 99/436 ([1999] OJ L176/17) adopted under Art. 2(1), para. 2 of the Schengen Protocol. For the practical problems associated with the integration of the Schengen *acquis*, see P. J. Kuijper, 'Some legal problems associated with the communitarization of policy on visas, asylum and immigration under the Amsterdam Treaty and incorporation of the Schengen acquis' (2000) 37 *CMLRev.* 345. In the absence of a legal basis being allocated the measures are deemed to be based on Title VI EU.

Even after the incorporation of the Schengen *acquis* into the EC and EU Treaties, it became obvious that there was a culture clash between the imperatives driving Schengen and those underpinning the single market. As Guild notes, the EC (and now EU) approach was rights-based, with the Court of Justice playing a leading role, privileging the rights of the individual to free movement over the security interests of the state to exclude individuals on public-policy, security, or health grounds. By contrast, the Schengen process has been led by interior ministries, distrustful of the Court of Justice, which are seeking to reclaim this policy area for national discretion, and so detaches immigration issues from a rights-based approach.

The situation was made yet more complex by the position taken by UK, Ireland and Denmark. The United Kingdom, which is opposed to the abolition of border controls envisaged by Schengen, and Ireland which harmonizes its position with that of the UK, were the only EU–15 Member States not to accede to the Schengen Agreements, and so they were not bound by the Schengen *acquis*. While their continued non-participation was confirmed by Article 4 of the Schengen Protocol, Article 4 also allowed them to take part in some or all of the existing Schengen *acquis*, but only with the unanimous agreement of the other states. Both states have taken advantage of this possibility[44] and, as with measures adopted under the protocol on Article 14 (now Article 26 TFEU), they have signed up to the flanking measures of the area without internal frontiers (police and judicial cooperation in criminal matters) but not those measures linked to the disappearance of internal border controls.

The Schengen Protocol also provides that, in respect of proposals and initiatives building on the Schengen *acquis* (i.e., measures adopted after Amsterdam), the UK and Ireland have a 'reasonable period'[45] in which to notify their desire to participate. In the absence of such notification, authorization for the Council to proceed without them is automatic.[46] Decisions approving the UK and Ireland's part participation in the Schengen *acquis* require the UK and Ireland to participate in further measures building on those aspects of that *acquis*. As Peers puts it, the UK and Ireland are 'locked out' of the Schengen building measure until they have opted into the underlying rules.[47] However, it seems that once they have opted into the underlying rules, the UK and Ireland cannot be regarded as locked into any participation in subsequent measures which build on them.[48]

The Schengen Protocol also made special provision for Denmark.[49] It acceded to Schengen in 1996 and so maintained its rights and obligations under the pre-Amsterdam Schengen *acquis*, even in respect of those measures which had a legal basis in Title IV EC from which, as we saw above, Denmark had an opt-out. However, in respect of *future*

---

[44] See Council Dec. 2000/365/EC ([2000] OJ L131/47) on the request of the UK to take part in some of the provisions of the Schengen *acquis* and Council Dec. 2002/192/EC ([2002] OJ L64/20) concerning Ireland's request to take part in some of the provisions of the Schengen *acquis*.

[45] Cf. three-month period under the Title IV Protocol. These protocols are mutually exclusive: Case C–77/05 *UK* v. *Council* [2007] ECR I–11459 and Case C–137/05 *UK* v. *Council* [2007] ECR I–11593, noted J. Rijpma (2008) 45 *CMLRev.* 835.                                                                    [46] Art. 5(1).

[47] 'In a world of their own? Justice and home affairs opt-outs' (2007–8) 10 *CYELS* 383, 389, citing Case C–77/05 *UK* v. *Council* [2007] ECR I–11459 and Case C–137/05 *UK* v. *Council* [2007] ECR I–11593.

[48] See below for a discussion of the changes introduced by the revised Schengen Protocol adopted under the Lisbon Treaty.

[49] Art. 3. See below for a discussion of the changes introduced by the revised Schengen Protocol adopted under the Lisbon Treaty.

Schengen *acquis*, the protocol on the position of Denmark allowed Denmark to decide whether it would implement the decision in its national law. If it decided to do so, this would create an obligation under *international law* between Denmark and the other Member States, not EU law,[50] and so the Court of Justice would have no jurisdiction.

## (c) The AFSJ after Amsterdam

In assessing the AFSJ in the aftermath of Amsterdam, Guild et al.[51] considered that the prevailing intergovernmental logic driving policymaking strategies led to the establishment of an AFSJ characterized by five factors: first, differentiation, flexibility and fragmentation illustrated by the opt-outs from Title IV by the UK, Ireland, and Denmark, and the diverging Schengen membership;[52] secondly, the first/third pillar divide; thirdly, alternative methods of cooperation, often not aiming at formal harmonization but at coordinating Member States' policies through the exchange of information and post evaluation mechanisms based on commonly agreed principles and goals. This approach falls outside traditional EU law, relying instead on 'new governance' mechanisms, in particular the open method of coordination (OMC).[53] The fourth characteristic of the AFSJ was the 'EU law of minimums' (i.e., standards set at the lowest common denominator driven by unanimous voting in Council) which, they argued, mirrored Member State interests too closely and offered wide discretion at times of domestic transposition.

Fifthly, they argued that fundamental rights and the rule of law were being taken for granted and put into a balancing relationship with the security of the state. They argue that the human rights of TCNs were too often neglected. They also expressed concerns about the exchange of information within and outside Europe[54] for the fundamental right of data protection. Despite the Data Protection Directive 95/46,[55] they argue that the mechanisms put into place to protect the individual from the misuse of their data are 'exceedingly weak and operate badly'. Douglas-Scott goes further, expressing concern about lack of accountability and judicial control.[56] Where the Court of Justice has had the chance to rule on related issues, it too has expressed concerns about the culture of secrecy. This can be seen in *Heinrich*.[57] A passenger was stopped at the security control of Vienna Airport as his cabin baggage contained tennis racquets, considered to be prohibited articles and

---

[50] Art. 5.

[51] E. Guild, S. Carrera, and A. Faure Atger, 'Challenges and prospects for the EU's area of freedom, security and justice: Recommendations to the European Commission for the Stockholm Programme', *CEPS Working Document* No. 313/Apr. 2009.

[52] See also K. Lachmeyer, 'European police cooperation and its limits: From intelligence–led to coercive measures' in C. Barnard and O. Odudu (eds.), *The Outer Limits of European Union Law* (Oxford: Hart Publishing, 2009).

[53] See, e.g., Commission, 'Communication on a common immigration policy for Europe, actions and tools', COM(2008) 359. For further discussion of OMC, see Ch. 16.

[54] See, e.g., the passenger name records, as revealed in Joined Cases C–317/04 and C–318/04 *Parliament* v. *Council (passenger name records)* [2006] ECR I–4721, discussed by S. Douglas-Scott, 'The EU's area of freedom, security and justice: A lack of fundamental rights, mutual trust and democracy' (2008–9) 11 *CYELS* 53, 63–73.

[55] [1995] OJ L281/31. See also Council Framework Decision 2008/977/JHA ([2008] OJ L350/60) on the protection of personal data processed in the framework of police and judicial cooperation in criminal matters. Although cf. the subsequent inclusion of Art. 16 TFEU on data protection by the Lisbon Treaty.

[56] S. Douglas-Scott, 'The rule of law in the European Union: Putting the security into the area of freedom, security and justice' (2004) 29 *ELRev.* 219, 239.

[57] Case C–345/06 *Heinrich* [2009] ECR I–1659, para. 43.

were listed as such in an unpublished annex to a Union regulation. The Court was robust: an act adopted by a Union institution could not be enforced against natural or legal persons in a Member State before they had an 'opportunity to make themselves acquainted with it by its proper publication in the Official Journal'. Because the annex had not been published it had no binding force on the passenger.[58]

Some, but not all, of the criticisms levelled at the EU's execution of its AFSJ policies have been addressed by the Lisbon Treaty.

### 1.4 The Lisbon Treaty

### (a) Overview

As this brief description of the Amsterdam Treaty shows, the communitarization of parts of the third pillar, the integration of the Schengen *acquis* into the (then) EC and EU Treaties, and the desire to accommodate the diverse interests of the UK, Ireland, and Denmark, have resulted in a complex web of legal provisions which created a serious challenge to the integrity of a single market for persons. The Lisbon Treaty attempted to deal with some of these problems, essentially by 'communitarizing' third-pillar criminal matters. There is now a single Title, Title V of Part Three TFEU, with a unified set of legal bases covering border checks, asylum and immigration, judicial cooperation in civil matters, judicial cooperation in criminal matters, and police cooperation. The effect of the change is that Union action under the new AFSJ is to be conducted through a newly unified set of legal acts;[59] the specific instruments under the third pillar are to be suppressed and measures adopted in the field of PJC are no longer prohibited *per se* from having direct effect.[60] The new AFSJ also sees a significant enhancement of the powers of the European Parliament and the use of qualified majority voting in Council: the ordinary legislative procedure[61] (broadly the old co-decision procedure under Article 251) becomes the standard. The role of national parliaments is also enhanced[62] and new governance

---

[58] Para. 63. In a similar vein, in respect of the accession states, see Case C–161/06 *Skoma-Lux sro* v. *Celní ředitelství Olomouc* [2007] ECR I–10841.

[59] M. Dougan, 'The Treaty of Lisbon 2007: Winning minds, not hearts' (2008) 45 *CMLRev.* 617, 680–1.

[60] Cf. Art. 34(2) EU. However, under the Transitional provisions set out in Protocol No. 36, the legal effects of pre-existing third-pillar acts, including the exclusion of direct effect, is preserved until those acts are repealed, annulled, or amended in accordance with the new Treaties. (However, under Decl. 50 the Union institutions are encouraged to adopt, in appropriate cases and as far as possible within the five-year period referred to in Art. 10(3) of the protocol (No. 36), legal acts amending or replacing the acts referred to in Art. 10(1) of Protocol No. 36.) The Commission will also not be able to bring any enforcement proceedings against defaulting Member States in respect of pre-existing third pillar acts for a period of five years (Art. 10(1) of Protocol No. 36). Special rules apply to the UK at the expiry of the five-year period. Art. 10(4) provides that at the latest six months before the expiry of the transitional period, the UK may notify the Council that it does not accept, with respect to the old third pillar acts, the powers of the institutions referred to in para. 1 as set out in the Treaties. If the UK makes that notification, all acts referred to in para. 1 will cease to apply to it as from the date of expiry of the transitional period referred to in para. 3. Art. 10(5) allows the UK to opt into acts which have ceased to apply to it under para. 4 in accordance with the Schengen Protocol or the Protocol on the Position of the UK and Ireland, as appropriate, with full powers of the Commission and the Court of Justice applicable to those acts. As Dougan points out (below n. 65, 683), this is the first time that a Treaty has allowed a Member State the right to opt out from not just the adoption of future measures but also to repudiate its obligations under an entire corpus of pre-existing measures.

[61] Art. 289 TFEU. The procedure is laid down in Art. 294 TFEU.

[62] Art. 69 TFEU then emphasizes the specific role of national parliaments in ensuring that all measures in the field of police and judicial cooperation in criminal matters comply with the principles of subsidiarity

methodology further entrenched.[63] In addition, the Lisbon Treaty extended the jurisdiction of the Court of Justice. First, the limitation on the Court hearing references only from courts of last resort under Title IV, Part Three EC has been removed, as have the more extensive restrictions on the Court's jurisdiction under the third pillar, although the Court's jurisdiction over pre-existing third-pillar acts are subject to the pre-Lisbon restrictions for five years following the entry into force of the Lisbon Treaty.[64]

Taken together, these changes lead Dougan[65] to conclude that the Lisbon reforms mean that the Union's power to act within the AFSJ is significantly strengthened and the quality of those new powers will considerably improve democratic accountability and individual rights, albeit that the transitional arrangements, particularly in respect of the Court's jurisdiction under the old third pillar, dilute the effectiveness of some of these changes at least initially.

## (b) The protocols

The four protocols considered above in section 1.3—now numbered No. 19 on the Schengen *acquis* integrated into the framework of the EU, No. 20 on the application of certain aspects of Article 26 TFEU to the UK and Ireland, No. 21 on the position of the UK and Ireland in respect of the AFSJ, and No. 22 on the position of Denmark—have been extended to the Lisbon Treaty. While all four protocols contain technical amendments reflecting the changes introduced by the Lisbon Treaty,[66] the Schengen Protocol (No. 19), Protocol No. 21 on the position of the UK and Ireland in respect of the AFSJ and the Danish Protocol (No.22) contain more substantial amendments.

The Schengen Protocol now includes the possibility of expelling the UK and Ireland from a pre-existing measure. Where the UK or Ireland has opted into an existing Schengen measure under Article 4, and a new proposal is made to build on that act, the UK or Ireland may decide, under Article 5(2), to opt out of that proposal.[67] In these

---

and proportionality in accordance with the protocol (No.2) on subsidiarity and proportionality (under Art. 7(2) of Protocol (No.2) on the application of the principles of subsidiarity and proportionality, the threshold for national parliaments showing a 'yellow card' to a legislative proposal in the field of PJC is lowered to one-quarter).

[63] The new Art. 70 TFEU authorizes the continuance of new governance methodology, in particular OMC. It allows the Council to establish a peer review mechanism of Member States' implementation of Union policies in this area. The Council must also adopt measures to ensure administrative cooperation between the relevant departments of the Member States and between those departments and the Commission: Art. 74 TFEU (ex Art. 66 EC). See, e.g., Council Dec. 2002/463/EC adopting an action programme for administrative cooperation in the fields of external borders, visas, asylum, and immigration (ARGO programme) ([2002] OJ L161/11). Measures ensuring administrative cooperation are to be adopted on a proposal from the Commission or on the initiative of a quarter of the Member States (Art. 76 TFEU). Cf. the original Art. 34(2) TEU which allowed any *one* Member State to make a proposal in the field of police and judicial cooperation.

[64] Art. 10(1) of Protocol No. 36. Art. 276 TFEU also imposes limits on the Court of Justice's jurisdiction in respect of PJC activities. See S. Peers, 'Finally "fit for purpose"? The Treaty of Lisbon and the end of the third pillar legal order' (2008) 28 *YEL* 47.

[65] M. Dougan, 'The Treaty of Lisbon 2007: Winning minds, not hearts' (2008) 45 *CMLRev.* 617.

[66] For a full discussion, see S. Peers, 'In a world of their own? Justice and home affairs opt-outs and the Treaty of Lisbon' (2007–8) 10 *CYELS* 383.

[67] See also Decl. 44 on Art. 5 of the Schengen Protocol which says that where a Member State has made a notification under Article 5(2) of the Protocol that it does not wish to take part in a proposal or initiative, that notification may be withdrawn at any moment before the adoption of the measure building upon the Schengen *acquis*. Decl. 45 on Art. 5(2) of the Schengen Protocol says that whenever the UK or Ireland

circumstances Article 5(3) provides that any measure already opted into 'shall, as from the date of entry into force of the proposed measure, cease to apply to the extent considered necessary by the Council', albeit that the Council must retain the widest possible measure of participation of the Member State concerned without seriously affecting the practical operability of the various parts of the Schengen *acquis* and respecting their coherence. If by the end of four months the Council fails to take a decision, the matter is referred to the European Council;[68] and if the European Council cannot agree, the Commission must take appropriate action.[69]

Protocol No. 21 on the position of the UK and Ireland in respect of the AFSJ also contains some significant revisions. First, and most importantly, it extends the UK opt-out/opt-in to all the areas covered by Title V, Part Three (i.e., the whole of the AFSJ) and not just the matters that were previously covered by Title IV of Part Three EC. So the UK and Ireland will be able to opt-out of areas where they are currently bound, most notably third-pillar (PJC) matters. Secondly, a new Article 4a extends the UK and Ireland's ability to opt-out of measures proposed or adopted under Title V of Part Three TFEU amending an existing measure by which they are bound. However, as with the Schengen Protocol, if the UK or Ireland does this, the Council has the power to exclude them from the existing act. Thirdly, Article 6a provides that the UK and Ireland are not bound by the EU's data protection rules as regards police and judicial cooperation in respect of acts in which they do not participate. Fourthly, Ireland has given up its right to apply the opt-out to matters listed in Article 75 TFEU (ex Article 60)[70] concerning freezing of funds of terrorists or equivalent.[71] The UK has merely declared its intention to opt-into such acts.[72]

The Danish Protocol has also been amended.[73] As with Protocol No. 21 on the UK and Ireland, Denmark's opt-out extends to the whole area of AFSJ and not just to matters previously covered by Title IV EC. Denmark also benefits from the same exclusion in respect of data protection matters. Perhaps most significantly, a new Article 8 allows Denmark to abandon its opt-out in favour of a system where it will be bound by all provisions of the Schengen *acquis* and the follow-on measures as a matter of Union, not international, law. In respect of all other measures adopted under Title V of Part Three, the Danish

---

indicates to the Council its intention not to participate in a measure building upon a part of the Schengen *acquis* in which it participates, the Council will have a full discussion on the possible implications of the non-participation of that Member State in that measure.

[68]  Art. 5(4).

[69]  See also Decl. 47 on Art. 5(3), (4), and (5) of the Schengen Protocol which provides that the Member State concerned shall bear the direct financial consequences, if any, necessarily and unavoidably incurred as a result of the cessation of its participation in some or all of the *acquis* referred to in any decision taken by the Council pursuant to Art. 4 of the said protocol.          [70]  See further Ch.15.

[71]  Art. 9 of the protocol.

[72]  Decl. 65 by the United Kingdom of Great Britain and Northern Ireland on Art. 75 TFEU: 'The United Kingdom fully supports robust action with regard to adopting financial sanctions designed to prevent and combat terrorism and related activities. Therefore, the UK declares that it intends to exercise its right under Article 3 of the Protocol on the position of the United Kingdom and Ireland in respect of the area of freedom, security and justice to take part in the adoption of all proposals made under Art. 75 TFEU.

[73]  See also Decl. 48 concerning the protocol on the position of Denmark: 'Denmark declares that it will not use its voting right to prevent the adoption of the provisions which are not applicable to Denmark.'

position will be equivalent to that of the UK and Ireland if Denmark opts to change its legal position.[74]

Returning to the criticisms levelled at the experience of the operation of the post Amsterdam version of the AFSJ by Guild et al, it can be said that while the Lisbon Treaty has more or less overcome the problems of the first/third pillar divide, differentiation, flexibility and fragmentation caused by the opt-outs for the UK, Ireland and Denmark and the diverging Schengen membership remain firmly entrenched. The emphasis on alternative methods of cooperation, noted by Guild et al have also spilled over into the Lisbon Treaty, as the next section will show.

## 2. THE POLITICAL STRATEGY

The newly introduced Article 68 TFEU reflects the primary role of the European Council in defining 'the strategic guidelines for legislative and operational planning' within the AFSJ. This confirms the role the European Council has long played of steering the direction of the AFSJ, first at Tampere, then at The Hague, and most recently at Stockholm.

### 2.1 The Tampere Programme

As we have seen, prior to the Amsterdam Treaty, the treatment of TCNs by (the then) Community law was somewhat ad hoc.[75] Title IV of Part Three EC offered a chance for greater coherence. A special European Council was held in Tampere in 1999 which considered, among other things, the implementation of Title IV of Part Three EC. It agreed on a common EU asylum and immigration policy, based on four principles. The first, partnership with the countries of origin, was intended to address political, human rights, and development issues in countries of origin and transit.[76] The idea behind this policy was that by reducing the 'push factors', countries of origin became more attractive to their own people. At Seville, the European Council introduced the stick of including a clause in any future cooperation or association agreement on joint management of migration flows and on compulsory readmission in the event of illegal immigration. It warned that '[i]nadequate cooperation by a country could hamper the establishment of closer relations between that country and the Union'.[77] The carrot comes in the form of financial and technical assistance to those third countries willing to cooperate.[78]

---

[74] See also Decl. 26 on non-participation by a Member State in a measure based on Title V of Part Three TFEU: 'the Council will hold a full discussion on the possible implications and effects of that Member State's non-participation in the measure'. It continues that any Member State may ask the Commission to examine the situation on the basis of Art. 116 TFEU.

[75] This was partly because there was an absence of clear competence for the (then) EEC to act. See, e.g., Joined Cases 281, 283–285/85 *Germany, France, Netherlands, Denmark and the United Kingdom v. Commission* [1987] ECR 3203, para. 10 on the use of Art. 118 EEC (Art. 156 TFEU).

[76] This requires combating poverty, improving living conditions and job opportunities, preventing conflicts, and consolidating democratic states. See Commission Communication, 'Integrating migration issues in the European Union's relations with third countries', COM(2002) 703. See also European Council: 'Global approach to migration: Priority actions focusing on Africa and the Mediterranean', Brussels, 15–16 Dec. 2005 and the Commission's follow-up: COM(2006) 735.

[77] Presidency Conclusions, Seville, 21–2 Jun. 2002, paras. 33 and 35. See also Commission Communication on the integration of migration issues in the EU's relations with third countries, COM(2003) 703.

[78] COM(2003) 355.

Secondly, the Tampere European Council envisaged a common European asylum system leading to a common asylum procedure and a uniform status for those granted asylum. This is based on the full and inclusive application of the Geneva Convention.

Thirdly, in order to integrate TCNs into the host state, the Tampere European Council insisted upon the principle of fair treatment of TCNs. This allowed TCNs admitted to the host state broadly the same rights and responsibilities as EU nationals[79] but, with the exception of a 'hard core' of rights available to migrants on their arrival,[80] these rights were to be incremental and related to the length of stay provided for in their entry conditions.[81] So, an individual would receive a (renewable) temporary work permit, followed by a permanent work permit, after a number of years to be determined, with the possibility of long-term residence status after a certain period[82] and even 'civic citizenship', comprising a common set of core rights and obligations based on the Charter of Fundamental Rights 2000, after a minimum period of years.[83]

Finally, the European Council wished to see a more efficient management of migration flows. This idea was subsequently fleshed out by the Commission in a Communication on a 'Community immigration policy'[84] which argued the case for a proactive immigration policy based on 'the recognition that migratory pressures will continue and that there are benefits that orderly immigration can bring to the EU, to the migrants themselves and to their countries of origin'.[85] At the heart of this approach lies the idea of creating a legislative framework for legal immigration into the EU by TCNs, and in particular a common policy on admission for economic reasons, backed up by information campaigns in countries of origin about the possibilities for legal immigration. Two factors influenced this policy. First, the Commission considered that the EU *needed* skilled and unskilled labour[86] to help ensure the success of the Lisbon strategy (of making the EU the most competitive and dynamic knowledge-based economy in the world),[87] to help address the demographic problems caused by an ageing population and a low birth rate,[88] and to help deal with a skills shortage in key industries.[89] Secondly, under the General Agreement on Trade in Services (GATS), the EU and the Member States committed themselves to allowing TCNs to pursue economic activities providing services in the EU, without there being any 'economic needs test'.[90]

The Tampere principles are reflected in Article 79(1) TFEU which provides:[91]

The Union shall develop a common immigration policy aimed at ensuring, at all stages, the efficient management of migration flows, fair treatment of third-country nationals residing

---

[79] See also Tampere Presidency Conclusions, 15 and 16 Oct. 1999, para. 3 and Commission's Communication on a 'Community immigration policy', COM(2000) 757, 3. See also its earlier Communication, 'Immigration and asylum policies', COM(94) 23.    [80] Ibid., 17.

[81] Ibid., 15.    [82] Ibid., 18.    [83] Ibid., 19.

[84] COM(2000) 757. See also 'On an EU approach to managing economic migration' (COM(2004) 811).

[85] Ibid., 13.    [86] COM(2000) 757, 15.

[87] This was emphasized in the Commission's Communication on immigration, integration, and employment: COM(2003) 336, 9–17.

[88] Commission, 'The demographic future of Europe: From challenge to opportunity': COM(2006) 571.

[89] According to figures prepared by Eurostat, and reproduced by the Commission in its Communication above n. 89, the dependency ratio, i.e. the number of people aged 65 relative to those aged from 16–64, is set to double and reach 51% by 2050, meaning that the EU will change from having four to only two persons of working age for each citizen over 65. Eurostat estimates that 40 million people will emigrate to the EU by 2050.    [90] COM(2000) 757, 15.

[91] See also Art. 67(2) TFEU.

legally in Member States, and the prevention of, and enhanced measures to combat, illegal immigration and trafficking in human beings.

This demonstrates just how the tone of the debate has begun to change in recent years,[92] with a shift in focus towards facilitating legal admission of 'desirable' TCNs (those coming for short visits as tourists or on business and those wishing to remain for the longer term with skills to offer), while keeping out 'undesirable' TCNs (those threatening the security of the EU such as drug and human traffickers, smugglers, and other criminals, along with those falsely claiming asylum). This is what is meant by 'managed' migration—the current vogue term.[93]

## 2.2 The Hague Programme

The balance that characterized the Tampere principles[94] was tipped in favour of the security agenda by the Hague Programme adopted five years later, laying down measures to be taken from 2004–9.[95] It said:[96]

The security of the European Union and its Member States has acquired a new urgency, especially in the light of the terrorist attacks in the United States on 11 September 2001 and in Madrid on 11 March 2004. The citizens of Europe rightly expect the European Union, while guaranteeing respect for fundamental freedoms and rights, to take a more effective, joint approach to cross-border problems such as terrorism, organised crime, irregular migratory flows and smuggling of human beings as well as the prevention thereof. Notably, in the field of security, the coordination and coherence between the internal and external dimension has been growing in importance and needs to continue to be vigorously pursued.

It continues:[97] 'A key element in the near future will be the prevention and repression of terrorism... [P]reserving national security is only possible in the framework of the Union as a whole.'[98] The EU is no longer just concerned with external security but also security within the EU: 'Freedom, justice, control at the external borders, internal security and the prevention of terrorism should henceforth be considered indivisible within the Union as a whole.' But, as the subsequent documentation makes clear, security is not just about terrorism but it is also about organized crime and drugs.[99] This shift in emphasis reflects a change in perception of TCNs—they are no longer a potential benefit to the EU economy but a threat to its security.

The Hague Programme was followed up by an Action Plan put forward by the Commission[100] identifying ten specific priorities on which the Commission believed

---

[92] See COM(2000) 757, 6.

[93] Commission, 'On an EU approach to managing economic migration': COM (2004) 811.

[94] For the Commission's review of Tampere: COM(2004) 401 final.

[95] EU Council, *The Hague Programme: Strengthening freedom, security and justice in the European Union*, Council Doc. 16054/04.                                                                                      [96] p. 3.

[97] p. 4.

[98] Although cf. Art. 72 TFEU (ex Art. 64 EC): 'This Title shall not affect the exercise of the responsibilities incumbent upon Member States with regard to maintenance of law and order and the safeguarding of internal security.'

[99] COM(2005) 184, introduction. See also the EU Action Plan on Drugs: COM(2005) 45, following the European strategy on drugs 2005.

[100] COM(2005) 184. See also Commission, 'Policy plan on legal migration' COM(2005) 669; Commission, 'Implementing the Hague Programme: The way forward' COM(2006) 331; and the Commission, 'Report on implementation of the Hague Programme for 2007' COM(2008) 373.

efforts should be concentrated. These included fundamental rights and citizenship; the fight against terrorism; managed migration; and integration.[101] Close on the heels of the Hague Programme came the Global Approach to Migration in 2005 and the European Migration Policy in 2006[102] based on 'solidarity, mutual trust and shared responsibility of the European Union and its Member States'. The emphasis was now on keeping out 'undesirable' TCNs through international cooperation and dialogue with third countries, strengthening cooperation among Member States in the fight against illegal immigration, improving the management of the EU's external border and only then to develop well-managed migration policies and promote integration. However, by 2008 the Commission's *Common European Immigration Policy*, showed some signs of rectifying the imbalance. Six of its ten common principles concerned non-security issues and focused on the themes of the need for clear, transparent and fair rules, matching skills with needs, integration and transparency, trust and cooperation.

### 2.3 The Stockholm Programme

Yet the security theme is continued through to the Stockholm Programme 2010–14.[103] In its Presidency Conclusions,[104] the European Council considers:

that the priority for the coming years should be to focus on the interests and needs of the citizens and other persons for whom the EU has a responsibility. The challenge will be to ensure respect for fundamental rights and freedoms and integrity while guaranteeing security in Europe. It is of paramount importance that law enforcement measures and measures to safeguard individual rights, the rule of law and international protection rules are coherent and mutually reinforcing.

The European Council then identified six areas of priority, broadly building on the areas identified by the Commission in its 2009 Communication *An Area of Freedom, Security and Justice Serving the Citizen*:[105] promoting citizenship and fundamental rights, creating a 'Europe of law and justice', a 'Europe that protects', and developing the role of Europe in a globalized world—the external dimension. For our purposes, the two strands of most relevance to this chapter are 'Access to Europe in a globalised world' and 'A Europe of responsibility, solidarity and partnership in migration and asylum matters'. The first concerns access to Europe for persons recognized as having a legitimate interest in accessing the EU territory. This has to be made more effective and efficient. It continues that 'At the same time, the Union and its Member States have to guarantee security for its citizens. Integrated border management and visa policies should be construed to serve these goals.' In other words, it should be made easier for desirable TCNs to have access to the EU but those who are not desirable should be kept out, a point picked up in the second strand: 'in order to maintain credible and sustainable immigration and asylum systems

---

[101] Commission, 'A common agenda for integration: Framework for the integration of third country nationals in the European Union', COM(2005) 389. See also the Council's 'Common basic principles for immigrant integration policy in the EU' (Council document 14615/04). In addition, a European Fund for Integration, with €825 millions allocated for 2007–13 (Council Dec. 2007/435/E (OJ [2007] L168/18). See also the Annual Reports on Migration and Integration, e.g. COM(2007) 512.

[102] Presidency Conclusions, Brussels European Council, 14–15 Dec. 2006, paras. 21 et seq.

[103] The full programme can be found in the minutes of the General Affairs Council, 2 Dec. 2009, doc. 17024/09, <http://www.se2009.eu/polopoly_fs/1.26419!menu/standard/file/Klar_Stockholmsprogram.pdf>. See also Commission Communication, 'Delivering an area of freedom, security and justice for Europe's citizens: Action plans implementing the Stockholm programme' COM(2010) 171.

[104] 11 Dec. 2009, para. 26.     [105] COM(2009) 262. See further Ch.12.

in the EU, it is necessary to prevent, control and combat illegal migration as the EU faces an increasing pressure from illegal migration flows and particularly the Member States at its external borders, including at its Southern borders'.

This policy strand also refers to the European Pact on Immigration and Asylum, introduced by the French presidency in 2008, as a tool to realizing well-managed migration. While the pact itself offers little that is new (it talks of organizing legal migration to take account of priorities, needs and reception capacities determined by each Member State, and encouraging immigration, controlling irregular immigration by ensuring the return of irregular aliens to their country of origin, making border controls more effective, constructing a Europe of asylum and creating a comprehensive partnership with the countries of origin and transit to encourage the synergy between migration and development), the techniques are, according to some commentators, driven more by nationalism and intergovernmentalism than by European supranationalism, prioritizing the competences of the Member States over those of an EU of 27.[106] This may not be altogether surprising given the intergovernmental antecedents of much policy in this area. However, the changes introduced by the Lisbon Treaty point somewhat in the opposite direction, with greater emphasis on the use of the 'Community', now Union method, and greater democratic input through the ordinary legislative procedure. We turn now to consider the legislation that has been proposed and adopted to date.

## C.  UNION LEGISLATION ON FREE MOVEMENT, RESIDENCE, EMPLOYMENT, AND FAMILY RIGHTS FOR TCNS

### 1.  INTRODUCTION

Title IV of Part Three EC provided the legal bases necessary to achieve the Tampere objectives and set a timetable by which the relevant measures should be adopted (in most cases five years from the date when the Treaty of Amsterdam came into force).[107] Both Title IV of Part Three EC and now Title V of Part Three TFEU envisage a three-pronged approach to immigration policy with separate legal bases:

(1)  measures concerning the physical movement of persons (i.e., travel) (Article 62 EC, Article 77 TFEU)

(2)  measures on asylum (Article 63(1) and (2) EC, Article 78 TFEU)

(3)  measures on immigration and integration (Article 63(3) and (4) EC, Article 79 TFEU).

Article 80 TFEU adds that EU policies in the area of asylum and immigration, together with their implementation, are to be governed by 'the principle of solidarity and fair sharing of responsibility, including its financial implications between the Member States'. Since asylum is a specialist area we shall not consider it further in this chapter.[108] Instead,

---

[106] S. Carrera and E. Guild, 'The French presidency's European Pact on Immigration and Asylum: Intergovernmentalism vs. Europeanisation? Security vs. rights?', *CEPS Policy Brief*, Sep. 2008, 4–5.

[107] The Lisbon Treaty removed this timeframe.

[108] See generally, Commission Communication, 'Towards a common asylum procedure and a uniform status, valid throughout the Union, for persons granted asylum' (COM(2000) 755), and the report COM(2003) 152; Commission Communication, 'Towards more accessible, equitable and managed asylum

we shall concentrate on the Union's approach to physical movement of persons and measures on immigration and integration.

## 2. BORDER CONTROL: ARTICLE 77 TFEU

There are 1,636 designated points of entry to the EU and about 900 million people cross those external frontiers a year. For the Commission, 'In an open world, with growing mobility, ensuring the effective management of the Union's external borders is a major challenge.[109] Article 77(1) (ex Article 62 EC) provides that the Union is to develop a policy with a view to:

(a) ensuring the absence of any controls on persons, whatever their nationality, when crossing *internal* borders

(b) carrying out checks on persons and efficient monitoring[110] of the crossing of *external* borders

(c) the gradual introduction of an integrated management system for external borders.

Article 77(2) then provides specific powers for the European Parliament and the Council, acting by the ordinary legislative procedure,[111] to adopt measures concerning:[112]

(a) the common policy on visas and other short-stay residence permits

(b) the checks to which persons crossing external borders are subject

---

systems', COM(2003) 315; Commission Communication, 'A policy action plan on asylum: An integrated approach across the EU' (COM(2008) 360). See now, e.g., Council Reg. 343/2003 establishing the criteria and mechanisms for determining the Member State responsible for examining an asylum application lodged in one of the Member States by a third-country national ('Dublin II') ([2003] OJ L50/1) adopted under Art. 63(1)(a) EC and the implementation rules: Reg. 1560/2003 ([2003] OJ L222/3). Ireland and the UK gave notice of their wish to participate in the adoption of this reg.; Denmark did not. See also Council Dir. 2003/9/EC laying down minimum standards on the reception of asylum seekers ([2003] OJ L31/18) adopted under Art. 63(1)(b) EC: the UK gave notice of its wish to participate in the directive. The directive does not apply to Ireland and Denmark. Dir. 2004/83 ([2004] OJ L304/12) on minimum standards for the qualification and status of TCNs and stateless persons as refugees or as persons who otherwise need international protection and the content of the protection granted (as interpreted in Joined Cases C–175/08–179/08 *Abdulla* v. *Germany* [2010] ECR I–000 and Case C–465/07 *Elgafaji* v. *Staatssecretaris van Justitie* [2009] ECR I–921): the UK and Ireland are participating in this measure; Denmark is not. In addition Council Dir. 2001/55/EC on minimum standards for giving temporary protection in the event of a mass influx of displaced persons and on measures promoting a balance of efforts between Member States in receiving such persons and bearing the consequences thereof ([2001] OJ L212/12) adopted under Art. 63(2)(a) and (b) EC: the UK and Ireland are participating; Denmark is not. Dir. 2005/85 ([2005] OJ L326/13) on minimum standards on procedures in Member States for granting and withdrawing refugee status, adopted under Art. 63(1)(d) EC: the UK and Ireland are participating in this measure; Denmark is not. Note the shift in language in Art. 78(1) TFEU from minimum standards to the development of a 'common asylum policy'.

[109] COM(2009) 262, 2.      [110] This reference is new in the Lisbon Treaty.

[111] Under the original EC Treaty the procedural requirements were unanimity and consultation with the European Parliament but the EC Treaty envisaged a phasing in of QMV and co-decision. This process was completed by 1 Jan. 2005 and this change is reflected in Art. 77(2) with its reference to the ordinary legislative procedure.

[112] A new Art. 77(4) adds that Art. 77 is not to 'affect the competence of the Member States concerning the geographical demarcation of their borders in accordance with international law'.

(c)   the conditions under which nationals of third countries shall have the freedom to travel within the Union for a short period

(d)   any measure necessary for the gradual establishment of an integrated management system for external borders[113]

(e)   the absence of any controls on persons, whatever their nationality, when crossing internal borders.

Finally, Article 77(3) introduces new default powers to adopt measures under the special legislative procedure (unanimity in council, consultation of the European Parliament) concerning passports, ID cards, residence permits, or any other such document to facilitate free movement of citizens.

A lot of the groundwork on border controls had already been done by the Schengen Agreement and Convention[114]. Article 2(1) of the Schengen Convention, subsequently based on Article 62(1) EC, provides that 'Internal borders may be crossed at any point without any checks on persons being carried out' but this is subject to a public-policy/national-security derogation.[115] Since Article 2(1) necessitated the harmonization of visa policy in respect of TCNs requiring visas, this was contained in Article 10 of the Schengen Convention, which provided for the introduction of a uniform visa—valid for the entire territory—for visits not exceeding three months. Visas issued for visits of more than three months are not subject to any common Schengen rules:[116] they are largely national visas issued under national law.[117] The Convention also lays down common rules making carriers responsible for ensuring that TCNs possess the correct travel documents.[118]

In order to compensate for the loss of internal border controls, the Convention provides for a range of additional measures at the external frontiers.[119] For example, Articles 3–8 introduce strict uniform rules about crossing external frontiers which are supplemented by detailed rules issued by the Executive Committee (now replaced by the Council), particularly a common manual on border checks,[120] now the borders code (see below), and common consular instructions (CCI),[121] now replaced by the visa code, on the procedures and conditions for issuing visas. In particular, Article 5 provides that for visits not exceeding three months, entry into Schengen territory will be granted to aliens provided:

•  they are in possession of a valid travel document and visa if required

•  they have documents substantiating the purpose of the visit and demonstrating sufficient means of support

•  they have not been reported in the Schengen Information System (SIS)[122] as a 'person not to be permitted entry'

---

[113]   This reference is new in the Lisbon Treaty.

[114]   [2000] OJ L239. The Implementing Agreement came into force in Sep. 1993 but was not applied for the purposes of abolishing border checks until 26 Mar. 1995.          [115]   Art. 2(2) of the Schengen Convention.

[116]   Art. 18.

[117]   Cf. Family Reunification Dir. 2003/86 considered below, and proposals for more harmonization: COM(2009) 90–1.          [118]   Art. 26.

[119]   D. O'Keeffe, 'The emergence of a European immigration policy' (1995) 29 *ELRev.* 20, 34.

[120]   Since declassification, the Common Manual appears at [2002] OJ C313/97 with all but three of its annexes.          [121]   [2000] OJ L239/317.

[122]   The SIS is a database of people who may pose a threat to security and of objects such as stolen cars and artworks. The legal basis for the SIS is found in Arts. 92–119. Although the UK (Dec. 2000/365/EC ([2000]

- they are not considered to be a threat to public policy or national security or the international relations of any contracting state.

There is a presumption that entry across one Schengen external border constitutes admission to the whole territory and an assumption that a short-stay visa issued by any participating state will be recognized for entry to the common territory.[123]

The Schengen system is based on the principle of mutual recognition of national decisions rather than harmonization. This has posed a number of problems. For example, Article 96 of the Schengen Implementing Agreement provides that individuals may be entered into the SIS database by a Member State if the state deems the individual to be 'a threat to public order or national security and safety'.[124] Since these matters are assessed according to national criteria,[125] different Member States have different conceptions of what constitutes risk. And as a result of the principle of mutual recognition, an individual may be excluded by all states even where he or she satisfies the exclusion criteria of only one.[126] Therefore, a Greenpeace activist and a New Zealand national was excluded from the Netherlands on the basis of an SIS entry against her by France even though many in the Netherlands did not consider her to pose such a risk.[127]

Since the incorporation of the Schengen *acquis* into the EC and EU Treaties by the Treaty of Amsterdam, the EU has adopted legislation concerning:

- the third countries whose nationals must be in possession of visas when crossing the external borders (and those who are exempt) for an intended stay in that Member State or in several Member States of no more than three months[128]

- a uniform format for visas[129]

- a legislative framework for the implementation and operation of the Visa Information System (VIS), facilitating checks at the external border crossing points and the exchange of visa data between Member States.[130]

---

L131/43) and Ireland (Dec. 2002/192 ([2002] OJ L64/20) participate in principle in the database, their participation has not yet been put into effect. See also EP and Council Reg. 1987/2006 ([2006] OJ L381/4) on the establishment, operation, and use of the second generation SIS. Council Reg. (EC) No. 1104/2008 ([2008] OJ L299/1) on the migration from the SIS I+ to the second generation Schengen Information System (SIS II). SIS II is not yet operational.

[123]  Guild, above n. 15, 305 and Arts. 19–20. This also applies to an alien holding a residence permit issued by one of the Member States. No detailed criteria are provided for the grant or renewal of a residence permit (Art. 21); cf. Art. 25 on a resident permit for a person on whom an alert has been issued.

[124]  See also Arts. 5–6 of the Schengen Convention. Cf. Case C–503/03 *Commission v. Spain (SIS)* [2006] ECR I–1097 considered in Ch. 13.                          [125]  See COM(2002) 233, 9–10.

[126]  Guild, above n. 15, 309. Although cf. Art. 16 of the Convention.        [127]  Ibid.

[128]  Council Reg. 539/2001 ([2001] OJ L81/1) (as amended). This does not apply to the UK and Ireland.

[129]  Council Reg. 334/2002 ([2002] OJ L53/7) based on Art. 62(2)(b)(iii) EC. This applies to the UK but not Ireland. The original Reg. 1683/95 ([1995] OJ L164/1) was adopted on the basis of Art. 100c EEC (now repealed). See also Council Reg. 333/2002 ([2002] OJ L53/4), adopted under 62(2)(b)(iii) EC on a uniform format for affixing the visa issued by Member States to persons holding travel documents not recognized by the Member State drawing up the form. This applies to the UK but not Ireland.

[130]  Reg. (EC) No. 767/2008 concerning the Visa Information System (VIS) ([2008] OJ L218/60) adopted under Art. 62(2)(b)(ii) EC. Denmark, the UK, and Ireland are not taking part. The VIS Reg. is not yet applied.

However, the two most important measures adopted are:

- a Community code on visas,[131] establishing the procedures and conditions for issuing visas for transit through or intended stays in the territory of the Member States for periods not exceeding three months in any six
- the Schengen Borders Code,[132] laying down standards and procedures states have to follow in controlling the movement of persons across internal and external EU borders. This measure allows TCNs to stay in the Member State for up to three months.

These measures all constitute a 'follow-on' from the Schengen *acquis* in accordance with the Schengen Protocol.

Secondary movement for short periods (the freedom for TCNs to travel between Member States) is also covered. According to Article 19 of the Schengen Convention, aliens who hold uniform visas and who have legally entered the territory of a Contracting Party may move freely within the territories of all the Contracting Parties during the period of validity of their visas. Article 20 provides that aliens not subject to a visa requirement may move freely within the territories of the Contracting Parties for a maximum period of three months during the six months following the date of first entry. Likewise, aliens with a valid residence permit can travel to another Member State for up to three months under Article 21. Recognizing the importance of these secondary mobility rights, the Commission had proposed a directive relating to the conditions in which TCNs would have had the freedom to travel in the territory of the Member States for periods not exceeding three months and determining the conditions of entry and movement for periods not exceeding six months.[133] However, this proposal was withdrawn.[134]

Finally, FRONTEX, the agency for coordinating border control cooperation between Member States, has been instrumental in the EU's response to securing its external borders.[135] While the responsibility for the control and surveillance of external borders lies with the Member States, the agency facilitates the application of existing and future Union measures relating to the management of external borders by ensuring the coordination of Member States' action in the implementation of those measures.[136]

---

[131] Reg. (EC) No. 810/2009 establishing a Community code on visas (the Visa Code) [2009] OJ L243/1 adopted under Art. 62(2)(a) and (b)(ii) EC. The UK, Ireland, and Denmark are not taking part.

[132] Reg. (EC) No. 562/2006 establishing a Community Code on the rules governing the movement of persons across borders ([2006] OJ L105/1), adopted under Art. 62(1) and (2)(a) EC. Denmark, the UK and Ireland are not taking part. This regulation was interpreted for the first time in Joined Case C–261/08 and 348/08 *Zurita Garcia v. Delegado del Gobierno en la Región de Murcia* [2009] ECR I–000 (a request for this case to be heard under the PPU was rejected). [133] COM(2001) 388.

[134] COM(2005) 462.

[135] Reg. (EC) No. 2007/2004 ([2004] OJ L349/1) establishing a European Agency for the Management of Operational Cooperation at the External Borders of the Member States of the EU, based on Arts. 62(2)(a) and 66 EC. The UK, Ireland, and Denmark are not taking part. See Case C–77/05 *UK v. Council* [2007] ECR I–11459 on the UK's unsuccessful attempt to opt-in (considered above). On the operation of FRONTEX, see Commission, 'Report on the evaluation and future development of the FRONTEX Agency': COM(2008) 67. See also Commission, 'Examining the creation of a European border surveillance system (EUROSUR)', COM(2008) 68; and Commission 'Preparing the next steps in border management in the EU', COM(2008) 69. [136] 4th recital.

## 3. MEASURES ON IMMIGRATION AND INTEGRATION: ARTICLE 79 TFEU

### 3.1 Legal Immigration

#### (a) Introduction

As the Tampere Council made clear, facilitating legal immigration is now a central tenet of current EU policy. The Amsterdam Treaty gave the EU the powers to achieve this. Under Article 63 EC the Council could act in the prescribed areas namely, under Article 63(3)(a) EC (now Article 79(2)(a) TFEU), immigration policy in the areas of the conditions of entry and residence, and standards on the issue of long-term visas and residence permits, including those for the purpose of family reunion;[137] and, under Article 63(4) EC (now Article 79(2)(b) TFEU), measures defining the rights of TCNs residing legally in a Member State, including the conditions under which legally resident TCNs could move and reside in other Member States.[138] While most of the provisions in Article 63 were subject to a requirement that the Council had to act within five years following the entry into force of the Amsterdam Treaty, this was not the case with the measures listed in Article 63(3)(a) and (4) EC. As a result, only a limited number of measures have actually been adopted so far: under Article 63(3)(a) regulations have been issued on long-term visas[139] and residence permits,[140] together with an important directive on family reunification (considered below);[141] under Article 63(4) EC, Regulation 1408/71 on social security (Regulation 883/04 from 1 March 2010) was extended to TCNs;[142] and under Article 63(3)(a) and (4) EC, the Long-term Residents Directive (also considered below) and the sectoral specific directives (students, researchers and highly qualified workers), all significant measures, were adopted.

The Lisbon Treaty introduced a further change: all measures taken in the areas listed in Article 79(2) are subject to the ordinary legislative procedure.[143] Finally, the new Article 79(4) allows the European Parliament and Council, again acting under the ordinary legislative procedure, to establish measures to provide incentives and support for the action of Member States with a view to promoting the integration of TCNs residing legally in their territories. Harmonization is expressly excluded under this provision.

---

[137] Art. 63(3)(a) EC.     [138] Art. 63(4) EC. There is no Schengen *acquis* under Art. 63(4) EC.

[139] Council Reg. 1091/2001 on giving rights to those TCNs wishing to move with a long-stay visa (but without a residence permit) ([2001] OJ L150/4) based on Arts. 62(2)(b)(ii) and 63(3)(a) EC. This constitutes a development of the Schengen *acquis* and does not apply to the UK or Ireland.

[140] Council Reg. 1030/2002 laying down a uniform format for residence permits for TCNs ([2002] OJ L157/1). This constitutes a development of the Schengen *acquis*. The UK and Ireland are participants.

[141] Council Dir. 2003/86/EC ([2003] OJ L251/12). The UK, Ireland, and Denmark are not participating in this directive.

[142] Council Reg. 859/2003 extending Reg. 1408/71 on social security to TCNs ([2003] OJ L124/1) based on Art. 63(4) EC. The UK and Ireland gave notice of their desire to be bound by the regulation; Denmark did not. Declaration 14 TFEU says that the interests of a Member State should also be taken into account where a proposal under Art. 79(2) TFEU would affect fundamental aspects of its social security scheme.

[143] Under the original EC Treaty the procedural requirements were unanimity and consultation with the European Parliament but the EC Treaty envisaged a phasing in of QMV and co-decision. This process was completed by 1 Jan. 2005 in respect of illegal immigration and residence. However, adoption of measures on legal migration required unanimity and simple consultation with the European Parliament after this date.

## (b) Family reunification

For the past twenty years, family reunification has been one of the main sources of immigration to the EU.[144] The Family Reunification Directive 2003/86[145] was the first of two measures put forward by the Commission aimed at integrating TCNs into the community of the host state and ensuring fair treatment of TCNs. The directive provides that a TCN ('the sponsor')[146] residing lawfully in the territory of a Member State, holding a residence permit issued by a Member State valid for a year or more, with reasonable prospects of obtaining the right of permanent residence, can apply for family reunification[147] (usually while the TCN family members are outside the territory).[148] As with Article 3(1) of the Citizens' Rights Directive (CRD) 2004/38, the Family Reunification Directive makes a distinction between those family members who must be admitted (spouse and minor children[149]) and those whom the Member State has a discretion whether to admit (first-degree relatives in the direct ascending line, where they are dependent on the TCN or his or her spouse and do not enjoy proper family support in the country of origin, adult unmarried children where they cannot support themselves, and an unmarried partner (in a duly attested long-term relationship or registered partnership).[150] The list of family members entitled to join the TCN is shorter than in the case of migrant workers under the CRD. The right to reunification is also dependent on evidence of the existence of 'normal' accommodation for a comparable family in the same region, sickness insurance for the TCN and the family members, and stable and regular resources which are higher than or equal to the level of resources which are sufficient to maintain the sponsor and the family members.[151]

If these conditions are not satisfied then the family may not be reunified with the paradoxical result that a so-called 'Family Reunification' Directive actually has the opposite effect.[152] Yet, in the Parliament's challenge to the validity of the directive in *EP v EU Council (Family Reunification Directive)*,[153] the Court upheld the validity of the directive, approving the margin of discretion given to the Member States. The European Parliament had argued that the directive's provisions enabling Member States to restrict family reunification (for example, where a child is aged over 12 years and arrives independently

---

[144] COM(2008) 610, 3.

[145] [2003] OJ L251/12 adopted under Art. 63(3)(a) EC. The UK, Ireland, and Denmark are not taking part in this measure. See also the Commission's report on the application of the directive: COM(2008) 610.

[146] The directive therefore does not apply to non-migrant nationals wanting to be joined by TCN family members (e.g., a German living in Germany wanting to be joined by his Chinese wife). This situation is covered by national law.

[147] Art. 1. Under Art. 8 Member States may require the sponsor to have stayed lawfully in their territory for a period not exceeding two years. This provision was unsuccessfully challenged in Case C–540/03 *EP v. Council (Family Reunification Directive)* [2006] ECR I–5769.          [148] Art. 5(3).

[149] Art. 4(1), 2nd para., contains a derogation for a child over 12 who arrives independently from the rest of his/her family.          [150] Art. 4(2).

[151] Art. 7(1)(c). In Case C–578/08 *Chakroun* [2010] ECR I-000, the Court ruled that it was contrary to the Dir., for the Member State to adopt rules resulting in family reunification being refused to a sponsor who has proved that he has stable and regular resources sufficient to maintain himself and his family but who, given the level of his resources, will nevertheless be entitled to claim special assistance to meet exceptional, individually determined, essential living costs, tax refunds granted by local authorities on the basis of his income or income support measures in the context of local authority minimum income policies.

[152] For a detailed discussion, see S. Peers, 'Family reunion and Community law' in N. Walker (ed.), *Europe's Area of Freedom, Security and Justice* (Oxford: OUP, 2004).

[153] Case C–540/03 [2006] ECR I–5769.

from the rest of his/her family, the Member State may, before authorizing entry and residence, verify whether he or she meets an integration condition provided for by its existing legislation on the date of implementation of the directive) were contrary to fundamental rights, in particular the right to respect for family life under Article 8 ECHR and the right to non-discrimination under the EU Charter. The Court dismissed the action but did stress that fundamental human rights are binding on Member States when they implement Union rules and that they had to apply the directive's rules in a manner consistent with the requirements governing human rights protection, especially regarding family life and the principle of protecting the best interests of the child.[154]

In order to ensure the integration of the family members the directive allows Member States to require the TCN family members to comply with integration measures, such as attending language courses.[155] It also provides for family members to enjoy access to employment and self-employment,[156] education, and vocational training,[157] but not social security or social assistance. After five years the spouse and children who have reached majority have the right to an autonomous residence permit independent of that of the sponsor.[158]

### (c) Rights of long-term residents

The Long-term Residents Directive 2003/109[159] was the second measure proposed by the Commission aimed at integrating TCNs into the community of the host state and ensuring their fair treatment.[160] The aim of this directive is to establish a common status of long-term resident for those TCNs who have resided 'legally and continuously' for five years in the territory of the Member State concerned.[161] A long-term residence permit, valid for at least five years, will be granted where the TCN has adequate resources and sickness insurance.[162] It is automatically renewable on expiry.[163] Member States can also require TCNs to comply with (unspecified) 'integration conditions',[164] before becoming long-term residents, tests which are usually reserved to granting an individual citizenship of a state, not merely long-term residence status.

Long-term residents enjoy not only a secure residence but also equal treatment with nationals as regards a number of matters, including access to employment (but not in

---

[154] Paras. 104–5.          [155] Art. 7(2).

[156] Art. 14(2) allows Member States to delay the exercise of employment/self-employment rights for up to 12 months.                                                                                       [157] Art. 14(1).

[158] Art. 15(1).

[159] [2003] L16/44, adopted under Art. 63(3)(a) and (4) EC. The directive does not apply to the UK, Ireland, and Denmark.                                                                        [160] COM (2001) 127.

[161] There is a long list of lawful residence in Art. 3(2) which will not entitle the TCN to long-term residence status: e.g., students, refugees, au-pairs.

[162] Cf. the CRD 2004/38 which does not impose the same obligations on EU citizens who have permanent residence.

[163] Art. 9 makes provision for the loss of long-term resident status including in the case of fraudulent acquisition of the status or absence from the territory for more than 12 consecutive months.

[164] Art. 5(2). See the 4th recital: 'The integration of third-country nationals who are long term resident in the Member States is a key element in promoting economic and social cohesion, a fundamental objective of the [Union] stated in the [Treaties].' Yet, K. Groenendijk suggests ('The Long Term Residents Directive, denizenship and integration' in A. Baldaccini, E. Guild, and H. Toner (eds.), *Whose Freedom, Security and Justice? EU immigration and asylum law and policy* (Oxford: Hart Publishing, 2007), 448) that some Member States have taken advantage of this possibility to create a new barrier to acquiring secure status for TCNs.

respect of activities which entail even occasional involvement in the exercise of public authority or activities that are reserved to nationals under laws in force on 25 November 2003), education and training (including study grants),[165] recognition of diplomas, social protection and social assistance (including social security),[166] and access to goods and services. The individual can be expelled only on the grounds of personal conduct but not, apparently, lack of resources.[167] In addition, the long-term resident 'with reasonable prospects of obtaining the right of permanent residence' will also enjoy the right to family reunion under Directive 2003/86.[168] Both the Family Reunification Directive and the directive on long-term residents are subject to derogations on the grounds of public policy, security, and health.[169]

Long-term residents with a long-term resident permit (and their families) will also enjoy the rights of free movement to other Member States (i.e. secondary mobility). The directive provides that long-term residents (and their families) can *reside* in (but makes no provision on entry into[170]) the territory of another Member State for more than three months[171] if they are exercising an economic activity as an employed or self-employed person or studying there and have adequate resources and sickness insurance, or simply have adequate resources and sickness insurance.[172] This directive demonstrates the increasing parallelism between the rights of legally resident TCNs and those of nationals of the Member States who are citizens of the Union.[173] The logical conclusion of this process of approximating the position of long-term legally resident TCNs to that of Member State nationals is the opportunity to obtain the nationality of the Member State in which they reside. This was endorsed by the European Council[174] and the Commission.[175]

### (d) The 'first admissions' directives

The two directives considered so far—on Family Reunification and Long-term Residents—focused on the integration of TCNs who had already been admitted to a Member State under *national* law. The Commission's other proposals have been concerned with managing legal migration flows and in particular giving certain groups a right of entry—under *Union* law—to the Member States. The first proposal, a directive on the conditions of entry and residence of TCNs for the purpose of paid employment and self-employed economic activities,[176] was seen as the 'cornerstone of immigration policy' and central to addressing

---

[165] Subject to limits in Art. 11(3).   [166] Although this can be limited: Art. 11(4).   [167] Art. 6.
[168] Art. 3(1).

[169] The 14th preambular para. of Dir. 2003/86 provides that the notion of public policy and public security covers cases in which a TCN belongs to an association which supports terrorism, supports such an association, or has extremist aspirations.

[170] S. Bolaert-Souminen, 'Non-EU nationals and Council Directive 2003/109/EC on the status of third country nationals who are long-term residents: Five paces forward and possibly three paces back' (2005) 42 *CMLRev.* 1011, 1030.

[171] This goes beyond the rights already provided in the Schengen *acquis* which merely gives rights to move for up to three months. See further S. Peers, 'Implementing equality? The directive on long term resident third country nationals' (2004) 29 *ELRev.* 437

[172] For criticism of these provisions, see A. Kocharov, 'What intra-Community mobility for third country nationals' (2008) 33 *ELRev.* 913, 919.   [173] COM(2001) 74, para. 1.7.

[174] However, access to nationality is a matter reserved solely for national powers: COM(2001) 127, para. 5.5.   [175] COM(2003) 323, 22.

[176] COM(2001) 386.

the 'shortage of skilled labour in certain sectors of the labour market'.[177] It provided for the grant of a renewable 'residence permit-worker' to a TCN, subject to certain formalities, valid for three years, where a job vacancy could not be filled by an EU citizen or other TCNs already legally resident in the EU (the 'economic needs test' or 'Union preference' test). Such a permit would have allowed the TCN to enter into, and reside in, the territory of the issuing state, exercise the activities authorized by the permit, and enjoy equal treatment with nationals in a number of areas, including working conditions, recognition of qualifications, social security including health care, and access to goods and services.

Given that this proposal was merely a 'first step' in achieving a Union policy, it did not affect Member States' responsibility for deciding whether to admit economic migrants, taking into account the needs of their labour markets and their overall capacity to integrate them (a point now enshrined in Article 79(5) TFEU[178]). Nevertheless, despite the professed importance of this directive, it could not be agreed upon and the proposal was withdrawn.[179]

The Commission therefore focused instead on sectoral specific measures as part of its approach to managing legal economic migration.[180] This led to the adoption of Directive 2004/114, on the conditions of entry and residence for TCNs for the purpose of studies, pupil exchange, vocational training, or voluntary service.[181] This measure is less market-oriented than the unsuccessful proposed directive on the conditions of entry and residence of TCNs for the purpose of paid employment and self-employment because the stay of migrants covered by Directive 2004/114 is temporary and viewed as a form of 'mutual enrichment for the migrants who benefit directly from it, both for their country of origin and for the host country, while helping mutual familiarity between cultures'.[182] Despite these worthy words, the directive does have a labour-market dimension since, as the Commission notes, many Member States provide certain TCNs with the opportunity to remain after their training 'so as to remedy shortages of skilled manpower'.[183] This directive requires those covered to have adequate resources and medical insurance. Students and unremunerated trainees can also have limited access to the employment market. The directive also provides for derogations on public-policy, security, and health grounds.

Directive 2004/114 was followed by Directive 2005/71 on a specific procedure for admitting third country nationals for the purposes of scientific research.[184] TCN researchers working with an approved research organization in the Member States are to be given a residence permit for a period of at least a year provided they have the relevant documentation and can show sufficient resources and medical insurance. Their family members can accompany them. The directive does allow the researchers to teach for a certain number

---

[177] Preambular paras. (3) and (6).

[178] 'This Article shall not affect the right of the Member States to determine volumes of admission of third-country nationals coming from third countries to their territory in order to seek work, whether employed or self-employed.'        [179] COM(2005) 462.

[180] See, e.g., the Commission's Green Paper COM(2004) 811.

[181] Council Dir. 2004/114/EC ([2004] OJ L375/12) adopted on the basis of Art. 63(3)(a) and (4) EC. The UK, Ireland, and Denmark are not taking part in the directive.        [182] COM(2002) 548, 2.

[183] Ibid., 3.

[184] [2005] OJ L289/15 adopted under Art. 63(3)(a) and (4) EC. Ireland has notified its wish to participate in this measure; the UK and Denmark are not participating.

of hours and to enjoy equal treatment with Member State nationals in respect of terms and conditions of employment, dismissal, and social security.

The directive also gives TCNs the right to carry out part of their research in another Member State. By allowing secondary mobility, these first admissions directives mark a new stage in the evolution of policy in respect of TCNs. The rationale for this is competition rather than principle: the EU was losing out to the US in attracting the brightest and the best from third countries. Secondary mobility rights are seen as a pull factor to make the EU more attractive as a destination.[185]

The final and perhaps most important of the first admissions directive is Directive 2009/50[186] on highly qualified workers (the so-called 'blue-card' directive). A TCN with a job offer for 'highly qualified' work (i.e., work requiring higher education qualifications or, where permitted by national law, five years' equivalent professional experience) in an EU Member State, who has sickness insurance and is not considered a threat to public policy, security or health, must be issued with an EU blue card.[187] Member States do not, however, need to issue a blue card where, for example, the vacancy could be filled by a member of the national or Union workforce, where the Member State deems the volume of admission of TCNs is too high, or where the job is in a sector suffering form a lack of qualified workers in the country of origin (e.g., healthcare).[188] Once in possession of a blue card, the TCNs must do the work they came for during the first two years; after that, Member States 'may grant' the persons concerned equal treatment with nationals as regards access to highly qualified employment.[189] Blue-card workers also enjoy equality in respect of other matters including working conditions, freedom of association, social security, and goods and services.[190] Directive 2003/86 also gives rights to the family members of the TCN blue-card holder. Finally, the directive allows for secondary mobility. It prescribes the right of residence (but not entry) in the second Member State for the TCN blue-card holder and their family members[191] after 18 months of legal residence in the first Member State in order to undertake highly qualified employment.

Complementing these three sectoral directives is a proposal for a Council directive on a single application procedure for a permit for TCNs to reside and work in the territory of a Member State and on a common set of rights for TCNs legally residing in a Member State.[192] There are thus two limbs to the proposal. The first, concerns those seeking to come to the EU to work. The proposal envisages a single application procedure, resulting in a single permit to work and stay. No additional permits (e.g., work permits) can then be required. The second limb of the proposal concerns those who are already legally residing in an EU Member State. Those legally working but not yet holding long-term resident status are to enjoy equal treatment in respect of employment related matters.

---

[185] S. Iglesias Sánchez, 'Free movement of third country nationals in the European Union? Main features, deficiencies and challenges of the new mobility rights in the area of freedom, security and justice' (2009) 15 *ELJ* 791, 799; A. Kocharov, 'What intra-Community mobility for third-country workers?' (2008) 33 *ELRev* 913, 915 who cites figures that the US attracts 55% of all skilled migrants worldwide, the EU attracts only 1/11th of that number.

[186] [2009] OJ L155/17 adopted under Art. 63(3)(a) and (4) EC. The UK, Ireland, and Denmark are not taking part.  [187] Arts. 5 and 7.

[188] Arts. 6 and 8.   [189] Art. 12.   [190] Art. 15.   [191] Arts. 18–19.

[192] COM(2007) 638.

### 3.2 Illegal Immigration, Residence, and Repatriation

Europol estimates that there are 500,000 illegal—or, using the more neutral term, irregular—immigrants entering the EU each year, many employed as undeclared workers.[193] Article 63(3)(b) EC (now Article 79(2)(c) TFEU) required the Council to take measures within five years of the coming into force of the Amsterdam Treaty to deal with illegal immigration and illegal residence, including repatriation of illegal residents. The Commission began by issuing a Communication on a common policy on illegal immigration[194] followed up by an Action Plan[195] which focused on keeping illegal immigrants out of the EU, particularly through the integrated management of external borders.[196] This has been complemented by a Union Return Policy on Illegal Residents[197] which was also followed up by an Action Plan.[198] The Commission recognizes the sensitive nature of the issue of forced return but stresses that it was essential for the credibility of any policy for fighting illegal immigration. It did, however, note that it had to fit 'smoothly into a genuine management of migration issues, requiring crystal clear consolidation of legal immigration channels'.[199]

In practical terms these policy statements led to the adoption of Directive 2001/40[200] on the mutual recognition of decisions on the expulsion of TCNs. The Schengen states have also agreed Directive 2001/51 on harmonizing financial penalties imposed on carriers transporting into Member States TCNs lacking the documents necessary for admission.[201] In addition, the European Parliament and Council adopted Directive 2008/115/EC[202] on common standards and procedures in Member States for returning illegally staying third-country nationals. This lays down 'clear, transparent and

---

[193] COM(2000) 757, 13. In COM(2009) 262 the Commission estimates that there about 8 million illegal immigrants.                                                                         [194] COM(2001) 672.

[195] 2002/C 142/23. Commission, 'Policy priorities in the fight against illegal immigration of third country nationals': COM(2006) 402.

[196] See, e.g., Commission, 'Reinforcing the management of the European Union's southern maritime borders' (COM(2006) 733) and on 'Strengthening the European neighbourhood policy', COM(2006) 726.

[197] COM(2002) 564 following on from the Green Paper COM(2002) 175.

[198] For a review of these measures see, e.g., the Commission's Communication on the development of a common policy on illegal immigration, smuggling, and trafficking of human beings, external borders, and the return of illegal immigrants, COM(2003) 323. There were further reviews in 2006 and 2009.

[199] COM(2002) 564, 4.

[200] [2001] OJ L149/34 adopted under Art. 63(3) EC. This is part of the Schengen *acquis*. The UK, but not Denmark, has agreed to participate in this measure.

[201] [2001] OJ L187/45, adopted under Art. 63(3)(b) EC. This is part of the Schengen *acquis*. The UK is participating in this directive but Ireland and Denmark are not. See also Council Dir. 2003/110/EC on assistance in cases of transit for the purposes of removal by air ([2003] OJ L 321/26) adopted under Art. 63(3)(b) EC as part of the Schengen *acquis*. The UK, Ireland, and Denmark are not participating. In addition, two further measures have been adopted, again to be applied by the Schengen states, on strengthening the penal framework to prevent the facilitation of unauthorized entry and residence for TCNs (Council Framework Dec. 2002/946/JHA [2002] OJ L328/1 based on Arts. 29, 31(e), and 34(2)(b) TEU—the UK and Ireland are taking part in this Framework Dec.) and defining the facilitation of unauthorized entry, transit, and residence (Council Dir. 2002/90/EC ([2002] OJ L328/17 based on Arts. 61 and 63(3)(b) EC). The UK and Ireland are taking part in this measure, Denmark is not.

[202] [2008] OJ L348/98, adopted under Art. 63(3)(b) EC and builds on the Schengen *acquis*. Denmark, the UK, and Ireland are not taking part in the adoption of this directive. This directive was interpreted by the Grand Chamber in Case C–357/09 PPU *Said Shamilovich Kazoev* [2009] ECR I–000.

fair rules'[203] for an effective return policy as a 'necessary element' of a well managed migration policy. The directive requires Member States to issue a return decision—usually accompanied by an entry ban—to any TCN staying illegally in their territory, subject to certain exceptions. The Member States must provide an appropriate period for voluntary departure, unless there is a risk of absconding or similar, followed up by enforced removal, with coercive measures, including detention, as a last resort. The directive lays down a number of procedural safeguards together with the requirement of an effective remedy.[204]

Article 79(3) TFEU gives the Union the power to conclude agreements with third countries for the readmission of TCNs to their country of origin where those TCNs do not, or no longer, fulfil the conditions for entry, presence or residence in the territory of one of the Member States. This is a new provision but reflect existing practice: readmission agreements have already been negotiated under the (then) Community's implied powers.

There is one further recent measure of considerable practical importance: Directive 2009/52/EC[205] which provides for minimum standards on sanctions against employers of illegally staying TCNs. This measure is seen as particularly important since the possibility of finding work is a pull factor for illegal immigration. Article 3(1) prohibits the employment of illegally staying TCNs. Non-compliance is subject to 'effective, proportionate and dissuasive sanctions against the employer'.[206] It is also to be a criminal offence when committed intentionally in certain circumstances.[207] To that end the directive obliges employers to require TCNs to hold a valid residence permit or authorization for their stay, to hold a copy of that document for inspection by the authorities and to notify the authorities of the employment of TCNs.

Finally, the Member States agreed a Framework Decision 2002/629/JHA under the third pillar on combating trafficking in human beings.[208] This is complemented by a directive designed to encourage the victims of people smugglers to come forward and cooperate with the authorities by giving information in return for a short-term residence permit.[209] As the Commission noted,[210] such steps were necessitated by tragic incidents, such as the one in Dover in June 2000 in which 58 Chinese nationals, trying to enter the UK illegally, died while left in a lorry exposed to the full sun with its refrigeration systems turned off. Various other measures taken under the third pillar also focus the efforts of the Member States and Europol on detecting and dismantling the criminal networks involved.[211] Competence for 'combating trafficking in persons, in particular women and children' has now been communitarized by the Lisbon Treaty and is found in Article 79(2)(d)[212] and subject to the ordinary legislative procedure.

---

[203] 4th recital.

[204] See also Dir. 2002/90 defining the facilitation of unauthorized entry, transit, and residence ([2002] OJ L328/17). The UK and Ireland are taking part, Denmark is not.

[205] [2009] OJ L168/24, proposed under Art. 63(3)(b) EC. The UK, Ireland, and Denmark are not taking part in this directive.                    [206] Art. 5(1).

[207] Art. 9.        [208] [2002] OJ L203/1.

[209] Council Dir. 2004/81 ([2004] OJ L261/19). The UK, Ireland, and Denmark are not participating in this legislation. There is a proposal to replace this measure: COM(2009) 136.        [210] COM(2000) 757, 6.

[211] Tampere Presidency Conclusions, para. 23.

[212] See also Art. 83(1) TFEU on criminal offences and sanctions.

## D. THE RIGHTS OF TURKISH WORKERS AND THEIR FAMILIES IN THE EU

### 1. INTRODUCTION

The EEC–Turkey Association Agreement of 1963 gives the most extensive rights to TCNs legally residing in the EU,[213] other than to EEA and Swiss nationals. While it does not affect the Member State's right to decide whether to admit a Turkish national,[214] nor the conditions under which they may take up their first employment, (subject to the application of the legislation outlined above in particular the Family Reunion Directive and the Long-term Residents Directive)[215] it does give Turkish workers an increasing number of rights the longer they are employed in the host state. The Agreement also does not give Turkish nationals the right to move between one EU state and another[216] but, unlike any other Union agreement (apart from the EEA and the EU/Swiss Treaty on free movement of persons), Article 12 of the Turkey Association Agreement envisages eventual free movement of persons between the Union and Turkey, guided by the principles laid down in Articles 45–7 TFEU.[217] This objective has influenced the Court's interpretation of the Agreement and the secondary legislation,[218] particularly Decision 1/80 of the Association Council on the development of the Association. This prompted the Court to observe in *Kurz*[219] that the aim and broad logic of Decision 1/80 is to 'seek to promote the integration of Turkish workers in the host Member State'. In this chapter we shall focus on the most litigated of the rules, those concerning the right to work for Turkish workers and their family members. We shall focus on these rules by way of comparison to the rights enjoyed by EU workers under Article 45 TFEU.

---

[213] For a full discussion, see M. Hedemann-Robinson, 'An overview of recent legal developments at Community level in relation to third country nationals resident within the European Union, with particular reference to the case law of the European Court of Justice' (2001) 38 *CMLRev.* 525.

[214] Case C–237/91 *Kus* v. *Landeshauptstadt Wiesbaden* [1992] ECR I–6781, para. 25; Case C–434/93 *Ahmet Bozkurt* v. *Staatssecretaris van Justitie* [1995] ECR I–1475, para. 21.

[215] Cf. the EU legislation outlined above which increasingly gives the EU competence over these matters. For discussion, see S. Peers, 'EC immigration law and EC association agreements: Fragmentation or integration?' (2009) *ELRev.* 628 discussing Case C–228/06 *Soysal* [2009] ECR I–1031.

[216] Case C–171/95 *Tetik* v. *Land Berlin* [1997] ECR I–329, para. 29; Case C–325/05 *Derin* v. *Landkreis Darmstadt-Dieburg* [2007] ECR I–6495, para. 66. See M. Cremona, 'Citizens of third countries: Movement and employment of migrant workers within the EU' [1995/2] *LIEI* 87, 94.

[217] Art. 12 is not directly effective since it sets out a programme and its provisions are not sufficiently precise and unconditional: Case 12/86 *Demirel* v. *Stadt Schwäbisch Gmünd* [1987] ECR 3719, paras. 23 and 25. Art. 36 of the additional protocol annexed to the Association Agreement lays down the timetable for the progressive attainment of freedom of movement of workers. This is also not directly effective: Case 12/86 *Demirel* [1987] ECR 3719, paras. 23 and 25.

[218] See, e.g., Case C–1/97 *Birden* v. *Stadtgemeinde Bremen* [1998] ECR I–7747. See also Case C–416/96 *El-Yassini* v. *Secretary of State for the Home Department* [1999] ECR I–1209 where the Court found that its interpretation of the EEC–Turkey Association Agreement did not apply to the EEC–Morocco agreement because the Morocco Agreement did not provide for consideration of Morocco's accession to the EU, nor was it aimed at progressively securing freedom of movement for workers.

[219] Case C–188/00 [2002] ECR I–10691, para. 45.

## 2. EMPLOYMENT RIGHTS

### 2.1 Introduction

For the purposes of this chapter the relevant secondary legislation is Decision 1/80[220] fleshing out the rights of Turkish workers already legally resident and employed in the EU. Article 6(1) provides that a Turkish worker, duly registered as belonging to the labour force of a Member State, is entitled to:

- the renewal of his permit to work for the same employer, if a job is available, after *one year's* legal employment

- respond to another offer of employment, with an employer of his choice, made under normal conditions and registered with the employment services of that state, for the same occupation, after *three years* of legal employment and subject to the priority to be given to workers of the Member States of the Union

- free access in that Member State to any paid employment of his choice, after *four years* of legal employment.

This shows that while Member States retain the competence to regulate both the entry to their territory and the conditions under which Turkish nationals take up their first employment,[221] Article 6(1) of Decision 1/80 applies after the first year's employment.[222] The basic premises under Article 6(1) is that the longer Turkish workers are employed, the more integrated they are considered in the host state and so the greater the rights they enjoy under that Decision. This means that after four years employment the individual is no longer dependent on the continuing existence of the conditions for access to the rights laid down in the three indents. This means s/he enjoys much greater freedom, including temporarily interrupting the employment relationship.[223] By contrast, those still building up the four years must be engaged in legal employment for one, three, or four years, without any interruption, except for that provided in Article 6(2). This provides that annual holidays and absences for reasons of maternity or an accident at work or short periods of sickness are treated as periods of legal employment. By contrast, periods of involuntary unemployment duly certified by the relevant authorities and long absences on account of sickness are not to be treated as periods of legal employment, but are not to affect rights acquired as the result of the preceding period of employment.[224]

---

[220] This is directly effective: Case C–192/89 *Sevince* v. *Staatssecretaris van Justitie* [1990] ECR I–3461, para. 26. For a statement of the supremacy of Dec. 1/80 see Case C–188/00 *Kurz* [2002] ECR I–10691, para. 68.

[221] Case C–294/06 *R (ex p. Payir)* v. *Secretary of State for the Home Department* [2008] ECR I–203.

[222] Case C–237/91 *Kus* [1992] ECR I–6781, para. 25; Case C–434/93 *Bozkurt* [1995] ECR I–1475, para. 21.

[223] Case C–230/03 *Sedef* v. *Freie und Hansestadt Hamburg* [2006] ECR I–157, para. 46.

[224] Case C–4/05 *Güzeli* v. *Oberbürgermeister der Stadt Aachen* [2006] ECR I–10279 confirms that if one of these situations occurs (i.e., involuntary unemployment or long-term sickness), this does not affect the rights that the Turkish worker has already acquired owing to preceding periods of employment. Note in Case C–230/03 *Sedef* [2006] ECR I–157 the lenient and practical approach the Court took to the phrase 'involuntary unemployment duly certified by the relevant authorities' in the case of a Turkish seaman employed in Germany for 15 years.

## 2.2 The Criteria under Article 6(1)

The rights laid down in Article 6(1) are conditional on (1) being a worker, (2) being 'duly registered as belonging to the labour force of a Member State', and (3) on a period of 'legal employment'. The Court enforces these specific requirements of Article 6(1) with some rigour so as not to 'undermine the coherence of the system set up by the Association Council with a view to gradually consolidating the position of Turkish workers in the host Member State'.[225]

The first condition, being a worker, is interpreted consistently with the equivalent term in Article 45 TFEU[226] and so we shall not discuss it further here. The second condition, 'duly registered as belonging to the labour force of a Member State', requires the national courts to consider whether the legal relationship of employment can be located within the territory of a Member State, or retains a sufficiently close link with that territory, taking account of the place where the person was hired, the territory on or from which the paid employment was pursued, and the applicable national legislation in the field of employment and social security law.[227]

In *Altun*[228] the Court elaborated further. It said the concept of being 'duly registered' as belonging to the labour force embraced all workers who have met the conditions laid down by law or regulation in the host Member State and who were thus entitled to pursue an occupation in its territory. It said that notwithstanding a temporary interruption of the employment relationship, a Turkish worker continued to be duly registered as belonging to the labour force in the host Member State during a period reasonably necessary for him to find other paid employment, regardless of the cause of the absence of the individual from the labour force, provided that that absence is temporary. Therefore workers and apprentices are considered duly registered as belonging to the labour force[229] as is an individual, like Mr Altun, who is involuntary unemployed following the declaration of insolvency of the undertaking in which he was working. A Turkish worker is excluded from the labour force only if he no longer has any chance of rejoining the labour force or has exceeded a reasonable time limit for finding new employment after the end of the period of inactivity.

In respect of the third condition, 'legal employment', the Court has said that the phrase 'presupposes a stable and secure situation as a member of the labour force'[230] and the existence of an undisputed right of residence.[231] The Court has so far found that there was no legal employment in two situations: first, in *Sevince*[232] where a Turkish worker

---

[225] Case C–230/03 *Sedef* [2006] ECR I–157, para. 37.

[226] See Ch. 9: Case C–1/97 *Birden* [1998] ECR I–7747, para. 23; Case C–188/00 *Kurz* [2002] ECR I–10691, para. 30; Case C–294/06 *ex p. Payir* [2008] ECR I–203; Case C–14/09 *Genc* v. *Land Berlin* [2010] ECR I–000, para. 27.

[227] Case C–98/96 *Ertanir* [1997] ECR I–5179, para. 39; Case C–4/05 *Güzeli* [2006] ECR I–10279, para. 37.

[228] Case C–337/07 *Altun* v. *Stadt Böblingen* [2008] ECR I–10323, paras. 23–6.

[229] Case C–188/00 *Kurz* [2002] ECR I–10691, para. 45.          [230] Ibid., para. 30.

[231] Ibid., para. 48. This even includes short periods during which the Turkish worker did not hold a valid residence or work permit: Case C–98/96 *Ertanir* [1997] ECR I–5179, para. 69.

[232] Case C–192/89 *Sevince* [1990] ECR I–3461, para. 32. In a similar vein, see also Case C–237/91 *Kus* [1992] ECR I–6781, para. 18 where the Court ruled that a worker did not fulfil the requirement of 'legal employment' where a right of residence was conferred on him only by the operation of national legislation permitting residence in the host country pending completion of the procedure for the grant of the residence permit, on the ground that he had been given the right to remain and work in that country pending a final decision on his right of residence.

was able to continue in employment only by reason of the suspensory effect deriving from his appeal against deportation and, secondly, in *Kol*[233] where a Turkish national was employed under a residence permit issued to him as a result of fraudulent conduct (he had entered a marriage of convenience with a German national), for which he was subsequently convicted.

The Court has also strictly enforced the periods of time laid down in the three indents of Article 6(1). This can be seen in *Eroglu*.[234] A Turkish worker worked lawfully for employer A for one year. She then worked for employer B. Subsequently, she sought an extension of her work permit in order to work for employer A again. The Court said that she was not entitled to do this under Article 6(1) because this would allow the worker to change employers under the first indent before the expiry of the three years prescribed in the second indent.[235]

The third indent of Article 6(1) concerns those Turkish workers who are duly integrated into the labour market. They have the right to give up one job to seek any other job.[236] The key feature here is that the worker must be deemed still to be a member of the labour force during any periods of absence from work. Therefore, in *Bozkurt*[237] the Court ruled that a Turkish national was not entitled to remain in the host state if he had reached retirement age or had suffered an industrial accident which left him totally and permanently unfit for further employment, since he was considered to have left the workforce for good. However, where the incapacity was only temporary and did not affect his fitness to continue exercising his right to employment he could still enjoy the right to join the labour force. In *Nazli*[238] the Court took this one stage further and said that a temporary break caused by detainment pending trial did not cause the Turkish worker to forfeit his rights under the third indent of Article 6(1), provided that he found a new job within a reasonable period after his release. In *Dogan*[239] the Court extended the ruling in *Nazli* to a Turkish worker imprisoned for four years. The Court said that the effectiveness of the rights to employment and residence conferred on Turkish workers by the third indent applied regardless of the cause of absence from the labour force, provided that the absence was temporary.[240]

The decision in *Bozkurt* highlights the unfavourable position in which Turkish nationals find themselves in the absence of express legislation, equivalent to what was Regulation 1251/70 on the right to remain for EU nationals (now the Citizens' Rights Directive (CRD)), which protects their position. While the Long-term Residents Directive 2003/109 may now cover some Turkish workers in this position, the rights of residence under the

---

[233] Case C–285/95 *Kol* v. *Land Berlin* [1997] ECR I–3069, para. 25. See in a similar vein Case C–37/98 *R.* v. *Secretary of State for the Home Department, ex p. Savas* [2000] ECR I–2927, para. 67 concerning a Turkish national unlawfully present in the host Member State.

[234] Case C–355/93 *Eroglu* v. *Land Baden-Württemberg* [1994] ECR I–5113, para. 14. See also Case C–386/95 *Eker* v. *Land Baden-Württemberg* [1997] ECR I–2697 where the Court ruled that if the worker left employer A before the expiry of one year to work for employer B, the worker had to work for a full year for employer B before he was entitled to the renewal of work and residence permits.

[235] See also Case C–4/05 *Güzeli* [2006] ECR I–10279, para. 45, where the Court said that eight months' employment was insufficient under the first indent.

[236] Case C–340/97 *Nazli* v. *Stadt Nürnberg* [2000] ECR I–957, para. 35.

[237] Case C–434/93 *Bozkurt* [1995] ECR I–1475, paras. 39–40.

[238] Case C–340/97 *Nazli* [2000] ECR I–957, para. 41.

[239] Case C–383/03 *Dogan* v. *Sicherheitsdirektion für das Bundesland Vorarlberg* [2005] ECR I–6237.

[240] Para. 20.

Turkey Association Agreement, while among the most extensive of all the Union agreements, are still firmly tied to the exercise of economic activity (actual employment) and are far from matching the general rights of residence available to Union citizens.[241]

Although the Court has been strict in the application of the criteria laid down in Article 6(1) to Turkish workers, it has also required the Member States to satisfy their side of the agreement. So, Member States cannot deprive Turkish workers of the rights laid down by Article 6(1) nor 'impede the exercise' of such rights.[242] So, in *Ertanir*[243] the Court said that a German rule permitting specialist chefs to reside in Germany for no more than three years was incompatible with Article 6(1).[244] In *Sevince*[245] the Court said that the employment rights of Turkish workers laid down by Article 6(1) necessarily implied a right of residence because, in the absence of such a right, access to the labour market and the right to work would be deprived of all legal effect.[246]

### 2.3  Other Rights

Once they are duly registered as belonging to the labour market of the host state, Turkish workers do enjoy equal treatment with Union workers in respect of remuneration and other conditions of work under Article 10 of Decision 1/80.[247] In *Wählergruppe Gemeinsam Zajedno*[248] the Court interpreted the phrase 'other conditions of work' to include the right for Turkish workers to stand as candidates in elections to bodies representing the legal interests of workers. Therefore, Austrian rules restricting eligibility for election to a body such as a chamber of workers to Austrians only breached Article 10.

Worker representation is one of three areas where Turkish workers have more rights than those TCNs covered by the Long-term Residents Directive 2003/109 (considered above). The other two areas are protection from expulsion and access to employment. However, in respect of access to social assistance and equal treatment, Directive 2003/109 offers more favourable rights than Decision 1/80. As Groenendijk points out,[249] the Long-term Residents Directive grants Turkish citizens and other TCNs the right to look for work, to live and work in other Member States and the Directive on Family Reunification gives them the right to family reunion. In this way the directives complement and supplement the provisions under Decision 1/80.

### 3.  FAMILY RIGHTS

### 3.1  The Right to Employment

The first paragraph of Article 7 of Decision 1/80 provides that the members of the family of a Turkish worker who is 'duly registered as belonging to the labour force of a Member

---

[241] Considered in Ch. 12.

[242] Case C–188/00 *Kurz* [2002] ECR I–10691, para. 67. The rights in Art. 6(1) are also directly effective: Case C–188/00 *Kurz* [2002] ECR I–10691, para. 26.

[243] Case C–98/96 *Ertanir* [1997] ECR I–5179, para. 34: despite the wording of Art. 6(3): 'The procedures for applying paragraphs 1 and 2 shall be those established under national rules.'

[244] See also Case C–36/96 *Günaydin v. Freiestaat Bayern* [1997] ECR I–5143, paras. 36–8.

[245] Ibid., para. 29.        [246] See also Case C–237/91 *Kus* [1992] ECR I–6781, para. 23.

[247] This provision is directly effective: Case C–171/01 *Wählergruppe Gemeinsam Zajedno/Birklikte Alternative und Grüne GewerkschafterInnen/UG* [2003] ECR I–4301, para. 57.        [248] Ibid.

[249] K. Groenendijk, above n. 164, 442.

State'[250] (with no reference this time to the concept of 'legal employment' which appears in Article 6(1) of Decision 1/80) and who have been 'authorized to join him' are, subject to the priority to be given to workers of Member States of the Union, entitled to:[251]

- respond to any offer of employment after they have been legally resident for at least three years in that Member State
- enjoy free access to any paid employment of their choice provided that they have been legally resident there for at least five years.[252]

According to *Kadiman*,[253] the purpose of this first paragraph is to 'create conditions conducive to family unity', first by enabling family members to be with a migrant worker and then by consolidating their position by granting them the right to obtain employment in the host state (and a concomitant right of residence[254]). Therefore, the host state could require actual cohabitation by the Turkish workers[255] and their family members during the first three years, even where there were accusations of domestic violence, subject to absences for a reasonable period and for legitimate reasons in order to take holidays or visit family in Turkey.[256] The Court said that the co-habitation requirement was intended to prevent Turkish nationals from evading the stricter requirements laid down in Article 6 by entering sham marriages and then taking advantage of the generous requirements of Article 7.[257]

However, the Court has made clear that cohabitation does not necessarily mean marriage (unlike the approach adopted under Article 10 of Regulation 1612/68, now Articles 2–3 CRD). In *Eyüp*[258] a Turkish couple living in Austria divorced but continued to live together. During this period of cohabitation they had a further four children. He was a worker and she looked after the children. They then remarried and continued to cohabit. Since they constantly maintained a common legal residence within the meaning of Article 7 the Court said that the period of cohabitation counted towards calculating the periods of legal residence. In *Ayaz*[259] the Court drew on the definition of family members under Regulation 1612/68 (now the CRD) to help determine the meaning of the equivalent term in Decision 1/80. It ruled that the phrase did not require a blood relationship: stepchildren were also covered.

However, Article 7 does not affect the power of the Member State to authorize family members to join the Turkish worker,[260] to regulate their stay until they become entitled to

---

[250] This is interpreted in the same was as the equivalent phrase in Art. 6(1): Case C–337/07 *Altun* [2008] ECR I–000, para. 28.

[251] The first para. of Art. 7 is directly effective: Case C–351/95 *Kadiman* v. *Freiestaat Bayern* [1997] ECR I–2133, para. 28. See, generally, G. Barratt, 'Family matters: European Community Law and third country family members' (2003) 40 *CMLRev.* 369.

[252] Case C–373/03 *Aydinili* v. *Land Baden-Württemberg* [2005] ECR I–6181: a Turkish national who has resided for five years did not forfeit rights under this provision due to prolonged absence from the labour market due to imprisonment.          [253] Case C–351/95 *Kadiman* [1997] ECR I–2133, para. 33.

[254] Case C–325/05 *Derin* [2007] ECR I–6495, para. 47.

[255] The Turkish workers themselves had to be duly registered as belonging to the labour force of that state: Case C–337/07 *Altun* [2008] ECR I–10323, para. 32.          [256] Ibid., para. 48.

[257] Ibid., para. 38.

[258] Case C–65/98 *Safet Eyüp* v. *Landesgeschäftsstelle des Arbeitsmarktservice Vorarlberg* [2000] ECR I–4747.          [259] Case C–275/02 *Ayaz* v. *Land Baden-Württemberg* [2004] ECR I–8765, para. 45.

[260] Case C–467/02 *Cetinkaya* v. *Land Baden-Württemberg* [2004] ECR I–10895, para. 26: Art. 7 also applies to family members actually born in the host state. The position of a Turkish worker's family members

respond to any offer of employment, and, if necessary, to allow them to take up employment before the expiry of the initial period of three years,[261] always subject to the provisions of the European Convention on Human Rights.[262] Union law requires only that during the three-year period members of the worker's family must be granted a right of residence.[263] Once those three years have expired, Member States can no longer attach conditions to the residence of a member of a Turkish worker's family.[264] Once five years have expired, the person derives 'an individual employment right directly from Decision 1/80' and 'a concomitant right of residence'.[265]

### 3.2 The Position of a Turkish Worker's Children

The second paragraph of Article 7,[266] which is more favourable than the first paragraph,[267] provides that children of Turkish workers who have completed a course of vocational training[268] in the host country may respond to any offer of employment there, irrespective of the length of time they have been resident in that Member State, provided that one of their parents has been legally employed in the Member State for at least three years. Since this paragraph is not intended to create conditions conducive to family unity, the Court said in *Akman*[269] that the child's right to respond to any offer of employment was not conditional on the Turkish worker parent residing in the host Member State at the time when the child wished to take up employment following vocational training. In *Eroglu*[270] the Court extended its rulings in *Sevince* and *Kus* to the second paragraph of Article 7, saying that 'any offer of employment necessarily implies the recognition of a right of residence for that person'.[271]

Finally, in *Derin*[272] the Court considered how the rights under Article 7 could be lost. One way would be because the individual constitutes, on account of his own conduct a 'genuine and sufficiently serious threat to public policy, public security or public health', in accordance with Article 14(1). The second way is that the individual has left the territory

---

is therefore less favourable than an EU worker's family members who enjoy an unconditional right to install themselves with the migrant Union workers under *Union* law, not national law: Case C–325/05 *Derin* [2007] ECR I–6495, paras. 61–3. However, the Family Reunification Dir. 2003/86 may now affect the Member State's powers.

[261] Case C–351/95 *Kadiman* [1997] ECR I–2133, para. 32.

[262] Case C–325/05 *Derin* [2007] ECR I–6495, para. 64.   [263] Ibid., para. 29.

[264] Case C–329/97 *Ergat* v. *Stadt Ulm* [2000] ECR I–1487.

[265] Ibid., para. 40. See also Case C–467/02 *Cetinkaya* [2004] ECR I–10895, paras. 32–3. Failure to obtain a residence permit in time can be punished, but only by penalties which are proportionate and comparable to those for minor offences committed by nationals but, as with Union nationals, this does not include deportation which would deny the very right of residence (Case C–467/02 *Cetinkaya* [2004] ECR I–10895, paras. 56–7). Therefore, administrative documents such as a residence permit are only 'declaratory of the existence of those rights and cannot constitute a condition for their existence' (Case C–434/93 *Bozkurt* [1995] ECR I–1475, para. 30).

[266] The 2nd para. of Art. 7 is directly effective: Case C–355/93 *Eroglu* [1994] ECR I–5113, para. 17.

[267] Case C–325/05 *Derin* [2007] ECR I–6495, para. 42.

[268] See also Art. 9, which gives Turkish children residing legally in a Member State access to education and training courses on the same terms as nationals as well as possible access to 'benefit from advantages provided for under the national legislation in that area'. According to Case C–374/03 *Gürol* v. *Bezirksregierung Köln* [2005] ECR I–6199, Art. 9 is directly effective and the 'advantages' include grants.

[269] Case C–210/97 *Akman* v. *Oberkreisdirektor des Rheinisch-Bergischen-Kreises* [1998] ECR I–7519, paras. 43–4. See also Case C–462/08 *Bekleyen* [2010] ECR I–000.

[270] Case C–355/93 *Eroglu* [1994] ECR I–5113.   [271] Para. 20.

[272] Case C–325/05 *Derin* [2007] ECR I–6495, para. 54.

of the host state for a significant length of time without legitimate reason. The Court has emphasized that these are the only ways that an individual can lose their rights under Article 7. Therefore, a Turkish national cannot be deprived of his rights either because he was unemployed on account of being sentenced to a term of imprisonment, even one of several years' duration, or because he never acquired rights relating to employment and residence pursuant to Article 6(1) of that decision, or because he was 'not active on the labour market for several years' (i.e., he attended various training course but never completed them).[273]

## 4. DEROGATIONS

Article 14(1) allows states to derogate from the rights provided on the grounds of public policy, public security, and public health.[274] The Court interprets these provisions consistently with those under the EU Treaties (e.g. Article 45(3) TFEU),[275] as far as possible.[276] In *Derin*[277] the Court set out the framework according to which the national authorities could act: they are 'obliged to assess the personal conduct of the offender and whether it constitutes a present, genuine and sufficiently serious threat to public policy and security, and in addition they must observe the principle of proportionality'. In particular, a measure ordering expulsion based on Article 14(1) may be taken only if the personal conduct of the person concerned indicates a specific risk of new and serious prejudice to the requirements of public policy. Consequently, such a measure cannot be ordered automatically following a criminal conviction and with the aim of general deterrence.

# E. CONCLUSIONS

This chapter started with the basic dichotomy of insiders versus outsiders, with insiders—nationals of one of the Member States—being in a favoured position. However, on closer examination the rules on EU citizens and those on TCNs show that this picture is less accurate than would at first appear. EU nationals who do not migrate or who are not economically active may find themselves marginalized by the application of rules which prioritize those who exercise their (economic) freedom of movement, while TCNs now may find that, as a result of developments under Title V of Part Three TFEU, they begin to enjoy something of a quasi- or civic citizenship.[278] Of course, this characterization

---

[273] Case C–453/07 *Er* v. *Wetteraukreis* [2008] ECR I–7299, para. 31.

[274] Art. 14(1). This is an exhaustive list: Case C–502/04 *Torun* v. *Stadt Augsburg* [2006] ECR I–1563.

[275] See further Ch. 13.

[276] Case C–467/02 *Cetinkaya* [2004] ECR I–10895, para. 39, which also confirms that the case law on derogations under Dir. 64/221 (now CRD) also applies to Dec. 1/80. Three cases are currently pending on whether the same applies to the provisions of the CRD. See also Case C–136/03 *Dörr* v. *Sicherheitsdirektion für das Bundesland Kärnten* [2005] ECR I–4759; Case C–349/06 *Polat* v. *Rüsselsheim* [2007] ECR I–8167, para. 29 Case C–97/05 *Gattoussi* v. *Stadt Rüsselsheim* [2006] ECR I–11917, para. 41 (in the context of the Eur-Mediterranean Agreement).

[277] Case C–325/05 *Derin* [2007] ECR I–6495, para. 74.

[278] COM(2003) 336, 30 and N. Reich, 'Union citizenship: Metaphor or source of rights?' (2001) 4 *ELJ* 4, 18.

is also not complete. Decisions of the Court of Justice, in particular in *Grzelczyk*[279] and *Baumbast*,[280] have done much to give rights to migrant citizens who are not economically active while the advent of the Charter and developments in the field of social, consumer, and environmental policy have benefited citizens who do not migrate. Meanwhile, the measures which have the most inclusive effect on TCNs still fall far short of Held's three-stranded definition of citizenship (considered in detail in Chapter 12): while legally resident TCNs have some rights, owing to the absence of any clear Union competence they have no ability to participate in the political process in the host state; nor do they have a strong sense of membership. As we have seen, it has already proved difficult for the EU to foster a sense of membership among EU nationals; this task may prove harder in respect of TCNs who come from extraordinarily diverse backgrounds.[281]

However, it is striking that two principles have been used to combat the sense of exclusion experienced by both EU nationals and TCNs: integration and, to a limited extent, solidarity. The language of integration underpinned the Court of Justice's justification for broadening the rights enjoyed by EU migrant workers and their families. It is the same language which has been used by the Heads of State at Tampere, by the Commission in its two Communications[282] and now by the Lisbon Treaty in the concept of 'fair treatment' in respect of TCNs. However, when considering the position of TCNs the Commission makes clear that integration entails bilateral commitments:[283]

integration should be understood as a two way process based on mutual rights and corresponding obligations of legally resident third country nationals and the host society which provides for full participation of the immigrant.

It continued that this implies on the one hand that it is the responsibility of the host society to ensure that the formal rights of immigrants are in place so that the individual can participate in economic, social, cultural, and civil life but, on the other, 'that immigrants respect the fundamental norms and values of the host society and participate actively in the integration process, without having to relinquish their own identity'. In this respect the Union is expecting more of TCNs than it does of migrant EU citizens.[284]

Solidarity has also been used to justify giving rights to both migrant citizens and TCNs.[285] The language of solidarity was used by the Court in *Grzelczyk* to justify giving limited social advantages to a migrant student. It is also used in the Commission's Communication on illegal immigration[286] to justify operational cooperation, and thus financial cooperation, between the Member States to keep illegal immigrants out of the EU or to return them to their Member States, language which is repeated in the strongest terms in the Lisbon Treaty.[287] In this way solidarity is being used to attain both inclusionary and exclusionary results.

---

[279] Case C–184/99 [2001] ECR I–6193.    [280] Case C–413/99 *Baumbast and R* [2002] ECR I–7091.

[281] For a critique, see N. Barber, 'Citizenship, nationalism and the European Union' (2002) 27 *ELRev.* 241.    [282] COM(2000) 757 and COM(2003) 336.

[283] COM(2003) 336, 17–18.

[284] See also EU Council, *The Hague Programme: Strengthening freedom, security and justice in the European Union*, Council Doc. 16054/04, 11.    [285] Ibid., 4.

[286] COM(2003) 323, 17.    [287] Art. 80 TFEU.

# PART IV

# FREE MOVEMENT OF CAPITAL

# 15

# FREE MOVEMENT OF CAPITAL AND ECONOMIC AND MONETARY UNION

## A. INTRODUCTION

Free movement of capital, the fourth fundamental freedom,[1] was for many years the poor relation to the other three. Because the movement of capital was not liberalized at the same rate as the other freedoms, the Court ruled that the original Treaty provision, Article 67 EEC (now Article 63 TFEU), was not directly effective and so Member States could restrict capital movements in a number of ways. The advent of the single market gave some muscle to this area of law when capital movements (i.e., those resources used for, or capable of, investment intended to guarantee revenue[2]) were finally liberalized. The free movement of capital was given renewed impetus by the establishment of economic and monetary union (EMU): the achievement of free capital movements was a condition for entry into the first stage of monetary union. This demonstrates the interconnection between monetary policy and free movement of capital, especially in respect of exchange rates. And since, in practice, free movement of capital and fixed exchange rates cannot be achieved in an economic area in which diverging economic and monetary policies are applied, economic *and* monetary union is the natural complement to the common market.

This chapter begins by examining the rules on capital (and payments) before outlining the basic structure of the economic and monetary union.

## B. FREE MOVEMENT OF CAPITAL

### 1. INTRODUCTION

According to Molle, capital can be considered free if entrepreneurs can satisfy their need for capital and investors can offer their disposable capital in the country where conditions

---

[1] Case C–483/99 *Commission* v. *France* [2002] ECR I–4781, para. 45; Case C–463/00 *Commission* v. *Spain* [2003] ECR I–4581, para. 68; Case C–302/97 *Klaus Konle* v. *Republik Österreich* [1999] ECR I–3099, para. 38.

[2] L. Flynn, 'Coming of age: The free movement of capital case law 1993–2002' (2002) 39 *CMLRev.* 773, 776.

are most favourable to them.[3] He summarizes the advantages of the integration of capital markets in the following terms:[4]

- It diminishes the risk of disturbances which tend to occur in small markets
- It increases the supply of capital, because better investing prospects mobilize additional savings
- It enables those who are in need of capital to raise larger amounts in forms better tailored to their needs
- It makes for equal production conditions and thus fewer disturbances of competition in the common market

He also lists the reasons why a Member State may wish to impede the export of capital:[5] the fear of capital drain-offs, reinforcing the economies of other states to the detriment of its own; the loss of currency reserves which may jeopardize its ability to meet its other international obligations; the need to maintain equilibria in the economy, both internally (a large outflow of capital may compel a high rate of interest when the state actually needs a low rate of interest) and externally (capital outflow may lead to devaluation of the currency, making imports more expensive, thereby importing inflation); and loss of confidence of the international markets in policy measures. Member States may also wish to impede the import of capital, again for reasons of internal and external disequilibria (avoiding an unnecessarily low rate of interest or an upward adaptation of the exchange rate), and also because capital is power, therefore capital in foreign hands means that the state loses some authority over its own economy.

In the EU the basic rule, contained in what is now Article 63(1) TFEU, is free movement of capital.[6] However, the interests of the Member States in impeding free movement are recognized by the express derogations found in Article 65 TFEU (ex Article 58 EC).

## 2. THE LEGAL CONTEXT

Because capital movements were closely linked to the stability of economic and monetary policy of the Member States, liberalization took longer for capital than for persons, services, and goods.[7] This was recognized in the original Treaty provisions on capital, which were drafted in more cautious, less 'imperative' terms[8] than the other three freedoms. The basic provision, Article 67(1) EEC, provided that:

During the transitional period and to the extent necessary to ensure the proper functioning of the common market, Member States shall progressively abolish between themselves all restrictions on the movement of capital belonging to persons resident in Member States and any discrimination based on the nationality or on the place of residence of the parties or on the place where such capital is invested.

---

[3] W. Molle, *The Economics of European Integration: Theory, practice, policy*, 5th edn (Aldershot: Ashgate, 2006). [4] Ibid., 218.

[5] Ibid.

[6] For a more detailed discussion, see J. Usher, *The Law of Money and Financial Services in the European Community* (Oxford: Clarendon Press, 2000). See also J. Usher, 'The evolution of the free movement of capital' (2008) 31 *Fordham Intl LJ* 1533. [7] Para. 9.

[8] Case 203/80 *Casati* [1981] ECR 2595, para. 19.

Article 68 EEC urged Member States to be 'as liberal as possible' in granting exchange authorizations. Article 69 EEC gave the Council powers to issue directives while Article 70 EEC required the Commission to propose to the Council measures for the progressive coordination of the exchange rate policies of the Member States.

Since Article 67(1) EEC did not abolish restrictions on the movement of capital by the end of the transitional period,[9] their abolition was left to the Council adopting directives on the basis of Article 69 EEC.[10] The first such directive was adopted in 1960,[11] followed by a second in 1963.[12] According to these directives, all movements of capital were divided into four lists (A, B, C, and D) annexed to the directives. In respect of the movements covered by lists A and B, the directives prescribed unconditional liberalization; for movements covered by list C, Member States could maintain or reimpose exchange restrictions if free movement of capital was capable of forming an obstacle to the achievement of its economic policy objectives. In the case of the movements referred to in list D (e.g., the physical importation and exportation of financial assets, including bank notes), the directives did not require the Member States to adopt any liberalizing measures.

Against this backcloth, the Court concluded in *Casati*[13] in 1981 (some years after its seminal judgments in cases such as *Dassonville*[14] and *Cassis de Dijon*,[15]) that complete freedom of movement of capital could undermine the economic policy of one of the Member States or create an imbalance in its balance of payments.[16] It therefore said that Article 67(1) differed from the provisions on goods, persons, and services in the sense that there was an obligation to liberalize capital movements only 'to the extent necessary to ensure the proper functioning of the common market'.[17] For this reason Article 67 was not directly effective.[18] As Snell points out,[19] the story of the historical development of the free movement of capital therefore differs significantly from that of the other freedoms. He continues, 'Instead of a determined Court and an enlightened Commission providing leadership for the reluctant Member States, in the early period the Member States were very much in the driving seat, with the Court silent and the Commission at times even an outright opponent of liberalization.' He concludes that from the perspective of the theoretical accounts of European integration (considered in Chapter 1), the free movement of capital displays features of liberal intergovernmentalism which is not the framework the four freedoms have traditionally been associated with.

---

[9] For background, see P. Oliver and J.-P. Baché, 'Free movement of capital between the Member States: Recent developments' (1989) 26 *CMLRev.* 61; J. Usher, 'Capital movements and the Treaty on European Union' (1992) 12 *YEL* 35.

[10] Case 203/80 *Casati* [1981] ECR 2595, paras. 8–13; Case C–484/93 *Svensson and Gustavsson* v. *Ministre du Logement et de l'Urbanisme* [1995] ECR I–3955, para. 5; Case C–222/95 *Société civile immobilière Parodi* v. *Banque H. Albert de Bary et Cie* [1997] ECR I–3899, paras. 11–12.

[11] First Dir. for the implementation of Art. 67 of the Treaty ([1959–62] OJ Spec Ed 49).

[12] Second Council Dir. 63/21/EEC ([1963–4] OJ Spec Ed 5).

[13] Case 203/80 *Casati* [1981] ECR 2595, paras. 9–10.  [14] Case 8/74 [1974] ECR 837.

[15] Case 120/78 [1979] ECR 649.  [16] Para. 9.  [17] Para. 10.

[18] Case 203/80 *Casati* [1981] ECR 2595.

[19] J. Snell, 'Free movement of capital: Evolution as a non-linear process' in P. Craig and G. De Búrca (eds.), *The Evolution of EU Law* (Oxford: OUP, forthcoming).

The most important measure adopted by the Council was Directive 88/361[20] which did bring about 'the full liberalization of capital movements'.[21] Article 1(1) of the directive provided that 'Member States shall abolish restrictions on movements of capital taking place between persons resident in Member States.' The directive contained a (non-exhaustive)[22] nomenclature of capital movements in the annex, but this was to facilitate the application of the directive and not to introduce distinctions in treatment.

The provisions on capital were complemented by those on payments. Article 106(1) EEC, first paragraph, originally provided that:

Each Member State undertakes to authorise, in the currency of the Member State in which the creditor or beneficiary resides, any payments connected with the movement of goods, services or capital, and any transfers of capital and earnings, to the extent that the movement of goods, services, capital and persons between Member States has been liberalised pursuant to this Treaty.

This required Member States to authorize means of payment as consideration for trade in goods, persons, services, or capital,[23] and for this reason the Court suggested that it was perhaps the most important provision in the (then) EEC Treaty for the purposes of attaining a common market.[24] As the Court put it in *ED Srl*,[25] the provision on payments was intended 'to enable a person liable to pay a sum of money in the context of a supply of goods or services to discharge that contractual obligation voluntarily without undue restriction and to enable the creditor freely to receive such a payment'. In *Luisi and Carbone*[26] the Court found Article 106(1) EEC to be directly effective.

Despite (or maybe because of) the importance of Article 106(1) EEC, the Court has traditionally adopted a rather cautious approach to its interpretation, as the early case of *Lambert*[27] shows. Lambert, a cattle dealer, was a Luxembourg national who accepted payment in cash for sales of cattle in other Member States contrary to Luxembourg laws requiring payment in foreign currency to be received only in the form of a bank transfer or a cheque (not cash) paid through a bank. The Court accepted that the requirements laid down by the Luxembourg law were legitimate[28] because they dealt solely with the *way* in which the exporter had to receive payment;[29] they did not impede either the importer making the payment in Luxembourg francs or the cattle dealer receiving that payment, and so were not a barrier to the liberalization of payments.

*Lambert* also clarified the distinction between Article 106 EEC and Article 67 EEC. It said that while Article 106 EEC covered current payments, i.e. the transfers of foreign exchange which constitute the consideration within the context of an underlying transaction (of goods, persons, services, or capital), Article 67 EEC covered movements

---

[20] [1988] OJ L178/5.

[21] Joined Cases C–358/93 and C–416/93 *Criminal Proceedings against Aldo Bordessa and others* [1995] ECR I–361, para. 17.

[22] Case C–222/97 *Manfred Trummer and Peter Mayer* [1999] ECR I–1661, para. 21.

[23] Case 308/86 *Ministère public* v. *Lambert* [1988] ECR 4369, para. 10; Joined Cases C–163/94, C–165/94 and C–250/94 *Criminal Proceedings against Sanz de Lera and others* [1995] ECR I–4830, para. 17.

[24] Case 7/78 *R.* v. *Thompson* [1978] ECR 2247, para. 22. Therefore means of payments are not goods within the meaning of Art. 34 TFEU (ex Art. 28 EC).

[25] Case C–412/97 *ED Srl* v. *Italo Fenocchio* [1999] ECR I–3845, para. 17.

[26] Cases 286/82 and 26/83 *Luisi and Carbone* [1984] ECR 377.

[27] Case 308/86 *Ministère public* v. *Lambert* [1988] ECR 4369, para. 10.   [28] Para. 16.   [29] Ibid.

of capital, i.e. financial operations essentially concerned with the investment of funds in question, rather than remuneration for a service. The significance of this distinction was reduced by the Maastricht Treaty which radically overhauled the provisions on capital and payments to coincide with the adoption of the new rules on the single currency. In a single Chapter, the Treaty on European Union brought together both the provisions on capital, which were amended largely to reproduce the contents of Directive 88/361,[30] and those on payments. Article 73b(1) EC (the Maastricht Treaty number), renumbered at Amsterdam as Article 56(1) EC and at Lisbon as Article 63(1) TFEU, provides that 'all restrictions on the movement of capital between Member States and Member States and third countries shall be prohibited'. Article 63(2) TFEU, replacing Article 106 EEC, prohibits 'all restrictions on payments'.

## 3. THE SCOPE OF THE PROVISION ON CAPITAL

### 3.1 The Definition of 'Capital'

While the Treaties do not define the term 'movements of capital' (or indeed 'payments' under Article 63(2)) in fact the Court often looks to the annex of Directive 88/361 for guidance as to what constitutes capital. As it noted in *Trummer and Meyer*,[31] inasmuch as Article 63(1) 'substantially reproduces' the contents of Article 1 of Directive 88/361, the nomenclature in respect of movements of capital annexed to Directive 88/361 still has 'the same indicative value', for the purposes of defining the notion of capital movements, as it did before the entry into force of Article 63 *et seq*.[32] On the facts of *Trummer and Meyer* the Court found that mortgages which 'represent the classic method of securing a loan linked to a sale of real property' was a transaction covered by the nomenclature[33] and so was 'inextricably linked to a capital movement'.[34] The Court has also recognized that investments in real property,[35] its administration,[36] and its sale[37] constituted a movement of capital. 'Direct investment' in a company by means of a shareholding with the view to effectively participating in the management and control of a company[38] constitutes a capital movement, as well as acquiring shares on the capital market solely with the intention of making a financial investment (a 'portfolio' investment[39]), and a resale of shares to the

---

[30] Case C–222/97 *Manfred Trummer and Peter Mayer* [1999] ECR I–1661, para. 21.      [31] Ibid.

[32] See Colomer AG's criticism of this interpretative approach in, e.g., Case C–98/01 *Commission* v. *UK* [2003] ECR I–4641, para. 39.

[33] Ibid., para. 23. Mortgages constitute an 'other guarantee' within the meaning of point IX of the nomenclature, headed 'Sureties, other guarantees and rights of pledge'.      [34] Ibid., para. 24.

[35] Ibid., para. 22; Case C–302/97 *Konle* [1999] ECR I–3099, para. 22; Case C–423/98 *Alfredo Albore* [2000] ECR I–5965, para. 14; Joined Cases C–515/99 and C–527/99 to C–540/99 *Hans Reisch and others* v. *Bürgermeister der Landeshauptstadt Salzburg* [2002] ECR I–2157, para. 30; Case C–364/01 *The Heirs of H. Barbier* v. *Inspecteur van de Belastingdienst Particulieren* [2003] ECR I–15013, para. 58; Case C–512/03 *Blanckaert* v. *Inspecteur van de Belastingdienst* [2005] ECR I–7685, para. 35; Case C–376/03 *D.* v. *Inspecteur van de Belastingdienst/Particulieren/Ondernemiingen buitenland te Heerlen* [2005] ECR I–5821, para. 24. See Point II of Annex I of the nomenclature.

[36] Case C–386/04 *Centro di Musicologia Walter Stauffer* [2006] ECR I–8203, para. 24.

[37] Case C–443/06 *Hollmann* v. *Fazenda Pública* [2007] ECR I–8491, para. 31.

[38] Case C–367/98 *Commission* v. *Portugal (Golden Share)* [2002] ECR I–4731, para. 38.

[39] Joined Cases C–282/04 and C–283/04 *Commission* v. *Netherlands* [2006] ECR I–9141, para. 19.

issuing company.[40] In addition, inheritances,[41] banknotes and coins,[42] gifts in money or in kind,[43] granting credit on a commercial basis,[44] and guarantees granted by non-residents to residents or by residents to non-residents[45] all constitute movements of capital.

Even where the transaction is not listed in the annex, it can still constitute a capital movement within the meaning of Article 63(1). Therefore in *Verkooijen*[46] the Court found that the receipt of dividends from a foreign company, although not listed in the annex, fell within the scope of the Treaties because it was linked to some of the measures in the annex.[47] On the other hand, in *Sanz de Lera*[48] the Court made clear that where individuals filled their car with money and tried to take it out of the country, this did not constitute a capital movement in the legal sense of the term.

One striking feature of the discussion so far is that, unlike the case law on free movement of persons, it is only very rarely that the Court has added the additional requirement that the capital movement be an 'economic activity':[49] the Court assumes that a movement of capital within Article 63 to be economic. In this way, free movement of capital has more in common with the free movement of goods.

### 3.2 The Territorial Scope

For Article 63 to apply, there must be a movement of capital between Member States. In most cases this is self-evident. However, in *Block*[50] the Court briefly considered the issue where a person resident in Germany at the date of death left to another person, also resident in Germany, capital claims against a financial institution in Spain on which inheritance tax was levied both in Germany and in Spain. The Court said that this was not a situation purely internal to a Member State and so Article 63 applied.

The striking feature that distinguishes Article 63 from the other fundamental freedoms is that it expressly applies not only to the abolition of all restrictions on capital and payments between Member States but also those between Member States and third countries.[51]

---

[40] Case C–265/04 *Bouanich* v. *Skatteverket* [2006] ECR I–923, para. 29.

[41] Case C–513/03 *Heirs of M.E.A. van Hilten-van der Heijden* v. *Inspecteur van de Belastingdienst/ Particulieren/Ondernemingen buitenland te Heerlen* [2006] ECR I–1957, paras. 41–2: 'An inheritance consists of the transfer to one or more persons of the estate left by a deceased person or, in other words, a transfer to the deceased's heirs of the ownership of the various assets, rights, etc., of which that estate is composed.'

[42] Joined Cases C–358/93 and C–416/93 *Criminal Proceedings against Aldo Bordessa and others* [1995] ECR I–361, para. 13.

[43] Case C–318/07 *Hein Persche* v. *Finanzamt Lüdenscheid* [2009] ECR I–359, para. 27.

[44] Case C–452/04 *Fidium Finanz AG* v. *Bundesanstalt für Finanzdienstleistungsaufsicht* [2006] ECR I–9521, para. 43.

[45] Case C–279/00 *Commission* v. *Italy* [2002] ECR I–1425, para. 36.

[46] Case C–35/98 *Staatssecretaris van Financiën* v. *Verkooijen* [2000] ECR I–4071. See also Case C–319/02 *Manninen* [2004] ECR I–7477.

[47] Paras. 28–9.

[48] Joined Cases C–163/94, C–165/94, and C–250/94 *Criminal Proceedings against Sanz de Lera and others* [1995] ECR I–4830, para. 33.

[49] Cf. Case C–326/07 *Commission* v. *Italy* [2009] ECR I–2291, para. 35 'Direct investments, that is to say, investments of any kind made by natural or legal persons which serve to establish or maintain lasting and direct link between the persons providing the capital and the undertakings to which that capital is made available in order to carry out an economic activity fall within the ambit of Article [63].'

[50] Case C–67/08 *Block* v. *Finanzamt Kaufbeuren* [2009] ECR I–883, para. 21.

[51] The Court confirmed this point in Case C–101/05 *Skatteverket* v. *A* [2007] ECR I–11531. Cf. Case C–102/05 *Skatteverket* v. *A and B*, Order of 10 May 2007, para. 29, which confirms that the scope of Art. 49 TFEU does not extend to situations concerning the establishment of a company of a Member State in a

Snell offers three reasons for the extension:[52] first, the free movement of capital between Member States would undermine capital controls towards third countries as investors would enter or exit the EU via the most liberal jurisdiction to access the target state. Secondly, the credibility of the single currency is bolstered by the liberalization. Thirdly, the extension contributes to the principle of an open market economy expressed in Article 119 TFEU (ex Article 4 EC).

However, the remaining provisions of Chapter 4 TFEU on free movement of capital make clear that the movement of capital and payments between Member States and third countries is actually more limited than the provisions of Article 63 would at first suggest. This is because, in addition to the derogations laid down in Article 65 (considered below), free movement of capital and payments to third countries are subject to four further potential restrictions. Peers describes these in the following terms.[53] The first, and in practice the most important, is historic: Article 64(1) grandfathers any restrictions existing at 31 December 1993[54] on four types of free movement of capital (but not payments) pursuant to EU or national law.[55] The second is potential: according to Article 64(2) the European Parliament and Council may adopt measures concerning the same four types of capital moving to and from third countries. In addition, Article 64(3) allows the Council, acting unanimously in accordance with the special legislative procedure and after consulting the European Parliament, to adopt measures which 'constitute a step backwards in Union law as regards the liberalization of the movement of capital to or from third countries'. The Lisbon Treaty added a further significant provision in Article 65(4). This allows the Commission or the Council, on an application from a Member State, to adopt a decision stating that 'restrictive tax measures adopted by a Member State concerning one or more third countries are to be considered compatible with the Treaties in so far as they are justified by one of the objectives of the Union and compatible with the proper functioning of the internal market'. This unusual provision allows the Council—not the Court—to rule on the legality of national measures.[56] It is seen as a rebuff to the Court that its 'restrictions' case law (see below) has been going too far.[57]

---

non-Member State. See also Case C–157/05 *Holböck* v. *Finanzamt Salzburg-Land* [2007] ECR I–4051, para. 28; Case C–524/04 *Thin Cap* [2007] ECR I–2107, para. 100. In addition, Case C–452/04 *Fidium Finanz AG* [2006] ECR I–9521, para. 25 confirms that Art. 56 TFEU cannot be relied on by a company established in a third country.

[52]  Above n. 19.

[53]  S. Peers, 'Free movement of capital: Learning lessons or slipping on spilt milk?' in C. Barnard and J. Scott (eds.), *The Law of the Single European Market: Unpacking the premises* (Oxford: Hart Publishing, 2002), 335–6. See also Case C–524/04 *Thin Cap Litigation* [2007] ECR I–2107, para. 171, where the Court of Justice suggested that additional justifications may be acceptable in the case of third-country restrictions.

[54]  For a discussion about how to determine whether the national legislation 'existed' on a particular date, see Case C–101/05 *A* [2007] ECR I–11531, paras. 47–9; Case C–157/05 *Holböck* [2007] ECR I–4051, paras. 41–2; Case C–541/08 *Fokus Invest AG* v. *FIAG* [2010] ECR I-000, para. 42.

[55]  I.e., direct investment, establishment, the provision of financial services, or the admission of securities to capital markets. The phrase 'Direct investment' concerns 'investments of any kind undertaken by natural or legal persons and which serve to establish or maintain lasting and direct links between the persons providing the capital and the undertakings to which that capital is made available in order to carry out an economic activity' and which allow the shareholder to participate effectively in he management of the company or its control: Case C–157/05 *Holböck* [2007] ECR I–4051, paras. 34–7. See also Case C–194/06 *Orange European Smallcap Fund* [2008] ECR I–3747, para. 102.

[56]  Cf. Art. 108(2), para. 3 TFEU on state aids.        [57]  J. Snell, above n. 19.

The third restriction concerns balance of payments: Article 66 allows the Council to take safeguard measures for up to six months '[w]here, in exceptional circumstances, movements of capital to or from third countries cause, or threaten to cause, serious difficulties for the operation of economic and monetary union'. The final provision is political: Article 75, as redrafted by the Lisbon Treaty and moved to Title V TFEU on the area of freedom, security, and justice, allows the European Parliament and Council to define a framework for administrative measures concerning capital or payments, such as freezing of funds, financial assets, or economic gains 'belonging to, or owned by or held by, natural or legal persons, groups or non-state entities'[58] in order to prevent and combat terrorism or related activities.[59]

### 3.3  Does Article 63 Apply to this Particular Defendant? The Direct Effect Question

As we have seen, the Court ruled that Article 67 EEC was not directly effective,[60] due to insufficient liberalization of the rules on capital at the time. However, in *Sanz de Lera* the Court ruled that Article 63(1) EC was directly effective.[61] In *A*[62] the Court said that Article 63(1) 'lays down a clear and unconditional prohibition for which no implementing measure is needed and which confers rights on individuals which they can rely on before the courts'. This rule also applies in respect of the movement of capital between Member States and third countries. As the Court put it in *A*, Article 63(1), in conjunction with Articles 64–5, 'may be relied on before national courts and may render national rules that are inconsistent with it inapplicable, irrespective of the category of capital movement in question'.[63]

These provisions will certainly be vertically directly effective. Since the majority of cases concern challenges to national legislation concerning, for example, taxation, the difficult questions as to the potential horizontal application of Article 63 have not be broached. However, given that the Court has not yet expressly ruled that Article 49 on freedom of establishment and Article 56 on free movement of services have full horizontal direct effect, it seems unlikely that Article 63 will do so either. There is some

---

[58]  This particular drafting, and that of Art. 215 TFEU, overcomes the problem of Art. 60(1) and 301 EC, identified in Joined Cases C–402/05 P and C–415/05 P *Kadi* v. *Council* [2008] ECR I–6351, para. 216, which provided the (then) EC with no competence to impose measures on addressees in no way linked to the governing regime of a third country. See also Decl. 25 on Arts. 75 and 215 TFEU on the rights of the individual or entities concerned by such measures. The Court of Justice has jurisdiction to hear judicial review actions brought by natural or legal persons against the Common Foreign and Security Policy (CFSP) measure identifying the individual/company and the implementing regulation imposing the restrictions: Art. 275(2) TFEU.

[59]  See Art. 9 of Protocol 21 for the position of Ireland in respect of this provision and Decl. 65 for the position of the UK. This is considered further in Ch. 14. Art. 60(2) EC empowered Member States to take unilateral action against a third country with regard to capital movements and payments 'for serious political reasons and on grounds of urgency', provided that the Council has not acted. The Council could subsequently override these restrictions. This was repealed by the Lisbon Treaty but Art. 215 TFEU (ex Art. 301 EC) allows for the imposition of economic and financial sanctions. Cf. Case C–124/95 *R.* v. *HM Treasury and Bank of England* [1997] ECR I–81 concerning the relationship between sanctions legislation limiting payment to third countries and the CCP (discussed in Ch. 7).          [60]  Case 203/80 *Casati* [1981] ECR 2595.

[61]  Joined Cases C–163/94, C–165/94 and C–250/94 *Criminal Proceedings against Sanz de Lera and others* [1995] ECR I–4830, para. 41; Joined Cases C–358/93 and C–416/93 *Criminal Proceedings against Aldo Bordessa and others* [1995] ECR I–361, para. 33 regarding Art. 1 of Dir. 88/361.

[62]  Case C–101/05 *Skatteverket* v. *A* [2007] ECR I–11531, para. 21.          [63]  Para. 27.

support for this view in *Commission v. Germany (Volkswagen).*[64] Germany argued that its Volkswagen law was not a measure within the meaning of the Court's case law because the law was based on a private agreement which was entered into in 1959 between workers and trade unions. In return for relinquishing their claim to a right of ownership over the company, the workers and the trade unions secured the assurance of protection against any large shareholder which might gain control of the company. If the Court had thought that Article 63 had horizontal direct effect, it could have dismissed Germany's argument on this basis. Instead, it said that the fact that the agreement had become the subject of a law, this sufficed for it to be considered as a national measure for the purposes of the free movement of capital.[65] It added: 'The exercise of legislative power by the national authorities duly authorised to that end is a manifestation *par excellence* of State power.'[66]

### 3.4 The Relationship between the Provisions on Capital and the Other Freedoms

According to the Court in *Casati*,[67] the free movement of capital constitutes, along with that of persons and services, one of the fundamental freedoms of the Union.[68] It continued:

Furthermore, freedom to move certain types of capital is, in practice, a precondition for the effective exercise of other freedoms guaranteed by the [Treaties], in particular the right of establishment.[69]

Thus, the provisions on capital have a close link with the other freedoms, especially the freedom of establishment. This is recognized in Article 65(2) TFEU, which says that 'The provisions of this chapter [on capital and payments] shall be without prejudice to the applicability of restrictions on the right of establishment which are compatible with the Treaties.' In addition, Article 50 TFEU (ex Article 44 EC), the legal basis for measures to attain freedom of establishment, expressly provides in paragraph (2)(e) that the European Parliament, Council, and the Commission are to carry out the duties devolved on them by enabling 'a national of one Member State to acquire and use land and buildings situated in the territory of another Member State'. The Court offers no clear guidance as to which Treaty provision it wishes to apply. In a number of cases in the late 1990s/early 2000s, the Court showed a preference for using Article 49 TFEU where possible,[70] followed by a period when it applied the capital provisions together with the rules on establishment.[71] This was not altogether surprising—with the liberalization of the capital provisions and a convergence of the tests to be applied to determine whether a restriction exists, the

---

[64] Case C–112/05 [2007] ECR I–8995. See also Case C–478/98 *Commission v. Belgium (Eurobond)* [2000] ECR I–7587 where the Belgian government tried to avoid liability by arguing that it was acting in its capacity as a private contractor (para. 20). The Court disputed this on the facts (paras. 22–5).

[65] Para. 26. Cf. the effect of the decision in Case C–438/05 *Viking* [2007] ECR I–10779.

[66] Para. 27.     [67] Case 203/80 *Criminal Proceedings against Guerrino Casati* [1981] ECR 2595.

[68] Para. 8.     [69] Ibid.

[70] See, e.g., Case C–200/98 *X and Y* [1999] ECR I–8261, para. 30; Joined Cases C–397/98 and C–401/98 *Metallgesellschaft* [2001] ECR I–1727, para. 75; Case C–251/98 *Baars* [2000] ECR I–2787. But see also Case C–414/06 *Lidl Belgium GmbH & Co.KG v. Finanzamt Heilbronn* [2008] ECR I–3601, para. 16.

[71] Case C–503/99 *Commission v. Belgium* [2002] ECR I–4809, para. 59. See also Case C–374/04 *ACT Group* [2006] ECR I–11673, paras. 37–8; and Case C–446/04 *FII Group Litigation* [2006] ECR I–11753. Cf. Case C–150/04 *Commission v. Denmark* [2007] ECR I–1163, para. 76, the Court, having applied Arts. 45, 49, and 56, said there was no need to look at Art. 63.

practical importance of the interaction between the different Treaty provisions became less significant. However, in the most recent cases the Court has attempted to identify the principal purpose of the rules—establishment or capital—and then apply the appropriate Treaty provision.[72]

In certain cases the Court has expressed a preference for applying Article 49. For example, in cases where the shareholding gives the holder a 'definite influence' over the company's decisions the provisions on freedom of establishment apply to any national restrictions.[73] Likewise, Article 49 applies to national rules which affect relations within a group of companies.[74] However, in cases where the legislation is 'not intended to apply only to stakes which enable the holder to have definite influence on a company's decisions and to determine the company's activities'—or where the Court is not sure that all the claimants satisfy the definite influence test—the Court examines the legislation in relation to both Article 49 and Article 63.[75]

A similar picture emerges in respect of freedom to provide services. The link between capital and services is recognized in Article 58(2) TFEU, which provides that the liberalization of banking and insurance services connected with movement of capital is to be effected in step with the liberalization of movement of capital. At first the Court was reluctant to apply the capital provisions,[76] but subsequently it applied the Treaty provisions on services together with those on capital.[77] However, most recently it has shown a greater willingness to examine the centre of gravity of the national rules and then applies either the Treaty provisions on services or those on capital, as appropriate .[78]

This change of approach—both in respect of establishment and services—can perhaps be explained by the fact that only Article 63 applies to transactions involving third countries. By keeping the Treaty provisions distinct, the Court avoided indirectly extending the territorial scope of the other freedoms. The Court made this clear in *Fidium Finanz*[79] where it said that if the 'predominant consideration' of the national legislation was freedom to provide services then a third-country company could not rely on Article 56. Therefore German rules which made the grant of credit on a commercial basis subject to prior authorization, which in turn depended on the company having its

---

[72] Case C–464/05 *Geurts v. Administratie van de BTW* [2007] ECR I–9325, para. 16; Case C–182/08 *Glaxo Wellcome* [2009] ECR I–000, para. 51: 'even if that legislation has restrictive effects on the freedom of establishment, they are the unavoidable consequence of any restriction on free movement of capital and, therefore, do not justify an independent examination of that legislation in the light of Article [49]'.

[73] Case C–231/05 *Oy AA* [2007] ECR I–6373, para. 20. See also, e.g., Case C–251/98 *Baars* [2000] ECR I–2787, paras. 21–2; Case C–436/00 *X, Y v. Riksskatteverket* [2002] ECR I–10829, para. 67.

[74] Case C–446/04 *FII Group Litigation* [2006] ECR I–11753, para. 118; Case C–231/05 *Oy AA* [2007] ECR I–6373, para. 23.

[75] Case C–531/06 *Commission v. Italy (pharmacists)* [2009] ECR I–000, para. 40. See also Case C–374/04 *ACT* [2006] ECR I–11673, para. 37.

[76] Case C–410/96 *Criminal Proceedings against André Ambry* [1998] ECR I–7875, para. 40; Case C–118/96 *Safir* [1998] ECR I–1897, para. 35.

[77] Case C–148/91 *Vereniging Veronica Omroep Organisatie v. Commissariaat voor de Media* [1993] ECR I–487, para. 15; Case C–279/00 *Commission v. Italy (temporary labour)* [2002] ECR I–1425, para.41; Case C–334/02 *Commission v. France (tax on investment income)* [2004] ECR I–2229, para. 25; Joined Cases C–155/08 and C–157/08 *X and E.H.A. Passenheim-van Schoot v. Staatssecretaris van Financiën* [2009] ECR I–000, para. 76.

[78] Case C–452/04 *Fidium Finanz* [2006] ECR I–9521, para. 34; Case C–42/07 *Liga Portuguesa* [2009] ECR I–000, para. 47.

[79] Case C–452/04 [2006] ECR I–9521.

central administration or branch in Germany, could not be challenged by a Swiss company under Article 56.

There has now been sufficient case law on Article 63 to identify five areas of national rules where the Court tends to apply the capital provisions alone:

- property purchase and investment[80]
- currency and other financial transactions[81]
- loans[82]
- investments in companies especially where the national rule affects those who do not have a dominant interest in the company[83]
- the 'golden share' cases[84]—i.e., cases involving newly privatized companies in sensitive sectors such as energy where the state's golden share enables it to retain a degree of influence over the activities of the company.

In addition, the Court has applied Article 63 to the tax treatment of certain capital movements, especially of property purchase, investment and charitable gifts.

## 4. WHAT IS PROHIBITED UNDER ARTICLE 63?

### 4.1 Introduction

Article 67 EEC talked of the abolition of 'all restrictions on the movement of capital' *and* 'any discrimination based on the nationality or on the place of residence of the parties or on the place where such capital is invested'. The Maastricht amendments to Article 67 EEC dropped the reference to discrimination and referred only to 'restrictions'. Yet, the Court has used both the discrimination model and the restrictions model to eliminate measures which interfere with the free movement of capital, even in respect of decisions based on the post-Maastricht version of Article 63(1).

### 4.2 National Rules which Discriminate

### (a) Direct and indirect discrimination

Article 67 EEC prohibited discrimination on three grounds:

- nationality
- the place of residence of the parties
- the place where capital was invested.

In this way Article 67 EEC anticipated subsequent developments in the field of services where the Court has now prohibited discrimination on all three grounds. Although

---

[80] Case C–302/97 *Konle* [1999] ECR I–3099, para. 39; Joined Cases C–515/99 and C–527/99 to C–540/99 *Reisch* [2002] ECR I–2157, para. 32, the *Golden Share* cases, e.g. Case C–483/99 *Commission* v. *France* [2002] ECR I–4781, para. 38, and Case C–364/01 *Barbier* [2003] ECR I–15013, para. 63.

[81] Joined Cases C–358/93 and C–416/93 *Bordessa and others* [1995] ECR I–361.

[82] Case C–478/98 [2000] ECR I–7587.

[83] Case C–531/06 [2009] ECR I–000, paras. 47–8.

[84] Case C–367/98 [2002] ECR I–4731; Case C–483/99 *Commission* v. *France* [2002] ECR I–4781, para. 41. Cf Case C–326/07 *Commission* v. *Italy* [2009] EER I–2291 where the Court considered the case under Arts 49 and 63.

Article 63(1) makes no reference to the language of discrimination, it seems likely that, following the model of the other three freedoms, Article 63(1) prohibits national measures which are both directly and indirectly discriminatory as well as non-discriminatory measures which (substantially) hinder access to the market.

In fact, most of the case law has concerned direct discrimination. Sometimes the national governments concede the discrimination issue. For example, in *Commission* v. *Portugal*,[85] one of the so-called golden share cases, it was 'common ground' that national rules precluding investors from other Member States from acquiring more than a given number of shares in certain newly privatized Portuguese companies in sensitive sectors involved 'unequal treatment of nationals of other Member States and restricts the free movement of capital'.

In other cases the Court examines the discrimination issue for itself. For example, in *Konle*[86] the Court said that an Austrian rule from 1993 which exempted Austrian—but not foreign—nationals from having to obtain authorization before acquiring a plot of land which was built on, and thus from having to demonstrate that the planned purchase would not be used to establish a secondary residence, created a 'discriminatory restriction against nationals of other Member States in respect of capital movements between Member States'.[87] Similarly, in *Albore*[88] an Italian law exempting Italians—but not foreign nationals—from the requirement of obtaining authorization before buying a property in areas designated as being of military importance was found to be discriminatory. In both *Konle* and *Albore* the Court then applied the orthodox rule that direct discrimination could be saved only by reference to the express derogations (see fig. 15.1).[89]

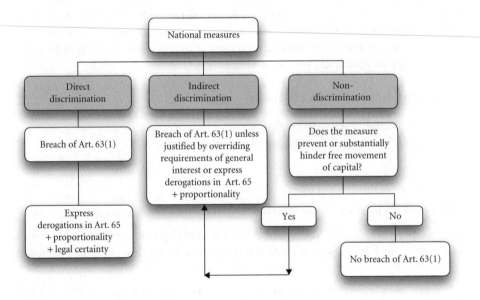

**Fig. 15.1** Discrimination and the free movement of capital

85  Case C–367/98 [2002] ECR I–4731, para. 40.
86  Case C–302/97 *Konle v. Republik Österreich* [1999] ECR I–3099.
87  Para. 23. The Court of Justice made this finding in respect of the pre-Accession law.
88  Case C–423/98 *Alfredo Albore* [2000] ECR I–5965, para. 16.
89  Case C–302/97 *Konle* [1999] ECR I–3099, para. 24; Case C–423/98 *Albore* [2000] ECR I–5965, para. 17.

Case law on indirect discrimination is harder to find but most of it arises in the field of tax rules which have a disparate impact on non-residents. This can be seen in *Hollman*.[90] Under Portuguese law, non-residents were subject to a higher rate of capital gains tax than residents. This was found to be an unjustified breach of Article 63. Outside the field of taxation, the EFTA Court found in *EFTA Surveillance Authority* v. *Norway*[91] a rule to be indirectly discriminatory which granted to private undertakings a time-limited concession for the acquisition of waterfalls for energy production, with an obligation to surrender all installations to the Norwegian state without compensation at the expiry of the concession period, while allowing Norwegian public undertakings to benefit from concessions for an unlimited period of time.[92] The EFTA Court said that 'The differentiation is liable to operate to a particular disadvantage for foreign investors, since the rules in fact exclude them from benefiting from the more favourable provisions applying to Norwegian public owners.'[93] The rules therefore breached the provisions on the free movement of capital (and establishment), could be justified on the grounds of environmental protection and the security of the energy supply but were not proportionate.

## (b) Non-discriminatory national rules

In the *Golden Share* cases of 2003[94] the Court appeared to follow *Alpine Investments*[95] and found that non-discriminatory measures which hinder access to the market breached Article 63(1) unless they could be objectively justified. For example, in *Commission* v. *UK*,[96] concerning the golden share in British Airports Authority (BAA), the Court said that although national rules limiting the acquisition of shareholdings over a certain level[97] applied without distinction to both residents and non-residents, 'it must nonetheless be held that they affect the position of a person acquiring a shareholding as such and are thus liable to deter investors from other Member States from making such investments and, consequently, affect access to the market'. This formulation also comes close to the restrictions model used in the other *Golden Share* cases (considered below).

The UK had argued in this case that the principle in *Keck*[98] applied, suggesting that rules requiring prior authorization from the national authorities before major structural changes occurred in newly privatized companies or before more than a certain number of shares in those companies were acquired, did not restrict access to the market and so did not affect the free movement of capital. The Court disagreed, arguing that '[t]he measures at issue do not have comparable effects to those of the rules which the judgment in *Keck and Mithouard* regarded as not falling within the scope of Article [34 TFEU]'.[99] It continued that the restrictions 'affect the position of a persons acquiring a shareholding as such and are thus liable to deter investors from other Member States from making such investments and, consequently, affect access to the market'.[100]

---

[90] Case C–443/06 *Hollmann* v. *Fazenda Pública* [2007] ECR I–8491, para. 36.

[91] Case E-2/06 [2007] *EFTA Court Reps.* 164.     [92] Para. 66.

[93] Para. 65. It could even be argued that the rules were directly discriminatory. The Court also used the language of 'restrictions' (para. 64).

[94] See, e.g., Case C–463/00 *Commission* v. *Spain* [2003] ECR I–4581, and Case C–98/01 *Commission* v. *UK* [2003] ECR I–4641.     [95] Case C–384/93 *Alpine Investments* [1995] ECR I–1141.

[96] Case C–98/01 [2003] ECR I–4641.

[97] Para. 47. See also Case C–463/00 *Commission* v. *Spain* [2003] ECR I–4581, para. 61.

[98] Joined Cases C–267/91 and C–268/91 [1993] ECR I–6097.     [99] Para. 59.     [100] Para. 61.

As with *Alpine Investments*,[101] the Court does not appear to be ruling out the possibility that *Keck*-style principles can apply to free movement of capital; rather it seems to be suggesting that in a case where prior authorization is at stake—a situation which the Court has ruled on numerous previous occasions constitutes a restriction on the movement of capital—there is a hindrance of market access and so there is a breach of Article 63(1). If, however, the breach is not substantial or is too remote from affecting inter-state capital movements, then the Court might argue that, following the case law on goods and persons, principles similar to those laid down in *Keck*, or in *Graf*[102] (the too-uncertain and indirect rule),[103] would apply and there would be no breach of Article 63(1) (see fig. 17.1).

### (c)  National rules which restrict or create an obstacle to the free movement of capital

In most cases, a discrimination model is difficult to apply to capital movements. As Peers points out, with the advent of the single currency it is not logical to assimilate foreign currencies with foreign nationals.[104] It may be for this reason—together with a desire for convergence with the other freedoms—that the Court is increasingly using a restrictions-based approach to free movement of capital. This change in direction was most clearly signalled by the *Golden Share* cases, decided in 2002, where the Court fully embraced the *Säger*[105] formulation developed in the context of services. For example, in *Commission* v. *Portugal*[106] the Court confirmed that the prohibition found in Article 63 'goes beyond the mere elimination of unequal treatment, on grounds of nationality, as between operators on the financial markets'.[107] It continued:[108]

> Even though the rules in issue may not give rise to unequal treatment, they are liable to impede the acquisition of shares in the undertakings concerned and to dissuade investors in other Member States from investing in the capital of those undertakings. They are therefore liable, as a result, to render the free movement of capital illusory.

Therefore, a Portuguese rule requiring potential shareholders to seek prior authorization from the Portuguese authorities to hold more than a specified number of shares in certain Portuguese companies constituted a restriction on the movement of capital,[109] even though it did not involve any discriminatory or particularly restrictive treatment of nationals of other Member States.[110] This shift reflects the language of Article 63(1) which prohibits 'all *restrictions* on the movement of capital'.[111] However, in some cases

---

[101]  Case C–384/93 [1995] ECR I–1141, considered in Ch. 11.

[102]  Case C–190/98 *Graf* v. *Filzmozer Maschinenbau GmbH* [2000] ECR I–493 considered in Ch. 8.

[103]  Case C–412/97 *ED Srl* v. *Italo Fenocchio* [1999] ECR I–3845, para. 11. For further discussion on this point, see Chs. 5 and 8.                              [104]  S. Peers, above n. 53.

[105]  Case C–76/90 [1991] ECR I–4221, considered in Chs. 8 and 11.

[106]  Case C–367/98 [2002] ECR I–4731; Case C–483/99 *Commission* v. *France* [2002] ECR I–4781, para. 41.                                                           [107]  Para. 44.

[108]  Para. 45.

[109]  Para. 46. See also Joined Cases C–282/04 and C–283/04 *Commission* v. *Netherlands* [2006] ECR I–9141, para. 24.                                                [110]  Para. 43.

[111]  The question of a minimum threshold which has concerned the Court in respect of the other freedoms has not yet troubled the Court in respect of capital. There is, however, one possible exception. In Case C–377/07 *Finanzamt Speyer-Germersheim* v. *STEKO Industriemontage* [2009] ECR I–299, para. 29 the Court said 'It is insignificant…that the difference in treatment exited only for a limited period of time…That fact alone does not preclude the difference in treatment from having *significant* effects…or, therefore, from giving rise to a *genuine* restriction on the free movement of capital' (emphasis added).

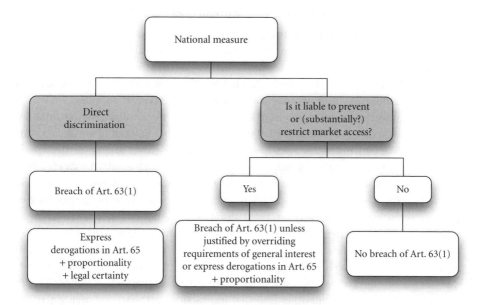

**Fig. 15.2** The free movement of capital: Restrictions/obstacles-based approach

the language of 'obstacles' is used[112]; in others, especially those involving a challenge to a home state rule, the Court continues to refer to measures which are liable to, for example, 'dissuade [home state] residents from obtaining loans or making investments in other Member States'.[113]

In other cases, the Court mixes language based on restrictions and obstacles with that based on discrimination. For example, in *Lenz*[114] the Court noted that the Austrian legislation produced 'a restrictive effect in relation to companies established in other Member States, inasmuch as it constitutes an obstacle to their raising capital in Austria'. The Court continued, 'To the extent that revenue from capital originating in another Member State receives less favourable tax treatment than revenue from capital of Austrian origin, the shares of companies established in other Member States are, for investors living in Austria, less attractive than the shares of companies established in that Member State.' Whichever formula is used, the Court usually finds that there is, in principle, a breach of Article 63(1). It then considers whether the national law can be justified either under the judicially developed public-interest requirements or, more commonly, under the broad express derogations, and whether the steps taken are proportionate.

---

[112] This term was used in Joined Cases C–282/04 and C–283/04 *Commission v. Netherlands* [2006] ECR I–9141, para. 20. In para. 27 the Court said that a possible refusal by the Dutch government of approving an important decision 'would be capable of depressing the value of the shares of that company and thus reduces the attractiveness of an investment in such shares'. As Snell points out (above, n. 19), 'Taken at face value, this [test] would open most national rules to challenge under the free movement of capital, as any interference with economic freedom is likely to depress the share prices in some companies.'

[113] Case C–478/98 *Commission v. Belgium (Eurobond)* [2000] ECR I–7587, para. 18. Case C–484/93 *Svensson and Gustavsson* [1995] ECR I–3955, para. 5.

[114] Case C–315/02 *Lenz v. Finanzlandesdirektion für Tirol* [2004] ECR I–7063, para. 21.

## 4.3 Examples of Restrictions on the Free Movement of Capital

Despite the problems with the restrictions model which we have already discussed in Chapters 1 and 8, it is now the norm for the free movement of capital. Therefore, we now turn to examine what sort of measures the Court has said constitute a restriction on free movement. The case law can broadly be divided up according to the five areas of national regulation (identified at heading 3.4 above) where Article 63 typically applies.

The first concerns property purchase and investment. Here, authorization rules are one of the most common requirements imposed by Member States and are always considered restrictions. This can be seen in *Konle*[115] where the Court said an Austrian rule of 1996 requiring prior authorization for the acquisition of land 'entails, by its very purpose, a restriction on the free movement of capital'. It could be regarded as compatible with Article 63 only if justified. Residence requirements connected with the purchase of property, often seen as indirectly discriminatory, are also more often described now as 'restrictions'. Thus in *Festersen*[116] the Court said that a Danish rule making it a condition for acquiring agricultural property that the acquirer take up his fixed residence on that property, 'while not discriminat[ing] between Danish nationals and nationals of other Member States... [nevertheless] restricts the free movement of capital'.

Cross-border currency and other financial transactions is the second area where the Treaty provisions on capital tend to apply. These currency transactions may take the form of physical movement of cash as in *Bordessa*,[117] where the Court said that a rule requiring the export of coins, banknotes, or bearer cheques conditional upon an administrative authorization would cause 'the exercise of the free movement of capital to be subject to the discretion of the administrative authorities and thus be such as to render that freedom illusory'. It continued that '[i]t might have the effect of impeding capital movements carried out in accordance with [Union] law'.

Alternatively, the movement may be electronic, as in *Trummer and Meyer*.[118] There the Court said that a national rule prohibiting the registration of a mortgage in the currency of another Member State weakened the link between the debt to be secured, payable in the currency of another Member State, and the mortgage, whose value could, as a result of subsequent currency exchange fluctuations, end up being lower than that of the debt to be secured, thereby reducing the effectiveness of the security, and thus its attractiveness. The Court therefore said that the national rule was 'liable to dissuade the parties concerned from denominating a debt in the currency of another Member State, and may thus deprive them of a right which constitutes a component element of the free movement of capital and payments'.[119] It added that the rules might also cause the parties to incur additional costs by requiring them, purely for the purpose of the

---

[115] Case C–302/97 *Klaus Konle* [1999] ECR I–3099, para. 39; Joined Cases C–515/99 and C–527/99 to C–540/99 *Reisch* [2002] ECR I–2157, para. 32; Case C–567/07 *Minister voor Wonen, Wijken en Integratie* v. *Woningstichting Sint Servatius* [2009] ECR I–000, para. 22.

[116] Case C–370/05 [2007] ECR I–1129, para. 25.

[117] Joined Cases C–358/93 and C–416/93 *Bordessa* [1995] ECR I–361, para. 25. Cf. Case 157/85 *Luigi Brugnoni and Roberto Ruffinengo* v. *Cassa di risparmio di Genova e Imperia* [1986] ECR I–2013, para. 22 for an early example of an authorization rule and the Court's more qualified approach.

[118] Case C–222/97 *Manfred Trummer and Peter Mayer* [1999] ECR I–1661, confirmed in Case C–464/98 *Westdeutsche Landesbank Girozentrale* v. *Friedrich Stefan and Republik Österreich* [2001] ECR I–173, para. 19.    [119] Para. 26.

registration, to value the debt in the national currency and formally register that currency conversion.[120]

In a different context, the Court ruled in *Commission v. Italy (temporary labour)*[121] that an Italian requirement that an out-of-state undertaking engaged in the provision of temporary labour in Italy had to establish a guarantee of 700 million lire with a credit institution having its registered office or a branch office in Italy was a restriction on capital movements.

Loans is the third area where Article 63 tends to apply. In *Svensson and Gustafsson*[122] the Court ruled that Luxembourg law requiring a bank to be established in Luxembourg for recipients of loans residing in its territory to obtain an interest rate subsidy from the State was 'liable to dissuade those concerned from approaching banks established in another Member State and therefore constitute[s] an obstacle to movements of capital such as bank loans' and could not be justified. In *Commission v. Belgium (Eurobond)*[123] the Belgian rule went even further because it prevented Belgian residents from subscribing to a loan issued in German marks on the Eurobond market. The Court said this rule went 'well beyond a measure which is intended to dissuade residents of a Member State from subscribing to a loan issued abroad' and thus 'all the more' constituted a restriction on the free movement of capital within the meaning of Article 63.[124]

Investments in companies and shares is the fourth area where Article 63 applies.[125] Once again, authorisation requirements are considered to be restrictions. So, in *Church of Scientology*[126] the Court said that 'A provision of national law which makes a foreign investment subject to prior authorization constitutes a restriction on the movement of capital'. *Commission v. Italy (pharmacists)*[127] concerned a different types of measure. The Court ruled that national legislation providing that members of companies and firms operating pharmacies had to be qualified pharmacists 'prevents investors from other Member States who are not pharmacists from acquiring stakes in companies and firms of that kind'. The national legislation therefore imposed restrictions within the meaning of Articles 49 and 63(1).

The *Golden Share* cases are the fifth area where Article 63 applies. Obligations imposed by the 'golden share' holder, usually the state acting as regulator albeit in the guise of a market participant, are considered restrictions on free movement of capital. So, as we saw in *Commission v. Portugal*,[128] the obligation to seek authorization from the state prior to holding more than a certain number of shares constituted a restriction on free movement of capital.[129] In *Federconsumatori*[130] a rule which gave public shareholders the right to participate in the board of directors in a more significant way than their status as shareholders would normally allow also constituted a restriction on the free movement of capital. Likewise, a golden shareholders' power to oppose the acquisition of certain

---

[120] Para. 27. Cf. Case C–168/01 *Bosal* [2003] ECR I–9409, para. 27 for even more relaxed language.
[121] Case C–279/00 [2002] ECR I–1425, para. 37.  [122] Case C–484/93 [1995] ECR I–3955, para. 10.
[123] Case C–478/98 [2000] ECR I–7587.  [124] Para. 19.
[125] Case C–531/06 *Commission v. Italy (pharmacists)* [2009] ECR I–000, para. 40.
[126] Case C–54/99 *Association Eglise de Scientologie de Paris v. The Prime Minister* [2000] ECR I–1335, para. 14.  [127] Case C–531/06 [2009] ECR I–000, paras. 47–8.
[128] Case C–367/98 [2002] ECR I–4731; Case C–483/99 *Commission v. France* [2002] ECR I–4781, para. 41.
[129] This was one of the three major obstacles to the free movement of capital identified by the Commission in its Communication on Certain Legal Aspects concerning intra-EU investment (OJ [1997] C220/15).
[130] Joined Cases C–463/04 and 464/04 *Federconsumatori v. Comune di Milano* [2007] ECR I–10419, paras. 23–4.

shareholdings or the conclusion of certain agreements by shareholders representing at least 5 per cent of voting rights, as in *Commission* v. *Italy*,[131] were considered restrictions on the free movement of capital. In *Commission* v. *Germany*[132] the Court said that a law capping voting rights of every shareholder in Volkswagen at 20 per cent, introducing a blocking minority at 20 per cent for important company decisions,[133] and allowing the federal government and the state of Lower Saxony to appoint two members each of the supervisory board,[134] thus enabling them to participate in a more significant manner in the activities of the supervisory board than their status as shareholders would normally allow, breached Article 63(1).

The discussion so far shows that, in the context of free movement of capital, Article 63(1) is less about the movement of capital itself than about facilitating other transactions requiring capital with a cross-border element. The Court finds relatively easily that any obstacle to such transactions is a restriction contrary to Article 63(c) unless justified. Does this case law apply equally to movements of capital between Member States and third countries? In *A*,[135] Germany and the Netherlands argued forcibly that it should not. Drawing on arguments which the Court itself has used to find that provisions of the WTO Agreements should not have direct effect,[136] the states said that by extending the restrictions case law to relations with third countries 'the [Union] would unilaterally open up the [Union] market to third countries without retaining the means of negotiation necessary to achieve liberalisation on the part of those countries'. The Court disagreed[137] and applied its restrictions case law. The case concerned a Swedish law which granted taxpayers living in Sweden an exemption from tax in respect of dividends distributed in the form of shares in a subsidiary by a limited liability company established in Sweden or in another state within the EEA but refused to grant them that exemption where such a distribution was made by a company established in a third country outside the EEA, unless that country had concluded a convention providing for the exchange of information with Sweden. The Court said that:

The effect of such legislation is to discourage taxpayers residing in Sweden from investing their capital in companies established outside the EEA. Since the dividends which such companies pay to Swedish residents receive less favourable tax treatment than dividends distributed by a company established in an EEA Member State, the shares of such companies are less attractive to investors residing in Sweden than shares in companies established in such a State.[138]

The Swedish law 'therefore entails a restriction of the movement of capital between Member States and third countries which, in principle, is prohibited by Article [63(1)]'.[139] However, the Court found that the Swedish rule could be justified on the grounds of fiscal supervision, particularly because the framework of cooperation between the competent authorities of the Member States established by Directive 77/799 does not exist in respect

---

[131] Case C–326/07 [2009] ECR I–2291, para. 40. See also the Commission's Communication on Certain Legal Aspects concerning intra-EU investment (OJ [1997] C220/15).

[132] Case C–112/05 *Commission* v. *Germany (Volkswagen)* [2007] ECR I–8995, paras. 56 and 68.

[133] Lower Saxony held 20 per cent of the shares. It therefore enjoyed an indirect veto on all major decisions of the company.

[134] The supervisory board is not a decision-making body but a monitoring body.

[135] Case C–101/05 *Skatteverket* v. *A* [2007] ECR I–11531, para. 38.        [136] See further Ch.2.

[137] Para. 38.      [138] Para. 42.      [139] Para. 43.

of relations with authorities of non-Member States.[140] This might suggest that while the Court is prepared to cast the Article 63 net widely to catch restrictions on the movement of capital with third countries so that it can scrutinize them, it might be more lenient in respect of accepting the justifications proposed by the Member States.[141]

### 4.4 Taxation

### (a) Introduction

While authorization and other similar requirements are classic examples of 'restrictions' on the free movement of capital, an increasing number of cases concern taxation of capital. Because of the special issues raised by national tax rules (discussed in Chapters 9 and 10) the taxation cases are considered separately. The story seen under Article 49 is repeated in respect of Article 63: up until the mid 2000s the cases focused on the question of whether the taxation rule constituted a restriction on free movement; later cases suggested a retreat to a discrimination-based analysis. However, the Court tends to paper over the cracks by describing any such discriminatory treatment as 'a restriction on the free movement of capital which is, in principle, prohibited by Article [63(1)]'.[142]

*Sandoz*[143] is a good example of the Court applying a restriction-based approach towards tax rules. It concerned stamp duty payable under Austrian law on a loan taken out by an Austrian company from a Belgian company. No tax was payable under Belgian law. The Court said that since the Austrian law deprived Austrian residents of the possibility of taking out a tax-free loan with a non-resident company 'such a measure is likely to deter such residents from obtaining loans from persons established in other Member States'.[144] It continued that 'such legislation constitutes an obstacle to the movement of capital' within the meaning of Article 63(1).[145] Thus, the mere imposition of tax was enough to constitute a restriction which had to be justified.

The approach adopted in this case now needs to be read in the light of the velvet revolution of late 2006/early 2007 in cases such as *FII Group Litigation*[146] and *ACT Group Litigation*,[147] considered in Chapter 10, where the Court was forced to re-examine its 'restrictions' jurisprudence. It will be recalled that, under the principles of international tax law the home state (State A) will always exercise tax jurisdiction over persons established within its territory (residents) in respect of their worldwide income. It will also tax non-residents on income received in State A (source).[148] Broadly speaking, the Court now applies the principle of equal treatment laid down in *FII*. Therefore, it has ruled that

---

[140] See also Case C–540/07 *Commission* v. *Italy* [2009] ECR I–000, paras. 70–1 where the Court extended the rule in *A* to EEA states.

[141] See also Case C–446/04 *FII* [2006] ECR I–11753, para. 121 where the Court said that 'it may be that a Member State will be able to demonstrate that a restriction on capital movements to or from non-member countries is justified for a particular reason in circumstances where that reason would not constitute a valid justification for a restriction on capital movements between Member States'.

[142] Case C–157/05 *Holböck* v. *Finanzamt Salzburg-Land* [2007] ECR I–4051, para. 30.

[143] Case C–439/97 *Sandoz GmbH* [1999] ECR I–7041. For another example, see Case C–35/98 *Verkooijen* [2000] ECR I–4071.

[144] Para. 19. Cf. Case E–1/00 *State Debt Management Agency* v. *Íslandsbanki–FBA hf.* [2000] EFTA Ct Rep 8, where the EFTA Court did not consider the imposition of a heavier burden on foreign transactions as being automatically a restriction, although it did on the facts (para. 26).

[145] Para. 20. See also Case C–484/93 *Svensson and Gustavsson* [1995] ECR I–3955, para. 8.

[146] Case C–446/04 *FII* [2006] ECR I–11753.      [147] Case C–374/04 *ACT* [2006] ECR I–11673.

[148] See B. J. M. Terra and P. J. Wattel, *European Tax Law*, 5th edn (Alphen aan den Rijn: Kluwer Law International, 2008), Ch. 17.

it is, in principle, contrary to Article 63 for State A to tax, for example, an inheritance received in State B,[149] income from property in State B,[150] or dividends from shares from companies established in State B[151] differently, and usually less favourably, than would be the case if the receipts came from inheritances received in State A, property in State A, or dividends payable by companies established in State A (these situations are considered in more detail below). Such difference in treatment based on the place of investment (or source[152]) breaches Article 63 unless saved by an express derogation or a public-interest justification.[153] However, given the existence of the Article 65(1)(a) derogation which expressly allows discrimination between residents and non-residents, the Court tends to be more willing to find a breach in principle of Article 63(1) using the restrictions approach,[154] even after *ACT* and *FII,* than it is of Article 49 where no equivalent derogation exists, but finds the measure lawful under Article 65(1)(a).

We shall now consider the application of Article 63 in the four main areas where national tax rules have been challenged: inheritances, property ownership, purchase of shares, and charitable gifts.

## (b) Inheritances

As regards inheritances, *Jäger*[155] provides a good example of the home state, State A, taxing property located in State B and received under an inheritance less favourably that property inherited in State A. The case concerned an inheritance consisting of agricultural land and forestry situated in France being subject, in Germany, to inheritance tax higher than that which would have been payable had the assets inherited been situated exclusively within Germany. The Court said that the German rule had the effect of restricting the movement of capital by reducing the value of an inheritance situated outside Germany. The rule therefore breached Article 63(1) and could not be saved by the Article 65(1)(a) derogation.

While *Jäger* concerned discrimination based on the location of the inherited property, *Eckelkamp*[156] concerned discrimination based on the residence of the deceased. Under Belgian law an inheritance consisting of immoveable property situated in Belgium was subject to transfer duties higher than inheritance duties that would have been payable had the deceased been residing in Belgium at the time of her death (she had been living in Germany). The Court said that the Belgian rule restricted the movement of capital in breach of Article 56 by reducing the value of an inheritance.[157] Once again, the Court said that the restriction could not be saved under Article 65(1)(a).

---

[149] Case C–256/06 *Jäger* v. *Finanzamt Kusel-Landstuhl* [2008] ECR I–123, para. 32. See also Case C–67/08 *Block* [2009] ECR I–883, para. 24 (although no discrimination was found on the facts).

[150] Case C–451/05 *ELISA* v. *Directeur general des impost* [2007] ECR I–8251.

[151] Case C–201/05 *Test Claimants in the CFC and Dividend Group Litigation* v. *Commissioners of Inland Revenue,* Order of 23 Apr. 2008, para. 55. The same applies to the sales of shares: Case C–436/06 *Grønfeldt* v. *Finanzamt Hamburg – AM Tierpark* [2007] ECR I–12357, paras. 13–14.

[152] Case C–157/05 *Holböck* [2007] ECR I–4051, para. 30. Since this case concerned dividends coming from a third country, the difference in treatment was permitted under Art. 64 (1) TFEU (ex Art. 57(1) EC) provided that the restrictions already existed on 31 Dec. 1993 (para. 39).

[153] Case C–436/06 *Grønfeldt* [2007] ECR I–12357, para. 14.

[154] See, e.g., Case C–11/07 *Eckelkamp* v. *Belgische Staat* [2008] ECR I–6845, paras. 54–6 and Case C–43/07 *Arens-Sikken* [2008] ECR I–6887, paras. 47–9. In neither case was the derogation made out on the facts. Cf. Case C–376/03 *D* [2005] ECR I–5821.          [155] Case C–256/06 *Jäger* [2008] ECR I–123, para. 32.

[156] Case C–11/07 *Eckelkamp* v. *Belgische Staat* [2008] ECR I–6845, para. 44.

[157] Para. 46. See also Case C–43/07 *Arens-Sikken* [2008] ECR I–6887, para. 40, decided the same day as *Eckelkamp.*

Where there is no discrimination, the national law is lawful, as *Van Hilten-van der Heijden*[158] shows. Dutch law provided that the estate of a national of a Member State who died within ten years of ceasing to reside in the Netherlands was to be taxed as if that national had continued to reside in the Netherlands, while providing for relief in respect of the taxes levied in the state to which the deceased had transferred her residence. The Court found that this law did not constitute a restriction on the movement of capital.[159] It reasoned that by enacting identical taxation provisions for the estates of nationals who transferred their residence abroad and for those who remained in the Netherlands, Dutch law did not discourage nationals who transferred their residence abroad from making investments in the Netherlands, nor those who remained in the Netherlands from investing in another Member State, nor did it diminish the value of the estate of nationals who had transferred their residence abroad.[160]

### (c) Property

The issue of differential tax treatment of residents and non-residents in respect of property arose in *Blanckaert*.[161] Blanckaert concerned a Belgian resident who had invested in property in the Netherlands. Dutch law provided that non-resident taxpayers, who received income in the Netherlands from savings and investments but who were not insured under the Dutch social security scheme, were not entitled to tax credits in respect of national insurance. By contrast, resident taxpayers, who were insured under the Dutch social security scheme but otherwise in the same situation as non-residents, were entitled to those credits. Had the case been decided under Articles 45 or 49 the Court may well have said that the situations of the resident and non-resident were not comparable and so there was no breach of Union law. However, since this case concerned free movement of capital, the Court said that 'Less favourable tax treatment for non-residents only might deter the latter from investing in property in the Netherlands. The legislation was therefore capable of hindering the free movement of capital.' However, the Court did take account the differences between the situation of residents and non-residents at the derogation stage and, considering that their situations were not comparable, found that the Dutch law could be justified under Article 65(1)(a).

### (d) Shares

The principle from *FII* also applies to differential tax treatment of shares by the home state depending on the place where the capital was invested. This can be seen in *STEKO Industriemontage*[162] where a resident company could not deduct from its taxable revenue reductions in profit resulting from the partial write-down of holdings in non-resident companies. By contrast, a resident company could deduct such reductions in profit from its taxable revenue where they related to holdings in resident companies. So, resident companies holding depreciated shares in non-resident companies were in a less favourable situation than those holding shares in resident companies. The national rule therefore constituted an 'obstacle' to free movement contrary to Article 63.[163]

---

[158] Case C–513/03 *van Hilten-van der Heijden* [2006] ECR I–1957.    [159] Para. 45.
[160] Para. 46.
[161] Case C–512/03 *Blanckaert* v. *Inspecteur van de Belastingdienst* [2005] ECR I–7685, para. 39.
[162] Case C–377/07 *Finanzamt Speyer-Germersheim* v. *STEKO Industriemontage* [2009] ECR I–299.
[163] Paras. 25–7.

While *STEKO* concerned treatment of residents' incoming income and losses, *Amurta SGPS*[164] concerned outgoing dividends. Dutch law provided for a withholding tax on dividends distributed by a company in the Netherlands to a company established in another Member State (Portugal) while exempting from that tax the dividends paid to a company liable to corporation tax in the Netherlands. The Court said that treating dividends paid to companies established in another Member State less favourably than dividends paid to companies established in the Netherlands was liable to deter companies established in another Member State from investing in the Netherlands and thus constituted a restriction on the free movement of capital prohibited by Article 63[165] which could not be justified.

As we saw with *Van Hilten-van der Heijden* above, where however there is no discrimination, then the national law is compatible with Article 63. This can be seen in *Kerckhaert-Morres*[166] where Belgian legislation did not make any distinction between dividends from companies established in Belgium and dividends from companies established in another Member State (France)—both dividends were taxed at the same rate and so there was no breach of Article 63(1).[167] The Court added that any adverse consequences arising from the Belgian system (the dividends had already been taxed in France, leading to 'juridical' double taxation—the taxation of the same income twice in the hands of the same person) were the result of the exercise in parallel by two Member States of their fiscal sovereignty.[168] In reaching this conclusion the Court acknowledged the point made by Advocate General Geelhoed in *ACT Group Litigation*[169] that 'quasi-restrictions' brought about by the coexistence of two systems of taxation should fall outside the Treaties.

### (e) Charitable gifts

The principle derived from *FII* also applies to tax relief on charitable donations, as *Persche*[170] shows. A German national claimed a tax deduction in respect of gifts (bed linen, towels, zimmer frames, and toys), valued at about €18,000, to a retirement home and a children's home in Portugal. He was refused the deduction on the basis of German law which allowed for the deduction for tax purposes of gifts to charitable bodies in Germany but excluded that tax advantage for gifts to bodies established and recognized as charitable in another Member State.

The Court said that since the possibility of obtaining a tax deduction could have 'a significant influence on the donor's attitude, the inability in Germany to deduct gifts to bodies recognised as charitable if they are established in other Member States is likely to affect the willingness of German taxpayers to make gifts for their benefit'.[171] The German legislation therefore constituted a restriction on the free movement of capital contrary to Article 63 which could not be justified.

---

[164] Case C–379/05 *Amurta SGPS v. Inspecteur van de Belastingdienst* [2007] ECR I–9569.
[165] Para. 28.     [166] Case C–513/04 *Kerckhaert-Morres v. Belgium* [2006] ECR I–10967, paras. 17–18.
[167] See also Case C–298/05 *Columbus Container Services* [2007] ECR I–10451, para. 40.
[168] Para. 21.     [169] Case C–374/04 [2007] ECR I–11673, considered in Ch. 10.
[170] Case C–318/07 *Persche* [2009] ECR I–359.     [171] Para. 38.

### 4.5 Public-interest Requirements and Proportionality

#### (a) Public-interest requirements

In *Commission* v. *Portugal*[172] the Court followed the approach adopted in *Gebhard*[173] in respect of justifications. It said:

The free movement of capital, as a fundamental principle of the [Treaties], may be restricted only by national rules which are justified by reasons referred to in Article [65(1)] of the [Treaties] or by overriding requirements of the general interest and which are applicable to all persons and undertakings pursuing an activity in the territory of the host Member State. Furthermore, in order to be so justified, the national legislation must be suitable for securing the objective which it pursues and must not go beyond what is necessary in order to attain it, so as to accord with the principle of proportionality.[174]

As with the other freedoms, the list of justifications is open-ended[175] and wide ranging. For example, in *Commission* v. *Italy (Golden Share)*[176] the Court recognized that certain restrictions on the free movement of capital could be justified by the need for 'the minimum supply of energy resources and goods essential to the public as a whole, the continuity of public service, national defence, the protection of public policy and public security and health emergencies'. In *A*[177] the Court recognized the justification of the need to guarantee the effectiveness of fiscal supervision;[178] and in *STEKO*[179] the Court contemplated as a possible justification the need for a seamless transition from an earlier system to its replacement.

A number of cases have concerned housing issues. For example, in *Konle*[180] the Court said that a Member States could justify its prior-authorization requirement for the acquisition of land by relying on a 'town and country planning objective such as maintaining, in the general interest, a permanent population and an economic activity independent of the tourist sector in certain regions'. In *Reisch*[181] the Court added that that finding could 'only be strengthened by other concerns which might underlie those same measures such as the protection of the environment'.[182] By analogy, in *Sint Servatius*[183] the Court recognized requirements relating to public-housing policy and to the financing of that policy could constitute overriding reasons in the general interest. And in *Ospelt*[184] the Court recognized that a prior-authorization requirement before purchasing agricultural land could be justified on the grounds of:

preserving agricultural communities, maintaining a distribution of land ownership which allows the development of viable farms and sympathetic management of green spaces and the

---

[172] Case C–367/98 *Commission* v. *Portugal* [2002] ECR I–4731.

[173] Case C–55/94 [1995] ECR I–4165, considered further in Ch. 12.

[174] See also Joined Cases C–515/99 and C–527/99 to C–540/99 *Reisch* [2002] ECR I–2157, para. 33: 'The national rules pursue, in a non-discriminatory way, an objective in the public interest and if they observe the principle of proportionality, that is if the same result could not be achieved by other less restrictive measures.'　　　　　　　　　　　　[175] See further the discussion of the list of justifications in Ch. 13.

[176] Case C–326/07 [2009] ECR I–2291, para. 45.　　　[177] Case C–101/05 *A* [2007] ECR I–11531.

[178] See also Art. 65(1)(b), considered below.

[179] Case C–377/07 *STEKO* [2009] ECR I–299, para. 50.

[180] Case C–302/97 *Konle* [1999] ECR I–3099. This part of the judgment concerned the post-Accession law.　　　[181] Joined Cases C–515/99 and C–527/99 to C–540/99 *Reisch* [2002] ECR I–2157.

[182] Para. 34.　　　[183] Case C–567/07 *Sint Servatius* [2009] ECR I–000, para. 30.

[184] Case C–452/01 *Ospelt* v. *Schlössle Weissenberg Familienstiftung* [2003] ECR I–9743.

countryside as well as encouraging a reasonable use of the available land by resisting pressure on land, and preventing natural disasters.[185]

As with the other freedoms, justifications of a purely economic nature are not permitted. So in *Manninen*[186] the Court rejected 'reduction in tax revenue' as an overriding reason in the public interest[187] and in *Verkooijn*[188] the Court rejected as an argument for a more favourable tax regime for companies established in the Netherlands 'the intention to promote the economy of the country by encouraging investment by individuals in companies with their seat in the Netherlands'.[189]

In practice the Court rarely finds that the justifications are made out on the facts.[190] For example, in *Trummer and Meyer*[191] the Court said that while a Member State was in principle entitled to take the necessary measures to ensure that a mortgage system clearly and transparently prescribed the respective rights of mortgagees *inter se*, as well as the rights of mortgagees as a whole vis-à-vis other creditors,[192] the need to achieve this was not made out on the facts.

### (b) Proportionality

Even if the justification is made out, the Court often finds that the national measure is not proportionate. This is particularly the case with a prior-authorization requirement. For example, in *Konle* the Court said that given the risk of discrimination inherent in a system of prior authorization for the acquisition of land and the other possibilities available to Austria for ensuring compliance with its town and country planning guidelines, the authorization procedure constituted a restriction on capital movements which was not essential to prevent infringements of the national legislation on secondary residences. It also added that the state could be liable in damages to individuals who had suffered a sufficiently serious breach of Union law.[193]

The Court did, however, say in *Konle* that a requirement of a *declaration* prior to the purchase of building plots, coupled with penalties for breach of the declaration,[194] would

---

[185] Para. 39. In a similar vein see also Case C–370/05 *Festersen* [2007] ECR I–1129, para. 27, where the Court accepted the Danish government's arguments based on the need 'first, to preserve the farming of agricultural land by means of owner-occupancy, which constitutes one of the traditional forms of farming in Denmark, and to ensure that agricultural property be occupied and farmed predominantly by the owners, second, as a town and country planning measure, to preserve a permanent agricultural community and, third, to encourage a reasonable use of the available land by resisting pressure on land'. However, the Court found the residence requirement disproportionate.

[186] Case C–319/02 *Manninen* [2004] ECR I–7477, para. 49.

[187] See also Case C–367/98 *Commission v. Portugal* [2002] ECR I–4731, para. 52 where the justification based on the 'need to safeguard the financial interest of the Portuguese republic' was also rejected. The Court also rejected the argument based on the need to preserve the Portuguese system of property ownership.

[188] Case C–35/98 *Verkooijn* [2000] ECR I–4071, paras. 47–8.

[189] Cf. Case C–194/06 *Orange European Smallcap Fund* [2008] ECR I–3747, para. 93, for hints to the contrary.

[190] Cf. Case C–101/05 *A* [2007] ECR I–11531 where the justification was made out but in a third country context where different rules may well apply in the absence of a framework of mutual cooperation between EU Member States and third countries. See also Case C–446/04 *FII* [2006] ECR I–11753, para. 121 considered above n. 141.      [191] Case C–222/97 *Trummer and Mayer* [1999] ECR I–1661.

[192] Para. 30.     [193] Paras. 58–9.

[194] Any penalties must themselves be proportionate: in Case C–213/04 *Burtscher v. Stauderer* [2005] ECR I–10309 the penalty provided was the retroactive invalidity of the property transaction and this was found incompatible with Art. 63.

comply with Union law.[195] In *Reisch* the Court added that the requirement of prior notification provided the acquirer of the title with an element of legal certainty and was better suited to preventing certain damage which was reparable only with difficulty, caused by hastily completed building projects.[196] For this reason, a declaration/notification requirement was compatible with Union law.

The question of authorization versus declaration has had a long history. It was first raised, not in respect of the acquisition of immovable property, but concerning national rules making currency exports conditional on prior authorization. For example, in *Bordessa*[197] an Italian leaving Spain by car was stopped at the French border and found to be carrying banknotes worth 50 million pesetas. Since he did not have the prior authorization required by Spanish law for the export of such a sum, he was arrested and the money confiscated. The Court said that because authorization had the effect of suspending currency exports and making them conditional on the consent of the administrative authorities, this might make the free movement of capital illusory.[198] For this reason, the Court usually finds that a prior declaration, giving 'useful information as to the nature of the planned operation and the actual identity of the declarant',[199] was more proportionate. Therefore, in *Bordessa* the Court said that a prior declaration might be one of the requisite measures which Member States were permitted to take since, unlike prior authorization, it did not entail suspension of the transaction but did still allow the national authorities to exercise effective supervision[200] to uphold public policy and effective supervision to prevent infringements of national law and regulations.[201]

However, the Court has recognized that in some circumstances there may be a role for prior authorization. For example, in *Commission v. Portugal*, one of the *Golden Share* cases, the Court acknowledged that[202] 'certain concerns'[203] could justify 'the retention by Member States of a degree of influence within undertakings that were initially public and subsequently privatised, where those undertakings are active in fields involving the provision of services in the public interest or strategic services' (variously in the banking, insurance, energy, and transport sectors).[204] Therefore, the Court suggested that a prior-authorization requirement could be justified provided it was proportionate, based on objective, non-discriminatory criteria which were known in advance to the undertakings concerned, and all persons affected by a restrictive measure had to have a legal remedy available to them.[205] Since this was not made out on the facts, the Portuguese law breached Article 63(1).

---

[195] Paras. 44–8.     [196] Para. 36.

[197] Joined Cases C–358/93 and C–416/93 *Bordessa* [1995] ECR I–361.     [198] Paras. 24–5.

[199] Joined Cases C–163/94, C–165/94, and C–250/94 *Sanz de Lera* [1995] ECR I–4830, para. 38.

[200] Para. 27.     [201] Para. 28.

[202] Citing the Commission's Communication on certain legal aspects concerning intra-EU investment 97/C 220/6 ([1997] OJ C220/15).

[203] But not those concerning systems of property ownership, referred to in Art. 345 TFEU (ex Art. 295 EC) (para. 48).

[204] Case C–367/98 *Commission v. Portugal* [2002] ECR I–4731, para. 47; Case C–483/99 *Commission v. France* [2002] ECR I–4781, para. 43, and Case C–503/99 *Commission v. Belgium* [2002] ECR I–4809, para. 43.

[205] Case C–205/99 *Analir* [2001] ECR I–1271, paras. 35 and 38; Case C–567/07 *Sint Servatius* [2009] ECR I–000, para. 35.

In *Commission* v. *Spain*,[206] another of the *Golden Share* cases, the Spanish government attempted to justify its prior-authorization requirement on the grounds of 'overriding requirements of the general interest linked to strategic imperatives and the need to ensure continuity in public services'. The Court rejected this on the ground that the companies concerned (a group of banks and a company producing tobacco) had no public-service objectives. In *Commission* v. *Germany (Volkswagen)*[207] the Court recognized protection of workers and minority shareholders as potential justifications but said that Germany had been unable to explain why, in order to meet these objectives, it was appropriate and necessary for the Federal and state authorities to maintain a strengthened and irremovable position in the capital of that company.[208]

In *Commission* v *Italy*[209] the Court was more demanding of the defendant state: to satisfy the proportionality principle, the state had to identify the public interest at stake and formulate in a specific and precise manner the connection between the criteria and the specific powers to which they relate. This level of scrutiny was also demonstrated in *Cibrian Fernandez*.[210] German law operated a taxation scheme intended to encourage the building of rental property in Germany (but not outside of Germany). The Court found that the scheme was not appropriate: instead of targeting places where the shortage of housing was particularly acute, the taxation scheme applied to all categories of rental property 'from the most basic to the most luxurious'. That being the case, the Court said it could not be assumed that 'private investors, who are motivated in particular by financial considerations, will meet the allegedly socio-political objective' of the German tax law.[211]

Proportionality also defeated the Dutch government's claim that its golden share in the privatized post office was necessary in *Commission* v. *Netherlands*.[212] The Court recognized that the guarantee of a service of general interest, such as a universal postal service, could constitute an overriding reason in the general interest justifying an obstacle to the free movement of capital.[213] However, the Court found that the special share went beyond what was necessary to safeguard the solvency and continuity of the provider of the universal post service: the special rights were not limited to the company's activities as provider of a universal postal service. The Court added that the exercise of those special rights was not based on any precise criterion and did not have to be backed up by any statement of reasons thereby making effective judicial review impossible.[214]

## 5. EXPRESS DEROGATIONS

### 5.1 Introduction

One explanation why there is less extensive case law on justifications in the field of capital than in respect of the other freedoms is because of the breadth of the express derogations and the fact that the derogations embrace some aspects of the public-interest

---

[206] Case C–463/00 [2003] ECR I–4581.     [207] Case C–112/05 [2007] ECR I–8995.

[208] Para. 74.

[209] See also Case C–326/07 *Commission* v. *Italy (Golden share)* [2009] ECR I–2291, para. 52.

[210] Case C–35/08 *Grundstücksgemeinschaft Busley and Cibrian Fernandez* v. *Finanzamt Stuttgart-Körperschaften* [2009] ECR I–000.     [211] Para. 32.

[212] Joined Cases C–282/04 and C–283/04 *Commission* v. *Netherlands* [2006] ECR I–9141, para. 19.

[213] Para. 38.     [214] Para. 40.

requirements found elsewhere. Article 65(1) contains two express derogations, one specific and one general. The specific one relates to tax. Article 65(1)(a) states that the provisions of Article 63 are without prejudice to the right of the Member States:

to apply the relevant provisions of their tax law which distinguish between taxpayers who are not in the same situation with regard to their place of residence or with regard to the place where their capital is invested.

Article 65(1)(b), replicating Article 4 of Directive 88/361,[215] contains the general derogation. It provides that the provisions of Article 63 shall be without prejudice to the right of Member States:

to take all requisite measures to prevent infringements of national law and regulations, in particular in the field of taxation and the prudential supervision of financial institutions, or to lay down procedures for the declaration of capital movements for purposes of administrative or statistical information, or to take measures which are justified on grounds of public policy or public security.

Thus, the express derogations contained in Article 65(1)(b) are a mixture of the standard public-policy/public-security derogations found elsewhere in the Treaties together with special provisions concerning taxation which reflect the mandatory requirements on the effectiveness of fiscal supervision.[216] Article 65(3) then adds:

The measures and procedures referred to in paragraphs 1 and 2 shall not constitute a means of arbitrary discrimination or a disguised restriction on the free movement of capital and payments as defined in Article 63.

This is the equivalent to the second sentence of Article 36 on goods.[217]

   Given the similarities and overlaps between the Article 65 derogations and the derogations found elsewhere in the Treaties, it is not surprising that the Court draws on its jurisprudence in respect of the other freedoms when interpreting the Article 65 derogations. For example, in *Casati*[218] the Court said that:

The administrative measures or penalties [imposed by Member States for breach of national rules] must not go beyond what is strictly necessary, the control procedures must not be conceived in such a way as to restrict the freedom required by the [Treaties] and they must not be accompanied by a penalty which is so disproportionate to the gravity of the infringement that it becomes an obstacle to the exercise of that freedom.

The Court offered a more detailed list of limitations on the use of the derogations in the *Church of Scientology*[219] case. It said that:

- Derogations from the fundamental principle of free movement of capital had to be interpreted strictly, so that their scope could not be determined unilaterally by each Member State without any control by the Union institutions.[220]
- Derogations could not be misapplied so as, in fact, to serve purely economic ends.[221]

---

215  Joined Cases C–358/93 and C–416/93 *Bordessa* [1995] ECR I–361, para. 22.
216  Case C–478/98 *Commission v. Belgium (Eurobond)* [2000] ECR I–7587.      217  See further Ch. 6.
218  Case 203/80 *Casati* [1981] ECR 2595, para. 27.
219  Case C–54/99 *Eglise de Scientologie* [2000] ECR I–1335, paras. 17–18.
220  Citing Case 36/75 *Rutili* [1975] ECR 1219, paras. 26–7.
221  Ibid., para. 30.

- Any person affected by a restrictive measure based on such a derogation had to have access to legal redress.[222]
- Derogations were subject to the principle of proportionality.

The Court then added that restrictions on free movement of capital also had to be subject to the principle of legal certainty. It said that individuals had to be 'apprised of the extent of their rights and obligations deriving from Article [63] of the [Treaties]'.[223] Although legal certainty is a general principle of law, only in respect of free movement of capital is the requirement so clearly stated.[224]

The limited nature of the Article 65 derogations was emphasized by the Court in *Commission* v. *Portugal*[225] where Portugal tried to justify its golden share rules on the ground of the need to safeguard Portuguese financial interests. The Court said that unless such reasons fell within the scope of Article 65(1) (for example, relating to tax law), 'the general financial interests of a Member State cannot constitute adequate justification'[226] because 'economic grounds can never serve as justification for obstacles prohibited by the [Treaties]'.[227] Therefore, the Court refused to accept 'the economic policy objectives' raised by the Portuguese government in justification, namely choosing a strategic partner, strengthening the competitive structure of the market, or modernizing and increasing the efficiency of means of production.

Having examined the general rules relating to the express derogations we shall now consider the derogations in turn, starting with the specific provision on tax.

### 5.2 Article 65(1)(a): Tax Provisions Distinguishing between Resident and Non-resident Taxpayers or the Place where their Capital Is Invested

Under this derogation, national laws can continue to distinguish between taxpayers according to their place of residence[228] or the place where their capital is invested.[229] However, as the Court emphasized in *Lenz*,[230] this provision had to be interpreted strictly and did not mean that any tax legislation making a distinction between taxpayers on the listed grounds was automatically compatible with the Treaties. This specific tax derogation is confined to tax laws which were already in existence at the end of 1993.[231]

The Court has had the opportunity of considering this provision in a number of cases including *Verkooijen*[232] and *Manninen*.[233] These cases establish that under Article 65(1)

---

[222] Case 222/86 *Unectef* v. *Heylens and Others* [1987] ECR 4097, paras. 14–15.     [223] Para. 22.

[224] On the importance of clarity of national rules restricting capital movements, see Flynn, above n. 2, 802.     [225] Case C–367/98 [2002] ECR I–4731.

[226] Para. 52.

[227] Ibid., citing Case C–265/95 *Commission* v. *France* [1997] ECR I–6959, para. 62 (as regards the free movement of goods) and Case C–398/95 *SETTG* [1997] ECR I–3091, para. 23 (in relation to freedom to provide services).     [228] Case C–512/03 *Blanckaert* [2005] ECR I–7685, para. 41.

[229] Case C–315/02 *Lenz* v. *Finanzlandesdirektion für Tirol* [2004] ECR I–7063, para. 24.

[230] Case C–315/02 *Lenz* [2004] ECR I–7063, para. 26.

[231] 'The Conference affirms that the right of Member States to apply the relevant provisions of their tax law as referred to in Article 73d(1)(a) of this Treaty will apply only with respect to the relevant provisions which exist at the end of 1993. However, this Declaration shall apply only to capital movements between Member States and to payments effected between Member States.' Decl. 7 on Art. 73d EC (now Art. 65 TFEU) annexed to the Final Act of the TEU. The Court rarely alludes to this limitation or dismisses reference to it: see, e.g., Case C–256/06 *Jäger* v. *Finanzamt Kusel-Landstuhl* [2008] ECR I–123, para. 39. See above n. 54 for the case law on an equivalent standstill clause in respect of movement of capital to third countries.

[232] Case C–35/98 *Verkooijen* [2000] ECR I–4071.

[233] Case C–319/02 *Manninen* [2004] ECR I–7477, para. 29.

(a)[234] the national court must consider (1) the comparability of the situations. If the situations are not objectively comparable, then the measure is lawful. If, on the other hand, the situations are comparable then the court has to consider (2) whether the different treatment can be justified by overriding reasons in the general interest and whether the steps taken are proportionate. If the differential treatment cannot be justified then the national measure is considered to be arbitrarily discriminatory contrary to Article 65(3).

Article 65(1)(a) therefore effectively codifies[235] the Court's decisions in *Schumacker*[236] (that national provisions which distinguish on the grounds of residence of taxpayers were compatible with Union law provided that they applied to situations which were not objectively comparable) and *Bachmann*[237] (that national tax law could be justified by overriding reasons in the general interest, in particular in relation to the cohesion of the tax system).[238] However, there is one major difference: in *Schumacker*, a case decided under the free movement of workers, the Court considered the question of comparability at the stage of establishing whether there was a breach of Article 45. Generally, in the free movement of capital case law, this question is considered at the defence stage, i.e. after it has been established that there is a breach of Article 63.[239]

In respect of the first question identified in *Verkooijn* and *Manninen*, comparability, the Court will look carefully to see whether the situations of the different taxpayers are objectively comparable. Its approach can be seen in *Blanckaert*,[240] concerning a Dutch law which favoured resident over non-resident taxpayers. The Court found that the situation of the resident and non-resident taxpayers was not comparable and so the national rules fell within the scope of the derogation.[241]

More usually, however, the Court does find that the two situations are comparable. For example, in *Persche*[242] the Court said that the Portuguese charity and Germany charities were in a comparable situation in terms of their tax treatment, as was the situation in *Hollman*[243] where the Court said that non-residents selling property in Portugal were in a comparable situation to a resident selling property. Likewise, in *Bouanich*[244] the Court said there was no objective difference between the situation of residents and non-residents as to justify different treatment where Swedish law provided that in respect of

---

[234] Or under the judicially developed public interest requirements: Case C–377/07 *STEKO* [2009] ECR I–299, para. 30.

[235] A point the Court itself noted in *Verkooijn*. It thus rejected the arguments of the intervening governments that it was a new invention.

[236] Case C–279/93 [1995] ECR I–225, considered further in Ch. 9.

[237] Case C–204/90 *Bachmann* [1992] ECR I–249.

[238] Cases such as Case C–118/96 *Safir* [1998] ECR I–1897 and Case C–136/00 *Danner* [2002] ECR I–8147 (considered in Ch. 11) which might have benefited from the provision, have been decided under the services provisions. See J. Usher, 'Financial services: Some taxing problems' [2001] *Zeitschrift für Europarechtliche Studien* 247.

[239] Although cf. Case C–376/03 *D* v. *Inspecteur van de Belastingdienst/Particulieren/Ondernemingen buitenland te Heerlen* [2005] ECR I–5821, paras. 34–8, where, following *Schumacker*, the question of comparability went to determining whether there had been a breach of Art. 63 in the first place. Since the Court considered the situations of the resident and the non-resident tax payer not to be comparable there was no breach of Art. 63.

[240] Case C–512/03 *Blanckaert* [2005] ECR I–7685, para. 39. The facts of the case are considered above at n. 161.          [241] See also Case C–194/06 *Orange European Smallcap Fund* [2008] ECR I–3747, para. 65.

[242] Case C–318/07 *Hein Persche* [2009] ECR I–359, para. 50, considered above at n. 170.

[243] Case C–443/06 *Hollmann* v. *Fazenda Pública* [2007] ECR I–8491, para. 53. See also Case C–562/07 *Commission* v. *Spain (taxation of capital gains)* [2009] ECR I–000, para. 59.

[244] Case C–265/04 *Bouanich* v. *Skatteverket* [2006] ECR I–923, para. 41.

a share repurchase by a company, payments made to resident shareholders were taxed as a capital gain with a right to deduct the cost of acquisition, while equivalent payments to non-residents were taxed as a dividend without there being a right to deduct the cost of acquisition.[245]

If the Court has found that the situations of the two groups of taxpayers are comparable, it then looks at the second question identified in *Verkooijn* and *Manninen,* namely whether the restriction can be justified by an overriding reason in the general interest which is supported by evidence.[246] The most common justification invoked is the threat to the cohesion of the national tax system. In *Weidert*[247] the Court repeated the *Bachmann*[248] principle that there needed to be a direct link between the tax advantage (the tax relief granted to the taxpayer resident in the home state) for the acquisition of shares in companies established in that Member State and an offsetting fiscal levy. As the Court pointed out, the tax advantage on the acquisition of shares was not offset by the taxation of the dividends which those companies subsequently paid, not least because there was no guarantee that the companies in which the investment was made giving rise to the tax benefit would pay dividends.[249] There was therefore no direct link between the tax advantage and the offsetting fiscal levy and so the Article 65(1)(a) derogation could not be relied on.

Another justification recognized by the Court is the effectiveness of fiscal supervision.[250] In *Stauffer* the Court said that a host Member State was entitled to ascertain in a clear and precise manner whether the body (in this case a charitable foundation) met the conditions imposed by national law to be entitled to the tax exemption available to equivalent national foundations and to monitor its effective management by, for example, requiring the submission of annual accounts and an activity report. However, while such checks might prove difficult in the case of foundations established in other Member States, disadvantages of a purely administrative nature were not sufficient to justify a refusal by the host state to grant tax exemptions to the out-of-state charitable foundation.

There are, however, a number of justifications which the Court has rejected.[251] For example, in *Lenz*[252] the Court said that a reduction in tax receipts could not be regarded as an overriding reason in the public interest;[253] and in *Commission* v. *France*[254] that a general presumption of tax avoidance or fraud was not sufficient to 'justify a fiscal measure which compromises the objectives of the [Treaties]'. There cases show that the Court adopts a fairly strict approach to justification and, even where it recognizes the public interest, usually finds it is not justified on the facts.

---

[245] Paras. 40–1. See also Case C–377/07 *STEKO* [2009] ECR I–299, para. 33; Case C–540/07 *Commission* v. *Italy* [2009] ECR I–000, paras. 51–4; Case C–182/08 *Glaxo Wellcome* [2009] ECR I–000, paras. 69–74.

[246] Case C–256/06 *Jäger* [2008] ECR I–123, para. 52.

[247] Case C–242/03 *Ministre des Finances* v. *Weidert and Paulus* [2004] ECR I–7379.

[248] Case C–204/90 *Bachmann* [1992] ECR I–249 considered in Ch. 9.　　[249] Para. 23.

[250] Case C–386/04 *Walter Stauffer* [2006] ECR I–8203, para. 47.

[251] See also the more detailed discussion on these justifications in Ch. 10, especially in respect of the justification concerning the fight against tax evasion (unsuccessfully raised in Case C–540/07 *Commission* v. *Italy* [2009] ECR I–000, paras. 58–9 in respect of intra-EU movement but successfully raised in respect of movements of capital between Italy and EEA countries).

[252] Case C–315/02 *Lenz* [2004] ECR I–7063, para. 40.

[253] See also Case C–318/07 *Persche* [2009] ECR I–359, para. 46 where the Court said that a Member State cannot introduce a difference in treatment in respect of taxation on charitable donations based on the fact that gifts made to a domestic charity absolve the taxing stage of some of its responsibilities while gifts made to a foreign charity do not.　　[254] Case C–334/02 *Commission* v. *France* [2004] ECR I–2229, para. 27.

Having considered the specific tax derogation we turn now to examine the general derogations.

## 5.3  Article 65(1)(b): General Derogations

### (a)  'All requisite measures to prevent infringements of national law and regulations, in particular in the field of taxation and the prudential supervision of financial institutions'

One of the (non-exhaustive) list of named areas in which Member States can take 'requisite measures' to prevent infringements of national law is the 'field of taxation'. As with Article 65(1)(a), this includes measures intended to ensure effective fiscal supervision and to combat illegal activities such as tax evasion.[255] This derogation was successfully relied on by the Austrian government in *Sandoz*.[256] It will be recalled that the case concerned stamp duty payable under Austrian law on a loan taken out by an Austrian company from a Belgian company. No tax was payable under Belgian law. The Court said that the main objective of the Austrian law was to ensure equal treatment for those natural or legal persons resident in Austria entering into a contract for a loan. The Court continued that since the effect of the measure was to compel individuals to pay the duty, 'it prevents taxable persons from evading the requirements of domestic tax legislation through the exercise of freedom of movement of capital' guaranteed by Article 63(1).[257] Turning to Article 65(3), the Court noted that since the Austrian rule applied to all borrowers resident in Austria without distinction as to nationality or the place where the loan was contracted, the Austrian legislation did not constitute a means of arbitrary discrimination. The Austrian rule was therefore lawful.

*Sandoz* can be compared with the *Eurobond* case[258] where the Court said that 'a general presumption of tax evasion or tax fraud cannot justify a fiscal measure' especially where the measure consists in 'an outright prohibition on the exercise of a fundamental freedom' guaranteed by Article 63.[259] Therefore, by prohibiting the acquisition by Belgian residents of securities of a loan issued abroad, Belgium breached Article 63.

While taxation and the prudential supervision of financial institutions are expressly listed as the grounds on which Member States can take all requisite measures to prevent infringements of national law and regulations, the non-exhaustive nature of the list in Article 65(1)(b) was emphasized in *Bordessa*[260] where the Court said that other measures were also permitted in so far as they were designed to prevent 'illegal activities of comparable seriousness, such as money laundering, drug trafficking or terrorism'.[261]

### (b)  To lay down procedures for the declaration of capital movements for the purposes of administrative or statistical information

There has been no case law on this provision giving guidance on how it is to be construed. However, it is remarkable for its breadth and for the fact that there is no equivalent provision in respect of the other freedoms.

---

[255]  Case C–478/98 *Commission* v. *Belgium (Eurobond)* [2000] ECR I–7587, para. 38;

[256]  Case C–439/97 *Sandoz* [1999] ECR I–7041.

[257]  Para. 24. See also Joined Cases C–155/08 and C–157/08 *Passenheim-van Schoot* [2009] ECR I–000 discussed in Ch. 9.          [258]  Case C–478/98 *Commission* v. *Belgium (Eurobond)* [2000] ECR I–7587.

[259]  Para. 45.          [260]  Joined Cases C–358/93 and C–416/93 *Bordessa* [1995] ECR I–361.

[261]  Para. 21.

### (c) Public policy and public security

The Court has drawn on the case law from the other freedoms to give meaning to the terms public policy and public security. For example, in *Church of Scientology*[262] it relied on the persons case law[263] to establish that while Member States were still, in principle, 'free to determine the requirements of public policy and public security in the light of their national needs', these grounds had to be interpreted strictly, which meant that public policy and public security could be relied on only if there was 'a genuine and sufficiently serious threat to a fundamental interest of society';[264] that the steps taken were necessary only for the protection of the interests which they were intended to guarantee; and that those objectives could not be attained by less restrictive measures.[265]

The case itself concerned a French rule making direct foreign investment subject to prior authorization. As we have seen, the Court often finds that systems of prior authorization are not necessary, favouring instead a system based on declarations.[266] However, where a genuine and sufficiently serious threat to public policy or public security is at stake, a system of prior declaration might prove inadequate to counter the threat.[267] The Court said that given the difficulty, in the case of direct foreign investments, of identifying and blocking capital once it has entered another Member State, this might make it necessary to prevent transactions which would adversely affect public policy or public security by using a system of prior authorization. However, because, on the facts, prior authorization was required for every direct foreign investment thought to represent a threat to public policy and public security, without any more detailed definition,[268] and investors were given no indication as to the specific circumstances in which prior authorization was required, the Court found the French system to contravene the principle of legal certainty and so breached Article 63(1).[269]

In *Albore*[270] the Court drew on its goods case law to define public security in the context of an Italian rule requiring foreigners to have authorization prior to living in certain areas of military importance. Having noted that public security included the external security of a Member State,[271] the Court said that a mere reference to the requirements of defence of the national territory was not sufficient to justify discrimination on grounds of nationality.[272] It continued that the position would be different only if it were demonstrated, for each area to which the restriction applied, that non-discriminatory treatment of the nationals of all the Member States would expose Italian military interests to real, specific, and serious risks which could not be countered by less-restrictive procedures.[273]

---

[262] Case C–54/99 *Association Eglise de Scientologie* [2000] ECR I–1335, para. 17.

[263] See further Ch. 14.

[264] Citing Case 36/75 *Rutili* [1975] ECR 1219, para. 28, and Case C–348/96 *Calfa* [1999] ECR I–11, para. 21.        [265] Case C–54/99 *Eglise de Scientologie* [2000] ECR I–1335, para. 18.

[266] Para. 19.

[267] Para. 20. Cf. Case C–567/07 *Sint Servatius* [2009] ECR I–000, para. 28, where the Court found that the need to promote social housing did not satisfy the public-policy derogation.        [268] Para. 21.

[269] Para. 22.        [270] Case C–423/98 [2000] ECR I–5965.

[271] Citing Case C–367/89 *Richardt* [1991] ECR I–4621, para. 22, considered in Ch. 6.

[272] Case C–423/98 [2000] ECR I–5965, para. 21.        [273] Para. 22.

The goods case law also inspired the Court in *Commission* v. *Belgium*[274] concerning the Belgian government's 'golden shares' in two energy companies.[275] These shares entitled it to oppose any transfer, use as security, or change in the intended destination of lines and conduits or of certain other strategic assets and certain management decisions regarded as contrary to the guidelines for the country's energy policy. The Belgian government justified its golden shares on the public-security ground of safeguarding energy supplies in the event of a crisis which, following the goods case *Campus Oil*,[276] the Court accepted as a legitimate public interest,[277] provided that the legislation enabled Belgium to ensure a minimum level of energy supplies in the event of a genuine and sufficiently serious threat,[278] and that the steps taken were proportionate.

On the facts, the Court found the Belgian rules to be justified and proportionate because the scheme was based, not on a prior authorization, but on *ex post facto* opposition. This procedure generally gave the energy companies a free hand in decision-making unless and until the government decided to intervene. Where the government did intervene—and the area for intervention was limited to cases in which the objectives of energy policy were jeopardized—the legislation provided that the government had to adhere to strict time limits, give reasons for intervention, and be subject to effective review by the courts.[279] Therefore, the Court said, the Belgian scheme made it possible to guarantee, on the basis of objective criteria which were subject to judicial review, the effective availability of the lines and conduits providing the main infrastructure for the domestic conveyance of energy products. This enabled Belgium to intervene with a view to ensuring compliance with the public-service obligations incumbent on the energy companies while at the same time observing the requirements of legal certainty.

This conclusion can be contrasted with the Court's decision in another golden share case, *Commission* v. *France* (*Elf-Aquitane*),[280] which concerned a French rule requiring prior authorization of any direct or indirect shareholding in Elf-Aquitane over and above certain limits. The Court said that because the investors were given no indication as to the specific, objective circumstances in which prior authorization would be granted or refused, the system was contrary to the principle of legal certainty.[281] It added that such a wide discretionary power constituted 'a serious interference with the free movement of capital, and may have the effect of excluding it altogether'.[282] Consequently, the Court found the French system disproportionate.

So far, we have concentrated on the free movement of capital, looking at it through the prism of the fourth of the four freedoms. However, free movement of capital is also a key pillar in the realization of economic and monetary union and it is to this subject that we now turn.

---

[274] Case C–503/99 *Commission* v. *Belgium* [2002] ECR I–4809.

[275] For a more detailed discussion on the background to the *Golden Share* cases, see D. Wyatt and A. Dashwood, *European Union Law*, 5th edn (London: Sweet and Maxwell, 2006), 854–63.

[276] Case 72/83 *Campus Oil* [1984] ECR 2727.     [277] Para. 46.     [278] Para. 48.

[279] Paras. 49–51. Cf. Case C–463/00 *Commission* v. *Spain* [2003] ECR I–4581, paras. 78–80, where these conditions were not satisfied.     [280] Case C–483/99 [2002] ECR I–4781.

[281] Para. 50. See also Case C–463/00 *Commission* v. *Spain* [2003] ECR I–4581, paras. 76–7.

[282] Para. 51.

# C. ECONOMIC AND MONETARY UNION

## 1. INTRODUCTION

Despite the fact that monetary policy was traditionally regarded as a key component of state sovereignty. In December 1969 the then six Heads of State agreed that a plan should be drawn up with a view to creating an economic and monetary union.[283] On the basis of a report prepared by a group chaired by the Luxembourg prime minister, Pierre Werner, the states agreed on a step-by-step plan to achieve economic and monetary union by 1980.[284] This deadline was not met, in part owing to the crisis caused by the collapse of the Bretton Woods Agreement, leading to a break up in the international monetary order.

Renewed impetus was given to the creation of economic and monetary union by Article 102a EEC, introduced by the SEA 1986, which recognized the European Monetary System (EMS)[285] as a valuable element of monetary cooperation. It also recognized the need for institutional changes in order to achieve further development in the field of economic and monetary policy. The aim of the EMS was to create a 'zone of monetary stability in Europe' based on a fixed but adjustable exchange rate system which allowed margins of fluctuation (normally 2.25 per cent) by participating states in the exchange rate mechanism (ERM). The system remained relatively stable for a number of years until a combination of market pressures in autumn 1992 drove the UK and Italy out of the ERM, although Italy rejoined in November 1996, and a significant broadening of the fluctuation bands (+/- 15 per cent) made the system almost meaningless.

Subsequently a high-level committee was set up, chaired by Jacques Delors, charged with providing a blueprint for the creation of economic and monetary union. It took as its starting point the view that the development of the single market necessitated a more effective coordination of economic policy between national authorities, pointing out that with full freedom of capital movements and integrated financial markets, incompatible national policies would translate into exchange rate tensions and put an increasing and undue burden on monetary policy.[286] EMU was therefore dependent on complete free movement (of goods, persons, services, and capital) together with fixed exchange rates and a single currency. This was to be achieved in three stages. The Maastricht Treaty contained the modifications necessary to attain stages two and three.[287]

Although the economic logic of Delors' plan convinced (most) Heads of State, EU citizens were still to be won over. What were the benefits of a single currency which could be used throughout the EU? The principal argument in favour was the absence of

---

[283] See, generally, C. Proctor, *The Euro and the Financial Markets: The legal impact of EMU* (Bristol: Jordans, 1999), Ch. 1; and L. Tsoukalis, 'Economic and monetary union: The primacy of high politics' in H. Wallace and W. Wallace (eds.), *Policy Making in the European Union*, 3rd edn (Oxford: OUP, 1996) and K. McNamara, 'Economic and monetary union: Innovation and challenges for the euro' in the 4th edn (Oxford: OUP, 2005); J. Usher, 'The legal background of the euro' in P. Beaumont and N. Walker (eds.), *Legal Framework of the Single European Currency* (Oxford: Hart Publishing, 1999).

[284] See Council Res. [1971] OJ C28/21.

[285] Established in 1978 by a Resolution of the European Council.

[286] *Agence Europe*, Documents Nos. 1550/1551, 20 Apr. 1989, paras. 10–12.

[287] For a detailed discussion, see, *inter alia*, R. Goebel, 'European economic and monetary union: Will the EMU ever fly?' (1998) 4 *Columbia Journal of European Law* 249; F. Snyder, 'EMU revisited: Are we making a constitution? What constitution are we making?' in P. Craig and G. de Búrca (eds.), *The Evolution of EU Law* (Oxford: OUP, 1999).

transaction costs of exchange from one currency to another. A single currency would also lead to transparency in the market place so that consumers could more easily compare prices, thereby reducing the chance of price discrimination. A single currency would also allow traders to set prices, safe in the knowledge that they would not need to hedge the risks in case of exchange rate fluctuations. In respect of larger companies which, prior to the single currency, would have scattered their plants across various states of the EU as another way of reducing the risk of exchange rate variation, a single currency would enable them to locate according to economies of scale, leading to more plants of an optimum size, bringing about a reduction in unit costs of production and an increase in efficiency. Finally, a strong monetary union would also be likely to attract foreign investment because the framework under which the single currency is managed should make it a stable currency with low inflation and low interest rates.

But what about the disadvantages? The principal cost of a single currency is to stop exchange rates from varying against rates of other member countries. This could be damaging because the purpose of letting the exchange rate vary is to act as a shock absorber for disturbances that impact on partner economies in different ways.[288] The loss of monetary autonomy means that the states lose the chance to regulate interest rates to promote or restrict growth. With countries in different economic cycles, a single currency would serve to accentuate differences, particularly if the EU as a whole is not an optimal monetary union.[289] Nevertheless, the majority of Member States calculated that the benefits of the single currency outweighed the disadvantages and agreed to go ahead.

## 2. MONETARY UNION

### 2.1 The Stages to Monetary Union

#### (a) Stage one

The first stage of monetary union was realized on the basis of existing Treaty provisions. The Madrid European Council meeting in June 1989 decided that the first stage should start on 1 July 1990, the date at which the free movement of capital was realized under Directive 88/361.[290] In essence, this stage involved closer coordination of economic policies and closer cooperation between central banks[291] as well as free movement of capital.

#### (b) Stage two

During the second stage Member States retained monetary sovereignty, but the coordination of economic and monetary policy was reinforced. The Maastricht Treaty provided that the second stage was to begin on 1 January 1994.[292] By that time, *all* Member States had to comply with, *inter alia*, the provisions of Article 63 on free movement of capital and put in place multiannual programmes to ensure the lasting convergence necessary to achieve EMU.[293] During the second stage Member States also had to avoid excessive

---

[288] M. Artis, 'European monetary union' in M. Artis and N. Lee, *The Economics of the European Union* (Oxford: OUP, 1994), 347–50.

[289] P. De Grauwe, *Economics of Monetary Union*, 6th edn (Oxford: OUP, 2005), 115; and De Grauwe, 'Monetary integration since the Maastricht Treaty' (2006) 44 *JCMS* 711.        [290] [1988] OJ L178/5.

[291] See Arts. 104–5 EEC.        [292] Art. 116(1) EC (now repealed by the Lisbon Treaty).

[293] Art. 116(2) EC (now repealed by the Lisbon Treaty).

government deficits[294] and had to start the process leading to the independence from government control of their central banks.[295] The European Monetary Institute (EMI), the precursor to the European Central Bank (ECB), was also established at the start of the second stage.[296] Its principal task was to prepare the instruments and procedures necessary for carrying out a single monetary policy in the third stage.

During the second stage, the Commission and the EMI were to report to the Council on the progress made by the Member States towards satisfying the EMU criteria.[297] These reports included an examination of (1) the compatibility of each Member State's national legislation, including the statutes of its national central bank, with Articles 130–1 TFEU (ex Articles 108–9 EC) (on the independence of the ECB and the national central banks and the statute of the European System of Central Banks (ESCB));[298] and (2) the achievement of 'a high degree of sustainable convergence' by reference to the fulfilment by each Member State of the following criteria:[299]

- the achievement of a high degree of price stability based on a rate of inflation which was close to that of the three best performing Member States[300]

- the sustainability of the government financial position, which means that its deficit must not be 'excessive', i.e. the government deficit could not exceed 3 per cent of GDP and government debt could not exceed 60 per cent of GDP[301]—these criteria were introduced to ensure the convergence of national economies not just on admission to the third stage but in perpetuity; the enforcement of these criteria is now subject to the Stability and Growth Pact (considered below)[302]

- the observance of the normal fluctuation margins provided for by the exchange rate mechanism of the Economic Monetary System for at least two years without devaluing against the euro

- the durability of convergence achieved by the Member State with a derogation and of its participation in the ERM being reflected in long-term interest levels.

In other words, the Commission and the EMI were to report to the Council on whether the states wishing to participate had low inflation, a sound budgetary situation, low interest rates, and stable exchange rates.[303] On the basis of these reports, the Council was to assess whether each Member State fulfilled the necessary conditions for adopting the single currency.

---

[294] Art. 116(4) EC (now repealed by the Lisbon Treaty).

[295] Art. 116(5) EC (now repealed by the Lisbon Treaty).

[296] Art. 117 EC. The Statute of the EMI was laid down in a separate protocol.

[297] Art. 140(1) TFEU, ex Art. 121(1) EC.

[298] Art. 129 TFEU (ex Art. 107 EC). ESCB comprises the ECB and the national central banks.

[299] Art. 140(1) TFEU (ex Art. 121(1) EC).

[300] The Protocol on Convergence Criteria (Protocol No. 13) referred to in Art. 140 TFEU defines closeness as not exceeding the best three states by 1.5%. The arithmetic average of the best performing states was 1.2% (Commission Recommendation of 25 Mar. 1998).

[301] For full details see Art. 126 TFEU (ex Art. 104 EC) and the Protocol (No.12) on Excessive Deficit Procedure.

[302] See Council Reg. 1466/97 on the strengthening of the surveillance of budgetary positions and coordination of economic policies ([1997] OJ L209/1) and Council Reg. 1467/97 on speeding up and clarifying the implementation of the excessive deficit procedure ([1997] OJ L209/6).

[303] For criticism of the reliance on 'nominal factors', see C. Hadjiemmanuil, 'Economic and monetary union' in Chalmers et al., *European Union Law* (Cambridge: CUP, 2006), 526–7.

## (c) Stage three

The Maastricht Treaty set the date for the start of the third stage as 1 January 1999[304] and the Protocol on the Transition to the Third Stage made clear that all Member States,[305] whether they fulfilled the necessary conditions for the adoption of the single currency, had to respect the will for the Union to enter the third stage swiftly and that no Member State could prevent the start of the third stage. From 1 January 1999, the Council set the 'irrevocably fixed rate' at which 'the ECU shall be substituted for these [national] currencies, and the ECU will become a currency in its own right'.[306] At first the ECU, now renamed the euro,[307] was used only for electronic payments. From 1 January 2002 euro coins and notes were put into circulation and on 28 February 2002 the national 'legacy' currencies were finally withdrawn.

The ECB and the ESCB started functioning fully on 1 January 1999.[308] The independence of the ECB and national central banks is guaranteed by Article 130 TFEU (ex Article 108 EC) which requires that neither the ECB nor national central banks can seek or take instructions from Union institutions or national governments.[309] The Union institutions and the Member States also undertake to respect the independence of these bodies and 'not to seek to influence the members of the decision-making bodies of the ECB or of the national central banks in the performance of their tasks'.[310]

According to Article 127(1) TFEU (ex Article 105(1) EC), the 'primary objective' of the ESCB is to maintain price stability. Here the hand of the German Bundesbank can be felt. Germany had one of the best post-war inflation records which was attributed to the Bundesbank's autonomous status and its mandate for price stability. The statutes of the ECB are largely modelled on those of the Bundesbank. Only to the extent that the objective of price stability is not jeopardized is the ESCB able to contribute to

---

[304] Art. 121(4) EC (now repealed by the Lisbon Treaty). See also the Declaration by the Council (Ecofin) and the ministers meeting in that Council issued on 1 May 1998 ([1998] OJ L139/28); Council Reg. 974/98 ([1998] OJ L139/1).

[305] D. R. R. Dunnett, 'Some legal principles applicable to the transition to the single currency' (1996) 33 *CMLRev.* 1133.

[306] Art. 123(4) EC (now repealed by the Lisbon Treaty). The conversion rates for the national currencies were fixed by Council Reg. 2866/98 ([1998] OJ L359/1).

[307] By Art. 2 of Reg. 1103/97 ([1997] OJ L162/1), not by Treaty amendment. This was challenged in Case T-207/97 *Berthu* v. *Council of the European Union* [1998] ECR II–509 but the action was declared manifestly inadmissible on the ground of lack of individual concern. Earlier, Berthu (a French MEP seeking to preserve the name ECU) had challenged the proposal for the regulation but this action was also declared inadmissible: Case T-175/96 *Berthu* v. *Commission* [1997] ECR II–811. See also Thomas Cook's unsuccessful challenge against the Commission for infringing its trade mark right due to the similarity between the symbol used by Thomas Cook and the official euro symbol: Case T-195/00 *Thomas Cook* v. *Commission* [2003] ECR II–1677.

[308] The institutional provisions governing the ECB are laid down in Arts. 283–4 TFEU (ex Arts. 112–15 EC). Protocol No. 4 lays down the Statute of the European System of Central Banks and of the European Central Bank. See C. Zilioli and M.Selmayr, 'The European Central Bank: An independent specialised organisation of Community Law' (2000) 37 *CMLRev.* 591 and the response by R. Torrent, 'Whom is the European Central Bank afraid of? Reaction to Zilioli and Selmayr' (1999) 36 *CMLRev.* 1229. L. Gormley and J. de Haan, 'The democratic deficit of the European Central Bank' (1996) 21 *ELRev.* 95; W. Buiter, 'Alice in Euroland' (1999) 37 *JCMS* 181, and, more generally, M. Andenas et al. (eds.), *European Economic and Monetary Union: The Institutional Framework* (The Hague: Kluwer, 1997).

[309] See also Arts. 7, 11, and 14 of the ESCB statute. See M. O'Connell, 'The Maastricht Treaty and aspects of monetary union' (1995) 1 *Irish Journal of European Law* 5, 13.

[310] Art. 130 TFEU (ex Art. 108 EC).

achieving the other objectives of the Union laid down in Article 3 TEU. Article 127(1) TFEU (ex Article 105 EC) continues that the ESCB is to act 'in accordance with the principle of an open market economy with free competition, favouring an efficient allocation of resources'.[311] It must also act in compliance with the principles laid down in Article 119 TFEU (ex Article 4 EC), notably 'stable prices, sound public finances and monetary conditions and a sustainable balance of payments'.[312]

Eleven Member States satisfied the convergence criteria[313] and entered the third stage. Greece joined in 2001. The UK has not joined, nor has Denmark. In September 2003 Sweden also voted in a referendum against joining the euro. According to the Protocol on Certain Provisions Relating to the UK,[314] the UK was not committed or obliged to move to the third stage of EMU without a separate decision of its government and Parliament. The protocol also made specific provision for dealing with the UK's failure to join the third stage, together with provision for the UK to opt in at a later date. A similar, but less detailed, protocol governs the position of Denmark.[315] They are described as 'Member States with a special status',[316] or the 'pre-ins' as they have been termed in Brussels,[317] in anticipation that they will eventually join (in which case the convergence criteria remain relevant[318]). In essence the second stage is prolonged for them, although in the UK's case the situation is more complex and certain second-stage rules do not apply to it, including provisions concerning the independence of the central bank under Article 130 TFEU (ex Article 108 EC).[319] Denmark's exchange rates continue to float against the euro within the bands laid down by EMS Mark II.[320] The UK and Sweden remain outside ERM II. None of the Accession states (the ten from 2004, the two from 2007) initially joined the eurozone but they were under a duty to pursue compliance with the convergence criteria. Subsequently, Slovenia (2007), Cyprus and Malta (2008), and Slovakia (2009) did adopt the euro. The euro is now the currency of the 329 million people living in the 16 euro-zone countries.[321] Estonia is likely to become the seventeenth member in 2011.

## 2.2 Monetary Policy

The details of monetary policy are laid down in Articles 127–33 TFEU (ex Articles 105–11 EC). The ESCB is responsible for monetary policy. Its principal tasks are to:[322]

- define and implement the monetary policy of the Union
- conduct foreign exchange operations
- hold and manage the official foreign reserves of the Member States
- promote the smooth operation of payment systems.

---

[311] See also Art. 119(1)–(2).     [312] Art. 119(3).

[313] Dec. 98/317 ([1998] OJ L139/30): namely Belgium, Germany, Spain, France, Ireland, Italy, Luxembourg, the Netherlands, Austria, Portugal, and Finland.

[314] Protocol No. 15, on certain provisions relating to the UK and Ireland.

[315] Protocol Nos. 16–17. See, generally, J. Usher, 'Economic and monetary union: A model for flexibility?' (1998) 1 *Cambridge Yearbook of European Legal Studies* 39.     [316] Art. 139(1) TFEU (ex Art. 122 EC).

[317] Usher, above n. 283, 15.

[318] For details about how they would join, see Art. 140 TFEU (ex Arts. 121–2 EC).

[319] For the difference between the UK and Danish opt-outs, see J.-V. Louis, 'A legal and institutional approach for building a monetary union' (1998) 35 *CMLRev.* 33, 64–7.     [320] [1997] OJ C236/5.

[321] See also Art. 137 TFEU and Protocol No. 14, on the Eurogroup. Art. 138 TFEU (ex Art. 111(4) EC) allows Eurozone Member States to concert at international level and, if they wish, to set up unified representation on economic and financial matters.     [322] Art. 127(2) TFEU (ex Art. 105(2) EC).

The ECB has the exclusive right to authorize the issue of euro banknotes;[323] Member States may issue coins subject to approval by the ECB of the volume of issue.[324]

## 3. ECONOMIC UNION

Certain states, particularly Germany (but not France),[325] feared that if monetary policy was integrated this would destabilize the economies of states with a high degree of price stability unless monetary policy was combined with a high degree of co-ordination of economic policy, especially in respect of budgetary matters. As a result, the Maastricht Treaty made the ESCB's principal objective the maintenance of price stability,[326] as well as requiring a high degree of economic convergence as a prerequisite for entering stage three of EMU.

The duties of economic coordination did not end on 1 January 1999. According to Article 121(1) TFEU (ex Article 99(1) EC), Member States have to regard their economic policies as a matter of common concern and must coordinate them in Council in accordance with the duties laid down in Article 120 TFEU (ex Article 98 EC). Article 120 requires Member States to conduct their economic policies with a view to contributing to the achievement of the Union's objectives as defined in Article 3 TEU, as well as in the context of the broad economic policy guidelines (BEPGs) laid down by the Council under Article 121(2) TFEU (ex Article 99(2) EC). Like the ESCB, the Member States and the Union must act in accordance with the principle of an open market economy with free competition favouring an efficient allocation of resources.[327]

The BEPGs referred to in Article 120 are drafted by the Commission, considered by the European Council[328] and then adopted by the Council in the form of a recommendation.[329] Member States must report to the Commission on developments in the field of economic policy; the Commission then reports to the Council. The Council monitors economic developments in the states and the Union. It also ensures the consistency of the economic policies with the broad economic guidelines.[330] If this 'multilateral surveillance procedure' reveals that the economic policies of a Member State are not consistent with the broad economic guidelines or 'risk jeopardising the attainment of the proper functioning of economic and monetary union', the Commission may address a 'warning' to the Member State concerned.[331] The Council has the power under Article 121(4) TFEU, acting on a qualified majority (excluding the vote of the state concerned[332]) on the basis of a recommendation from the Commission, to make a recommendation to the Member State concerned.

In addition to this multilateral surveillance procedure, Article 126 TFEU (ex Article 104 EC) requires Member States to avoid excessive levels of national debt and excessive budget

---

[323] Art. 128(1) TFEU (ex Art. 106(1) EC).    [324] Art. 128(2) TFEU (ex Art. 106(2) EC).

[325] Dunnett, above n. 309, 136.    [326] Art. 127(1) TFEU (ex Art. 105(1) EC).

[327] Art. 120 TFEU. This provision is not directly effective: Case C–9/99 *Echirolles Distribution* v. *Association du Dauphiné* [2000] ECR I–8207, para. 25: 'What is involved is a general principle whose application calls for complex economic assessments which are a matter for the legislature or the national administration.'    [328] Art. 121(2) TFEU, 2nd para.

[329] Art. 121(2) TFEU, 3rd para. See also the newly introduced Art. 136 TFEU, which allows Member States who have adopted the euro to adopt measures relating to the BEPGs and the excessive deficit procedure affecting them only.    [330] Art. 121(3) TFEU.

[331] Art. 121(4) TFEU. This possibility was introduced by the Treaty of Lisbon.

[332] This was also introduced by the Lisbon Treaty.

deficits.[333] It also sets up a monitoring and reporting process which, in the last resort, can result in sanctions being applied to a Member State; these include requiring the Member State to make a non-interest-bearing deposit 'of an appropriate size' with the Union until the budget deficit in question has been cleared, and, in the last resort, the levying of a fine on the Member State.[334]

These Treaty-based procedures are supplemented by the Stability and Growth Pact (SGP), agreed by the Member States at the Amsterdam European Council in 1997, to answer concerns about the continuation of budgetary discipline once economic and monetary union was underway.[335] The SGP is contained in two regulations[336] and a Council resolution.[337] The Council resolution is a political commitment by the Commission, Council, and the Member States to the full implementation of the budget surveillance process. Although not legally binding, the resolution is based on the idea that peer pressure can be used to ensure that Member States live up to their commitments.[338]

The hard-law measures, the regulations, are intended to achieve complementary functions. Regulation 1466/97 on the strengthening of the surveillance of the budgetary procedures and the surveillance and coordination of economic policies[339] serves a preventive function.[340] It puts in place an 'early warning system' designed to alert the Council to the possibility that a Member State participating in the third stage of EMU may be running up an excessive deficit (i.e., one going above the 3 per cent reference value). Regulation 1467/97 on speeding up and clarifying the implementation of the excessive deficit procedure[341] serves a dissuasive function. It concerns the situation where, in the event of the 3 per cent reference value being breached, Member States must take immediate corrective action. If necessary the regulation allows for sanctions to be imposed.[342] It provides that if the Member State has not rectified the situation within two years of the decision to require it to make the deposit,[343] the deposit shall be converted into a fine, a sanction condemned as not credible: 'to threaten a deficit-ridden country with huge fines is like chastising a man hanging on to a cliff by treading on his fingers'.[344]

To date, the power to fine has not been used, despite the fact that most Member States, including both France and Germany, have persistently breached the 3 per cent

---

[333] See also the Excessive Deficit Protocol (EDP) (No.12) which lays down the same reference values as are contained in the convergence criteria. In addition to the limits on public spending laid down in Art. 126 TFEU, Arts. 123–5 TFEU (ex Arts. 101–2 EC) set out limits on government financing.

[334] Art. 126(11) TFEU (ex Art. 104(11) EC).

[335] See generally H. Hahn, 'The Stability Pact for European monetary union: Compliance with deficit limit as a constant legal duty' (1998) 35 CMLRev. 77.

[336] Council Reg. 1466/97 ([1997] OJ L209/1) and Council Reg. 1467/97 ([1997] OJ L209/6).

[337] Res. 97/C 236/01 ([1997] OJ C236/1).

[338] Alongside this measure, the Council issued a further resolution on growth and employment (Res. 97/C 236/02, [1997] OJ C236/3) which calls for the coordination of economic policies with the procedure laid down in the Employment Title (para. 6).       [339] [1997] OJ L209/1.

[340] This is now accompanied by the Code of Conduct on the content and format of the stability and convergence programmes, endorsed by the ECOFIN Council on 11 Oct. 2005. It incorporates the essential elements of Council Reg. 1466/97 into guidelines to assist the Member States in drawing up their programmes. It also aims at facilitating the examination of the programmes by the Commission, the Economic and Financial Committee, and the Council.       [341] [1997] OJ L209/6.

[342] Ibid., Art. 12.       [343] The annual amount of the deposit cannot exceed 0.5% GDP.

[344] Reg. 1467/97 Art. 13, discussed in 'The Euro and the future of Europe' The Ecconomist, 15 May 2010.

limit.[345] While critics have argued that the failure to fine France and Germany jeopardizes the euro's credibility and undermines the SGP, others say that the SGP itself needs
to be re-examined so as to allow countries to increase their deficits in order to achieve
structural reforms. This latter group has won the day: in the light of the Commission's
successful challenge to Ecofin's decision to suspend the excessive deficit procedure
against France and Germany,[346] even though their net borrowing exceeded 4 per cent
of GDP, the SGP was reformed to provide greater flexibility or rather, as the Ecofin
Council report of 20 March 2005 put it, 'effectiveness', based on a greater emphasis on
economic developments and an increased focus on safeguarding the sustainability of
public finances.[347] This led to the two regulations being amended[348] and the inclusion of
the Ecofin report itself in the SGP.[349] The result of these changes are that more attention
should be paid to a state's medium-term debt objectives rather than simply an annual
evaluation and more account should be paid to the economic circumstances of any
individual state. In other words discretion prevails over rigidity.

However in the relaxation of the criteria for budget deficits lay the seed of budget
irresponsibility in countries such as Greece which almost brought the eurozone to its
knees in early May 2010. This led to a massive €750 billion plan to defend the single currency[350] and calls for urgent reform of economic governance. Writing in the *Financial
Times*,[351] the German Minister of Finance, Wolfgang Schäuble, said that 'The euro has
shown itself to be a reliable anchor of stability in the crisis. It has protected us from intra-
European currency turbulence that would otherwise have aggravated the situation in
Europe.' Nevertheless, he admits that 'The fallout from the crisis is becoming ever more
visible, labour markets in some countries are languishing and government debt almost
everywhere is far in excess of permissible deficit limits.' He recognizes that economic
and fiscal policy surveillance in the eurozone was insufficient to prevent 'undesirable
trends in a timely manner' and that 'monetary union is unprepared for extremely severe
situations of the type we are now seeing and that demand a comprehensive intervention
to avert greater systemic risks'. He concludes that 'There is only one course of action: all
eurozone members must return to adherence to the stability and growth pact as rapidly
as possible.'

---

[345] M. Buti and L. Pench, 'Why do large countries flout the Stability Pact? And what can be done about
it?' (2004) 42 *JCMS* 1025.

[346] Case C–27/04 *Commission v. Council (EDP)* [2004] ECR I–4829. The Court quashed the Council's
conclusions that the procedures against France and Germany should be suspended as long as they continued
to act in accordance with their public commitments to implement certain deficit reduction, without going
so far as to require the Council to take enforcement action against the defaulting states under Art. 126(8)–(9)
TFEU (ex Art. 104(8)–(9) EC).

[347] Presidency Conclusions, Brussels European Council, 22 and 23 Mar. 2005, Annex II, 'Improving the
implementation of the Stability and Growth Pact'. This endorsed the Ecofin Council's 2005 report. See the
earlier Commission Communication 'Strengthening economic governance and clarifying the implementation of the Stability and Growth Pact' COM(2004) 581.

[348] Reg. 1466/97 was amended by Council Reg. 1055/2005 (OJ [2005] L174/1); Reg. 1467/97 was amended
by Council Reg. 1056/2005 (OJ [2005] L174/5). For a full discussion of the amendments, see J.-V. Louis, 'The
review of the Stability and Growth Pact' (2006) 43 *CMLRev.* 85.

[349] See the 2nd recital in the preamble to Reg. 1055/2005 and the Conclusions of the Brussels European
Council 22–3 Mar. 2005, para. 3.

[350] See eg. Reg (EU) 407/210 establishing a European financial stabilization mechanism (OJ [2010] L
118/1).

[351] 'Why Europe's monetary union faces its biggest crisis', *Financial Times*, 11 Mar. 2010.

## D. CONCLUSIONS

With the advent of EMU, capital is no longer the poor relation. It is starting to attract the judicial and academic attention that might be expected of a provision so central to the creation of the internal market. Since 1992 the number of cases decided under Article 63(1) has increased significantly. The striking feature of this case law is the Court's willingness to apply principles developed in respect of the other freedoms, notably the freedom to provide services, to shape its jurisprudence on capital.

Free movement of capital is the fourth and final 'freedom'. However, negative integration can only go so far. A single market needs positive integration to ensure that it works effectively. The final chapter of the book examines the problems facing the Union in deciding whether to regulate, what form that regulation might take, and how best to deliver on particular policy goals.

# PART V

# COMPLETING THE SINGLE MARKET

# 16

# REGULATING THE
# INTERNAL MARKET

## A. INTRODUCTION

In 1957 the European Economic Community set itself the task of creating a common market with the attainment of the four freedoms at its core. This book has concentrated on the Treaty provisions intended to achieve this objective and their interpretation by the Court of Justice. While in theory these Treaty provisions should have been sufficient to allow for successful regulatory competition—where states compete to attract products and factors of production—in practice regulatory competition has not produced the result anticipated, owing to the absence of the necessary conditions for such competition to function. This market failure, together with the derogations provided by the Treaties and the mandatory requirements developed by the Court, has meant that there would always be a need for harmonization legislation enacted by the Union institutions. Such harmonization would help the market to function properly while at the same time protecting vital public interests such as consumer protection and public health. Harmonization was always envisaged by the Treaty of Rome, which gave wide-ranging powers to the (then) Community to enact secondary legislation.

By setting harmonized standards, EU law enables goods, persons, services, and capital to move freely. When viewed from this perspective, harmonization is the complement of the four freedoms. However, it remains a sensitive matter both legally and politically. For example, to what extent should a single harmonized standard set by the EU replace diverse national standards? And at what level should that standard be set—at the standard of the lowest state in the EU, at the highest, or somewhere in between? The aim of this chapter is to examine the power to harmonize, the different approaches to harmonization adopted by the Union, and the problem of implementation and enforcement of Union standards.

## B. THE POWER TO HARMONIZE:
## ARTICLE 114 TFEU

### 1. INTRODUCTION

The 1985 Single Market White Paper proposed the adoption of about 300 measures to eliminate the three principal barriers to trade (physical, technical, and fiscal) identified in the White Paper.[1] The problem facing the EU was how to realize these measures within a relatively short time frame when the principal legal bases provided by the EEC Treaty (Article 100 EEC (Article 94 EC and now Article 115 TFEU) and Article 235 EEC (Article 308 EC and now Article 352 TFEU)) required unanimous voting. The Single European Act 1986 provided an answer. It introduced a new legal basis, Article 100a EEC (Article 95 EC and now Article 114 TFEU), with qualified-majority voting (QMV). Given the importance of Article 114 to the attainment of the single market, it is this legal basis that we shall focus on.[2]

Article 114(1) provides 'Save where otherwise provided in the Treaties' the European Parliament and Council, acting in accordance with the ordinary legislative procedure, are to adopt 'measures' (not just directives[3]) 'for the approximation of the provisions laid down by law, regulation, or administrative action in Member States which have as their object the establishment and functioning of the internal market' as defined in Article 26 TFEU (ex Article 14 EC).[4] There are therefore two limits to the use of Article 114. First, resort to Article 114 can be made where no other specific legal basis applies.[5] In other words Article 114, a general provision, is a residual legal basis (although at times this seems to be honoured more in the breach than the observance). The importance of this limitation was, however, emphasized in *Commission* v. *Council (VAT)*[6] where the Court said that if the Treaties contained a more specific provision that was capable of consti-tuting the legal basis for the measure, the measure had to be founded on that provision. Therefore, on the facts, the Court ruled that two Union measures intended to consoli-date and strengthen administrative cooperation in the field of VAT should not have been adopted under Article 114(1) but under the (more specific) tax legal bases, Articles 113 TFEU (ex Article 93 EC).

The second limit on the use of Article 114 is that the measures adopted under Article 114 must be for approximation of laws (also known as harmonization).[7] Therefore measures

---

[1] See further Ch. 1.

[2] The internal market is identified as an area of 'shared' competence by Art 4(2) TFEU. According to Art. 2(2) TFEU, 'When the Treaties confer on the Union a competence shared with the Member States in a specific area, the Union and the Member States may legislate and adopt legally binding acts in that area. The Member States shall exercise their competence to the extent that the Union has not exercised its competence. The Member States shall again exercise their competence to the extent that the Union has decided to cease exercising its competence.' See also Decl. 18.

[3] Although a Declaration annexed to the SEA requires the Commission to give precedence to the use of directives. In practice this is not always the case (see, e.g., the regulation at issue in Case C–66/04 *UK* v. *EP and Council (smoke flavourings)* [2005] ECR I–10553). Cf. Art. 115 TFEU, which allows for the use of direc-tives only.

[4] See also Art. 26(3) TFEU giving the Council the power, on a proposal from the Commission, to deter-mine the guidelines and conditions necessary to ensure balanced progress in all the sectors concerned, and the Commission's duty in Art. 27 TFEU (ex Art. 15 EC) to take into account the extent of the effort that certain economies showing differences in development will have to sustain for the establishment of the internal market. It may propose appropriate provisions. If these provision take the form of derogations, they must be of a temporary nature and must cause the least possible disturbance to the functioning of the inter-nal market.

[5] The Lisbon Treaty removed the reference in Art. 95 EC to 'By way of derogation from Article 94'. The reordering of Arts. 94–5 EC (Art. 95 EC has become Art. 114 TFEU and Art. 94 EC has become Art. 115 TFEU) reflects what happened in practice: Art. 95 EC (now Art. 114 TFEU) had become the principal legal basis of the two.

[6] Case C–533/03 *Commission* v. *Council (VAT)* [2006] ECR I–1025, para. 45.

[7] The Court appears to use the two terms interchangeably: see, e.g., Case C–217/04 *UK* v. *EP and Council (European Network and Information Security Agency (ENISA))* [2006] ECR I–3771, para. 43.

which do not harmonize cannot be adopted under Article 114. This can be seen in the *ECS* case[8] where the Parliament and the Commission argued that a regulation establishing a European Cooperative Society should have been adopted on the basis of Article 114 and not Article 352. The Court disagreed, reasoning that because the national laws remain unchanged by the regulation (the aim of the measure was to create a new form of cooperative society in addition to national forms) the regulation did not lead to 'approximation' of national laws and so Article 114 could not be used.

In its original version, the procedure laid down by Article 114(1) was QMV and cooperation with the European Parliament; since Maastricht the co-decision procedure has applied, now called the ordinary legislative procedure. However, Article 114(2) expressly provides that Article 114(1) cannot be used to adopt fiscal measures,[9] nor measures relating to the free movement of persons, nor measures relating to the rights and interests of employed persons—areas considered to be too sensitive to be the subject of QMV.[10]

The Union has adopted a large number of directives under Article 114. Case Study 16.1 shows how Article 114 has been used to regulate tobacco production and advertising and the problems this has generated.

**Case Study 16.1** REGULATING TOBACCO PRODUCTION AND ADVERTISING

The health risks associated with smoking have long been a matter of concern for the Member States.[11] Even before the EU was given express powers over public health by the Maastricht Treaty, the Council, and the Representatives of the Governments of the Member States issued a resolution on a programme of action against cancer in 1986.[12] This led to the adoption of Directives 89/622/EEC on tobacco labelling[13] and 90/239/EEC on the maximum tar yield of cigarettes,[14] both based on Article 114 and supported by references to the Council resolution. According to the preambles to the directives, Article 114 was used because the differences between the laws, regulations, and administrative provisions were likely 'to constitute barriers to trade and to impede the establishment and operation of the internal market'.[15]

Directive 89/622 on tobacco labelling required the health warning 'Tobacco seriously damages health' to be displayed on all packets of tobacco products. This warning had to cover at least 4 per cent of each large surface of the packet. Directive 90/239

---

[8] See, e.g., Case C–436/03 *EP and Commission* v. *Council (ECS)* [2006] ECR I–3733.

[9] In Case C–533/03 *Commission* v. *Council (VAT)* [2006] ECR I–1025, para. 47 the Court said that the words 'fiscal measures' covered not only all areas of taxation, without drawing any distinction between the types and duties or taxes concerned, but also all aspects of taxation, whether material rules or procedural rules.

[10] Pre-Lisbon, measures adopted in these fields were assumed to be subject to unanimous vote under Art. 94 EC due to the reference in Art. 95(1) EC to the phrase 'By way of derogation from Article 94'. However, it may well be that the expansion of Union competence in the areas listed in Art. 114(2) TFEU means that specific legal bases should be applied instead.

[11] For a fuller account see T. Hervey, 'Up in smoke? Community (anti)-tobacco law and policy' (2001) 26 *ELRev.* 101.                                                                    [12] [1986] OJ C184/19.

[13] [1989] OJ L158/30.        [14] [1990] OJ L137/36.

[15] See preamble to Dir. 89/622 [1989] OJ L158/30.

on tar yield provided that the tar yield could not be greater than 15 mg per cigarette as from 31 December 1992 and 12 mg from 31 September 1997, with Greece being given a special exemption until 31 December 2006. Since both directives laid down minimum standards, Member States could require a physically larger warning or lower levels of tar for domestically produced cigarettes. However, if a Member State did impose stricter standards on its own producers, the 'free movement' clause[16] required the state to allow cigarettes produced in other Member States which complied only with the minimum standards laid down in the directive to be sold in its country.

Both directives were amended a number of times and were eventually repealed, recast, and amended by Directive 2001/37/EC[17] on the manufacture, presentation, and sale of tobacco products (the Tobacco Control Directive), which was based on both Article 114 TFEU and Article 207 TFEU (ex Article 133 EC) on the common commercial policy.[18] This directive reduced maximum tar yields still further (to 10 mg), for the first time set maximum nicotine and carbon monoxide levels,[19] and imposed stricter labelling requirements, including an increase in size of the health warning: the general warning (e.g., 'Smoking kills/Smoking can kill') now had to cover at least 30 per cent of the surface area of the packet,[20] and an additional warning (e.g., 'Smokers die younger') had to cover at least 40 per cent of the surface area.[21] Like its predecessors, Directive 2001/37 also contained a free movement clause.[22] As we shall see, the validity of this directive, or at least parts of it, was unsuccessfully challenged in *Ex p. BAT*,[23] *Swedish Match*,[24] and *Arnold André*.[25]

At much the same time as the original tobacco labelling and tar yield directives were adopted, the 'Television without Frontiers' (TWF) Directive 89/552/EEC was also enacted[26] (now called the Audiovisual Media Services Directive (AVMS) 2010/13/EU) which, according to Article 9(1)(d), prohibited 'all forms of audiovisual commercial communications for cigarettes and other tobacco products'.[27] With the TWF/AVMS

---

[16] Considered further in Case C–11/92 *R. v. Secretary of State for Health, ex p. Gallaher Ltd* [1993] ECR I–3545 discussed below n. 266.

[17] [2001] OJ L194/26. See also Commission Dec. 2003/641/EC on the use of colour photographs or other illustrations as health warnings on tobacco packages ([2003] OJ L226/24). This directive is complemented by Council Recommendation on the 'Prevention of smoking and on initiatives to improve tobacco control' ([2003] OJ L22/31).

[18] For a heated assault on Art. 114 as a legal basis of this directive, see S. Crosby, 'The new Tobacco Control Directive: An illiberal and illegal disdain for the law' (2002) 27 *ELRev*. 177.　　　　[19] Art. 3(1)–(2).

[20] Art. 5(2)(a) and (5).　　　[21] Art. 5(2)(b) and (5).　　　[22] Art. 13.

[23] Case C–491/01 *The Queen v. Secretary of State for Health, ex p. British American Tobacco (Investments) Ltd and Imperial Tobacco Ltd (BAT)* [2002] ECR I–11453. The German government was out of time in its own challenge to the directive: Case C–406/01 *Germany v. Parliament and Council* [2002] ECR I–4561. See also Case T–311/00 *British American Tobacco (Investments) Ltd v. Commission* [2002] ECR II–2181 on access to the Commission's documents on which it based its proposal.

[24] Case C–210/03 *R v. Secretary of State for Health, ex p. Swedish Match* [2004] ECR I–11893.

[25] Case C–434/02 *Arnold André GmbH & Co KG v. Landrat des Kreises Herford* [2004] ECR I–11825.

[26] [1989] OJ L298/23 repeated and replaced by Dir. 2010/13/EU ([2010] OJ L 95/1). See Case Study 11.2 for further details about this directive. The directive was based on Art. 53(1) TFEU (ex Art. 47(2) EC) on the free movement of persons and Art. 62 TFEU (ex Art. 55 EC). The ban on radio advertising of tobacco was introduced by Dir. 2003/33 ([2003] OJ L152/16), considered below, to mirror the television ban and this was an influential factor in persuading the Court to uphold the validity of Dir. 2003/33 in Case C–380/03 *Germany v. European Parliament and Council (Tobacco Advertising II)* [2006] ECR I–11573, paras. 64 and 70.

[27] As a result of changes introduced by Dir. 2007/65 to Dir. 89/552, audiovisual media services or programmes are not to be sponsored by undertakings whose principal activity is the manufacture or sale of

Directive in place, campaigners called for a ban on other forms of cigarette and tobacco advertising that took place away from the point of sale (e.g., on the radio, posters, billboards, and in newspapers and magazines)[28] as well as a ban on sponsorship by tobacco companies (especially sports sponsorship). This was the essence of Directive 98/43/EC on Tobacco Advertising.[29] The directive, which was adopted by a majority of Member States (Austria and Germany voted against, Denmark and Spain abstained[30]), set a (high) minimum standard,[31] banning all forms of advertising and sponsorship of tobacco products.[32] However, unlike Directive 89/622 on tobacco labelling and Directive 90/289 on tar yield, Directive 98/43 did not contain a free movement clause for products which met its provisions. The directive was due to have been implemented by 30 July 2001 but it made provision for delayed implementation for specific sectors: one year for the press, two years for sponsorship, and, 'in exceptional circumstances' existing tobacco sponsorship of events or activities organized at world level (primarily formula one racing) would have continued until 2006.[33]

Although Directive 98/43 was adopted under the internal-market legal bases Articles 53(1), 62, and 114 TFEU (ex Articles 47(2), 55, and 95 EC), it was widely thought to be a public-health measure. Article 168 TFEU (ex Article 152 EC) had been introduced by the Maastricht Treaty to provide the Union with express competence in the field of public health.[34] The competence was, however, specifically limited by the then Article 152(4)(c) EC (now Article 168(5) TFEU) which provided that the Council can adopt 'incentive measures designed to protect and improve human health, *excluding any harmonisation of the laws and regulations of the Member States'*.[35]

The Union's competence to act in this sensitive area and its choice of legal basis lay at the heart of Germany's successful challenge to Directive 98/43 in *Tobacco Advertising I*,[36] where the Court said that Article 152(4)(c) EC did not mean that harmonizing measures adopted on the basis of other provisions of the (then) EC Treaty could not have any impact on the protection of human health.[37] Some support for this view can

cigarettes and other tobacco products (Art. 10(2) of Dir. 2010/13/EU). In addition, Art. 11(4) provides that where states allow product placement in programmes, these are not to contain product placement of tobacco products or cigarettes or product placement from undertakings whose principal activity is the manufacture or sale of cigarettes and other tobacco products.

[28] Hervey, above n. 11, 106.     [29] [1998] OJ L213/9.

[30] D. Khanna, 'The defeat of the European Tobacco Advertising Directive: A blow for health' (2001) 20 *YEL* 113, 115. See also F. Duina and P. Kurzer, 'Smoke in your eyes: The struggle over tobacco control in the European Union' (2004) 11 *JEPP* 57.

[31] Art. 5. Minimum standards directives are considered in more detail below nn. 251–82.

[32] Art. 5(1).     [33] Art. 6(3).

[34] Art. 168(1) TFEU (ex Art. 152(1) EC) provides that 'A high level of human health protection shall be ensured in the definition and implementation of all Union policies and activities.'

[35] Emphasis added. This provision has been revised by the Lisbon Treaty. Art. 168(5) TFEU says that the Parliament and the Council may also adopt incentive measures designed to protect and improve public health 'and measures which have as their direct objective the protection of public health regarding tobacco and abuse of alcohol, excluding any harmonisation of the laws and regulations of the Member States'.

[36] Case C–376/98 *Germany* v. *European Parliament and Council* [2000] ECR I–8419 and Case C–74/99 *R.* v. *Secretary of State for Health and others, ex p. Imperial Tobacco* [2000] ECR I–8599. A direct challenge under Art. 230(4) EC (now Art. 263(4) TFEU) could not be brought by the tobacco companies because they lacked *locus standi*: Joined Cases T–172, 175–177/98 *Salamander AG* v. *European Parliament and Council* [2000] ECR II–2487, para. 54.     [37] Para. 78.

be found in Article 114(3)[38] which provides that the Commission, when making proposals, must 'take as a base a high level of protection, taking account in particular of any new development based on scientific facts'.[39] In subsequent cases, the Court went further, saying that the Union legislature could not be prevented from relying on Article 114 'on the ground that public health protection is a *decisive* factor in the choices to be made'.[40] However, the Court added in *Tobacco Advertising I* that other Articles of the Treaties could not be used 'as a legal basis in order to circumvent the express exclusion of harmonization laid down in Article Article 152(4)(c) EC (now Article 168(5) TFEU)'.[41]

Having implied that the directive might have been a disguised health measure,[42] the Court made no further reference to the public-health provision.[43] Instead, it focused on the question of the circumstances in which Article 114 could be used to adopt EU legislation.[44] It said that where the Union measure was genuinely[45] intended to improve the conditions for the establishment and functioning of the internal market,[46] and actually had that effect,[47] then Article 114(1) could be used in two, alternative[48] situations:

- where the legislation contributes to the elimination of likely obstacles to the exercise of fundamental freedoms

- where the legislation contributes to the removal of appreciable distortions of competition which are likely to arise from the diverse national rules.[49]

---

[38] On the legal effects of Art. 114(3): Case C–350/03 *Schulte* v. *Deutsche Bausparkasse Badenia AG* [2005] ECR I–9215, para. 61.

[39] Though this does not necessarily have to be the highest standard that is technically possible. Case C–284/95 *Safety HI-Tech* v. *S&T* [1998] ECR I–4301, para. 49. See also Art. 9 TFEU which requires the Union to take a range of values into account, including public health.

[40] See, e.g., Case C–380/03 *Germany* v. *European Parliament and Council (Tobacco Advertising II)* [2006] ECR I–11573, para. 39 (emphasis added) and paras. 92–8 and the earlier cases on which it relied: Case C–491/01 *Ex p. BAT* [2002] ECR I–11453, paras. 62 and 75; Case C–210/03 *Swedish Match* [2004] ECR I–11893; Case C–434/02 *Arnold André* [2004] ECR I–11825.                    [41] Para. 79.

[42] For a discussion on why the Member States agreed to a measure which apparently exceeded the limits they had chosen to lay down in Art. 152(4)(c) EC (now Art. 168(5) TFEU), see G. de Búrca, 'The tobacco judgment: Political will versus constitutional limits' in *The ECJ's Tobacco Advertising Judgment*, CELS Occasional Paper No. 5, 2000, 13–15.

[43] Case C–380/03 *Tobacco Advertising II* [2006] ECR I–11573.

[44] Case C–376/98 [2000] ECR I–8419, paras. 83–4 and 95.

[45] Case C–376/98 *Tobacco Advertising I* [2000] ECR I–8419, para. 84. See generally, M. Kumm, 'Constitutionalising subsidiarity in integrated markets: The case of tobacco regulation in the European Union' (2006) 12 *ELJ* 503.

[46] Case C–376/98 *Tobacco Advertising I* [2000] ECR I–8419, para. 83. See S. Weatherill, 'Competence creep and competence control' (2004) 23 *YEL* 1.

[47] Although not very clearly stated in *Tobacco Advertising I*, it can be seen in paras. 84, 102, 104, and 107–8.

[48] Case C–380/03 *Germany* v. *European Parliament and Council (Tobacco Advertising II)* [2006] ECR I–11573, para. 67.

[49] See Poiares Maduro AG's view in Case C–58/08 *Vodaphone* v. *Secretary of State for Business, Enterprise and Regulatory Reform*, Opinion of 1 Oct. 2009, that a proper reading of Art. 114 had to distinguish between what triggers Union harmonization (the risk of obstacles to free movement or distortions of competition) and the scope and content of that harmonization. In respect of scope and content, he argued that the Union should be able to pursue a variety of policy goals, not limited to market integration, policy goals usually pursued by national measures which are to be replaced by Union harmonization (para. 8).

We examine in more detail the circumstances in which Article 114 can be used below. However, on the facts of *Tobacco Advertising I* the Court found that a number of the provisions in Directive 98/43 could not be adopted under Article 114 and, because these measures were so interconnected with the directive as whole, the Court annulled the whole directive rather than simply severing the offending Articles. The Council and the EP subsequently readopted the directive with the offending parts removed[50] and this directive was again challenged by Germany in *Tobacco Advertising II*.[51] This time Germany was unsuccessful.

## 2. THE CIRCUMSTANCES IN WHICH ARTICLE 114(1) CAN BE USED

### 2.1 Elimination of Obstacles to the Exercise of Fundamental Freedoms

As we have seen from Case Study 16.1, in *Tobacco Advertising I* the Court said that Article 114(1) could be used to adopt EU measures in two situations. The first is where those measures contribute to the elimination of obstacles to the exercise of fundamental freedoms. The following example illustrates this point. State B has stricter rules than State A on the quantity of additives that can be used in a product. State B's rules, although justified on public-health grounds, create an obstacle to the free movement of goods because State A's goods need to be adapted before they can be imported into State B. The solution to this problem would be to enact a common standard under Article 114 to eliminate these obstacles to trade.[52]

In *Tobacco Advertising I* the Court made clear that not only could Article 114(1) be used to adopt measures dealing with actual obstacles to trade, as in the additives example above, but it could also be used to address future obstacles to trade which might emerge due to the 'multifarious development of national laws'.[53] In this case, the emergence of such obstacles had to be 'likely' and the measure in question had to be 'designed to prevent them'.[54] Therefore, in *Tobacco Advertising I*[55] the Court said that Directive 98/43's ban on advertising of tobacco products in (the confusingly named) 'non-static advertising media' (periodicals, magazines, and newspapers) could be adopted on the basis of Article 114(1), since this would help to ensure the free movement of press products. The Court said that, even though the obstacles to trade were potential rather than actual, it was 'probable' that the obstacles would arise in the future.[56]

The obstacles to free movement also have to be appreciable. For this reason, the Court found in *Tobacco Advertising I* that Article 114(1) could not be used to ban advertising in 'static advertising media' (eg posters, parasols, ashtrays, and other articles used in hotels, restaurants, and cafés). This was because the effect on free movement of goods was too

---

[50] EP and Council Dir. 2003/33 on the approximation of laws relating to advertising and sponsorship of tobacco products ([2003] OJ L152/16).

[51] Case C–380/03 *Germany v. European Parliament and Council* [2006] ECR I–11573.

[52] Case C–491/01 *Ex p. BAT* [2002] ECR I–11453, paras. 64–5.

[53] This language is actually taken from Case C–491/01 *Ex p. BAT* [2002] ECR I–11453, para. 61.

[54] Ibid.      [55] Case C–376/98 *Tobacco Advertising I* [2000] ECR I–8419, para. 98.

[56] Ibid., para. 97.

uncertain and indirect:[57] the prohibition on advertising could not be justified by the need to eliminate obstacles to the free movement of advertising media or the freedom to provide services in the field of advertising.[58] This view was reinforced by the fact that the directive did not contain a free movement clause.[59] By contrast, Directive 2001/37 on tobacco control did contain such a clause, and for this reason the Court said in *Ex p. BAT* that because Member States could not prevent the import, sale, or use of tobacco products which did comply with the directive, the directive did improve the conditions for the functioning of the internal market.[60] Therefore Directive 2001/37 was correctly adopted under Article 114(1).

## 2.2 Removal of Appreciable Distortions of Competition

According to *Tobacco Advertising I*, the second situation in which Article 114(1) can be used is where the Union adopts measures to remove distortions of competition arising from the diverse national rules. To a certain extent this second ground overlaps with the first: any obstacle to trade is also likely to distort competition. However, this second ground is broader, covering situations where, owing to the absence of regulation in State A, the producers or service providers established there enjoy a competitive advantage in terms of production costs over their competitors in State B who face substantial regulation. A harmonization directive would iron out these cost differences.[61]

Once again, Article 114(1) can be used to address actual, as well as potential, distortions of competition. The Court made this clear in *Titanium Dioxide* where it said that the Union could also legislate where the distortions were 'likely' to arise from the diverse national rules.[62] Moreover, the distortions had to be 'appreciable'.[63] In *Tobacco Advertising I* the Court explained that it was not sufficient for the EU legislature to rely on single market legal bases 'with a view to eliminating the smallest distortions of competition';[64] i.e., where the effects on competition were 'remote and indirect'.[65] It explained that in the absence of such a requirement 'the powers of the [Union] legislature would be practically unlimited',[66] and that would be incompatible with the principle embodied in Article 5(2) TEU[67] that the powers of the Union are limited to those specifically conferred on it.[68] For this reason the Court said that the adoption of Directive 98/43 under Article 114(1) could

---

[57] D. Wyatt, 'Constitutional significance of the tobacco advertising judgment of the European Court of Justice' in *The ECJ's Tobacco Advertising Judgment*, CELS Occasional Paper No. 5, 2000. It is, however, rather puzzling why posters, ashtrays, and parasols were classified as static rather than non-static since the arguments made about non-static media seem equally applicable to these so-called static media.

[58] Case C–376/98 *Tobacco Advertising I* [2000] ECR I–8419, para. 99.          [59] Ibid., para. 101.

[60] Ibid., para. 74.

[61] For arguments to this effect see Case C–300/89 *Commission* v. *Council (titanium dioxide)* [1991] ECR I–2867.          [62] Ibid., para. 15.

[63] Case C–376/98 *Tobacco Advertising I* [2000] ECR I–8419, para. 106.

[64] Ibid., para. 107. See also para. 84: 'If a mere finding of disparities between national rules and of the abstract risk of obstacles to the exercise of fundamental freedoms or of distortions of competition liable to result therefrom were sufficient to justify the choice of Article [114] as a legal basis, judicial review of compliance with the proper legal basis might be rendered nugatory.'

[65] Ibid., para. 109. Cf. Case C–190/98 *Graf* [2000] ECR I–493, para. 25, considered in Ch. 8.

[66] Para. 107.

[67] See also Art. 5(1) TEU: 'The limits of Union competences are governed by the principle of conferral.' For the avoidance of doubt, Art. 4(1) TEU states 'In accordance with Article 5, competences not conferred upon the Union in the Treaties remain with the Member States.' This is reiterated again in Art. 5(2), 2nd sentence.          [68] Case C–376/98 [2000] ECR I–8419, para. 83.

not be justified on the ground of the distortion of competition caused to the advertising industry. It recognized that while advertising agencies and producers of advertising media established in Member States which imposed fewer restrictions on tobacco advertising were at an advantage in terms of economies of scale and increase in profits, the effects of such advantages on competition were 'remote and indirect' and did not 'constitute distortions which could be described as appreciable'.[69]

The Court also rejected the justification based on the distortions of competition in the marketing of tobacco products. The Commission had argued that, in Member States where advertising was restricted, producers and sellers of tobacco products had to resort to price competition to influence their market share. The Court dismissed these arguments, saying that in these states the national laws constituted a '*restriction* of forms of competition which applied to all economic operators in those Member States'[70] and not a distortion. Because the national laws merely *restricted* competition rather than distorted it, no harmonization was possible under Article 114(1).[71] To some commentators, this distinction between *distortions* of competition (which justify Union measures under Article 114(1)) and *restrictions* (which do not) reflects the distinction drawn in *Keck*[72] between product requirements (to which Article 34 TFEU applies) and non-discriminatory measures such as selling arrangements (to which Article 34 does not apply).[73]

Finally, the Court considered whether Article 114(1) could be used to harmonize national rules concerning sports sponsorship by tobacco companies. It noted that prohibiting sponsorship in some Member States and authorizing it in others caused certain sports events to be moved, affecting the conditions of competition for undertakings associated with such events.[74] Since this gave rise to an appreciable distortion on competition, it did justify an EU measure adopted under Article 114 but not an outright ban on advertising of the kind proposed by the directive.[75]

## 2.3 The Follow-up to *Tobacco Advertising I*

Given that the Court could not separate those parts of the directive which had been validly adopted and those which had not, it annulled the directive in its entirety.[76] The Council and Parliament then adopted a new, more tailored measure, Directive 2003/33[77] on advertising and sponsorship of tobacco products, covering those areas of Directive 98/43 which the Court had said could be validly adopted under the internal-market legal bases.[78] Article 3 of Directive 2003/33 bans advertising in the press and other printed publications ('non-static' advertising media), except for publications intended exclusively for

---

[69] Para. 109.  [70] Para. 113, emphasis added.

[71] See also Case C–412/93 *Leclerc–Siplec* [1995] ECR I–179 considered in Ch. 7 where restrictions on advertising applied equally to all traders operating in the state and did not make a distinction, in law or in fact, between domestic and imported goods. These were certain selling arrangements which did not breach Art. 34 TFEU.  [72] Joined Cases C–267 and 268/91 *Keck and Mithouard* [1993] ECR I–6097.

[73] See also Geelhoed AG's Opinion in Case C–434/02 *Arnold André* [2004] ECR I–11825, para. 65. See also the direct links between the Art. 34 TFEU case law (e.g., Case C–405/98 *Gourmet International Products* [2001] ECR I–1795) and the Art. 114 TFEU case law made in Case C–380/03 *Tobacco Advertising II* [2006] ECR I–11573, para. 42. Cf. G. Davies, 'Can selling arrangements be harmonised?' (2005) 30 *ELRev*. 371 and Poiares Maduro AG's views on parallelism in Case C–58/08 *Vodaphone*, Opinion of 1 Oct. 2009, paras. 21–4.  [74] Para. 110.

[75] Para. 111.  [76] Para. 117.  [77] [2003] OJ L152/16.

[78] EP and Council Dir. 2003/33 on the approximation of laws relating to advertising and sponsorship of tobacco products ([2003] OJ L152/16).

professionals in the tobacco trade and for publications not intended for the Union market. According to the preamble, this ban was justified by the need to overcome 'an appreciable risk of obstacles to free movement' created by diverse national laws.[79] Article 4 prohibits all forms of radio advertising for tobacco products as well as tobacco sponsorship of radio programmes. Article 5 prohibits tobacco sponsorship of events taking place in more than one Member State. This was justified by the need to address national rules giving rise to 'an appreciable risk of distortion of the conditions of competition'.[80] The directive also contains a free movement clause.[81]

In *Tobacco Advertising II*[82] the Court upheld the validity of Articles 3–4 of the directive. Having analysed the existing national law on tobacco advertising and the risks of new barriers arising as a result of the accession of the new Member States, the Court said the barriers and risks of distortions of competition warranted intervention by the Union legislature on the basis of Article 114,[83] and that Articles 3–4 were in fact designed to eliminate or prevent obstacles to the free movement of goods/services or to remove distortions of competition, not least because of the existence of the free movement clause.[84]

In the light of the decisions in *Tobacco Advertising I* and *Ex p. BAT* it is clear that the Union does not have the power to intervene in all cases where the market does not function optimally, since this would be tantamount to providing the Union with a general legislative power.[85] However, the Union can legislate to overcome the geographic fragmentation of the EU market. As Bernard puts it, the Union does not have the power under Article 114(1) to ensure the functioning of the common *market* (i.e., the market in general) but does have the power to regulate matters to ensure the functioning of the *common* market (i.e., the creation of a single, unified market).[86]

### 2.4 The Case Law after *Tobacco Advertising I*

#### (a) Departing from *Tobacco Advertising I*

Although the Court sent out a strong message in *Tobacco Advertising I* that there were limits to the use of Article 114 and that it could not be used to regulate all aspects of economic life,[87] subsequent cases suggest that the Court might be relaxing its tough stance,

---

[79] 4th recital.  [80] 5th recital.

[81] According to Art. 8 'Member States shall not prohibit or restrict the free movement of products which comply with this Directive'.

[82] Case C–380/03 *Germany* v. *European Parliament and Council (Tobacco Advertising II)* [2006] ECR I–11573.  [83] Para. 68.

[84] Para. 73.  [85] Cf. M. Ludwigs note on *Tobacco Advertising II*, (2007) 44 *CMLRev.* 1159, 1176.

[86] N. Bernard, 'The future of European economic law in the light of the principle of subsidiarity' (1996) 33 *CMLRev.* 633, 640–1.

[87] See also the politically important decision in Joined Cases C–317/04 and C–318/04 *Parliament* v. *Council (passenger name records)* [2006] ECR I–4721 where the Court ruled that Art. 114 TFEU, read in conjunction with Art. 25 of Dir. 95/46/EC on the protection of individuals with regard to the processing of personal data and on the free movement of such data, could not justify (then) Community competence to conclude an agreement between the EC and the USA on the processing and transfer of passenger name record (PNR) data by air carriers to the US Department of Homeland Security. Because the agreement related to data-processing operations which were excluded from the scope of the directive, the decision implementing the agreement could not be adopted under Art. 114. Any internal market objective was purely incidental; the real objectives of the agreement (prevention of terrorism, organized crime, and protection of privacy) were objectives of the then EU, not EC, Treaty.

upholding a number of uses of Article 114 which might not apparently satisfy either the detail or the spirit of the *Tobacco Advertising I* ruling.[88] For example, the Court has since made clear that the phrase 'measures for the approximation' in Article 114 conferred on the legislature a broad discretion as regard the method most appropriate for achieving the desired result, in particular in areas characterized by complexity.[89] Measures adopted can consist of requiring all Member States to authorize the marketing of products, subjecting any such authorization to certain conditions, or even *prohibiting* the marketing of products.[90] Therefore, in *Swedish Match* and *Arnold André*[91] the Court said that a total ban on the marketing of oral tobacco products such as snuff (finely ground tobacco consumed by placing it between the gum and the lip) in the Tobacco Control Directive 2001/37 could be adopted under Article 114,[92] even though a *ban* might appear to fly in the face of a single market in goods.[93] And in *Österreichischer Rundfunk*[94] the Court said that the Data Protection Directive could be adopted under Article 114 even though it applied to a wholly internal situation. The Court said that 'recourse to Article [114] as a legal basis does not presuppose the existence of an actual link with free movement between Member States in every situation referred to by the measure founded on that basis'. It was sufficient that the measure adopted under Article 114 was actually intended to improve the conditions for the establishment and functioning of the internal market.[95]

### (b) Indirect harmonization

Subsequent cases raised other difficulties for the Court. For example, can Article 114 be used to create legal forms which help the internal market to run smoothly but are not about harmonization *per se*? Two Advocate Generals thought not[96] but the Court disagreed. In *UK v. EP and Council (European Network and Information Security Agency (ENISA))*[97] the Court said that Article 114 could be used to establish a Union body responsible for contributing to the implementation of a process of harmonization where, for example,

---

[88] See S. Weatherill, 'Competence and legitimacy' in C. Barnard and O. Odudu (eds.), *The Outer Limits of European Union Law* (Oxford: Hart Publishing, 2009), 19–20 who argues that the Court's approach is now 'competence-enhancing and not competence-restricting'. He also argues that the result of Case C–176/03 *Commission v Council (Criminal Penalties)* [2005] ECR I–7879 hints at the use of Art. 114 to make a harmonized criminal law. Although see Case C–301/06 *Ireland* v. *European Parliament and Council (data processing)* [2009] ECR I–593 for a straight application of the principles in *Tobacco Advertising I*, albeit in the context of a cross-pillar dispute. The Court did refer to Art. 47 EU which provided that none of the provisions of the then EC Treaty could be affected by the provisions of the EU Treaty (now replaced by Art. 40 TEU). [89] Case C–380/03 *Tobacco Advertising II* [2006] ECR I–11573, para. 42.

[90] Ibid., para. 43.

[91] Case C–210/03 *Swedish Match* [2004] ECR I–11893; Case C–434/02 *Arnold André* [2004] ECR I–11825.

[92] *Arnold André*, para. 35. See also the discussion of the proportionality of the ban in para. 54.

[93] See also Reg. (EC) No. 1007/2009 ([2009] OJ L286/36) on trade in seal products which essentially banned the import of seal products. This has now been contested by Canadian and Greenlandic Inuit groups: L. Philips, 'Inuit sue EU over seal ban', *euobserver.com*, 15 Jan. 2010.

[94] Case C–465/00 [2003] ECR I–4989, para. 41. Case C–101/01 *Lindqvist* [2003] ECR I–12971, paras. 40–1 noted by Coudray (2004) 41 *CMLRev.* 1361, 1369.

[95] Case C–380/03 *Germany* v. *Council and European Parliament (Tobacco Advertising II)* [2006] ECR I–11573, para. 80.

[96] Stix-Hackl AG in Case C–436/03 *ECS* [2006] ECR I–3733; Kokott AG in Case C–217/04 *UK* v. *EP and Council (ENISA)* [2006] ECR I–3771.

[97] Case C–217/04 *ENISA* [2006] ECR I–3771, noted V. Randazzo (2007) 44 *CMLRev.* 155.

the Union body provided services to national authorities and/or operators which affected the homogenous implementation of harmonizing instruments and was likely to facilitate their application.[98] The Court added that the tasks conferred on such a body did, however, have to be closely linked to the subject matter of the harmonization legislation.[99] Therefore, ENISA[100] could be established on the basis of Article 114 since its aim was to assist the Commission and the Member States with meeting the requirements of network and information security, as part of a wider package of measures,[101] thereby ensuring the smooth functioning of electronic communications services.

In *Smoke Flavourings*[102] the Court also upheld the use of Article 114 as a legal basis for a regulation which did not harmonize laws but established procedures (then the regulatory procedure laid down by the Comitology decision,[103] now the regulatory procedure with scrutiny) for the approval of lists of authorized products which could be used in 'smoked' foods. The UK had argued that Article 114 could be used only to harmonize national laws—i.e., Article 114 could be used to achieve at Union level what Member States could have achieved at national level on their own (direct harmonization); it could not be used to establish Union bodies, confer tasks on these bodies or establish authorization procedures such as those in *Smoke Flavourings* (indirect harmonization). However, Advocate General Kokott said that Article 114 could be used to approximate laws both directly *and* indirectly in a 'multi-stage model with intermediate steps'[104] and the Court appeared to accept her view. It said that Article 114 could be used to adopt a measure which merely defines the basic provisions essential for achieving the objective which then confers power on the Commission to adopt the harmonization measures needed for the implementation of the legislative act in question.[105] In other words, Article 114 could be used to establish a parent measure which delegates implementing power to the Commission.

The Court also said that where the Union legislature provided for harmonization which comprised several stages, for instance the fixing of a number of essential criteria set out in a basic (parent) regulation followed by scientific evaluation of the substances concerned and the adoption of a positive list of substances authorized throughout the Union (the subordinate measure), two conditions had to be satisfied:

- the Union legislature had to determine in the basic act the essential elements of the harmonizing measure in question

- the mechanism for implementing those elements had to be designed in such a way that it led to a harmonization within the meaning of Article [114].

In particular, the Court said the parent measure had to establish detailed rules for making decisions at each stage of an authorization procedure, and determine and circumscribe precisely the powers of the Commission as the body which had to take the final decision.[106] That applied in particular where the harmonization in question consisted

---

[98] Paras. 44–5.     [99] Para. 45.

[100] *ENISA* is an example of the relatively recent phenomenon of establishing an Agency to facilitate decision-making by ensuring independence and expertise.     [101] Para. 60.

[102] Case C–66/04 *UK v. EP and Council (smoke flavourings)* [2005] ECR I–10553.

[103] See below n. 225.     [104] Para. 33.     [105] Para. 50.

[106] Art. 290 (1) TFEU now articulates this point in respect of *delegated* power (but not the implementation power which is covered by Art. 291 TFEU): 'A legislative act may delegate to the Commission the power to adopt non-legislative acts of general application to supplement or amend certain non-essential elements of the legislative act. The objectives, content, scope and duration of the delegation of power shall be explicitly

of drawing up a list of products authorized throughout the Union to the exclusion of all other products.[107]

Given the emphasis in *Smoke Flavourings* on the need for the parent measure to prescribe carefully and in detail the relevant procedure for adopting subordinate measures, the Court's decision in the earlier case of *Alliance for Natural Health*[108] came as something of a surprise. *Alliance for Natural Health* concerned the Food Supplements Directive 2002/46,[109] a classic single-market measure in the sense that it had been introduced to harmonize the rules on food supplements, such as vitamins and minerals, which had been the subject of much (diverse) national legislation which in turn had been challenged by traders under Article 34 TFEU. States invariably, and often successfully, invoked Article 36 TFEU to defend their rules,[110] and in so doing created (legitimate) obstacles to trade. Directive 2002/46 was intended to address these obstacles by creating an EU-wide regime. It envisaged a two-stage approach to the harmonization of the rules in this area. By 1 August 2003 Member States had to permit trade in foods containing vitamins and minerals which had been 'positive listed' (i.e., approved). This obligation was ensured through a free movement clause. By 1 August 2005 Member States had to prohibit trade in products that did not comply with the requirements of the directive.

While Advocate General Geelhoed and the Court recognized that the directive had an internal-market dimension and so was correctly adopted on the basis of Article 114, the Advocate General was much concerned about the proportionality of the measure.[111] He said that the legal instruments which put the positive list system into effect had to be designed with care since they had far-reaching impact on the freedom of market operators: they impeded the continuation of activities previously regarded as lawful and subjected new developments to a prior assessment by the Commission before they could be positive-listed.[112] He argued that the directive failed in three respects:[113]

- the directive, in delegating power to the Commission and the comitology committee, provided no substantive norm for the decision-makers to follow as a guiding principle to decide whether a product should appear on the positive list[114]

- the directive did not make clear whether private parties themselves could submit substances for evaluation[115]

- if they could, then the directive failed to provide a clear procedure to provide minimum guarantees for protecting the parties' interests.

---

defined in the legislative acts. The essential elements of an area shall be reserved for the legislative act and accordingly shall not be the subject of a delegation of power.' See further COM(2009) 673.

[107] Paras. 47–9.

[108] Joined Cases C–154/04 and C–155/04 *Alliance for Natural Health* [2005] ECR I–6451.

[109] OJ [2002] L183/51.

[110] E.g., Case C–192/01 *Commission v. Denmark* [2003] ECR I–9693, Case C–24/00 *Commission v. France (nutrients)* [2004] ECR I–1277, Case C–95/01 *Greenham and Abel* [2004] ECR I–1333. See further Ch. 6.

[111] Para. 38.      [112] Para. 66.      [113] Para. 68.

[114] This, he emphasized was particularly serious: para. 69. The Court disagreed: it said that the procedure for modifying the positive list was linked to recitals in the directive which made clear that the Commission had to use public health as the yardstick for modification.

[115] There was an internal conflict in the directive between the preamble which said that private operators could do so and the body of the directive which said that it was for the Member States.

He concluded, 'this procedure, in so far as it may exist and in so far as it may deserve this title, has the transparency of a black box'.[116] He therefore considered the directive invalid. The Court agreed that it would have been 'desirable' for the directive to have contained provisions which ensured that the application process be completed transparently and within a reasonable time[117] but, unlike the Advocate General, the Court thought that this was not sufficient to jeopardize the validity of the directive because of the Commission's general duty, under the principle of sound administration, to act transparently and within a reasonable time. It therefore upheld the validity of the directive.

The cases considered so far concern delegation. The *Vodaphone*[118] case raises a further difficult question for the Court: can Article 114 be used as a legal basis for a measure affecting the conduct of private parties, *in casu* a regulation establishing Union-wide maximum prices for roaming on public mobile phone networks? The Advocate General thought it could. While he doubted that the EU had shown that the risk of possible future differences in national price controls created obstacles to trade justifying regulation under Article 114,[119] he did think that the EU legislator could regulate roaming prices under Article 114 to remove 'restrictions to free movement arising from the behaviour of private parties which disfavours cross-border economic activity'.[120] In so doing, he asked the Court to apply 'the logical consequences of its case-law on the horizontal application of free movement rules to its analysis of Article [114]'.[121]

## 3. CHOICE OF LEGAL BASIS

So far we have focused on the question of whether the Union has the competence at all to adopt measures under Article 114. We turn now to the question of where a secondary measure could have been adopted on one of a number of legal bases. In addition to the general legal bases (Articles 114–15 and 352), there are various specific legal bases which could be used for measures which might have implications for the internal market, in particular Article 43 TFEU (ex Article 37 EC) (agriculture), Article 173 TFEU (ex Article 157 EC) (industrial policy), and Article 192 TFEU (ex Article 175 EC) (environment). This can lead to the situation where the proposed measure appears to raise single-market issues as well as issues covered by another legal basis. What rules should apply? As we have seen, Article 114(1) is supposed to be a residual legal basis, only to be used where there is no other suitable provision.[122] Yet, in *Titanium Dioxide*[123] the Court favoured the use of Article 114 over (the more specific) Article 192 on the environment as the choice of legal basis for adopting a directive on disposing of waste by the titanium dioxide industry.[124] It argued that, since environmental and health measures were a burden on undertakings, competition could be appreciably distorted in the absence of harmonization; thus Article 114(1) applied. If this logic was accepted, then *Titanium Dioxide* would have had the effect of marginalizing all other legal bases since nearly all Union measures have some cost implication.

---

[116] Para. 85.      [117] Para. 81.      [118] Case C–58/08, AG's Opinion of 1 Oct. 2009.
[119] Para. 18.      [120] Para. 19.      [121] Para. 21.
[122] For criticisms of the misuse of Art. 114, see S. Crosby, 'The single market and the rule of law' (1991) 16 *ELRev*. 451.          [123] Case C–300/89 [1991] ECR I–2867.
[124] Dir. 89/428/EEC ([1989] OJ L201/56).

In reality, the Court's judgment may have disguised a policy preference for Article 114 at a time when Article 114 required the more democratic cooperation procedure,[125] allowing for a greater involvement of the European Parliament, while other Treaty provisions, like the environmental basis (Article 130s EEC as it then was), required only simple consultation. However, such reasoning was much criticized because it allowed procedural rules to determine the choice of legal basis rather than the substantive content of the measure,[126] and significant doubt has now been cast on elements of *Titanium Dioxide* by the *Waste Directive*[127] and *Beef Labelling*[128] cases. In the *Waste Directive* case the Court said that recourse to Article 114 was not justified where the measure to be adopted had 'only the incidental effect of harmonizing market conditions within the [Union]'.[129] In *Beef Labelling* the Court refused to countenance an argument that Article 114 should be used due to its more democratic procedures.

Therefore, it can now be said that if an examination of a Union act shows that it has a twofold purpose, one of which is identifiable as main or predominant and the other merely incidental, the act must be founded on the sole, predominant, legal basis.[130130] Exceptionally, the Court will accept a dual basis. As the Court said in *Ex p. BAT*,[131] if it is established that the act simultaneously pursues a number of objectives, indissociably linked, without one being secondary and indirect in relation to the other, such an act may be founded on the various corresponding legal bases.[132] On the facts of the case, the Court said that because the directive had been properly adopted on the basis of Article 114 it could not simultaneously have Articles 114 and 207 for a legal basis: the provisions affecting tobacco products exported to non-EU states were secondary to the aim and content of the directive as a whole, which was primarily designed to improve the conditions for the functioning of the internal market.[133] However, since the reference to Article 207 was a formal defect only, it did not invalidate the directive because the procedures under the two bases were essentially similar.[134]

With a greater use of the ordinary legislative procedure following the Lisbon Treaty, these Treaty-base disputes should become less common. However, the residual legal basis in Article 352 TFEU (ex Article 308 EC) is not subject to the ordinary legislative procedure. In its revised form it provides that if action by the Union should prove necessary, within the framework of the policies defined in the Treaties, to attain one of the objectives set out in the Treaties (thereby broadening the scope of the original Article 308 EC which was limited to action necessary to attain the common market),[135] and the Treaties have not provided the necessary powers, the Council, acting unanimously on a proposal from the Commission and after obtaining the consent of the European Parliament, must adopt the appropriate measures. Those measures may be legislative in character in which case they are deemed to have been adopted by the special legislative procedure.

---

[125] Para. 20.     [126] S. Crosby, above n. 122, 464.

[127] Case C–155/91 *Commission v. Council (Waste Directive)* [1993] ECR I–939.

[128] Case C–269/97 *Commission and Parliament v. Council (beef labelling)* [2000] ECR I–2257.

[129] Para. 19.     [130] Case C–491/01 *Ex p. BAT* [2002] ECR I–11453, para. 94.     [131] Ibid.

[132] *Opinion 2/00* [2001] ECR I–9713, para. 23.     [133] Paras. 95–6.

[134] Cf. Case C–211/01 *Commission v. Council (carriage of goods by road and combined transport)* [2003] ECR I–8913, para. 52.

[135] Note the additional safeguard in Art. 352(2): 'Using the procedure for monitoring the subsidiarity principle referred to in Article 5(3) of the Treaty on European Union, the Commission shall draw national Parliaments' attention to proposals based on this Article.'

Perhaps in a nod to the problems generated by *Tobacco Advertising I* and the Court's cavalier approach to the non-harmonization provision in Article 152(4)(c) EC, as it then was, Article 352(2) provides 'Measures based on this Article shall not entail harmonisation of Member States' laws or regulations in cases where the Treaties exclude such harmonisation.'[136]

## 4. THE APPLICATION OF THE PRINCIPLES OF SUBSIDIARITY AND PROPORTIONALITY TO MEASURES ADOPTED UNDER ARTICLE 114

In areas, such as the internal market, where the Union's competence is not exclusive,[137] measures adopted must respect the principle of subsidiarity[138] (i.e., they should be taken at the lowest appropriate level[139]). If an application of the subsidiarity principle reveals that the Union should act, any measure adopted must also be proportionate (no more extensive than necessary to achieve the objective).[140] For many years the Court has been reluctant to engage in a detailed examination of the compatibility of a Union act with the principles of subsidiarity and proportionality because, as it explained in *Ex p. BAT*,[141] 'the [Union] legislature must be allowed a broad discretion in an area such as that involved in the present case, which entails political, economic, and social choices on its part, and in which it is called upon to undertake complex assessments'. Consequently, the legality of a measure adopted can be affected 'only if the measure is manifestly inappropriate having regard to the objective which the competent institution is seeking to pursue'.[142]

Subsidiarity has proved a particularly sensitive issue.[143] In the past, the Court has been reluctant to review the merits of complaints alleging breach of subsidiarity, viewing subsidiarity more as a political than as a legal principle. In particular, it has refused to examine whether the criteria laid down in Article 5(3) TEU (i.e., whether the action can be sufficiently achieved by the Member States or, whether by reason of the scale or

---

[136] See also the limit in Art. 352(4): 'This Article cannot serve as a basis for attaining objectives pertaining to the common foreign and security policy and any acts adopted pursuant to this Article shall respect the limits set out in Article 40, 2nd para., of the Treaty on European Union.' See also Decls. 41–2 annexed to the final act and the discussion by A. Dashwood, 'Article 308 EC as the outer limit of expressly conferred Community competence' in C. Barnard and O. Odudu (eds.), *The Outer Limits of European Union Law* (Oxford: Hart Publishing, 2009).

[137] Art. 5(3) TEU. See also Case C–491/01 *Ex p. BAT* [2002] ECR I–11453, para. 179.

[138] As Case C–491/01 *Ex p. BAT* [2002] ECR I–11453 indicates, subsidiarity will also apply to situations where the Union has already exercised its shared competence, with at least some pre-emptive effects, and replaces that legislation with revised rules (the Tobacco Control Dir.).

[139] This is reflected in the revised language (in italics) of Art. 5(3) TEU which provides that the 'Union shall act only if and in so far as the objectives of the proposed action cannot be sufficiently achieved by the Member States, either at *central level or at regional and local level*'.

[140] Art. 5(4) TEU. For a fuller discussion, see A. Dashwood, 'The relationship between the Member States and the European Union/European Community' (2004) 41 *CMLRev.* 355.

[141] Case C–491/01 [2002] ECR I–11453, para. 123.      [142] Para. 123.

[143] See generally, A. Toth, 'A legal analysis of subsidiarity' in D. O'Keeffe and P. Twomey (eds.), *Legal Issues of the Maastricht Treaty* (Chichester: Chancery, 1994). See also the essays by Steiner and Emiliou in the same volume as well as N. Emiliou, 'Subsidiarity: An effective barrier against "the enterprises of ambition"' (1992) 17 *ELRev.* 383; A. Toth, 'The principle of subsidiarity in the Maastricht Treaty' (1992) 29 *CMLRev.* 1079.

effects of the proposed action, it could be better achieved by the Union) have been met.[144] Instead, the Court has been content to focus on the procedural aspects of the subsidiarity principle, checking to see whether the Union institutions have actually considered the implications for the principle of subsidiarity of the proposed measure;[145] it has not been prepared to look behind those reasons to see whether they were justified. For example, in *Working Time*[146] the Court simply observed that if harmonization was at issue this 'necessarily' presupposed Union-wide action,[147] without examining the prior question of whether there was a need for harmonization in this area. Similarly, in *Biotechnological Inventions*[148] the Court argued that the objective pursued by the directive, to ensure the smooth operation of the internal market by preventing or eliminating differences between the legislation and practice of the various Member States, could not be achieved by action taken by the Member States alone. As the scope of the protection of biotechnological inventions had immediate effects on trade and on intra-Union trade, it was clear that 'given the scale and the effects of the proposed action, the objective in question could be better achieved by the [Union]'.[149]

However, in *Ex p. BAT*[150] the Court showed itself a little more willing to consider the merits of the subsidiarity principle in deciding whether the Community should have adopted the Tobacco Control Directive 2001/37. It began by considering 'whether the objective of the proposed action could be better achieved at [Union] level'.[151] It said that since the directive's objective was to eliminate the barriers raised by the differences which still existed between the laws of the Member State on the manufacture, presentation, and sale of tobacco products, 'such an objective cannot be sufficiently achieved by the Member States individually and calls for action at [Union] level, as demonstrated by the multifarious development of national laws in this case'. It therefore considered that the objective of the directive could be better achieved at Union level.[152] In effect this is a clearer articulation of the point made in *Working Time* and *Biotechnological Inventions* that harmonization requires EU action. Rather curiously, the Court then appeared to merge the tests of subsidiarity and proportionality. It said that:

the intensity of the action undertaken by the [Union] in this instance was also in keeping with the requirements of the principle of subsidiarity in that . . . it did not go beyond what was necessary to achieve the objective pursued.[153]

The Court also found the Tobacco Control Directive's provisions proportionate. For example, when considering the obligation to give information on the tar, nicotine, and carbon monoxide levels and to print health warnings on the packets, it noted that these were appropriate measures for attaining a high level of health protection when the barriers raised by national laws on labelling were removed.[154] The Court continued that although the directive required more of the surface area of the packaging to be used for

---

[144] N. Bernard, 'The future of European economic law in the light of the principle of subsidiarity' (1996) 33 *CMLRev.* 633, 653.

[145] Case C–233/94 *Germany v. Parliament and Council (deposit guarantee schemes)* [1997] ECR I–2405.

[146] Case C–84/94 *UK v. Council* [1996] ECR I–5755.     [147] Para. 47.

[148] Case C–377/98 *Netherlands v. Parliament and Council* [2001] ECR I–7079.     [149] Para. 32.

[150] Case C–491/01 [2002] ECR I–11453. See also Joined Cases C–154/04 and C–155/04 *Alliance for Natural Health* [2005] ECR I–6451, paras. 105–6.     [151] Para. 180.

[152] Paras. 181–3. See also Case C–103/01 *Commission v. Germany (PPE)* [2003] ECR I–5369, para. 47.

[153] Para. 187.     [154] Para. 131.

warnings, it also allowed for sufficient space to be left for the manufacturers to affix other material, in particular trade marks. For this reason, the Court concluded, 'the [Union] legislature has not overstepped the bounds of the discretion which it enjoys in this area'.[155]

Similarly, in *Tobacco Advertising II*[156] the Court made clear that a tailored ban on tobacco advertising (the ban did not apply to publications intended for professionals in the tobacco trade or published in third countries) was proportionate. It was also compatible with Article 10 ECHR on the freedom of expression. As the Court said, the discretion enjoyed by the competent authorities in determining the balance to be struck between freedom of expression in Article 10(1) and objectives in the public interest referred to in Article 10(2) varies for each of the goals justifying restrictions on that freedom and depends on the nature of the activities in question. When a certain amount of discretion is available, 'review is limited to an examination of the reasonableness and proportionality of the interference. This holds true for the commercial use of freedom of expression in a field as complex and fluctuating as advertising.'[157]

Amendments introduced by the Lisbon Treaty are intended to improve the monitoring and enforcement of the subsidiarity principle through *ex ante* control by national parliaments, the bodies that stand to lose most by Union action, rather than by *ex post* review by the Court.[158] Article 5(3) TEU says that the Union's institutions must apply the principle of subsidiarity in accordance with Protocol No. 2 on the principles of subsidiarity and proportionality. National parliaments are to ensure compliance with the principle of subsidiarity in accordance with Protocol No. 1 on the role of national parliaments in the European Union.[159] Protocol No. 2 introduces the so-called 'yellow card' procedure under which any national parliament or chamber thereof can object to a proposed EU measure, on the grounds that it does not comply with the principle of subsidiarity, by issuing a reasoned opinion. Where one-third of the national parliaments object, the proposal must be formally reviewed by the EU institutions.[160] Heightened scrutiny applies to a proposal under the ordinary legislative procedure which is objected to by a simple majority of votes allocated to national parliaments.

## 5. DEROGATIONS FROM MEASURES ADOPTED UNDER ARTICLE 114(1)

Perhaps the most striking and controversial feature of Article 114 is that Articles 114(4)–(5) make express provision for Member States to derogate from a measure adopted under Article 114(1).[161] This was the price for the introduction of QMV into

---

[155] Para. 132.

[156] Case C–380/03 *Germany* v. *European Parliament and Council* [2006] ECR I–11573, para. 148.

[157] Para. 155, citing the controversial decision in Case C–71/02 *Karner* [2004] ECR I–3025, para. 51.

[158] Although Art. 8 of Protocol No. 2 on the principles of subsidiarity and proportionality confirms that 'The Court of Justice of the European Union shall have jurisdiction in actions on grounds of infringement of the principle of subsidiarity by a legislative act', brought in accordance with the rules laid down in Art. 263 TFEU by 'Member States, or notified by them in accordance with their legal order on behalf of their national Parliament or a chamber thereof'. See generally, M. Kumm, 'Constitutionalising subsidairity in integrated markets: The case of tobacco regulation in the European Union' (2006) 12 *ELJ* 503.

[159] See also Art. 12(a)–(b) TEU.

[160] For a full explanation of the procedure, see M. Dougan, 'The Treaty of Lisbon 2007: Winning minds, not hearts' (2008) 45 *CMLRev.* 617, 657–61.

[161] This is the only way that derogation can occur: Joined Cases C–281/03 and C–282/03 *Cindu Chemicals* v. *College voor de Toelating van bestrijdingsmiddelen* [2005] ECR I–8069, para. 47. For a detailed analysis see

Article 114(1).[162] Initially the possibility of opting out of Article 114(1) measures was confined, by Article 114(4), to national measures existing at the time when the harmonization measure was adopted (i.e., pre-existing national measures).[163] Article 114(4) says:

If, after the adoption of a harmonisation measure by the European Parliament and the Council, by the Council or by the Commission, a Member State deems it necessary to *maintain* national provisions on grounds of major needs referred to in *Article 36*, or relating to the protection of the environment or the working environment, it shall notify the Commission of these provisions as well as the grounds for maintaining them.[164]

The Amsterdam Treaty extended the possibility of derogating from measures adopted under Article 114(1) to national rules adopted *after* the enactment of the harmonization measure. So Article 114(5) allows a Member State 'to *introduce* national provisions based on new scientific evidence...on grounds of a problem specific to that Member State arising *after* the adoption of the harmonisation measure'.[165] This scientific evidence—which must be both new and raising a problem specific to the applicant Member State—can relate only to the protection of the environment or the working environment. Thus, unlike Article 114(4), the grounds listed in Article 36 cannot be invoked to justify a national derogation under Article 114(5).[166] This is because, as the Court explained in *Commission v. Denmark*[167] in respect of Article 114(4), the EU institutions already know of the national provisions but choose not to take them into account, while the adoption of new national legislation under Article 114(5) is more likely to jeopardize harmonization. For this reason the grounds under which Article 114(5) can be invoked are more limited.

The Amsterdam Treaty also elaborated on the procedure to be followed once a Member State has notified either an existing or a new national measure. On receipt of a notification, Article 114(6) provides that the Commission has six months (or 12 in the case of complexity) to approve or reject the national provisions 'after having verified whether or not they are a means of arbitrary discrimination or a disguised restriction on trade between Member States and whether or not they shall constitute an obstacle to the functioning of the internal market'.[168] If the Commission does not respond within the six-month period

---

C. D. Ehlermann, 'The internal market following the Single European Act' (1987) 24 *CMLRev.* 361, 389–98 and J. Flynn, 'How will Article 100A(4) work? A comparison with Article 93' (1987) 24 *CMLRev.* 689. See also Commission's Communication, 'Article 95 (paragraphs 4, 5 and 6) of the Treaty Establishing the European Community', COM(2002) 760 final.

[162] The opt-out applies only to measures adopted under Art. 114(1) and not to those adopted under any other legal basis: Case C–183/00 *González Sánchez* v. *Medicina Asturiana SA* [2002] ECR I–3901, para. 23.

[163] E.g., Sweden applied for a derogation under Art. 114(4) from Dir. 94/36 ([1994] OJ L237/4) to maintain its prohibition on the use of E124 (cochineal red) in foodstuffs. The Commission then failed to respond to the notification. However, in Case C–319/97 *Criminal Proceedings against Kortas* [1999] ECR I–3143 the Court ruled that Sweden could not apply its national rules until authorized to do so by the Commission (para. 28). Cf. Case C–194/94 *CIA* [1996] ECR I–2201, considered in Ch. 6.

[164] Emphasis added.

[165] Emphasis added. On the need to produce new scientific evidence, see Commission Dec. 2003/1/EC relating to 'national provisions on limiting the importation and placement on the market of certain NK fertilizers of high nitrogen content and containing chlorine notified by France pursuant to Art. [114(5) TFEU]' ([2003] OJ L1/72).

[166] This distinction was recognized by the Court in Case C–512/99 *Germany* v. *Commission* [2003] ECR I–845, paras. 40–1, and again in Case C–3/00 *Denmark* v. *Commission* [2003] ECR I–2643, paras. 57–8.

[167] Case C–3/00 *Commission* v. *Denmark* [2003] ECR I–2643, para. 57.

[168] For an example of this process see the Dutch notification on maintaining national provisions concerning the use of short-chain chlorinated paraffins (SCCP) (2003/C 100/07).

the national provisions are deemed to have been approved.[169] If the Commission does respond and authorizes a Member State to maintain or introduce national provisions derogating from a harmonization measure, the Commission can examine whether to propose an adaptation of the harmonization measure,[170] especially when the national provisions approved by the Commission offer a level of protection which is higher than the harmonization measure.[171] Article 114(9) then provides an expedited procedure, by way of derogation from Articles 258–9 TFEU (ex Articles 226–7 EC), to bring a Member State directly before the Court of Justice if the Commission or another Member State considers that a Member State is making improper use of the derogation procedure.

Despite the initial fears of some commentators,[172] Article 114(4)–(5) has not been much invoked by Member States,[173] except in the area of GMOs. The most notorious case was a derogation obtained by Germany from Directive 91/173 on dangerous substances[174] enabling it to maintain stricter standards for PCPs (pentachlorophenol) than those provided in the directive.[175] But the case's notoriety arose not from Germany's abuse of the procedure but from the Commission's procedural failings in respect of the decision granting the derogation to Germany.[176] As the Court said in *France* v. *Commission*,[177] the Commission had merely described in general terms the content and aim of the German rules and then stated that those rules were compatible with Article 114(4) 'without explaining the reasons of fact and law on account of which the Commission considered that all the conditions contained in Article [114(4)] were to be regarded as fulfilled in the case in point'.[178] In particular, the Court said, the Commission should have checked whether the German provisions were justified on the grounds of the major needs mentioned in Article 114(4) and were not a means of arbitrary discrimination or a disguised restriction on trade.[179]

---

[169] This will prevent the problem that arose in Case C–319/97 *Kortas* [1999] ECR I–3143, above n. 163, from recurring. See also Case C–439/05 P *Land Oberösterreich* v. *Commission* [2007] ECR I–7141, para. 41 where the Court of Justice emphasized that the authors of the Treaties intended, in the interests of both the notifying Member State and the proper functioning of the internal market, that the procedure laid down in Art. 114 should be swiftly concluded. It added that this objective would be difficult to reconcile with a requirement for prolonged exchanges of information and observations. Therefore there was no right to a hearing. See generally, N. De Sadeleer, 'Procedures for derogations from the principle of approximation of laws under Article 95' (2003) 40 *CMLRev.* 889.

[170] Art. 114(7). Art. 114(8) makes specific provision regarding Member State difficulties in the public health field where that area has already been the subject of harmonization.

[171] Case C–3/00 *Commission* v. *Denmark* [2003] ECR I–2643, para. 65.

[172] P. Pescatore, 'Some critical remarks on the "Single European Act"' (1987) 24 *CMLRev.* 9, 12.

[173] Hitherto the Commission's decisions have concerned PCP, creosote, mineral wool, food colourings, sulphates and nitrites, and nitrates used in foodstuffs. See J. Scott and E. Vos, 'The juridification of uncertainty: Observations on the ambivalence of the precautionary principle within the EU and the WTO' in C. Joerges and R. Dehousse (eds.), *Good Governance in Europe's Integrated Market* (Oxford: OUP, 2002), 267–71.    [174] [1991] OJ L85/34.

[175] This directive had been the result of a German notification in 1987 under Dir. 98/34 of a draft regulation restricting PCP concentration in wood-treatment preparations.

[176] Dec. of 2 Dec. 1992, not published in the OJ but summarized in a Communication ([1992] OJ C334/8).    [177] Case C–41/93 *France* v. *Commission* [1994] ECR I–1829.

[178] Ibid., para. 36.

[179] Para. 27. The Commission remade the decision authorizing the German government to maintain its stricter rules. The Danish government was also authorized to maintain stricter rules on PCPs after having notified its draft national laws under Art. 114(4) (Dec. 96/211 ([1996] OJ L68/32)). At first it had argued that Dir. 91/173 represented a minimum rather than complete harmonization. The Commission disagreed.

The Court has also been prepared to take a tough line under Article 114(5), requiring Member States to show that they have satisfied the conditions prescribed. This can be seen in the Austrian GMO case. The provincial government of Upper Austria wanted to ban GMOs, on the basis of a scientific report, in order (1) to safeguard organic and traditional farming which is characteristic of the region, and (2) to protect natural bio-diversity, particularly in sensitive ecological areas, as well as genetic resources, from 'contamination' by GMOs. Since this ban would contravene the controversial Directive 2001/18 on the deliberate release of GMOs into the environment,[180] the Austrian government notified the Commission of its draft legislation, in accordance with Article 114(5). The Commission referred the matter to the European Food Safety Authority,[181] which found that (1) there was no new scientific evidence, in terms of risk to human health and the environment, to justify the prohibition;[182] (2) there were no new data that would change the environmental risk assessment conducted on GMOs that currently held marketing consent in the EU; and (3) there was no scientific evidence to indicate that Upper Austria had unusual or unique ecosystems that required separate risk assessments from those carried out for Austria as a whole.[183] The Commission therefore rejected the Austrian application.[184]

The Land of Upper Austria unsuccessfully sought judicial review of the Commission's decision.[185] The General Court (formerly the Court of First Instance) emphasized that, in order to avoid prejudicing the binding nature and uniform application of Union law, the procedures laid down in Article 114(4)–(5) were both intended to ensure that no Member State applied national rules derogating from the harmonized legislation without obtaining prior approval from the Commission. In that respect, the rules applicable to national measures notified under Article 114(4) did not differ significantly from those which applied to national measures still in draft form notified under Article 114(5).[186] In respect of Austria's application under Article 114(5), the Court noted that Austria had failed to satisfy the burden of proof that there existed specific problems faced by Upper Austria[187] and, since one of the cumulative conditions laid down in Article 114(5) had not been satisfied, Austria could not derogate from Directive 2001/18.[188] The Court of Justice upheld the General Court's decision.[189]

---

Eventually Denmark was persuaded to make an application under Art. 114(4) to maintain the stricter national rules, and the measure was considered under the Dir. 98/34 procedure.

[180] [2001] OJ L106/1.

[181] <http://www.efsa.europa.eu/en.html>. The reference was made in accordance with Reg. 178/2002 ([2002] OJ L31/1).

[182] If the Commission itself does not properly analyse the relevant scientific evidence this is 'apt to vitiate not only its determination as to whether there was a specific problem but the entirety of its determination of the conditions for applying Articles [114(5)–(6)], and, particularly, that of the proportionality of the measure notified': Case C–405/07 P *The Netherlands* v. *Commission* [2008] ECR I–8301, para. 77.

[183] Opinion of the Scientific Panel on Genetically Modified Organisms on a question from the Commission related to the Austrian notification of national legislation governing GMOs under [Art. 114(5) TFEU] (2003) 1 *The EFSA Journal* 1.

[184] Commission Dec. 2003/653 ([2003] OJ L230/34). See also Commission Dec. 2008/62/EC ([2008] OJ L16/17) where the Commission rejected a similar request from Poland on the grounds of the absence of any new scientific evidence relating to the protection of the environment or the working environment.

[185] Joined Cases T–366/03 and T–235/04 *Land Oberösterreich* v. *Commission* [2005] ECR II–4005.

[186] Para. 44.    [187] Paras. 64–5.    [188] Para. 69.

[189] Case C–430/05 P *Land Oberösterreich* v. *Commission* [2007] ECR I–7141.

## C. DIFFERENT APPROACHES
## TO HARMONIZATION

### 1. INTRODUCTION

Having considered the Union's power to harmonize national rules, we turn now to consider the different approaches adopted by the Union to harmonization. In essence, harmonization involves replacing the multiple and divergent national rules on a particular
subject with a single EU rule. This rule is intended to protect certain beneficial interests,
which would otherwise be protected by national law and justified on the ground of one of
the express derogations or a public-interest requirement (e.g., consumer protection and
public health), while at the same time advancing free trade and market integration. The
Union has long faced the problem of how to realize a harmonized, uniform standard and
thus a level playing field upon which firms can compete, while at the same time respecting (even fostering) the diversity of the national systems. The EU has experimented with
different types of harmonization measure—exhaustive, optional, partial, minimum,
reflexive—which we shall examine in turn. However, we begin by examining the situation where no harmonization is necessary at all: mutual recognition.

### 2. MUTUAL RECOGNITION

The principle of mutual recognition means that products/services lawfully put on the
market in one Member State can and should be allowed access to the markets in other
Member States because they have already satisfied home-state controls. This principle—
found in the Treaties[190] and confirmed by *Cassis de Dijon*[191]—lies at the heart of the single
market where standard-setting and enforcement are decentralized, thus removing the
need for harmonization. The result of this approach is to put the national systems of regulation into competition.[192]

Mutual recognition goes beyond the simple requirement that the host state must not
discriminate on the ground of nationality. As Armstrong puts it, it requires host states to
be 'other-regarding' in the sense that they must recognize and give meaning to information about the regulatory history of a product, service, or worker coming from another
Member State.[193] Host state *administrators* need to be open to the regulatory systems of
other Member States and active in their assessment of equivalence. The duty to be 'other-
regarding' also applies to *legislators*. National legislation must not foreclose the possibility of accepting products complying with equivalent standards made in other Member
States. Therefore, in *Foie Gras*[194] France was condemned by the Court for adopting a law
on the use of the term '*foie gras*' without including a mutual recognition clause in its legislation. Such a clause would permit *foie gras* produced to equivalent standards in other
Member States to be sold in France. The Commission now requires mutual recognition

---

[190] Art. 53 TFEU (ex Art. 47 EC) on the mutual recognition of diplomas and Art. 293 EC (repealed by
Treaty of Lisbon) on the mutual recognition of companies and legal persons.

[191] Case 120/78 [1979] ECR 649.     [192] This is considered further in Chs. 1 and 4.

[193] K. Armstrong, 'Mutual recognition' in C. Barnard and J. Scott (eds.), *The Law of the Single European
Market: Unpacking the premises* (Oxford: Hart Publishing, 2002), 231.

[194] Case C–184/96 *Commission* v. *France* [1998] ECR I–6197.

clauses to be included in all technical regulations to alert economic operators to the existence of the principle,[195] although *Commission v. France (nutrients)*[196] cast doubt on the validity of this requirement, especially in legislation which is not susceptible to having such a clause imposed (e.g., legislation requiring authorization such as that at issue in the *Nutrients* case).[197]

However, despite the promise offered by the principle of mutual recognition as a vehicle for ensuring both market access and national regulatory diversity, its full potential has been limited by administrators who are reluctant to recognize the equivalence of foreign products.[198] As we saw in Chapters 4 and 6, the Mutual Recognition Regulation 764/2008, laying down procedures relating to the application of certain national technical rules to products lawfully marketed in another Member State, attempts to overcome this problem. The effect of this regulation is to make clear that the burden of proof is on the host state as to why it is denying market access rather than on the trader as to why its goods should be admitted.

The role of mutual recognition has also been limited by the Court, first by the introduction of mandatory requirements which can rebut the presumption of mutual recognition,[199] and, secondly, by the development of the principle of functional equivalence[200] which requires those making an assessment of equivalence to take into account not only the foreign standards but also the broader context in which the goods/services are to be used. This can be seen in *Commission v. France (woodworking)*[201] concerning woodworking machines manufactured in Germany according to standards which took account of the fact that those (Germans) operating them would have a high level of training. However, in France, standards were premised on the fact that (French) users of the machines had to be protected from their own mistakes and so presupposed a low (or non-existent) level of training. Given these differences between the systems, the Court allowed France to apply its own standards to the imported German goods.

While the principle of mutual recognition is attractive and continues to be a key pillar of the single-market programme, the serious limits on its use have meant that it is not a miracle solution and that there is still a need for harmonization legislation to ensure

---

[195] The *Foie Gras* case came to the Commission's attention as a result of France's notification of its draft legislation under the Technical Standards Dir. 98/34 [1998] OJ L204/37. This directive is seen by the Commission as an important instrument to promote mutual recognition because the Member States can have their own rules recognized when the draft national legislation is sent to other Member States: Commission's Communication, 'Management of the mutual recognition of national rules after 1992', 93/C 353/04, para. 36.     [196] Case C–24/00 *Commission v. France (nutrients)* [2004] ECR I–1277, para. 28.

[197] For more detailed discussion, see M. Jarvis (2004) 41 *CMLRev.* 1395, 1401–5.

[198] Commission's Communication, 'Mutual recognition in the context of the follow-up to the action plan for the single market', Jun. 1999, 5, and Council Res. of 28 Oct. 1999 on mutual recognition (2000/C 141/02, para. 12). See also Commission's Communication, 'Internal market strategy. Priorities 2003–2006', COM(2003) 238, 7, on ways to improve the effectiveness of the operation of the mutual recognition principle.     [199] See further Ch. 6.

[200] J. H. H. Weiler, 'The constitution of the common market place: Text and context in the evolution of the free movement of goods' in P. Craig and G. de Búrca (eds.), *The Evolution of EU Law* (Oxford: OUP, 1999), 366–7.

[201] Case 188/84 *Commission v. France* [1986] ECR 419. Cf. Case 124/81 *Commission v. UK (UHT milk)* [1983] ECR 203 where the Court obliged Member States to recognize regulations and controls which provided equivalent guarantees to their own. See, further, N. Bernard, 'Flexibility in the European Single Market' in Barnard and Scott (eds.), above n. 193.

free movement.[202] This can take a number of forms: exhaustive, optional, minimum, and reflexive. We start by examining exhaustive harmonization.

## 3. EXHAUSTIVE HARMONIZATION

### 3.1 What is It?

As the name suggests, exhaustive (or full) harmonization concerns situations where diverse national rules are replaced by a single EU rule, leaving no room for Member State action. A number of such directives have been adopted in the field of goods and all impose a twofold obligation on the Member States:[203]

- to permit the goods complying with the directive to be freely imported and marketed (the free movement clause)
- to prohibit the sale of goods not complying with the directive, even when manufacture and sale take place wholly inside one Member State (the exclusivity clause).

Directive 76/768,[204] concerning the content of cosmetics together with their packaging and labelling, provides a good example of exhaustive harmonization in the field of goods. Article 7(1) of Directive 76/768 contains the free movement clause:

Member States may not, for reasons related to the requirements laid down in this Directive and the Annexes thereto, refuse, prohibit or restrict the marketing of any cosmetic products which comply with the requirements of this Directive and the Annexes thereto.

Article 3 of Directive 76/768 contains the exclusivity clause:

Member States shall take all necessary measures to ensure that only cosmetic products which conform to the provisions of this Directive and its Annexes may be put on the market.

Once the Union has adopted an exhaustively harmonized standard[205] Member States cannot unilaterally impose stricter standards because their action is *pre-empted*. For example, Article 6(1) of the Cosmetics Directive 76/768 and its annexes list the information which must appear on the packaging of cosmetics. Because this list is 'exhaustive',[206] the Court said in *Provide*[207] that Germany could not require further information concerning the quantity and quality of a particular product.[208]

The UK also discovered the full effects of pre-emption in *Dim-dip Headlights*.[209] The annex to Directive 76/756/EEC[210] contained a list of all the lighting and light-signalling

---

[202] Commission, 'Second biennial report on the application of the principle of mutual recognition in the single market', COM(2002) 419, para. 3.

[203] P. Oliver with M. Jarvis, *Free Movement of Goods in the European Community*, 4th edn (London: Sweet and Maxwell, 2003), 478.

[204] [1976] OJ L262/169, as amended on numerous occasions. The directive has now been repealed and replaced by Reg. (EC) No. 1223/2009 ([2009] OJ L342/59 with effect from 1 Dec. 2010. The original directive is used, by way of illustration here, since its terminology is more straightforward.

[205] As with Dir. 2001/37 which imposed stricter standards concerning maximum tar yields of cigarettes: Case C–491/01 *Ex p. BAT* [2002] ECR I–11453, paras. 77–8.                    [206] N. 190, para. 17.

[207] Case 150/88 *Parfümerie-Fabrik* v. *Provide* [1989] ECR 3891, para. 28.        [208] Ibid.

[209] Case 60/86 *Commission* v. *UK* [1988] ECR 3921. In the environmental field see Case C–2/90 *Commission* v. *Belgium (Walloon waste)* [1992] ECR I–4431, paras. 20–1.

[210] [1976] OJ L262/1. The directive has been repealed and replaced by Reg. (EC) No. 661/2009 ([2009] OJ L200/1).

devices that were permitted on motor vehicles. This list did not include the dim-dip device which, for safety reasons, British law required vehicles to have. The Court said that because the annex contained an exhaustive list of all the lighting devices considered necessary or acceptable for motor vehicles,[211] the UK could not unilaterally require manufacturers who had satisfied the harmonized technical rules set out in Directive 76/756/EEC to comply with this additional British requirement. Thus, in the name of free movement, the UK was deprived of the possibility of imposing additional safety standards. If the area had not been harmonized and the matter had been dealt with by the Court solely under Articles 34 and 36 TFEU, such additional requirements might well have been justified. However, as the Court said in *Van Bennekom*,[212] when EU directives made provision for the full harmonization of all the measures needed to ensure, *inter alia*, the protection of human and animal health and life, then recourse to Article 30 ceased to be justified.

Given the pre-emptive effects of exhaustive harmonization, the Court will check to see whether the directive does in fact fully harmonize the field. This can be seen in *Crespelle*,[213] a case concerning the unlikely subject of trade in deep-frozen bovine semen. Directive 88/407[214] on health requirements of bovine semen made provision for the collection and processing of semen in the Member State of dispatch and transport to the state of destination. It did not, however, address the question of the storage or use of semen in the state of destination. The Court therefore said that since health conditions in intra-Union trade in bovine semen had not yet been fully harmonized at EU level, the state of destination (France) could take unilateral action and, relying on the health grounds in Article 36, require importers of bovine semen to store it in an authorized insemination and production centre.[215]

## 3.2 The Problem with Exhaustive Harmonization

Exhaustively harmonized rules have their attractions for producers: by developing a clear set of rules which manufacturers can apply, they create a level playing field for competition, thereby reducing transactions costs.[216] However, negotiating the content of those rules can take years[217] because, given the pre-emptive effects of any Union rule, Member States are determined to ensure that their own national interests are protected (see Case Study 4.1 Jam and Chocolate) and, where the legal basis requires unanimous voting in Council, any unpopular proposal can be blocked almost indefinitely. And, once adopted, the same obstacles make such legislation difficult to amend to take account of innovation or other unforeseen circumstances, making harmonization conservative and inflexible.

---

[211] Paras. 9 and 11.

[212] Case 227/82 *Criminal Proceedings against Leendert van Bennekom* [1983] ECR 3883, para. 35. See also the discussion of the Unfair Commercial Practices Directive 2005/29 [2005] OJ L149/22 in Ch. 5.

[213] Case C–323/93 *Société Civile Agricole du Centre d'Insémination de la Crespelle* v. *Coopérative d'Elevage et d'Insémination Artificielle du Département de la Mayenne* [1994] ECR I–5077.

[214] [1988] OJ L194/10.     [215] Paras. 34–5.

[216] This now seems to be the driving philosophy behind the Commission's current approach to consumer protection: see, e.g. COM(2002) 208, 7; COM(2007) 99, 7. For criticism, see S. Weatherill, 'Maximum or minimum harmonsation: What kind of "Europe" do we want' in K. Boele-Woelki and W. Grosheide (eds.), *The Future of European Contract Law: Essays in honour of Ewoud Hondius* (Utrecht: Kluwer, 2007).

[217] E.g., the Architects Dir. took 17 years to agree and the Pharmacists Dir. 16 years: Lord Cockfield, *The European Union: Creating the single market* (Chichester: Wiley Chancery, 1994), 79.

Furthermore, by its very nature, exhaustive harmonisation eliminates the chance for diversity and experimentation at national level[218] and so raises the spectre of creating Euro-products (sausages, beer, cheese), fears exacerbated by certain parts of the (British) press vigilant for a good Euro-scandal. This has resulted in scare stories about the demise of the prawn-cocktail crisp,[219] and tales of European bans on matters as diverse as home-made jam, round cheese, the sale of plants at church fetes, donkeys from beaches, and darts from pubs.[220] Yet this is a caricature of exhaustive harmonization: as Case Study 16.1 demonstrates, harmonization legislation has helped accommodate national differences through derogations,[221] opt-outs, and phased implementation.[222]

### 3.3 Comitology

Further flexibility is introduced into exhaustive harmonization measures by provisions allowing for adaptation to technical progress through the comitology procedures. Comitology refers to the work of committees comprising representatives of Member States chaired by the Commission which scrutinize Commission proposals made under powers conferred on it by the Council under Article 202 EC, third indent, for the implementation of the rules which the Council lays down (now Article 290 TFEU on delegated acts and Article 291 TFEU on implementing acts[223]). Depending on the type of comitology procedure prescribed (see below), the Commission must take more or less account of the comitology committee's views. The advantage of the power to delegate is that decisions can be taken more quickly by the Commission, thus avoiding the Commission having to go through the full legislative process each time it wants to make a technical amendment to a piece of legislation. However, the Commission is not given a free reign; the comitology committee, while offering expertise, is at the same time also

---

[218] See the discussion by J. Stuyck, E. Terryn, and T. Van Dyck, 'Confidence through fairness? The new directive on unfair business-to-consumer commercial practices in the internal market' (2006) 43 *CMLRev.* 107, 116–17.

[219] According to the *Daily Telegraph* (1 May 1991, 19), 'Herr Martin Bangemann, the corpulent crisp-hating German who has apparently been the architect of European attempts to scupper the slightly kinky-flavoured crisps we British so enjoy, has been an easy target. On Tuesday he was pursued around Luxembourg by journalists inviting him to try a prawn cocktail crisp or tomato ketchup or Worcestershire sauce.' In fact this scare was caused by an oversight—the crisps had been left off a catalogue of permissible foods containing artificial sweeteners.

[220] Taken from, *inter alia*, 'Hurd highlights myths and lunacies of Brussels', *Herald*, 7 Nov. 1992, 7; P. Kingsnorth, 'Yes, we have no rules about abnormally bent bananas', *Independent*, 3 Jul. 1995, 4; 'Why Brussels sprouts', *Economist*, 26 Dec. 1992, 70. Although cf. Z. Casey, 'EU scraps rules on veg to reduce waste: Misshapen fruit and vegetables set to return to European tables despite opposition from most European states', *EuropeanVoice.com*, 12 Nov. 2008.

[221] See, in particular, the use of Art. 114(4)–(5) (considered above nn. 161–89), as the Court pointed out in Joined Case C–281/03 and C–282/03 *Cindu Chemicals BV* v. *College voor de toelating van bestrijdingsmiddelen* [2005] ECR I–8069, para. 47, or derogations expressly provided for in the directive itself, as the Court recognized in Case C–439/06 *Citiworks* v. *Flughafen Leipzig* [2008] ECR I–3913, para. 63.

[222] See G. de Búrca, 'Differentiation within the core: The case of the Common Market' in G. de Búrca and J. Scott (eds.), *Constitutional Change in the EU: From uniformity to flexibility* (Oxford: Hart Publishing, 2000). As she notes, such differentiation did not begin with the SEA but at least at a 'meso-level' had been found in directives dating back to the 1970s. See also N. Bernard, 'Flexibility in the European single market' in Barnard and Scott (eds.), above n. 193.

[223] The new legal basis for comitology is found in Art. 291(3) only. See M. Dougan, above n. 160, 649–50 on the problems of where comitology fits into this new structure and Commission Communication, *Implementation of Article 290 TFEU*, COM(2009) 673.

looking over the Commission's shoulder. Some describe comitology as the Council in the Commission.

Article 202 EC required the Council to lay down procedures in advance for the conferral of powers on the Commission.[224] These procedures are contained in the 1999 Comitology Decision 99/468,[225] which was amended in 2006.[226] The 1999 decision envisages three procedures by which the committees can act:

- *advisory*—the fall back position[227] where the Commission is required to take 'the utmost account' of the opinion delivered by the committee[228]

- *management*—for measures relating to the CAP and fisheries or the implementation of programmes with substantial budgetary implications.[229] Under this procedure, if the committee votes against a Commission proposal, the Commission is obliged to defer application of the proposed measure for a period laid down in the relevant parent legislation, giving the Council time to adopt, by qualified majority, a different measure to that proposed by the Commission.[230]

- *regulatory*—for measures of general scope designed to apply essential provisions of basic instruments.[231] The Commission can submit its proposal to the Council if the committee does not deliver an opinion or delivers an unfavourable opinion. The Council then has to confirm by qualified-majority vote whether it adopts the proposal or opposes it. If it opposes the proposal the Commission must re-examine it and submit an amended proposal to the Council, resubmit its proposal or present a legislative measure under the Treaties. If, however, the Council does not either adopt or oppose the proposal within three months, the Commission can adopt the measure.

A fourth procedure was added in 2006:

- *regulatory procedure with scrutiny*—intended to enable the legislator, especially the European Parliament, to scrutinize the adoption of 'quasi-legislative' measures amending non-essential elements of a basic instrument adopted by co-decision, including deleting some of those elements or adding new non-essential elements.[232] If the committee's opinion is unfavourable or no opinion is delivered, the Council has to confirm by QMV whether it adopts or opposes the proposal. If it plans to adopt the proposal then it must send the draft measure to the European Parliament, which has four months to oppose the measure. If the EP or Council opposes the

---

[224] The Court will scrutinize whether the Commission has respected the conditions under which delegation has been made: Joined Cases C–14/06 and C–295/06 *European Parliament* v. *Commission (DecaBDE)* [2008] ECR I–1649.

[225] [1999] OJ L184/23. See generally K. Armstrong, *Regulation, Deregulation, Re-regulation* (London: Koogan Page, 2000), Ch. 3; K. Lenaerts and A. Verhoeven, 'Towards a legal framework for executive rule making in the EU? The contribution of the new comitology decision' (2000) 37 *CMLRev.* 645. On rule by committee, see C. Joerges, 'The law's problems with the governance of the single European market' in C. Joerges and R. Dehousse (eds.), *Good Governance in Europe's Integrated Market* (Oxford: OUP, 2002), 18.

[226] Council Dec. 2006/512/EC ([2006] OJ L200/11).     [227] Art. 2(c).     [228] Art. 3.

[229] Art. 2(a). The content of Art. 2 is to help guide the institutions; it is not binding but where the [Union] legislature departs from those criteria in the choice of a committee procedure, it must give reasons for its choice: Case C–378/00 *Commission* v. *Parliament and Council (LIFE)* [2003] ECR I–937, paras. 49 and 56. Cf. Case C–122/04 *Commission* v. *EP and Council (Forest Focus)* [2006] ECR I–2001, para. 45.

[230] Art. 4.     [231] Art. 2(b).     [232] Art. 2(2).

measure the Commission cannot adopt it in its current form and must submit a revised proposal to the committee or submit a legislative proposal.

This new procedure is particularly intended to ensure democratic scrutiny by the European Parliament of measures adopted in the financial services field (the so-called Lamfalussy instruments, which are considered below).[233] However, this procedure sits uncomfortably with the new wording of Article 291(3) TFEU which talks only of Member State (not European Parliament) control of the Commission (not the Council),[234] and the fact that the comitology legal basis is in Article 291 on implementing acts, not Article 290 on delegated acts, albeit that the definition of delegated acts in Article 290(1) is similar to that of acts subject to the regulatory procedure with scrutiny.[235] It may well be that the Comitology Decision will have to be reconsidered following the Lisbon Treaty.[236] However, it will continue to apply in respect of existing acts.

In *Alliance for Natural Health*[237] the Court recognized the value of the comitology procedure:[238]

[It] is intended to reconcile, on the one hand the requirement for effectiveness and flexibility arising from the need regularly to amend and update aspects of [Union] legislation in the light of developments in scientific understanding in the area of protection of human health and safety and, on the other, the need to take account of the respective powers of the [Union] institutions.

An example of the application of the comitology procedures can be found in Article 10 of the original Cosmetics Directive 76/768. This provided that the Standing Committee on Cosmetic Products (comprising representatives of the Member States) would assist the Commission[239] under the regulatory committee procedure in amending the lists of substances which cannot be used in cosmetics. Scientific expertise is provided by the Scientific Committee on Consumer Safety.[240] The role of this committee was emphasized in *Angelopharm*,[241] where the Court said that since the purpose of consulting the Scientific Committee was to ensure that measures adopted at EU level were necessary and

---

[233] Statement by the European Parliament, the Council and the Commission concerning the Council decision of 17 Jul. 2006 amending Dec. 1999/468/EC laying down the procedures for the exercise of implementing powers conferred on the Commission (2006/512/EC) ([2006] OJ C255/1).

[234] Dougan, above n. 160, 651.

[235] Although cf. Decl. 39 on Art. 290 TFEU which says that the Commission has the 'intention to continue to consult experts appointed by the Member States in the preparation of draft delegated acts in the financial services area' which might suggest that the Commission expects comitology-style procedures will continue to apply under Art. 290. See also COM(2009) 673.

[236] See H. Hofman, 'Legislation, delegation and implementation under the Treaty of Lisbon: Typology meets reality' (2009) 15 *ELJ* 482, 500.     [237] Joined Cases C–154/04 and C–155/04 [2005] ECR I–6451.

[238] Para. 78.

[239] Art. 10. This is still the case under Art. 32 of the Cosmetics Reg. 1223/2009.

[240] Art. 8(2).

[241] Case C–212/91 *Angelopharm GmbH* v. *Freie Hansestadt Hamburg* [1994] ECR I–171. See generally J. Scott and D. Trubeck, 'Mind the gap: Law and new approaches to governance in the European Union' (2002) 8 *ELJ* 1, esp. 9–14 , and K. St J. Bradley, 'Institutional aspects of comitology: Scenes from the cutting room floor' in C. Joerges and E. Vos (eds.), *EU Committees, Social Regulation, Law and Politics* (Oxford: Hart Publishing, 1999), 81–3; J. Corkin, 'Science, legitimacy and the law: Regulating risk regulation judicially in the European Community' (2008) 33 *ELRev.* 359, 366–7.

adapted to the objective pursued by the Cosmetics Directive of protecting human health, 'consultation of the Committee must be mandatory in all cases'.[242]

## 3.4 Conclusions

Despite the various techniques to ensure flexibility, hostility to exhaustive European regulation was acute. In the UK the so-called 'Metric Martyrs' case, *Thoburn*,[243] demonstrated this most clearly. According to Directive 80/181/EC[244] as amended, metric measures had to be the primary indicators for goods sold loose from 31 December 2000. Imperial measures could be used until January 2010 but only as secondary indicators.[245] Steve Thoburn, a British greengrocer, was successfully prosecuted for using scales calibrated only in imperial measures. He and four others, backed by the anti-EU UK Independence Party, appealed to the Divisional Court, unsuccessfully invoking the doctrine of implied repeal to challenge the validity of the UK's implementation of the EU directives.[246] They were bitter in defeat and used their new-found celebrity to challenge the legitimacy of EU lawmaking.[247] Against this backcloth of hostility it is not surprising that the EU increasingly looked to other types of harmonization.

## 4. OPTIONAL HARMONIZATION

One such alternative is optional harmonization, where directives provide a harmonized standard which manufacturers can *choose* whether to follow. Such directives therefore have a free movement clause but not an exclusivity clause.[248] This means that if manufacturers wish to trade goods across frontiers, then the harmonized standard must be applied; if they wish to operate on a local market only, they can decide whether to apply the harmonized standard or continue to apply national rules. Directive 71/316 on measuring instruments[249] provides an example of such harmonization. The preamble makes it clear that initially EU standards would complement national standards and later, after the required conditions develop, national standards would be replaced by Union standards.

While optional harmonization offers some advantages, by avoiding the disruption to existing markets and preventing technical progress from being stifled, it does

---

[242] Para. 38.      [243] *Thoburn* v. *Sunderland City Council* [2003] QB 151.      [244] [1980] OJ L39/40.

[245] After public consultation, the Commission agreed to lift the sundown clause for the UK and Ireland and to permit the use of supplementary indications indefinitely: Commission 'Pints and miles will not disappear due to Commission proposal', IP/07/1297, now Dir. 2009/3/EC ([2009] OJ L114/10).

[246] *Thoburn* [2002] EWHC 195 (Admin), [2002] 1 WLR 247, noted by A. Perreau-Saussine (2002) 61 *CLJ* 527, A. Arnull (2002) 27 *ELRev.* 239, and S. Boyron (2002) 27 *ELRev.* 771. Had the Metric Martyrs tried to challenge the validity of the directive instead of raising points of UK constitutional law, they might have enjoyed more success, since it could be argued that a directive regulating loose, over-the-counter sales could not be justified on the grounds of removing obstacles to intra-Union trade under Art. 114, nor was such a measure compatible with the principles of subsidiarity and proportionality.

[247] Neil Herron of the Metric Martyrs Defence Fund expressed his disgust at the ruling: 'It shows our laws can be overturned by a gathering of unelected bureaucrats over which we have no democratic control.' P. Crosbie and M. Davill, 'Death of pounds and ounces', *Sun*, 19 Feb. 2002, 8. The front-page story is headed 'SURRENDER. Pound of bananas banned as our judges cave in to Europe. So who's running Britain now? BRUSSELS'.      [248] Oliver, above n. 203, 478.

[249] Council Dir. 71/316/EEC of 26 Jul. 1971 on the approximation of the laws of the Member States relating to common provisions for both measuring instruments and methods of metrological control ([1971] OJ L202/1), repealed by Dir. 2009/34 ([2009] OJ L106/7).

raise problems in respect of trade in non-conforming products and difficulties with Articles 34–6 TFEU.[250] It has therefore been little used.

## 5. MINIMUM HARMONIZATION

### 5.1 What is It?

Minimum harmonization is one of the most common forms of approximation used today. As the name suggests, the Union sets minimum standards but Member States are free to impose higher standards on their own goods and services. This partly explains the popularity of minimum standards directives: they help to reconcile the need for a level playing field for competition (the minimum standards) with space to accommodate national diversity (above those minima). This is particularly important in more welfare-orientated areas such as social and consumer policy that merely interface with, rather than serve, the economic demands of the single market.[251]

Although minimum harmonization directives have been around since the early days of the EU,[252] their use was constitutionalized by the Single European Act 1986 when certain new legal bases expressly provided that the Union should adopt directives laying down 'minimum requirements'[253] but that these directives did not 'prevent any Member State from maintaining or introducing more stringent protective measures compatible with the Treaties'.[254] Even though Articles 114–15 do not contain an express minimum standards clause, minimum harmonization directives have also been adopted under these bases,[255] as the Tobacco Labelling Directive 89/622 and the Tobacco Control Directive 2001/37 (considered in Case Study 16.1) both show.

Minimum harmonization directives therefore provide the floor below which national legislation cannot fall. This floor is exhaustively harmonized and may be set at a relatively high level. As the Court explained in the *Working Time* case, minimum standards do not mean minimal standards: the term minimum requirements 'does not limit [Union] action to the lowest common denominator, or even the lowest level of protection established by the Member States'.[256] Over and above the floor, Member States are free to

---

[250] J. Currall, 'Some aspects of the relation between Articles 30–36 and Article 100 of the EEC Treaty, with a closer look at optional harmonisation' (1984) 4 *YEL* 169, 179–80.

[251] M. Dougan, 'Minimum harmonisation and the internal market' (2000) 37 *CMLRev.* 853, 860.

[252] For an early example see Art. 11 of Council Dir. 69/466/EEC and the discussion in Case 4/75 *Rewe-Zentralfinanz GmbH* v. *Landwirtschaftskammer* [1975] ECR 843; more recently see Case C–44/01 *Pippig Augenoptik GmbH & Co. KG* v. *Hartlauer Handelsgesellschaft mbH* [2003] ECR I–3095, para. 40.

[253] E.g., Art. 153(2)(b) TFEU (ex Art. 137(2) EC).

[254] Art. 153(4) TFEU (ex Art. 137 EC). Similar provisions appear in Art. 193 TFEU (ex Art. 176 EC) on environmental protection, also introduced by the SEA 1986, and in Art. 169(4) TFEU (ex Art. 153(5) EC) on consumer protection, introduced by the Maastricht Treaty.

[255] Under Art. 115: e.g., Art. 5 of Council Dir. 98/59/EC ([1998] OJ L225/16) on collective redundancies. Under Art. 114: e.g., Art. 8 of Dir. 93/13 on unfair terms in consumer contracts ([1993] OJ L95/29). See also the Edinburgh European Council's conclusions in 1992 that where it is necessary to set standards at Union level, 'consideration should be given to setting minimum standards, with freedom for the Member States to set higher standards, not only in the areas where the [Treaties] so require...but also in other areas where this would not conflict with the objectives of the proposed measure or with the [Treaties].' See generally, P. Rott, 'Minimum harmonisation for the completion of the internal market? The example of consumer sales law' (2003) 40 *CMLRev.* 1107.

[256] Case C–84/94 *UK* v. *Council* [1996] ECR I–5755, para. 56.

choose whether to adopt more stringent measures than those resulting from EU law.[257] The only constraints on that freedom are the provisions of the EU Treaties.[258] *Buet*,[259] concerning doorstep selling, provides a good example of how the Treaties set the ceiling beyond which national legislation cannot go.

Doorstep selling is regulated by Directive 85/577/EEC on the protection of the consumer in respect of contracts negotiated away from business premises.[260] The directive does not prohibit doorstep selling; rather it aims to protect the consumer from the surprise element associated with such contracts by giving the consumer a right of cancellation.[261] However, Article 8 of the directive allows Member States to adopt or maintain more favourable provisions to protect the consumers[262] which, according to the preamble, may include 'a total or partial prohibition on the conclusion of contracts away from business premises'.[263] This was the approach adopted by French law. The question in *Buet* was whether the French provisions were compatible with Article 34 TFEU. The Court acknowledged that the French law constituted an obstacle to imports and breached Article 34 but found that it could be justified on the grounds of protecting consumers, especially those who were particularly vulnerable, against the risk of ill-considered purchases. Thus, the French prohibition on door-to-door selling, which gave consumers more protection than that laid down by the floor in the directive, was also compatible with the ceiling provided by the Treaty provisions (Articles 34–6 TFEU).

## 5.2 Reverse Discrimination

Laws protecting consumers are territorial in nature. Not only do they apply to all companies established in the state which sets standards above the directive's minima (e.g., France) but they also apply to those companies wishing to trade in France but established in another Member State where only the minimum standards laid down by the directive have been implemented. So, if a company wishes to leave France in order to avoid the ban on doorstep selling and set up in Belgium where it can engage in doorstep selling, it will nevertheless have to respect France's standards when trading in France. Therefore, in

---

[257] See also *Opinion 2/91* [1993] ECR I–1061, para. 16, and Case C–2/97 *Società Italiana Petroli SpA v. Borsana* [1998] ECR I–8597.

[258] Case C–1/96 *ex p. Compassion in World Farming* [1998] ECR I–1251, para. 63, considered below nn. 274–77 and Case C–169/89 *Criminal proceedings against Gourmetterie van den Burg* [1990] ECR I–2143, para. 9. As to whether fundamental rights might also constitute a 'ceiling', see F. De Cecco, 'Room to move minimum harmonisation and fundamental human rights' (2006) 43 *CMLRev*. 9.

[259] Case 382/87 *Buet v. Ministère public* [1989] ECR 1235, para. 8, also considered in Ch. 6. In the field of services, see, e.g., Joined Cases C–34–36/95 *De Agostini* [1997] ECR I–3843 concerning the TWF Dir. 89/552 ([1989] OJ L298/23) now AVMS Dir. 2010/13 ([2010] OJ L 95/1), considered in Case study 11.2, where the Court found that the national rule could in principle be justified and so did not breach Art. 56 TFEU, although ultimately this was a matter for the national court to decide. Cf. Case C–410/96 *André Ambry* [1998] ECR I–7875 where the Court found that the national rule did breach the Art. 56 ceiling.

[260] [1985] OJ L372/31. See the proposal for repeal in COM(2008) 614.

[261] Preamble to the directive.

[262] Cf. the Product Liability Dir. 85/374/EEC ([1985] OJ L210/29) which does not contain the equivalent clause and so is an exhaustive harmonization directive: Case C–183/00 *González Sánchez* [2002] ECR I–3901.

[263] Cf. Case C–376/98 *Tobacco Advertising I* [2000] ECR I–8419, paras. 101–5 where the presence in a directive of a clause permitting Member States to introduce stricter rules that impede imports complying with the requirements of the harmonization directive may be relevant in determining whether the use of Art. 114 is valid.

respect of *consumer protection* rules, when a Member State sets higher standards than the directive's minima its businesses do not suffer a competitive disadvantage and consumers benefit.

The situation may be different in respect of minimum standards directives which regulate *products*. For example, if French law requires goods manufactured in France to be produced according to standards above the directive's minima, the French manufacturer may be placed at a competitive disadvantage when exporting its goods to Belgium,[264] where the manufacturer has to comply only with the minimum standards laid down by the directive. This disadvantage also extends to sales within France. If, due to the free movement clause, the directive requires that France admits Belgian goods manufactured according to the minimum requirements laid down by the directive, while French goods have to be manufactured according to the higher French standards, French producers may suffer a competitive disadvantage when faced with competition from their Belgian rivals. The disadvantage experienced by national producers forced to comply with 'superior' national laws is known as 'reverse discrimination'.[265]

The compatibility of reverse discrimination with Union law was considered by the Court in *Gallaher*,[266] a case concerning the UK's implementation of Directive 89/622[267] on tobacco labelling (see Case Study 16.1). The directive required that indications of tar and nicotine levels and health warnings should cover 'at least 4%' of the surface area of the packet. Although the UK voted against the directive, arguing that it represented an undue incursion into national competence,[268] the British implementing rules actually exceeded the minimum requirements laid down by the directive since they required that the warnings cover 'at least 6%' of the surface of the packet.[269] However, in accordance with the free movement clause in Article 8 of the directive,[270] the UK regulations provided that an importer of cigarettes from another Member State was to be regarded as complying with the requirements of UK law if the packets carried the warnings in English and those warnings complied with the rules of the state of origin (normally 4%).[271] Various tobacco companies argued that this different treatment led to reverse discrimination and inequalities in conditions of competition[272] but the Court rejected their argument, saying that the reverse discrimination was the consequence of 'the degree of harmonization sought by the provisions in question, which lay down minimum requirements'.[273]

---

[264] As Dougan points out, above n. 251, 867, even in respect of domestic producers or service providers, more stringent national measures must respect primary Treaty rules on free movement *from* the Member State: see, e.g., Case C–6/98 *ARD* v. *PRO Sieben Media* [1999] ECR I–7599.

[265] According to Weatherill, the application of stricter rules against *imports* is constitutionally preempted as in *Dim-dip headlights*: S. Weatherill, *Law and Integration in the European Union* (Oxford: Clarendon Press, 1995).                                    [266] Case C–11/92 [1993] ECR I–3545.

[267] Now Dir. 2001/37.

[268] S. Weatherill, 'Regulating the internal market: Result orientation in the Court of Justice' (1994) 19 *ELRev.* 55, 57.

[269] Even though the directive did not state explicitly that any of its provisions set minimum standards only, the Court accepted that some of the provisions in the directive laid down minimum requirements: the expression 'at least' gave the Member States the liberty to decide that the indications and warnings were to cover a greater surface area in view of the level of public awareness of the health risks associated with tobacco consumption.

[270] Art. 8(1) provides: 'Member States may not, for reasons of labelling, prohibit or restrict the sale of products which comply with this Directive.'                                    [271] Para. 20.

[272] Para. 22.

[273] Ibid. See also Case C–128/94 *Hans Hönig* v. *Stadt Stockach* [1995] ECR I–3389, para. 17; Case C–14/00 *Commission* v. *Italy (chocolate)* [2003] ECR I–513, paras. 72–3. However, in Case C–222/91 *Ministero delle*

The same rule about reverse discrimination applies equally to exports, as *Compassion in World Farming (CWF)* demonstrates.[274] Directive 91/629/EEC[275] laid down minimum standards for the protection of fattening calves, including minimum provisions on housing space and diet. Article 11(2) provided that 'Member States may, in compliance with the general rules of the [Treaties], maintain or apply *within their territories* stricter provisions for the protection of calves than those laid down in this Directive'.[276] Stricter standards were applied in the UK. The Court confirmed that the UK could not, as CWF had advocated, ban exports of calves for rearing in veal crates to countries which had implemented the directive but which did not have the same high standards as the UK. Such a result would have given extraterritorial effect to UK law and undermined the harmonization achieved by the directive. The Court said that:

the fact that the Member States are authorised to adopt within their own territory protective measures stricter than those laid down in a directive does not mean that the Directive has not exhaustively regulated the powers of the Member States in the area of the protection of veal calves.[277]

In other words, the floor laid down by the directive was exhaustively harmonized regarding imported/exported goods. The UK was free to insist upon higher standards, but only in respect of British calves.

The effect of these rulings might be to prompt a company to move to a Member State which requires only the (cheaper) minimum standards laid down by the directive and then, relying on the directive's free movement clause, import products into the UK, thereby circumventing the higher British standards.[278] Faced with the prospect of an exodus of companies (and thus the loss of British employment), the UK might decide to drop its higher standards and require only the directive's minima. In this way a minimum rule risks becoming a maximum rule. If this is the case then the level at which that minimum is set becomes an important issue for the purpose of consumer protection.

However, some commentators can see commercial advantages for producers manufacturing in states which do insist on higher standards. For example, Scharpf argues that national regulations setting standards above the minima may serve as a certificate of superior quality.[279] Where this is the case, high levels of regulation imposed by France or the UK may create a competitive advantage for the companies subjected to them, and thus exert a competitive pressure on other governments to raise their own level of regulation. These national product regulations may then induce a race to the top, particularly if the French or British market is considered attractive and big enough, with governments of

---

*Finanze and Ministero della Sanità* v. *Philip Morris Belgium SA* [1993] ECR I–3469 the Court recognized that not all of the provisions of the directive laid down minimum standards: e.g., Art. 4(2) of the directive provided for the use of only a single specific health warning. Since this provision did not lay down a minimum requirement the Member State could not require more than one warning (para. 28).

[274] Case C–1/96 [1998] ECR I–1251.

[275] [1991] OJ L340/28. This has now been repealed and replaced by Dir. 2008/119/EC ([2009] OJ L10/7).

[276] Emphasis added.      [277] Case C–1/96 *CWF* [1998] ECR I–1251, para. 63.

[278] These problems could be avoided if there was no free movement clause, although following *Tobacco Advertising I* the legality of such directives adopted under Art. 114 is uncertain because they do not assist in the process of market integration: manufacturers still have to comply with the different standards of the Member States. See M. Dougan (2000) 37 *CMLRev.* 853; and Case C–389/96 *Aher-Waggon* v. *Germany* [1998] ECR I–4473.

[279] F. Scharpf, 'Introduction: The problem-solving capacity of multi-level governance' (1997) 2 *JEPP* 520.

other Member States being persuaded to regulate at French/British levels (or at least their producers voluntarily manufacturing according to French/British standards) so that they do not lose out competitively. This is sometimes referred to as the 'California effect',[280] where states in the USA copied the stricter environmental standards of California in order to enable their producers to trade on the Californian market.

Minimum harmonization is inevitably a compromise between market integration and ensuring sufficient flexibility for Member States. In terms of market integration, the free movement clause has the advantage of ensuring that out-of-state traders will have to comply with only one set of rules across the EU, even if producers in a state which requires higher standards may suffer a competitive disadvantage. From the perspective of diversity and regulatory autonomy, minimum harmonization also has merits because Member States are free to experiment above the minima, if they so choose. Member States must inform the Commission of the steps they have taken to implement the directive[281] which gives the Commission a large database of comparative national practice to inform any proposed amendments to the directive.[282]

## 6. THE NEW APPROACH TO TECHNICAL HARMONIZATION AND STANDARDIZATION

### 6.1 Introduction

The old vertical approach to harmonization was based on common, detailed, technical rules applying to individual sectors. However, the 1980s witnessed a renaissance of a simpler method of regulation known as the 'new approach', which formed a key pillar in the Commission's White Paper on completing the internal market.[283] These new-approach directives are horizontal,[284] applying throughout an industry as a whole rather than to specific groups within that industry. Given their broad field of application, these directives set out general principles rather than detailed rules, leaving wide latitude for interpretation,[285] and rely on private bodies to set voluntary standards. In fact, this 'new' approach is not so new. It was first tried in the Low Voltage Directive 73/23/EEC[286] and the experience gained formed the basis of a Commission Communication,[287] approved by the Council

---

[280] D. Vogel, 'Trading up and governing across: Transnational governance and environmental protection' (1997) 4 *JEPP* 556, 571.

[281] Directives now contain a fairly standard clause requiring Member States to 'communicate to the Commission the texts of the provisions of national law which they adopt in the field governed by the Directive': e.g., Art. 10 of Dir. 93/13 on unfair terms in consumer contracts.

[282] S. Weatherill, 'Pre-emption, harmonisation and the distribution of competence to regulate the internal market' in Barnard and Scott (eds.), above n. 193, cites an example from the environmental field: a four-year concession made on accession allowing Austria, Finland, and Sweden to apply stricter environmental and health standards generated a review that led to the adoption of higher EU-wide standards in a number of relevant areas (COM(98) 745). [283] COM(85) 310 final, 19–20.

[284] See Case C–359/92 *Germany v. Council (product liability)* [1994] ECR I–3681, paras. 23–4.

[285] N. Burrows and H. Hiram, 'Legal articulation of policy in the EC' in T. Daintith (ed.), *Implementing EC Law in the UK: Structures for indirect rule* (Chichester: Wiley, 1995), 45.

[286] Council Dir. 73/23/EEC on the harmonization of the laws of Member States relating to electrical equipment designed for use within certain voltage limits ([1973] OJ L77/29) now repealed and replaced by Dir. 2006/95 ([2006] OJ L374/10). For a full discussion of the 1973 directive see T. Hartley, 'Consumer safety and the harmonisation of technical standards: The Low Voltage Directive' (1982) 7 *ELRev*. 55.

[287] COM(85) 19.

in a 'Resolution on a new approach to technical harmonisation and standards', which contained a 'model' new-approach directive.[288] This was followed up by a Commission Communication and a Council Resolution 'Enhancing the implementation of the new approach directives'. More significant revisions have occurred with the Requirements for Accreditation and Market Surveillance (RAMS) Regulation 765/2008,[289] which has laid down general principles on the accreditation of conformity assessment bodies, on CE marking, and on market surveillance, and Decision 768/2008/EC[290] on a common framework for the marketing of products which provides common principles and reference provisions for the purposes of legislation based on the new-approach principles. Both of these measures, which formed part of the Commission's 2007 Goods Package,[291] will apply to all the new-approach directives which are being revised to take account of the changes they introduce.

## 6.2 The Fundamental Principles

The Commission summarizes the new approach in the following terms: it ensures free movement of goods on condition that a manufacturer guarantees that they are safe. The legislation sets out the level of protection to be achieved but does not prejudge the choice of technical solution to achieve the levels.[292] The new approach is based on five fundamental principles.[293] First, legislative harmonization is limited to the adoption of essential safety standards with which products placed on the market must conform. Once goods conform to those standards and a CE marking is placed on the goods, they must enjoy free movement throughout the Union without the need for verification.[294] Secondly, the task of drawing up the technical specifications which satisfy the essential requirements is entrusted to specialist standardization organizations, CEN,[295] CENELEC,[296] and ETSI,[297] acting by QMV,[298] on a mandate from the Commission.[299] Thirdly, these technical standards are voluntary, and the producer has the choice of either manufacturing in accordance with the standards set by the voluntary bodies or manufacturing according to other standards and then proving that they conform with the essential requirements

---

[288] 85/C 136/01. Commission, *Enhancing the Implementation of New Approach Directives* (COM(2003) 240, 5) and Council Res. of 10 Nov. 2003. For details, see <http://www.newapproach.org>.

[289] [2008] OJ L218/30. See L. Gorywoda, 'The New European Legislative Framework for the Marketing of Goods' (2009–10) 16 *Columbia J Eur. L.* 161.

[290] [2008] OJ L218/82. It covers the general obligations of economic operators, the presumption of conformity, formal objections against harmonized standards, rules for the CE marking, requirements for conformity assessment bodies and notification procedures and the provisions concerning procedures dealing with products presenting a risk should be aligned to that Decision.    [291] This was considered in Ch. 4.

[292] Commission, 'Package on internal market for goods', MEMO/07/54.

[293] 'Guidelines for a new approach to technical harmonisation and standards' in Annex II of Council Res. 85/C 136/01; and Commission, *Enhancing the Implementation of New Approach Directives* (COM(2003) 240, 5).    [294] See also Case 123/76 *Commission* v. *Italy* [1977] ECR 1449, para. 13.

[295] *Comité Européen de Normalisation.*    [296] *Comité Européen de Normalisation Electronique.*

[297] European Telecommunications Standards Institute.

[298] The use of QMV was challenged in Case 123/76 *Commission* v. *Italy* [1977] ECR 1449. Although the Court did not discuss the point, Warner AG said that national standards organizations could decide 'by common agreement' to be bound by QMV.

[299] See General Guidelines for the Cooperation between CEN, CENELEC, and ETSI and the European Commission and EFTA ([2003] OJ C91/7), supplementing the General Guidelines for Cooperation adopted in 1984 (CEN/CENELEC Memo. 4) which confer a monopoly of standard setting on CEN, CENELEC, and now ETSI.

of the directive through a system of tests and certificates.[300] Fourthly, products manufactured in conformity with harmonized standards are presumed to conform to the essential requirements established by the directive.[301] Finally, Member States must take all appropriate enforcement measures, including market surveillance to ensure that non-conforming products are withdrawn from the market.

### 6.3 The Toy Safety Directive

The paradigm example of a new-approach directive is the Toy Safety Directive 2009/48.[302] This updates and replaces the original Toy Safety Directive 88/378[303] which itself was considered a key test for the new approach to harmonization[304] because it unblocked proposals for a directive on toy safety based on the old approach which had dragged on since the mid 1970s. A proposed directive put forward in 1979 contained over 80 pages of technical annexes.[305] By contrast, the new-approach proposal (what became Directive 88/378) took less than two years to adopt, had 15 articles and 4 relatively short annexes covering 7 pages. Directive 2009/48 is somewhat longer (57 Articles and 5 annexes) but is based on broadly similar principles, albeit revised to take account of the RAMS Regulation and the Decision on marketing of products.

According to the directive, any toy, defined as a product designed or intended for use in play by children of under 14,[306] may be placed on the market, but only if it meets essential safety requirements. These safety requirements are both general, as set out in Article 10(2) ('Toys, including the chemicals they contain, shall not jeopardise the safety or health of users or third parties when they are used as intended or in a foreseeable way, bearing in mind the behaviour of children'), and particular, as set out in Annex II to the directive. The onus is on the Member States to ensure that toys cannot be placed on the market unless they meet these essential safety requirements.[307] The annex identifies six specific risks: physical and mechanical, flammability, chemical, electrical, hygiene, and radioactivity. In some cases the requirements are drafted in general terms, setting objectives to be achieved rather than specifying detailed technical rules. For example, the annex provides '[t]oys, and their parts must not present a risk of strangulation'. Other requirements are more technical and prescriptive, including the requirement that 'Toys shall not be powered by electricity of a nominal voltage exceeding 24 volts direct current (DC) or the equivalent alternating current (AC) voltage, and their accessible parts shall not exceed 24 volts DC or the equivalent AC voltage.'

A manufacturer has two ways to ensure that toys satisfy these essential safety requirements. The first is to manufacture the toy according to harmonized standards produced

---

[300] This was facilitated by the Global Approach to Testing and Certification aimed at coordinating the different practices and procedures across Europe: COM(89)209. See further Egan, below n. 304, 126–9; and Commission, *Guide to the Implementation of Directives Based on the New Approach and the Global Approach* (Luxembourg: OPEC, 2000). There is now a dedicated website to the new approach: <http://www.ec.europa.eu/enterprise/newappraoch/index_en.htm>.

[301] Case 815/79 *Criminal Proceedings against Gaetano Cremonini and Maria Luisa Vrankovich* [1980] ECR 3583, para. 13.          [302] [2009] OJ L170/1.

[303] [1988] OJ L187/1.          [304] M. Egan, *Constructing a European Market* (Oxford: OUP, 2001), 169.

[305] Ibid., 171.

[306] Art. 2(1). Certain exceptions to this definition are listed in Annex I which broadly covers products not intended for children, such as scale models for adult collectors and those requiring supervision such as fireworks. Further exceptions (e.g., playground equipment for public use) can be found in Art. 1(2).

[307] Art. 10(1).

by CEN and CENELEC[308] in accordance with Directive 98/34.[309] Conformity with harmonized standards[310] provides a presumption of conformity with the essential safety requirements of the directive.[311] The manufacturer[312] is then entitled to affix the CE mark (the French acronym for EC) confirming that the toys comply with the essential safety requirements laid down by the directive.[313] This process of self-certification is a central feature of the directive. Contrary to popular belief,[314] the CE mark does not represent a guarantee of quality, nor does it indicate prior approval of the toy. It merely shows that the manufacturer declares that it has applied all applicable EU directives.[315] The Commission has recognized that the function of CE marking is misunderstood but has not made significant changes. Article 30 of the RAMS Regulation 765/2008 merely reiterates that 'The CE marking shall be the only marking which attests the conformity of the product with the applicable requirements of the relevant [Union] harmonisation legislation providing for its affixing.' The Commission also intends to run an information campaign explaining the true meaning of the CE marking.[316] It also makes provision for Member States to take action against improper use of the CE marking.

The second method of ensuring compliance with essential safety standards is to manufacture the toy in accordance with a model which has been 'EC-type examined' by an approved, conformity assessment body (referred to as a notified body) in the state of manufacture.[317] In essence, the notified body will test a sample of the toy to see whether it satisfies the essential safety requirements laid down by the directive. The testing body then issues an 'EC-type examination certificate'[318] which means that the manufacturer can attach the CE mark to each production toy as a self-declaration that the toy has been manufactured in accordance with the sample which has been the subject of an EC-type examination certificate. This second route for compliance was introduced to encourage innovation in new toys where the existing standards are inadequate to establish compliance with the essential safety requirements.[319]

Once the toy complies with the directive and bears the CE mark, it enjoys free movement. The host Member State must assume compliance with the essential safety requirements and cannot impede the toy from being placed on its market[320] (unless the state's market surveillance authorities consider that it presents a risk to health and safety[321]). The host state certainly cannot require products with the CE marking from other Member States to undergo a prior-authorization procedure or any other procedure designed to

---

[308] CEN/CENELEC's role is referred to in the preamble only.     [309] [1998] OJ L204/37.

[310] In addition, the manufacturer must use the internal production control procedure set out in Module A of Annex II to Decision 768/2008/EC (Art. 19(2) of Dir. 2009/48).

[311] Art. 13. See also Case C–14/02 *ATRAL* [2003] ECR I–4431, para. 51).

[312] Or his authorized representative within the EU or the person responsible for placing the apparatus on the market.     [313] Art. 8(1). The manufacturer must also keep certain specified information available.

[314] S. Weatherill, 'Playing safe: The United Kingdom's implementation of the Toy Safety Directive' in Daintith (ed.), above n. 285. See also Commission Communication, 'Enhancing the implementation of the new approach directive', COM(2003) 240.     [315] COM(2007) 35, 9.

[316] MEMO/07/54.

[317] An application for 'EC–type' examination, performance of that examination and issue of the 'EC–type' examination certificate are to be carried out in accordance with the procedures set out in Module B of Annex II to Decision No 768/2008/EC. 'EC–type' examination shall be carried out in the manner specified in the 2nd indent of point 2 of that Module: Art. 20(1).     [318] Art. 20.

[319] In a similar vein, in the context of Art. 34, see Joined Cases C–388/00 and 429/00 *Radiosistemi* [2002] ECR I–5845 and Case C–13/01 *Safalero Srl v. Prefetto di Genova* [2003] ECR I–8679.     [320] Art. 12.

[321] Art. 42. See further below nn. 437–40.

multiply the number of people required to affix the conformity marking.[322] From this perspective the directive is a total harmonization measure:[323] once the manufacturer[324] complies with the essential requirements its goods will have free access to the markets of all the Member States, with the CE mark acting as a kind of passport. The Member States certainly cannot invoke any Treaty provisions (e.g., Article 36 TFEU) to justify any national measures which derogate from the provisions of the directive.[325] However, the principle of mutual recognition also plays a role: the host state must assume that, for example, the certificates issued by the notified body in the state of origin after testing the toy, are equivalent to the host state's standards or tests.[326] The accreditation rules introduced by the RAMS Regulation are intended to enhance confidence in the genuine equivalence of conformity assessment testing by the 1,800 or so testing bodies in the Member States.[327]

Finally, Member States must organize and perform surveillance of toys placed on the market in accordance with the provisions of the RAMS Regulation. This includes performing physical checks on samples of the toy.[328] Where they consider that the product presents a serious risk requiring rapid intervention, they can order the recall of the product.[329] The RAPEX mechanism (considered in Section D below) is used for exchanging information with other Member States.

### 6.4 Assessment

While some commentators have expressed concerns that the new approach may actually reduce protection given to consumers due to the absence of specific detailed standards,[330] Pelkmans believes that the new approach is 'qualitatively an enormous improvement over the traditional approach'.[331] He argues that it is a serious attempt to achieve coherence by 'combining *total harmonization* of the objectives at issue (safety etc.) with a flexible approach of the means (standardization)'.[332] At the heart of the new approach lie the harmonized standards adopted by CEN, CENELEC, and ETSI. Some have questioned whether this constitutes an impermissible delegation of power by the

---

[322] Case C–132/08 *Lidl Magyarország Kereskedelmi bt* v. *Nemzeti Hírközlési Hatóság Tanácsa* [2009] ECR I–000, para. 28.

[323] See Annex II, B, II.1 of Council Res. 85/C 136/01 and Case C–288/08 *Kemikalieinspektionen* v. *Nordiska Dental AB* [2009] ECR I–000, para. 44; Case C–132/08 *Lidl Magyarország Kereskedelmi bt* [2009] ECR I–000, para. 43. The absence of a minimum standards clause nearly jeopardized the adoption of the 1988 directive. Several Danish MEPs proposed rejecting the directive on the ground that the individual Member States could not impose stricter rules than those outlined in the legislation (Egan, above n. 304, 173).

[324] The directive also imposes obligations on other economic operators, such as importers and distributors: Arts. 4–9.       [325] Case C–132/08 *Lidl Magyarország Kereskedelmi bt* [2009] ECR I–000, para. 42.

[326] This is what Armstrong (above n. 193) describes as 'passive mutual recognition': the active work of recognizing equivalence has already been carried out by the adoption of EU legislation which requires that test results are to be regarded as equivalent to those in the host state.

[327] See also the detailed requirements imposed on the notified bodies by Art. 26 of Dir. 2009/48.

[328] Art. 19 RAMS Reg.       [329] Art. 20 RAMS Reg.

[330] Cf. the discussion in Ch. 6 about the effects of the judgment in Case 120/78 *Cassis de Dijon* [1979] ECR 649.

[331] J. Pelkmans, 'The new approach to technical harmonization and standardization' (1987) 25 *JCMS* 249, 259.       [332] Ibid., 257.

Commission.[333] But the Commission argues that no delegation is involved because the standards (as opposed to the essential safety requirements) are voluntary codes and therefore independent of EU law.[334] Others have questioned the legitimacy and accountability of CEN, CENELEC, and ETSI. For example, Burrows expresses concerns that decision-making can be slow[335] and lacks transparency, prompting concerns of capture by the industry to be regulated and thus the risk of dilution of the pre-existing national standards and the exclusion of the consumer's voice.[336] These standards bodies are also not bound by Treaty obligations such as the duty to give reasons in Article 296 TFEU (ex Article 253 EC) or other principles of good government,[337] nor have they been subject to review by the Court of Justice.[338]

There is some recognition of these problems by the EU institutions,[339] but, in the context of the wider debate about the quality of governance in the EU,[340] reforming the standard-setting process is not a priority.[341] This may be because the process actually works. As De Búrca puts it, one of the possible explanations for the acceptance of such 'non-democratic' bodies and networks in the EU is that elite or technocratic modes of governance have always been central to the European integration project, and the EU has never been more than a weakly democratic polity whose legitimacy has been based on factors such as the success of the single market project.[342]

---

[333] E. Previdi, 'The organisation of public and private responsibilities in European risk regulation: An institutional gap between them' in C. Joerges, K.-H. Ladeur, and E. Vos (eds.), *Integrating Scientific Expertise into Regulatory Decision-Making: National traditions and European innovations* (Baden-Baden: Nomos Verlagsgesellschaft, 1997), considered in C. Joerges, H. Schepel, and E. Vos, 'The law's problems with the involvement of non-governmental actors in Europe's legislative processes: The case of standardisation under the new approach', EUI Working Paper Law No. 99/9.

[334] Burrows and Hiram, above n. 285, 44, and L. Gormley, 'Some reflections on the internal market and free movement of goods' [1989/1] *LIEI* 9, 13. Cf. R. H. Lauwaars, 'The "model" directive on technical harmonisation' in R. Bieber et al. (eds.), *One European Market? A critical analysis of the Commission's internal market strategy* (Baden-Baden: Nomos Verlagsgesellschaft, 1988), 165–7.

[335] See, e.g., Council Res. of 28 Oct. 1999 (2000/C 141/02), para. 29; Council Conclusions of 1 Mar. 2002 on Standardization (2002/C 66/01) and Kellaway, *Financial Times*, 5 May 1990, cited in Burrows and Hiram, above n. 285. This is caused in part by lack of resources: J. Pelkmans, 'The new approach to technical harmonization and standardization' (1987) 25 *JCMS* 249, 263.

[336] A. McGee and S. Weatherill, 'The evolution of the single market: Harmonisation or liberalisation' (1990) 53 *MLR* 578, 585.

[337] R. Dehousse, '1992 and beyond: The institutional dimension of the internal market programme' [1989/1] *LIEI* 109, 126.

[338] Although the Court may have an ancillary role in ensuring that these committees are involved in the standardization process: cf. Case C–212/91 *Angelopharm* [1994] ECR I–171. Cf. the Lisbon revisions to Art. 263(1): the Court of Justice shall review 'the legality of acts of bodies, offices or agencies of the Union intended to produce legal effects vis-à-vis third parties'

[339] See, e.g., Commission, 'Efficiency and accountability in European standardisation under the new approach' (COM(98) 291); Council Res. 2000/C141/01 which 'Confirms that standardisation is a voluntary, consensus driven activity, carried out by and for the interested parties themselves, based on openness and transparency'; Parliament Res. ([1999] OJ C150/624) and the follow up Commission Report COM(2001) 527.

[340] See the European Governance White Paper, COM(2001) 428.

[341] See COM(2001) 527, para. 4.1.

[342] G. de Búrca, 'Institutional development of the EU' in P. Craig and G. de Búrca (eds.), *The Evolution of EU Law* (Oxford: OUP, 1999), 79.

## 7. 'NEW GOVERNANCE' APPROACHES

### 7.1 Introduction

Of the approaches to harmonization considered so far, the law has been used to 'perfect' the market in the sense of reproducing the outcome which the parties would have arrived at in the absence of transaction costs. Such a substantive approach to regulation presupposes that there is 'optimal' legislation which can be identified by legislators. In practice the information problems facing legislators are such that it is very difficult to identify an 'optimal' solution. For this reason there has been a growing interest in a more procedural approach to regulation whereby the law does not seek to achieve its ends by direct prescription (e.g., an exhaustive harmonization directive) but instead empowers local actors to promote diverse local-level approaches to regulatory problems. This has been described as 'reflexive harmonization',[343] by analogy to the idea of reflexive law,[344] where the law seeks to devolve or confer rule-making powers to self-regulatory processes.

### 7.2 Reflexive Harmonization and the Open Method of Coordination

This reflexive quality can be seen in minimum-standards directives which allow Member States or other actors to exceed the minimum standards, taking into account national interests. The European Works Councils (EWC) Directive[345] provides a good example. It requires the creation of an EWC or a similar information and consultation procedure in transnational companies over a certain size. Management and labour, the so-called social partners, are encouraged to set up their own EWCs or equivalent and to negotiate the terms and conditions under which they operate. If they fail to do so, the default rules found in the annex apply. These default rules induce the more powerfully placed party (the employer) to enter into a bargaining process when it otherwise would lack an incentive to do so.[346] The success of this model has been extended to the worker participation provisions in a European company (Societas Europea).[347] The standard rules contained in the annex, as laid down by the legislation of the Member State in which the registered office of the SE is to be situated, apply from the date of the registration of the SE where either the parties so agree or no agreement has been concluded at the end of the six-month deadline.

---

[343] C. Barnard and S. Deakin, 'Market access and regulatory competition' in Barnard and Scott (eds.), above n. 193, and S. Deakin, 'Two types of regulatory competition: Competitive federalism versus reflexive harmonisation. A law and economics perspective on *Centros*' (1999) 2 *CYELS* 231. See also M. Dougan, 'Vive la différence? Exploring the legal framework for reflexive harmonisation within the single European market' in M. R. Miller and P. Zumbansen (eds.), *Annual of German and European Law* (Oxford: Berghahn Books, 2003).

[344] See generally G. Teubner, *Law as an Autopoietic System* (Oxford: Blackwell, 1993); R. Rogowski and T. Wilthagen (eds.), *Reflexive Labour Law* (Deventer: Kluwer, 1994).

[345] Dir. 2009/38/EC ([2009] OJ L122/28).

[346] I. Ayres and R. Gertner, 'Filling gaps in incomplete contracts: A theory of default rules' (1989) 99 *Yale LJ* 87.

[347] See Council Reg. No. 2157/2001 on the Statute for a European Company ([2001] OJ L294/1) supplemented by Council Dir. 2001/86 with regard to the involvement of employees ([2002] OJ L294/22). For a further example of reflexive law, see EP and Council Dir. 2002/14 on the general framework for informing and consulting employees in the European company ([2002] OJ L80/29).

The open method of coordination (OMC) provides another, softer example of reflexive harmonization. OMC involves:

fixing guidelines for the Union, establishing quantitative and qualitative indicators and benchmarks as a means of comparing best practice, translating these European guidelines into national and regional policies by setting specific targets, and periodic monitoring, evaluation and peer review organised as 'mutual learning processes'.[348]

The OMC process is explicitly about experimentation and learning. Most commentators agree that it should, at least in theory, increase democracy in the EU through the enhanced role for deliberation among policymakers and participation of a broad range of actors at different levels.[349]

OMC was first tried and tested in the policies supporting EMU.[350] It then spilled over into the Luxembourg employment strategy where guidelines are set which are then reflected in national action plans (now national reform programmes).[351] OMC now peppered the Lisbon strategy 2000 (which set the over-ambitious target of making the European economy the most competitive in the world by 2010). For example, in the context of modernizing the European social model, targets were set (e.g., raising the employment rate from an average of 61 per cent in 2000 to as close as possible to 70 per cent by 2010[352]), and comparing best practice was encouraged (e.g., Member States were to exchange experiences and best practices on improving social protection and to gain a better understanding of social exclusion[353]). The follow-on programme, Europe 2020,[354] still relies on OMC techniques, albeit with fewer targets.

In the context of free movement of goods and persons the Commission's Communication on immigration[355] provides an illustration of how OMC may function in the internal market. The Commission suggests that OMC will complement EU legislation by providing a framework for reviewing the Member States' implementation. The Communication provides the example of admission of migrants.[356] It suggests that national measures will be adopted taking account of the criteria laid down in the directive, including the number of migrants to be admitted and the duration of residence permits. The Commission believes that it would then be helpful to discuss the national implementing measures to 'evaluate their efficacity and identify practice which might be useful in other national situations'.[357]

Advocates of OMC argue that it offers a 'third way' for European policy between regulatory competition (with the risk of a race to the bottom) and harmonization (with the risk of ill-suited uniformity). According to the Commission,[358] OMC has greater

---

[348] Presidency Conclusions, Lisbon European Council, 23 and 24 Mar. 2000, para. 37.

[349] Although, for a sceptical view based on a case study taken from the Occupational Health and Safety sector, see S. Smismans, 'New modes of governance and the participatory myth', *European Governance Papers* (EUROGOV) No. N–06–01. [350] See further Ch. 15.

[351] Discussed further in C. Barnard, *EC Employment Law* (Oxford: OUP, 2006), Ch. 3; and D. Ashiagbor, *The European Employment Strategy: Labour market regulation and new governance* (Oxford: OUP, 2005).

[352] Presidency Conclusions, Lisbon European Council, 23 and 24 Mar. 2000, para. 30. It also envisages that the number of women in employment will increase from an average of 51% today to more than 60% by 2010. [353] Ibid., paras 31 and 33.

[354] European Council Presidency Conclusions 25/26 March 2010.

[355] Commission's Communication on an open method of coordination for the Community immigration policy, COM(2001) 387 final. [356] Ibid., 6.

[357] Ibid. [358] <http://www.qec-eran.org/projects/lapsraps_index.htm>.

visibility, encourages a strategic and integrated approach, puts a particular issue in the mainstream, mobilizes all relevant actors, and encourages mutual learning. It can also be used in areas which are not so easily susceptible to regulation either because of the subject matter (e.g., employment policy) or because of a lack of clear Union competence (e.g., education). It can sit alongside a legislative approach, in areas such as employment and social policy, or it can stand alone, adding 'value' at a European level where there is little scope for legislative solutions (e.g., work at a European level defining future objectives for national education systems).[359]

Detractors of OMC say that it allows the EU to encroach into policy areas largely reserved for the Member States; that it is more opaque and unaccountable[360] than the 'classic Community method';[361] and that its success is still dependent on Member State action. If—or when—states do not fulfil their commitments, the credibility of the process is undermined. It certainly seems not to have the impact that its proponents had hoped for and the ambitious Lisbon targets are a long way from being achieved. This was the case even before the financial crisis.

Even if OMC worked perfectly, it is clear that there would still be a role for hard-law harmonization. As Von Sydow bluntly observes, it will be possible to buy an electrical appliance in any part of the EU and to take it across the border without restriction, but at home it may still prove impossible to plug it into the wall socket.[362]

### 7.3 The Lamfalussy Process

Another example of these 'new governance' techniques with a 'harder' edge than OMC is the Lamfalussy process. A committee of 'wise men', under the chairmanship of Baron Lamfalussy, identified the problems associated with the traditional approach to regulation, especially in the field of financial services.[363] It noted that blockages occur at four levels:[364]

- in the Commission itself—over-stretched, sometimes slow off the mark
- most notably in the Council of Ministers where there is far too often a tendency to add unnecessary levels of complexity to straightforward Commission proposals (often in an attempt to try to fit 15 (now 27) sets of national legislation into one Union framework)
- in the European Parliament, although much less than in the past
- in the Member States where transposition and implementation are often late and frequently incomplete.

---

[359] Governance White Paper, COM(2001) 428, 22.

[360] C. de la Porte and Nanz, 'The OMC: A deliberative-democratic mode of governance? The cases of employment and pensions' (2004) 11 *JEPP* 267. As Hepple puts it in *Rights at Work* (London: Sweet and Maxwell, 2005), 32, the employment guidelines are phrased in 'the mumbo-jumbo of modern management speak'.

[361] Cf. the principles of good governance set out in the Commission's *White Paper on Governance* (COM(2001) 428).

[362] See H. Schmitt von Sydow, 'The basic strategies of the Commission's White Paper' in R. Bieber et al. (eds.), above n. 334.

[363] Final Report of the Committee of Wise Men on the Regulation of European Securities Market (Brussels, 2001). [364] p. 14.

The Lamfalussy report therefore concluded that the current regulatory system was too slow (e.g., the European Company Statute took more than 30 years to agree), too rigid (every change, however small or technical, required a full-blown Commission proposal to be negotiated by co-decision), and produced too much ambiguity both in the substance of the directive and the way the texts were implemented.[365] It also complained that the system failed to distinguish between core, enduring, essential framework principles and practical, day-to-day, implementing rules with the result that directives were too detailed and could not be adjusted expeditiously at a time when the pace of change in financial markets, global and Europe-wide, was accelerating. Lamfalussy therefore proposed a four-level approach to regulation designed to overcome the defects it had identified:[366]

- Level 1: *Framework principles*—the core political principles—to be decided by normal EU legislative procedures (i.e., the ordinary legislative procedure). Level 1 principles should clearly specify the nature and the extent of the technical implementing measures and the limits within which the resulting provisions can be adapted and updated at that level without requiring a change of framework legislation.

- Level 2: *Detailed technical measures*—comitology through the establishment of two new committees: an EU Securities Committee (ESC) and an EU Securities Regulators Committee (ESRC) to assist the European Commission in determining how to implement the details of the Level 1 framework.

- Level 3: *Enhanced cooperation and networking*—among EU securities regulators coordinated by the ESRC to ensure consistent and equivalent transposition of Level 1 and 2 legislation through issuing guidelines and common standards.

- Level 4: *Strengthened enforcement*—notably with more vigorous action by the European Commission to enforce Union law, underpinned by enhanced cooperation between the Member States, their regulators, and the private sector.

This Lamfalussy process therefore recognizes two layers: (1) legislative and (2) implementation/enforcement. The legislative layer is subdivided into two: basic political choices that are translated into broad but sufficiently precise framework norms (Level 1)[367] and then operationalized through more detailed technical measures (Level 2) which are to be adopted on a faster track. More controversially, Level 2 measures can make technical amendments to Level 1 principles.[368] At Level 2 the preparatory work is done by the ESRC,[369] comprising heads of the national regulatory authorities. On the basis of this work, the Commission puts forward a proposal to the ESC, a committee composed of high-level representatives of Member States chaired by the Commission,[370] which, acting initially as a regulatory committee (and, subsequently, a regulatory committee by scrutiny) under the comitology procedure, decides whether to approve the draft. The

---

[365] p. 15.    [366] p. 19.

[367] See the Market Abuse Dir. 2003/6/EC ([2003] OJ L96/16); the Prospectus Dir. 2003/71 ([2003] OJ L345/64); the Markets in Financial Instruments Dir. 2004/39/EC ([2004] OJ L145/1); the Transparency Dir. 2004/109/EC ([2004] OJ L390/38) for examples of Level 1 measures.

[368] A number of Level 2 measures have been adopted, using regulations where this is legally possible to avoid problems of transposition; where not possible, directives have been adopted.

[369] Commission Dec. 2001/527/EC ([2001] OJ L191/43).

[370] Commission Dec. 2001/528/EC ([2001] OJ L191/45).

implementation/enforcement layer is also subdivided into two: Level 3 concerns practical implementation, with greater consistency in implementation using the ESRC to achieve this,[371] and more robust enforcement (Level 4).[372]

One concern with the Lamfalussy process is the constitutionality of Level 2. While, in theory, the divide between framework principles and technical implementing measures is clear, in practice it risks infringing the distinction drawn in the case law between (1) implementing measures which can be delegated to the Commission under Article 202 EC (now Articles 290–1 TFEU considered above), and (2) the essential elements which must be included in the basic legislation[373] because what might be described as a technical implementing measure might in fact broaden or narrow the Level 1 basic instrument. The European Parliament was particularly concerned that it was being marginalized from the process: while it had co-decision in Level 1 measures, its involvement in the Level 2 comitology was minimal. It therefore called for the right to 'call back' its powers if it was unhappy with the proposals (see now Article 290(2)(a) TFEU). While it did not win this particular argument at the time, following the failure of the Constitutional Treaty various safeguards were included to protect the role of the European Parliament, including the introduction of the new 'regulatory committee with scrutiny', within the meaning of Article 5a of the amended comitology procedure.[374] This enabled the Parliament to object to the Commission's draft on the grounds that it exceeds the implementing powers provided for in the basic instrument or that the draft is not compatible with the aim or content of the basic instrument or does not respect the principles of subsidiarity or proportionality.

---

[371] Three committees exist at the EU level in the financial services sector, with advisory powers, the Committee of European Banking Supervisors (CEBS), the Committee of European Insurance and Occupational Pensions Committee (CEIOPS) and the Committee of European Securities Regulators (CESR). These are often known as the 'Lamfalussy Level 3 Committees'. In Feb. 2009 a report by a high-level group chaired by J. de Larosière (<http://www.ec.europa.eu/internal_market/finances/docs/de_larosiere_report_en.pdf>) recommended transforming the three Committees into European Authorities, with commensurately increased powers to, inter alia: coordinate the work of national supervisors; arbitrate between national supervisors in supervisory colleges in cases of disagreement on supervisory issues regarding a cross-border financial institution; take steps to harmonize national regulatory rules and move towards a common European rulebook; and directly supervise certain pan-European institutions which are regulated at EU level, such as Credit Rating Agencies. The Commission took on board these recommendations (COM(2009) 252) and proposed the establishment of a new European System of Financial Supervisors (ESFS) composed of three new European supervisory authorities, based on the old committees but with greater powers, working in a network with national supervisory authorities to develop common supervisory approaches to the supervision of all financial firms, to protect consumers of financial services, and to contribute to the development of a single set of harmonized rules. The ESFS should draw up technical standards, help ensure the consistent application of Union law, and resolve disputes between supervisors. The Commission also proposed the establishment of a European Systemic Risk Council (ESRC), chaired by the ECB President and including governors of national central banks, the chairpersons of the three European Supervisory Authorities, and a member of the European Commission. The ESRC will be charged with continuously assessing the stability of the financial system as a whole and be given the necessary authority to issue timely warnings/recommendations for remedial action and to monitor responses. This was followed up by a legislative package published in Sep. 2009: <http://www.ec.europa.eu/internal_market/finances/committees/index_en.htm#communication>.

[372] The process was approved by the Stockholm European Council in Mar. 2001 ([2001] OJ C138/1).

[373] See, e.g., Case 25/70 *Einfuhr- and Vorratstelle für Getreide und Futtermittel* v. *Köster* [1971] ECR 1161, para. 6.

[374] [2006] OJ C255/1 discussed above at n. 226.

In assessing the effects of the Lamfalussy process, Hadjiemmanuil writes that the Level 1 directives have indeed all included significant comitology mandates, asking the Commission to clarify and adapt certain basic definitions found in the main instrument.[375] He also notes that the detailed character of the Level 2 instruments signals a drastic departure from the minimum harmonization principle. More controversially, he identifies the practice of preparing Level 2 measures while the content of the Level 1 measure has not been finalized, thereby risking pre-empting the political decisions at Level 1. He concludes that while the Lamfalussy process is complex and not as quick as originally envisaged, it has streamlined rule-making and strengthened cooperation between regulators and the coherent and equivalent application of norms by the Member States[376] with the result that the Lamfalussy process has now been extended to banking, insurance, and pensions.

# D. COMPLETING THE INTERNAL MARKET: BEYOND 1992

## 1. INTRODUCTION

Most of the Commission's 282 proposals put forward in the Single Market White Paper of 1985 were adopted by the end of 1992[377] (although crucial elements such as utilities, taxation, and corporate law were still missing[378]). The question then was where to go next. In its 1999 Internal Market Strategy,[379] the Commission outlined the objectives for the internal market[380] together with four strategic targets, the first of which was 'Making the rules more effective'. The 1999 Strategy document was in turn followed by the Commission's Internal Market Strategy, setting priorities for 2003–6.[381] These emphasized the need to coordinate three related policies: the internal market strategy, the broad economic policy guidelines,[382] and the employment guidelines[383] in line with the Lisbon strategy of 2000. The priorities identified included dealing with the seemingly intractable barriers to the attainment of the single market, national taxation and public procurement, along with the need to simplify the regulatory environment and to enforce the rules, a theme again

---

[375] See D. Chalmers et al., *European Union Law* (Cambridge: CUP, 2006), 815–17.

[376] This broadly favourable view is repeated in the Commission's own review of the Lamfalussy process: COM(2007) 727, with the exception of the operation of the Level 3 committees which is considered above.

[377] The Commission noted in 1992 that 32 out of the 282 measures proposed still awaited adoption, of which 9 were of low priority: COM(92) 383.

[378] A. Young 'The single market' in H. Wallace, W. Wallace, and M. Pollack (eds.), *Policy-Making in the European Union*, 5th edn (Oxford: OUP, 2005), 102.

[379] Commission's Communication, *The Strategy for Europe's Internal Market*, COM(99) 624. This followed on from the Single Market Action Plan CSE(97) 1 final which followed on from the Commission's Communication 'The impact and effectiveness of the single market', COM(96) 520. The Action Plan is considered in detail in K. Mortelmans, 'The common market, the internal market and the single market, what's in a market?' (1998) 35 *CMLRev.* 101, 108–13 and K. Armstrong, 'Governance and the single European market' in P. Craig and G. de Búrca (eds.), *Evolution of EU Law* (Oxford: OUP, 1999), 753–6.

[380] Namely, to improve the quality of life of citizens; to enhance the efficiency of Union product and capital markets; to improve the business environment; and to exploit the achievement of the internal market in a changing world. [381] COM(2003) 238.

[382] COM(2003) 170. [383] COM(2003) 176.

repeated by those contributing to the debate on a Future Single Market Policy 2006[384] which led to the most significant policy document in recent years: the Single Market Review 2007.[385]

The aim of the review is to foster 'flexibility and adaptability while maintaining the legal and regulatory certainty necessary to preserve a well-functioning single market'.[386] It combines this with a general recognition of 'effective universal access to key services, high social and environmental standards, and high levels of investment in research and education'. This is an important recognition of valves going beyond the hegemony of the market, now buttressed by the horizontal clause in Article 9 TFEU. In practical terms, the Review outlines a number of proposals to 'empower consumers', including consumer contractual rights and collective redress, together with measures to help small businesses, such as a Small Business Act, cutting red tape and increasing access by small and medium enterprises (SMEs) to European programmes. In addition, the review identifies a 'fifth freedom' in the single market, 'free movement of knowledge and innovation'. Despite its professed 'new approach to the single market', the review shows remarkable continuity with the earlier programmes, albeit without a 'classic legislative action programme' and a greater emphasis on a more 'impact-driven', economic approach. There is, however, one difference: the fact that business and the consumer have been put on the same footing is intended as a direct riposte to the critics of the 1992 programme who saw it as a measure of benefit for business only. Nevertheless, the Month Review of May 2010, 'A New Strategy for the Single Market, recognises 'integration fatigue', eroding the appetite among citizens for a *single* market' and 'market fatigue', with a reduced confidence in the role of the market. It is to be followed up with another relaunch of the single market in Autumn 2010.

The majority of the 2007 review is, however, devoted to 'Delivering results' which includes focusing on areas where the EU matters most, taking action where markets do not deliver and where the EU will have maximum impact; using a 'smarter mix' of policy tools (legally binding instruments as well as guidance, self-regulation, training or advocacy) combined with better implementation and enforcement of EU rules; and requiring action by authorities and stakeholders at all levels of governance, ensuring that single market rules are known, understood, applied and enforced. This idea of a 'coordinated and cooperative approach'—in partnership between the Commission and the Member States who must assume 'shared responsibility for and therefore a more pro-active role in managing the single market'—with a 'common objective of improved transposition, application and enforcement of single market rules', is further emphasized by the Commission in its Recommendation 2009/524/EC[387] on measures to improve the functioning of the single market. It is this aspect of the post-1992 internal-market strategy—described by Weatherill as 'market management'[388]—that we shall focus on, looking in

---

[384] SEC(2006) 1215/2 following up on the consultation document. The issue of enforcement also comes up in *Citizen's Agenda: Delivering results for Europe* COM(2006) 211. See the Commission: 2007 Goods Package COM(2007) 35 discussed in Ch. 6.

[385] COM(2007) 724. It was preceded by an interim report COM(2007) 60 which set out the Commission's vision for the 21st-century single market: 'a strong, innovative and competitive market, which maximizes the potential of services, directly benefits consumers and entrepreneurs and positions Europe to better respond to and shape globalization'. See further I. Govaere, 'The Future Direction of the EU Internal Market: On Vested Values and Fashionable modernism' (2009–10) 16 *Columb. J. Eur. L. 67.*

[386] COM(2007) 724, 4.        [387] [2009] OJ L176/17.

[388] S. Weatherill, 'New strategies for managing the EC's internal market' (2000) 53 *CLP* 595, 598.

particular at simplification/improving the quality of legislation, implementation of that legislation and enforcement.

## 2. MARKET MANAGEMENT

### 2.1 Simplification/Improving Quality of Legislation

According to the Commission, €50 billion could be saved by better-quality legislation.[389] This emphasis on better lawmaking has been a preoccupation for the EU for 15 years or so. The 'Better Lawmaking' programme[390] has now been replaced by the Better Regulation for Growth and Jobs Agenda, following the relaunch of the Lisbon strategy in March 2005.[391] It has three strands. First, *pending* legislative proposals are screened to ensure their consistency with the objectives of the revised Lisbon strategy to check they meet with the better regulation standards and to ensure they are not outdated. As a result, a total of 108 proposals have been withdrawn, including 30 in 2008.[392]

Secondly, *existing* legislation is to be simplified. This strand builds on the earlier 'SLIM'[393] initiatives. The case for simplification is a strong one.[394] For example, there were 38 directives on agricultural tractors, 13 on dangerous substances, and 11 on fertilizers.[395] The Commission launched a series of actions to simplify the content of the *acquis*,[396] update it, and reduce its volume (through consolidation, codification, and removal of obsolescent legislation) as well as improving its organization and presentation. This resulted in a simplification rolling programme of 185 initiatives to be repealed, codified, recast, or reviewed.[397] As the Commission admits,[398] although initial progress was slow, the Commission has now tabled proposals to simplify 132 of them. Seventy-five of these proposals have been adopted, and a further 50 are pending before the Council and Parliament.

As well as simplifying, the Commission has been codifying its legislation, bringing the basic law and subsequent amendments into one text. This has made laws clearer and reduced the volume of legislation. In 2008, the Commission finalized the codification of 229 acts out of a total of 436. One hundred and forty-two acts were adopted

---

[389] <http://www.europa.eu.int/comm/internal_market/en/update/score/busisum9.htm>. See, e.g., H. Xanthaki, 'The problem of quality in EU legislation: What on earth is really wrong?' (2001) 38 *CMLRev.* 651.

[390] COM(96) 559, <http://www.europa.eu.int/comm/internal_market/en/update/slim/index.htm>. See the Better Lawmaking reports (e.g., COM(2003) 770). This is based on the idea of legislating less to legislate better and the Commission's Action Plan, 'Simplifying and improving the regulatory environment' (COM(2002) 278) followed up by the Commission's Communication, 'Updating and simplifying the Community *acquis*' (COM(2003) 71). See also the Inter-Institutional Agreement on Better Law-Making ([2003] OJ L321/1), 4.

[391] Commission Communication, 'Better regulation for growth and jobs in the European Union' COM(2005) 97. This was supported by various documents designed to help assess administrative costs imposed by individual pieces of legislation: SEC(2005) 175, COM(2005) 518, SEC(2005) 1329.

[392] 'Third strategic review for better regulation': COM(2009) 15.

[393] Simpler Legislation for the Internal Market.

[394] Council Resolution of 8 Jul. 1996 on legislative and administrative simplification in the field of the internal market ([1996] OJ C224/5).

[395] Sutherland Report, *The Internal Market after 1992: Meeting the challenge*, Report to the EEC Commission by the High Level Group on the Operation of Internal Market 1992, 10. See also the Molitor Report on Legislative and Administrative Simplification (COM(95) 288 and its review COM(2000) 104).

[396] COM(2003) 71.     [397] For the first progress report, see COM(2006) 690.

[398] COM(2009) 15.

and published in the Official Journal. By simplifying and codifying legislation, the Commission has taken action which will reduce the *acquis* by almost 10 per cent—about 1,300 legal acts and 7,800 pages of the Official Journal.[399] The Commission is moving towards a more integrated approach to simplification where the aim is to examine the entire body of legislation that affects a policy area to identify overlaps, gaps, inconsistencies, obsolete measures, and potential for reducing regulatory burdens.[400]

The third strand of the Commission's Better Regulation Agenda concerns better quality of *new* Commission proposals, in particular through the systematic use of impact assessment[401] and public consultation[402] in the development of proposals. Despite all these initiatives, the problem remains that legislation, like the Services Directive,[403] adopted under the co-decision procedure (now the ordinary legislative procedure) is the result of a large-scale political compromise which inevitably means that there are provisions, inserted in the middle of the night to accommodate a particular interest, whose meaning is not clear or certain. As we saw in *Alliance for Natural Health*,[404] the Court has tried to use general principles of law to paper over some of the cracks.

## 2.2 Implementation

Even with better-quality legislation, the question is whether the Member States will actually implement it.[405] The Lamfalussy reports this is a major issue. In order to assist states with the task of implementation, the Commission issued a recommendation on the transposition of directives affecting the internal market.[406] This contains practical advice to Member States on how to address transposition problems, in particular through the appointment of a senior member of the government to take responsibility for monitoring transposition. The Commission has also set up an Internal Market scoreboard documenting the levels of implementation of directives by each Member State.[407] This has shown that implementation has been steadily improving (the EU average deficit has fallen from 6.3 per cent in 1997 to 1.0 per cent in July 2009) with Denmark and Malta at the top of the table, having failed to implement only three internal-market directives, and with the Czech Republic, Portugal, Poland, and Greece at the bottom, having failed to implement ten times that number.[408] However, while these league tables have had some success in naming and shaming, they do not reveal the quality of implementation, the level of actual compliance with the national laws, or the means of enforcement.[409] This is something

---

[399] Ibid.      [400] Ibid.

[401] See the Commission's *Impact Assessment Guidelines* (SEC(2005) 791).

[402] Commission, 'Towards a reinforced culture of consultation and dialogue—General principles and minimum standards for consultation of interested parties by the Commission' (COM(2002) 704).

[403] Dir. 2006/123 ([2006] OJ L376/36) discussed in Ch. 14.

[404] Joined Cases C–154/04 and C–155/04 *Alliance for Natural Health* [2005] ECR I–6451, above n. 108.

[405] See also the Inter-Institutional Agreement on Better Law-Making ([2003] OJ L321/1), p. 4.

[406] Commission Recommendation 2005/309/EC ([2005] OJ L98/47).

[407] <http://www.ec.europa.eu/internal_market/score/index_en.htm>.

[408] Internal Market Scoreboard: Member States still on target but need to focus on correct application of the rules: IP/09/1149.

[409] In fact there has been remarkably little empirical work on such questions generally. M. Jarvis, *The Application of EC Law by National Courts: The free movement of goods* (Oxford: OUP, 1998) and Daintith (ed.), above n. 285, are exceptions to this.

that the EU is trying to address through its annual reports monitoring the application of EU law.[410]

## 2.3 Enforcement

Enforcement has proved to be the greatest challenge. It has two elements: (1) the enforcement of EU rules by Member States against their own nationals; and (2) the enforcement of EU rules by nationals and the Commission against Member States. Both types of enforcement are essential to ensure the continuation of confidence in the single market.[411] The first element requires states to enforce national laws implementing EU law. If the EU measure is premised on the idea of home-state control (e.g., the Toy Safety Directive) this leads to the intriguing result that the home state is enforcing legislation largely for the benefit of the host state's consumers.[412] This raises the paradox of why home states would act against the interests (and votes) of home-state producers to protect largely out-of-state consumers. For domestic political reasons the home state might have the incentive not to enforce the law, raising the spectre of a race to the bottom—not in terms of *setting* rules at national level but in respect of enforcing EU rules.

However, in *Muñoz*[413] the Court made clear that individuals as well as states have the power to enforce Union standards. The case concerned a trader wishing to bring civil proceedings against a competitor to enforce Union rules on quality standards laid down in two regulations. The Court recognized that the possibility of bringing proceedings 'strengthens the practical working of the [Union] rules on quality standards'. It continued that as a 'supplement' to the action of the Member States' authorities, proceedings brought by competitors 'helps to discourage practices, often difficult to detect, which distort competition'.[414]

The second type of enforcement—of EU rules by individuals and the Commission against Member States—is more familiar territory. Individuals enforce Union law by relying on their directly effective rights,[415] and the Court has required conflicting national laws to be set aside.[416] The Commission can bring enforcement proceedings under Article 258 TFEU (ex Article 226 EC) against a defaulting state.[417] The weakness of this type of enforcement is

---

[410] See, e.g., COM(2008) 777. This was also emphasized in the Commission's Recommendation 2009/524/EC: 'Regular monitoring and evaluation of national legislation is important as it allows verification of how effectively single market rules are applied in practice.'

[411] COM(2003) 238, 28. In Case C–5/94 *ex p. Hedley Lomas* [1996] ECR I–2553, para. 20, the Court glossed over this point, blithely noting that 'Member States must rely on trust in each other to carry out inspections on their respective territories' (para. 19). See further G. Majone, 'Mutual trust, credible commitments and the evolution of rules for a single European market', EUI Working Paper RSC No. 95/1. See also Council Resolution on the development of administrative cooperation in the implementation and enforcement of [Union] legislation in the internal market ([1994] OJ C179/1); Council Resolution on cooperation between administrations for the enforcement of legislation on the internal market ([1996] OJ C224/3). Both resolutions call upon the Member States to identify contact points in the national administration.

[412] Weatherill, 'Pre-emption, Harmonisation and the Distribution of Competence to Regulate the Internal Market' in Barnard and Scott (eds) above n. 193. 66–9.

[413] Case C–253/00 *Antonio Muñoz y Cia SA* v. *Frumar Ltd* [2002] ECR I–7289, noted A. Biondi (2003) 40 *CMLRev.* 1241.　　　　　　　　　　　　　　　　　　　　　　　　　[414] Para. 31.

[415] Case 26/62 *Van Gend en Loos* [1963] ECR 1.

[416] Case C–213/89 *Factortame (No. 1)* [1990] ECR I–2433.

[417] See also Commission's Communication, 'Better monitoring of Community law', COM(2002) 725. See also the SOLVIT initiative, complementary to infringement proceedings, which is an attempt through administrative cooperation to make it easier to obtain redress where internal market rules are misapplied in practice: Commission, 'Effective problem solving in the internal market (SOLVIT)' COM(2001) 702, Commission Rec. ([2001] OJ L331/79).

that that it is lengthy[418] and depends on the Commission's discretion. In its Communication, *A Europe of Results: Applying [Union] law*,[419] the Commission commits itself to improving the current situation, in particular by involving better integration of implementation issues throughout the policy cycle—from design of laws through the adoption process to evaluation of results—so as to reduce the need for enforcement actions. Where such proceedings are necessary, the Commission aims to streamline its processes, giving priority to cases which have the greatest impact on citizens and businesses.[420] It intends to provide particular time limits for priority cases (12 months in cases of non-communication of transposition measures, 12–24 months for cases involving the non-respect by a state of an earlier judgment of the Court of Justice). The simplification of the enforcement proceedings provisions introduced by the Lisbon Treaty will help in this respect.[421]

However, litigation, by its nature, is uncoordinated[422] and will have only limited effect in the case of a truly recalcitrant state, as the BSE crisis showed. Following the discovery of a probable link between a variant of Creutzfeldt-Jakob disease (CJD), a disease affecting human beings, and bovine spongiform encephalopathy (BSE), which was then widespread in the UK, the Commission adopted Decision 96/239/EC,[423] prohibiting the UK from exporting beef to other Member States and third countries. The ban was subsequently lifted for Northern Ireland and then the UK as a whole[424] subject to strict conditions based on various factors including the eligibility and traceability of the origins of the beef which were laid down in Decision 98/256 on the so-called 'date-based export scheme' (DBES).[425] France nevertheless continued to refuse to allow British beef imports on public-health grounds, due largely to concerns raised by the French Food Standards Agency (AFSSA) about the traceability of the imported beef, a disregard of the precautionary principle,[426] and the risks still associated with British meat.

---

[418] COM(2007) 502.      [419] Ibid.      [420] Ibid.

[421] Under Art. 260(2) TFEU, where a Member State has been found to be in breach, the Commission does not need to issue a reasoned opinion. Instead, the Member State is given the chance to submit its opinion. Art. 260(3) introduces a further change. When the Commission brings a case before the Court pursuant to Art. 258 on the grounds that the Member State has failed to fulfil its obligation to notify measures transposing a directive adopted under a legislative procedure, it may, in it is initial application to the Court, specify the amount of the lump sum or penalty payment to be paid by the Member State which it considers appropriate in the circumstances.

[422] For a detailed discussion see S. Weatherill, 'Addressing problems of imbalanced implementation in EC law: Remedies in an institutional perspective', in C. Kilpatrick, T. Novitz, and P. Skidmore (eds.), *The Future of Remedies in Europe* (Oxford: Hart Publishing, 2000), esp. 99–104.

[423] [1996] OJ L78/47. This decision was unsuccessfully challenged in Art. 263 TFEU (ex Art. 230 EC) judicial review proceedings brought by the British government (Case C–180/96 *UK* v. *Commission* [1998] ECR I–2265). The UK also unsuccessfully sought interim measures under Arts. 278–9 TFEU (ex Arts. 242–3 EC) (Case C–180/96 *UK* v. *Commission* [1996] ECR I–3903). In addition, the decision was unsuccessfully challenged in an Art. 267 TFEU (ex Art. 234 EC) reference on invalidity brought by, *inter alia*, the National Farmers' Union (Case C–157/96 *R.* v. *Ministry of Agriculture, Fisheries and Food (MAFF), ex p. NFU* [1998] ECR I–2211). See also Case T–149/96 *Confederazione Nazionale Coltivatori Divetti (Coldiretti) and 110 Farmers* v. *Council* [1998] ECR II–3841 concerning the inadequacy of the EU's response to the BSE crisis, considered in J. Wakefield, 'BSE: A lesson in containment? Avoiding responsibility and accountability in the compensation action' (2002) 27 *ELRev*. 426.

[424] From 1 Aug. 1999: Dec. 99/514 ([1999] OJ L195/42). France unsuccessfully brought proceedings under Arts. 263 and (effectively) 265 TFEU (ex Arts. 230 and 232 EC respectively) challenging the Commission's failure to amend this decision despite new evidence: Case C–514/99 *France* v. *Commission* [2000] ECR I–4705.

[425] [1998] OJ L113/32 as amended. It was subsequently repealed when the UK proved that it was no longer a high risk country: Reg. 657/2006 [2006] OJ L116/9.

[426] See further the Commission's Communication on the precautionary principle, COM(2000) 1.

Despite an agreement that all British meat would be distinctively marked, France persisted in its refusal. As a result, the Commission successfully brought Article 258 TFEU (ex Article 226 EC) enforcement proceedings against France,[427] arguing that it could not rely on the Article 36 TFEU (ex Article 30 EC) derogations to justify its conduct since the decisions lifting the ban on the export of British beef achieved full harmonization.[428] The French, traumatized by their own scandal of contaminated blood,[429] still refused to allow British beef imports.[430] Further proceedings were then initiated by the Commission, this time with a view to having a fine imposed on France under Article 228 EC (now the somewhat amended Article 260 TFEU[431]). The British National Farmers' Union (NFU) also started proceedings in the French courts to enforce the rights of free movement. The case was referred to the Court of Justice.

On 2 October 2002, more than three years after the initial ban on the export of British beef had been lifted by the EU, France finally agreed to lift its own ban on the import of British beef, following an AFSSA report which concluded that British beef imports posed 'a negligible risk' of causing variant CJD.[432] The Commission then withdrew the second round of its enforcement proceedings.[433] Shortly before that, the Court of Justice gave judgment in the *NFU* case,[434] where it again confirmed that, since the DBES decision laid down the rules necessary for the protection of public health regarding the export of British veal, France could not invoke Article 36 TFEU to prevent the resumption of beef imports from the UK.

In the UK, the BSE saga substantially undermined confidence in the effectiveness of Article 258 as a means of protecting the rights of free movement. As NFU President Ben Gill said, 'the French have cynically exploited false consumer protection in a shameless attempt to protect their own beef producers'.[435] He added that it was unacceptable that an illegal ban had been imposed for such a lengthy time and that France could 'walk away from this disgraceful situation at the last possible moment before fines are imposed'.[436]

## 3. MARKET SURVEILLANCE

Once EU legislation has been transposed into national law and importers and producers are making use of its provisions, Member States must fulfil their obligations to ensure that only compliant goods are allowed onto the market ('market surveillance'). Certain specific directives, such as the General Product Safety Directive 2001/95,[437] make provision for coordination between the Member States to remove dangerous products

---

[427] Case C–1/00 *Commission v. France* [2001] ECR I–3493.     [428] Para. 112.

[429] C. Joerges, 'Law, science and the management of risks to health at the national, European and international level: Stories on baby dummies, mad cows and hormones in beef' (2001) 7 *Columbia Journal of European Law* 1, 8.

[430] At the same time as refusing to admit British beef, an EU report revealed that France's own controls on meat did not meet EU standards to protect consumers from BSE: L. Roberts, 'Toothless EU allows France to get away with illegal beef ban', *Western Mail*, 16 Apr. 2002, 6, and 'French BSE hypocrisy', *Farmers Guardian*, 12 Apr. 2002, 1.

[431] Art. 260 TFEU has simplified the process of imposing a lump sum or penalty payment against a defaulting state.

[432] J. Henley, 'France lifts ban on British beef after six-year dispute', *Guardian*, 3 Oct. 2002, 6.

[433] IP/02/1671, 13 Nov. 2002.

[434] Case C–241/01 *NFU v. Secrétariat général du gouvernement* [2002] ECR I–9070.

[435] Reported in R. Graham, M. Mann, and J. Mason, 'France heads off sanctions and lifts embargo on British beef', *Financial Times*, 3 Oct. 2002, 1.     [436] Reported in Henley, above n. 432.

[437] [2002] OJ L11/4.

form the market. Most successful has been RAPEX,[438] the EU's rapid alert system for dangerous consumer products (but not food, pharmaceutical and medical devices, which are covered by other mechanisms). It facilitates the rapid exchange of information between Member States and the Commission on measures taken to prevent or restrict the marketing or use of products posing a serious risk to the health and safety of consumers. The importance of such procedures can be seen in Case Study 16.2 (below). The RAMS Regulation 765/2008 extends the RAPEX system to all products which present a serious risk. In addition, it improves the traceability of products and clarifies the obligations for economic operators.[439] It also makes provision for border controls on products from non-EU sources which, if they do not comply with Union harmonization legislation or if the product poses a serious risk, will not be authorized for release for free circulation.[440]

---

**Case Study 16.2** PRODUCT SAFETY, TOY SAFETY, AND BABIES' DUMMIES[441]
......................................................................................................

Babies chew things. Teething babies chew more and are often given teething rings, dummies, and rattles to chew on. These are made out of PVC which, in the past, was softened by the addition of plasticizers (phthalates) which have been linked to damage to the kidneys, liver, and testicles. During the 1990s, a high-profile campaign was run by certain consumer groups, such as Greenpeace,[442] arguing that phthalates can leach from products and this has a particularly serious effect on children who chew and suck over prolonged periods. This chewing can break down the plastic, which accelerates the release of the phthalates into the saliva.[443]

On 23 April 1997 the Danish authorities notified the Commission of an 'emergency situation', in accordance with Article 12 of the General Product Safety (GPS) Directive 2001/95[444] (and Article 42 of the Toy Safety Directive[445]), concerning phthalates in teething rings made in China for the Italian company Chicco. Their concerns were based on a study produced for the Danish Environmental Protection Agency which found that a baby who chewed a Chicco Softy Vinyl Sweets ring for three hours would ingest 2,219 micrograms of phthalates per kilogram of body weight—44 times the

---

[438] For full details, see <http://www.ec.europa.eu/consumers/safety/rapex/index_en.htm>. Commission Dec. 2010/15/EU ([2010] OJ L22/1) lays down guidelines on the management of RAPEX.

[439] MEMO/07/54.          [440] On the meaning of free circulation, see further Ch. 7.

[441] The following draws on Joerges, above n. 429.

[442] <http://www.greenpeaceusa.org/media/factsheets/toxic_fact_english.htm>. Greenpeace's research was strongly contested by manufacturers in the industry: see, e.g., <http://www.vinyltoys.com/docs/pl/cmapep3.html>; <http://www.ecpi.org/>. See also B. Durodié, 'Plastic Panic', *Wall Street Journal Europe*, 6 Sep. 1999 and 'Calculating the cost of caution', *Chemistry and Industry*, 6 Mar. 2000, 170.

[443] Opinion of ECOSOC ([2000] OJ C117/59), para. 2.2.

[444] [2002] OJ L11/4, originally Dir. 92/59 [1992] OJ L228/24. This directive requires producers to place only safe products on the market (Art. 3). As with the Toy Safety Dir., the GPS Dir. lists only general safety requirements (Art. 2(b)). Goods manufactured according to 'voluntary national standards transposing European standards' are 'presumed safe' (Art. 3(2), para. 2 of Dir. 2001/95). This directive also lays down procedures for dealing with dangerous products. Art. 8 concerns emergency situations. For further details see G. Argiros, 'The EEC Directive on General Product Safety' [1994/1] *LIEI* 125.

[445] The GPS Dir. was invoked on 'childcare articles' ('any product designed to facilitate sleep, relaxation, the feeding of children or sucking on the part of children'); the Toy Safety Dir. covered 'toys' (any product designed or clearly intended for use in play by children).

maximum amount permitted in food under EU law.[446] Although Chicco argued that the rings did not constitute any risk and conformed with the Toy Safety Directive,[447] it nevertheless withdrew the products from the market pending the results of its own tests.

In 1998 the Spanish government notified the Commission under Article 8 of the GPS Directive of the steps it was taking against phthalates. The Greek, Austrian, Swedish, Finnish, Italian, French, and German governments also took steps against the phthalates, most of which were notified to the Commission under Directive 98/34/EC on the provision of information in the field of technical standards and regulations.[448] The Commission referred the matter to the relevant scientific committee on Toxicity, Ecotoxicity, and the Environment (CSTEE),[449] which confirmed that a precautionary approach[450] was justified. This enabled the Commission to take preventive action where evidence was 'insufficient, inconclusive or uncertain' but where failure to act would result in excessive risk to public health or the environment. This was only the third time that the principle had been invoked.[451] As an interim measure, the Commission issued a recommendation[452] that Member States had to adopt the measures required to ensure a high level of child health protection in regard to phthalate-containing soft PVC childcare articles and toys intended to be placed in the mouth.

When scientific evidence showed that this approach was not sufficient to ensure consistent,[453] high-level protection, the Commission issued a decision under Article 13 of the GPS Directive,[454] banning the use of certain phthalates in toys altogether.[455] This, the Commission argued, was a proportionate response; merely setting limits on the migration of these phthalates was not possible because there were no reliable means of testing their migration. This decision, as amended, remained in operation until amendments to the Dangerous Substances Directive 76/769 were adopted.[456] Based on the precautionary principle, these amendments distinguished, in the name of

---

[446] D. MacKenzie, 'Alarm sounds over toxic teething rings', *New Scientist*, 14 Jun. 1997, 10.

[447] Joerges, above n. 429, 4.   [448] See further Ch. 6.

[449] <http://www.ec.europa.eu/health/scientific_committees/environmental_risks/opinions/sctee/index_en.htm>.   [450] See ibid.

[451] Opinion of ECOSOC ([2000] OJ C117/59), para. 1.2.5.1.

[452] Commission Rec. 98/485/EC on childcare articles and toys made of soft PVC containing certain phthalates intended to be placed in the mouths of children under three years of age ([1998] OJ L217/35). The then Commissioner Emma Bonino had wanted the phthalates to be banned. Some reports of her intervention continued to reflect the theme of 'mad Brussels bureaucrats' interfering where they are not wanted: see, e.g., T. Harrison and J. Palmer, 'Eurocrats plan to ban baby dummies: But Britain says there is no risk', *Mirror*, 15 May 1998, 13; 'Rubber ducks win Euro reprieve', *The Times*, 15 May 1998.

[453] Cf. B. Durodié, 'Plastic panics European risk regulation in the aftermath of BSE' in J. Morris (ed.), *Rethinking Risk and the Precautionary Principle* (Leicester: Perpetuity Press, 2000), who contests much of the scientific evidence.

[454] This provision had been unsuccessfully challenged in Case C–359/92 *Germany v. Council* [1994] ECR I–3681.

[455] Commission Dec. 1999/815/EC adopting measures prohibiting the placing on the market of toys and childcare articles intended to be placed in the mouths of children under three years of age made of soft PVC containing one or more of the substances dI–iso-nonyl phthalate (DINP), di(2-ethylhexyl) phthalate (DEHP), dibutyl phthalate (DBP), dI–iso-decyl phthalate (DIDP), dI–n-octyl phthalate (DNOP), and butyl-benzyl phthalate (BBP) (notified under Doc. No. C(1999)4436) ([1999] OJ L315/46).

[456] Dir. 2005/84/EC ([2005] OJ L344/40).

proportionality, between two groups of phthalates: (1) DEHP, DBP, BBP; and (2) DINP, DIDP, and DNOP. The first group is banned altogether in toys and childcare articles; the second is banned but only in respect of 'toys and childcare articles, which can be placed in the mouth by children' (e.g. dummies and teething rings). No age limitation is specified in the directive.

## E.  CONCLUSIONS

The discussion in this chapter suggests that, far from the Union being a 'market without a state',[457] in Joerges' words, the EU market is increasingly heavily regulated by the central authorities. However, this is not a case of straightforward re-regulation, with a shift of regulation from the national level to the EU,[458] but rather a blending of the national and the Union—this is multilevel governance.[459] Modern regulatory techniques which aim to combine the benefits of centralization together with local autonomy—minimum harmonization, the new-approach directives, reflexive harmonization, and OMC—rely on a mix of centralized and decentralized regulation together with the involvement of a wide range of actors, both public and private. For this reason it may be more appropriate to talk about co-regulation or self-regulation than re-regulation.[460] This approach to regulation represents a seismic shift away from the caricature of exhaustive harmonization and the basic philosophy of 'if it moves (or even if it doesn't) harmonize it' and a far greater sensitivity to the values of diversity and local autonomy. Given the limits of the EU's powers, as *Tobacco Advertising I* makes so clear,[461] together with the political unacceptability of doing more, such meshing of decision-making is the only viable option for the EU as it expands to 27 states and possibly beyond.

The reliance on national and sub-national actors is particularly true in the case of enforcement. The absence of an effective range of enforcement mechanisms at EU level means that the EU is dependent on enforcement at national level, and it is here that the Court of Justice has been instrumental in strengthening the hand of one of the most important defenders of the Union's interests, the individual (both natural and legal persons). And here we come full circle—the four freedoms are intended to benefit the individual and it is ultimately up to the individual to ensure that they work.

---

[457] C. Joerges, 'European economic law, the nation state and the Treaty of Maastricht' in R. Dehousse (ed.), *Europe After Maastricht: An ever closer union* (Munich: Law Books in Europe, 1994).

[458] K. Armstrong, *Regulation, De-regulation, Re-regulation* (London: Kogan Page, 2000), 2.

[459] L. Hooghe and G. Marks, *Multi-level Governance and European Integration* (Lanham, Md: Rowman and Littlefield, 2001).

[460] COM(2003) 238, 26.

[461] Although cf. S. Weatherill, 'Why harmonise?' in T. Tridimas and P. Nebbia, *European Union Law for the Twenty-first Century* (Oxford: Hart Publishing, 2004), who expresses concerns about 'false harmonization' on the internal-market legal bases where the impetus to integrate markets brought with it incidental incursion into new areas of regulatory activity.

# INDEX